Lecture Notes in Computer Science 10878

Commenced Publication in 1973
Founding and Former Series Editors:
Gerhard Goos, Juris Hartmanis, and Jan van Leeuwen

More information about this series at http://www.springer.com/series/7407

Tingwen Huang · Jiancheng Lv
Changyin Sun · Alexander V. Tuzikov (Eds.)

Advances in Neural Networks – ISNN 2018

15th International Symposium on Neural Networks, ISNN 2018
Minsk, Belarus, June 25–28, 2018
Proceedings

 Springer

Editors
Tingwen Huang (ID)
Texas A&M University at Qatar
Doha
Qatar

Changyin Sun
Southeast University
Nanjing
China

Jiancheng Lv
Sichuan University
Chengdu
China

Alexander V. Tuzikov
United Institute of Informatics Problems
Minsk
Belarus

ISSN 0302-9743   ISSN 1611-3349 (electronic)
Lecture Notes in Computer Science
ISBN 978-3-319-92536-3   ISBN 978-3-319-92537-0 (eBook)
https://doi.org/10.1007/978-3-319-92537-0

Library of Congress Control Number: 2018944404

LNCS Sublibrary: SL1 – Theoretical Computer Science and General Issues

Printed on acid-free paper

This Springer imprint is published by the registered company Springer International Publishing AG
part of Springer Nature
The registered company address is: Gewerbestrasse 11, 6330 Cham, Switzerland

Preface

This volume of *Lecture Notes in Computer Science* constitutes the proceedings of the 15th International Symposium on Neural Networks (ISNN 2018) held during June 25–28, 2018, in Minsk, Belarus. Thanks to the success of the previous events, ISNN has become a well-established series of popular and high-quality conferences on the theory and methodology of neural networks and their applications. This year's symposium was held in Minsk, the capital and largest city of Belarus with a population of over two million. ISNN aims at providing a high-level international forum for scientists, engineers, educators, and students to gather so as to present and discuss the latest progress in neural network research and applications in diverse areas. This symposium encouraged open discussion and exchange of ideas. No doubt it promoted research in the fields of neural networks and applications.

Based on the rigorous peer reviews by the Program Committee members and reviewers, 97 high-quality papers from 32 countries and regions were selected for publication in the LNCS proceedings. These papers cover many topics of neural network-related research including intelligent control, neurodynamic analysis, bio-signal, bioinformatics and biomedical engineering, clustering, classification, forecasting, models, algorithms, cognitive computation, machine learning, optimization. In addition to the contributed papers, the ISNN 2018 technical program included three keynote and plenary speeches by renowned scholars: Jose Principe (University of Florida, USA), Leszek Rutkowski (Czestochowa University of Technology, Poland), and Dacheng Tao (University of Sydney, Australia).

Many organizations and volunteers made great contributions toward the success of this symposium. We would like to express our sincere gratitude to Belarusian State University, Dalian University of Technology, and City University of Hong Kong for their sponsorship, the IEEE Computational Intelligence Society, the International Neural Network Society, Polish Neural Network Society, and Russian Neural Network Society for their technical co-sponsorship. We would also like to sincerely thank all the committee members for all their great efforts in organizing the symposium. Special thanks to the Program Committee members and reviewers whose insightful reviews and timely feedback ensured the high quality of the accepted papers and the smooth flow of the symposium. We would also like to thank Springer for their cooperation in publishing the proceedings in the prestigious *Lecture Notes in Computer Science* series. Finally, we would like to thank all the speakers, authors, and participants for their support.

April 2018

Tingwen Huang
Jiancheng Lv
Changyin Sun
Alexander V. Tuzikov

Organization

General Chairs

Sergey V. Ablameyko   Belarusian State University, Minsk, Belarus
Jun Wang   City University of Hong Kong, Hong Kong, China

Advisory Chairs

Witali L. Dunin-Barkowski   Moscow Institute of Physics and Technology, Moscow, Russia
Robert Kozma   University of Memphis, Memphis, USA
Boris V. Kryzhanovsky   Center for Optical Neural Technologies, Scientific Research Institute for System Analysis, Russian Academy of Sciences, Moscow, Russia
Derong Liu   University of Illinois – Chicago, Chicago, USA
Leszek Rutkowski   Technical University of Czestochowa, Czestochowa, Poland

Steering Chairs

Haibo He   University of Rhode Island, Kingston, USA
Derong Liu   University of Illinois – Chicago, Chicago, USA
Jun Wang   City University of Hong Kong, Hong Kong, China

Organizing Chairs

Fengyu Cong   Dalian University of Technology, Dalian, China
Shuhong Guo   Dalian University of Technology, Dalian, China
Shunying Ji   Dalian University of Technology, Dalian, China
Dmitri Medvedev   Belarusian State University, Minsk, Belarus

Program Chairs

Tingwen Huang   Texas A&M University – Qatar, Doha, Qatar
Jiancheng Lv   Sichuan University, Chengdu, China
Changyin Sun   Southeast University, Nanjing, China
Alexander V. Tuzikov   United Institute of Informatics, National Academy of Sciences of Belarus, Minsk, Belarus

Special Sessions Chairs

Long Cheng	Institute of Automation, Chinese Academy of Sciences, Beijing, China
Shukai Duan	Southwest University, Chongqing, China
Valeri Gromak	Belarusian State University, Minsk, Belarus
Tieshan Li	Dalian Maritime University, Dalian, China

Publicity Chairs

Jinde Cao	Southeast University, Nanjing, China
Min Han	Dalian University of Technology, Dalian, China
Xiaofeng Liao	Southwest University, Chongqing, China
Jun Zhang	South China University of Technology, Guangzhou, China
Nian Zhang	University of District of Columbia, Washington, USA

Publications Chairs

Yuejiao Gong	South China University of Technology, Guangzhou, China
Xinyi Le	Shanghai Jiao Tong University, Shanghai, China
Sitian Qin	Harbin Institute of Technology – Weihai, Weihai, China
Zheng Yan	University Technology Sydney, Sydney, Australia

Registration Chairs

Shenshen Gu	Shanghai University, Shanghai, China
Chengan Guo	Dalian University of Technology, Dalian, China
Qingshan Liu	Southeast University, Nanjing, China
Ka Chun Wong	City University of Hong Kong, Hong Kong, China

Local Arrangements Chairs

Tatiana Dick	Belarusian State University, Minsk, Belarus
Yuri Metelsky	Belarusian State University, Minsk, Belarus
Dmitri Malinin	Belarusian State University, Minsk, Belarus

Secretary

Ying Qu	Dalian University of Technology, Dalian, China

Webmasters

Hangjun Che	City University of Hong Kong, Hong Kong, China
Man Fai Leung	City University of Hong Kong, Hong Kong, China

Program Committee

Zhaohui Cen
Jie Chen
Long Cheng
Zheru Chi
Fengyu Cong
Jose Alfredo Ferreira Costa
Ruxandra Liana Costea
Mingcong Deng
Jianchao Fan
Wai-Keung Fung
Jianping Gou
Zhishan Guo
Ping Guo
Zhenyuan Guo
Wangli He
Zhenan He
Xing He
Bill Howell
Jin Hu
Xiaolin Hu
Jinglu Hu
Junjian Huang
He Huang
Mahdi Jalili
Sungshin Kim
Chiman Kwan
Michael Li
Yongming Li
Zhen Li
Chuandong Li
Huaqing Li
Jie Lian
Hualou Liang
Qiuhua Lin

Ju Liu
Zhi-Wei Liu
Jianquan Lu
Wenlian Lu
Dmitry Malinin
Dmitri Medvedev
Nankun Mu
Seiichi Ozawa
Xi Peng
Dezhong Peng
Sitian Qin
Hong Qu
Qiankun Song
Norikazu Takahashi
Yang Tang
Ke Tang
Qing Tao
Christos Tjortjis
Feng Wan
Huiwei Wang
Dianhui Wang
Jin-Liang Wang
Guanghui Wen
Ailong Wu
Yong Xu
Shaofu Yang
Yin Yang
Wen Yu
Wenwu Yu
Chi Zhang
Lei Zhang
Jie Zhang
Xiaojun Zhou
Bo Zhou

Contents

Clustering, Classification, Learning, and Forecasting

Neurodynamics, Complex Systems, and Chaos

Multi-agent Systems and Game Theory

Signal, Image and Video Processing

Intelligent Control, Robotics and Hardware

Bio-signal, Bioinformatics and Biomedical Engineering

Cognition Computation

Fast Convergent Capsule Network
with Applications in MNIST

Xianli Zou[1], Shukai Duan[1(✉)], Lidan Wang[2], and Jin Zhang[3]

[1] College of Electronic and Information Engineering, Southwest University,
Chongqing 400415, China
duansk@swu.edu.cn
[2] National and Local Joint Engineering Laboratory of Intelligent Transmission
and Control Technology, Southwest University, Chongqing 400415, China
[3] Brain-Inspired Computing and Intelligent Control of Chongqing Key Lab,
Southwest University, Chongqing 400415, China

Abstract. Capsule network is a new neural network architecture, which avoids
the problem of location information loss due to the pool operation of the convolution neural network. The capsule network uses vector as input and output
and dynamic routing updates parameters, which has better effect than convolution neural network. In this paper, a new activation function is proposed for
the capsule network and the least weight loss is added to the loss function. The
experiment shows that the improved capsule network improves the convergence
speed of the network, increases the generalization ability, and makes the network more efficient.

Keywords: Capsule network · Activation function · Loss function
Generalization

1 Introduction

In recent years, deep learning has been widely used and has made great breakthrough in
Speech Recognition [1], Image Processing [2], natural language processing [3] and
other direction. Convolution neural network has become one of the most important
hotspots of deep learning [4].

Convolution neural network is a common deep learning architecture inspired by the
cognitive mechanism of biological natural vision. In the 2012 ILSVRC competition,
Hinton et al. [5] won the competition by using the AlexNet model built by CNN and
took second place with absolute superiority over that of SVM. Since then, CNN
occupied a dominant position in image recognition. Subsently, models such as GoogLeNet [6], VGGNet [7], ResNet [8] and DenseNet [9] were proposed continuously to
refresh the game records and exceeded the human recognition accuracy on the ImageNet dataset.

However, in the training process, the convolution neural network needs to add the
deformation of the image to adapt to some rotating or distorted images. In addition, the
convolution kernel of 5×5, 3×3 is often used in convolutional neural networks.
Convolutional layers always understand local features. When combined by the previous

multi-layer features into later complex and abstract features, we need to use pooling to reduce the size of output feature maps. The pooling generally adopts the maximum pooling and the average pooling.

Convolutional layers always understand local features. When combined by the previous multi-layer features into later complex and abstract features, a pooling operation is needed to reduce the size of the output feature map. The pooling generally adopts the maximum and the average pooling. But pooling will lose the location information in the image.

In response to this problem, Hinton et al. proposed a new network structure, capsule network (CapsNet), which is different from the convolution neural network in 2017. The capsule network removes the pooling layer in the convolutional neural network and will not discard the location information of the entities within the area. The neurons in the capsule network are expressed in the form of vector. Compared with the scalar used by the convolution neural network, it is closer to the abstract of the objective world. At the same time, the capsule network adopts the method of dynamic routing to selectively conduct activation from bottom to top, which can better realize the segmentation of highly overlapping images. The capsule network has achieved better results than the basic convolutional neural network in handwritten digit recognition.

This section introduces the excess of convolution to capsule, the benefits of the capsule network and the improvement of this article.

2   CapsNet Architecture [10]

The capsule network is actually improved on the basis of Convolutional neural network. The CapsNet architecture is composed of two convolutional layers and one fully connected layer. The architecture of the convolution part is shown in Fig. 1. The input is a 28×28 handwritten digital image. After convolution with a 9×9 convolution kernel and a stride of 1, 256 characteristic images with a size of 20×20 pixels are obtained. Then convolution with a convolution kernel of 9×9 and a stride of 2 gets 256 characteristic maps of 6×6 pixels. It can be seen as a combination of 32 feature maps of 6×6 pixels and 8 channels. Transform it into 1152 vectors with a length of 8. These vectors will be used as all inputs. That is to say, the first and second layers are traditional convolution layers, but only second layer of output can be transformed into vector form by reshape and then input to the third level (DigitCaps layer).

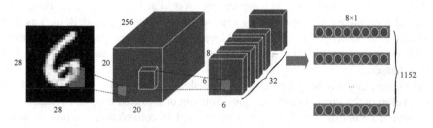

Fig. 1. CapsNet convolutional network structure

The full connection of capsule (DigitCaps) uses dynamic routing mechanism to update the parameters. Capsule full connection dynamic routing mechanism parameters update.

The network structure shown in Fig. 2. The input u_i is a multi-column vector, and output v_j is a multi-column vector. The transformation process is described as follows:

$$\hat{u}_{j|i} = W_{ij}u_i \tag{1}$$

$$c_{ij} = \frac{\exp\left(b_{ij}\right)}{\sum_k \exp(b_{ik})} \tag{2}$$

$$s_j = \sum_i c_{ij}\hat{u}_{j|i} \tag{3}$$

$$v_j = \frac{||s_j||^2}{1 + ||s_j||^2} \frac{s_j}{||s_j||} \tag{4}$$

As shown in Fig. 2, the spread and distribution of the entire hierarchy is divided into two parts. The first part is the linear combination of u_i and $\hat{u}_{j|i}$. The second part is the Routing process between $\hat{u}_{j|i}$ and s_j. The input vectors u_1, u_2, u_3, and u_4 are capsule units containing a set of neurons. They are multiplied by different weight W_{ij} respectively to get the prediction vector $\hat{u}_{j|i}$. The predictive vector $\hat{u}_{j|i}$ multiplied the coupling coefficient c_{ij} and passed into the next layer of capsule unit. The input s_j of the different capsule units in the next layer is the sum of the products of all the predicted vectors $\hat{u}_{j|i}$ passed into the previous layer and the coupling coefficient c_{ij}. The different input vector s_j obtains the output vector v_j of the latter layer through the non-linear function squashing Eq. (4). The coupling coefficient c_{ij} is iteratively updated and determined by the dynamic routing process. The routing process is the update process

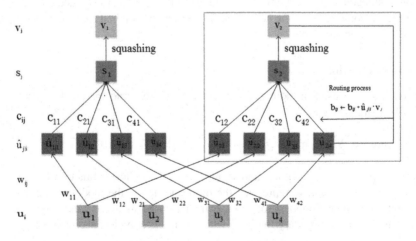

Fig. 2. Routing process (update process)

on the right of Fig. 2. Calculate the product of v_j and $\hat{u}_{j|i}$ and add it to the original b_{ij} to update b_{ij}, and then use softmax (b_{ij}) Eq. (2) to update c_{ij} to further correct the input s_j of the next layer. When the new v_j is output, the c_{ij} can be updated iteratively, so that the update can be recycled multiple times.

3   Improvement of the Network

3.1   Activation Function

The previous part $\frac{||s_j||^2}{1+||s_j||^2}$ is the scale of the input vector s_j, and the second part $\frac{s_j}{||s_j||}$ is the unit vector of the input vector s_j. This non-linear function not only retains the direction of the input vector, but also compresses the length of the input vector to the interval [0, 1). The nonlinear function can be regarded as a kind of compression and redistribution of the length of the vector. So it can also be seen as a way to get an output vector by activating an input vector. This article presents a better activation function, as shown in Eq. (5).

$$v_j = \left(1 - \exp^{-a||s_j||^b}\right) \frac{s_j}{||s_j||} \tag{5}$$

The activation function proposed in this paper is divided into two parts $1 - \exp^{-a||s_j||^b}$ and $\frac{s_j}{||s_j||}$. The first part can compress the length of the input vector s_j into the interval [0, 1), and the latter part is the unit vector of the input vector s_j. In the activation function, a and b both numbers over zero, and the actual needs can be changed as needed.

In this paper, the activation function has many advantages compared to the activation function in the original capsule network. Firstly, the use of exponential function is more conducive to the derivation. Second, there is a faster convergence rate. Thirdly, it is easier to converge than the activation function in the original capsule network, and can get higher accuracy.

3.2   Loss Function

The loss function used in the capsule network is divided into margin loss and recon loss. The margin loss is

$$\text{Mloss} = \sum_k T_k \max(0, m^+ - ||v_k||)^2 + \lambda(1 - T_k)\max(0, ||v_k|| - m^-)^2 \tag{6}$$

Where k represents the category, and T_k represents the indicator function (1 if class k exists, 0 otherwise), and v_k represents the output vector of the model prediction. m^+ represents the upper boundary of $||v_k||$, which is used to avoid false negative. m^- represents the lower boundary of $||v_k||$, which is used to avoid false positive.

The calculation process of reconfiguration error Recon is shown in Fig. 3. The output (v_j) of the model in Fig. 2 (10 vectors of length 16) is used as input. After two full connections, a vector with a length of 1024 is obtained. Here the activation function is ReLU. Then through the full connection layer of the activation function to Sigmoid, a vector with an output length of 784 can be get. At the same time, the input image of the model is 28×28 pixels, which is compressed into a vector of length 784 through Flatten. Two vectors are used to do SSE (sum of square error) and variance to get the reconfiguration error. Reconfiguration error can try to reconstruct the actual image represented by the category by predicting categories, which is conducive to adjusting parameters to make the model achieve higher accuracy.

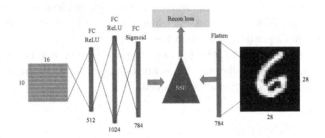

Fig. 3. Recon loss

Based on the two parts of the loss function Mloss (margin loss) and Rloss (Recon loss) in the capsule network, we add the weight attenuation function Wloss (weights loss). Wloss's calculation is as follows:

$$\text{Wloss} = \sum_w ||w||^2 \tag{7}$$

In Eq. (8), w denotes the weight matrix of the capsule network in the full connection of the capsule version in Fig. 2. Wloss can try to minimize the weight during training so that the network prefers to learn smaller weights and reduce overfitting. In summary, the loss function used in this paper is shown in Eq. (8).

$$\text{loss} = \alpha\text{Mloss} + \beta\text{Rloss} + (1 - \alpha - \beta)\text{Wloss} \tag{8}$$

The loss function contains three parts: Mloss (margin loss), Rloss (Recon loss) and Wloss (weights loss). Both α and β are numbers between [0, 1], and $0 < \alpha + \beta \leq 1$. The proportion of different parts of the loss function can be adjusted by adjusting the coefficients α and β.

4 Experiment and Effect

All experiments in this article are completed in the experimental environment shown in Table 1.

Table 1. Experimental environment

Operating system	CPU	RAM	Graphics-card	Programming language	Frame
Ubuntu 14.04	i7-7700 K	16 GB	GTX 1080 8 GB	Python 2.7	Keras

In this paper, the MNIST handwritten digit set is used for training and testing. The MNIST dataset contains 60000 training samples and 10000 test samples. The optimization algorithm uses Adam [11], and the initialization learning rate is 0.0005.

In this paper, the activation function squashing of the capsule network is changed to the activation function exping (set the parameters as a = 10 and b = 1), and the improved capsule network is identified on the handwritten digital data set MNIST. Under the same conditions such as optimization algorithm and learning rate, 20 epochs were trained on the MNIST dataset by using the capsule network with activation function exping and squashing activation function respectively.

As shown in Fig. 4, the activation function exponential proposed in this paper has a faster convergence rate than the activation function squashing. In the case of fewer training times, higher accuracy can be obtained.

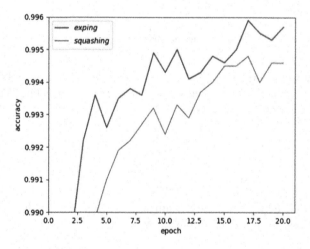

Fig. 4. Test accuracy distribution of different activation functions at epoch <20

In this paper, when other parameters are the same, we use a capsule network with the activation function squashing, activation function exping (Eq. (5), parameters set to a = 10, b = 1) and activation function exping + Wloss (Eq. (8), parameter set to $\alpha = 0.5$, $\beta = 0.4$) respectively.

Figure 5 shows the accuracy of recognition in handwritten digit set MNIST. The green curve represents the recognition accuracy of the capsule network using the squashing function on the MNIST test set, with an accuracy of 99.71%. The purple curve represents the recognition accuracy of the capsule network using the exping function on the MNIST test set, with an accuracy of 99.72%. The red curve represents the recognition accuracy of the capsule network using exping activation function and the proposed loss function Wloss on the MNIST test set, with an accuracy of 99.75%.

It can be seen from Fig. 5 that the exponential activation function Eq. (5) proposed in this paper can converge faster and obtain higher accuracy. In the loss function, adding Wloss to minimize the loss of weight can increase the generalization ability of the model and improve the recognition accuracy.

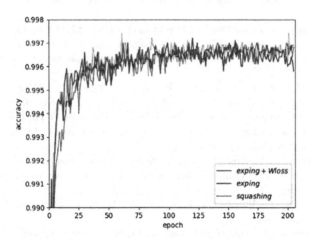

Fig. 5. The recognition accuracy of MNIST test sets by different methods (Color figure online)

5 Conclusions

In this paper, a new activation function is proposed for the capsule network, which improves the convergence speed and accuracy of the network training, and has a great use value. At the same time, properly adding the weight minimization loss in the loss function can increase the generalization ability of the capsule network model. Exceeds all current recognition accuracy.

Acknowledgements. This work was supported by the National Natural Science Foundation of China under Grant 61571372, 61672436, 61372139 and 61601376, the Natural Science Foundation of Chongqing under Grant cstc2017jcyjBX0050, and the Fundamental Research Funds for the Central Universities under Grant XDJK2017A005 and XDJK2016A001.

References

1. Zhang, P., Ma, X.H., Ding, S.X.: Audio source separation from a monaural mixture using convolutional neural network in the time domain. In: Cong, F., Leung, A., Wei, Q. (eds.) ISNN 2017. LNCS, vol. 10262, pp. 388–395. Springer, Cham (2017). https://doi.org/10.1007/978-3-319-59081-3_46

2. Jia, S., Liu, H., Sun, F.: Aerial scene classification with convolutional neural networks. In: Hu, X., Xia, Y., Zhang, Y., Zhao, D. (eds.) ISNN 2015. LNCS, vol. 9377, pp. 258–265. Springer, Cham (2015). https://doi.org/10.1007/978-3-319-25393-0_29

3. Kim, Y.: Convolutional Neural Networks for Sentence Classification. University of Waterloo (2015)

4. LeCun, Y., Bengio, Y., Hinton, G.: Deep learning. Nature **521**(7553), 436–444 (2015)

5. Krizhevsky, A., Sutskever, I., Hinton, G.E.: ImageNet classification with deep convolutional neural networks. In: 26th Annual Conference on Neural Information Processing Systems (NIPS), pp. 1097–1105 (2012)

6. Szegedy, C., Liu, W., Jia, Y., Sermanet, P., Reed, S., Anguelov, D., Erhan, D., Vanhoucke, V., Rabinovich, A.: Going deeper with convolutions. In: Proceedings of the IEEE Conference on Computer Vision and Pattern Recognition (CVPR), pp. 1–9 (2015)

7. Simonyan, K., Zisserman, A.: Very deep convolutional networks for large-scale image recognition. arXiv (2014)

8. He, K.M., Zhang, X.Y., Ren, S.Q., Sun, J.: Deep residual learning for image recognition. In: Proceedings of the IEEE Conference on Computer Vision and Pattern Recognition (CVPR), pp. 770–778 (2016)

9. Huang, G., Liu, Z., Weinberger, K.Q., Maaten, L.: Densely connected convolutional networks. arXiv (2016)

10. Sabour, S., Frosst, N., Hinton, G.: Dynamic routing between capsules. In: Advances in Neural Information Processing Systems (NIPS), pp. 3859–3869 (2017)

11. Kingma, D.P., Ba, J.: Adam: a method for stochastic optimization. arXiv (2014)

A Neurodynamic Approach to Multiobjective Linear Programming

Man-Fai Leung[1,2(✉)] and Jun Wang[1,2]

[1] Department of Computer Science, City University of Hong Kong,
Kowloon Tong, Hong Kong
manfleung7-c@my.cityu.edu.hk, jwang.cs@cityu.edu.hk
[2] City University of Hong Kong, Shenzhen, Guangdong, China

Abstract. In this paper, a neurodynamic approach is proposed for solving multiobjective linear programming problems. Multiple objectives are firstly scalarized using a weighted sum technique. Recurrent neural networks are then adopted to generate Pareto-optimal solutions. To diversify the solutions along Pareto fronts, particle swarm optimization is used to optimize the weights of the scalarized objective function. Numerical results are presented to illustrate the effectiveness of the proposed approaches.

Keywords: Multiobjective optimization · Linear programming
Neurodynamic optimization · Recurrent neural network

1 Introduction

Multiobjective optimization (MOP) involves optimizing functions with more than one objective simultaneously, under a set of constraints. When the objective functions and constraints of a MOP problem are linear, it is regarded as a multiobjective linear programming (MOLP) problem. MOLP is an important research topic which has been studied extensively and applied in different fields such as science and engineering (see [1,2], and references therein).

A Pareto-optimal solution is the one that none of the objective functions can be improved without sacrificing others. By solving an MOLP problem, a set of Pareto-optimal solutions is obtained. Over the past few decades, numerous proposals have been made for MOLP problems (e.g., see [1], and references therein). Scalarization is one of the most popular methods for MOLP problems. It transforms the MOLP problem into scalarized single-objective optimization problems. Then the problem is solved with different weights and the solutions constitute a Pareto front.

This work was supported in part by the Research Grants Council of the Hong Kong Special Administrative Region of China, under Grants 14207614 and 11208517, and in part by the National Natural Science Foundation of China under grant 61673330.

© Springer International Publishing AG, part of Springer Nature 2018
T. Huang et al. (Eds.): ISNN 2018, LNCS 10878, pp. 11–18, 2018.
https://doi.org/10.1007/978-3-319-92537-0_2

Over the years, many efforts have been made on neurodynamic approaches to single-objective optimization. It is a promising brain-like approach based on neural networks and widely applied to various areas. Early research on recurrent neural networks can be traced back to Hopfield and Tank's pioneer work [3]. After that, various neural network models were proposed to solve different types of single-objective optimization problems (e.g., linear programming problems [4,6], constrained optimization problems [5], pseudoconvex optimization problems [7], global optimization problems [9] and so on).

Recently, attention has been drawn to MOP using neurodynamic optimization: a neurodynamic approach was proposed to multiobjective distributed optimization [10]; a collaborative neurodynamic approach was proposed to MOP [11].

Particle swarm optimization (PSO) [12] is an efficient technique among the metaheuristics-based algorithms. It simulates the behaviors of swarms and it has the property of fast convergence. Due to this reason, different variants were proposed and experiments showed that they perform well in global optimization (see [13], and references therein).

Based on the above discussions, a PSO-based neurodynamic approach is presented to solve multiobjective linear programming problems. A weighted sum technique is adopted to scarlarize a multiobjective problem into a set of single-objective problems. Then multiple recurrent neural networks are employed to seek for Pareto-optimal solutions. Besides, a weight optimization approach is presented to diversify the solutions by maximizing the hypervolume metric.

2   Preliminaries

2.1   Multiobjective Linear Programming

An MOLP problem is written as follows:

$$\min c_i^T x, \quad i = 1, 2, \dots, k,$$
$$\text{subject to } x \in X = \left\{ x \in \mathbb{R}^n \mid Ax \geq b, x \geq 0 \right\} \tag{1}$$

or equivalently

$$\min Cx$$
$$\text{subject to } x \in X \tag{2}$$

where C is a $k \times n$ matrix with $k \geq 2$; A is an $m \times n$ constraint matrix; $b \in \mathbb{R}^n$.

A solution $x^* \in X$ is called a Pareto-optimal solution if there does not exist $x \in X$ such that $Cx \leq Cx^*$ and $Cx \neq Cx^*$. All the Pareto-optimal solutions of an MOLP problem are called Pareto-optimal set (PS).

Weighted sum scalarization [1] is a popular technique to convert an MOLP problem to scalarized single-objective optimization problems. Let $W = \{ w \in \mathbb{R}^k \mid w \geq 0, \sum_{i=1}^{k} w_i = 1 \}$. By means of weighted sum, problem (2) is reformulated as follows:

$$\min w^T Cx$$
$$\text{subject to } x \in X = \left\{ x \in \mathbb{R}^n \mid Ax \geq b, x \geq 0 \right\} \tag{3}$$

The set of Pareto-optimal solutions of the MOLP problem can be characterized as optimal solutions of the problem with a convex combination of objectives c_i, $i = 1, 2, \ldots, k$ and a proof can be found in [15].

2.2   Performance Measures

Hypervolume (HV) [14] is one of the most popular indicators used in literature. It is employed to assess the performance of MOP algorithms by considering the precision of the obtained solutions as well as their distribution over the objective space. Let $r = (r_1, ..., r_m)^T$ be a reference vector dominated by the PS. The HV value of a solution set (denoted as $\mathcal{SS}$) is the non-overlapped region of all the hypercubes formed by r and a member s in $\mathcal{SS}$. The indicator is defined as:

$$\text{HV}(\mathcal{SS}, r) = L\left(\bigcup_{s \in \mathcal{A}} [f_1(s), r_1] \times \ldots \times [f_m(s), r_m] \right) \tag{4}$$

where L is the Lebesgue measure. A larger of the value indicates the set of obtained solutions has higher precision and is more well-distributed.

2.3   Neurodynamic Optimization

Consider a linear programming problem (single-objective):

$$\begin{aligned} \min \ & c^T x \\ \text{subject to } \ & x \in X = \left\{ x \in \mathbb{R}^n | Ax \geq b, x \geq 0 \right\} \end{aligned} \tag{5}$$

A one-layer recurrent neural network (RNN) for solving (5) is presented in [8]:

$$\epsilon \frac{dx}{dt} = -\sigma A^T g_{[0,1]}(Ax - b) - c \tag{6}$$

where ϵ is a positive time constant; σ is a nonnegative gain parameter; $g_{[0,1]}(x)$ is a piecewise linear activation function. It is proved that the RNN is globally convergent to the optimum when σ is larger than a derived lower bound [8].

2.4   Particle Swarm Optimization

PSO simulates fish schooling for solving optimization problems. Particles move towards global optimum of an optimization problem iteratively. Each particle moves to the target based on its past experience (pbest) and a leader among the group (gbest). After reaching the termination condition, the gbest leader is the solution of the optimization problem.

Let $x^i = (x_1^i, x_2^i, \ldots, x_n^i)^T$ and $v^i = (v_1^i, v_2^i, \ldots, v_n^i)^T$ be the position and velocity of ith particle respectively, where n is the dimension of the particle. The velocity and position of the particle are updated as follows:

$$\begin{cases} v^i \leftarrow \psi v^i + c_1 r_1 (\tilde{x}^i - x^i) + c_2 r_2 (\hat{x} - x^i) \\ x^i \leftarrow x^i + v^i \end{cases} \tag{7}$$

where ψ is inertia weight; c_1 and c_2 are the learning factors; r_1 and r_2 are two random variables ranging from 0.0 to 1.0; $\tilde{x}^i$ is the pbest of the ith particle; $\hat{x}$ is the gbest. A larger value of ψ encourages global search ability, while a smaller value favours local search ability of the algorithm.

3   The Neurodynamic Approach

There are two ultimate goals for solving MOLP problems. The first one is to generate a set of Pareto-optimal solutions and the second one is to diversify the solutions. To achieve the goals, two approaches are proposed: neurodynamic optimization is for the first goal and a particle swarm optimization approach is for the second goal.

As mentioned above, an MOLP problem is scalarized to a single-objective optimization problem by using weighted sum. A group of RNN from different initial states are used to generate a set of Pareto-optimal solutions. Based on the neural network model (6), the ith RNN is described as follows:

$$\epsilon \frac{dx^i}{dt} = -\sigma A^T g_{[0,1]}(Ax^i - b) - C^T w \tag{8}$$

The Pareto-optimal solutions depends on the weights of the scalarized objective function. As a set of uniformly distributed weights may not lead to a set of well-distributed Pareto-optimal solutions in objective space, a PSO-based weight optimization approach is proposed to diversify the solutions. Specifically, the PSO algorithm is used to update the weights by optimizing the HV metric stated in (4):

$$\begin{cases} \varphi^i \leftarrow \omega \varphi^i + c_1 r_1(\tilde{w}^i - w^i) + c_2 r_2(\hat{w}^j - w^i) \\ w^i \leftarrow w^i + \varphi^i \end{cases} \tag{9}$$

where φ^i is the velocity; $\tilde{w}^i$ is the personal best weight vector; $\hat{w}^j$ is the global best and the index j is generated in the following way: before updating w^i, it selects the nearest weight vector from the global best group. The weight optimization approach terminates until the HV value of the global best group is larger than a threshold. Figure 1 shows the interaction between the neurodynamic and particle swarm optimization. By using the neurodynamic and particle swarm optimization, both the Pareto optimality and solution diversity can be achieved.

4   Illustrative Examples

This section presents three examples to illustrative the PSO-based neurodynamic approach for solving MOLP problems. Both c_1 and c_2 are set to 2 and the number of RNNs is set to 9. As a comparison, a set of Pareto-optimal solutions generated

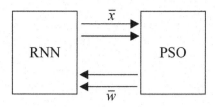

Fig. 1. Interaction between the neurodynamic optimization and particle swarm optimization.

by the neural network model (8) with fixed weights is also provided, where the weights are uniformly generated using the simplex-lattice design [16] as follows:

$$W = \begin{bmatrix} 0.000 \ 0.125 \ 0.250 \ 0.375 \ 0.500 \ 0.625 \ 0.750 \ 0.875 \ 1.000 \\ 1.000 \ 0.875 \ 0.750 \ 0.625 \ 0.500 \ 0.375 \ 0.250 \ 0.125 \ 0.000 \end{bmatrix}.$$

Example 1: Consider the following bi-objective MOLP problem with two decision variables [1]:

$$\max \ x_1, \ \max \ x_2$$
$$\text{subject to } 5x_1 + 9x_2 \geq 45, \ 2x_1 + x_2 \leq 18, \ x_1 + x_2 \leq 10, \ x_1, x_2 \geq 0. \tag{10}$$

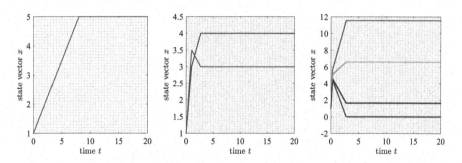

Fig. 2. Transient behaviors of state vector x in Example 1 (left), Example 2 (middle) and Example 3 (right) with weight vectors $[0.5, 0.5]^T$, $[0.4, 0.6]^T$ and $[0.4, 0.6]^T$ respectively.

The left subplot of Fig. 2 shows the convergence of state vector x of the neurodynamic approach to $[5.00, 5.00]^T$ in the decision space corresponding to $[5.00, 5.00]^T$ in the objective space in Example 1, where the weight vector is $[0.5, 0.5]^T$. Figure 3 shows the generated solutions with weight optimization (left), and fixed weights (right).

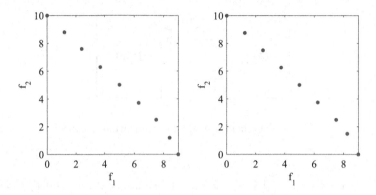

Fig. 3. Pareto-optimal solutions in objective space obtained by the proposed approach with weight optimization (left), and fixed weights (right) in Example 1.

Example 2: Consider the following bi-objective MOLP problem with two decision variables [17]:

$$\max \ 3x_1 + x_2, \ \max \ x_1 + 4x_2$$
$$\text{subject to} \ -x_1 + x_2 \le 2, \ x_1 + 2x_2 \le 10, \ x_1 + x_2 \le 7, \ x_1, x_2 \ge 0. \tag{11}$$

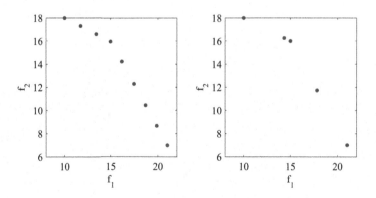

Fig. 4. Pareto-optimal solutions in objective space obtained by the proposed approach with weight optimization (left), and fixed weights (right) in Example 2.

The middle subplot of Fig. 2 shows the convergence of state vector x of the neurodynamic approach to $[3.99, 2.99]^T$ in the decision space corresponding to $[14.98, 15.97]^T$ in the objective space in Example 2, where the weight vector is $[0.4, 0.6]^T$. Figure 4 shows the generated solutions with weight optimization (left), and fixed weights (right).

Example 3: Consider the following bi-objective MOLP problem with four decision variables [17]:

$$\max \; -6x_1 + 30x_2 + 6x_3 + 12x_4, \; \max \; 30x_1 + 10x_2 + 20x_3 + 10x_4$$
$$\text{subject to } 2x_1 + x_2 + 4x_3 + 3x_4 \leq 60, \; 3x_1 + 4x_2 + x_3 + 2x_4 \leq 60 \quad (12)$$
$$x_1 + 2x_2 + 3x_3 + 4x_4 \leq 50, \; 4x_1 + 3x_2 + 2x_3 + x_4 \leq 50$$
$$x_1, x_2, x_3, x_4 \geq 0.$$

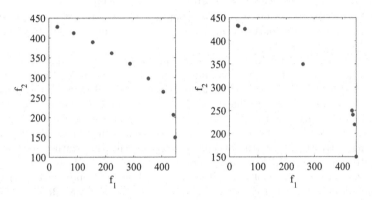

Fig. 5. Pareto-optimal solutions in objective space obtained by the proposed approach with weight optimization (left), and fixed weights (right) in Example 3.

The right subplot of Fig. 2 shows the convergence of state vector x of the neurodynamic approach to $[0.01, 11.55, 6.60, 1.65]^T$ in the decision space corresponding to $[405.84, 264.30]^T$ in the objective space in Example 3, where the weight vector is $[0.4, 0.6]^T$. Figure 5 shows the generated solutions with weight optimization (left), and fixed weights (right).

The results show that the proposed neurodynamic with weight optimization can well characterize the efficient frontiers of the MOLP problems but the frontiers cannot be well characterized with fixed weights as duplicated Pareto-optimal solutions are generated. As a result, the Pareto-optimal solutions computed by the proposed approach with weight optimization are more evenly distributed than that with fixed weights.

5   Conclusions

In this paper, a PSO-based neurodynamic approach is proposed for MOLP. An MOLP problem is scalarized to a single-objective optimization problem by means of weighted sum. Multiple neural networks are applied to generate Pareto-optimal solutions and PSO is adopted to diversify the Pareto-optimal solutions by optimizing the weights of the scalarized objective function. Further investigations focus on PSO-based neurodynamic approaches to multiobjective nonlinear optimization [11], and applications in business intelligence.

References

1. Steuer, R.E.: Multiple Criteria Optimization: Theory, Computation, and Applications. Wiley, Hoboken (1986)
2. Ogryczak, W.: Multiple criteria linear programming model for portfolio selection. Ann. Oper. Res. **97**(1), 143–162 (2000)
3. Hopfield, J.J., Tank, D.W.: Computing with neural circuits: a model. Science **233**(4764), 625–633 (1986)
4. Wang, J.: Analysis and design of a recurrent neural network for linear programming. IEEE Trans. Circuit Syst. I. **40**(9), 613–618 (1993)
5. Xia, Y., Leung, H., Wang, J.: A projection neural network and its application to constrained optimization problems. IEEE Trans. Circuits Syst. I. **49**(4), 447–458 (2002)
6. Liu, Q., Wang, J.: A one-layer recurrent neural network with a discontinuous activation function for linear programming. Neural Comput. **20**(5), 1366–1383 (2008)
7. Guo, Z., Liu, Q., Wang, J.: A one-layer recurrent neural network for pseudoconvex optimization subject to linear equality constraints. IEEE Trans. Neural Netw. **22**(12), 1892–1900 (2011)
8. Liu, Q., Wang, J.: Finite-time convergent recurrent neural network with a hard-limiting activation function for constrained optimization with piecewise-linear objective functions. IEEE Trans. Neural Netw. **22**(4), 601–613 (2011)
9. Yan, Z., Fan, J., Wang, J.: A collective neurodynamic approach to constrained global optimization. IEEE Trans. Neural Netw. Learn. Syst. **28**(5), 1206–1215 (2017)
10. Yang, S., Liu, Q., Wang, J.: A collaborative neurodynamic approach to multiple-objective distributed optimization. IEEE Trans. Neural Netw. Learn. Syst. **29**(4), 981–992 (2018). https://doi.org/10.1109/TNNLS.2017.2652478
11. Leung, M.F., Wang, J.: A collaborative neurodynamic approach to multiobjective optimization. IEEE Trans. Neural Netw. Learn. Syst. https://doi.org/10.1109/TNNLS.2018.2806481
12. Eberhart, R., Kennedy, J.: A new optimizer using particle swarm theory. In: Proceedings of the 1995 IEEE International Symposium on Micro Machine and Human Science, pp. 39–43 (1995)
13. Del Valle, Y., Venayagamoorthy, G.K., Mohagheghi, S., Hernandez, J.C., Harley, R.G.: Particle swarm optimization: basic concepts, variants and applications in power systems. IEEE Trans. Evol. Comput. **12**(2), 171–195 (2008)
14. Bader, J., Zitzler, E.: HypE: an algorithm for fast hypervolume-based many-objective optimization. Evol. Comput. **19**(1), 45–76 (2011)
15. Geoffrion, A.M.: Proper efficiency and the theory of vector maximization. J. Math. Anal. Appl. **22**(3), 618–630 (1968)
16. Das, I., Dennis, J.E.: Normal-boundary intersection: a new method for generating the Pareto surface in nonlinear multicriteria optimization problems. SIAM J. Optimiz. **8**(3), 631–657 (1998)
17. Antunes, C.H., Alves, M.J., Climaco, J.: Multiobjective Linear and Integer Programming. Springer, Cham (2016). https://doi.org/10.1007/978-3-319-28746-1

Neural Network Model of Unconscious

Alexandr A. Ezhov[(✉)]

Troitsk Institute for Innovation and Fusion Research, 108840 Troitsk, Moscow,
Russia
ezhov@triniti.ru

Abstract. We describe neural network model of unconscious processing as it
defined by the symmetrical logic of Matte Blanco. The model system consists of
hierarchy of ensembles of Hopfield network representing definite classes of
objects. Patterns in each of a network are considered as in some sense identical
representatives of given class. These networks generate their self-reproducible
descendants which can exchange patterns with each other and generate
self-reproducible networks of a higher level representing wider classes of
objects. We also give some examples of applications of this model.

Keywords: Unconscious · Symmetrical logic
Self-reproducible neural networks

1 Introduction

Unconscious now is one of the central theme in cognitive science. Historically in
psychoanalysis it is considered as related to *primary* process (in contrast to *secondary*
conscious process) [1]. There is a big amount of papers devoted to the role of
unconscious in decision making. From the dual system point of view [2] unconscious
can be related to the operation of so called System 1. This fast energy free system [3] or
mode of operation is also in contrast to *conscious* lazy System 2 and is connected to
emotions. Unconscious is also in the center of the studies of creativity. Its role in the
incubation period which follows after hard conscious attempts to solve difficult
problem and finished by insight (*Aha*-process) and relation of these processes with
neural activity including brain oscillations is extensively studied [4].

There are many studies which connect unconscious with emotions. Emotions are
considered as unconscious itself or as a measure of proportion between unconscious
and conscious part of mind operation. On the other hand, emotions can control the
proportion between conscious and unconscious thinking, e.g., in decision making.
Belavkin [5] demonstrated that this control process can be interpreted using simulated
annealing analogy. This analogy can be used however with different interpretation
which can also indicate not only the features of mode of System 1 [2] operation but also
its connection with the possible brain structure. Indeed in [6] we showed that *symmetrical algorithm is connected with model right brain dominant agent*. This indicated
that this part of brain can be related to the symmetrical timeless and spaceless logic of
unconscious described by Matte Blanco [7]. This is in the contrast to the approach [5]
which considers unconscious as type of operation at high temperatures where real

© Springer International Publishing AG, part of Springer Nature 2018
T. Huang et al. (Eds.): ISNN 2018, LNCS 10878, pp. 19–28, 2018.
https://doi.org/10.1007/978-3-319-92537-0_3

asymmetry governs agent's rule of behavior and where left brain dominant agents are time confident. Note that the last interpretation contradicts to the well known phenomena when problem solving starts with conscious attempts and then follows by unconscious search for the solutions [8].

The relation of unconscious with brain laterality e.g. with right brain hemisphere is discussed e.g. in [9]. There are also evidences that unconscious processes are connected with the operation of so called brain *default mode network* [10] and also decision making unconscious processes is accompanied with holding the activity of *right dorsolateral prefrontal cortex and left intermediate visual cortex* activated preliminary during the encoding of complex decision information [11]. Note, however, that the brain structures involved in unconscious emotion information connected with unconscious processes are not known yet. Sometimes they can be roughly attributed to subcortical structures, while consciousness ones to neocortex. But it is known that as unconscious is related to some neocortex regions the consciousness is related to subcortical ones such as e.g. hippocampus [12]. Nevertheless, the connection of emotions and unconscious to right brain structures seems to be rather plausible.

Earlier we have considered two types of agents in our model of unequal society [6] – left and right dominant ones – and are interested in elaboration of this model, in particular to introduce some neural model of unconscious or emotional processing in it. In spite of this goal it is interesting to formulate some simple neural network model of unconscious which uses symmetrical logic formulated by Matte Blanco [7]. In this paper we propose such a model which uses a set of Hopfield networks [13] able to produce their replicated descendants which can exchange information with each other producing sets of identical networks which reflects the ability of unconscious to create a hierarchical structure of homogeneous classes of identical objects.

In the second section we briefly outline Matte Blanco model of unconscious. In the third section we observe the earlier proposed interpretation of Hopfield net memorized and also stable states. In the fourth section we remind the model of self-reproduced Hopfield neural networks able to replicate their interconnection structure [14, 15]. In the fifth section we outline neural model of unconscious processing and in the last one we remind briefly one biological analog of the model.

2   Matte Blanco Theory of Unconscious

In the theory developed by Chilean psychologist Matte Blanco it is suggested that human mind uses two logics – conscious and unconscious ones [7]. The first ordinary (Aristotelian) logic of conscious has been realized with artificial neural networks by McCulloch and Pitts [16]. The second logic of (unrepressed) unconscious has main features described by Freud [17] – the presence of contradictions and the absence of negation and also of the space and time ordering [7]. Matte Blanco supposed that these two logics are *asymmetrical* and *symmetrical* correspondingly.

According to ordinary logic the relation "*Neuron is a part of a network*" is asymmetrical, because its reverse form "*Network is a part of a neuron*" seems to be wrong. Of course, there are also symmetrical relations in ordinary logic such as "*Warren McCulloch is the co-author of Walter Pitts*", but in general their statements have some order and are asymmetrical ones. The second logic considers all relations of ordinary logic as reversible. In fact, it symmetrizes them. For example, *"all dragons are dangerous entities"* is transformed by unconscious to *"all dangerous entities are dragons"* and both of them are considered true. This permits to explain why in dreams we can see dangerous man in the form of dragon. According to Matte Blanco this is not a consequence of associations as Freud asserted but the result of inference of symmetrical (and also asymmetrical) logic. Note, that the action of symmetrical logic can be rather fruitful. For example, the statement *"Network is a part of a neuron"* is not nonsense if we remind that as every cell it contains cytoskeleton made on microtubule which can be considered as interconnected network consisting of tubulin dimers [18, 19]. However, this *Principle of Symmetry* is only the second one of two main Matte Blanco principles of the logic of unconscious.

The first principle of this logic is the *Principle of Generalization*. It declares that unconscious treats every object as belonging to some set. The last one is the element of other set, etc. Hence Matte Blanco theory of unconscious uses not only notions of logic but also of set theory, especially the theory of infinite sets. According to him human mind uses two logics – asymmetrical and symmetrical or bi-logic at the same time.

In bi-logic Matte Blanco actually formalizes Freud view on unconscious [17], but not in suppressed form. He suggests that both conscious and unconscious are present in human awaked states and their proportion can determine the emotional part of thinking. The problem of emotion analysis of texts is widely explored. We can refer to the works of Murtagh [20] and Khrennikov [21] who used the ultrametric analysis adequate to unconscious studies [22].

Here we will propose a neural network model of Matte Blanco theory of unconscious treating it as possible perspective application of neural networks for problem solving. In the next section we consider the basic element of this model – the Hopfield network with specially interpreted stable states and consequently special interpreted functioning.

3   Hopfield Model: Attractors Interpretation

Hopfield model of content-addressable memory has been comprehensively studied for many years. One of review of studies of memory capacity of Hopfield network has been made by Sulheria and Zhang [23]. The authors, however, noted that approach to attractors interpretations used in [24] "may also affect change in the scenario for capacity research". In fact, this approach which eliminated division of memory on true and spurious has been presented by us earlier, e.g. in [25]. It considers *all networks attractors* as prototype versions of *single pattern* which Hopfield network can store properly. This conclusion follows from probabilistic interpretation of network state energy. Let us briefly outline this approach as it was presented in [26].

Consider the situation in which single pattern $\boldsymbol{m} = (m_1, \ldots, m_N)$, where $m_i \in \{\pm 1\}$ is memorized in a N-neurons Hopfield network with Hebbian interconnections $w_{j \to i} = m_i m_j$, $w_{j \to i} = w_{i \to j}$, $w_{i \to i} = 0$. Pattern $\boldsymbol{m}$ (and its mirror negative) will be only stable state of such a network. Moreover, in this state all synaptic connections will be non-frustrated, i.e. for all of them

$$w_{j \to i}(\pm m_i)(\pm m_j) = (m_i)^2 (m_j)^2 > 0. \tag{1}$$

Assume that *Alice* (a metavariable of information theory) want to send to *Bob* a *message* coded by the vector $\boldsymbol{m}$. Before doing this, she creates her own Hopfield network Net$_A$, and memorizes this message in it. Surely, the probability to find frustrated bond in the net Net$_A$, which is in the state $\boldsymbol{m}$, equals to zero. Now *Alice* send her message to *Bob* but because she knows, that transmission channel is noisy, she repeats this procedure P times. *Bob* after receiving the corrupted messages $\boldsymbol{x}^{(\alpha)}$, $\alpha = 1, \ldots, P$ can only estimate *a probability* of correlation (+) or anticorrelations (−) of neurons i and j bipolar states in the *Alice* message $\boldsymbol{m}$:

$$p_{ij}^{\pm} = (2P)^{-1} \sum_{\alpha=1}^{P} (1 \pm x_i^{(\alpha)} x_j^{(\alpha)}), \quad p_{ij}^{+} + p_{ij}^{-} = 1 \tag{2}$$

Then Hebbian interconnections in the network Net$_B$

$$w_{j \to i} = (P)^{-1} \sum_{\alpha=1}^{P} x_i^{(\alpha)} x_j^{(\alpha)}, \quad w_{j \to i} = w_{i \to j}, \quad i \neq j, \quad w_{i \to i} = 0 \tag{3}$$

can be expressed in terms of these probabilities as

$$w_{j \to i} = p_{ij}^{+} - p_{ij}^{-} \quad w_{j \to i} = w_{i \to j}, \quad i \neq j, \quad w_{i \to i} = 0 \tag{4}$$

and an energy of arbitrary state $\boldsymbol{x}$ in this network takes the form

$$E = -1/2 \sum_{ij} w_{j \to i} x_i x_j = -1/2 \sum_{ij} (p_{ij}^{+} - p_{ij}^{-}) x_i x_j$$

$$= -1/2 \sum_{\substack{i,j \neq i \\ x_i x_j = 1}} (1 - 2p_{ij}^{-}) + 1/2 \sum_{\substack{i,j \neq i \\ x_i x_j = -1}} (2p_{ij}^{+} - 1) = -\frac{N(N-1)}{2} + \left(\sum_{\substack{i,j \neq i \\ x_i x_j = 1}} p_{ij}^{-} + \sum_{\substack{i,j \neq i \\ x_i x_j = -1}} p_{ij}^{+} \right). \tag{5}$$

Taking into account that *Bob* estimation of the probability to find frustrated bond in the *Alice* network placed in this state equals to

$$p^f = \frac{2}{N(N-1)} \left(\sum_{\substack{i,j \neq i \\ x_i x_j = 1}} p_{ij}^{-} + \sum_{\substack{i,j \neq i \\ x_i x_j = -1}} p_{ij}^{+} \right) \tag{6}$$

the final form of energy takes the form:

$$E = \frac{N(N-1)}{2} (p^f - 1) \tag{7}$$

If state x in *Bob*'s network is stable, then the energy takes its local minimal value. This means that in this state *Bob* can also estimate that the probability to find a random frustrated bond in *Alice*'s network put in the same state x, is locally *minimal*. Because this probability really equals to zero for the correct message m, *Bob* can conclude that any stable state of his network gives him the locally most plausible version of *Alice*'s correct message. It also means that all stable states in Hopfield network with Hebbian bonds can be treated in the same manner without dividing them into any subsets (as *memorized* patterns and *spurious* memories). This means that all network states are *in some sense equivalent* (though their energies are different) and can be named *message* or *prototype versions*. Moreover, all patterns stored in a network gives equal (i.e. symmetrical) input in Hebbian matrix of connections. Such *imaginable identification* of all stored patterns and also of all network's attractors is not too artificial. Just placing obviously different patterns *in the same network* implicitly suggests that *they are preliminary identified in definite sense*. This idea which clearly is in parallel with Matte Blanco interpretation of equivalence of class members in symmetrical logic of unconscious has been used in our further considerations.

4 Self-reproducible Neural Networks

A simple model of self-reproducible neural networks has been introduced in [14, 15].

Two decades later the idea of the existence of replicators in brain has been extensively discussed (see review [27]) from the point of view of selectionist approach to brain functioning. It is possible to present many arguments for existence of replicators in a brain. We prefer to guess that as a brain is a complex system its creative activity indicates that it operates at the edge of chaos. This view has been supported by experimental studies [28]. But it is just this functioning zone where replicators ordinary arise [29].

Our model implies the existence of the mechanism of synchronously changing threshold of all neurons in Hopfield networks [14]. It is suggested that ancestor Hopfield network has arbitrary matrix of interconnections and corresponding set of attractors for zero neuron thresholds. This network is placed in a network ensemble (e.g., one or two dimensional) consisting of the untrained networks having zero synaptic matrix. The ancestor network can force neighbor network neurons to take values of their neuron states in quasi-stable attractors through one-to-one interconnections in the course of information transmission [14]. The signal of the start of this transmission arises when ancestor network puts all the thresholds of their neurons to the very low negative values at once. In this case all states of ancestor network neurons take maximal values (+1 for spin state coding). This maximally excited state of ancestor network opens the channel of information transmission to neighbor network. Then all thresholds of ancestor network start to grow synchronously and adiabatically, taking the same values. At some threshold level the state of some neurons become unstable and neural dynamics starts until equilibrium state at this threshold will be reached (note, that threshold grow is very slow to permit this process to terminate). This equilibrium state is transmitted to the neighbor network forcing it to learn this pattern with Hebbian rule [13]. Then, the growth of thresholds in ancestor network continues and it transmits its quasi stable attractors arisen at different threshold levels to a neighbor network which learns all of them. When the threshold level becomes high enough all neurons becomes passive (their states tales values −1) and this passive network state is interpreted by neighbor network as the signal of the finish of information transmission. After this course the neighbor network learns all quasi stable (stable in given threshold interval) states of ancestor network and becomes a new ancestor network able to transmit information to its untrained neighbor network. So, for example, in linear chain of networks a one-directional wave of learning can be organized. The remarkable phenomena observed in such a system [14] is that after few steps of transmission a special network arises in a chain which transmit further *just those patterns which it learned from its neighbor*. In other words, this network produces its *exact copy*, or is self-reproducible. In effect, identical networks arise and spread through the system. The self-reproducible networks are absolutely transparent ones - in contrast to ordinary Hopfield nets having very complicated relation between learned patterns and formed attractors they show as quasi attractors all learned patterns during the cycle of threshold growth. In two-dimensional array of networks having the possibility to transmit information in two directions clusters of self-reproducible networks arise. Detailed study of different cluster structures and also generalization of the model to other learning rules have been earlier presented in [15]. One important characteristic of self-reproducible network is that the set of patterns forming its matrix is in general hierarchically organized: the first switching of neuron points to the feature which can be considered as representing most general class patterns belong to. The second switched of one refines the narrower class, etc. Actually, each feature of pattern vectors indicates to specific class this pattern belongs to (this class is defined by this given property). Initially all these properties have equal right to represent patterns and define it in symmetrical manner. But in self-reproducible descendants this symmetry breaks and properties hierarchy arises. The fact that patterns in self-reproducible network have different level of generalization and nevertheless are stored in the same network which made them identical in the sense defined earlier opens the way to use such network for representing unconscious information processing.

Other remarkable and rather trivial characteristics of self-reproducible networks which is important to our consideration here is that if two such networks are permitted to exchange their stored patterns with each other, then *their interconnections become identical*!

5   Neural Network Model of Unconscious

Here we propose a neural model which has main features of symmetrical logic of unconscious. According to the principle of generalization suggested by symmetrical logic this model implies the creation of hierarchical structures of network ensembles corresponding to the hierarchy of object classes – from specific to final superclass. Each hierarchy level contains two regions: the first one contains a set of ensembles corresponding to given class in each of them formation of self-reproducible networks from the specific seed Hopfield network is realized. The second region is a region where these self-reproducible networks can *interact* i.e. exchange patterns with each other by forming new identical seed network of wider class. The first region can be simple chain of networks starting from the seed one which is long enough to permit formation of replicator.

Below we illustrate this general and abstract scheme by simple example reflecting debated definition of polygon classes in mathematics. Table 1 contains properties of classes of parallelograms (rhombus, rectangles and squares) and of trapezoids, which in *exclusive definition* includes only quadrilaterals having *exactly one pair* of parallel sides (acute or abuse, right and isosceles trapezoids – see Fig. 1). These two classes of objects are joined in wider class of trapezoids which are defined using *inclusive definition (at least one pair* of sides are parallel). Note, that the property *at least two sides are parallel* can be used to define exclusive trapezoids because in fact the list of them in the Table 1 does not include parallelograms. Of course, each of the low level objects – rhombus, rectangle etc. are also the names of classes. For parallelograms and exclusive trapezoids two Hopfield networks are built correspondingly with the Hebbian connections defined by 3 patterns with components defined by 6-component vectors (columns in the Table 1). It is easy to verify, that both for parallelograms and trapezoid (exclusive) networks only one threshold growth cycle is needed to form self-reproducible descendant: for parallelogram network it has most primitive form – it is formed by only pattern (1, 1, 1, 1, 1, −1, 1) which corresponds to the presence of property *diagonals are perpendicular* which is a property of both rhombus and squares. On the other hand, trapezoid (exclusive) self-reproducible descendant is formed by three patterns (1, −1, 1, 1, 1, 1), (1, −1, −1, 1, 1, 1) and (1, −1, −1, 1, −1, 1) which corresponds to the two real classes of "acute and obtuse" and also of "right" trapezoid and to one of impossible class for trapezoid but belonging to parallelograms, actually to "squares"! Now, in interaction phase these two self-reproducible networks exchange information with each other and form two identical networks with four patterns in Hebbian network (Fig. 1).

Table 1. Polygon features: −1 means that given property is present while +1 means that it is absent

Property	Trapezoids (inclusive)					
	Parallelograms			Trapezoids (exclusive)		
	Rhombus	Rectangle	Square	Acute or obtuse	Right	Isosceles
At least two sides are congruent	−1	−1	−1	1	1	−1
At least two sides are parallel	−1	−1	−1	−1	−1	−1
At least two angles are right angles	1	−1	−1	1	−1	1
Diagonals are congruent	1	−1	−1	1	1	−1
Diagonals are perpendicular	−1	1	−1	1	1	1
At least two consecutive angles are supplementary	−1	−1	−1	1	1	−1

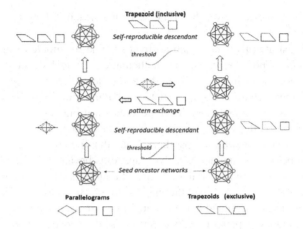

Fig. 1. The scheme of unconscious processing of polygon sets

Again, it is necessary to use only threshold growth cycle to find self-reproducible descendant representing joint class of parallelograms and inclusive trapezoids. It is remarkable, that is coincides with the self-reproducible network representing exclusive trapezoids (it is built again using the same three patterns). In some sense the unconscious system identifies the classes of parallelograms and of exclusive trapezoids to the wider class of inclusive trapezoids which is not only in accordance with the Matte Blanco symmetrical logic of unconscious but also with the ordinary intuition. Also, self-reproducible network representing inclusive trapezoids includes patterns corresponding to different level of generalizations: acute or abuse class includes the class of right trapezoids etc. This means that this higher level's network identifies the objects of different classes just in the accordance to Matte Blanco theory of unconscious.

Identification of objects belonging to the class to the class itself is considered as the cause of emotions it opens the way to use this model to describe emotional agents.

One remark should be made. Asynchronous dynamic of Hopfield network can govern to different self-reproducible descendants. In this case additional exchanges of patterns between different descendants can be added. In the examples presented in the Table 2 five actresses representing the class "Elena Andreevna" (a character of Chekhov's play "Uncle Vanya") are characterized by 7 features listed in its first column. The last feature means that the actress seems to be more attractive than other woman Sonya (this is not in all performances). Two different self-reproducible networks are generated for 7-neuron ancestor Hopfield network. The first one is formed by two consistently arisen pattern classes: "More attractive than Sonya" (MATS) and MATS - "theater actress" {(111111-1); (1, 1, 1, 1, −1, 1, −1)}; while the second one is built on four pattern classes: MATS, MATS-"blonde", MATS-"blonde"-"Russian" and MATS-"blond"-"Russian"-"beauty" {(11111-1); (111-111-1); (111-11-1-1); (1-11-11-1-1)}. But after pattern exchange and single threshold growth cycle a unique self-reproducible network is generated which coincides with the second one.

Table 2. Binary features of actresses playing the role of Elena Andreevna

	Irina Miroshnichenko	Natalia Vdovina	Natalia Danilova	Michelle Dockery	Sarah Sarandon
Woman	−1	−1	−1	−1	−1
Beauty	−1	−1	−1	−1	1
Young	−1	−1	−1	−1	−1
Blonde	−1	−1	1	1	1
Theater actress	1	−1	−1	−1	−1
Russian	−1	−1	−1	1	1
More attractive than Sonya	1	1	−1	−1	1

6   Conclusions

We present neural network model of unconscious information processing as it was formulated by Matte Blanco. Apart from its application to solving problems such as illustrated by examples presented above (and many other ones) it is possible to apply this approach to build more realistic models of memory possessing agents which can be used in computational social science [30]. Remind, that this is one of the main motivation of present study. Is it also possible to ask if this model has any relation to the real brain structures and functioning involved in unconscious information processing? We can note that at least the structure of memory sets in self-reproducible networks resembles one found by Tsien in mouse hippocampus [31]. It really consists of patterns of different hierarchy levels as typical for self-reproducible descendants of Hopfield networks. So unconscious information processing can be responsible for such joining of patterns of different generality in the same memory structures.

References

1. McLaughlin, J.T.: Primary and secondary process in the context of cerebral hemispheric specialization. Psychoanal. Q. **47**, 237–266 (1978)
2. Stanovich, K.E.: Who is Rational? Studies of Individual Differences in Reasoning. ErlBaum, Mahwah (1999)
3. Kahneman, D.: Thinking, Fast and Slow. Straus and Giroux, New York (2011)
4. Sprugnoli, G., et al.: Neural correlates of Eureka moment. Intelligence **62**(C), 99–118 (2017)
5. Belavkin, R.V.: The role of emotion in problem solving. In: Proceedings of the AISB 2001 Symposium on Emotion, Cognition and Affective Computing, England, pp. 49–57 (2001)
6. Ezhov, A.A., Khrennikov, A.Yu.: Agents with left and right dominant hemispheres and quantum statistics. Phys. Rev. E. **71**, 016138:1–016138:8 (2005)
7. Matte Blanco, I.: The Unconscious as Infinite Sets: An Essay in BiLogic. Karnac Books, London (1975)
8. Poincare, H.: The Foundations of Science: Science and Hypothesis, the Value of Science, and Science and Method. Science Press, New York (1921)
9. Gainotti, G.: Unconscious processing of emotions and the right hemisphere. Neuropsychologia **50**, 205–218 (2012)

10. Kühn, S., Ritter, S.M., Müller, B.C.N., van Baaren, R.B., Brass, M., Dijksterhuis, A.: The importance of unconscious processes in creativity – a structural MRI study. J. Creat. Behav. **48**(2), 152–163 (2014)

11. Creswell, J.D., Bursley, J.K., Satpute, A.B.: Neural reactivation links unconscious thought to decision-making performance. Soc. Cogn. Affect. Neurosci. **8**, 863–869 (2013)

12. Evans, J.St.B.T., Stanovich, K.E.: Dual-process theories of higher cognition: advancing the debate. Perspect. Psychol. Sci. **8**(3), 223–241 (2013)

13. Hopfield, J.J.: Neural networks and physical systems with emergent computational abilities. PNAS USA **79**, 2554–2558 (1982)

14. Ezhov, A.A., Vvedensky, V.L., Khromov, A.G., Knizhnikova, L.A.: Self-reproducible neural networks with synchronously changing neuronal threshold. In: Holden, A.V., Kryukov, V.I. (eds.) Neurocomputers and Attention II: Connectionism and Neurocomputers, pp. 523– 534. Manchester University Press (1991)

15. Ezhov, A.A., Khromov, A.G., Knizhnikova, L.A., Vvedensky, V.L.: Self-reproducible networks: classification, antagonistic rules and generalization. Neural Netw. World **1**, 52–57 (1991)

16. McCulloch, W.S., Pitts, W.: A logical calculus of the ideas immanent in nervous activity. Bull. Math. Biophys. **5**, 113–115 (1943)

17. Freud, S.: The unconscious. SE **14**, 159–204 (1915)

18. Behrman, E.C., Gaddam, K., Steck, J.E., Skinner, S.R.: Microtubules as a quantum Hopfield network. In: Tuszynski, J.A. (ed.) The Emerging Physics of Consciousness, pp. 351–370. Springer, Heidelberg (2006). https://doi.org/10.1007/3-540-36723-3_10

19. Srivastava, D.P., Sahni, V., Satsangi, P.S.: Modelling microtubules in the brain as n-qudit quantum Hopfield network and beyond. Int. J. Gen. Syst. **45**, 41–54 (2016)

20. Murtagh, F.: Ultrametric model of mind, II: application to text content analysis. p-Adic Numbers Ultrametric Anal. Appl. **4**, 207–221 (2012)

21. Khrennikov, A.Yu.: Human subconscious as a p-adic dynamical system. J. Theor. Biol. **193**, 179–196 (1998)

22. Lauro-Grotto, R.: The unconscious as an ultrametric set. Am. Imago **64**, 535–543 (2008)

23. Sulehria, H.M., Zhang, Y.: Study on the capacity of Hopfield neural networks. Inf. Technol. J. **7**, 684–688 (2008)

24. Ezhov, A.A., Vvedensky, V.L.: Object generation with neural networks (when spurious memories are useful). Neural Netw. **9**, 1491–1495 (1996)

25. Ezhov, A.A., Kalambet, Ya.A., Knizhnikova, L.A.: Neural networks: general properties and particular applications. In: Holden, A.V., Kryukov, V.I. (eds.) Neural Networks – Theory and Architecture, pp. 39–47. Manchester University Press (1990)

26. Ezhov, A.A., Berman, G.P.: Introduction to Quantum Neural Technologies. Rinton Press, Princeton (2003)

27. Fernando, C., Szathmáry, E., Husbands, P.: Selectionist and evolutionary approaches to brain function: acritical appraisal. Front. Comput. Neurosci. **6**, 24 (2012)

28. Kitzbichler, M.G., Smith, M.L., Christensen, S.R., Bullmore, E.: Broadband criticality of human brain network synchronization. PLoS Comput. Biol. **5**(3), e1000314 (2009)

29. Bilotta, E., Lafusa, A., Pantano, P.: Is self-replication an embedded characteristic of artificial/living matter? In: Artificial Life VIII: Proceedings of the Eighth International Conference on the Simulation and Synthesis of Living Systems (2002)

30. James, A., Pierowicz, J., Moskal, M., Hanratty, T., Tuttle, D., Sensenig, B., Hedges, B.: Assessing consequential scenarios in a complex operational environment using agent-based simulation. ARL-TR-7954 (2017)

31. Tsien, J.: The memory code. Sci. Am. **297**, 52–59 (2007)

Formal Aspects of Streaming Recurrent Neural Networks

Vasiliy Osipov and Viktor Nikiforov[✉]

St. Petersburg Institute for Informatics and Automation of Russian Academy of
Sciences, 14 Liniya 39, St. Petersburg 199178, Russia
nik@iias.spb.su

Abstract. Streaming recurrent neural networks with linear and spiral space-
time structures are analyzed. Formal aspects of the construction and operation of
such networks are considered. Four types of synapses are identified in such
networks. One of them is the track synapses, which ensure the advancement of
signals over the network. Three other types are synapses of dynamic memory.
Additionally to traditional synapse weights the attenuation functions of
diverging and converging signals are taken into account. The results of simulation of signal processing by streaming recurrent networks with different
structures of their layers are presented.

Keywords: Neural network structure · Synapses · Signals
Associative memory

1 Introduction

Perfection of artificial neural network technologies is a promising trend in intellectual
data processing. Artificial neural networks as means of data processing attract significant attention of scientists and engineers. In the nearest future some key solutions shall
be determined in the area of neural network that will bring real-time intellectual data
processing to a new level.

The artificial neural networks are used for discovering various properties of input
data. There are two kinds of the artificial neural networks—direct propagation networks
and recurrent networks.

Direct propagation networks are employed primarily for classification and recognition of digit sample objects, represented by incoming data.

Recurrent neuron networks (RNN) operate by accumulating information about
input sample objects during processing of their complete forms—*patterns*. In *learn
mode* all possible patterns are fed through network to memorize information about the
patterns features in *synaptic weights*. In *restore mode* memorized data are used to
restore the complete form of sample during alteration some incomplete sample.

Such restoration is achieved by advancement the incomplete sample form through
network. The information about complete forms of samples is kept in appropriately
tuned synaptic weights. Synapses with their weights play the role of associative
memory. Features of pattern, that are not present in incomplete sample, are restored by
associations with the features, which are supplied by incoming sample object. Classic

© Springer International Publishing AG, part of Springer Nature 2018
T. Huang et al. (Eds.): ISNN 2018, LNCS 10878, pp. 29–36, 2018.
https://doi.org/10.1007/978-3-319-92537-0_4

examples of recurrent networks that accumulate the features of some sample set and then restore full fledged sample via associative mechanism are suggested since 1980-th years [1, 2].

In recent years a special form of dual-layer recurrent networks is suggested in papers [3–5]. The main distinction of these networks is that they accumulate features not of isolated incoming samples, but of incoming data streams (this mode of operation has prompted their description as "*streaming networks*") that contains series of such samples. The stream of samples arrives to network *input module* as a sequence of sample forms, moves through the network, accumulating the pattern features or restoring data that is missing in incomplete samples.

In such dual-layer recurrent networks an advancement of signals between layers involves changing of corresponding network spatial characteristics with taking into account layers current state. Particularly, some changeable logical structures may be providing in RNN as the results of some spatial shifts of signals. These logical structures are determined by parameters of spatial shifts of signals that are sending between the layers in the control process of associative signal interaction.

The synaptic weights in such RNN are determined with taking into account additional control functions of weakening of diverging and converging signals.

Results of experiments that demonstrate restoring pattern features by streaming recurrent networks that are processing incomplete sample forms are offered in papers [6–8]. However, the features of such RNN are not investigated in full. For example, it is unknown to date, in what structures and in what forms the information about data stream is accumulated by the set of synapses in streaming recurrent networks. Subset of synapses that plays main role of associative memory and which subset of synapses does not involved in this process and, therefore, may be removed from the network structure are not identified. This paper represents the result of experiments that offer answer to these questions.

2 Architecture of Streaming Recurrent Networks

2.1 Neuron Layers

The refined block diagram of the streaming RNN is shown in Fig. 1. Input signals before the supply to the network are decomposed, in general, into space-frequency components.

In this case, each component is transformed into a sequence of single pulses with a frequency and a repetition phase as functions of the frequency and phase of the component. At the output of the streaming RNN, inverse transformations are realized. The feature of the RNN in Fig. 1 is to control not only the synapses, but also the characteristics of the neurons in the layers of the network. Depending on the control actions, this network can be endowed with different logical structures of layers and the various functional capabilities.

Some of these logical structures have been partially investigated in [4, 5]. Figure 2 shows one more possible variant of the structure of the streaming RNN with the sizes $J \cdot K$ of layers, where 1 is lines of division of layers into logical fields with the size

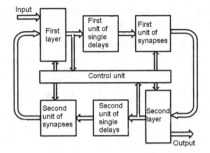

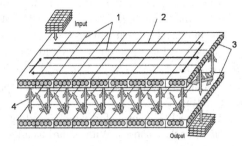

Fig. 1. Block scheme of the streaming RNN

Fig. 2. An example of the logical structure of the streaming RNN in the form of a loop

$d \cdot q$ neurons; 2 - directions of advancement of input sets of single pulses (SSPs) along layers; 3 - neurons; 4 - directions of transfer of SSPs between layers. In this network, each row includes $m = J/d$ of fields, and each column: $z = B/q$ of fields. Each $N_{i,j,k}$ neuron is characterized by its digital coordinates $0 < i < 2$, $0 < j < J$, $0 < k < K$.

Endowment such networks by logical structures is provided by spatial shifts of SSPs transmitted from layer to layer taking into account their current states. The neurons $N_{i,j,k}$ in this network can be in three states $S_t(N_{i,j,k})$: standby $(S_t(N_{i,j,k}) = 0)$, excitation $(S_t(N_{i,j,k}) = 1)$ and refractoriness $(S_t(N_{i,j,k}) = -1)$. In this case, the delay time of single pulses in the formed two-layer network contours is less than the time of the neuron refractoriness after excitation.

The existence of specifically two identical layers of neurons is the distinctive feature of streaming recurrent networks. A special kind of streaming networks constitute the *linear networks* with a single row of fields ($z = 1$). Other streaming networks ($z > 1$) constitute the *multi-coil* (or *spiral*) networks. Variants of spiral networks are described in [7, 8]. The variant of spiral networks with $z = 3$ in Fig. 2 is *loop* network.

2.2 Synaptic Links

Two neurons $N_{i,j,k}$ and $N_{i',j',k'}$ with $i \neq i'$ may be linked by directed *synaptic link— synapse* $(N_{i,j,k}, N_{i',j',k'})$: exciting pulses are passed from $N_{i,j,k}$ to $N_{i',j',k'}$ through *synapse* $(N_{i,j,k}, N_{i',j',k'})$. In the link $(N_{i,j,k}, N_{i',j',k'})$ the neuron $N_{i,j,k}$ is a *sending* neuron. The neuron $N_{i',j',k'}$ in synaptic link $(N_{i,j,k}, N_{i',j',k'})$ is a *receiving* neuron, i.e., it may be excited by sending exciting pulse through synapse $(N_{i,j,k}, N_{i',j',k'})$. Synapse $(N_{i,j,k}, N_{i',j',k'})$ is the *input* synapse for $N_{i',j',k'}$. For $N_{i,j,k}$ this synapse is the *output* synapse.

The set of synapses comply with the following fundamental restriction: it shall not include synapses where sending and receiving neurons belong to the same neuron layer.

At moment of time t each synapse $(N_{i,j,k}, N_{i',j',k'})$ is characterized by a dynamic parameter, its weight $w_t(N_{i,j,k}, N_{i',j',k'})$. The weight varies from 0 to 1.

There are two kinds of synapses in streaming recurrent networks: *memory synapses* and *track synapses*.

The track synapses, vertical and diagonal ones, are forming the path of single pulses advance through the network. The role of each track link is to move single pulses on one step. Each neuron $N_{0,j,k}$ of upper layer has one output *vertical track link* $(N_{0,j,k}, N_{1,j,k})$. Each neuron $N_{1,j,k}$ of lower layer with $0 \leq j < (J - d)$ has one output *diagonal track link* $(N_{1,j,k}, N_{0,(j+fl),k})$. Vertical and diagonal track links provide advancement of processed SSPs from the input module along all fields to the output module (Fig. 2).

Two track synapses for which sending neurons belong to the same field are *neighbor* track synapses. With regard to a specific SSP it can be stated that each field has a stamp of neurons that corresponds to this SSP. The subset of neighbor track synapses, which sending neurons belong to the stamp, makes up the *sheaf* of track synapses for this SSP. This sheaf of track synapses joins two neuron stamps, corresponds to this SSP: the stamp of neurons in sending field with the stamp of neurons in receiving field.

All synapses that are not track synapses are memory synapses.

3   Rules of Network Operation

Streaming recurrent network is working in discrete style: changing of their dynamic parameters (*states* $S_t(N_{i,j,k})$ of neurons and values $w_t(N_{i,j,k}, N_{i',j',k'})$ of *synaptic weights*) may occur only at the time moments $t_0, t_1, \ldots, t_x, \ldots$ (*beats* of the network running). If the beats of network running follow with equal time intervals, duration being equal to 1 time unit. So, symbols t_x and t_y may be regarded as digits: $(t_y - t_x) = (y - x)$.

3.1   Rules for Changing Neuron States

At every beat t_x of data processing by the network some neurons work as sending ones. If for the beat t_x neuron N plays a role of sending neuron and synapses (N, N') exists, than for t_x neuron N' plays a role of receiving neuron. In streaming recurrent network the neurons of subsets L_0 and L_1 play the roles of sending or receiving neurons by turns. If x is an even number, than at beat t_x neurons $\{N_{0,j,k}\}$ play the role of sending neurons, neurons $\{N_{1,j,k}\}$ play the role of receiving neurons. If x is an odd number, than at beat t_x neurons $\{N_{0,j,k}\}$ play the role of receiving neurons, neurons $\{N_{1,j,k}\}$ play the role of sending ones.

The state $S_t(N_{i,j,k})$ of each neuron may be changed at every beat t_x. With respect to any t_x the state $S_t(N_{i,j,k})$ is a *previous state* if $(t_x - 1) < t \leq t_x$; it is a *subsequent state* if $t_x < t \leq (t_x + 1)$. Similar terms *previous weight* and *subsequent weight* are used for the weight $w_t(N_{i,j,k}, N_{i',j',k'})$ of a synapse.

The subsequent state of a receiving neuron $N_{i',j',k'}$ with respect to t_x depends on three affecting factors:

- Previous states of $N_{i,j,k}$ that play the role of sending neurons according to $N_{i',j',k'}$.
- Previous weights $w_t(N_{i,j,k}, N_{i',j',k'})$ of synapses that are input synapses to $N_{i',j',k'}$;
- The value B of threshold for excitement that is determined for the network.

The subsequent state of receiving neuron $N_{i',j',k'}$ depends on the summary exciting force $I_t(N_{i,j,k})$, applied to $N_{i,j,k}$ at the moment t:

$$I_t(N_{i,j,k}) = \Sigma_{0 \leq j' \leq J} \Sigma_{0 \leq k' \leq K} \, w_t(N_{i,j,k}, N_{i',j',k'}) \, \Delta V_t(N_{i,j,k}, N_{i',j',k'}),$$

where $\Delta V_t(N_{i,j,k}, N_{i',j',k'})$—potential drop between $(N_{i,j,k})$ and $(N_{i,j,k})$.

The subsequent state of a sending neuron $N_{i,j,k}$ may be changed, if this neuron has been participating in exciting any neuron of the opposite layer. If such participation occurs, then the subsequent state is "refractoriness", else the subsequent state is "standby".

3.2   Determination of Synaptic Weights

The weights w_t of track synapses $(N_{0,j,k}, N_{1,j,k})$ and $(N_{1,j,k}, N_{0,j+lf,k})$, that are initialized by value 1, stay unchanged during entire period of operation of the network. The weights $w_t(N_{i,j,k}, N_{i',j',k'})$ of memory synapses are changed when the network is working in the learn mode. The purpose of such changes is accumulation of information about the patterns features in the network associative memory that is the set of synapses. An approach, suggested in [3, 7] implies the following formula for synaptic weight:

$$w_t(N_{i,j,k}, N_{i',j',k'}) = \pi_t(N_{i,j,k}, N_{i',j',k'}) \bullet \beta\,(N_{i,j,k}, N_{i',j',k'}) \bullet \eta\,(N_{i,j,k}, N_{i',j',k'}),$$

where $\pi_t(N_{i,j,k}, N_{i',j',k'})$ is the weight coefficient; $\beta\,(N_{i,j,k}, N_{i',j',k'})$ is a function of diverging signals from $N_{i,j,k}$, to $N_{i',j',k'}$; $\eta(N_{i,j,k}, N_{i',j',k'})$ is a attenuation function of converging signals to $N_{i',j',k'}$ [7].

The value of π_t may be changed from 0 to 1. If memory synapse $(N_{i,j,k}, N_{i',j',k'})$ has not been used for exciting $N_{i',j',k'}$ by $N_{i,j,k}$ during time interval $[0, t)$, then the value $\pi_t(N_{i,j,k}, N_{i',j',k'})$ remains zero.

The value of factor β_t depends on the distance $D(N_{i,j,k}, N_{i',j',k'})$ between neurons $N_{i,j,k}$ and $N_{i',j',k'}$ in the network, it is determined by equation

$$\beta(N_{i,j,k}, N_{i',j',k'}) = h(\alpha \bullet D(N_{i,j,k}, N_{i',j',k'})), \quad 0 < \alpha < 1,$$

where $D(N_{i,j,k}, N_{i',j',k'})$ is the distance between $N_{i,j,k}$ and $N_{i',j',k'}$), $h(x)$—non-increasing function $0 < f(x) < 1$. As long as distance $D\,(N_{i,j,k}, N_{i',j',k'})$ does not changed, factor β_t is constant—it does not change during network function.

4   Experiments with Streaming Networks

A set of experiments was carried out with streaming recurrent networks. Figure 3 shows results of processing input data by linear network with $m = 7$, $d = 8$, $q = 5$. Figure 3a and b represent input data—four SSPs and corresponding incomplete SSPs. The SSPs depict symbols 'C', 'E', 'T', and 'Ъ'. If the synapse weights are properly tuned during learn mode, the incomplete SSP will be restored in the course of their advancement through the network. This is the reason for watching during learn mode after dynamic of synapse weights changing.

The number of learn cycles lc should be chosen carefully for properly tuning the weights of synapses during learn mode. If lc is too small, then memory synapses could not accumulate enough weights to recreate the complete form of processed incomplete SSPs. If lc is too large, then superfluous elements will appear in output module.

Figure 3c and d shows results of processing incomplete SSPs Fig. 3b by the same streaming network with too small (Fig. 3c) and too large (Fig. 3d) lc values. With small lc incomplete SSP for each symbol does not restored in fool. With large lc superfluous output elements occur by processing SSP for symbol 'C'.

Another set of experiments was carried out with spiral networks. Spiral networks are able to restore not only separate symbols, but also sequences of symbols. In Fig. 4 the input data is given that was processed by three-coil streaming network with architecture Fig. 2. SSPs sequence Fig. 4a was used in learning mode to tune properly network synapses. The network with $z = 14$ was restored in full the SSPs by processing of its incomplete form Fig. 4b.

Fig. 3. Variant of (a) pattern set, (b) incomplete samples; results of the samples processing (c) with too small number of learn cycles, (d) with too large number of learn cycles

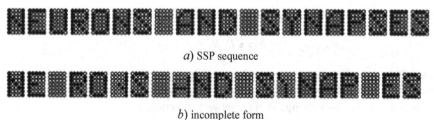

Fig. 4. Input data for loop network in Fig. 2

Network successfully restores not only incomplete SSPs symbols 'N', 'A', and 'Y', but also SSPs 'U' and 'S', that are missing entirely in the incomplete form.

Three varieties of memory synapses were identified by observing dynamics of synapse weights change: *step*, *opposite* and *extend* synapses.

If for memory synapse $(N_{i,j,k}, N_{i',j',k'})$ a track synapse $(N_{i,j,k}, N_{i^*,j^*,k^*})$ exists with receiving neuron N_{i^*,j^*,k^*} in same field that contain neuron $N_{i',j',k'}$, then it is step synapse.

A memory synapse $(N_{i,j,k}, N_{i',j',k'})$ is the opposite synapse, if $(N_{i',j',k'}, N_{i,j,k})$ is a step synapse or if $(N_{i',j',k'}, N_{i,j,k})$ is a track synapse.

A memory synapse $(N_{i,j,k}, N_{i',j',k'})$ is the extend synapse, if it is neither step synapse no opposite synapse.

4.1   Sheaf of Step Synapses

For every track synapse $(N_{i,j,k}, N_{i^*,j^*,k^*})$ the number of step synapses $(N_{i,j,k}, N_{i',j',k'})$ is exactly $(d \cdot q) - 1$. In Sect. 2 the special notion is introduced: sheaf of track synapses for specific pattern. Similar notion has place for step synapses: sheaf of step synapses for specific pattern.

If track synapses $(N_{i,j,k}, N_{i',j',k'})$ and $(N_{l,x,y}, N_{l',x',y'})$ belong to a sheaf for specific SSP, then step synapses $(N_{i,j,k}, N_{l',x',y'})$ and $(N_{l,x,y}, N_{i',j',k'})$ belong to *sheaf of step synapses* for this SSP. On the other words, sheaf of step synapses unites all step synapses $(N_{i,j,k}, N_{i',j',k'})$, in which $N_{i,j,k}$, belongs to the stamp of specific SSP in the layer L_i and $N_{i',j',k'}$ belongs to the stamp of the same SSP in the layer $L_{i'}$.

In linear streaming networks information about a SSP is memorized mainly in sheaves of step synapses.

4.2   Opposite Synapses

While observing behavior of the weights of opposite synapses during learn mode the authors have discovered, that such weights always equal to zero, i.e., opposite synapses never participate in processing data under the rules that are described in Sect. 3. When this fact came into notice, it became clear, that such futility of opposite synapses may be proven theoretically. This is an important observation. It allows avoiding of inclusion redundant memory resources for network implementation.

4.3   Extend Synapses

SSPs that are moving step by step through the chain of fields in streaming network reach the fields in the sequence, presented in Sect. 2. If some SSP enters field $F_{0,0}$ at the beat t_x, then it reaches field $F_{l,j}$ at the beat t_{x+l+2j}. The value $T(F_{l,j}, F_{l',j'}) = l' + 2j' - l + 2j$ may be regarded as "time distance" between fields $F_{i,j}$ and $F_{i',j'}$. The value of time distance may be either positive or negative. If it is positive, then the synapse $T(F_{i,j}, F_{i',j'})$ is future-oriented, if it is negative, the synapse $T(F_{i,j}, F_{i',j'})$ is past-oriented.

The definition of distance $D(N_{i,j,k}, N_{i',j',k'})$ between neurons in Sect. 3 may be regarded as space (geometry) distance. Additional characteristic for a couple $(N_{i,j,k}, N_{i',j',k'})$ is time distance $T(N_{i,j,k}, N_{i',j',k'}) = T(F_{z,x}, F_{z',x'})$, where $N_{i,j,k}$ belongs to $F_{z,x}$ and $N_{i',j',k'}$ belongs to $F_{z',x'}$. If a couple $(N_{i,j,k}, N_{i',j',k'})$ is track synapse, or step synapse, or opposite synapse, then the absolute value of $T(N_{i,j,k}, N_{i',j',k'})$ is always 1. All other synaptic links correspond to memory synapses with grater absolute value of time distance. This is a reason to name such synaptic links *extend synapses*.

Experiments carried out by the authors demonstrate that these are extend synapses who are responsible for causing superfluous elements to appear at the output module (like those which are present in result of processing of SSP 'C' in Fig. 3d). Such effects occur when extend synapses exist in linear network or inside of a separate coil in multi-coil network. Therefore, extend synapses in linear network or in a separate coil in multi-coil network are a harmful structural element of streaming networks. Conversely, inter-coil extend synapses (synapses, whose sending neuron and receiving neuron belong to different coils) are indispensable elements of multi-coil network—they play the role of associative memory of multi-coil network.

5 Conclusion

The set of synapses is used as associative memory of streaming recurrent networks. SSPs are processed by network in learning mode with tuning this associative memory for memorizing SSP features. Incomplete SSP is processed by network with restoring all SSP features due to response of associative memory. Three varieties of memory synapses were identified – step, opposite and extend synapses. These types of synapses operate differently. It is revealed that step synapses play the main role in linear streaming networks. Extend synapses, that are harmful to linear streaming networks are pivotal for multi-coil design. It is revealed also, that opposite synapses are useless in both forms of streaming networks – linear or multi-coil. Incorporation of those synapses into streaming networks architecture has no sense.

References

1. Hopfield, J.J.: Neural networks and physical systems with emergent collective computational abilities. Proc. Nat. Acad. Sci. USA **79**(8), 2554–2558 (1982)
2. Kosko, B.: Bidirectional associative memories. IEEE Trans. Syst. Man Cybern **18**(1), 49–60 (1988)
3. Osipov, V.Yu.: Associative intellectual machine. Technol. Comput. Mach. **2**, 59–67 (2010). (in Russian)
4. Osipov, V.Yu.: Space-time structures of recurrent networks with controlled synapses. In: Cheng, L., Liu, Q., Ronzhin, A. (eds.) Advances in Neural Networks – ISNN 2016. LNCS, vol. 9719, pp. 177–184. Springer, Cham (2016). https://doi.org/10.1007/978-3-319-40663-3_21
5. Osipov, V.: Method for intelligent information processing in neural network. RU Patent 2427914 (2011), RU Patent 2502133 (2013)
6. Osipov, V.: Direct and inverse signal transformation in associative intelligent systems. Mekhatronika avtomatizatsiya u pravlenie (Mechatron. Autom. Control) **7**, 27–32 (2010). (in Russian)
7. Osipov, V.: Associative and spatial addressing to memory of recurrent neural networks. Inf. Tehnol. **21**(8), 631–637 (2015)
8. Osipov, V.: Structure and basic functions of cognitive neural network machine. In: 12th International Scientific-Technical Conference on Electromechanics and Robotics "Zavalishin's Readings", pp. 1–5 (2017)

Approaches to Modeling of Nontrivial Cognitive Behavior

Vladimir G. Red'ko$^{(\boxtimes)}$ and Galina A. Beskhlebnova

Scientific Research Institute for System Analysis,
Russian Academy of Sciences, Moscow, Russia
vgredko@gmail.com, beskhlebnova@gmail.com

Abstract. The approaches to modeling of nontrivial cognitive behavior of animals have been analyzed. We consider this modeling in the context of investigation of cognitive evolution. Cognitive evolution is evolution of animal cognitive abilities. The important result of cognitive evolution is the human thinking, which is used in the scientific cognition of nature. The modeling of animal cognitive behavior should be based on the corresponding biological experiments. This paper characterizes briefly the results of biological experiments on cognitive behavior of New Caledonian crows. Schemes of modeling and some results of modeling of cognitive behavior of crows have been characterized. The general relations of our approach with other researches have been also analyzed.

Keywords: Modeling of animal cognitive abilities · New Caledonian crows
Neurobiological theories · Evolutionary origin of human thinking

1 Introduction

The current work discusses the approaches to modeling of nontrivial cognitive behavior of animals. The basic suggestions of our approach are the following:

- The most serious cognitive processes are the processes of scientific cognition.
- We should take into account the biological experiments on cognitive properties of animals.
- We can also use our original approaches to modeling of cognitive evolution [1–3]. Modeling of cognitive evolution is investigation of the evolution of cognitive abilities of biological organisms by means of mathematical and computer models. We will consider such schemes of modeling of animal cognitive abilities, which are directed to analyze the evolutionary roots of human thinking.

There are two important concepts that can be used in the analysis of the cognitive evolution: model and prediction [4]. We consider here the "internal models" (briefly "models"), which are formed in the "knowledge database" of animals. These models allow animals to predict future situations and to use adequately the prediction for decision-making in a changing external world.

Humans also have models of the external world. Moreover, the scientific picture of the world can be regarded as a set of models. Basing on the scientific models, we can

© Springer International Publishing AG, part of Springer Nature 2018
T. Huang et al. (Eds.): ISNN 2018, LNCS 10878, pp. 37–43, 2018.
https://doi.org/10.1007/978-3-319-92537-0_5

make predictions of future events in the external world. So, using the concept "model" and analyzing the methods of using models, we can attempt to trace the evolution of cognitive abilities at different stages: from simple animal cognitive properties to the processes of the scientific cognition.

The structure of the current paper is the following. Section 2 outlines some interesting biological experiments on cognitive abilities of animals (mainly experiments on New Caledonian crows). Section 3 describes schemes and models that characterize our approach. Section 4 considers general relations of our approach with other researches.

2   Overview of Some Biological Experiments

Interesting biological experimental investigations on cognitive properties of animals were performed in recent years. These experiments demonstrated that not only higher animals, but also rather simple animals, for example, insects (bees, ants) and birds, have nontrivial mental abilities. The work [5] contains the good review of interesting cognitive properties of corvids (crows, jays, and so on). Our schemes of modeling of animal cognitive abilities are based mainly on the most concrete biological experiments on New Caledonian crows. This section describes briefly these experiments.

2.1   New Caledonian Crows Can Invent a Method of Manufacturing Tools

In the wild nature, New Caledonian crows can prepare simple tools (sharpened sticks or hooks) from twigs. Using these tools, the crow can get its food. By means of sharpened sticks, the crow can get the insect larvae by sticking them; using a hook, the crow can pull out the larvae that are under the bark of trees.

The researchers of the University of Oxford investigated the behavior of New Caledonian crows, which were a long time in captivity [6]. The researchers offered two crows (the young female and older male) to get a small bucket with food from the bottom of a transparent vertical cylinder. The straight wire and the wire, which was bent into the hook, were near the cylinder. The bucket could be pulled out from the cylinder by the hook, but not by the straight wire. The crows did not deal with the wire before. However, they quickly recognized that the bucket can be pulled out by the hook.

The surprise came when the male dragged away the hook. Then the female at first tried to pull out the bucket by means of the straight piece of wire; this was unsuccessful. Further, she guessed to make the hook from the straight wire by pinching one end of the wire in some crack of the experimental setup and bending the wire. Then she used this hook to pull out the bucket with food. Further, when the hook was removed, the female made again the new hook from the straight wire and obtained the food. It should be noted that the male did not use the experience of the female; he watched her and sometimes took her food.

Thus, the crow itself, without any training, without any instructions, invented the method of manufacturing the tool.

2.2   New Caledonian Crows Can Mentally Plan Purposeful Actions

The researchers from New Zealand investigated experimentally another interesting cognitive behavior of New Caledonian crows [7]. The experiment included two parts. In the first part, the crows were preliminary trained to execute particular elements of a rather complex task. The task was to execute a purposeful behavior that include these particular elements. In the second part, the task was presented to the crows. In order to solve this task, the crows should form mentally the plan of solution of the task, using knowledge about particular elements of the whole behavior. The experiment demonstrated that the crows can form mentally the plan of rather complex behavior.

3   Schemes of Modeling, Example of Modeling

We consider the following main concepts that can be included into models of nontrivial animal abilities: internal model, situations, actions, prognosis of results of action, knowledge database, learning, memory, goal situation.

Below we characterize the schemes of modeling for the biological experiments outlined above.

3.1   Approaches to Modeling of the Crow Making the Hook

Consider the female crow making the hook from the straight piece of wire [6]. We should take into account that New Caledonian crows prepare tools from twigs in the wild nature. Thus, we can conclude that the female crow could guess the method of wire bending, using her *associative memory*. Also, we can suppose that because the female crow observes both the straight wire and wired hook, she can mentally represent that it is possible to create the wired hook from the straight wire. We can imagine that the crow can prognose results of the hook preparation and check this *prognosis* by means of real action: the hook was made and used, the bucket with food was pulled out from the cylinder. Consequently, the action of hook preparation was successful, the goal was reached, therefore, the prognosis was correct. Thus, we can try to understand the mental processes in the crow mind and represent these processes in some computer model. We have described above the mental processes qualitatively; however, it is not difficult to characterize these processes using some quantitative dynamics, e.g., we can consider the dynamics of assurances in predictions made by the crow.

3.2   Main Features of Model of Planning by New Caledonian Crows

Now we consider the second experiment on New Caledonian crows [7]. In this case, we outline our model [8].

We assume that each crow memorizes results of the preliminary training in the form of prediction of results of actions. We suppose that *the prognosis* of results of action has the form:

$$\{S_{current}, A_{current}\} \rightarrow S_{next}, \tag{1}$$

where $S_{current}$ and $A_{current}$ are the current situation and action, S_{next} is the next situation.
The main situations and actions are the following:

S_1: the short stick is tied to the end of the string; the long stick is in the barred toolbox; the food is in the deep hole;
S_2: the short stick is free; the long stick is in the barred toolbox; the food is in the deep hole;
S_3: the long stick is free; the food is in the deep hole;
S_4: the food is free;
A_1: to pull up the string and to release the short stick tied to the end of the string;
A_2: to extract the long stick from the barred toolbox by means of the short stick;
A_3: to extract the food from the deep hole by means of the long stick;
S_1 is the starting situation; S_4 is the goal situation.

These situations and actions correspond to the biological experiment [7].

In order to reach the food, the crow should execute the following sequence of actions: $A_1 \rightarrow A_2 \rightarrow A_3$. See [7] for details.

Crows memorize some predictions after the preliminary training and generate other needed predictions during plan formation by means of mental imagination or real experimental testing. Assurances in prognoses are increased during training and planning.

Note that considered predictions (1) are similar to simple functional systems in Petr Anokhin's theory of functional systems [9]. The next situation S_{next} can be considered as the acceptor of the result of the current action at these predictions.

We suppose that the mechanism of plan formation includes the following steps (Fig. 1):

(1) The forward mental movement (until the correct path to the goal is mentally reached).
(2) The testing of this path.
(3) The generation of the stereotype of the goal-directed behavior after the testing of results.

At the forward mental movement, the crow analyzes ways to reach the goal situation S_4 from the starting situation S_1. At this forward movement, the crow guesses possible results of its action. The crow mentally represents the forward movement several times, until it finds the scheme of reaching of the goal situation S_4. This process of the reiterative forward movement is shown by the upper loop in Fig. 1. After reaching mentally the goal situation, the crow mentally checks the way to reach the goal by means of testing (see the block "Testing of results" in Fig. 1).

At testing of results, the crow estimates the distance ρ between the considered situations and the goal situation S_4; this distance is the number of actions needed to reach the goal situation S_4 from the considered situation (Table 1).

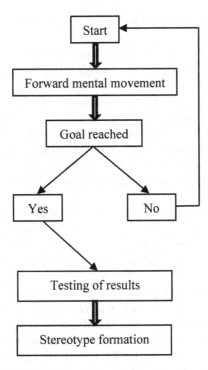

Fig. 1. The scheme of plan formation

Table 1. Knowledge database.

Current situation, $S_{current}$	Current action, $A_{current}$	Next situation, S_{next}	$\rho(S_{current}, S_4)$	$\rho(S_{next}, S_4)$
S_1	A_1	S_2	3	2
S_2	A_2	S_3	2	1
S_3	A_3	S_4	1	0

$\rho(S_{current}, S_4)/\rho(S_{next}, S_4)$ in this table is the distance between the situation $S_{current}/S_{next}$ and the goal situation S_4.

The described scheme of the mechanism of plan formation was analyzed by means of computer simulation [8]. Results of computer simulations are in qualitative agreement with the biological experiment [7]. The considered mechanism is based on the particular biological experiment; however, the mechanism is rather general, so some parts of this mechanism could be applicable for different processes of planning the goal-directed behavior.

We can also note that the processes of the mental testing of results are analogous to the replay of behavioral sequences in hippocampal place cells [10, 11].

4   Discussion and Conclusion

Below we consider general relations of our approach with other researches.

We selected only the most concrete biological experiments to illustrate possible models of cognitive features of animals. It is possible to formalize directly these concrete experiments in models. However, there are many biological data on animal cognitive abilities. For example, many important cognitive properties of corvids have been characterized in the work [5]. These properties include: imagining the past and future, planning of future events, using cognitive abilities at social relations, understanding of causal interrelations, some forms of stimulus generalization. It is interesting to formalize these properties and usage of these properties at animal intelligent behavior.

We can also use the neurobiological theories at modeling of animal cognitive abilities. For example, it is possible use the theory of functional systems, this theory was developed by Petr Anokhin in the 1930-70th [9]. The most important particularity of Anokhin's theory is the orientation of operation of any functional system to the achievement of a final needful result. The work [12] describes the operation of functional systems and an initial model that is based on functional systems.

It is important to use methods of cognitive architectures [13] to model animal cognitive abilities. In our opinion, the SOAR (from State, Operator And Result) cognitive architecture [14, 15] can be effectively used in modeling animal cognitive abilities. The SOAR system was created by specialists in the field of artificial intelligence as a certain attempt to construct a unified theory of cognition. Biologically Inspired Cognitive Architectures (BICA), which are intensively investigated in recent years [16], also have a good potential for using in modeling of nontrivial animal cognitive behavior.

We can also consider approaches to modeling of an autonomous agent with certain scientific abilities [17]. The autonomous agent can try to cognize elementary laws of mechanics in the following manner. The agent observes movements and collisions of rigid bodies. Basing on these observations, the agent can cognize regularities of mechanical interactions. Using computer modeling, we can analyze, how the autonomous agent discovers laws of mechanics.

Thus, the approaches to modeling of nontrivial cognitive behavior of animals have been proposed and analyzed.

Acknowledgements. This work was carried out within the framework of the state task, project no. 0065-2018-0002. The authors thank anonymous reviewers for useful comments.

References

1. Red'ko, V.G.: Modeling of cognitive evolution: perspective direction of interdisciplinary investigation. Procedia Comput. Sci. **71**, 215–220 (2015)
2. Red'ko, V.G.: Modeling of cognitive evolution: agent-based investigations in cognitive science. In: Cheng, L., Liu, Q., Ronzhin, A. (eds.) ISNN 2016. LNCS, vol. 9719, pp. 720–730. Springer, Cham (2016). https://doi.org/10.1007/978-3-319-40663-3_83

3. Red'ko, V.G.: Epistemological foundations of investigation of cognitive evolution. Biol. Inspired Cogn. Archit. **18**, 105–115 (2016)
4. Turchin, V.F.: The Phenomenon of Science: A Cybernetic Approach to Human Evolution. Columbia University Press, New York (1977)
5. Taylor, A.H.: Corvid cognition. Wiley Interdisc. Rev.: Cogn. Sci. **5**(3), 361–372 (2014)
6. Weir, A.A.S., Chappell, J., Kacelnik, A.: Shaping of hooks in New Caledonian crows. Science **297**(5583), 981–983 (2002)
7. Taylor, A.H., Elliffe, D., Hunt, G.R., Gray, R.D.: Complex cognition and behavioural innovation in New Caledonian crows. Proc. R. Soc. B. **277**(1694), 2637–2643 (2010)
8. Red'ko, V.G., Burtsev, M.S.: Modeling of mechanism of plan formation by New Caledonian crows. Procedia Comput. Sci. **88**, 403–408 (2016). https://www.sciencedirect.com/science/article/pii/S1877050916317124
9. Anokhin, P.K.: Biology and Neurophysiology of the Conditioned Reflex and its Role in Adaptive Behavior. Pergamon Press, Oxford (1974)
10. Foster, D.J., Matthew, A., Wilson, M.A.: Reverse replay of behavioural sequences in hippocampal place cells during the awake state. Nature **440**(7084), 680–683 (2006)
11. Diba, K., Buzsaki, G.: Forward and reverse hippocampal place-cell sequences during ripples. Nat. Neurosci. **10**(10), 1241–1242 (2007)
12. Red'ko, V.G., Anokhin, K.V., Burtsev, M.S., Manolov, A.I., Mosalov, O.P., Nepomnyashchikh, V.A., Prokhorov, D.V.: Project "animat brain": designing the animat control system on the basis of the functional systems theory. In: Butz, M.V., Sigaud, O., Pezzulo, G., Baldassarre, G. (eds.) ABiALS 2006. LNCS (LNAI), vol. 4520, pp. 94–107. Springer, Heidelberg (2007). https://doi.org/10.1007/978-3-540-74262-3_6. https://www.niisi.ru/iont/ni/rvgpubl/Redkoetal2007.pdf
13. Langley, P., Laird, J.E., Rogers, S.: Cognitive architectures: research issues and challenges. Cogn. Syst. Res. **10**(2), 141–160 (2009)
14. Laird, L.E.: The Soar Cognitive Architecture. The MIT Press, Cambridge (2012)
15. Website of Soar Research Groups. https://soar.eecs.umich.edu/
16. Samsonovich, A.V.: On a roadmap for the BICA challenge. Biol. Inspired Cogn. Archit. **1**, 100–107 (2012)
17. Red'ko, V.G.: Principles of functioning of autonomous agent-physicist. In: Chella, A., Pirrone, R., Sorbello, R., Johannsdottir, K.R. (eds.) Biologically Inspired Cognitive Architectures 2012. AISC, vol. 196, pp. 265–266. Springer, Heidelberg (2012). https://doi.org/10.1007/978-3-642-34274-5_46

Competitive Hyperparameter Balancing on Spiking Neural Network for a Fast, Accurate and Energy-Efficient Inference

Jeongho Kim and Dae-Shik Kim[✉]

School of Electrical Engineering, KAIST,
291, Daehak-ro, Yuseong-gu, Daejeon, Republic of Korea
{causaljh,daeshik}@kaist.ac.kr
http://brain.kaist.ac.kr

Abstract. The Spiking Neural Network (SNN) is currently considered as a next generation neural network model. However, its performance often lags that of classical Artificial Neural Networks. Although there has been a wide range of research to improve the accuracy of SNNs, their performance is determined not only by accuracy, but also by speed and energy efficiency. In this study, we analyzed the relationship between hyperparameters, accuracy, speed and energy of SNN, set a new criterion to estimate the comprehensive performance and applied the Neuro-evolutionary algorithm to balance the hyperparameters without the need for manually setting them. The optimized model showed better performance in all terms of our criteria.

Keywords: Spiking Neural Network · Spiking neuron
Evolutionary algorithm · Tournament Selection · Hyperparameter

1 Introduction and Related Work

Due to its powerful performance, artificial neuron based Artificial Neural Network (ANN) has been developed in various machine learning fields such as computer vision, natural language processing and robotics. However, the large amount of computations and the resulting high power consumption remain to be improved in ANN. As a candidate for solving this problem, spiking neuron model is considered as a next-generation neuron model [1]. Unlike artificial neuron model Eq. 1, spiking neuron model Eq. 2 has time term internally, which enable the Spiking Neural Networks (SNNs) to perform inferences using both spatial and temporal information. In particular, when a Neuromorphic chip is fabricated in SNN architecture, energy efficiency improvements of several orders of magnitude may be possible compared to ANN operating in von Neumann architecture [2].

The mathematical descriptions for artificial neuron and spiking neuron are as follows.

$$y = f(\sum_l W^k x^l + b^k), \tag{1}$$

© Springer International Publishing AG, part of Springer Nature 2018
T. Huang et al. (Eds.): ISNN 2018, LNCS 10878, pp. 44–53, 2018.
https://doi.org/10.1007/978-3-319-92537-0_6

where inputs x^l and bias b^k from the previous layer are summed up with weights W^k and then fed to activation function f.

$$dv_{mem}(t)/dt = \sum_i \sum_s w_i \delta(t - s), \tag{2}$$

where w_i is synaptic weight and δ is a pulse from the previous layer. Input spikes s are weighted-summed up with w_i at each time step. When the membrane voltage v_{mem} exceeds threshold voltage, it produces a spike and reset to the resting potential. [3] showed that replacing the reset mechanism with subtraction by the threshold voltage value reduces the forward error propagation from the low layer to higher layer.

SNNs, however, are not replacing ANNs because improvements are still needed. Because of the non-differentiated discrete output of spiking neuron models, it is difficult to do powerful learning using backpropagation which is possible for ANNs. Several methods have been proposed to train SNN [4–6].

Among these, the method of transplanting the trained weights of ANN to SNN has recently shown high accuracies in [3,7,8]. These methods analyze the relationship between artificial neuron model and biologically plausible 'Integrate-and-Fire' spiking neuron model Eq. 2 and transplant firing rate-based weights to SNN. [7] performed nearly loss-less conversion with weight normalization in MNIST classification [9] using Convolutional Neural Network and Fully Connected Neural Network. [8] converted Recurrent Neural Network (RNN) to SNN and mapped it to a Neuromorphic chip. [3] synthesizes and refines the previous theories and verifies the effect of the conversion on problems that only the Deep Neural Network can handle, such as ImageNet dataset [10].

Because of this conversion method, the accuracy of SNN is greatly increased, but in order to reach those high accuracies after the conversion, several hyperparameters existing in the SNN must be manually set. It is time consuming and inefficient search to set those hyperparameters manually. In addition, it is dangerous to compare the performances of SNNs using only accuracy because accuracy, speed and power consumption are in the relationship of trade-off. Setting a threshold voltage higher and an Inference Time longer increases accuracy but decreases speed and energy efficiency. Therefore, the performance of SNN should not be judged only by accuracy, but by the comprehensive performance including accuracy, speed and energy.

In the case of ANN, there are studies in which hyperparameters are successfully set without hand-tuning using reinforcement learning and evolutionary algorithm [11,12]. In this study, we analyzed the relationship between hyperparameters, accuracy, speed and energy efficiency of SNN converted from ANN. We defined a new performance criterion including not only accuracy but also speed and energy efficiency based on the observations from SNN. Using this criterion, by applying neuro-evolutionary algorithm, Tournament Selection, we were able to find an improved model in terms of comprehensive performance without the need for manually setting them.

2   Conversion from ANN to SNN

We performed an experiment in the task [13], 'Classifying Names with a Character-Level RNN'. ANN was trained on about 16,000 surnames from 18 languages of origin and the test was done on 4000 examples. The trained model predicted which language a name is from based on the spelling.

2.1   ANN Architecture

Character level RNN receives a one-hot encoded vector from a character as input and performs sequential inference using its recurrent structure. We used Rectified Linear Unit (ReLU) instead of hyperbolic tangent function which is the most typical activation function of RNN as an activation function for ANN to SNN conversion. The reason for using ReLU is described in Sect. 2.2. The network architecture is shown in Fig. 1a.

We got 78.65% top-2 accuracy on the training dataset and 73.18% top-2 accuracy on the test dataset.

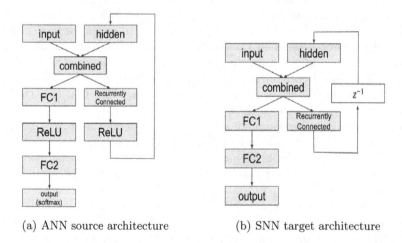

(a) ANN source architecture   (b) SNN target architecture

Fig. 1. Network architectures. In ANN, input encoded into one-hot vector is fed to FC1 layer with hidden input from the previous character input. In SNN, the one-hot vector is encoded again to poisson spike train.

2.2   SNN Conversion and Architecture

As a conversion method, [3,7,8] were mixed. In [7], the input is converted into a poisson spike train and put into the network. [3] argues that it is better to use ANN to the first layer, judging that the encoding method used in [7] has no merit. However, we followed the input encoding of [7] because a SNN chip following this input encoding does not need a multiplier which occupies a large area within the chip. Conversion from ANN to SNN was done in the following order.

(1) ReLU activation function
Since typical RNN uses hyperbolic tangent activation function, negative activation values are required in the inference. In SNN, it is difficult to express such a negative value because information is transmitted only by 0 and 1. ReLU only outputs non-negative activation values, thus negative values could be avoided.

(2) Training ANN using backpropagation
We used backpropagation, the most common training method, to train ANN.

(3) Weight Normalization from training dataset
After converted to SNN, a performance loss occurs when the post synaptic potential values are too large or too small compared to the threshold voltage value. As [7] did to solve this problem, we scaled the weights by finding the maximum activation value of each layer in the training dataset.

(4) Transplant weights from ANN to SNN
Finally, we transplanted the scaled weights to SNN. The input of SNN, a poisson spike train according to hyperparameter input rate f_{input}, given as a one-hot vector was fed to the network during n time steps T_{infer}. We assumed that the unit time step is 1ms. *Reset by subtraction (RBS)* [3] was used for the voltage reset mechanism after spike generation instead of *reset to zero (RTZ)* because our neuron model is discretized in time term. Real neuron model is based on a continuous time. Thus, Using RBS reduces the approximation error caused by the adoption of discretization [3].

The target SNN architecture is in Fig. 1b. According to [8] did, the spikes stored in the hidden memory was fed to the network after n time steps T_{infer}. The conversion result and the effect of weight normalization are in the Table 1 and Fig. 2. There was no accuracy loss after the conversion.

To visualize how recurrent SNN performs inference, we used raster plots Fig. 3.

Table 1. After applying weight normalization, the accuracy of SNN was slightly higher than that of ANN, but it seems to be error caused by noise rather than improvement of performance after conversion.

Model	V_{th}	f_{input}	T_{infer}	Training accuracy	Test accuracy
ANN trained using backpropagation	-	-	-	78.65%	73.19%
raw SNN after conversion	0.35	500 Hz	70 ms	-	52.92%
SNN after weight normalization	0.35	500 Hz	70 ms	-	73.50%

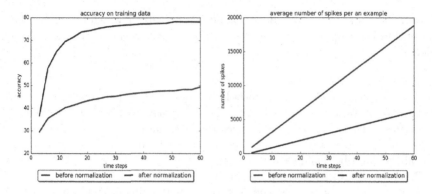

Fig. 2. After applying weight normalization, inference time, accuracy and the number of spikes are improved. The improved network performs inference with higher accuracy within a shorter time than the raw SNN and the number of spikes required for the inference was also reduced.

3   Hyperparameter Balancing

The main goal of this study is to find the balanced hyperparameters after conversion. Although we achieved a lossless conversion result, we had to try many different combinations of hyperparameters such as voltage threshold, input firing rate, and inference time in order to get this result and the hand-tuned model did not guarantee that it is energy-efficient and fast enough because there was no rule to set these parameters. We observed relationships between the hyperparameters and performances of the model, set a hypothesis based on the relationship and did an experiment to validate our hypothesis.

3.1   Observation and Hypothesis

In addition to accuracy, the criterion for determining SNN performance should include inference speed and the number of spikes. As shown in [2], if the number of spikes increases in a neuromorphic chip, the energy consumption also increases. So we need to design a model with high accuracy with less energy and short inference time. We check the relationship between the input firing rate and accuracy per spike for the model we got in the Sect. 3.

If the input firing rate f_{input} increases, the accuracy per energy decreases logarithmically as Fig. 4. And in Fig. 2, accuracy and inference time T_{infer} are also in the logarithmic relationship, which means that longer inference time no longer guarantees higher accuracy from a certain moment.

Voltage threshold V_{th} also matters. If it is high, a long inference time and many spikes are required for high accuracy. Or if it is too low, it is impossible to get high accuracy. As accuracy, speed and power consumption are in a trade-off relationship, it is not so easy to find a fast, accurate and energy-efficient model by manually setting these parameters, V_{th}, f_{input} and T_{infer}.

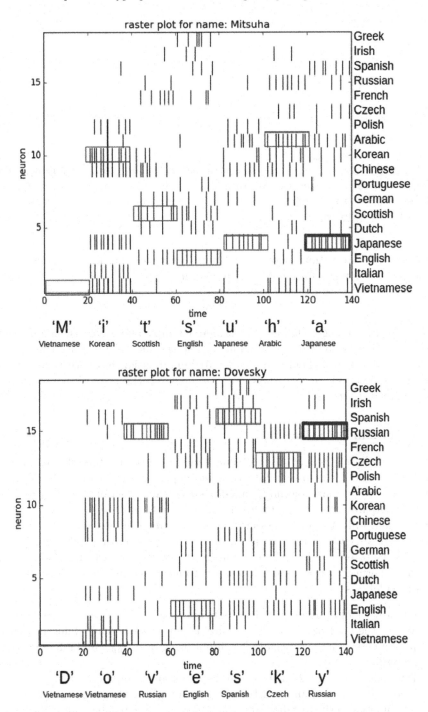

Fig. 3. Examples of SNN inferences. Each character was presented for 20 ms in these examples. When n_{th} character input is given, the network infers the class of inputs based on the characters from 1_{th} input to n_{th} input. At the final character input, the network determines which origin the name belongs to based on the number of accumulated spikes in the last layer.

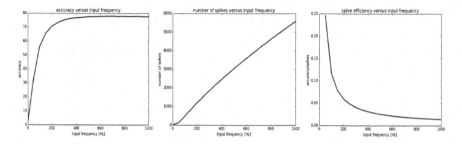

Fig. 4. Relationships between accuracy, number of spikes and accuracy/spike per input firing rate. Accuracy is improved logarithmically as the input firing rate increases. The number of spikes, which is directly related to the power consumption, also increases as the frequency increases.

From the observations above, we defined a criterion Formula 3 to determine the comprehensive performance P of a SNN model.

$$P = Accuracy/\log(\sqrt{S \cdot T_{infer}}) \tag{3}$$

where S is the average number of spikes per example and T_{infer} is the inference time. Accuracy is divided by the number of spikes and the inference time in log scale because each of them is in the logarithmic relationship with accuracy. In the next subsection, we will show how we improved the network based on this performance criterion.

3.2   Tournament Selection

We applied the method of [11] to balance the hyperparameters of SNN, which was used to find the neural architecture and hyperparameters of ANN. We used this neuro-evolutionary method, called Tournament Selection, to find the best set of hyperparameters by making various combinations of sets compete. In this competition, only the most powerful entities remain at the final step by the principle of survival of the fittest. In order to apply Tournament Selection, it is necessary to establish criterion to judge the fitness of each individual. As a criterion, Formula 3 was used. Details of Tournament Selection algorithm we used is as follows

(1) Create a pool of different-valued entities.
    We set the pool size as 5 and initialized 5 entities who have different hyperparameters: voltage threshold V_{th}, input firing rate f_{input} and inference time steps T_{infer}.
(2) Randomly take out 2 entities from the pool and compare them.
    The entities were compared based on Formula 3 on the training dataset.
(3) The inferior entity is killed and the superior one is put back into the pool.
(4) In the vacant space of the pool due to (3), a new entity which a mutation operator was applied to from the superior entity is inserted.

The entities in the pool evolves using this mechanism. Because we removed one entity from the pool, there is one vacancy. For this seat, a new entity is necessary. We can use the superior entity to make a new one. By applying a mutation operator below, the entities in the pool get chances to compete with more superior entities and the pool get evolved from the superior entity. We designed this mutation operator to make the new entity have good and similar, but slightly different parameters with the superior entity.

(5) Define (2)–(4) as 'one round' and repeat.
  We repeated 100 rounds to get an optimized entity.

```
Mutation Operator (entity)
Randomly apply one operation among the following 3 operations.
1) Vth    := Vth + N(0,0.1);
2) Tinfer := Tinfer + N(0,10);
3) finput := finput + N(0,100);
```

3.3   Optimization Result

After 100 round matches, we got an improved entity in all terms of speed, energy consumption and accuracy. The average performance of the pool increased steadily in a step-shaped trend during the hyperparameter balancing Fig. 5a. Optimization results Fig. 5b show improved results both in terms of accuracy and speed. Examples of the improved performance are listed in Table 2.

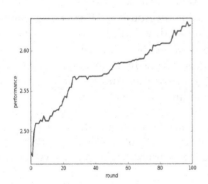
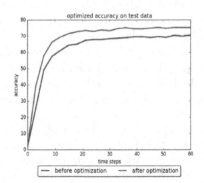

(a) Performance growth during the Tournament Selection.

(b) Accuracy improvement after optimization.

Fig. 5. (a) The average performance of the entities in the pool increased steadily in a step-shaped trend during the hyperparameter balancing. (b) The optimized network converged faster and showed higher accuracy compared to the initial setting.

Table 2. Performance of SNN before and after Tournament Selection. To reach the same accuracy, 70%, the optimized model got 3 times faster convergence than the initial one. On the fixed the number of spikes for the inference, the optimized one showed higher accuracy within the shorter time.

To get about 70% accuracy		
-	T_{infer}	spikes number
Before TS	54 ms	18,770,734 spikes
After TS	15 ms	5,981,044 spikes
With about 21,000,000 spikes		
-	T_{infer}	Accuracy
Before TS	60 ms	70.49%
After TS	48 ms	75.26%

4   Conclusion

In this study, we analyzed the relationship between hyperparameters and comprehensive performance of Spiking Neural Network, defined a new performance criterion and applied the neuro-evolutionary method to show that it is possible to balance the hyperparameters without manual-setting. The optimized model showed faster, more accurate and more energy-efficient performance compared to the initial setting.

In future work, there remains many spaces to be improved in the method. We did simulation with a relatively small-sized network because typical evolutionary algorithm requires a lot of computational resources. Of course, because evolutionary algorithms are easy to be parallelized, we will be able to try larger scale of simulations if we have lots of individual computing resources. It will be also possible to take individual threshold voltage layer-by-layer into account. We applied only one threshold voltage to all layers *en bloc*. And it is left to set up other hyperparameters related to network architecture and learning.

Acknowledgments. This work was supported by the KIST Institutional Program (Project No. 2E27330-17-P026), and by the ICT R&D program of MSIP/IITP. [R-20161130-004520, Research on Adaptive Machine Learning Technology Development for Intelligent Autonomous Digital Companion]

References

1. Maass, W.: Networks of spiking neurons: the third generation of neural network models. Neural Netw. **10**(9), 1659–1671 (1997)
2. Merolla, P.A., Arthur, J.V., Alvarez-Icaza, R., Cassidy, A.S., Sawada, J., Akopyan, F., Jackson, B.L., Imam, N., Guo, C., Nakamura, Y., et al.: A million spiking-neuron integrated circuit with a scalable communication network and interface. Science **345**(6197), 668–673 (2014)

3. Rueckauer, B., Hu, Y., Lungu, I.-A., Pfeiffer, M., Liu, S.-C.: Conversion of continuous-valued deep networks to efficient event-driven networks for image classification. Front. Neurosci. **11**, 682 (2017)
4. Lee, J.H., Delbruck, T., Pfeiffer, M.: Training deep spiking neural networks using backpropagation. Front. Neurosci. **10**, 508 (2016)
5. Kheradpisheh, S.R., Ganjtabesh, M., Thorpe, S.J., Masquelier, T.: STDP-based spiking deep neural networks for object recognition. arXiv preprint arXiv:1611.01421 (2016)
6. Wiklendt, L., Chalup, S.K., Seron, M.M.: Simulated 3D biped walking with an evolution-strategy tuned spiking neural network. Neural Netw. World **19**(2), 235 (2009)
7. Diehl, P.U., Neil, D., Binas, J., Cook, M., Liu, S.-C., Pfeiffer, M.: Fast-classifying, high-accuracy spiking deep networks through weight and threshold balancing. In: 2015 International Joint Conference on Neural Networks, pp. 1–8 (2015)
8. Diehl, P.U., Zarrella, G., Cassidy, A., Pedroni, B.U., Neftci, E.: Conversion of artificial recurrent neural networks to spiking neural networks for low-power neuromorphic hardware. In: IEEE International Conference on Rebooting Computing, pp. 1–8 (2016)
9. LeCun, Y., Cortes, C., Burges, C.: MNIST handwritten digit database. AT&T Labs, vol. 2 (2010). http://yann.lecun.com/exdb/mnist
10. Deng, J., Dong, W., Socher, R., Li, L.-J., Li, K., Fei-Fei, L.: Imagenet: a large-scale hierarchical image database. In: IEEE Conference on Computer Vision and Pattern Recognition, pp. 248–255 (2009)
11. Real, E., Moore, S., Selle, A., Saxena, S., Suematsu, Y.L., Le, Q., Kurakin, A.: Large-scale evolution of image classifiers. arXiv preprint arXiv:1703.01041 (2017)
12. Zoph, B., Le, Q.V.: Neural architecture search with reinforcement learning. arXiv preprint arXiv:1611.01578 (2016)
13. Robertson, S.: PyTorch Tutorial (2017). http://pytorch.org/tutorials/intermediate/char_rnn_classification_tutorial.html

Automatic Inference of Cross-Modal Connection Topologies for X-CNNs

Laurynas Karazija[(✉)], Petar Veličković, and Pietro Liò

Computer Laboratory, University of Cambridge, Cambridge, UK
laurynas.karazija@cantab.net, {pv273,pl219}@cam.ac.uk

Abstract. This paper introduces a way to learn cross-modal convolutional neural network (X-CNN) architectures from a base convolutional network (CNN) and the training data to reduce the design cost and enable applying cross-modal networks in sparse data environments. Two approaches for building X-CNNs are presented. The base approach learns the topology in a data-driven manner, by using measurements performed on the base CNN and supplied data. The iterative approach performs further optimisation of the topology through a combined learning procedure, simultaneously learning the topology and training the network. The approaches were evaluated agains examples of hand-designed X-CNNs and their base variants, showing superior performance and, in some cases, gaining an additional 9% of accuracy. From further considerations, we conclude that the presented methodology takes less time than any manual approach would, whilst also significantly reducing the design complexity. The application of the methods is fully automated and implemented in Xsertion library (Code is publicly available at https://github.com/karazijal/xsertion).

Keywords: Deep learning · Model selection and structure learning
Optimisation algorithms · Evolutionary neural networks

1 Introduction

In recent years, deep learning has become a popular approach, revolutionising various fields, including computer vision [1], agent control [2] and natural language processing [3]. However, training such deep neural nets requires vast amounts of labeled data, a limiting factor in many fields. An example of this is biomedical research, where few data examples can be obtained because the number of patients taking part in clinical studies is limited.

A proposal by Veličković et al. [4] has introduced cross-modal convolutional networks (X-CNNs) that use several constituent CNNs to process parts of wide data. This architecture has shown performance improvements in sparse data environments [5], offering a new way to handle different types of data present (different *modalities*). In X-CNNs, separate CNN super-layers are utilised to process each modality individually, producing specialised feature detectors. The

© Springer International Publishing AG, part of Springer Nature 2018
T. Huang et al. (Eds.): ISNN 2018, LNCS 10878, pp. 54–63, 2018.
https://doi.org/10.1007/978-3-319-92537-0_7

classifier part of the network is shared between super-layers. Additionally, *cross-modal connections* are established between super-layers to share information between modalities. However, this architecture carries a significant overhead – the number of design decisions concerning the network composition grows at least quadratically with the number of different types of data available. This means that such a technique is not well suited for widespread application.

This paper proposes a solution to this problem by introducing two methods to construct cross-modal architectures automatically, learning the required architecture from a base untrained convolutional network and a portion of the training data. This serves to both reduce the design effort and facilitate easy application by non-expert practitioners. Furthermore, the evaluation of the approaches showed that not only are the automatically constructed models better than hand-constructed ones, but also the additional time and design effort requirements are superior to those of the manual approaches. The next section discusses related work, followed by explanation of the methods, evaluation and conclusions.

2   Related Work

The idea to learn neural network architectures is not new and there has been substantial previous work on this. Initially, this was primarily achieved through the use of evolutionary algorithms and meta-heuristic optimisation approaches such as particle swarm optimisation [6], evolutionary programming net by Yao and Liu [7], neuroevolution of augmenting topologies by Stanley et al. [8] as well as variants of neural trees by Zhang et al. [9] and Chen et al. [10] to name a few. However, all these approaches were aimed at a single MLP problem, and involved constructing ensembles of models through time-consuming runs of cross-validation whilst still operating in low-dimensional problem spaces.

Initial attempts at adjusting deep neural nets algorithmically were primarily focused on reducing the computational complexity. Molchanov et al. [11] used train-prune iterations to remove connections from CNN models. Similarly, Hu et al. [12] utilised a more data-driven approach to remove whole neurons. Wen et al. [13] proposed structured sparsity learning as a way to regularise CNNs to produce a more compact form. However, all these approaches relied on having a trained CNN and aimed to simplify its structure by removing elements for computational- and energy- efficiency with a minimal reduction in performance. This project, instead, aims to adjust and add topological elements to the CNNs algorithmically to increase performance.

Work by Zoph et al. [14], Real et al. [15] and Baker et al. [16] revisited ideas of evolutionary algorithms, applying them to deep learning by training an agent to design NNs using reinforcement learning. The approaches showed competitive results but search space could not include cutting-edge topological modifications, and came with extensive computational, data and time costs. Work presented here concentrates on introducing one such novel topology automatically and could be used in conjunction with their work to achieve state-of-the-art results in low-data availability environments.

3   Methodology

Two methods, the base and iterative approach, take as input an untrained CNN to use as a blueprint for the sort of network that would be appropriate for the dataset. Then, a portion of training data is used to infer and introduce two topological aspects of X-CNNs: separation into super-layers and introduction of cross-modal connections. The methods produce networks with similar number of parameters to the input CNN, maintaining similar computational complexity.

It should be noted that the separation of data into different modalities falls outside the scope of these approaches, and could be handled either through unsupervised methods such as clustering or done manually through domain knowledge. To carry out work here, we utilised known modalities for visual data of *luminance* and *chroma difference*, drawing inspiration from the human visual system.

3.1   Base Approach

We conducted a series of ablation experiments to investigate important aspects of X-CNN architecture. This allowed decomposing the problem of CNN → X-CNN transform into several steps that can be carried out algorithmically. In short, the base approach constructs the cross-modal architecture using measures of generalisation accuracy of each modality, to calculate hyper-parameters for each super-layer and connections between them, whilst a heuristically guided search is used to find connection positions. This reduces the design complexity from a quadratic of a number of modalities to two hyper-parameters α, β. The following details the key steps (Fig. 1) in the base approach with relevant findings from the experiments.

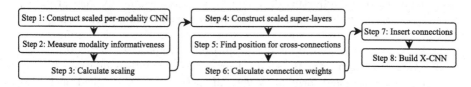

Fig. 1. The steps of the base automatic approach to creating X-CNN topology.

Modality Informativeness (Steps 1 and 2). To perform CNN → X-CNN transformation some notion of how informative modality is was required. In deep learning, near-raw data is used in the models, so existing methodologies, such as feature selection and ranking, are not suited to examine the significance of modalities. Here, we found accuracy measures performed on the base CNN using only one modality to be suitable for the task, giving a modality informativeness measure n_{l_i} for modality i.

Super-Layers (Steps 3 and 4). Super-layers are instantiated as copies of the base CNN, which take as input only one modality and share the classifier part of the network. However, experiments have shown that giving more feature maps to a more informative data split allows appropriate feature representation to be constructed whilst keeping the overall complexity of the network low. To support a variety of architectures and not be bound by dimensional constraints required by certain operations, a scaling multiplier, parametrised as follows, is used:

$$s_{l_1} = \frac{n_{l_1}^\alpha}{\sum_i n_{l_i}^\alpha}. \tag{1}$$

where α is a hyper-parameter used to tune how much higher informativeness is prioritised. This multiplier scales appropriate hyper-parameters of layers within the super-layers, such as controlling number of kernels.

Cross-Modal Connections. The experiments have shown that cross-modal connections are key to capturing cross-modal interactions, without which model performance is severely degraded. The algorithm approaches building connections in three steps: firstly, finding a position where the connections could be placed, secondly, determining how super-layers should connect and, finally, determining the composition of the connection.

Position (Step 5). The place where cross-modal connections should be established in the network is more dependent on the CNN topology rather than data. We introduced a heuristic that places cross-modal connections at the ends of blocks or modules, such as commonly used downsampling operations following convolution [1,17] or various merge points used in other architectures [18–20]. This approach was verified using linear probe[1] methodology in [21]. Such points were shown to have a large ratio of accuracy to feature volume suggesting that a suitably dense representation exists that could be used as extra context by other modalities.

Connectivity (Step 7). The problem of placing cross-modal connections is modelled as a directed graph where nodes are points from super-layers and edges are connections (Fig. 2). It is reasonable to assume that at the same depth feature extractors of similar complexities are formed.[2] We therefore always connect points at the same depth. This also allows circumventing the problems of projection such as those encountered by the authors of [19,20], which limited their ability to optimise the computational efficiency of the network. Additionally, since the connections are concatenated rather than summed, the network maintains the ability to utilise the information passed through the connections at

---

[1] A linear classifier is trained using outputs of frozen intermediate layers as inputs, measuring generalisation performance.

[2] For example, it is known that nearly always the initial convolutional layers in CNNs learn to be edge extractors [22].

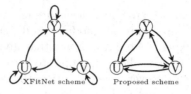

Fig. 2. Problem of placing cross-modal connections shown as a directed graph.

lower depths if that is optimal. Experiments have shown that a fully-connected graph allows learning appropriate connections between each pair of modalities and sharing information between all. This leads to better performance than a more restricted variant used in XKerasNet and XFitNet [4].

Composition (Step 6). To abstract from specifics of operations performed on the connection, we introduced a concept of a connection *weight*[3], which controls hyper-parameters of these operations. The experiments showed that connections with equal weights did not perform as well as connections that were weighted more heavily for originating in a more informative node. This is because the connections implement a mapping accomplishing three things. Firstly, they *compress* the information transferred along the connection through weighted combinations of outputs from the origin super-layer, reducing the parameter cost of destination super-layer. Secondly, they implement an *affine transformation* of features. Finally, they provide *gating* during training, which prevents gradients of a highly informative super-layer from propagating too much into a less informative one. Intermediate computations on the cross-connection soak up much of the transferred gradient to train the connection itself, enabling each super-layer to learn to be an optimal feature extractor for its respective modality.

The connection weight controls this behaviour. Thus, a desired weight $w_{l_1,l_2} \in [0,1]$ of a connection between super-layers $l_1 \leadsto l_2$ is such a number $w_{l_1,l_2} > 0.5$ for connecting a node from a more informative position to a less informative one. A sensible parametrisation of this is

$$w_{l_1,l_2} = \frac{n_{l_1}^{\beta}}{n_{l_1}^{\beta} + n_{l_2}^{\beta}}, \tag{2}$$

where β is a hyper-parameter controlling the discounting of lower informativeness. With $\beta \to 0$ all nodes are treated equally. When $\beta \to \infty$, most of the weight is assigned to the features transferred from the informative super-layer. If the weight is set to zero, the connection is dropped.

3.2 Iterative Approach

The iterative approach (Fig. 3) extends the previous methodology by adopting a learning procedure for the connection weights. It works by constructing

---

[3] This should not be confused with parameters of the layers themselves, in other literature sometimes referred to as weights as well.

successive generations of X-CNN models, where each generation contains models for each pair of modalities. The first generation uses equal-weighted connections, whilst second-generation uses the base approach calculations. Afterwards, a gradient ascent procedure on connection weights is performed. We adapt ideas behind Nasterov accelation for Adam optimiser [23,24] to construct an update procedure based on the generalisation measures for the connection weights. We also add weight-decay regularisation to ensure that resulting X-CNN does not grow too complex.

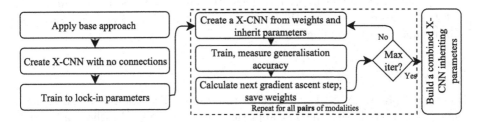

Fig. 3. Iterative approach for producing a trained X-CNN

Parameter Inheritance. To make this approach viable in practice, additional technique is needed to reduce the time requirements. An initial pre-training step is conducted where X-CNN without connections is trained for several epochs to lock parameter positions. Alternatively, the same random seed value can used for initialisation across models. This enables inheriting layer parameters between successive generations, making training of each generation require only a small number of updates to adapt to new connections, greatly reducing time requirement.

Combined Learning. The parameter inheritance transforms the gradient ascent procedure for connection-weights into a combined learning procedure for a full X-CNN, where both the connection-weights and model parameters are learned simultaneously. Effectively, the search is performed not in the parameter space of the resulting X-CNN, but across a combined parameter space of all potential X-CNNs with different connection weights. This is only possible because the search performed is inherently *greedy*. It assumes that a better minima can be found using better connections weights rather than by continuing to optimise parameters. In other words, combined learning only takes steps on a subset of axes at once. This could lead to a problem where parameters become too finely tuned for a particular connection configuration, "poisoning" future generations. To counteract this, we introduce a slight perturbation to the parameters between generations, by averaging across a couple of generations, which acts an additional regularisation against this type of overfitting.

4 Evaluation

The approaches were evaluated against hand-optimised X-CNNs from [4]: XKerasNet based on KerasNet [25] and XFitNet based on Fitnet4 [17]. The datasets used were CIFAR-10/100 [26]. All models were trained using a learning rate of 10^{-3} utilising Adam optimiser [23]. Training was done using batch size of 32/128 for 200/230 epochs for Keras/Fitnet based models. Xsertion library built X-CNN topologies using KerasNet and FitNet4 as blueprints, using 80% of the training set for internal training for 80 epochs and 20% of the training set as a validation set for internal metrics. Hyper-parameters α of 1 and 2 and β of 2 and 4 were used, respectively. At each datapoint, $p\%$ of *per-class* samples were retained in the training set.

4.1 Results

Base Approach. Tables 1 and 2 detail the results. The evaluation shows that models constructed using the base approach outperform their baseline and hand-constructed counterparts on all data availability points. A significant margin is maintained between 95% confidence intervals. It is important to consider time requirements as well. In theory, the time requirement for the base approach is $O(nk)$, where n is the number of modalities and k is a function showing the time taken to train the base model. However, all models used to take measurements are scaled down by $1/n$, thus the time commitment in practice is closer to that of training the base CNN. However, if the topology were to be constructed by hand, either through a grid search or through trial and error, it would take more than a single try to arrive at a peak performing topology. Similarly, the number of hyper-parameters is reduced from $O(n^2)$ of all pair-wise connections to only two.

Table 1. Comparison of accuracies of KerasNet based models

CIFAR-10					
$Model\backslash p\%$	20% (%)	40% (%)	60% (%)	80% (%)	100% (%)
KerasNet	70.02 ± 0.14	76.57 ± 0.16	79.28 ± 0.17	81.40 ± 0.10	82.55 ± 0.11
XKerasNet	71.00 ± 0.23	76.92 ± 0.10	79.62 ± 0.16	81.32 ± 0.10	82.68 ± 0.15
Xsertion	$\mathbf{72.02 \pm 0.70}$	$\mathbf{77.29 \pm 0.16}$	$\mathbf{79.92 \pm 0.07}$	$\mathbf{81.54 \pm 0.10}$	$\mathbf{82.93 \pm 0.09}$
CIFAR-100					
$Model\backslash p\%$	20% (%)	40% (%)	60% (%)	80% (%)	100% (%)
KerasNet	28.20 ± 0.13	36.28 ± 0.24	42.14 ± 0.56	45.40 ± 0.33	48.53 ± 0.35
XKerasNet	30.41 ± 0.32	39.32 ± 0.39	43.95 ± 0.40	47.08 ± 0.23	48.96 ± 0.22
Xsertion	$\mathbf{31.31 \pm 0.49}$	$\mathbf{40.01 \pm 0.11}$	$\mathbf{44.74 \pm 0.20}$	$\mathbf{47.75 \pm 0.27}$	$\mathbf{50.29 \pm 0.53}$

Table 2. Comparison of accuracies of FitNet based models

CIFAR-10

$Model \backslash^{p\%}$	20% (%)	40% (%)	60% (%)	80% (%)	100% (%)
FitNet	75.47 ± 0.32	82.02 ± 0.18	84.98 ± 0.20	86.22 ± 0.19	87.42 ± 0.05
XFitNet	76.56 ± 0.24	82.43 ± 0.07	85.11 ± 0.19	86.23 ± 0.18	87.42 ± 0.08
Xsertion	$\mathbf{77.35 \pm 0.15}$	$\mathbf{82.66 \pm 0.09}$	$\mathbf{85.43 \pm 0.12}$	$\mathbf{86.78 \pm 0.16}$	$\mathbf{87.77 \pm 0.22}$

CIFAR-100

$Model \backslash^{p\%}$	20% (%)	40% (%)	60% (%)	80% (%)	100% (%)
FitNet	29.29 ± 1.69	40.91 ± 2.48	50.94 ± 0.51	55.47 ± 0.96	58.92 ± 0.60
XFitNet	36.17 ± 0.27	48.02 ± 0.72	54.18 ± 0.36	57.98 ± 0.33	60.32 ± 0.29
Xsertion	$\mathbf{38.59 \pm 0.37}$	$\mathbf{50.11 \pm 0.30}$	$\mathbf{55.48 \pm 0.41}$	$\mathbf{59.06 \pm 0.63}$	$\mathbf{61.67 \pm 0.31}$

Iterative Approach. The iterative approach was further applied to optimise the automatically constructed networks. 15 iterations were used, training each model for a maximum of 30 epochs. On CIFAR-100 with KerasNet base CNN, the accuracy was observed to jump to 51.07% roughly 0.3% above the upper 95% confidence bar. Similarly, on CIFAR-10, the accuracy jumped to 83.36%, again roughly 0.3% above the upper 95% confidence bar. In the base approach, luminance modality Y was deemed significantly more important than V, which in turn was slightly more important than U. The iterative approach strengthened Y⤳U connection and weakened U⤳Y. However, the converse was true for Y⤳V. It seems that it is important to transfer information from Y to U and from V to Y. Whilst connections between U and V did not disappear, they became significantly weakened both ways. For FitNet on CIFAR-10/100, the iterative approach did not yield any significant improvements. The learned connection weights were very close to those of the base approach.

Application to Residual Learning. The base approach was further applied to networks utilising residual learning [19], to see how it performs with state-of-art architectures. A variant of residual in residual network [27] was used here, which utilised pre-activations and contained 12 residual blocks. It was trained for 200 epochs, with a batch size of 64, using Adam optimiser [23], with learning rate schedule of $10^{-3}, 10^{-4}, 10^{-5}$ transitioning at 50 and 75 epochs. The layers were initialised as in [28] with 10^{-4} L_2 regularisation applied to all parameters. The base network achieved 85.72% on CIFAR-10 and 55.43% on CIFAR-100 datasets. When the base approach was applied to architecture, with $\alpha = 2, \beta = 2$, 80 epochs, the final networks achieved 88.81% and 61.33% on CIFAR-10/100, respectively, showing value and validity of methodology even for the latest networks.

5 Conclusion

We presented an way to apply the ideas of cross-modality and a library that helps to facilitate that. The results show that the automatically constructed topologies perform better than the baseline networks and hand-optimised X-CNNs, without adding additional parameters and reducing the time required to produce such topologies. The base approach successfully introduces difficult modification of CNN architecture using a data-driven procedure, which removes vast amounts of hyper-parameters that need to be considered. In that respect, the presented work reduces the complexity of applying a state-of-the-art advance in CNN design to a library call. Ideas behind combined learning procedure can be transferred to other work focused on building networks automatically from scratch, speeding up traversal of the vast search space. Hopefully, this shows that the bleeding-edge results in deep learning need not to exist in a vacuum. The ideas behind the work here can be transferred and applied to other research, resulting in a more automated field, which invites further adoption.

References

1. Krizhevsky, A., Sutskever, I., Hinton, G.E.: Imagenet classification with deep convolutional neural networks. In: Advances in Neural Information Processing Systems, pp. 1097–1105 (2012)
2. Mnih, V., Kavukcuoglu, K., Silver, D., Rusu, A.A., Veness, J., Bellemare, M.G., Graves, A., Riedmiller, M., Fidjeland, A.K., Ostrovski, G., et al.: Human-level control through deep reinforcement learning. Nature **518**(7540), 529–533 (2015)
3. Hinton, G., Deng, L., Yu, D., Dahl, G.E., Mohamed, A.R., Jaitly, N., Senior, A., Vanhoucke, V., Nguyen, P., Sainath, T.N., et al.: Deep neural networks for acoustic modeling in speech recognition: the shared views of four research groups. IEEE Sig. Process. Mag. **29**(6), 82–97 (2012)
4. Veličković, P., Wang, D., Laney, N.D., Liò, P.: X-CNN: cross-modal convolutional neural networks for sparse datasets. In: 2016 IEEE Symposium Series on Computational Intelligence (SSCI), pp. 1–8. IEEE (2016)
5. Velickovic, P., Karazija, L., Lane, N.D., Bhattacharya, S., Liberis, E., Lio, P., Chieh, A., Bellahsen, O., Vegreville, M.: Cross-modal recurrent models for weight objective prediction from multimodal time-series data. arXiv e-prints (2017)
6. Yao, X.: Evolving artificial neural networks. Proc. IEEE **87**(9), 1423–1447 (1999)
7. Yao, X., Liu, Y.: EPNet for chaotic time-series prediction. In: Yao, X., Kim, J.-H., Furuhashi, T. (eds.) SEAL 1996. LNCS, vol. 1285, pp. 146–156. Springer, Heidelberg (1997). https://doi.org/10.1007/BFb0028531
8. Stanley, K.O., Bryant, B.D., Miikkulainen, R.: Real-time neuroevolution in the nero video game. IEEE Trans. Evol. Comput. **9**(6), 653–668 (2005)
9. Zhang, B.T., Ohm, P., Mühlenbein, H.: Evolutionary induction of sparse neural trees. Evol. Comput. **5**(2), 213–236 (1997)
10. Chen, Y., Yang, B., Dong, J., Abraham, A.: Time-series forecasting using flexible neural tree model. Inf. Sci. **174**(3), 219–235 (2005)
11. Molchanov, P., Tyree, S., Karras, T., Aila, T., Kautz, J.: Pruning convolutional neural networks for resource efficient transfer learning. CoRR abs/1611.06440 (2016)

12. Hu, H., Peng, R., Tai, Y., Tang, C.: Network trimming: a data-driven neuron pruning approach towards efficient deep architectures. CoRR abs/1607.03250 (2016)
13. Wen, W., Wu, C., Wang, Y., Chen, Y., Li, H.: Learning structured sparsity in deep neural networks. In: Advances in Neural Information Processing Systems, pp. 2074–2082 (2016)
14. Zoph, B., Vasudevan, V., Shlens, J., Le, Q.V.: Learning transferable architectures for scalable image recognition. CoRR abs/1707.07012 (2017)
15. Real, E., Moore, S., Selle, A., Saxena, S., Suematsu, Y.L., Le, Q.V., Kurakin, A.: Large-scale evolution of image classifiers. CoRR abs/1703.01041 (2017)
16. Baker, B., Gupta, O., Naik, N., Raskar, R.: Designing neural network architectures using reinforcement learning. CoRR abs/1611.02167 (2016)
17. Romero, A., Ballas, N., Kahou, S.E., Chassang, A., Gatta, C., Bengio, Y.: FitNets: hints for thin deep nets. CoRR abs/1412.6550 (2014)
18. Szegedy, C., Liu, W., Jia, Y., Sermanet, P., Reed, S., Anguelov, D., Erhan, D., Vanhoucke, V., Rabinovich, A.: Going deeper with convolutions. In: The IEEE Conference on Computer Vision and Pattern Recognition (CVPR), June 2015
19. He, K., Zhang, X., Ren, S., Sun, J.: Deep residual learning for image recognition. In: Proceedings of the IEEE Conference on Computer Vision and Pattern Recognition, pp. 770–778 (2016)
20. Srivastava, R.K., Greff, K., Schmidhuber, J.: Highway networks. CoRR abs/1505.00387 (2015)
21. Alain, G., Bengio, Y.: Understanding intermediate layers using linear classifier probes. arXiv preprint arXiv:1610.01644 (2016)
22. Zeiler, M.D., Fergus, R.: Visualizing and understanding convolutional networks. In: Fleet, D., Pajdla, T., Schiele, B., Tuytelaars, T. (eds.) ECCV 2014. LNCS, vol. 8689, pp. 818–833. Springer, Cham (2014). https://doi.org/10.1007/978-3-319-10590-1_53
23. Kingma, D.P., Ba, J.: Adam: A method for stochastic optimization. CoRR abs/1412.6980 (2014)
24. Dozat, T.: Incorporating nesterov momentum into adam (2016). http://cs229.stanford.edu/proj2015/054_report.pdf
25. Chollet, F., et al.: Train a simple deep CNN on the CIFAR10 small images dataset (2015). https://github.com/keras-team/keras/blob/master/examples/cifar10_cnn.py
26. Krizhevsky, A., Hinton, G.: Learning multiple layers of features from tiny images (2009). https://www.cs.toronto.edu/~kriz/learning-features-2009-TR.pdf
27. Targ, S., Almeida, D., Lyman, K.: Resnet in resnet: Generalizing residual architectures. CoRR abs/1603.08029 (2016)
28. He, K., Zhang, X., Ren, S., Sun, J.: Delving deep into rectifiers: Surpassing human-level performance on imagenet classification. In: Proceedings of the IEEE International Conference on Computer Vision, pp. 1026–1034 (2015)

Complex-Valued Stacked Denoising Autoencoders

Călin-Adrian Popa[(✉)]

Department of Computer and Software Engineering,
Polytechnic University Timişoara,
Blvd. V. Pârvan, No. 2, 300223 Timişoara, Romania
calin.popa@cs.upt.ro

Abstract. Stacking layers of denoising autoencoders, which are trained to reconstruct corrupted versions of their inputs, results in a type of deep neural network architecture called stacked denoising autoencoders. This paper introduces a model of complex-valued stacked denoising autoencoders, which can be used to build complex-valued deep neural networks. Experiments done using the MNIST and FashionMNIST datasets show superior performance of the complex-valued stacked denoising autoencoders with respect to their real-valued counterparts, both in terms of reconstruction error, and in terms of classification error.

Keywords: Complex-valued neural networks
Stacked denoising autoencoders · Deep neural networks

1 Introduction

The recent availability of computational resources and parallel computing on graphics processors (GPUs), together with advancements in the design of neural network models, gave rise to the deep learning domain [3,4,8,17]. It is currently a very active area of research, and has been also successfully adopted by the industry.

One of the first papers in the deep learning domain was [11], which has shown that Restricted Boltzmann Machines (RBMs) can be stacked to form a deep belief network, which could then in turn be used as an unsupervised pretraining procedure for deep neural networks. The idea was that greedy layer-wise pretraining [5] can be used to initialize deep architectures [7], which can then be fine-tuned via supervised learning to produce better results than the ones using random weight initialization. The random weight initialization prevented deep models from obtaining better performance than shallow ones.

Autoencoders are networks that learn to generate a representation of the input called a code, which can be then used to reconstruct the original input. Denoising autoencoders [19] are a special type of autoencoders which learn to reconstruct the original input from a corrupted version of it. Stacking denoising autoencoders is a similar idea to stacking RBMs to form deep belief networks,

© Springer International Publishing AG, part of Springer Nature 2018
T. Huang et al. (Eds.): ISNN 2018, LNCS 10878, pp. 64–71, 2018.
https://doi.org/10.1007/978-3-319-92537-0_8

and was introduced by [20]. It has been shown in [20] that stacked denoising autoencoders match and even surpass the performance attained by deep belief networks.

On the other hand, the complex-valued deep learning domain has only appeared in the very recent years. An important paper in the domain of complex-valued convolutional neural networks is [18], which gives a formulation of these networks as nonlinear multiwavelet packets, making the mathematical analysis in the signal processing domain available for studying convolutional networks. A wavelet scattering network which uses complex numbers was proposed in [6]. Complex-valued recurrent neural networks were introduced in the form of unitary networks in [1], and were later developed in [12,21]. Learning time series representations using complex-valued recurrent networks was undergone by [16], with similar if not superior results than the real-valued ones. Also, these networks display certain interesting properties that do not appear in the real-valued case.

In the complex domain, complex-valued linear autoencoders were proposed by [2], which also gave a training algorithm for them. But the most interesting types of autoencoders are nonlinear. Following the success of complex-valued convolutional neural networks for real-valued image classification [15], and the above observations, we considered a promising idea to introduce complex-valued stacked denoising autoencoders in this paper.

The remainder of the paper is organized as follows: Sect. 2 is dedicated to presenting complex-valued stacked denoising autoencoders, with emphasis on their specific complex domain characteristics. Experimental results of training real- and complex-valued stacked denoising autoencoders on the MNIST and FashionMNIST datasets are discussed in Sect. 3. The conclusions of the paper are formulated in Sect. 4.

2 Complex-Valued Stacked Denoising Autoencoders

A complex-valued autoencoder is composed of two parts: the encoder, which transforms the input into a representation called a code, and the decoder, which transforms this code into a reconstruction of the input. The goal of the autoencoder is thus to obtain a representation of its input, which, upon reconstruction, is as close as possible to the original. The following deduction of the complex-valued stacked denoising autoencoders follows its real-valued counterpart given in [20].

For a complex-valued encoder, we denote by $f(x)$ the mapping that transforms the input vector x of dimension d into its representation y of dimension d'. Let W denote the $d' \times d$ complex-valued weight matrix of the encoder and b its d'-dimensional bias. Then, the representation y is given by:

$$
\begin{aligned}
y &= y^R + iy^I \\
&= f(x) \\
&= \mathrm{ReLU}_{\mathbb{C}}(Wx + b) \\
&= \mathrm{ReLU}(W^R x^R - W^I x^I + b^R) + i\mathrm{ReLU}(W^R x^I + W^I x^R + b^I),
\end{aligned}
$$

where $z = z^R + \imath z^I$, which means that z^R and z^I respectively denote the real and imaginary parts of complex matrix z, and $\imath$, with $\imath^2 = -1$, represents the complex imaginary unit. The above writing of the complex-valued representation y is necessary because the common computational frameworks that are used in the deep learning field mainly deal with real-valued operations, and thus we need to express all complex-valued relations using only real-valued operations.

The nonlinearity used is the split complex ReLU$_\mathbb{C}$ nonlinearity, which applies the ReLU function to the real and imaginary parts of a complex number separately:

$$\text{ReLU}_\mathbb{C}(x^R + \imath x^I) = \text{ReLU}(x^R) + \imath \text{ReLU}(x^I)$$
$$= \max(0, x^R) + \imath \max(0, x^I).$$

Because of its popularity in real-valued deep learning, we also use it in the complex domain. Other variants of the ReLU nonlinearity are possible, such as modReLU [1], defined by

$$\text{modReLU}(x) = \begin{cases} (|x| + b)\frac{x}{|x|} & \text{if } |x| + b \geq 0 \\ 0 & \text{otherwise} \end{cases},$$

where $b \in \mathbb{R}$ is a learnable parameter, and zReLU [9], defined by

$$\text{zReLU}(x) = \begin{cases} x & \text{if } x^R,\ x^I \geq 0 \\ 0 & \text{otherwise} \end{cases},$$

but they exhibited worse performance on preliminary experiments than the split complex ReLU nonlinearity, defined above.

For the complex-valued decoder, we denote by z the d-dimensional reconstruction of the representation y, and by $g(y)$ the mapping that does this reconstruction. We have that:

$$z = z^R + \imath z^I$$
$$= g(y)$$
$$= \sigma_\mathbb{C}(W'y + b')$$
$$= \sigma(W'^R y^R - W'^I y^I + b'^R) + \imath \sigma(W'^R y^I + W'^I y^R + b'^I),$$

where W' represents the $d \times d'$ complex-valued weight matrix of the decoder, b' its d-dimensional weight, and $\sigma_\mathbb{C}$ represents the split complex sigmoid function:

$$\sigma_\mathbb{C}(x^R + \imath x^I) = \sigma(x^R) + \imath \sigma(x^I)$$
$$= \frac{1}{1 + e^{-x^R}} + \imath \frac{1}{1 + e^{-x^I}}.$$

We will consider that $x \in [0,1]^d + \imath[0,1]^d$. We can also easily see that, because of the sigmoid nonlinearity, we also have $z \in [0,1]^d + \imath[0,1]^d$. The loss function which measures the reconstruction error is given by the cross-entropy loss:

$$L(x, z) = - \sum_j \left[x_j^R \log z_j^R + (1 - x_j^R) \log(1 - z_j^R) \right]$$
$$- \sum_j \left[x_j^I \log z_j^I + (1 - x_j^I) \log(1 - z_j^I) \right].$$

If a good reconstruction of the input is given by the representation, then it has retained much of the information presented as input. But it is possible that the autoencoder simply learns the identity mapping, without discovering a more useful representation than the input, especially in the case when $d' > d$. Usually, autoencoders produce an under-complete representation in the case $d' < d$, and so we say that they produce a lossy compressed representation of the input. On the other hand, it is possible to avoid the learning of the identity mapping by an over-complete but sparse representation ($d' > d$).

A different approach to avoid the simple copying of the input by the autoencoder is to change the reconstruction criterion in order for it to perform a different task: to reconstruct the input from a corrupted version of it. This approach is called denoising, and was proposed by [20] for the real-valued case. The idea behind the approach is that, while learning to reconstruct the input, the autoencoder will also extract features that capture useful structure in the input.

Thus, a denoising autoencoder is trained to reconstruct the input x from a corrupted version $\tilde{x}$ of x. As a consequence, the encoder becomes $y = f(\tilde{x})$, and the decoder remains the same: $z = g(y)$. The observation is that, in this case, we are interested that the reconstruction z be as close as possible to the original input x, and not to the corrupted input $\tilde{x}$. For this reason, the loss function is the same cross-entropy loss $L(x, z)$, defined above. Each time an input x is presented, the autoencoder will use a different corrupted version $\tilde{x}$ of it, generated by the corruption process.

We consider two types of corruption processes:

– Additive Gaussian Noise (GN), in which $\tilde{x}$ is given as $\tilde{x} = \tilde{x}^R + \imath \tilde{x}^I \sim \mathcal{N}(x^R, \sigma^2/2) + \imath \mathcal{N}(x^I, \sigma^2/2)$;
– Masking Noise (MN), in which $\tilde{x}$ is obtained by setting a fraction ν of the elements of x to $0 + 0\imath = 0$, randomly chosen for each example.

It has been shown that stacking Restricted Boltzmann Machines (RBMs) to form deep belief networks and autoencoders to form stacked autoencoders can be used as unsupervised pretraining procedures for deep neural networks [10,11]. Likewise, denoising autoencoders can be stacked to form stacked denoising autoencoders. In such networks, each layer is trained separately, using greedy layer-wise training [5]. We must mention that the corrupted input to each individual layer is only used in the training phase, and after the mapping f has been learned, it is used on the uncorrupted layer input.

After all the mappings f have been learned for each of the layers of the stacked denoising autoencoder, a logistic regression layer can be added on top of the encoders, giving rise to a complex-valued deep neural network, which can be used for classification. The weights learned through unsupervised pretraining can then be fine-tuned using supervised training via gradient descent.

3   Experimental Results

In our experiments, we train real-valued and complex-valued stacked denoising autoencoders, like the ones described in Sect. 2. The 28×28 pixel images are linearized as 784-dimensional vectors to be given to the networks. Each encoder is then pretrained using the greedy layer-wise procedure described above. The number of neurons for each complex-valued encoder is 1.41 times smaller then for its real-valued counterpart, to ensure approximately the same number of parameters in the two networks, and, as such, a fair comparison between them.

After the greedy layer-wise pretraining has learned the weights of each layer, a logistic regression layer which consists of the softmax function and the negative log likelihood loss function is added on top of the last encoder in the network. Learning then continues in a supervised manner, like in a deep neural network.

The Adam [13] algorithm with minibatches of 128 images was used for training. The learning rate was 0.001 and the number of epochs was 50 both for pretraining and for fine-tuning. The two types of noise used for corrupting the layer inputs were: Gaussian noise (GN) with standard deviation of $1/\sqrt{2}$ for the complex case, and of 1 for the real case; and masking noise (MN), for which a fraction of $\nu = 0.25$ (25%) of the inputs to the layers were set to 0.

3.1   MNIST

The MNIST dataset was created by [14], and is formed of 28×28 pixel grayscale images representing handwritten digits. The training set consists of 60,000 images and was used without any augmentations. The test set contains 10,000 images.

The experimental results are given in Table 1. The first column in the table shows the architecture of the complex-valued network which has 1.41 times less neurons than the real-valued one. In the second and third columns, the value of the cross-entropy loss for the pretraining part computed on the test set is given for the complex-valued and real-valued autoencoders, respectively. Then, in the last two columns, the error (computed on the test set) after fine-tuning is given for the two types of networks. It can be seen from the table that the complex-valued networks have better performance than their real-valued counterparts both in terms of reconstruction loss and in terms of classification error.

Also, the reconstructed images by the real-valued and complex-valued stacked denoising autoencoders are given in Fig. 1, along with the original images. It can be seen that the quality of the images reconstructed by the complex-valued network is better than that of the images reconstructed by the real-valued network.

3.2   FashionMNIST

A dataset that appeared recently is the FashionMNIST dataset [22]. Its characteristics are very similar to the MNIST dataset, from which it was inspired, but it is more complicated. The grayscale 28×28 pixel images pertain to the following 10 classes: t-shirt/top, trouser, pullover, dress, coat, sandal, shirt, sneaker, bag, ankle boot. There are 60,000 training samples and 10,000 test samples.

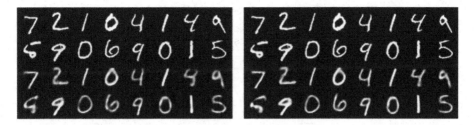

Fig. 1. MNIST images reconstructed by the real-valued (left) and complex-valued (right) stacked denoising autoencoders, along with the original images

Table 1. Experimental results for MNIST

Architecture	Complex loss	Real loss	Complex error	Real error
784-128-64-32 (GN)	**10.88e − 4**	11.33e − 4	**1.44%**	1.49%
784-128-64-32 (MN)	**9.24e − 4**	9.67e − 4	**1.71%**	1.91%
784-256-128-64 (GN)	**10.70e − 4**	10.88e − 4	**1.18%**	1.26%
784-256-128-64 (MN)	**8.96e − 4**	9.19e − 4	**1.35%**	1.63%
784-1024-512-256-128 (GN)	**10.64e − 4**	10.83e − 4	**1.19%**	1.21%
784-1024-512-256-128 (MN)	**8.69e − 4**	9.15e − 4	**1.18%**	1.24%

The experimental results are given in the same way as with the above experiment in Table 2. It can be seen that the task is more complicated, both in terms of reconstruction error as well as in terms of classification error. Nonetheless, the conclusion of the set of experiments is the same: complex-valued networks have better reconstruction error and better classification error then the real-valued networks.

The reconstructed images for the two types of networks are given in Fig. 2, along with the original images. In this case too, the complex-valued reconstructed images have a better quality.

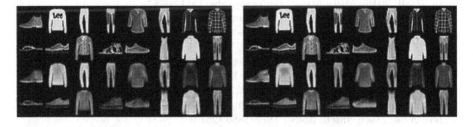

Fig. 2. FashionMNIST images reconstructed by the real-valued (left) and complex-valued (right) stacked denoising autoencoders, along with the original images

Table 2. Experimental results for FashionMNIST

Architecture	Complex loss	Real loss	Complex error	Real error
784-128-64-32 (GN)	$24.32e - 4$	$24.54e - 4$	**10.37%**	10.72%
784-128-64-32 (MN)	$23.07e - 4$	$23.47e - 4$	**10.15%**	10.82%
784-256-128-64 (GN)	$24.21e - 4$	$24.30e - 4$	**10.30%**	10.37%
784-256-128-64 (MN)	$22.82e - 4$	$23.07e - 4$	**10.21%**	10.45%
784-1024-512-256-128 (GN)	$24.23e - 4$	$24.29e - 4$	**10.01%**	10.09%
784-1024-512-256-128 (MN)	$22.84e - 4$	$22.89e - 4$	**9.97%**	10.05%

4   Conclusions

A model of complex-valued stacked denoising autoencoders was proposed, by highlighting the specifics of learning in the complex domain. The model allowed the construction of deep complex-valued neural networks.

Testing the proposed architecture on the MNIST and FashionMNIST datasets revealed better performances of the complex-valued stacked denoising autoencoders with respect to their real-valued counterparts, both in terms of reconstruction error, and in terms of classification error. The quality of the reconstructed images was also better for the complex-valued networks.

The present paper represents another step done towards complex-valued deep learning. Many ideas remain to be explored in order to fully use the properties of the complex domain representation to enhance the capabilities of the network models. This represents an interesting future work direction.

Acknowledgement. This work was supported by research grant no. PCD-TC-2017-41 of the Polytechnic University Timişoara, Romania.

References

1. Arjovsky, M., Shah, A., Bengio, Y.: Unitary evolution recurrent neural networks. In: ICML 2016 (2016). https://arxiv.org/abs/1511.06464
2. Baldi, P., Lu, Z.: Complex-valued autoencoders. Neural Netw. **33**, 136–147 (2012)
3. Bengio, Y.: Learning deep architectures for AI. Found. Trends Mach. Learn. **2**(1), 1–127 (2009)
4. Bengio, Y., LeCun, Y., Hinton, G.: Deep learning. Nature **521**, 436–444 (2015)
5. Bengio, Y., Lamblin, P., Popovici, D., Larochelle, H.: Greedy layer-wise training of deep networks. In: NIPS 2006, pp. 153–160 (2006)
6. Bruna, J., Mallat, S.: Invariant scattering convolution networks. IEEE Trans. Pattern Anal. Mach. Intell. **35**(8), 1872–1886 (2013)
7. Erhan, D., Bengio, Y., Courville, A., Manzagol, P.A., Vincent, P., Bengio, S.: Why does unsupervised pre-training help deep learning? J. Mach. Learn. Res. **11**, 625–660 (2010)
8. Goodfellow, I., Bengio, Y., Courville, A.: Deep Learning. MIT Press, Cambridge (2016)

9. Guberman, N.: On complex valued convolutional neural networks. Master's thesis, School of Computer Science and Engineering, The Hebrew University of Jerusalem (2016). https://arxiv.org/abs/1602.09046

10. Hinton, G.E., Salakhutdinov, R.R.: Reducing the dimensionality of data with neural networks. Science **313**(5786), 504–507 (2006)

11. Hinton, G.E., Osindero, S., Teh, Y.W.: A fast learning algorithm for deep belief nets. Neural Comput. **18**(7), 1527–1554 (2006)

12. Jing, L., Shen, Y., Dubcek, T., Peurifoy, J., Skirlo, S., LeCun, Y., Tegmark, M., Soljacic, M.: Tunable efficient unitary neural networks (EUNN) and their application to RNNs. In: ICML 2017 (2017). https://arxiv.org/abs/1612.05231

13. Kingma, D.P., Ba, J.: Adam: a method for stochastic optimization. In: ICLR 2015 (2015)

14. LeCun, Y., Bottou, L., Bengio, Y., Haffner, P.: Gradient-based learning applied to document recognition. Proc. IEEE **86**(11), 2278–2324 (1998)

15. Popa, C.A.: Complex-valued convolutional neural networks for real-valued image classification. In: 2017 International Joint Conference on Neural Networks (IJCNN). IEEE, May 2017

16. Sarroff, A.M., Shepardson, V., Casey, M.A.: Learning representations using complex-valued nets (2015). https://arxiv.org/abs/1511.06351

17. Schmidhuber, J.: Deep learning in neural networks: an overview. Neural Netw. **61**, 85–117 (2015)

18. Tygert, M., Bruna, J., Chintala, S., LeCun, Y., Piantino, S., Szlam, A.: A mathematical motivation for complex-valued convolutional networks. Neural Comput. **28**(5), 815–825 (2016)

19. Vincent, P., Larochelle, H., Bengio, Y., Manzagol, P.A.: Extracting and composing robust features with denoising autoencoders. In: ICML 2008 (2008)

20. Vincent, P., Larochelle, H., Lajoie, I., Bengio, Y., Manzagol, P.A.: Stacked denoising autoencoders: learning useful representations in a deep network with a local denoising criterion. J. Mach. Learn. Res. **11**, 3371–3408 (2010)

21. Wisdom, S., Powers, T., Hershey, J.R., Roux, J.L., Atlas, L.: Full-capacity unitary recurrent neural networks. In: NIPS 2016 (2016). https://arxiv.org/abs/1611.00035

22. Xiao, H., Rasul, K., Vollgraf, R.: Fashion-MNIST: a Novel Image Dataset for Benchmarking Machine and Learning Algorithms (2017). https://arxiv.org/abs/1708.07747

Complex-Valued Deep Belief Networks

Călin-Adrian Popa[✉]

Department of Computer and Software Engineering, Polytechnic University
Timişoara, Blvd. V. Pârvan, No. 2, 300223 Timişoara, Romania
calin.popa@cs.upt.ro

Abstract. Deep belief networks were among the first models in the deep learning paradigm. Their use for unsupervised pretraining allowed deep neural network architectures to perform better than shallow ones. This paper introduces complex-valued deep belief networks, which can be used for unsupervised pretraining of complex-valued deep neural networks. Experiments on the MNIST dataset using different network architectures show better results of the complex-valued networks compared to their real-valued counterparts, when complex-valued deep belief networks are used for pretraining them.

Keywords: Complex-valued neural networks · Deep belief networks
Deep neural networks

1 Introduction

The domain of deep learning [2,3,7,14] is currently a very active area of research and has also been successfully adopted by the industry. Its development was also nurtured by the increase in computational power in the form of parallel computing done on graphics processing units (GPUs).

Among the first models in this paradigm were deep belief networks. It was shown in [8] that Restricted Boltzmann Machines (RBMs) can be stacked to form a deep belief network, which, after training, can be used to initialize learning in a feedforward neural network [6]. Because deep belief networks are trained in an unsupervised manner, using the greedy layer-wise technique [4], the resulted networks can then be fine-tuned using supervised learning. As it turns out, this unsupervised pretraining of deep neural networks allows them to have better results than with random weight initialization.

On the other hand, the domain of complex-valued deep learning is only beginning to emerge. Complex-valued convolutional neural networks seen as nonlinear multiwavelet packets were proposed in [15]. Neural synchrony in a complex-valued neural network was discussed in [12], in which it is shown that complex-valued networks have more interesting properties than their real-valued counterparts. A wavelet scattering network which uses complex numbers was introduced in [5]. Unitary recurrent networks, which use complex-valued weights, were developed in [1], and were later discussed in [9,16]. Learning time series

© Springer International Publishing AG, part of Springer Nature 2018
T. Huang et al. (Eds.): ISNN 2018, LNCS 10878, pp. 72–78, 2018.
https://doi.org/10.1007/978-3-319-92537-0_9

representations using complex-valued recurrent networks was undergone by [13], with similar if not superior results than the real-valued ones.

On the footsteps of these papers, also taking into account the success of complex-valued convolutional neural networks for real-valued image classification [11], we introduce complex-valued deep belief networks in this paper.

The rest of the study is organized as follows: Sect. 2 presents the full deduction of the complex-valued deep belief networks, with emphasis on the characteristics of learning in the complex domain. The experimental results of different network architectures of real- and complex-valued deep belief networks trained on the MNIST dataset are shown and discussed in Sect. 3. Section 4 concludes the paper.

2 Complex-Valued Deep Belief Networks

Restricted Boltzmann Machines (RBMs) are part of the larger family of energy-based models, which associate a scalar energy to each configuration of the variables of interest. Learning corresponds to modifying the energy function so that it has some desired properties. Usually, we would want the energy to be as low as possible. The following deduction of the properties of complex-valued RBMs follows that of [2] for the real-valued case.

For Boltzmann Machines (BMs), the energy function is linear in its free parameters. To increase the representational power of the Boltzmann Machines in order for them to be able to represent more complicated input distributions, some variables are considered to never be observed, and that is why they are called hidden variables. Restricted Boltzmann Machines (RBMs) restrict the BM model by not allowing visible-visible and hidden-hidden connections. If we denote the visible variables by v and the hidden variables by h, in the case of complex-valued RBMs, the energy function is defined by

$$
\begin{aligned}
\mathcal{E}(v,h) &= -(b^H v)^R - (c^H h)^R - (h^H W v)^R \\
&= -(b^R)^T v^R - (b^I)^T v^I - (c^R)^T h^R - (c^I)^T h^I \\
&\quad -(h^R)^T (Wv)^R - (h^I)^T (Wv)^I \\
&= -(b^R)^T v^R - (b^I)^T v^I - (c^R)^T h^R - (c^I)^T h^I \\
&\quad -(v^R)^T (W^H h)^R - (v^I)^T (W^H h)^I,
\end{aligned} \tag{1}
$$

where z^R and z^I are the real and imaginary parts, respectively, of the complex-valued matrix z, z^H is the Hermitian (complex-conjugate) transpose of matrix z, a^T is the transpose of real-valued matrix a, and we used the property that $(x^H y)^R = (y^H x)^R$. Also, W represents the weights connecting the visible and hidden layers, b represents the bias of the visible layer, and c represents the bias of the hidden layer.

With the above notations, the probability distribution of complex-valued RBMs can be defined as

$$
P(v) = \sum_h P(v,h) = \sum_h \frac{e^{-\mathcal{E}(v,h)}}{Z},
$$

where Z is called the partition function by analogy with physical systems.

If we denote by

$$\mathcal{F}(v) = -\log \sum_h e^{-\mathcal{E}(v,h)},$$

which is called free energy (a notion also inspired from physics), we have that

$$P(v) = \frac{e^{-\mathcal{F}(v)}}{Z},$$

and Z is given by

$$Z = \sum_v e^{-\mathcal{F}(v)}.$$

Now, from (1), we have that

$$
\begin{aligned}
\mathcal{F}(v) = &-(b^R)^T v^R - (b^I)^T v^I \\
&- \sum_i \log \sum_{h_i^R} e^{h_i^R(c_i^R + (W_i v)^R)} - \sum_i \log \sum_{h_i^I} e^{h_i^I(c_i^I + (W_i v)^I)} \\
= &-(b^R)^T v^R - (b^I)^T v^I \\
&- \sum_i \log \sum_{h_i^R} e^{h_i^R(c_i^R + W_i^R v^R - W_i^I v^I)} - \sum_i \log \sum_{h_i^I} e^{h_i^I(c_i^I + W_i^R v^I + W_i^I v^R)}, \quad (2)
\end{aligned}
$$

where h_i is the ith element of vector h and W_i is the ith column of matrix W.

We can also obtain an expression for the conditional probabilities $P(h^R|v)$ and $P(h^I|v)$:

$$
\begin{aligned}
P(h^R|v) &= \frac{e^{(b^R)^T v^R + (b^I)^T v^I + (c^R)^T h^R + (c^I)^T h^I + (h^R)^T (Wv)^R + (h^I)^T (Wv)^I}}{\sum_{\widetilde{h}^R} e^{(b^R)^T v^R + (b^I)^T v^I + (c^R)^T \widetilde{h}^R + (c^I)^T h^I + (\widetilde{h}^R)^T (Wv)^R + (h^I)^T (Wv)^I}} \\
&= \frac{\prod_i e^{c_i^R h_i^R + h_i^R (W_i v)^R}}{\prod_i \sum_{\widetilde{h}_i^R} e^{c_i^R \widetilde{h}_i^R + \widetilde{h}_i^R (W_i v)^R}} \\
&= \prod_i \frac{e^{h_i^R(c_i^R + (W_i v)^R)}}{\sum_{\widetilde{h}_i^R} e^{\widetilde{h}_i^R(c_i^R + (W_i v)^R)}} \\
&= \prod_i P(h_i^R|v),
\end{aligned}
$$

$$
\begin{aligned}
P(h^I|v) &= \frac{e^{(b^R)^T v^R + (b^I)^T v^I + (c^R)^T h^R + (c^I)^T h^I + (h^R)^T (Wv)^R + (h^I)^T (Wv)^I}}{\sum_{\widetilde{h}^I} e^{(b^R)^T v^R + (b^I)^T v^I + (c^R)^T h^R + (c^I)^T \widetilde{h}^I + (h^R)^T (Wv)^R + (\widetilde{h}^I)^T (Wv)^I}} \\
&= \frac{\prod_i e^{c_i^I h_i^I + h_i^I (W_i v)^I}}{\prod_i \sum_{\widetilde{h}_i^I} e^{c_i^I \widetilde{h}_i^I + \widetilde{h}_i^I (W_i v)^I}} \\
&= \prod_i \frac{e^{h_i^I(c_i^I + (W_i v)^I)}}{\sum_{\widetilde{h}_i^I} e^{\widetilde{h}_i^I(c_i^I + (W_i v)^I)}} \\
&= \prod_i P(h_i^I|v).
\end{aligned}
$$

This means that the visible and hidden neurons are conditionally independent given one another.

If we assume that h_i^R, $h_i^I \in \{0, 1\}$, we obtain

$$P(h_i^R = 1|v) = \frac{e^{c_i^R + (W_i v)^R}}{1 + e^{c_i^R + (W_i v)^R}} = \sigma(c_i^R + (W_i v)^R) = \sigma(c_i^R + W_i^R v^R - W_i^I v^I),$$

$$P(h_i^I = 1|v) = \frac{e^{c_i^I + (W_i v)^I}}{1 + e^{c_i^I + (W_i v)^I}} = \sigma(c_i^I + (W_i v)^I) = \sigma(c_i^I + W_i^R v^I + W_i^I v^R),$$

where σ is the real-valued sigmoid function: $\sigma(x) = \frac{1}{1+e^{-x}}$. The above expressions, together with (2), prove that a complex-valued RBM can be implemented only using real-valued operations. This is important, because the computational frameworks used in the deep learning domain mainly deal with real-valued operations.

Because of the symmetry in the expression of the energy function between the visible and hidden neurons, assuming that v_j^R, $v_j^I \in \{0, 1\}$, the following relations can also be deduced:

$$P(v^R|h) = \prod_j P(v_j^R|h),$$

$$P(v^I|h) = \prod_j P(v_j^I|h),$$

$$P(v_j^R = 1|h) = \sigma(b_j^R + (W_j^H h)^R) = \sigma(b_j^R + (W_j^R)^T h^R + (W_j^I)^T h^I),$$

$$P(v_j^I = 1|h) = \sigma(b_j^I + (W_j^H h)^I) = \sigma(b_j^I + (W_j^R)^T h^I - (W_j^I)^T h^R).$$

The free energy for an RBM with binary neurons can be further simplified to

$$\mathcal{F}(v) = -(b^R)^T v^R - (b^I)^T v^I$$
$$- \sum_i \log(1 + e^{c_i^R + W_i^R v^R - W_i^I v^I}) - \sum_i \log(1 + e^{c_i^I + W_i^R v^I + W_i^I v^R}).$$

Samples from the distribution $P(x)$ can be obtained by running a Markov chain to convergence, using as transition operator the Gibbs sampling procedure. Gibbs sampling for N joint random variables $S = (S_1, \ldots, S_N)$ is done in a sequence of N sampling steps of the form $S_i \sim P(S_i|S_{-i})$, where S_{-i} denotes the other $N - 1$ variables that are not S_i. In the case of an RBM, this means that first we sample h^R, h^I from $P(h^R|v)$, $P(h^I|v)$, and then we sample v^R, v^I from $P(v^R|h)$, $P(v^I|h)$. By doing this procedure a sufficient amount of time, it is guaranteed that (v, h) is an accurate sample of $P(v, h)$. This would however be very computationally expensive, and so different algorithms have been devised to sample from $P(v, h)$ efficiently during learning.

One such algorithm is contrastive divergence, which we use in our experiments. It is based on two ideas to speed up the sampling process. First, because we want to have $P(v) \approx P_{\text{train}}(v)$, i.e., the true distribution of the training data, we initialize the Markov chain described above with a training sample, which will speed up convergence. The second idea is that contrastive divergence doesn't wait for the Markov chain to converge, but only does k steps of Gibbs sampling. Surprisingly, $k = 1$ gives good results in practice.

Now that we have all the ingredients for constructing and training a complex-valued RBM, we can stack several complex-valued RBMs to form a complex-valued deep belief network. This type of network is trained one layer at a time, using the greedy layer-wise procedure [4]. After training the first layer to model the input, the following layers are trained as complex-valued RBMs to model the outputs of the previous layers. After learning the weights for all the RBMs in the deep belief network, a logistic regression layer is added on top of the last RBM in the deep belief network, thus forming a complex-valued deep neural network. This network can then be fine-tuned in a supervised manner, using gradient-based methods. Thus, the deep belief network is used to initialize the parameters of the deep neural network.

3 Experimental Results

The MNIST dataset was created by [10], and is formed of 28×28 pixel grayscale images representing handwritten digits. The training set consists of $60,000$ images and was used without any augmentations. The test set contains $10,000$ images.

In the experiments, we use real-valued and complex-valued deep belief networks for the unsupervised pretraining of deep neural networks. The 28×28 images were linearized into 784-dimensional vectors, which constitute the inputs of the networks. The number of neurons in every hidden layer of the complex-valued networks is given in the first column of Table 1. The real-valued networks had 1.41 times more neurons in the hidden layers, to ensure the same number of real parameters between the two types of networks, and thus a fair comparison. Each layer was trained in an unsupervised manner, and then the learned weights were used to initialize the weights of the deep networks. These networks were then fine-tuned using stochastic gradient descent.

The number of pretraining epochs was 100, and the number of fine-tuning epochs was 50. The learning rate was 0.01 for the unsupervised learning, and 0.1 for the supervised learning.

The experimental results on the MNIST dataset are given in Table 1. It can be seen from the table that we tested different architectures, and the results were consistent: complex-valued neural networks pretrained using complex-valued deep belief networks attained better classification results than real-valued networks using their real-valued counterparts.

Table 1. Experimental results for MNIST

Hidden layer sizes	Real-valued error	Complex-valued error
1000	1.42%	**1.40%**
1000, 500	1.36%	**1.32%**
1000, 1000	1.38%	**1.23%**
1000, 1000, 1000	1.31%	**1.20%**
1000, 1000, 1000, 1000	1.38%	**1.37%**
2000, 1500, 1000, 500	1.64%	**1.34%**
2500, 2000, 1500, 1000, 500	1.45%	**1.31%**

4   Conclusions

The full deduction of the complex-valued deep belief networks and their training algorithm was given, with special emphasis on the characteristics of learning in the complex domain.

Different network architectures were pretrained using real- and complex-valued deep belief networks on the MNIST dataset. The experimental results show an improvement in classification error of the complex-valued deep neural networks when pretrained using complex-valued deep belief networks, than the same type of networks with real values.

These results give an insight into the potential of complex-valued neural networks following the deep learning paradigm. More work needs to be done in order to fully harness the representational power of complex numbers for the deep neural network domain, which constitutes a challenging future work direction.

Acknowledgement. This work was supported by research grant no. PCD-TC-2017-41 of the Polytechnic University Timişoara, Romania.

References

1. Arjovsky, M., Shah, A., Bengio, Y.: Unitary evolution recurrent neural networks. In: ICML 2016 (2016). https://arxiv.org/abs/1511.06464
2. Bengio, Y.: Learning deep architectures for AI. Found. Trends Mach. Learn. **2**(1), 1–127 (2009)
3. Bengio, Y., LeCun, Y., Hinton, G.: Deep learning. Nature **521**, 436–444 (2015)
4. Bengio, Y., Lamblin, P., Popovici, D., Larochelle, H.: Greedy layer-wise training of deep networks. In: NIPS 2006, pp. 153–160 (2006)
5. Bruna, J., Mallat, S.: Invariant scattering convolution networks. IEEE Trans. Pattern Anal. Mach. Intell. **35**(8), 1872–1886 (2013)
6. Erhan, D., Bengio, Y., Courville, A., Manzagol, P.A., Vincent, P., Bengio, S.: Why does unsupervised pre-training help deep learning? J. Mach. Learn. Res. **11**, 625–660 (2010)

7. Goodfellow, I., Bengio, Y., Courville, A.: Deep Learning. MIT Press, Cambridge (2016)
8. Hinton, G.E., Osindero, S., Teh, Y.W.: A fast learning algorithm for deep belief nets. Neural Comput. **18**(7), 1527–1554 (2006)
9. Jing, L., Shen, Y., Dubcek, T., Peurifoy, J., Skirlo, S., LeCun, Y., Tegmark, M., Soljacic, M.: Tunable efficient unitary neural networks (EUNN) and their application to RNNs. In: ICML 2017 (2017). https://arxiv.org/abs/1612.05231
10. LeCun, Y., Bottou, L., Bengio, Y., Haffner, P.: Gradient-based learning applied to document recognition. Proc. IEEE **86**(11), 2278–2324 (1998)
11. Popa, C.A.: Complex-valued convolutional neural networks for real-valued image classification. In: 2017 International Joint Conference on Neural Networks (IJCNN). IEEE, May 2017
12. Reichert, D.P., Serre, T.: Neuronal synchrony in complex-valued deep networks. In: ICLR 2014 (2014). https://arxiv.org/abs/1312.6115
13. Sarroff, A.M., Shepardson, V., Casey, M.A.: Learning representations using complex-valued nets (2015). https://arxiv.org/abs/1511.06351
14. Schmidhuber, J.: Deep learning in neural networks: an overview. Neural Netw. **61**, 85–117 (2015)
15. Tygert, M., Bruna, J., Chintala, S., LeCun, Y., Piantino, S., Szlam, A.: A mathematical motivation for complex-valued convolutional networks. Neural Comput. **28**(5), 815–825 (2016)
16. Wisdom, S., Powers, T., Hershey, J.R., Roux, J.L., Atlas, L.: Full-capacity unitary recurrent neural networks. In: NIPS 2016 (2016). https://arxiv.org/abs/1611.00035

Modeling of the Cognitive Activity of Simultaneous Interpretation Using the Theory of Information Images

Alexandr Y. Petukhov$^{(\boxtimes)}$ and Sofia A. Polevaya

Lobachevsky Nizhny Novgorod State University, Novgorod, Russia
Lectorr@yandex.ru

Abstract. This article reviews cognitive activity of the brain during the simultaneous interpretation from foreign language into Russian, as well as during a number of additional professional tasks (shadowing). From the experimental point of view, using the technology of event-related telemetry (ERT) of heart rate, we investigated the features of mobilization of vegetative resources for a record-breaking activity in terms of energy efficiency and stressogenic load-simultaneous interpretation (SI). The results have been analyzed from the point of view of the Information Images Theory. The main provisions of this theory are given along with overview of the hierarchy of information images in the mind of an individual, which determines his real and virtual activity. This paper provides a model of the dynamics of information images in the mind of individuals during simultaneous interpretation.

Keywords: Interpretation · Communicative field · Information image
The information images space · Virtual particles

1 Introduction

The problem that arises from the need to describe the processes of transmission and processing of information by an individual is fundamental to modern cognitive science. Relatively recently there appeared unique natural-science models of information transfer from an individual to an individual [1], and some others in other fields of biology and cognitive psychology [2–5] and others. These methods have cleared a path to studying the physiological mechanisms of the individual stages of the information processing: sensory analysis, mobilization of attention, image formation, extraction of memory patterns, decision making, etc.

The study of time parameters of electrophysiological reactions to stimuli of different types and under different conditions for the first time made it possible to apply chronometry, i.e. an estimation of the duration of individual stages in the course of processing the information directly at the brain substrate level. Many fundamental facts were also obtained using classical methods of psychology in the study and analysis of the behavior of subjects in various social situations. Along with cognitive psychophysiology, a relatively new field of neuroscience - neuroinformatics - has emerged. Similar to cognitive psychophysiology, neuroinformatics in fact represents an

© Springer International Publishing AG, part of Springer Nature 2018
T. Huang et al. (Eds.): ISNN 2018, LNCS 10878, pp. 79–88, 2018.
https://doi.org/10.1007/978-3-319-92537-0_10

application of a computer metaphor to the analysis of mechanisms of creating and processing information in the brain of humans and animals.

However, many of the presented models are either poorly scalable or not sufficiently formalized and therefore do not lead to fundamental explaination of the processes of information transfer and its distortion as a result of interaction with the external communicative environment.

The proposed theory is based on the idea of the universal cognitive unit [2] of the information in the human mind - the information image, a space, in which it exists, its topology and properties. Information images (hereinafter IIs) can be defined as the display of objects and events in any feature space.

Accordingly, the Information Images Theory (hereinafter IIT) can serve as a method of describing information interactions of individuals, as well as a number of cognitive functions of a person.

From the point of view of cognitive loads, the activity of simultaneous interpreters is one of the most energy-intensive and stressful ones for the brain [6]. Therefore, this type of activity can be indicative for recording the activity of information images.

In view of the limitations of the size of the article, it is more effective to get acquainted with the theory of information images in these work – [7].

2   Experiment

The experimental studies can be correlated with the IIT through the reaction time to the perturbation (i.e., impact) of the individual. The reaction time will correspond to the image activation time, i.e. its transition to a higher level in the II space. Therefore, we chose an experiment based on the information technology of event-related telemetry (ERT) of the heart rate [8]. A WEB-platform Apway.ru developed by our team was used for the study of cognitive functions. This platform provides a universal infrastructure for designing and conducting various psycho-physiological tests.

The idea of the experiment is as follows: interpreters working in succession performed professional tasks: shadowing the text in Russian, simultaneous interpretation of the text from foreign language to Russian, shadowing the text in a foreign language, simultaneous interpretation of the text from foreign language to Russian. In addition, before and after the professional activity, the interpreters were to pass the projective test to determine the level of emotional deconditioning (LED), the sensorimotor activity test and the Stroop test (10 subjects - Russian version, 6 - bilingual) using the Apway platform [9]. During the whole experiment, a telemetric registration of the cardiointervalogramm was conducted to identify the features of the mobilization of vegetative and energy resources for all types of activities of interpreters and to determine the level of stress load induced by each type of activity. The following methods were used for the statistical analysis: ANOVA (method of repeated measurements) and correlation analysis.

Sixteen (16) simultaneous interpreters (13 women and 3 men, ages 21 to 28) took part in the experiments. Each test subject had been specifically trained (educated) for this kind of activity.

Monitoring the variability of RR-intervals in the process of experimental modeling of the professional activity of a simultaneous interpreter (Fig. 1) fully confirmed the widespread opinion about the high degree of its stress load. This manifested both in a distinctive decrease in native RR-intervals, and in the corresponding changes in the parameters of vegetative regulation: a drop in the overall range of the spectrum of heart rate variability against a sharp increase in the dominance of sympathetic activity over the parasympathetic one.

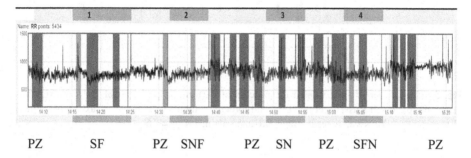

Fig. 1. A typical example of recording a cardiointervalogramm of a subject during two shadowing sessions (1 in German, 3 in Russian) and two simultaneous interpreting sessions (2 from Russian into German, 4 from German into Russian).

Statistical analysis of the results of heart rate monitoring allowed to identify the least (shadowing the text in the native language) and the most (simultaneous interpretation, especially from a foreign language into the native language) stressful activities of simultaneous interpreters (Fig. 2).

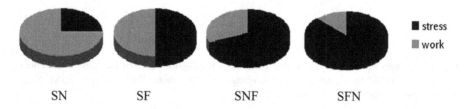

Fig. 2. The ratio of the time of the normal functional state and the periods of stress in the course of performance of professional work (n = 64) by simultaneous interpreters (n = 16). The abbreviations are the same as in Fig. 1

The lower mobilization of energy resources was predictably manifested when working with the Russian language (Fig. 3). Particularly suprising was the result of the analysis of the dynamics of changes in the RR-intervals in relation to the type of work (Fig. 4): the stress during the simultaneous interpretation statistically was significantly higher (compared to shadowing) only in the first 100 s of the task, and then the differences became unreliable.

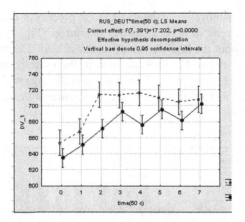

Fig. 3. Changes in RR-intervals in the process of performing professional tasks for simultaneous interpreters in Russian (dotted line) and foreign (solid lines) language. X axis denotes time (1 step = 50 s); Y-axis denotes average RR-intervals in ms; n = 16

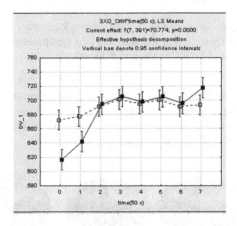

Fig. 4. Changes in RR-intervals during the shadowing sessions (dotted line) and simultaneous interpretation (solid lines), regardless of language. X axis denotes time (1 step = 50 s); Y-axis denotes average RR-interval in ms; n = 16

Abbreviations: STR - Stroop test (Russian version), STF- Stroop test (foreign version), SMA- sensorimotor activity test, LED- level of emotional deconditioning, SF- shadowing of a foreign text, PZ - pause in the activity, SNF- simultaneous interpretation from native language to foreign language, SN- shadowing the text in the native language, SFN - simultaneous interpretation from a foreign language into the native language.

Thus, the maturity factor of the functional system, which determines the proficiency in native or foreign language, was clearly manifested in comparison of energy costs when working with native and foreign languages. To clarify the role of the time factor (the ability to maintant and follow the speaker's speech tempo), the results of the test for simple sensorimotor activity were analyzed (Fig. 5). Increasing inter-stimulus intervals (from 600 to 5000 ms), leads to the significant increase in the response time (Fig. 5A) and RR-intervals (Fig. 5B), which indicates the expected drop in the energy expenditures along with the decrease in the tempo of stimuli presentation (Fig. 5C)

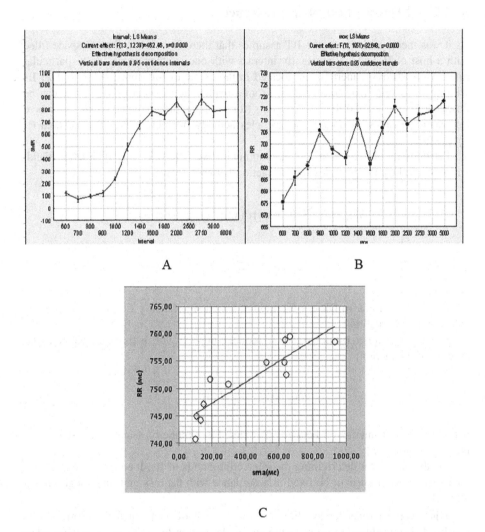

Fig. 5. Correlation between the reaction time and heart rate during the simple sensorimotor activity. A is the dynamics of the reaction time against the interstimulus interval changes during the simple sensorimotor activity; B is the dynamics of RR-intervals against the interstimulus interval changes during the simple sensorimotor activity; C is the direct correlation between the reaction time and the mean RR interval against the interstimulus interval changes.

Thus, it is necessary to analyze the obtained results from the point of view of the information images theory, as well as to compare the experimental data with the simulation data.

3 Model Description of the II Space

As it was mentioned above, the IIT assumes that there is a certain limited space filled with a host of IIs, which constantly interact with one another according to particular rules. More "heavy", inert IIs are located in the center of this space, while lighter IIs with higher energy tend to its edges. From a mathematical point of view, this can be described by means of diffusion equations (for example, the Langevin equation), where information images are likened to particles actively interacting in a limited area (II space) [9].

Let us write the equation for the communicative field (CF), i.e. Interaction Field, which is used by the particles for interaction between them:

$$\frac{\partial}{\partial t} h(x_i, t) = \sum_{j=1}^{N} f(x_i, x_j) \vartheta(x_i, x_j) \overline{\delta}_{k_c^j, k_c^i} + D \Delta h(x_i, t),$$

$$\vartheta(x_i, x_j) = \frac{1}{u\sqrt{\pi}} e^{\frac{-(x_i - x_j)^2}{u^2}}$$

when $u \to 0$ is similar to Dirac's δ-function, which significantly simplifies the process of computer simulation;

k_c is coefficient determining the conditional complexity of IIs that can change in the process of interaction;

$$f(x_i, x_j) = \frac{1}{v\sqrt{\pi}} e^{\frac{-(x_1 - x_2)^2}{v^2}},$$

is the function of interaction between particles. For simplicity, Gauss was used as the interaction function;

v is the parameter determining the interaction radius of IIs. It can either depend on other system parameters or be fixed in accordance with the task and time length of the research;

$\overline{\delta}$ is inverse Kronecker symbol (i.e. the inverse of a classical two-dimensional matrix). It is introduced in order to prevent an II from influencing itself in the model.

The movement is described by the following equation:

$$\frac{dx_i}{dt} = k_c^i \left(\sum_{j=1, j \neq i}^{N} \frac{\partial}{\partial x_j} h(x_j, t) \right) + \sqrt{2D} \xi_i(t),$$

Here, stochastic force is also given by Gauss:

$$\xi_i(t) = \frac{1}{o\sqrt{\pi}}e^{\frac{-(t_1-t_2)^2}{o^2}},$$

where o – is the parameter determining the effect of the stochastic (i.e. random) force. Taking into account the field potential $\vec{U} = \nabla\Psi$,

$$\vec{F}(\vec{r},t) = -\nabla U(\vec{r},t),$$

Thus, the II movement can be described as the following:

$$\frac{dx_i}{dt} = k_c^i\left(\sum_{j=1,j\neq i}^{N}\frac{\partial}{\partial x_j}h(x_j,t)\right) + \sqrt{2D}\xi_i(t) - \int\nabla U(x_i,t),$$

where $\varepsilon_i(t)$– stochastic force.

Information images interact with each other in a similar way as the particles in the Brownian motion; the only difference is that the clash happens with the changes of not only in parameters of kinetic energy and the speed vector, but also in the specific II parameters.

4   The Results of Modeling from the Point of View of IIT

The simulation was conducted using the MatLab 2009b and MatLab 2011a software packages.

The developed model was used to build dependencies of the activation of information images for the experiment with simultaneous interpreters.

During the numerical simulation, the simultaneous interpretation was interpreted as the emergence of two simultaneous information disturbances (i.e., interaction and transition of two information images - the primary and its analogue in another language) – Fig. 6.

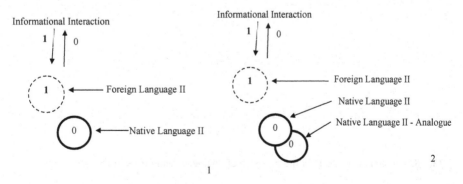

Fig. 6. Schematic representation of the impact. 1 - regular interpretation. 2 - with a choice between II analogs (synonyms, deformed IIs, etc.)

The following series of graphs refers to the display of the distinctive dependency of activation (activation of the II means its transition from the zone where it was before the introduction of an external stimulus into the zone of interaction with the new information stimulus; this, as a rule, leads to a shift to a higher level in the space of the II) for an individual II.

The dynamics of an individual II in this case is reduced to sequential activation and relaxation until the next activation (possibly erroneous, as a result of associative links, cognitive errors, etc.).

Numerically the first case - the regular interpretation - looks as follows – Fig. 7. X-axis represents time intervals, y - the cumulative change of coordinates in the space of information images.

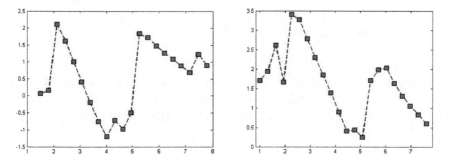

Fig. 7. Two variants of the activity of an individual language II during the simultaneous interpretation.

We can clearly see the sequential activations of images - a sharp increase in the curves followed by a relatively slow relaxation, caused by a shift of "attention" of cognitive activity.

For interpretation with errors and analogues – Fig. 8.

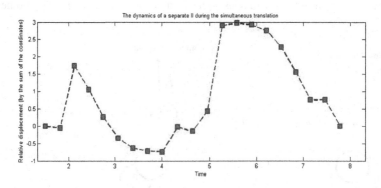

Fig. 8. Dynamics of the II in the presence of analogues and errors in the interpretation.

In the presence of errors and analogues in the simultaneous interpretation, the time between the activation of images increases significantly, the relaxation is slower, which indicates a sharp "overload" of the individual's brain by the information activity.

5   Conclusion

Thus, our study managed to verify experimentally and partially confirm the hypothesis of the three-factor psychophysiological mechanism responsible for a high complexity of simultaneous interpretation, which require the interpreter to have a high level of maturity of the functional system that determines the knowledge of native or foreign language ("competence"); ability to keep up with the pace of speech of the speaker; and an optimally built architecture of the interaction of information images in solving problems that require simultaneous activation of neuronal modules that enter not only into synergistic, but also into antagonistic interactions. (shadowing - interpretation, native language - foreign language).

From the point of view of the Information Images Theory, these processes are characterized by a high degree of activity in terms of the dynamics of information interactions, increase in cognitive errors and, as a consequence, increased load on the decision-making centers of the individual, increased cardio activity, etc. The multidi-rectional consecutive disturbance of the II space in presence of cognitive deformations caused by excessive activity of individual images and corresponding subsequent shifts in the overall structure leads to a distinctive pattern of the variation of the RR-intervals.

Funding. This study was funded by grants from the Board President of the Russian Federation (Project MK-328.2017.6) (Theoretical part).

This study was funded by RHSF grant № 15-06-10894_a, RFFR grants № 16-06-00501_a and № 17-06-00640_a (Experimental part).

Compliance with Ethical Standards
Ethical approval: All procedures performed in studies involving human participants were in accordance with the ethical standards of the institutional and/or national research committee and with the 1964 Helsinki declaration and its later amendments or comparable ethical standards. This article does not contain any studies with animals performed by any of the authors.

Informed consent: Informed consent was obtained from all individual participants included in the study.

Declaration of Conflicting Interests
The author(s) declared no potential conflicts of interest with respect to the research, authorship, and/or publication of this article.

References

1. Aleksandrov, Y.: Laws actualization of individual experience, and the reorganization of its system structure: a comprehensive study. Proc. ISA RAS **61**(3), 3–12 (2011)
2. Anokhin, K.V.: The genetic probes for mapping the neural network during training. The Principles and Mechanisms of the Human Brain, Leningrad Science (1989)

3. Ashby, F.G., Helie, S.: Tutorial on computational cognitive neuroscience: modeling the neurodynamics of cognition. J. Math. Psychol. **55**, 273–289 (2011)
4. Rutt, B.T., Oehlert, M.E., Krieshok, T.S., Lichtenberg, J.W.: Effectiveness of cognitive processing therapy and prolonged exposure in the department of veterans affairs. Psychol. Rep. **121**(2), 282–302 (2017). https://doi.org/10.1177/0033294117727746
5. Chernavskii, D.S.: Synergetics and Information. Dynamic Information Theory. URSS (2009)
6. Chernigovskaya, T.V.: Simultaneous interpreting and stress: pilot experiment. Int. J. Psychophysiol. **108**, 165 (2016)
7. Petukhov, A.Y., Polevaya, S.A.: Modeling of communicative individual interactions through the theory of information images. Curr. Psychol. **36**(3), 428–433 (2017)
8. Polevaia, S.A., Parin, S.B., Eremin, E.V., Bulanov, N.A., Chernova, M.A., Parina, I.S., Chernigovskaya, T.V.: Event-related telemetry (ERT) technology for study of cognitive functions. Int. J. Psychophysiol. **108**, 87–88 (2016)
9. Petukhov, A.Y., Polevaya, S.A.: The bilingual stroop test from the view of the information images theory. Procedia Comput. Sci. **88**, 415–422 (2016)

Models, Methods and Algorithms

Development of a Sensory-Neural Network for Medical Diagnosing

Igor Grabec[1(✉)], Eva Švegl[2], and Mihael Sok[2]

[1] Slovenian Academy of Sciences and Art, Ljubljana, Slovenia
igor.grabec@fs.uni-lj.si
[2] Faculty of Medicine, University of Ljubljana, Ljubljana, Slovenia
eva.svegl@gmail.com, miha.sok@kclj.si

Abstract. Performance of a sensory-neural network developed for diagnosing of diseases is described. Information about patient's condition is provided by answers to the questionnaire. Questions correspond to sensors generating signals when patients acknowledge symptoms. These signals excite neurons in which characteristics of the diseases are represented by synaptic weights associated with indicators of symptoms. The disease corresponding to the most excited neuron is proposed as the result of diagnosing. Its reliability is estimated by the likelihood defined by the ratio of excitation of the most excited neuron and the complete neural network.

Keywords: Sensory-neural network · Disease symptoms
Medical diagnosing

1 Introduction

Medical diagnosing can be treated as a mapping of symptoms to characteristics of diseases [1,2]. Our goal is to develop a sensory-neural network (SNN) by which this mapping could be performed automatically by a PC [3–5]. With this aim we first transform data about patient's condition into a proper form for the numerical processing. This transformation corresponds to sensing of symptoms by sensors at the input layer of the SNN shown in Fig. 1. Similarly as data of patients, the characteristics of diseases are transformed and utilized to specify the synaptic weights of neurons in the next layer [6]. At this specification we take into account the performance of a doctor at the diagnosis assessment. The doctor collects symptoms of the treated patient and compares them with the properties of diseases. At the comparison he considers certain symptoms as more significant than others and so assesses the agreement between given symptoms and those describing diseases [6,7]. The disease with the highest correlation is then selected as a result of diagnosis. We describe such treatment by characterizing the significance of symptoms by synaptic weights connecting the sensors to neurons that correspond to various diseases. A signal from a particular sensor thus contributes different amounts to excitation of various neurons. The excitation of

© Springer International Publishing AG, part of Springer Nature 2018
T. Huang et al. (Eds.): ISNN 2018, LNCS 10878, pp. 91–98, 2018.
https://doi.org/10.1007/978-3-319-92537-0_11

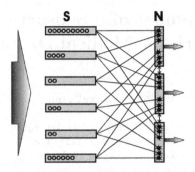

Fig. 1. Schematic drawing of the sensory-neural network. Bold arrows demonstrate input and output information flow, o - denote symptom indicators, ∗ - show synapses, ↔ - represent connections between SNN elements.

a particular neuron therefore represents the correlation between the symptoms of a patient and the properties of the disease represented by the neuron. The disease corresponding to the most excited neuron in the NN layer determines the result of diagnosis. We describe the reliability of such assessment by expressing the output of the neuron relatively with respect to the mean value of all outputs. The corresponding estimator represents the likelihood of the diagnosis. At the specification of the SNN we first select a set of diseases and specify their symptoms as well as synaptic weights of neurons. In terms of them we next define the agreement and likelihood estimators.

2   Properties of Data Bases

2.1   Symptoms and Diseases

According to the suggestion of the research initiator [5] we apply the set of 15 most frequent diseases denoted by the name and index $D(d)$: (1) *Anemia*, (2) *Urinary tract infection*, (3) *Diabetes-2*, (4) *Atrial fibrillation*, (5) *Acute hemorrhagic stroke*, (6) *Obstructive sleep apnea*, (7) *Tuberculosis*, (8) *Chronic obstructive pulmonary disease*, (9) *Pneumonia*, (10) *Otitis media*, (11) *Leukocytosis*, (12) *Hepatitis-A*, (13) *Hypertension*, (14) *Throat inflammation*, (15) *No disease*. Their properties are characterized by $N_s = 46$ symptoms $S(s)$ shown in Table 1 and used to describe the sensory layer of the SNN [3,4]. A symptom $S(s)$ is described by up to $N_i = 9$ possible indicators $I(s, i)$ shown in Table 2.

A particular disease is characterized by various symptom indicators. The presence or absence of a symptom indicator can be generally denoted by 0 or 1, but such indication leads to a very rough assessment of diagnosis. For a better assessment we describe the importance of the symptom indicator $I(s, i)$ of the disease $D(d)$ by a synaptic weight $W(d, s, i)$. A non- important indicator is assigned the weight $W = 0$, while the other weights are positive or negative. A negative weight points to the absence of the disease. To avoid problems related

Table 1. Symptoms used for characterization of diseases

s	Symptom name - $S(s)$	s	Symptom name - $S(s)$	s	Symptom name - $S(s)$
1	No symptoms	17	Sleep disturb.- night walk	33	Difficulty when speaking
2	Sudden onset of illness	18	Distorted vision	34	Difficulty moving one side
3	Hyperthermia	19	Frequent urination	35	Sudden infertility
4	Malaise, tiredness	20	Tinnitus	36	Difficult verbal expression
5	Age over 70	21	Bleeding	37	Vomiting
6	Headache	22	Dark urine in last 2 weeks	38	Snoring during sleep
7	Sudden headache	23	Thirst, dry mouth	39	Smelly urine
8	Cough	24	Nervousness, depression	40	Heart rate
9	Dizziness	25	Throat irritation	41	Arterial hypertension
10	Trouble breathing	26	Pharyngeal dryness	42	Pulse rhythmicity
11	Pain	27	Hoarseness	43	O satur. - pulse oxim.
12	w. loss in last 1/2 y	28	Obstruction in the throat	44	Breathing frequency
13	Loss of appetite	29	Jaundice of skin & Sclera	45	Body height
14	Irregular pulse	30	Light feces	46	Body weight
15	Sweating	31	Frequent infections		
16	Difficult concentrating	32	Ability to lift both arms		

Table 2. Indicators of symptoms

s	Indicators $I(s,:)$
3	{fever, y, n}
6	{y, n, in the morning, daily persistent}
8	{y-in the morning, y-with sputum, y-daily persistent, y-without sputum,n}
10	{at rest, on exertion, n}
11	{chest, ear, abdomen, pharynx, at swallowing, at speaking, at urinating, shoulder, n}
15	{daily persistent, nocturnal,n}
18	{y, n, one eye only}
19	{y, n, at night}
21	{from the nose, in the sputum, in the urine, n}
31	{urinary tract, tongue, corners of the mouth, lung, n}
40	{<50, 51–70, 71–90, >90}
41	{<100, 100–140, >140}
42	{rhythmic, arrhythmic}
43	{≤ 90, >90}
44	{<10, 11–15, >15}
45	{<150, 151–160, 161–170, 171–180, 181–190, >190} cm
46	{<50, 51–60, 61–70, 71–80, 81–90, 91–100, >100} kg

All other possible indicators are specified by: $I(s,:) = \{\text{yes}, \text{no}\} = \{\text{y}, \text{n}\}$.
Components missing in Table 2 correspond to empty space $\emptyset$, for example: $I(s,:) = \{\text{fever}, \text{y}, \text{n}\} \equiv \{\text{fever}, \text{y}, \text{n}, \emptyset, \emptyset, \emptyset, \emptyset, \emptyset, \emptyset\}$.

Table 3. Statistical weights describing importance of symptom indicators

d	The values denote: (symptom index s, indicator index i, weight $W(d,s,i)$)
1	(2,2,1) (3,3,1) (4,1,1) (6,1,1) (9,1,1) (10,1,1) (14,1,1) (16,1,1) (17,1,1) (20,1,1) (31,1,1) (31,3,2) (40,4,1) (44,3,2)
2	(2,1,1) (3,1,3) (3,2,1) (11,3,2) (11,8,4) (19,1,3) (22,1,3) (39,1,3)
3	(2,2,2) (3,3,2) (4,1,1) (12,2,2) (18,1,1) (19,1,2) (31,1,2)
4	(2,1,3) (3,2,3) (5,1,3) (10,2,2) (11,1,2) (14,1,3) (41,2,1) (41,3,3) (42,2,3)
5	(2,1,2) (3,3,1) (7,1,2) (9,1,1) (18,3,2) (32,2,2) (33,1,2) (34,2,2) (35,1,2) (36,1,2) (37,1,1)
6	(2,2,1) (4,1,1) (6,3,1) (16,1,1) (17,1,3) (23,1,1) (24,1,2) (41,3,1) (46,6,2) (46,7,3)
7	(2,2,1) (3,2,1) (4,1,1) (8,3,3) (11,1,1) (12,1,1) (13,1,1) (15,2,3) (21,2,3)
8	(2,2,2) (3,3,1) (8,1,3) (8,2,3) (8,5,-3) (31,4,2)
9	(2,1,2) (3,1,3) (3,2,1) (4,1,2) (8,2,1) (8,3,1) (8,4,1) (10,1,1) (10,2,1) (11,1,1)
10	(2,1,2) (3,2,1) (4,1,1) (6,4,2) (11,2,3) (29,1,1)
11	(2,2,1) (3,2,1) (4,1,1) (9,1,1) (10,1,1) (10,2,1) (12,1,1) (13,1,1) (15,1,1) (18,1,1)
12	(2,1,2) (3,2,1) (4,1,3) (11,3,2) (13,1,2) (29,1,3) 22,1,3) (30,1,3) (37,1,2)
13	(2,2,1) (3,3,2) (5,1,1) (6,4,2) (9,1,1) (21,1,1) (41,3,6)
14	(2,1,2) (3,1,1) (11,4,3) (25,1,2) (26,1,1) (27,1,1) (28,1,1)
15	(1,1,1) (2,2,1) (3,3,1) (4,2,1) (6,2,1) (8,5,1) (11,9,1) (13,2,1) (16,2,1) (18,2,1) (21,4,1) (22,2,1) (23,2,1) (24,2,1) (25,2,1) (26,2,1) (27,2,1) (28,2,1) (29,2,1) (30,2,1) (31,5,1) (32,2,1) (33,2,1) (34,2,1) (35,2,1) (36,2,1) (37,2,1) (38,2,1) (39,2,1)

Weights at other indices are 0.

with network training we apply a set of fixed weights specified by a clinical research. Their values mostly lie in the interval $(1,3)$. By the set $\{W(d,s,i); 1 \leq d \leq 15; 1 \leq s \leq 46; 1 \leq i \leq 9\}$ shown in Table 3 we describe quantitatively the properties of diseases. For this purpose we treat the weights $W(d,s,i)$ as the transmission parameters of synaptic joints on the neuron with index d. To provide for equivalent treatment of all diseases at the assessment of a diagnosis, it is reasonable to normalize the weights so that the sum of their positive values equals 1. By using the Heaviside function: $\{H(x) = 0 \text{ for } x \leq 0 \; ; \; H(x) = 1 \text{ for } x > 0\}$ we include just positive weights into the total positive weight: $W_t(d) = \sum_{s=1}^{N_s} \sum_{i=1}^{N_i} W(d,s,i)H(W(d,s,i))$, and define the normalized weight by the fraction: $W_n(d,s,i) = W(d,s,i)/W_t(d)$.

2.2   Algorithm of Diagnosis

At a diagnosis, the patient first completes the questionnaire containing names of symptoms and their indicators. A confirmed item is represented by the value 1 in the response matrix $\{R(s,i); s = 1 \ldots N_s; i = 1 \ldots N_i\}$, while all other non-confirmed terms are 0. This matrix represents the signals of values 0/1 supplied from the sensory to neural layer of the network. We next assume that the signal from $I(s,i)$ excites the $neuron(d)$ over the synaptic weight $W_n(d,s,i)$ and adds to its output the amount $W_n(d,s,i)R(s,i)$. The complete output of the $neuron(d)$ is then given by the sum:

$$A(d) = \sum_{s=1}^{N_s} \sum_{i=1}^{N_i} W_n(d, s, i) R(s, i) \qquad (1)$$

The distribution $\{A(d); d = 1, \ldots, N_d\}$ describes the excitation of the complete NN, while $A(d)$ is the estimator of the agreement between the patient's symptoms and the symptoms of the disease $D(d)$. If all symptoms of $D(d)$ coincide with the symptoms confirmed by the patient, the $neuron(d)$ is maximally excited and we get $A(d) = 1$ (or 100%). As the result of the diagnosis assessment, we propose the disease $D(d_o)$ with the maximal agreement: $A(d_o) = \max\{A(d); d = 1 \ldots N_d\}$.

To support our decision we determine the mean value $<A> = \sum_{d=1}^{N_d} A(d)/N_d$ and the standard deviation $\sigma_A = \sqrt{\mathrm{var}(A)}$ of $A(d)$, and then determine the relative deviation: $\Delta_A(d) = (A(d) - <A>)/\sigma_A$. In the case when $\Delta_A(d_o) \gg 1$ we conclude that the corresponding $D(d_o)$ is significantly outstanding and can be considered as a reliable quantitative result of the diagnosis. Such reasoning is possible when the symptoms of a particular disease are well exhibited. However, this is not always the case, since several diseases share similar symptoms. This leads to similar stimulations and consequently, a question arises as how to infer when $\Delta_A(d_o)$ is not outstanding. To address this possibility we divide $A(d)$ by the sum: $\sum_{d=1}^{N_d} A(d)$ and define the disease likelihood estimator $L(d)$ as:

$$L(d) = \frac{A(d)}{\sum_{d'=1}^{N_d} A(d')} \qquad (2)$$

This estimator describes the relative stimulation of the $neuron(d)$ in the layer of neurons and represents the reliability of our decision. A high value of $L(d)$ corresponds to a firm argument for selecting the corresponding disease as a reliable result of the diagnosis. It is important that both $A(d)$ and $L(d)$ are quantitative in character and thus can be treated as the supplement of other quantitative data in clinical tests.

3   Performance of SNN

3.1   Characterization of the Performance

For a wide application we have developed a program that interacts with a user over a graphic interface [3,4]. At the start the graphic interface presents the user with three options: (1) Identifying a diagnosis based on completing the questionnaire, (2) Testing the program performance based on internally stored data sets of *formal symptoms* for all diseases, (3) Changing the weights of symptom indicators. All options can be repeated.

In the first option a new window with instructions for the user appears together with a window to enter the patient's name. After accepting the name, the program shows sequentially 46 windows with the symptom names and their indicators. Confirmed data are translated into the response matrix R that is led from the sensory to the neural layer of SNN, where the distributions of the agreement A and likelihood L are determined. The results are transferred to the user over various channels. The most informative is the displayed diagram of $A(d)$ and $L(d)$ distribution versus the disease index d. The lines at the levels of $<A>$, $<A> + \sigma_A$ and $<A> + 2\sigma_A$ are used as references for a visual assessment of the diagnosis. Two examples are shown in Fig. 2. In addition to such diagram, the files with the patient's responses and corresponding numerical data are available for printing.

In the second option the program displays the set of diseases. After one of them is selected, the program applies the corresponding formal set of symptoms and uses it instead of the patient's symptoms in the same procedure as in the first option. This step shows the optimal possibility of the selected disease diagnosis.

The third option allows specialists to examine how a variation of synaptic weights influences the diagnosis process. By adjusting the weights and further testing the diagnosis using the second option, the performance of the complete program can be gradually improved. With this aim, the program allows modification of weights. This option provides for NN *training*, while the changing of the set of symptoms provides for *evolution* of the complete SNN.

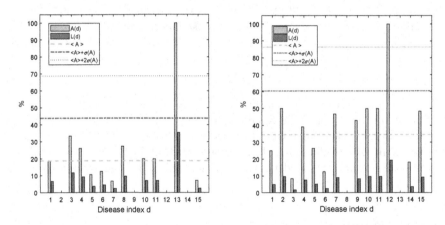

Fig. 2. Left: Distribution of A and L in testing the program performance based on formal symptoms of $D(13)$ - *hypertension*. Right: Distribution of A and L based on the answers to the questionnaire by a patient suffering from $D(12)$ - *hepatitis A*.

3.2   Testing of the Program Performance

To demonstrate the performance of developed SNN we first present results of its testing performed with the formal symptoms of the typical disease $D(13)$ - *hypertension*. In this test, we get the diagram shown on the left of Fig. 2.

The value of the corresponding optimal agreement estimator is in this case $A_o(4) = 100\%$, and it surpasses the mean value $<A>$ for $3.25\,\sigma_A$. This outstanding deviation from the mean value indicates a correct assessment of the diagnosis. But the value of A corresponding to several other diseases also surpasses the mean value $<A>$. This outcome indicates that the symptoms of these diseases are in a sense similar to those of *hypertension*. In spite of this property, the distribution of $A(d)$ suggests selecting *hypertension* as the result of the diagnosis. Although the agreement with its symptom indicators is $A_o = 100\%$, the likelihood value of *hypertension* disease is only $L_o = 35\%$; the other values, however, are still appreciably smaller: $L(d) \ll L_o; d \neq d_o$.

Similar performance of the program as in testing the diagnosis of *hypertension* is observed when using formal symptoms of other diseases. The corresponding optimal likelihood values $\{L_o(d); d = 1, \ldots 15\}$ are:

$$L_o = (29, 32, 34, 32, 37, 33, 29, 48, 24, 32, 28, 28, 35, 48, 41)\% \qquad (3)$$

The mean value of the set of optimal values $\{L_o(d); d = 1, \ldots, 15\}$ is similar as in the demonstrated case of *hypertension*, amounting to $<L_o> = 34, 6\%$. The corresponding standard deviation is $\sigma_L = 7\%$ while the maximal and minimal values are $L_{o,max} = L_o(8) = L_o(14) = 48\%$ and $L_{o,min} = L_o(9) = 24\%$, respectively. These data indicate that the likelihood value of $L_o \approx 35\%$ yields a rather firm quantitative argument for accepting the result of the automatic diagnosing.

To demonstrate performance of SNN in the clinical practice we perform diagnosis of the disease $D(12)$ - *hepatitis A* by data obtained from a patient. The diagram is shown on the right of Fig. 2. In this case the value of the relative agreement is also $A(12) = 100\%$ and surpasses the mean value $<A>$ of the agreement distribution by $2.53\,\sigma_A$. All other values $\{A(d); d \neq 12\}$ are essentially below the value $A(12)$; therefore, we accept as the rather reliable result of diagnosis the $D(12)$ - *hepatitis A*. This conclusion is supported by the value $L(12) = 19\%$ that is smaller as $L_o(12) = 28\%$ obtained at testing by formal indicators, but still approximately two times greater than all other values. Such result is obtained when all significant symptom indicators in the questionnaire are confirmed by a patient. Other characteristic examples are published elsewhere [3,4].

4 Conclusions

Our testing has indicated that the selected sets of symptoms and synaptic weights provide a proper basis for the specification of a sensory-neural network applicable for an automatic diagnosing of selected diseases. The advantage of the developed method is the quantitative expression of the agreement between patient symptoms and properties of diseases. By using this estimator various subjective errors could be avoided at the assessment of a diagnosis. Moreover, its reliability can be described by the disease likelihood estimator. Consequently, the developed SNN could be widely applied by medical doctors and patients outside the professional environment.

At the development of our SNN we have utilized synaptic weights determined by doctors. However, in the interest of refining the diagnosing the corresponding data could also be automatically created and even improved during the application of the corresponding computer program. Various methods developed for training artificial neural networks could be applied for this purpose [1,6]. Such an adaptation would in fact allow for the acquisition of new medical knowledge and also for its storage.

We are aware that our procedure corresponds to a rather crude simplification of the professional performance of doctors. To improve it one should take more symptoms as well as diseases into account. However, making such an improvement requires more in-depth descriptions of the corresponding sets. We expect that for this purpose applying a hierarchic structure could be advantageous.

Acknowledgments. This research was supported by the Slovenian Academy of Sciences and Art, Ljubljana and Amanova Ltd, Technology Park of Ljubljana, Slovenia.

References

1. Wagholikar, K.B., Sundararajan, V., Deshpande, A.W.: Modeling paradigms for medical diagnostic decision support: a survey and future directions. J. Med. Syst. **36**(5), 3029–3049 (2012)
2. Balogh, E.P., Miller, B.T., Ball, J.R. (eds.): Improving Diagnosis in Health Care. Committee on Diagnostic Error in Health Care; Board on Health Care Services; Institute of Medicine; The National Academies of Sciences, Engineering, and Medicine. The National Academic Press, Washington DC (2015)
3. Sok, M., Švegl, E., Grabec, I.: Statistical diagnosis of diseases. In: International Conference Applied Statistics, Ribno (Bled), Slovenia, 18–21 September 2016
4. Sok, M., Švegl, E., Grabec, I.: A sensory-neural network for medical diagnosis. In: IEEE Conference on Evolving and Adaptive Intelligent Systems, Ljubljana, Slovenia (2017). https://doi.org/10.1109/EAIS.2017.7954819, http://ieeexplore.ieee.org/document/7954819/
5. Project proposals call. https://en.wikipedia.org/wiki/Tricorder_X_Prize
6. Grabec, I., Sachse, W.: Synergetics of Measurement, Prediction and Control. Springer, Berlin (1997). https://doi.org/10.1007/978-3-642-60336-5
7. Zhou, X.H., Obuchowski, N.A., McClish, D.K.: Statistical Methods in Diagnostic Medicine, 2nd edn. Wiley Series in Probability and Statistics, Hoboken (2011)

Review of Pseudoinverse Learning Algorithm for Multilayer Neural Networks and Applications

Jue Wang[1,3], Ping Guo[1,2(✉)], and Xin Xin[1]

[1] School of Computer Science and Technology,
Beijing Institute of Technology, Beijing 100083, China
{3120160445,xxin}@bit.edu.cn, pguo@bnu.edu.cn
[2] School of Systems Science, Beijing Normal University, Beijing 100875, China
[3] School of Space Information,
Space Engineering University, Beijing 101400, China

Abstract. In this work, we give an overview of pseudoinverse learning (PIL) algorithm as well as applications. PIL algorithm is a non-gradient descent algorithm for multi-layer perception. The weight matrix of network can be exactly computed by PIL algorithm. So PIL algorithm can effectively avoid the problem of low convergence and local minima. Moreover, PIL does not require user-selected parameters, such as step size and learning rate. This algorithm has achieved good application in the fields of software reliability engineering, astronomical data analysis and so on.

Keywords: Back propagation · Pseudoinverse learning
Multi-layer perception · Deep neural network · Stacked auto-encoder

1 Introduction

Multi-layer perception (MLP) is a kind of feedforward neural networks, which is most studied in mid-eighties of last century. Now with more than three hidden layers, it is called deep neural network, and it has already been found to be successful for various supervised learning tasks. Both theoretical and empirical studies have shown that the network is of powerful capabilities for pattern classification and universal approximation [1–4].

When there are few hidden layers, weight parameters of network can be learned by the gradient descent learning algorithm, namely the well-known error back propagation (BP) algorithm. With the increase of network depth, the disadvantages of BP algorithm become more and more obvious. These algorithms usually have two disadvantages. One is poor convergence rate and local minima [5]. Convergence to local minima can result from less hidden neurons and improper initial weight settings. Another disadvantage is the selection of hyperparameters, such as learning rate, momentum constant and so on. The ideal learning algorithm just takes a dataset and outputs a function, without requiring hand-tuning of hyperparameters [6]. Because of no theory guidance how to choose these parameters except rich experience, so the selection of hyperparameters is crucial for the success of the BP algorithm.

© Springer International Publishing AG, part of Springer Nature 2018
T. Huang et al. (Eds.): ISNN 2018, LNCS 10878, pp. 99–106, 2018.
https://doi.org/10.1007/978-3-319-92537-0_12

In order to solve these problems, Guo et al. [7–9] proposed pseudoinverse learning (PIL) algorithm. Unlike BP algorithm, PIL algorithm is a non-gradient descent algorithm. It could exactly calculate the network's weights rather than iterative optimization. PIL algorithm only adopted generalized linear algebraic methods. Moreover, it didn't explicitly set any control parameters, which were usually specified empirically. For two decades, PIL algorithm has been developed and applied in many fields.

In this paper, we give an overview of PIL algorithm as well as applications. The rest of the paper is organized as follows. In Sect. 2, we summarize the development of PIL algorithm. In Sect. 3, we sort applications of PIL algorithm in various fields. In Sect. 4, we discuss the characteristics of PIL algorithm. Finally, we draw a conclusion about this work in Sect. 5.

2   Learning Algorithm

BP algorithm, which is a kind of gradient decent algorithm, has a few of disadvantages, such as slow convergence and local minima. So it is worth to develop the non-gradient descent algorithm. PIL algorithm is a non-gradient descent algorithm for MLP.

As mentioned earlier, hyperparameters need to be pre-considered in BP algorithms. The choices of hyperparameter are more difficult for the average user. In 1995, Guo et al. [7] proposed PIL algorithm to train a single hidden layer neural network (SHLN). This algorithm is a non-gradient descent algorithm, and does not require the setting of hyperparameters. In this work, the sum of square error function was adopted and can be denoted as

$$minimize[E] = minimize \, \|\mathbf{H} \cdot \mathbf{W}_2 - \mathbf{B}\|^2, \qquad (1)$$

where $\mathbf{H} = Tanh \, (\mathbf{X} \cdot \mathbf{W}_1)$ is the output matrix of the hidden layer, $\mathbf{B} = ArcTanh \, (\mathbf{O})$, $\mathbf{X}$ is the input matrix consisting of N input vectors as its rows and d columns, and $\mathbf{O}$ is the target label matrix which consists of N label vectors as its rows and m columns.

Equation (1) is formally a problem of least squares in linear algebra. However, only the $\mathbf{B}$ matrix is known at present. The weights $\mathbf{W}_1$ connecting input and hidden neurons, and the weights $\mathbf{W}_2$ connecting the hidden and output neurons, are not yet known.

A formal solution to $\mathbf{W}_2$ in Eq. (1) is $\mathbf{W}_2 = \mathbf{H}^+ \cdot \mathbf{B}$, where $\mathbf{H}^+$ is the pseudoinverse of $\mathbf{H}$. To bring this formal solution to Eq. (1), we can also get the following form:

$$\mathbf{H}\mathbf{H}^+ \mathbf{B} - \mathbf{B} = 0, \qquad (2)$$

If Eq. (2) holds, an intuitive explanation is that $\mathbf{H}\mathbf{H}^+ = \mathbf{I}$ satisfies the requirement. So $\mathbf{H}^+$ is the final solution.

For values of $\mathbf{W}_1$, it is a simple way to choose random values [7, 10–14]. In practice, it is found that if no constraints are applied to random generated value, the solution will become unstable. There are many ways to solve this problem, such as the common data normalization method. PIL sets the pseudoinverse of the input matrix as $\mathbf{W}_1$ matrix. In doing so, it is obviously theoretically possible to avoid this problem.

At that time, PIL algorithm achieve perfect learning for some data, and it is also fast learning compared with BP algorithm. But for some other data, the accuracy of learning cannot meet the requirements. In 2001, Guo and Lyu [8] proposed a new solution that extended the structure of neural network from single hidden layer to multiple hidden layers.

For given training data set $D = \{\mathbf{x}^i, \mathbf{o}^i\}_{i=1}^N$, $\mathbf{x}^i = (x_1, x_2, \ldots, x_d) \in R^d$ is the input signal vector and $\mathbf{o}^i = (o_1, o_2, \ldots, o_m) \in R^m$ is the corresponding target output vector. The training task of neural networks is to find a set of network parameters by minimizing the following error function

$$E = \sum_{i=1}^N \sum_{j=1}^m \left\| g_j(\mathbf{x}^i, \mathbf{\Theta}) - \mathbf{o}^i \right\|^2, \tag{3}$$

where $g(\mathbf{x}, \mathbf{\Theta})$ is the mapping function of network, and $\mathbf{\Theta}$ is a collection of network parameters. The samples are propagated along the network in the forward direction. In this case, the optimization problem of neural network becomes

$$\min \left\| \mathbf{H}^L \mathbf{W}^L - \mathbf{O} \right\|^2, \tag{4}$$

where L denotes the last layer. According to the knowledge of linear algebra, we know that the inverse of $\mathbf{H}^l$ exists, when $\mathbf{H}^l$ is full rank. $\mathbf{H}^l$ is the output of l layer. In this case, a complete learning of given training sample can be achieved. So PIL algorithm termination condition is set as $\left\| (\mathbf{H}^l)^{-1} \mathbf{H}^l - \mathbf{I} \right\|^2 < \epsilon$, where ϵ is a user-specified value that can be set to a very small value.

For the PIL algorithm, overfitting is easy to happen and reduces generalized performance. In 2004, Guo and Lyu [9] developed the PIL with stacked generalization to overcome the overfitting problem. The complete set D of available data is partitioned. The single data sample from D is treated as a validation sample, and the remainder of D is treated as a training set. All level-0 networks are then trained by PIL on the training partition and their outputs are measured using the validation data point. Let z_j denote the validation output of the model M_j on x_j. The data set $D_{CV} = \{\mathbf{z}^j, \mathbf{o}^j\}_{j=1}^N$ is used to train level-1 model.

In order to better solve the problem of deep learning, Wang et al. [15] proposed a pseudoinverse learning algorithm for stacked auto-encoder (PILAE) and a fast incremental learning algorithm which extended the original PIL algorithm in 2016. The basic idea of PILAE is to pre-train the basic elements of a deep architecture analytically, such as an auto-encoder, without any iterative optimization process.

In the study of deep learning, how to design a good network structure is an important research question. In 2017, Wang et al. [16] proposed a fast and fully automated method to train stacked auto-encoders. The presented method trains the stacked auto-encoders adopting the PILAE with the low rank approximation. In this process, the rank of the input matrix can be used to guide the setting the hidden layer neuron number. The depth of the stacked auto-encoder neural network can be determined with a criterion when the output matrix of the hidden layer was close to full rank matrix.

3 Development and Applications

After two decades of development, MLP with PIL algorithm has made a lot of progress. Its application area also is extended from software reliability engineering to astronomy and image processing.

3.1 Software Reliability Engineering

In software engineering field, software reliability is an important part of software quality. Compared with hardware reliability, it is more difficult to evaluate the software reliability. The neural networks have been used for the last few decades in a broad variety of applications because of their better predictions [17, 18]. BP algorithm is one of the most widely used neural network paradigms and has been applied successfully in application studies in a broad range of areas [19, 20]. To overcome the problem of BP algorithm, PIL algorithm is used to improve the speed and accuracy of software reliability predictions. Guo and Lyu [9] develop PIL algorithm with stacked generalization. The software reliability data sets, Sys1 and Sys3, are used to test the proposed method. The experimental results indicate that PIL only requires less than 0.1% computation time to achieve the same accuracy as the BP algorithm.

In order to improve the predictability of software reliability, Zhang and Guo [18] propose a feedforward neural network hybrid learning method. The method consists of a pattern extraction algorithm (Alopex) and PIL algorithm. In this method, the learning task is decomposed into two parts. One part is that the weights of hidden layer are given randomly and perturbed continuously by Alopex algorithm. Another part is the weights of output layer are trained by PIL algorithm. The proposed method not only inherits the advantages of fast convergence and good generalization performance from the PIL algorithm, but also can significantly improve the prediction accuracy of software reliability. Experimental results show that compared with the method of Renate Sitte [21], the method of Zhang can reduce the prediction error by 55%.

3.2 Astronomy Application

With the technology advancement of observational instruments in astronomy, huge volumes of spectral data have been and will be generated in modern spectroscopic surveys. The huge amount of data and the high rate of data acquisition makes the efficiency of BP algorithm lower. Therefore, aimed to time-consuming problem of BP algorithm, especially when the network structure is complicated, Wang et al. [22] employ 'divide and conquer' strategy to design a locally connected network structure to decrease the network complexity. This network forces the basic units of the deep architecture to extract local features in an analytical way without iterative optimization and assemble these local features into a unified feature. Then the network is trained by PIL algorithm. This method is applied in astronomical spectrum recognition application. The results demonstrate that, compared with conventional deep learning technique, this method only needs 0.3% computation time in LAMOST data, and is superior in the comprehensive performance.

In order to quickly and accurately carry out spectral classification and defective spectra recovery, Wang et al. [23] presents a new efficient and automated feature-extraction method for large-scale astronomical spectral datasets. The proposed method learns the features by using deep neural network, which is trained with PIL algorithm layer by layer. Each layer of the network is associated with a PILAE, which is trained to extract the features from its input. The performance is evaluated on real-world spectral data, and the results show that this method has comprehensive performance and lower computational cost. But this method doesn't study the fake features problem.

3.3   Image Processing

PIL algorithm can also be applied in the field of image processing, such as image stitching and image annotation. Yan et al. [24] present a novel image stitching method, which utilizes scale-invariant feature transform (SIFT) feature and SHLN to get higher precision of parameter estimation. To get fast speed and high efficiency, PIL algorithm is used to train SHLN. The SIFT descriptor is used as the input data, and the perspective transformation parameters are used as the output. The results show that, compared with RANSAC, the proposed method not only improves the matching accuracy by 11%, but also reduces the running time by 16%.

In image annotation area, Li et al. [25] propose an automatic image annotation method based on data grouping (ABDG). The samples are mapped into a new space as well as grouped. Then the classifier is trained on the partitioned dataset. This classifier consists of softmax gate network and multiple experts. Each expert is a SHLN, and is trained by PIL algorithm. Experiment results on three image annotation benchmark datasets show that ABDG achieves better automatic image annotation results.

3.4   Other Applications

In addition to the applications mentioned above, MLP with PIL algorithm can be applied elsewhere. Mohammadi et al. [26] implement scalable hardware architectures for training the learning parameters of radial basis function neural network (RBFNN). They provide a generic hardware solution for classification using RBFNN on a reconfigurable data path that overcomes the major drawback of fixed-function hardware data paths. In this process, PIL algorithm is used to obtain the weights of RBFNN. The input data is presented to the network one at a time, and the weights of RBFNN are iteratively adjusted. The results of experiment show that scalability of this hardware architecture makes it favorable solution for classification of extremely large data sets.

Li and Guo [27] developed marginalizing out hidden layer noise (MHLN), in which the predictor of SHLN is trained with infinite samples. MHLN adopts PIL algorithm to obtain the model parameters. Because PIL algorithm can obtain the analytical solutions of the model parameters, MHLN can effectively avoid the problem of slow convergence for training SHLN with BP algorithm. Moreover, PIL algorithm also has potential applications in the field of chemistry [28].

One of the thing should be noted is that extreme learning machine is a simple variant of ours single hidden layer neural network with PIL algorithm.

4 Discussion and Further Work

In PIL algorithm, the number of hidden neurons is an important parameter. If the number of hidden layer neurons is too large, low training error and high generalization error will be obtained. That is overfitting and high variance. If the number of hidden layer neurons is too small, training errors and generalization errors will be larger. That is underfitting and high bias. Therefore, PIL algorithm avoids excessive variance by controlling the number of hidden neurons, which could also be seen as the number of features. At the same time, the generalization error is reduced by adding hidden layer to gradually reduce the bias, until less than the expected value. Therefore, PIL algorithm achieves the balance of bias and variance by adopting early stop regularization technique.

Different number of hidden layer neurons and number of network layers produce different models. Our goal is to choose the best model, that is, to be able to achieve the best between bias and variance. Therefore, the number of hidden layer neurons and the number of network layers are two important hyper-parameters in model selection. In PIL algorithm, the number of network layers is dynamical determined by minimizing the generalization error, and the number of hidden layer neuron is related to the rank of input data matrix.

In the future work, PIL algorithm can be combined with CNN. For image data, the better features can be effectively extracted from the two-dimensional information by CNN, and then are used to train network by PIL algorithm. The difference is that the pseudoinverse of matrix is transformed into the inverse of tensor.

5 Conclusions

For thirty years, BP algorithm has achieved great success in machine learning. However, with the emergence of deep learning, gradient descent based optimizing algorithms has also exposed many problems, such as the selection of hyperparameters, local minima, gradient vanish and so on. These problems can be exactly solved by PIL algorithm. PIL algorithm is a non-gradient learning method for training feedforward neural network. The algorithm is based on generalized linear algebra, matrix inner product and pseudoinverse matrices. In the procedure of training model, the learning error propagates feedforward only without gradient descent. After more than two decades of development, PIL algorithm has made great progress and can also get better performance. In addition, PIL algorithm has been applied in many fields, such as software reliability, astronomy, image processing, and has achieved remarkable results. In the future research work, non-gradient learning method will become a hot research topic, it is worth for more researchers to explore.

Acknowledgements. This work is fully supported by the grants from the Joint Re-search Fund in Astronomy (Grant No. U1531242) under cooperative agreement between the National Natural Science Foundation of China (NSFC) and Chinese Academy of Sciences (CAS), Prof. Ping Guo is the author to whom all correspondence should be addressed.

References

1. Lecun, Y., Boser, B., Denker, J.S., Henderson, D., Howard, R.E., Hubbard, W., Jackel, L.D.: Handwritten digit recognition with a back-propagation network. In: Advances in Neural Information Processing Systems, vol. 2, pp. 396–404. Morgan Kaufman, San Francisco (1990)
2. Haykin, S., Deng, C.: Classification of radar clutter using neural networks. IEEE Trans. Neural Netw. **2**, 589–600 (1991)
3. Bishop, C.M.: Neural Networks for Pattern Recognition. Clarendon Press, Oxford (1995)
4. Broomhead, D.S., Lowe, D.: Multivariable functional interpolation and adaptive networks. Complex Syst. **2**, 321–355 (1988)
5. Wessels, L.F.A., Barnard, E.: Avoiding false local minima by proper initialization of connections. IEEE Trans. Neural Netw. **3**, 899–905 (1992)
6. Goodfellow, I., Bengio, Y., Courville, A.: Deep Learning. MIT Press, Cambridge (2016)
7. Guo, P., Chen, C.P., Sun, Y.: A exact supervised learning for a three-layer supervised neural network. In: Proceedings of 1995 International Conference on Neural Information Processing, pp. 1041–1044. Publishing House of Electronics Industry, Beijing (1995)
8. Guo, P., Lyu, M.R.: Pseudoinverse learning algorithm for feedforward neural networks. In: Advances in Neural Networks and Applications, pp. 321–326 (2001)
9. Guo, P., Lyu, M.R.: A pseudoinverse learning algorithm for feedforward neural networks with stacked generalization applications to software reliability growth data. Neurocomputing **56**, 101–121 (2004)
10. Pao, Y.H., Takefuji, Y.: Functional-link net computing: theory, system architecture, and functionalities. IEEE Comput. **25**, 76–79 (1992)
11. Pao, Y.H., Park, G.H., Sobajic, D.J.: Learning and generalization characteristics of the random vector functional-link net. Neurocomputing **6**, 163–180 (1994)
12. Wang, D.: Editorial: randomized algorithms for training neural networks. Inf. Sci. **364–365**, 126–128 (2016)
13. Wang, D., Li, M.: Stochastic configuration networks: fundamentals and algorithms. IEEE Trans. Cybern. **47**, 3466–3479 (2017)
14. Scardapane, S., Wang, D.: Randomness in neural networks: an overview. WIREs Data Mining Knowl. Discov. **7** (2017)
15. Wang, K., Guo, P., Yin, Q., Luo, A.L., Xin, X.: A pseudoinverse incremental algorithm for fast training deep neural networks with application to spectra pattern recognition. In: 2016 International Joint Conference on Neural Networks, pp. 3453–3460. IEEE Press, New York (2016)
16. Wang, K., Guo, P., Xin, X., Ye, Z.: Autoencoder, low rank approximation and pseudoinverse learning algorithm. In: 2017 IEEE International Conference on Systems, Man, and Cybernetics, pp. 948–953. IEEE Press, New York (2017)
17. Aggarwal, G., Gupta, D.V.: Neural network approach to measure reliability of software modules: a review. Int. J. Adv. Eng. Sci. **3**, 1–7 (2013)
18. Zhang, X., Guo, P.: A study on software reliability prediction based on ensemble neural network (in Chinese). J. Beijing Normal Univ. (Nat. Sci.) **41**, 599–603 (2005)
19. Mehrotra, K., Mohan, C.K., Ranka, S.: Elements of Artificial Neural Networks. MIT Press, Cambridge (1996)
20. Wang, G., Li, W., Xu, Y.: Research of software reliability assessment based on neural net combination model (in Chinese). Comput. Simul. **27**, 176–180 (2010)
21. Sitte, R.: Comparison of software-reliability-growth predictions: neural networks vs parametric-recalibration. IEEE Trans. Reliab. **48**, 285–291 (1999)

22. Wang, K., Guo, P., Luo, A.-L., Xin, X., Duan, F.: Deep neural networks with local connectivity and its application to astronomical spectral data. In: 2016 IEEE International Conference on Systems, Man, and Cybernetics, pp. 2687–2692. IEEE Press, New York (2016)
23. Wang, K., Guo, P., Luo, A.-L.: A new automated spectral feature extraction method and its application in spectral classification and defective spectra recovery. Mon. Not. Roy. Astron. Soc. **465**, 4311–4324 (2016)
24. Yan, M., Yin, Q., Guo, P.: Image stitching with single-hidden layer feedforward neural networks. In: 2016 International Joint Conference on Neural Networks, pp. 4162–4169. IEEE Press, New York (2016)
25. Li, Y., Guo, P., Xin, X.: A divide and conquer method for automatic image annotation. In: 2016 International Conference on Computational Intelligence and Security, pp. 660–664. IEEE Press, New York (2016)
26. Mohammadi, M., Krishna, A., Nalesh, S., Nandy, S.: A hardware architecture for radial basis function neural network classifier. IEEE Trans. Parallel Distrib. Syst. (2017)
27. Li, Y., Guo, P.: Training neural networks by marginalizing out hidden layer noise. Neural Comput. Appl. (2017)
28. Curteanu, S., Cartwright, H.: Neural networks applied in chemistry. I. Determination of the optimal topology of multilayer perceptron neural networks. J. Chemometr. **25**, 527–549 (2011)

Identification of Vessel Kinetics
Based on Neural Networks
via Concurrent Learning

Nan Gu[1], Lu Liu[1], Dan Wang[1(✉)], and Zhouhua Peng[1,2]

[1] School of Marine Electrical Engineering, Dalian Maritime University,
Dalian 116026, People's Republic of China
`gunandlmu@gmail.com`, `wendaoerji@163.com`, `dwangdl@gmail.com`,
`zhpeng@dlmu.edu.cn`
[2] Control Science and Engineering, Dalian University of Technology,
Dalian 116024, People's Republic of China

Abstract. This paper is concerned with system identification for autonomous surface vehicles subject to unknown kinetics. The considered unknown kinetics stems from model uncertainties, unmodeled dynamics and external disturbances caused by wind, waves and ocean currents. The identification method is developed based on neural networks owing to its universal approximation property. In the adaptive weight law design, a concurrent learning method is involved to utilize the instantaneous data and the recorded data for adaptation. By using the proposed identification approach, the output weights will approach and stay bounded within a small neighborhood of ideal weights without a persistence of excitation condition. Finally, by resorting to the Lyapunov theory, the performance of the proposed kinetics identification method is analyzed.

Keywords: Neural networks · Concurrent learning
Kinetics identification · Autonomous surface vehicles

1 Introduction

Recently, autonomous surface vehicles (ASVs) play a critical role in the exploitation and development of marine environment for their low cost and high autonomy [1]. While in the marine environment, because of the model uncertainties,

The work of D. Wang was supported in part by the National Natural Science Foundation of China under Grants 61673081, and in part by the Fundamental Research Funds for the Central Universities under Grant 3132016313, and in part by the National Key Research and Development Program of China under Grant 2016YFC0301500.

The work of Z. Peng was supported in part by the National Natural Science Foundation of China under Grant 51579023, and in part by High Level Talent Innovation and Entrepreneurship Program of Dalian under Grant 2016RQ036, and in part by the Hong Kong Scholars Program under Grant XJ2015009, and in part by the China Post-Doctoral Science Foundation under Grant 2015M570247.

© Springer International Publishing AG, part of Springer Nature 2018
T. Huang et al. (Eds.): ISNN 2018, LNCS 10878, pp. 107–114, 2018.
https://doi.org/10.1007/978-3-319-92537-0_13

unmodeled dynamics and environment disturbances induced by wind, waves and ocean currents, the unknown kinetics of ASVs are unavoidable. Thus, in order to achieve autonomous control more accurately, reasonable kinetics model parameters of the ASVs have to be identified. In this setting, many model identification approaches have been proposed, which can be divided into off-line identification and on-line identification. For the off-line identification, the methods such as frequency domain methods [2], time domain methods [3], hybrid-extended Kalman filtering [4], onboard sensor-based identification [5] have been used. However, the above methods need to collect numerous data from onboard sensor and conduct extensively experiments.

In contrary to the off-line identification, many on-line identification method such as disturbances observer [6–9], extended state observer [10–12], fuzzy-logic based identification method [13,14], neural network (NN) -based identification method [15–23] have been carried out to cope with system identification. In particular, NNs takes the advantage of inherent universal approximation property to nonlinear systems as long as sufficient number of NN nodes are available. However, if the input signals are not persistence of excitation (PE), traditional NN weight adaptation laws do not guarantee that the output weights will converge to the ideal weights. Besides, the condition on PE reference input is restrictive and often infeasible to implement on ASVs.

Taking into account the aforementioned problems, this paper is dedicated to present an NN-based identification approach combining with a concurrent learning method to identify the unknown kinetics of ASVs. The concurrent learning method was proposed for the adaptation law design in [24,25]. The concurrent learning method combines the current and recorded data which was saved when the nodes of NN under a relaxed finite excitation. Through the concurrent learning technique, the PE condition can be eliminated. Finally, based on the Lyapunov theory and input-to-state stable (ISS) theory, the effectiveness of the proposed identification method is analyzed.

The remainder of the paper is organized as follows. The definition of NNs and the kinetics model of ASV are given in the Sect. 2. In Sect. 3, an NN-based kinetics identification method is established and analyzed. Conclusions are given in Sect. 4.

2   Preliminaries and Problem Formulation

2.1   Notation

In this paper, the following notations are used. $\|\cdot\|$ denotes the Euclidean norm of a vector; $\|\cdot\|_F$ is the Frobenius norm of a matrix; $(\cdot)^T$ is the transposing of a matrix; $\lambda_{\min}(\cdot)$ and $\lambda_{\max}(\cdot)$ represent the smallest and the largest eigenvalue of a matrix, respectively; $\Re^n$ represents the n-dimensional Euclidean Space.

2.2   Neural Networks

Considering an unknown continuous function $f(x) : \Re^n \to \Re$, the NN takes the form of $W^T \sigma(x)$ where $W \in \Re^{l \times m}$ denotes weight matrix with l being the number of nodes; $\sigma(x) \in \Re^l$ is a known activation function with x being the input vector of NN. There exist positive constants σ^* and W^* such that $\|\sigma(x)\| \leq \sigma^*$ and $\|W\|_F \leq W^*$. Using the NN learning ability to nonlinear system, the unknown function $f(x)$ can be approximated as follows

$$f(x) = W^T \sigma(x) + \varepsilon(x), \quad \forall x \in \Omega, \tag{1}$$

where $\|\varepsilon(x)\| \leq \varepsilon^*$ is the approximation error with ε^* being positive constant and Ω is a compact set.

2.3   Kinetics Model of ASV

According to [26], a 3 degrees of freedom kinetics of an ASV is expressed by (Fig. 1)

$$M\dot{\nu} = -C(\nu)\nu - D(\nu)\nu - g(\nu, \eta) + \tau + \tau_w(t), \tag{2}$$

where $M \in \Re^{3\times3}$ denotes the rigid-body system inertial matrix and added mass matrix which is unique and satisfies $M = M^T > 0$; $C(\nu) \in \Re^{3\times3}$ is a skew-symmetric matrix of Coriolis and centripetal terms including added mass; $D(\nu) \in \Re^{3\times3}$ is a hydrodynamic damping matrix; $g(\eta, \nu)$ represents the unmodeled dynamics including gravitational/buoyancy forces and moments; $\tau_w = [\tau_{wu}, \tau_{wv}, \tau_{wr}]^T \in \Re^3$ means a vector of external environment disturbances induced by wind, waves and currents and τ_w is assumed to be bounded; $\nu = [u, v, r]^T \in \Re^3$ is a vector denoting surge velocity, sway velocity, and yaw rate expressed in the body-fixed reference frame, respectively; $\tau = [\tau_u, \tau_v, \tau_r]^T \in \Re^3$ denotes the control inputs in surge, sway and yaw directions.

The objective is to present an NN-based identification method such that the unknown kinetics in (2) can be identified.

3   NN-based Kinetics Identification Design and Analysis

Rewrite vehicle kinetics (2) as follows

$$M\dot{\nu} = \tau + f(\cdot), \tag{3}$$

where $f(\cdot) = -C(\nu)\nu - D(\nu)\nu - g(\nu, \eta) + \tau_w(t)$.

By using NN, the unknown kinetics in (3) can be approximated as follows

$$M\dot{\hat{\nu}} = -F(\hat{\nu} - \nu) + \hat{W}^T \sigma(\xi) + \tau, \tag{4}$$

where $\hat{\nu} = [\hat{u}, \hat{v}, \hat{r}]^T \in \Re^3$ and $\hat{W} \in \Re^{n\times3}$ are the estimation of ν and W, respectively; $F = \text{diag}\{k_1, k_2, k_3\} \in \Re^{3\times3}$ is a control gain matrix with k_1, k_2 and k_3 being positive constants; $\xi = [\bar{\nu}^T(t), \tau^T(t)]^T \in \Re^6$ with $\bar{\nu} = \nu(t) - \nu(t - t_d)$, t_d is the sample time.

In what follows, the concurrent learning method is introduced and the subscript $(\cdot)_j$ denotes the data need to be saved at the time instance t_j. To facilitate the concurrent learning method, the following Assumption on the recorded data is used.

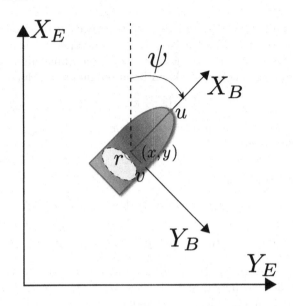

Fig. 1. A geometrical illustration of reference frames

Assumption 1 [27]. The recorded data has as many linearly independent elements $\sigma(\xi_j) \in \Re^m$ as the dimension of the basis of the uncertainty. That is, if $Z = [\sigma(\xi_1), ..., \sigma(\xi_p)]$ denotes the recorded data, then $rank(Z) = m$.

The update law for $\hat{W}$ is designed based on the concurrent learning method as follows

$$\dot{\hat{W}}(t) = -\Gamma \left\{ \sigma(\xi)\tilde{\nu}^T + \sum_{j=1}^{p} \sigma(\xi_j)\Delta_j^T \right\}, \tag{5}$$

where $\tilde{\nu} = \hat{\nu} - \nu$ denotes the estimation error; $\Gamma \in \Re$ is an adaptation gain; $\sigma(\xi_j)$ is the jth recorded regressor vector data.

Δ_j is defined in the following form

$$\Delta_j = \hat{W}^T \sigma(\xi_j) - f_j(\cdot) - M\dot{\tilde{\nu}}_j = \tilde{W}^T \sigma(\xi_j) - M\dot{\tilde{\nu}}_j, \tag{6}$$

where $\tilde{W} = \hat{W} - W$ and $f_j(\cdot)$ is the jth recorded unknown kinetics.

The unknown kinetics $f_j(\cdot)$ at the time instant t_j can be observed by the following equation

$$f_j(\cdot) = M\dot{\nu}_j - \tau_j = -M\dot{\tilde{\nu}}_j + M\dot{\hat{\nu}}_j - \tau_j. \tag{7}$$

In this case, the update law (5) forces the $\hat{W}$ to a ball around the ideal weights, the size of which is decided by $\dot{\tilde{\nu}}_j$. Thus, it is desirable to drive $\dot{\tilde{\nu}}$ to the origin such that a higher identification performance can be achieved.

Recorded data include the regressor vector $\sigma(\xi_j)$ and the unknown kinetics $f_j(\cdot)$. A selection criteria for choosing appropriate data to be saved is important for concurrent learning method. For simplicity, the following criteria can be used

$$\frac{\|\sigma(\xi) - \sigma(\xi_p)\|^2}{\|\sigma(\xi)\|} \geq \iota, \tag{8}$$

where ι is a positive constant.

According to (3) and (4), the error dynamics of $\tilde{\nu}$ and $\tilde{W}$ are expressed by

$$\begin{cases} M\dot{\tilde{\nu}} = -F\tilde{\nu} + \tilde{W}^T \sigma(\xi) - \varepsilon, \\ \dot{\tilde{W}} = -\Gamma\left\{\sigma(\xi)\tilde{\nu}^T + \sum_{j=1}^{p} \sigma(\xi_j)\Delta_j^T\right\}. \end{cases} \tag{9}$$

The following theorem presents the stability of the system (9) once the Assumption 1 on the recorded data is satisfied.

Theorem 1. Under the Assumption 1, using the recorded data selection criteria (8), the system (9) viewed as a system with states being $\tilde{\nu}$ and $\tilde{W}$, the input being ε, is ISS.

Proof. Construct the Lyapunov candidate as follows,

$$V = \frac{1}{2}\left\{\tilde{\nu}^T M\tilde{\nu} + \mathrm{tr}(\tilde{W}^T \Gamma^{-1}\tilde{W})\right\}.$$

It follows that V is bounded by

$$\frac{1}{2}\lambda_{\min}(P)\|E\|^2 \leq V \leq \frac{1}{2}\lambda_{\max}(P)\|E\|^2, \tag{10}$$

where $P = \mathrm{diag}\{M, \Gamma^{-1}\}$ and $E = [\|\tilde{\nu}\|, \|\tilde{W}\|_F]^T$.

By differentiating V with respect to time and using (6), (9), one has

$$\dot{V} = -\tilde{\nu}^T F\tilde{\nu} - \tilde{\nu}^T\varepsilon - \mathrm{tr}\left\{\tilde{W}^T \sum_{j=1}^{p} \sigma(\xi_j)\Delta_j^T\right\},$$

$$= -\tilde{\nu}^T F\tilde{\nu} - \tilde{\nu}^T\varepsilon - \mathrm{tr}\left\{\tilde{W}^T \sum_{j=1}^{p} \sigma(\xi_j)\left\{\sigma(\xi_j)^T \tilde{W} - \dot{\tilde{\nu}}_j^T M\right\}\right\}. \tag{11}$$

Under the Assumption 1, letting

$$\Theta_1 = \sum_{j=1}^{p} \sigma(\xi_j)\sigma(\xi_j)^T, \tag{12}$$

$$\Theta_2 = \sum_{j=1}^{p} \sigma(\xi_j)\dot{\tilde{\nu}}_j^T M, \tag{13}$$

we have $\Theta_1 > 0$ and $\Theta_2 > 0$.

From (11), we can obtain the following inequality

$$\dot{V} \leq -\lambda_{\min}(F)\|\tilde{\nu}\|^2 + \|\tilde{\nu}\|\|\varepsilon\| - \lambda_{\min}(\Theta_1)\|\tilde{W}\|_F^2 + \lambda_{\min}(\Theta_2)\|\tilde{W}\|_F. \tag{14}$$

It follows that

$$\dot{V} \leq -\zeta_1\|E\|^2 + (\|\varepsilon\| + \lambda_{\min}(\Theta_2))\|E\|, \tag{15}$$

where $\zeta_1 = \min\{\lambda_{\min}(F), \lambda_{\min}(\Theta_1)\}$.

Since

$$\|E\| \geq \frac{\|\varepsilon\| + \lambda_{\min}(\Theta_2)}{\delta\zeta_1}, \tag{16}$$

it renders

$$\dot{V} \leq -(1-\delta)\zeta_1\|E\|^2, \tag{17}$$

where $0 < \delta < 1$.

It follows that the system (9) is ISS. There exists a $\mathcal{KL}$ function $\kappa_1(\cdot)$ and a $\mathcal{K}_\infty$ function $\kappa_2(\cdot)$, such that

$$\|E(t)\| \leq \max\{\kappa_1(E(0), t), \kappa_2(\|\varepsilon\|)\}, \tag{18}$$

where $\kappa_2 = \sqrt{\frac{\lambda_{\max}(P)}{\lambda_{\min}(P)}}(\frac{\lambda_{\min}(\Theta_2)+s}{\delta\zeta_1})$.

Theorem 1 shows the ISS stability of the system (9) and the bound of the error signals are given by $\sqrt{\frac{\lambda_{\max}(P)}{\lambda_{\min}(P)}}(\frac{\lambda_{\min}(\Theta_2)+\|\varepsilon\|}{\delta\zeta_1})$. It is noted that the NN approximation error $\|\varepsilon\|$ is bounded by ε^* which can be chosen arbitrary small. Θ_2 is determined by the estimation error $\tilde{\nu}$ which can be taken arbitrary small by using large enough control gain F. It follows that the NN output weights can converge to an arbitrary close neighborhood around the ideal weights. Thus, the NN-based kinetics identification method for ASVs is achieved.

4   Conclusions

This paper presented a kinetics identification technique for ASVs suffering from uncertainties and disturbances. The identification method is developed by combing the NN with the concurrent learning approach. By using the proposed identification method, the current and recorded data are both used to design the NN weight adaptation law and the PE condition can be eliminated. Finally, the ISS stability is given and it shows that the NN output weights can converge to the ideal weight with an arbitrary small neighborhood.

References

1. Liu, Z., Zhang, Y., Yu, Y., Yuan, C.: Unmanned surface vehicles: an overview of developments and challenges. Annu. Rev. Control **41**, 71–93 (2016)
2. Selvam, R.P., Bhattacharyya, S.K.: A frequency domain system identification method for linear ship maneuvering. Int. Shipbuild. Prog. **52**(1), 5–28 (2005)
3. Mišković, N., Vukić, Z., Bibuli, M., Bruzzone, G., Caccia, M.: Fast in-field identification of unmanned marine vehicles. Field Rob. **28**(1), 101–120 (2010)
4. Yoon, H.K., Rhee, K.P.: Identification of hydrodynamic coefficients in ship maneuvering equations of motion by estimation-before-modeling technique. Ocean Eng. **30**(18), 2379–2404 (2003)
5. Caccia, M., Bruzzone, G., Bono, R.: A practical approach to modeling and identification of small autonomous surface craft. IEEE J. Ocean Eng. **33**(2), 133–145 (2008)
6. Zheng, Z., Feroskhan, M.: Path following of a surface vessel with prescribed performance in the presence of input saturation and external disturbances. IEEE/ASME Trans. Mechatron. (2018, in press)
7. Peng, Z., Wang, D., Wang, J.: Cooperative dynamic positioning of multiple marine offshore vessels: a modular design. IEEE/ASME Trans. Mechatron. **21**(3), 1210–1221 (2016)
8. Hall, C.E., Shtessel, Y.B.: Sliding mode disturbance observer-based control for a reusable launch vehicle. J. Guid. **29**, 1315–1328 (2006)
9. Chen, M., Shao, S., Jiang, B.: Adaptive neural control of uncertain nonlinear systems using disturbance observer. IEEE Trans. Cybern. **47**(10), 3110–3123 (2017)
10. Cui, R., Chen, L., Yang, C., Chen, M.: Extended state observer-based integral sliding mode control for an underwater robot with unknown disturbances and uncertain nonlinearities. IEEE Trans. Ind. Electron. **64**(8), 6785–6795 (2017)
11. Peng, Z., Wang, J.: Output-feedback path-following control of autonomous underwater vehicles based on an extended state observer and projection neural networks. IEEE Trans. Syst., Man, Cybern. Syst. (2018, in press)
12. Liu, L., Wang, D., Peng, Z.: ESO-based line-of-sight guidance law for path following of underactuated marine surface vehicles with exact sideslip compensation. IEEE J. Ocean Eng. **42**(2), 477–487 (2017)
13. Xiang, X., Yu, C., Lapierre, L., Zhang, J., Zhang, Q.: Survey on fuzzy-logic-based guidance and control of marine surface vehicles and underwater vehicles. Int. J. Fuzzy Syst. **37**(1), 1–15 (2017)
14. Xiang, X., Yu, C., Zhang, Q.: Robust fuzzy 3D path following for autonomous underwater vehicle subject to uncertainties. Comput. Oper. Res. **84**, 165–177 (2017)
15. Moreira, L., Guedes Soares, C.: Dynamic model of manoeuvrability using recursive neural networks. Ocean Eng. **30**(13), 1669–1697 (2003)
16. Peng, Z., Wang, J., Wang, D.: Distributed maneuvering of autonomous surface vehicles based on neurodynamic optimization and fuzzy approximation. IEEE Trans. Control Syst. Technol. (2018, in press)
17. Peng, Z., Wang, J., Wang, D.: Containment maneuvering of marine surface vehicles with multiple parameterized paths via spatial-temporal decoupling. IEEE/ASME Trans. Mechatron. **22**(2), 1026–1036 (2017)
18. Peng, Z., Wang, D., Wang, J.: Predictor-based neural dynamic surface control for uncertain nonlinear systems in strict-feedback form. IEEE Trans. Neural Netw. Learn. Syst. **28**(9), 2156–2167 (2017)

19. Peng, Z., Wang, D., Shi, Y., Wang, H., Wang, W.: Containment control of networked autonomous underwater vehicles with model uncertainty and ocean disturbances guided by multiple leaders. Inf. Sci. **316**(20), 163–179 (2015)
20. Cui, R., Yang, C., Li, Y., Sharma, S.: Adaptive neural network control of AUVs with control input nonlinearities using reinforcement learning. IEEE Trans. Syst. Man Cybern. Syst. **47**(6), 1019–1029 (2017)
21. Dai, S., Wang, C., Luo, F.: Identification and learning control of ocean surface ship using neural networks. IEEE Trans. Ind. Electron. **8**(4), 801–810 (2012)
22. Yuan, C., Licht, S., He, H.: Formation learning control of multiple autonomous underwater vehicles with heterogeneous nonlinear uncertain dynamics. IEEE Trans. Cybern. (2018, in press)
23. Peng, Z., Wang, J., Wang, D.: Distributed containment maneuvering of multiple marine vessels via neurodynamics-based output feedback. IEEE Trans. Ind. Electron. **64**(5), 3831–3839 (2017)
24. Chowdhary, G., Yucelen, T., Mühlegg, M., Johnson, E.: Concurrent learning adaptive control of linear systems with exponentially convergent bounds. Int. J. Adapt. Control Sig. Process. **27**(4), 280–301 (2012)
25. Chowdhary, G., Johnson, E.: Theory and flight-test validation of a concurrent-learning adaptive controller. J. Guid. Control Dyn. **34**(2), 592–607 (2011)
26. Fossen, T.I.: Handbook of Marine Craft Hydrodynamics and Motion Control. Wiley, Hoboken (2011)
27. Chowdhary, G. Johnson, E.: Concurrent learning for convergence in adaptive control without persistency of excitation. In: IEEE Conference Decision Control, pp. 3674–3679 (2011)

Method to Improve the Performance
of Restricted Boltzmann Machines

Jing Yin[1,2], Qingyu Mao[3], Dayiheng Liu[1], Yong Xu[1], and Jiancheng Lv[1(✉)]

[1] Machine Intelligence Laboratory, College of Computer Science, Sichuan University,
Chengdu 610065, People's Republic of China
lvjiancheng@scu.edu.cn
[2] College of Computer Science and Engineering,
Chongqing University of Technology, Chongqing 400054, People's Republic of China
[3] Archives, Sichuan University, Chengdu 610065, People's Republic of China

Abstract. Restricted Boltzmann machines (RBMs) are widely applied
to solve many machine learning problems. Usually, the cost function of
RBM is log-likelihood function of marginal distribution of input data,
and the training method involves maximizing the cost function. Distribution of the trained RBM is identical to that of input data. But the
reconstruction error always exists even the distributions are almost identical. In this paper, a method to train RBM by adding reconstruction
error to the cost function is put forward. Two categories of trials are
performed to validate the proposed method: feature extraction and classification. The experimental results show that the proposed method can
be effective.

Keywords: Restricted Boltzmann machine · Feature learning
Reconstruction error · Classification

1 Introduction

Restricted Boltzmann machines (RBMs) [1] have been successfully used to many
tasks of machine learning, including collaborative filtering [2], feature extraction [3], dimensionality reduction [4], object recognition [5], classification [6],
and many others. RBMs usually extract features by unsupervised learning. The
RBMs could be initializers of other neural networks [7], solve classification problems with other classifiers [7,8], or form deep belief nets (DBNs) [9] and deep
Boltzmann machines (DBMs) [10].

RBM is an undirected graph model based on energy function, which consists
of two layers. The training objective of RBM is maximizing the log-likelihood
function of marginal distribution of input data. When the distribution learned
by RBM is identical to the distribution of input data, the training is complete.
However, reconstruction error always exists even if the distributions are almost
identical. So, a method which adds reconstruction error to the cost function
of RBM is presented to improve the performance of RBM. In fact, there are

© Springer International Publishing AG, part of Springer Nature 2018
T. Huang et al. (Eds.): ISNN 2018, LNCS 10878, pp. 115–123, 2018.
https://doi.org/10.1007/978-3-319-92537-0_14

some literatures that use reconstruction error to improve the performance of RBM [11–15]. [11] uses reconstruction error as the criterion for cutting down the learning rate. [12] proposes an approach for RBM training. The approach used a normalized reconstruction error to determine increment necessity and compute the number of additional features for the increment. [13] proposes a new training technique for deep belief neural network, which based on minimizing the reconstruction error. [14] trains a new model by selecting a subset of the training set through reconstruction errors. [15] trains a new model by using reconstruction errors themselves. However, we use the reconstruction error as the part of the cost function of RBM. In the case of ensuring that the distribution learned by the model is identical to the distribution of input data, the reconstruction error is as small as possible to achieve better performance. We make experiments on several public databases to verify the effectiveness of the proposed method. Compared with RBM, the proposed method could be better on feature extraction and classification.

In the rest of this paper, we give an outline of the RBM in Sect. 2, introduce the proposed method in Sect. 3, implement several experiments and analyze the experimental results in Sect. 4, and provide the conclusion in final section.

2   Restricted Boltzmann Machines

RBM is a random neural network model, which consists of two layers: visible layer and hidden layer shown in Fig. 1. Visible layer with $|\mathbf{v}|$ neurons represents input data, and hidden layer with $|\mathbf{h}|$ neurons is representation of the input data. $\mathbf{W}$ is the connections weight between the visible layer and the hidden layer.

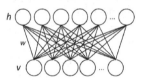

Fig. 1. Restricted Boltzmann machine.

Energy function of RBM takes following form:

$$E(\mathbf{v}, \mathbf{h}|\theta) = -\sum_{m=1}^{|\mathbf{v}|} a_m v_m - \sum_{n=1}^{|\mathbf{h}|} c_n h_n - \sum_{m=1}^{|\mathbf{v}|}\sum_{n=1}^{|\mathbf{h}|} W_{mn} h_n v_m, \qquad (1)$$

where θ denotes the real-valued parameters a_m, c_n and W_{mn}, and $v_m \in \{0,1\}$, $h_n \in \{0,1\}$. According to the energy function, the joint distribution of the RBM is defined by

$$p(\mathbf{v}, \mathbf{h}) = \frac{1}{Z} e^{-E(\mathbf{v},\mathbf{h})}, \qquad (2)$$

where $Z = \sum_{\mathbf{v},\mathbf{h}} e^{-E(\mathbf{v},\mathbf{h})}$ is a normalization constant. Conditioned on $\mathbf{v}$, the probability of hidden neuron n with the value of 1 has the form

$$p(h_n = 1|\mathbf{v}) = \sigma(c_n + \sum_{m=1}^{|\mathbf{v}|} W_{mn} v_m), \tag{3}$$

where $\sigma(y) = 1/(1 + e^{-y})$ is the logistic sigmoid function. Conditioned on $\mathbf{h}$, the probability of visible neuron m with the value of 1 has the form

$$p(v_m = 1|\mathbf{h}) = \sigma(a_m + \sum_{n=1}^{|\mathbf{h}|} W_{mn} h_n), \tag{4}$$

Given the marginal probability $p(\mathbf{v})$, the cost function of the RBM is given by $L(\theta) = \frac{1}{|T|} \sum_{t=1}^{|T|} logp(\mathbf{v}^{(t)}; \theta)$, and θ could be optimized by gradient ascent on the log-likelihood. $|T|$ is the quantity of training data. In this formula, calculating partial derivative of $l(\theta) = logp(\mathbf{v}^{(t)}; \theta)$ is the key. For any input data $(\mathbf{v}^{(t)})$, the gradient of θ has the form:

$$\frac{\partial l(\theta)}{\partial \theta} = -\sum_{\mathbf{h}} p(\mathbf{h}|\mathbf{v}^{(t)}) \frac{\partial E(\mathbf{v}^{(t)}, \mathbf{h}|\theta)}{\partial \theta} + \sum_{\mathbf{v},\mathbf{h}} p(\mathbf{v},\mathbf{h}) \frac{\partial E(\mathbf{v},\mathbf{h}|\theta)}{\partial \theta}. \tag{5}$$

From Eq. 5, partial derivative of the parameter W_{mn} can be obtained by

$$\frac{\partial l(\theta)}{\partial W_{mn}} = p(h_n = 1|\mathbf{v}^{(t)}) v_m^{(t)} - \sum_{\mathbf{v}} p(\mathbf{v}) p(h_n = 1|\mathbf{v}) v_m. \tag{6}$$

Because of the existence of normalization constant $Z(\theta)$, the computational complexity of the gradient is very high. In order to reduce the computational complexity, approximate calculations are usually used, such as the contrastive divergence (CD) [16] algorithm. The connection weight $\mathbf{W}$ learns the features of the input data, and its gradients are relevant to the probability of $\mathbf{h}$. Given $\mathbf{h}$, we can compute the active probability of $\mathbf{v}$, then get reconstructions by sampling.

3   Improved Training Method

The objective of RBM is updating model parameters to make model distribution and input data distribution as identical as possible. In fact, the difference between the input data and the reconstructions always exists, even if the distributions are almost identical. The difference is called reconstruction error, we define the reconstruction error as $\varepsilon = \|\mathbf{v}' - \mathbf{v}\|^2$, where $\mathbf{v}$ is any one of the input data, $\mathbf{v}'$ is a reconstruction of $\mathbf{v}$. Here we propose a method to make the distributions as identical as possible, while the reconstruction error as small as possible. The basic idea of the improved training method is to add the reconstruction error into the cost function of RBM and generate a new cost function. The new cost function of RBM could be defined as

$$L(\theta) = \frac{1}{|T|} \sum_{t=1}^{|T|} \left(logp(\mathbf{v}^{(t)}; \theta) - \frac{1}{2} \|\mathbf{v}' - \mathbf{v}^{(t)}\|^2 \right), \qquad (7)$$

where $\mathbf{v}'$ can be computed by $v'_m = \sigma(a_m + \sum_{n=1}^{|\mathbf{h}|} W_{mn}h_n)$. In order to distinguish, RBM with the new cost function is called reRBM. To train the reRBM, we should maximize $L(\theta)$. The same as RBM, we define $l(\theta) = logp(\mathbf{v}^{(t)}; \theta) - \frac{1}{2}\|\mathbf{v}' - \mathbf{v}^{(t)}\|^2$, the updating formula of θ is:

$$\frac{\partial l(\theta)}{\partial \theta} = -\sum_{\mathbf{h}} p(\mathbf{h}|\mathbf{v}^{(t)})\frac{\partial E(\mathbf{v}^{(t)}, \mathbf{h}|\theta)}{\partial \theta} + \sum_{\mathbf{v},\mathbf{h}} p(\mathbf{v},\mathbf{h})\frac{\partial E(\mathbf{v},\mathbf{h}|\theta)}{\partial \theta} - (\mathbf{v}' - \mathbf{v}^{(t)})\frac{\partial(\mathbf{v}' - \mathbf{v}^{(t)})}{\partial \theta}.$$
$$(8)$$

The reRBM uses CD-1 algorithm similar to RBM does. Specifically, the updating formulas of the parameters W_{mn}, c_n and a_m are:

$$W_{mn} = W_{mn} + \epsilon(p(h_n = 1|\mathbf{v}^{(t)})v_m^{(t)} - p(h'_n = 1|\mathbf{v}')v'_m - (v'_m - v_m^{(t)})\dot{\sigma}(a_m + \sum_{n=1}^{|\mathbf{h}|} W_{mn}h_n)h_n),$$
$$(9)$$

$$a_m = a_m + \epsilon((v_m^{(t)} - v'_m) - (v'_m - v_m^{(t)})\dot{\sigma}(a_m + \sum_{n=1}^{|\mathbf{h}|} W_{mn}h_n)), \qquad (10)$$

$$c_n = c_n + \epsilon(p(h_n = 1|\mathbf{v}^{(t)}) - p(h'_n = 1|\mathbf{v}')). \qquad (11)$$

where $\dot{\sigma}(a_m + \sum_{n=1}^{|\mathbf{h}|} W_{mn}h_n) = \sigma(a_m + \sum_{n=1}^{|\mathbf{h}|} W_{mn}h_n)[1 - \sigma(a_m + \sum_{n=1}^{|\mathbf{h}|} W_{mn}h_n)]$, ϵ is the learning rate of the reRBM. The model keeps learning until the gradients do not change or runs to the fixed number of epochs.

4   Experimental Results and Analysis

To evaluate the performance of the proposed method, we conducted two categories of experiments on several databases: one was carried out to extract features on standard MNIST database and AR face database, the other was carried out to classify on standard MNIST database, variation of MNIST database and OCR letters database. The experimental results showed that the reRBM could be more effective than RBM.

4.1   Features Extracted by ReRBM

We verified the efficiency of the reRBM using standard MNIST database and AR face database. Standard MNIST database contains 28×28 images which contains a training set with 60000 examples and a test set with 10000 examples, each image is handwritten digit number from 0 to 9 with white character on a black background. AR face database contains 100 people's faces which contains a training set with 700 images and a test set with 699 images, each image is of 60 by 43 pixels with different facial expressions, illumination conditions. In this part, we only compare the features of input data extracted by reRBM and RBM, the experiments were performed on the training sets of two databases.

Comparison of Features on Standard MNIST Database. We compared the efficacy of reRBM and RBM on standard MNIST database. For fair comparison, the parameters of the two models were the same. We set initial values of bias to zero and set weight matrices to random values from uniform distribution $[-b^{-0.5}, b^{-0.5}]$, where b is the maximum value between the numbers of rows and columns of the matrix, and set learning rate to 0.005. For a better illustration of the features extracted by reRBM, we carried out the experiments using reRBM and RBM with different number of hidden neurons. Because the initial values of the weight matrices were random and the values of visible and hidden neurons are sampled, the experimental results were processed 10 times to ensure the effectiveness.

Figure 2 shows reconstructions for five examples. The results in row 1 were generated by two models with 64 hidden neurons, the results in row 2 were generated by the models with 128 hidden neurons, and the last row were generated by the models with 256 hidden neurons. The left displays the reconstructions generated by the RBM, and the right is the results produced by the reRBM. From Fig. 2, we could find that the reconstructions of the reRBM are better than those of RBM, especially, the reconstructions in row 1 generated by the reRBM. But as the number of hidden neurons increases, the difference between the two models is getting smaller and smaller. In short, it indicates that the reRBM obtains a better performance on extracting features compared to the RBM.

Fig. 2. Reconstructions for five examples from standard MNIST database (The left generated by the RBM, while the right generated by the reRBM).

Figure 3 shows the energy of two models with 1024 hidden neurons, the mean and standard deviation of reconstruction errors of two models with 6000 hidden neurons. In order to illustrate the difference between the two models, the figure only shows the result of the first 20 epochs. From Fig. 3, we can see that the convergence rate of the reRBM is faster than that of the RBM, and the reRBM could be more competitive with the RBM when the number of hidden neurons was small.

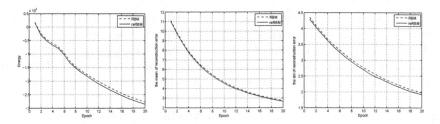

Fig. 3. Two models on standard MNIST. (left) the energies. (middle) the mean of reconstruction errors. (right) the standard derivation of reconstruction errors.

Comparison of Features on AR Face Database. We compared the performance of reRBM and RBM on AR face database. Because the face database is continuous data, the visible neurons of models are replaced by Gaussian units, and the hidden neurons remain binary. The value of visible neuron m is to sample from a normal distribution with unit variance and mean $a_m + \sum_{n=1}^{|\mathbf{h}|} W_{mn} h_n$, and the reconstruction data $\mathbf{v}'$ is defined as $v'_m = a_m + \sum_{n=1}^{|\mathbf{h}|} W_{mn} h_n$.

The network is trained using the gradient ascent method (the learning rate was set to 0.001, the weight matrices were initialized to $W_{mn} \sim 0.1 \times N(0,1)$, and all initial values of biases were set to zero). Similarly, we performed the experiments with different number of hidden neurons and carried out ten times to ensure the effectiveness of the experimental results.

Figure 4 shows the reconstruction data for three examples. The faces in row 1 are generated by two models with 256 hidden neurons, the faces in row 2 are generated by the models with 1024 hidden neurons, and the last row are generated by the models with 3000 hidden neurons. We could conclude that the reconstruction results of the reRBM with Gaussian units are better than those of RBM with Gaussian units from Fig. 4.

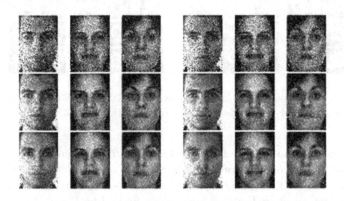

Fig. 4. Reconstructions for three examples from AR face database (The left generated by the RBM with Gaussian units, while the right generated by the reRBM with Gaussian units).

Figure 5 shows the energy of two models with 1024 hidden neurons, the mean and standard deviation of reconstruction errors of two models with 3000 hidden neurons. From Fig. 5, we can conclude that the reRBM with Gaussian units obtains better performance on extracting features compared to the RBM with Gaussian units.

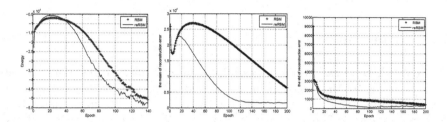

Fig. 5. Two models on AR. (left) the energies. (middle) the mean of reconstruction errors. (right) the standard derivation of reconstruction errors.

4.2   Classification Performance of ReRBM

For a classification problem, a label layer should be added on the RBM, and matrix **U** denotes the connections among the label layer and hidden layer. In the classification results, we focused on whether the reRBM could outperform the RBM.

We verify the classification performance of the proposed method using standard MNIST database, variation of MNIST database and OCR letters database. Each image of variation of MNIST database is handwritten digit number from 0 to 9 with black character on a white background, and the rest is the same as standard MNIST database. OCR letters database contains images of handwritten letters from a to z. All training sets were divided into two parts: one part is used for training and the other is used to validate. In this part, the number of validation part of the three databases was set to 10, 000, and the remaining part of the training set is used for training.

The parameters of the two models were the same as those in the experimental setting used by Larochelle [6]. The results of the experiments are shown in Table 1. Owing to the random initial values of the matrices and random sampling, the trials were executed 10 times. The experimental result for the RBM on standard MNIST database is 3.39% [6], the classification error rate of the RBM on variation MNIST is 3.16% [15]. The rest values in Table 1 are given by the mean of ten results. Table 1 shows that the classification results of reRBM are better than those of RBM.

Table 1. Classification error rates for three databases.

	RBM	reRBM
Standard MNIST	3.39%	**2.52%**
Variation MNIST	3.16%	**2.68%**
OCR	15.33%	**13.36%**

5   Conclusions

The RBMs have already been successfully applied to many tasks. Usually, the objective of the RBMs is maximizing the log-likelihood to make the distribution learned by the RBM as identical as the distribution of the input data. But reconstruction error always exists even the distribution learned by the RBM is identical as that of the input data. In this paper, a method to improve the performance of the RBM by adding the reconstruction error to the cost function of RBM was proposed. Two categories of experiments on several databases were carried out, the experimental results on standard MNIST and AR showed that reconstruction performance of the reRBM was better than that of the RBM, and classification results on standard MNIST, variation of MNIST and OCR letters showed that the reRBM was more competitive than the RBM. In future work, we intent to use the proposed method to more databases or other applications and apply the idea to other models.

Acknowledgments. This work was Supported by National Natural Science Fund for Distinguished Young Scholar Grant No. 61625204).

References

1. Fischer, A., Igel, C.: Training restricted Boltzmann machines: an introduction. Pattern Recogn. **47**(1), 25–39 (2014)
2. Salakhutdinov, R., Mnih, A., Hinton, G.: Restricted Boltzmann machines for collaborative filtering. In: International Conference on Machine Learning, vol. 227, pp. 791–798. ACM (2007)
3. Xie, G.S., Zhang, X.Y., Zhang, Y.M., Liu, C.L.: Integrating supervised subspace criteria with restricted Boltzmann machine for feature extraction. In: International Joint Conference on Neural Networks, pp. 1622–1629. IEEE Press, New York (2014)
4. Zhang, K., Liu, J., Chai, Y., Qian, K.: An optimized dimensionality reduction model for high-dimensional data based on restricted Boltzmann machines. In: Control and Decision Conference, pp. 2939–2944. IEEE Press, New York (2015)
5. Salakhutdinov, R., Tenenbaum, J.B., Torralba, A.: Learning with hierarchical-deep models. IEEE Trans. Pattern Anal. Mach. Intell. **35**(8), 1958–1971 (2013)
6. Larochelle, H., Mandel, M., Pascanu, R., Bengio, Y.: Learning algorithms for the classification restricted Boltzmann machine. J. Mach. Learn. Res. **13**(1), 643–669 (2012)

7. Hinton, G.E., Salakhutdinov, R.R.: Reducing the dimensionality of data with neural networks. Science **313**(5786), 504–507 (2006)
8. Hinton, G.E.: To recognize shapes, first learn to generate images. Prog. Brain Res. **165**, 535–547 (2007)
9. Ji, N.N., Zhang, J.S., Zhang, C.X.: A sparse-response deep belief network based on rate distortion theory. Pattern Recogn. **47**(9), 3179–3191 (2014)
10. Srivastava, N., Salakhutdinov, R.: Multimodal learning with deep Boltzmann machines. In: International Conference on Neural Information Processing Systems, pp. 2222–2230. IEEE Press, New York (2012)
11. Luo, L., Wang, Y., Peng, H., Tang, Z., You, S., Huang, X.: Training restricted Boltzmann machine with dynamic learning rate. In: International Conference on Computer Science & Education. IEEE (2016)
12. Yu, J., Gwak, J., Lee, S., Jeon, M.: An incremental learning approach for restricted Boltzmann machines. In: International Conference on Control, Automation and Information Sciences, pp. 113–117. IEEE Press, New York (2015)
13. Golovko, V., Kroshchanka, A., Turchenko, V., Jankowski, S., Treadwell, D.: A new technique for restricted Boltzmann machine learning. In: International Conference on Intelligent Data Acquisition and Advanced Computing Systems: Technology and Applications, vol. 1, pp. 182–186. IEEE Press, New York (2015)
14. Huang, W., Hong, H., Bian, K., Zhou, X., Song, G., Xie, K.: Improving deep neural network ensembles using reconstruction error. In: 2015 International Joint Conference on Neural Networks (IJCNN), pp. 1–7. IEEE Press, New York (2015)
15. Yin, J., Lv, J., Sang, Y., Guo, J.: Classification model of restricted Boltzmann machine based on reconstruction error. Neural Comput. Appl. 1–16 (2016)
16. Hinton, G.E.: Training products of experts by minimizing contrastive divergence. Neural Comput. **14**(8), 1771–1800 (2002)

Modeling Hysteresis Using Non-smooth Neural Networks

Yonghong Tan[1] and Ruili Dong[2(✉)]

[1] College of Mechanical and Electrical Engineering,
Shanghai Normal University, Shanghai, China
tany@shnu.edu.cn
[2] College of Information Science and Technology, Donghua University,
Shanghai, China
ruilidong@dhu.edu.cn

Abstract. A non-smooth neural network is proposed for modeling of hysteresis with non-smooth characteristic and multi-valued mapping. In the proposed non-smooth neural network, the non-smooth neurons with multi-valued mapping are constructed for depicting the non-smoothness and multi-valued mapping of hysteresis inherent in piezo-actuators. For parameter estimation, the training algorithm based on non-smooth iterative technique is proposed. In this case, the parameters of the non-smooth neurons can be determined automatically based on the optimization of the cost function. Finally, the experimental results are illustrated to demonstrate the modeling performance of the proposed modeling method.

Keywords: Hysteresis · Iterative training · Non-smooth neural networks

1 Introduction

The actuators using smart materials such as piezoceramic, ionic polymer-metal composite, memory alloy and electromagnetic mechanism are usually used in positioning systems [1–5]. It is also known that the nonlinear hysteresis inherent in these smart materials will usually affect the dynamic performance and positioning accuracy of actuators. Accurate modeling of hysteresis in smart materials based actuators is important for the design of a model based compensator to reduce the effect of hysteresis on the performance of smart material based actuators. By considering the hysteresis is a complex system with multi-valued mapping and non-smoothness [4], it motivates us to apply neural networks to the modeling of hysteresis since neural networks have the well-known capability of universal approximation. However, most of the neural networks such as feedforward neural networks [11], radial basis function neural networks [12] and Elman neural networks [12] etc. are only applicable for modeling the systems with one-to-one mapping between the input and output [7, 8, 10]. Those neural networks will not be able to model the hysteresis which has the features of non-smoothness and multi-valued mapping between the input and output. Therefore, it is a real challenge for modeling hysteresis with neural networks. For tackling the problem of hysteresis with non-smoothness and multi-valued mapping, Refs. [7, 8, 10, 12] proposed the so-called expanded input space based neural network hysteresis models. In these methods, an expanded input space with an introduced hysteresis operator is constructed. Then, the multi-valued mapping between the input and output of hysteresis can be transformed into a one-to-one mapping on the constructed expanded input space. Afterward, the neural networks can be applied to modeling of hysteresis on the expanded input space.

Although Refs. [6, 11, 13] developed different forms of neural networks for modeling hysteresis, these neural networks just used smooth basis functions to approximate non-smooth hysteresis and may result in larger modeling errors. On the other hand, it should note that the hysteresis is a nonlinear system with multi-valued mapping. How to handle the modeling of the systems with multi-valued mapping is still a problem needs to be solved.

For describing the hysteresis involved with non-smooth characteristic and multi-valued mapping, a neural network consisting of non-smooth neurons with multi-valued mapping will be developed in this paper. Firstly, a non-smooth neuron with multi-valued mapping used as the basis function of neural network is developed. Then, the non-smooth neural network involved with the non-smooth neurons is constructed. Afterward, a learning algorithm is developed to determine the parameters of non-smooth neural network based hysteresis model. Moreover, the experiments to test the proposed modeling method are presented.

2 Non-smooth Neural Network

For describing the non-smooth characteristic of hysteresis, a non-smooth neural network is proposed in this section. Note that the hysteresis to be described has the features of non-smoothness and multi-valued mapping between the input and output. It motivates us to develop a basis function or neuron with the characteristics of multi-valued mapping and local non-smoothness. Then, based on the non-smooth basis function, a non-smooth neural network which is the sum of weighted non-smooth basis functions is constructed.

Suppose the non-smooth basis function is defined by

$$
z_i(k) = \begin{cases} m_{1i}(x(k) - r_{1i}), & x(k) \geq a_{ri} \\ z_i(k-1), & a_{li} < x(k) < a_{ri} \\ m_{2i}(x(k) + r_{2i}), & x(k) \leq a_{li} \end{cases} \tag{1}
$$

where $x(k)$ is the input of hysteresis; $z_i(k)$ is the output of ith non-smooth neuron; m_{1i} and m_{2i} are gains; r_{1i} and r_{2i} are thresholds; as well as a_{li} and a_{ri} are lower and upper bounds, namely

$$
a_{ri} = \frac{z_i(k-1)}{m_{1i}} + r_{1i} \text{ and}
$$

$$
a_{il} = \frac{z_i(k-1)}{m_{2i}} - r_{2i}.
$$

Then, the corresponding non-smooth neural network can be described by

$$y(k) = W^T \cdot Z[x(k), z_0, m_1, m_2, r_1, r_2] \tag{2}$$

where y is the output of neural network, $W^T = [\, w_0 \quad \cdots \quad w_n \,]$ is the weight vector, n is the number of the non-smooth neurons; $z_0 = [\, z_{00} \quad \cdots \quad z_{0n} \,]^T$ is the initial state vector; $m_1 = [\, m_{10} \quad \cdots \quad m_{1n} \,]^T$; $\quad m_2 = [\, m_{20} \quad \cdots \quad m_{2n} \,]^T$; $\quad r_1 = [\, r_{10} \quad \cdots \quad r_{1n} \,]^T \quad$ and $r_2 = [\, r_{20} \quad \cdots \quad r_{2n} \,]^T$. As the non-smooth neurons have multi-valued mapping between input and output, (2) is much convenient for hysteresis modeling.

3   Training of Non-smooth Neural Network

For determining the parameters of non-smooth neural network, we define the following criterion for neural network training:

$$\{\hat{W}, \hat{m}, \hat{r}\} = \underset{\hat{W}, \hat{m}, \hat{r}}{\arg \min} \frac{1}{N} \sum_{k=1}^{N} \left(y(k) - \hat{W}^T Z[x(k), z_0, \hat{m}, \hat{r}] \right)^2 \tag{3}$$

Where N is the number of the data for modeling; $\hat{W}, \hat{m}$, and $\hat{r}$ are the estimations of the parameter vectors W, m, and r. Then, the iterative algorithm used for above-mentioned minimization is derived based on the following steps:

(1) Initialize the parameters to be estimated, i.e. $\hat{m}(0) = [\hat{m}_1(0), \hat{m}_2(0)]^T$ and $\hat{r}(0) = [\hat{r}_1(0), \hat{r}_2(0)]^T$.
(2) Estimate $\hat{W}(k)$, $\hat{m}(k)$ and $\hat{r}(k)$ according to

$$\hat{w}_i(k) = \hat{w}_i(k-1) + \lambda \frac{1}{2N} \sum_{k=1}^{N} [y(k) - \hat{W}^T(k-1)Z(k-1)]z_i(k-1) \tag{4}$$
$$i = 0, \dots, n$$

$$\hat{m}_{1i}(k) = \hat{m}_{1i}(k-1) + \lambda \frac{1}{2N} \sum_{k=1}^{N} [y(k) - \hat{W}^T(k-1)Z(k-1)]\hat{w}_i \partial_{\hat{m}_{1i}(k-1)} z_i(k-1) \tag{5}$$
$$i = 0, \dots, n$$

$$\hat{m}_{2i}(k) = \hat{m}_{2i}(k-1) + \lambda \frac{1}{2N} \sum_{k=1}^{N} [y(k) - \hat{W}^T(k-1)Z(k-1)]\hat{w}_i \partial_{\hat{m}_{2i}(k-1)} z_i(k-1) \tag{6}$$
$$i = 0, \dots, n$$

$$\hat{r}_{1i}(k) = \hat{r}_{1i}(k-1) + \lambda \frac{1}{2N} \sum_{k=1}^{N} [y(k) - \hat{W}^T(k-1)Z(k-1)] \hat{w}_i \partial_{\hat{r}_{1i}(k-1)} z_i(k-1) \tag{7}$$

$$i = 0, \ldots, n$$

and

$$\hat{r}_{2i}(k) = \hat{r}_{2i}(k-1) + \lambda \frac{1}{2N} \sum_{k=1}^{N} [y(k) - \hat{W}^T(k-1)Z(k-1)] \hat{w}_i \partial_{\hat{r}_{2i}(k-1)} z_i(k-1) \tag{8}$$

$$i = 0, \ldots, n$$

where λ is the optimizing step size. Moreover,

$$\partial_{\varphi_{ji}(k-1)} z_i(k-1) = \begin{cases} \partial z_i(k-1)/\partial \varphi_{ji}(k-1), & smooth \ region \\ \partial_{\varphi_{ji}(k-1)} z_i(k-1), & non-smooth \ region \end{cases} \tag{9}$$

$$\varphi_{ji}(k-1) \in \{\hat{m}_{ji}(k-1), \hat{r}_{ji}(k-1)\}, j = 1, 2; i = 0, \ldots, n$$

is the generalized gradient [9] of the neuron output with respect to the parameters $\hat{m}_{1i}$, $\hat{m}_{2i}$, $\hat{r}_{1i}$ or $\hat{r}_{2i}$. Note that $\partial_{\varphi_{ji}(k-1)} z_i(k-1)$ equals the normal gradient when x locates in smooth region otherwise equals the sub-gradient.

(3) Update the iteration index k by $k+1$ and the process is repeated until the mean squared estimated error is less than the expected error bound.

4   Experimental Results

In this section, the proposed approach is applied to the modeling of a set of data measured from a piezoceramic actuator (PZT-753.21C). The output of the hysteresis of the piezoceramic actuator has a nominal expansion of 0–20 μm under the input voltage within 0–10 v and the sampling frequency is 1 kHz. The input signal shown in Fig. 1 is applied to the excitation of the piezo-actuator to acquire the data for modeling. It is shown that the amplitude and frequency of the input signal is attenuate with time.

Then, the input signal: $u(t) = Ae^{-0.0013k}sin(2\pi f e^{-0.0003k}k) + B$ is used to excite the actuator to derive data for model validation, where A is the amplitude is 2.5 v, B is 0.5 v, and $f = 600$ Hz is the frequency of the input signal. The non-smooth neural network containing 60 non-smooth neurons is used for modeling. For comparison, the

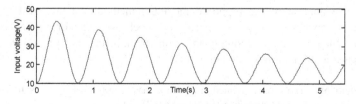

Fig. 1. Input signals for exciting piezo-actuator

Prandtl–Ishilinski model [4] with 100 play operators is also implemented to model the hysteresis.

Figure 2 illustrates the model validation results of the experiments. Figure 2(a) and (b) respectively show the model validation results of the PI model and the proposed method while Fig. 2(c) and (d) show the corresponding modelling errors of the PI model and the proposed method. It can be seen that the proposed modeling scheme has derived better modelling performance than the Prandtl–Ishilinski modelling method.

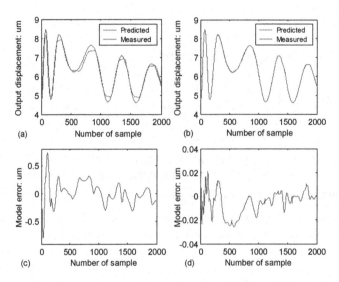

Fig. 2. (a) Model validation of PI model; (b) Model validation of the proposed method; (c) Model error of PI model; (d) Model error of the proposed method.

5   Conclusions

In this paper, the non-smooth neuron with multi-valued mapping is constructed. Then, the non-smooth neural network consisting of non-smooth neurons is proposed for modeling of hysteresis. For the training of non-smooth neural network, an iterative algorithm is proposed. As the non-smooth neural network is involved with non-smooth neurons, the gradients do not exist at non-smooth points of the neural network. Thus, the generalized gradients are applied to the estimation of gradients at the non-smooth points.

For the evaluation of the proposed modeling method, the proposed method is applied to the modeling of the hysteresis of a piezoelectric actuator. The experimental results show the proposed modeling method can obtain better modeling results than the well-known Prandtl–Ishilinski modeling method.

Acknowledgments. The work presented in this paper has been funded by the National Science Foundation of China under Grants 61671303 and 61571302.

References

1. Hu, H: Compensation of hysteresis in Piezoceramic actuators and control of nanopositioning system. Ph.D. thesis of University of Toronto, Canada (2003)
2. Ge, P., Jouaneh, M.: Modeling hysteresis in piezoceramic actuators. Precis. Eng. **17**, 211–221 (1995)
3. Mayergoyz, I.D.: Dynamic Preisach models of hysteresis. IEEE Trans. Magn. **24**(6), 2925–2927 (1988)
4. Su, C., Wang, Q., Chen, X., Rakheja, S.: Adaptive variable structure control of a class of nonlinear systems with unknown Prandtl-Ishlinskii hysteresis. IEEE Trans. Autom. Control **50**(12), 2069–2074 (2005)
5. Kugi, A., Thull, D., Kuhnen, K.: An infinite-dimensional control concept for piezoelectric structures with complex hysteresis. Struct. Control Health Monit. **13**, 1099–1119 (2006)
6. Selmic, R., Lewis, F.L.: Neural net backlash compensation with Hebbian tuning using dynamic inversion. Automatica **37**, 1269–1277 (2001)
7. Dong, R., Tan, Y., Chen, H., Xie, Y.: A neural networks based model for rate-dependent hysteresis for piezoceramic actuators. Sens. Actuators A: Phys. **143**(2), 370–376 (2008)
8. Zhang, X., Tan, Y.: A hybrid model for rate-dependent hysteresis in piezoelectric actuators. Sens. Actuators A: Phys. **157**(1), 54–60 (2010)
9. Clarke, F.: Optimization and Nonsmooth Analysis. Wiley, New York (1983)
10. Xie, Y., Tan, Y., Dong, R.: Nonlinear modeling and decoupling control of XY micropositioning stages with piezoelectric actuators. IEEE/ASME Trans. Mechatron. **18**(3), 821–832 (2013)
11. Liu, W., Cheng, L., Hou, Z., Yu, J., Tan, M.: An inversion-free predictive controller for piezoelectric actuators based on a dynamic linearized neural network model. IEEE/ASME Trans. Mechatron. **21**(1), 214–226 (2016)
12. Dang, X., Tan, Y.: RBF neural networks hysteresis modelling for piezoceramic actuator using hybrid model. Mech. Syst. Sig. Process. **21**(1), 430–440 (2007)
13. Saghafifar, M., Kundu, A., Nafalski, A.: Dynamic magnetic hysteresis modelling using Elman recurrent neural network. Int. J. Appl. Electromagnet. Mech. **13**(1–4), 209–214 (2002)

The Implementation of a Pointer Network Model for Traveling Salesman Problem on a Xilinx PYNQ Board

Shenshen Gu[1]([✉]), Tao Hao[1], and Shaofu Yang[2]

[1] School of Mechatronic Engineering and Automation, Shanghai University,
Shanghai 200072, China
gushenshen@shu.edu.cn
[2] School of Computer Science and Engineering, Southeast University,
Nanjing 211189, China

Abstract. In this paper, a pointer network model for traveling salesman problem (TSP) was implemented on a Xilinx PYNQ board which supports Python and Jupyter notebook and is equipped with ZYNQ SOC. We implement a pointer network model for solving TSP with Python and Theano firstly, then train the model on a GPU platform, and eventually deploy the model on a PYNQ board. Unlike traditional neural network implementation, hardware libraries on PYNQ (Overlays) are used to accelerate the pointer network model application. The experimental results show that the pointer network model for TSP can be deployed on the embedded system successfully and achieve good performance.

Keywords: Pointer networks · Traveling salesman problem · Theano
PYNQ · FPGA

1 Introduction

In recent years, deep neural networks (DNNs) are widely used in many artificial intelligence applications, particularly tasks involving computer vision [1], speech recognition [2], and robotics [3]. Currently, DNN models usually require a Graphics Processing Unit (GPU) to accelerate computation, so they mostly have been developed and applied on large machines with powerful computation capacity. With increasingly need of DNN models deployed in mobile devices, there is a growing concern in deep learning area about how to deploy powerful and cost-effective DNN models in an embedded system. DNN on embedded system projects have been launched by some researchers [4]. A TensorFlow-on-Raspberry-pi Project was issued by Sam Abrahahms. In addition, a Binary Neural Network project that converts the floating-point parameters into binary values on an FPGA [5] has been published by a Xilinx research group. Deep learning models can be trained off-line and then implemented onto embedded system, so that the system only needs to focus on improving the throughput of forward propagation.

© Springer International Publishing AG, part of Springer Nature 2018
T. Huang et al. (Eds.): ISNN 2018, LNCS 10878, pp. 130–138, 2018.
https://doi.org/10.1007/978-3-319-92537-0_16

Meanwhile, DNNs have made remarkable achievements in solving combinatorial optimization problems. For instance, Vinyals solves the traveling salesman problem (TSP) with recurrent neural networks (RNNs) [6]. TSP is a classical example of combinatorial optimization arising in many areas of theoretical computer science. It can be described as follows. Given a set of city coordinates, one needs to search the space of permutations to find an optimal sequence of nodes with minimal total tour length. TSP plays an important role in microchip design, DNA sequencing, and robot path planning. In [6], a new architecture termed as Pointer network is proposed for solving large scale TSPs. In this network, attention mechanism is used as a pointer to select a position from the input sequence as an output symbol. The pointer network is shown as a simple and effective model for solving TSPs. Therefore, it is meaningful to deploy the pointer network in an embedded system for various wearable applications.

FPGA is very suitable for parallel computing, and have been widely used to accelerate the neural network and machine learning algorithm [7]. Nowadays, most embedded devices are composed of ARM-based processor and the hardware programmability of an FPGA, such as Xilinx Zedboard, ZYBO, and so on. Python has more advantages in scientific computation and data processing than other programming languages. Due to the fact that a lot of software libraries in Python exist, which make data sampling, analysis, and processing very convenient. Python has consistently been ranked the top of Lists of Programming languages for deep learning. Motivated by the release of PYNQ from Xilinx which aids in the interfacing with custom hardware in the FPGA fabric and providing many useful utilities, such as downloading bitstreams from within the application, we consider how to use Python in an FPGA development environment.

Currently, many popular open-source deep learning framework programming tools such as TensorFlow, Theano, Caffe all support Linux platform, and all support Python interface. Comparing these neural network framework tools, we found that Theano is the most suitable for PYNQ development board. Because Theano can be installed on PYNQ easily and runs well under a 32bit Linux Operation System (OS). What's more, the support of Theano for customized layer is very high.

The rest of this paper is organized as follows. In Sect. 2, recurrent neural network and architecture of pointer network are introduced briefly. Section 3 introduces how to implement the pointer network model for TSP based on Theano and FPGA accelerator Overlay design in detail. Next, in Sect. 4, the training process of the model and performance on PYNQ board are shown. Finally, a conclusion is drawn to summarize this work in Sect. 5.

2   Recurrent Neural Network and Pointer Network Model

In this section, we first introduce RNNs, especially Long Short Term Memory (LSTM) which is the basic cell of pointer networks. And then, the architecture of the pointer network model will be described.

2.1   Recurrent Neural Network

RNNs are becoming an increasingly popular way to process and predict sequences of data. RNNs have shown excellent performance in problems such as speech recognition, machine translation and scene analysis. RNNs are recurrent because they perform the same computations for all the elements of a sequence of inputs, and the output of each element depends on not only the current input but also all the previous computations.

As a special RNN architecture, LSTM implements a learned memory controller for avoiding vanishing or exploding gradients [8]. LSTM is a network that consists of cells (LSTM blocks) linked to each other. Each LSTM block contains three types of gate: Input gate, Output gate and Forget gate, respectively, which perform the functions of writing, reading, and resetting on the cell memory. There are some variations on the LSTM architecture and all those variations have similar performance as shown in [9]. This is the vanilla LSTM [10], which can be formulated as follows:

$$i_t = \sigma \left(W_{xi} x_t + W_{hi} h_{t-1} + b_i \right) \tag{1}$$

$$f_t = \sigma \left(W_{xf} x_t + W_{hf} h_{t-1} + b_f \right) \tag{2}$$

$$o_t = \sigma \left(W_{xo} x_t + W_{ho} h_{t-1} + b_f \right) \tag{3}$$

$$\tilde{c}_t = \tanh \left(W_{xc} x_t + W_{hc} h_{t-1} + b_c \right) \tag{4}$$

$$c_t = f_t * c_{t-1} + i_t * \tilde{c}_t \tag{5}$$

$$h_t = o_t * \tanh \left(c_t \right) \tag{6}$$

where i, f and o represent input, forget, and output gate respectively, x is the input vector of the layer, W is the model paraments, c is memory cell activation, $\tilde{c}$ is the candidate memory cell gate, h is the layer output vector, σ is the logistic sigmoid function, and $*$ is element wise multiplication. And $t - 1$ represents results from the previous time step.

2.2   Architecture of Pointer Networks

The architecture of pointer networks in [6] is applied to solve TSP. Given an input sequence, this type of deep neural architecture (see Fig. 1) combines the popular sequence-to-sequence learning framework [11] with a modified Attention Mechanism [12] to learn the conditional probability of an output whose values correspond to positions in an input sequence.

To solve the problem that the encoder output dictionary size depends on the length of the input sequence, the pointer network adjusts the standard attention mechanism to create pointers to elements in the input sequence. The following modification to the attention model was proposed:

$$u_j^i = v^T \tanh(W_1 e_j + W_2 d_i) \qquad j \in \{1, 2, \cdots, n\} \tag{7}$$

$$p \left(C_i | C_1, \cdots, C_{i-1}, P \right) = \text{softmax} \left(u^i \right) \tag{8}$$

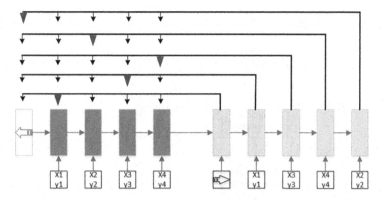

Fig. 1. Architecture of the pointer network (encoder in blue, decoder in yellow) (Color figure online)

where softmax normalizes the vector u^i (of length n) to be an output distribution over the dictionary of inputs, and v, W_1, W_2 are learnable parameters. Note that unlike the standard attention mechanism, the pointer network model does not use the encoder states to propagate extra information to the decoder, but instead uses u^i_j as pointers to the input sequence elements [13].

Figure 1 illustrates the architecture of the pointer network, which mainly consists of encoder network and decoder network. An encoder converts the input sequence to a code (blue) that is fed to a decoder (yellow). The input/output pairs (P, C^P) for TSP are illustrated in detail. The input sequence $P = \{P_1, \ldots, P_n\}$ is the cartesian coordinates representing the cities. $C^P = \{C_1, \ldots, C_n\}$ is a permutation of integers from 1 to n representing the optimal path.

3   Implementation

In this section, the pointer network model for TSP design, training, and deployment methods and procedures will be concretely described. The training of the neural network will consume much computing resource and time, so we use a GPU to train the network, and then deploy the model on PYNQ board.

3.1   Implementation of Pointer Network Model for TSP Based on Theano

Figure 2 shows the procedure of implementing a pointer network model. The first step is to generate TSP training dataset, preprocess the data and then load it. We set the maximum and minimum number of nodes in a set of data, then generate the random number between maximum and minimum as the number of nodes, and then generate randomly plane coordinates in the $[0, 1] \times [0, 1]$ square. Without loss of generality, in the training dataset, we always start from the first

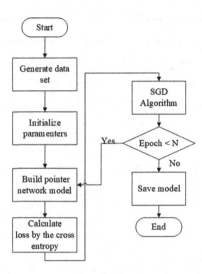

Fig. 2. Scheme of implementing a pointer network model

city in order to keep consistency. For small scale TSP, dynamic programming algorithm are implemented to obtain exact solutions. For large scale TSP, due to the importance of TSP, many good and efficient algorithms have provided reasonable approximate solutions, so we can use benchmark for TSP to create samples. The training data is saved as tsp.pkl.gz.

The second step is to make parameter initialization module. The initial value for the weights and biases of the neural network need to be configured. The next step is to build the pointer network model. We first define the LSTM cell function module, and then according to the architecture of pointer network in Sect. 2.2, make an encoder network and a decoder network with LSTM cell. The softmax function, used in the output layer, is a kind of normalization function that can convert a vector into a probability distribution form and give every element a probability, whose definition is described as follows.

$$\sigma(z)_j = \frac{\exp(z_j)}{\sum_{k=1}^{K} \exp(z_k)} \quad j \in 1, \ldots, K \tag{9}$$

The cross-entropy is more suitable for training RNN, which is used as loss function to calculate the gap between the prediction and the actual values. The definition of the cross-entropy function is described as follows.

$$H(p, q) = -\sum_{i=1}^{n} p(x) \log(q(x)) \tag{10}$$

Stochastic Gradient Descent (SGD) algorithm is used to update the weights of the neural network according to loss function. Above functions can be implemented conveniently with Python and Theano. The final step is to train the model and save the trained pointer network model. The trained model will be saved in a npz file, which saves several arrays into a single file in uncompressed format. Then the trained model can be used to predict results.

3.2   FPGA Accelerator Overlay Design

PYNQ provides an Overlay framework to support interfacing with the board's IO. However, any custom logic must be created and integrated by the developer. A Vivado project for a Zynq design consists of the PL design and the PS configuration settings. For PS configuration, it covers settings for system clocks and the clocks used in the PL. And, the PS settings in their Vivado project should be ensured to match the PYNQ image settings. The PL clock configuration are set as Table 1.

Table 1. PL clock configuration

PL Clock	FCL_CLK0	FCL_CLK1	FCL_CLK2	FCL_CLK3
Frequency	100.00 MHz	142.86 MHz	200.00 MHz	166.67 MHz

The schedule of creating a PYNQ overlay is described as follows. Hardware accelerators should be first designed and implemented to an IP through Vivado HLS, a high-level synthesis tool. Based on a base design which includes most of the peripheral interface overlay provided by the PYNQ project, a Vivado project is created and IPs are added to a block design and the design is synthesized, implemented, and a bitstream is generated, a tcl file of the block design is exported.

The communication between the PL and PS depends on an AXI interface. An IP with AXI interface can be easily created in Vivado Design Suite. In addition, PYNQ includes the MMIO Python class to simplify communication between the Zynq PS and PL. Once the overlay has been created, and the memory map can be known through Address Editor in Vivado, the MMIO can be used to access memory mapped locations in the PL. Matrix multiplication operations are the most frequent operation in the neural network, so a matrix multiplication accelerator is designed in this paper. Figure 3 shows the connection between the matrix multiplication and the Zynq processor.

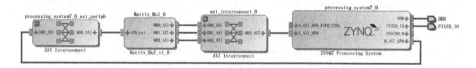

Fig. 3. The connection between the matrix multiplication and the Zynq processor

4   Experimental Results

To test the effectiveness of the implementation, a pointer network model for TSP was trained by supervised learning. The weights of neural networks were updated by SGD algorithm with a learning rate of 0.01. All the parameters were initialized obeying random distribution in $[-0.08, 0.08]$.

We obtained the loss values of 1000 epochs in the training process. As is shown in Fig. 4, the loss values are gradually reducing with the increase of training epochs, which means the training algorithms works well.

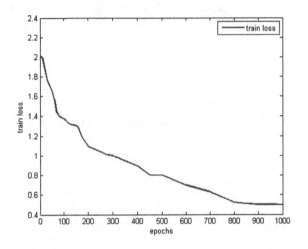

Fig. 4. The loss values of 1000 epochs

The PYNQ board should be configured as required. After booting up the linux system in the PYNQ board, we could view and run the notebooks interactively through our browser. The final size of the trained model is about 5 MB, which needed to be copied to the board file system, and loaded in Jupyter notebook. Then the model on PYNQ board can be used to predict the result of the TSP.

After installing the essential package, the trained model was deployed successfully on the PYNQ board. In our experiment, the PYNQ's CPU was clocked at frequency of 665 MHz. For different scale of TSP, the inference time of running pointer network models on the PC (equipped with Intel i5-2450M CPU @ 2GHz and 4 GB RAM), PYNQ board without Overlay and PYNQ board with Overlay respectively is shown in Table 2. It is found that the performance of the pointer network model deployed on PYNQ board is nearly comparable to that on conventional PC. In addition, Overlay can promote the performance of PYNQ board to some degree.

Table 2. Performance of the pointer network model

Number of nodes	10	20	30	40	50
Inference time on PC (sec.)	0.21	0.35	0.61	0.72	0.82
Inference time on PYNQ without Overlay (sec.)	0.29	0.44	0.71	0.83	0.96
Inference time on PYNQ with Overlay (sec.)	0.24	0.38	0.65	0.76	0.85

The core chip of PYNQ is a ZYNQ SOC XC7Z020-1CLG400C, which has plentiful programmable logic resource. The FPGA resource utilization is shown in Table 3. In our experiment, BRAM and LUT are mainly used. BRAM resource is used to restore the weights. LUT resource is consumed to register and routing.

Table 3. FPGA resource utilization

Resource	Utilization	Available	Utilization%
LUT	32414	53200	60.93
LUTRAM	2619	17400	15.05
FF	39252	106400	36.89
BRAM	74.50	140	53.21
DSP	11	220	5.0
IO	96	125	76.80
BUFG	6	32	18.75
MMCM	2	4	50.00

5   Conclusions

In this paper, a pointer network model for TSP is implemented with python and Theano and trained on a GPU platform. Furthermore, the trained model is deployed on PYNQ board through Jupyter notebook. As deep neural networks have delivered state-of-the-art performances in the fields of speech recognition, machine translation and machine vision, the deployment of well-trained neural networks to embedded equipment is a trend of future development. FPGA is a very promising accelerator for deep neural network due to its strong parallel-process capability, reconfigurability and low power consumption. Experimental results show that the implementation of pointer network for TSP is successful and the performance is promising which suggests that it can be applied to various models and fields.

Acknowledgments. The work described in the paper was supported by the National Science Foundation of China under Grant 61503233.

References

1. LeCun, Y., Bengio, Y., Hinton, G.: Deep learning. Nature **521**(7553), 436–444 (2015). Nature Publishing Group
2. Li, S., Wu, C., Li, H., Li, B., Wang, Y., Qiu, Q.: FPGA acceleration of recurrent neural network based language model. In: Proceedings of the IEEE 23rd Annual International Symposium on Field-Programmable Custom Computing Machines (FCCM), pp. 111–118. IEEE Press (2015)
3. Lenz, I., Lee, H., Saxena, A.: Deep learning for detecting robotic grasps. Int. J. Robot. Res. **34**(4–5), 705–724 (2015). SAGE Publications Sage UK, London
4. Hao, Y., Quigley, S.: The implementation of a deep recurrent neural network language model on a Xilinx FPGA. arXiv preprint arXiv:1710.10296 (2017)
5. Umuroglu, Y., Fraser, N.J., Gambardella, G., Blott, M., Leong, P., Jahre, M., Vissers, K.: Finn: a framework for fast, scalable binarized neural network inference. In: Proceedings of the 2017 ACM/SIGDA International Symposium on Field-Programmable Gate Arrays, pp. 65–74 (2017)
6. Vinyals, O., Fortunato, M., Jaitly, N.: Pointer networks. In: Advances in Neural Information Processing Systems, pp. 2692–2700 (2015)
7. Guan, Y., Yuan, Z., Sun, G., Cong, J.: FPGA-based accelerator for long short-term memory recurrent neural networks. In: Proceedings of the 22nd Asia and South Pacific Design Automation Conference (ASP-DAC), pp. 629–634. IEEE Press (2017)
8. Hochreiter, S., Schmidhuber, J.: Long short-term memory. Neural Comput. **9**(8), 1735–1780 (1997)
9. Greff, K., Srivastava, R.K., Koutník, J., Steunebrink, B.R., Schmidhuber, J.: LSTM: a search space odyssey. IEEE Trans. Neural Netw. Learn. Syst. **28**(10), 2222–2232 (2017)
10. Chang, A.X.M., Martini, B., Culurciello, E.: Recurrent neural networks hardware implementation on FPGA. arXiv preprint arXiv:1511.05552 (2015)
11. Sutskever, I., Vinyals, O., Le, Q.V.: Sequence to sequence learning with neural networks. In: Advances in Neural Information Processing Systems, pp. 3104–3112 (2014)
12. Bahdanau, D., Cho, K., Bengio, Y.: Neural machine translation by jointly learning to align and translate. arXiv preprint arXiv:1409.0473 (2014)
13. Milan, A., Rezatfighi, S.H., Garg, R., Dick, A.R., Reid, I.D.: Data-driven approximations to NP-hard problems. In: Proceedings of the 31st AAAI Conference on Artficial Intelligence (AAAI 2017), pp. 1453–1459 (2017)

Generalized Affine Scaling Trajectory Analysis for Linearly Constrained Convex Programming

Xun Qian and Li-Zhi Liao$^{(\boxtimes)}$

Department of Mathematics, Hong Kong Baptist University, Kowloon Tong,
Kowloon, Hong Kong, PRC
`13479784@life.hkbu.edu.hk`, `liliao@hkbu.edu.hk`

Abstract. In this paper, we propose and analyze a continuous trajectory, which is the solution of an ordinary differential equation (ODE) system for solving linearly constrained convex programming. The ODE system is formulated based on a first-order interior point method in [Math. Program., **127**, 399–424 (2011)] which combines and extends a first-order affine scaling method and the replicator dynamics method for quadratic programming. The solution of the corresponding ODE system is called the generalized affine scaling trajectory. By only assuming the existence of a finite optimal solution, we show that, starting from any interior feasible point, (i) the continuous trajectory is convergent; and (ii) the limit point is indeed an optimal solution of the original problem.

Keywords: Continuous trajectory · Convex programming
Interior point method · Ordinary differential equation

1 Introduction

We consider the following convex programming with linear constraints

$$
\begin{aligned}
\min \ & f(x) \\
\text{s.t.} \ & Ax = b, \ x_i \geq 0, \ i = 1, ..., s,
\end{aligned}
\tag{1}
$$

where $x \in \mathbb{R}^n$, $0 \leq s \leq n$, $f(x)$ is convex over the feasible set, and $A \in \mathbb{R}^{m \times n}$ with rank m. The following notations are used in this paper:

$$
\mathbb{R}^n_{s+} = \{x \in \mathbb{R}^n | x_i \geq 0, \ 1 \leq i \leq s\}, \ \mathbb{R}^n_{s++} = \{x \in \mathbb{R}^n | x_i > 0, \ 1 \leq i \leq s\},
$$
$$
\mathcal{P}^+ = \{x \in \mathbb{R}^n_{s+} | Ax = b\}, \quad \text{and} \quad \mathcal{P}^{++} = \{x \in \mathbb{R}^n_{s++} | Ax = b\}.
$$

It is conventional to assume that $\mathcal{P}^{++}$ is nonempty.

We are particularly interested in the (interior point) continuous solution trajectory of the following ordinary differential equation (ODE) system

$$
\frac{dx}{dt} = -DP_{AD}D\nabla f(x), \ x(t_0) = x^0 \in \mathcal{P}^{++},
\tag{2}
$$

© Springer International Publishing AG, part of Springer Nature 2018
T. Huang et al. (Eds.): ISNN 2018, LNCS 10878, pp. 139–147, 2018.
https://doi.org/10.1007/978-3-319-92537-0_17

where

$$\frac{1}{2} \leq \gamma < 1, \ t_0 > 0, \ x \in \mathbb{R}^n_{s++},$$

$$d \in \mathbb{R}^n, \ \{d_i\}_{i=1}^s = \{x_i^\gamma\}_{i=1}^s, \ d_i = 1 \text{ for } i = s+1, \dots, n,$$

$$D = \text{diag}(d) \in \mathbb{R}^{n \times n}, \ P_{AD} = I_n - DA^T(AD^2A^T)^{-1}AD,$$

and I_n is the $n \times n$ identity matrix. We require $\nabla f(x) \in C^1$ on $\mathbb{R}^n_{s+}$.

First we explain where the ODE system comes from when $s = n$. The right-hand side (**RHS**) of the ODE system (2) was used by Tseng *et al.* in [12], who proposed a first-order interior point method for linearly constrained smooth optimization which combines and extends the first-order affine scaling method and the replicator dynamics method (see [1]) for quadratic programming. In [12], the objective function is not necessarily convex. It was proved in [12] that every accumulation point is a stationary point under nondegeneracy assumption and that the sequence will converge in the quadratic case without nondegeneracy assumption if $\gamma < 1$. In this paper, we restrict the power γ to be in $[\frac{1}{2}, 1)$. As a matter of fact, when the power γ equals 1, the RHS of the ODE system (2) is just the primal affine scaling direction for problem (1) when $s = n$. The affine scaling algorithm was first introduced by Dikin [4] in 1967. However the solution curve of the ODE system (2) does not contain the affine scaling trajectory since we require $\gamma < 1$. Hence we call the solution curve of the ODE system (2) as the generalized affine scaling trajectory. When $s = n$, the affine scaling trajectory and the generalized affine scaling trajectory are contained in the Cauchy trajectories for convex semidefinite programming in [6], but there were no strong convergence results for the Cauchy trajectories there. It should be noticed that, when $s = n$, the primal affine scaling continuous trajectory for problem (1) was studied in [9] recently.

Now we explain where the ODE system comes from when $s < n$. When $s = n$, the matrix D^γ is like a barrier to prevent the trajectory from going into the nonpositive region. Hence for $s < n$, it is natural that we replace x_i^γ with 1 for $i = s+1, \dots, n$. As a result we can get the ODE system (2) for problem (1). In fact, when the power γ equals 1, the RHS of the ODE system (2) is also the search direction in primal affine scaling algorithm for problem (1) when $s < n$ which was studied in [5]. But in order to get the optimality of the algorithm, the nondegeneracy assumption is needed in [5].

For simplicity, in what follows, $\|\cdot\|$ denotes the 2-norm. C^k stands for the class of the kth order continuously differentiable functions. Unless otherwise specified, $e = (1, \cdots, 1)^T$ and e_i are the conventional vectors whose dimensions are clear from the context, and $x_i = e_i^T x$.

The rest of this paper is organized as follows. In Sect. 2, we (i) introduce a potential function for the ODE system (2); (ii) verify that the ODE system has a unique solution in $[t_0, +\infty)$; and (iii) show that the RHS of the ODE system (2) approaches zero. In Sect. 3, we show that every accumulation point of the continuous trajectory of the ODE system (2) solves problem (1). In Sect. 4, we first show the strong convergence of the continuous trajectory and then verify that the limiting point has the maximal number of the positive components in $\{x_1, \ldots, x_s\}$ among the optimal solutions. At last, some conclusions are drawn in Sect. 5.

2   Properties of the Continuous Trajectories

The following assumption is made throughout this paper.

Assumption 1 *There exists a point* $x^* \in \mathcal{P}^+$ *such that* $f(x^*)$ *is the optimal value of problem (1).*

The following Lemmas 1 and 3 reveal some smoothness properties for the RHSs of the ODE system (2), and they are Lemmas 3, and 4 in [8] respectively.

Lemma 1. *For any* $\gamma > 0$, $(AD^2 A^T)^{-1} \in C^1$ *on* $\mathbb{R}^n_{s++}$.

Lemma 2. *If* $A, B \in \mathbb{R}^{n \times n}$ *are both symmetric and positive semidefinite, then all eigenvalues of* AB *are nonnegative.*

Lemma 3. *For any* $\gamma > 0$, *if* $\nabla f(x) \in C^1$, *then* $DP_{AD}D\nabla f(x) \in C^1$ *on* $\mathbb{R}^n_{s++}$.

Proof. For any $\gamma > 0$ and $x \in \mathbb{R}^n_{s++}$, from Lemma 1, we know that

$$P_{AD} = I - DA^T (AD^2 A^T)^{-1} AD \in C^1.$$

Thus the proof is completed.

Theorems 1 and 2 below guarantee the existence, uniqueness, and feasibility for the solutions of the ODE system (2).

Theorem 1. *For the ODE system (2), there exists a unique solution* $x(t)$ *with a maximal existence interval* $[t_0, \alpha)$, *in addition,* $x_i(t) > 0$ *for* $i = 1, \ldots, s$ *on the existence interval.*

Proof. By Lemma 3, $DP_{AD}D\nabla f(x)$ is locally Lipschitz continuous on $\mathbb{R}^n_{s++}$. From Theorem IV.1.2 in [2], there exists a unique solution $x(t)$ of the ODE system (2) on the maximal existence interval $[t_0, \alpha)$, for some $\alpha > t_0$ or $\alpha = +\infty$. Because the RHSs of the ODE system (2) is defined on the open set $\mathbb{R}^n_{s++}$, the solution of the ODE system is of course in the open set $\mathbb{R}^n_{s++}$, hence it must satisfy $x_i(t) > 0$ for $i = 1, \ldots, s$ on the existence intervals. The proof is completed.

Later in this section, it will be shown that $\alpha = +\infty$ (Theorem 3). For simplicity, in the following discussions, $x(t)$ and $D(t)$ will be replaced by x and D whenever no confusion would occur.

Theorem 2. *For the solution of the ODE system (2)* $x(t)$ *on the maximal existence interval* $[t_0, \alpha)$, *we have* $Ax(t) = b \ \forall t \in [t_0, \alpha)$.

Proof. We know

$$x(t) = x^0 - \int_{t_0}^t (DP_{AD}D\nabla f(x)|_{t=\tau})d\tau,$$

for any $t \in [t_0, \alpha)$. Noticing

$$ADP_{AD} = AD - AD^2A^T(AD^2A^T)^{-1}AD \equiv 0,$$

we can get

$$Ax(t) = Ax^0 - \int_{t_0}^t (ADP_{AD}D\nabla f(x)|_{t=\tau})d\tau = b.$$

Thus the theorem is proved.

The next four lemmas lay the foundation for our potential function which will be introduced in (4)–(6).

Lemma 4. *For any fixed $\gamma \geq \frac{1}{2}$, if $0 < x_i \leq M$ for $i = 1, \ldots, s$ and $|x_i| \leq M$ for $i = s+1, \ldots, n$, and $\nabla f(x) \in C^1$ on $\mathbb{R}^n_{s+}$, then there exists some positive constant $\hat{M}$ such that $\|\nabla f(x)\| \leq \hat{M}$, moreover, every entry of $DP_{AD}D\nabla f(x)$ and $D^{1-\frac{1}{\gamma}}P_{AD}D\nabla f(x)$ is bounded, and the bound depends only on A, M, n, and $\hat{M}$.*

Proof. It is Lemma 8 in [8].

Lemma 5. *([3]) Suppose f is differentiable (i.e., its gradient ∇f exists at each point in $\text{dom} f$). Then f is convex if and only if $\text{dom} f$ is convex and*

$$f(y) \geq f(x) + \nabla f(x)^T(y-x) \tag{3}$$

holds for all x, $y \in \text{dom} f$.

Proof. See Sect. 3.1.3 in [3].

Lemma 6. *Let a be any positive constant. Then for any scalar $x > 0$, $g(x) = x - a - a \cdot \ln \frac{x}{a} \geq 0$ and $g(x) = 0$ if and only if $x = a$. Furthermore, $g(x) \to +\infty$ as $x \to 0^+$ or $x \to +\infty$.*

Proof. Obvious and omitted.

Lemma 7. *Let a be any positive constant and $1 < r < 2$. Then for any scalar $x > 0$, $g(x) = \frac{1}{2-r}(x^{2-r} - a^{2-r}) - \frac{a}{1-r}(\frac{1}{x^{r-1}} - \frac{1}{a^{r-1}}) \geq 0$ and $g(x) = 0$ if and only if $x = a$. Furthermore, $g(x) \to +\infty$ as $x \to 0^+$ or $x \to +\infty$.*

Proof. This can be shown by basic calculus and the proof is omitted.

Next we introduce a potential function for the ODE system (2). With the help of the potential function, the boundedness of the optimal solution set is no longer needed in the convergence proof for the solution of the ODE system (2). Instead, only the weaker Assumption 1 is needed. In 1983, Losert and Akin [7] introduced a potential function for both the discrete and continuous dynamical systems in a classical model of population genetics. Their potential function can be extended for our purpose. In order to define our potential function, we first introduce some notations. For any $y \in \mathbb{R}^n_{s+}$, $B(y) = \{i \mid y_i > 0, \ i = 1, \ldots, s\}$ and $N(y) = \{i \mid y_i = 0, \ i = 1, \ldots, s\}$. Obviously, for any $y \in \mathbb{R}^n_{s+}$, $B(y) \cap N(y) = \emptyset$ and $B(y) \cup N(y) = \{1, \ldots, s\}$. Then the potential function $I(x, y)$ for the ODE system (2) can be defined as

$$I(x, y) = \sum_{i=s+1}^{n} \frac{1}{2}(x_i - y_i)^2 +$$

$$\begin{cases} \sum_{i=1}^{s}(x_i - y_i) - \sum_{i \in B(y)} y_i \cdot \ln \frac{x_i}{y_i} & \text{if } \gamma = \frac{1}{2}, B(y) \subseteq B(x), \quad (4) \\ \sum_{i=1}^{s} \frac{x_i^{2-2\gamma} - (y_i)^{2-2\gamma}}{2-2\gamma} \\ \quad - \sum_{i \in B(y)} \frac{y_i}{1-2\gamma}\left(\frac{1}{x_i^{2\gamma-1}} - \frac{1}{y_i^{2\gamma-1}}\right) & \text{if } \frac{1}{2} < \gamma < 1, B(y) \subseteq B(x), \quad (5) \\ +\infty & \text{if } B(y) \nsubseteq B(x), \quad (6) \end{cases}$$

where $x \in R^n_{s+}$ is the variable, $y \in \mathbb{R}^n_{s+}$ is a parameter.

The proofs of Lemma 8 and Theorem 3 below are similar to Lemma 14 and Theorem 15 in [8] respectively.

Lemma 8. *Let $x(t)$ be the solution of the ODE system (2) on the maximal existence interval $[t_0, \alpha)$. Then there exists an $M > 0$ which depends only on x^0 and x^* such that $|x_i(t)| \leq M \ \forall t \in [t_0, \alpha)$ for $i = 1, \ldots, n$.*

Theorem 3. *Let the maximal existence interval of the solution $x(t)$ of the ODE system (2) be $[t_0, \alpha)$. Then $\alpha = +\infty$.*

From Theorem 3, we can define the limit set for the solution of the ODE system (2). Let $x(t)$ be the solution of the ODE system (2), the limit set of $\{x(t)\}$ can be defined as follows

$$\Omega^1(x^0) = \left\{ p \in R^n \mid \exists \ \{t_k\}_{k=0}^{+\infty} \text{ with } \lim_{k \to +\infty} t_k = +\infty \text{ such that } \lim_{k \to +\infty} x(t_k) = p \right\}.$$

Theorem 4. *The limit set $\Omega^1(x^0)$ is nonempty and contained in $\mathcal{P}^+$.*

Proof. From Theorems 1, 2, and 3, we know that the limit set $\Omega^1(x^0)$ is contained in $\mathcal{P}^+$. From the proof of Theorem 3, it is evident that the solution $x(t)$ is contained in a bounded closed set. Hence the limit set $\Omega^1(x^0)$ is also nonempty.

In the rest of this section, we will show that the RHS of the ODE system (2) approaches zero. First, we reveal some fundamental properties for the solution of the ODE system (2).

Theorem 5. *Let $x(t)$ be the solution of the ODE system (2), then $f(x(t))$ is a nonincreasing function on $[t_0, +\infty)$. Furthermore, if $x^0 \in P^{++}$ is an optimal solution for problem (1), then $x(t) \equiv x^0$ on $[t_0, +\infty)$; otherwise $f(x(t))$ is a strictly decreasing function on $[t_0, +\infty)$.*

Proof. Similar to the proof of Theorem 17 in [8].

Lemma 9 (Barbalat's Lemma [10]). *If the differentiable function $f(t)$ has a finite limit as $t \to +\infty$, and $\dot{f}$ is uniformly continuous, then $\dot{f} \to 0$ as $t \to +\infty$.*

Lemma 10. *For any fixed $\gamma \geq \frac{1}{2}$, if $0 < x_i \leq M$ for $i = 1, \ldots, s$ and $|x_i| \leq M$ for $s + 1 \leq i \leq n$ with $M > 0$ and $\nabla f(x) \in C^1$ on $\mathbb{R}^n_{s+}$, then there exists some positive constant $\tilde{M}$ such that $\|\nabla f(x)\| \leq \tilde{M}$, moreover, for every $i \in \{1, \ldots, n\}$, every entry of*

$$\frac{\partial DP_{AD}D\nabla f(x)}{\partial x_i}$$

is bounded, and the bound depends only on A, M, n, and $\tilde{M}$.

Proof. If $0 < x_i \leq M$ for $i = 1, \ldots, s$ and $|x_i| \leq M$ for $i = s + 1, \ldots, n$, then x belongs to a closed bounded subset of $\mathbb{R}^n_{s+}$. Along with the assumption that $\nabla f(x) \in C^1$ on $\mathbb{R}^n_{s+}$, there must exist some positive constant $\tilde{M}$ such that $\|\nabla f(x)\| \leq \tilde{M}$ and $\|\nabla f(x)\|^2 \leq \tilde{M}$. Let $Q = (AD^2A^T)^{-1}AD^2$. From

$$DP_{AD}D = D^2 - D^2A^T \left(AD^2A^T\right)^{-1} AD^2,$$

we know that for $i = 1, \ldots, s$

$$\frac{\partial DP_{AD}D}{\partial x_i} = \frac{\partial D^2}{\partial x_i} - \frac{\partial D^2 A^T}{\partial x_i}Q - D^2A^T\frac{\partial(AD^2A^T)^{-1}}{\partial x_i}AD^2 - Q^T\frac{\partial AD^2}{\partial x_i},$$

and for $i = s + 1, \ldots, n$

$$\frac{\partial DP_{AD}D}{\partial x_i} = 0.$$

From Lemma 3 and the Remark in [11], we know that when $x \in \mathbb{R}^n_{k++}$, every entry of Q and Q^T is bounded, and the bound depends only on A and n.
From

$$\frac{\partial(AD^2A^T)^{-1}}{\partial x_i} = -2\gamma x_i^{2\gamma-1}(AD^2A^T)^{-1}(Ae_ie_i^TA^T)(AD^2A^T)^{-1},$$

for $i = 1, \ldots, s$ we have

$$D^2A^T\frac{\partial(AD^2A^T)^{-1}}{\partial x_i}AD^2 = -2\gamma x_i^{2\gamma-1}Q^T(Ae_ie_i^TA^T)Q.$$

Therefore when $0 < x_i \leq M$ for $i = 1, \ldots, s$ and $|x_i| \leq M$ for $s + 1 \leq i \leq n$, every entry of

$$\frac{\partial DP_{AD}D}{\partial x_i}$$

is bounded, and the bound depends only on A, M, and n. Hence it is evident that for every $i \in \{1, \ldots, n\}$, every entry of

$$\frac{\partial DP_{AD}D\nabla f(x)}{\partial x_i}$$

is bounded, and the bound depends only on A, M, n, and $\tilde{M}$.

Theorem 6. *Let $x(t)$ be the solution of the ODE system (2). Then*

$$\lim_{t \to +\infty} DP_{AD}D\nabla f(x) = 0.$$

Proof. From Lemma 8, there exists an $M > 0$ such that the solution $x(t)$ is contained in the bounded closed set $\{x \in \mathbb{R}^n | 0 \le x_i \le M, \ for \ i = 1, \ldots, s, \ |x_i| \le M \ for \ i = s+1, \ldots, n\}$. From Lemma 4, there exists some constant $L > 0$ such that

$$\left\| \frac{dx}{dt} \right\| \le L, \tag{7}$$

and L depends on A, x^0, x^*, n, and $\hat{M}$ only. Since $\nabla f(x) \in C^1$ on $\mathbb{R}^n_{s+}$, from Theorem 1 and Lemma 10, there exists a constant L_1 such that for every $i \in \{1, \ldots, n\}$, every entry of

$$\frac{\partial \nabla f(x)^T DP_{AD}D\nabla f(x)}{\partial x_i} \tag{8}$$

is bounded by L_1, and L_1 depends only on A, n, x^0, x^*, and $\tilde{M}$.

From Theorem 5, we know that $f(x(t))$ is a nonincreasing function and $f(x(t)) \ge f(x^*)$ on $[t_0, +\infty)$. Thus $f(x(t))$ has a finite limit as $t \to +\infty$. From (7) and (8), we have

$$\left| \frac{df(x(t))}{dt} \Big|_{t=t_1} - \frac{df(x(t))}{dt} \Big|_{t=t_2} \right|$$

$$= \left| \int_0^1 \frac{\partial \nabla f(x)^T DP_{AD}D\nabla f(x)}{\partial x} \Big|_{x=x(t_2)+\tau(x(t_1)-x(t_2))} (x(t_1) - x(t_2)) d\tau \right|$$

$$\le \sqrt{n}L_1 \cdot \|x(t_1) - x(t_2)\| = \sqrt{n}L_1 \cdot \left\| \int_{t_1}^{t_2} \frac{dx}{d\tau} d\tau \right\| \le \sqrt{n}L_1 L |t_1 - t_2|.$$

Thus, $\frac{df(x(t))}{dt}$ is uniformly continuous. From Barbalat's Lemma, we have

$$\lim_{t \to +\infty} \frac{df(x(t))}{dt} = -\lim_{t \to +\infty} \|P_{AD}D\nabla f(x)\|^2 = 0.$$

Therefore

$$\lim_{t \to +\infty} DP_{AD}D\nabla f(x) = 0.$$

Thus the proof is completed.

3   Optimality of the Limit Point(s)

In this section, we will show that every accumulation point of the solution of the ODE system (2) is an optimal solution for problem (1).

Theorem 7. *For any $x^{(1)} \in \Omega^1(x^0)$, $x^{(1)}$ is an optimal solution for problem (1).*

Proof. Similar to the proof of Theorem 18 in [8].

4   Convergence of the Continuous Trajectories

Now, it comes to a key result of the paper. Theorems 8 below shows that the solution of the ODE system (2) converges as $t \to +\infty$. The proofs of Theorems 8 and 9 below are similar to Theorems 19 and 20 in [8] respectively.

Theorem 8. *The limit set $\Omega^1(x^0)$ only contains a single point.*

Interestingly, we can show that the limit point of the solution of the ODE system (2) has the maximal number of the positive components in $\{x_1, \ldots, x_k\}$ among the optimal solutions.

Theorem 9. *The limit point of the solution of the ODE system (2) has the maximal number of the positive components in $\{x_1, \ldots, x_s\}$ among the optimal solutions.*

5   Conclusions

In this paper, an interior point generalized affine scaling continuous trajectory for solving convex programming with general linear constraints is introduced and discussed. Under a very mild assumption on the existence of an optimal solution, we have shown that the solution of the ODE system (2) will converge to the optimal solution set. In the ODE system (2), the projection matrix P_{AD} involves the matrix inversion, however, this can be calculated by some neural networks (for example, see [13] or [14]). Hence, if the calculation of $\nabla f(x)$ could be realized by hardware, the ODE system (2) can be achieved by hardware implementation.

References

1. Bomze, I.M.: Regularity versus degeneracy in dynamics, games, and optimization: a unified approach to different aspects. SIAM Rev. **44**, 394–414 (2002)
2. Bourbaki, N.: Functions of a Real Variable. Springer, Heidelberg (2004). https://doi.org/10.1007/978-3-642-59315-4
3. Boyd, S., Vandenberghe, L.: Convex Optimization. Cambridge University Press, Cambridge (2004)

4. Dikin, I.I.: Iterative solution of problems of linear and quadratic programming. Soviet Math. Doklady **8**, 674–675 (1967). (in Russian)
5. Gonzaga, C.C., Carlos, L.A.: A primal affine-scaling algorithm for linearly constrained convex programs (2002). http://www.optimization-online.org/DB_HTML/2002/09/531.html
6. López, J., Ramírez C., H.: On the central paths and Cauchy trajectories in semidefinite programming. Kybernetika **46**, 524–535 (2010)
7. Losert, V., Akin, E.: Dynamics of games and genes: discrete versus continuous time. J. Math. Biology **17**, 241–251 (1983)
8. Qian, X., Liao, L.-Z., Sun, J., Zhu, H.: The convergent generalized central paths for linearly constrained convex programming. SIAM J. Optim. (Accepted)
9. Qian, X., Liao, L.-Z.: Analysis of the primal affine scaling continuous trajectory for convex programming. Pac. J. Optim. (Accepted)
10. Slotine, J.J.E., Li, W.: Applied Nonlinear Control. Prentice Hall, New Jersey (1991)
11. Sun, J.: A convergence proof for an affine scaling algorithm for convex quadratic programming without nondegeneracy assumptions. Math. Program. **60**, 69–79 (1993)
12. Tseng, P., Bomze, I.M., Schachinger, W.: A first-order interior point method for linearly constrained smooth optimization. Math. Program. **127**, 399–424 (2011)
13. Wang, J.: A recurrent neural network for real-time matrix inversion. Appl. Math. Comput. **55**, 89–100 (1993)
14. Wang, J.: Recurrent neural networks for computing pseudoinverses of rank-deficient matrices. SIAM J. Sci. Comput. **18**, 1479–1493 (1997)

Drift Compensation for E-Nose Using QPSO-Based Domain Adaptation Kernel ELM

Yulin Jian[1], Kun Lu[2], Changjian Deng[1], Tailai Wen[1], and Jia Yan[1(✉)]

[1] College of Electronic and Information Engineering, Southwest University,
Chongqing 400715, China
yanjia119@swu.edu.cn
[2] High Tech Department, China International Engineering Consulting
Corporation, Beijing 100048, China

Abstract. A novel theoretical framework for drift compensation and classification of an electronic nose (E-nose), called QPSO-based domain adaptation kernel extreme learning machine (QDA-KELM) is presented in the work. The kernel method combines with domain adaption extreme learning machine (DAELM) to remove the drift in E-nose and enhance the classification performance. A swarm intelligent algorithm is utilized for the optimization of the model parameters. In order to evaluate the performance of our approach, three types of common kernels are used to form the composite kernel function. In addition, ELM and DAELM are compared with the proposed method. Finally, we also applied Analysis of Variance (ANOVA) to demonstrate our results are significantly better than the control methods.

Keywords: Electronic nose · Drift compensation · Kernel method
Multiple kernel learning · DAELM

1 Introduction

An artificial olfactory system, also known as electronic nose (E-nose), which consists of gas sensors and pattern recognition algorithms, is regarded as an intelligent instrument for various odors. However, due to the intrinsic variability of gas sensors and longtime service of the gas sensors, the gradual and unpredictable variation of the chemo-sensory signal responses of an E-nose when exposed to the constant external conditions reduces the accuracy and repeatability of sensors severely. That is caused by unknown dynamic changes which are known as sensor drift [1]. Sensor drift impairs the reliability of gas sensors, deteriorates the performance and remains to be the most serious limitation of E-nose system. Therefore, renewal training has to be implemented on the classifier for calibration regularly leveraging new samples in a specific period. However, it seems to be virtually impossible to retrain the classifier and acquire newly labeled samples regularly because of the complicated experiments and high labor costs.

Extreme learning machine (ELM), which was first brought up for single-hidden layer feedforward neural networks (SLFNs) in 2004 [2], has been proven to have exceedingly fast learning speed and reliable performance for classification and regression in distinct fields. ELM is also a new name of single hidden neural network trained with pseudoinverse learning algorithm (PIL) [3–5]. In the past few years, researchers have contributed a lot to ELM theories and applications in various fields. However, along with the growing of big data, the probability distribution of the data acquired in distinct phases with distinct experiment parameters probably changes, i.e., from different domains. As is known to all, the unlabeled data are far more than the labeled data for the training of the E-nose in practical large-scale application. The classifiers trained by small amounts of labeled data can be not robust and may result in poor extrapolation effect and generalizability. However, it is extremely time-consuming and laborious to acquire and label data. In order to increase the transferring capability of ELM with a few labeled samples from the target domain, a domain adaptation ELM (DAELM) framework for the sake of compensating sensor drift was proposed by Zhang et al. [6], which is inspired by ELM and domain-adaptation methods.

On the other hand, the kernel method has stimulated great interest in improving the performance of ELM. More recently, kernel ELM (KELM) was also applied to classify gas sensor array data, which markedly achieved high efficiency [7] Moreover, multiple kernel learning (MKL), which takes multiple feature spaces into consideration, can obtain better generalization ability and robustness than a single kernel due to the various forms and a relatively broader mapping range of multiple kernels [8] and widely applied in the machine learning field [9–12].

In this paper, we extend the DAELM to realize the feature nonlinear mapping by virtue of kernel matrix rather than the activation functions of hidden-layer neurons, and overcome the generalization and robustness disadvantages of DAELM on account of the fixed form of activation functions and thus a relatively narrow range of variation of the outputs. In addition, multiple kernels are leveraged to constitute the composite kernel function and the quantum-behaved particle swarm optimization (QPSO) is utilized for the optimization of the kernel parameters and the combination coefficients of each base kernel. This overcomes the stability disadvantage of DAELM that it is easier to be influenced by the number of the hidden-layer neurons. In particular, we dedicate to compensate the sensor drift utilizing the presented kernel approach. Combined with DAELM and MKL, we propose a QPSO-based domain adaptation kernel extreme learning machine (QDA-KELM) framework to compensate sensor drift. The main contribution of the work including: (1) To the best of our knowledge, combining domain adaptation with KELM framework in machine learning community has not been explored; (2) Integrating a novel methodology, i.e. QDA-KELM, for sensor drift compensation and gas identification of E-nose in practical application. The proposed QDA-KELM is a uniform classifier learning framework which addresses the sensor drift and gas identification issues well.

2 Methodology

In this section, first of all, we review the principle of ELM, which was proposed by Huang [2] in Subsect. 2.1. Then, the formulation of QDA-KELM framework containing two approaches, K-DAELM and MK-DAELM, is demonstrated in Subsect. 2.2.

2.1   Principle of ELM

ELM randomly chooses the input weights and hidden-layer biases and analytically determines the output weights of SLFNs. Its learning speed can be thousands of times faster than traditional feedforward network learning algorithms [2].

Assuming that there are N arbitrary distinct samples $\mathbf{X} = \{x_i|i = 1, \ldots, N\}$, where $x_i \in \mathbf{R}^n$ is the i-th sample and its corresponding ground truth is $t_i \in \mathbf{R}^m$, m and n are the number of neurons in the output and input layers, respectively. Then the output of hidden layer neurons can be denoted as $\mathcal{H}(x_i) \in \mathbf{R}^{1 \times L}$ where L is the number of the hidden nodes and $\mathcal{H}(\cdot)$ is the activation function of the hidden layer.

According to the generalized ELM, it aims to minimize the training error and the norm of the output weights. This objective function, for classification with multi-output nodes can be expressed as follows:

$$\underset{\boldsymbol{\beta}}{minimize}\ \mathcal{L}_{ELM} = \frac{1}{2}\|\boldsymbol{\beta}\|^2 + \frac{C}{2}\sum_{i=1}^{N}\|\boldsymbol{\xi}_i\|^2,$$
$$s.t.\ \mathcal{H}(x_i)\boldsymbol{\beta} = t_i - \boldsymbol{\xi}_i,\ i = 1, \cdots, N \tag{1}$$

where C is the penalty constant and $\boldsymbol{\xi}_i = [\xi_{i1}, \xi_{i2}, \cdots, \xi_{im}]^T$ is the training error of training sample x_i.

Then Eq. (1) can be redefined as Eq. (2) when $\boldsymbol{\xi}_i$ is substituted by the constraint term:

$$\underset{\boldsymbol{\beta}}{minimize} : \mathcal{L}_{ELM} = \frac{1}{2}\|\boldsymbol{\beta}\|^2 + \frac{C}{2}\|\mathbf{T} - \mathbf{H}\boldsymbol{\beta}\|^2, \tag{2}$$

where $\mathbf{H} = [\mathcal{H}(x_i); \mathcal{H}(x_2); \cdots; \mathcal{H}(x_N)] \in \mathbf{R}^{N \times L}$ and $\mathbf{T} = [t_1, t_2, \cdots, t_N]^T$.

Two different solutions are shown in Eq. (3) when calculating the weight vector β of the output layer in terms of the sample size N and hidden nodes L:

$$\tilde{\boldsymbol{\beta}} = \left(\mathbf{H}^T\mathbf{H} + \frac{\mathbf{I}_L}{C}\right)^{-1}\mathbf{H}^T\mathbf{T}, N \geq L$$
$$\tilde{\boldsymbol{\beta}} = \mathbf{H}^T\left(\mathbf{H}\mathbf{H}^T + \frac{\mathbf{I}_N}{C}\right)^{-1}\mathbf{T}, N < L, \tag{3}$$

where $\mathbf{I}_L$ and $\mathbf{I}_N$ are denoted as the identity matrix.

2.2   DAELM with Kernel Methods

Principle of DAELM. The DAELM aims to utilize all labeled samples from the source domain (assume that all the samples from the source domain are labeled) as well as a quite small number of labeled samples from the target domain to learn the output layer weight vector $\boldsymbol{\beta}$ of the classifier. Hence, for the DAELM, the objective function is generally defined as:

$$minimize_{\boldsymbol{\beta}} \; \mathcal{L}_{DAELM} = \tfrac{1}{2}\|\boldsymbol{\beta}\|^2 + \tfrac{C_S}{2}\sum_{i=1}^{N_S}\|\xi_i^S\|^2 + \tfrac{C_T}{2}\sum_{j=1}^{N_T}\|\xi_j^T\|^2 \tag{4}$$

$$s.t.\,\mathcal{H}\left(x_i^S\right)\boldsymbol{\beta} = t_i^S - \xi_i^S,\; i=1,\cdots,N_S;\, \mathcal{H}\left(x_j^T\right)\boldsymbol{\beta} = t_j^T - \xi_j^T,\, j=1,\cdots,N_T$$

where N_S and C_S denote the number and the penalty coefficient of the labeled training data from source domain, respectively; N_T and C_T denote the number and the penalty coefficient of the guide samples from target domain, respectively.

According to [6], Lagrange multiplier equation can solve the Eq. (4). Denote the output matrix of hidden layer to the labeled data from source and target domains as $\mathbf{H}_S$ and $\mathbf{H}_T$, respectively. Firstly, if $N_S < L$, it means $\mathbf{H}_S$ is row full rank, resulting in underdetermined least square problem, and we can calculate the $\boldsymbol{\beta}$ by:

$$\begin{aligned}\boldsymbol{\beta} =&\mathbf{H}_S^T(\mathcal{C}\mathcal{B}^{-1}\mathcal{A} - \mathcal{D})^{-1}(\mathcal{C}\mathcal{B}^{-1}t^T - t^S)\\ &+ \mathbf{H}_T^T[\mathcal{B}^{-1}t^T - \mathcal{B}^{-1}\mathcal{A}(\mathcal{C}\mathcal{B}^{-1}\mathcal{A} - \mathcal{D})^{-1}(\mathcal{C}\mathcal{B}^{-1}t^T - t^S)]\end{aligned} \tag{5}$$

where $\mathbf{I}$ is a N_S-dimensional identity matrix. $\mathbf{H}_T\mathbf{H}_S^T$, $\mathbf{H}_T\mathbf{H}_T^T + \mathbf{I}/C_T$, $\mathbf{H}_S\mathbf{H}_T^T$ and $\mathbf{H}_S\mathbf{H}_S^T + \mathbf{I}/C_S$ are represented by $\mathcal{A}$, $\mathcal{B}$, $\mathcal{C}$ and $\mathcal{D}$, respectively.

Second, if $N_S \geq L$, $\mathbf{H}_S$ is column full rank, resulting in overdetermined least square problem, the output weights $\boldsymbol{\beta}$ can be calculated as follows:

$$\boldsymbol{\beta} = (\mathbf{I} + C_S\mathbf{H}_S^T\mathbf{H}_S + C_T\mathbf{H}_T^T\mathbf{H}_T)^{-1}(C_S\mathbf{H}_S^T t^S + C_T\mathbf{H}_T^T t^T), \tag{6}$$

where $\mathbf{I}$ is a L-dimensional identity matrix with size. Finally, we can calculate the predicted output y_k^{Tu} by:

$$y_k^{Tu} = \mathcal{H}\left(x_k^{Tu}\right)\boldsymbol{\beta},\; k=1,\cdots,N_{Tu} \tag{7}$$

where $\mathcal{H}\left(x_k^{Tu}\right)$ denotes the output of the hidden nodes with respect to the k-th unlabeled sample from target domain. N_{Tu} is the number of unlabeled samples in target domain.

DAELM with Single Kernel. The DAELM learns a robust classifier based on the source domain using a limited number of labeled samples from target domain. It inherit superiorities of ELM, which can effectively overcome the inherent flaws of traditional neural networks. However, determining the number of hidden layer nodes is an arduous task, which is a crucial parameter of ELM affecting the performance of prediction model. For avoiding the hidden nodes selection problem and better feature mapping, DAELM is developed by substituting kernel function mapping for the hidden layer mapping $\mathcal{H}(\cdot)$. Consequently, the replaced feature nonlinear mapping $\mathcal{H}(\cdot)$ can be unknown.

The DAELM with a kernel (K-DAELM) can be constructed exclusively while using a kernel function without explicitly knowing the mapping $\mathcal{H}(\cdot)$. If the hidden nodes are unknown, one may prefer to extend Eq. (5) to application of kernel instead. So, the output of K-DAELM can be written as:

$$y_k^{Tu} = \mathcal{H}(x_k^{Tu})\beta = \begin{bmatrix} \mathcal{H}(x_k^{Tu})\mathcal{H}(x_i^S)^T \\ \vdots \\ \mathcal{H}(x_k^{Tu})\mathcal{H}(x_{N_S}^S)^T \end{bmatrix}^T (CB^{-1}\mathcal{A} - \mathcal{D})^{-1}(CB^{-1}t^T - t^S)$$

$$+ \begin{bmatrix} \mathcal{H}(x_k^{Tu})\mathcal{H}(x_i^T)^T \\ \vdots \\ \mathcal{H}(x_k^{Tu})\mathcal{H}(x_{N_T}^T)^T \end{bmatrix}^T [\mathcal{B}^{-1}t^T - \mathcal{B}^{-1}\mathcal{A}(CB^{-1}\mathcal{A} - \mathcal{D})^{-1}(CB^{-1}t^T - t^S)] \tag{8}$$

where $\mathcal{A}$, $\mathcal{B}$, $\mathcal{C}$ and $\mathcal{D}$ have the same definitions as Eq. (5), t^S and t^T denote the label vectors of the training data from source domain and the guide samples from the target domain, respectively.

For two arbitrary input samples x_p and x_q, assuming that $k(x_p, x_q) = \mathcal{H}(x_p)\mathcal{H}(x_q)^T$ is a kernel function, by which the non-linear mapping are implicitly defined. $\mathbf{K} = \mathbf{HH}^T$ is a kernel matrix, which consists of the inner products of two arbitrary input samples in the feature space. Let $\mathbf{K}_{TS} = \mathbf{H}_T\mathbf{H}_S^T$, $\mathbf{K}_T = \mathbf{H}_T\mathbf{H}_T^T$, $\mathbf{K}_{ST} = \mathbf{H}_S\mathbf{H}_T^T$, $\mathbf{K}_S = \mathbf{H}_S\mathbf{H}_S^T$ and thus we obtain the final output of K-DAELM as:

$$y_k^{Tu} = \begin{bmatrix} \mathbf{K}(x_k^{Tu}, x_i^S) \\ \vdots \\ \mathbf{K}(x_k^{Tu}, x_{N_S}^S) \end{bmatrix}^T [\mathbf{K}_{ST}(\mathbf{K}_T + \tfrac{1}{C_T})^{-1}\mathbf{K}_{TS} - (\mathbf{K}_S + \tfrac{1}{C_S}))^{-1}(\mathbf{K}_{ST}(\mathbf{K}_T + \tfrac{1}{C_T})^{-1}t^T - t^S)]$$

$$+ \begin{bmatrix} \mathbf{K}(x_k^{Tu}, x_i^T) \\ \vdots \\ \mathbf{K}(x_k^{Tu}, x_{N_T}^T) \end{bmatrix}^T [(\mathbf{K}_T + \tfrac{1}{C_T})^{-1}t^T - (\mathbf{K}_T + \tfrac{1}{C_T})^{-1}\mathbf{K}_{TS}(\mathbf{K}_{ST}(\mathbf{K}_T + \tfrac{1}{C_T})^{-1}\mathbf{K}_{TS}$$

$$- (\mathbf{K}_S + \tfrac{1}{C_S}))^{-1}(\mathbf{K}_{ST}(\mathbf{K}_T + \tfrac{1}{C_T})^{-1}t^T - t^S)] \tag{9}$$

DAELM with Multiple Kernel. Three common kernels (Gaussian kernel, polynomial kernel and wavelet kernel) are utilized to constitute the multiple kernel DAELM model (MK-DAELM) with the kernel parameters Θ and the combination coefficients λ, which seriously affect the performance of the model and have to be optimized.

The multiple kernel function is constructed by adding two base kernels possessing the identical form by a weighting technique as follows:

$$\mathbf{K}(x_p, x_q; \lambda, \Theta) = \lambda_1 \mathbf{K}_1(x_p, x_q; \theta_p) + \lambda_2 \mathbf{K}_2(x_p, x_q; \theta_q)$$
$$\text{s.t. } \lambda_1 + \lambda_2 = 1; \lambda_1 > 0, \lambda_2 > 0 \tag{10}$$

where $\mathbf{K}_1(\cdot)$ and $\mathbf{K}_2(\cdot)$ are the afore-mentioned base kernels and possess the same form. $\Theta = \{\theta c_p, \theta_q\}$ is the set of kernel parameters, and $\lambda = \{\lambda_1, \lambda_2\}$ is the combination coefficients of the base kernel combination. For one hand, the kernel parameters of base kernels Θ have a strong impact on the spatial distribution of the data in the implicitly defined feature space. On the other hand, the combination coefficients λ can be regarded as measures of relative importance considered in the composition.

Consequently, taking into account the effect of the model parameters, an effective swarm intelligent algorithm should be incorporated for optimization these key parameters. In our method, the combination coefficients and the kernel parameters are optimized by the QPSO.

3 Results and Discussion

3.1 Description of Dataset and Experimental Setup

In this paper, a big data which was released in UCI Machine Learning Repository [13] is exploited and studied for evaluating the proposed K-DAELM and MK-DAELMS models. The details of the datasets have been described in previous work [14].

For proving the effectiveness of the proposed methods, two experimental settings according to [6] are given as follows:

Setting 1: Take batch 5 (source domain) as fixed training set and tested on batch M ($M = 1,...,4$) (target domains).

Setting 2: The training set (source domain) is dynamically changed with batch $M + 1$ and tested on batch M ($M = 2,...,5$) (target domains).

Following the two settings, we implement the proposed framework, which combines the DAELM, kernel technique as well as QPSO. We also compare it with ELM with RBF as the activation function (ELM-rbf) and the DAELM based source domain [6]. K-DAELM and MK-DAELM methods are evaluated under the same experimental setup in [6]. The activation function is RBF function with $\sigma = 1$. The L is 1000. The penalty coefficients $C_S = 0.01$ and $C_T = 10$, respectively. Twenty labeled samples from target domain are chosen as the guide samples for training in source domain. The same operation process is implemented ten times of which average results are given.

3.2 Results and Discussion

Following the mentioned two settings, Tables 1 and 2 display the results of K-DAELM based on three types of single kernel and the results of MK-DAELM, respectively. As it can be seen from the two tables, all of the DAELM combined with kernel method get the excellent results, which can be reflected from the average value which can obtain 95.00% at least. And the weighted-Polynomial kernel shows the best performance while the Gaussian-kernel and Wavelet-kernel presents the same worst performance for both settings.

For further certifying the advantages of DAELM with the kernel method in drift compensation and make it visually observed, the recognition accuracy of all methods are showed in Tables 3 and 4 successively. From Tables 3 and 4, we can see that ELM shows the worst performance under both two settings, which only attain 61.00% and 55.10% accuracies, respectively. Moreover, the accuracies of K-DAELM and MK-DAELM far outdistance other methods and both approximate 100%.

Table 1. Classification results of K-DAELM and MK-DAELM under the experimental setting 1

Kernel type	Accuracy rate (%)				
	Batch 1	Batch 2	Batch 3	Batch 4	Average
Gaussian	97.14	85.00	97.86	100.00	95.00
Polynomial	100.00	98.57	100.00	100.00	99.64
Wavelet	97.14	85.00	97.86	100.00	95.00
Weighted-Gaussian	97.14	86.07	97.86	100.00	95.27
Weighted-Polynomial	100.00	99.00	100.00	100.00	99.75
Weighted-Wavelet	97.28	86.29	98.43	100.00	95.50

Table 2. Classification results of K-DAELM and MK-DAELM under the experimental setting 2

Kernel type	Accuracy rate (%)				
	$2 \rightarrow 1$	$3 \rightarrow 2$	$4 \rightarrow 3$	$5 \rightarrow 4$	Average
Gaussian	97.14	85.00	97.86	100	95.00
Polynomial	100.00	98.71	100.00	100.00	99.68
Wavelet	97.14	85.00	97.86	100	95.00
Weighted-Gaussian	97.14	86.21	97.86	100	95.30
Weighted-Polynomial	100.00	99.07	100.00	100.00	99.77
Weighted-Wavelet	97.28	86.57	98.50	100	95.59

Table 3. Classification results of different models under the experimental setting 1

Kernel type	Accuracy rate (%)				
	Batch 1	Batch 2	Batch 3	Batch 4	Average
ELM-rbf	62.50	56.44	56.44	68.63	61.00
DAELM(20)	88.63	85.88	98.69	98.25	92.86
K-DAELM(20)	100.00	98.57	100.00	100.00	99.64
MK-DAELM(20)	100.00	99.00	100.00	100.00	99.75

Table 4. Classification results of different models under the experimental setting 2

Kernel type	Accuracy rate (%)				
	$2 \rightarrow 1$	$3 \rightarrow 2$	$4 \rightarrow 3$	$5 \rightarrow 4$	Average
ELM-rbf	58.19	61.69	31.88	68.63	55.10
DAELM(20)	91.06	86.00	98.56	98.25	93.47
K-DAELM(20)	100.00	98.71	100.00	100.00	99.68
MK-DAELM(20)	100.00	99.07	100.00	100.00	99.77

We applied the hypothesis testing to verify if all of the classification models have huge impact on the recognition. Obviously, the values of F statistic are 1920.425 and 2132.743, respectively, by which we reject the null hypothesis and consider that distinct classification models have huge distinctions in accuracies under the level of significance $\alpha = 0.05$ (Tables 5 and 6).

Table 5. ANOVA for the experimental setting 1

	Sum of squares	df	Mean square	F	Sig.
Between groups	10257.444	3	3419.148	1920.425	0.000
Within groups	64.095	36	1.780		
Total	10321.539	39			

Table 6. ANOVA for the experimental setting 2

	Sum of squares	df	Mean square	F	Sig.
Between groups	13834.287	3	4611.429	2132.743	0.000
Within groups	77.839	36	2.162		
Total	13912.127	39			

4 Conclusions

In this paper we presented a theoretical framework for drift compensation of E-nose, which is based on DAELM combined with the kernel technique, to improve the performance of multi-class classification. Moreover, the crucial parameters in the model including combination coefficients and kernel parameters of base kernels were optimized by QPSO. In order to further testify the effectiveness of the proposed approach in classification and drift compensation of E-nose, ELM and DAELM were applied as control methods for the same dataset. The results achieved with the experiments have shown that both K-DAELM and MK-DAELM can compensate the sensor drift and obviously enhance the classification performance of E-nose.

Acknowledgments. The work was supported by National Natural Science Foundation of China (Grant Nos. 61571372, 61672436), Undergraduate Students Science and Technology Innovation Fund Project of Southwest University (Grant No. 20171803005).

References

1. Holmberg, M., Davide, F.A.M., Natale, C.D., D'Amico, A., Winquist, F., Lundström, I.: Drift counteraction in odour recognition applications: lifelong calibration method. Sens. Actuators B Chem. **42**, 185–194 (1997)
2. Huang, G.B., Zhu, Q.Y., Siew, C.K.: Extreme learning machine: a new learning scheme of feedforward neural networks. In: 2004 IEEE International Joint Conference on Neural Networks, pp. 985–990. IEEE Press, Budapest (2004)
3. Guo, P., Chen, C.L.P., Sun, Y.G.: An Exact supervised learning for a three-layer supervised neural network. In: International Conference on Neural Information Processing, pp. 1041–1044. Springer, Beijing (1995)

4. Guo, P., Lyu, M.: A pseudoinverse learning algorithm for feedforward neural networks with stacked generalization applications to software reliability growth data. Neurocomputing **56**, 101–121 (2004)
5. Wang, K., Guo, P., Xin, X., Ye, Z.B.: Autoencoder, low rank approximation and pseudoinverse learning algorithm. In: 2017 IEEE International Conference on Systems, Man, and Cybernetics, pp. 948–953. IEEE Press, Canada (2017)
6. Zhang, L., Zhang, D.: Domain adaption extreme learning machines for drift compensation in e-nose systems. IEEE Trans. Instrum. Measur. **64**, 1790–1801 (2015)
7. Peng, C., Yan, J., Duan, S.K., Wang, L.D., Jia, P.F., Zhang, S.L.: Enhancing electronic nose performance based on a novel QPSO-KELM model. Sensors **16**, 520 (2016)
8. Gönen, M., Alpaydın, E.: Multiple kernel learning algorithms. J. Mach. Learn. Res. **12**, 2211–2268 (2011)
9. Li, X.D., Mao, W.J., Jiang, W.: Multiple-kernel-learning-based extreme learning machine for classification design. Neural Comput. Appl. **27**, 175–184 (2016)
10. Jian, Y.L., Huang, D.Y., Yan, J., Lu, K., Huang, Y., Wen, T.L., Zeng, T.Y., Zhong, S.J., Xie, Q.L.: A novel extreme learning machine classification model for e-Nose application based on the multiple kernel approach. Sensors **17**, 1434 (2017)
11. Zhu, C.Z., Liu, X.W., Liu, Q., Ming, Y.W., Yin, J.P.: Distance based multiple kernel ELM: a fast multiple kernel learning approach. Math. Probl. Eng. **2015**, 372748 (2015)
12. Jia, P., Tian, F., He, Q., Fan, S., Liu, J., Yang, S.X.: Feature extraction of wound infection data for electronic nose based on a novel weighted KPCA. Sens. Actuators B Chem. **201**, 555–566 (2014)
13. UC Irvine Machine Learning Repository. http://archive.ics.uci.edu/ml/datasets/Twin+gas+sensor+arrays
14. Fonollosa, J., Fernández, L., Gutiérrez-Gálvez, A., Huerta, R., Marco, S.: Calibration transfer and drift counteraction in chemical sensor arrays using direct standardization. Sens. Actuators B Chem. **236**, 1044–1053 (2016)

Convergence Analysis of Self-adaptive Immune Particle Swarm Optimization Algorithm

Jingqing Jiang[1,2], Chuyi Song[2], Huan Ping[2(✉)],
and Chenggang Zhang[1]

[1] College of Computer Science and Technology,
Inner Mongolia University for Nationalities, Tongliao 028043, China
jiangjingqing@aliyun.com
[2] College of Mathematics, Inner Mongolia University for Nationalities,
Tongliao 028043, China
729573903@qq.com

Abstract. The self-adaptive immune particle swarm optimization (SAIPSO) algorithm is a hybrid algorithm based on immune algorithm and particle swarm optimization algorithm. SAIPSO algorithm has been implemented and achieved better result compared with the classical particle swarm optimization algorithm. However, the theoretical support of the algorithm is equally important as the implementation of the algorithm. Therefore, this paper mainly uses the convergence theorem of random search algorithm and the mathematical induction to prove the convergence of SAIPSO algorithm, which will help the improvement and application of the algorithm in the future.

Keywords: Immune algorithm · Particle swarm optimization algorithm
Self-adaptation · Convergence

1 Introduction

The convergence of the algorithm provides theoretical support for the algorithm. Many scholars have analyzed the convergence of the algorithm by using mathematical knowledge. For example, Solis and Wets gave the convergence theorem of random search algorithm in 1981 [1], and Tang gave the global convergence theorem of artificial immune algorithm by using Markov Chain theory in 2004 [2], and Cui gave the convergence theorem of particle swarm optimization algorithm by matrix analysis in 2007 [3]. For the self-adaptive immune particle swarm optimization (SAIPSO) algorithm, it combines the advantages of immune algorithm and particle swarm optimization algorithm. It guarantees the stability of the algorithm and increases the diversity of the particle. Therefore, proving the convergence of (SAIPSO) algorithm is very important. At the beginning of the study, the immune particle swarm algorithm only added the immune mechanism to the particle optimization swarm algorithm [4]. Then, the immune particle swarm optimization algorithm was proposed by Han [5]. She concatenated immune algorithms and particle swarm algorithms. The series combination of the immune algorithm and particle swarm optimization algorithm reduced the diversity of the particles. The parallel combination of the immune

© Springer International Publishing AG, part of Springer Nature 2018
T. Huang et al. (Eds.): ISNN 2018, LNCS 10878, pp. 157–164, 2018.
https://doi.org/10.1007/978-3-319-92537-0_19

algorithm and particle swarm optimization algorithm is proposed by Zhang [6]. In this paper, we use the mathematical induction to analyze the convergence of the self-adaptive immune particle swarm optimization algorithm proposed by Chao Zhang.

2 The Convergence Theorem of Random Search Algorithm

Now we introduce the random search algorithm that proposed by Solis and Wets [1]. The random search algorithm includes the immune algorithm, particle swarm optimization algorithm, genetic algorithm, and so on. The SAIPSO algorithm satisfies the condition of the random search algorithm.

We consider the following problems:

Given a function f which map R^n to R. S is a measurable subset of R^n. We will seek a point x in S, which minimizes f on S or approaches the infimum of f on S in an acceptable approximation.

The steps of the random search algorithm are as follows:

Step 1. Randomly select x^0 in S and set $t = 0$.
Step 2. Generate ξ^t from the solution space according to μ_t.
Step 3. Set $x^{t+1} = H(x^t, \xi^t)$, choose μ_{t+1}, set $t = t+1$ and go to Step 2.

where H presents an iterative function, and μ_t is the conditional probability measure corresponding to the distribution functions defined on R^n. $\mu_t = P(x^t) = P(x^t | x^0, x^1, x^2, \cdots x^{t-1})$. M_t denotes the support set of μ_t, i.e. M_t is the smallest closed subset of R under measure 1.

The algorithm satisfies the following conditions:

(H1) $f(H(x, \xi)) \leq f(x)$ and if $\xi \in S$, $f(H(x, \xi)) \leq f(\xi)$

This condition indicates that the new individual produced by the iterative function H is superior to the current individual, that is, the function value is monotone decreasing. By monotone bounded theorem, the function or sequence of continuous space is convergent.

(H2)   For any Borel subset G of S with $v(G) > 0$, we have

$$\prod_{t=0}^{\infty} (1 - \mu_t(G)) = 0 \tag{1}$$

This condition indicates that the probability is 0 for the random optimization algorithm can't find the point that belongs to subset G in consecutive infinite iterations.

Next we give the convergence theorem.

CONVERGENCE THEOREM: Suppose that f is a measurable function, S is a measurable subset of R^n and (H1) and (H2) are satisfied. Let $\{x_t\}_{t=0}^{+\infty}$ is a solution sequence generated by the algorithm. Then

$$\text{Lim}_{t \to \infty} P\big[x^t \in R_{\varepsilon,M}\big] = 1 \tag{2}$$

Where $P\big[x^t \in R_{\varepsilon,M}\big]$ is the probability at step t, and the point x^t is generated by the algorithm in $R_{\varepsilon,M}$.

3 Self-adaptive Immune Particle Swarm Optimization Algorithm

The self-adaptive immune particle swarm optimization algorithm (SAIPSO) combines the particle swarm optimization algorithm and the immune algorithm in parallel. Compared with the combination of the particle swarm optimization algorithm and the immune algorithm in series, it avoids reducing the diversity of particles at the beginning. And the algorithm self-adaptive selects the evolutionary strategy according to the particle concentration.

Now we give the SAIPSO algorithm steps:

(1) Creating the initial population which includes N particles. The velocity V_i and the position x_i are initialized randomly.
(2) Calculating the fitness values $f(x_i)$ for all N particles.
(3) Using the r-bits consecutive method to calculate the affinity between particles, which is the particle concentration $d(x_i)$. The formula is

$$\rho(x_i) = \sum\nolimits_{j=1}^{N} \begin{cases} 1, & 0.95 \le \frac{x_i}{x_j} \le 1.01 \\ 0, & else. \end{cases} \tag{3}$$

$$d(x_i) = \frac{\rho(x_i)}{N}, \quad i = 1, 2, \cdots, N. \tag{4}$$

d_{max} denotes the maximum value of $d(x_i)$ in each generation.
(4) Calculating the expecting reproduction rate $P(x_i)$ for each particle. The formula is

$$P(x_i) = \lambda f(x_i) + (1 - \lambda)d(x_i) \tag{5}$$

λ is the weight coefficient.
(5) Sorting the particles by $P(x_i)$, and then taking the first $popA$ particle as the subset A, the remaining $popB$ particles as the subset B. At the same time, sorting the global optimal value P_g.

$$popA = d_{max}N \tag{6}$$

$$popB = N - popA \tag{7}$$

The subset A includes some particles with high fitness and poor concentration. The following formulas are used to update the speed and location of the particles.

$$V(t+1) = \omega V(t) + c_1 r_1(t)(P_i(t) - x(t)) + c_2 r_2(t)\left(P_g(t) - x(t)\right) \tag{8}$$

$$x(t+1) = x(t) + v(t+1) \tag{9}$$

The subset B contains some particles with poor fitness and high concentration. The following formulas are used to vaccinate the particle.

$$Vaccine(x_i) = P_g + range(t), i = 1, 2, \cdots, popB \tag{10}$$

$$range(t) = rand \times R(t) \tag{11}$$

P_g is the searching center and $R(t)$ is the searching radius. $Vaccine(x_i)$ is the location of the particles after vaccination. $rand$ is a random number on the interval 0 to1. The initial value $R(1)$ is V_{max}, then $R(t)$ is updated by the following formula

$$R(t) = R(t-1)\frac{1 + \frac{n(t)}{t_{max}}}{1 + \frac{m(t)}{t_{max}}} \tag{12}$$

Where m and n are two parameters for adjusting the search radius. The adjusting formula is

$$n(t) = \begin{cases} n(t-1)+2, & d_{max} > 0.8 \\ n(t-1)+1, & 0.8 \geq d_{max} > 0.6 \\ n(t-1), & d_{max} \leq 0.6 \end{cases} \tag{13}$$

$$m(t) = \begin{cases} m(t-1)+2, & d_{max} \leq 0.2 \\ m(t-1)+1, & 0.2 < d_{max} \leq 0.4 \\ m(t-1), & d_{max} > 0.4 \end{cases} \tag{14}$$

4   The Convergence of the SAIPSO Algorithm

Now we will use the mathematical induction to prove the SAIPSO algorithm satisfies the H1 and H2. Then we will prove this algorithm satisfies the convergence theorem.

Lemma 1: The ASIPSO algorithm satisfies condition 1 (H1).

Proof. Suppose

$$H\left(P_g, x_i^A, x_i^B\right) = \begin{cases} P_g, & f\left(P_g\right) \leq \min\left(f\left(x_i^A\right), f\left(x_i^B\right)\right) \\ x_i^A, & f\left(x_i^A\right) \leq \min\left(f\left(x_i^B\right), f\left(P_g\right)\right) \\ x_i^B, & f\left(x_i^B\right) \leq \min\left(f\left(x_i^A\right), f\left(P_g\right)\right) \end{cases} \tag{15}$$

x_i^A belongs to the subset A, x_i^B belongs to the subset B. According to iterative function H, we know that the algorithm satisfies the condition 1. This completes the proof.

Lemma 2: The ASIPSO algorithm satisfies condition 2 (H2).

Liang Sun proposed a novel stochastic particle swarm optimization algorithm, which is global convergence [7]. Literature [7] showed that the condition 2 (H2) is satisfied as long as the condition 3 is satisfied.

(H3)   For each generation in the algorithm, it needs to satisfy the following formula

$$M_t = \bigcup_{i=1}^{N} M_{i,t} = S \qquad (16)$$

Where $M_{i,t}$ is the support set of the antibody x_i in the tth generation.

Lemma 3: The SAIPSO algorithm satisfies condition 3 (H3).

Proof: The mathematical induction is used to prove.

For $t = 1$:

At beginning, the algorithm initializes N initial particles which are randomly selected from the set. It satisfies following formula.

$$S = (a,b)^1 \times (a,b)^2 \times \cdots \times (a,b)^D \qquad (17)$$

$$S \subseteq S = \bigcup_{i=1}^{N} M_{i,1} \qquad (18)$$

Where D is the dimension of the solution. And $M_{i,1}$ is the support subset of the particle i while t is equal to 1.

So the algorithm satisfies the condition 3 while t is equal to 1.

We suppose that the algorithm satisfies the condition 3 when the algorithm runs to $t - 1$ generation.

Now we prove the algorithm satisfies the condition 3 when it runs to t generation.

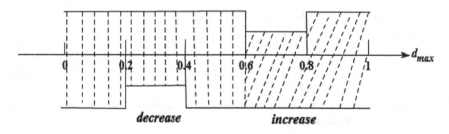

Fig. 1. The change of radius R

According to the Fig. 1, the radius $R(t)$ can be divided into two situations: increase and decrease controlled by the particle's concentration d_{max}.

We will discuss these two cases.

Case 1: Considering the radius $R(t)$ increases:

When the concentration of particles is high and the diversity is poor, the search radius will increase.

Because the algorithm satisfies the condition 3 when it runs to $R(t)$ generation, the following formulas can be proved.

$$R(t) > R(t-1) \tag{19}$$

$$P_{g,j,t-1} \geq P_{g,j,t-2} \tag{20}$$

$$P_{g,j,t-2} + R(t-1) \geq b \tag{21}$$

Then we have the following result.

$$P_{g,j,t-1} + R(t) > P_{g,j,t-2} + R(t-1) \geq b \tag{22}$$

According to the immune vaccination formula of the SAIPSO algorithm, we have the following formulas.

$$0 < range(t) = rand \times R(t) < R(t) \tag{23}$$

$$Vaccine(x_{i,j}) = P_{g,j,t-1} + range(t) < P_{g,j,t-1} + R(t) \tag{24}$$

We know that $Vaccine(x_i)$ contains left boundary b of the interval (a,b).

Because the algorithm satisfies the condition 3 when it runs to $t-1$ generation, the following formula can also be proved.

$$P_{g,j,t-2} - R(t-1) \leq a \tag{25}$$

$$P_{g,j,t-1} \rightarrow P_{g,j,t-2} \tag{26}$$

We can also have the following results.

$$P_{g,j,t-1} - R(t-1) \leq a \tag{27}$$

$$P_{g,j,t-2} - R(t) \leq a \tag{28}$$

Because the randomness of the immune algorithm, the following inequalities are true in a certain probability.

$$P_{g,j,t-1} - R(t) \leq a \tag{29}$$

$$P_{g,j,t-1} - R(t) < P_{g,j,t-1} - range(t) = Vaccine(x_{i,j}) \tag{30}$$

We know that $Vaccine(x_i)$ contains right boundary a of the interval (a, b). In summary, in this case, the algorithm satisfies condition 3.

Case 2: Considering the radius $R(t)$ decreases.

When the concentration is moderate and the diversity is moderate, the search radius will decrease.

Literature [8] has proved that the classical particle swarm optimization algorithm did not satisfy the condition 3. The main reason is that the diversity of the particles is very low when the algorithm converges to $(c_1 P_i + c_2 P_g)/(c_1 + c_2)$.

According to the velocity formula and position formula of the particle, we have the formula of $M_{i,t}$.

$$M_{i,t} = x_{i,j,t-1} + \omega(x_{i,j,t-1} - x_{i,j,t-2}) + \phi_1(P_i - x_{i,j,t-1}) + \phi_2(P_g - x_{i,j,t-1}) \tag{31}$$

In the formula, ϕ_1 and ϕ_2 satisfy the following inequalities.

$$0 \leq \phi_1 \leq c_1 \tag{32}$$

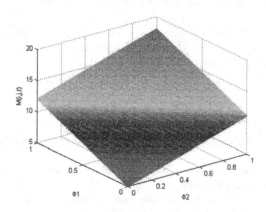

Fig. 2. The figure of super rectangle

$$0 \leq \phi_1 \leq c_1 \tag{33}$$

So $M_{i,k}$ represents a super rectangle shown in the Fig. 2 which is determined by ϕ_1 and ϕ_2.

When the particle x_i converges to $(c_1 P_i + c_2 P_g)/(c_1 + c_2)$, we have the following formula.

$$\lim_{t \to \infty} v(M_{i,t}) = 0 \tag{34}$$

So the classical particle swarm optimization algorithm does not satisfy the condition 3.

But for the ASIPSO algorithm, it adopts case 1 when the diversity of the population is poor, and it adopts particle swarm optimization algorithm when the population diversity is moderate.

So in this case, the algorithm satisfies condition 3.

In summary, the SAIPSO algorithm satisfies the condition 2 by mathematical induction.

Combined case 1 and 2, the SAIPSO algorithm satisfies the condition 1 and 2. According to the convergence theorem of random search algorithm, we know the ASIPSO algorithm is global convergent.

5   Conclusion

This paper proves the convergence of SAIPSO algorithm, and it will provide theoretical support for this algorithm in the future. At the same time, it plays an important role for the improvement and application of this algorithm, and provides a new idea for the convergence of hybrid algorithm. Therefore, it is necessary to further study and discuss the improvement and application of hybrid algorithm.

Acknowledgement. This work was supported by The National Natural Science Foundation of China (Project No. 61662057, 61672301) and Higher Educational Scientific Research Projects of Inner Mongolia Autonomous Region (Project No. NJZC17198).

References

1. Solis, F., Wets, R.: Minimization by random search techniques. Math. Oper. Res. **6**, 19–30 (1981)
2. Tang, F., Li, M., Luo, A.: Global convergence analysis of an artificial immune algorithm. J. Changsha Univ. Electr. Pow. **19**, 1–4 (2004)
3. Cui, H., Zhu, Q.: Convergence analysis and parameter selection in particle swarm optimization. Comput. Eng. Appl. **43**, 89–91 (2007)
4. Zhang, H., Wang, H., Zhijun, H.: Analysis of particle swarm optimization algorithm global convergence method. Eng. Appl. **47**, 61–63 (2011)
5. Han, L.: The study of immune particle swarm optimization algorithm and its application. Xi'an Polytechnic University (2008)
6. Zhang, C., Li, Q.: Immune particle swarm optimization algorithm based on the adaptive search strategy. Chin. J. Eng. **39**, 125–132 (2017)
7. Sun, L., Hailang, X., Ge, H.: Novel global convergence stochastic particle swarm optimization optimizers. J. Jilin Univ. **47**, 615–621 (2017)
8. Xie, Z., Zhong, S., Wei, Y.: Modified particle swarm optimization algorithm and its convergence analysis. Comput. Eng. Appl. **47**, 46–49 (2011)

An Improved Artificial Fish Swarm Algorithm to Solve the Cutting Stock Problem

Chunying Cheng[1(✉)] and Lanying Bao[2]

[1] College of Computer Science and Technology,
Inner Mongolia University for Nationalities, Tongliao 028043, China
chengchunying_80@163.com
[2] College of Mathematics, Inner Mongolia University for Nationalities,
Tongliao 028043, China

Abstract. In order to improve the utilization rate of sheet,an improved artificial fish swarm algorithm is proposed in this paper, which improved the preying behavior and swarming behavior, meanwhile set upper and lower limit for the Congestion factor of swarming behavior. Furthermore, the proposed algorithm is used to solve the cutting stock problem. After comparing the results of the simulation experiment with the improved particle swarm algorithm in the literature and the basic artificial fish swarm algorithm, it shows that the optimal solution obtained by the improved artificial fish swarm algorithm is better than the algorithm in the literature, thus improves the utilization rate of sheet.

Keywords: Artificial fish swarm algorithm · Cutting stock problem
Improved preying behavior · Improved congestion factor · Utilization rate

1 Introduction

The cutting stock problem can be described as a process of cutting square, rectangular and other small regular pieces as much as possible from given flat raw materials with a certain amount of methods. It's about how to place small rectangles of pre-determined size on a large, limited rectangular sheet which can achieve the highest utilization rate of sheet. The goal of the cutting stock problem is to minimize the area that might be dumped. Due to the requirements of saving raw materials, the cutting stock problem has become a very important research topic in the industrial production process of glass, paper, wood and steel. So far, many valuable methods have been proposed as solutions to the cutting stock problem, such as simulated annealing [1], genetic algorithm [2] and particle swarm optimization [3]. Artificial Fish Swarm Algorithm (AFSA) is a new random searching algorithm proposed by Li [4] in 2002 by observing the habits of fish swarms. This algorithm is a new idea of seeking the global optimal solution based on animal behaviors, which is a typical application of behavioral artificial intelligence. The algorithm starts with constructing simple underlying behaviors of animals and finally makes the global optimal value emerge in the group through the local optimization behavior of individual animals.

Artificial fish swarm algorithm is featured for its good ability to overcome the local optimal and obtain the global optimal solution, and the realization of the algorithm does

© Springer International Publishing AG, part of Springer Nature 2018
T. Huang et al. (Eds.): ISNN 2018, LNCS 10878, pp. 165–172, 2018.
https://doi.org/10.1007/978-3-319-92537-0_20

not need gradient values of the objective function, so it has some adaptive ability to the search space. However, the main application of artificial fish swarm algorithm is still focused on solving continuous optimization problems. When solving the combinatorial optimization problems, it will appear "premature" or fall into the local optimal solution, or the convergence speed is too slow. Therefore, in this paper improved preying behavior, swarming behavior and improved congestion factor are introduced into the basic artificial fish school algorithm, which can prevent the artificial fish from falling into the local extremum effectively and accelerate the search speed. Meanwhile, the artificial fish can jump out of the local extremum and make the population converge quickly to the global maximum in the end and reach the solution with high precision.

2 Basic Artificial Fish Swarm Algorithm

In an area of waters, where fishes appear most is often rich in nutrients in this area. So, artificial fish swarm algorithm is based on this character to imitate the preying behavior of fishes, in order to achieve the optimization of the solution.

(1) Related definitions

Individual status of the artificial fish can be expressed as a vector, where $x_i(i = 1, 2, \cdots, n)$ are variables for optimization, the food concentration where the artificial fish currently locates is expressed as $Y = f(X)$, Y means the objective function value, the distance between individuals artificial fishes is expressed as $d_{ij} = \|X_i - X_j\|$, Visual means the perception distance of the artificial fish, Step means the moving step of the artificial fish, δ means the congestion factor.

(2) Description of the fish behavior

① Preying behavior

Let the current status of the artificial fish be X_i, we randomly select a status X_j within the scope of its perception. If the problem is for the search of the maximal value $Y_i < Y_j$ (or for the search of the minimal value, $Y_i > Y_j$, because the maximum problem and minimum problem can be converted to each other), then move a step in this direction. On the contrary, it will randomly select the status X_j again, and determine whether it can meet the conditions of moving forward. If it still cannot meet the conditions of moving forward after repeating several times, then it moves a step randomly.

② Swarming behavior

Let the current status of the artificial fish be X_i, it will explore the number n_f of partners in the current neighboring area (i.e. $d_{ij} < Visual\ d_{ij} < Visua$) and its center position X_c, and if $Y_c/n_f > \delta Y_i$, it indicates that the partner center has more food and is less congested, then the artificial fish will proceed one step closer to the partner's center position, otherwise it will execute its preying behavior.

③ Following behavior

Let the current status of the artificial fish be X_i, it will explore whether Y_j is the largest one X_j among partners who are in the current neighboring area. If $Y_c/n_f > \delta Y_i$, it indicates the partner X_j has a higher food concentration and it is not crowded around, move one step further toward the partner X_j, otherwise it will execute its preying behavior.

④ Stochastic behavior

The implementation of stochastic behavior is simpler and it can be performed as follows: select a status randomly within the field of view and then move in that direction, which is actually a default behavior of preying behavior.

(3) Choice of behavior

According to the characteristics of the problem to be solved, assess the current situation of the artificial fish in order to choose a behavior. The easiest way to find the maximum is to use heuristics. The implementation is as follows: simulate the swarming, following and other behaviors, and then evaluate the value after the action, select the largest of them to execute the actual implementation, and the default behavior is the preying behavior.

(4) Bulletin board

The bulletin board records the current status of the best individual artificial fish. After every action, each artificial fish is compared with the individual status of the artificial fish on the bulletin board. If it is better than individual status of artificial fishes on the bulletin board, it will update individual status of the artificial fish on the bulletin board with its own status.

3   The Proposed Algorithm to Solve the Cutting Stock Problem

3.1   Encoding

In this paper, the sheet and the small pieces to be placed are encoded with free coordinates. The lower left corner of the large sheet is placed at the coordinate origin, each small pieces to be placed are represented by a 4-dimensional vector (x_k, y_k, l_k, w_k), where (x_k, y_k) is the position coordinates of the lower left corner of small pieces on the sheet, (l_k, w_k) is the length and the width of small pieces. That is, $0 \leq x_k, l_k \leq X_{max}$, $0 \leq y_k, w_k \leq Y_{max}$, where X_{max} and Y_{max} represent the length and the height of raw materials. Each individual in the artificial fish swarm represents a cutting stock pattern, and each cutting stock pattern consist a sequence of small pieces. The established coordinate system is as follows (Fig. 1):

The algorithm of cutting stock is about how to place the pieces to be cut in the right place on the sheet. Here the conversion is performed with a method similar to the Bottom Left Algorithm (BL) [5]. This method is called coordinate-based Bottom Left Algorithm (CBL). According to the rules of the Bottom Left algorithm, the pieces to be cut are placed in the upper right corner of the coordinate system. In order to reduce the amount of effort of moving back and forth when cutting the sheet, it is arranged in advance in the fixed order of x_k which is described by the encoding method of cutting sheet. The actual operation of the algorithm is as follows:

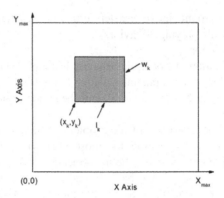

Fig. 1. Coordinate system of cutting stock

Step 1: Sort each small piece x_k ascendingly.

Step 2: The movement rule of small pieces to be cut is as follows: place small pieces according to the remarks of x_k and y_k, the left side and the top of the small pieces is placed inside the big sheet absolutely, and they will move on the direction of "first left then down" when they do not overlap other sheets. "First left then down" means it will move to the left as much as possible. And then move down when reaching the right side of the large sheet or the left side of other small sheet. Move based on the principle of "first left then down" again as much as possible when reaching the side of the large sheet or a small sheet. If there is a piece of sheet overlapping a placed sheet, then arrange it into the order of the sheet to be cut. After each small piece is placed, go to following step.

Step 3: The sheet where small pieces are not placed in Step 2 moves according to the principle of "first left then down". When the cut sheet cannot move further to the left and down and the surrounding edges are completely placed inside or the edge is aligned with the raw material, it is its final position, otherwise, this one should be abandoned.

3.2   Improvement of Artificial Fish Swarm Algorithm

The solution to the cutting stock problem is to find a place of higher concentration of food, which is described with $Y = f(X)$, where represents the artificial fish status, d_{ij} represents the length between the artificial fish X_i and X_j, the distance between the two fishes, max *number* represents the iteration number of the artificial fish, *Visual* represents the visual field of artificial fish, *Step* represents the distance each time artificial fish moves, N represents the number of individuals of artificial fish swarm.

(1) Design of fitness function

In the improved cutting stock algorithms of artificial fish swarm, the sheet utilization rate is used to represent the fitness function. Therefore, the fitness function *fitness*(x) can be designed as:

$$fitness(x) = f(M) \tag{1}$$

Therefore, the utilization rate of the improved algorithm can be expressed as:

$$f(x) = \frac{r(M)}{S} \tag{2}$$

In formula (2), M represents each completed process in the actual design, a cutting stock pattern, $r(M)$ represents the total area of the small pieces cut by the algorithm, and S represents the area of the raw material.

(2) Improvement of preying behavior

Implement the optimal individual retention strategy on preying behavior to avoid the degradation of optimal artificial fish status. Set the current status of artificial fish as X_i, randomly select a status X_j within the perception range of the artificial fish. If the food concentration is $Y_i < Y_j$, then move forward in this direction. On the other hand, randomly select the status X_j again to determine whether the conditions for moving forward are satisfied. If the conditions for moving forward are still not satisfied after repeating several times and the current status X_i is not the optimal status in the current group, then move one step randomly. If it is the optimal status in the current group, do not move.

(3) Improvement of swarming behavior and congestion factor

Set the upper limit δ_{max} and the lower limit δ_{min} of the congestion factor δ, so as to restrict the conditions for swarming behavior to occur at $[\delta_{min}, \delta_{max}]$ and forbid the swarming behavior of $\delta < \delta_{min}$ or $\delta > \delta_{max}$ at the same time. When the congestion factor exceeds δ_{max}, let the other fish swarms in the range $1 - \delta_{max}$ perform improved preying behavior. When the congestion factor is lower than δ_{min}, dismiss the congested fish swarm forcibly and let them perform the preying behaviors individually. This congestion behavior can prevent the occurring of "premature", and thus improve the ability of global optimization.

(4) Realization of the algorithm

$X_i = (q_{i1}, q_{i2}, \cdots, q_{in})$ represents a fish, where $i = 1, 2, \cdots, N$. N represents the number of fish swarms. q_{ik} represents a small piece that can be cut. The position of the coordinate system describes the raw materials and the small sheet to be cut. The lower left corner of a large sheet is placed at the origin of coordinates, each small piece to be placed is represented by a 4-dimensional vector $q_{ik} = (x_{ik}, y_{ik}, l_{ik}, w_{ik})$, where $k = 1, 2, \cdots, n$. n represents the number of sheet to be cut. (x_{ik}, y_{ik}) is the position of x axis and y axis of the sheet to be cut, (l_{ik}, w_{ik}) represents the length of the cut piece on the horizontal line and the height of the vertical line. The distance between the artificial fish X_i and the current X_j can be represented as:

$$d_{ij} = \|X_i - X_j\| = \frac{1}{n} \sum_{k=1}^{n} \|q_{ik} - q_{jk}\| = \frac{1}{n} \sum_{k=1}^{n} \sqrt{(x_{ik} - x_{jk})^2 + (y_{ik} - y_{jk})^2} \tag{3}$$

In the artificial fish swarm algorithm, the food concentration at the current position of the artificial fish is represented as the utilization rate of the sheet. That is, among $f(M) = \frac{r(M)}{S}$, M means the time when the specific setting of artificial fish swarm algorithm for the cutting stock problem is completed, $r(M)$ is the sum of areas of small pieces which could be cut from the raw materials, $S = Length * Width$ is the area of the raw material.

The steps for the improved artificial fish swarm algorithm for the cutting stock problem are described below:

> Step 1: Initialize each artificial fish randomly, that is, each piece placed on the sheet is at the lower left corner.
>
> Step 2: Calculate the food concentration value of the artificial fish and its partners. Compare the food concentration value with that on the bulletin board, and put the artificial fish with higher food concentration onto the bulletin board.
>
> Step 3: Each artificial fish performs following behavior, improved swarming behavior and improved preying behavior respectively. After each execution, the food concentration at the new position is compared to the record on the bulletin board. Update the bulletin board when the current value is better than that on the bulletin board, and go to step 4. Otherwise, choose the next action based on the current behavior. The specific behaviors are as follows: If the food concentration in the new position is lower than the record on the bulletin board after the following behavior, perform the improved swarming behavior; if the food concentration in the new position is lower than the record on the bulletin board after the swarming behavior, perform the improved preying behavior.
>
> Step 4: Stop the iterations if the maximum number of iterations or the threshold is reached. Otherwise, go to step 3 to continue.

(5) Selection of numerical examples and parameters

In this paper, 10 experiments were carried out, the number of sheets to be cut are ranged from 10 to 30 pieces. In this paper, Visual C++ language is used as a programming tool, the experimental environment is as follows: AMD Phenom (tm)II X6 1065T Processor, 2.9 GHz CPU, 4 GB memory, Windows 7 operating system. In order to verify the effectiveness of the improved artificial fish swarm algorithm to solve the cutting stock problem, in this paper the improved artificial fish swarm algorithm is used to solve the experimental cases in [3, 6]. The parameters were set as follows: the number of artificial fishes is 50, trying number *trynumber* in preying behavior is 20, congestion factor δ_{max} is 0.6, δ_{min} is 0.2, the maximum number of iterations is 2000, field view *Visual* of artificial fish in Example 1 to Example 5 are valued as 20, 30, 20, 30, 50 respectively.

Table 1 shows the properties of the test cases used in [3, 6]. Figure 2 shows the cutting results of the example 5 through the improved artificial fish swarm algorithm. Table 2 shows the loss rate of experimental cutting in the actual example.

Table 1. The size of the test cases.

No.	Number of pieces	Size of stock plate	Size of pieces
1	10	(30 × 40) × 2, (10 × 40), (20 × 40) × 3, (20 × 50), (20 × 30), (30 × 20) × 2	100 × 80
2	10	(20 × 4), (16 × 4), (10 × 6) × 2, (16 × 6), (4 × 10), (10 × 5) × 2, (10 × 10), (20 × 10)	40 × 20
3	15	(5 × 6) × 4, (10 × 3), (12 × 5) × 2, (10 × 7) × 2, (20 × 4) × 2, (10 × 5) × 3, (8 × 10)	40 × 20
4	20	(11 × 15) × 4, (17 × 5) × 4, (12 × 4) × 4, (3 × 9) × 4, (5 × 15) × 4	40 × 40
5	30	(17 × 6), (6 × 9) × 3, (6 × 12) × 5, (9 × 12) × 4, (9 × 6) × 2, (17 × 12), (14 × 9), (12 × 9) × 2, (6 × 15) × 2, (9 × 15), (11 × 12), (9 × 18), (9 × 9), (15 × 9), (15 × 6), (15 × 12), (6 × 6), (14 × 6)	65 × 45

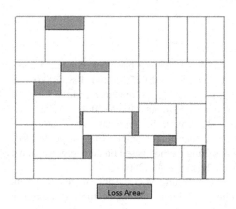

Fig. 2. Cutting results running hybrid artificial fish swarm algorithm

Table 2. Comparison of experimental results

No.	1	2	3	4	5
PSO loss rate (%)	0	0	7.5	6.3	7.1
Literature [3] loss rate (%)	0	0	0	6.3	6.8
Literature [6] loss rate (%)	0	0	0	3	6.6
IAFSA loss rate (%)	0	0	0	3	5.53

(6) Results analysis of numerical experiment

In this paper, 10 experiments are carried out. In Fig. 2, the experimental results of the improved artificial fish swarm algorithm are given. With the improved artificial fish swarm algorithm, 29 blocks can be cut out, and the shaded area represents the area which cannot be used. Table 2 shows the contrast of the loss rates of the cutting stock problem with the same data through the improved particle swarm optimization algorithm, the basic artificial fish swarm algorithm and the improved artificial fish swarm algorithm in this paper. Looking upon the simulation results, it is obvious that the improved artificial fish swarm algorithm has a better performance in solving the cutting stock problem.

4   Conclusion

Through the simulation experiment, it is feasible to use the improved artificial fish swarm algorithm to solve the cutting stock problem. After comparing it with the improved particle swarm algorithm and with the basic artificial fish swarm algorithm in the literature, the experimental results show that the improved algorithm can obtain the most optimal solution better than the algorithm in the literature, and solve the problem about the utilization of sheets.

References

1. Changzheng, X.: Optimal board cutting based on simulated annealing genetic algorithm. J. LiaoNing Tech. Univ. (Nat. Sci. Ed.) **25**(3), 406–408 (2006)
2. Xingfang, Z., Yaodong, C., Ying, Y.: A genetic algorithm for the rectangular strip packing problem. J. Comput.-Aid. Des. Comput. Graph. **20**(4), 540 (2008)
3. Qijinbao, B., Jingqing, J., Chuyi, S.: Optimal stock cutting based on particle swarm optimization and simulated annealing. Comput. Eng. Appl. **44**(26), 246–248 (2008)
4. Li, X., Shao, Z.: An optimizing method based on autonomous animals: fish-swarm algorithm. Syst. Eng. Theory Pract. **22**(11), 2–38 (2002)
5. Leung, T.W., Yung, C.H., Troutt, M.D.: Applications of genetic search and simulated annealing to the two-dimensional non-guillotine cutting stock problem. Comput. Ind. Eng. **40**, 201–214 (2001)
6. Bao, L., Jiang, J., Song, C., Zhao, L., Gao, J.: Artificial fish swarm algorithm for two-dimensional non-guillotine cutting stock problem. In: Guo, C., Hou, Z.-G., Zeng, Z. (eds.) ISNN 2013. LNCS, vol. 7952, pp. 552–559. Springer, Heidelberg (2013). https://doi.org/10.1007/978-3-642-39068-5_66

A Hyper Heuristic Algorithm for Low Carbon Location Routing Problem

Zhenyu Qian, Yanwei Zhao$^{(\boxtimes)}$, Shun Wang, Longlong Leng, and Wanliang Wang

Key Laboratory of Special Equipment and Advanced Processing Technology, Ministry of Education, Zhejiang University of Technology, Hangzhou, China
{qzy,zyw,ws,cyxll,wwl}@zjut.edu.cn

Abstract. In this paper, the carbon emission factor is taken into account in the Location Routing Problem (LRP), and a multi-objective LRP model combining carbon emission with total cost is established. Due to the complexity of the proposed problem, a generality-oriented and emerging Multi-Objective Hyper Heuristic algorithm (MOHH) is proposed. In the framework of MOHH, the LRP related operates are constructed as the low level heuristics, and the different high level strategies are designed. Compared with the NSGA-II algorithm, the MOHH can better solve the multi-objective problem of LRP, and can quickly find the better solution, and achieve higher search efficiency and stability of the algorithm.

Keywords: Location Routing Problem · Carbon emission · Multi-Objective Hyper Heuristic algorithm

1 Introduction

With the emergence of environmental problems such as global warming, low carbon economy has gradually become the focus of attention in the world. As logistics industry is one of the main sources of CO_2 emission, Location Routing Problem (LRP) under low carbon environment is concerned by scholars. In the actual logistic and distribution systems, the optimization objective function is often more than one. In the existing literature, Jemai et al. [1] and Sawik et al. [2] studied the multi-objective Vehicle Routing Problem (VRP) by minimizing transportation distance and CO_2 emission. Ghaffarinasab et al. [3] and Golmohammadi et al. [4] proposed a LRP model for minimizing the transportation cost, number of vehicles and times. There are not much literature studied multi-objective LRP by considering CO_2 emission. Though existing search-based approaches (e.g. linear weighting method, NSGA-II, SPEA-II) have been effectively adopted to solve the multi-objective VRP or LRP, they are generally domain-dependent, resulting in a hard task for tester without a deep knowledge in the domain. A corresponding search strategy must be designed for a kind of LRP problem,

Y. Zhao—The research direction is the intelligent distribution and optimal dispatch of logistics system, modern design theory and method of digital products.

© Springer International Publishing AG, part of Springer Nature 2018
T. Huang et al. (Eds.): ISNN 2018, LNCS 10878, pp. 173–182, 2018.
https://doi.org/10.1007/978-3-319-92537-0_21

so it is a hotspot to design a universal algorithm so that it can be applied to a similar problem domain. In this paper, a generality-oriented and emerging heuristic algorithm is proposed to solve multi-objective LRP by balancing two objective functions in the multi-objective combinatorial optimization problem.

2 Mathematical Formulation

2.1 Problem Description

The mathematical formulation of multi-objective LRP can be defined as follows: Given the demand of each customer, depot will distribute the goods to each customer, the completion of the established distribution mission to return to the depot, each customer by the delivery vehicle has and only be serviced once. The impact of CO_2 emission on distribution route is analyzed. At the same time, the total cost is as small as possible through the route planning, and the total CO_2 emissions generated in the distribution process are as small as possible.

The LRP can be defined as a complete and directed graph $G = (V, E)$, where V denotes a vertex set and E is an edge set. The former is composed of two subsets: C of n customers and M of m candidate depots, $S = (C \cup M)$ is the sum of the depots and the customers. Each customer, indexed by $i \in C$, has a non-negative demand d_i, and is served by a potential depot $m \in M$ with capacity Q_m and fixed operating cost C_m. Q_{ij} is the total amount of goods to be delivered to the customer j after leaving customer i. A set of an unlimited fleet of homogeneous vehicles $k \in V$ with capacity Q_k and fixed working cost C_v are assigned to serve these customers. Concerning each edge $(i, j) \in E$, there are traveling cost C_r, vehicle depreciation cost C_d, the unit CO_2 emission cost C_c, the unit fuel consumption cost C_f.

2.2 Computation of Fuel Consumption and Total CO_2 Emission

According to the literature [5], The CO_2 emissions formula for calculating fuel consumption is as follows:

$$F = G \times D \times (a \times Q + b) \tag{1}$$

Where, F is the fuel consumption in the transportation process; G is the terrain slope factor; taking on the value 1; D is the vehicle transportation distance; Q is vehicle load; a and b are the fuel consumption parameters.

Therefore, CO_2 emission can be written as:

$$E_{CO_2} = F \times \eta \tag{2}$$

Where: E_{CO_2} is CO_2 emission; η is fuel conversion factor.

2.3 Multi-objective LRP Mathematical Model

$$\min \psi_1 = \eta \sum_{i \in S} \sum_{j \in S} \sum_{k \in K_m} D_{ij} X_{ijk} [aQ_{ij} + b] \tag{3}$$

$$\min \quad \psi_2 = C_m \sum_{m \in M} Z_m + C_v \sum_{m \in M} \sum_{i \in C} \sum_{k \in K_m} X_{mik} + (C_r + C_d) \sum_{i \in S} \sum_{j \in S} \sum_{k \in K_m} D_{ij} X_{ijk} +$$
$$C_f \sum_{i \in S} \sum_{j \in S} \sum_{k \in K_m} D_{ij} X_{ijk} [aQ_{ij} + b] + C_c \eta \sum_{i \in S} \sum_{j \in S} \sum_{k \in K_m} D_{ij} X_{ijk} [aQ_{ij} + b] \tag{4}$$

s.t.

$$\sum_{m \in M} \sum_{k \in K_m} \sum_{j \in S} X_{ijk} = 1, \ \forall i \in C \tag{5}$$

$$\sum_{j \in S} X_{mjk} = 1, \ \forall m \in M, \ k \in K_m \tag{6}$$

$$\sum_{i \in S} X_{imk} = 1, \ \forall m \in M, \ k \in K_m \tag{7}$$

$$\sum_{m \in M} \sum_{j \in C} X_{mjk} \leq 1, \ \forall k \in K_m \tag{8}$$

$$\sum_{m \in M} \sum_{j \in C} X_{mjk} + \sum_{j \in C} \sum_{n \in M} X_{jnk} \leq 1, \ \forall k \in K_m \tag{9}$$

$$\sum_{i \in S} X_{ihk} - \sum_{j \in S} X_{hjk} = 0, \ \forall h \in C, \ k \in K_m \tag{10}$$

$$\sum_{k \in K_m} \sum_{i \in C} d_i \sum_{j \in S} X_{ijk} \leq Q_m Z_m, \ \forall m \in M \tag{11}$$

$$\sum_{i \in C} d_i \sum_{j \in S} X_{ijk} \leq Q_k, \forall k \in K_m \tag{12}$$

The objective function (3) minimizes the CO_2 emission. The second objective function (4) minimizes total costs composed of fixed lease cost of depots and vehicles and travelling cost of edges. Constraint (5) ensures that each customer is visited only once. Constraints (6) and (7) guarantee that each vehicle must return to the departure depot at the end of the route. Constraint (8) ensures that the route is removed from a depot at most. Constraint (9) specifies that the vehicles in any two depots are not on the same route. Constraint (10) requires that entering and leaving the edge to each node is equal. Constraint (11) forbids that total delivery and pickup demands of clients exceed the depot's capacity. Constraint (12) ensures that the load of the vehicle is not greater than its load capacity.

3 Proposed Approach

3.1 Hyper Heuristic Algorithm

Hyper heuristic algorithm is an emerging heuristic algorithm developed in recent years [6, 7]. It provides a high level strategy to solve a variety of combinatorial optimization problems by managing or manipulating a series of low level heuristics which directly modify the space of solutions.

Figure 1 gives the framework of the Hyper-heuristic algorithm, which is divided into two parts: high level strategy and low level heuristic (LLH). In the control domain, high level strategies are designed by intelligent computing expert, including how to construct a feasible solution or improve the quality of the solution by using the LLHs. In the problem domain, the application domain experts provide a series of LLHs and problem definition, objective function and other information.

This paper presents a tabu search hyper heuristic algorithm to solve the multi-objective LRP model, which provides a reference for the further application of the hyper heuristic algorithm in the field of LRP.

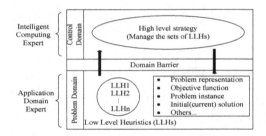

Fig. 1. The framework of hyper heuristic algorithm

3.2 Hyper Heuristic Algorithm Based on Tabu Search

In this paper, tabu search is adopted as a high level strategy and leverages on the strength of each LLHs.

3.2.1 Low Level Heuristics

In the LRP model, the LLHs based on the classification criteria in the literature [8]: Mutational heuristics; Ruin & recreate heuristics; Local search heuristics; Crossover heuristics. Details of the heuristics are as follows.

Mutational heuristics.

LLH_1: 2-opt. Swap the locations of two consecutive customers within a single route.
LLH_2: Or-opt. Move two consecutive customers to a different location within a single route.
LLH_3: Interchange. Select two customers from two different routes and swap them.
LLH_4: Replace. Randomly select one customer and move it to a different route.

LLH_5: Shift. Select a route and use a new depot to replace the depot for this route.
LLH_6: Interchange. Select two depots from two different routes and swap them.

Ruin & recreate heuristics

LLH_7: Location-based Radial Ruin. Removes [1%–10%] of customers from the solution, based on the proximity of their location to a randomly chosen customer.

Local search heuristics

LLH_8: Interchange. Same as LLH3, and only accept the improved solution.
LLH_9: Shift. Same as LLH4, and only accept the improved solution.
LLH_{10}: 2-opt*. Takes the end sections of two routes, and swap them to create two new routes.
LLH_{11}: GENI. A customer is moved between two adjacent customers on a different route that is closest to it.

Crossover heuristics

LLH_{12}: Combine. Select two parent solutions, [25%, 75%] of routes are copied from one parent to create a single offspring route, add non-conflicting routes from another parent and randomly insert the remaining customers.
LLH_{13}: Longest Combine. Select two parent solutions, all routes are considered in the order of the number of service customers, and any route that does not repeat the customer is added to generate a single offspring route and randomly inserted into the remaining customers.

3.2.2   High Level Strategy

The high level strategy mainly considers the selection strategy of the LLHs, that is, deciding which heuristics should be selected to modify the current solution in each iteration. Tabu search is adopted as high level strategy by monitoring the performance of each LLH and assigning score to each LLH [9]. Each low level heuristic has the same initial score, and reinforcement learning method is used to update the score. When the heuristic improves the current solution, it adds points to the heuristic and vice versa. Finally, according to the score, the greedy method is utilized to select the heuristic with the highest score.

3.3   Solving the LRP Process

In the LRP model, a gravity center method is designed to locate the depot and the customer groups firstly, and then to solve distribution routes of different customer groups. The specific process is as follows:

Step 1: Initialize the population.
Step 2: Each individual in the population is converted into a feasible route. According to the constraint conditions (vehicle capacity and depot inventory), each customer is incorporated into the vehicle routes in turn. When a customer violates the constraints, a new route is reopened and the customer is added to it.

Step 3: Select the location of the depot. For the location of multiple depots, in order to simplify the model, it can be changed into a number of single depot location problem to deal with [10].

Step 4: The routes of each chromosome in the initial population P are optimized by the high level strategy designed in Sect. 3.2.2.

Step 4.1: Set the relevant algorithm parameters. It includes the initial score of the low level heuristics, the tabu length, and the tabu list empty.

Step 4.2: Select the objective function. In the two objective functions (u, v), randomly select an objective function u with equal probability.

Step 4.3: Select the low level heuristic. Select a LLH_k heuristic according to the score of the low level heuristic.

Step 4.4: Calculate the value of the objective function. Use the selected LLH_k by step 4.3 to calculate the function value of the selected objective u by step 4.2.

Step 4.5: The difference of objective function value is calculated as Δ_u, if $\Delta_u > 0$, then the score of LLH_k is increased by 1, e.g. $r_k(u) = r_k(u) + 1$. Otherwise, the score is reduced by 1, e.g. $r_k(u) = r_k(u) - 1$, and the LLH_k is put into the tabu list, and the low level heuristic in the tabu list is pardoned according to the 'first in, first out' mechanism.

Step 4.6: Calculating the objective function Δ_v, if $\Delta_v > 0$, $r_k(v) = r_k(v) + 1$, otherwise, $r_k(v) = r_k(v) - 1$.

Step 4.7: Non dominated sorting, update the non-dominated solution set.

Step 4.8: If the termination criteria are met, turn to step 4.2;

Step 4.9: Return non-dominated solutions set.

4   Experimental Results and Analysis

The Multi-Objective Hyper Heuristic algorithm based on Tabu Search (MOHH_TS) in this paper is programmed by MATLAB and runs on Intel Core i5, 2.6 GHz, 4G memory computer platforms. The Barreto benchmarks are used as computation instance to evaluate the proposed algorithm. The parameters are set as follows [5]: Population size is 50, the algorithm iteration number is 1000, the fuel consumption parameter a = 6.208×10^{-3}, b = 0.2125, the fuel conversion factor η = 2.68.

4.1   Comparative Analysis

Using the MOHH_TS selection strategies, compared with the existing high level strategies: Simple Random (SR); Random Descent (RD); Random Permutation Descent (RPD) [11]. A better strategy is obtained by experiment and the number of Pareto solutions is obtained.

The evaluation of the Pareto solution set includes two indexes:

(1) The advantages and disadvantages of Pareto solution set are evaluated by the following methods.

It is assumed that according to two different algorithms, two final Pareto solution sets are obtained, and the minimum values of two objective functions is f_{1min} and f_{2min}, over Point (f_{1min}, f_{2min}) to make a curve $y = \frac{1}{kx}$. The definition of the optimal solution shows that all the Pareto solutions are one side of the curve, then the Pareto of the Point (f_1, f_2) of the solution set to the shortest distance is

$$d^i_{min} = min\sqrt{\left(f^i_1 - x\right)^2 + \left(f^i_2 - y\right)^2} = min\sqrt{\left(f^i_1 - x\right)^2 + \left(f^i_2 - \frac{1}{kx}\right)^2}.$$ The optimal

exponential $Opt = \sqrt{\frac{1}{n}\sum_{i=1}^{n}(d^i_{min})^2}$, and n is the number of solutions for the Pareto

solution. The smaller the Opt value, the closer to the curve, the better the quality of the solution.

(2) To measure the Pareto solution on the standards proposed in the literature [12]

$$Sp \triangleq \sqrt{\frac{1}{n-1}\sum_{i=1}^{n}(d/4 - d_i)^2} \tag{13}$$

$$d_i = min\left(\left|f^i_1(\vec{x}) - f^j_1(\vec{x})\right| + \left|f^i_2(\vec{x}) - f^j_2(\vec{x})\right|\right), \quad i,j = \dots,n; \quad d/4 = \frac{1}{n}\sum_{i=1}^{n}d_i \tag{14}$$

The smaller the Sp value, the more uniform the distribution of the solution. The data obtained from the above experiments are shown in Table 1.

Table 1. Comparison results of different combinations

Instance	MOHH_SR			MOHH_RD			MOHH_RPD			MOHH_TS		
	n	Opt	Sp	n	Opt	Sp	n	Opt	Sp	n	Opt	Sp
Christ50x5be	3	82.0958	146.8202	2	41.8317	34.9874	5	35.018	26.154	6	26.6999	20.0667
Christ75x10ba	3	130.7183	67.0881	4	75.1317	61.3404	3	88.8589	42.6662	6	55.8708	21.429
Christ75x10be	1	37.9738	0	1	32.5661	0	2	155.6977	27.3087	6	33.7205	12.9934
Christ100x10	2	80.1097	36.8927	1	170.9825	0	2	219.3673	12.5862	5	5.2279	1.7714
Gaskell21x5	4	41.0958	4.0415	4	38.6173	40.2555	3	54.5368	50.8068	5	18.1242	2.4156
Gaskell29x5	4	72.8844	60.1288	1	35.0327	0	4	55.7298	35.5636	6	43.2548	33.1038
Gaskell36x5	4	23.7231	26.2117	2	47.3591	20.5537	6	20.4345	88.1087	6	24.6368	12.5299
Min27x5	2	27.6277	9.0067	3	26.6383	7.8977	5	49.6941	9.006	7	16.2665	3.5707
Perl55x15	6	35.6619	96.4175	3	143.6436	397.0438	5	43.0842	162.7707	9	35.5837	79.8786
Perl85x7	8	94.5996	72.1594	4	112.7248	41.5911	8	102.5197	93.2832	10	64.0709	21.022

Among them, the depth value represents the optimal value, 0 represents the number of Pareto solution is 1.

It is shown from Table 1 that the effect of TS selection strategy is more obvious and the result is better than that of the other three selection strategies.

Comparing the MOHH_TS with the NSGA-II, the performance comparison of MOHH_TS and NSGA-II in solving the multi-objective LRP is analyzed: Pareto number, convergent algebra, Opt and Sp. The convergent algebra takes the average convergent algebra of 10 times, and the convergence criterion is as follows: no more excellent individuals appear in successive ten generations. The results of the algorithm comparison are shown in Table 2.

Table 2. Comparison results of different algorithms

Instances	MOTH_TS					NSGA- II					
	n	Convergent algebra	Opt	Sp	Time (s)	n	Convergent algebra		Opt	Sp	Time (s)
		Avg	std					Avg	Std			
Christ50x5be	6	96.3	16.7	26.6999	20.0667	299.89	3	126.8	18.4	18.2349	19.7661	379.79
Christ75x10ba	6	81.7	13.7	55.8708	21.429	421.07	4	140	25.1	119.856	37.0876	400.32
Christ75x10be	6	122	20.9	33.7205	12.9934	417.38	2	167.3	27.7	57.4873	53.405	430.97
Christ100x10	5	112.3	26.8	5.2279	1.7714	593.46	3	185.2	25.9	139.2023	9.9304	635.3
Gaskell21x5	5	69.7	15.2	18.1242	2.4156	187.12	6	107.7	19.9	46.3794	0.6197	200.39
Gaskell29x5	6	94.9	17.8	43.2548	33.1038	234.33	3	160.3	18.9	105.9522	230.9978	230.71
Gaskell36x5	6	102.3	22.3	24.6368	12.5299	290.13	2	92.7	21.3	62.0312	41.1651	305.15
Min27x5	7	97.4	18.6	16.2665	3.5707	228.18	3	119	18.5	19.2207	8.3138	229.32
Perl55x15	9	201.1	32.1	35.5837	79.8786	340.71	6	218.7	35.4	38.3095	245.4893	407.36
Perl85x7	10	210.8	29.8	64.0709	21.022	450.27	9	212.1	30.2	63.3493	47.4976	430.04

As can be seen from Table 2, the optimal solution can be found in both the MOHH_TS and NSGA-II. However, the MOHH_TS has less convergence algebra than the NSGA-II in most benchmark instances, indicating that compared with the NSGA-II. The convergence rate of the MOHH_TS is faster and the efficiency is higher, which will be more obvious when solving the larger scale problem. Meanwhile, the Std value of the convergence algebra of the MOHH_TS is smaller than that of the NSGA-II, indicating that the MOHH_TS is more stable. At the same time, the running time of the MOHH_TS is shorter than that of NSGA-II for most instances.

4.2   Computational Results

The Pareto optimal solution sets of the other instances are shown in Fig. 2. It can be seen that the Pareto optimal solution set obtained by each instance is a satisfactory solution set. It can be seen that the MOHH algorithm can effectively solve the multi-objective LRP optimization model.

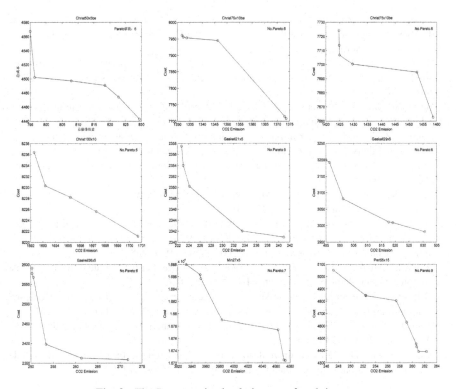

Fig. 2. The Pareto optimal solution set of each instance

5   Conclusion

This paper considered a model for multi-objective Location Routing Problem by minimizing both the CO_2 emission and total cost, a multi-objective hyper heuristic algorithm with tabu search as the high level strategy was designed. The simulation experiment proved that the hyper heuristic algorithm can effectively solve the proposed multi-objective LRP model. The Pareto optimal solution is also beneficial for the decision maker to choose the most suitable distribution scheme from the actual needs. As the hyper heuristic algorithm has good generality, it can be applied to other combinatorial optimization problems, without changing the framework, just providing a set of low level heuristics related to the problem.

Acknowledgement. This work supported by the National Natural Science Foundation, China (No. 61572438).

References

1. Jemai, J., Zekri, M., Mellouli, K.: An NSGA-II algorithm for the green vehicle routing problem. In: Hao, J.-K., Middendorf, M. (eds.) EvoCOP 2012. LNCS, vol. 7245, pp. 37–48. Springer, Heidelberg (2012). https://doi.org/10.1007/978-3-642-29124-1_4

2. Tunga, H., Bhaumik, A.: A method for solving bi-objective green vehicle routing problem (G-VRP) through genetic algorithm. In: International Conference on Frontiers in Optimization, pp. 1–19. Springer, Berlin (2017)
3. Ghaffarinasab, N., Jabalameli, M., Saboury, A.: Multi-objective capacitated location-routing problem: modelling and a simulated annealing heuristic. Int. J. Serv. Oper. Manag. **15**(2), 140–156 (2013)
4. Golmohammadi, A., Bonab, S., Parishani, A.: A multi-objective location routing problem using imperialist competitive algorithm. Int. J. Ind. Eng. Comput. **7**(3), 481–488 (2016)
5. Yanwei, Z., Wen, L.: Low carbon for a multi-vehicle routing problem with simultaneous pickups and deliveries. J. Zhejiang Univ. Technol. **43**(1), 18–23 (2015)
6. Kheiri, A., Özcan, E.: An iterated multi-stage selection hyper-heuristic. Eur. J. Oper. Res. **250**(1), 77–90 (2016)
7. Burke, K., Gendreau, M., Hyde, M.: Hyper-heuristics: a survey of the state of the art. J. Oper. Res. Soc. **64**(12), 1695–1724 (2016)
8. Marshall, R.J., Johnston, M., Zhang, M.: Hyper-heuristic operator selection and acceptance criteria. In: Ochoa, G., Chicano, F. (eds.) EvoCOP 2015. LNCS, vol. 9026, pp. 99–113. Springer, Cham (2015). https://doi.org/10.1007/978-3-319-16468-7_9
9. Zamli, Z., Alkazemi, B., Kendall, G.: A Tabu search hyper-heuristic strategy for t-way, test suite generation. Appl. Soft Comput. **44**(1), 57–74 (2016)
10. Mehrjerdi, Z., Nadizadeh, A.: Using greedy clustering method to solve capacitated location-routing problem with fuzzy demands. Eur. J. Oper. Res. **229**(1), 75–84 (2013)
11. Zcan, E., Bilgin, B., KorkmazE, E.: A comprehensive analysis of hyper-heuristics. Intell. Data Anal. **12**(1), 3–23 (2018)
12. Xu, J., Huang, D.: Research on multi-objective vehicle routing based on hybrid particle swarm optimization. Comput. Integr. Manuf. Syst. 573–579+584 (2007)

Pulse Neuron Supervised Learning Rules for Adapting the Dynamics of Synaptic Connections

Vladimir Bondarev$^{(\boxtimes)}$

Sevastopol State University, Sevastopol, Russia
bondarev@sevsu.ru

Abstract. In this study, we propose a discrete time vector-matrix model of a pulse neuron and novel supervised learning rules. We assumed that the synaptic connections of the neuron model are characterized by linear dynamic behavior. A distinctive feature of the considered approach is that for the training of the neuron model we do not adjust the synaptic weights, instead we adapt the impulse responses of the synaptic connections.

We propose two types of supervised learning rules. They are driven by the values of the total postsynaptic potential or by the time moments when the output pulses are emitted. The quantitative changes in the values of the impulse responses are proportional to the values of the matrix of binary vectors that fix the recent time history of input pulse trains. We demonstrate the properties of rules by computer simulation of pulsed neural networks that mimic linear dynamic reference systems.

Keywords: Pulse neuron · Pulse train · Supervised learning
Synaptic dynamics

1 Introduction

In recent years, much attention has been paid to pulsed (spike) neural networks (PNN) since they have more powerful computational capacity for processing spatio-temporal information [1–3]. In PNN the stimulus and signals are encoded by pulse trains (sequences). This creates difficulties in the development of learning rules for such networks that actually perform computation with time and map the input pulse trains to the desired output pulse trains. The development of supervised temporal learning rules for PNN, suitable for approximation of functions and online processing of sensory information, is an important problem in computational neuroinformatics [4].

There have been many studies on supervised learning rules for PNN. A number of supervised learning rules based on precise time of pulses were proposed in [5–9]. However, in most cases they focus on the problems of pattern classification and do not focus directly on approximation of functions or on online signal processing, where the variables are represented by multi-pulse trains.

The model of pulse neuron (PN) and temporal supervised learning rules applicable to solving of various problems of online signal processing were considered in [10, 11].

© Springer International Publishing AG, part of Springer Nature 2018
T. Huang et al. (Eds.): ISNN 2018, LNCS 10878, pp. 183–191, 2018.
https://doi.org/10.1007/978-3-319-92537-0_22

The learning rules proposed in [11] are pulsed-based and allow the adaptation of synaptic weights during the online training process. As noted in [12] the intrinsic dynamics of synapses also plays an important role in neural computation. Therefore, the development of pulses-based learning rules that adapt the dynamics of synapses can provide additional possibilities in constructing PNN.

The purpose of this paper is to expand the scope of the proposed approach [10, 11] by developing supervised learning rules that adapt the entire dynamics of PN synaptic connections. Adaptation of synapse dynamics will expand the domain of applications of pulsed neuron models in solving problems of online signal processing.

2 Model of Pulse Neuron

For our study, we will use the model of PN considered in [10]. It is assumed that input and output pulse trains of the PN are bipolar. Therefore input pulse trains $u_i(t)$ generated by the encoding presynaptic neurons can be represented as the sum of the signed Dirac delta functions

$$u_i(t) = \sum_j \lambda_i^j \delta(t - t_i^j), \; t_i^j \leq t, \tag{1}$$

where t is the current time, t_i^j is the time corresponding to the occurrence of the pulse j at the output of presynaptic neuron i, $\lambda_i^j = \pm 1$ is the sign of the pulse. Dynamic properties of the PN synaptic connections are modelled by linear filters with pulse responses $h_i(t)$. Since the filter output is determined by convolution integral, the reaction of the filter to the input (1) can be written as

$$x_i(t) = \sum_j \lambda_i^j h_i(t - t_i^j). \tag{2}$$

The filter reactions $x_i(t)$ are weighted by synaptic weights w_i and summed to form the total postsynaptic potential $y_o(t)$ of the PN

$$y_o(t) = \sum_{i=0}^{I-1} w_i x_i(t), \tag{3}$$

where I is the number of the PN inputs.

The state of the neuron o is determined by the membrane potential $v_o(t)$. The evolution of the $v_o(t)$ over time interval $t \in (t_o^{f-1}, t_o^f]$ between output pulses is given by the equation

$$v_o(t) = \int_{t_o^{f-1}}^{t} h_o(t - \tau) y_o(\tau) d\tau, \tag{4}$$

where $h_o(t)$ is the pulse response of neuron membrane, t_o^{f-1} is the time of the previous output pulse. If the module of $v_o(t)$ reaches the firing threshold *Thr* the neuron generates the pulse at time moment t_o^f. After the pulse the membrane potential is reset to zero. The sign of the output pulse is determined as follows

$$\lambda_o^f = sign \left(\int_{t_o^{f-1}}^{t_o^f} h_o(t_o^f - \tau) y_o(\tau) d\tau \right). \tag{5}$$

Generally, the specified chain of conversions corresponds to the LIF-neuron, if $h_o(t) = \exp(-t/\tau_m)$, where τ_m is the time constant, or to the IF-neuron, if $h_o(t)$ is the Heaviside step function.

To calculate the values of formulas (2–5) we need to perform a sampling. Let pulse responses $h_i(t)$ be characterized by finite duration T and all values are calculated at discrete times $t_n = n\Delta t$, where Δt is the time sampling step, n is the step number. Following the approach outlined in [10], we introduce the sliding binary vector $\mathbf{b}_i(n)$ whose elements are equal to

$$b_i(n-k) = \begin{cases} \lambda_i^j, & t_n - (k+1)\Delta t < t_i^j \le t_n - k\Delta t \\ 0, & else \end{cases}, \tag{6}$$

where $k = 0,1,...,K-1$ and $K = [T/\Delta t]$. Then the reaction of the filter to the input pulse train at a discrete instant of time will be written in the form

$$x_i(n) = \mathbf{b}_i^T(n)\mathbf{h}_i, \tag{7}$$

where $\mathbf{h}_i = (h_i(0), h_i(1), \ldots, h_i(K-1))^T$ denotes the impulse response vector. Hence

$$y_o(n) = \sum_{i=0}^{I-1} w_i \mathbf{b}_i^T(n)\mathbf{h}_i = \sum_{i=0}^{I-1} \mathbf{b}_i^T(n)\mathbf{h}_i^*, \tag{8}$$

where $\mathbf{h}_i^* = w_i \mathbf{h}_i$ is the scaled impulse response vector.

Taking into account the scale factor, Eqs. (7) and (8) can be rewritten in a convenient matrix form

$$\mathbf{x}^*(n) = diag(\mathbf{B}(n)\mathbf{H}), \tag{9}$$

$$y_o(n) = \mathbf{1}^T diag(\mathbf{B}(n)\mathbf{H}), \tag{10}$$

where *diag* denotes the main diagonal of the matrix product $\mathbf{B}(n)\mathbf{H}$. The rows of the matrix $\mathbf{B}(n)$ are sliding binary input vectors (6), the columns of the matrix $\mathbf{H}$ are scaled impulse response vectors $\mathbf{h}_i^*$, $\mathbf{1}^T$ is the unit vector of a suitable size.

3 Supervised Learning Rules for Adapting Synaptic Dynamics

Let us consider the scheme of adaptive modeling of a linear dynamical system acting as a reference system and performing the specified linear transformation of the input dynamic variable $u(t)$ to the output variable $y_d(t)$, which is also encoded as a sequence of pulses $s_d(t)$. We want to build a PNN model that reproduces the dynamics of the reference system based on the output variable $y_d(t)$ or on the sequence of pulses $s_d(t)$, called desired or reference signals.

A distinctive feature of the considered approach is that we want to solve the problem not by adapting the synaptic weights of the pulsed neuron, but by adapting the dynamics of synaptic connections. To solve the problem in such a general formulation, it is necessary to determine the pulse responses of the neuron synaptic connections (matrix $\mathbf{H}$), which ensure a minimum of the functional

$$J(\mathbf{H}) = E\{F(e(n))\}, \tag{11}$$

where E is the mathematical expectation, F is the convex function (for example, the quadratic function), $e(n)$ is an error that can be calculated as the difference $e(n) = y_d(n) - y_o(n)$ or otherwise, when the pulse train $s_d(t)$ is used as the desired signal.

To find the quasi-optimal values of the impulse response vectors, we apply the standard descending gradient method. If we consider $y_o(n)$ as the output of the pulsed neuron and $y_d(n)$ as the desired signal, then, taking into account (10), the estimation of the gradient of the quadratic functional (11) over the matrix $\mathbf{H}$ will be equal to

$$\nabla J(\mathbf{H}^{\mathrm{T}}) = -2E\{e(n)\mathbf{B}(n)\}. \tag{12}$$

Having performed the stochastic approximation, we obtain the matrix learning rule that provides the necessary adaptation of the dynamic properties of synaptic connections

$$\mathbf{H}^{\mathrm{T}}(n) = \mathbf{H}^{\mathrm{T}}(n-1) + \mu(n)e(n)\mathbf{B}(n) \tag{13}$$

or in vector form

$$\mathbf{h}_i^*(n) = \mathbf{h}_i^*(n-1) + \mu(n)e(n)\mathbf{b}_i(n), \tag{14}$$

where $\mu(n)$ is the learning rate. These rules assume that the PN input signals are pulse sequences and the output signal of the PN is represented by total postsynaptic potential. Therefore, the rules (13) and (14) cannot be used directly for training of a PNN where not only the input signals, but also the output signals are represented by pulse sequences.

Let us derive supervised PN learning rules for the case when the desired output signal $y_d(n)$ of the reference dynamic system (reference PNN) and the actual output signal $y_o(n)$ of the PN model (10) are represented by pulse trains. These rules will be driven by the time of pulses and belong to temporal rules.

The actual and desired output sequences can be represented as a sum of delta functions

$$s_o(t) = \sum_f \lambda_o^f \delta(t - t_o^f), \quad s_d(t) = \sum_l \lambda_d^l \delta(t - t_d^l), \tag{15}$$

where t_o^f and t_d^l are the time moments of the pulses in the actual and desired pulse sequences. To determine the similarity of these pulse sequences and to calculate the error $e(n)$, we perform their convolution with some positive local kernel $h_r(t)$[13]. Then, by analogy with (6) and (7), we get

$$\tilde{y}_o(n) = \mathbf{b}_o^T(n)\mathbf{h}_r, \quad \tilde{y}_d(n) = \mathbf{b}_d^T(n)\mathbf{h}_r, \tag{16}$$

where $\mathbf{h}_r$ is the vector of samples of the kernel $h_r(t)$, $\mathbf{b}_o^T(n)$ and $\mathbf{b}_d^T(n)$ are the binary sliding vectors containing M elements that correspond to the pulse sequences $s_o(t)$ and $s_d(t)$.

The variables $\tilde{y}_o(n)$ and $\tilde{y}_d(n)$ approximate the variables $y_o(n)$ and $y_d(n)$. By replacing the last variables in the learning rule (13) with $\tilde{y}_o(n)$ and $\tilde{y}_d(n)$, we get the following temporal learning rule

$$\mathbf{H}^T(n) = \mathbf{H}^T(n-1) + \mu(n)[(\mathbf{b}_d(n) - \mathbf{b}_o(n))\mathbf{h}_r]\mathbf{B}(n). \tag{17}$$

Comparing (13) and (17), we come to the conclusion that in the rule (17) the error e (n) corresponds to the weighted (with the weight $\mathbf{h}_r$) difference of the binary vectors representing the actual and desired pulse sequences (15). As this temporal rule for adapting the impulse response matrix $\mathbf{H}$ is based on comparing the filtered binary vectors, we will call it HB-FILT.

If the length of the window $\mathbf{h}_r$ is limited to one sample with the value of one then from (17) we will derive the simple learning rule

$$\mathbf{H}^T(n) = \mathbf{H}^T(n-1) + \mu(n)[b_d(n) - b_o(n)]\mathbf{B}(n), \tag{18}$$

where $b_d(n)$ and $b_o(n)$ are the elements of binary vectors. This temporal rule uses the instantaneous error value which is the difference of the elements of the corresponding binary vectors. We will call it HB-INST.

4   Computer Simulation

During simulation the model of the bipolar pulse neuron with a single input was used as the model for encoding neurons. The dynamic properties of the encoding neurons were described by equations analogous to (4) and (5). In all our computational experiments, we integrated (4) and (5) with a simple rectangular formula and replaced $h_o(t)$ with the stepwise Heaviside function.

Encoding neurons were used to convert analog input signals to pulse trains. There were two encoding neurons. One neuron was used to encode the input signal $u(t)$ and the other was used to encode the desired output signal $y_d(t)$. The input pulse sequences $u_i(t)$ were formed with the help of delay line taps. For this purpose, a sequence of output pulses of the first encoding neuron was applied to the delay line input. The delay time step was equal to the sampling step Δt. As an initial pulse response $\mathbf{h}_i(0)$ of synaptic connections we used a step function with small amplitude. The initial value of the learning rate was equal to 0.5 and decreased as $1/\sqrt{n}$.

The finite damped symmetric exponent function (with the time constant τ_r) was used as the kernel function $\mathbf{h}_r$ to keep the waveform of signals. The kernel function has been shifted by half of its length to provide a linear phase response. Such kernel function creates the time delay equal to $(M-1)/2$ (if M is odd) that requires correction of the rule (17):

$$\mathbf{H}^{\mathrm{T}}(n) = \mathbf{H}^{\mathrm{T}}(n-1) + \mu(n)[(\mathbf{b}_d(n) - \mathbf{b}_o(n))\mathbf{h}_r]\mathbf{B}(n - (M-1)/2). \qquad (19)$$

The parameters used in the computational experiments are listed in the Table 1.

Table 1. Parameters of the PNN model.

Parameters	I	K	M	τ_r, ms	Δt, ms	Thr
Experiment 1	400	128	129	10	0.5	1×10^{-3}
Experiment 2	2000	16	65	160	10	2×10^{-3}

In the first computational experiment, we investigated the properties of the learning rule (13) when solving the problem of the original signal reconstruction from the input pulse train and suppressing additive noise. We assumed here that the input signal is equal to $u(t) = s(t) + \xi(t)$, where $s(t)$ is the original signal, $\xi(t)$ is stochastic stationary uncorrelated noise. The original signal was a harmonic oscillation with the frequency of 20 Hz, and additive noise was presented as a sum of harmonic signal with the frequency of 10 Hz and white noise with normal distribution and unit variance. The output signal of the reference system was equal to $y_d(t) = s(t)$. The PN has to reconstruct the original signal from its mixture with additive noise using the sequence of encoding input pulses.

Diagrams of the input $u(t)$, reference $y_d(t) = s(t)$ and output $y_o(t)$ signals, as well as the visualization of the matrix $\mathbf{H}$ after training the PN with the help of rule (13) are shown in Fig. 1. The simulation results showed that the PN reconstructs the original signal well and effectively suppresses the noise. If the signal-to-noise ratio for the input signal $u(t)$ was equal to -4.74 dB, then for the output signal $y_o(t)$ it reached a value of 22.64 dB, i.e. the signal-to-noise ratio as a result of adaptation of the synaptic dynamics increased up to 27.38 dB.

The purpose of the second experiment was to analyze the properties of the temporal learning rules (18–19). These rules are driven by the time of pulses of the output pulse train $s_o(t)$ of the PN and the reference system $s_d(t)$. We trained the PN to mimic the dynamics of the reference system that realizes the double integration of the input signal $u(t)$. The similar problem arises in the case of processing accelerometers signals [14].

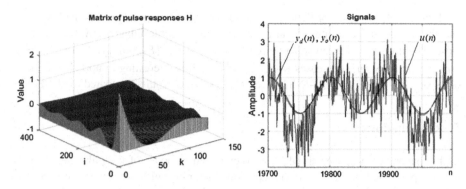

Fig. 1. Signal reconstruction and noise suppression with learning rule (13).

To train the PN we used an input signal $u(t)$ equal to the sum of sinusoidal signals with multiple frequencies. The signal $y_d(t)$ was calculated using the normalized frequency response of the reference double integrator [14]. The frequency response was set at 30 points uniformly distributed in the frequency range [0, 1.5] Hz.

The results of the PN training based on the HB-FILT rule (19) are shown in Fig. 2(a) and based on the HB-INST rule (18) in Fig. 2(b). The results include the visualization of the pulse response matrix of synaptic connections, the diagram of the reconstructed output signals of the PN $\tilde{y}_o(n)$ and the reference double integrator $\tilde{y}_d(n)$, the dependence of the normalized mean square errors (NMSE) on the number of iterations.

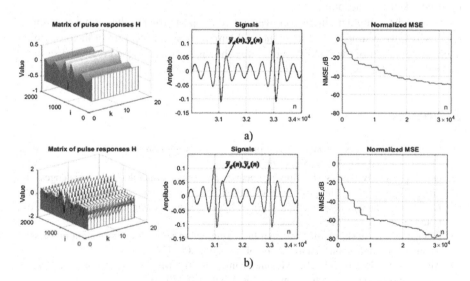

Fig. 2. Results of the PN training with HB-FILT (a) and HB-INST (b) rules.

Figure 2 shows that, for both rules the reconstructed output signal of the PN $\tilde{y}_o(n)$ and the reconstructed output signal of the reference double integrator $\tilde{y}_d(n)$ are very close. The normalized mean square error ($NMSE = 10\log(E\{\tilde{e}^2(n)\}/E\{\tilde{y}_d^2(n)\}$, where $\tilde{e}(n) = \tilde{y}_d(n) - \tilde{y}_o(n)$) decreases with increasing n. It is interesting to note that, despite of its simplicity, the rule HB-INST gives more accurate results compared to HB-FILT.

5 Conclusions

In this paper, we proposed the discrete vector-matrix model of the pulse neuron and novel supervised learning rules. The developed learning rules are driven either by the values of the total postsynaptic potential or by the time of appearance of the output impulses. The quantitative changes of the values of the impulse responses in all the proposed rules are proportional to the values of the matrix of binary vectors, which fixes the recent time history of the input pulse sequences. The matrix of binary vectors may serve as a dynamic memory of synapses.

For the rule (13), it is assumed that the PN input signals are pulse sequences, and the output signal is represented by samples of the total postsynaptic potential. This rule is focused on training of readout neurons for reservoir networks.

The HB-FILT and HB-INST rules, which are driven by time of pulses, along with the necessary adaptation of the dynamics of the synaptic connections, provide the desired mapping of the input pulse sequences to the output pulse sequences. In order to measure the similarity of the output pulse sequence to the desired one, the HB-FILT rule uses the kernel function. The kernel function can introduce some time delay, which must be taken into account.

During the computer simulation, we studied the properties of the proposed learning rules, which were supposed to solve the problem of noise suppression or the problem of double integration of the input signal. It was shown that all proposed rules successfully solve these problems.

References

1. Maass, W.: Networks of spiking neurons: the third generation of neural network models. Neural Netw. **10**(9), 1659–1671 (1997)
2. Grüning, A., Bohte, S.M.: Spiking neural networks: principles and challenges. In: Proceedings of 22nd European Symposium on Artificial Neural Networks, Computational Intelligence and Machine Learning (ESANN 2014), Bruges (Belgium), 23–25 April 2014. Louvain-La-Neuve (2014). i6doc.com
3. Ponulak, F., Kasiński, A.: Introduction to spiking neural networks: information processing, learning and applications. Acta Neurobiol. Exp. **71**, 409–433 (2011)
4. Abbott, L.F., DePasquale, B., Memmesheimer, R.-M.: Building functional networks of spiking model neurons. Nat. Neurosci. **19**(3), 350–355 (2016)
5. Memmesheimer, R.-M., Rubin, R., Ölveczky, B.P., Sompolinsky, H.: Learning precisely timed spikes. Neuron **82**(4), 925–938 (2014). https://doi.org/10.1016/j.neuron.2014.03.026

6. Ponulak, F., Kasinski, A.: Supervised learning in spiking neural networks with ReSuMe: sequence learning, classification, and spike shifting. Neural Comput. **22**(2), 467–510 (2010). https://doi.org/10.1162/neco.2009.11-08-901
7. Mohemmed, A., Schliebs, S., Matsuda, S., Kasabov, N.: SPAN: spike pattern association neuron for learning spatio-temporal spike patterns. Int. J. Neural Syst. **22**(4), 1–17 (2012). https://doi.org/10.1142/S0129065712500128
8. Yu, Q., Tang, H., Tan, K.C., Li, H.: Precise-spike-driven synaptic plasticity: learning hetero-association of spatiotemporal spike patterns. PLoS ONE **8**(11), 1–16 (2013). https://doi.org/10.1371/journal.pone.0078318
9. Gardner, B., Grüning, A.: Supervised learning in spiking neural networks for precise temporal encoding. PLoS ONE **11**(8), 1–28 (2016). https://doi.org/10.1371/journal.pone.0161335
10. Bondarev, V.: Vector-matrix models of pulse neuron for digital signal processing. In: Cheng, L., Liu, Q., Ronzhin, A. (eds.) ISNN 2016. LNCS, vol. 9719, pp. 647–656. Springer, Cham (2016). https://doi.org/10.1007/978-3-319-40663-3_74
11. Bondarev, V.: Pulse neuron learning rules for processing of dynamical variables encoded by pulse trains. In: Kryzhanovsky, B., Dunin-Barkowski, W., Redko, V. (eds.) NEUROINFORMATICS 2017. SCI, vol. 736, pp. 53–58. Springer, Cham (2018). https://doi.org/10.1007/978-3-319-66604-4_8
12. Maass, W., Markram, H.: Synapses as dynamic memory buffers. Neural Netw. **15**, 155–161 (2002)
13. Rusu, C.V., Florian, R.V.: A new class of metrics for spike trains. Neural Comput. **26**(2), 306–348 (2014). https://doi.org/10.1162/NECO_a_00545
14. Bondarev, V.N., Smetanina, T.I.: Digital pulse neuron model for processing of wave accelerometer sensor signals. Sistemy Kontrolya Okruzhayuschey Sredy. **8**(28), 16–23 (2017). (in Russian)

An Artificial Neural Network for Solving Quadratic Zero-One Programming Problems

Wen Han[1], Su Yan[1], Xingnan Wen[1], Sitian Qin[1(✉)], and Guocheng Li[2]

[1] Department of Mathematics, Harbin Institute of Technology, Weihai, China
qinsitian@163.com
[2] Department of Mathematics,
Beijing Information Science and Technology University, Beijing, China

Abstract. This paper proposes a neurodynamic approach for solving the quadratic zero-one programming problem with linear constraints. Based on the basic idea of the Scholtes' relaxation scheme, the original quadratic zero-one programming problem can be approximated by a parameterized nonlinear program. Then, an artificial neural network is proposed to solve the related parameterized nonlinear programming. It is certified that the presented artificial neural network is stable in the sense of Lyapunov. Some numerical experiments are introduced to illustrate our results in the end.

Keywords: Quadratic zero-one programming problem
Relaxation scheme · Parameterized nonlinear programming
Artificial neural network

1 Introduction

Quadratic zero-one programming problems are essential in many applications of science, engineering and management, such as location decision, strategic planning situations, quadratic assignment and dynamic set covering, etc. [1,7]. The quadratic zero-one programming problem was meant as:

$$\begin{aligned}
\min \quad & f(x) = \frac{1}{2}x^T Q x + c^T x \\
\text{s.t.} \quad & Ax = a \\
& x \in \{0,1\}^n.
\end{aligned} \tag{1}$$

where $Q \in \mathbb{R}^{n \times n}$ is a symmetric and positive semi-definite matrix, $c \in \mathbb{R}^n$, $A \in \mathbb{R}^{m \times n}$, $a \in \mathbb{R}^m$.

Before the 1980s, most of the methods used to solve problem (1) were branch-and-bound type [2,9]. Hereafter, a reformulation-linearization technique was proposed by Sherali and Adams in [13], and this technology is dedicated to optimizing formulations, but the size of the problem is limited.

© Springer International Publishing AG, part of Springer Nature 2018
T. Huang et al. (Eds.): ISNN 2018, LNCS 10878, pp. 192–199, 2018.
https://doi.org/10.1007/978-3-319-92537-0_23

However, the traditional numerical methods for quadratic zero-one programming problem are computationally intensive and inefficient, especially for large-scale algorithms. Compared with traditional numerical methods, the neurodynamic approaches to solve problem (1) have the advantage of parallel and quick property. Due to the highly interconnected performance of its information processing unit, neural network method can solve the optimization problem faster than the traditional optimization algorithm [4,19,20].

Since the pioneering research in [14] by Tank and Hopfield, many neural networks have been reported for linear, nonlinear programming problems and zero-one programming problems [5,8,10–12,15–18]. A neural network model was proposed in [3], which uses the generalized Fischer-Burmeister to solve nonlinear complementarity problems. In order to solve quadratic zero-one programming problem with linear constraints, Ranjbar et al. [12] constructed an artificial neural network, by transforming the quadratic zero-one programming problem into a quadratic programming problem under nonlinear constraints.

Inspired by the above researches, this paper presents a novel neural network for solving quadratic zero-one programming problem. The rest of this paper is arranged as follows. We introduce several related preliminaries and present a neural network model, then study the stability of the equilibrium point of recurrent neural network in Sect. 2. Some numerical examples are given to illustrate our results in Sect. 3, and Sect. 4 concludes this paper.

2   Problem Description and Main Results

In this paper, we discuss the following problem:

$$
\begin{aligned}
\min \quad & f(x) = \frac{1}{2} x^{\mathrm{T}} Q x + c^{\mathrm{T}} x \\
\text{s.t.} \quad & A x = a \\
& x = (x_1, x_2, \cdots, x_n)^T \in \{0,1\}^n.
\end{aligned}
$$

We assume that there has at least one optimal solution for the problem (1) in this paper. From $x_i \in \{0,1\}$, we can get $\mid x_i - \frac{1}{2} \mid = \frac{1}{2}$. Next introduce two parameters , $u_i = x_i/2$, $v_i = (1-x_i)/2$. Then $x = (x_1, x_2, \cdots, x_n)^T \in \{0,1\}^n$ if and only if $u_i v_i = 0$, $i = 1, 2, \cdots, n$.

Then the above problem can be converted to the problem as follows:

$$
\begin{aligned}
\min \quad & f(x) = \frac{1}{2} x^{\mathrm{T}} Q x + c^{\mathrm{T}} x \\
\text{s.t.} \quad & A x = a \\
& u_i = x_i/2 \\
& v_i = (1-x_i)/2 \\
& u_i v_i = 0, u_i, v_i \geq 0 \quad i = 1, 2, \cdots, n.
\end{aligned}
\tag{2}
$$

Let $h_j(x) = \sum\limits_{i=1}^{n} a_{ji}x_i - a$, $G_i(x) = \dfrac{x_i}{2}$, $H_i(x) = \dfrac{1-x_i}{2}$. Then, (2) is equivalent to the following problem:

$$
\begin{aligned}
\min \quad & f(x) = \frac{1}{2}x^{\mathrm{T}}Qx + c^{\mathrm{T}}x \\
\text{s.t.} \quad & h_j(x) = 0 \quad \forall j = 1, 2, \cdots, m \\
& G_i(x) \geq 0 \quad \forall i = 1, 2, \cdots, n \\
& H_i(x) \geq 0 \quad \forall i = 1, 2, \cdots, n \\
& G_i(x)H_i(x) = 0 \quad \forall i = 1, 2, \cdots, n.
\end{aligned}
\tag{3}
$$

By the basic idea of the Scholtes' relaxation scheme [6], (3) can be approximated by the following parameterized nonlinear program:

$$
\begin{aligned}
\min \quad & f(x) = \frac{1}{2}x^{\mathrm{T}}Qx + c^{\mathrm{T}}x \\
\text{s.t.} \quad & h_j(x) = 0 \quad \forall j = 1, 2, \cdots, m \\
& G_i(x) \geq 0 \quad \forall i = 1, 2, \cdots, n \\
& H_i(x) \geq 0 \quad \forall i = 1, 2, \cdots, n \\
& G_i(x)H_i(x) \leq \frac{1}{k} \quad \forall i = 1, 2, \cdots, n.
\end{aligned}
\tag{4}
$$

Lemma 1 [6]. *Let x^k be a stationary point of (4) with $x^k \to x^*$, and such that mathematical programs with equilibrium constraint-Mangasarian-Fromovitz constraint qualification holds at x^*, then x^* is a C-stationary point of (2).*

Next, we construct the neurodynamic approach to study the stationary point of (4). Let

$$
g(x) = \begin{pmatrix} g_1(x) \\ \vdots \\ g_n(x) \end{pmatrix}, g_i(x) = \begin{pmatrix} -x_i/2 \\ x_i/2 \\ x_i(1-x_i)/4 \end{pmatrix}, b^k = \begin{pmatrix} b_1 \\ \vdots \\ b_n \end{pmatrix}, b_i = \begin{pmatrix} 0 \\ 1/2 \\ 1/k \end{pmatrix}.
$$

Then the problem (4) is equivalent to the problem as follows:

$$
\begin{aligned}
\min \quad & f(x) = \frac{1}{2}x^{\mathrm{T}}Qx + c^{\mathrm{T}}x \\
\text{s.t.} \quad & Ax = a \\
& g(x) \leq b^k.
\end{aligned}
\tag{5}
$$

The derivative of g_i can be calculated as follows:

$$
\nabla g_i(x) = (-\frac{1}{2}e_i, \frac{1}{2}e_i, \frac{1}{4}e_i - \frac{1}{2}e_i^{\mathrm{T}}xe_i).
$$

Since (1) has one optimal solution at least, the feasible set of the problem (5) is nonempty. x is an optimal solution of (5) if there exist $\lambda = (\lambda_1, \lambda_2, \cdots, \lambda_n), \lambda_i = (\lambda_i^{(1)}, \lambda_i^{(2)}, \lambda_i^{(3)}), \nu \in \mathbb{R}^m$, such that

$$0 = Qx + c + \sum_{i=1}^{n} \nabla g_i(x)\lambda_i + A^{\mathrm{T}}\nu \tag{6}$$

$$b_i \geq g_i(x) \quad 0 \leq \lambda \tag{7}$$

$$0 = -\sum_{i=1}^{n} \lambda_i^{\mathrm{T}}(g_i(x) - b_i) \tag{8}$$

$$a = Ax. \tag{9}$$

According to (6), we can get

$$-\sum_{i=1}^{n} \nabla g_i(x)\lambda_i = Qx + c + A^{\mathrm{T}}\nu. \tag{10}$$

After simple calculation, it is obtained that

$$\begin{aligned}
\lambda_i^{\mathrm{T}}(g_i(x) - b_i) = {}& -\frac{1}{2}\lambda_i^{(1)}x_i + \frac{1}{2}\lambda_i^{(2)}x_i + \frac{1}{4}\lambda_i^{(3)}x_i - \frac{1}{4}\lambda_i^{(3)}x_i^2 \\
& -\frac{1}{2}\lambda_i^{(2)} - \frac{1}{k}\lambda_i^{(3)}.
\end{aligned} \tag{11}$$

$$x^{\mathrm{T}}\nabla g_i(x)\lambda_i = -\frac{1}{2}\lambda_i^{(1)}x_i + \frac{1}{2}\lambda_i^{(2)}x_i + \frac{1}{4}\lambda_i^{(3)}x_i - \frac{1}{2}\lambda_i^{(3)}x_i^2. \tag{12}$$

Combining with (11) and (12) we have

$$\begin{aligned}
\sum_{i=1}^{n} -\lambda_i^{\mathrm{T}}(g_i(x) - b_i) &= x^{\mathrm{T}}\sum_{i=1}^{n} \nabla g_i(x)\lambda_i - \frac{1}{4}\sum_{i=1}^{n} \lambda_i^{(3)}x_i^2 + \sum_{i=1}^{n} \lambda_i^{\mathrm{T}}b_i \\
&= x^{\mathrm{T}}Qx + cx + a^{\mathrm{T}}\nu + \lambda^{\mathrm{T}}b^k - \frac{1}{4}\sum_{i=1}^{n} \lambda_i^{(3)}x_i^2.
\end{aligned} \tag{13}$$

Then (10) is equivalent to the following equality

$$x^{\mathrm{T}}Qx + cx + a^{\mathrm{T}}\nu + \lambda^{\mathrm{T}}b^k - \frac{1}{4}\sum_{i=1}^{n} \lambda_i^{(3)}x_i^2 = 0.$$

From the above analysis, x is an optimal solution of (5) if there exist $\lambda \in \mathbb{R}^{3n}, \lambda_i \in \mathbb{R}^3, \nu \in \mathbb{R}^m$, such that

$$0 = x^{\mathrm{T}}Qx + cx + a^{\mathrm{T}}\nu + \lambda^{\mathrm{T}}b^k - \frac{1}{4}\sum_{i=1}^{n} \lambda_i^{(3)}x_i^2 \tag{14}$$

$$g_i(x) \leq b_i, \lambda \geq 0, a = Ax.$$

For convenience, let

$$z = (x^{\mathrm{T}}, \lambda^{\mathrm{T}}, \nu^{\mathrm{T}})^{\mathrm{T}},$$

and define an appropriate energy function as follows:

$$E(z) = \sum_{i=1}^{n}((g_i(x) - b_i)^+)^2 + ((-\lambda)^+)^2$$

$$+ (x^{\mathrm{T}}Qx + cx + a^{\mathrm{T}}\nu + \lambda^{\mathrm{T}}b^k - \frac{1}{4}\sum_{i=1}^{n}\lambda_i^{(3)}x_i^2)^2 \qquad (15)$$

$$+ (Ax - a)^{\mathrm{T}}(Ax - a).$$

Lemma 2. *If x^* is an optimal solution of (5), then z^* a local minimum of $E(z)$.*

We next propose the following neural network to solve the problem (5):

$$\frac{d}{dt}z(t) = -\beta\nabla E(z(t)). \qquad (16)$$

β is a positive scaling constant.

Theorem 1. *If z^* is a local minimum of $E(z)$, then z^* is an equilibrium point of neural network (16), and the equilibrium point of (16) is stable in the sense of Lyapunov.*

Proof. Since z^* is the local solution of $E(z)$, from the necessary condition for optimality, we can get $\nabla E(z^*) = 0$. Then by using (16), $\frac{d}{dt}z(t) = 0$, z^* is an equilibrium point of (16).

By the construction of E, we have $E(z) \geq 0$,

$$\frac{d}{dt}E(z(t)) \leq \nabla E(z(t)), \dot{z}(t) \geq -\beta \parallel \nabla E(z(t)) \parallel^2 \leq 0.$$

We conclude that $E(z)$ is a Lyapunov function of the model (16) and the equilibrium point of (16) is stable in the sense of Lyapunov.

Remark 1. For any equilibrium point of (16), we can determine whether it is the maximum or minimum value by calculating the Hessian matrix of E at that equilibrium point.

3   Numerical Examples

In this section, we will give two numerical examples to illustrate our results.

Example 1. Consider the following zero-one quadratic programming problem (Table 1):

$$\begin{aligned} \min \quad & f(x) = x_1 + 2x_2 + 3x_3 \\ \text{s.t.} \quad & x_1 + x_3 = 1 \\ & x_2 + x_3 = 1 \\ & x_i \in \{0, 1\} \quad i = 1, 2, 3. \end{aligned}$$

Table 1. Relation between limit point and k

k	Limit point
$k_1 = 1$	$(4.3751, 4.6868, -1.8734)$
$k_2 = 10$	$(3.5714, 3.8421, -1.2109)$
$k_3 = 10^4$	$(1.0000, 1.0000, 0.0000)$
$k_4 = 10^6$	$(1.0000, 1.0000, 0.0000)$

$x^* = (1, 1, 0)$ is an optimal solution of this problem. Using neural network (16) to solve the related (5) of this problem with $\beta = 100$. We adopt the initial values $(x_1(0), x_2(0), x_3(0)) = (2, 5, -4)$ and different k, the limit points can be obtained as follows:

It's obvious that the equilibrium point of neural network (16) approximate the optimal solution $x^* = (1, 1, 0)$ for sufficiently large k. The transient behaviors of $x_1(t), x_2(t), x_3(t)$ with $k = 10^4$ based on neural network (16) is plotted in Fig. 1.

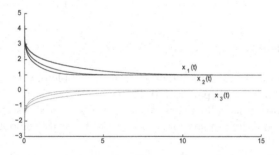

Fig. 1. The transient behaviors of $x_1(t), x_2(t), x_3(t)$ with $k = 10^4$ based on (16).

Example 2. Consider the following zero-one quadratic programming problem:

$$\min \quad f(x) = \frac{1}{2}(x_1^2 + x_2^2 + x_3^2) + 3x_1 + 2x_2 + x_3$$
$$\text{s.t.} \quad 2x_1 + x_2 = 1$$
$$x_1 + x_3 = 1$$
$$x_i \in \{0, 1\} \quad i = 1, 2, 3.$$

This problem has an optimal solution $x^* = (0, 1, 1)$. We solve the related (5) of the above problem by using the proposed neural network (16) with $\beta = 100$. We obtain the following limit points with different k and initial values $(x_1(0), x_2(0), x_3(0)) = (0, 1, 3)$.

Obviously, the equilibrium point of (16) closes to the optimal solution $x^* = (0, 1, 1)$ for sufficiently large k. Figure 2 displays the transient behaviors of the neural network with the above initial values with $k = 10^4$ (Table 2).

Table 2. Relation between limit point and k

k	Limit point
$k_1 = 1$	$(-1.6814, 4.6234, 4.4502)$
$k_2 = 10$	$(-0.9861, 3.0514, 3.1528)$
$k_3 = 10^4$	$(0.0000, 1.0000, 1.0000)$
$k_4 = 10^6$	$(0.0000, 1.0000, 1.0000)$

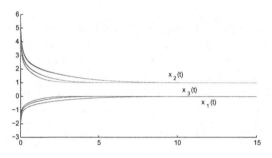

Fig. 2. The transient behaviors of $x_1(t), x_2(t), x_3(t)$ with $k = 10^4$ based on (16).

4   Conclusions

In order to solve quadratic zero-one programming problem, we proposed an artificial neural network in this paper, and discussed the stability of the equilibrium point of the proposed neural network. We obtain the related results by Lyapunov function theory, and give some numerical results to verify the obtained result.

Acknowledgments. This research is supported by the National Natural Science Foundation of China (61773136, 11471088) and the NSF project of Shandong province in China with granted No. ZR2014FM023.

References

1. Billionnet, A., Costa, M.C., Sutter, A.: An efficient algorithm for a task allocation problem. J. ACM **39**(3), 502–518 (1992)
2. Billionnet, A., Sutter, A.: Persistency in quadratic 0–1 optimization. Math. Program. **54**(1–3), 115–119 (1992)
3. Chen, J.S., Ko, C.H., Pan, S.: A neural network based on the generalized Fischer-Burmeister function for nonlinear complementarity problems. Inf. Sci. **180**, 697–711 (2010). Elsevier Science Inc.
4. Effati, S., Mansoori, A., Eshaghnezhad, M.: An efficient projection neural network for solving bilinear programming problems. Neurocomputing **168**(C), 1188–1197 (2015)
5. Feng, J., Ma, Q., Qin, S.: Exponential stability of periodic solution for impulsive memristor-based cohen-grossberg neural networks with mixed delays. Int. J. Pattern Recognit Artif Intell. **31**(7), 1750022 (2017)

6. Hoheisel, T., Kanzow, C., Schwartz, A.: Theoretical and numerical comparison of relaxation methods for mathematical programs with complementarity constraints. Math. Program. **137**(1–2), 257–288 (2013)
7. Krarup, J., Pisinger, D., Plastria, F.: Discrete location problems with push–pull objectives. Discret. Appl. Math. **123**(1), 363–378 (2002)
8. Nazemi, A.R.: A dynamic system model for solving convex nonlinear optimization problems. Commun. Nonlinear Sci. Numer. Simul. **17**(4), 1696–1705 (2012)
9. Pardalos, P.M., Rodgers, G.P.: Computational aspects of a branch and bound algorithm for quadratic zero-one programming. Computing **45**(2), 131–144 (1990)
10. Qin, S., Yang, X., Xue, X., Song, J.: A one-layer recurrent neural network for pseudoconvex optimization problems with equality and inequality constraints. IEEE Trans. Cybern. **47**(10), 3063–3074 (2017)
11. Qin, S., Xue, X.: A two-layer recurrent neural network for nonsmooth convex optimization problems. IEEE Trans. Neural Netw. Learn. Syst. **26**(6), 1149 (2015)
12. Ranjbar, M., Effati, S., Miri, S.M.: An artificial neural network for solving quadratic zero-one programming problems. Neurocomputing **235**, 192–198 (2017)
13. Sherali, H.D., Adams, W.P.: A hierarchy of relaxations between the continuous and convex hull representations for zero-one programming problems. SIAM J. Discret. Math. **3**(3), 411–430 (2006)
14. Tank, D.W., Hopfield, J.J.: Simple 'neural' optimization networks: an A/D converter, signal decision circuit, and a linear programming circuit. IEEE Trans. Circ. Syst. **33**(5), 533–541 (1986)
15. Vidyasagar, M.: Minimum-seeking properties of analog neural networks with multilinear objective functions. IEEE Trans. Autom. Control **40**(8), 1359–1375 (1995)
16. Wang, Y., Cheng, L., Hou, Z.G., Yu, J., Tan, M.: Optimal formation of multirobot systems based on a recurrent neural network. IEEE Trans. Neural Netw. Learn. Syst. **27**(2), 322–333 (2016)
17. Wu, H., Li, R., Yao, R., Zhang, X.: Weak, modified and function projective synchronization of chaotic memristive neural networks with time delays. Neurocomputing **149**(PB), 667–676 (2015)
18. Wu, H., Zhang, X., Xue, S., Wang, L., Wang, Y.: LMI conditions to global Mittag-Leffler stability of fractional-order neural networks with impulses. Neurocomputing **193**(c), 148–154 (2016)
19. Xia, Y., Wang, J.: A recurrent neural network for solving nonlinear convex programs subject to linear constraints. IEEE Trans. Neural Netw. **16**(2), 379–386 (2005)
20. Xia, Y., Wang, J.: A general projection neural network for solving monotone variational inequalities and related optimization problems. IEEE Trans. Neural Netw. **15**(2), 318–328 (2004)

A New Parameter Identification Method for Type-1 TS Fuzzy Neural Network

Tao Gao[1(✉)], Long Li[2], Zhen Zhang[3], Zhanquan Sun[4], and Jian Wang[3]

[1] College of Information and Control Engineering, China University of Petroleum, Qingdao 266580, China
gaotao_1989@126.com
[2] College of Mathematics and Statistics, Hengyang Normal University, Hengyang 421000, China
long_li1982@163.com
[3] College of Science, China University of Petroleum, Qingdao 266580, China
zhang_zhen1995@163.com, wangjiannl@upc.edu.cn
[4] Shandong Provincial Key Laboratory of Computer Networks, Shandong Computer Science Center, Jinan 250014, China
sunzhq@sdas.org

Abstract. Conjugate gradient methods can be used with advantages such as fast convergence and low memory requirement in real applications. A conjugate gradient-based neuro-fuzzy learning algorithm for zero-order Takagi-Sugeno inference systems is proposed in this paper. Compared with the existing gradient-based algorithm, this method enhances the learning performance.

Keywords: Takagi-Sugeno · Gaussian · Softmin · Conjugate gradient

1 Introduction

Corresponding to the classical back-propagation (BP) algorithm in training feed forward networks, the gradient-based supervised learning algorithm (GNF) has been widely employed to tune the parameters of neuro-fuzzy systems, whose parameter updating formula can be described as below:

$$\mathbf{w}^{k+1} = \mathbf{w}^k + \eta^k \mathbf{d}^k, \tag{1}$$

where $\mathbf{d}^k = -E_\mathbf{w}(\mathbf{w}^k)$, which denotes the negative gradient direction of error function $E(\mathbf{w})$ (see Eq. (6)), $k = 0, 1, \cdots$ and it represents the iteration epochs, $\eta^k > 0$ is the learning rate. For convenience, we write $E_\mathbf{w}^k = E_\mathbf{w}(\mathbf{w}^k)$

This work was supported in part by the National Natural Science Foundation of China (No. 61305075), the Natural Science Foundation of Shandong Province (No. ZR2015AL014, ZR201709220208) and the Fundamental Research Funds for the Central Universities (No. 15CX08011A, 18CX02036A).

© Springer International Publishing AG, part of Springer Nature 2018
T. Huang et al. (Eds.): ISNN 2018, LNCS 10878, pp. 200–207, 2018.
https://doi.org/10.1007/978-3-319-92537-0_24

Inspired by the learning algorithm, GNF, for neuro-fuzzy systems, a modification of GNF, MGNF, is proposed in [1]. To avoid the singularity, the form of the error function has been revised by considering the reciprocals of the widths of Gaussian membership functions as independent variables. Consequently, the updating formulas for the weight sequence are adjusted in a simple way. Unfortunately, it still belongs to common gradient descent method, for it calculates the descent search direction by $\mathbf{d}^k = -E_{\mathbf{w}}(\mathbf{w}^k)$. So it is with the disadvantages such as slow convergence rate, local minimum.

Conjugate gradient (CG) methods are probably the most famous iterative methods for efficiently training neuro-fuzzy system in scientific and engineering computation compared with gradient method [2]. Differ from the steepest descent search direction, $\mathbf{d}^k = -E_{\mathbf{w}}(\mathbf{w}^k)$, the search direction of conjugate gradient methods can be presented as below:

$$\mathbf{d}^k = \begin{cases} -E_{\mathbf{w}}^k, & k = 0, \\ -E_{\mathbf{w}}^k + \gamma^k \mathbf{d}^{k-1}, & k \geq 1, \end{cases} \tag{2}$$

where γ^k is defined by different formulas. Three expressions of original conjugate gradient methods, Hestenes-Stiefel (HS) [3], Fletcher-Reeves (FR) [4] and Polak-Ribière-Polyak (PRP) [5,6], are given as follows:

$$\gamma_{HS}^k = \frac{(E_{\mathbf{w}}^k)^T (E_{\mathbf{w}}^k - E_{\mathbf{w}}^{k-1})}{(\mathbf{d}^{k-1})^T (E_{\mathbf{w}}^k - E_{\mathbf{w}}^{k-1})}, \gamma_{FR}^k = \frac{\| E_{\mathbf{w}}^k \|^2}{\| E_{\mathbf{w}}^{k-1} \|^2}, \gamma_{PRP}^k = \frac{(E_{\mathbf{w}}^k)^T (E_{\mathbf{w}}^k - E_{\mathbf{w}}^{k-1})}{\| E_{\mathbf{w}}^{k-1} \|^2}, \tag{3}$$

where subscripts in Eq. (3) indicate inventors of the corresponding method, respectively. We note that the descent directions, $\mathbf{d}^k$, in the Eq. (3) satisfies $(E_{\mathbf{w}}(\mathbf{w}^k))^T \mathbf{d}^k < 0$, and the subsequent variant of three original CG methods follows this strategy. From Eq. (2), for CG method, the search direction $(\mathbf{d}^k)$ is determined by current negative gradient direction $(-E_{\mathbf{w}}^k)$ and previous iteration direction $(\mathbf{d}^{k-1})$ when $k \geq 1$. But for descent gradient method, $\mathbf{d}^k = -E_{\mathbf{w}}(\mathbf{w}^k)$, for $k \geq 1$.

In addition, in [1], the specific T-norm, product, is used. But when we use product and ignore the denominator, even for moderate number of inputs, say 25, the firing strength could be very low, although each atomic antecedent clause might be satisfied to a great extent. So this could be problematic. One way to solve this problem is to employ other T-norms such as minimum [7], but it is not differentiable, and we need differentiability of T-norm to exploit gradient based techniques. Therefore, in this paper, a softer version of minimum, softmin, is borrowed to compute the value of firing strength. The softmin function is differentiable and can deal with a large number of features [8].

In this paper, a novel neuro-fuzzy algorithm has been presented in terms of the Polak-Ribière-Polyak (PRP) conjugate gradient method (PCGNF). One numerical simulation has been performed, which demonstrates that our proposed algorithm, PCGNF, shows a better performance than MGNF.

The structure of the paper is outlined as below. We give a concise description of zero-order Takagi-Sugeno (TS) neuro-fuzzy system in Sect. 2. Section 3 shows one supporting simulation result. The concise conclusion is presented in Sect. 4.

2 Zero-Order TS Fuzzy Neural Inference System

In this section, we present the architecture of zero-order Takagi-Sugeno (TS) fuzzy neural system and describe its conjugate gradient based learning algorithm. Assume we obtain a set of training data, $\{\mathbf{x}_j, o_j\}_{j=1}^{J} \subset \mathbb{R}^m \times \mathbb{R}$, where $\mathbf{x}_j = (x_{j1}, x_{j2}, \cdots, x_{jm}) \in \mathbb{R}^m$ is the jth input sample to the network and o_j is the jth corresponding ideal output of the network. The aim of the system is to find a functional relationship, f, that maps the input to the output: $f(\mathbf{x}_j, o_j)$.

2.1 Architecture

The zero-order TS fuzzy neural system, which is realized with a four-layer network. The topological structure of the network is shown in Fig. 1. A detailed description of each layer is described herein.

The zero-order TS fuzzy neural system possesses a set of fuzzy rules of the following form:

$$\mathbf{R}_i : \mathbf{IF}\ x_{j1}\ \text{is}\ A_{i1}\ \text{and}\ x_{j2}\ \text{is}\ A_{i2}\ \text{and}\ \cdots\ \text{and}\ x_{jm}\ \text{is}\ A_{im}\,\mathbf{THEN}\ y_j\ \text{is}\ y_i,$$

where i ($i = 1, 2, \cdots, n$) denotes the ith fuzzy rule, A_{il} is a fuzzy subset of x_{jl}, which can be characterized by membership function $\mu_{A_{il}}(x_{jl})$.

Layer 1: In Layer 1, each node represents one input variable (linguistic variable). Each node in this layer just fans out its input to a set of nodes in membership layer (Layer 2), with which it is connected.

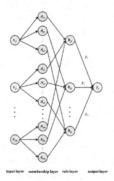

input layer   membership layer   rule layer   output layer

Fig. 1. Structure of the zero-order Takagi-Sugeno neuro-fuzzy system.

Layer 2: Each node of this layer represents a linguistic value or membership function defined on an input variable. For each feature x_{jl}, there are k_{jl} number of nodes in Layer 2, where k_{jl} is the total number of linguistic values defined on x_{jl}. Although other choices are possible, we use the Gaussian membership function in (4).

$$\mu_{A_{il}}(x_{jl}) = \exp(-(x_{jl} - a_{il})^2/\sigma_{il}^2). \tag{4}$$

Layer 3: In this layer, nodes are called rule nodes. For the ith fuzzy rule, in Layer 3, there is one node representing the antecedent of the ith rule and it computes the firing strength of the ith rule using softmin as:

$$h_{ji} = \Big(\sum_{l=1}^{m} \mu_{A_{il}}(x_{jl})e^{\beta \mu_{A_{il}}(x_{jl})}\Big) / \Big(\sum_{l=1}^{m} e^{\beta \mu_{A_{il}}(x_{jl})}\Big), \tag{5}$$

where β is a constant. Note that, $\lim\limits_{\beta \to -\infty} h_{ji}(\beta) = \min\{\mu_{A_{il}}(x_{jl})\}$.

Layer 4: It denotes the output layer, which computes the actual output, y, as follows: $y_j = \sum\limits_{i=1}^{n} h_{ji}y_i$, where y_i serves as the connection weight linking the firing strength value of the ith fuzzy rule to the output layer.

Next, we shall describe the CG based learning algorithm for zero-order TS fuzzy neural system.

2.2 PRP CG-Based Fuzzy Neural Learning Algorithm

For convenience, we write $\mathbf{a}_0 = (y_1, y_2, \cdots, y_n)$, $\mathbf{a}_i = (a_{i1}, a_{i2}, \cdots, a_{im})$, $\mathbf{b}_i = (b_{i1}, b_{i2}, \cdots, b_{im}) = (\frac{1}{\sigma_{i1}}, \frac{1}{\sigma_{i2}}, \cdots, \frac{1}{\sigma_{im}})$. To simplify the presentation, we combine $\mathbf{a}_0$, $\mathbf{a}_i$ with $\mathbf{b}_i$, and write a long weight vector: $\mathbf{w} = (\mathbf{a}_0, \mathbf{a}_1, \cdots, \mathbf{a}_n, \mathbf{b}_1, \cdots, \mathbf{b}_n) \in \mathbb{R}^{(2m+1)n}$. Let $\mathbf{h}_j = (h_{j1}, h_{j2}, \cdots, h_{jn})$, on account of $\mathbf{w}$, we define error function of the neuro-fuzzy network as below:

$$E(\mathbf{w}) = \frac{1}{2}\sum_{j=1}^{J}(y_j - o_j)^2 = \sum_{j=1}^{J} E_j(\mathbf{a}_0 \cdot \mathbf{h}_j) = \frac{1}{2}\sum_{j=1}^{J}(\mathbf{a}_0 \cdot \mathbf{h}_j - o_j)^2. \tag{6}$$

Using the notation, $b_{il} = \frac{1}{\sigma_{il}}; \sigma_{il} \neq 0$, we get $\mu_{A_{il}}(x_{jl}) = \exp(-(x_{jl}-a_{il})^2 b_{il}^2)$. Employing (5), for $q = 1, 2, \cdots, n$, we can obtain that

$$h_{jq} = \Big(\sum_{l=1}^{m} \mu_{A_{ql}}(x_{jl})e^{\beta \mu_{A_{ql}}(x_{jl})}\Big) / \Big(\sum_{l=1}^{m} e^{\beta \mu_{A_{ql}}(x_{jl})}\Big). \tag{7}$$

Based on (6) and $\mathbf{w} = (\mathbf{a}_0, \mathbf{a}_1, \cdots, \mathbf{a}_n, \mathbf{b}_1, \cdots, \mathbf{b}_n)$, we can get the gradient expression: $E_{\mathbf{w}}(\mathbf{w}) = (E_{\mathbf{a}_0}(\mathbf{w}), E_{\mathbf{a}_1}(\mathbf{w}), \cdots, E_{\mathbf{a}_n}(\mathbf{w}), E_{\mathbf{b}_1}(\mathbf{w}), \cdots, E_{\mathbf{b}_n}(\mathbf{w}))$, where $E_{\mathbf{a}_0}(\mathbf{w}) = \sum\limits_{j=1}^{J} E_j'(\mathbf{a}_0 \cdot \mathbf{h}_j)\mathbf{h}_j$. For the sake of computing the gradient $E_{\mathbf{a}_i}(\mathbf{w})$, the following expression is given

$$\frac{\partial h_{jq}}{\partial \mathbf{a}_i} = \begin{cases} 0, & \forall q \neq i, \\ 2h_{ji}((\mathbf{x}_j - \mathbf{a}_i) \odot \mathbf{b}_i \odot \mathbf{b}_i \odot \mathbf{c}_i), & \forall q = i. \end{cases} \tag{8}$$

We note the operator "$\odot$" is defined by $\mathbf{u} \odot \mathbf{v} = (u_1 v_1, u_2 v_2, \cdots, u_n v_n) \in \mathbb{R}^n$, where $\mathbf{u} = (u_1, u_2, \cdots, u_n) \in \mathbb{R}^n$, $\mathbf{v} = (v_1, v_2, \cdots, v_n) \in \mathbb{R}^n$, and

$$
\begin{aligned}
\mathbf{c}_i &= (c_{i1}, c_{i2}, \cdots, c_{im}) \\
&= \left(\frac{\mu_{A_{i1}}(x_{j1})(1 + \beta\mu_{A_{i1}}(x_{j1}))e^{\beta\mu_{A_{i1}}(x_{j1})}}{\sum\limits_{l=1}^{m} \mu_{A_{il}}(x_{jl})e^{\beta\mu_{A_{il}}(x_{jl})}} - \frac{\beta\mu_{A_{i1}}(x_{j1})e^{\beta\mu_{A_{i1}}(x_{j1})}}{\sum\limits_{l=1}^{m} e^{\beta\mu_{A_{il}}(x_{jl})}}, \right. \\
&\quad \frac{\mu_{A_{i2}}(x_{j2})(1 + \beta\mu_{A_{i2}}(x_{j2}))e^{\beta\mu_{A_{i2}}(x_{j2})}}{\sum\limits_{l=1}^{m} \mu_{A_{il}}(x_{jl})e^{\beta\mu_{A_{il}}(x_{jl})}} - \frac{\beta\mu_{A_{i2}}(x_{j2})e^{\beta\mu_{A_{i2}}(x_{j2})}}{\sum\limits_{l=1}^{m} e^{\beta\mu_{A_{il}}(x_{jl})}}, \cdots, \\
&\quad \left. \frac{\mu_{A_{im}}(x_{jm})(1 + \beta\mu_{A_{im}}(x_{jm}))e^{\beta\mu_{A_{im}}(x_{jm})}}{\sum\limits_{l=1}^{m} \mu_{A_{il}}(x_{jl})e^{\beta\mu_{A_{il}}(x_{jl})}} - \frac{\beta\mu_{A_{im}}(x_{jm})e^{\beta\mu_{A_{im}}(x_{jm})}}{\sum\limits_{l=1}^{m} e^{\beta\mu_{A_{il}}(x_{jl})}} \right). \quad (9)
\end{aligned}
$$

Using (6) and (8), the gradient, $E_{\mathbf{a}_i}(\mathbf{w})$, is written as follows

$$
\begin{aligned}
E_{\mathbf{a}_i}(\mathbf{w}) &= \sum_{j=1}^{J} E_j'(\mathbf{a}_0 \cdot \mathbf{h}_j) \left(\sum_{q=1}^{n} y_q \frac{\partial h_{jq}}{\partial \mathbf{a}_i} \right) \\
&= 2\sum_{j=1}^{J} E_j'(\mathbf{a}_0 \cdot \mathbf{h}_j) h_{ji} y_i ((\mathbf{x}_j - \mathbf{a}_i) \odot \mathbf{b}_i \odot \mathbf{b}_i \odot \mathbf{c}_i). \quad (10)
\end{aligned}
$$

Similar to $E_{\mathbf{a}_i}(\mathbf{w})$, for $1 \le i \le n$, it is easy to obtain the gradient $E_{\mathbf{b}_i}(\mathbf{w})$:

$$
E_{\mathbf{b}_i}(\mathbf{w}) = -2\sum_{j=1}^{J} E_j'(\mathbf{a}_0 \cdot \mathbf{h}_j) h_{ji} y_i ((\mathbf{x}_j - \mathbf{a}_i) \odot (\mathbf{x}_j - \mathbf{a}_i) \odot \mathbf{b}_i \odot \mathbf{c}_i). \quad (11)
$$

Beginning with the initial weight value $\mathbf{w}^0$, the weight vector $\mathbf{w}$ is updated iteratively by PRP conjugate gradient method:

$$
\mathbf{w}^{k+1} = \mathbf{w}^k + \eta\mathbf{d}^k, \mathbf{d}^k = -E_{\mathbf{w}}^k + \gamma^k \mathbf{d}^{k-1}, \ k \in \mathbb{N}, \quad (12)
$$

where $\mathbf{d}^{-1} = 0$, η is the positive step size during training process, and

$$
\gamma^k = \begin{cases} 0, & k = 0, \\ \frac{(E_{\mathbf{w}}^k)^T (E_{\mathbf{w}}^k - E_{\mathbf{w}}^{k-1})}{\|E_{\mathbf{w}}^{k-1}\|^2}, & k \ge 1. \end{cases} \quad (13)
$$

In the next section, we present the performance of CG TS system on Auto MPG Regression Data Set.

3 Results

3.1 Initialization of the Network

Before discussing our results, we explain how the fuzzy neural system will be initialized. To initialize the neuro-fuzzy network we first find a set of crude fuzzy rules using clustering as in [10] and use it to obtain the initial network. To understand the procedure let us consider an example with two inputs and one output.

Suppose $\mathbf{X} = \{\mathbf{x}_1, \mathbf{x}_2 \cdots \mathbf{x}_J\}$, where $\mathbf{x}_j \in \mathbb{R}^2$, $\mathbf{Y} = \{o_1, o_2 \cdots o_J\}$, where $o_j \in \mathbb{R}$, let $\mathbf{X}^* = \{\mathbf{x}_1^*, \mathbf{x}_2^* \cdots \mathbf{x}_J^*\}$, where $\mathbf{x}_j^* = (\mathbf{x}_j \; o_j) \in \mathbb{R}^3$. Suppose we cluster $\mathbf{X}^*$ by the K-means algorithm producing a set of centroids. Let $\mathbf{v}_i^*$ $(i = 1, 2, \cdots, n)$ be the centroids of the clusters obtained by the K-means [9] on $\mathbf{X}^*$, where $\mathbf{v}_i^* = (\mathbf{v}_i^x \; \mathbf{v}_i^o) \in \mathbb{R}^3$. The ith cluster can be translated into a TS rule [11]: $\mathbf{R}_i$: **IF x is CLOSE** to $\mathbf{v}_i^x$ then $y = \mathbf{u}_i(\mathbf{x}, \mathbf{v}_i^o)$. Note that, "**x is CLOSE** to $\mathbf{v}_i^x$ " is an antecedent clause with 2 components in this example. For a better interpretability of a fuzzy rule, we can rewrite the fuzzy rule as follows: $\mathbf{R}_i$: **IF** x_1 **is CLOSE** to v_{i1}^x **and** x_2 **is CLOSE** to v_{i2}^x then $y = \mathbf{u}_i(\mathbf{x}, \mathbf{v}_i^o)$. We emphasize that although the two forms are equivalent, they are not equal always. Since $o \in \mathbb{R}$, $\mathbf{R}_i$ can be viewed as one rule [10]. If we assume TS model of 0th order, then the rule $\mathbf{R}_i$ can be rewritten as follows: $\mathbf{R}_i$: **IF** x_1 **is** A_{1i} **and** x_2 **is** A_{2i} **THEN** y **is** y_i, where $\mathbf{R}_i$ can be viewed as one rule, for $o_j \in \mathbb{R}$.

So the ith cluster will be represented by two nodes in Layer 2 of the network: (i) one corresponding to x_1 is CLOSE to v_{i1}^x and this node will be connected to the input layer node corresponding to x_1; and (ii) the other node representing x_2 is CLOSE to v_{i2}^x and this node will be connected to the input layer node for x_2. These two nodes in Layer 2 will be connected to one node in Layer 3. Similarly, for each of the clusters, we have to add nodes in Layer 2 and Layer 3.

In addition, we note that, the parameter β in (7) is set to -50 for all our experiments. We also compare the performance of PCGNF with MGNF using the commonly used average square error: $D = \frac{1}{J} \sum_{j=1}^{J} (y_j - o_j)^2$.

3.2   Numerical Example

This is a more complex real world data set, called auto MPG, on city-cycle fuel consumption. The auto MPG dataset was retrieved from the UCI machine learning repository at http://archive.ics.uci.edu/ml/datasets/Auto+MPG. The data contains 392 samples, and every sample is with seven input features and one output feature. In this simulation, the network is trained by using randomly chosen 196 samples and the remaining 196 samples constitute the testing set.

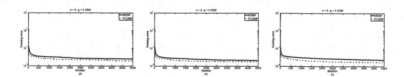

Fig. 2. Average training error for different η when $n = 6$ (the number of rules).

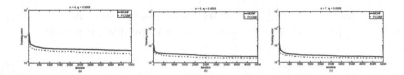

Fig. 3. Average training error for different n (the number of rules) when $\eta = 0.0008$.

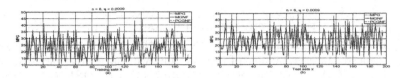

Fig. 4. The training and test regression results for auto MPG data when $n = 6, \eta = 0.0009$.

Two experiments are done: one to show the effect of the learning rate, and the other to show the effect of the number of fuzzy rules. Seven trials are carried out for the both learning algorithms.

Table 1. Example results for identifying auto MPG data set when $n = 6$ (the number of fuzzy rules).

Learning rate	Learning algorithms	Numbers of epochs	Average error of training sets	Average error of test sets
$\eta = 0.0006$	MGNF	5,000	0.0256	0.0286
$\eta = 0.0006$	PCGNF	5,000	0.0191	0.0235
$\eta = 0.0008$	MGNF	5,000	0.0210	0.0273
$\eta = 0.0008$	PCGNF	5,000	0.0177	0.0258
$\eta = 0.0009$	MGNF	5,000	0.0230	0.0258
$\eta = 0.0009$	PCGNF	5,000	0.0170	0.0229

Table 1 summarizes the results with different learning coefficients while Table 2 shows the summary of performance with different number of rules. From Tables 1 and 2, it is easy to visualize that the performance of PCGNF is consistently better than MGNF for all cases. Figs. 2 and 3 provide pictorial representation of the test results for some typical runs of the two algorithms.

In Fig. 4, we display, a typical approximation result for the auto MPG data (for $n = 6$, $\eta = 0.0009$). From these figures we find that both methods perform almost equally well, at least visually.

Table 2. Example results for identifying auto MPG data set when $\eta = 0.0008$.

Numbers of rules	Learning algorithms	Numbers of epochs	Average error of training sets	Average error of test sets
$n = 4$	MGNF	5,000	0.0298	0.0312
$n = 4$	PCGNF	5,000	0.0228	0.0279
$n = 6$	MGNF	5,000	0.0235	0.0274
$n = 6$	PCGNF	5,000	0.0186	0.0253
$n = 7$	MGNF	5,000	0.0213	0.0267
$n = 7$	PCGNF	5,000	0.0175	0.0262

4   Conclusion

A PRP conjugate gradient-based algorithm (PCGNF) is proposed to train a neuro-fuzzy network model in this paper. Based on a real function approximation type problem, using the zero-order Takagi-Sugeno fuzzy neural system, we have demonstrated that PCGNF indeed preforms better than MGNF.

References

1. Wu, W., Li, L., Yang, J., Liu, Y.: A modified gradient-based neuro-fuzzy learning algorithm and its convergence. Inf. Sci. **180**, 1630–1642 (2010)
2. Wang, J., Wu, W., Zurada, J.M.: Deterministic convergence of conjugate gradient method for feedforward neural networks. Neurocomputing **74**, 2368–2376 (2011)
3. Hestenes, M.R., Stiefel, E.L.: Method of Conjugate Gradients for Solving Linear Systems. National Bureau of Standards, Washington (1952)
4. Fletcher, R., Reeves, C.M.: Function minimization by conjugate gradients. Comput. J. **7**, 149–154 (1964)
5. Polak, E., Ribiere, G.: Note sur la convergence de directions conjugates. Revue Fran. d'Info. et de Rech. Oper. **16**, 94–112 (1969)
6. Polyak, B.T.: The conjugate gradient method in extremal problems. USSR Comput. Math. Math. Phys. **9**, 94–112 (1969)
7. Ghosh, A., Pal, N.R., Das, J.: A fuzzy rule based approach to cloud cover estimation. Remote Sens. Environ. **100**, 531–549 (2006)
8. Chen, Y.C., Pal, N.R., Chung, I.F.: An integrated mechanism for feature selection and fuzzy rule extraction for classification. IEEE Trans. Fuzzy Syst. **20**, 683–698 (2012)
9. Bezdek, J.C., Keller, J., Krishnapuram, P., Pal, N.R.: Fuzzy Models and Algorithms for Pattern Recognition and Image Processing. Kluwer, Norwell (1999)
10. Pal, N.R., Eluri, V.K., Mandal, G.K.: Fuzzy logic approaches to structure preserving dimensionality reduction. IEEE Trans. Fuzzy Syst. **10**, 277–286 (2002)
11. Takagi, T., Sugeno, M.: Fuzzy identification of systems and its application to modeling and control. IEEE Trans. Syst. Man Cybern. **SMC-15**, 116–132 (1985)

Performance Enhancement of Deep Reinforcement Learning Networks Using Feature Extraction

Joaquin Ollero$^{(\boxtimes)}$ and Christopher Child$^{(\boxtimes)}$

City, University of London, London, UK
joaquinollerogarcia@gmail.com, C.Child@city.ac.uk

Abstract. The combination of Deep Learning and Reinforcement Learning, termed Deep Reinforcement Learning Networks (DRLN), offers the possibility of using a Deep Learning Neural Network to produce an approximate Reinforcement Learning value table that allows extraction of features from neurons in the hidden layers of the network. This paper presents a two stage technique for training a DRLN on features extracted from a DRLN trained on a identical problem, via the implementation of the Q-Learning algorithm, using TensorFlow. The results show that the extraction of features from the hidden layers of the Deep Q-Network improves the learning process of the agent (4.58 times faster and better) and proves the existence of encoded information about the environment which can be used to select the best action. The research contributes preliminary work in an ongoing research project in modeling features extracted from DRLNs.

Keywords: Reinforcement Learning · Neural Networks
Deep Learning · Feature extraction · TensorFlow

1 Introduction

Deep Learning is a class of Machine Learning algorithms based on learning data representations based on Artificial Neural Networks (ANN). By using an architecture such as a Deep Neural Network [1], it is possible to extract information from neurons placed in the hidden layers of the network that automatically encode valuable features from the raw data used as inputs. Reinforcement Learning algorithms, as opposed to supervised and unsupervised learning, present a mechanism to train an artificial agent in the learning process of how to solve a specific problem. Overall, a Reinforcement Learning algorithm maps every state/action combination within a given environment to a specific value. This value will inform the agent how good or bad taking each action is in relation to the next state that the agent will experience straight afterwards. Q-Learning is a popular Reinforcement Learning technique, used to produce optimal selections of actions for any Markov Decision Process [2]. Reinforcement Learning using Deep Learning Neural Networks is currently receiving intense media attention. There

© Springer International Publishing AG, part of Springer Nature 2018
T. Huang et al. (Eds.): ISNN 2018, LNCS 10878, pp. 208–218, 2018.
https://doi.org/10.1007/978-3-319-92537-0_25

is growing interest in this area of artificial intelligence since [3] introduced Deep Q-Networks (DQNs) and the research was published in the multidisciplinary scientific journal Nature. The presented work proved that the proposed model achieved a higher level of expertise than that of a professional human game player in a set of 49 Atari 2600 games [4]. The field of Machine Learning is evolving rapidly in terms of revolutionary applications and groundbreaking research that is leading the area to tremendous popularity. Along with this, open source tools that allow scientists to experiment with algorithms and structures are becoming more accessible and straightforward to learn and use. One of the Machine Learning libraries that is experiencing the biggest growth is TensorFlow [5], an open-source software library for Machine Intelligence developed by Google.

The objective of this paper is the training of a DRLN on features extracted from an DRLN trained to solve a similar problem with the Q-Learning algorithm. Emphasis have been given to the detailed study of this structure by extracting features from its hidden layers in order to use them in an environment modelling algorithm. The state space can be reduced by predicting the future states of these features and using this as a model, replacing the original environment. The system will model features extracted from an initial level of a Deep Neural Network, using them as inputs of a reduced Deep Neural Network (in terms of number of layers) to prove that the information of the inputs is automatically encoded and preserved and can be used to increase the speed of learning of the agent. Performing feature extraction from a later level of a Deep Neural Network will allow the system to classify the codifications and verify if they can be used to predict future states of the features.

The rest of the paper is structured as follows. A literature review that covers research on Deep Reinforcement Learning Networks is presented in the next section. The problem statement, the Q-Learning algorithm and the structures in which the technique is implemented, a Deep Q-Network and a Deep Q-Network using Feature Extraction, are presented on Sect. 3. Results, introduced on Sect. 4, are stated in terms of testing the behaviour of the agent and if the overall learning process is improved in terms of time. A thorough analysis of the model, overall considerations and a set of extensions that would improve and contribute to the research are discussed in the last section of this paper.

2 Context

The renaissance of Reinforcement Learning is largely due to the emergence of Deep Q-Networks [3]. The Deep-Q Network framework [3] was motivated due to the limitations of Reinforcement Learning agents when solving real-world complex problems, because they must obtain efficient representations from the inputs and use these to relate past experiences to the next situations the agent will be presented with. The developed framework, a combination of Reinforcement Learning with Deep Neural Networks, was able to effectively learn policies directly from the inputs. More precisely, the agent was tested on 49 classic Atari 2600 games [4], receiving only the pixels of the image and the game score as inputs, performing with a level comparable to the one of a professional human player. The research introduced the first intelligent agent that was able to learn how to solve a set of different tasks with groundbreaking results.

Several extensions have been proposed to the work presented in [3]. The adaptation of the Deep Q-Network framework using the Double Q-Learning algorithm has reduced observed overestimations [6]. By prioritizing experience replay, a technique that lets the agent review important transitions more frequently, the learning process of the agent can be improved in terms of efficiency [7]. In contrast to architectures such as Convolutional Neural Networks or Autoencoders, a new structure, termed Dueling Network Architecture, was introduced to prove the generalization of learning across actions without performing any change to the Reinforcement Learning algorithm [8]. All these works have produced agents that perform better in the Atari 2600 games domain in comparison with the original Deep Q-Network. Finally, the original authors of Deep Q-Networks [3], introduced four different asynchronous methods for Reinforcement Learning: one-step Q-Learning, one-step Sarsa, n-step Q-Learning and advantage actor-critic [9]. Advantage actor-critic was the algorithm that performed best overall.

In an early stage of combining Reinforcement Learning with neural networks, TD-Gammon [10] showed that an agent could learn how to play the board game Backgammon by playing against itself and learning from the results it was obtaining while playing. AlphaGo, a computer program that plays the game of Go, defeated the European Go champion by 5 games to 0 on a full-sized 19×19 board, becoming the first computer program to defeat a human professional player in this game [11]. Later, AlphaGo Zero achieved superhuman performance, mastering Go without human knowledge [12]. DeepMind researchers have recently produced further groundbreaking results. For example, a research has taught digital creatures to learn how to navigate across complex environments [13]. StarCraft II is a highly technical real-time strategy video game released in 2010. Blizzard Entertainment, the company that developed the video game, and DeepMind have published a joint paper that presents the StarCraft II Learning Environment, a challenging environment for testing Deep Reinforcement Learning algorithms and architectures on this game [14]. Another work poses the task for an agent to push boxes onto red target squares to successfully complete a level [15]. The challenge for the agent is that some actions might lead to irreversible mistakes resulting in the level being impossible to complete. The agent uses imagination, which is a routine to choose not only one action, but entire plans consisting of several steps to ultimately select the one that has best expected reward.

"Inceptionism" [16] and "DeepDream" [17] proved that after training a Deep Neural Network with a high number of related images and adjusting the network parameters, each layer progressively contains higher-level features of the image, until reaching the output layer, that ultimately makes a decision on what the image shows. Therefore, it was proven that the first hidden layers of a Deep Neural Network trained under these circumstances, contained low-order features, such as edges or corners. Then, the intermediate hidden layers contained information about simple shapes, such as doors or leaves and the last hidden layers put together this information to form complete figures such as buildings or trees.

3   Methods

A structured set of methods will be followed to undertake this research. First, the problem to solve and the environment in which the agent will operate will be defined. The cornerstone of the research is the Reinforcement Learning algorithm that will teach the agent how to learn over time the specifics of the environment: the states, actions and reward values. Specifically, the Q-Learning technique will be implemented using a Deep Neural Network, a structure that will ultimately allow the feature extraction to occur. Features are going to be extracted from the initial level of the Deep Q-Network with the objective of improving the overall learning process of the agent and from the later level of the Deep Q-Network to predict which actions will lead to the next best states.

The Deep Reinforcement Learning Networks and the Q-Learning algorithm have been implemented using the programming language Python 3.5 and have been built using TensorFlow 1.2 [5], an open-source software library for Machine Intelligence. The project has been developed using the Python API of Tensor-Flow with CPU support.

3.1   Problem Statement and Environment

The agent must learn how to solve a pathfinding problem, which is to find the shortest route between two states. It will start in an initial state and its objective will be to learn over time how to arrive at a goal state (+1 reward) with the addition of learning how to avoid a set of states ("holes", −1 reward) that are present in the environment. In order to represent this pathfinding problem, an environment composed by a set of states, actions and rewards in relation to the states is defined. The description of the environment used throughout the implementation is a 4 × 4 matrix composed by the letters 'A' to 'P' in alphabetical order, inspired by the Frozen Lake environment [18]. To complete the environment definition, the initial, goal and hole states are designated (Fig. 1). Given this environment, a 16 × 4 matrix (R) that contains, every state, the next state resulting in taking all of the available actions (move up, down, right or left) is automatically generated.

Fig. 1. Environment. Initial state: 'A', goal state: 'P' and hole states: 'F', 'H', 'L', 'M'.

3.2   Q-Learning

The Q-Learning algorithm [19] works by learning an action-value function that ultimately gives the expected utility of taking a given action in a given state and consequently following the optimal policy thereafter. The agent will have a maximum of 2000 episodes to learn how to find the shortest path from the initial to the goal state, and in each of these episodes it will have 99 steps to move through the environment in search of the goal and to continuously adjust the values for the weights of the Deep Neural Network. An episode will end if the agent consumes all the steps or if it reaches the goal state. It starts by picking one action from the state it is in at the moment. This action will be either the best one as calculated until that moment or a random one. This decision is taken based on a ϵ-greedy policy ($\epsilon = 0.1$), which keeps a balance between exploration (taking random actions) and exploitation (taking best actions at that moment) in the discovery process of the environment. Once the action has been selected, using the R matrix, the next state that the agent will be in is extracted along with its related reward (neutral, positive or negative). Using the next state, the Q-values associated with that state are generated by feeding the state through the whole neural network. Therefore, it is possible to calculate the maximum Q-value that will be used in the fundamental Q-Learning formula, computed by the multiplication of the discount factor (γ) times the maximum Q-value plus the reward (Eq. 1). Overall, for each state, the value that has been reinforced the most, corresponding to the best action, is chosen in order to determine the next state that the agent will be in. The algorithm will ultimately replace all the random initialized values of the weights and these will represent the minimum path from any state to the goal state.

$$Q(s, a) = r + \gamma(max(Q(s', a'))). \tag{1}$$

3.3   Deep Q-Network and Feature Extraction

The Deep Q-Network takes every state encoded in a unique 1×16 vector, and produces a vector of 4 values in its output layer, one for each action. In order to have a Deep Neural Network, it is necessary to include hidden layers between the input and output layers. In relation to the number of inputs and outputs and to have a representative number of hidden layers, a first hidden layer with 12 neurons was added, connected to a second hidden layer composed by 8 neurons, which is finally connected to the last hidden layer composed by 2 neurons ($2^2 = 4$, the number of total actions) (Fig. 2).

The method of updating the values of the weights of the Deep Neural Network will be achieved by using backpropagation and a loss function. The loss function is defined as the sum-of-squares loss, where the difference between the output and the predicted output is computed. In this case, the target Q-value for the chosen action is the equivalent to the new Q-value computed in the Q-Learning algorithm. Finally, the agent is trained, using the target and predicted Q-values, with a gradient descent optimizer in order to minimize the loss. With a Deep Neural Network the information is propagated through the weights of the whole network.

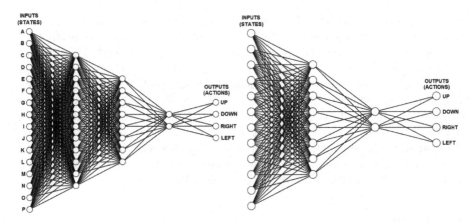

Fig. 2. The DQN with 12 input neurons (right) will be trained using as inputs features extracted from the first hidden layer of the DQN with 16 input neurons (left).

The parameters used to configure the neural network are the following. Learning rate $(\alpha) = 0.05$, discount factor $(\gamma) = 0.99$, the hyperbolic tangent (tanh) activation function for hidden and output neurons, the $\sum((Y - Ypredicted)^2)$ loss function and the gradient descent optimizer. The weights of the Deep Q-Network are initialized randomly to normalize the variance of the output of each neuron to 1. This is achieved by scaling its weight vector by the square root of the number of inputs $(\sim \bigcup[-1/\sqrt{numStates}, 1/\sqrt{numStates}])$, where $\bigcup[-a, a]$ is the uniform distribution in the interval $(-a, a)$ and numStates is the number of inputs of the algorithm [20]. The biases are initially set to 0, because the symmetry between hidden units of the same layer is broken by initializing the weights randomly in the indicated range.

Features can be extracted from the neurons of the hidden layers of a Deep Neural Network trained with a Reinforcement Learning algorithm. A neuron is considered activated if its activation value is greater than 0, and not activated if its activation value is less than 0. More precisely, features are going to be extracted from the first hidden layer of the $16 \times 12 \times 8 \times 2 \times 4$ Deep Q-Network, by having each available state encoded in a 1×12 vector, to be used as inputs for a different $12 \times 8 \times 2 \times 4$ Deep Q-Network (Fig. 2). Features extracted from the last hidden layer of these two Deep Q-Networks, and encoded in 1×2 vectors, are going to be used to demonstrate that these codifications can be used to predict the best action to take in each state.

4   Results

This research was approached using a number of discrete steps. First, a testing phase was undertaken to demonstrate that the trained agent was capable of learning how to behave in the proposed environment. This was achieved by checking whether the agent reaches the goal state in an optimum number of steps from each state. Parallelly, the training time, the accumulated reward over time, the first episode in which the agent receives a reward equal to 1 and the average number of steps per episode were also obtained. These values define the performance of the agent in a specific training process and are used to make observations about the behaviour of the agent following the Q-Learning algorithm in the different Deep Q-Networks. Lastly, by using features extracted from the last hidden layer of a specific Deep Q-Network, we demonstrate that these can be used to predict the best actions to take from each state to reach the goal state. 30 different and independent experiments were run on a MSI GE63VR 7RE Raider laptop (Windows 10 Home 64 bits, Intel Core i7-7700HQ CPU @ 2.80 GHz, 16.0 GB RAM, GeForce GTX 1060).

4.1   Testing

The experiments demonstrated that the agent was able to find the shortest path from any state to the goal state without traversing through a hole. Because the Q-Learning algorithm does not end an episode if the agent enters a hole state, these states have related values that can lead the agent to the goal state. The agent has great difficulty to find the goal state from either states 'D' and 'H'. This occurs because these two states are not on the optimal path to the goal state from any state and when exploring the environment, the agent usually does not reach states that are slightly further apart. The Deep Q-Networks that uses features extracted from the original Deep Q-Network as inputs shows marginally better results in finding the optimum path from each starting square (Fig. 3).

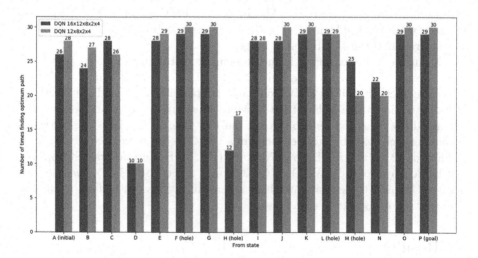

Fig. 3. Number of times that the agent finds an optimum path from each state of the environment to the goal state without entering a hole state.

4.2   Performance

The performance of the agent is tested on both Deep Q-Networks, with the objective of concluding in which one the agent performs the best. The results show that training an agent in the $16 \times 12 \times 8 \times 2 \times 4$ Deep Q-Network takes an average training time of 66.73 s, with an accumulated reward of -0.09%, that it will receive its first reward equal to 1 in the episode 570, and that it takes 47.93 steps per episode on average. On the other hand, it can be seen that the training process of the agent on the $12 \times 8 \times 2 \times 4$ Deep Q-Network is considerably improved by using as inputs features extracted from the first hidden layer of the original Deep Q-Network. In this case, the average training time is 26.06 s, the accumulated reward over time is 0.63%, the episode in which it first receives a reward equal to 1 is 117 and that it only takes 16.36 steps per episode to reach the goal state for each episode on average. The performance of the agent using the $12 \times 8 \times 2 \times 4$ Deep Q-Network against using the original Deep Q-Network is 2.56 times faster in terms of training time, 8 times better regarding the accumulated reward over time, 4.87 times faster on finding the first episode with reward equal to 1, and 2.92 times better on the average number of steps it consumes per episode (Fig. 4). Overall, the agent using $12 \times 8 \times 2 \times 4$ Deep Q-Network performs 4.58 times faster and better than using the $16 \times 12 \times 8 \times 2 \times 4$ Deep Q-Network.

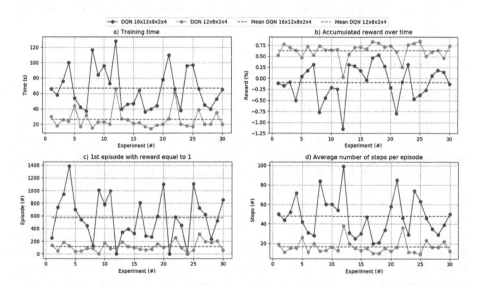

Fig. 4. Comparison of the performance of the agent between using $16 \times 12 \times 8 \times 2 \times 4$ DQN and the $12 \times 8 \times 2 \times 4$ DQN trained on features extracted from the original DQN.

4.3   Prediction of Next States

After training both Deep Q-Networks (Fig. 2) on every experiment, features are extracted from the last hidden layers using the activation of neurons. These features, encoded in 1×2 vectors, contain information regarding the best action to take from each state, so they can be used to predict the best state/action combinations without accessing the values contained in the output layers of both Deep Neural Networks. The $16 \times 12 \times 8 \times 2 \times 4$ Deep Q-Network has been able to predict the best actions to take from each state 13.33% of times, while the $12 \times 8 \times 2 \times 4$ Deep Q-Network has achieved correct predictions 3.33% of times. This is due to several factors. For a prediction to be succesful it is fundamental that the training process has firstly been succesful and that from every state, the agent is capable of reaching the goal state in an optimum number of steps (from Fig. 3, at maximum 10 times, the number of times that optimum paths were effectively calculated from 'D'). In addition, the activation threshold is established on 0 and it has been observed that this threshold is sometimes displaced by a factor of $-0.15/+0.15$ from 0. Due to the training process, the activation values for the neurons are not always centered exactly on 0 because the hyperbolic tangent function is not a step function. When a prediction is correct, different groups of states will share the same codification indicating that all the states that belong to a group will take the same action in order to reach the goal state in an optimum set of steps. This demonstrates that the extracted features can be used to make predictions about the future states in which the agent will be in.

5   Conclusions

This work has presented an analysis of DRLNs focused primarily on the features that are automatically encoded in the hidden layers of this type of neural network. To achieve this, an environment to be discovered by an intelligent agent has been defined and the Q-Learning algorithm has been implemented using a Deep Q-Network. 30 experiments have been run in order to test if the agent is able to solve an established pathfinding problem within the defined environment and to compare the effectiveness of the different Deep Q-Networks. The research has produced two results: features extracted from the initial stage of a Deep Q-Network can be used in a different Deep Q-Network in order to improve the performance of an intelligent agent by a factor of 4.58 on average (Fig. 4). And secondly, features extracted from the later stage of a Deep Q-Network contain information regarding the best action to take from a specific state. We have also shown that the information of the states is lost in later levels of the neural network, as the information regarding the states is transformed into decisions about which taken actions will lead to the best next states.

This research could be improved with the implementation of various extensions. First, to determine if the initialization of the weights of the Deep Q-Network and the activation functions and thresholds used are the optimal ones. Second, to implement a decaying ϵ-greedy policy, which would improve the way the agent discovers the environment. Third, to define a metric that would measure how long does it takes to learn the optimal policy. Fourth, to test the agent in different environments. Fifth, to obtain an optimal topology for a Deep Q-Network by consecutively extracting features from the first hidden layers of successive Deep Q-Networks. Lastly, to obtain a model built from a table of features and actions to features and rewards then to unseen states. As it stands, the model cannot work without the original environment, as it is only possible to extract rewards by relating them to the states.

References

1. Hinton, G.E., Salakhutdinov, R.R.: Reducing the dimensionality of data with neural networks. Science **313**(5786), 504–507 (2006)
2. Bellman, R.: A Markovian decision process. J. Math. Mech. **6**, 679–684 (1957)
3. Mnih, V., Kavukcuoglu, K., Silver, D., Rusu, A.A., Veness, J., Bellemare, M.G., Graves, A., Riedmiller, M., Fidjeland, A.K., Ostrovski, G., et al.: Human-level control through deep reinforcement learning. Nature **518**(7540), 529–533 (2015)
4. Bellemare, M.G., Naddaf, Y., Veness, J., Bowling, M.: The arcade learning environment: an evaluation platform for general agents. J. Artif. Intell. Res. **47**, 253–279 (2012)
5. Abadi, M., Agarwal, A., Barham, P., Brevdo, E., Chen, Z., Citro, C., Corrado, G.S., Davis, A., Dean, J., Devin, M., et al.: Tensorflow: large-scale machine learning on heterogeneous distributed systems. arXiv preprint arXiv:1603.04467 (2016)
6. Van Hasselt, H., Guez, A., Silver, D.: Deep reinforcement learning with double q-learning. In: AAAI, pp. 2094–2100 (2016)
7. Schaul, T., Quan, J., Antonoglou, I., Silver, D.: Prioritized experience replay. In: International Conference on Learning Representations (ICLR) (2016)
8. Wang, Z., Schaul, T., Hessel, M., van Hasselt, H., Lanctot, M., de Freitas, N.: Dueling network architectures for deep reinforcement learning. arXiv preprint arXiv:1511.06581 (2015)
9. Mnih, V., Badia, A.P., Mirza, M., Graves, A., Lillicrap, T.P., Harley, T., Silver, D., Kavukcuoglu, K.: Asynchronous methods for deep reinforcement learning. In: International Conference on Machine Learning (2016)
10. Tesauro, G.: TD-Gammon, a self-teaching backgammon program, achieves master-level play. Neural Comput. **6**(2), 215–219 (1994)
11. Silver, D., Huang, A., Maddison, C.J., Guez, A., Sifre, L., Van Den Driessche, G., Schrittwieser, J., Antonoglou, I., Panneershelvam, V., Lanctot, M., et al.: Mastering the game of go with deep neural networks and tree search. Nature **529**(7587), 484–489 (2016)
12. Silver, D., Schrittwieser, J., Simonyan, K., Antonoglou, I., Huang, A., Guez, A., Hubert, T., Baker, L., Lai, M., Bolton, A., et al.: Mastering the game of go without human knowledge. Nature **550**(7676), 354 (2017)
13. Heess, N., Sriram, S., Lemmon, J., Merel, J., Wayne, G., Tassa, Y., Erez, T., Wang, Z., Eslami, A., Riedmiller, M., et al.: Emergence of locomotion behaviours in rich environments. arXiv preprint arXiv:1707.02286 (2017)
14. Vinyals, O., Ewalds, T., Bartunov, S., Georgiev, P., Vezhnevets, A.S., Yeo, M., Makhzani, A., Küttler, H., Agapiou, J., Schrittwieser, J., et al.: Starcraft II: a new challenge for reinforcement learning. arXiv preprint arXiv:1708.04782 (2017)

15. Weber, T., Racanière, S., Reichert, D.P., Buesing, L., Guez, A., Rezende, D.J., Badia, A.P., Vinyals, O., Heess, N., Li, Y., et al.: Imagination-augmented agents for deep reinforcement learning. arXiv preprint arXiv:1707.06203 (2017)
16. Mordvintsev, A., Olah, C., Tyka, M.: Inceptionism: going deeper into neural networks. Google Research Blog, p. 14, Retrieved 20 June 2015
17. Mordvintsev, A., Olah, C., Tyka, M.: DeepDream - a code example for visualizing neural networks. Google Research (2015)
18. Brockman, G., Cheung, V., Pettersson, L., Schneider, J., Schulman, J., Tang, J., Zaremba, W.: OpenAI gym. arXiv preprint arXiv:1606.01540 (2016)
19. Watkins, C.J., Dayan, P.: Q-learning. Mach. Learn. 8(3–4), 279–292 (1992)
20. Glorot, X., Bengio, Y.: Understanding the difficulty of training deep feedforward neural networks. In: Proceedings of 13th International Conference on Artificial Intelligence and Statistics, pp. 249–256 (2010)

Clustering, Classification, Learning, and Forecasting

Online GRNN-Based Ensembles
for Regression on Evolving Data Streams

Piotr Duda[1(✉)], Maciej Jaworski[1], and Leszek Rutkowski[1,2]

[1] Institute of Computational Intelligence, Czestochowa University of Technology,
Al. Armii Krajowej 36, 42-200 Czestochowa, Poland
`piotr.duda@iisi.pcz.pl`
[2] Information Technology Institute, Academy of Social Sciences, 90-113 Łódź, Poland

Abstract. In this paper, a novel procedure for regression analysis in
the case of non-stationary data streams is presented. Despite numerous
applications, the regression task is rarely considered in a scientific literature, e.g. compared to classification task. The proposed method applies
an ensemble technique to deal with data streams (especially with concept
drift). As weak learners, a nonparametric estimator of regression is used.
Every single weak model (weak learner) is able to track a specific type
of the non-stationarity. The experimental section demonstrates that the
proposed algorithm allows for tracking different types nonstationarities
and increases accuracy with respect to a single estimator.

Keywords: Regression analysis · Ensemble methods · Data streams

1 Introduction

One of the most important tasks in the field of machine learning is regression
analysis [5]. The regression estimators are applied to find a relationship between
dependent and independent variables, to predict future values of random variables [1] or to interpolation tasks. Applications of those techniques are daily used
in the financial market, in weather forecasting, in security systems, etc. Current
development of the big data analysis and spreading of the internet of things,
highlighted the new challenges for regression analysis. In particular, one of the
most important tasks is a regression analysis in a time-varying environment.

Parametric methods are the widely quoted techniques, see e.g. [2], however,
they require a priori knowledge to find an optimal model and to satisfy its many
assumptions. The other techniques, allowing tracking more general relationships,
are called nonparametric methods [6]. The problem of non-stationary regression
can be formalized in the following way. Let us assume that we obtain a pair of
data (X_i, Y_i), where X_i, Y_i are related to independent and dependent variables,
respectively. We assume that both random variables are continuous and they
depend on each other as follows

$$Y_i = m_i(X_i) + Z_i \qquad i = 1, 2, \ldots,$$

(1)

© Springer International Publishing AG, part of Springer Nature 2018
T. Huang et al. (Eds.): ISNN 2018, LNCS 10878, pp. 221–228, 2018.
https://doi.org/10.1007/978-3-319-92537-0_26

where $\{m_i(\cdot)\}_{i \in \mathbf{N}}$ is a sequence of functions, and Z_i is a measurement error. In a stationary case all the functions $m_i(\cdot)$ are identical. In the non-stationary case, our task is not only to find the best estimation of the function for a certain number of data but also to track its changes. Contrary to the parametric methods we do not assume in advance any shape of the functions $m_i(\cdot)$.

One of the most promising research areas in big data analysis in the non-stationary environment is known in the literature under the name Stream Data Mining (SDM). A properly designed SDM algorithm has to fulfill the following criteria [16]:

- the data cannot be stored and considered as a whole. The data elements should be analysed as fast as it is possible, and the memory should be released for a newly coming data,
- the processing time should be as limited as it is possible, as the number of the new coming data can be arbitrarily large,
- the distribution of the data can change during processing of the stream. Such event is called a concept-drift and it can occur in every moment. The algorithm should be able to adjust to time-varying environment.

Intuitively the types of the non-stationary can be seen as one of the following cases or as their combinations:

i. the abrupt changes - this type is related to the case when the probability density function of generated data changes suddenly from one pattern to the another,
ii. the incremental changes - this type is related to the case when the probability density function of generated data is changing permanently in some specific manner, e.g. the data are generated from a normal distribution with fixed standard deviation, but expected value increases by some fixed value with every new data element,
iii. the gradual changes - this type occurs when one state (probability distribution of data) is replaced by the other state by the gradual disappearance of data generated by the first one in favor of the second one,
iv. the reoccurring changes - we say about this case when data are generated by a few different states, which can exchange in an undetermined manner.

The illustration of the aforementioned types can be seen in Fig. 1. It is also worth to mention that the performance of classifiers depends both on a distribution of the feature variables and distribution of the target variable. If the changes occur

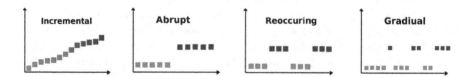

Fig. 1. Different types of concept-drift.

only in the feature variables, such change is called virtual. If decision boundaries or fraction of classes are non-stationary, then such change is called real.

One of the most promising approaches which can handle various stream data problems are ensemble methods, see e.g. [14]. However, as the authors of the up-to-date survey on the ensemble methods for data streams emphasized [13]: "Many ensemble methods can be found in the literature for solving classification tasks on streams, but only a few exist for regression tasks".

To address this problem we decided to propose a novel method for regression analysis in a time-varying environment. The method creates an ensemble of the regression estimators based on the chunks of data. Each component of the ensemble, which is an asymptotically convergent estimator developed in our recent paper [4], is responsible for tracking a specific concept drift.

The rest of the paper is organized as follows. In Sect. 2 a short description of regression analysis methods for data streams is presented. Section 3 introduces in details the proposed algorithm. The applied type of the weak learner, studied by us in [4], is recalled in a Subsect. 3.1 and the general scheme of a new ensemble algorithm is given in Subsect. 3.2. The experimental results are provided in Sect. 4 and finally the conclusions are presented in Sect. 5.

2   Related Works

In [17] the author explained how to apply the bagging and boosting mechanisms to deal with a non-stationary data stream. The paper presented the online versions of this mechanism. The proposed method can be applied both to classification and regression tasks. In [12] is proposed an algorithm where each component of the ensemble has its own weight. The prediction was made as a weighted average of the weak learners outputs. The weights of the component are multiplied by a factor dependent on the obtained error. In [11] two-phase adaption of the model to the changing environment is proposed. The first phase allows for an adaptation of the local model. The second one adapts the weights of the ensemble. The ensemble of the regression trees was proposed in [7]. The leaves of the tree are incorporated in linear regression models. The application of the option trees is presented in [8]. The application of the Hoeffding-based regression trees in studied in [9]. Moreover, that paper analyses application of the random forest. In paper [3] a streaming rule learning algorithm for regression problem, called Adaptive Model Rules algorithm (AMRules), is proposed. The AMRules algorithm uses the Page-Hinkley test to react to the changes in the environment. The Gaussian process approximation scheme for on-line regression is presented in [18]. The authors reduced the computational demand of the Gaussian Process regression by updating only some selecting subset of the initial base model. The subset is selected by optimization of a submodular function. In [4] the properties of the General Regression Neural Network to tracking different types of non-stationarity are studied. The paper presents various types of non-stationarities that can be tracked by a proposed procedure. The application of sliding windows and forgetting mechanism is considered in [10].

3   The E-GRNN Algorithm

The proposed algorithm applies an ensemble technique to deal with non-stationary data streams. As weak learners, a nonparametric estimator of regression, developed in our previous paper [4], is implemented. In the next subsections, the description of the weak learner will be recalled and the general procedure will be presented.

3.1   Weak Learner

The Incremental General Regression Neural Network $IGRNN$ algorithm, proposed in our previous paper [4], is applied as a weak learner. The method is a type of the General Regression Neural Network based on the so-called Parzen kernels [15]. The scheme of the weak learner ϕ^n is described by the following incremental formulas

$$\hat{f}_n(x) = \hat{f}_{n-1}(x) + \frac{1}{n}\left[K'_n(x, X_n) - \hat{f}_{n-1}(x)\right] \tag{2}$$

$$\hat{R}_n(x) = \hat{R}_{n-1}(x) + a_n\left[Y_n K_n(x, X_n) - \hat{R}_{n-1}(x)\right], \tag{3}$$

$$\phi^n(x) = \frac{\hat{R}_n(x)}{\hat{f}_n(x)} \tag{4}$$

where $K_n(\cdot, \cdot)$ and $K'_n(\cdot, \cdot)$ are the so-called Parzen kernels [6] and a_n is a learning rate.

The $IGRNN$ algorithm allows tracking changes in a model only if they occur to a limited extent. In particular, if the character of the changes can be defined as an incremental, the $IGRNN$ will track changes only if they do not exceed a certain degree of changes, e.g. if $|m_i(x)| = O(i^\alpha)$ then α should be less than $1/3$, see [4]. If the type of non-stationarity would change, the $IGRNN$ algorithm cannot adjust automatically.

3.2   The General Procedure

To fulfill this gap we propose a novel algorithm called Ensemble General Regression Neural Network $E\text{-}GRNN$ which combines the $IGRNN$ algorithm with the ensemble approach. The general scheme of the proposed procedure is depicted in Fig. 2.

At the beginning, a new ensemble component (called model in scheme 2) is initialized with the parameters fixed by the user. In particular, the user has to determine the value of the learning rate a_i and chunk size N. Next, until the whole chunk would not be filled, the first component is updated (according to (2) and (3)) and the residuals are computed. When the chunk reaches its maximum size, the grade of usability of the weak model $\phi^t(x)$ (component of the ensemble) is computed according to the following formula

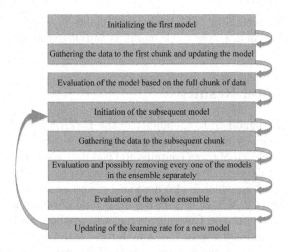

Fig. 2. General scheme of the proposed procedure.

$$FVU^t = \frac{\sum\limits_{i=1}^{n} \left(Y_i - \phi_i^t(X_i)\right)^2}{\sum\limits_{i=1}^{n} \left(\overline{Y} - Y_i\right)^2},$$
(5)

where $\phi_i^t(X_i)$ is a prediction of the t-th component in the step i and $\overline{Y}$ is a mean of the all dependent values from the gathered chunk. The obtained grades are stored in memory. Contrary to the parametric model, the FVU^t does not have to be in the interval $[0, 1]$. However, still, its low value indicates better fits of the estimator. Next, a new chunk and a new component are initialized. When new data are coming to the system, every component of the ensemble is updated. When the chunk will be filled, every component is evaluated according to (5). If differences between its current and previous values exceed some threshold, then such a component is rejected. In another case, the stored grades FVU^t of the models are replaced. The next step is an evaluation of the whole ensemble. Based on an independent variable, the target variable is indicated as a weighted sum of the outputs of every single component. The weights are determined based on the previously obtained grades, according to the formula

$$\hat{m}_i(X_i) = \frac{\sum\limits_{j=1}^{E} \phi_i^j(X_i) \cdot (FVU^j)^{-1}}{\sum\limits_{j=1}^{E} (FVU^j)^{-1}},$$
(6)

where E is a number of components in the ensemble. The evaluation of the ensemble is made analogously to the single component (ϕ_i^t should be replaced by $\hat{m}_i$). Based on the obtained value, a subsequent weak model is initialized with increased or decreased learning rate. The higher value of a_i ensures faster convergence of the estimator. The lower value makes it enable to track a wider range of changes. Then a new weak model is initialized and the procedure is repeated.

4   Experimental Results

In this section, we demonstrate the ability of the E-$GRNN$ algorithm to adjust to a non-stationary environment. For this purpose, we will use three different training sets, where each of them contains $100'000$ data elements. The size of the chunk was set to 1250 elements. The proposed procedure will be compared with the $IGRNN$ algorithm, which is also used as a weak learner in an ensemble. The application of the $IGRNN$ algorithm requires some parameters defined by the user. In each simulation, the Gaussian kernel was applied, and the parameters related to kernel bandwidth were the same for the estimators (2) and (3).

In the first experiment, we demonstrate fit of the model in the case of incremental concept drift. The X_i value (independent variable) were randomly generated from the uniform distribution in the interval $(0, 6)$. The value of Y_i was obtained as a sum of the following function

$$m_i(x) = i^{0.1} 2 \sin(x + 2) \cos(2x - 3), \tag{7}$$

and the noise (Z_i) randomly generated from the normal distribution with expected value equal to 0 and standard deviation equal to 2. The initial learning rate is set to $a_i = i^{-0.69}$ and the kernel bandwidth $h_i = 2i^{-0.4}$. The exact meaning of the parameters is explained in [4]. To evaluate the fit of the models, values of FVU^t were compared for every chunk of data. The obtained results are depicted in Fig. 3. The red and blue lines show obtained values for the E-$IGRNN$ and single $IGRNN$ algorithms, respectively.

One can see that both algorithms demonstrate similar results, and the models improve the accuracies. It is worth to mention that assumed value of parameters ensures convergence with the probability of the $IGRNN$ algorithm, for details see [4].

The second experiment demonstrates fit of the regression in the case of abrupt concept drift. The synthetic data were generated analogous to the first experiment, except that the dependent variable meets the following model

$$m_i(x) = \begin{cases} 2 \sin(x + 2) \cos(2x - 3), & \text{if } i > 50'000, \\ 5 \arctan(x^2), & \text{otherwise.} \end{cases} \tag{8}$$

In this case, the data represents the stationary model until $50'000$-th data element, when the sudden change of the model occurred. The learning rate is set to $a_i = i^{-0.9}$ and the kernel bandwidth is set to $h_i = 2i^{-0.5}$. The obtained FVU^t are depicted in Fig. 4.

The presented result demonstrates that the ensemble gives better results for the stationary case. Similar trends in FVU^t changes indicate that one component plays a key role in the ensemble.

To show possibility of an application to the case of gradual concept drift, function (8) was replaced by the following one

$$m_i(x) = \begin{cases} 2\sin(x+2)\cos(2x-3), & \text{with probability } \frac{i}{100000}, \\ 5\arctan(x^2), & \text{with probability } 1 - \frac{i}{100000}. \end{cases} \qquad (9)$$

The dependent values are generated from two different models. The data from the first one appear very rarely at the beginning of the stream. Next the frequencies of their appearance increases. To get results depicted in Fig. 5 the learning rate was set to $a_i = i^{-0.75}$ and the kernel bandwidth is set to $h_i = i^{-0.6}$.

The E-$GRNN$ presents significantly better results. One can also see that the variance of FVU^t seems to be lower in this case.

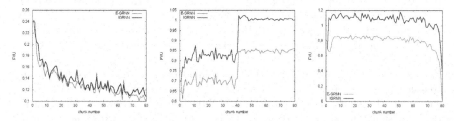

Fig. 3. The FVU in the case of incremental concept drift for the subsequent chunks (Color figure online)

Fig. 4. The FVU^t in the case of abrupt concept drift for the subsequent chunks

Fig. 5. The FVU^t in the case of gradual concept drift for the subsequent chunks

5 Conclusions

In this paper we presented the E-$GRNN$ algorithm, to deal with non-stationary data. The algorithm creates the ensemble of the non-parametric regression models. The proposed procedure is able to track the incremental drift, adjust the model to a new environment after abrupt drift and maintain various models in the case of gradual drift. The algorithm can react both to real and virtual concept drifts. The simulation result shows that the proper choice of the parameters allows for a significant improvement of the obtained accuracy with respect to a single, convergent in probability, estimator. In the future work, an attempt should be made to automatization of the choice of the parameters. Combining the proposed procedure with sliding windows and drift detection methods will be also a very interesting issue which can provide satisfactory results.

Acknowledgments. This work was supported by the Polish National Science Centre under Grant No. 2014/15/B/ST7/05264.

References

1. Akdeniz, E., Egrioglu, E., Bas, E., Yolcu, U.: An ARMA type Pi-Sigma artificial neural network for nonlinear time series forecasting. J. Artif. Intell. Soft Comput. Res. **8**(2), 121–132 (2018)
2. Chatterjee, S., Hadi, A.S.: Regression Analysis by Example. Wiley, Hoboken (2015)
3. Duarte, J., Gama, J., Bifet, A.: Adaptive model rules from high-speed data streams. ACM Trans. Knowl. Discov. Data (TKDD) **10**(3), 30 (2016)
4. Duda, P., Jaworski, M., Rutkowski, L.: Int. J. Neural Syst. **28**, 1750048 [23 pages] (2018). https://doi.org/10.1142/S0129065717500484
5. Fox, J.: Applied Regression Analysis and Generalized Linear Models. Sage Publications, Thousand Oaks (2015)
6. Greblicki, W., Pawlak, M.: Nonparametric System Identification, vol. 1. Cambridge University Press, Cambridge (2008)
7. Ikonomovska, E., Gama, J., Dzeroski, S.: Learning model trees from evolving data streams. Data Min. Knowl. Disc. **23**(1), 128–168 (2011)
8. Ikonomovska, E., et al.: Speeding-up Hoeffding-based regression trees with options. In: Proceedings of 28th International Conference on Machine Learning. Omnipress (2011)
9. Ikonomovska, E., Gama, J., Dzeroski, S.: Online tree-based ensembles and option trees for regression on evolving data streams. Neurocomputing **150**, 458–470 (2015)
10. Jaworski, M., Duda, P., Rutkowski, L., Najgebauer, P., Pawlak, M.: Heuristic regression function estimation methods for data streams with concept drift. In: Rutkowski, L., Korytkowski, M., Scherer, R., Tadeusiewicz, R., Zadeh, L.A., Zurada, J.M. (eds.) ICAISC 2017. LNCS (LNAI), vol. 10246, pp. 726–737. Springer, Cham (2017). https://doi.org/10.1007/978-3-319-59060-8_65
11. Kadlec, P., Gabrys, B.: Local learning based adaptive soft sensor for catalyst activation prediction. AIChE J. **57**(5), 1288–1301 (2011)
12. Kolter, J.Z., Maloof, M.A.: Using additive expert ensembles to cope with concept drift. In: Proceedings of 22nd International Conference on Machine Learning. ACM (2005)
13. Krawczyk, B., et al.: Ensemble learning for data stream analysis: a survey. Inf. Fusion **37**, 132–156 (2017)
14. Pietruczuk, L., Rutkowski, L., Jaworski, M., Duda, P.: How to adjust an ensemble size in stream data mining? Inf. Sci. **381**, 46–54 (2017)
15. Specht, D.F.: A general regression neural network. IEEE Trans. Neural Netw. **2**(6), 568–576 (1991)
16. Susheela, D.V., Meena, L.: Parallel MCNN (PMCNN) with application to prototype selection on large and streaming data. J. Artif. Intell. Soft Comput. Res. **7**(3), 155–169 (2017)
17. Oza, N.C.: Online bagging and boosting. In: IEEE International Conference on Systems, Man and Cybernetics, vol. 3, pp. 2340–2345. IEEE (2005)
18. Xiao, H., Eckert, C.: Lazy Gaussian process committee for real-time online regression. In: AAAI (2013)

A Broad Neural Network Structure
for Class Incremental Learning

Wenzhang Liu[1], Haiqin Yang[2], Yuewen Sun[1], and Changyin Sun[1(✉)]

[1] School of Automation, Southeast University, Nanjing 210096, China
{wzliu,amber_sun,cysun}@seu.edu.cn
[2] Department of Computing, Hang Seng Management College, Shatin, Hong Kong
hqyang@ieee.org

Abstract. Class Incremental Learning, learning concepts over time, is
a promising research topic. Due to unknowing the number of output
classes, researchers have to develop different methods to model new
classes while preserving pre-trained performance. However, they will
meet the catastrophic forgetting problem. That is, the performance will
be deteriorated when updating the pre-trained model using new class
data without including old data. Hence, in this paper, we propose a novel
learning framework, namely Broad Class Incremental Learning System
(BCILS) to tackle the above issue. The BCILS updates the model when
there are training data from unknown classes by using the deduced iterative formula. This is different from most of the existing fine-tuning
based class incremental learning algorithms. The advantages of the proposed approach including (1) easy to model; (2) flexible structure; (3)
pre-trained performance preserved well. Finally, we conduct extensive
experiments to demonstrate the superiority of the proposed BCILS.

Keywords: Class incremental learning · Neural network
Broad learning · Catastrophic forgetting

1 Introduction

Reflecting the human growing experience, it is obviously that the learning process is progressive because it is impossible to get all the data at one-time to
train our brain. For instance, a child can learn various animals like dolphins,
seals in aquarium without forgetting the tigers, lions saw before in a zoo, and
he will also preserve the existing knowledge to learn more other new species in
future. The child never knew how many categories to learn, so he learns them
incrementally. For most existing machine learning systems, they can only learn
from the data in known classes at one-time, thus are lack of the incremental
learning ability like the child. In most practical cases, the labeled data cannot
be obtained at one-time, and it would also be inefficient if a learning system
does not work until all the labeled training data being collected. To address this
issue, it is important to develop a more practical machine learning algorithm
which learns the concepts incrementally.

© Springer International Publishing AG, part of Springer Nature 2018
T. Huang et al. (Eds.): ISNN 2018, LNCS 10878, pp. 229–238, 2018.
https://doi.org/10.1007/978-3-319-92537-0_27

This learning strategy is called class incremental learning [1,2] or continual learning [3], whose learning process is dynamic and progressive along with the data stream in various classes being input (See Fig. 1). There are three principles when training an incremental classifier: (i) The model should be updated without catastrophic forgetting [4,5]; (ii) There should be no re-training process; (iii) The additional learning process is not time-consuming. These three principles coincide with human learning process well, however, are not provided with most existing machine learning algorithms.

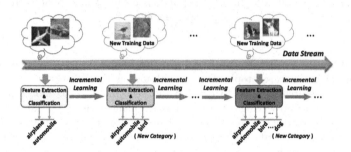

Fig. 1. Illustration of class incremental learning system.

In recent decades, machine learning algorithms, especially deep learning technologies, have made significant progress. Although deep neural networks [7] play an important role in many artificial applications nowadays, most of them, like deep Boltzmann machine (DBM) [8], VGG-Net [10], residual networks (ResNet) [11], etc., are hard to satisfy those three principles mentioned above in class incremental learning scenario, hence limit their application in practice. For mitigating catastrophic forgetting problem, relevant researchers consider metric learning for new instances [14], which need much computation of the metric between instances for large volume of input data. Some other researchers consider adding knowledge distillation loss functions for novel classes and fine-tuning the network [1,17], or using fisher information matrix to preserve the pre-trained performance [19], etc. These technologies try to find the optimal parameters nearby that of pre-trained model, and therefore are easy to convergence on local minimum when more unseen classes are input.

In this paper, we apply the broad learning system [12] to class incremental learning, namely Broad Class Incremental Learning System (BCILS). The broad learning system (BLS) is extended from random vector functional-link neural networks (RVFLNN) [13]. The BLS is flexible since it extends the topological structure in the horizontal level. The BLS is more efficient to train than traditional deep learning models because it does not need to back propagate the errors to each layer. Most notably, the BLS is more applicable in some real-time systems and successive learning processes, because the optimal solution can be found using an appropriate iterative method or a closed-form solution. Back to class incremental learning, once there comes new class, an additional output node is added and then only an iterative formula is needed for model updating. Due to unknowing the number of classes, fixed model structure like deep neural network, is hard to adapt new classes while the flexible BCILS is not.

Some important work about class incremental learning and broad learning system will be presented in Sect. 2. Then we introduce the progressive learning algorithm (BCILS) minutely in Sect. 3, including BLS and BCILS. To express the performance of our algorithm, experiment results on MNIST dataset are showed in Sect. 4. Finally, we conclude in Sect. 5.

2 Related Work

The BCILS is built on broad learning system [12]. This learning system can mitigate the catastrophic forgetting well for class incremental learning. In this section, we first introduce some relevant research in the literature about class incremental learning. Then some recent work on BLS is explained.

2.1 Class Incremental Learning

As described in Sect. 1, most of the existing machine learning algorithms suffer catastrophic forgetting [4,5], which has been existing along with the development of the artificial intelligence. As to classification, existing classifiers like multi-layer perceptron (MLP), support vector machine (SVM), deep neural network (DNN), etc. cannot address the catastrophic forgetting well directly for class incremental learning.

In recent years, there are several researches about class incremental learning with mitigated catastrophic forgetting. Mensink *et al.* proposed a class incremental learning system based on metric leaning approach in [14]. They explored two techniques: nearest class mean classifier (NCM) and k-NN classifier, to implement their approach. Ristin *et al.* introduced a random forests where the decision nodes are designed based on nearest class mean (NCM) classification [16]. These approaches will be computed costly when the samples are high-dimensional and non-linear, and therefore the computation of the distance between samples is time-consuming. Kuzborskij *et al.* addressed this issue based on a Least-Square Support Vector Machine (LSSVM) formulation in [15]. For additional class, they modified the objective function of conventional SVM. To achieve the performance on both target $(N+1)$-th class and previous N classes, they used distance-based regularizers.

In [17], Li *et al.* used feature extraction and fine-tuning adaption techniques in Convolutional Neural Network with cross entropy and knowledge distillation loss. And Triki *et al.* proposed autoencoders based lifelong learning system in a similar formulation [18]. But these methods are easy to fall into the local minimum point and the performance would decline along with the continuous input of new training data. For mitigating catastrophic forgetting, [1] considered preserving some old data under a memory size constraint. They built an iCaRL learning system based on the Nearest Class Mean (NCM) classification and fine-tuning the CNN with both cross entropy loss and distillation loss for representation updating. However, their incremental algorithm has to reselect the exemplars dynamically because of the memory limitation and therefore is time-consuming. Kirkpatrick *et al.* represented their recent work on mitigating catastrophic forgetting in neural networks using elastic weight consolidation (EWC) [19]. They indicated that the solution for new task could be found near the solution of old task in a Bayesian update formulation. In addition, the Fisher information matrix was used to update the model, and thus will be time-consuming when the architecture of neural networks is complex.

2.2   Broad Learning System

Recently, Chen *et al.* proposed an efficient and effective incremental learning system, called broad learning system (BLS), without the need for deep architecture [12]. This learning strategy can update the architecture of the neural networks dynamically whenever new data stream is input. Its learning structure was built on the random vector functional-link neural networks (RVFLNN) [13], and the original topological structure is showed in Fig. 2.

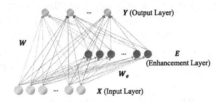

Fig. 2. The random vector functional-link neural network (RVFLNN)

As shown in Fig. 2, RVFLNN initializes the weights from input layer (X) to enhancement layer (E) randomly and only the pseudo-inverse of the input matrix $[X; E]$ needs to be calculated to find the optimal solution for the network, which is similar to Extreme Learning Machine (ELM) [6]. This results in the fast training and testing processes of the neural network and can be very efficient in embedded learning system like robot. Although the RVFLNN can speed up the learning rate and promote the performance by adding the enhancement nodes significantly, it can't work well on big, time-series data because of its limited capacity and static structure. In [20], Chen *et al.* proposed a dynamic stepwise updating algorithm and applied it on time-series prediction. The proposed algorithm in [20] is able to incrementally deal with new training data in seen classes easily by the deduced iterative formulas, which is different from ELM [6].

As for broad learning system (BLS) [12], Chen *et al.* extend their neural network based on [20] and made it more flexible to train. Thanks for the incremental learning essence of BLS, we find it is possible to update the pre-trained model using new class data without performance reducing, and therefore can mitigate the catastrophic forgetting. Details of our work will be introduced in Sect. 3.

3   Proposed Algorithm

In this section, we first introduce the details of the BLS in Sect. 3.1, then the proposed BCILS will be introduced in Sect. 3.2.

3.1   Broad Learning System (BLS)

The BLS consists of feature map layer, enhancement layer and ouput layer. Unlike traditional RVFLNN, the BLS first maps the raw data to construct a set of mapped features (feature map layer, see Fig. 3) [12].

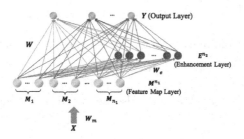

Fig. 3. The broad neural network

Let $\boldsymbol{X} \in \mathbb{R}^{d \times N}$ denotes the raw input set, $\boldsymbol{X} = [\boldsymbol{x}^{(1)}, \boldsymbol{x}^{(2)}, \ldots, \boldsymbol{x}^{(N)}]$, d is the dimension of $\boldsymbol{x}^{(i)}$ and N is the cardinality of $\boldsymbol{X}$. We first generate the feature map layer, $\boldsymbol{M}^{n_1} = [\boldsymbol{M}_1; \ldots; \boldsymbol{M}_{n_1}]$, where $\boldsymbol{M}_i = \phi_i(\boldsymbol{W}_{m_i}\boldsymbol{X} + \boldsymbol{\beta}_{m_i})$, $i = 1, \ldots, n_1$, ϕ_i is an activation function (sigmoid, Tanh, etc.). $\boldsymbol{W}_{m_i}, \boldsymbol{\beta}_{m_i}$ are weights and bias generated randomly, one can also use sparse coding method for generating these nodes. Then we create the enhancement layer using feature map nodes with random weights, $\boldsymbol{E}^{n_2} = [\boldsymbol{E}_1; \ldots; \boldsymbol{E}_{n_2}]$, where $\boldsymbol{E}_i = \varphi_i(\boldsymbol{W}_{e_i}\boldsymbol{M}^{n_1} + \boldsymbol{\beta}_{e_i})$, $i = 1, \ldots, n_2$, φ_i is an activation function (Sigmoid, Tanh, etc.) too. $\boldsymbol{W}_{e_i}, \boldsymbol{\beta}_{e_i}$ are weights and bias generated randomly [12].

As we finish the generation of the two layers, let $\boldsymbol{A} = [\boldsymbol{M}^{n_1}; \boldsymbol{E}^{n_2}]$, and $\boldsymbol{Y} = [\boldsymbol{y}^{(1)}, \ldots, \boldsymbol{y}^{(N)}]$ is the label matrix. Then the objective function could be

$$\min_{\boldsymbol{W}} ||\boldsymbol{W}\boldsymbol{A} - \boldsymbol{Y}||_p^2 + \lambda ||\boldsymbol{W}||_p^2, \tag{1}$$

where $|| \cdot ||_p$ denotes the p-norm, λ is the regularization coefficient, $\boldsymbol{W}$ is the weights should be solved and by taking $p = 2$, $\boldsymbol{W} = \boldsymbol{Y}\boldsymbol{A}^\dagger$, where $\boldsymbol{A}^\dagger = \lim_{\lambda \to 0}(\lambda \boldsymbol{I} + \boldsymbol{A}\boldsymbol{A}^T)^{-1}\boldsymbol{A}^T$. Unlike deep neural networks, this broad neural network (as showed in Fig. 3) promotes its performance by adding feature map nodes and enhancement nodes dynamically rather than stacking the hidden layers [12].

Taking enhancement layer as an example, let $\boldsymbol{E}_{n_2+1} = \varphi(\boldsymbol{W}_{e_{n_2+1}}\boldsymbol{M}^{n_1} + \boldsymbol{\beta}_{e_{n_2+1}})$ be the added nodes, where $\boldsymbol{W}_{e_{n_2+1}}$ and $\boldsymbol{\beta}_{e_{n_2+1}}$ are new parameters generated randomly. In this case, let $\boldsymbol{A}^n = [\boldsymbol{M}^{n_1}; \boldsymbol{E}^{n_2}]$, then $\boldsymbol{A}^{n+1} = [\boldsymbol{A}^n; \boldsymbol{E}_{n_2+1}]$, and the new object function would be

$$\min_{W} ||WA^{n+1} - Y||_p^2 + \lambda ||W||_p^2. \tag{2}$$

Then $W^{n+1} = Y(A^{n+1})^\dagger$ will be the new solution. Notice that A^{n+1} contains A^n, and the $(A^n)^\dagger$ has been calculated before, we have

$$(A^{n+1})^\dagger = \left[(A^n)^\dagger - BD^T, B \right], \tag{3}$$

where $D^T = E_{n_2+1}(A^n)^\dagger$, let $C = E_{n_2+1} - D^T A^n$, then

$$B = \begin{cases} C^\dagger & \text{if } C \neq O, \\ (A^n)^\dagger D(I + D^T D)^{-1} & \text{if } C = O. \end{cases} \tag{4}$$

The O in Eq. (4) is zero matrix. Then the new weights can be deduced as

$$W^{n+1} = Y \left[(A^n)^\dagger - BD^T, B \right] = \left[W^n - YBD^T, YB \right]. \tag{5}$$

The nodes in feature map layer can also be added in a same way (see Fig. 4) [12].

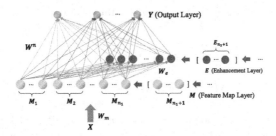

Fig. 4. The node incremental learning strategy of broad neural network

3.2   Broad Class Incremental Learning Approach

The BLS introduced above can also learn new data in seen classes incrementally. This is practical in real-time learning like robot system [12]. In this paper, we study how does it train new instances in unseen classes incrementally. In this case, let $X^{new} = [x^{(N+1)}, \ldots, x^{(N+L)}]$ denotes the new data set contains L instances and each of them belongs to $(K+1)$-th class, which is unseen before. As is showed in Fig. 5, for each unseen class, a new node in output layer is needed.

Firstly, we calculate the feature map layer for X^{new} in $(K+1)$-th class as $(M^{n_1})^{new} = [M_1^{new}; \ldots; M_{n_1}^{new}]$, where $M_i^{new} = \phi_i(W_{m_i} X^{new} + \beta_{m_i})$, $i = 1, \ldots, n_1$. As to enhancement layer, $(E^{n_2})^{new} = [E_1^{new}; \ldots; E_{n_2}^{new}]$, where $\boldsymbol{E}_i^{new} = \varphi_i(\boldsymbol{W}_{e_i}(\boldsymbol{M}^{n_1})^{new} + \boldsymbol{\beta}_{e_i})$, for $i = 1,\ldots,n_2$. Then $\boldsymbol{A}^{new} = [(\boldsymbol{M}^{n_1})^{new}; (\boldsymbol{E}^{n_2})^{new}]$. Let $\boldsymbol{A}^n$ denotes the input matrix of current neural network, $\boldsymbol{A}^{new}$ is the additional input matrix, then the new input matrix of the incremental neural network is $\boldsymbol{A}^{n+1} = [\boldsymbol{A}^n, \boldsymbol{A}^{new}]$. Beside that, the new output matrix $\boldsymbol{Y}^{n+1}$ should be reconstructed as

$$\boldsymbol{Y}^{n+1} = \begin{bmatrix} \boldsymbol{Y}^n & \boldsymbol{O}_{K \times L} \\ \boldsymbol{O}_{1 \times N} & \boldsymbol{1}_{1 \times L} \end{bmatrix}. \tag{6}$$

Thus, we get the new objective function,

$$\min_{W} ||\boldsymbol{W}\boldsymbol{A}^{n+1} - \boldsymbol{Y}^{n+1}||_p^2 + \lambda ||\boldsymbol{W}||_p^2, \tag{7}$$

and the new solution is $\boldsymbol{W}^{n+1} = \boldsymbol{Y}^{n+1}(\boldsymbol{A}^{n+1})^{\dagger}$.

We can also deduce the $(\boldsymbol{A}^{n+1})^{\dagger}$ as

$$(\boldsymbol{A}^{n+1})^{\dagger} = [(\boldsymbol{A}^n)^{\dagger} - \boldsymbol{D}\boldsymbol{B}^T; \boldsymbol{B}^T], \tag{8}$$

where $\boldsymbol{D} = (\boldsymbol{A}^n)^{\dagger}\boldsymbol{A}^{new}$. Let $\boldsymbol{C} = \boldsymbol{A}^{new} - \boldsymbol{A}^n \boldsymbol{D}$, then

$$\boldsymbol{B}^T = \begin{cases} \boldsymbol{C}^{\dagger} & \text{if } \boldsymbol{C} \neq \boldsymbol{O}, \\ (\boldsymbol{I} + \boldsymbol{D}^T\boldsymbol{D})^{-1}\boldsymbol{D}^T(\boldsymbol{A}^n)^{\dagger} & \text{if } \boldsymbol{C} = \boldsymbol{O}. \end{cases} \tag{9}$$

and

$$\boldsymbol{W}^{n+1} = [\boldsymbol{W}^n(\boldsymbol{I} - \boldsymbol{A}^{new}\boldsymbol{B}^T); \boldsymbol{1}_{1 \times L} \cdot \boldsymbol{B}^T]. \tag{10}$$

From Eq. (10), we find there is no need to retrain the neural network for new incoming data with unseen class labels, and the performance can be maintained because the important information for seen classes was preserved in matrix $\boldsymbol{B}$, thus the catastrophic forgetting was mitigated.

In summary, Eq. (10) are the key iterative formulas for class incremental learning. As introduced in Sects. 3.1 and 3.2, the flexible BCILS is easy to model with mitigated catastrophic forgetting, and therefore is more practical.

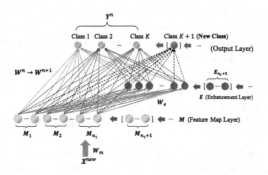

Fig. 5. The broad neural network for class incremental learning

4   Experiment

In this section, experiment results on MNIST dataset show the performance of the proposed algorithm, we compared our method with NCM [14] and iCaRL [1].

The MNIST handwritten digit dataset contains 60,000 training and 10,000 testing instances [9] and each of them is a grayscale image with 28 × 28 pixels (Fig. 6(a)). As introduced in Sect. 3.1, we first input the raw image data and map them into feature map layer using sparse coding, and continually map the feature map layer into enhancement layer with random weights. Then, we concatenate both feature map layer and enhancement layer as input matrix for broad neural network, and calculate the solution of the classification problem of Eq. (1). In our experiment setting for BCILS (Fig. 6(b)), we first model the BLS for two classes, then update this pre-trained BLS on the third class using Eq. (10), and next the fourth, etc. To analyze how the performance of BCILS influenced by the number of nodes in two layers (feature map layer and enhancement layer), we set different number of feature map nodes and enhancement nodes. The experiment results are showed in Fig. 7.

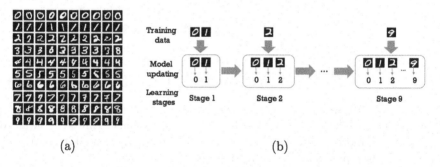

(a)   (b)

Fig. 6. The illustration of the experiments: (a) The MNIST dataset; (b) The experiment setting of our BCILS on MNIST dataset.

As showed in Figs. 7(a) and (b), one can get better performance along with the increasing of feature map nodes and enhancement nodes. However, we can also find that the speed of performance increase will get slower and slower. The best performance is achieved when there's 900 feature map nodes for fixed enhancement layer (Fig. 7(a)) and 4500 enhancement nodes for fixed feature map layer (Fig. 7(b)) respectively. Considering the trade-off between learning accuracy and computational cost, it is found that (900, 4500) nodes for feature map layer and enhancement layer respectively can get almost best performance on MNIST dataset.

Furthermore, we have compared our method with existing class incremental learning algorithms, they are Nearest Class Mean (NCM) [14] and iCaRL [1] in Fig. 7(c). The NCM can add new class mean easily but it is a metric

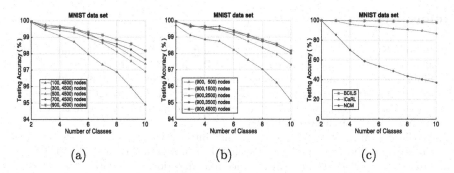

Fig. 7. Experiment results: (a) different number of feature map nodes with enhancement layer fixed; (b) different number of enhancement nodes with feature map layer fixed; (c) comparison results of different methods.

based method, so is hard to solve non-Gaussian distributed data. As to iCaRL, although some old data is preserved for feature representation, it can't mitigate catastrophic forgetting thoroughly because it uses NCM based classification but lacks the guarantee of Gaussian distributed features. Unlike to those methods, the reasons for the great performance of BCILS are listed as follows:

- BCILS is very easy to model, and there is no need to stack a deep architecture, hence is more controllable than deep neural networks;
- The width of BCILS is very easy to change, so its structure is more flexible for unseen classes than that of other neural networks;
- Important information for pre-trained BCILS is preserved for class incremental learning, hence the catastrophic forgetting is mitigated well, which is a key difference from existing class incremental learning methods.

Additionally, the experiment result in Fig. 7(c) shows that the BCILS performs best and hence demonstrates our inference.

5 Conclusion

The proposed BCILS is built on broad learning system (BLS). For the issue of catastrophic forgetting in class incremental learning, we improve the BLS by adding the output nodes incrementally and deducing an iterative formula for model updating when there comes unseen classes, and the performance can be maintained simultaneously. In future work, we will improve the algorithm performance on bigger data sets and explore the combination of broad learning and deep learning. Further more, we will consider the scenario where new training instances are from different feature spaces, e.g., the dimension of the input data might be different, which makes the incremental learning system more general and thus the BLS can learn more broadly.

References

1. Rebuffi, S.-A., Kolesnikov, A., Sperl, G., Lampert, C.H.: iCaRL: incremental classifier and representation learning. In: CVPR, pp. 5533–5542 (2017)
2. Shmelkov, K., Schmid, C.: Incremental learning of object detectors without catastrophic forgetting. In: ICCV, pp. 3420–3429. Karteek Alahari (2017)
3. Lopez-Paz, D., Ranzato, M.A.: Gradient episodic memory for continual learning. In: NIPS 2017, pp. 6470–6479 (2017)
4. McCloskey, M., Cohen, N.J.: Catastrophic interference in connectionist networks: the sequential learning problem. Psychol. Learn. Motiv. **24**, 109–165 (1989)
5. French, R.M.: Catastrophic interference in connectionist networks: can it be predicted, can it be prevented? In: NIPS 1993, pp. 1176–1177 (1993)
6. Huang, G.-B., Zhu, Q.-Y., Siew, C.K.: Extreme learning machine: theory and applications. Neurocomputing **70**(1–3), 489–501 (2006)
7. LeCun, Y., Bengio, Y., Hinton, G.E.: Deep learning. Nature **521**(7553), 436–444 (2015)
8. Salakhutdinov, R., Hinton, G.E.: Deep Boltzmann machines. In: AISTATS, pp. 448–455 (2009)
9. LeCun, Y., Bottou, L., Bengio, Y., Haffner, P.: Gradient-based learning applied to document recognition. Proc. IEEE **86**(11), 2278–2324 (1998)
10. Simonyan, K., Zisserman, A.: Very deep convolutional networks for large-scale image recognition. CoRR abs/1409.1556 (2014)
11. He, K., Zhang, X., Ren, S., Sun, J.: Deep residual learning for image recognition. In: CVPR, pp. 770–778 (2016)
12. Chen, C.L.P., Liu, Z.: Broad learning system: an effective and efficient incremental learning system without the need for deep architecture. IEEE Trans. Neural Netw. Learn. Syst. **29**(1), 10–24 (2018)
13. Pao, Y.-H., Takefuji, Y.: Functional-link net computing: theory, system architecture, and functionalities. IEEE Comput. **25**(5), 76–79 (1992)
14. Mensink, T., Verbeek, J., Perronnin, F., Csurka, G.: Metric learning for large scale image classification: generalizing to new classes at near-zero cost. In: Fitzgibbon, A., Lazebnik, S., Perona, P., Sato, Y., Schmid, C. (eds.) ECCV 2012. LNCS, pp. 488–501. Springer, Heidelberg (2012). https://doi.org/10.1007/978-3-642-33709-3_35
15. Kuzborskij, I., Orabona, F., Caputo, B.: From N to N+1: multiclass transfer incremental learning. In: CVPR 2013, pp. 3358–3365 (2013)
16. Ristin, M., Guillaumin, M., Gall, J., Van Gool, L.J.: Incremental learning of NCM forests for large-scale image classification. In: CVPR 2014, pp. 3654–3661 (2014)
17. Li, Z., Hoiem, D.: Learning without forgetting. In: Leibe, B., Matas, J., Sebe, N., Welling, M. (eds.) ECCV 2016. LNCS, vol. 9908, pp. 614–629. Springer, Cham (2016). https://doi.org/10.1007/978-3-319-46493-0_37
18. Triki, A.R., Aljundi, R., Blaschko, M.B., Tuytelaars, T.: Encoder based lifelong learning. In: ICCV, pp. 1329–1337 (2017)
19. Kirkpatrick, J., Pascanu, R., Rabinowitz, N., Veness, J., Desjardins, G., Rusu, A.A., Milan, K., Quan, J., Ramalho, T., Grabska-Barwinska, A., Hassabis, D.: Overcoming catastrophic forgetting in neural networks. Proc. Natl. Acad. Sci. **114**, 3521–3526 (2017). 201611835
20. Chen, C.L.P., Wan, J.Z.: A rapid learning and dynamic stepwise updating algorithm for flat neural networks and the application to time-series prediction. IEEE Trans. Syst. Man Cybern. Part B **29**(1), 62–72 (1999)

WeiboCluster: An Event-Oriented Sina Weibo Dataset with Estimating Credit

Shiping Wen[1](✉), Guanghua Ren[1], Yuting Cao[2], Zhenyuan Guo[2], Qiang Xiao[1], Zhigang Zeng[1], and Tingwen Huang[3]

[1] Huazhong University of Science and Technology, Wuhan 430074, China
`wenshiping226@126.com`
[2] College of Mathematics and Econometrics, Hunan University, Changsha, China
[3] Texas A&M University at Qatar, Doha 23874, Qatar

Abstract. The earliest and the most famous micro-blogging platform is Twitter, which was created in 2006. But in China, Sina Weibo, the latecomer, has become bigger than Twitter and plays a vital role in the social media. With eight times more users than Twitter [1], the problems about rumor are more severe for Sina Weibo. In recent years, deep learning has been used into the natural language processing (NLP). For example, a contextual LSTM model, which is a kind of recurrent neural networks, was employed to solve large scale NLP tasks [2]. NLP technology aims to extract the potential information of the text, which is appropriate for detecting rumor. The basis of neural networks is data set to be trained. Unfortunately, there is no suitable data set of Sina Weibo for NLP. To solve this problem, this paper proposed a process to collection data source of micro-blogs used for rumor detecting. The process here is event-oriented and introduced the concept of credit (or confidence) into the final dataset, which makes the dataset different and useful.

Keywords: Sina Weibo · NLP · Dataset · Event-oriented

1 Introduction

Sina Weibo is popular in China, particularly among Chinese young people. Sina Weibo is an useful media for its' users to offer ideas of their own, express emotions of themselves and share their daily lives. In micro-blogging platforms, the basic operation is sending a micro-blog, which can be called as weibo, and the sender or other users can comment, forward or like this weibo. A weibo usually can't exceed 140 words, this makes weibo difficult to deliver complete information but easy to propagate. The convenience and immediacy of weibo have subverted the information dissemination of the traditional media. According to the China Internet Network Information Center (CNNIC), users of Sina Weibo have reached 249 million as early as 2014.

© Springer International Publishing AG, part of Springer Nature 2018
T. Huang et al. (Eds.): ISNN 2018, LNCS 10878, pp. 239–246, 2018.
https://doi.org/10.1007/978-3-319-92537-0_28

The rumor is a special language phenomenon. With the growth of users in Sina Weibo, the dissemination of information becomes more and more difficult to manage. Due to the "butterfly effect", a wrong message also has a great potential in affecting our lives. The spread of false rumours during emergencies can jeopardise the well-being of citizens as they are monitoring the stream of news from social media to stay abreast of the latest updates [3]. So the rumor detection problem on social network has attracted considerable attention in recent years [4].

Deep learning is an emerging technology. This technology has obtained rapid development and widespread application in different fields. Recurrent neural network (RNN), as one of deep learning technologies, has an excellent ability to handle time series problems [5–9]. It is generally known that the result of deep learning is hugely dependent on the dataset to be used for training. But for rumor detecting, there is no uniform, published and suitable dataset for researchers to use. This paper tries to provide a whole process to collect appropriate weibo dataset for rumor detecting, the process is referred as WeiboCluster. Noting that the paper doesn't offer the final dataset. For existed studies about rumor detecting, these authors often detailed the methods used in their papers, they hardly put energy to illustrate dataset. Ref. [10] used a dataset, which does not include enough information for neural networks. Jain et al. employed clustering to collect tweets based on topics in [11]. The method used by Jain et al. does not take into account senders of tweets, so it is one-sided.

Weibos are firstly divided into different groups by event, this pattern is named as event-oriented collection in the process. Sina Weibo exposes a set of APIs, which can be utilized for collecting raw data. Then the user's information of the weibo is gathered. On the basis of these information, the credit (or confidence) of the user is automatic estimated with an algorithm. In this paper, we propose a process to normalize the dataset used by rumor detecting—WeiboCluster. The process getting WeiboCluster is very convenient. WeiboCluster contains information that satisfies requirements of machine learning as much as possible, such as users' information, weibos' information and so on.

The rest of this paper is organized as follows. Section 2 is about how to build WeiboCluster. Section 3 describes the advantages of WeiboCluster. And Sect. 4 draws the conclusions.

2   Building WeiboCluster

In this section, the whole process and some concepts of WeiboCluster will be detailed. The event-oriented concept used in this process can be interpreted simply as cluster. So the dataset is called WeiboCluster.

2.1   Event-Oriented Collection

The main goal of this dataset is to detect rumor with deep learning technology, more specifically, for methods using neural networks. Neural networks are

Fig. 1. The official account for spiking rumors in Sina Weibo.

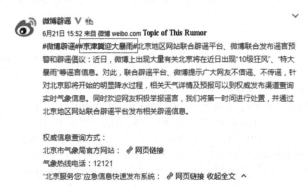

Fig. 2. The explanatory weibo sent by the official account.

dependent on weights among neurons to mine potential knowledge of data. For rumor detecting, different events are obvious not to be mixed. The most reasonable state is that an event corresponds to a set of weights, that means a trained neural network should be retrained when other weibos about a new event are inputted into this neural network.

Considering the above main reason, the process has to adopt event-oriented collection. There is a official account for spiking rumors in Sina Weibo, shown in Fig. 1. This account regularly publishes some weibos to clarify rumors. So it's easy to find out keywords indicating rumors. For example, Fig. 2 is a weibo claiming the rumor that there would be a heavy rain in Beijing, note that this weibo has a topic in Fig. 1, which can be used as event label. Using search function of Sina Weibo with this event label, weibos related about heavy rain of Beijing could be gathered quickly.

After finding these weibos, special codes written by Python to parse contents of weibos could come in handy. Web pages containing target weibos are treated as a tree consisted of HTML elements by these codes, taking weibos' information from this tree is a easy thing. Finally, these information is summarized into a table.

2.2 Cluster Based on Relational Mapping

This subsection will detail how the data are organized by relationship. Figure 3 shows one of the searching results with keyword–"Shandong" and "turning round

Fig. 3. Search results with keyword: "Shandong" and "turning round but not going back to the past".

but not going back to the past". The necessary information is made up of two parts: the current weibo's information and the current sender's information.

The current weibo's information contains user name, user id, content, forwarding number, commenting number and liking number. The process ignores the client that the sender uses and sending time of the weibo. The current sender's information contains user name, user id, gender, province, city, location, followers count, friends count, statuses count, favourites count, user's creating time and validated or not. The process would put these information into a table, too.

Using these information, each weibo corresponds to an user and an event. And the process give a mark to each user to evaluate user's credit, which will be described in next subsection. The credit of each user is still put into a table.

Up to now, four tables have been used here, as shown in Table 1. These tables are all stored in MySQL, which is the world's most popular open source database.

Table 1. Tables used in the process.

Table name	Table description
weibodicevent	The mapping among event id, event name and search keyword
weibodetail	The detailed information of each weibo
user	The detailed information of each user
user_score	The credit grade of each user

Sina Weibo has provided application program interfaces (APIs) for Java developers to obtain users' information, and then the designed codes are called to store these information into tables in MySQL.

2.3 The Algorithm for Estimating Credit

The biggest difference between WeiboCluster and other datasets is that each user in WeiboCluster has a credit rating. The reason for evaluating users will narrate in Sect. 4. This subsection mainly discussed how to evaluate users' credit.

Table 2. The groups of table user.

Group	Field	Total score
Name group	Username	50
Gender group	Gender	10
Location group	Province	20
	City	
	Location	
Relationship group	followersCount	75
	friendsCount	
statusesCount group	followersCount	50
	friendsCount	
	statusesCount	
favoritesCount group	favoritesCount	20
Creating group	Createtime	25
	Verified	
—	—	250

The algorithm for estimating credit involves two tables—Table user and Table user_score. The total score of credit is 250 inside the algorithm, and the final score of credit is converted to the range of 0 and 1.

The algorithm firstly divides user's information into eight groups, as shown in Table 2. The score of the user is set as 0 at the beginning of the algorithm, and then is added up for each group. After analysing a large number of microblog users, we find out that a reliable user usually doesn't contain more than four consecutive numbers. Sometimes, the user may append his/her year of birth, which is four digits, to the username. When registering a new account in Sina Weibo, the first option of user's gender is male, users with low credit are more likely not to choose the second option–female or even leave it vacant, so the gender group gives more weight to female. For the same reason, the location group prefers to domestic users with complete location information, code 1000 means the loss of city information and code 400 indicates that the user is overseas. The relationship group is evaluating by a followersCount-to-friendsCount ratio. In general, users with low credit tend to follow a lot of accounts (friendsCount) but have a few followers (followersCount), and the condition of stars in Sina Weibo is opposite. For ordinary users, the ratio of followers number to friends number falls in a specific range. Owing to stars and some user with low credit have the same behavior that both of them would send quantities of weibos, the statusesCount group depends on not only statusesCount but also followersCount and friendsCount. the evaluation criterion for the favoritesCount group and the creating group is not complex, because the information of the three fields has limited effect.

(a) Profile of the high credit user.   (b) Content of the weibo that this user sent.

Fig. 4. One of high credit users. This user gets the score of 0.888, the information in his profile is complete, and weibos sent by this user are about education.

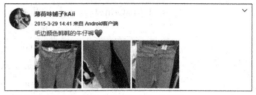

(a) Profile of the low credit user.   (b) Content of the weibo that this user sent.

Fig. 5. One of low credit users. This user gets the score of 0.432, the information in his profile is incomplete, and weibos sent by this user are ads.

3   Advantages of WeiboCluster

The previous sections have illustrated how to build each part of WeiboCluster. The algorithm of evaluating users' credit can be implemented as a stored procedure in MySQL, then the stored procedure is done automatically after inserting a new record into Table user by adding in a trigger.

In Sina Weibo, there are plenty of online water army, which refers to the hordes of people that are paid to post comments on the Internet. An important step is how to distinguish such users from legitimate users. This is one of the reasons why the algorithm of evaluating users' credit is proposed here. The other reason for this algorithm is that inactive users usually take less responsibility for their own words. This algorithm can effectively recognize users with low credit. The Fig. 6 shows the result of the algorithm. The user in the first red box is an example of low credit, the details of this user are shown in Fig. 5. The user in the second red box is an example of high credit, the details of this user are shown in Fig. 4. Information of the lower credit user is less than the higher credit user's, and contents of weibos are different, the lower one prefers to send ads.

By this result, the algorithm is proved to have an ability to effectively identify inactive users and online water army. In addition to this, all collected information is stored in database—MySQL, which makes interaction of the data layer and the logical function layer easier.

5404681472	_相志惠	0.84
5443990665	塞外晴格格201412	0.572
5508681587	睿商女王大人	0.624
5520022526	朱心语yoooo	0.664
5538023876	吾生莫沉亦可旭	0.568
5540246503	橘子味儿的大晨	0.688
5547631227	薄荷味铺子kAii	0.432
5567264660	李瑟心	0.756
5580013569	泰安校园头条	0.888
5648588122	莄寂	0.82

Fig. 6. Part of the evaluating result computed by the algorithm. The user in the first red box is an example of low credit, the details of this user are shown in Fig. 5. The user in the second red box is an example of high credit, the details of this user are shown in Fig. 4. (Color figure online)

4   Conclusion

In other fields of machine learning, there are established datasets for researching, but in the field of rumor detecting, researchers often ignored the study of dataset. This paper tried to solve this problem and proposed a process (or a method) to collect dataset of weibos. Information collected by this process is organized according to relational mapping and weibos are grouped by event. The main contribution is that the process in this paper contains a algorithm which can effectively distinguish users.

The higher score one user gets, the less probability this user claims a rumor. So in the future work, the final credit of each user can be used into neural network as a weight.

Acknowledgments. This work was supported by the Natural Science Foundation of China under Grant 61403152, 61402218, 61673187 and 61673188. The Research Grants Council of Hong Kong under General Research Fund Grant 106140120. This publication was made possible by NPRP grant: NPRP 8-274-2-107 from the Qatar National Research Fund (a member of Qatar Foundation). The statements made herein are solely the responsibility of the author[s].

References

1. Yang, F., Liu, Y., Yu, X., Yang, M.: Automatic detection of rumor on Sina Weibo, pp. 1–7. ACM (2012)
2. Ghosh, S., Vinyals, O., Strope, B., Roy, S., Dean, T., Heck, L.: Contextual LSTM (CLSTM) models for large scale NLP tasks. arXiv.org (2016)

3. Zubiaga, A., Liakata, M., Procter, R., Bontcheva, K., Tolmie, P.: Towards detecting rumours in social media. In: AAAI Workshop on AI for Cities (2015)
4. Zhang, Q., Zhang, S., Dong, J., Xiong, J., Cheng, X.: Automatic detection of rumor on social network. In: Li, J., Ji, H., Zhao, D., Feng, Y. (eds.) NLPCC 2015. LNCS (LNAI), vol. 9362, pp. 113–122. Springer, Cham (2015). https://doi.org/10.1007/978-3-319-25207-0_10
5. Huang, T., Chan, A., Huang, Y., Cao, J.: Stability of Cohen-Grossberg neural networks with time-varying delays. Neural Netw. 20, 868–873 (2007)
6. Huang, T., Li, C., Yu, W., Chen, G.: Synchronization of delayed chaotic systems with parameter mismatches by using intermittent linear state feedback. Nonlinearity 22, 569–584 (2009)
7. Huang, T., Li, C., Duan, S., Starzyk, J.: Robust exponential stability of uncertain delayed neural networks with stochastic perturbation and impulse effects. IEEE Trans. Netw. Learn. Syst. 23, 866–875 (2012)
8. Wen, S., Zeng, Z., Chen, M.Z.Q., Huang, T.: Synchronization of switched neural networks with communication delays via the event-triggered method. IEEE Trans. Neural Netw. Learn. Syst. 28(10), 2334–2343 (2017)
9. Wen, S., Zeng, Z., Huang, T., Meng, Q., Yao, W.: Lag synchronization of switched neural networks via neural activation function and applications in image encryption. IEEE Trans. Neural Netw. Learn. Syst. 26(7), 1493–1502 (2015)
10. Dayani, R., Chhabra, N., Kadian, T., Kaushal, R.: Rumor detection in Twitter: an analysis in retrospect. In: IEEE International Conference on Advanced Networks and Telecommunications Systems, pp. 1–3 (2015)
11. Jain, S., Sharma, V., Kaushal, R.: Towards automated real-time detection of misinformation on Twitter. In: International Conference on Advances in Computing, Communications and Informatics, pp. 2015–2020 (2016)
12. Heilbron, F.C., Escorcia, V., Ghanem, B., Niebles, J.C.: ActivityNet: a large-scale video benchmark for human activity understanding. In: Computer Vision and Pattern Recognition, pp. 961–970 (2015)
13. Rohrbach, A., Rohrbach, M., Tandon, N., Schiele, B.: A dataset for movie description. In: IEEE Computer Society, pp. 3202–3212 (2015)

Robust Neural Networks Learning: New Approaches

Z. M. Shibzukhov$^{(\boxtimes)}$

Institute of Applied Mathematics and Automation KBSC RAS, Nalchik, Russia
szport@gmail.com

Abstract. The paper suggests an extended version of principle of empirical risk minimization and principle of smoothly winsorized sums minimization for robust neural networks learning. It's based on using of M-averaging functions instead of the arithmetic mean for empirical risk estimation (M-risk). Theese approaches generalize robust algorithms based on using median and quantiles for estimation of mean losses. An iteratively reweighted schema for minimization of M-risk is proposed. This schema allows to use weighted version of traditional back propagation algorithms for neural networks learning in presence of outliers.

Keywords: Neural network · Averaging aggregation function
Empirical risk minimization · Winsorized sum · Robust learning

1 Introduction

The solution to the most common machine learning tasks is based on the principle of empirical risk minimization [1]. This principle implies a minimization of the averaged loss resulted from the erroneous functioning of the system trained on finite set of precedents. The value of empirical risk is estimated as the arithmetic average of losses:

$$ER(\mathbf{w}) = \frac{1}{N} \sum_{k=1}^{N} \ell_k(\mathbf{w}), \tag{1}$$

where $\ell_k(\mathbf{w})$ is a loss function associated with k-th precedent.

The required set of the parameters $\mathbf{w}^*$ minimizes the empirical risk:

$$ER(\mathbf{w}^*) = \min_{\mathbf{w}} ER(\mathbf{w}). \tag{2}$$

Usually $\ell_k(\mathbf{w}) = \varrho(r_k(\mathbf{w}))$, where $\varrho(r)$ is nonnegative function. In regression problems $r_k(\mathbf{w})$ is an error function, in classification problems $r_k(\mathbf{w})$ is a margin function for k-th precedent.

Most of algorithms for neural networks (NN) learning are based on this principle. In particular back propagation (BP) algorithm is based on minimization of arithmetic mean squared errors.

© Springer International Publishing AG, part of Springer Nature 2018
T. Huang et al. (Eds.): ISNN 2018, LNCS 10878, pp. 247–255, 2018.
https://doi.org/10.1007/978-3-319-92537-0_29

However, presence of outliers in the empirical loss distribution may bias the estimate of (1). Traditional M-regression approach [2] tries to treat this problem using a such function $\varrho(r)$, which could be able to "suppress" outliers. Here is the representation of the empirical risk in the M-regression approach:

$$\mathsf{ER}(\mathbf{w}) = \frac{1}{N} \sum_{k=1}^{N} \varrho(r_k(\mathbf{w})).$$ (3)

In order to understand why the function $\varrho(r)$ is able to "suppress" outliers let us consider equation $|\varrho(r + \Delta) - \varrho(r)| = \varrho'(\tilde{r})\Delta$, where Δ is a magnitude of distortion, $\tilde{r}$ is a value between of r and $r + \Delta$. In order to "suppress" outliers the function $\varrho'(r)$ should be bounded. Ideally the function $\varrho(r)$ should be bounded (i.e. $\lim_{r \to \infty} |\varrho'(r)| \to 0$).

However, there are a number of cases when the M-regression method isn't able to overcome the outliers problem. For example, when data contains large amount of significant outliers (till 50%). The main reason for the failure of M-regression approach is that the estimation of the distortions introduced by outliers contains factor Δ. So if there are many greater outliers then the distortion of estimation of the empirical risk is large enough in order to damage optimal parameters $\mathbf{w}^*$. In such cases a different approach has been used based on estimations of the average empirical losses, which are resistant to the outliers. For example median [8,9] or quantiles [11] are resistant to the outliers. But since median and quantiles are not differentiable, then gradient based approaches are not applicable for solving (2). Consequently NN could not be trained by gradient based algorithms.

In this paper, we consider general approach where for estimation of average empirical losses it will be used M-averaging aggregation functions (M-averages). This approach generalizes M-regression method and provides universal technique for solving the problem of the empirical risk minimization in presence of outliers. It allows to use differentiable M-averages that could be treated as a sort of approximations of median and quantiles. In such cases a general gradient based procedure could be constructed for NN robust training.

2   M-Averaging Functions

M-averaging functions are examples of averaging aggregation functions (AF) [3,4]. Any averaging AF under certain conditions can be defined on the base of corresponding penalty function [5,6]. AF M_P based on the penalty function $P(z_1, \ldots, z_N, u)$ is defined as follows:

$$\mathsf{M}_P\{z_1, \ldots, z_N\} = \arg\min_u P(z_1, \ldots, z_N, u).$$ (4)

If $\mathbf{M}_{z_1 \ldots z_N} = \{u \colon P(z_1, \ldots, z_N, u) = \min_u P(z_1, \ldots, z_N, u)\}$ is a singleton and

$$\mathsf{M}_P\{z_1, \ldots, z_N\} = \frac{a+b}{2},$$

if $\mathbf{M}_{z_1\ldots z_N}$ is a segment with the endpoints a and b.

To define M-averaging functions, let us consider penalty functions of the following kind:

$$P(z_1,\ldots,z_N,u) = \sum_{k=1}^{N} \rho(z_k,u), \tag{5}$$

where $\rho(z,u)$ is a dissimilarity function [6]. If $\rho(z,u) = g(h(z) - h(u))$, where g is nonnegative and convex, $g(0) = 0$ and h is a reversible monotonic function, then M_P is averaging aggregation function. We will denote M_ρ AF based on (5). M-averaging functions are sufficiently a broad class for calculation of averaged values.

3   Empirical M-Risk Minimization Principle

Let M_ρ be some M-averaging function. We define empirical M-risk based on M-averaging function M_ρ, as follows:

$$\mathsf{ER}_\rho(\mathbf{w}) = \mathsf{M}_\rho\{\ell_1(\mathbf{w}),\ldots,\ell_N(\mathbf{w})\}. \tag{6}$$

The classical empirical risk (1) is a special case of (6), when M_ρ is arithmetical mean. The best set of the parameters for $\mathbf{w}^*$ have to minimize the function with respect to the M-risk minimization principle [14]:

$$\mathsf{ER}_\rho(\mathbf{w}^*) = \min_{\mathbf{w}} \mathsf{M}_\rho\{\ell_1(\mathbf{w}),\ldots,\ell_N(\mathbf{w})\}. \tag{7}$$

This method have already been applied in [12,13] to determine the aggregation functionals. In [8,9] for estimating the mean squared error in regression problem the median has been used since it is a robust estimator of the mean. In the robust version of SVM [11] median and α-quantile have been used to estimate average losses.

Assume that $\rho(z,u)$ has second derivatives $\rho''_{uz}(z,u)$ and $\rho''_{uu}(z,u)$. If gradients $\ell_1(\mathbf{w}),\ldots,\ell_N(\mathbf{w})$ are exist then

$$\mathrm{grad}\,\mathsf{ER}_\rho(\mathbf{w},\bar{z}) = \sum_{k=1}^{N} \alpha_k(\mathbf{w},\bar{z})\,\mathrm{grad}\,\ell_k(\mathbf{w}), \tag{8}$$

where $\bar{z} = \mathsf{M}_\rho\{\ell_1(\mathbf{w}),\ldots,\ell_N(\mathbf{w})\}$,

$$\alpha_k(\mathbf{w},\bar{z}) = \frac{-\rho''_{uz}(\ell_k(\mathbf{w}),\bar{z})}{\rho''_{uu}(\ell_1(\mathbf{w}),\bar{z}) + \cdots + \rho''_{uu}(\ell_N(\mathbf{w}),\bar{z})}.$$

The optimal parameter set $\mathbf{w}^*$ (7) and the minimum risk value u^* can be calculated numerically using gradient descent methods. An Iteratively Reweighted Empirical Risk Minimization (IR-ERM) method [14] is proposed for solving (7):

procedure IR-ERM($\mathbf{w}$)

  $t \leftarrow 0$

  repeat

    $z_1, \ldots, z_N \leftarrow \ell_1(\mathbf{w}_t), \ldots, \ell_N(\mathbf{w}_t)$

    $u_t \leftarrow M_p\{z_1, \ldots, z_N\}$

    $(v_1, \ldots, v_N) = \operatorname{grad} M_p\{z_1, \ldots, z_N\}$

    $\mathbf{w}_{t+1} \leftarrow \mathbf{w} : \displaystyle\sum_{k=1}^{N} v_k \operatorname{grad} \ell_k(\mathbf{w}) = 0.$

    $t \leftarrow t + 1$

  until $\{u_t\}$ and $\{\mathbf{w}_t\}$ not stabilizes

end procedure

4 Robust Empirical M-Risk Estimations

Since the median and quantile are not differentiable, the gradient procedures for minimization of the risk functional are not possible. However, instead of median we can use differentiable parametric family of M-average functions based on the dissimilarity function $\rho_\varepsilon(z - u)$ that satisfy the following requirements:

(1) $\lim_{\varepsilon \to 0} \rho_\varepsilon(z - u) = |z - u|$;

(2) $\lim_{\varepsilon \to 0} \rho'_\varepsilon(z - u) = \operatorname{sign}(z - u)$;

(3) $\lim_{\varepsilon \to 0} \rho''_\varepsilon(z - u) = \delta(z - u)$.

For example, for $\varepsilon \geqslant 0$: 1) $\rho_\varepsilon(x) = |x| - \varepsilon \ln(\varepsilon + |x|) + \varepsilon \ln \varepsilon$; 2) $\rho_\varepsilon(x) = \sqrt{\varepsilon^2 + x^2} - \varepsilon$.

Similarly, it can be built parameterized M-averaging function that converge to the function $|x|_\alpha$ as $\varepsilon \to 0$ and establishes the quantile. For example, the following family

$$\rho_{\alpha,\varepsilon}(x) = \begin{cases} \alpha \rho_\varepsilon(x), & \text{if } x > 0 \\ \alpha \rho_\varepsilon(+0) + (1 - \alpha)\rho_\varepsilon(-0), & \text{if } x = 0 \\ (1 - \alpha)\rho_\varepsilon(x), & \text{if } x < 0. \end{cases} \tag{9}$$

could be considered as a sort of approximation of quantiles.

Linear regression example (Fig. 1). There is artificially generated example that demonstrate the robust capabilities of the proposed approach. To design a robust technique for solving linear regression problem it used $M_{\rho_{\alpha,\varepsilon}}$ with $\rho_\varepsilon(x) = \sqrt{\varepsilon^2 + x^2} - \varepsilon$, $\varepsilon \approx 10^{-2} \div 10^{-3}$, where $\rho_{\alpha,\varepsilon}$ is dissimilarity function introduced above.

We have sampled such data that within the least-squares method and the M-method turned left the straight line. The exact linear relationship is $y = 3x$. The distortions are caused by uniform noise with an amplitude of 2 and by 33% and 44% of big outliers. These examples demonstrate ability to fit the correct model in presence of large number of big outliers.

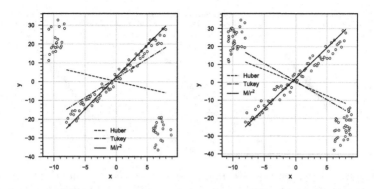

Fig. 1. Data with outliers, which are able to turn straight line if Least of Squares (LS) or Least of Absolute Deviations (LAD) methods are used. Here r^2 denote LS, $|r|$ denote LAD, M/r^2 denote Least of M-average of Squares methods, correspondingly.

5 Minimization of Winsorized Sums of Losses

Another approach to construct robust training procedures is LTS (Least Trimmed Sums) [8,9]:

$$\mathsf{TS}_p(\mathbf{w}) = \sum_{k=1}^{N-p} \ell_{(k)}(\mathbf{w}),$$

Here $z_{(1)}, \ldots, z_{(N)}$ denotes ascending ordered sequence $z_1, \ldots, z_N$, $p < N/2$ is number of trimmed values.

In this paper we consider another robust summing method:

$$\mathsf{WS}_\rho\{z_1, \ldots, z_N\} = \sum_{k=1}^{N} \frac{1}{2}\big(z_k + \bar{z} - \rho(z_k - \bar{z})\big),$$

where $\bar{z} = \mathsf{M}_\rho\{z_1, \ldots, z_N\}$, ρ is dissimilarity function and M_ρ is M-average function based on ρ. It could be considered as a sort of Winsorized summing mentioned in [9] together with LTS.

Further let us consider the following principle of minimization smoothed winsorized mean:

$$\mathcal{Q}(\mathbf{w}) = \frac{1}{N}\mathsf{WS}_\rho\{\ell_1(\mathbf{w}), \ldots, \ell_N(\mathbf{w})\}.$$

Gradient of $\mathcal{Q}$ has the following form:

$$\operatorname{grad} \mathcal{Q}(\mathbf{w}) = \sum_{k=1}^{N} v_k(\mathbf{w}) \operatorname{grad} \ell_k(\mathbf{w}),$$

where

$$v_k(\mathbf{w}) = \frac{1}{2N}\big(1 - \rho'(z_k - \bar{z})\big) + \frac{1}{2}\frac{\partial \mathsf{M}_\rho}{\partial z_k},$$

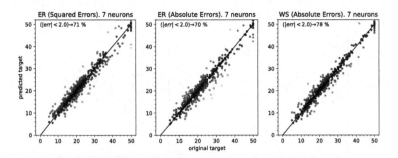

Fig. 2. Errors distributions for NN training by boston dataset using three approaches: Least Squares (ER), Least Absolute Errors (ER) and Least Winsorized Squares (WS).

$z_k = \ell_k(\mathbf{w})$, $\bar{z} = \bar{z}(\mathbf{w})$.

It is completely analogous to construct an algorithm IR-SWSM (Iteratively Reweighted Smoothly Winsorized Sum Minimization):

procedure IR-SWSM($\mathbf{w}$)
$\quad t \leftarrow 0$
$\quad$**repeat**
$\quad\quad z_1, \ldots, z_N \leftarrow \ell_1(\mathbf{w}_t), \ldots, \ell_N(\mathbf{w}_t)$
$\quad\quad u_t \leftarrow \mathsf{M}_p\{z_1, \ldots, z_N\}$
$\quad\quad$**for** $k = 1, \ldots, N$ **do**
$\quad\quad\quad v_k = \frac{1}{2N}\left(1 - \rho'(z_k - u_t)\right) + \frac{1}{2}\frac{\partial \mathsf{M}_\rho}{\partial z_k}$
$\quad\quad$**end for**
$\quad\quad \mathbf{w}_{t+1} \leftarrow \mathbf{w}: \sum_{k=1}^{N} v_k \operatorname{grad} \ell_k(\mathbf{w}) = 0.$
$\quad\quad t \leftarrow t + 1$
$\quad$**until** $\{u_t\}$ and $\{\mathbf{w}_t\}$ not stabilizes
end procedure

There are several examples of application of IR-SWSM procedure for training of NN with single hidden layer:

$$y = w_0 + w_1 u_1 + \cdots + w_m u_m$$
$$u_j = \mathsf{softplus}(w_{j0} + w_{j1}x_1 + \cdots + w_{jn}x_n),$$

where $\mathsf{softplus}(s) = \ln(1 + e^s)$.

Boston example. Consider boston dataset. Neural network has 12 neurons in the hidden layer. This example is used to demonstrate the ability of robust learning to decrease greater number of errors. First NN is trained to minimize sum of squared errors. Then NN is trained to minimize sum of absolute values of errors. Last it is trained using IR-SWSM with $\rho_{\alpha,\varepsilon}$ (9), where $\alpha = 0.9$, $\rho_\varepsilon(r) = \sqrt{\varepsilon^2 + r^2} - \varepsilon$, $\varepsilon = 0.001$. Figure 2 demonstrates distribution of pairs plot: predicted target value vs. original target value. So this example demonstrates the ability of IR-SWSM to decrease absolute errors on 80% of training data.

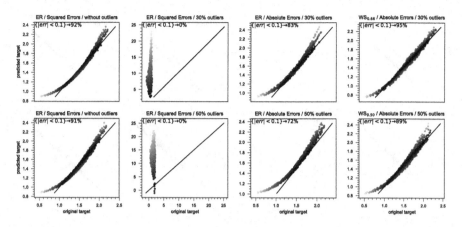

Fig. 3. Errors distributions for NN training by example 1 dataset using three approaches: Least Squares (ER), Least Absolute Deviation (ER) and Least Winsorized Absolute Deviation (WS).

Further there are 2 artificially generated datasets by [15]. They represents some function $f(\mathbf{x})$, where $\mathbf{x} \in \mathbb{R}^3$. Training and testing data are generated uniformly and randomly on the cube $[-2, 2]^3$, number of points in training and testing data are 1000 and 1000, correspondingly. In addition uniformly distributed noise $\varepsilon \in [-0.1, 0.1]$ is added. Outliers are added to the training data using the following schema. They are chosen uniformly and randomly by 30% and 50% of training data, correspondingly. These examples clearly demonstrate that minimization of smoothed winsorized sum of absolute errors on data with outliers produce error distribution, which is not worse than error distribution that produced by minimization of sum of squared error on data without outliers. They are also demonstrate that minimization of sum of absolute errors is not able to achieve such a result.

Example 1. In this example the function $f(\mathbf{x}) = \|\mathbf{x}\|^{2/3}$. For all outlier points in the training datasets each target value is replaced by 20 (note that $\max f(\mathbf{x}) < 3$ on $[-2, 2]^3$). Figure 3.

Example 2. In this example the function $f(\mathbf{x}) = \sin\|\mathbf{x}\|/(\|\mathbf{x}\| + 10^{-8})$, where $\mathbf{x} \in \mathbb{R}^3$. For all outlier points in the training datasets each target value is also replaced by 20 (note that $\max f(\mathbf{x}) < 1$ on $[-2, 2]^3$). Figure 4.

The algorithms IR-ERM and IR-SWSM are implemented in the library mlgrad[1]. All numerical calculation implementation are performed with the help of mlgrad.

---

[1] http://bitbucket.org/intellimath/mlgrad.

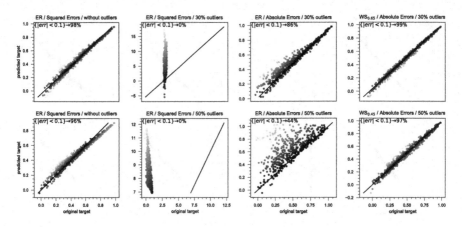

Fig. 4. Errors distributions for NN training by example 2 dataset using three approaches: Least Squares (ER), Least Absolute Deviation (ER) and Least Winsorized Absolute Deviation (WS).

6   Conclusion

A new approach to NN robust learning on data, which contains significant number of outliers is considered. It is based on minimization of differentiable robust analogs of median, quantiles and winsorized sums of loss functions. The above approaches is preferable in the cases when application of gradient based minimization procedures are preferable. For example these approaches made possible application of weighted variants of back propagation algorithms for NN robust learning. In particular an iteratively reweighted procedures are proposed. In these procedures at each step a weighted variant of back propagation algorithm is used. Examples presented above clearly show that proposed approaches and algorithms can be resistant to large amount of outliers.

Acknowledgments. This work is supported by the RFBR grant 18-01-00050.

References

1. Vapnik, V.: The Nature of Statistical Learning Theory. Information Science and Statistics. Springer, New York (2000). https://doi.org/10.1007/978-1-4757-3264-1
2. Huber, P.J.: Robust Statistics. John Wiley and Sons, Hoboken (1981)
3. Mesiar, R., Komornikova, M., Kolesarova, A., Calvo, T.: Aggregation functions: a revision. In: Bustince, H., Herrera, F., Montero, J. (eds.) Fuzzy Sets and Their Extensions: Representation Aggregation and Models. Springer, Heidelberg (2008). https://doi.org/10.1016/j.fss.2009.05.012
4. Grabich, M., Marichal, J.-L., Pap, E.: Aggregation Functions. Encyclopedia of Mathematics and its Applications. Series (Book 127). Cambridge University Press, Cambridge (2009)

5. Beliakov, G., Bustince Sola, H., Calvo Sánchez, T.: A Practical Guide to Averaging Functions. SFSC, vol. 329. Springer, Cham (2016). https://doi.org/10.1007/978-3-319-24753-3
6. Calvo, T., Beliakov, G.: Aggregation functions based on penalties. Fuzzy Sets Syst. **161**(10), 1420–1436 (2010). https://doi.org/10.1016/j.fss.2009.05.012
7. Yohai, V.J.: High breakdown-point and high efficiency robust estimates for regression. Ann. Stat. **15**, 642–656 (1987). https://doi.org/10.1214/aos/1176350366
8. Rousseeuw, P.J.: Least median of squares regression. J. Am. Stat. Assoc. **79**, 871–880 (1987)
9. Rousseeuw, P.J., Leroy, A.M.: Robust Regression and Outlier Detection. John Wiley and Sons, Hoboken (1987)
10. Newey, W., Powell, J.: Asymmetric least squares estimation and testing. Econometrica. **55**(4), 819–847 (1987)
11. Ma, Y., Li, L., Huang, X., Wang, S.: Robust support vector machine using least median loss penalty. In: IFAC Proceedings Volumes (18th IFAC World Congress), vol. 44, no. 1, pp. 11208–11213 (2011). https://doi.org/10.3182/20110828-6-IT-1002.03467
12. Shibzukhov, Z.M.: Correct aggregate operations with algorithms. Pattern Recogn. Image Anal. **24**(3), 377–382 (2014). https://doi.org/10.1134/S1054661814030171
13. Shibzukhov, Z.M.: Aggregation correct operations on algorithms. Doklady Math. **91**(3), 391–393 (2015). https://doi.org/10.1134/S1064562415030357
14. Shibzukhov, Z.M.: On the principle of empirical risk minimization based on averaging aggregation functions. Doklady Math. **96**(2), 494–497 (2017). https://doi.org/10.1134/S106456241705026X
15. Beliakov, G., Kelarev, A., Yearwood, J.: Robust artificial neural networks and outlier detection. Technical report. arxiv:1110.0169v1 [math.OC] 20 Oct 2011. https://doi.org/10.1080/02331934.2012.674946

Data Cleaning and Classification
in the Presence of Label Noise
with Class-Specific Autoencoder

Weining Zhang[1], Dong Wang[1], and Xiaoyang Tan[1,2(✉)]

[1] Department of Computer Science and Technology,
Nanjing University of Aeronautics and Astronautics, Nanjing 210016, China
x.tan@nuaa.edu.cn
[2] Collaborative Innovation Center of Novel Software Technology
and Industrialization, Nanjing 210016, China

Abstract. We present a simple but effective method for data cleaning
and classification in the presence of label noise. The key idea is to treat
the data points with label noise as outliers of the class indicated by the
corresponding noisy label. However, finding such dubious observations
is challenging in general. We therefore propose to reduce their potential
influence using feature learning method by class-specific autoencoder.
Particularly, we learn for each class a feature space using all the samples
labeled as that class, including those with noisy labels. Furthermore, in
the case of high label noise, we propose a weighted class-specific autoencoder by considering the effect of each data point. To fully exploit the
advantage of the learned feature space, we use a minimum reconstruction error based method for testing. Experiments on several datasets
show that the proposed method achieves state-of-the-art performance
on the related tasks with noisy labels.

Keywords: Class-specific autoencoder · Label noise · Classification
Data cleaning · Outliers

1 Introduction

Classification is one of the most basic and core tasks in pattern recognition and
machine learning. A classifier is first trained based on a labeled training set and is
then used to predict the label of the test set. Since collecting reliably labeled data
is often expensive and time-consuming, nowadays people tend to use alternative
simple and convenient methods, such as crowdsourcing [1], Amazon Mechanical
Turk [2] and some other non-expert methods. However, the data collected in this
way may result in a certain degree of label noise, i.e., some of labels are labeled
incorrectly. When the data set is polluted by label noise, it directly affects the

This work is partially supported by National Science Foundation of China (61672280,
61373060, 61732006), Jiangsu 333 Project (BRA2017377) and Qing Lan Project.

© Springer International Publishing AG, part of Springer Nature 2018
T. Huang et al. (Eds.): ISNN 2018, LNCS 10878, pp. 256–264, 2018.
https://doi.org/10.1007/978-3-319-92537-0_30

performance of the classifier. Moreover, inaccurate label information can seriously deteriorate the data quality, making the learning algorithm unnecessarily complex. Due to the above reasons, label noise problem has recently attracted a lot of attention from researchers [3].

Typically, to reduce the influence of noisy labels, one can clean the data first. [4] learns a neural network by using the data set with label noise and removes the instances that are misclassified by the classifier. A similar attempt is proposed in [5] for SVM classifier. However, it may remove some correctly labeled instances and only minority mislabeled instances are removed because of the misclassification of the classifier. To solve this problem, based on the fact that support vectors of an SVM contain most of the mislabeled data, [6] introduces a human expert to check the suspicious instances from the support vectors and relabel the mislabeled instances. Although the human expert based methods get a good cleaning results, human expert which may be hard to get in most of the applications. Alternatively, one may make those data points with noisy labels less harmful using various robust statistics techniques, e.g., robust loss functions [7] or optimization methods [8,9]. These are mainly supervised methods in which the effect of each data point on the postulated model is carefully controlled by design but at the risk of reduced learning efficiency.

In this paper, we present a novel, simple but effective method to solve label noise problem. Our key idea is based on the observations that the data points with label noise are likely to be outliers of the class indicated by the corresponding noisy label. This conceptual connection between label noise and outliers essentially allows us to deal with the traditional supervised problem of classification with label noise as an unsupervised one, i.e., outliers analysis. Particularly, we learn a feature space by using autoencoder for each class - note that although each class contains some portion of points that actually do not belong to it due to label noise, the influence of these points is supposed to be reduced. For cases with higher label noise, we also propose a weighted autoencoder by robust optimization. To fully exploit the advantage of the learned class-specific feature space, a minimum reconstruction error based method is used to find out outliers (label noise) and classify the data. Experiments on several datasets show that the proposed method is effective for data cleaning and classification task.

2   The Proposed Method

2.1   Label Noise as Outliers

To reduce the influence of those with label noise, a natural idea is to identify them and separate them from the normal data. From a global perspective, the label generation process is complicated and it is hard to distinguish normal labels from noisy labels. However, if we think it locally (i.e., in a class-specific), distribution of data points with label noise in each class would be much simpler - they are just like outliers as they would be different from the normal distribution of that class, although they have the same annotations as the rest of the samples in the same class. This inspires us to treat the label noise problem as one that handles

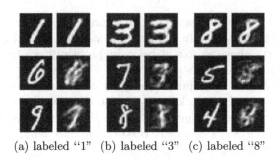

(a) labeled "1" (b) labeled "3" (c) labeled "8"

Fig. 1. The reconstruction results for correct labeled images and mislabeled ones respectively. Each pair of the images is the digit image and its reconstruction. Images in the first row are the correct labeled images, while the others are the mislabeled ones.

outliers. One major advantage of this point of view lies in that it essentially allows us to deal with the traditional supervised problem (classification) as an unsupervised one, i.e., outliers analysis [10].

2.2 Class-Specific Autoencoder

Assuming that we have a set of training samples $\mathbf{X} = \{\mathbf{x}_1, \mathbf{x}_2, \ldots, \mathbf{x}_n\}$, where $\mathbf{x}_i \in R^d$ and each of the sample have the same label (note that some of the samples actually do not belong to it due to label noise), a class-specific autoencoder first encodes an input $\mathbf{x}$ to a hidden representation, and then decodes it back to a reconstruction $\hat{\mathbf{x}}$. The $\hat{\mathbf{x}}$ can be formulated as

$$\hat{\mathbf{x}} = g(\mathbf{W}_2 f(\mathbf{W}_1 \mathbf{x} + \mathbf{b}_1) + \mathbf{b}_2) \tag{1}$$

where $\mathbf{W}_1$ and $\mathbf{W}_2$ are weight matrices, $\mathbf{b}_1$ and $\mathbf{b}_2$ are biases for encoder and decoder. The activation function for $f(x)$ and $g(x)$ is sigmoid function.

To learn the class-specific autoencoder which can well reconstruct the training samples, we define the loss function based on reconstruction error as

$$L(\theta; \mathbf{X}) = \frac{1}{n} \sum_{i=1}^{n} ||\hat{\mathbf{x}}_i - \mathbf{x}_i||^2 \tag{2}$$

where $\theta = \{\mathbf{W}, \mathbf{b}\}$. Moreover, to reduce the sensitivity of the model, an extra L2 regularization is added.

Then we do a toy example to prove that the proposed class-specific autoencoder is effective and robust to label noise problem. Totally 1000 images with 100 per class are randomly selected in MNIST dataset [11]. We inject 10% label noise into these images following the method introduced in [3]. Digits which are labeled "1", "3" and "8" are chosen to learn three class-specific autoencoder. The reconstruction results are visualized in Fig. 1. It can be shown that the correct labeled images are well reconstructed, although it exists 10% label noise. However, the reconstruction of mislabeled images is blurry and inaccurate.

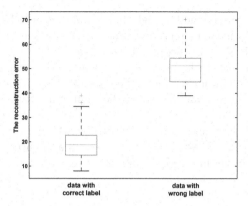

Fig. 2. The distribution of reconstruction error for images with correct label and wrong label respectively.

Furthermore, we also analyze the distribution of reconstruction error by using boxplot from a statistical perspective and the result is shown in Fig. 2. It can be seen that the reconstruction error for the correct labeled images is much lower than the error for mislabeled images.

When the noise level is relatively high, simply learning a feature space by class-specific autoencoder is not enough. One can further improve the quality of the learned feature space using label noise-robust methods [7,12,13]. Considering the effect of each data point on the postulated model, we propose a weighted class-specific autoencoder. Specifically, when updating the parameters of the class-specific autoencoder, a weighted mini-batch gradient descent is used as

$$\theta_{j+1} = \theta_j - \alpha \sum_{k=1}^{m} w_k \nabla_\theta f(\mathbf{x}_k) \qquad (3)$$

where θ is the parameter of an autoencoder, α is the learning rate, m is the batch size, f is the loss function, and w_k is the importance weight for $\mathbf{x}_k$, which is calculated by

$$w_k = \frac{e^{-||\hat{\mathbf{x}}_k - \mathbf{x}_k||^2}}{\sum_{i=1}^{m} e^{-||\hat{\mathbf{x}}_i - \mathbf{x}_i||^2}}. \qquad (4)$$

The greater the reconstruction error of an $\mathbf{x}$, the more it likely to be a data with noisy label which should get a lower importance in updating the gradient. By introducing the importance weight, the impact of label noise will be further reduced, thus getting a more reliable feature space.

2.3 Data Cleaning and Classification with Reconstruction Error

After feature learning by class-specific autoencoder, we obtain two sets of mappings. Each of the first set of mappings $f_j(\mathbf{x}), j = 1, \ldots, K$ projects a new point $\mathbf{x}$ into the j−th feature spaces, while each of the second set of mappings

$g_j(\mathbf{z}), j = 1, \ldots, K$ reconstructs a high-dimensional sample from the point $\mathbf{z}$ in the latent space, which can be regarded as compact representation of some proto-types of the j−th class. As the proposed class-specific autoencoder has effectively reduced the influence of the label noise, meanwhile, the reconstruction error can distinguish outliers from normal data, the data cleaning and classification tasks can be solved in a unified way based on the minimum reconstruction error cri-terion.

Particularly, for classification task, we predict the label y_t of a test data $\mathbf{x}_t$ by simply calculating the reconstruction error on each autoencoder and then assign it to the class with minimum reconstruction error, as follows,

$$y_t = argmin_{j=1,2,3\ldots,K} \ ||g_j(f_j(\mathbf{x}_t)) - \mathbf{x}_t||^2. \tag{5}$$

For data cleaning task, whether a data contains label noise can be judged by an indicator function,

$$I(\mathbf{x}) = \begin{cases} 1 & y \neq \hat{y} \\ 0 & otherwise \end{cases} \tag{6}$$

where y is the label of the data and $\hat{y}$ is the predicted label by (6).

3   Experiments and Analysis

3.1   Parameter Setting

In the implementation of the proposed methods, we use class-specific autoen-coder and weighted class-specific autoencoder for feature learning, which are respectively denoted as CS-AE and CS-WAE. Parameter settings are mainly related to the model of autoencoder and its training process. The hidden layer comprised 200 neurons. We set 0.1 for regularization weight λ and 0.01 for learn-ing rate α. Batch size is equal to the number of training samples in each class and epochs for training process is 100. Particularly, CS-WAE is used to fine-tuning the model of CS-AE in our follow-up experiments.

3.2   Data Cleaning

In this section, we verify the performance of the proposed method in data clean-ing task. Particularly, we follow the experimental protocol outlined in [6] and carry out the experiments on the MNIST digit dataset. 1,000 instances per class are chosen from digits "7" and "9" respectively, which are the two visually con-fusing classes. Label-noise is randomly injected at the amount of 10%, 20%, and 30% respectively. In order to exclude the possibility of a biased result caused by the instances of those two classes, we repeated the experiment 30 times and randomly selected the instances each time.

The proposed methods are compared with three state-of-the-art label noise removing methods where the hyper-parameters are based on related papers.

Table 1. Noise removal performance (%) on MNIST dataset with different label noise.

Noise level (%)	ICCN-SMO [14]	TC-SVM [6]	ALNR [15]	CS-AE (ours)	CS-WAE (ours)
10	71.38	**98.83**	95.84	97.32	98.65
20	78.60	97.21	96.01	95.25	**97.30**
30	82.49	95.03	95.69	94.57	**96.24**

Note that these three methods learn from the annotation from human expert to determine which samples are outliers, while in this respect, our method is completely 'unsupervised' in the sense that we do not assume the existence of such supervised information. Table 1 gives the average results, where only the outlier detection accuracy is given. It can be seen that although no human expert correction, our proposed method achieves comparable results with the state-of-the-art methods. This shows that the proposed method captures well the characteristics of digits "7" and "9" in spite of the deliberate disturbance imposed on. Moreover, the proposed CS-WAE method gets a higher accuracy compared with the CS-AE method which shows that the optimization method proposed in CS-WAE can reduce the effect of label noise on the feature space.

3.3 Classification in the Presence of Label Noise

We conduct our classification experiments on the MNIST digit dataset [11] and the Caltech-10 image dataset [16], which are two popular classification benchmarks with ten classes. Totally 600 images with 60 per class are randomly selected in both datasets, and they are partitioned into training set and test set with equal number. We inject label noise at three levels, i.e., 10%, 20% and 30%.

In the implementation of the proposed methods, we try three methods based on CS-WAE which are: (1) directly classification by the minimum reconstruction (2) removing the label noise before classification and (3) relabeling the label noise before classification. These methods are denoted as WAE, WAE-Remove, WAE-Relabel respectively. Note that WAE-Remove and WAE-Relabel methods need twice feature learning by CS-WAE, while WAE method just needs once.

We also learn a global PCA subspace using the whole training set (without partition for each class) and classify the test set in it using K-NN. This naive method is named PCA-KNN and is used as the baseline method. Besides these, we also compare our method with two types of methods, which are:

1. **Filter based cleaning methods:** including the classical PCA-based outlier detection method (PCA-Outlier) [17] and Complementary Fuzzy SVM based noise cleaning method (FSVM-Clean) [5].
2. **Label noise-robust methods:** including L1-norm metric learning (L1-norm) [18], Bayesian metric learning (BML) [19], and Robust Neighbourhood Component Analysis (RNCA) [13].

Table 2. Comparative classification performance (%) on two datasets with different label noise.

Dataset	MNIST				Caltech-10			
Noise level(%)	0	10	20	30	0	10	20	30
PCA-KNN	89.12	87.49	85.15	80.96	80.12	79.02	76.15	68.96
PCA-Outlier [17]	89.12	88.35	86.13	81.15	80.12	79.14	76.22	69.24
FSVM-Clean [5]	91.57	90.34	87.17	82.41	81.13	80.06	77.81	70.29
L1-norm [18]	92.10	89.65	86.09	78.63	81.36	79.30	75.84	65.66
BML [19]	90.68	89.11	86.53	80.31	80.68	79.21	76.53	68.31
RNCA [13]	92.51	91.62	86.47	81.97	81.77	80.14	77.27	69.72
WAE (ours)	**96.10**	92.17	86.28	81.03	**86.31**	81.37	77.63	69.05
WAE-Remove (ours)	95.61	92.33	87.35	81.78	83.92	81.76	78.14	70.85
WAE-Relabel (ours)	95.76	**92.86**	**87.71**	**82.98**	83.21	**81.84**	**78.39**	**71.02**

In our experiments, the related hyper-parameters of these methods are selected by cross-validation. We repeat thirty times for each experiment and report the mean of the classification accuracy in Table 2. It shows that the WAE-Relabel method achieves the best performance among the compared methods consistently at both low-level noise and high-level noise. When the training set is clean, our WAE method gets the best classification accuracy which shows that the minimum reconstruction error based classifier is a suitable choice. On the other hand, the baseline PCA-KNN method tolerates label noise to some degree when the noise level is relatively low, but its performance decreases significantly when the noise is high. The PCA-Outlier and FSVM-Clean method achieve higher accuracy compared with the baseline method, as they have some built-in mechanism to deal with outliers and mislabeled instances. As for the second type of methods, they achieve better results at 10% noise level compared with the state of the art first type methods. However, these methods perform worse at higher noise levels, especially in 30% label noise, highlighting the difficulty of obtaining reliable point estimation under the high-level label noise.

4   Conclusion

In this paper, we proposed a simple but novel and effective method to deal with the label noise problem. The key idea of our method is to address the label noise problem from the perspective of feature learning by class-specific autoencoder. This is based on our observation of the connection between two conceptually different problems: although one is the data contamination problem in the output space (label noise) while the other is in the input space (outliers), locally data points with noisy labels in some class are likely to be outliers of that class. We wish that this simple observation could help to inspire more methods to deal with the less-studied label noise problem. Extensive experiments show that our proposed method is effective in data cleaning and classification task.

References

1. Krishna, R.A., Hata, K., Chen, S., Kravitz, J., Shamma, D.A., Fei-Fei, L., Bernstein, M.S.: Embracing error to enable rapid crowdsourcing. In: Proceedings of the 2016 CHI Conference on Human Factors in Computing Systems, pp. 3167–3179. ACM (2016)
2. Ipeirotis, P.G., Provost, F., Wang, J.: Quality management on amazon mechanical turk. In: Proceedings of the ACM SIGKDD Workshop on Human Computation, pp. 64–67. ACM (2010)
3. Frénay, B., Verleysen, M.: Classification in the presence of label noise: a survey. IEEE Trans. Neural Netw. Learn. Syst. **25**(5), 845–869 (2014)
4. Jeatrakul, P., Wong, K.W., Fung, C.C.: Data cleaning for classification using misclassification analysis. J. Adv. Comput. Intell. Intell. Inform. **14**(3), 297–302 (2010)
5. Pruengkarn, R., Wong, K.W., Fung, C.C.: Data cleaning using complementary fuzzy support vector machine technique. In: Hirose, A., Ozawa, S., Doya, K., Ikeda, K., Lee, M., Liu, D. (eds.) ICONIP 2016. LNCS, vol. 9948, pp. 160–167. Springer, Cham (2016). https://doi.org/10.1007/978-3-319-46672-9_19
6. Fefilatyev, S., Shreve, M., Kramer, K., Hall, L., Goldgof, D., Kasturi, R., Daly, K., Remsen, A., Bunke, H.: Label-noise reduction with support vector machines. In: 2012 21st International Conference on Pattern Recognition (ICPR), pp. 3504–3508. IEEE (2012)
7. Liu, T., Tao, D.: Classification with noisy labels by importance reweighting. IEEE Trans. Pattern Anal. Mach. Intell. **38**(3), 447–461 (2016)
8. Wang, D., Tan, X.: Robust distance metric learning via bayesian inference. IEEE Trans. Image Process. **27**(3), 1542–1553 (2018)
9. Wang, D., Tan, X.: Bayesian neighborhood component analysis. IEEE Transactions on Neural Networks and Learning Systems (2017)
10. Aggarwal, C.C.: Outlier analysis. Data Mining, pp. 237–263. Springer, Cham (2015). https://doi.org/10.1007/978-3-319-14142-8_8
11. LeCun, Y., Bottou, L., Bengio, Y., Haffner, P.: Gradient-based learning applied to document recognition. Proc. IEEE **86**(11), 2278–2324 (1998)
12. Wang, D., Tan, X.: Label-denoising auto-encoder for classification with inaccurate supervision information. In: 2014 22nd International Conference on Pattern Recognition (ICPR), pp. 3648–3653. IEEE (2014)
13. Wang, D., Tan, X.: Robust distance metric learning in the presence of label noise. In: AAAI, pp. 1321–1327 (2014)
14. Rebbapragada, U.D.: Strategic targeting of outliers for expert review. Ph.D. thesis, Tufts University (2010)
15. Ekambaram, R., Fefilatyev, S., Shreve, M., Kramer, K., Hall, L.O., Goldgof, D.B., Kasturi, R.: Active cleaning of label noise. Pattern Recogn. **51**, 463–480 (2016)
16. Qian, Q., Hu, J., Jin, R., Pei, J., Zhu, S.: Distance metric learning using dropout: a structured regularization approach. In: Proceedings of the 20th ACM SIGKDD International Conference on Knowledge Discovery and Data Mining, pp. 323–332. ACM (2014)

17. Vidal, R., Ma, Y., Sastry, S.: Generalized principal component analysis (GPCA). IEEE Trans. Pattern Anal. Mach. Intell. **27**(12), 1945–1959 (2005)
18. Wang, H., Nie, F., Huang, H.: Robust distance metric learning via simultaneous l1-norm minimization and maximization. In: International Conference on Machine Learning, pp. 1836–1844 (2014)
19. Yang, L., Jin, R., Sukthankar, R.: Bayesian active distance metric learning. arXiv preprint arXiv:1206.5283 (2012)

Using the Wide and Deep Flexible Neural Tree to Forecast the Exchange Rate

Jing Xu[1,2], Peng Wu[1,2(✉)], Yuehui Chen[1,2(✉)], Hassan Dawood[3],
and Qingfei Meng[1,2]

[1] School of Information Science and Engineering, University of Jinan, Jinan, China
734007433@qq.com, {ise_wup,yhchen}@ujn.edu.cn, mqingfei@mail.ujn.edu.cn
[2] Shandong Provincial Key Laboratory of Network Based Intelligent Computing,
Jinan, China
[3] Software Engineering Department UET, Taxila, Pakistan
Hassan.dawood@uettaxila.edu.pk

Abstract. Forecasting exchange rate plays an important role in the financial market. It has become a hot research topic and many methods have been proposed. In this paper, a wide and deep flexible neural tree (FNT) is proposed to forecast the exchange rate. The wide component has the function to memorize the original input features, while the deep component can automatically extract unseen features. By balancing the width and depth of flexible neural tree, the structure of FNT is optimized from the experiments to forecast the exchange rate. Experiments have been conducted on four different kinds of exchange rate daily data to check the performance of the FNT. The architecture of the wide and deep FNT is developed by grammar guided genetic programming (GGGP) and the parameters are optimized by the particle swarm optimization algorithm (PSO). Proposed method performs well as compared to the autoregressive moving average model and neural networks.

Keywords: Flexible neural tree · Wide and deep learning
Exchange rates forecasting · Neural networks

1 Introduction

The exchange rate is a significant factor in financial markets, which directly affects the import and export of a country also influences the commodity price [1,2], so it is closely related to consumers like people living in that particular country. The research on prediction of exchange rate can help investors to obtain more profits. There are lots of researches work done to find the potential rules according to the fluctuation [3–5]. Since the change in exchange rate is nonlinear, that makes the prediction process very difficult. In recent years, many ways have been put forward to predict the exchange rate, including autoregressive moving average (ARMA) models, logistic regression, and multiple regressions [6–8]. However, the precision of those linear model to predict the exchange rate is not good enough [9].

© Springer International Publishing AG, part of Springer Nature 2018
T. Huang et al. (Eds.): ISNN 2018, LNCS 10878, pp. 265–272, 2018.
https://doi.org/10.1007/978-3-319-92537-0_31

Back-propagation (BP) algorithm made a drastic change to forecast the exchange rate [10], artificial neural networks (ANN) are often applied for forecasting exchange rate [11–13]. They observed that the ANNs combined with BP algorithm perform better than the traditional statistical ways.

Although neural networks can deal with the nonlinear problems, neural networks also have many disadvantages. For example, the structure of neural networks do not have accurate algorithm to design and the structure has closely relationship with performance. Then, it suffers from the convergence and over-fitting problem.

Chen [14–16] has proposed an architecture called flexible neural tree (FNT). The flexible neural tree (FNT) is a particular type of neural network that allows over-layer connections and input variables selection. FNT has successfully solved the problems of designing the architecture of neural networks [17]. The structure of FNT is automatically selected by the evolutionary algorithm.

In this paper, we propose a model called wide and deep flexible neural tree to forecast the exchange rate. The wide component has the function to memorize the original input features and it can be regarded as a linear model. While the deep component can automatically extract unseen features, which shows the generalization of a model. To combine the advantages of memorization and generalization of a model, the wide and deep FNT is put forward [18–20]. The proposed method automatically design the structure and can be trained faster to get a better value. The experimental results show that wide and deep FNT performs better than ARMA model and neural networks.

2   Methodology

The chapter firstly introduces the autoregressive moving average model (ARMA) which were often used to forecast exchange rates before, then two optimization algorithms involved is declared, and finally the description of wide and deep FNT we proposed is mentioned.

2.1   Autoregressive Moving Average Model

In the statistical analysis of time series, autoregressive moving average (ARMA) models are widely used to forecast [3]. It is composed of two polynomials, one is Autoregressive (AR) and another is moving average (MA).

There is a time series X_t, the ARMA can understand and predict future values. The model is generally expressed as ARMA (p, q) where p is the order of the AR and q is the order of MA. The ARMA (p, q) model is written below:

$$X_t = c + \varepsilon_t + \sum_{i=1}^{p} \varphi_i X_{t-i} + \sum_{i=1}^{q} \theta_i \varepsilon_{t-i} \tag{1}$$

where φ_i, θ_i are parameters, c is a constant. The ε_t and ε_{t-i} are white noise.

2.2   Grammar Guided Genetic Programming

Genetic programming (GP) overcome the limitations of traditional genetic algorithms by operating groups using independent computer programs rather than fixed-length binary strings. The individuals in the initial population is evaluated by fitness function. The fitness function is chosen according to the specific problem. For example, if the problem to be solved is in the field of time series prediction, the root mean square error (RMSE) is usually selected as an evaluation function of the fitness. From the initial generation, individuals are randomly produced and then the program with the best fitness value is copied into the next generation, following application of a genetic operator: (1)With reproduction, the program is directly copied without changes; (2)With mutation, a part of the program is randomly modified; (3)With crossover, two programs are selected to produce a new program.

GP requires that the contents of the function sets and the terminator character sets be of the same type. Otherwise, an invalid representation tree may be easily generated during the crossover and mutation operations. This limitation triggers a grammar guided genetic programming (GGGP). A context-free grammar G is defined by the 4 tuple: $G = \{N, T, P, \sum\}$, where N is called nonterminal characters, and T symbolizes terminals characters. The members of P are called rules of the grammar. $\sum$ is the start symbol and an element of N. The rules of the grammar are expressed as x→y, where x belongs to N and y belongs to $N \cup T$.

There are four basic steps to generate grammar guided genetic programming, listed as below:

```
(1) Generate an initial population:
This process is to randomly produce individual trees,
the production of trees is based on the grammar model.
(2) Evaluate each tree in the current generation:
Each tree has a specific value,
these values are the fitness of individuals.
(3) Apply one of three genetic operators to produce next generation:
three genetic operators: reproduction, mutation and crossover,
Then evaluate all trees in the new generation.
(4) Repeat until the best tree is found or termination criteria are met.
```

2.3   Particle Swarm Optimization Algorithm

The particle swarm optimization (PSO) algorithm searches the best solution using particles. The initial particles are randomly produced. Each particle represents a possible solution and has a value called position vector s_i. A population of particles in the problem space has the moving velocity represented by a vector a_i. At each step, a function f_i representing a fitness score. Each particle keeps track of its own best position, and the best fitness of particle is in a vector p_i. Moreover, the best position among all the particles is kept track of as p_g. At each time step t, a new velocity for particle i is calculated by

$$a_i(t+1) = a_i(t) + c_1\varphi_1(p_i(t) - s_i(t)) + c_2\varphi_2(p_g(t) - s_i(t)) \tag{2}$$

where φ_1 and φ_2 are random number in $[0,1]$, c_1 and c_2 are limited factors of position. In view of the changed velocities, each particle changes its position according to the following equation:

$$s_i(t+1) = s_i(t) + a_i(t+1) \tag{3}$$

In experiments, parameters in wide and deep flexible neural tree are optimized by PSO.

2.4   Wide and Deep Flexible Neural Tree

The wide and deep flexible neural tree is a special type of neural network. To generate the wide and deep FNT, the flexible activation function is in the following.

$$f(u_i, v_i, x) = exp(-(\frac{x - u_i}{v_i})^2) \tag{4}$$

Where two parameters u_i and v_i are randomly generated as flexible activation parameters. The output of a flexible neuron $+_n$ is produced as follows:

$$net_n = \sum_{j=1}^{n}(w_j * x_j) \tag{5}$$

Where $x_j(j = 1, 2, \ldots, n)$ are the inputs. The output of the node $+_n$ is calculated by:

$$out_n = f(u_n, v_n, net_n) = exp(-(net_n - u_n/v_n)^2) \tag{6}$$

The wide component acts as a linear model of the form $y = w^T x + b$, which includes raw input features and transformed features [20]. If a model only has the deep component, the original input features can be lost during the process of training, but sometimes it has a significant effect on the final output.

The deep component of our model is a FNT, which automatically extracts features. The parameters are changed to minimize the loss function during training process. The wide component and deep component are combined using a weighted sum of their output, which is then fed to one loss function for joint training. And then the wide and deep FNT has both the merits of memorization and generalization. The common structure of wide and deep FNT is illustrated in Fig. 1.

Using grammar guided genetic programming to automatically choose the best architecture of wide and deep FNT. As for the parameters of FNT, it can be specified by particle swarm optimization algorithm.

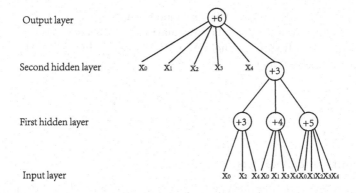

Fig. 1. A typical representation of wide and deep FNT

3 Experimental Results and Analysis

3.1 Experimental Design

Four data sets as in the experiments as US dollar (USD), Euro (EURO), British Pound Sterling (GBP) and Japanese yen (JPY), and all exchange rates are converted into RMB. These data are taken from the state administration of foreign exchange website http://www.safe.gov.cn/wps/portal/sy/tjsj_hlzjj_inquire. In the experiments, we both used 667 data from 1st January 2015 to 1st October 2017 in four different kinds of daily rates. These data are separated into two parts: 500 training data and 167 test data. The exchange rate was firstly transformed to the interval [0,1] before entering the model.

In the experiments, we have used grammar guided genetic programming to optimize the architecture of individual trees. As for the parameters of trees, it can be specified by PSO algorithm. The corresponding parameters are listed in Table 1.

Table 1. Parameter settings

Population size	50	Crossover probability	0.1
Mutation probability	0.01	C1	2.0
C2	2.0	Vmax	2.0

The input of the model is the data of first five days and the result calculated by wide and deep FNT as the forecasting value. The instruction sets of wide and deep FNT is $S = F \cup T = \{+_2, +_3, \ldots, +_N\}\{x_1, \ldots, x_n\}$.

To verify the efficiency of proposed model, the experiments have been done on the ARMA and NN. The number of inputs for ARMA, NN and wide and deep FNT is five, and the forecasting values can be obtained by the outputs of the three models. In addition, the parameters in ARMA are set to 1 and the structure of the NN is 5–10-1. The evaluation parameter is standard as root mean square error (RMSE). Where Y_i is the actual value, Y_i' is the predicted value, and n is the number of data samples.

$$RMSE = \sqrt{\frac{\sum\limits_{i=1}^{n} (Y_i - Y_i')^2}{n}} \tag{7}$$

3.2   Results and Analysis

Figure 2 shows the results on ARMA, NN and wide and deep FNT forecasting the exchange rate of USD, EURO, GBP, JPY, respectively. It can be observed that the changing tendency of the exchange rate can be clearly seen. It is obvious that the trend of the three curves are roughly the same, but the curves of wide and deep FNT model and NN is closer to actual output compared with ARMA. The wide and deep FNT model effectively predicts the exchange rate, the NN also forecast exchange rate accurately, but the performance of ARMA is less than the other two models. It demonstrated that due to the complexity of the change of exchange rate, the linear models like ARMA cannot forecast it well.

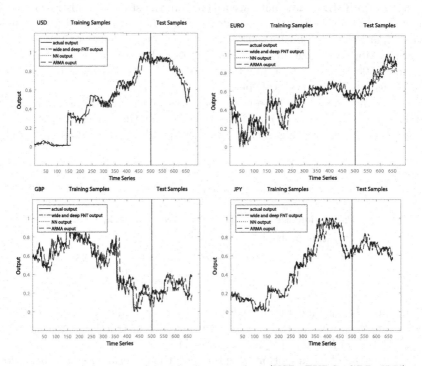

Fig. 2. The time series of 4 exchange rates data (USD, EURO, GBP, JPY)

The wide and deep FNT forecasting results of RMSE compared with traditional linear model ARMA and most widely used NN is illustrated in the Table 2, including both training set and test set on 4 kinds of exchange rates. From the Table 2, it can be observed that the wide and deep FNT has the less RMSE than the other two models whether in the training set or test set. The reason why it performs better than the NN is that the structure of NN is selected according to the experience, which effects the results greatly. However the proposed can automatically choose the architecture, and the balancing between the width and depth improves the performance of memorization and generalization.

Table 2. Models performance

Model	USD		EURO		GBP		JPY	
	Train	Test	Train	Test	Train	Test	Train	Test
ARMA	0.0192	0.0180	0.0304	0.0317	0.0374	0.0249	0.0225	0.0196
NN	0.0174	0.0167	0.0297	0.0290	0.0356	0.0240	0.0199	0.0186
FNT	0.0158	0.0151	0.0279	0.0195	0.0331	0.0220	0.0204	0.0170

4   Conclusion

In this paper, wide and deep flexible neural tree is put forward to forecast the exchange rate. The wide component has the function to memorize the original input features, while the deep component can automatically extract unseen features. The experiments show that the wide and deep FNT model is superior to that of ARMA and NN. The architecture of the wide and deep FNT is developed by grammar guided genetic programming (GGGP) and parameters are optimized by particle swarm optimization algorithm (PSO). The experimental results depicts that the predicted values of FNT approximate the true values, so the wide and deep FNT is an efficient method to forecast exchange rates.

In future, we intend to do further research on using other methods to optimize the architecture and parameters of the wide and deep FNT.

Acknowledgments. This work was supported by the National Natural Science Foundation of China (Grant No. 61671220, 61640218, 61201428), the National Key Research and Development Program of China (2016YFC106000) the Shandong Distinguished Middle-aged and Young Scientist Encourage and Reward Foundation, China (Grant No. ZR2016FB14), the Project of Shandong Province Higher Educational Science and Technology Program, China (Grant No. J16LN07), the Shandong Province Key Research and Development Program, China (Grant No. 2016GGX101022), the Doctoral Foundation of University of Jinan.

References

1. Liu, C., Hou, W., Liu, D.: Foreign exchange rates forecasting with convolutional neural network. Neural Process. Lett. **2**, 1–25 (2017)
2. Deng, S., Yoshiyama, K., Mitsubuchi, T., et al.: Hybrid method of multiple kernel learning and genetic algorithm for forecasting short-term foreign exchange rates. Comput. Econ. **45**(1), 49–89 (2015)
3. Cheng, H.: Autoregressive modeling of canadian money and income data. Am. Stat. Assoc. **74**(367), 553–560 (2012)
4. Finn, M.G.: Forecasting the exchange rate: a monetary or random walk phenomenon? J. Int. Money Finance **5**(2), 181–193 (1986)
5. Bui, L.T., Truong, V.V., Huong, D.T.T.: A novel evolutionary multi-objective ensemble learning approach for forecasting currency exchange rates. Data Knowl. Eng. **114**, 40–66 (2017)
6. Moscarola, J., Roy, B.: Financial ratios, discriminant analysis and the prediction of corporate bankrunptcy (1977)
7. Laitinen, E.K., Laitinen, T.: Bankruptcy prediction: application of the Taylor's expansion in logistic regression. Int. Rev. Financ. Anal. **9**(4), 327–349 (2000)
8. Taylor, S.J.: Forecasting volatility of exchange rates. Int. J. Forecast. **3**(1), 159–170 (1987)
9. Chiarella, C., Peat, M., Stevenson, M.: Detecting and modelling nonlinearity in flexible exchange rate time series. Asia Pac. J. Manag. **11**(2), 159–186 (1994)
10. Werbos, P.J.: Generalization of backpropagation with application to a recurrent gas market model. Neural Netw. **1**(4), 339–356 (1988)
11. Hann, T.H., Steurer, E.: Much ado about nothing? exchange rate forecasting: neural networks vs. linear models using monthly and weekly data. Neurocomputing **10**(4), 323–339 (1996)
12. Leung, M.T., Chen, A.S., Daouk, H.: Forecasting exchange rates using general regression neural networks. Comput. Oper. Res. **27**(11–12), 1093–1110 (2000)
13. Shen, F., Chao, J., Zhao, J.: Forecasting exchange rate using deep belief networks and conjugate gradient method. Neurocomputing **167**(C), 243–253 (2015)
14. Chen, Y., Yang, B., Dong, J., et al.: Time-series forecasting using flexible neural tree model. Inf. Sci. **174**(34), 219–235 (2005)
15. Chen, Y., Yang, B., Abraham, A.: Flexible neural trees ensemble for stock index modeling. Neurocomputing **70**(46), 697–703 (2007)
16. Wang, L., Yang, B., Chen, Y., et al.: Modeling early-age hydration kinetics of Portland cement using flexible neural tree. Neural Comput. Appl. **21**(5), 877–889 (2012)
17. Chen, Y., Yang, B., Meng, Q.: Small-time scale network traffic prediction based on flexible neural tree. Appl. Soft Comput. **12**(1), 274–279 (2012)
18. Chen, C.L.P., Liu, Z.: Broad learning system: a new learning paradigm and system without going deep. In: Automation, pp. 1271–1276. IEEE Press (2017)
19. Chen, C., Liu, Z.: Broad learning system: an effective and efficient incremental learning system without the need for deep architecture. IEEE Trans. Neural Netw. Learn. Syst. **PP**(99), 1–15 (2017)
20. Cheng, H.T., Koc, L., Harmsen, J., et al.: Wide and deep learning for recommender systems. In: The Workshop on Deep Learning for Recommender Systems, pp. 7–10. ACM (2016)

An Immune Genetic K-Means Algorithm for Mongolian Elements Clustering

Chun Hua[1,2(✉)] and Chun Ying Cheng[1]

[1] School of Computer Sciences and Technology, Inner Mongolia University for Nationalities, Tongliao 028043, People's Republic of China
chunhua99018074@163.com
[2] School of Mathematical Sciences, Dalian University of Technology, Dalian 116024, People's Republic of China

Abstract. Text clustering is an important area in artificial intelligence. Production of the some character recognitions have been transformed into commercial soft-ware, but the research on Mongolian elements is now just beginning. There are many characters in Mongolian structure and written pattern in contrast with other kinds of characters. In this paper, we proposed a novel clustering technique that combined genetic K-Means algorithm and immune algorithm. The proposed technique clustered the Mongolian elements to the better result. Experiment show that the accurate clustering rate of this method is over 98% and this technique is efficient and feasible.

Keywords: Immune algorithm · Genetic algorithm
Mongolian element clustering · K-Means

1 Introduction

Mongolian nationality is gathering in some provinces and autonomous regions in China, such as, Xinjiang, Gansu, and Heilongjiang. In which, the Inner Mongolia Autonomous Region is the most concentrated area of Mongolian nationalities and its main language is Mongolian. The input, storage and processing of Mongolian information is a key issue. Text clustering is a new technique which combines image processing and clustering analysis. Which groups the elements according to similar characteristics such as similar structure or similar expression, so that the elements in the same group have the greatest similarity, while the elements in different groups have the greatest dissimilarity.

This paper is organized as follows. In Sect. 2, we describe the immune optimization algorithm, genetic algorithms and our proposed algorithm (IGKM). In Sect. 3, numerical experiments are shown on IGKM algorithms, some short conclusions are drawn in Section 4.

This research work was supported by project of Inner Mongolia University for Nationalities (NMDYB15080).

2 IGKM Algorithm

In this section, we first describe the Immune optimization algorithm and genetic algorithm. Then, we combine the Immune optimization algorithm with genetic K-Means mechanism obtain our IGKM algorithm.

2.1 Immune Optimization Algorithm

Artificial immune algorithm is a new intelligent optimization algorithm inspired by biological immune system. In which, the antigen and antibody corresponded to the objective function and the feasible solution of the optimization problem respectively. Affinity for antibody and antigen presents matching degree of feasible solution and objective function. And affinity between antibodies ensures the diversity of feasible solutions. Furthermore, fitness value of antibodies promotes the inheritance and variation of superior antibodies. Memory cell unit preserved optimal solution and inhibited from producing similar feasible solutions, which accelerate search for global optimal solution.

2.2 The Basic Concept of the Genetic Algorithm

The genetic strategy consists of an initialization step and the iterative generations.

In iteration step, user defined the number of generations that he or she wants. The genetic algorithm will run this number of generations and retain the chromosome with the best fitness. This string represents the solution obtained by the genetic algorithm. In the next, selection operator is implemented by using a roulette wheel strategy according to fitness. For each chosen pair of chromosomes, crossover operator is applied by probability Pc. Mutation process changed the bits of the chromosomes strings with probability Pm.

2.3 The Proposed Hybrid Algorithm

In this section, the immune genetic algorithm is described.

Initialization: each chromosome of population is randomly generated for possible solutions within the range of design values. Each chromosome represents a possible solution of the problem. To avoid empty clusters, we initialize the population $\{S_w^j, j = 1, 2, \ldots, N\}$ in two steps. First, the top K components of S_w^j is randomly assigned as permutations of the $\{1, 2, \ldots, N\}$. Secondly, the rest components of S_w^j are assigned as a random cluster number selected from the uniform distribution of the set $\{1, 2, \ldots, N\}$.

Crossover: In this phase, we adopt single point crossover strategy. If a pair of chromosome S_{wi} and S_{wj} are chosen for applying the crossover operator, a random number p are generated to decide where position of the chromosomes are to be interchanged. For each chosen pair of chromosomes, the crossover operator is done with probability Pc.

Mutation: In this phase, each bit of selected chromosome will be changed to random number between 1 and K and each chromosome will be chosen with probability Pm, if the fitness value of the new chromosome is better than that of original value, then the new chromosome is stored in the place of the original one, otherwise the old chromosome is kept in population.

Immune operation: this phase include vaccine and immunity selection operation. First, the current population is vaccinated with a certain probabilities, and then immune selection is employed (Fig. 1).

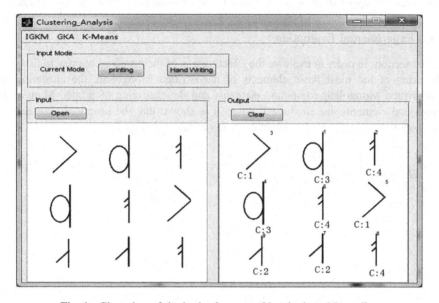

Fig. 1. Clustering of the basic elements of handwritten Mongolian

K-Means: K-Means is applied for rapid convergence. For an individual S_w, reassign each gene to the cluster with the closest cluster center to form a new individual S_w.

Let us introduce some notations. Our aim is to cluster n elements $\{x_i, i = 1, 2, \ldots, n\}$ into K clusters. And we define

$$w_{ik} = \begin{cases} 1 & \text{if the } i - \text{th element belongs to the } k - \text{th cluster,} \\ 0 & \text{otherwise.} \end{cases}$$

and we define the label matrix, $W = [w_{ik}]$,

$$\sum_{k=1}^{K} w_{ik} = 1, i = 1, 2, \ldots, n, \tag{1}$$

$$1 \leq \sum_{i=1}^{n} w_{ik} < n, \quad k = 1, 2, \ldots, K. \tag{2}$$

Objective function is as follows:

$$\min F = \sum_{i=1}^{n} \sum_{k=1}^{K} d_{ik} w_{ik} \tag{3}$$

Where $d_{ij} \leq s$, represents the distance from $i - th$ point to the nearest cluster center; S denoted the upper limit of the distance $i - th$ element belongs to the k-th cluster.

2.4   Experimental Evaluation

In this section, in order to evaluate the effectiveness of the proposed approach, first, the clustering of the most basic elements of handwritten Mongolian, the clustering of handwritten Mongolian compound elements and the clustering of printed Mongolian compound elements are conducted. After, it is shown that the proposed approach is successful to cluster the Mongolian elements accurately (Fig. 2).

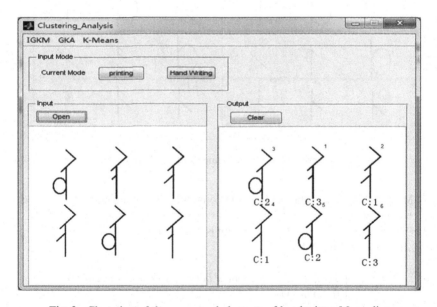

Fig. 2. Clustering of the compound elements of handwritten Mongolian

The basic elements are the most basic units of the Mongolian characters. The recognition and classification of basic Mongolian elements is simpler than that of compound elements because of complexity of structure. For hand writing elements, each person writes in a different size and shape, therefore, the same character written by the same person may be different. But on the premise of a fixed font and size, the same printed text has nothing to do with the typist (Fig. 3).

Each algorithms is conducted fifty times, the average accuracy is as follows (Table 1):

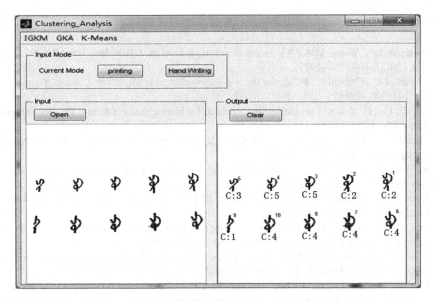

Fig. 3. Clustering of the elements of printed Mongolian elements

Table 1. The accuracy of proposed clustering algorithm

Algorithm	Hand–basic	Hand–compound	Printed
K-Means	89.5%	89.3%	90.4%
GKA	92.8%	91.6%	92.2%
IGKM	99.7%	98.9%	99.8%

3 Conclusion

In this paper, we combine the Immune algorithm with the genetic K-Means algorithm to get a novel algorithm called IGKM algorithm for Mongolian elements clustering. Our algorithm includes four operations: immune selection for the population to have a good evolution direction; K-Means for local search for better individuals; vaccination and mutation for the ergodicity of the evolution process, which guarantees the appearance of a global optimal individual in the evolution process; and updating of the super individual for catching forever the global optimal individual once it appears. The IGKM algorithm is evaluated and compared with K-Means, GKA-Mean. The experimental results demonstrate that IGKM algorithm outperforms other algorithms.

References

1. Hartigan, J.A., Wong, M.A.: A k-means clustering algorithm. J. Roy. Stat. Soc.: Ser. C (Appl. Stat.) **28**(3), 100–108 (1979)
2. Bezdek, J.C., Ehrlich, R.: FCM: the fuzzy c-means clustering algorithm. Comput. Geosci. **10**(1), 191–203 (1984)
3. Du, Z., Lin, F.: A novel parallelization approach for hierarchical clustering. Parallel Comput. **31**(5), 523–527 (2005)
4. Maulik, U., Bandyopadhyay, S.: Genetic algorithm based clustering technique. Pattern Recogn. **33**(9), 1455–1465 (2000)
5. de Castro, L.N., Timmis, J.I.: Artificial immune systems as a novel soft computing paradigm. Soft Comp. **7**(8), 526–544 (2003)
6. Khoo, L.P., Alisantoso, D.: Line balancing of PCB assembly line using immune algorithms. Comp. Eng. **19**(2), 92–100 (2003)
7. Luh, G.C., Chueh, C.H.: Multi-modal topological optimization of structure using immune algorithm. Comp. Methods Eng. **193**(36), 4035–4055 (2004)
8. Luh, G.C., Chueh, C.H.: Multi-objective optimal design of truss structure with immune algorithm. Comp. Strut. **82**(11), 829–844 (2004)
9. Haifeng, D., Moaguo, G., Licheng, J., Ruochen, L.: A novel algorithm of artificial immune system for high-dimensional function numerical optimization. Prog. Nat. Sci. **15**(5), 463–471 (2005)

Classification of Concrete Strength Grade Using Nearest Neighbor Partitioning

Xuehui Zhu[1], Lin Wang[1(✉)], Bo Yang[1,2(✉)], Jin Zhou[1], Shiyuan Han[1],
Yu Liu[3], Jifeng Guo[1], and Shuangrong Liu[1]

[1] Shandong Provincial Key Laboratory of Network Based Intelligent Computing,
University of Jinan, Jinan 250022, China
`wangplanet@gmail.com, yangbo@ujn.edu.cn`
[2] School of Informatics, Linyi University, Linyi 276000, China
[3] Shenzhen Gangchuang Building Material Co., Ltd., Shenzhen, China

Abstract. Concrete is an important building material in the field of civil engineering. As an important factor, the strength of concrete affects its quality directly. Although conventional methods are made to forecast concrete strength, the classification of its grade is still an important issue in terms of non-uniformity of mortar and the complexity of curing condition. In this study, the classification of strength grade is implemented by employing the nearest neighbor partitioning method-based neural network classifier, which not only produces flexible decision boundaries but also eliminates centroid-based constraints and further enlarges the opportunity for finding optimal solutions. Experimental results manifest that the adopted method improves the performance of concrete grade classification.

Keywords: Neural network · Nearest neighbor partitioning
Concrete strength

1 Introduction

With the development of concrete technology in terms of performance, concrete is widely used in industrial and civil buildings, as well as in railways, highways, bridges, tunnels, various types of underwater applications, marine and other special projects; thus, concrete is an indispensable composite material of modern civil engineering. Concrete is a general term for composite materials that are completely consolidated by cementitious materials, that is, it is obtained by mixing, forming and water curing (adding or not adding admixtures) in a certain proportion. Concrete has the advantages of simple production process, low cost, and rich raw materials. In comparison other engineering materials, concrete has higher durability and compressive strength.

Cement is an important raw material in producing concrete. The performance of concrete quality and production will be stable and qualified if the raw materials, especially the quality of cement, are of high quality and standards.

© Springer International Publishing AG, part of Springer Nature 2018
T. Huang et al. (Eds.): ISNN 2018, LNCS 10878, pp. 279–288, 2018.
https://doi.org/10.1007/978-3-319-92537-0_33

Therefore, concrete performance is influenced by the performance of cement, which is a challenging task.

The strength of concrete is formed by the coagulation of chemical and physical reactions due to the mixture of inorganic cementitious materials with water. Concrete strength includes compressive, tensile, shear, bending, folding and grip. In addition, concrete grade is classified by the standard value of the compressive strength of concrete cubes. Factors that affect concrete strength are mainly the grade of cement and water-cement ratio, aggregate, age, curing temperature, and humidity. Furthermore, concrete specimens are got out at a certain age to measure their average strength. However, this traditional method takes considerable time and consumes substantial raw materials.

Many types of computation methods, such as support vector machine [1], neural network [2], and gene expression programming [3], can predict cement and concrete strength directly. However, the classification of concrete strength grade remains an important issue in terms of non-uniformity of mortar and the complexity of curing condition. Classification plays an important role in data mining. The classification model is established through training of data set, which is then used to test new sample categories. Among all types of classification techniques, the neural network classifier has been successfully applied in solving practical problems.

Concrete strength grade was successfully predicted [4], and the best results were obtained using the floating centroids method (FCM) [5], which uses the way of centroids clustering [6]. However, FCM cannot produce flexible decision boundaries, thereby reducing the probabilities in building the best neural network. Therefore, the nearest neighbor partitioning (NNP) [7] method is proposed to solve the above problem. This method can find the best neural networks whose quality is evaluated by the nearest neighbor criteria evaluation. In addition, for traditional methods, the high cost of concrete strength prediction limits the execution of the process. Thus, the NNP neural network classifier is used to the classification of concrete strength grade.

This paper is organized as follows. Section 2 presents the related works. Section 3 presents the NNP method and its application in the classification of concrete strength grade. Section 4 discusses and describes the experimental results, followed by the conclusion in Sect. 5.

2   Related Works

Researchers have done a lot of works on concrete strength prediction. Trtnik et al. [8] established a mathematical model in the environment of Matlab using the artificial neural network and the model is able to estimate the compressive strength of concrete easily by the analysis of the relationship between ultrasonic pulse velocity and strength of concrete. Lee [9] developed a "i-precons" (concrete strength intelligent prediction system) using artificial neural networks, which can effectively predict the compressive strength of concrete. Kim et al. [10] proposed the probabilistic method of concrete compressive strength prediction based on concrete mix proportions. By using the probability neural network, the strength is estimated effectively.

Gupta et al. [11] obtained more accurate concrete strength prediction based on concrete mixing ratio by using ANN model. In addition, in order to overcome the bottleneck of complex knowledge acquisition, expert system has been established for the problem as a mechanism, which convert project experience into useful knowledge through the rule-based knowledge representation technology.

Rajasekaran et al. [12] developed a intelligent system for prediction of concrete strength through the functional network in order to provide concrete location strength information for concrete demolition and construction scheduling. Jongjae et al. [13] used support vector regression (SVR) to estimate the strength of concrete. Compared with the estimation performance of NN, SVR method is very efficient in computation time and estimation accuracy. Lai and Serra [14] established a model based on neurocomputing and predicted the compressive strength of cement enterprises in a sufficient approximation. Severcan [15] proposed a formula for predicting the tensile strength of concrete through gene expression programming (GEP), and the GEP formula has good performance in predicting the tensile strength of concrete.

3 Methodology

3.1 Nearest Neighbor Partitioning

In NNP method, training data are mapped in the partition space, and the distribution of samples in the partition space is then used to evaluate the neural network quality, in which the samples with the same class are close to each other and the samples with different classes are away from each other. In addition, the k-nearest neighbor(KNN) [16] algorithm is used to predict the new samples in the partition space.

Particle swarm optimization (PSO) [17] algorithm is applied for NNP optimization. It is adopted to optimize the weights and biases of the neural network and it aims to obtain the best fitness and guide the evolution direction. In the training process of NNP, the individual is randomly initialized at the beginning of evolution. Each individual is encoded as a vector of weights. The samples are initially mapped in the partition space through the neural network, and are further normalized using Z-score [18]. The normalized samples are constrained into a hypersphere with a radius of 1 using

$$F_1(\mathbf{x}) = \mathbf{x} \frac{1 - e^{-|\mathbf{x}|/2}}{|\mathbf{x}| + |\mathbf{x}| \cdot e^{-|\mathbf{x}|/2}} \tag{1}$$

where F_1 is an function of hypersphere mapping, $\mathbf{x}$ represents a normalized point. Thereafter, the similarity of the within-class and the similarity of the current point and other points in the neighborhood are calculated. And the maximum distance between any two points is 2. Then, the similarity formula is described as follows

$$s(\mathbf{x_1}, \mathbf{x_2}) = 2 - |F_1(\mathbf{x_1}) - F_1(\mathbf{x_2})| \tag{2}$$

where $\mathbf{x_1}$ and $\mathbf{x_2}$ stand for two normalized points. Then, the fitness value of particles is then acquired using the optimization target function, which is described as follows

$$F_2 = \sum_{i=1}^{n} \{\omega(\mathbf{x}_i)(S_{nonself}(\mathbf{x}_i) - \alpha S_{self}(\mathbf{x}_i))\} \tag{3}$$

where $\omega(\mathbf{x}_i)$ represents the weight of current sample (Same class has the same weight, that is, the weight of each sample is equal to the total number of samples divided by the number of classes of the current sample.) and α is a adjustment coefficient. $S_{nonself}(\mathbf{x}_i)$ is the sum of similarities between current sample and samples from the other classes in neighborhood of current sample. $S_{self}(\mathbf{x}_i)$ is the sum of similarities between current sample and samples from the same class. Finally, an optimal neural network is established. Algorithm 1 shows the training process of NNP.

Algorithm 1. Training Process of NNP

---

1 Initialize the population;
2 Calculate the weight for each class in the data set;
3 **while** *maximum generation has not been reached* **do**
4   **for** *every individual in the population* **do**
5   Decode the current individual as a vector of a neural network;
6   **for** *each sample in the data set* **do**
7 | Map the current sample to partition space;
8   **end**
9   **for** *mapped points in the partition space* **do**
10 | Normalize the points using Z-score;
11   **end**
12   **for** *normalized points in the partition space* **do**
13   Calculate the sum of within-class similarities in neighborhood of current point;
14   Calculate the sum of similarities between current point and points from the other classes in neighborhood of current point;
15   **end**
16   Compute the fitness value of current individual using (3);
17   **end**
18   Individuals reproduce the next generation according to their fitness;
19 **end**
20 Return the best neural network and its partition space.

Figure 1 explains the NNP example in three categories. If a sample is predicted as a class, then it is marked as the same class in its neighborhood. Compared with the data space, there is a clear decision boundary between classes in the partition space. Thus, the advantage of NNP is the production of flexible decision boundary among different classes based on mapping points. Moreover, NNP removes constraint from a centroid-based typical spherical method and

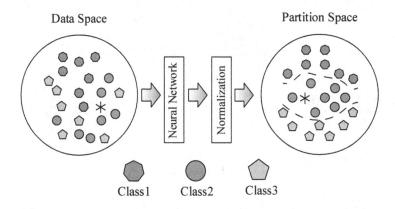

Fig. 1. Data space and partition space for classification into three classes using NNP

generate arbitrary shape boundaries compared with one-per-class, SoftMax [19], ECOC [20] and FCM. This method expands the scope in building a best neural network.

3.2   Classification of Concrete Strength Grade

The data set is able to be acquired by extracting the concrete image features using the differential equations [21–23]. Each sample has eight input features, including Age (day), Fine Aggregate (kg in a m^3 mixture), Coarse Aggregate (kg in a m^3 mixture), Blast Furnace Slag (kg in a m^3 mixture), Superplasticizer (kg in a m^3 mixture), Water (kg in a m^3 mixture), Fly Ash (kg in a m^3 mixture) and Cement (kg in a m^3 mixture). The final output is the strength grade. The training data are applied in NNP learning process to find the best solution. The general procedure is shown in Fig. 2.

If the strength grade of a new sample is categorized, its features are initially mapped in the partition space through the optimal neural network. The category is then predicted by the weighted KNN. Figure 3 shows the sample categorization with a certain strength grade using NNP.

4   Experiments

Training accuracy (TA) [5], generalization accuracy (GA) [5], and average F-measure (Avg.FM) [5] are used as measurement standards to assess the NNP's performance in concrete strength grade classification in this study. TA is a method that measures training data sets, whereas GA measures testing data sets. TA and GA values will be high if a classifier has good performance. Avg.FM is the weighted harmonic mean of precision and recall. Recall refers to the relevant files retrieved by the system divided by the total number of relevant files in the system, which measures the recall rate of the retrieval system. Precision

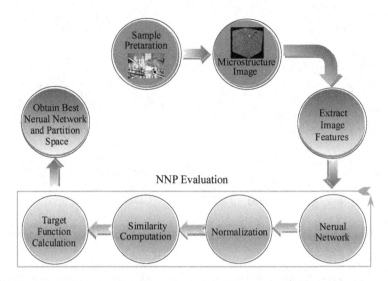

Fig. 2. The procedure of concrete strength grade classification

refers to the relevant files retrieved by the system divided by the total number of files retrieved by the system, which measures the precision rate of the retrieval system. Recall and precision values are between 0 and 1. If the value is close to 1, recall and precision rates are high. Avg.FM is a combination of two indexes that are used to reflect the overall index.

The compressive strength data set of concrete is obtained from the web site http://archive.ics.uci.edu/ml/. The data set includes 1030 samples, and the last value of each sample is the concrete compressive strength (Mpa). The samples are segmented into three categories. The first category is made up of samples with concrete strength less than $30Mpa$. The second category comprises samples with concrete strength between $30Mpa$ and $60Mpa$. The third category is composed of samples with concrete strength greater than $60Mpa$.

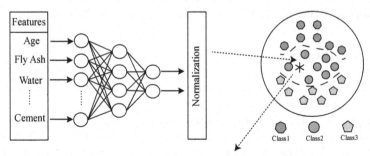

The grade of this concrete sample is categorized as Class 2.

Fig. 3. Categorize a new concrete sample

The data set should be standardized with min-max normalization [7] to address the comparability among the data indexes, thereby eliminating the dimensional impact among the indexes. After the original data are standardized, the indexes are on the same order of magnitude, which is suitable for comprehensive comparison evaluation.

The 10-fold cross-validation is applied to test the accuracy of the algorithm. This method splits the data set into ten subsets, takes nine subsets as training data, and selects the remaining subset as testing data. Each experiment yields corresponding accuracy. The average of the ten results is then used as the performance evaluation. A three layers feedforward neural network with five neurons in its hidden layer is applied in this experiment. The number of nearest neighbors L and K is set to 30 and 8, respectively; the discrimination weight α is set to 1. In PSO, Max Generation is 1000, population size is 20, $\varphi 1$ and $\varphi 2$ are set to 1.8, and $Vmax$ is set to 0.4.

In order to show the distribution of mapped points, the dimension of partition space m is set to 2 so that the partition space can be visualized. Figure 4 shows the distribution of mapped points in partition space for each validation after optimization. The points with the same class are clustered together, whereas the points with different classes are away from each other.

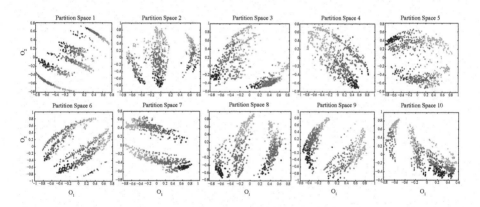

Fig. 4. The point distribution in partition space on all validations. Each of them corresponds to a neural network. The blue points represent the first category. The green points represent the second category. The red points represent the third category. (Color figure online)

In order to test the effectiveness of the proposed method, the dimension of partition space m is increased to 3 to increase redundancy. Table 1 shows the TA of NNP and other methods in terms of concrete grade classification. It can be seen that the NNP has the best training accuracy compared with other methods. Moreover, NNP has a smaller standard deviation, indicating that the stability of NNP training is better. Figure 5 shows the change in the TA of concrete strength grade classification for each validation. The curve shape indicates that the evolution process converges after 600 generations.

Table 1. Results of training accuracy

Validation	Traditional	SoftMax	ECOC	FCM	NB	SVM	NNP
1	82.96	80.37	83.17	83.5	80.15	81.55	86.73
2	84.90	82.85	82.09	86.41	80.47	83.17	85.87
3	82.74	52.21	83.28	83.93	80.26	82.74	85.01
4	81.45	83.17	69.47	83.82	80.37	83.6	85.22
5	65.26	84.03	83.17	84.14	81.34	81.45	86.08
6	83.28	82.09	61.06	84.90	80.58	82.31	83.93
7	83.71	83.39	83.06	86.3	80.26	81.88	85.35
8	83.60	63.86	72.49	84.47	79.94	82.96	84.79
9	84.47	69.26	83.28	86.62	80.91	82.52	86.41
10	82.85	81.98	81.23	84.36	79.29	83.17	86.84
MEAN	81.52	76.32	78.23	84.84	80.36	82.54	85.62
STD	5.79	10.89	7.83	1.17	0.55	0.73	0.93

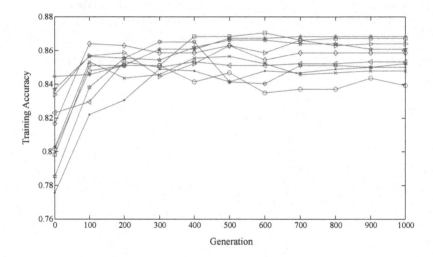

Fig. 5. The training accuracy of concrete strength grade classification on all validations

Figure 6 describes the GA and Avg. FM of NNP and other methods in terms of concrete grade classification. NNP achieves a significant result on the measures. In particular, the result of F-measure shows that NNP is more stable than the traditional method, SoftMax, ECOC, FCM, NB and SVM. Therefore, the performance of NNP is the best among all compared methods. The proposed NNP method enlarges the scope in building an optimal neural network classifier, and further improves the performance in classifying concrete strength grade.

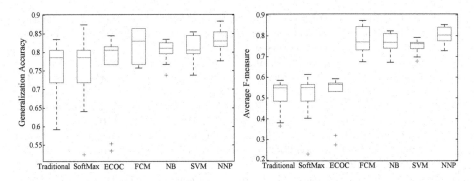

Fig. 6. Results of the generalization accuracy and average F-measure

5 Conclusion

In this paper, the nearest neighbor partitioning neural network classifier is applied to the classification of concrete strength grade, which produces arbitrary shape boundaries, eliminates centroid-based constraints, and expends the probability of discovering the optimal solutions. In this method, NNP converts the concrete sample features into a strength grade according to the concrete sample input. The strength grade for each concrete sample is predicted by the number of its nearest neighbors. In addition, the concrete compressive strength data is applied to evaluate NNP performance by comparing several measurements with other methods. Experimental results indicate that the nearest neighbor partition method improves the classification performance. In future works, more experiments will be performed in evaluating the application of concrete quality. Furthermore, its applications in more fields will be studied to evaluate NNP performance.

Acknowledgments. This work was supported by National Natural Science Foundation of China under Grant No. 61573166, No. 61572230, No. 81671785, No. 61472164, No. 61472163, No. 61672262. Science and technology project of Shandong Province under Grant No. 2015GGX101025. Project of Shandong Province Higher Educational Science and Technology Program under Grant no. J16LN07. Shandong Provincial Key R&D Program under Grant No. 2016ZDJS01A12, No. 2016GGX101001.

References

1. Shi, X.C., Dong, Y.F.: Support vector machine applied to prediction strength of cement. In: 2nd International Conference on Artificial Intelligence, Management Science and Electronic Commerce, pp. 1585–1588 (2011)
2. Yeh, I.C.: Modeling of strength of high-performance concrete using artificial neural networks. Cem. Concr. Res. **28**, 1797–1808 (1998)
3. Wang, L., Yang, B., Wang, S., Liang, Z.: Building image feature kinetics for cement hydration using gene expression programming with similarity weight tournament selection. IEEE Trans. Evol. Comput. **19**, 679–693 (2015)

4. Wang, L., Yang, B., Abraham, A.: Prediction of concrete strength using floating centroids method. In: 2013 IEEE International Conference on Systems, Man, and Cybernetics. Manchester, pp. 988–992 (2013)

5. Wang, L., Yang, B., Chen, Y., Abraham, A., Sun, H., Chen, Z., Wang, H.: Improvement of neural network classifier using floating centroids. Knowl. Inf. Syst. **31**, 433–454 (2012)

6. Zhou, J., Chen, L., Chen, C.L.P., Zhang, Y., Li, H.X.: Fuzzy clustering with the entropy of attribute weights. Neurocomputing **198**, 125–134 (2016)

7. Wang, L., Yang, B., Chen, Y., Zhang, X., Orchard, J.: Improving neural-network classifiers using nearest neighbor partitioning. IEEE Trans. Neural Netw. Learn. Syst. **28**, 2255–2267 (2017)

8. Trtnik, G., Kavcic, F., Turk, G.: Prediction of concrete strength using ultrasonic pulse velocity and artificial neural networks. Ultrasonics **49**, 53–60 (2009)

9. Lee, S.C.: Prediction of concrete strength using artificial neural networks. Eng. Struct. **25**, 849–857 (2003)

10. Kim, D.K., Lee, J.J., Lee, J.H., Chang, S.K.: Application of probabilistic neural networks for prediction of concrete strength. J. Mater. Civil Eng. **17**, 353–362 (2005)

11. Gupta, R., Kewalramani, M.A., Goel, A.: Prediction of concrete strength using neural-expert system. J. Mater. Civil Eng. **18**, 462–466 (2006)

12. Rajasekaran, S., Lee, S.C.: Prediction of concrete strength using serial functional network model. Struct. Eng. Mech. **16**, 83–99 (2003)

13. Jongjae, L., Dookie, K., Seongkyu, C., Jangho, L.: Application of support vector regression for the prediction of concrete strength. Comput. Concr. **4**, 299–316 (2007)

14. Lai, S., Serra, M.: Concrete strength prediction by means of neural network. Constr. Build. Mater. **11**, 93–98 (1997)

15. Severcan, M.H.: Prediction of splitting tensile strength from the compressive strength of concrete using gep. Neural Comput. Appl. **21**, 1937–1945 (2012)

16. Yu, Z., Liu, Y., Yu, X., Pu, K.Q.: Scalable distributed processing of k nearest neighbor queries over moving objects. IEEE Trans. Knowl. Data Eng. **27**, 1383–1396 (2015)

17. Wang, L., Yang, B., Orchard, J.: Particle swarm optimization using dynamic tournament topology. Appl. Soft Comput. **48**, 584–596 (2016)

18. Booth, H.S., Maindonald, J.H., Wilson, S.R., Gready, J.E.: An efficient z-score algorithm for assessing sequence alignments. J. Comput. Biol. J. Comput. Mol. Cell Biol. **11**, 616–625 (2004)

19. Bridle, J.S.: Probabilistic interpretation of feedforward classification network outputs, with relationships to statistical pattern recognition. In: Soulié, F.F., Hérault, J. (eds.) Neurocomputing. NATO ASI Series (Series F: Computer and Systems Sciences), vol. 68, pp. 227–236. Springer, Berlin, Heidelberg (1990)

20. Dietterich, T.G., Bakiri, G.: Solving multiclass learning problems via error-correcting output codes. J. Artif. Intell. Res. **2**, 263–286 (2012)

21. Li, T., Rogovchenko, Y.V.: Oscillation of second-order neutral differential equations. Mathematische Nachrichten **288**, 1150–1162 (2015)

22. Li, T., Rogovchenko, Y.V.: Oscillation criteria for even-order neutral differential equations. Appl. Math. Lett. **61**, 35–41 (2016)

23. Han, S.Y., Chen, Y.H., Tang, G.Y.: Fault diagnosis and fault-tolerant tracking control for discrete-time systems with faults and delays in actuator and measurement. J. Franklin Inst. **354**, 4719–4738 (2017)

An Efficient Extreme Learning Machine for Robust Regression

Decai Li and Yuqing He[✉]

Shenyang Institute of Automation, the Chinese Academy of Sciences (CAS),
Nanta Street, 110016 Shenyang, China
{lidecai,heyuqing}@sia.cn

Abstract. In this paper, we intend to build a robust extreme learning machine (RELM) with the advantage of both Bayesian framework and Huber loss function. The new method inherits the basic idea of training ELM in a Bayesian framework and replacing the original quadratic loss function by Huber loss function when estimating output weights, in order to enhance the robustness of model. However, the introduction of Huber loss function also yields the prior distribution of model output no longer Gaussian, which makes it difficult to estimate model parameters by using Bayesian method directly. To solve this problem, the iteratively re-weighted least squares (IRWLS) is employed and the Huber cost function can be equivalently transformed into the form of quadratic loss function, which results in an efficient Bayesian method for parameter estimation and remains robust to outliers. We demonstrate with experimental results that the proposed method can effectively increase the robustness of model.

Keywords: Extreme learning machine · Robust regression · Bayesian method
Huber loss function

1 Introduction

Recently, a novel single-hidden layer feed-forward network (SLFN), which is known as extreme learning machine (ELM) [1–3], has received much interest in wide applications [4–7]. Different from the traditional feed-forward networks (FNNs), the input weights and hidden layer biases in ELM can be randomly assigned. Hence, determination of the readout weights is the only trainable part of ELM, which can be obtained by a simple linear regression algorithm. As shown in [1], the ELM can provide competitive generation performance with BP and SVM at extremely fast learning speed.

Because of no gradient-based method is required in the model training, ELM is dramatically faster than many other traditional FNNs and easily implemented. But there are still some problems in ELM for feed-forward application. The ELM network usually has a large number of hidden nodes. However, a relatively large reservoir may easily lead to ill-posed problem and accompanies very large output weights, which will weaken the generalization performance of ELM [8]. To avoid this problem, regularization method for output weights leaning is needed, such as truncated singular value

© Springer International Publishing AG, part of Springer Nature 2018
T. Huang et al. (Eds.): ISNN 2018, LNCS 10878, pp. 289–299, 2018.
https://doi.org/10.1007/978-3-319-92537-0_34

decomposition [9] and Tikhonov-type regularization [10], which will keep the modeling performance from deteriorating.

Apart from regularization method, Bayesian method is also an alternative choice to improve the properties of ELM solutions. Compared with the regularization method, the Bayesian method can automatically estimate model parameters by using training data along and avoid the usage of computational expensive cross validation to estimate the regularization parameter [11 and 12]. Therefore, it seems that the Bayesian method is more suitable for ELM training. In [13], a Bayesian ELM (BELM) is proposed, which has the advantage of both ELM and Bayesian models and performs well on several benchmark datasets. However, the BELM assumes the model errors as Gaussian noise, which is usually not robust to outliers [14]. Hence, the generalization capability of the BELM may be significantly influenced when outliers are included.

To solve the problem that mentioned above, this paper proposes a robust extreme learning machine (RELM) by combing the advantage of Bayesian framework and Huber loss function. The basic idea of RELM is to employ Bayesian method for model training. Then, in order to increase the robustness to outliers, the original quadratic loss function is replaced by Huber loss function when estimating output weights. Moreover, to facilitate the computation process, iteratively re-weighted least squares (IRWLS) is employed and the Huber loss function can be equivalently transformed into the form of quadratic loss function. Based on which, an efficient training method can be obtained following Bayesian framework and estimate model parameters in a fully automatic way. Comparisons with the BELM are included, and several examples demonstrate that the proposed method is more effective when outliers are included.

This paper is organized as follows. In Sect. 2, the basics of the ELM and BELM are revisited. Section 3 will present the main results and shows the details of the proposed RELM estimator. In Sect. 4, we will give two illustration examples to show the performance of the RELM estimator. Section 5 presents the conclusions of this paper.

2 The Basics of Bayesian Extreme Learning Machine

2.1 Extreme Learning Machine (ELM)

The preliminary ELM is a large-scale feed-forward neural, which originates from the single-hidden layer feed-forward network with randomly generated hidden nodes and hidden layer biases. Consider N arbitrary distinct samples (x_i, t_i). Then, the equations of the ELM with L hidden nodes can be written as follows

$$\sum_{j=1}^{L} w_j g\left(\tilde{\mathbf{w}}_j^T \mathbf{x}_i + b_j\right) + \varepsilon_i = t_i, \quad i = 1, \ldots, N \tag{1}$$

where $\tilde{w}_j$ is the input weights connecting the jth hidden node and the input nodes, b_j is the bias of jth hidden node, $g(\cdot)$ denotes the hidden layer activation function, ε_i is assumed to be zero-mean Gaussian noise with variance β. Rigorous proof has been shown that $\tilde{w}_j$ and b_j can be randomly assigned if $g(\cdot)$ is infinitely differentiable, piecewise continuous. Thus, output weights w_j is the only trainable part in ELM.

Equation (1) can be written compactly as

$$\mathbf{t} = \mathbf{\Phi}\,\mathbf{w} + \mathbf{\varepsilon} \tag{2}$$

where

$$
\mathbf{\Phi}(\tilde{\mathbf{w}}_1, \ldots, \tilde{\mathbf{w}}_L, b_1, \ldots, b_L, \mathbf{x}_1, \ldots, \mathbf{x}_N)
$$
$$
= \begin{bmatrix} g(\tilde{\mathbf{w}}_1^T \mathbf{x}_1 + b_1) & \cdots & g(\tilde{\mathbf{w}}_L^T \mathbf{x}_1 + b_L) \\ \vdots & \cdots & \vdots \\ g(\tilde{\mathbf{w}}_1^T \mathbf{x}_N + b_1) & \cdots & g(\tilde{\mathbf{w}}_L^T \mathbf{x}_N + b_L) \end{bmatrix}_{N \times L} \tag{3}
$$

$$
\mathbf{w} = \begin{bmatrix} w_1^T \\ \vdots \\ w_L^T \end{bmatrix}_{L \times 1}, \mathbf{t} = \begin{bmatrix} t_1^T \\ \vdots \\ t_N^T \end{bmatrix}_{N \times 1}, \mathbf{\varepsilon} = \begin{bmatrix} \varepsilon_1 \\ \vdots \\ \varepsilon_N \end{bmatrix}_{N \times 1} \tag{4}
$$

It is clear that, determination of the output weights $\mathbf{w}$ is to minimize the following objective function:

$$\min_{\mathbf{w}} \| \mathbf{t} - \mathbf{\Phi}\,\mathbf{w} \|^2 \tag{5}$$

and $\mathbf{w}$ can be obtained by the Moore-Penrose's generalized inverse.

$$\mathbf{w} = \left(\mathbf{\Phi}^T \mathbf{\Phi}\right)^{-1} \mathbf{\Phi}^T \mathbf{t} = \mathbf{\Phi}^\dagger \mathbf{t} \tag{6}$$

Where $\mathbf{\Phi}^\dagger$ is the pseudoinverse matrix of $\mathbf{\Phi}$.

2.2 ELM Based on Bayesian Method

A Bayesian extreme Learning machine (BELM) is proposed in [13]. It takes the advantage of both ELM and Bayesian models. Compared with the regularization method, the BELM can achieve competitive accuracy by reducing the probability of ill-posed problem and takes the additional advantage, namely, automatically estimate model parameters by using training data along and avoid the usage of computational expensive cross validation to estimate the regularization parameter.

In the BELM, by assuming the model errors ε as independent zero-mean Gaussian noise with the variance β, the likelihood function of the model output $\mathbf{t}$ can be written as:

$$p(\mathbf{t}|\mathbf{w}, \beta) = \left(\frac{\beta}{2\pi}\right)^{N/2} \exp\left\{-\frac{\beta}{2}(\mathbf{t} - \mathbf{\Phi}\,\mathbf{w})^2\right\} \tag{7}$$

Then, the prior distributions of the output weights $\mathbf{w}$ are commonly assumed as Gaussian prior with hyperparameter α:

$$p(\mathbf{w}|\alpha) = \left(\frac{\alpha}{2\pi}\right)^{L/2} \exp\left\{-\frac{\alpha}{2}\mathbf{w}^{\mathsf{T}}\mathbf{w}\right\}. \tag{8}$$

As the likelihood function of $\mathbf{t}$ and the prior distribution of $\mathbf{w}$ are both following Gaussian prior, the posterior distribution $p(\mathbf{w}|\alpha)$ over $\mathbf{w}$ is also Gaussian [15], which allows us to write down the mean value μ and the variance Σ of $p(\mathbf{w}|\mathbf{t})$ directly as:

$$\mu = \beta \sum \Phi^T \mathbf{t} \tag{9}$$

$$\Sigma = \left(\alpha \mathbf{I} + \beta \Phi^T \Phi \mathbf{I}\right)^{-1} \tag{10}$$

where $\mathbf{I}$ is the identity matrix.

The hyperparameters α and β can be estimated by using Evidence Procedure [15]:

$$\alpha = \frac{\gamma}{\mu^T \mu} \tag{11}$$

$$\beta = \frac{N - \gamma}{\|\mathbf{t} - \Phi\mu\|^2} \tag{12}$$

$$\gamma = Q - \alpha \cdot trace(\Sigma) \tag{13}$$

where Q denotes the number of parameters.

3   Robust Extreme Learning Machine (RELM)

3.1   Extreme Learning Machine Based on Huber Loss Function

In the BELM, the estimation of output weights w is achieved by using the results that provided by [15]. In fact, this is corresponds to the maximization of the logarithm of the posterior distribution $p(\mathbf{w}|\mathbf{t})$ with respect to $\mathbf{w}$, which equivalent to the minimization of the quadratic loss function with the addition of l_2-norm regularization term:

$$L(\mathbf{w}) = -\ln p(\mathbf{w}|\mathbf{t}) = \frac{1}{2}\|\mathbf{y} - \Phi\mathbf{w}\|^2 + \frac{\lambda}{2}\|\mathbf{w}\|_2 \tag{14}$$

where $\lambda = \alpha/\beta$ corresponding to the regularization coefficient.

As shown in (14), because of assuming the prior distribution of model output $\mathbf{t}$ as Gaussian prior, the corresponding error function in the $\ln p(\mathbf{w}|\mathbf{t})$ is quadratic loss function, which is usually not robust to outliers. Hence, the generalization capability of the BELM may be significantly influenced when outliers are included.

Huber loss function is a commonly used robust loss function, which can be given by (15):

$$l_H(\varepsilon_i) = \begin{cases} \frac{1}{2}\varepsilon_i^2 & |\varepsilon_i| < \tau \\ \tau|\varepsilon_i| - \frac{\tau^2}{2} & others \end{cases} \tag{15}$$

where parameter τ is called a tuning constant and selected by user, and ε_i is the model error at ith sample, $i = 1,2,...N$. Therefore, it seems that we can replace the quadratic loss function in (14) by the Huber loss function in order to enhance the robustness of model and (14) can be rewritten as:

$$L_H(\mathbf{w}) = l_H(\boldsymbol{\varepsilon}) + \frac{\lambda}{2}\|\mathbf{w}\|_2 \tag{16}$$

3.2 Robust Extreme Learning Machine Based on IRWLS

Although the introduction of the Huber loss function in (17) may increase the robustness of model, it also yields the prior distribution of model output t no longer Gaussian, which makes it difficult to estimate model parameters by using Bayesian method directly. To solve this problem, iteratively re-weighted least squares (IRWLS) is employed. As we shall see that the Huber loss function can be equivalently transformed into the form of quadratic loss function, while remaining robust to outliers. Based on this operation, we can train the RELM by using Bayesian method and estimate model parameters in a fully automatic way.

A detail discussion of the IRWLS for Huber loss function training is provided in [16]. Here, we extend it to the situation when a regularization term is added.

The gradient of the error function (16) takes the form as:

$$\frac{\partial L_H(\mathbf{w})}{\partial \mathbf{w}} = \frac{\partial L_{H_1}(\mathbf{w})}{\partial \boldsymbol{\varepsilon}}\frac{\partial \boldsymbol{\varepsilon}}{\partial \mathbf{w}} + \frac{\partial L_{H_2}(\mathbf{w})}{\partial \mathbf{w}} = -\boldsymbol{\Phi}^T \boldsymbol{\varphi} + \lambda\mathbf{w} \tag{17}$$

where

$$L_{H_1}(\mathbf{w}) = l_H(\mathbf{w}) \tag{18}$$

$$L_{H_2}(\mathbf{w}) = \frac{\lambda}{2}\mathbf{w}^T\mathbf{w} \tag{19}$$

$$\boldsymbol{\varphi} = \left[\frac{\partial L_{H_1}(\mathbf{w})}{\partial \varepsilon_1}, \frac{\partial L_{H_1}(\mathbf{w})}{\partial \varepsilon_2}, \ldots, \frac{\partial L_{H_1}(\mathbf{w})}{\partial \varepsilon_N}\right]^T \\ = [\varphi(\varepsilon_1), \varphi(\varepsilon_2), \ldots, \varphi(\varepsilon_N)]^T \tag{20}$$

where $\varphi(\varepsilon_i)$ is the derivative of with respect to ε_i.

Setting the gradient (17) to zero, we have:

$$-\boldsymbol{\Phi}^T\boldsymbol{\Lambda}\boldsymbol{\varepsilon} + \lambda\mathbf{w} = \mathbf{0} \tag{21}$$

where

$$\Lambda = diag\{\omega_1, \omega_2, \ldots, \omega_N\} \tag{22}$$

$$\omega_i = \frac{\varphi(\varepsilon_i)}{\varepsilon_i} = \begin{cases} 1 & |\varepsilon_i| < \mu \\ \frac{\mu}{|\varepsilon_i|} & others \end{cases} \tag{23}$$

$$\varepsilon = t - \Phi w \tag{24}$$

By combing (21)–(24), the solution of the model output w can be obtained as following:

$$w = \left(\Phi^T \Lambda \Phi + \lambda I\right)^{-1} \Phi^T \Lambda t \tag{25}$$

It is noted that, due to the model error ε cannot be determined primarily, the iteratively re-weighted least squares (IRWLS) is employed. Set n is the iteration step, and initialize $n = 1$ and $\Lambda^{(n)} = I$. Then, (28) at nth iteration can be written as:

$$w^{(n)} = \left(\Phi^T \Lambda^{(n)} \Phi + \lambda I\right)^{-1} \Phi^T \Lambda^{(n)} t \tag{26}$$

where

$$\omega_i^{(n)} = \frac{\varphi\left(\varepsilon_i^{(n-1)}\right)}{\varepsilon_i^{(n-1)}} = \begin{cases} 1 & \left|\varepsilon_i^{(n-1)}\right| < \mu \\ \frac{\mu}{\left|\varepsilon_i^{(n-1)}\right|} & others \end{cases} \tag{27}$$

$$\Lambda^{(n)} = diag\left\{\omega_1^{(n)}, \omega_2^{(n)}, \ldots, \omega_N^{(n)}\right\} \tag{28}$$

3.3   Parameter of Robust Extreme Learning Machine

According to (27) and (28), we can see that $\Lambda^{(n)}$ is a diagonal matrix and each element of $\Lambda^{(n)}$ is non-negative. Hence, Eq. (26) can be rewritten as:

$$w = \left(\tilde{\Phi}^{(n)T} \tilde{\Phi}^{(n)} + \lambda I\right)^{-1} \tilde{\Phi}^{(n)T} \tilde{t}^{(n)} \tag{29}$$

where

$$\tilde{\Phi}^{(n)} = \tilde{\Lambda}^{(n)} \Phi \tag{30}$$

$$\tilde{t}^{(n)} = \tilde{\Lambda}^{(n)} t \tag{31}$$

$$\tilde{\Lambda}^{(n)} = \sqrt{\tilde{\Lambda}^{(n)}} = diag\left\{\sqrt{\omega_1^{(n)}}, \sqrt{\omega_2^{(n)}}, \ldots, \sqrt{\omega_N^{(n)}}\right\} \tag{32}$$

It is clear that, (29) is the solution of the following objective function:

$$\tilde{L}^{(n)}(\mathbf{w}) = \frac{1}{2}\left\|\tilde{\mathbf{t}}^{(n)} - \tilde{\mathbf{\Phi}}^{(n)}\mathbf{w}\right\|^2 + \frac{\lambda}{2}\|\mathbf{w}\|_2 \tag{33}$$

Equation (33) shows that the Huber loss function in (16) can be equivalently transformed into the form of the quadratic loss function by introducing the weighted least squares. This allows us to assume the prior distribution of model output t as Gaussian and the Bayesian method can be used for parameter estimation. Moreover, compared with (14), the error function in (33) is more robust when outliers are included. For a training sample contaminated by outlier, the Huber loss function is used and a small weight is added to $\mathbf{\Phi}$, which will reduce the influence of the contaminated sample to the model.

According to (33), the likelihood function of the model output $\mathbf{t}^{(n)}$ can be assumed as Gaussian, which takes the form as:

$$p\left(\tilde{\mathbf{t}}^{(n)}|\mathbf{w},\beta\right) = \left(\frac{\beta}{2\pi}\right)^{N/2}\exp\left\{-\frac{\beta}{2}\left(\tilde{\mathbf{t}}^{(n)} - \tilde{\mathbf{\Phi}}^{(n)}\mathbf{w}\right)^2\right\} \tag{34}$$

The prior over the output weights w is still given as (11).

Similar to the BELM, as the likelihood function (34) and the prior distribution of (8) are both following Gaussian prior, the posterior distribution $p(\mathbf{w}|\mathbf{t}^{(n)})$ over w is also Gaussian, with the mean value $\mathbf{m}^{(n)}$ and the variance $\mathbf{\Sigma}^{(n)}$ as:

$$\mathbf{\mu}^{(n)} = \beta\mathbf{\Sigma}^{(n)}\tilde{\mathbf{\Phi}}^{(n)T}\tilde{\mathbf{t}}^{(n)} \tag{35}$$

$$\mathbf{\Sigma}^{(n)} = \left(\alpha^{(n)}\mathbf{I} + \beta^{(n)}\tilde{\mathbf{\Phi}}^{(n)T}\tilde{\mathbf{\Phi}}^{(n)}\mathbf{I}\right)^{-1} \tag{36}$$

where $\mathbf{I}$ is the identity matrix.

The hyperparameters $\alpha^{(n)}$ and $\beta^{(n)}$ can be estimated by using Evidence Procedure:

$$\alpha^{(n)} = \frac{\gamma^{(n)}}{\mathbf{\mu}^{(n)T}\mathbf{\mu}^{(n)}} \tag{37}$$

$$\beta^{(n)} = \frac{N - \gamma^{(n)}}{\left\|\tilde{\mathbf{t}}^{(n)} - \tilde{\mathbf{\Phi}}^{(n)}\mathbf{\mu}^{(n)}\right\|^2} \tag{38}$$

$$\gamma^{(n)} = Q - \alpha^{(n)} \cdot trace\left(\mathbf{\Sigma}^{(n)}\right) \tag{39}$$

where Q denotes the number of parameters.

4 Simulations

In this section, we will use examples to evaluate the performance of the RELM. The first example is the SinC function approximation problem, and the other is the identification of a nonlinear dynamic system. Before the datasets are used, all the input vectors are normalized into the range $[-1, 1]$, while the target outputs are normalized to $[0, 1]$. For each example, Totally 50 trials of simulations are conducted and the prediction performance is measured by the root-mean-squared error (RMSE), which reflects the absolute deviation between the predicted value and the observed value and takes the form as:

$$\text{RMSE} = \left(\frac{1}{N-1}\sum_{i=1}^{N}(t_i - \hat{t}_i)^2\right)^{1/2} \tag{40}$$

where t_i is the target value, $\hat{t}_i$ is the predicted value and N is the number of testing samples.

Example:
In this example, the performance of the proposed RELM is evaluated on the benchmark testing of SinC function, which takes the form as follows.

$$y(x) = \begin{cases} \frac{\sin(x)}{x} & x \neq 0 \\ 1 & x = 0 \end{cases} \tag{41}$$

The training set $\{x_i, y_i\}$ is created from $y(x)$ with 200 data, where the input xi is uniformly distribution on the interval $(-10, 10)$. Then, the uniform noise distributed in the range $[-0.2, 0.2]$ has been added to all the training samples as shown in Fig. 1. A testing set $\{x_i, y_i\}$ is also created from $y(x)$ with 200 noise free data, in which xi is equally spaced in $(-10, 10)$.

(1) Approximating SinC function without outliers

In order to illustrate the performance of the proposed RELM, the BELM is employed for comparison and the numbers of hidden nodes of both the methods are chosen as 100 by using cross validation. Figure 2 shows the true and the testing curve of SinC function with RELM and BELM. Because of no training samples are contaminated by outliers, both the methods can approximate the SinC function well. Totally 50 trials of simulations are conducted for RELM and BELM, and the average testing RMSE are 0.0301 and 0.0276. It indicated that the assumption of Gaussian prior is more suitable to the clean training samples without outliers and the proposed RELM can achieve a competitive performance with the BELM.

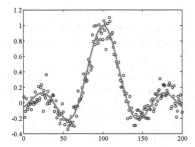

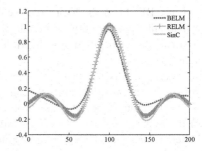

Fig. 1. The training samples without outliers

Fig. 2. The true and testing curves without outliers

(2) Approximating SinC function with constant outliers

To further demonstrate the performance of the proposed RELM, 25 outliers that have constant value of 0.5 are added to the training samples, as shown in the Fig. 3.

Both the RELM and BELM are applied to the contaminated training samples and in order to explore the influence on the performance of RELM by different model structures, the number of hidden nodes is set to be 25, 50, 100, 150 and 200. Totally 50 trials of simulations are conducted for each method and the average training RMSE, average testing RMSE and the standard deviation of the RMSE are presented in Table 1.

For the BELM, because of assuming the prior distribution of the model output **t** as Gaussian, it is not robust when outliers are included. As shown in the Table 1, the testing errors of the BELM in each case of hidden nodes are significantly influenced by the outliers. In contrast, due to the introduction of Huber loss function when estimating output weighs, the RELM is not sensitive to the outliers and the testing errors are smaller than that of the BELM for each number of hidden nodes.

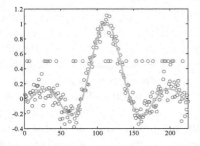

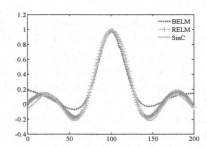

Fig. 3. The training samples with outliers

Fig. 4. The true and testing curves without outliers

The testing curves of both the RELM and BELM are depicted in Fig. 4 and the numbers of hidden nodes for each method are chosen the same as 150. In the Fig. 4, the solid line represents the true curve of the SinC function and the testing curves of the

RELM and BELM methods are represented by '+' and dash line, respectively. It is clear that, although the outliers are added to the training samples, the RELM can still approximate the SinC function well, while the curve of BELM obviously deviates from the true one.

Moreover, as discussed above, estimating the output weights **w** is equivalent to optimize an error loss function with regularization term in the Bayesian method. This can prevent a model from ill-posed problem, which may occur in the preliminary ELM when the number of hidden nodes is large. Therefore, as shown in the Table 1, the testing errors are stable for each method during the number of hidden nodes varies from 25 to 200.

Table 1. Performance comparison between the BELM [13] and the proposed RELM with constant outliers

Hidden nodes	Algorithms	Training RMSE		Testing RMSE	
		Mean	Dev)	Mean	Dev.
25	BELM	0.0476(0.0115)		0.0929(0.0118)	
	RELM	0.0922(0.0071)		**0.0476**(0.0115)	
50	BELM	0.0406(0.0078)		0.0922(0.0071)	
	RELM	0.0925(0.0067)		**0.0406**(0.0078)	
100	BELM	0.0383(0.0064)		0.0925(0.0067)	
	RELM	0.0909(0.0096)		**0.0383**(0.0064)	
150	BELM	0.0370(0.0087)		0.0909(0.0096)	
	RELM	0.0925(0.0071)		**0.0370**(0.0087)	
200	BELM	0.0384(0.0067)		0.0925(0.0071)	
	RELM	0.1822(0.0070)		**0.0384**(0.0067)	

5   Conclusion

In this paper, a robust extreme learning machine (RELM) is proposed by combining the advantage of Bayesian framework and Huber loss function. The basic idea is to replace the quadratic loss function by Huber loss function, which makes it difficult to directly apply Bayesian method for parameter estimation. The iteration re-weighted least squares is applied to solve this problem and an effective training method is derived. The performance of the proposed RELM is evaluated by SinC function. Simulation results indicate that, RELM can enhance the robustness of model and performs well when outliers are included. Moreover, by employing the iteration re-weighted least squares, the Huber loss function is equivalently transformed to the form of quadratic loss function, which leads to a fully automatic method for model parameters estimation.

References

1. Huang, G.B., Zhu, Q.Y., Siew, C.K.: Extreme learning machine: theory and applications. Neurocomputing. **70**(1–3), 489–501 (2006)
2. Huang, G.B., Wang, D.H., Lan, Y.: Extreme learning machines: a survey. Int. J. Mach. Learn. Cybern. **2**(2), 107–122 (2011)
3. Rong, H.J., Ong, Y.S., Tan, A.H., Zhu, Z.: A fast pruned-extreme learning machine for classification problem. Neurocomputing. **72**(1–3), 359–366 (2008)
4. Wang, G.R., Zhao, Y., Wang, D.: A protein secondary structure prediction framework based on the extreme learning machine. Neurocomputing. **72**(1–3), 262–268 (2008)
5. Sun, Z.L., Au, K.F., Choi, T.M.: A neuro-fuzzy inference system through integration of fuzzy logic and extreme learning machines. IEEE Trans. Syst. Man Cybern. Part B Cybern. **37**(5), 1321–1331 (2007)
6. Rong, H.J., Huang, G.B., Sundararajan, N.: Online sequential fuzzy extreme learning machine for function approximation and classification problems. IEEE Trans. Syst. Man Cybern. Part B Cybern. **39**(4), 1067–1072 (2009)
7. Nizar, A.H., Dong, Z.Y., Wang, Y.: Power utility nontechnical loss analysis with extreme learning machine method. IEEE Trans. Power Syst. **23**(3), 946–955 (2008)
8. Tang, X.L., Han, M.: Partial Lanczos extreme learning machine for single-output regression problems. Neurocomputing. **72**, 3066–3076 (2009)
9. Hansen, P.C.: The truncated SVD as a method for regularization. BIT Numer. Math. **27**(4), 534–553 (1987)
10. Colinas, J., Goussard, Y., Laurin, J.J.: Application of the Tikhonov regularization technique to the equivalent magnetic currents near-field technique. IEEE Trans. Antennas Propag. **52**(11), 3122–3132 (2004)
11. Gao, J.B., Zhang, J., Tien, D.: Relevance units latent variable model and nonlinear dimensionality reduction. IEEE Trans Neural Netw. **21**(1), 123–135 (2010)
12. Cawley, G.C., Talbot, N.L.C., Janacek, G.J., Peck, M.W.: Sparse Bayesian kernel survival analysis for modeling the growth domain of microbial pathogens. IEEE Trans. Neural Netw. **17**(2), 471–481 (2006)
13. Olivas, E.S., Sanchis, J.G., Martin, J.D., Martínez, M., Magdalena, J.R., Serrano, A.J.: BELM: Bayesian extreme learning machine. IEEE Trans. Neural Netw. **22**(3), 505–509 (2011)
14. Tipping, M.E., Lawrence, N.D.: Variational inference for Student-t models robust Bayesian interpolation and generalised component analysis. Neurocomputing. **69**, 123–141 (2005)
15. Bishop, C.M.: Pattern Recognition and Machine Learning. Springer, New York (2007)
16. Hong, X., Chen, S.: M-estimator and D-optimality model construction using orthogonal forward regression. IEEE Trans. Syst. Man Cybern.-Part B: Cybern. **35**(1), 155–162 (2005)
17. Chuan, C.C., Lee, Z.J.: Hybrid robust support vector machines for regression with outliers. Appl. Soft Comput. **11**, 64–72 (2011)

Fourier Transform-Based Image Classification Using Complex-Valued Convolutional Neural Networks

Călin-Adrian Popa[(⊠)] and Cosmin Cernăzanu-Glăvan

Department of Computer and Software Engineering,
Polytechnic University Timişoara,
Blvd. V. Pârvan, No. 2, 300223 Timişoara, Romania
calin.popa@cs.upt.ro

Abstract. Although complex-valued convolutional neural networks (CVCNNs) have shown an improvement over their real-valued counterparts (RVCNNs) when trained on real-valued images, in order to harness the full potential of CVCNNs, they should be used with fully complex-valued inputs. Because every image has one and only one Fourier transform, the problem of classifying real-valued images is equivalent to the problem of classifying their complex-valued Fourier transforms. Experiments done using the MNIST, SVHN, and CIFAR-10 datasets show an improved performance of CVCNNs trained on Fourier-transformed images over CVCNNs trained on real-valued images (for which the imaginary part of the input is considered to be zero), and over RVCNNs.

Keywords: Complex-valued neural networks
Convolutional neural networks · Discrete Fourier Transform

1 Introduction

Convolutional neural networks have become one of the most successful models for solving a variety of image recognition-related tasks. Since they were first proposed in their most popular form by [13], they began having increasing success in solving virtually any image recognition problem, starting from handwritten digit recognition to state-of-the-art sophisticated large-scale tasks. Their development was nurtured by the increased power of the available computational resources, and their implementation using parallel computing on graphics processors (GPUs). This model, together with other models for which it was proved that increased depth translated into increased performance, gave rise to the deep learning domain [2, 3, 7, 18].

The complex-valued deep learning domain, however, is only beginning to appear. One of the most important papers in the domain of complex-valued convolutional neural networks (CVCNNs) is [19], in which CVCNNs are formulated as nonlinear multiwavelet packets, paving the way for the mathematical

© Springer International Publishing AG, part of Springer Nature 2018
T. Huang et al. (Eds.): ISNN 2018, LNCS 10878, pp. 300–309, 2018.
https://doi.org/10.1007/978-3-319-92537-0_35

analysis from the signal processing domain to be used in order to give a rigorous formulation of the properties of CVCNNs.

Some imaging devices produce complex-valued images. Synthetic Aperture Radars (SAR) are imaging systems that produce complex-valued images of the ground [4,5,17]. Single layer CVCNNs were used in [9] for object detection in Polarimetric Synthetic Aperture Radar (PolSAR) images, which are a special type of SAR images. Also, more recently, CVCNNs were used for wide angle SAR automatic target recognition in [21]. On the other hand, functional Magnetic Resonance Imaging (fMRI) also collects the data in complex form, but, until recently, only the amplitude of this data was used, ignoring the frequency information [10,11,22]. Fully connected complex-valued neural networks were used for MRI fingerprinting in [20], showing superior performance to their real-valued counterparts. These results support the idea that the full potential of complex-valued neural networks is harnessed when used with complex-valued inputs.

Although these applications are interesting, they are limited to complex-valued images, whereas the majority of images of interest are real-valued. Beside these uses in complex-valued imaging, CVCNNs were rarely used for real-valued image recognition. In [16], CVCNNs have shown better performance than their real-valued counterparts (RVCNNs) on real-valued image classification.

It is possible, however, to obtain a unique complex-valued representation of any real-valued image. This representation is given by the Discrete Fourier Transform (DFT) of an image. Based on this bijective correspondence between real-valued images and their complex-valued DFTs, it can be deduced that the problem of classifying real-valued images is equivalent with the problem of classifying their complex-valued DFTs.

Taking all the above observations into account, this paper introduces complex-valued Fourier transform-based image classification using CVCNNs. The rest of the paper is organized as follows: Sect. 2 presents the Fourier transform in the context of image processing, and its most important properties. Section 3 is dedicated to describing CVCNNs, with emphasis on their specific complex domain characteristics. Experimental results using the proposed CVCNNs architecture on the MNIST, SVHN, and CIFAR-10 datasets are discussed in Sect. 4. Lastly, Sect. 5 is dedicated to presenting the conclusions of the paper.

2   The Fourier Transform

The French mathematician Jean-Baptiste Joseph Fourier proved that any periodic function can be expressed as a sum of sines and cosines of different frequencies, each multiplied by different coefficients, which is called the Fourier series. Based on it, the Fourier transform decomposes any function into its different frequencies. In the domain of image processing, the function represents a digital image, and thus we are concerned only with the Discrete Fourier Transform (DFT). The DFT has a wide range of applications in image processing, such as image analysis, image filtering, image denoising and reconstruction, and image compression. Our presentation of the main properties of the DFT mainly follows that of [6].

For an $M \times N$ image denoted by $f(x, y)$, with spatial coordinates $x = 0, 1, 2, \ldots, M - 1$ and $y = 0, 1, 2, \ldots, N - 1$, the Discrete Fourier Transform (DFT) is defined as

$$F(u, v) = \sum_{x=0}^{M-1} \sum_{y=0}^{N-1} f(x, y) e^{-i2\pi(ux/M+vy/N)},$$

where $i^2 = -1$ is the complex imaginary unit, $u = 0, 1, 2, \ldots, M - 1$ and $v = 0, 1, 2, \ldots, N - 1$. One of the most important properties of the Fourier transform is that it is a bijective function on the space of images, which means that we can define the Inverse Discrete Fourier Transform (IDFT) of $F(u, v)$ by:

$$f(x, y) = \frac{1}{MN} \sum_{u=0}^{M-1} \sum_{v=0}^{N-1} F(u, v) e^{i2\pi(ux/M+vy/N)},$$

for $x = 0, 1, 2, \ldots, M - 1$ and $y = 0, 1, 2, \ldots, N - 1$. This means that each image has one and only one Fourier transform, and the Fourier transform of an image can be used to retrieve the original image. The two form a discrete Fourier transform pair, and we will write

$$f(x, y) \leftrightarrow F(u, v).$$

As it can be easily seen, in general, the Fourier transform of a real-valued image is complex-valued because of the Euler formula: $e^{ix} = \cos x + i \sin x$. Thus, we can write

$$F(u, v) = R(u, v) + iI(u, v) = |F(u, v)| e^{i\phi(u,v)},$$

where

$$|F(u, v)| = \sqrt{R^2(u, v) + iI^2(u, v)},$$

is the Fourier (or frequency) spectrum and

$$\phi(u, v) = \arctan \left[\frac{I(u, v)}{R(u, v)} \right],$$

represents the phase angle, for $u = 0, 1, 2, \ldots, M - 1$ and $v = 0, 1, 2, \ldots, N - 1$.

The DFT of an image satisfies the following properties:

$$f(x, y) e^{i2\pi(u_0 x/M+v_0 y/N)} \leftrightarrow F(u - u_0, v - v_0),$$

and

$$f(x - x_0, y - y_0) \leftrightarrow F(u, v) e^{-i2\pi(ux_0/M+vy_0/N)}.$$

Based on these properties, the Fourier transform of an image can be shifted so that $F(0, 0)$ is at the point $(u_0, v_0) = (M/2, N/2)$, using the transformation

$$f(x, y)(-1)^{x+y} \leftrightarrow F(u - M/2, v - N/2).$$

Because of the periodicity of the DFT, which states that

$$F(u,v) = F(u + k_1 M, v + k_2 N),$$

for any integers k_1, k_2, the transform $F(u - M/2, v - N/2)$ contains the exact information that the original $F(u,v)$ contains, but organized in a different way.

Taking all of the above properties of the Fourier transform into account, the problem of classifying real-valued images is equivalent with the problem of classifying their complex-valued Fourier transforms. Because the Fourier transform offers a richer representation of an image, it can constitute the basis for classification algorithms that could potentially work better than their real-valued counterparts on the original images.

3   Complex-Valued Convolutional Neural Networks

Complex-valued convolutional neural networks (CVCNNs) have been introduced [16] to handle complex-valued data organized as a (2D) grid, for example a complex-valued image. They are particularizations of feedforward neural networks, in which the matrix multiplication of the inputs and weights is replaced by convolution:

$$h(x,y) = (f \bigstar g)(x,y) = \sum_{m=0}^{M-1} \sum_{n=0}^{N-1} f(m,n)g(x-m, y-n),$$

for $x = 0, 1, 2, \ldots, M - 1$ and $y = 0, 1, 2, \ldots, N - 1$.

A convolutional neural network is, generally, composed of three types of layers: convolutional, pooling, and fully connected layers.

For convolutional layers of CVCNNs, the inputs of a layer are complex-valued images organized into channels. The weights of the convolutional layers are represented by relatively small convolution kernels. In order to perform complex-valued convolution using computational frameworks that can mainly handle real-valued operations, we can write the complex convolution in terms of two real-valued convolutions, as follows:

$$k \bigstar x = (k^R + \imath k^I) \bigstar (x^R + \imath x^I) = k^R \bigstar x^R - k^I \bigstar x^I + \imath (k^R \bigstar x^I + k^I \bigstar x^R),$$

from which we have that

$$(k \bigstar x)^R = k^R \bigstar x^R - k^I \bigstar x^I$$
$$(k \bigstar x)^I = k^R \bigstar x^I + k^I \bigstar x^R,$$

where x represents an input, k represents a convolution kernel, x^R is the real part, and x^I is the imaginary part of complex matrix x. After the convolution operation, a nonlinearity is applied. Different choices are possible for the nonlinearity in the complex domain, but preliminary experiments done with CVCNNs have shown that the best results are obtained using the split-complex ReLU non-linearity, which applies the ReLU function separately on the real and imaginary components of a complex number:

$$\text{ReLU}(x^R + \imath x^I) = \text{ReLU}(x^R) + \imath\text{ReLU}(x^I) = \max(0, x^R) + \imath\max(0, x^I).$$

Different variants of the ReLU nonlinearity were proposed for the complex domain, such as modReLU [1]:

$$\text{modReLU}(x) = \begin{cases} (|x| + b)\frac{x}{|x|} & \text{if } |x| + b \geq 0 \\ 0 & \text{otherwise} \end{cases},$$

where $b \in \mathbb{R}$ is a learnable parameter, and zReLU [8]:

$$\text{zReLU}(x) = \begin{cases} x & \text{if } x^R, x^I \geq 0 \\ 0 & \text{otherwise} \end{cases},$$

but, unfortunately, the performance in the context of CVCNNs of these nonlinearities is worse than that of the split-complex ReLU defined above.

The second type of layer in convolutional networks is the pooling or subsampling layer, which is used to reduce the dimensionality of the input and obtain a more abstract representation of it. The most known types of pooling layers are max pooling and average pooling. In the max pooling layer, any neighborhood of small dimension in an image is replaced by the pixel with the maximum value from that neighborhood. The average pooling layer replaces the neighborhood with the average of the pixels in that neighborhood. In the context of CVCNNs, these pooling operations can only be done separately on the real and imaginary components of the complex-valued inputs.

For the max pooling operation, this could mean that the real part of the output of the max pooling operation can come from one complex-valued pixel, and the imaginary part of the output from a different complex-valued pixel, thus introducing unwanted distortions in the final subsampled image. Preliminary experiments done using max pooling have shown that this can be an issue which degrades the performance of CVCNNs. For this reason, a better choice is the average pooling, because the average of a set of complex numbers is just the complex number whose real part is the average of the real parts and whose imaginary part is the average of the imaginary parts of the numbers in the set.

Lastly, the fully connected layers are the same as the hidden layers in a feedforward neural network. In order to use real-valued operations, the complex-valued matrix multiplication can be expressed similarly as the convolution:

$$(Wx)^R = W^R x^R - W^I x^I$$
$$(Wx)^I = W^R x^I + W^I x^R,$$

where x is the input to the fully connected layer, and W is the weight matrix of the fully connected layer. The nonlinearity used for the fully connected layers is the same split-complex ReLU nonlinearity, defined above.

Usually, the output of a convolutional network is represented by class scores assigned to each class using the softmax function, in conjunction with the negative log likelihood loss function. In the complex domain, a separate softmax function is applied to the real and imaginary parts of the last fully connected layer, and the final class scores are considered to be the average of the two softmax scores given by the real and imaginary parts. Also, the negative log likelihood loss is applied to the real and imaginary parts separately. This novel formulation of CVCNNs has shown slightly better results in preliminary experiments than the one using only the real part of the last fully connected layer for defining the class scores and as input to the negative log likelihood loss.

CVCNNs can be applied to real-valued image classification, by considering the imaginary part of the input to such networks as being zero, and have shown better results than their real-valued counterparts [16]. However, the full potential of CVCNNs can be harnessed for complex-valued image classification. Although there exist naturally complex-valued images, such as SAR and fMRI images, the majority of the images of interest are real-valued. Nonetheless, their Fourier transform, as shown above, is complex-valued and unique for each image. This means that CVCNNs can be used to perform Fourier transform-based image classification of real-valued images.

4 Experimental Results

All the experiments were done using the same network architectures for the real-valued convolutional neural networks (RVCNNs), complex-valued convolutional neural networks (CVCNNs) trained on the real-valued images (for which the imaginary part of the input was set to zero), and complex-valued convolutional networks trained on the complex-valued Discrete Fourier Transform (DFT) of the real-valued images.

The architecture consists of two (or three) convolutional layers, each followed by an average pooling layer. The number of input channels of the first convolutional layer was 1 or 3, depending on whether the input images were grayscale or RGB images. The number of input and output channels of the rest of the convolutional layers was 64 for the RVCNNs. For the CVCNNs trained on the real-valued images, this number was 45, which is approximately 1.41 times smaller than 64, thus assuring the same number of real parameters for the two networks. Because the CVCNNs trained on Fourier-transformed images have to deal with fully complex-valued inputs, the number of input and output channels for the convolutional layers was also 64, to ensure a fair comparison with the other networks. Thus, they have twice the number of real parameters, but also twice the number of real inputs. The average pooling was done over neighborhoods of 2×2 pixels.

The last average pooling layer was followed by two fully connected layers, which had 6 times, and 3 times, respectively, more units than the output channels of the convolutional layers (384, and 192, respectively, for RVCNNs and CVC-NNs trained on Fourier-transformed images, and 270, and 135, respectively, for

CVCNNs trained on real-valued images). The rest of the details of the CVCNNs are the ones mentioned in Sect. 3, which were similarly applied to the RVCNNs.

Training was done using stochastic gradient descent for 200 epochs, with the learning rate starting from 0.01, which was then divided by 10 two times, first after 100 epochs, and then after 50 epochs. One important aspect is that the DFTs of the input images were also shifted so that $F(0,0)$ is at the center of the image, as mentioned in Sect. 2. This is usually a standard procedure in the image processing domain, and preliminary experiments have shown that training on the unshifted images has worse results than training on shifted ones.

4.1   MNIST

The MNIST dataset is formed of images representing handwritten digits, and was created by [14]. The images are grayscale and their size is 28 × 28 pixels. The full training set of 60,000 was used for training the three types of networks described above, with no augmentations.

The experimental results are given in Table 1. The first column represents the dimensions of the convolution kernels for the first two (or three) convolutional layers. The second column represents the errors measured on the full 10,000 image test set for the CVCNNs trained on the Discrete Fourier Transform (DFT) of the original images. Next, the errors on the test set for the CVCNNs trained on the original images are reported, for which the imaginary parts of the network inputs are considered to be zero. Lastly, the errors of the RVCNNs are given.

It can be seen that, although these last two types of networks have approximately the same number of parameters, CVCNNs perform better than RVCNNs. But even better performance than the CVCNNs trained on real-valued images was attained by the CVCNNs trained on the Fourier-transformed images. This shows that, in order to fully harness the power of complex-valued neural networks, they must be used with complex-valued inputs.

Table 1. Experimental results for MNIST

Kernel sizes	Complex DFT	Complex	Real
3, 2	**0.69**%	0.89%	0.98%
3, 4	**0.63**%	0.73%	0.79%
5, 3	**0.56**%	0.78%	0.96%
5, 5	**0.55**%	0.82%	0.88%
5, 3, 2	**0.54**%	0.65%	0.87%

4.2   SVHN

The Street View House Numbers (SVHN) dataset was created by [15], and consists of RGB images of digits cropped from house numbers in Google Street View images. The dataset contains 73,257 images for training, 26,032 images for testing, and $531, 131$ additional, somewhat less difficult samples, for use as extra training data. We only use the standard training and testing images, with no data augmentation. The size of each sample in the dataset is 32×32 pixels. It is a more difficult task than MNIST, because the images are RGB, and may also contain distracting digits to the sides of the digit of interest.

The three types of networks described above were trained on this dataset, and the errors on the test set are reported in Table 2. The structure of the table is the same as the one in the previous experiment: first the kernel sizes of the convolutional layers are given, then the errors attained by the CVCNNs trained on the Fourier-transformed images, by the CVCNNs trained on the original images, and by the RVCNNs, respectively, are shown. The Fourier transform of an RGB image is computed separately for the three RGB channels, thus providing three complex-valued inputs for the CVCNNs.

The errors show that CVCNNs trained on the original images obtain better results than the RVCNNs trained on the same inputs. But the best performance was attained by the CVCNNs trained on the Fourier-transformed images.

Table 2. Experimental results for SVHN

Kernel sizes	Complex DFT	Complex	Real
$3, 2$	**8.66%**	10.97%	12.17%
$3, 4$	**8.42%**	10.61%	11.21%
$5, 3$	**7.94%**	9.40%	10.45%
$5, 5$	**8.16%**	9.10%	9.91%
$5, 3, 3$	**8.69%**	8.81%	9.27%

4.3   CIFAR-10

Lastly, the CIFAR-10 dataset contains RGB images of 32×32 pixels, belonging to 10 classes, such as airplane, cat, frog, or truck, for example, and was created by [12]. Training was done on the full $50, 000$ image training set, which were only randomly flipped before being given to the networks. No other types of data augmentation were used.

The results of training the three types of networks are given in the same format as above, in Table 3. The errors are reported for the full $10, 000$ image test set. The conclusion of the experiment is consistent with the ones of the above experiments: the CVCNNs perform better than their real-valued counterparts, but the CVCNNs trained on the Fourier-transformed images perform best.

Table 3. Experimental results for CIFAR-10

Kernel sizes	Complex DFT	Complex	Real
3, 2	**22.26%**	24.81%	27.13%
3, 4	**21.51%**	24.86%	24.97%
5, 3	**21.77%**	25.64%	25.99%
5, 5	**21.25%**	25.24%	25.68%
5, 3, 3	**21.61%**	21.88%	22.32%

5   Conclusions

Taking into account the one to one correspondence between real-valued images and their complex-valued Fourier transforms, complex-valued Fourier transform-based image classification was introduced using CVCNNs.

Experimental results on three very known and used datasets, i.e., MNIST, SVHN, and CIFAR-10 have shown that CVCNNs with real-valued inputs (for which the imaginary part is zero) perform better than RVCNNs with the same inputs. But, most importantly, the experiments showed that CVCNNs trained using Fourier-transformed images performed even better than CVCNNs with real-valued inputs.

The present paper constitutes a first step done towards complex-valued image classification of real-valued images. The complex-valued CVCNNs architecture still needs improvements in order to fully take advantage of the complex-domain representation, which constitutes a very interesting and challenging future work direction.

Acknowledgement. This work was supported by research grant no. PCD-TC-2017-41 of the Polytechnic University Timişoara, Romania.

References

1. Arjovsky, M., Shah, A., Bengio, Y.: Unitary evolution recurrent neural networks. In: ICML 2016 (2016). https://arxiv.org/abs/1511.06464
2. Bengio, Y.: Learning deep architectures for AI. Found. Trends Mach. Learn. **2**(1), 1–127 (2009)
3. Bengio, Y., LeCun, Y., Hinton, G.: Deep learning. Nature **521**, 436–444 (2015)
4. Chaturvedi, A., Sharma, R., Wadekar, D., Bhandwalkar, A., Shitole, S.: Adaptive parametric estimator for complex valued images. In: International Conference on Technologies for Sustainable Development (ICTSD) (2015)
5. Eichel, P., Ives, R.: Compression of complex-valued SAR images. IEEE Trans. Image Process. **8**(10), 1483–1487 (1999)
6. Gonzalez, R.C., Woods, R.E.: Digital Image Processing. Pearson Prentice Hall, Upper Saddle River (2008)
7. Goodfellow, I., Bengio, Y., Courville, A.: Deep Learning. MIT Press, Cambridge (2016)

8. Guberman, N.: On Complex Valued Convolutional Neural Networks. Master's thesis, School of Computer Science and Engineering. The Hebrew University of Jerusalem (2016). https://arxiv.org/abs/1602.09046
9. Hansch, R., Hellwich, O.: Complex-valued convolutional neural networks for object detection in PolSAR data. In: European Conference on Synthetic Aperture Radar (EUSAR) (2010)
10. Hernandez-Garcia, L., Vazquez, A., Rowe, D.: Complex-valued analysis of arterial spin labeling based FMRI signals. Magn. Reson. Med. **62**(6), 1597–1608 (2009)
11. Hui, Y., Smith, M.: MRI reconstruction from truncated data using a complex domain backpropagation neural network. In: Pacific Rim Conference on Communications, Computers, and Signal Processing (PACRIM) (1995)
12. Krizhevsky, A.: Learning multiple layers of features from tiny images. Technical report (2009)
13. LeCun, Y., Boser, B., Denker, J.S., Henderson, D., Howard, R.E., Hubbard, W., Jackel, L.D.: Handwritten digit recognition with a back-propagation network. In: Advances in Neural Information Processing Systems (NIPS) (1989)
14. LeCun, Y., Bottou, L., Bengio, Y., Haffner, P.: Gradient-based learning applied to document recognition. Proc. IEEE **86**(11), 2278–2324 (1998)
15. Netzer, Y., Wang, T., Coates, A., Bissacco, A., Wu, B., Ng, A.Y.: Reading digits in natural images with unsupervised feature learning. In: NIPS Workshop on Deep Learning and Unsupervised Feature Learning (2011)
16. Popa, C.A.: Complex-valued convolutional neural networks for real-valued image classification. In: 2017 International Joint Conference on Neural Networks (IJCNN). IEEE May 2017
17. Samadi, S., Cetin, M., Masnadi-Shirazi, M.: Sparse signal representation for complex-valued imaging. In: Digital Signal Processing Workshop and Signal Processing Education Workshop (DSP/SPE), pp. 365–370 (2009)
18. Schmidhuber, J.: Deep learning in neural networks: an overview. Neural Netw. **61**, 85–117 (2015)
19. Tygert, M., Bruna, J., Chintala, S., LeCun, Y., Piantino, S., Szlam, A.: A mathematical motivation for complex-valued convolutional networks. Neural Comput. **28**(5), 815–825 (2016)
20. Virtue, P., Yu, S.X., Lustig, M.: Better than real: complex-valued neural nets for MRI fingerprinting. In: ICIP 2017 (2017). https://arxiv.org/abs/1707.00070
21. Wilmanski, M., Kreucher, C., Hero, A.: Complex input convolutional neural networks for wide angle SAR ATR. In: 2016 IEEE Global Conference on Signal and Information Processing (GlobalSIP). IEEE, DEC 2016
22. Yu, M.C., Lina, Q.H., Kuang, L.D., Gong, X.F., Cong, F., Calhoun, V.: ICA of full complex-valued fMRI data using phase information of spatial maps. J. Neurosci. Methods **249**, 75–91 (2015)

MHFlexDT: A Multivariate Branch Fuzzy Decision Tree Data Stream Mining Strategy Based on Hybrid Partitioning Standard

Xin Song[1,2(✉)], Han Wang[1], Huiyuan He[1], and Yakun Meng[2]

[1] School of Computer Science and Engineering, Northeastern University,
Shenyang, China
bravesong@163.com
[2] Computer Center, Northeastern University at Qinhuangdao,
Northeastern University, Qinhuangdao, China
244544786@qq.com

Abstract. Because of the inability to take a multi-pass scanning algorithm for random access to fast data streams and traditional data mining algorithms can't sample all samples of the data stream, research of data stream mining algorithm based on fuzzy decision tree theory that fuzzy decision tree combines the understandability of decision tree and the ability of representation of fuzzy set to deal with the fuzziness and uncertainty information is very valuable to improve the accuracy of data mining. This paper presents a fuzzy decision tree data mining strategy based on hybrid partitioning standard for the problem that the method has a low accuracy when we deal with low-membership samples with missing values by dividing the samples into leaf nodes according to their membership. The multivariate branch fuzzy decision tree data stream mining strategy based on hybrid partitioning standard(MHFlexDT) is used to construct the multivariate branch fuzzy tree structure. The data fitting problem is solved by adding temporary branches to the uncertain data. At the same time, the decision tree depth is effectively limited by using the McDiarmid bound threshold. The experimental results show that MHFlexDT strategy compared with fuzzy decision tree data mining strategy is more effective in large-scale data stream mining to reduce system computation, control decision tree depth, and ensure a high accuracy when we deal with missing values, data over-fitting and noisy data problems.

Keywords: Data streams mining · Fuzzy decision tree
Hybrid partitioning standard · Classification learning

1 Introduction

With the development of network technology, dealing with the issue of data stream became more and more important. Data in the data stream (ie, streaming data) is ordered, continuous and constantly changing, even infinite [1]. So, the cost of data mining algorithms for high accuracy is very high. The data stream mining algorithm should process the samples in the data stream within the system control time and take a fixed memory space for data processing with real-time and incremental updating of the

© Springer International Publishing AG, part of Springer Nature 2018
T. Huang et al. (Eds.): ISNN 2018, LNCS 10878, pp. 310–317, 2018.
https://doi.org/10.1007/978-3-319-92537-0_36

processing capacity. Decision tree algorithm is a kind of classification algorithm with explanatory and less input parameters [2, 3], but the traditional discriminant decision tree algorithm model is not suitable for data stream mining. The thesis presents a fuzzy decision tree data mining algorithm which combines the understandability of decision tree and the ability of representation of fuzzy set to deal with the fuzziness and uncertainty information based on hybrid partitioning standard. This paper proposes a hybrid decision tree partitioning model based on based on Gini index and misclassification error to divide the features. Then we propose using hybrid partitioning standard to deal with low-membership samples. And we propose a method for controlling growth of a fuzzy decision tree's depth based on McDiarmid bound thresholds.

The rest of this paper is organized as follows: in Sect. 2, we briefly review some closely related works. Section 3 elaborates building and running the method of MHFlexDT. The feasibility analysis and performance evaluation of the algorithm through experiments is presented in Sect. 4. Finally, the conclusions and future work directions are described in Sect. 5.

2   Related Works

The traditional decision tree algorithm is generally used for static data. In the implementation of data mining model, we need to adjust the traditional classification model based on decision tree to adapt to dynamic, continuous and diversity features of the data stream mining system [4]. In 2000, Domingos and Hulten et al. proposed Very Fast Decision Tree (VFDT) and first applied the decision tree learning to data stream mining [5], which solves the problem of insufficient training in the process of constructing the decision tree. However, the VFDT only can process discrete attributes and has not been designed for continuous attributes. In 2003, Gama et al. proposed the VFDTc algorithm based on VFDT algorithm which can not only process discrete data but also process continuous data [6]. H Yang proposed two lightweight pre-pruning mechanisms for stream mining [7]. Anagnostopoulo et al. proposed a data stream classification algorithm based on probability estimation, but the result of the estimation is often biased by the data [8]. Although there were many disadvantages of the early VFDT algorithm, the data stream classification gradually became a hot research topic.

To adapt to the diversity and uncertainty of data and to establish a robust model, Hulten et al. proposed the CVFDT algorithm [9]. However, the CVFDT algorithm can't solve the problem of concept drift. Therefore, Hashemi and Yang proposed a Flexible Decision Tree (FlexDT) model based on the problem of noise and missing values by using incremental algorithms [10]. Kuncheva and Ludmila found that the accuracy of the classification model is not only affected by data quality but also related to the sliding window [10]. In 2007, Wang et al. proposed an incremental fuzzy decision tree classification method for data streams mining based on threaded binary search trees (fVFDT) [11]. Isazadeh et al. proposed a multi-flexible fuzzy decision tree (MFlexDT) algorithm to handle data stream classification [12]. However, the accuracy of the algorithm constructed by single partitioning is low in the early training. Thus, there is still much room for research to improve the accuracy, reduce the complexity and enhance the ability of processing data with missing values.

3 MHFlexDT: A Data Mining Strategy Based on Multivariate Branch Hybrid Partitioning Fuzzy Decision Tree

3.1 Building Classification Model Based on Hybrid Partitioning

The strategy adopts hybrid partitioning standard to decide the feature selection and then determines whether the classification conditions are satisfied by McDiarmid bound [13]. The traditional Gini-based classification model [5, 14, 15] should be adjusted for fuzzy attributes. As shown in Eqs. (1)–(3), S is a fuzzy data set, S_L and S_R are fuzzy subsets of left and right branch divided by attribute α. S^i represents a subset of the ith class in S, and | S | represents the sum of membership degree of S:

$$Gini_a(S) = \frac{|S_L|}{|S|} Gini_a(S_L) + \frac{|S_R|}{|S|} Gini_a(S_R) \tag{1}$$

$$Gini_a(S_L) = 1 - \sum_{i=1}^{C} (\frac{|S_L^i|}{|S_L|})^2 \tag{2}$$

$$Gini_a(S_R) = 1 - \sum_{i=1}^{c} \left(\frac{|S_R^i|}{|S_R|}\right)^2 \tag{3}$$

In the same way, the fuzzy set is processed according to the standard membership function based on the Misclassification error method as shown in Eq. (4):

$$\Delta g_a^M(S) = g^M(S) - \sum_{q\in\{L,R\}} \frac{|S_{q,a}|}{|S_q|} (1 - \max_{k\in\{1,\cdots K\}} \frac{|S_{q,a}^k|}{|S_{q,a}|}) \tag{4}$$

The hybrid partitioning standard method based on Gini gain and its Misclassification error [16] is based on McDiarmid inequality operation respectively to decide whether the attribute is classified and increase the nodes of the tree. Let $S = S_1,\ldots\ldots, S_n$ be a set of random variable data elements where $\Delta Gini_{a,best}(S)$ and $\Delta Gini_{b,2th\_best}(S)$ are the value attribute α with the highest Gini gain based on the Gini coefficient and the attribute b with the second largest Gini gain value. In addition, $\Delta g_{c,best}^M(S)$ and $\Delta g_{d,2th\_best}^M(S)$ are the attribute c (the maximum misclassification value) and the attribute d (the second largest misclassification value) according to the Misclassification error standard respectively.

If the condition of Eq. (5) is satisfied, the attribute a with the largest information gain will be considered as a cut point. And if the condition of Eq. (6) is satisfied, the attribute c will be selected. If neither of the conditions is satisfied, no classification is made.

$$\Delta Gini_{a,best}(S) - \Delta Gini_{b,2th\_best}(S) > 8\sqrt{\frac{\ln(1/\delta)}{n}} \qquad (5)$$

$$\Delta g^M_{c,best}(S) - \Delta g^M_{d,2th_{best}}(S) > z(1-\delta)\sqrt{\frac{1}{2n}} \qquad (6)$$

3.2   Building Multivariate Branch Fuzzy Decision Tree

The structure of a fuzzy decision tree is shown in Fig. 1 where X_j is a feature node based on α_j partitioned by feature j, α_j and σ_j are the center deviation and standard deviation of the sigmoid fuzzy membership function, μ_{jk} is the membership degree in the class kth at the current jth node, β_{jk} is the membership degree in the class kth at the jth leaf node. If the received instance has a particularly low membership in the related node partitioned by α, in other words the feature node X_j received the new feature of the instance, a new α'_{ji} will be temporarily created at the related node. That is, this new feature forms a new temporary node X'_{ji} based on α'_{ji} and the corresponding μ'_{jk} and β'_{jk} represent the degree of membership and category of the new branch being built. If this new variable is used to make decision for new instance, the new subtree of α will be added to the current tree. Therefore, each node may contain a range $\left\{\alpha_j, \alpha'_{j1}, \ldots\ldots, \alpha'_{jn}\right\}$ of new values. Whether a new subtree becomes a new branch of the current tree will be verified by McDiarmid bound. When the condition is satisfied, a new node based on the new α value partition will be replaced by the original leaf node. And the node is classified as an internal node from the leaf node, then it will split on the attribute and recursively process new leaf nodes. The life cycle of the temporary branch is determined by the threshold of McDiarmid bound. If the number of instances in a temporary branch can't meet the defined threshold, the branch will be pruned. This pre-pruning scheme allows the MHFlexDT algorithm to better control the depth.

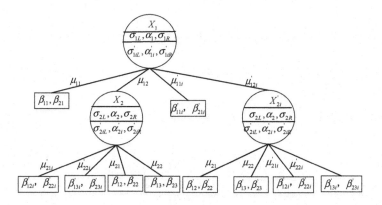

Fig. 1. The structure of MHFlexDT fuzzy decision tree

The MHFlexDT is an incremental algorithm that increases the coverage of classification space by identifying new range values by adding temporary branches. It can effectively process data that can't match the existing feature nodes based on the cut point α and data with low membership degree. When a model processes noise data and data whose concept is changed, it is not necessary to update the parameter values for each instance. This means that the data in the temporary branch is not updated so that the computation of the model is reduced. When the method of adding temporary branch is used to process unknown data, it is ensured that there is no noise data in the fixed branch of the fuzzy decision tree and the accuracy of model mining processing is improved.

4   Experiments and Analysis

In the experiments, we use a synthetic dataset (WaveformGeneratorDrift dataset) and a real dataset (Airlines dataset). the experimental deploys main parameter setting used by each algorithm's corresponding paper. η=0.1 is the learning rate, $n_{min} = 200$ is the least sufficient number of instances for determining each node partition. To assume desired δ=0.01, the probability 1-δ ensures that the attributes chosen by using a small portion of data are the same as the attributes chosen by using entire data stream. The difference between the attribute with the highest information gain and the attribute with the second highest information gain at the leaf node passes the Hoeffding bound due to arrival of the new instance. Given a predefined threshold τ=0.05, 0<τ<1, for assigning each membership degree β_{kl} to the kth class at the lth leaf $(0 \le \beta_{kl} \le 1)$, the node portioning is processed when $\tau \le \beta_{kl} \le 1 - \tau$.

The experiment compares the experimental results of accuracy and tree depth growth changes among the two data sets in MHFlexDT model based on hybrid partitioning, HFlexDT model based on the binary branch and classical HAT processing model.

In experiments for synthetic dataset, we present the tree depth and accuracy results for WaveformGeneratorDrift dataset of the three models in Figs. 2 and 3. It can be seen

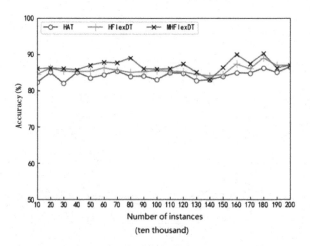

Fig. 2. Accuracy results of three algorithms for WaveformGeneratorDrift dataset

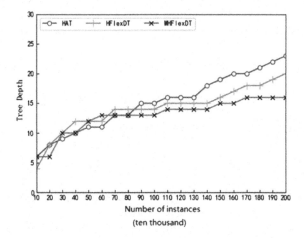

Fig. 3. Tree depth results of three algorithms for WaveformGeneratorDrift dataset

from the experimental results that the MHFlexDT model improves the accuracy of about 5%–10% compared with the other two models, but the depth of the fuzzy decision tree is only about 60% of the HAT model when the amount of data increases to 2 million, which reduces the time complexity of model processing.

In experiments for real dataset, we present the tree depth and accuracy results for Airlines dataset of running the three models in Figs. 4 and 5. From the experimental results, we can see that the MHFlexDT model improves the accuracy of the HAT model by 10%, but the depth of the fuzzy decision tree is only increased by 2 layers compared with the HAT model as the amount of data increases. However, the fuzzy decision tree depth of MHFlexDT model reduced by two levels while maintaining a high accuracy compared with the HFlexDT model.

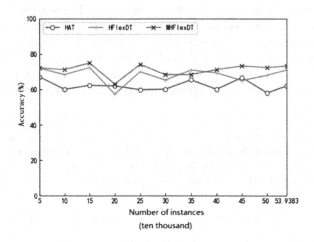

Fig. 4. Accuracy results of three algorithms for Airlines dataset

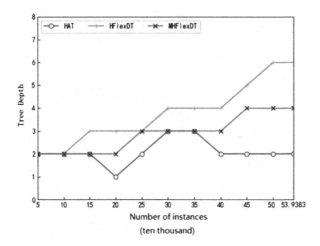

Fig. 5. Tree depth results of three algorithms for Airlines dataset

In conclusion, the MHFlexDT can effectively control the depth of the tree while maintaining a high processing accuracy both in the synthetic dataset experiment and the real dataset experiments, and reduces the time complexity of the model running.

5 Conclusion

MHFlexDT is a data stream mining processing model of a multivariate branch fuzzy decision tree based on hybrid partitioning, which can obtain a higher accuracy while reducing the depth of fuzzy decision tree. The algorithm makes the range of attribute operating values more flexible and improves the classification responsiveness. MHFlexDT can add new feature at different levels of the decision tree, which can make the construction of the fuzzy decision tree more flexible. The new method is provided for the data with low membership by the using temporary branches and the method reduces data computations compared to the binary HFlexDT algorithm. On the other hand, it is more easily to find the data of the concept change and to creates a new branch as the result of the use of temporary branches. In conclusion, MHFlexDT algorithm based on incremental learning facilitates self-learning in complex environments with unstructured data.

Acknowledgment. The research work was supported by the National Natural Science Foundation of China under Grant No. 61403069 and 61603083, the Fundamental Research Funds of the Central Universities under Grant No. N162304009, the Major Project of Science and Technology Research of Hebei University under Grant No. ZD2017303.

References

1. Wei G.: Research & Development of Distributed Stream Real-time Computing Framework. Zhejiang Sci-Tech University (2013)
2. Han, J., Kamber, M.: Data Mining: Concepts and Techniques. Data Mining Concepts Models Methods & Algorithms Second Edition **5**(4), 1–18 (2011)
3. Rokach, L., Maimon, L.: Data Mining with Decision Trees: Theory and Applications. World Scientific Publishing Company, Singapore (2014)
4. Yao Y., Zhang J.X., Xu G.K.: The Methods of Dynamic Data Stream Classification and Its Applications in Data Mining of Ethnic Information, pp. 43–45. Publishing House of Electronics Industry, Beijing (2014)
5. Jaworski, M., Rutkowski, L., Pawlak, M.: Hybrid splitting criterion in decision trees for data stream mining. In: Rutkowski, L., Korytkowski, M., Scherer, R., Tadeusiewicz, R., Zadeh, Lotfi A., Zurada, Jacek M. (eds.) ICAISC 2016. LNCS (LNAI), vol. 9693, pp. 60–72. Springer, Cham (2016). https://doi.org/10.1007/978-3-319-39384-1_6
6. Gama, J., Fernandes, R., Rocha, R.: Decision trees for mining data streams. Intell. Data Anal. **10**(1), 23–45 (2006)
7. Yang, H., Fong, S.: Moderated VFDT in stream mining using adaptive tie threshold and incremental pruning. In: Cuzzocrea, A., Dayal, U. (eds.) DaWaK 2011. LNCS, vol. 6862, pp. 471–483. Springer, Heidelberg (2011). https://doi.org/10.1007/978-3-642-23544-3_36
8. Anagnostopoulos, C., Tasoulis, D.K., Adams, N.M., et al.: Temporally adaptive estimation of logistic classifiers on data streams. Adv. Data Anal. Classif. **3**(3), 243–261 (2009)
9. Hulten G., Spencer L., Domingos, P.: Mining Time-changing Data Streams. In: ACM SIGKDD International Conference on Knowledge Discovery and Data Mining, pp. 97–106 (2001)
10. Hashemi, S., Yang, Y.: Flexible decision tree for data stream classification in the presence of concept change, noise and missing values. Data Min. Knowl. Disc. **19**(1), 95–131 (2009)
11. Kuncheva, Ludmila I.: Classifier ensembles for changing environments. In: Roli, F., Kittler, J., Windeatt, T. (eds.) MCS 2004. LNCS, vol. 3077, pp. 1–15. Springer, Heidelberg (2004). https://doi.org/10.1007/978-3-540-25966-4_1
12. Wang, T., Li, Z., Yan, Y., Chen, H.: An incremental fuzzy decision tree classification method for mining data streams. In: Perner, P. (ed.) MLDM 2007. LNCS (LNAI), vol. 4571, pp. 91–103. Springer, Heidelberg (2007). https://doi.org/10.1007/978-3-540-73499-4_8
13. Isazadeh, A., Mahan, F., Pedrycz, W.: MFlexDT: multi flexible fuzzy decision tree for data stream classification. Soft. Comput. **20**(9), 3719–3733 (2016)
14. Rutkowski, L., Pietruczuk, L., Duda, P., et al.: Decision trees for mining data streams based on the McDiarmid. IEEE Trans. Knowl. Data Eng. **25**(6), 1272–1279 (2013)
15. Rutkowski, L., Jaworski, M., Pietruczuk, L., et al.: The CART decision tree for mining data streams. Inf. Sci. **266**(5), 1–15 (2014)
16. Matuszyk, P., Krempl, G., Spiliopoulou, M.: Correcting the usage of the hoeffding inequality in stream mining. In: Tucker, A., Höppner, F., Siebes, A., Swift, S. (eds.) IDA 2013. LNCS, vol. 8207, pp. 298–309. Springer, Heidelberg (2013). https://doi.org/10.1007/978-3-642-41398-8_26

Developments on Solutions
of the Normalized-Cut-Clustering
Problem Without Eigenvectors

Leandro Leonardo Lorente-Leyva[1], Israel David Herrera-Granda[1],
Paul D. Rosero-Montalvo[1,2], Karina L. Ponce-Guevara[1,3],
Andrés Eduardo Castro-Ospina[4(✉)], Miguel A. Becerra[4],
Diego Hernán Peluffo-Ordóñez[5,6], and José Luis Rodríguez-Sotelo[7]

[1] Universidad Técnica del Norte, Ibarra, Ecuador
{lllorente,idherrera,pdrosero,klponceg}@utn.edu.ec
[2] Instituto Tecnológico Superior 17 de Julio, Ibarra, Ecuador
[3] Universidade Federal de Pernambuco, Recife, Brazil
klpg@cin.ufpe.br
[4] Instituto Tecnológico Metropolitano, Medellín, Colombia
{andrescastro,miguelbecerra}@itm.edu.co
[5] Yachay Tech, Urcuquí, Ecuador
dpeluffo@yachaytech.edu.ec
[6] Corporación Universitaria Autónoma de Nariño, Pasto, Colombia
[7] Universidad Autónoma de Manizales, Manizales, Colombia
jlrodriguez@autonoma.edu.co

Abstract. Normalized-cut clustering (NCC) is a benchmark graph-based approach for unsupervised data analysis. Since its traditional formulation is a quadratic form subject to orthogonality conditions, it is often solved within an eigenvector-based framework. Nonetheless, in some cases the calculation of eigenvectors is prohibitive or unfeasible due to the involved computational cost – for instance, when dealing with high dimensional data. In this work, we present an overview of recent developments on approaches to solve the NCC problem with no requiring the calculation of eigenvectors. Particularly, heuristic-search and quadratic-formulation-based approaches are studied. Such approaches are elegantly deduced and explained, as well as simple ways to implement them are provided.

Keywords: Eigenvectors · Graph-based clustering
Normalized cut clustering · Quadratic forms

1 Introduction

In pattern recognition scenarios, the graph-partitioning-based clustering are discriminative approaches to grouping homogeneous nodes (representing data points) within a fully unsupervised framework, that is to say, with no assumptions about the global structure of data. Instead, it is considered local evidence

© Springer International Publishing AG, part of Springer Nature 2018
T. Huang et al. (Eds.): ISNN 2018, LNCS 10878, pp. 318–328, 2018.
https://doi.org/10.1007/978-3-319-92537-0_37

on the pairwise relationship between data points –known as similarity– which provides an estimate of the probability that two data points belong to the same cluster. Accordingly, the clustering procedure is carried out by splitting the graph into disjunct subgraphs or subsets following similarity-based criteria which are mostly formulated to keep accurate relationship among nodes regarding a lower-dimensional representation space of the original input data. In this connection, to solve the graph-based clustering problems, eigenvector decomposition results appealing when seeking for continuous solutions by following a relaxed formulation [1,2]. Among other reasons, this is due to the fact that eigenvectors can be interpreted as geometric coordinates and therefore a feasible grouping procedure is via directly clustering them by means of any conventional technique (such as k-means) as suggested in [3,4]. As well, there are spectral relaxations and kernel formulations [5].

Nonetheless, given the complexity and computational cost that involves the computation of eigenvectors, spectral clustering approaches may be prohibitive or unfeasible for some problems, such as those involving high-dimensional data or large data sets. In the scientific literature, there have been reported some papers to deal with this issue by providing approaches that approximate spectral solutions without using eigenvectors, being among them: multi-level schemes [6], heuristic search with pre-clustering stages [7,8], or formulating simple quadratic problems with linear constraints [9–11]. In this study is presented an overview of alternative approaches to solve the NCC problem by using heuristic searches and quadratic problem formulations. Particularly, to yield the alternative solutions, we set as benchmark method the so-called multi-cluster spectral clustering (MCSC) introduced in [1], forasmuch as it estimates binary cluster indicators from the space spanned by the eigenvectors through a discretization process without requiring extra clustering procedures.

This paper presents a complete explanation and different solutions for the formulation of normalized cut clustering problem. First, a brief outlining the MCSC method is encompassed in Sect. 2, taking advantage of some matrix algebra properties proposing a muticluster partitioning criterion based on graph theory. In Sects. 3 and 4, the alternative solutions based on heuristic searches and quadratic problem formulations are respectively presented. Finally, some concluding remarks are drawn in Sect. 5.

2   Normalized Cuts Based-Clustering

Given the topological nature of the conventional NCC formulation, it can be readily understood from graph theory concepts. In this work, we study a weighted-graph-based NCC approach that naturally yields a quadratic matrix formulation as detailed in [1].

For further statements, consider the following notation: A weighted non-directed graph is defined as $\mathbb{G} = (\mathbb{V}, \mathbb{E}, \boldsymbol{W})$, where $\mathbb{V} = [N]$ are the N nodes and the notation $[m]$ ($m \in \mathbb{N}$) stands for the set of numbers less than or equal to m ($[m] = \{1, \cdots, m\}$), the set of edges is noted as $\mathbb{E}$, and matrix $\boldsymbol{W} \in \mathbb{R}^{N \times N}$

stands for the affinity matrix. Since the graph $\mathbb{G}$ is a weighted undirected graph, the affinity matrix $\boldsymbol{W} = [W]_{ij}$ is a positive semi-definite symmetric matrix. NCC aims to split the set $\mathbb{V}$ into a pre-established number C of disjoint sub-graphs or groups. Mathematically, we can write $\mathbb{V} = \cup_{c=1}^{C} \mathbb{V}_c$, where $\mathbb{V}_l \cap \mathbb{V}_c = \emptyset \; \forall l \neq c$. Here, input instances to be clustered are in $\boldsymbol{X} \in \mathbb{R}^{N \times d} = (\boldsymbol{x}_1, \ldots, \boldsymbol{x}_N)^\top$, where vector $\boldsymbol{x}_i \in \mathbb{R}^d$ is the i-th data point feature vector associated with node i and represented with d variables. To pose a convex matrix optimization problem, NCC can be formulated as the computation of a membership indicator matrix $\boldsymbol{B} \in \{0,1\}^{N \times C}$, with $\boldsymbol{B} = (\boldsymbol{b}^{(1)}, \ldots, \boldsymbol{b}^{(C)})$, such that $\boldsymbol{b}^{(c)}$ denotes the c-th column vector as the membership of every instance to cluster c. Each entry ic of matrix $\boldsymbol{B}$ is defined as $b_{\ell c} = m_{\ell}^{(c)} = 1$ if $\ell \in \mathbb{V}_c$, otherwise, with $c \in [C]$, and $\ell \in \mathbb{V}$. Additionally, to ensure the membership of each node to a unique group or sub-graph, the following condition must be met:

$$\sum_{c=1}^{C} b_{\ell}^{(c)} = (b_{\ell}^{(1)}, \ldots, b_{\ell}^{(C)})^\top \mathbf{1}_C = 1, \; \ell \in [N] \; \therefore \; \boldsymbol{B}\mathbf{1}_C = \mathbf{1}_N, \tag{1}$$

where $\mathbf{1}_C$ is a C-dimensional vector of all ones. Considering the duality of weighted undirected graph problems [1], computed sub-graphs can be determined by either maximizing within or minimizing between-cluster similarities, i.e., maximizing or minimizing the cuts. By considering the maximization scenario, we can write a matrix cost function as follows:

$$\sum_{\ell, r \in \mathbb{V}_c, c \in [C]} W_{\ell r} = \mathrm{tr}(\boldsymbol{B}^\top \boldsymbol{W} \boldsymbol{B}) = \sum_{c=1}^{C} \boldsymbol{b}^{(c)\top} \boldsymbol{W} \boldsymbol{b}^{(c)} \tag{2}$$

As demonstrated in [1], optimization of associations and cuts occurs simultaneously when normalizing their formulations regarding the graph degree. Also, such normalization make suitable solutions to lie into a unit hyper-sphere space. The graph degree matrix $\boldsymbol{D} \in \mathbb{R}^{N \times N}$ is a diagonal matrix whose entries are given by $d_{\ell\ell} = \sum_{r \in [N]} W_{\ell r}$. For short, we can write it in matrix terms as $\boldsymbol{D} = \mathrm{Diag}(\boldsymbol{W}\mathbf{1}_N)$, where $\mathrm{Diag}(\cdot)$ stands for the diagonal matrix formed by its argument. Taking into account the above, the K-way-normalized-cut-based clustering criterion is written as:

$$\max_{\boldsymbol{B}} f(\boldsymbol{B}) = \max_{\boldsymbol{b}^{(c)}} f(\boldsymbol{b}^{(c)}) = \frac{1}{C} \frac{\mathrm{tr}(\boldsymbol{B}^\top \boldsymbol{W} \boldsymbol{B})}{\mathrm{tr}(\boldsymbol{B}^\top \boldsymbol{D} \boldsymbol{B})} = \frac{1}{C} \frac{\sum_{c=1}^{C} \boldsymbol{b}^{(c)\top} \boldsymbol{W} \boldsymbol{b}^{(c)}}{\sum_{c=1}^{C} \boldsymbol{b}^{(c)\top} \boldsymbol{D} \boldsymbol{b}^{(c)}} \tag{3}$$

s. t. $\boldsymbol{B} \in \{0,1\}^{N \times C}$, $\boldsymbol{B}\mathbf{1}_C = \mathbf{1}_N$.

As can be noticed, the formulation (3) is clearly a quadratic problem dependent of $\boldsymbol{B}$ (also $\boldsymbol{b}^{(c)}$), and given its convexity and continuous orthogonality conditions, a continuous solution can be obtained by the eigenvector decomposition of the normalized similarity matrix (Lapacian of similarity matrix, as well). Then, to generate the binary membership indicators, a discretization process can be performed as explained in [1].

3   Alternative Solutions Based on Heuristic Searches Within the Graph

To heuristically determine the binary cluster indicators $\boldsymbol{B}$, it is possible to perform a search within the graph-based representation space aimed at identifying the data points holding the maximum pairwise similarity. The methods explored here are lower-computational-cost alternatives to typical eigenvector-based solutions of MCSC –named MCSC method based on a heuristic search (in short, MCSChs). As reported in literature, MCSChs may significantly outperform traditional spectral clustering techniques for solving the NCC problem regarding the processing time while reaching a comparable performance [7,8]. Briefly put, the aim of this approach is to formulate a novel simpler loss function by rewriting the MCSC quadratic expressions given in Eq. (3) so that a solution can be obtained by means of an intuitive searching process on the graph similarity representation space starting from given a few initial nodes. Moreover, to avoid a trivial solution, i.e. where all elements belong to a single cluster, it is incorporated an initialization stage using prior knowledge, i.e., exploit the original targets to initialize data points for starting a pre-clustering and grouping stages to ensure suitable initial nodes.

3.1   Rewriting the NCC Problem

Recalling Eq. (3), the NCC problem can be expressed as:

$$\max_{\boldsymbol{B}} \frac{1}{C} \frac{\operatorname{tr}(\boldsymbol{B}^\top \boldsymbol{W} \boldsymbol{B})}{\operatorname{tr}(\boldsymbol{B}^\top \boldsymbol{D} \boldsymbol{B})}; \quad \text{s. t. } \boldsymbol{B} \in \{0,1\}^{N \times C}, \quad \boldsymbol{B} \boldsymbol{1}_C = \boldsymbol{1}_N$$

Consider the following mathematical development and analysis. Let $\boldsymbol{H} = \boldsymbol{B}^\top \boldsymbol{D} \boldsymbol{B}$, with $\boldsymbol{H} \in \mathbb{R}^{C \times C}$, then each corresponding entry ℓr is

$$h_{\ell r} = (b_{1\ell}, \ldots, b_{N\ell}) \begin{pmatrix} d_1 & 0 & \cdots & 0 \\ 0 & d_2 & \cdots & 0 \\ \vdots & \vdots & \ddots & \vdots \\ 0 & 0 & \cdots & d_N \end{pmatrix} \begin{pmatrix} b_{1r} \\ b_{2r} \\ \vdots \\ b_{Nr} \end{pmatrix} = \sum_{s=1}^{N} b_{s\ell} b_{sr} d_s,$$

where $\boldsymbol{D} = \operatorname{Diag}(\boldsymbol{d})$ and $\boldsymbol{d} = [d_1, \ldots, d_N] = \boldsymbol{W} \boldsymbol{1}_N$. Thus,

$$\operatorname{tr}(\boldsymbol{B}^\top \boldsymbol{D} \boldsymbol{B}) = \sum_{\ell=1}^{C} h_{\ell\ell} = \sum_{\ell=1}^{C} \sum_{s=1}^{N} b_{s\ell}^2 d_s = \sum_{\ell=1}^{C} \left(b_{1\ell}^2 d_1 + b_{2\ell}^2 d_2 + \cdots + b_{N\ell}^2 d_N\right) = \sum_{\ell=1}^{N} d_\ell$$

however $d_\ell = \sum_{r=1}^{N} W_{\ell r}$, thus:

$$\operatorname{tr}(\boldsymbol{B}^\top \boldsymbol{D} \boldsymbol{B}) = \sum_{\ell=1}^{N} \sum_{r=1}^{N} W_{\ell r} = ||W||_{L_1} = \text{const.} \tag{4}$$

On the other hand, let $\boldsymbol{G} \in \mathbb{R}^{N \times N}$ be an auxiliary matrix with $\boldsymbol{G} = \boldsymbol{B}^{\top} \boldsymbol{W} \boldsymbol{B}$, thereby, each ℓr-th entry of $\boldsymbol{G}$ is:

$$
g_{\ell r} = (b_{1\ell}, \ldots, b_{N\ell}) \, \boldsymbol{W} \begin{pmatrix} b_{1r} \\ \vdots \\ b_{Nr} \end{pmatrix} = \sum_{s=1}^{N} b_{sr} \sum_{t=1}^{N} b_{t\ell} W_{ts} = \sum_{s=1}^{N} \sum_{t=1}^{N} b_{sj} b_{ti} W_{ts}.
$$

Therefore,

$$
\begin{aligned}
\operatorname{tr}(\boldsymbol{B}^{\top} \boldsymbol{W} \boldsymbol{B}) &= \sum_{\ell=1}^{C} g_{\ell\ell} = \sum_{\ell=1}^{C} \sum_{s=1}^{N} \sum_{t=1}^{N} b_{s\ell} b_{t\ell} W_{ts} \\
&= \sum_{\ell=1}^{C} \sum_{s=1}^{N} b_{s\ell} \left(b_{1\ell} W_{1s} + b_{2\ell} W_{2s} + \cdots + b_{N\ell} W_{Ns} \right) \\
&= \sum_{\ell=1}^{C} b_{1\ell} \left(b_{1\ell} W_{11} + b_{2\ell} W_{21} + \cdots + b_{N\ell} W_{N1} \right) \\
&\quad + b_{2\ell} \left(b_{2\ell} W_{12} + b_{2\ell} W_{22} + \cdots + b_{N\ell} W_{N2} \right) + \cdots \\
&\quad + b_{N\ell} \left(b_{1\ell} W_{1N} + b_{2\ell} W_{2N} + \cdots + b_{N\ell} W_{NN} \right).
\end{aligned}
$$

Besides, considering that matrix $\boldsymbol{W}$ is symmetric, then:

$$
\operatorname{tr}(\boldsymbol{B}^{\top} \boldsymbol{W} \boldsymbol{B}) = W_{11} \sum_{\ell=1}^{C} b_{1\ell}^{2} + W_{21} \sum_{\ell=1}^{C} (b_{1\ell} b_{2\ell} + b_{2\ell} b_{1\ell}) + \cdots + W_{NN} \sum_{\ell=1}^{C} b_{N\ell}^{2}.
$$

Considering that $\sum_{\ell=1}^{C} b_{n\ell}^{2} = 1, \quad \forall n \in [N]$, we can write

$$
\operatorname{tr}(\boldsymbol{B}^{\top} \boldsymbol{W} \boldsymbol{B}) = W_{11} + W_{22} + \cdots + W_{NN} + 2 \sum_{p>q} \sum_{\ell=1}^{N} W_{pq} b_{p\ell} b_{q\ell}
$$

$$
\operatorname{tr}(\boldsymbol{B}^{\top} \boldsymbol{W} \boldsymbol{B}) = \operatorname{tr}(W) + 2 \sum_{p>q} W_{pq} \delta_{pq}, \tag{5}
$$

where $\delta_{pq} = 1$ if $p = q$, otherwise 0.

Notice that the membership operator δ_{pq} becomes 0 when the dot product between the rows p and q is equal to 0, i.e., when such rows are orthogonal. On the other hand, it is equal to 1 ensuring that both row vectors are equivalents, i.e., containing 1 in the same entry. Finally, in accordance with Eq.(5), since $\operatorname{tr}(\boldsymbol{W})$ is constant, the term to be maximized is only $\sum_{p>q} W_{pq} \delta_{pq}$.

3.2 Heuristic Search for Solving MCSC (MCSChs)

The so-called MCSChs groups data naturally by following a heuristic search criterion, which uses prior knowledge beforehand of data and incorporates a pre-clustering stage. It consists of three main stages: initial nodes setting, grouping by a heuristic search, and pre-clustering.

Initial Nodes Setting Using Prior Knowledge: When maximizing $\sum_{p>q} W_{pq}\delta_{pq}$, a trivial solution may be achieved where all nodes are clustered together into the same sub-graph. To evade this problem, few prior knowledge is taken into account, by using the ground truth to randomly assign the C data points (one per class) into the membership matrix $\boldsymbol{B}$, by setting $b_{\ell c}$ as 1 if the ℓ-th entry is chosen as a seed node and 0 for the remaining row entries. Let the indexes related to initial nodes be noted as $\boldsymbol{q} = (q_1, \ldots, q_C)$ where $q_c \in \mathbb{V}$. Starting from these seed nodes, the remaining clusters are completed by assigning each datum to the cluster which has the maximum value of similarity.

Pre-clustering Stage: In this sense, to prevent the misassignment of closer data points, a pre-clustering stage is carried out. A low proportion of the N data points, noted as ϵ, are appended to the previously assigned seed nodes whose value of similarity is maximum, i.e., when the initial nodes are selected, the $\epsilon\%$ of data points per node with maximum similarity are identified and these are assigned to their respective node. By doing this, the initial C seed clusters are completed.

Heuristic-search-based Grouping: Once the pre-clustering stage is performed and the C initial clusters are established, a heuristic procedure were proposed to assign the remaining data points as members of the previously assigned data with which presents the greatest similarity. The complete procedure works as follows: To avoid the reuse of data previously assigned, at each iteration, where an entry $W_{\ell r}$ of similarity matrix is chosen and assigned, its value is set to zero, i.e., $W_{\ell r} = 0$. The assignment process is performed until all the data is assigned to any cluster, mathematically the L_1-norm is used since all entries of $\boldsymbol{B}$ are positive, thus, when the expression $\sum_{\ell=1}^{N} \sum_{c=1}^{C} b_{\ell c} = ||\boldsymbol{B}||_{L_1} = N$ is fulfilled, the heuristic search process is completed. A graphic explanation of the heuristic search is depicted in Fig. 1.

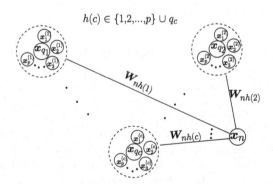

Fig. 1. Heuristic search within a graph-similarity-representation space.

It can be seen how the seed nodes $\{\boldsymbol{x}_{q_1}, \ldots, \boldsymbol{x}_{q_C}\}$ corresponds to the coordinates noted as $q_1, q_2, \ldots, q_C$. Then, C seed or initial clusters are formed by adding P (the integer closest to $\epsilon\%$ of N) data points to the most similar seed node at the pre-clustering stage. Finally, the remaining points are added following the heuristic-search-based proposed previously. At this step, the term $h(c)$ stands for the set of indexes of the data points belonging to the c-th cluster, including its seed node q_c. As expected, this set is incremented every time a new datum is added to cluster c.

In the example shown in Fig. 1, x_n is the datum to be grouped. For this purpose, the similarity between itself, i.e., x_n, and the formed clusters at the actual iteration, i.e., $W_{nh(c)}, \forall c \in [C]$ are used to assign it by following the rule: x_n is assigned to the c-th cluster in such a way that $\arg\max_c W_{nh(c)}$, s. t. $c \in [C]$. A complete algorithm for heuristic search is detailed in [12].

3.3 Alternative Initialization of Seed Nodes

As any other discriminative/parametric pattern recognition approach, the initialization is a crucial stage. In the heuristic search (MCSChs) an inadequate selection of the C initial seed nodes $q = (q_1, \ldots, q_C)$, may lead the clustering to converge to a local optimum, distant from the global one. Therefore, initializations of seed nodes remains as an important issue. An initialization technique named KDE-Centers was proposed in [7] based on the bivariate kernel density estimator (KDE) from [13]. KDE-Centers works as follows: *(i)* as a first step, a bidimensional distribution is generated by applying the bivariate KDE estimator onto the first two dimensions of the feature matrix X; *(ii)* the local maxima of the generated distribution are found, noted as $\xi_h \in \mathbb{R}^2$, $h = 1, \ldots, H, H \geq C$. Each ξ_h is seen as an initial candidate node; *(iii)* C initial nodes are established by grouping the previously computed candidates by using a hierarchical clustering technique; *(iv)* since the estimated distribution may generates overlapping clusters, a data count inside a sphere of radius ϵ_q centered at each centroid is performed. Afterwards, if the overlapping number is greater than the proportion γN, a new couple of dimensions is chosen from step *(i)* and a new set of initial nodes is generated; *(v)* iterate until convergence.

4   Alternative Solutions Based on Quadratic Formulations

If a sufficient number of linear constraints are introduced, the NCC formulation can be posed as a quadratic problem. To do so, the function f in Eq. (3) can be rewritten by taking advantage of what has been demonstrated in Eq. (4) at Sect. 3.1, thus, eliminating the denominator. Furthermore, conditions introduced in Eq. (1) ensure that each cluster has as members at least one node and it can be upper bounded by $N - C + 1$ in order to prevent all vertices from being assigned to a single cluster. By following a vector notation, previous constraints can be summarized as $0 < b^{(c)\top} 1_N < N - C$. Additionally, let N_c for $c \in [C]$ be the number of nodes to grouped into the cluster c. Thus, all membership vectors will fulfill $||b^{(c)}||_{L_2}^2 = b^{(c)\top} b^{(c)} = N_c$. Finally, the optimization problem stated in Eq. (3) along with the above given conditions, gives rise to the following new problem:

$$\max_{\boldsymbol{b}^{(c)}} \sum_{c=1}^{C} \boldsymbol{b}^{(c)\top} \boldsymbol{W} \boldsymbol{b}^{(c)}$$

$$\text{s. t. } \boldsymbol{b}^{(c)} > 0, 0 < \boldsymbol{b}^{(c)\top} \boldsymbol{1}_N < N - C, \text{ with } c \in [C], \tag{6}$$

$$\sum_{c=1}^{C} \boldsymbol{b}^{(c)\top} \boldsymbol{D} \boldsymbol{b}^{(c)} = ||\boldsymbol{W}||_{L_1}, \sum_{c=1}^{C} \boldsymbol{b}^{(c)\top} \boldsymbol{b}^{(c)} = N_1 + \cdots + N_c = N.$$

4.1 Simplified Approach

A simplified approach is achieved when problem Eq. 6 is relaxed by incorporating the quadratic constraints in the functional, as follows:

$$f(\boldsymbol{b}^{(c)} | \lambda, \mu) =$$

$$\sum_{c=1}^{C} \left(\boldsymbol{b}^{(c)\top} \boldsymbol{W} \boldsymbol{b}^{(c)} + \lambda \boldsymbol{b}^{(c)\top} \boldsymbol{D} \boldsymbol{b}^{(c)} + \mu \boldsymbol{b}^{(c)\top} \boldsymbol{b}^{(c)} \right) - \lambda ||\boldsymbol{W}||_{L_1} - \mu N,$$

where μ and λ are additional parameters added for regularization purposes. Therefore, by eliminating constant terms and introducing the matrix $\boldsymbol{P}_{\lambda,\mu} \in \mathbb{R}^{N \times N}$ defined by $\boldsymbol{P}_{\lambda,\mu} = \boldsymbol{W} + \lambda \boldsymbol{D} + \mu \boldsymbol{I}_N$, the new functional becomes

$$f(\boldsymbol{b}^{(c)}) = \sum_{c=1}^{C} \boldsymbol{b}^{(c)\top} \boldsymbol{P}_{\lambda,\mu} \boldsymbol{b}^{(c)}. \tag{7}$$

Then, to formulate a purely quadratic problem, we can write the following vectorized problem (recalling membership matrix $\boldsymbol{B}$):

$$\max_{\boldsymbol{B}} \ f(\boldsymbol{B}) = \text{vec}(\boldsymbol{B})^{\top} (\boldsymbol{P} \otimes \boldsymbol{I}_C) \, \text{vec}(\boldsymbol{B})$$

$$\text{s. t. } \text{vec}(\boldsymbol{B}) > 0, \quad 0 < \left(\boldsymbol{1}_N^{\top} \otimes \boldsymbol{I}_C \right) \text{vec}(\boldsymbol{B}) < N - C, \tag{8}$$

where $\otimes$ denotes the Kronecker product and $\text{vec}(\boldsymbol{B})$ is the vectorization of $\boldsymbol{B}$ given by $\text{vec}(\boldsymbol{B}) = (\boldsymbol{b}^{(1)\top}, \ldots, \boldsymbol{b}^{(c)\top})^{\top}$. Now, since the constraints are linear and its functional is quadratic, it is noticeable that the problem Eq. (8) –in its dual formulation– can be addressed by means of a traditional quadratic programming algorithm.

4.2 Forcing Orthogonality: A Better Alternative

To this extend, by constraining the formulation with $\sum_{c=1}^{C} \boldsymbol{b}^{(c)\top} \boldsymbol{b}^{(c)} = \text{tr}(\boldsymbol{B}^{\top} \boldsymbol{B}) = N$, posed optimization problem still produces infinite solutions being highly likely to be local optima. Typically, this issue requires some additional binaryzing processes [10]. Instead, the alternative here outlined is to explore the information provided by $\boldsymbol{B}^{\top} \boldsymbol{B}$ in its out-diagonal elements mainly. Let us consider the following statements: On one hand, given the binary nature of matrix $\boldsymbol{B}$, condition $\boldsymbol{B}^{\top} \boldsymbol{B} = \text{Diag}(N_1, \ldots, N_c)$ is naturally fulfilled, and therefore desired solutions can be searched into a space wherein column vectors $\boldsymbol{b}^{(c)}$ are orthogonal. On the other hand, since condition $\text{vec}(\boldsymbol{B}) > 0$ is already taken into consideration, the complete orthogonality constraint can be expressed as: $\sum_{c \neq s} \boldsymbol{b}^{(c)\top} \boldsymbol{b}^{(s)} = 0$. Next, to incorporate such constraint into the original problem statement (see Eq. (6)), we use a Kronecker's delta δ_{sc} given by $\delta_{sc} = 1$ if $s = c$ and 0 otherwise, the modified functional becomes

$$f(\boldsymbol{b}^{(c)}|\lambda, \mu, \gamma) = \sum_{c=1}^{C} \sum_{s=1}^{C} \boldsymbol{b}^{(c)\top} \delta_{sc} \left(\boldsymbol{W} - \lambda \boldsymbol{D} - \mu \boldsymbol{I}_N\right) \boldsymbol{b}^{(s)}$$

$$- \gamma \sum_{c=1}^{C} \sum_{s=1}^{C} (1 - \delta_{sc}) \boldsymbol{b}^{(c)\top} \boldsymbol{b}^{(s)} + \lambda \left\|\boldsymbol{W}\right\|_{L_1} + \mu N,$$

being γ a regularization parameter. Again, by removing constant terms and rearranging the functional, we can write:

$$\sum_{c=1}^{C} \sum_{s=1}^{C} \boldsymbol{b}^{(c)\top} \left(\delta_{sc} \left(\boldsymbol{W} - \lambda \boldsymbol{D} - (\mu - \gamma) \boldsymbol{I}_N\right) - \gamma \boldsymbol{I}_N\right) \boldsymbol{b}^{(s)} \tag{9}$$

$$= \sum_{c=1}^{C} \boldsymbol{b}^{(c)\top} \boldsymbol{P}_{\lambda,\mu} \boldsymbol{b}^{(c)} - \gamma \sum_{c=1}^{C} \sum_{s=1}^{C} \boldsymbol{b}^{(c)\top} \boldsymbol{b}^{(s)}.$$

Then, in terms of membership matrix $\boldsymbol{B}$, the problem can be stated as follows:

$$f(\boldsymbol{B}|\gamma) = \text{tr}\left(\boldsymbol{B}^\top \boldsymbol{P}_{\lambda,\mu} \boldsymbol{B}\right) - \frac{\gamma}{(C-1)!} \sum_{i=1}^{L} \text{tr}(\boldsymbol{Z}_\pi^{(i)} \boldsymbol{B}^\top \boldsymbol{B}),$$

where the permutation of C elements is noted as $\pi : \{1, \ldots, C\} \rightarrow \{1, \ldots, C\}$, $\boldsymbol{Z}_\pi^{(i)}$ is the i-th $C \times C$ dimensional permutation matrix and $L = C!$ is the total number of permutations. Let us define an auxiliary matrix $\boldsymbol{H} \in \mathbb{R}^{NC \times NC}$ as:

$$\boldsymbol{H} = (\boldsymbol{I}_C \otimes \boldsymbol{P}_{\lambda,\mu}) - \frac{\gamma}{(C-1)!} \sum_{i=1}^{L} \left(\boldsymbol{Z}_\pi^{(i)} \otimes \boldsymbol{I}_N\right).$$

Finally, $f(\boldsymbol{B}|\gamma)$ can be vectorized as follows:

$$\max_{\boldsymbol{B}} \ f(\boldsymbol{B}) = \text{vec}\left(\boldsymbol{B}\right)^\top \boldsymbol{H} \, \text{vec}\left(\boldsymbol{B}\right)$$

$$\text{s. t. } \text{vec}(\boldsymbol{B}) > 0, \quad 0 < \left(\boldsymbol{1}_N^\top \otimes \boldsymbol{I}_C\right) \text{vec}\left(\boldsymbol{B}\right) \prec N - C. \tag{10}$$

Just as the other approaches discussed in this paper, functional $f(\boldsymbol{B})$ is a quadratic form in terms of the vectorization of $\boldsymbol{B}$. Also, Eq. (10) can be solved by minimizing its corresponding dual formulation given by:

$$g(\boldsymbol{B}) = \text{vec}\left(\boldsymbol{B}\right)^\top \left(\boldsymbol{I}_{NC} - \boldsymbol{H}\right) \text{vec}\left(\boldsymbol{B}\right) = \text{vec}\left(\boldsymbol{B}\right)^\top \text{vec}\left(\boldsymbol{B}\right) - f(\boldsymbol{B}). \tag{11}$$

Since $\boldsymbol{I}_{NC} - \boldsymbol{H}$ is a positive semi-definite matrix and function g ensures maximal variance of matrix $\boldsymbol{B}$, then the problem of minimizing g is convex when considering the same linear constraints stated in Eq. (10). Therefore, any quadratic programming algorithm suffices to find a solution.

As explained in [11], when ensuring a proper initialization as those explained here, considered quadratic programming algorithms reduces the complexity regarding typical conventional spectral methods, since each iteration can be performed in $O(N^2)$. In contrast, the conventional MCSC in $O(N^3)$. Also, kernel k-means approaches involve a maximum complexity of $O(N^3 + N^{dC+1} \log N)$ due to the calculation of eigenvector decomposition along with the iterations of the k-means procedure.

5   Conclusions

Despite being an appealing alternative when dealing with complex data, spectral clustering may be unfeasible for some problems wherein the computation of eigenvectors might involve a significantly high computational cost.

In this overview, we outlined two alternative approaches to solve the normalized-cut-clustering (NCC) problem. Starting from the NCC conventional formulation, alternatives problem formulations can be stated. Particularly, we study two approaches: one based on a constrained similarity and another aimed at formulating quadratic functional with suitable linear constraints. We explore possible solutions followed from heuristic search procedures as well as quadratic programming algorithms.

References

1. Yu, S.X., Shi, J.: Multiclass spectral clustering. In: Proceedings of Ninth IEEE International Conference on Computer Vision, ICCV 2003, vol. 1, pp. 313–319. IEEE (2003)
2. Langone, R., Mall, R., Alzate, C., Suykens, J.A.K.: Kernel spectral clustering and applications. In: Celebi, M.E., Aydin, K. (eds.) Unsupervised Learning Algorithms, pp. 135–161. Springer, Cham (2016). https://doi.org/10.1007/978-3-319-24211-8_6
3. Zelnik-Manor, L., Perona, P.: Self-tuning spectral clustering. In: Advances on Neural Information Processing Systems, vol. 2, pp. 1601–1608. MIT Press (2004)
4. Dhillon, I.S., Guan, Y., Kulis, B.: Kernel k-means, spectral clustering and normalized cuts. In: Proceedings of the 2004 ACM SIGKDD International Conference on Knowledge Discovery and Data Mining, KDD 2004, pp. 551–556. ACM (2004)
5. Li, T., Dou, Y., Liu, X.: Joint diversity regularization and graph regularization for multiple kernel k-means clustering via latent variables. Neurocomputing 218, 154–163 (2016)
6. Dhillon, I.S., Guan, Y., Kulis, B.: Weighted graph cuts without eigenvectors a multilevel approach. IEEE Trans. Pattern Anal. Mach. Intell. 29(11), 1944–1957 (2007)
7. Castro-Ospina, A.E., Castro-Hoyos, C., Peluffo-Ordonez, D., Castellanos-Dominguez, G.: Novel heuristic search for ventricular arrhythmia detection using normalized cut clustering. In: 2013 35th Annual International Conference of the IEEE Engineering Medicine and Biology Society, pp. 7076–7079. IEEE (2013)

8. Peluffo-Ordóñez, D.H., Castro-Ospina, A.E., Chavez-Chamorro, D., Acosta-Medina, C.D., Castellanos-Domínguez, G.: Normalized cuts clustering with prior knowledge and a pre-clustering stage. In: ESANN 2013 proceedings, 21st European Symposium on Artificial Neural Networks, Computational Intelligence and Machine Learning (2013)
9. Xu, L., Li, W., Schuurmans, D.: Fast normalized cut with linear constraints. In: 2009 IEEE Conference on Computer Vision and Pattern Recognition, pp. 2866–2873. IEEE (2009)
10. Peluffo-Ordóñez, D.H., Acosta-Medina, C.D., Castellanos-Domínguez, C.G.: An Improved multi-class spectral clustering based on normalized cuts. In: Alvarez, L., Mejail, M., Gomez, L., Jacobo, J. (eds.) CIARP 2012. LNCS, vol. 7441, pp. 130–137. Springer, Heidelberg (2012). https://doi.org/10.1007/978-3-642-33275-3_16
11. Peluffo-Ordóñez, D.H., Castro-Hoyos, C., Acosta-Medina, C.D., Castellanos-Domínguez, G.: Quadratic problem formulation with linear constraints for normalized cut clustering. In: Bayro-Corrochano, E., Hancock, E. (eds.) CIARP 2014. LNCS, vol. 8827, pp. 408–415. Springer, Cham (2014). https://doi.org/10.1007/978-3-319-12568-8_50
12. Peluffo-Ordóñez, D.H.: Dynamic spectral clustering based on kernels. Ph.D. thesis, Universidad Nacional de Colombia (2013)
13. Botev, Z.I., Grotowski, J.F., Kroese, D.P.: Kernel density estimation via diffusion. Ann. Stat. **38**(5), 2916–2957 (2010)

Neurodynamics, Complex Systems, and Chaos

Dynamical Behavior Analysis
of a Neutral-Type Single Neuron System

Qiuyu Lv, Nankun Mu$^{(\boxtimes)}$, and Xiaofeng Liao$^{(\boxtimes)}$

The Chongqing Key Laboratory of Nonlinear Circuits and Intelligent Information
Processing, Southwest University, Chongqing 400715, People's Republic of China
nankun.mu@qq.com, xfliao@swu.edu.cn

Abstract. In this paper, the equation used to describe a single neuron system of neutral-type with one delay is studied. By using a suitable Lyapunov function, we derive sufficient conditions of globally asymptotic stability of the zero equilibrium point of this equation. Moreover, the criterions of the existence of Hopf bifurcation that gives rise to self-sustained oscillation are obtained. Finally, the perturbation theory is used to acquire the expansion of oscillation to any order on the basis of the coefficient of the fundamental frequency, and the frequency-amplitude relations about the second order are carefully discussed.

Keywords: Neutral-type differential system · Lyapunov function
Asymptotic stability · Hopf bifurcation · Perturbation theory

1 Introduction

The existence of delay arises naturally in many scientific areas, such as the network connection delays in biology, neurosciences [1], the translation and transcription delays during synapses in neurophysiology [3], the transmission of information from one neuron to another and so on. In [5–7], we have known if the connection matrices are symmetric or antisymmetric, neural networks without time delays are always either a convergent gradient network or a stable network. But, if the delays are presented, their convergences and stability properties may be lost even for very small delays, and oscillations or chaos may occur. So, in recent years, delay differential equations have been studied by many scholars and experts at home and abroad, and there are many monographs published. In these monographs, the oscillation of delay differential equations are systematically studied and summarized in [8]. In this paper, we study the dynamical behavior of a single neuron system of neutral-type with one delay based on the Lyapunov function approach and the perturbation theory, with the following form:

$$\frac{d}{dt}\left[x(t) + px(t-\tau)\right] = -ax(t) + b\tanh(x(t) + cx(t-\tau)), t \geq 0, \qquad (1)$$

where a, b, c are positive constants, p, c are real constants with $|p| < 1$.

© Springer International Publishing AG, part of Springer Nature 2018
T. Huang et al. (Eds.): ISNN 2018, LNCS 10878, pp. 331–338, 2018.
https://doi.org/10.1007/978-3-319-92537-0_38

2   Stability Analysis

Let $v(t) = x(t) + cx(t - \tau)$, then Eq. (1) can become as

$$\frac{d\left[v(t) + pv(t - \tau)\right]}{dt} = -av(t) + b\tanh v(t) + bc\tanh v(t - \tau). \tag{2}$$

Let $Dv_t = v(t) + pv(t - \tau)$, its very easy to see that the operator Dv_t which associated with Eq. (1) is stable if $|p| < 1$. Obviously, we find that the equilibrium point of the functional differential Eq. (1) in $x(t)$ is zero. Next, we will find criterions for the non-existence of oscillation on the neutral-type system (1) by analyzing the equations asymptotic behavior.

Theorem 1. *If $a \geq 2b$ and $c^2 \leq \frac{a^2\left(1-2p^2\right)}{4b^2}$, then the zero solution of Eq. (1) is globally asymptotical stability.*

Proof. In order to study the asymptotic behavior of the system (1), we construct a Lyapunov functional

$$V(v_t) = (Dv_t)^2 + \frac{1}{2}a\int_{t-\tau}^{t} v^2(s)ds, t \geq 0, \tag{3}$$

where a is a positive number. Furthermore, we have $\tanh^2 x \leq x^2$, so we can obtain $\tanh^2 v(t) \leq v^2(t)$, and $\tanh^2 v(t - \tau) \leq v^2(t - \tau)$.

Now, we calculate the derivative of V along the solution of Eq. (1)

$$\dot{V}(v_t)$$
$$= 2Dv_t\left(\dot{D}v_t\right) + \frac{1}{2}av^2(t) - \frac{1}{2}av^2(t - \tau)$$
$$\leq 2Dv_t\left(\dot{D}v_t\right) + \frac{1}{2}av^2(t) - \frac{1}{2}av^2(t - \tau) + \frac{1}{2}av^2(t) - \frac{1}{2}a\tanh^2 v(t)$$
$$= 2\left(v(t) + pv(t - \tau)\right)\left(-av(t) + b\tanh v(t) + bc\tanh v(t - \tau)\right) + \frac{1}{2}av^2(t)$$
$$- \frac{1}{2}av^2(t - \tau) + \frac{1}{2}av^2(t) - \frac{1}{2}a\tanh^2 v(t)$$
$$= -a\left(v^2(t) + \frac{2b\tanh v(t) + 2bc\tanh v(t - \tau) - 2apv(t - \tau)}{-a}v(t)\right)$$
$$+ 2bpv(t - \tau)\tanh v(t) + 2bcpv(t - \tau)\tanh v(t - \tau) - \frac{1}{2}av^2(t - \tau)$$
$$- \frac{1}{2}a\tanh^2 v(t)$$
$$= -a\left(v(t) + \frac{b\tanh v(t) + bc\tanh v(t - \tau) - apv(t - \tau)}{-a}\right)^2$$
$$+ a\left(\frac{b\tanh v(t) + bc\tanh v(t - \tau) - apv(t - \tau)}{-a}\right)^2$$

$$+ 2bpv(t-\tau)\tanh v(t) + 2bcpv(t-\tau)\tanh v(t-\tau) - \frac{1}{2}av^2(t-\tau)$$

$$- \frac{a}{2}v^2(t-\tau) - \frac{a}{2}\tanh^2 v(t)$$

$$\leq \frac{b^2\tanh^2 v(t) + b^2c^2\tanh^2 v(t-\tau) + a^2p^2v^2(t-\tau)}{a}$$

$$+ \frac{2b^2c\tanh v(t)\tanh v(t-\tau)}{a} - \frac{a}{2}v^2(t-\tau) - \frac{a}{2}\tanh^2 v(t)$$

$$+ \frac{2b^2c^2}{a}\left(v^2(t-\tau) - \tanh^2 v(t-\tau)\right)$$

$$= -\frac{b^2c^2}{a}\left(\tanh v(t-\tau) + \frac{1}{-c}\tanh v(t)\right)^2 + \frac{b^2c^2}{a}\left(\frac{1}{-c}\tanh v(t)\right)^2$$

$$+ \frac{2b^2-a^2}{2a}\tanh^2 v(t) + \frac{2a^2p^2 - a^2 + 4b^2c^2}{2a}v^2(t-\tau)$$

$$\leq \frac{4b^2-a^2}{2a}\tanh^2 v(t) + \frac{2a^2p^2 - a^2 + 4b^2c^2}{2a}v^2(t-\tau).$$

Because of $a \geq 2b$, we have $\frac{4b^2-a^2}{2a} \leq 0$, and $c^2 \leq \frac{a^2(1-2p^2)}{4b^2}$, we can see that $\frac{2a^2p^2-a^2+4b^2c^2}{2a} \leq 0$. Thus we can testify $\dot{V}(v_t) \leq 0$, that is the zero solution of Eq. (1) is globally asymptotical stability. The proof is complete.

3   Bifurcation Analysis

3.1   The Characteristic Equation of the Linearized System

In the system (1), the linearized equation is

$$L(v) = [v'(t) + pv'(t-\tau)] + (a-b)v(t) - bcv(t-\tau) = 0.$$

Note that $\tanh x = x - \frac{x^3}{3} + \frac{2x^5}{15} + \dots$, by simple calculation, we obtain the following characteristic equation:

$$\lambda(s) = (s + pse^{-s\tau}) + (a-b) - bce^{-s\tau} = 0. \qquad (4)$$

An oscillation occurs when a root of the characteristic equation crosses the imaginary axis. Therefore, in order to find the condition of c satisfying that characteristic equation has an imaginary root, we suppose $s = i\omega$, with $\omega > 0$. Substituting s into Eq. (4), we have

$$\lambda(i\omega) = [i\omega + pi\omega\exp(-i\omega\tau)] + (a-b) - bc\exp(-i\omega\tau) = 0. \qquad (5)$$

Separating the real part and imaginary part in Eq. (5), we have

$$\begin{cases} p\omega\sin(\omega\tau) + (a-b) - bc\cos(\omega\tau) = 0, \\ \omega + p\omega\cos(\omega\tau) + bc\sin(\omega\tau) = 0. \end{cases} \qquad (6)$$

By Eq. (6), we can immediately obtain $\omega^2 = \frac{b^2c^2 - (a-b)^2}{1-p^2}$ and $\tan(\omega\tau) = \frac{(bc-ap+bp)\omega}{p\omega^2 - bc(a-b)}$. To guarantee these equations, it is necessary to make $|b|\,|c| \geq |a-b|$ and $|p| < 1$.

By simple calculation, we obtain that if $|p| < 1$, $|c| \geq \frac{|a-b|}{|b|}$, the intersections of $\tan(\omega\tau)$ and $\frac{(bc-ap+bp)\omega}{p\omega^2-bc(a-b)}$ would be roots.

By [12], it is easy to show that all other characteristic roots have negative real parts, that is, $\mathrm{Re}(s) < 0$. We can shift the whole spectrum to the right area by increasing c^2 in some methods. We note that c_0 is the value of c where a pair of characteristic roots that cross the imaginary axis for the first time, and at $c = c_0$, ω is ω_0. By simple analysis, when $c = c_0$, oscillation starts, and the frequency of initial oscillation is ω_0. Through the above analysis, a Hopf-bifurcation in system (2) only occurs.

3.2   Perturbation Expansion Analysis

As we know $\tanh v(t)$ can be replaced by $\tanh v(t) = v(t) - \frac{v^3(t)}{3} + ...$, and $\tanh v(t - \tau)$ can be replaced by $\tanh v(t - \tau) = v(t - \tau) - \frac{v^3(t-\tau)}{3} + ...$ at the zero equilibrium point. Letting $v = \beta y$ and $\omega t = s$, Eq. (2) becomes

$$\omega\left[y'(s) + py'(s - \omega\tau)\right] + (a - b)y(s) - bcy(s - \omega\tau) = -\frac{b}{3}\varepsilon y^3(s) - \frac{b}{3}c\varepsilon y^3(s - \omega\tau),$$
(7)

where $\varepsilon = \beta^2$ and ε is small.

Now, we look for a periodic solution of Eq. (7) in the following form

$$\begin{cases} y(s) = y_0(s) + \varepsilon y_1(s) + \varepsilon^2 y_2(s) + ..., \\ \omega = \omega_0(s) + \varepsilon\omega_1(s) + \varepsilon^2\omega_2(s) + ..., \\ c = c_0(s) + \varepsilon c_1(s) + \varepsilon^2 c_2(s) + ... \end{cases}$$

Substituting the above forms into Eq. (7), we can obtain

$$\begin{aligned} &\left(\omega_0 + \varepsilon\omega_1 + \varepsilon^2\omega_2 + ...\right)\left[y'(s) + py'(s - \omega\tau)\right] + (a - b)y(s) \\ &-b(c_0 + \varepsilon c_1 + \varepsilon^2 c_2 + ...) \times y(s - \omega\tau) \\ &= -\frac{b}{3}\varepsilon y^3(s) - \frac{b}{3}(c_0 + \varepsilon c_1 + \varepsilon^2 c_2 + ...)\varepsilon y^3(s - \omega\tau). \end{aligned}$$
(8)

According to the knowledge of Taylor series, we have

$$\begin{aligned} y'(s - \omega\tau) &= y'(s - (\omega_0 + \varepsilon\omega_1 + \varepsilon^2\omega_2 + ...)\tau), \\ &= y'(s - \omega_0\tau) - (\varepsilon\omega_1 + \varepsilon^2\omega_2 + ...)\tau y''(s - \omega_0\tau) + ... \end{aligned}$$
(9)

$$\begin{aligned} y(s - \omega\tau) &= y(s - (\omega_0 + \varepsilon\omega_1 + \varepsilon^2\omega_2 + ...)\tau) \\ &= y(s - \omega_0\tau) - (\varepsilon\omega_1 + \varepsilon^2\omega_2 + ...)\tau y'(s - \omega_0\tau) + ... \end{aligned}$$
(10)

Substituting Eqs. (9), (10) into (8), we can note that the coefficient of ε^0 in the right part of the equation is zero. Therefore, we have the following equation

$$\omega_0\left[y'(s) + py'(s - \omega_0\tau)\right] + (a - b)y(s) - bc_0 y(s - \omega_0\tau) = 0.$$
(11)

Subtracting Eqs. (7) and (11), we have

$$
\begin{aligned}
&\omega_0 \left[y'(s) + py'(s - \omega_0\tau) \right] + (a - b)y(s) - bc_0 y(s - \omega_0\tau) \\
&= (\omega - \omega_0)y'(s) + \left[\omega py'(s - \omega\tau) - \omega_0 py'(s - \omega_0\tau) \right] \\
&\quad - \left[bcy(s - \omega\tau) - bc_0 y(s - \omega_0\tau) \right] \\
&\quad + \frac{b}{3}\varepsilon y^3(s) + \frac{b}{3}c\varepsilon y^3(s - \omega\tau) = 0 .
\end{aligned}
\tag{12}
$$

Note that we define a linear differential-difference operator $L(.)$ by Eq. (7), if $c = c_0$, $\omega = \omega_0$, $s = \omega_0 t$. We denote this operator by $L_0(.)$, and denote its characteristic equation by $\lambda_0(s) = 0$. Furthermore, we define a non-linear differential-difference operator $F(y, \varepsilon)$ of order $o(\varepsilon)$ by the right-hand side of Eq. (11). That is, Eq. (12) can be written as

$$
L_0(y) = F(y, \varepsilon) .
\tag{13}
$$

Taylor series expansion of the operator $F(y, \varepsilon)$ at $\varepsilon = 0$, by expanding and equating coefficients of $\varepsilon^i (i = 0, 1, 2, ...)$, we obtain the following infinite set of equations

$$
\begin{cases}
L_0(y_0) = 0, \\
L_0(y_1) = \frac{dF}{d\varepsilon}(y_0, \varepsilon)|_{\varepsilon=0} , \\
L_0(y_2) = \frac{d^2 F}{2! d\varepsilon^2}(y_0 + \varepsilon y_1, \varepsilon)|_{\varepsilon=0} , \\
\cdots \\
L_0(y_n) = \frac{d^n F}{n! d\varepsilon^n}(y_0 + \varepsilon y_1 + ... + \varepsilon^{n-1} y_{n-1}, \varepsilon)|_{\varepsilon=0} , \\
\cdots
\end{cases}
\tag{14}
$$

Thus, y is a periodic solution of Eq. (13) with period ω in t, if $y = y_0 + \varepsilon y_1 + \varepsilon^2 y_2 + ...$ is converged and $y_0, y_1, y_2, ...$ are periodic solutions of Eq. (14). From [11, 12], we know that in order to satisfy these conditions, one asks that each of Eq. (14) has a 2π- period solution. According to the knowledge of Fredholm alternative, we know that the right-hand sides of Eq. (14) must be orthogonal to the periodic solution of the adjoint equation of L_0.

$$
\begin{cases}
L_0^*(u) = -\omega_0 \left[u'(s) + pu'(s + \omega_0\tau) \right] + (a - b)u(s) - bc_0 u(s + \omega_0\tau) = 0, \\
\lambda_0^*(s) = -\omega_0 \left[s + pse^{s\omega_0\tau} \right] + (a - b) - bc_0 e^{s\omega_0\tau} = 0.
\end{cases}
\tag{15}
$$

Obviously, we can see that $\lambda_0(s) = 0$ and $\lambda_0^*(s) = 0$ have the same purely imaginary roots and multiplicity. Furthermore, we can choose $\sin\phi$, $\cos\phi$ to span the space of periodic solutions of the adjoint Eq. (15). Thus, for all n, we require that

$$
\begin{aligned}
&\int_0^{2\pi} \frac{d^n F}{d\varepsilon^n}(y_0 + \varepsilon y_1 + ... + \varepsilon^{n-1} y_{n-1}, \varepsilon)|_{\varepsilon=0} \sin\phi \, d\phi \\
&= \int_0^{2\pi} \frac{d^n F}{d\varepsilon^n}(y_0 + \varepsilon y_1 + ... + \varepsilon^{n-1} y_{n-1}, \varepsilon)|_{\varepsilon=0} \cos\phi \, d\phi \\
&= 0 .
\end{aligned}
\tag{16}
$$

In order to solve the Eq. (16), we expand each left-hand side of Eq. (14) as a Fourier series. For all n, we have $L_0(y_n) = \sum_{k=n+2}^{\infty} (a_k e^{ik\phi} + \bar{a}_k e^{-ik\phi})$, and we find a solution $y_n = \sum_{k=n+2}^{\infty} (d_k e^{ik\phi} + \bar{d}_k e^{-ik\phi})$. For all n, we can choose c_k to satisfy the conditions of $L_0(d_k e^{ik\phi}) = a_k e^{ik\phi}$ term by term, that reduces to $d_k \lambda_0(ik) = a_k$. Thus, Eq. (14) can be solved for periodic solutions of period 2π.

3.3 Computations for the Frequency-Amplitude Relation

For the sake of simplicity, we only solve the first two equations of Eq. (14). The first equation of Eq. (14) is $L_0(y_0) = 0$, and we can easily see $y_0(\phi) = \cos\phi$ is the solution of Eq. (14). With this value of y_0, Eq. (13) can be written as

$$
\begin{aligned}
L_0(y) =\ & (\omega_0 + \varepsilon\omega_1 + \varepsilon^2\omega_2 + \ldots - \omega_0)\left(-\sin\phi + \varepsilon y'_1(\phi) + \varepsilon^2 y''_2(\phi) + \ldots\right) \\
& + (\omega_0 + \varepsilon\omega_1 + \varepsilon^2\omega_2 + \ldots)\,p\left(-\sin(\phi - \omega\tau) + \varepsilon y'_1(\phi - \omega\tau) + \varepsilon^2 y''_2(\phi - \omega\tau) + \ldots\right) \\
& - \omega_0 p\left(-\sin(\phi - \omega_0\tau) + \varepsilon y'_1(\phi - \omega_0\tau) + \varepsilon^2 y''_2(\phi - \omega\tau) + \ldots\right) \\
& - b(c_0 + \varepsilon c_1 + \varepsilon^2 c_2 + \ldots)(\cos(\phi - \omega\tau) + \varepsilon y_1(\phi - \omega\tau) + \varepsilon^2 y_2(\phi - \omega\tau) + \ldots) \\
& + bc_0\left(\cos(\phi - \omega_0\tau) + \varepsilon y_1(\phi - \omega_0\tau) + \varepsilon^2 y_2(\phi - \omega_0\tau) + \ldots\right) \\
& + \frac{b}{3}\varepsilon(\cos\phi + \varepsilon y_1(\phi) + \varepsilon^2 y_2(\phi) + \ldots)^3 + \frac{b}{3}(c_0 + \varepsilon c_1 + \varepsilon^2 c_2 + \ldots)\varepsilon\times \\
& (\cos(\phi - \omega\tau) + \varepsilon y_1(\phi - \omega\tau) + \varepsilon^2 y_2(\phi - \omega\tau) + \ldots)^3,
\end{aligned}
\tag{17}
$$

and the second equation of Eq. (14) is

$$
\begin{aligned}
L_0(y_1) =\ & -\omega_1\sin\phi - \omega_1 p\sin(\phi - \omega_0\tau) + \omega_0\omega_1 p\tau\cos(\phi - \omega_0\tau) \\
& -bc_1\cos(\phi - \omega_0\tau) - bc_0\omega_1\tau\sin(\phi - \omega_0\tau) + \frac{b}{3}\cos^3\phi + \frac{b}{3}c_0\cos^3(\phi - \omega_0\tau) \\
=\ & -\omega_1\sin\phi - (\omega_1 p + bc_0\omega_1\tau)\sin(\phi - \omega_0\tau) - (bc_1 - \omega_0\omega_1 p\tau)\cos(\phi - \omega_0\tau) \\
& + \frac{1}{3}\left(\frac{3b}{4}\cos\phi + \frac{b}{4}\cos 3\phi + \frac{3bc_0}{4}\cos(\phi - \omega_0\tau) + \frac{bc_0}{4}\cos 3(\phi - \omega_0\tau)\right),
\end{aligned}
\tag{18}
$$

where $\cos^3\phi = \frac{3\cos\phi + \cos 3\phi}{4}$. By analyzing the bifurcation Eq. (16), the real and the imaginary part must be zero. We have the following equations

$$
\begin{cases}
-\omega_1 - (\omega_1 p + bc_0\omega_1\tau)\cos\omega_0\tau - \left(bc_1 - \omega_0\omega_1 p\tau - \frac{bc_0}{4}\right)\sin\omega_0\tau = 0, \\
(\omega_1 p + bc_0\omega_1\tau)\sin\omega_0\tau - \left(bc_1 - \omega_0\omega_1 p\tau - \frac{bc_0}{4}\right)\cos\omega_0\tau + \frac{b}{4} = 0.
\end{cases}
\tag{19}
$$

Multiplying i in the first equation of Eq. (19) and subtracting the second equation, through simple reorganizing, we can obtain

$$
-\left(\frac{b}{4} + i\omega_1\right) - \left(\left(\omega_0\omega_1 p\tau + \frac{bc_0}{4}\right) + i\omega_1\,(p + bc_0\tau)\right)e^{-i\omega_0\tau} = -bc_1 e^{-i\omega_0\tau}.
\tag{20}
$$

From Eq. (20), by simple analysis, we know the relation of ω_1, c_1 is determined.

Furthermore, multiplying $\sin\phi$ in the first equation of Eq. (19) and adding the second equation with multiplying $\cos\phi$, we have

$$
-\omega_1 \sin\phi + \frac{b}{4}\cos\phi - (\omega_1 p + bc_0\omega_1\tau)\sin(\phi - \omega_0\tau)
$$
$$
-\left(bc_1 - \omega_0\omega_1 p\tau - \frac{bc_0}{4}\right)\cos(\phi - \omega_0\tau) = 0 . \tag{21}
$$

From the above analysis, we have the expression

$$
L_0(y_1) = \frac{b}{12}\cos 3\phi + \frac{bc_0}{12}\cos 3(\phi - \omega_0\tau)
$$
$$
= \frac{b}{24}\left[\left(1 + c_0 e^{-i3\omega_0\tau}\right)e^{i3\phi} + \left(1 + c_0 e^{i3\omega_0\tau}\right)e^{-i3\phi}\right] . \tag{22}
$$

From the above analysis, $y_1(\phi)$ can be written as $y_1(\phi) = d_3 e^{i3\phi} + \bar{d}_3 e^{-i3\phi}$, and we can obtain

$$
d_3 = \frac{a_3}{\lambda_0(i3)} = \frac{\frac{b}{24}\left(1 + c_0 e^{-i3\omega_0\tau}\right)}{i3\omega_0\left(1 + pe^{-i3\omega_0\tau}\right) + (a - b) - bc_0 e^{-i3\omega_0\tau}} . \tag{23}
$$

Through the above analysis, we can find that $y_1(\phi)$ can be determined completely, that is the conditions of Eq. (16) are satisfied.

Now we calculate the relation of frequency-amplitude. As we know, $\lambda_0(i) = i\omega_0\left(1 + pe^{-i\omega_0\tau}\right) + (a - b) - bc_0 e^{-i\omega_0\tau} = 0$. Multiplying Eq. (20) by ε and through simple calculation, we can obtain, within an error $o(\varepsilon^2)$,

$$
0 = -\varepsilon\left(\frac{b}{4} + i\omega_1\right) - \varepsilon\left(\left(\omega_0\omega_1 p\tau + \frac{bc_0}{4}\right) + i\omega_1\left(p + bc_0\tau\right)\right)e^{-i\omega_0\tau}
$$
$$
+ \varepsilon bc_1 e^{-i\omega_0\tau} - i\omega_0\left(1 + pe^{-i\omega_0\tau}\right) - (a - b) + bc_0 e^{-i\omega_0\tau} \tag{24}
$$
$$
\approx -\left(i\omega + (a - b) + \frac{b\varepsilon}{4}\right) - \left(i\omega p - bc + \frac{\varepsilon bc}{4}\right)e^{-i\omega\tau} .
$$

We regard $\hat{\lambda}(i\omega) = \left(i\omega + a - b(1 - \frac{\varepsilon}{4})\right) + \left(i\omega p - bc(1 - \frac{\varepsilon}{4})\right)e^{-i\omega\tau} = 0$. Through analyzing the equation and separating its real part and its imaginary part, we can have

$$
\begin{cases} a - b(1 - \frac{\varepsilon}{4}) + p\omega\sin\omega\tau - bc(1 - \frac{\varepsilon}{4})\cos\omega\tau = 0 , \\ \omega + p\omega\cos\omega\tau + bc(1 - \frac{\varepsilon}{4})\sin\omega\tau = 0 . \end{cases} \tag{25}
$$

Solving Eq. (25), the equation can be reduced to

$$
\tan(\omega\tau) = \frac{\left(b\left(1 - \frac{\varepsilon}{4}\right)c - ap + b\left(1 - \frac{\varepsilon}{4}\right)p\right)\omega}{p\omega^2 - b\left(1 - \frac{\varepsilon}{4}\right)c\left(a - b\left(1 - \frac{\varepsilon}{4}\right)\right)} ,
$$

which is the relation of frequency-amplitude with $o\left(\varepsilon^2\right)$.

4 Conclusion

In this paper, we have studied the globally asymptotical stability of a single neuron system of a neutral type with one delay, and verified the accuracy through numerical examples. What's more, we have found the conditions of Hopf bifurcation that give rise to the self-sustained oscillations, and verified the existence of periodic solutions by numerical simulations.

Acknowledgments. This work is supported by National Key Research and Development Program of China (Grant no. 2016YFB0800601), Natural Science Foundation of China (Grant no. 61472331, 61772434).

References

1. Hopfield, J.J.: Neurons with graded response have collective computational properties like those of two-state neurons. Proc. Nat. Acad. Sci. **81**(10), 3088–3092 (1984)
2. Gopalsamy, K.: Stability and Oscillations in Delay Differential Equations of Population Dynamics. Kluwer Academic, Dordrecht (1992)
3. Field, M.J.: Heteroclinic networks in homogeneous and heterogeneous identical cell systems. J. Nonlinear Sci. **25**(3), 779–813 (2015)
4. Wang, S.S., Kloth, A.D., Badura, A.: The cerebellum, sensitive periods, and autism. Neuron **83**(3), 518–532 (2014)
5. Dong, T., Hu, W., Liao, X.F.: Dynamics of the congestion control model in underwater wireless sensor networks with time delay. Chaos Soliton Fract. **92**, 130–136 (2016)
6. Liao, X., Wong, K.W., Wu, Z.: Novel robust stability criteria for interval-delayed Hopfield neural networks. IEEE Trans. Circuits Syst. I Fundam. Theory Appl. **48**(11), 1355–1359 (2001)
7. Baldi, P., Atiya, A.F.: How delays affect neural dynamics and learning. IEEE Trans. Neural Netw. **5**(4), 612–621 (1994)
8. Györi, I., Ladas, G.: Oscillation Theory of Delay Differential Equations: with Applications. Clarendon Press, Oxford (1991)
9. Erbe, L.H., Kong, Q., Zhang, B.G.: Oscillation Theory for Functional Differential Equations. Dekker, New York (1995)
10. Liao, X.F.: Dynamical behavior of Chua's circuit with lossless transmission line. IEEE Trans. Circuits Syst. I: Reg. Pap. **63**(2), 1–11 (2016)
11. Hale, J.K., Lunel, S.M.V.: Introduction to Functional Differential Equations. Springer, New York (1993). https://doi.org/10.1007/978-1-4612-4342-7
12. Bellman, R., Cooke, K.L.: Differential-Difference Equations. Academic Press, New York (1963)

Recurrent Neural Network with Dynamic Memory

Jiaqi Bai$^{(\boxtimes)}$, Tao Dong$^{(\boxtimes)}$, Xiaofeng Liao, and Nankun Mu

College of Electronic and Information Engineering, Southwest University,
Chongqing 400715, China
swu.bjq@gmail.com, david_312@126.com

Abstract. Recurrent neural network presents great performance and learning capability in dealing with sensory processing, sequence learning and reinforcement learning. However, the memory ability of the RNNs is limited because of the gradient vanishing problem, the memory conflict and the very limited memory capability. In order to overcome these defects, we propose a novel RNN model, which is called RNN-DM. The proposed model has two types of memory: internal memory and external memory. The internal memory exists in the neuron unit of hidden layer, which is used to solve the memory conflict problem and reduce the influence of gradient vanishing problem during network learning. The external memory is a memory matrix, which is used to store the complex data structure and variable, it has ability to solve the limited memory capacity problem.

Keywords: Recurrent neural networks · Internal memory
External memory

1 Introduction

Recurrent neural network, as one of the important artificial neural networks, has self-feedback connections, which means that it can maintain temporal memory information. This ability makes the RNN presents stronger performance and learning capability in dealing with language understanding [1,2], sequence learning [3,4], and machine translation [5,6]. However, the traditional RNNs show less ability to keep steady and useful long term memory information, because of the input weight conflict [7], output weight conflict [7], memory conflict [7], gradient vanishing problem [8] and very limited storage capacity of the memory [9]. The input weight conflict occurs in the connection weights between the input neuron and the hidden neuron. The recurrent unit not only need store the input information, but also has to prevent this information from being interfered by the irrelevant later inputs. The output weight conflict happens in the connection weights between the hidden neuron and the output neuron. The recurrent unit need transmit information to other neurons, meanwhile, it has to not disturb these neurons at different times. The memory conflict is defined as a conflict

© Springer International Publishing AG, part of Springer Nature 2018
T. Huang et al. (Eds.): ISNN 2018, LNCS 10878, pp. 339–345, 2018.
https://doi.org/10.1007/978-3-319-92537-0_39

between the output and the memory in a recurrent unit. The recurrent unit need not only maintain the input information in the output, but also neglect it in the memory in the meantime, vice versa. Gradient vanishing problem refers to the large decrease in the norm of the gradient during training process. This problem is due to the sharp decrease of the long term components, which will decrease exponentially more than short term gradients when long term gradients are exponentially close to zero. The limited memory capability problem is that the RNN are limited in their ability to represent variables and data structures and to store data over long timescales.

In order to overcome these problems, many RNN models have been investigated [10–12]. In [13], by applying the output gates and input gates to control the reading and writing operations of the recurrent neuron, the authors have proposed the long short-term memory RNN model (LSTM), which can overcome both the input and output weight conflicts. In [14], by using the forget gate, the authors have modified the LSTM. The modified model allows the network to forget the unnecessary information, therefore it can avoid the indefinitely growing of internal state values. In [15], the authors have proposed a gated recurrent unit (GRU), which introduces a leaky-integration mechanism by integrating the update gates and reset gates into the recurrent unit. In [7], the authors have proposed a recurrent unit with auxiliary memory. The memory unit and neuron unit of the proposed unit are decomposed, which can eliminate the memory conflict easily. In [16], the authors have proposed the neural turing machine (NTM). NTM is composed of the read-write external memory and a neural network. The NTM can largely improve the memory capability. In [17], based on the NTM, the authors have also proposed a differentiable neural computers (DNC). The DNC improve the read and write mechanism of external memory and further enhance the write and read efficiency.

However, the existing works dont solve the memory conflicts, gradient vanishing problem and the limited memory capacity problem, simultaneously. To address the above problems, in this paper, a novel neural network model is proposed, namely, RNN-DM. The main contributions of this paper are as follows: Firstly, by combining the internal memory units and external memory matrix, a novel RNN model is proposed, which is named as RNN-DM. Secondly, the specifics of our proposed RNN-DM is given and described in detail.

2   The Architecture of RNN-DM

2.1   Model Description

In this section, a novel neural network model with internal memory unit and an external memory matrix is proposed. There are four layers of our model: input layer, hidden layer, processing layer and output layer. The input layer is used to obtain the input data. There are two types of input data: input vector $x_t \in R^X$ from the data set and the content vector $c_{t-1} \in R^W$ read from the external memory. The hidden layer is used to computation. The processing layer is used to receive the information from the hidden layer and construct the output z

and ξ. ξ is used to interact with the external memory. The output layer is used to construct a network output y by combining z and the content c read from external memory.

2.2 Internal Memory

The internal memory is in the neuron unit of hidden layer. Each neuron of hidden layer connects to an internal memory unit. Different from traditional RNN and LSTM, our framework separates the memory and output of each neuron unit, which can avoid the memory conflict problem [7]. The memory unit can be considered as a linear neuron, which has a feedback connection. The weight of feedback connection is constant 1, which can deal with the gradient vanishing problem during network learning.

2.3 External Memory

The external memory is composed of a memory matrix, which can be denoted as $M \in R^{N \times W}$, where N is the memory slots and each slot has W elements. Each element of memory matrix is a real number, which makes the external memory has ability to train using gradient descend method. Like the traditional computers, the external memory can be iteratively modified and read through the update and read operations. But, traditional computers use unique addresses to read and write memory contents, the proposed RNN-DM uses a differentiable attention mechanism [17] to define the weights over the N slots in the external memory, where the weights represent the degree to which each location is involved in a read or update operation.

3   The Details of RNN-DM Model

3.1 Model Input and Output

The network inputs of model contains an input vector $x_t \in R^X$ from the data set and a content vector $c_{t-1} \in R^W$ read from the external memory. The hidden layer activity is computed as follows:

$$
\begin{cases}
h_t\left[a\right] = f\left(net_t^h\left[a\right]\right) \\
net_t^h\left[a\right] = \sum_{u=1}^{H} w_{au} h_{t-1}\left[u\right] + \sum_{p=1}^{X} w_{ap} x_t\left[p\right] \\
\quad + \sum_{j=1}^{W} w_{aj} c_{t-1}\left[j\right] + w_{as_a} s_{t-1}\left[a\right] \\
s_t\left[a\right] = s_{t-1}\left[a\right] + h_t\left[a\right]
\end{cases}
\tag{1}
$$

where a is the index of the ath neuron unit in hidden layer. $h_t\left[a\right]$ is the output of a-th hidden layer neuron and $net_t^h\left[a\right]$ is its input, $f\left(\cdot\right)$ is activation function. H is the number of nonlinear neurons. $x_t\left[p\right]$ is the input neuron that corresponds to the p-th element of the input vector x_t, X is the dimension of input vector x_t. Similarly, $c_{t-1}[j]$ is the neuron that corresponds to the j-th element of the content c_{t-1} and W is its dimensions. The state of memory unit in a-th neuron unit is denoted as $s_t[a]$, which can use equation $s_t[a] = s_{t-1}[a] + h_t[a]$ to update.

The processing layer activity is computed as follows:

$$
\begin{aligned}
z_t[k] &= \sum_{a=1}^{H} w_{ka}^{p,z} h_t[a] \\
\xi_t[k] &= \sum_{a=1}^{H} w_{ka}^{p,\xi} h_t[a]
\end{aligned}
\tag{2}
$$

where $z_t \in R^{Z \times 1}$ is the output vector, $z_t[k]$ is the k-th element of z_t. $w_{ka}^{p,z}$ is the weight that connect from $h_t[a]$ to $z_t[k]$. $\xi_t[k]$ is the k-th element of ξ_t, and $\xi_t \in R^{(3W+2) \times 1}$ is the parameter vector of external memory, which can be divided as:

$$
\xi_t = [k_t, e_t, v_t, \beta_t, g_t]
\tag{3}
$$

where $k_t = W_k h_t$ is the key vector and scalar $\beta_t = \log(1 + \exp(W_\beta h_t))$ is the key strength, they are both used in the content-based addressing. $g_t = 1/(1 + \exp(-W_g h_t))$ is interpolation gate, which is used to tradeoff between two items. $e_t = 1/(1 + \exp(-W_e h_t))$ are write vector and erase vector respectively, which are both used in the external memory update.

The output from this model is fed into the output layer as follows:

$$
y_t[n] = f_y \left(\sum_{k=1}^{Z} w_{nk}^{yc} z_t[k] + \sum_{j=1}^{W} w_{nj}^{yc} c_t[j] \right)
\tag{4}
$$

where $y_t \in R^{Y \times 1}$ is the output of output layer, and $y_t[n]$ represents the n-th neuron of output layer, c_t is the content vector, and $c_t[j]$ is the j-th element of c_t. $f_y(\cdot)$ is the activation function. Particularly, this arrangement allows the RNN-DM to incorporate the processing layer output with the memory that has been read.

3.2   External Memory Read

In this subsection, we present the mechanisms of external memory read. First, the address of the content should be obtained. The key vector k_t is used to search the contents of external memory. we use cosine similarity $K(u, v) = (u \cdot v)/(|u| \cdot |v|)$ to compare the resemblance between the key vector and the contents of external memory. The content-based addressing weight for the i-th slot $M_t[i, :]$ in the memory M_t is computed as follows:

$$
\hat{w}_t[i] = \frac{\exp \beta_t K(k_t, M_t[i, :])}{\sum_q \exp \beta_t K(k_t, M_t[q, :])}
\tag{5}
$$

where the cosine similarity between the key vector k_t and the memory content of i-th slot $M_t[i,:]$ is represented as:

$$K\left(k_t, M_{t-1}[i,:]\right) = \frac{\sum\limits_{m=1}^{W} k_t[m] \cdot M_{t-1}[i,:]}{\sqrt{\left(\sum\limits_{m=1}^{W} (k_t[m])^2\right) \cdot \left(\sum\limits_{m=1}^{W} (M_{t-1}[i,m])^2\right)}} \qquad (6)$$

then, the above weight estimating with the past weight is integrated to obtain the read weight:

$$w_t[i] = (1 - g_t) w_{t-1}[i] + g_t \hat{w}_t[i] \qquad (7)$$

the interpolation gate $g_t \in [0,1]$ tradeoff between the read weight w_{t-1} at previous time and the content-based addressing weight $\hat{w}_t$. Intuitively, when $g_t = 1$, the read weight at current time will be fully determined by content-based addressing weight $\hat{w}_t$.

The memory content can be retrieved from the external memory using:

$$c_t[j] = \sum_{i=1}^{N} M_t[i,j] \cdot w_t[i] \qquad (8)$$

where $c_t[j]$ is the j-th element of the content vector c_t, it is also the output of j-th neuron in the read layer. From the Eq. (8), we can infer that the content vector c_t is a weighted sum over all memory locations. The updated process of external memory matrix M is introduced in following section.

3.3 External Memory Update

In this subsection, we present the mechanisms of external memory update. First, the update locations of external memory should be determined by using the update gate. For convince, we simply let:

$$u_t = w_t \qquad (9)$$

therefore, memory is only updated if it is to be read.

Then, we use forget gate f_t to control what and where to forget in the external memory matrix, which is defined by:

$$f_t[i,j] = 1 - w_t[i] e_t[j] \qquad (10)$$

where $f_t[i,j]$ is the j-th element of i-th slot in forget gate. e_t is the erase vector emitted by the neural network. Notice that $f_t[i,j]$ is equal to zero only if both $w_t[i]$ and $e_t[j]$ are set to one. Furthermore, memory will not be forgotten if it is not read.

Then, the memory is updated by using the following equation:

$$M_t[i,j] = M_{t-1}[i,j] \cdot f_t[i,j] + w_t[i] v_t[j] \qquad (11)$$

344   J. Bai et al.

where $M_t[i,j]$ is the j-th element of i-th slot in external memory matrix, v_t is the write vector emitted by the neural network. It is worth noting that $M_{t-1}[i,j] \cdot f_t[i,j]$ represent the forgotten information and $w_t[i]\,v_t[j]$ is the information that is written to memory.

4   Conclusion

In this paper, we propose a novel recurrent neural network model called RNN-DM, which is composed of internal memory units and external memory matrix. The proposed model fully utilize the merits of internal and external memory, furthermore, the internal memory units has ability to reduce the influence of gradient vanishing problem during network learning, and can also be used to overcome the memory conflict problem; the external memory matrix can store the past information structurally thus improve the memory capability of the network. Finally, the specifics of RNN-DM are introduced and formally described in detail.

References

1. Dauphin, Y., Yao, K., Bengio, Y., Deng, L., Hakkani-Tur, D., He, X., Heck, L., Tur, G., Yu, D., Zweig, G.: Using recurrent neural networks for slot filling in spoken language understanding. IEEE Trans. Audio Speech Lang. Process. **23**(3), 530–539 (2015)
2. Korpusik, M., Glass, J.: Spoken language understanding for a nutrition dialogue system. IEEE Trans. Audio Speech Lang. Process. **25**(7), 1450–1461 (2017)
3. Chien, J.T., Ku, Y.C.: Bayesian recurrent neural network for language modeling. IEEE Trans. Neural Netw. Learn. Syst. **27**(2), 361 (2016)
4. Arena, P., Patane, L., Stornanti, V., Termini, P.S., Zapf, B., Strauss, R.: Modeling the insect mushroom bodies: application to a delayed match-to-sample task. Neural Netw. **41**(6), 202–211 (2013)
5. Zhang, J., Zong, C.: Deep neural networks in machine translation: an overview. IEEE Intell. Syst. **30**(5), 16–25 (2015)
6. Chherawala, Y., Roy, P.P., Cheriet, M.: Feature set evaluation for offline handwriting recognition systems: application to the recurrent neural network model. IEEE Trans. Cybern. **46**(12), 2825–2836 (2016)
7. Wang, J., Zhang, L., Guo, Q., Yi, Z.: Recurrent neural networks with auxiliary memory units. IEEE Trans. Neural Netw. Learn. Syst. **PP**(99), 1–10 (2017)
8. Gustavsson, A., Magnuson, A., Blomberg, B., Andersson, M., Halfvarson, J., Tysk, C.: On the difficulty of training recurrent neural networks. In: International Conference on Machine Learning, p. III–1310 (2013)
9. Weston, J., Chopra, S., Bordes, A.: Memory networks. Eprint Arxiv (2014)
10. Botvinick, M.M., Plaut, D.C.: Short-term memory for serial order: a recurrent neural network model. Psyc. Rev. **113**(2), 201–233 (2006)
11. Chung, J., Gulcehre, C., Cho, K., Bengio, Y.: Gated feedback recurrent neural networks. In: Computer Science, pp. 2067–2075 (2015)
12. Chung, J., Gulcehre, C., Cho, K.H., Bengio, Y.: Empirical evaluation of gated recurrent neural networks on sequence modeling. Eprint Arxiv (2014)

13. Hochreiter, S., Schmidhuber, J.: Long short-term memory. Neural Comput. **9**(8), 1735–1780 (1997)
14. Gers, F.A., Schmidhuber, J., Cummins, F.: Learning to forget: continual prediction with lstm. Neural Comput. **12**(10), 2451–2471 (2000)
15. Cho, K., Van Merrienboer, B., Gulcehre, C., Bahdanau, D., Bougares, F., Schwenk, H., Bengio, Y.: Learning phrase representations using RNN encoder-decoder for statistical machine translation. In: Computer Science (2014)
16. Graves, A., Wayne, G., Danihelka, I.: Neural turing machines. In: Computer Science (2014)
17. Graves, A., Wayne, G., Reynolds, M., Harley, T., Danihelka, I., Grabskabarwiska, A., Colmenarejo, S.G., Grefenstette, E., Ramalho, T., Agapiou, J.: Hybrid computing using a neural network with dynamic external memory. Nature **538**(7626), 471 (2016)

Missing Link Prediction in Social Networks

Jin Zhou and Chiman Kwan[✉]

Signal Processing, Inc., Rockville, MD, USA
ferryzhou@gmail.com, chiman.kwan@signalpro.net

Abstract. This paper summarizes our effort of applying matrix completion techniques to a popular social network problem: link prediction. The results of our matrix completion algorithm are comparable or even better than the results of state-of-the-art methods. This means that matrix completion is a promising technique for social network problems. In addition, we customize our algorithm and developed a recommender system for Github. The recommender can help users find software tools that match their interest.

Keywords: Link prediction and recovery · Social networks
Recommender system · Github

1 Introduction

Social networks such as users' connections in Facebook, Wechat, Linkedin, etc. can be viewed as a graph and the links/edges can be represented by a binary matrix. For instance, suppose the matrix is M, then $M(i, j)$ represents the link from node i to node j. If there is a link from i to j, $M(i, j)$ is 1, otherwise 0. If the edges are un-directional, the matrix is symmetric; otherwise the matrix is not symmetric. From the matrix point of view, the link prediction problem is the same as matrix completion problem, i.e. given some known elements in the matrix, predict the unknown elements. However, this problem is challenging due to: (1) the matrix is binary, (2) the links are sparse, and (3) the dimension of the matrix can be very large such as million by million.

Matrix completion is a branch of sparsity based algorithms [1–4] and has found wide range of applications [5–9]. The basic idea is to determine missing elements in matrices.

We developed an efficient imputation based matrix completion algorithm which can handle very large scale link prediction problems. Two real world datasets were used to demonstrate the effectiveness of our algorithm. The first one was from [10] whose task is predicting the co-authorship. The second one was from Kaggle [11] which has millions of nodes and links. For the first dataset, our result is significantly better than the state-of-the-art result. For the second one, our result ranks top 5 out of 119 teams. In addition to the above experiments, we also developed a recommender for Github by using the same link prediction algorithm.

The paper is organized as follows. In Sect. 2, we summarize the line prediction algorithm. Section 3 summarizes two applications of the prediction algorithm for social networks. In Sect. 4, we will describe in detail the development of a recommender system that utilizes the link prediction algorithm. Finally, we conclude the paper in Sect. 5.

© Springer International Publishing AG, part of Springer Nature 2018
T. Huang et al. (Eds.): ISNN 2018, LNCS 10878, pp. 346–354, 2018.
https://doi.org/10.1007/978-3-319-92537-0_40

2 Link Prediction Algorithm

We present an efficient and high performance link prediction algorithm, which is shown below. The input is the mask (Ω) of known values and the initial matrix Y_0. Suppose the known values are C, then $Y_0(\Omega) = C$ and $Y_0(\sim\Omega) = 0$. The output is the final iteration of the predicted matrix Y. The algorithm starts with Y_0 and performs a set of iterations. Each iteration contains three steps: (1) perform low rank approximation (or called factorization) of matrix M_i; (2) set the approximation as the prediction; (3) adjust the prediction with known values.

Algorithm: IMPUTE

Input: Ω, Y_0

Output: Y_n

Algorithm

1. $M_1 = Y_0$,

2.   Iterate

3. $(U_i, V_i) = f(M_i)$ // factorize or low rank approximation

4. $Y_i = U_i V_i$

5. $M_{i+1} = Y_i + \alpha(Y_0 - Y_i) \circ \Omega$ //adjust with known values

---

The factorization is done by singular value decomposition (SVD),

$$
\begin{aligned}
[U, S, V] &= svd(M_i), \\
U_i &= U(:, 1:r), \\
V_i &= S(1:r, 1:r)V(:, 1:r)^T
\end{aligned}
\tag{1}
$$

If the matrix is symmetric, we use

$$
V_i = S(1:r, 1:r)U(:, 1:r)^T
\tag{2}
$$

For very large matrices, we cannot explicitly generate Y_i and M_i by applying SVD. To overcome this issue, we use the lansvd method from PROPACK [12], which is a software package for large and sparse SVD. The lansvd algorithm uses two function handles to perform SVD of sparse matrix:

$$
yf(M, x) = Mx \text{ and } yt(M, x) = M^T x
\tag{3}
$$

where M is the input matrix and x is a vector. In our algorithm, we design the function handles as follows:

$$
Mx = U(
\tag{4}
$$

$$M^T x = V^T(U^T x) + \alpha Y_\Delta^T x \qquad (5)$$

where $Y_\Delta = (Y_0 - U_i V_i) \circ \Omega$ is a sparse matrix if the number of known elements (or links) is small compared to the whole matrix. This is true for social network since the links are always very sparse.

By using function handles, we only need to store U_i and V_i in memory, whose sizes are $m \times r$ and $r \times m$ respectively. Here m is the number of nodes and r is the number of rank (or hidden features) we use. Usually, r is set to be less than 100. In this way, it is easy to handle millions of nodes with a normal PC. The convergence speed is relatively fast (fewer than 100 iterations).

3   Experiments

3.1   Predicting NIPS Coauthorship

In the first example, we used the coauthorship data from the NIPS dataset compiled in [10]. This dataset contains a list of papers and authors information from NIPS 1–7. Similar to [13], we took 234 authors who had published with other people and constructed the coauthorhip matrix, which is symmetric. For testing the algorithm, we randomly extract 20% of the matrix elements for testing and the rest 80% for learning. In the experiment, we set $r = 50$ and $\alpha = 0.05$. The results are shown in Table 1, in which results of two other state-of-the-art methods (LFRM [13] and LFL [14]) are also shown. We can see that our results are significantly better than the other two state-of-the-art methods in terms of area under the curve (AUC) metric.

Table 1. AUC scores of different methods on NIPS data

	LFRM	LFL	Ours
AUC	0.9509	0.9424	**0.9673**

3.2   Predicting Links of a Large Online Social Network

In the second experiment, we used an online challenge data and compared our results with others. The data set was the 2011 IJCNN social network challenge. The data were downloaded from a social network (Flickr). There are 7.2 million contacts/edges of 38 k users/nodes. They have been drawn randomly ensuring a certain level of closeness. The training data contain 7,237,983 contacts/edges. There are 37,689 outbound nodes and 1,133,518 inbound nodes. Most outbound nodes are also inbound nodes so that the total number of unique nodes is 1,133,547. The test dataset contains 8,960 edges from 8,960 unique outbound nodes. Of those 4,480 are true and 4,480 are false edges. The task is to predict which are true (1) and which are false (0).

Since we do not have the ground truth of the test data, we generate our own test data from the training samples, with the same 4,480 true and false edges. The testing

Table 2. AUC scores of Kaggle data. 10 runs. Our results.

#	1	2	3	4	5	6	8	8	9	10	Mean
AUC	0.934	0.930	0.931	0.936	0.932	0.933	0.930	0.937	0.930	0.933	0.9326

Table 3. Top 5 AUC scores on the leader board (the first one is not included due to de-normalization algorithm). Our result in Table 2 ranked just below Jeremy.

Team	wcuk	vsh	Jeremy	grec	hans
AUC	0.96954	0.95272	0.94506	0.92712	0.92613

edges are randomly selected for 10 times and our algorithm is applied for each testing data. Our results are shown in Table 2. The mean AUC of our results is 0.9326, which ranks **4th out of 119 teams** (see the top AUC scores in Table 3). This is promising since we did not perform any tricks like blending results of lots of different approaches or perform any problem-specific algorithm tuning.

4 Application of Link Prediction to the Development of a Recommender for GITHUB

4.1 Overview

This section summarizes our effort on applying the matrix completion technique in Sect. 2 to a real world problem, i.e. Github repository recommendation. We developed a commercial software product and the product has attracted quite a lot of initial users.

Github is a web-based hosting service for software development projects [15] launched in April 2008. It is the most popular open source code repository site [15]. The slogan of the site is "Social Coding" as the site provides social networking functionality such as feeds, followers and stars [15]. On January 16, 2013, Github hit 3 million users and about 5 million repositories. Today, Github has 64 M repositories and 23 M developers worldwide, see https://github.com/.

It is well known that a core feature of any social network site is recommendation. For instance, Facebook recommends friends, Twitter recommends followees, and LinkedIn recommends contacts. Actually, recommendation service is also a core feature for e-business website. The most famous one is Amazon, it is the earliest company who developed a recommendation system to recommend products for users. Recommendation can bring more traffic and more revenue for a website. It can also significantly improve the user experience. For instance, Amazon provides service like "Customers who bought this item also bought" and "Amazon.com recommends". However, as the most popular open source code repository website, Github does not provide a recommendation service. In this performance period, we developed a commercial software product called Github Repository Recommendation, which aimed at providing recommendation service for Github users. Similar to Amazon, this product provides the following service:

1. Coders who like this repo also like…
2. Signalpro recommend repos for "a user" based on his history.

The two features are implemented as two web apps which are hosted on our company's website [16]. One screenshot of the web app is shown in Fig. 1.

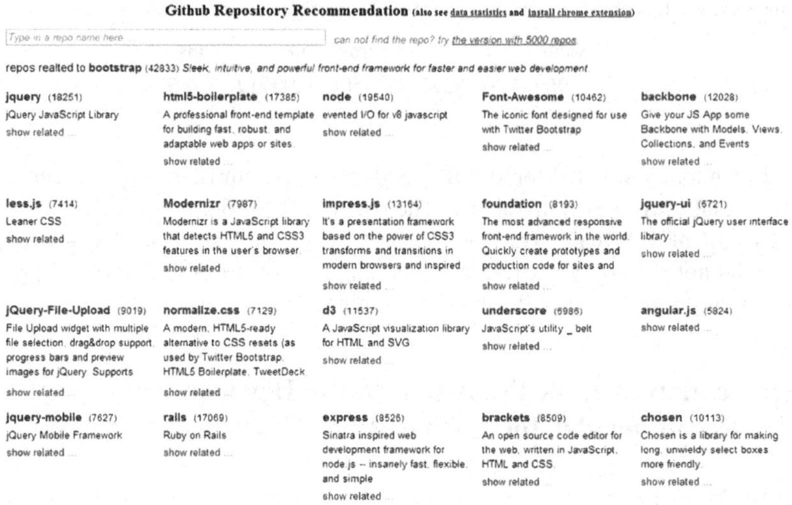

Fig. 1. Screenshot of recommendation service (recommend by repository)

We also developed a Google Chrome extension [17] which injects the recommendations to Github website.

4.2 Implementation

Data Acquisition. We use the data from Github Archive [18], an open source project which record the public Github timeline. The data can be retrieved from Google BigQuery. The timeline is a series of event logs. There are 18 event types. We only use the star event to do repository recommendation. A star event means a user is interested in and bookmarked a repository.
The query is shown below:

```
SELECT repository_name, actor, created_at
FROM [githubarchive:github.timeline]
WHERE type="WatchEvent" and created_at >='2012-04-01 00:00:00'
GROUP BY repository_name, actor, created_at
ORDER BY created_at ASC;
```

After running the query, we cannot directly download the data as it is too large. We need to save the results as a table and export the table data to Google cloud storage.

Data Preprocessing. The raw data we collect is a sequence of records. Each record has three items: username, reponame and time. Before using the data, we do the following preprocessing tasks:

1. Index username and reponame, i.e. convert each username and reponame to an integer
2. Convert time to an integer number
3. Removing repetitive records
4. Reorder/reindex user and repo index based on star count, in descend order.

Data Statistics. After data preprocessing, we have a big sparse binary matrix, whose columns represent repos and rows represent users. A nonzero value at (i, j) indicates the user i starred repo j. From the star events from 04/01/2012 to 01/10/2013, we got 344,120 users, 317,128 repos and 3,253,207 stars. The total number of matrix elements is about 0.1 billion and sparse level is 1/33545.

Tables 4 and 5 show how many users/repos have a certain number of stars. The tables show the following facts:

1. About half users starred only 1 repo and about half repos has only one starred user.
2. About 5000 repos have more than 100 stars
3. About 90% repos have less than 10 stars.
4. About 10 thousands repos have more than 50 stars.

Table 4. The number of repos that has stars.

Star count	# of repos	Percentage
1	162399	51.2%
<=5	259335	81.8%
<=10	281935	88.9%
>10	35193	11.1%
>50	9509	3.0%
>100	5061	1.6%
>1000	254	0.08%

Table 5. The number of users that has stars.

Star count	# of repos	Percentage
1	141639	41.2%
<=5	246617	71.7%
<=10	282384	82.1%
>10	61736	17.9%
>50	12468	3.6%
>100	4341	1.3%
>1000	32	0.01%

Repository Recommendation. We try to answer two questions: 1. coders who like this repo like? 2. from your history, what repos you may like? The first question can be answered using nearest neighbors. From user-repo star matrix M, we compute similarity between two repos with the normalized cross correlation

$$S(i,j) = \frac{M(:, i)^T M(:,j)}{||M(:,i)|| \times ||M(:,j)||} \tag{6}$$

With similarity scores, we can find closest K repos for any given repo and thus the first question is answered. In matrix form, the equation is

$$S = \hat{M}^T \hat{M} \tag{7}$$

where $\hat{M}$ is normalized M such that the norm of each column is equal to 1.

For the second question, we need to do matrix completion, i.e. estimate a user-repo score for all user repo interactions. Once we have the scores, we can sort the repo scores for each user and recommend the repos with highest scores to the user. In our system, the user-repo scores are computed based on following equation:

$$R(i,:) = \sum_{k \in M(i,:)} S(k,:) \tag{8}$$

Basically, it is equivalent to

$$R = MS \tag{9}$$

The interpretation is intuitive: if a user starred repo A and repo B, then we first collect similar repos to A and similar repos to B and then merge the similar repos.

Based on the data statistics, we picked the first 5000 repos for recommendation.

Evaluation. We first split data into training set and testing set based on time. From training set, we compute repo similarities. For each user in testing set, we first compute 20 recommendations for the user and see how many of them are actually hit in the testing data. Average hit rate is used as a metric to measure the performance. We compared our method with a baseline method, i.e. recommend purely based on repo popularity. For evaluation data, we picked first 10,000 users and 1,000 repos. The baseline method's average hit rate is 9.2% and ours is 10.4%, which means about 15% performance boost. We plan to implement a c version of the recommender system for algorithm evaluation. We noticed that if we choose only 1000 users, then our results are very close to baseline method. This means that baseline method is more biased to very active users. When more (not so active) users are used for comparison, our results should perform much better than the baseline method.

Software Development. We implemented our recommendation software as a web application, so that there is no need to download and install, and everyone can easily use our service. The front-end is static html files using javascript/html/css techniques. The backend is implemented with Ruby and deployed to Heroku. The backend provides web service of repo recommendation and the front-end use jsonp to communicate with backend. Currently, no database is used. All data is loaded into memory in the beginning. For space efficiency, we only load S matrix. When a user submits a repo recommendation request for a given username, we first crawl Github to get the user's star repos and then compute the user-repo scores on the fly. We also developed chrome extension which injects recommendations to Github's website.

Now we have 1800 users for the web app. This is a good sign which shows the potential of the product.

5 Conclusions

In this paper, we present a high performance link recovery algorithm for predicting missing links in social networks. The approach has been applied to a recommender for Github. Currently, the recommender has been widely used in Github. Comparison with other recommenders [19–21] will be carried out in the future.

Acknowledgments. This research was supported by Office of Naval Research under contract # N00014-12-C-0079. Distribution Statement A. Approved for public release; distribution is unlimited.

References

1. Candes, E.J., Recht, B.: Exact matrix completion via convex optimization. Found. Comput. Math. **9**, 717–772 (2008)
2. Dao, M., Kwan, C., Ayhan, B., Tran, T.: Burn scar detection using cloudy MODIS images via low-rank and sparsity-based models. In: IEEE Global Conference on Signal and Information Processing, pp. 177–181 (2016)
3. Dao, M., Kwan, C., Koperski, K., Marchisio, G.: A joint sparsity approach to tunnel activity monitoring using high resolution satellite images. In: IEEE Ubiquitous Computing, Electronics and Mobile Communication Conference, pp. 322–328 (2017)
4. Kwan, C., Budavari, B., Dao, M., Zhou, J.: New sparsity based pansharpening algorithm for hyperspectral images. In: IEEE Ubiquitous Computing, Electronics and Mobile Communication Conference, pp. 88–93 (2017)
5. Zhou, J., Kwan, C., Ayhan, B.: A high performance missing pixel reconstruction algorithm for hyperspectral images. In: 2nd International Conference on Applied and Theoretical Information Systems Research (2012)
6. Kwan, C., Zhou, J.: Method for Image Denoising. Patent #9,159,121 (2015)
7. Zhou, J., Kwan, C.: High performance image completion using sparsity based algorithms. In: SPIE Commercial + Scientific Sensing and Imaging Conference (2018)
8. Zhou, J., Kwan, C., Tran, T.: ATR performance improvement using images with corrupted or missing pixels. In: SPIE Defense + Security Conference (2018)
9. Dao, M., Suo, Y., Chin, S., Tran, T.: Video frame interpolation via weighted robust principal component analysis. In: International Conference on Acoustics, Speech and Signal Processing (2013)
10. NIPS data. http://ai.stanford.edu/~gal/Data/NIPS
11. Kaggle data. http://www.kaggle.com/c/socialNetwork/Data
12. Propac. http://soi.stanford.edu/~rmunk/PROPACK/
13. Miller, K., Griffiths, T., Jordan, M.: Nonparametric latent feature models for link prediction. In: Advances of Neural Information Processing Systems, pp. 1276–1284 (2009)
14. Menon, A., Elkan, C.: Dyadic Prediction Using a Latent Feature Log-Linear Model. arXiv: 1006.2156v1 10 June 2010
15. Github. http://en.wikipedia.org/wiki/GitHub
16. Github Repository Recommendation by Repo. http://signalpro.net/github/repo_rec.htm
17. Github Repository Recommendation Chrome Extension. https://chrome.google.com/webstore/detail/github-repository-recomme/dpmjlcnijpnkklopinedkkhmjcchecia
18. Github Achieve. http://www.githubarchive.org/

19. Rezaeimehr, F., Moradi, P., Ahmadiana, S., Qader, N.N., Jalili, M.: TCARS: time- and community-aware recommendation system. Future Gener. Comput. Syst. **78**, 419–429 (2018)
20. Azadjalal, M.M., Moradi, P., Abdollahpouri, A., Jalili, M.: A trust-aware recommendation method based on pareto dominance and confidence concepts. Knowl.-Based Syst. **116**, 130–143 (2017)
21. Ranjbar, M., Moradi, P., Azami, M., Jalili, M.: An imputation-based matrix factorization method for improving accuracy of collaborative filtering systems. Eng. Appl. Artif. Intell. **46**, 58–66 (2015)

Dynamical Behaviors of Discrete-Time Cohen-Grossberg Neural Networks with Discontinuous Activations and Infinite Delays

Jinling Wang[1], Haijun Jiang[1(✉)], Tianlong Ma[2], and Cheng Hu[1]

[1] College of Mathematics and System Sciences, Xinjiang University,
Urumqi 830046, Xinjiang, China
jianghaijunxju@163.com

[2] Department of Basic Research, Qinghai University, Xining 810016, Qinghai, China

Abstract. The dynamical behaviors of discrete-time Cohen-Grossberg neural networks (DCGNNs) with discontinuous activations and infinite delays are further considered in this paper. Based on the functional differential inclusions theory, criteria for DCGNNs are derived to ensure the existence and uniqueness of the solution. In addition, we obtain some novel sufficient conditions for the asymptotic stability of discontinuous DCGNNs via applying the Lyapunov approach. Finally, several examples with numerical simulation are carried out to demonstrate the validity and effectiveness of the obtained results.

Keywords: Discrete-time Cohen-Grossberg neural networks
Discontinuous activations · Infinite delays · Stability

1 Introduction

Neural networks (NNs) have been explored in depth due to their widespread applications, such as, speech synthesis, signal processing, combinatorial optimization and other scientific areas [1,2]. In fact, Cohen-Grossberg neural networks (CGNNs) contain various models, while most CGNNS are considered with continuous-time systems and many nice results have been derived [3–9]. Recently, monographs find that discrete-time NNs are essential to implement continuous-time NNs in the practice. Hence, a multitude of numerical schemes are proposed to acquire discrete-time counterparts of continuous-type NNs, for instance, Euler scheme, Runge-Kutta scheme [10,11]. To be more specific, it has been a deserved research to study how to keep the dynamic characteristics of DCGNNs.

H. Jiang—This was supported in part by the Excellent Doctor Innovation Program of Xinjiang University under Grant XJUBSCX-2016004, in part by the National Natural Science Foundation of People's Republic of China (Grant NO. 61164004 and U1703262).

T. Huang et al. (Eds.): ISNN 2018, LNCS 10878, pp. 355–363, 2018.
https://doi.org/10.1007/978-3-319-92537-0_41

As far as we known, discontinuous activations existed in many practical NNs can be caused by engineering tasks [12,13]. So, it is necessary to overcome these difficulties for the DCGNNs with discontinuous activations. Based on the Filippov differential inclusion [14], the analysis has been done on discontinuous NNs [15–17]. In [18,19], authors studied the NNs based on Leray-Schauder alternative theorem, matrix theory. In [20], authors investigated the periodicity of CGNNs via functional differential inclusions. In [21], authors introduced a discrete-time CGNN, while the activation function was continuous. So, it's high time to analyze the stability of DCGNNs with discontinuous activations.

With this motivation, solutions of discrete-time CGNNs with discontinuous activations and infinite delays are introduced into the different inclusion based on the differential inclusions theory, and the dynamical behaviors are investigated.

2   Preliminary Notes

The continuous-time CGNN with infinite delays and discontinuous activation functions is defined:

$$\frac{dx_i(t)}{dt} = -a_i(x_i(t))[b_i(x_i(t)) - \sum_{j=1}^{l} c_{ij} f_j(x_j(t)) - \sum_{j=1}^{l} d_{ij} f_j(x_j(t - \tau_{ij}))$$

$$- \sum_{j=1}^{l} e_{ij} f_j \left(\int_0^\infty K_{ij}(s) x_j(t - s) ds \right) + I_i], \tag{1}$$

where $L = \{1, 2, ..., l\}$; $x_i(t)$ represents the state with the i-th neuron; $a_i(x_i(t))$ denotes the amplification function; $b_i(t)$ is an behaved function; c_{ij}, d_{ij}, e_{ij} call the connection weights of unit j to unit i; $f_i(\cdot)$ is the activation to its incoming potential; $\tau_{ij} > 0$ means the transmission delay, $K_{ij}(v)$ corresponds to the delay kernel and I_i is the constant external input. Moreover, we assume that $a_i > 0, 0 < \Phi(t) \leq \frac{a_i(u)b_i(u) - a_i(v)b_i(v)}{u - v} \leq \Gamma(t)$, where $\Phi(t), \Gamma(t)$ are continuous functions. Moreover, the neuron activation functions of system (1) are assumed to be piecewise continuous.

From the measurable selection theorem [22], the concept of the Filippov solutions is defined as follows:

Definition 1. A function $x : (-\infty, b) \to R^l, b \in [0, +\infty)$ is a state solution of system (1) if x is continuous on $(-\infty, 0)$ and absolutely continuous on $[0, b)$, there exists a measurable function $\gamma = (\gamma_1, \gamma_2, \cdots, \gamma_l,)^T : (-\infty, b) \to R^l$ such that $\gamma(\cdot) \in \overline{co}[f(\cdot)]$ for a.e.$t \in (-\infty, b)$ and

$$\frac{dx_i(t)}{dt} = -a_i(x_i(t))[b_i(x_i(t)) - \sum_{j=1}^{l} c_{ij} \gamma_j(x_j(t)) - \sum_{j=1}^{l} d_{ij} \gamma_j(x_j(t - \tau_{ij}))$$

$$- \sum_{j=1}^{l} e_{ij} \gamma_j \left(\int_0^\infty K_{ij}(s) x_j(t - s) ds \right) + I_i], \tag{2}$$

where $\overline{co}[X]$ is the closure of the convex hull of X.

Let $\mathbb{R}, \mathbb{Z}$ denote the set of real number and all integers, respectively. Denote $\mathbb{Z}_0^+ = \{0, 1, 2, ...\}$. $\|x\|_p = (\sum_{i=1}^{l} |x_i|^p)^{\frac{1}{p}}$, $\|x\|_\infty = \max_{1 \le i \le l} |x_i|$, where $x = (x_1, x_2, ..., x_l)^T$. For $a, b \in \mathbb{Z}$ and $a \le b$, $[a, b]_\mathbb{Z} = \{a, a+1, ..., b-1, b\}$. $[\frac{t}{h}] = n$, $[\frac{\tau_{ij}}{h}] = v_{ij}, [\frac{s}{h}] = v$. Based on the semi-discretization technique, a discrete-time CGNN is acquired as

$$x_i(n+1) = x_i(n) - \xi_i(h)a_i(x_i(n))\{b_i(x_i(n)) - \sum_{j=1}^{l} c_{ij} f_j(x_j(n)) - \sum_{j=1}^{l} d_{ij}$$

$$\times f_j(x_j(n - v_{ij})) - \sum_{j=1}^{l} e_{ij} f_j(\sum_{v=1}^{\infty} K_{ij}(v)x_j(n-v)) + I_i\}, \qquad (3)$$

where $i \in L, n \in \mathbb{Z}_0^+$, h is a fixed positive real number denoting a uniform discretization step-size, and $\xi_i(h) = \frac{1-e^{-\frac{\Gamma_i(n)+\Phi_i(n)}{2}h}}{\frac{\Gamma_i(n)+\Phi_i(n)}{2}}$. System (3) is the discrete-time analogue of continuous-time system (1) which the activation function f_i is bounded and has a finite number of discontinuous points d_k.

(H_1) f_i is piecewise continuous, and there exist finite right and left limits, $f_i^+(x_i(d_k))$ and $f_i^-(x_i(d_k))$, while $\overline{co}[f_i(x_i(d_k)] = \{\min\{f_i^-(x_i(d_k)), f_i^+(x_i(d_k))\}, \max\{f_i^-(x_i(d_k)), f_i^+(x_i(d_k))\}\}$ (see Forti and Nistri [23]).

(H_2) There exists constant k_i, h_i such that $|\overline{co}[f_i(x_i)]| \le k_i|x_i| + h_i, i \in L$.

(H_3) There exists constants $l_i > 0$ such that $|\overline{co}[f_i(u)] - \overline{co}[f_i(v)]| \le l_i|u - v|$.

(H_4) $K_{ij}(u) \in [0, \infty)$ and it is bounded for $u \in \mathbb{Z}_0^+$, $\sum_{u=1}^{\infty} K_{ij}(u) = 1$, and there exist ς such that $\sum_{u=1}^{\infty} K_{ij}(u)\varsigma^u < \infty$.

(H_5) For any $i \in L$, there exist constants $\underline{a}_i, \overline{a}_i, \rho_i$ such that

$$0 < \underline{a}_i \le a_i(n) \le \overline{a}_i, \frac{b_i(x) - b_i(x)}{x - y} \ge \rho_i, x \ne y, \rho_i \ge 0.$$

For an initial value problem associated (IVP) with the system (3), the follow definition are introduced [23].

Definition 2. For any function $\varphi : (-\infty, 0]_\mathbb{Z} \to R^l$ and any measurable selection $\phi : (-\infty, 0]_\mathbb{Z} \to R^l$, such that $\phi(\eta) \in \overline{co}[f(\varphi(\eta))]$ for a.e. $\eta \in (-\infty, 0]_\mathbb{Z}$ by an initial value problem associated to (3) with initial condition $[\varphi, \phi]$, we mean the following problem: find a couple of functions of $[x, \gamma] : (-\infty, b)_\mathbb{Z} \to R^l \times R^l$, such that x is a solution of (3) on $(-\infty, b)_\mathbb{Z}$ for some $b > 0$, γ is an output solution associated to x, and

$$\begin{cases} x_i(n+1) = x_i(n) - \xi_i(h)a_i(x_i(n))\{b_i(x_i(n)) - \sum_{j=1}^{l} c_{ij}\gamma_j(x_j(n)) - \sum_{j=1}^{l} d_{ij} \\ \qquad \times \gamma_j(x_j(n - v_{ij})) - \sum_{j=1}^{l} e_{ij}\gamma_j(\sum_{v=1}^{\infty} K_{ij}(v)x_j(n-v)) + I_i\}, \\ \gamma_i(x(n)) \in \overline{co}[f_i(x_i(n))], \quad n \in [0, b)_\mathbb{Z}, \\ x_i(\eta) = \varphi_i(\eta), \quad \eta \in (-\infty, 0]_\mathbb{Z}, \\ \gamma_i(\eta) = \phi_i(\eta), \quad \eta \in (-\infty, 0]_\mathbb{Z}. \end{cases} \qquad (4)$$

3   Main Results

The aim of this section is to investigate the viability existence of solutions of IVP for system (3) with discontinuous activation functions.

Theorem 1. Suppose $(H_1), (H_3)$ and (H_4) are satisfied, then the IVP of system (3) has at least a solution on $[0, +\infty)_Z$.

Proof. From (H_1), there is at least a local solution $x(n)$ of (3) with initial condition. Furthermore, any solution $x(n)$ is bounded and hence defined on $[0, +\infty)_Z$. Next, suppose $x(n)$ is unbounded and is defined on a maximal interval $[0, b)_Z$.
Let

$$x(n + 1) = \Xi(n)x(n) + F(n, x(n), x(n - u)),$$

where

$$x(\cdot) = (x_1(\cdot), x_1(\cdot), \cdots, x_l(\cdot))^T,$$
$$\Xi(n) = \operatorname{diag}(e^{-\frac{\Gamma_1(n)+\Phi_1(n)}{2}h}, e^{-\frac{\Gamma_2(n)+\Phi_2(n)}{2}h}, \dots, e^{-\frac{\Gamma_l(n)+\Phi_l(n)}{2}h}),$$
$$F(n, x(n), x(n - u)) = (F_1(n, x_1(n), x_1(n - u)), \cdots, F_l(n, x_l(n), x_l(n - u)))^T,$$
$$F_i(n, x_i(n), x_i(n - u)) = (\Gamma_i(n) + \Phi_i(n)/2)\xi_i(h)x_i(n) - \xi_i(h)a_i(x_i(n))\{b_i(x_i(n))$$
$$-\sum_{j=1}^{l} c_{ij}\gamma_j(x_j(n)) - \sum_{j=1}^{l} d_{ij}\gamma_j(x_j(n - v_{ij})) - \sum_{j=1}^{l} e_{ij}\gamma_j(\sum_{v=1}^{\infty} K_{ij}(v)x_j(n - v)) + I_i\}.$$

Hence, the solution of system (4) with initial condition satisfies

$$x(n) = \Phi(n, \eta)\varphi(\eta) + \sum_{s=0}^{n-1} \Phi(s + 1, \eta)F(s, x(s), x(s - u)),$$

where $\Phi(n, \eta)$ is the fundamental-solution matrix. Since the condition of (4), we claim that $\|F(s, x(s), x(s - u))\| \le \overline{M}\|x(s)\|_C + M$, where $\xi(h) = \operatorname{diag}(\xi_1(h), \xi_2(h), \dots, \xi_l(h))$, $\Gamma(n) = \operatorname{diag}(\Gamma_1(n), \Gamma_2(n), \dots, \Gamma_l(n))$, $\Phi(n) = \operatorname{diag}(\Phi_1(n), \Phi_2(n), \dots, \Phi_l(n))$, $A(0) = \operatorname{diag}(a_1(0), a_2(0), \dots, a_l(0))$, $B(0) = \operatorname{diag}(b_1(0), b_2(0), \dots, b_l(0))$, $C = (c_{ij})_{l \times l}, D = (d_{ij})_{l \times l}, E = (e_{ij})_{l \times l}, I = (I_1, I_2, \dots, I_l)^T, \overline{M} = \|\xi(h)\|(3/2\|\Gamma(n)\| + \|\Phi(n)\| + \|k\|(\|C\| + \|D\| + \|E\|)))$, $M = (\|A(0)\|\|B(0)\| + \|h\|(\|C\| + \|D\| + \|E\|)\| + \|I\|)\|\xi(h)\|$.
Then, we claim that $\|x(n + 1)\|_C \le q(n + 1) + \sum_{s=0}^{n} u(s)\|x(s)\|_C$, and $q(n + 1) = \|\Phi(n+1, \eta)\|\|\varphi(\eta)\| + \sum_{s=0}^{n} \|\Phi(s+1, \eta)\|\|M\|$, $u(s) = \|\Phi(s+1, \eta)\|\overline{M}$. Clearly, we have $\|x(n)\| \le q_n + \sum_{s=n_0}^{n-1} q_s u_s \exp\{\sum_{r=s+1}^{n-1} u_r\}$. Note that if $b < +\infty$ implies that $x(n)$ is bounded which is in contradiction with the hypothesis. Hence, we have shown that $b = +\infty$. It means that the IVP of system (3) has at least a solution on $[0, +\infty)_Z$.

Next, we investigate the existence of an equilibrium of system (3).

Theorem 2. For the neural network defined by (3), assume that the network parameters satisfy $(H_1), (H_3) - (H_5)$. Then, the system (3) has an unique equilibrium point, if the following condition holds: there exist real numbers $\sigma_i, \sigma_j > 0, i, j \in L$, and p is a positive integer, such that

$$\rho_i - \frac{p-1}{p} \sum_{j=1}^{l} (|c_{ij}| + |d_{ij}| + |e_{ij}|) l_j - \frac{1}{p} \sum_{j=1}^{l} \frac{\sigma_j}{\sigma_i} (|c_{ji}| + |d_{ji}| + |e_{ji}|) l_i > 0.$$

Proof. To show the existence of an unique equilibrium point of the system (3), we consider the mapping $H(x)$ associated with

$$H_i(x) = b_i(x_i) - \sum_{j=1}^{l} c_{ij} \gamma_j(x_j) - \sum_{j=1}^{l} d_{ij} \gamma_j(x_j) - \sum_{j=1}^{l} e_{ij} \gamma_j(x_j) + I_i, i, j \in \mathbb{L}.$$

First, let $H_i(u) = H_i(v), u, v \in \Phi$. Then, it follows that $\sum_{i=1}^{l} \sigma_i \varepsilon |u_i - v_i|^p \leq 0$, where ρ_i are positive constants, p is a positive integer, and ε is defined as

$$\varepsilon = \min_{1 \leq i \leq l} \{\rho_i - \frac{p-1}{p} \sum_{j=1}^{l} (|c_{ij}| + |d_{ij}| + |e_{ij}|) l_j - \frac{1}{p} \sum_{j=1}^{l} \frac{\sigma_j}{\sigma_i} \sigma_j (|c_{ji}| + |d_{ji}| + |e_{ji}|) l_i \} > 0.$$

Consequently, we obtain $u_i = v_i$, that is $u = v$. Hence the map H is injective.

Next, we will show that $\|H(x)\|_p \to \infty$ as $\|x\|_p \to \infty$. Define function $\mathbb{F}(x)$

$$\mathbb{F}(x) = \sum_{i=1}^{l} \sigma_i |x_i|^{p-1} sgn(x_i)(H_i(x) - H_i(0)) \geq \varepsilon \min_{1 \leq i \leq l} \{\sigma_i\} \sum_{i=1}^{l} |x_i|^p.$$

Then, we have $\|x\|_p \leq \frac{\max_{1 \leq i \leq l} \{\sigma_i\}}{\varepsilon \min_{1 \leq i \leq l} \{\sigma_i\}} \|H(x) - H(0)\|_p, i, j \in L$. It shows that $\|H(x)\|_p \to \infty$ as $\|x\|_p \to \infty$ for any positive integer p. So, the system (3) has an unique fixed point $\bar{x}$.

In the next part, we will get the system (3) has an uniqueness equilibrium point under the infinite norm.

Corollary 1. For the neural network defined by the system (3), assume that the network parameters satisfy $(H_1), (H_3) - (H_5)$, Then, system (3) has an unique equilibrium point, if the following condition holds

$$\exists t \in L, \max_{1 \leq i \leq l} |u_i - v_i| = |u_t - v_t|, s.t. \rho_t - \sum_{j=1}^{l} (|c_{tj}| + |d_{tj}| + |e_{tj}|) L_j > 0.$$

Remark 1. From the above discussion, it shows that we can use the homeomorphism mapping properties to prove that the discrete-time system has a uniqueness equilibrium point under commonly used vector norms just like infinite norm, p-norm, instead of Brouwer fixed point theorem which only can ensure the existence and uniqueness of equilibrium point under infinite norm or 2-norm [21].

To obtain stability of the system (3), we will first shift the equilibrium point $\bar{x}$ of the system (3). Set $z(n) = x(n) - \bar{x}$, then we transform the system (3) to

$$z_i(n+1) = z_i(n) - \xi_i(h)\tilde{a}_i(z_i(n))[\tilde{b}_i(z_i(n)) - \sum_{j=1}^{l} c_{ij}\tilde{\gamma}_j(z_j(n))$$

$$- \sum_{j=1}^{l} d_{ij}\tilde{\gamma}_j(z_j(n - v_{ij})) - \sum_{j=1}^{l} e_{ij}\tilde{\gamma}_j(\sum_{v=1}^{\infty} K_{ij}(v)z_j(n-v))], i,j \in L.$$

where $\tilde{a}_i(z_i(n)) = a_i(z_i(n) + \bar{x}_i), \tilde{b}_i(z_i(n)) = b_i(z_i(n) + \bar{x}_i) - b_i(\bar{x}_i), \tilde{\gamma}(\cdot) \in \overline{co}[F(\cdot)]$, $F_j(z_j(n)) = f_j(z_j(n) + \bar{x}_j) - \bar{\gamma}_j, F_j(z_j(n - v_{ij})) = f_j(z_j(n - v_{ij}) + \bar{x}_j) - \bar{\gamma}_j$, $F_j(\sum_{v=1}^{\infty} K_{ij}(v)z_j(n-v)) = f_j(\sum_{v=1}^{\infty} K_{ij}(v)(z_j(n-v) + \bar{x}_j)) - \bar{\gamma}_j$.

Theorem 3. Under the assumptions (H_1), (H_3), suppose:

(i) There exists $\mu_i > 0$ such that $x\tilde{b}_i(x) \geq \mu_i x^2$, and $\underline{a}\mu_i < 1$ for $i \in L$.
(ii) $\underline{a}_i\mu_i - \bar{a}_j l_i \sum_{j=1}^{l}(|c_{ji}| + |d_{ji}| + |e_{ji}|) \geq 0$.

Then, the equilibrium point $\bar{x}$ of system (3) is globally asymptotically stable.

Proof. Define the Lyapunov functional

$$V_i(Z_i(n)) = \sum_{j=1}^{l} Z_i(n) + \bar{a}_i \sum_{j=1}^{l} \xi_j(h)|d_{ij}|l_j\lambda^{v_{ij}+1} \sum_{v=n-v_{ij}}^{n-1} Z_j(v) + \bar{a}_i \sum_{j=1}^{l} \xi_j(h)|e_{ij}|$$

$$\times l_j \sum_{v=1}^{\infty} K_{ij}(v)\lambda^{v+1} \sum_{r=n-v}^{n-1} Z_r^j,$$

where $Z_i(n) = \lambda^n \frac{|z_i(n)|}{\xi_i(h)}$. Consider the function $\tilde{G}_i(\cdot)$

$$\tilde{G}_i(\tilde{\lambda}) = 1 - \tilde{\lambda} + \tilde{\lambda}\underline{a}_i\mu_i\xi_i(h) - \tilde{\lambda}\xi_i(h)\bar{a}_j \sum_{j=1}^{l} |c_{ji}|l_i - \xi_i(h)\bar{a}_j \sum_{j=1}^{l} |d_{ji}|l_i\tilde{\lambda}^{v_{ji}+1}$$

$$- \xi_i(h)\bar{a}_j \sum_{j=1}^{l} |e_{ji}|l_i\tilde{\lambda}^{v+1},$$

where $\tilde{\lambda} \in [1, +\infty)$, and $\tilde{G}_i(1) > 0$. Since $\tilde{G}_i(\cdot)$ is continuous on $[1, +\infty)$, there exists a real number $\lambda > 1$ such that $\tilde{G}_i(\lambda) \geq 0$. Hence, we assert that $\Delta V \leq 0$, and $V_i(Z_i(n)) \leq V_i(Z_i(0))$. That is to say $\sum_{i=1}^{l} |z_i(n)| \leq \sup_{l \in (-\infty, 0]_{\mathbb{Z}}} |z_i(l)|(1/\lambda)^n \mathcal{M}$, where $\mathcal{M} = 1 + \bar{a}_j \sum_{j=1}^{l} |d_{ji}|l_i\lambda^{v_{ji}+1} + \bar{a}_j \sum_{j=1}^{l} |e_{ji}|l_i\lambda^{v+1}$.

Next, we consider the exceptional case of system (3) without infinite delays.

Corollary 2. Under the conditions (H_1) and (H_3), suppose

(i) There exists $\mu_i > 0$ such that $x\tilde{b}_i(x) \geq \mu_i x^2$, and $\underline{a}\mu_i < 1$ for $i \in L$.

(ii) $\underline{a}_i\mu_i - \bar{a}_j l_i \sum_{j=1}^{l}(|c_{ji}| + |d_{ji}|) \geq 0$.

Then, the equilibrium point $\bar{x}$ of system without infinite delays is globally asymptotically stable.

Remark 2. Although there are some results on the stability of continuous-time neural networks with discontinuous activation functions [16,18,24], there is little work on discrete-time CGNNs with discontinuous activation functions. Main challenges to guarantee the stability of DCGNNs are how to deal with the amplification function, discontinuous activation functions and infinite delays, while we overcome these problem in Theorem 3.

4   Examples

Example 1. Consider the two-dimensional CGNNs without infinite delays. Assume $a_1(x_i(t)) = 1 + 0.1\sin(x_1(t)), a_2(x_2(t)) = 1 + 0.1\cos(x_2(t))$, $b_1(x_1(t)) = 0.1x_1(t)$, $b_2(x_2(t)) = 0.1x_2(t)$, $c_{11} = d_{12} = -0.004$, $c_{12} = d_{11} = 0$, $c_{21} = d_{22} = 0$, $c_{22} = 0.015$, $d_{21} = -0.05, \tau = 2, I_i = 0$, and

$$f(x_i(n)) = \begin{cases} x_i(n) + 1, & x_i(n) > 0, \\ x_i(n), & x_i(n) \leq 0, \end{cases} \quad i = 1, 2.$$

Furthermore, the conditions of Corollary 2 can be satisfied, and the solution of the system is asymptotic stability (see Fig. 1).

Example 2. Consider the following two-dimensional CGNNs with discontinuous activations and infinite delays. Assume $a_1(x_i(t)) = 1 + 0.1\sin(x_1(t))$, $a_2(x_2(t)) = 1 + 0.1\cos(x_2(t))$, $b_1(x_1(t)) = 0.1x_1(t)$, $b_2(x_2(t)) = 0.1x_2(t)$, $c_{ij} = 0, (i, j = 1, 2)$, $d_{11} = e_{12} = -0.003$, $d_{12} = e_{11} = 0, d_{21} = e_{22} = 0, d_{22} = 0.021$, $e_{21} = -0.02, \tau = 2, I_i = 0, K_{ij}(s) = 2^{-s}, f(x_i(n) = \text{sgn}(x_i(n)), i = 1, 2$.

Furthermore, the conditions of the Theorem 3 can be satisfied, and the solution is asymptotic stability(see Fig. 2).

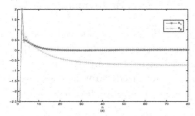

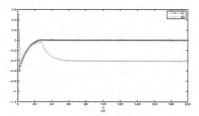

Fig. 1. The response curves of system without infinite delays.

Fig. 2. The response curves of system with infinite delays.

5   Conclusions

In this paper, we aim to seek methods for studying the existence, uniqueness and stability of the discontinuous discrete-time CGNNs. From what have been discussed above, we apply the functional differential inclusions theory and homeomorphism mapping principle to achieve the existence of an equilibrium point of system. At the same time, we find an appropriate Lyapunov function to guarantee the stability of discrete-time neural networks system with discontinuous activations.

References

1. Chua, L., Yang, L.: Cellural neural networks theory. IEEE Trans. Circuits Syst. **35**, 1257–1272 (1988)
2. Zhang, C., He, Y., Jiang, L., Wang, Q., Wu, M.: Stability analysis of discrete-time neural networks with time-varying delay via an extended reciprocally convex matrix inequality. IEEE Trans. Cybern. **99**, 1–10 (2017)
3. Wan, Y., Cao, J., Wen, G., Yu, W.: Robust fixed-time synchronization of delayed Cohen-Grossberg neural networks. Neural Netw. **73**, 86–94 (2016)
4. Cai, Z., Huang, L.: Finite-time synchronization by switching state-feedback control for discontinuous Cohen-Grossberg neural networks with mixed delays. Int. J. Mach. Learn. Cyb. **8**, 1–13 (2017)
5. Cui, N., Jiang, H., Hu, C., Abdurahman, A.: Finite-time synchronization of inertial neural networks. J. Assoc. Arab Univ. Basic Appl. Sci **24**, 300–309 (2017)
6. Su, W., Chen, Y.: Global robust stability criteria of stochastic Cohen-Grossberg neural networks with discrete and distributed time-varying delays. Commun. Nonlinear Sci. Numer. Simul. **14**, 520–528 (2009)
7. Li, R., Cao, J., Alsaedi, A., Ahmad, B.: Passivity analysis of delayed reaction-diffusion Cohen-Grossberg neural networks via Hardy-Poincar inequality. J. Frankl. I **354**, 3021–3038 (2017)
8. Luo, W., Zhong, S., Yang, J.: Global exponential stability of impulsive Cohen-Grossberg neural. Chaos Solitons Fract. **42**, 1084–1091 (2009)
9. He, W., Chu, L.: Exponential stability criteria for fuzzy bidirectional associative memory Cohen-Grossberg neural networks with mixed delays and impulses. Adv. Differ. Equ. **2017**, 61–77 (2017)
10. Mohamad, S., Gopalsamy, K.: Exponential stability of continuous-time and discrete-time cellular neural networks with delays. Appl. Math. Comput. **135**, 17–38 (2003)
11. Wang, J., Jiang, H., Hu, C., Ma, T.: Convergence behavior of delayed discrete cellular neural network without periodic coefficients. Neural Netw. **53**, 61–68 (2014)
12. Aubin, J., Frankowska, H.: Set-valued Analysis. Birkauser, Boston (1990)
13. Forti, M., Grazzini, M., Nistri, P., Pancioni, L.: Generalized lyapunov approach for convergence of neural networks with discontinuous or non-lipschitz activations. Physica D **214**, 88–89 (2006)
14. Filippov, A.: Differential Equations with Discontinuous Right-hand Side. Mathematics and its Applications. Springer, Netherlands (1988). https://doi.org/10.1007/978-94-015-7793-9

15. Wang, L., Shen, Y., Sheng, Y.: Finite-time robust stabilization of uncertain delayed neural networks with discontinuous activations via delayed feedback control. Neural Netw. **76**, 46–54 (2016)
16. Qin, S., Cheng, Q., Chen, G.: Global exponential stability of uncertain neuralnetworks with discontinuous Lurie-type activation and mixed delays. Neurocomputing **198**, 12–19 (2016)
17. Cai, Z., Huang, L., Zhang, L.: New exponential synchronization criteria for time-varying delayed neural networks with discontinuous activations. Neural Netw. **65**, 105–114 (2015)
18. Wang, J., Huang, L., Guo, Z.: Dynamical behavior of delayed Hopfield neural networks with discontinuous activations. Appl. Math. Model. **33**, 1793–1802 (2009)
19. Cai, Z., Huang, L.: Existence and global asymptotic stability of periodic solution for discrete and distributed time-varying delayed neural networks with discontinuous activations. Neurocomputing **74**, 3170–3179 (2011)
20. Wang, D., Huang, L.: Periodicity and multi-periodicity of generalized Cohen-Grossberg neural networks via functional differential inclusions. Nonlinear Dyn. **85**, 67–86 (2016)
21. Li, W., Pang, L., Su, H., Wang, K.: Global stability for discrete Cohen-Grossberg neural networks with finite and infinite delays. Appl. Math. Lett. **25**, 2246–2251 (2012)
22. Aubin, J., Cellina, A.: Differential Inclusions. Springer-Verlag, Berlin (1984). https://doi.org/10.1007/978-3-642-69512-4
23. Forti, M., Nistri, P.: Global convergence of neural networks with discontinuous neuron activations. IEEE Trans. Circuits Syst. I Fundam. Theory Appl. **50**, 1421–1435 (2003)
24. Bao, G., Zeng, Z.: Global asymptotical stability analysis for a kind of discrete-time recurrent neural network with discontinuous activation functions. Neurocomputing **193**, 242–249 (2016)

Analysis and Circuit Implementation of a Novel Memristor Based Hyper-chaotic System

Dengwei Yan, Lidan Wang$^{(\boxtimes)}$, and Shukai Duan

School of Electronics and Information Engineering, Southwest University,
Chongqing 400715, China
ldwang@swu.edu.cn

Abstract. The memristor shares the best features of both memory function intrinsically and nonlinear characteristics, which is seen as a potential candidate to reduce system power consumption and circuit size. In this paper, a novel four-dimensional hyper-chaos system containing a memristor has been put forward, and the hyper-chaos characteristic of the system was verified through the Lyapunov index calculation. Moreover, Standard nonlinear diagnostic tools such as dissipation and system stability, power spectrum, time domain spectrum and Poincare map are employed to investigate its complex dynamic characteristics. Subsequently the system is simulated by the SPICE circuit. A fully good agreement is observed between Spice simulation results and the theoretical analysis, which verify the feasibility of the memristive hyper-chaotic system.

Keywords: Memristor · Hyper-chaotic system · Dynamic behavior
Circuit implementation

1 Introduction

In 2008, the Hewlett-Packard (HP) laboratory research team developed the first memristor [1] model, which the resistance is related to the charge or flux. The memristor exists encouraging applications in Computer Science [2], Bioengineering [3], Neural Networks [3], Electrical Engineering [4], and Communication Engineering [5].

The memristor, as an adjustable nonlinear element, is an easy to use nonlinear partial chaotic generator. Furthermore, the memristor has the characteristics of small volume and low power consumption, and it has become an ideal choice for nonlinear elements in the chaotic circuit, therefore, various kinds of chaotic systems based on memristors have been widely concerned by the researchers. Itoh and Chua [6], in 2008, derived two kinds of memristor chaotic oscillations by applying the flux-controlled piece-wise linear memristor model to replace the non-linear elements in Chua's circuit. Muthuswamy and Kokate [7] applied a piece-wise linear model of memristors to replace Chua's diodes and analyzed the dynamic characteristics of the system, which the results show that the chaotic characteristics are more complex than the classical Chua's circuits. Subsequently, Bharathwaj and Chua [8] proposed the simplest structure of the third-order memristive chaotic circuit so far. The key feature of the circuit is

© Springer International Publishing AG, part of Springer Nature 2018
T. Huang et al. (Eds.): ISNN 2018, LNCS 10878, pp. 364–371, 2018.
https://doi.org/10.1007/978-3-319-92537-0_42

the simple structure, which consists of an inductor, a capacitor and a memristor connected in series. The above researches have greatly promoted the development of the memristive chaotic circuits, which give us a detailed introduction about the new chaotic dynamical characteristics. How to better use the memristor non-linear and design various new chaotic circuits have become the focus.

The role played by the memristive hyper-chaotic system behavior will be clearly analyzed in the following. A novel hyper-chaotic system based on HP memristor model is proposed and the basic dynamic characteristics of the system are analyzed, such as the Lyapunov exponent and the dimension, dissipation and system stability, time domain spectrum and the Poincare section will be described in Sect. 2. The SPICE circuit of the system is established in Sect. 3. Finally, conclusions are drawn in Sect. 4.

2 A Hyper-chaotic System Based on Memristor

2.1 The Memristive Hyper-chaotic System Model

The new hyper-chaotic system is presented by the following autonomous nonlinear system of differential equations:

$$
\begin{aligned}
\dot{x} &= ay + bxz; \\
\dot{y} &= -cx + yz - w; \\
\dot{z} &= d - y^4; \\
\dot{w} &= -w + ef(-|x|);
\end{aligned}
\tag{1}
$$

where x, y, z and w are the states of the hyper-chaotic system. a, b, c, d and e are parameters. The function $f(\cdot)$ [9] refers to the charge of the memristor, and accurately indicated as follows:

$$
f(x) =
\begin{cases}
\dfrac{x - c_3}{R_{off}} & x < c_5, \\[2mm]
\dfrac{\sqrt{2kx + M^2(0)} - M(0)}{k} & c_5 \leq x < c_6, \\[2mm]
\dfrac{x - c_4}{R_{oN}} & x \geq c_6,
\end{cases}
\tag{2}
$$

where,

$$
c_3 = -\frac{(R_{off} - M(0))^2}{2k}, \quad c_4 = -\frac{(R_{on} - M(0))^2}{2k}, \quad c_5 = \frac{R_{off}^2 - M(0)^2}{2k},
$$
$$
c_6 = \frac{R_{on}^2 - M(0)^2}{2k}
\tag{3}
$$

And, x is the magnetic flux of the memristor, and the memristor model parameters are set as follows: $M(0) = 16000$, $R_{off} = 20$ kΩ, $R_{on} = 100$ Ω, $D = 10$ nm, $u_v = 10^{-14}$ m^2 s^{-1} v^{-1}, and the initial conditions $(x, y, z, w) = (0.1, 0.1, 0.1, 0.1)$ are chosen. One efficacious set of parameter values of the system which can generate chaotic dynamics behavior are $a = 55$, $b = 0.4$, $c = 5$, $d = 1$, $e = 10000$. Typical hyper-chaotic attractors are formed, which are shown in Fig. 1.

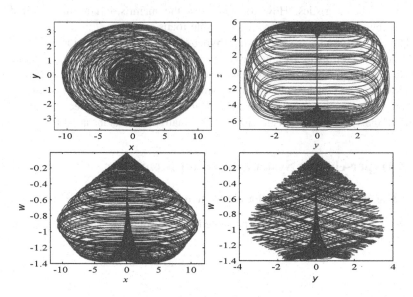

Fig. 1. Various projections of the chaotic attractor codified system (1)

2.2   The Lyapunov Exponents and the Lyapunov Dimension

The Lyapunov exponents of the system (1) are determined numerically, which are shown in Fig. 2. With the parameters chosen as $a = 55$, $b = 0.4$, $c = 5$, $d = 1$ and $e = 10000$, and the initial state chosen as $x(0) = (0.1, 0.1, 0.1, 0.1)$, the corresponding Lyapunov exponents are obtained as $L_1 = 0.045$, $L_2 = 0.043$, $L_3 = -0.034$, $L_4 = -1.004$. Therefore, the Lyapunov dimension of the system (1) is given by

$$d_L = j + (1/|L_{j+1}|) \sum_{i=1}^{j} L_i \approx 3.054 \tag{4}$$

We conclude that the Lyapunov dimension of the system is fractional, which further proves that the system is in a hyper-chaotic state.

2.3   Sensitivity to Initial Conditions and Power Spectrum

Sensitivity to initial conditions means that any arbitrarily small perturbations of the initial state of the system can lead to the significantly distant behavior of the future state of the chaotic system. This dependence on initial conditions in the system makes the

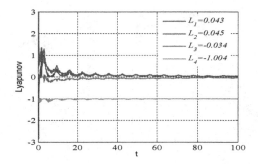

Fig. 2. Lyapunov exponents of the system (1)

long-term prediction impossible. Obtained time domain spectrum using ode45 function for $x = 0.1$ and $x = 0.100001$ have given in Fig. 3. It means that the evolution of the chaotic trajectories is very sensitive to initial conditions. Moreover, in the experimental observation, the power spectrum is given Fig. 4. A familiar feature of chaotic motion can be found that the spectrum is broadened with some broad peaks from the Fig. 4.

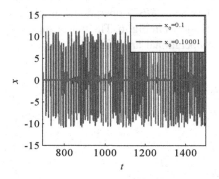

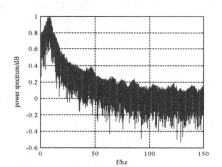

Fig. 3. Time domain waveform of the state variables $y(t)$

Fig. 4. Power spectrum

2.4 Poincare Map

Poincare map has laid a foundation for the understanding of the formation of attractors and the horseshoe mapping of the chaotic system, which is identified as a chaotic system if the point on the Poincare Map is a piece of dense point with fractal structure, on the contrary, it is not a chaotic system. The Poincare map of the system (1) is illustrated in Fig. 5. A conclusion can be drawn that the system has extremely rich dynamic characteristics because the map shows a continuous curve.

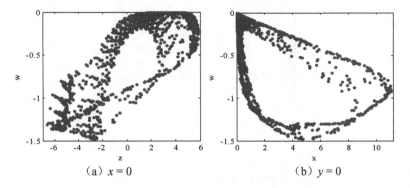

(a) $x = 0$ (b) $y = 0$

Fig. 5. Poincare section of the system (1)

3 The SPICE Circuit Implementation

A circuit is designed to validate hyper-chaotic characteristics of the system (1), which consists of four analog operation circuits, and the voltages at the nodes are marked as x, y, z and w corresponding to the states of system (1). The circuit is constructed of the memristor, multiplier, diodes, resistors, capacitors and $LM675$ operational amplifiers. The $SPICE$ simulation circuit of the system (1) is shown in Fig. 6. The power supply to the system is $Vcc = +30$ V, $V_{EE} = -30$ V. The operational amplifiers $U5$ and $U6$ are used to realize the following formula:

$$v_x = -\frac{1}{R_7 C_1} \int \left(-\frac{R_9 R_{11} R_6}{R_8 R_{10} R_{12}} v_y - \frac{R_2 R_4 R_6}{R_1 R_3 R_5} v_x v_z \right) dt \tag{5}$$

or equivalently,

$$\dot{v}_x = \frac{1}{R_7 C_1} \left(\frac{R_9 R_{11} R_6}{R_8 R_{10} R_{12}} v_y + \frac{R_2 R_4 R_6}{R_1 R_3 R_5} v_z v_x \right) \tag{6}$$

Compare with system (1) and set $R_1 = R_3 = R_5 = R_6 = R_8 = R_9 = R_{10} = R_{12} = 1$ KΩ, $R_2 = 55$ KΩ, $R_{11} = 0.4$ KΩ, $R_7 = 1$ MΩ, $C_1 = 1$ uF, and the Eq. (8) becomes $\dot{v}_x = 55y + 0.4xz$. Similarly, the operational amplifiers $U11$ and $U12$ are used to realize the formula:

$$v_y = -\frac{1}{R_{17} C_2} \int \left(\frac{R_{14} R_{16}}{R_{13} R_{15}} v_x + \frac{R_{24} R_{16}}{R_{23} R_{25}} v_w - \frac{R_{19} R_{21} R_{16}}{R_{18} R_{20} R_{22}} v_y v_z \right) dt \tag{7}$$

then lead to:

$$\dot{v}_y = \frac{1}{R_{17} C_2} \left(-\frac{R_{14} R_{16}}{R_{13} R_{15}} v_x - \frac{R_{24} R_{16}}{R_{23} R_{25}} v_w + \frac{R_{19} R_{21} R_{16}}{R_{18} R_{20} R_{22}} v_y v_z \right) \tag{8}$$

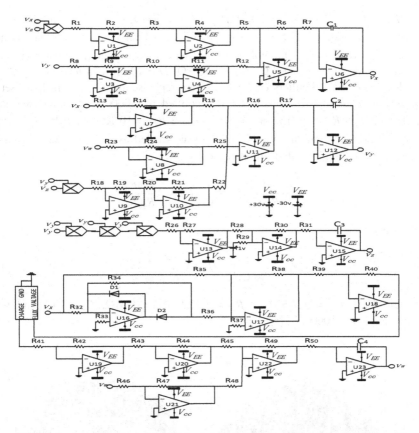

Fig. 6. Analog SPICE implementation of the memristive hyper-chaotic system (1)

Compare with system (1) and set $R_{13} = R_{15} = R_{18} = R_{19} = R_{20} = R_{21} = R_{22} = R_{23} = R_{24} = R_{25} = 1$ KΩ, $R_{14} = 5$ KΩ, $R_{17} = 1$ MΩ, $C_2 = 1$uF, and then get $\dot{v}_y = -x + yz$. Similarly, $\dot{v}_z = 1 - y^4$.

The operational amplifiers $U16$ and $U17$ are used to implement the absolute value circuit, where D120NQ045 diode models are used. When $v_x \leq 0$, D1 is conductive while D2 is cut-off, the inverting "$-$" port is virtually shortened. The output voltage of $U16$ is v_{U16}, and $U17$ is and adder, and the output voltage of $v_{U13} = -\frac{R_{38}}{R_{35}} v_x$. When $v_x \geq 0$, operational amplifiers $U16$ output voltage is less than zero, D2 is conductive while D1 is cut-off. As long as $U16$ is -0.7 v, D2 is turned on, and at this time $U16$ is equivalent to an inverting input of the proportional amplifier, and the output voltage of $U16$ is $v_{U16} = -\frac{R_{34}}{R_{32}} v_x$, the output voltage $v_{U17} = -(\frac{R_{38}}{R_{35}} v_x + \frac{R_{38}}{R_{36}} v_{U16})$, which $U17$ is an adder, namely: $v_{U17} = -\frac{R_{38}}{R_{35}} v_x + \frac{R_{34}R_{38}}{R_{36}R_{32}} v_x$. We can yield:

$$v_{U17} = \begin{cases} -\frac{R_{38}}{R_{35}} v_x + \frac{R_{25}R_{29}}{R_{23}R_{27}}, & v_x \geq 0 \\ -\frac{R_{38}}{R_{35}}, & v_x < 0 \end{cases} \tag{9}$$

When $R_{32} = R_{34} = R_{35} = R_{38} = 1$ KΩ, $R_{33} = R_{37} = 500\Omega$, $v_{U17} = |v_x|$, and the output voltage $v_{U18} = -\frac{R_{40}}{R_{39}}|v_x|$. Set $R_{39} = R_{40} = 1$ KΩ, and then $v_{U17} = -|v_x|$. The output voltage $U18$ is used as the input voltage of the memristor, the memristor parameters are set to $R_{on} = 100$ Ω, $R_{off} = 20$ kΩ, $M(0) = 16$ kΩ, $D = 10$ nm and $u_v = 10^{-14}$ m^2 s^{-1} v^{-1}. The operational amplifiers $U19$ and $U20$ are rephrase amplifiers, which are set to 100, and the charge of the memristor is amplified by 10000 times after two-stage amplification. Set $R_{41} = 100$ Ω, $R_{43} = 10$ Ω, $R_{42} = R_{44} = 10$ KΩ, we get:$v_{U20} = \frac{R_{42}R_{44}}{R_{41}R_{43}}$ $f(-|x|)$. Operational amplifiers $U17$ and $U18$ are treated as an adder and integrator, $U21$ is a reverse amplifier, the following holds

$$v_w = -\frac{1}{R_{50}C_3} \int (-\frac{R_{49}}{R_{45}}U20 + \frac{R_{49}R_{47}}{R_{48}R_{46}})dt; \tag{10}$$

or equivalently,

$$\dot{v}_w = \frac{R_{49}}{R_{50}C_3R_{45}}U20 - \frac{R_{49}R_{47}}{R_{48}R_{46}C_3}, \tag{11}$$

Substitute $R_{46} = R_{47} = R_{45} = R_{48} = R_{49} = 1$ KΩ, $R_{50} = 1$ MΩ, $C_4 = 1$ uF and v_{U20} obtain $\dot{v}_w = -w + 10000f(-|x|)$.

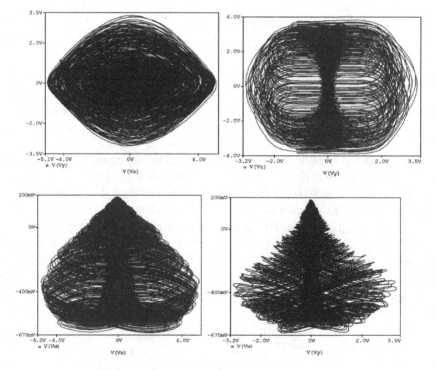

Fig. 7. SPICE simulation results of the system (1)

The *SPICE* simulation time is set to 200 s, and the maximum simulation step size is 0.05 s. Figure 7 shows the phase diagram of the analog realization of the memristive hyper-chaotic system by *SPICE*.

4 Conclusion

A novel memristor-based hyper-chaotic system is proposed and studied in this paper. A series of computer simulations have been presented, including the Lyapunov exponent spectrum, Power spectrum and Poincare map. The hyper-chaotic system is simulated by the *SPICE* circuit, and the simulation results and numerical analysis are consistent. This paper provides an experimental basis for further research on the application in speech secure communication and information processing.

References

1. Bu, S., Wang, B.: Improving the security of chaotic encryption by using a simple modulating method. Chaos, Solitons Fractals **19**(4), 919–924 (2004)
2. Gai, R., Xia, X., Chen, G.: Complex dynamics of systems under Delta-modulated feedback. IEEE Trans. Autom. Control **51**(12), 1888–1902 (2006)
3. Pershin, Y., Di Ventra, M.: Experimental demonstration of associative memory with memristive neural networks. Neural Netw. **23**(7), 881–886 (2010)
4. Shin, S., Kim, K., Kang, S.: Memristor applications for programmable analog ICs. IEEE Trans. Nanotechnol. **10**(2), 266–274 (2011)
5. Witrisal, K.: Memristor-based stored-reference receiver-the UWB solution. Electron. Lett. **45**(14), 713–714 (2009)
6. Itoh, M., Chua, L.: Memristor oscillators. Int. J. Bifurcat. Chaos **18**(11), 3183–3206 (2008)
7. Muthuswamy, B., Kokate, P.: Memristor-based chaotic circuits. IETE Tech. Rev. **26**(6), 415–426 (2009)
8. Bharathwaj, M., Chua, L.: Simplest chaotic circuit. Int. J. Bifurcat. Chaos **20**(05), 1567–1580 (2010)
9. Wang, L., Li, H., Duan, S., Huang, T., Wang, H.: Pavlov associative memory in a memristive neural network and its circuit implementation. Neurocomputing **171**, 23–29 (2016)

Lag Synchronization of Complex Networks via Decentralized Adaptive Control

Fan Yang and Nankun Mu[✉]

The Chongqing Key Laboratory of Nonlinear Circuits and Intelligent Information Processing, Southwest University, Chongqing 400715, People's Republic of China
nankun.mu@qq.com

Abstract. Take into account the fact that the transmission delay of communication channel and the traditional self-node time-varying delays generally coexist. A lag synchronization (LS) problem of the heterogeneous dynamical delayed complex networks (HDDCNs) by using a decentralized adaptive control (DAC) scheme is investigated in this paper. Besides this, the nodes are divided into clusters based on their dynamics characteristic, each cluster is considered as a whole. Firstly, several sufficient criteria are proposed to guarantee a lag synchronization. Secondly, we employ a DAC scheme to reduce the cost of control while achieving lag synchronization. Thirdly, one typical simulation is conducted to illustrate the correctness of the results that we obtained.

Keywords: Lag synchronization · Decentralized control
Adaptive control

1 Introduction

Synchronization/consensus, an interesting branch in the complex network field, is an important phenomenon in the investigations of dynamics behavior for complex networks. Hitherto, various types of synchronization have been proposed and studied, such as complete synchronization [27], lag synchronization [24,31], generalized synchronization [2,20,28], phase and imperfect phase synchronization, those were first presented in [6], and also projective synchronization [3,25,26]. The related control problems also have stirred ever-increasing research attention [8,10,22]. It not only can explain many biological phenomenon well, but also have potential application value in the areas of mechanical engineering [1], image processing [21], etc. Certainly, many important and interesting results have already obtained. See e.g. [14,19,33].

It is worth mentioning that, the synchronous behavior particularly relies on the time delay. As a critical factor, the time delay is of interest to many researchers recently in [7,9,14,15]. And there are many works investigated the synchronization problem with time-varying delays. For instance, in [16], the author has investigated a robust synchronization problem with the mixed time-varying delays which has also been analyzed in an exponential synchronization

© Springer International Publishing AG, part of Springer Nature 2018
T. Huang et al. (Eds.): ISNN 2018, LNCS 10878, pp. 372–379, 2018.
https://doi.org/10.1007/978-3-319-92537-0_43

problem [8]. However, majority of the work in network synchronization focus on the inner synchronization, i.e., the time delay in self-dynamics. In many practical situations, it is not only the inner delays but also the transmission delay, namely, the signal transmitted from the source at the time t is always received at the time $t + \sigma$. Therefore, the investigation of lag synchronization problem has very vital significance in practice and theory.

For several decades, in the network control problem, the classical control theory would suggest that feedback control inputs be applied to each network node to independently redirect its state to the desired trajectory. Unfortunately, researchers find that it often turns out being impossible to implement this requirement in actual applications. The reason is that the size of network which to be controlled is too large. So the decentralized control be proposed and applied with great advantage. The controllers only need to be added on a part of nodes. In [17], it made use of the decentralized event-triggered strategy to analysis a consensus problem. In addition, a robust decentralized control was proposed for a synchronization control problem in the study conducted by [5].

It is unrealistic to implement a controller continuously since that is extremely expensive. Therefore, discontinuous control technologies attracts more attention than continuous control, and have been widely used in practice. In [30], the authors investigated the synchronization problem of neural networks via a discontinuous Lyapunov functional approach. One of the discontinuous control technologies was used in [4] for a robust synchronization of a class of uncertain complex networks. And a periodical intermittent control technique is one of the popular strategies. With this control scheme, the control interval is assumed to be periodic, and each period T is composed of work hours δ and rest period $T - \delta$. It has become an enormously successful technology.

Besides this, adaptive strategy has also been used in practical applications [11,34]. In recent years, there have a lot of works about the adaptive control technology. For example, an adaptive control has been designed to deal with the uncertainties of system parametric in [12]. In [10], it adopted this control scheme for the problem of system disturbances. But unlike the above research, there is not much research on how to reduce control costs by using this technique.

Inspired by the above discussion, the purpose of this paper is to investigate the LS of HDDCNs (heterogeneous complex networks with non-identical delayed dynamical nodes), and presents several criteria to guarantee the LS. In addition, an intermittent DAC scheme has also been proposed to reduce control costs. Then, we introduce a valid controlled clustering options scheme to guide what kind of group should be priority control.

2   Problem Statement and Preliminaries

In this paper, for a network model that contains N non-identical dynamical nodes, consider the following complex networks, where each node represents an n-dimensional dynamical delayed system, assuming that all nodes can be divided into m clusters:

$$\begin{cases} \dot{x}_i(t) = f_k(\cdot) + c \sum_{q=1}^{m} \sum_{j \in C_q} b_{ij} \Gamma x_j(t) + u_i(t), & i \in \bar{C}, \\ \dot{x}_i(t) = f_k(\cdot) + c \sum_{q=1}^{m} \sum_{j \in C_q} b_{ij} \Gamma x_j(t), & i \in C - \bar{C}. \end{cases} \tag{1}$$

where $x_i(t) = (x_{i1}(t), x_{i2}(t), ..., x_{in}(t))^{\mathrm{T}} \in \mathbf{R}^n$ denotes the state vector of the i-th node. $f_k(\cdot) = f_k(x_i(t), \tau_k(t)) : \mathbf{R}^n \times \mathbf{R}^n \to \mathbf{R}^n$ are continuous vector-valued function, representing the evolution of the nodes in the k-th cluster while $\tau_k(t)$ denotes the time-varying delays, and the delays may be unknown but be known constraints. i.e., $0 \leq \tau_k(t) \leq \tau_k$. And c is the coupling strength. $B = (b_{ij}) \in \mathbf{R}^N$ denotes the coupling matrix which will be carefully defined later. $\Gamma = \mathrm{diag}(\gamma_1, \gamma_2, ..., \gamma_n) > 0$ denotes the inner-coupling matrix. $u_i(t) \in \mathbf{R}^n$ represents the external control that will be added on the i-th node, and its specific form will be introduced later. $C_k = \{r_{k-1} + 1, ..., r_k\}$ indicates the index set of all the nodes in the k-th cluster, and $r_{k-1} < r_k$, where $r_0 = 0$, $r_m = N$, $k \in \Re = \{1, ..., m\}$. For convenience, we suppose $\bar{C}$ denotes the clusters that being selected and controlled to achieve the LS of the decentralized-controlled HDDCN (1), and then $C - \bar{C}$ denotes the rest of the clusters.

In this paper, we pay attention to using the DAC scheme to drive the network (1) to the LS. For this purpose, we give some definitions, propositions and lemma about the LS of a dynamical network.

Definition 1. *The synchronization error $e_{ik}(t, \sigma)$ denotes $x_i(t) - s_k(t - \sigma)$, $i \in C_k$ and $k \in \Re$. $\sigma > 0$ is the transmission delay and $s_k(t - \sigma)$ denotes the synchronous state in the cluster. $s(t) = (s_1(t), s_2(t), ... s_m(t))$ is called the expected lag synchronous state of network (1).*

Definition 2. *A LS of the network which has been divided into m clusters is realizable iff any node $i \in C_k$, $k \in \Re$ have $\lim_{t \to +\infty} \|e_{ik}(t, \sigma)\| = 0$ and $\lim_{t \to +\infty} \|s_k(t) - s_j(t)\| \neq 0$, $j \neq k$ holds.*

Definition 3. *Let $E^k(t) = (E_1^k(t), E_2^k(t), ..., E_n^k(t))^{\mathrm{T}}$ denotes the LS errors, and for $k, j \in \Re$, have $E_i^k(t) = \sqrt{\frac{1}{r_k - r_{k-1}} \sum_{j \in C_k} \|e_{jk,i}(t, \sigma)\|^2}$.*

Proposition 1. *Assume that the coupling matrix $B = (b_{ij}) \in \mathbf{R}^N$ of network (1) has the following form:*

$$B = \begin{pmatrix} B_{11} & \cdots & B_{1m} \\ \vdots & \ddots & \vdots \\ B_{m1} & \cdots & B_{mm} \end{pmatrix}.$$

Each block matrices $B_{uv} = (b_{ij}) \in \mathbf{R}^{r_u \times r_v} (u, v \in \Re)$ has the same sum of row, i.e., there are some constants $\beta_{uv}, u, v \in \Re$, so that $\sum_{j \in C_v} b_{ij} = \beta_{uv}, i \in C_u$. And for $i = 1, 2, ..., N$, have $\sum_{j=1}^{N} b_{ij} = 0$.

Under Proposition 1, the lag synchronous form of a network with cluster characteristic can be described as follows:

$$\dot{s}_k(t) = f_k(\cdot) + c \sum_{q=1}^{m} \beta_{kp} \Gamma s_q(t). \tag{2}$$

where $f_k(\cdot) = f_k(s_k(t), \tau_k(t))$.

Clearly, the LS states are sets of un-decoupled trajectories instead of decoupled ones, which is different from mostly previous work in [18, 23, 29].

Proposition 2. *Suppose there are some constants L_k^0 and $L_k^\tau \geq 0$, so that for any $x(t), y(t) \in \mathbf{R}^n$ and $k \in \Re$, the vector-valued function $f_k(\cdot)$ have the following inequality holds:*

$$S_t^{\mathrm{T}} F_k(\cdot) \leq L_k^0 S_t^{\mathrm{T}} \Gamma S_t + L_k^\tau (x^{\tau_k}(t) - y^{\tau_k}(t))^{\mathrm{T}} \Gamma (x^{\tau_k}(t) - y^{\tau_k}(t)),$$

where S_t denotes $x(t) - y(t)$, $F_k(\cdot) = f_k(x(t), \tau_k(t)) - f_k(y(t), \tau_k(t))$, and $x^{\tau_k}(t) = x(t - \tau_k(t))$, $y^{\tau_k}(t) = y(t - \tau_k(t))$.

Lemma 1. *[32] The linear matrix inequality as follow:*

$$\begin{pmatrix} Q(x) & Z(x) \\ Z(x)^{\mathrm{T}} & R(x) \end{pmatrix} < 0,$$

where $Q(x) = Q(x)^{\mathrm{T}}$, $Z(x)$ is a suitable-dimensions matrix, and $R(x) = R(x)^{\mathrm{T}}$, can be represented by one of the following situations:

(1) $Q(x) < 0, R(x) - Z(x)^{\mathrm{T}} Q(x)^{-1} Z(x) < 0$;

(2) $R(x) < 0, Q(x) - Z(x) R(x)^{-1} Z(x)^{\mathrm{T}} < 0$.

3   Model Description

A DAC scheme with intermittent control effect is proposed to realize the LS of the HDDCN (1). The controllers for the LS are designed as:

$$u_i(t) = \begin{cases} -cd_k(t)\Gamma e_{ik}(t, \sigma), & t \in [\omega T, (\omega + \theta)T], i \in \bar{C}, \\ 0, & \text{otherwise}, \end{cases} \tag{3}$$

and for $t \in [\omega T, (\omega + \theta)T]$, $\omega = 0, 1, 2, \cdots$, under the adaptive laws, we have:

$$\dot{d}_k(t) = h_k \sum_{i \in C_k} e_{ik}(t, \sigma)^{\mathrm{T}} \Gamma e_{ik}(t, \sigma), \tag{4}$$

where the control rate $\theta = \delta/T$ denotes the ratio of the control width δ to the control period T. Then for the cluster C_k, $d_k(t)$ denotes the adaptive intermittent feedback control gain. And for $k = 1, 2, ..., l$, $d_k(0) \geq 0, k = 1, 2, ..., l$ represents the initial conditions. l is the number of the clusters which is rearranged and controlled for the LS of the HDDCN, by using the selection scheme which has been proposed in [13]. The positive constant $h_k > 0$ is relatively small. Without loss of generality, we assume that the positive constant $d_k(t_\omega^-) = \lim_{t \to t_\omega^-} d_k(t)$ exists and $d_k((\omega + 1)T) = d_k(t_\omega^-)$, where $t_\omega = (\omega + \theta)T$.

Clearly, the control time of controllers (3) is cyclical, and each period consists of time of work and breaks. As a result, the control behavior is intermittent rather than continuous, and it can reduce the cost of control.

From the control law (3) and the (1), the following error dynamical system $\dot{e}_{ik}(t, \sigma)$ is obtained:

$$
\begin{cases}
\tilde{f}_k^{\tau_k}(\cdot) + c \sum\limits_{q=1}^{m} \sum\limits_{j \in C_q} b_{ij} \Gamma e_{jq}(t, \sigma) - c d_k \Gamma e_{ik}(t, \sigma), \\
\qquad\qquad\qquad\qquad t \in [\omega T, (\omega + \theta)T], i \in \bar{C}, \\
\tilde{f}_k^{\tau_k}(\cdot) + c \sum\limits_{q=1}^{m} \sum\limits_{j \in C_q} b_{ij} \Gamma e_{jq}(t, \sigma), \qquad \text{otherwise.}
\end{cases}
\tag{5}
$$

where $\tilde{f}_k^{\tau_k}(\cdot) = f_k(x_i(t), \tau_k(t)) - f_k(s_k(t - \sigma), \tau_k(t))$.

Obviously, if the dynamic error system (5) has a globally exponentially stable zero solution, then the global LS is achievable for the decentralized-controlled HDDCN (1).

We define a block diagonal matrix $G = \text{diag}(G_{11}, ..., G_{mm}) \in \mathbf{R}^{N \times N}$, for $k \in \Re$, let $r_0 = 0$, and for each $i \in C_k$, let $a_i^k = \sum_{j \in C_k}(b_{ij} + b_{ji})$, $\xi_i^k = \sum_{j=1}^{N} b_{ji}$, $A_k = \text{diag}\left(a_{r_{k-1}+1}^k, ..., a_{r_k}^k\right)$ and $\Xi_k = \text{diag}\left(\xi_{r_{k-1}+1}^k, ..., \xi_{r_k}^k\right)$. Let $\Pi_k = \lambda_{\max}(B_{kk}^s + \frac{1}{2}\Xi_k - \frac{1}{2}A_k + \frac{L_k^0}{c})$, where $B_{kk}^s = \frac{1}{2}(B_{kk} + B_{kk}^{\mathrm{T}})$.

Theorem 1. *Suppose $a_1^0 > q_1/(2\lambda_{\min}(\Gamma))$, and there have l clusters being controlled such that the condition holds. Under Propositions 1 and 2, if*

$$
\Pi_k < -\frac{a_1^0}{c}, l + 1 \leq k \leq m,
\tag{6}
$$

$$
1 - \frac{\phi(a_1^0)}{p_1 + p_2} < \theta < 1,
\tag{7}
$$

where $p_1 = 2a_1^0 \lambda_{\min}(\Gamma)$, $p_2 = 2c\lambda_{\max}(G)\lambda_{\max}(\Gamma)$, $q_1 = 2(\max_{1 \leq k \leq m} L_k^\tau)\lambda_{\max}(\Gamma)$. $\phi(a_1^0) = \lambda > 0$ denotes the unique solution of the equation $\lambda - p_1 + q_1 e^{\lambda\tau} = 0$, which is obtained by substituting $a_1 = a_1^0$ into the equation. Then, under the discontinuous DAC strategy as mentioned above, the LS of the decentralized controlled HDDCN (1) is reliable.

Proof. In the ensuing proof process, $\omega = 0, 1, 2, ...$.

A piecewise Lyapunov candidate function is constructed as follows:

$$
W(t) = \frac{1}{2} \sum_{k=1}^{m} \sum_{i \in C_k} e_{ik}^{\mathrm{T}}(t, \sigma)e_{ik}(t, \sigma) + \frac{1}{2}\Psi(t) \sum_{k=1}^{l} c e^{-p_1 t} \frac{(d_{k(t)} - d_k^*)^2}{h_k}
\tag{8}
$$

where for $k = 1, 2, ..., l$, the constants d_k^* are positive, and the piecewise function $\Psi(\cdot)$ is defined by us as:

$$\Psi(s) = \begin{cases} 1, & s \in [-\tau, 0], \\ e^{p_1 \omega T}, & s \in [\omega T, (\omega + 1)T), \end{cases}$$

With Propositions 1, and 2, calculate the time derivative of W (t) along the trajectory of (5) as follows.

When $t \in [\omega T, (\omega + \theta)T]$, with (8) and Lemma 1, we can deduce that

$$\dot{W}(t) \leq -p_1 W(t) + q_1 \left(\sup_{t-\tau \leq s \leq t} W(s) \right).$$

Similarly, when $t \in [(\omega + \theta)T, (\omega + 1)T]$, one has

$$\dot{W}(t) \leq p_2 W(t) + q_1 \left(\sup_{t-\tau \leq s \leq t} W(s) \right).$$

The condition (7) means

$$\dot{W}(t) \leq \left(\sup_{-\tau \leq s \leq 0} W(s) \right) e^{-\varpi t}, t \geq 0,$$

where $\varpi = [\lambda - \theta(1 - \theta)]$.

Therefore, the proof is completed. Based on this Theorem 1, the LS for the network (1) is realizable.

4   Conclusion

The lag synchronization (LS) of HDDCNs via DAC is investigated in this paper. We design and generalize a DAC scheme from the synchronization to the LS involving both the inner time delays and the transmission delay σ. Meanwhile, we regard each cluster as a whole in the investigation of the LS problem. The expected lag synchronization states are selected as a set of the un-decoupled trajectories. By making some mild propositions, the main theorem and the criteria is obtained for the LS, and the results demonstrate the correctness of the DAC control scheme that we proposed.

Acknowledgments. This work is supported by National Key Research and Development Program of China (Grant no. 2016YFB0800601), Natural Science Foundation of China (Grant no. 61472331, 61772434).

References

1. Aghababa, M., Aghababa, H.: Robust synchronization of a chaotic mechanical system with nonlinearities in control inputs. Nonlinear Dyn. **73**(1–2), 363–376 (2013)
2. Bao, H., Cao, J.: Finite-time generalized synchronization of nonidentical delayed chaotic systems. Nonlinear Anal.: Model. Control **21**, 306–324 (2016)
3. Bao, H., Cao, J.: Projective synchronization of fractionalorder memristor-based neural networks. Neural Netw. **63**, 1–9 (2015)
4. Barajas-Ramírez, J.G.: Robust synchronization of a class of uncertain complex networks via discontinuous control. Comput. Math. Appl. **64**(5), 956–964 (2012)
5. Bechlioulis, C.P., Rovithakis, G.A.: Decentralized robust synchronization of unknown high order nonlinear multi-agent systems with prescribed transient and steady state performance. IEEE Trans. Autom. Control **62**(1), 123–134 (2016)
6. Boccaletti, S., Kurths, J., Osipov, G., Valladares, D.L., Zhou, C.S.: The synchronization of chaotic systems. Phys. Rep. **366**(1), 1–101 (2002)
7. Cai, G., Jiang, S., Cai, S., Tian, L.: Cluster synchronization of overlapping uncertain complex networks with time-varying impulse disturbances. Nonlinear Dyn. **80**(1), 503–513 (2015)
8. Cheng, J., Park, J., Liu, Y., Liu, Z., Tang, L.: Finite-time h_∞ fuzzy control of nonlinear markovian jump delayed systems with partly uncertain transition descriptions. Fuzzy Sets Syst. **314**, 99–115 (2017)
9. Cheng, J., Park, J., Zhang, L., Zhu, Y.: An asynchronous operation approach to event-triggered control for fuzzy Markovian jump systems with general switching policies. IEEE Trans. Fuzzy Syst. **pp**(99), 1 (2016)
10. He, W., Chen, Y., Yin, Z.: Adaptive neural network control of an uncertain robot with full-state constraints. IEEE Trans. Cybern. **46**(3), 620–629 (2016)
11. He, W., Ge, S.: Vibration control of a flexible beam with output constraint. IEEE Trans. Ind. Electron. **62**(8), 5023–5030 (2015)
12. He, W., Zhang, S., Ge, S.: Robust adaptive control of a thruster assisted position mooring system. Automatica **50**(7), 1843–1851 (2014)
13. Hu, C., Jiang, H.: Cluster synchronization for directed community networks via pinning partial schemesm. Chaos Solitons Fractals **45**(11), 1368–1377 (2012)
14. Karimi, H.: A sliding mode approach to h_∞ synchronization of master-slave time-delay systems with Markovian jumping parameters and nonlinear uncertainties. J. Franklin Inst. **349**(4), 1480–1496 (2012)
15. Karimi, H., Gao, H.: New delay-dependent exponential h_∞ synchronization for uncertain neural networks with mixed time delays. IEEE Trans. Syst. Man Cyberne. Part B Cybern. **40**(1), 173–185 (2010)
16. Karimi, H., Luo, N.: Robust synchronization and fault detection of uncertain master-slave systems with mixed time-varying delays and nonlinear perturbations. Int. J. Control Autom. Syst. **9**(4), 671–680 (2011)
17. Li, H., Chen, G., Dong, Z., Xia, D.: Consensus analysis of multiagent systems with second-order nonlinear dynamics and general directed topology. Inf. Sci. **370**(C), 598–622 (2016)
18. Liu, X., Chen, T.: Synchronization of linearly coupled networks with delays via aperiodically intermittent pinning control. IEEE Trans. Neural Netw. Learn. Syst. **26**(10), 2396–2407 (2015)
19. Lu, W., Chen, T.: Cluster synchronization in networks of coupled nonidentical dynamical systems. Chaos: Interdisc. J. Nonlinear Sci. **20**(1), 013120 (2010)

20. Ouannas, A., Odibat, Z.: Generalized synchronization of different dimensional chaotic dynamical systems in discrete time. Nonlinear Dyn. **81**, 765–771 (2015)
21. Prakash, M., Balasubramaniam, P., Lakshmanan, S.: Synchronization of markovian jumping inertial neural networks and its applications in image encryption. Neural Netw. **83**, 86–93 (2016)
22. Shi, L., Zhu, H., Zhong, S., Shi, K., Cheng, J.: Cluster synchronization of linearly coupled complex networks via linear and adaptive feedback pinning control. Nonlinear Dyn. **88**(2), 859–870 (2017)
23. Su, H., Rong, Z., Chen, M.: Decentralized adaptive pinning control for cluster synchronization of complex dynamical networks. IEEE Trans. Cybern. **43**(1), 394–399 (2013)
24. Sun, W., Wang, S.: Lag synchronization via pinning control between two coupled networks. Nonlinear Dyn. **79**, 2659–2666 (2015)
25. Vaidyanathan, S.: Generalized projective synchronization of vaidyanathan chaotic system via active and adaptive control. In: Vaidyanathan, S., Volos, C. (eds.) Advances and Applications in Nonlinear Control Systems. SCI, vol. 635, pp. 97–116. Springer, Cham (2016). https://doi.org/10.1007/978-3-319-30169-3_6
26. Vaidyanathan, S., Pakiriswamy, S.: Generalized projective synchronization of a novel chaotic system with a quartic nonlinearity via adaptive control. In: Vaidyanathan, S., Volos, C. (eds.) Advances and Applications in Chaotic Systems. SCI, vol. 636, pp. 427–446. Springer, Cham (2016). https://doi.org/10.1007/978-3-319-30279-9_18
27. Vaidyanathan, S., Sampath, S.: Complete synchronization of hyperchaotic systems via novel sliding mode control. In: Taher Azar, A., Vaidyanathan, S. (eds.) Advances in Chaos Theory and Intelligent Control. SFSC, vol. 337, pp. 327–347. Springer, Cham (2016). https://doi.org/10.1007/978-3-319-30340-6_14
28. Wang, X., Fang, J., Mao, H., Dai, A.: Finite-time global synchronization for a class of Markovian jump complex networks with partially unknown transition rates under feedback control. Nonlinear Dyn. **79**, 47–61 (2015)
29. Wang, Y., Cao, J.: Cluster synchronization in nonlinearly coupled delayed networks of non-identical dynamic systems. Nonlinear Anal.: Real World Appl. **14**(1), 842–851 (2013)
30. Wu, Z.G., Ju, H.P., Su, H., Chu, J.: Discontinuous lyapunov functional approach to synchronization of time-delay neural networks using sampled-data. Nonlinear Dyn. **69**(4), 2021–2030 (2012)
31. Wu, Z., Fu, X.: Cluster lag synchronization in community networks via linear pinning control with local intermittent effects. Phys. A **395**, 487–498 (2014)
32. Xia, W., Cao, J.: Pinning synchronization of delayed dynamical networks via periodically intermittent control. Chaos **19**(1), 013120 (2009)
33. Zhang, J., Ma, Z., Zhang, G.: Cluster synchronization induced by one-node clusters in networks with asymmetric negative couplings. Chaos: Interdiscip. J. Nonlinear Sci. **23**(4), 043128 (2013)
34. Zhao, Z., He, W., Yin, Z., Zhang, J.: Spatial trajectory tracking control of a fully actuated helicopter in known static environment. J. Intell. Robot. Syst. **85**(1), 127–144 (2017)

Crossbar-Based Hamming Associative Memory with Binary Memristors

Mikhail S. Tarkov[✉]

Rzhanov Institute of Semiconductor Physics SB RAS, Novosibirsk, Russia
tarkov@isp.nsc.ru

Abstract. The Hamming associative memory hardware realization based on the use of a crossbar with binary memristors (binary resistors with memory) and CMOS circuitry is proposed. It is shown that the binary memristors crossbar realizes the Hamming network first layer properties according to which the first layer neuron output signal is non-negative. This signal is maximal for a neuron with the reference vector closest to the input vector. For a given reference vector dimension, the relationship between the maximum and minimum binary memristors resistances is obtained. It guarantees the Hamming network first layer correct operation. The simulation in the LTSPICE system of the proposed Hamming memory scheme confirmed its operability.

Keywords: Associative Hamming memory · Memristor · Crossbar
CMOS-technology · LTSPICE

1 Introduction

An artificial neural network typically uses a weighting coefficients matrix to represent a set of neurons layer synapses. Accordingly, the computation of the layer neurons activations can be considered as the weighting matrix multiplication by the input layer signals vector. The neural network hardware implementation requires a lot of memory for storing the weights matrix of the neurons layer and it is expensive.

Solving this problem is simplified by using the device called "memristor" as a memory cell. The memristor was predicted theoretically in 1971 by Chua [1]. The first physical implementation of the memristor was demonstrated in 2008 by a laboratory from Hewlett Packard as a thin film structure TiO_2 [2]. The memristor has many advantages, such as non-volatile storage media, low power consumption, high density integration and excellent scalability. The unique ability of retaining the traces of the device excitation makes it an ideal candidate for the implementation of electronic synapses in neural networks [3].

The memristor behaves like a synapse: it "remembers" the total electric charge passed through it [4]. The memristor-based memory can reach a very high integration degree of 100 Gbits/cm^2, several times higher than that based on flash memory technology [5]. These unique properties make the memristor a promising device for creating massively parallel neuromorphic systems [6–8].

Binary memristors [9, 10], based on the mechanism of switching filaments, are distributed more widely than the analog memristors, the materials for which they are

T. Huang et al. (Eds.): ISNN 2018, LNCS 10878, pp. 380–387, 2018.
https://doi.org/10.1007/978-3-319-92537-0_44

encountered much less often and require a more complex processing. When switching a filament, the memristors can have either high resistance (HR) or low resistance (LR). Thus, we can store only 1 or 0 (−1) when switching the filament of a binary memristor. Binary memristors are much more stable for statistical fluctuations compared to analog memristors. This is due to the fact that HR is much higher than LR despite the large number of fluctuations in resistances.

The memristor resistance (memristance) (Fig. 1) can be represented [2] as

$$M(p) = p \cdot R_{on} + (1 - p) \cdot R_{off}$$

where $0 \leq p \leq 1$ is the doping front position relative to the total film thickness h of TiO$_2$, R_{on} is the minimum memristance, R_{off} is the maximum memristance. When a voltage V above a certain threshold V_{th} is applied to the memristor, its memristance decreases due to the expansion of the doped band D, which has a low resistance, and reducing zone U of pure oxide having a high resistance. Accordingly, the memritance is increased by applying a voltage V lower $-V_{th}$ due to the zone D reduction and the zone U expansion. After the voltage switching off, the current memristance is preserved.

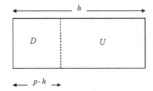

Fig. 1. Memristor structure: D is the low resistance region, U is the high resistance region

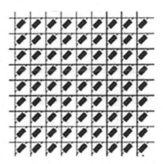

Fig. 2. Example of memristor crossbar

An example of the memristor crossbar which can be used to implement the weighting coefficient matrix of a neurons layer is shown in Fig. 2. The weighing factors are set by the memristor conductivities located at the wires intersection. The memristor crossbar is interesting for the implementation of coupling matrices in neural networks, since it can provide a large number of signal links and calculate a weighed combination of input signals. The crossbar vertical bars are fed with the input signal vector components. Each crossbar horizontal bus allows us to calculate the scalar product of the input signals vector by a vector of weights given by the conductivities of the corresponding crossbar row memristors.

The Hamming associative memory hardware realization based on the use of a crossbar with binary memristors (binary resistors with memory) and CMOS circuitry is proposed in this paper. The approach proposed to constructing the associative Hamming memory makes it possible to halve the number of memristors used in comparison with the implementation proposed in [11].

2 Programming of Binary Memristors Crossbar

The setting of the crossbar binary memristors resistances is carried out by the technique proposed in [10]. Let us consider the memristor setting in the state +1 (low resistance) using the crossbar fragment example shown in Fig. 3. To be certain, consider the memristor M11. To make the memristor resistance low, we will make the voltage settings shown in the Table 1.

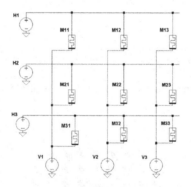

Fig. 3. Crossbar fragment

Table 1. The voltages for setting the low resistance of memristor M11 (Fig. 3)

H1	H2	H3	V1	V2	V3
+7	0	0	−7	+7	+7

The experiment in LTSPICE shows that, with such voltage settings, the memristor M11 resistance sets to a minimum value (100 Ω) for 2 ns. The memristors M12 and M13 resistances remain unchanged, and the remaining memristors (M21, M22, M23, M31, M32, M33) resistances change insignificantly (no more than 0.5%). To set the memristor M11 to the state −1 (high resistance 100 kΩ), we change the polarity of the Table 1 voltages. In this case the setting time is increased to 5 ns.

3 Hamming Network and Its Implementation Using the Memristor Crossbar

In the Hamming network [12], the first layer neurons calculate the Hamming distances between the vector x supplied to the network input and the weight vectors (reference vectors) x^i, $i = 1, 2, \ldots, P$ of the layer neurons, P is the reference vectors number. The Hamming distance $d_H(x^i, x)$ between the vector x and reference vector x^i is the number of noncoinciding components of these vectors. The output signal values of the first layer neurons are determined by the formula

$$y_i = 1 - \frac{d_H(x^i, x)}{N} \tag{1}$$

where N is the vector x components number. It follows from (1) that $y_i \in [0, 1]$, and for $x = x^i$ the equality $y_i = 1$ (the maximum possible value) is satisfied.

The signals y_i become the initial states of the second layer neurons functioning in accordance with the WTA ("Winner takes all") principle. This layer determines the winner among the first layer neurons, i.e. a neuron which output signal is close to 1. This neuron corresponds to a reference vector x^i with the minimum Hamming distance $d_H(x^i, x)$ to the input vector x.

We put into one-to-one correspondence to the Hamming network reference vector x^i, $i = 1, \ldots, P$ the weight vector w^i given by the crossbar row memristors conductances $g_H > g_L$ according to the rule

$$w^i_j = \begin{cases} g_L, & \text{if } x^i_j = -1 \\ g_H, & \text{if } x^i_j = 1 \end{cases}$$

Let w be an arbitrary vector of dimension N with components g_L and g_H.

Theorem 1

$$(x^i, w^i) - (x^i, w) \geq g_H - g_L > 0 \text{ if } w \neq w^i.$$

Proof. Let m components of the vector w^i be equal to g_H and n components of the same vector are equal to g_L, $m + n = N$. According to the vector x^i definition, we have $(x^i, w^i) = mg_H - ng_L$.

To obtain a vector $w \neq w^i$ we need to replace $k \in \{1, \ldots, m\}$ components g_H in w^i by g_L and/or $l \in \{1, \ldots, n\}$ components g_L by g_H, $k + l \in \{1, \ldots, m + n\}$. Then we have

$$(x^i, w) = (x^i, w^i) - (k + l)(g_H - g_L)$$

and

$$(x^i, w^i) - (x^i, w) = (k + l)(g_H - g_L) \geq g_H - g_L > 0$$

because $g_H > g_L$. Theorem 1 is proved.

It follows from theorem 1 that the computations according to the formula (1) can be replaced by calculating the scalar product (x, w^i) which can be realized on a memristor crossbar. The memristor crossbar with the above properties does not realize the formula (1) of the Hamming network first layer, but it realizes the layer required property: a neuron with a weight vector w^i implemented by the i-th crossbar row gives the maximum output signal $y_i = (x^i, w^i)$ for the reference vector x^i.

We call vector w nontrivial if, at least, one of its components is equal to g_H. Then $(x^i, w) \geq g_H - (N - 1)g_L$. From here we have

Theorem 2

$(x^i, w) \geq 0$ for the nontrivial w if $g_L \leq g_H/(N - 1)$.

Theorem 2 specifies the restriction on the ratio between the maximum g_H and minimum g_L conductances of the crossbar memristors, which ensures the Hamming network first layer output signal non-negativity.

4 The Hamming Network Implementation Example

The symbols L, T, and X images with the pixel size 3×3 are presented in Fig. 4. These images can be described by the reference vectors (progressive scan of images).

$$L = (1, -1, -1, 1, -1, -1, 1, 1, 1)$$
$$T = (1, 1, 1, -1, 1, -1, -1, 1, -1)$$
$$X = (1, -1, 1, -1, 1, -1, 1, -1, 1)$$

where 1 corresponds to the white pixel and -1 corresponds to the black one.

These images memorization in the Hamming memory is realized by the memristor crossbar shown in Fig. 5, where each crossbar row corresponds to one of the images. In the crossbar, the reference vector component 1 corresponds to a memristor with a minimum resistance of $R_H = 100\ \Omega$ (maximum conductivity $g_H = 1/R_H$), and component -1 corresponds to a memristor with a maximum resistance of $R_L = 100\ k\Omega$ (minimum conductivity $g_L = 1/R_L$). Denoting the weight vectors by w^L, w^T and w^X, we can write the crossbar rows output signals (Fig. 5) as

$$SumL = (x, w^L)$$
$$SumT = (x, w^T)$$
$$SumX = (x, w^X)$$

where x is an input signals vector which components are the voltages of 0.3 V (corresponding to 1) and -0.3 V (corresponding to -1).

The first layer input voltages are presented for the image T in Table 2. The voltages absolute value is selected below the binary memristor threshold in order to exclude the possibility of changing the crossbar memristors conductivity during its operation.

The Hamming network second layer (Fig. 6) is implemented on the CMOS technology basis [13] and converts the input signal vector according to the WTA ("Winner

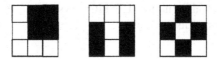

Fig. 4. The character images *L*, *T*, and *X* with 3 × 3 pixels

Fig. 5. The first layer of the Hamming network

Table 2. The first layer input voltages for image *T*

V1	V2	V3	V4	V5	V6	V7	V8	V9
0.3	0.3	0.3	−0.3	0.3	−0.3	−0.3	0.3	−0.3

takes all") principle, i.e. the maximum input component corresponds to 1 at the layer output (high voltage, for the circuit in Fig. 6 it is about 4.5 V), and the remaining input components are put in correspondence with 0 (the voltage close to zero, for the circuit in Fig. 6 it is about 10^{-4} V).

For example, in Fig. 5, $SumT > SumL$ and $SumT > SumX$. In this case, on the second layer output (Fig. 6), we obtain $OutT \approx 4.5$ V and $OutL = OutX \approx 10^{-4}$ V. The Hamming memory scheme (Figs. 5, 6) is implemented in the LTspice modeling

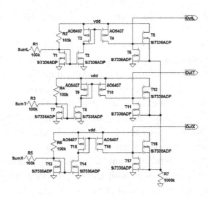

Fig. 6. The second layer of the Hamming network (vdd = +7 volts)

system [14]. The simulation in the LTSPICE system of the proposed Hamming memory scheme confirmed its operability.

5 Conclusion

The Hamming associative memory hardware realization based on the use of a binary memristors crossbar and CMOS circuitry is proposed. The computations in the Hamming network first layer we realized as a scalar product of the input vector and the reference vectors stored in the memristor crossbar. The maximum binary memristor resistance corresponds to the stored reference vector component value −1, and the minimum resistance corresponds to the value +1. It is shown that the binary memristors crossbar realizes the Hamming network first layer properties according to which the output first layer neuron signal is non-negative. This signal is maximal for a neuron with the reference vector closest to the input vector. For a given reference vector dimension, the relationship between the maximum and minimum binary memristors resistances is obtained. It guarantees the Hamming network first layer correct operation. The approach proposed to constructing the associative Hamming memory makes it possible to halve the number of memristors used in comparison with the implementation proposed earlier. The simulation in the LTSPICE system of the proposed Hamming memory scheme confirmed its operability.

References

1. Chua, L.: Memristor – the missing circuit element. IEEE Trans. Circ. Theory **18**, 507–519 (1971)
2. Strukov, D.B., Snider, G.S., Stewart, D.R., Williams, R.S.: The missing memristor found. Nature **453**, 80–83 (2008)
3. Pershin, Y., Di Ventra, M.: Experimental demonstration of associative memory with memristive neural networks. Neural Netw. **23**(7), 881–886 (2010)
4. Chua, L.: Resistance switching memories are memristors. Appl. Phys. A: Mater. Sci. Process. **102**(4), 765–783 (2011)
5. Ho, Y., Huang, G.M., Li, P.: Nonvolatile memristor memory: device characteristics and design applications. In: Proceedings of International Conference on Computer-Aided Design (ICCAD), pp. 485–490 (2009)
6. Jo, S.H., Chang, T., Ebong, I., Bhadviya, B.B., Mazumder, P., Lu, W.: Nanoscale memristor device as synapse in neuromorphic systems. Nano Lett. **10**(4), 1297–1301 (2010)
7. Kavehei, O.: Memristive devices and circuits for computing, memory, and neuromorphic applications. Ph.D. thesis. The University of Adelaida, Australia (2011)
8. Lehtonen, E.: Memristive Computing. University of Turku, Finland (2012)
9. Truong, S.N., Ham, S.-J., Min, K.-S.: Neuromorphic crossbar circuit with nanoscale filamentary-switching binary memristors for speech recognition. Nanoscale Res. Lett. **9**, 629 (2014). http://www.nanoscalereslett.com/content/9/1/629
10. Yakopcic, C., Taha, T.M., Subramanyam, G., Pino, R.E.: Memristor SPICE model and crossbar simulation based on devices with nanosecond switching time. In: Proceedings of International Joint Conference on Neural Networks, Dallas, Texas, USA, 4–9 August 2013 (2013)

11. Zhu, X., Yang, X., Wu, C., Wu, J., Yi, X.: Hamming network circuits based on CMOS/memristor hybrid design. IEICE Electron. Express **10**(12), 1–9 (2013)
12. Lippmann, R.: An introduction to computing with neural nets. IEEE ASSP Mag. **4**, 4–22 (1987)
13. Lazzaro, J., Ryckebusch, S., Mahowald, M.A., Mead, C.A.: Winner-take-all networks of O(n) complexity. In: Advances in Neural Information Processing Systems, pp. 703–711 (1989)
14. LTspice XVII. http://www.linear.com/designtools/software/#LTspice

Continuous Attractors of 3-D Discrete-Time Ring Networks with Circulant Weight Matrix

Jiali Yu[1](✉), Zhang Yi[2], Yong Liao[3], De-An Wu[1], and Xiong Dai[1]

[1] School of Mathematics Science,
University of Electronic Science and Technology of China,
Chengdu, People's Republic of China
yujiali@uestc.edu.cn
[2] College of Computer Science, Sichuan University, Chengdu, China
[3] School of Information and Software Engineering,
University of Electronic Science and Technology of China,
Chengdu, People's Republic of China

Abstract. A continuous attractor of a recurrent neural network is a set of connected stable equilibrium points. The continuous attractors of neural networks with symmetric connection weights have been studied widely. However, most of the matrixes are asymmetric. In this paper, the continuous attractors of 3-D discrete-time ring networks with circulant weight matrix are studied. The circulant matrix is asymmetric. The eigenvalues of asymmetric matrix may be complex. Based on the complex eigenvalues, the conditions that guarantee the networks with circulant weight matrix to have continuous attractors are obtained.

Keywords: Continuous attractors · Ring networks · 3-D ·
Discrete-time · Circulant matrix · Asymmetric

1 Introduction

Based on the distribution of the stationary state, neural networks can have discrete attractors or continuous attractors [1,2]. Continuous attractor is a connected stable stationary state set [3]. Different from the discrete attractor network, continuous attractor neural network can store and manipulate continuous variables such as the population coding information [4,5], eye position [6,7], head direction [8], path integrator [9–11], moving direction [12–14], working memory [15] and cognitive map [16].

From a mathematical point of view continuous attractor is a low-dimensional manifold embedded in the high-dimensional state space [12,17,18]. It can be a line, a plane, a bump curve and a surface. It's dimension can be one or more. The

J. Yu—This work is supported by National Natural Science Foundation of China under Grant 61572112, 61103041, 61432012, the Fundamental Research Funds for the Central Universities under Grant ZYGX2016J136.

© Springer International Publishing AG, part of Springer Nature 2018
T. Huang et al. (Eds.): ISNN 2018, LNCS 10878, pp. 388–396, 2018.
https://doi.org/10.1007/978-3-319-92537-0_45

one-dimensional continuous attractor is also called line attractor. Line attractor is the most important kind of continuous attractors and it has been used to explain the mystery of how the brain can keep the eyes still successfully [19].

Our brain may sense the world through multiple sensory modules [20–22]. Recently, there has been increasing interest in ring network [23,24]. In ring network, all the neurons are arranged on a ring. Ring network can explain contrast invariant tuning of V1 cells [25] and multiplicative response modulation of parietal cells. The connection matrix in ring network is asymmetric generally because the weight matrix is a circulant matrix. Circulant matrix is a class of asymmetric matrix which is a special kind of Toeplitz matrix where each row vector is rotated one element to the right relative to the preceding row vector.

The continuous attractor study is focused on those symmetric networks [3]. When the reciprocal connections between two neurons are not always equal, the synaptic weight is asymmetric. The continuous attractor of a parameterized 2-D asymmetric network was studied in [26]. For more higher dimensional asymmetric network, it is hard to analyze the continuous attractor problem. Motivated by the above discussions, in this paper, the continuous attractors of asymmetric ring networks are studied. The connection matrix in ring network is circulant matrix. It is easy to see that only when the circulant matrix is a 2×2 matrix, it is a symmetric matrix. Otherwise, the matrix is asymmetric. On the other hand, when the order of the connection matrix is more than three, we can't visualize the trajectories of the network clearly in R^3. Based on these issues, we study the continuous attractors of 3-D ring network with circulant weight matrix. By using the complex eigenvalues and eigenvectors, ring network with circulant matrix is investigated and the continuous attractors are obtained.

This paper is organized as follows. Preliminaries are given in Sect. 2. The continuous attractor of a ring network with circulant matrix is analyzed in Sect. 3. Simulations are given in Sect. 4. Conclusions are drawn in the final Section.

2 Preliminaries

In this paper, we study the ring network whose synaptic connection matrix is a circulant matrix:

$$s(t + 1) = f(Ws(t)) + h \tag{1}$$

for $t \geq 0$, where $s \in R^N$, $f : R^N \to R^N$ is some continuous mapping. $h = (h_1, \cdots, h_N)^T$ denotes the external input.

All the neurons are aligned on a ring (Fig. 1 shows the network).

The $N \times N$ circulant matrix W takes the following form

$$W = \begin{bmatrix} w_1 & w_2 & w_3 & \cdots & w_N \\ w_N & w_1 & w_2 & \cdots & w_{N-1} \\ w_{N-1} & w_N & w_1 & \cdots & w_{N-2} \\ \vdots & \vdots & \vdots & \ddots & \vdots \\ w_2 & w_3 & w_4 & \cdots & w_1 \end{bmatrix},$$

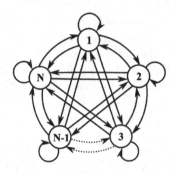

Fig. 1. Ring network structure.

where $w_k(k = 1, \cdots, N)$ are real entries. It is easy to see that the circulant matrix is a symmetric matrix only when it is 2×2, otherwise, the matrix is asymmetric.

Definition 1. *A vector $s^* \in R^N$ is called an equilibrium point of (1), if it satisfies $s^* = f(Ws^*) + h$.*

Definition 2. *An equilibrium point s^* is said to be stable, if given any constant $\epsilon > 0$, there exists a constant $\delta > 0$ such that*

$$\|s(0) - s^*\| \leq \delta$$

implies that

$$\|s(t) - s^*\| \leq \epsilon$$

for all $t \geq 0$.

Definition 3. *An equilibrium point s^* is said to be asymptotically stable, if there exist a $\delta > 0$ such that*

$$\|s(0) - s^*\| \leq \delta$$

implies that

$$\lim_{t \longrightarrow +\infty} s(t) = s^*$$

for all $t \geq 0$.

Definition 4. *A set of stationary points C is called a continuous attractor if it is a connected set and each point $s^* \in C$ is stable.*

Definition 5. *A set of equilibrium points C is called an asymptotical continuous attractor if it is connected and each point $s^* \in C$ is asymptotically stable.*

3 Continuous Attractor of networks with Circulant Connection Matrix

For network (1), in order to analyze the continuous attractors in ring network substantively, we take $f(s) = s$. On the other hand, when the order of the connection matrix is more than three, we can't visualize the trajectories of the network clearly in R^3. Based on these issues, we study the continuous attractors of 3-D ring network.

The 3×3 connection matrix W takes the form

$$W = \begin{bmatrix} w_1 & w_2 & w_3 \\ w_3 & w_1 & w_2 \\ w_2 & w_3 & w_1 \end{bmatrix}.$$

Denote

$$\lambda_1 = w_1 + w_2 + w_3$$

$$\lambda_2 = w_1 + (w_2 + w_3)\cos(\frac{2\pi}{3}) + i(w_2 - w_3)\sin(\frac{2\pi}{3})$$

$$\lambda_3 = w_1 + (w_2 + w_3)\cos(\frac{2\pi}{3}) - i(w_2 - w_3)\sin(\frac{2\pi}{3})$$

where $i = \sqrt{-1}$, and

$$S_1 = \begin{bmatrix} 1 \\ 1 \\ 1 \end{bmatrix}, \quad S_2 = \begin{bmatrix} 1 \\ \cos(\frac{2\pi}{3}) \\ \cos(\frac{2\pi}{3}) \end{bmatrix}, \quad S_3 = \begin{bmatrix} 0 \\ \sin(\frac{2\pi}{3}) \\ -\sin(\frac{2\pi}{3}) \end{bmatrix}$$

for $k = 1, 2, 3$.

It is easy to prove that

$$W S_k = \lambda_k S_k,$$

so S_k is the eigenvector of W corresponding to eigenvalue λ_k.

Form an 3×3 matrix

$$P = \begin{bmatrix} S_1, & S_2, & S_3 \end{bmatrix},$$

$$P = \begin{bmatrix} 1 & 1 & 1 \\ 1 & \cos(\frac{2\pi}{3}) & \sin(\frac{2\pi}{3}) \\ 1 & \cos(\frac{2\pi}{3}) & -\sin(\frac{2\pi}{3}) \end{bmatrix} = \begin{bmatrix} 1 & 1 & 1 \\ 1 & -\frac{1}{2} & -\frac{\sqrt{3}}{2} \\ 1 & -\frac{1}{2} & \frac{\sqrt{3}}{2} \end{bmatrix}.$$

P is invertible, S_1, S_2, S_3 are independent. There exist a diagonal matrix D such that

$$D = P^{-1}WP,$$

where

$$D = \begin{bmatrix} \lambda_1 & & \\ & \lambda_2 & \\ & & \lambda_3 \end{bmatrix}.$$

Denote $s(t) = Pu(t)$, where $u(t) = (u_1(t), u_2(t), u_3(t))^T$, that is $u(t) = P^{-1}s(t)$, and $h = Pb$.

Theorem 1. *Suppose* $w_1 + w_2 + w_3 = 1$, $|w_1^2 + w_2^2 + w_3^2 - w_1 w_2 - w_1 w_3 - w_2 w_3| < 1$, *and the external input h is orthogonal to* $(1, 1, 1)^T$, *then the ring network (1) has a asymptotical continuous attractor and the continuous attractor can be represented by*

$$C = \left\{ u_1(0)S_1 + \frac{b_2}{1 - \lambda_2} S_2 + \frac{b_3}{1 - \lambda_3} S_3 | u_1(0) \in R \right\}.$$

Proof. Network (1) is changed from the change of variable $s(t) = Pu(t)$ to

$$u(t + 1) = Du(t) + b \tag{2}$$

for $t \geq 0$.

So we have

$$u_k(t + 1) = \lambda_k u_k(t) + b_k \tag{3}$$

for $k = 1, 2, 3$.

Case 1: $k = 1$:

Because h is orthogonal to the S_1, we have $b_1 = 0$.

Since $w_1 + w_2 + w_3 = 1$, then $\lambda_1 = 1$, then

$$u_1(t + 1) = u_1(t),$$

so

$$u_1(t) = u_1(0).$$

Case 2: $k = 2, 3$:

$$u_k(t) = \lambda_k^t u_k(0) + \sum_{r=1}^{t} . \lambda_k^{r-1} b_k.$$

Since

$$|\lambda_k| = |w_1^2 + w_2^2 + w_3^2 - w_1 w_2 - w_1 w_3 - w_2 w_3|,$$

and

$$|w_1^2 + w_2^2 + w_3^2 - w_1 w_2 - w_1 w_3 - w_2 w_3| < 1,$$

so

$$|\lambda_k| < 1,$$

then

$$\lim_{t \longrightarrow +\infty} u_k(t) = \frac{b_k}{1 - \lambda_k}.$$

So

$$\begin{bmatrix} u_1(t) \\ u_2(t) \\ u_3(t) \end{bmatrix} \longrightarrow \begin{bmatrix} u_1(0) \\ \frac{b_2}{1-\lambda_2} \\ \frac{b_3}{1-\lambda_3} \end{bmatrix} = u^*,$$

when $t \longrightarrow +\infty$.

Then when $t \longrightarrow +\infty$, we have

$$s(t) \longrightarrow s^* = Pu^*$$
$$= u_1(0)S_1 + \frac{b_2}{1 - \lambda_2} S_2 + \frac{b_3}{1 - \lambda_3} S_3.$$

Here the sum of the second part and third part of s^* is a constant point, because W and h of a network are given. While the first part of s^* is dependent on the initial point, for different initial points, we may have different first parts. Hence after a long range, the convergent points will form a line which is parallel to S_1 going through the point $\frac{b_2}{1-\lambda_2} S_2 + \frac{b_3}{1-\lambda_3} S_3$. Therefore network (1) has a one dimensional continuous attractor, Moreover, the continuous attractor is asymptotical stable.

The proof is complete.

4   Simulations

Consider a ring network with three neurons:

$$s(t+1) = \begin{bmatrix} 0.7 & 0.2 & 0.1 \\ 0.1 & 0.7 & 0.2 \\ 0.2 & 0.1 & 0.7 \end{bmatrix} s(t) + \begin{bmatrix} 0.1 \\ 0 \\ 0.1 \end{bmatrix}. \tag{4}$$

Denote

$$W = \begin{bmatrix} 0.7 & 0.2 & 0.1 \\ 0.1 & 0.7 & 0.2 \\ 0.2 & 0.1 & 0.7 \end{bmatrix}, \quad h = \begin{bmatrix} 0.1 \\ 0 \\ 0.1 \end{bmatrix}.$$

It can be checked that $0.7 + 0.2 + 0.1 = 1$, W has three eigenvalues, 1, $0.55 +$ $0.0866i$ and $0.55 + 0.0866i$. 1 is the only real eigenvalue with multiplicity 1, and $|0.55 + 0.0866i| = |0.55 - 0.0866i| = 0.5568$ which is less than 1. Moreover, external input h is orthogonal to $(1, 1, 1)^T$. By Theorem 1, the network possesses a one-dimensional continuous attractor. The red line in Fig. 2 is the continuous attractor. The trajectories (black curves) starting from the initial points (circles) close to the continuous attractor are attracted to the continuous attractor (red line).

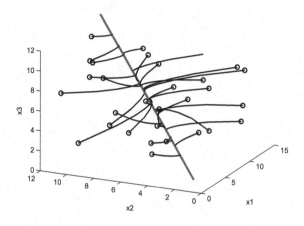

Fig. 2. Continuous attractor of ring network (4). The red line is the continuous attractor which is one dimensional in R^3. (Color figure online)

5   Conclusions

In continuous attractors field, it is short of the research for neural networks with asymmetric connection weights. In this paper, the continuous attractors of ring networks with asymmetric connection weights have been investigated. By using eigenvector theory we obtained the conditions to guarantee the asymmetric ring network to have a continuous attractor. Moreover, the explicit expression of continuous attractor is obtained. The methods of this paper could be further developed to study continuous attractors of more general networks.

References

1. Amari, S.: Dynamics of pattern formation in lateral-inhibition type neural fields. Biol. Cybern. **27**(2), 77–87 (1977)
2. Yi, Z., Zhang, L., Yu, J., Tan, K.K.: Permitted and forbidden sets in discrete-time linear threshold recurrent neural networks. IEEE Trans. Neural Netw. **20**, 952–963 (2009)

3. Yu, J., Yi, Z., Zhang, L.: Representations of continuous attractors of recurrent neural networks. IEEE Trans. Neural Netw. **20**, 368–372 (2009)
4. Pouget, A., Dayan, P., Zemel, R.: Information processing with population codes. Nat. Rev. Neurosci. **1**, 125–132 (2000)
5. Yu, J., Mao, H., Yi, Z.: Parameter as a switch between dynamical states of a network in population decoding. IEEE Trans. Neural Netw. Learn. Syst. **28**(4), 911–916 (2017)
6. Seung, H.S.: How the brain keeps the eyes still. Proc. Nat. Acad. Sci. U.S.A. **93**, 13339–13344 (1996)
7. Lee, D.D., Reis, B.Y., Seung, H.S., Tank, D.W.: Nonlinear network models of the Oculomotor integrator. In: Bower, J.M. (ed.) Computational Neuroscience. Springer, Boston (1997). https://doi.org/10.1007/978-1-4757-9800-5_60
8. Zhang, K.C.: Representation of spatial orientation by the intrinsic dynamics of the head-direction cell ensemble: a theory. J. Neurosci. **16**, 2112–2126 (1996)
9. Robinson, D.A.: Integrating with neurons. Ann. Rev. Neurosci. **12**, 33–45 (1989)
10. Koulakov, A., Raghavachari, S., Kepecs, A., Lisman, J.E.: Model for a robust neural integrator. Nat. Neurosci. **5**(8), 775–782 (2002)
11. Stringer, S.M., Trappenberg, T.P., Rolls, E.T., de Araujo, I.E.T.: Self-organizing continuous attractor networks and path integration: one-dimensional models of head direction cells. Netw.: Comput. Neural Syst. **13**, 217–242 (2002)
12. Seung, H.S., Lee, D.D.: The manifold ways of perception. Science **290**, 2268–2269 (2000)
13. Stringer, S.M., Rolls, E.T., Trappenberg, T.P., de Araujo, I.E.T.: Self-organizing continuous attractor networks and motor function. Neural Netw. **16**, 161–182 (2003)
14. Yu, J., Tang, H., Li, H.: Dynamics analysis of a population decoding model. IEEE Trans. Neural Netw. Learn. Syst. **24**(3), 498–503 (2013)
15. Wimmer, K., Nykamp, D.Q., Constantinidis, C., Compte, A.: Bump attractor dynamics in prefrontal cortex explains behavioral precision in spatial working memory. Nat. Neurosci. **17**(3), 431–439 (2014)
16. Samsonovich, A., McNaughton, B.L.: Path integration and cognitive mapping in a continuous attractor neural network model. J. Neurosci. **17**, 5900–5920 (1997)
17. Miller, P.: Analysis of spike statistics in neuronal systems with continuous attractors or multiple, discrete attractor states. Neural Comput. **18**, 1268–1317 (2006)
18. Yoon, K., Buice, M.A., Barry, C., Hayman, R., Burgess, N., Fiete, I.R.: Specific evidence of low-dimensional continuous attractor dynamics in grid cells. Nat. Neurosci. **16**(8), 1077–1084 (2013)
19. Seung, H.S.: Continouuous attractors and oculomotor control. Neural Netw. **11**, 1253–1258 (1998)
20. Skaggs, W.E., Knierim, J.J., Kudrimoti, H.S., Mcnaughton, B.L.: A model of the neural basis of the rat's sense of direction. Neural Comput. **7**(7), 173–180 (1995)
21. Zhang, W., Wu, S.: Reiprocally coupled local estimator implement bayesian information integration distibutively. In: Advances in Neural Information Processing System, pp. 19–27 (2013)
22. Wu, S., Wong, K.Y., Fung, C.C., Mi, Y., Zhang, W.: Continuous attractor neural networks: candidate of a canonical model for neural information representation. F1000research **5**(16), 209–226 (2016)
23. Machens, C.K., Brody, C.D.: Design of continuous attractor networks with monotonic tuning using a symmetry principle. Neural Comput. **20**, 452–485 (2008)

24. Hahnloser, H.R., Sarpeshkar, R., Mahowald, M.A., Douglas, R.J., Seung, H.S.: Digital selection and analogue amplication coexist in a cortex-inspired silicon circuit. Nature **405**, 947–951 (2000)
25. Ben-Yishai, R., Bar-Or, R.L., Sompolinsky, H.: Theory of orientation tuning in visual cortex. Proc. Nat. Acad. Sci. U.S.A. **92**, 3844–3848 (1995)
26. Zou, L., Tang, H., Tan, K.C., Zhang, W.: Analysis of continuous attractors for 2-D linear threshold neural networks. IEEE Trans. Neural Networks **20**, 175–180 (2009)

Hopf-Pitchfork Bifurcation Analysis
of a Coupled Neural Oscillator System
with Excitatory-to-Inhibitory Connection
and Time Delay

Lei Yang$^{1(\boxtimes)}$, Tao Dong^1, and Tingwen Huang^2

^{1} School of Electronics and Information Engineering, Southwest University,
Chongqing 400715, China
yanglei9872@163.com
^{2} Texas A&M University, Doha 23874, Qatar

Abstract. In this paper, a coupled neural oscillator system with excitatory-to-inhibitory connection and time delay is considered. First, the existence of pitchfork bifurcation and the equilibrium patterns are investigated. It is found that the system has one, three and five equilibria with self-connection weight increasing. Then, by choosing the self-connection weight and communication delay as the two bifurcation parameters, the conditions where Hopf-pitchfork bifurcation occurs are obtained. Analyzing the bifurcation diagram, we find that the system exhibits many complex phenomena such as co-existence of two synchronous equilibria or two anti-synchronous equilibria, two stable periodic solutions, and two quasi-periodic attractors, which are validated by numerical simulations.

Keywords: Hopf-pitchfork bifurcation · Neural oscillator system
Excitatory-to-inhibitory connection

1 Introduction

Neural oscillation is the normal and universal neural activity in the central nervous system. Besides, the oscillation as the important part of dynamic behaviors, plays an important player in modern scientific research such as in sensory, self-adaption, optimization and so on. Because of these unique properties and advantages, different types of networks are put forward by researchers [1–3].

In biological nervous system, time delay widely exists. The variable or constant time delay usually makes the neural oscillator system present complicated dynamic behaviors such as equilibria unstable, bifurcation, periodic orbits, even chaos and so on. In order to study the effect of the time delay on the neural networks, there are many meaningful works by the excellent researchers [4–8]. For example, in [6], the stability and the Hopf bifurcation are researched in a type of two delay-coupled neural oscillators system. In [7], the hybrid effects of uncertain time delay, stochastic perturbation, and impulses on global stability of delayed neural networks are well studied. In [8], by using intermittent linear state feedback control, synchronization of delayed chaotic systems is investigated.

© Springer International Publishing AG, part of Springer Nature 2018
T. Huang et al. (Eds.): ISNN 2018, LNCS 10878, pp. 397–404, 2018.
https://doi.org/10.1007/978-3-319-92537-0_46

On the other hand, the network structure also play a vital role for the dynamic behaviors evolution of neural networks due to the synaptic coupling can alter through learning. To study the influence of connection weights on dynamic behavior of oscillator neural system, many connection structures of oscillatory neural network are proposed [9, 10]. In fact, it is essential to consider the effect of multiple bifurcation parameters on the system, such as connection weight and time delay. Therefore, it is necessary to study the codimension two bifurcation of biological nervous system.

Based on the above discussion and the work of [3], in this paper, we propose a class of coupled neural oscillator system with time delay and excitatory-to-inhibitory connection and investigate the Hopf-pitchfork bifurcation. The architecture of our proposed neural oscillator system is list as Fig. 1. In our model, we assume the excitatory neuron connect to the inhibitory neuron. Then, this system can be described as follows:

$$
\begin{aligned}
\dot{E}_1(t) &= -E_1(t) - bf(I_1(t-\tau)) + \alpha f(E_1(t-\tau)) \\
\dot{I}_1(t) &= -I_1(t) + af(E_1(t-\tau)) - cf(E_2(t-\tau)) - \beta f(I_1(t-\tau)) \\
\dot{E}_2(t) &= -E_2(t) - bf(I_2(t-\tau)) + \alpha f(E_2(t-\tau)) \\
\dot{I}_2(t) &= -I_2(t) + af(E_2(t-\tau)) - cf(E_1(t-\tau)) - \beta f(I_2(t-\tau))
\end{aligned}
\tag{1}
$$

where $E_1(t)$ and $E_2(t)$ describe the neural activities of excitatory populations at time t; $I_1(t)$ and $I_2(t)$ are the inhibitory neural activities; $a > 0, b > 0$ denote the inner coupled weights of neural oscillator; $c > 0$ is the cross-interaction weight of neural oscillator by excitatory-to-inhibitory connection; $\alpha > 0, \beta > 0$ are the self-connection weights of excitatory and inhibitory populations; $\tau > 0$ is the delay of cross- and self-interaction; the neural activation function is considered as the hyperbolic tangent function $f(x) = \tanh(x)$, which implies that $f(0) = 0$, $f'(0) = 1$, $f(x) = -f(x)$ and $f(x) \in (-1, 1)$ for $x \in R$. For this model, first, the pitchfork bifurcation and the patterns of equilibria are investigated. It is found that the system has one, three and five equilibria when the coupled weight increasing. Then, by choosing the connection weight and time delay as the bifurcation parameters, the conditions where Hopf-pitchfork bifurcation occurs are obtained. Analyzing the bifurcation diagram, we find that the system exhibits many complex phenomena such as two stable periodic orbits, and two attractive quasi-periodic motions.

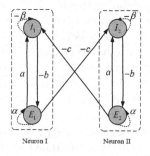

Neuron I   Neuron II

Fig. 1. The model of neural network with excitatory-to-inhibitory connection

The rest paper is organized as follows. In the Sect. 2, the existence of pitchfork bifurcation and equilibrium patterns analysis are given. In the Sect. 3, the existence of Hopf-pitchfork bifurcation is obtained. In Sect. 4, the bifurcation analyses and numerically simulations based on the bifurcation diagram are presented.

2 The Existence of Pitchfork Bifurcation and Equilibrium Patterns Analysis

In this section, the existence of pitchfork bifurcation and equilibria properties analysis are presented. The characteristic equation for the system (1) is

$$\Delta(\lambda) = \begin{bmatrix} A & be^{-\lambda\tau} & 0 & 0 \\ -ae^{-\lambda\tau} & B & ce^{-\lambda\tau} & 0 \\ 0 & 0 & A & be^{-\lambda\tau} \\ ce^{-\lambda\tau} & 0 & -ae^{-\lambda\tau} & B \end{bmatrix} = 0 \qquad (2)$$

where $A = \lambda + 1 - \alpha e^{-\lambda\tau}$, $B = \lambda + 1 + \beta e^{-\lambda\tau}$.

Then, we can obtain:

$$\Delta(\lambda) = \Delta_1(\lambda)\Delta_2(\lambda) = 0, \qquad (3)$$

Where

$$\Delta_1(\lambda) = \left(\lambda + 1 - \alpha e^{-\lambda\tau}\right)\left(\lambda + 1 + \beta e^{-\lambda\tau}\right) + (ab + bc)e^{-2\lambda\tau},$$
$$\Delta_2(\lambda) = \left(\lambda + 1 - \alpha e^{-\lambda\tau}\right)\left(\lambda + 1 + \beta e^{-\lambda\tau}\right) + (ab - bc)e^{-2\lambda\tau}.$$

Let $\alpha_1 = 1 + (ab + bc)/(1 + \beta)$, $\alpha_2 = 1 + (ab - bc)/(1 + \beta)$. We have

Lemma 1. If $\alpha = \alpha_1$ or $\alpha = \alpha_2$ holds, the Eq. (3) has a single zero root.

Theorem 1.

(1) If $\alpha = \alpha_1$ holds, the system will undergoes a pitchfork, which means the system (1) has one zero equilibrium and two nontrivial synchronous equilibrium when $\alpha > \alpha_1$ is satisfied.

(2) If $\alpha = \alpha_2$ holds, the system will undergoes a pitchfork, which means the system (1) has one zero equilibrium and two nontrivial anti-synchronous equilibrium when $\alpha > \alpha_2$ is satisfied.

3 The Existence of Hopf-Pitchfork Bifurcation

If $\alpha_1 < \alpha_2$, the system generates pitchfork bifurcation at $\alpha = \alpha_1$ and generates multi-pitchfork bifurcation at $\alpha = \alpha_2$. In order to investigate the Hopf-pitchfork, we assume $\alpha_1 < \alpha_2$ and consider the case that (3) has $\lambda = 0$ and $\lambda = \pm i\omega$ when $\alpha = \alpha_1$. It is not hard to see $\Delta_1(\lambda)$ and $\Delta_2(\lambda)$ cannot have $\pm i\omega$ simultaneously. First, we consider $\Delta_1(\lambda)$ has $\pm i\omega$ besides zero root with $\alpha = \alpha_1$. Multiply both sides of $\Delta_1(\lambda)$ by $e^{\lambda\tau}$, we can obtain:

$$(\lambda+1)^2 e^{\lambda\tau} + (\beta - \alpha)(\lambda+1) - (1+\beta - \alpha)e^{-\lambda\tau} = 0. \tag{4}$$

Let $\lambda = i\omega(\omega > 0)$, then we have:

$$(i\omega + 1)^2 e^{i\omega\tau} + (\beta - \alpha)(i\omega + 1) - (1+\beta - \alpha)e^{-i\omega\tau} = 0. \tag{5}$$

then

$$\cos \omega\tau = \frac{\alpha - \beta}{\omega^2 + \alpha - \beta}, \sin \omega\tau = -\frac{(\alpha - \beta)\omega}{\omega^2 + \alpha - \beta}. \tag{6}$$

Then, we can obtain:

$$\omega^4 + \left(2(\alpha - \beta) - (\alpha - \beta)^2\right)\omega^2 = 0. \tag{7}$$

Let $z = \omega^2$, (7) can be rewritten as

$$z^2 + l_1 z = 0, \tag{8}$$

where

$$l_1 = 2(\alpha - \beta) - (\alpha - \beta)^2.$$

If $l_1 < 0$, (8) has a positive root $z = -l_1$. By (6), we can obtain

$$\tau_1 = \frac{1}{\omega_1}\arccos\frac{\alpha - \beta}{\omega_1^2 + \alpha - \beta} + \frac{2i\pi}{\omega_1}, i = 1, 2, 3. \ldots \tag{9}$$

In the following, we investigate the case $\Delta_2(\lambda)$ has a pair of purely imaginary root $\pm i\omega$ with $\alpha = \alpha_1$, multiply both sides of $\Delta_2(\lambda)$ by $e^{\lambda\tau}$, we can obtain:

$$(\lambda+1)^2 e^{\lambda\tau} + (\beta - \alpha)(\lambda+1) + (1+\beta - \alpha)e^{-\lambda\tau} = 0. \tag{10}$$

Let $\lambda = i\omega(\omega > 0)$, then we have:

$$(i\omega + 1)^2 e^{i\omega\tau} + (\beta - \alpha)(i\omega + 1) + (1+\beta - \alpha)e^{-i\omega\tau} = 0. \tag{11}$$

then

$$\cos \omega\tau = \frac{\alpha - \beta}{\omega^2 + \alpha - \beta + 2}, \sin \omega\tau = -\frac{(\alpha - \beta)\omega}{\omega^2 + \alpha - \beta + 2}. \tag{12}$$

According to $\sin^2 \omega\tau + \cos^2 \omega\tau = 1$, we can obtain:

$$\omega^4 + e_1\omega^2 + e_2 = 0, \tag{13}$$

Where $e_1 = 4 + 2(\alpha - \beta) - (\alpha - \beta)^2$, $e_2 = 4(1 + \alpha - \beta)$.

Let $z = \omega^2$, (13) can be rewritten as:

$$z^2 + e_1 z + e_2 = 0. \tag{14}$$

Lemma 2.

(1) If $e_1^2 - 4e_2 > 0$, $e_1 < 0$, there are at least has one positive root of Eq. (14).
(2) If $e_1^2 - 4e_2 > 0$, $e_1 \geq 0$, $e_2 < 0$, there are only one positive root of Eq. (14).

Supposing that $z_j (j = 1, 2)$ are the positive roots of (14), $\omega_2 = \sqrt{z_1}$, $\omega_3 = \sqrt{z_2}$, then we can obtain

$$\tau_j = \frac{1}{\omega_j} \arccos \frac{\alpha - \beta}{\omega^2 + \alpha - \beta + 2} + \frac{2i\pi}{\omega_j}, i = 1, 2, 3 \ldots, j = 2, 3. \tag{15}$$

Defining $\tau_0 = \min\{\tau_1, \tau_2, \tau_3\}$, let $m_1 = m_2 = 2 - \alpha + \beta$, $m_3 = -2bc$.

Lemma 3. If $m_{1,2} > 0$ and $m_3 > 0$, all roots of (4) have negative real parts except the zero root when $\alpha = \alpha_1$ and $0 < \tau < \tau_0$.

Theorem 2. From Theorem 1 and Lemmas 2, 3, we have:

(1) If $\alpha = \alpha_1$ and $\tau < \tau_0$ is satisfied, then system (1) undergoes a pitchfork bifurcation at origin.
(2) If $\alpha = \alpha_1$, $\tau = \tau_0$, $m_1 < 0$, $m_{2,3} > 0$ and one of the following conditions are satisfied,
  (a). $l_1 < 0$
  (b). $e_1^2 - 4e_2 > 0$, $e_1 < 0$
  (c). $e_1^2 - 4e_2 > 0$, $e_1 \geq 0$, $e_2 < 0$

then, we can say that, the system (1) experiences a Hopf-pitchfork bifurcation at the zero equilibrium.

4 Hopf-Pitchfork Bifurcation Analysis and Numerical Simulation

To obtain a clear bifurcation diagram, let $a = 1$, $b = 2$, $c = 0.2$, $\beta = 0.2$. Then we can obtain $\alpha_1 = 2.3333$ and $\tau_0 = 0.9187$. Let $\alpha = \alpha_1$ and $\tau = \tau_0$, from Theorem 1, we know the Hopf-pitchfork bifurcation occurs at the zero equilibrium. By a simple calculation, following with [10], the following critical bifurcation lines are obtained: $L_0 : \mu_2 = -1.0502\mu_1$, $L_1 : \mu_2 = -9.2269\mu_1$, $L_2 : \mu_2 = -21.6389\mu_1$. Then the bifurcation diagram is given in Fig. 2.

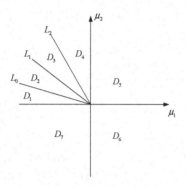

Fig. 2. The bifurcation set and phase portraits

Based on the Fig. 2, we obtain the details of Hopf-pitchfork bifurcation, from the region D_1 to the region D_7. In D_1, there are three equilibria, the unstable zero equilibrium and two stable nontrivial equilibria. From D_1 to D_2, the periodic solution is occurred at trivial equilibrium, which is unstable. In D_3, the above unstable periodic solution becomes a saddle from a source. In region D_4, two quasi-periodic attractors appear. In D_5, there are two periodic solutions at nontrivial equilibrium. In D_6, there exists a trivial equilibrium, which is unstable. In D_7, there exists trivial equilibrium, which is stable.

In the following simulations, four sets of different parameter values are chosen:

(1) If $\mu_1 = -0.03$, $\mu_2 = -0.03 \in D_7$, then the system has one zero equilibrium point, and is asymptotically stable, which is shown in Fig. 3.

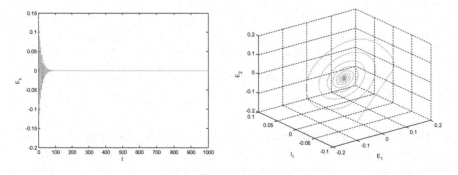

Fig. 3. The stable trivial equilibrium

(2) If $\mu_1 = 0.03$, $\mu_2 = -0.03 \in D_6$, then the system has one zero equilibrium point, and is unstable, which is shown in Fig. 4.

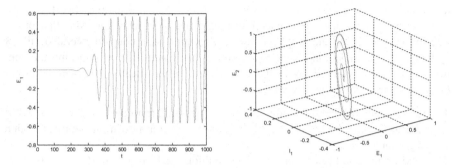

Fig. 4. The bifurcation occurs at the trivial equilibrium

(3) If $\mu_1 = -0.03$, $\mu_2 = 0.03 \in D_1$, then the system has one zero equilibrium point and two nonzero equilibrium, and is asymptotically stable, which is shown in Fig. 5.

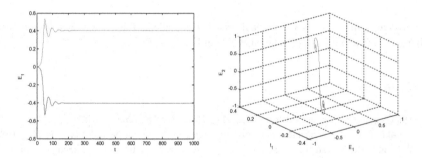

Fig. 5. Two stable nontrivial equilibria points and unstable trivial equilibrium.

(4) If $\mu_1 = 0.03$, $\mu_2 = 0.03 \in D_5$, there are there are two periodic solutions, which is shown in Fig. 6.

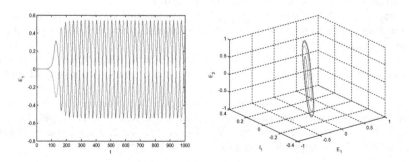

Fig. 6. Two unstable nontrivial periodic orbits at different equilibrium point.

5 Conclusions

In biological nervous system, the connection weight and time delay play a key role in dynamic behavior evolution. However, there are very few works investigate the dynamic behaviors when the connection weight and time delay vary simultaneously. This paper investigate the Hopf-pitchfork bifurcation of a coupled neural oscillator system with time delay and excitatory-to-inhibitory connection by choosing the connection weight and time delay as the two bifurcation parameters. The main contributions are concluded in the following:

1. The existence of pitchfork bifurcation and the equilibrium patterns are obtained. It is found that the system has one, three and five equilibria with the self-connection weight increasing.
2. Based on the equilibrium pattern, the conditions of Hopf-pitchfork bifurcation are given.
3. Analyzing the bifurcation diagram, the complex phenomena are found such as co-existence of two synchronous equilibria or two anti-synchronous equilibria, two stable periodic solutions, and two quasi-periodic attractors, which are validated by numerical simulations.

Acknowledgments. This paper is partially funded by National Priority Research Project NPRP 9 166-1-031, funded by Qatar National Research Fund.

References

1. MacGregor, R.: Neural and Brain Modeling. Elsevier, New York (2012)
2. Kryukov, V.: The metastable and unstable states in the brain. Neural Netw. **1**, 264 (1988)
3. Wilson, H.R., Cowan, J.D.: Excitatory and inhibitory interactions in localized populations of model neurons. Biophys. J. **12**(1), 1–24 (1972)
4. Dong, T., Liao, X., Wang, A.: Stability and Hopf bifurcation of a complex-valued neural network with two time delays. Nonlinear Dyn. **82**(1–2), 173–184 (2015)
5. Dong, T., Liao, X.: Hopf-Pitchfork bifurcation in a simplified bam neural network model with multiple delays. J. Comput. Appl. Math. **253**, 222–234 (2013)
6. Song, Z., Xu, J.: Stability switches and multistability coexistence in a delay-coupled neural oscillators system. J. Theor. Biol. **313**, 98–114 (2012)
7. Huang, T., Li, C., Dusan, S., Starzyk, J.: Robust exponential stability of uncertain delayed neural networks with stochastic perturbation and impulse effects. IEEE Trans. Neural Netw. Learn. Syst. **23**, 866–875 (2012)
8. Huang, T., Li, C., Yu, W., Chen, G.: Synchronization of delayed chaotic systems with parameter mismatches by using intermittent linear state feedback. Nonlinearity **22**, 569–584 (2009)
9. Jia, B., Gu, H., Xue, L.: A basic bifurcation structure from bursting to spiking of injured nerve fibers in a two-dimensional parameter space. Cogn. Neurodyn. **11**(2), 189–200 (2017)
10. Carr, J.: Applications of Centre Manifold Theory. Springer Science & Business Media, Heidelberg (2012). https://doi.org/10.1007/978-1-4612-5929-9

Multi-agent Systems and Game Theory

Adaptive Consensus Tracking of First-Order Multi-agent Systems with Unknown Control Directions

Yajun Zheng, Qingling Wang$^{(\boxtimes)}$, and Changyin Sun$^{(\boxtimes)}$

School of Automation, Southeast University, Nanjing, China
{yjzheng,qlwang,cysun}@seu.edu.cn

Abstract. A novel control algorithm based on Nussbaum function is proposed to settle the adaptive consensus tracking for first-order multi-agent systems with completely non-identical unknown control directions (UCDs) and uncertainties under connected undirected graphs or balanced and weakly connected digraphs in this paper. The Nussbaum function is introduced in the distributed control law to settle the UCDs of multi-agent systems. Then, it is proven that multi-agent systems with UCDs and uncertainties can achieve asymptotic consensus and reach the target state under the assumption that the underlying topology is undirected graphs or balanced and weakly connected graphs. Finally, theoretical and simulation results has verified the validity of our proposed algorithm.

Keywords: Consensus tracking · Multi-agent system
Unknown control direction · Nussbaum function

1 Introduction

The researches on multi-agent systems have received more and more attention of many scholars. The definition of multi-agent system is that agents form a network and exchange information through the network [1]. The consensus tracking of multi-agent describes that all agents in the network update their states based on information exchange and run as common as the leader's state [2], which has important applications in many fields, such as distributed sensor network systems, robotic teams, formation control of unmanned robots, underwater vehicles [3–5].

The problem of multi-agent systems with UCDs has received numerous attention recently. There are many applications which the control directions are unknown [6], such as autopilot design of time-varying ships [7] and uncalibrated visual servoing [8]. If the knowledge about signs of control gains is lacking, the adaptive contr ol problem is more hard to solve, because we cannot determine the control direction [9]. Nussbaum first introduced the Nussbaum-type function to control the first-order continuous-time adaptively in 1983 [11].

© Springer International Publishing AG, part of Springer Nature 2018
T. Huang et al. (Eds.): ISNN 2018, LNCS 10878, pp. 407–414, 2018.
https://doi.org/10.1007/978-3-319-92537-0_47

Inspired by the pioneering papers [6,10], we research the consensus tracking problem of first-order linearly multi-agents with UCDs. The main contributions of this paper are summarized as follows. Compared with the work in [6], where the unknown control directions are identical and the consensus can only reach zero, in this paper, the unknown control directions are non-identical and the consensus can reach the target state. Compared with [10], this paper considers uncertainties of the multi-agent systems.

The rest of this paper is arranged as follows. In Sect. 2, we introduce some preliminaries and lemmas. In Sect. 3, we formulate a problem about linearly first-order multi-agent systems with UCDs and uncertainies. In Sect. 4, we propose the main theorems with Nussbaum function. In Sect. 5, the simulation results verify these theorems. The final section concludes this work.

2   Preliminaries

2.1   Notions

R represents the set of real numbers. $R^{N \times N}$ and I_n denote the $N \times N$ real matrices and the set of $n \times n$ identity matrices respectively. $sup(\cdot)$ and $inf(\cdot)$ represent the least upper bound and the greatest lower bound respectively.

2.2   Nussbaum-Type Function

Definition 1. *If the function $N(\cdot)$ is even and differentiable and satisfies the following properties, it is Nussbaum function [11]:*

$$\lim_{k \to \infty} = sup(\frac{1}{k}) \int_0^k N(\tau)d\tau = +\infty$$
$$\lim_{k \to \infty} = inf(\frac{1}{k}) \int_0^k N(\tau)d\tau = -\infty \tag{1}$$

These functions including $e^{k^2}cos(k)$, $k^2cos(k)$ and $k^2sin(k)$ are Nussbaum-type function. We choose $N_0 = k^2sin(k)$ in this paper.

2.3   Graph Theory

This section introduces some graph terminologies which you can find in [12]. Denote a weighted graph as $\mathscr{G} = (V, \varepsilon)$, where $V = (1, \cdots, N)$ is a finite nonempty node set and $\varepsilon \subseteq V \times V$ is an edge set. The edge (i, j) in the undirected graph says that agents i and j can communicate with each other. If every pair of different nodes has an undirected path, we denote the undirected graph is connected. But in directed graph, the edge (i, j) does not equal (j, i) and denotes the agent j can accept messages from the agent i. If a directed graph's underlying graph is connected, we call the directed graph is weakly connected.

If the in-degree of every node i is equal to the out-degree in a directed graph, the directed graph is balanced.

The adjacency matrix $A = [a_{ij}] \in R^{N \times N}$ of a graph $\mathscr{G} = (V, \varepsilon)$ is defined such that $a_{ij} = 1$, if $(i, j) \in \varepsilon$ and $a_{ij} = 0$, if $(i, j) \notin \varepsilon$. In undirected graph, $a_{ij} = a_{ji}$ for all $i \neq j$ and $a_{ii} = 0, \forall i$.

Define the matrix $L = [l_{ij}] \in R^{N \times N}$ as

$$l_{ii} = \sum_{j=1, j \neq i}^{N} a_{ij}, l_{ij} = -a_{ij}, i \neq j \tag{2}$$

Matrix holds

$$l_{ij} \leq 0, i \neq j, \sum_{j=1}^{N} l_{ij} = 0, i = 1, \ldots, N \tag{3}$$

L is called the Laplacian matrix. If a graph is undirected, the Laplacian matrix is symmetrical.

2.4 Main Lemmas

Lemma 1. *(Barbalats Lemma): If there is a uniformly continuous function $f : R \to R, \forall t \geq 0, t \in R$ and if $\lim_{t \to \infty} \int_0^t f(\lambda) d\lambda$ exists and is finite, then $\lim_{t \to \infty} f(t) = 0$ [13].*

Lemma 2. $V(\cdot)$ *and $k(\cdot)$ are smooth functions where both of them are defined on $[0, t_f)$ and $V(t) \geq 0, \forall t \in [0, t_f)$. $N(\cdot)$ be an even smooth Nussbaum-type function. If there exists the following inequality [14]:*

$$V(t) \leq \int_0^t (bN(k) + 1)\dot{k} d\tau + c, \forall t \in [0, t_f) \tag{4}$$

where c is a appropriate constant, then $V(t)$, $k(t)$ and $\int_0^t (bN(k) + 1)\dot{k} d\tau$ must be bounded on $[0, t_f)$.

Lemma 3. *A directed graph is balanced and weakly connected which means $L + L^T \geq 0$ [15].*

Lemma 4. *Let the undirected graph be connected and there exists at least $g_i > 0$ and $G = diag\{g_i\}$, then $H = L + G \in R^{N \times N}$ is a positive definite matrix [16].*

3 Problem Formulation

We consider the class of first-order linearly multi-agent systems with uncertainties and UCDs as follows:

$$\dot{x}_i = b_i u_i + \phi_i(x_i)\theta_i, i = 1, 2, \cdots, N \tag{5}$$

where x_i, b_i, u_i and $\theta_i \in R$ are the state, control inputs, control gain with unknown signs and unknown constant, respectively. ϕ_i is known continuous function.

Assumption 1: All unknown control directions b_i are unknown and nonzero constant with unknown sign.

There exists following assumption for the applicable topology graph.

Assumption 2: We only consider the connected undirected graph or the balanced and weakly connected directed graph.

For each agent, we design a distributed controller under Assumptions 1–2 to achieve the control objective that $lim_{t \to \infty} x_i(t) = x_0$ for $i \in \{1, 2, \cdots, N\}$, where x_0 is constant and $x_0 \in R$. We introduce Lemma 5 for the following Theorem 1's demonstration.

Lemma 5. *Considering a network of N agents, $\xi_i = \sum_{j=1}^{N} a_{ij}(x_i - x_j) + g_i(x_i - x_0)$ is the error of agent i for $x_0 \in R$. Then, $H\tilde{X}(t) = \sum_{i=1}^{N} \xi_i$ with $\tilde{X}(t) = [x_1(t) - x_0(t), \cdots, x_1(t) - x_0(t)]^T$.*

Proof.

$$H\tilde{X}(t) = (L + G)(X(T) - X_0(t))$$
$$= LX(t) - LX_0(t) + G(X(t) - X_0(t))$$

by (3), we can obtain $LX_0 = 0$

$$H\tilde{X}(t) = LX(t) + G(X(t) - X_0(t)) = \sum_{i=1}^{N} \xi_i$$

Hence, $H\tilde{X}(t) = \sum_{i=1}^{N} \xi_i$ with $\tilde{X}(t) = [x_1(t) - x_0(t), \cdots, x_1(t) - x_0(t)]^T$, which completes the prove.

4   Main Results

An adaptive controller based on Nussbaum-type function will be designed to achieve consensus for each agent in the system.

Theorem 1. *Consider a system composed by a N-agent network which is given by (5), there is a distributed adaptive control law as follows.*

$$u_i = N_0(k_i)(\xi_i + \phi_i(x_i)^T \hat{\theta}_i), i = 1, 2, \cdots, N \tag{6}$$

where $\xi_i = \sum_{j=1}^{N} a_{ij}(x_i - x_j) + g_i(x_i - x_0)$ is the error of agent i with k_i and $\hat{\theta}_i$ respectively updated by

$$\dot{k}_i = \gamma_i \xi_i (\xi_i + \phi_i(x_i)^T \hat{\theta}_i) \tag{7}$$

and

$$\dot{\hat{\theta}}_i = \zeta_i \phi_i(x_i) \xi_i \tag{8}$$

with γ_i and ζ_i chosen by positive constant.

Proof. Let $\tilde{\theta}_i = \hat{\theta}_i - \theta_i$ and $H = L + G$. Denote $x = [x_1, \cdots, x_N]^T$ and $\tilde{\theta} = [\tilde{\theta}_i, \cdots, \tilde{\theta}_N]$. Notice that G is a connected undirected graph, so L is symmetric. Select the following Lyapunov-candidate-function for the overall system

$$V = \frac{1}{2}\tilde{x}^T H \tilde{x} + \frac{1}{2}\tilde{\theta}^T \left(diag\{\varsigma\}^{-1} \otimes I\right)\tilde{\theta} \tag{9}$$

where $\varsigma = [\varsigma_i, \cdots, \varsigma_N]^T$. Differentiating (9) yields

$$\dot{V} = \tilde{x}^T H \dot{x} + \tilde{\theta}^T (diag\{\varsigma\}^{-1} \otimes I)\dot{\tilde{\theta}}$$

$$= -\sum_{i=1}^N \xi_i^2 + \sum_{i=1}^N \frac{1}{\gamma_i}\dot{k}_i + \sum_{i=1}^N \frac{b_i}{\gamma_i}N_0(k_i)\dot{k}_i \tag{10}$$

$$= -\sum_{i=1}^N \xi_i^2 + \sum_{i=1}^N \frac{1}{\gamma_i}(b_iN_0(k_i) + 1)\dot{k}_i$$

Integrating both sides of (11) form 0 to t, we get

$$V(t) = -\sum_{i=1}^N \int_0^t \xi_i^2 d\tau + \sum_{i=1}^N \frac{1}{\gamma_i}\int_0^t (b_iN_0(k_i) + 1)\dot{k}_i + c \tag{11}$$

$$\leq \sum_{i=1}^N \frac{1}{\gamma_i}\int_0^t (b_iN_0(k_i) + 1)\dot{k}_i + c$$

where c is a constant.

By Lemma 2, we can know that $V(t)$, $\dot{k}(t)$ and $\int_0^t(b_iN_0(k_i) + 1)\dot{k}d\tau$ are bounded on $[0, t_f]$. Thus, ξ_i^2 is integrable on $[0, \infty]$. Based on Lemma 1, $\lim_{t\to\infty}\xi_i^2(t) = 0, 1 \leq i \leq N$, which follows that $\lim_{t\to\infty}\xi_i(t) = 0, 1 \leq i \leq N$ and $\lim_{t\to\infty}\sum_{i=1}^N \xi_i(t) = 0, 1 \leq i \leq N$. By Lemmas 3 and 5, we can know that $\lim_{t\to\infty}\tilde{X}(t) = 0$, which finishes the proof.

Corollary 1. *Consider a multi-agent system which is composed by N agents given in (5), there is a distributed adaptive controller (6) with adaptive update law (7) and (8), such that $\lim_{t\to\infty} x_i = x_0$, $x_0 \in R$ if the directed graph is weakly connected and balanced.*

Proof. As a similar way in the proof for Theorem 1, it can be known that $\int_0^t(b_iN_0(k_i) + 1)\dot{k}d\tau$, $V(t)$ are bounded and $\lim_{t\to\infty}\xi_i(t) = 0, 1 \leq i \leq N$. When the directed graph is balanced and connected, $\hat{L} = L + L^T$

$$\lim_{t\to\infty}\sum_{i=1}^N \xi_i(t) \times 2 = (H + H^T)\tilde{X}(t) \tag{12}$$

$$= (L + L^T + G + G^T)\tilde{X}(t) \tag{13}$$

$$= [\hat{L} + 2G]\tilde{X}(t) = 0 \tag{14}$$

Hence, when the directed graph is balanced and weakly connected, $\lim_{t\to\infty}\tilde{X}(t) = 0$, which completes the proof.

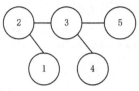

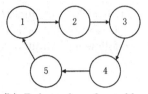

(a) 5-agent graph that is   (b) Balanced and weakly
undirected and connected   connected directed graph
                                   for 5 agents

Fig. 1. Two kinds of multi-agent systems topology

5   Simulation Results

This section shows some simulation graphs to verify the effectiveness of the
designed controllers in Theorem 1 and Corollary 1. Select a group of 5 agents
where the interconnection topology is undirected and connected shown as
Fig. 1(a). For simplicity, we set that $a_{ij} = 1$ if agent i can acquire messages from
agent j and $a_{ij} = 0$ otherwise, $i, j = 1, 2, 3, 4, 5$. To be more specific, we set system parameters b as $[2.1, -4.5, 1, 4.1, -1.3]$ and the functions $\phi_i(x_i)$ are taken as
$\phi_1(x_1) = \sin(x_1)$, $\phi_2(x_2) = \cos(x_2)$, $\phi_3(x_4) = x_3$, $\phi_4(x_4) = x_4^2$ and $\phi_4(x_4) = x_5$.
The unknown parameters θ are specified as $[-1.1, -2.3, -1.8, 1.5, 0.4]$ and the ini-
tial values of agents are chosen as $[4, 2.5, -2.6, -3.4, 0.6]$. The distributed control
law (6) with the adaptive updaters (7) and (8) are synthesized to solve the consensus problem when the network topology is shown as the Fig. 1(a). The design
parameters ζ and γ are chosen as $[0.6, 1.6, 2.3, 1.1, 1.3]$ and $[0.5, 1.7, 2.9, 1.1, 2.3]$
respectively. The x_0 is chosen as 10 and $g_1 = 1, g_2 = g3 = g_4 = g_5 = 0$. All
the other initial values start from 0. The simulation has verified our theory and
Fig. 2 shows its results. Similarly, a group of 5 agents is considered where the
interconnection topology is directed, balanced and weakly connected shown as
Fig. 1(b) and set the parameters as the above. As shown in Fig. 3, we can see all
x_i achieve consensus and reach x_0 eventually from the simulation results.

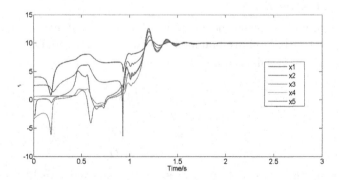

Fig. 2. Trajectories of $x_i, i = 1, 2, 3, 4, 5$ in undirected graph.

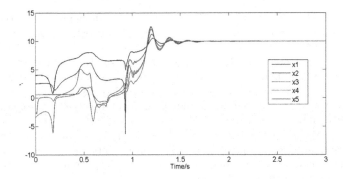

Fig. 3. Trajectories of $x_i, i = 1, 2, 3, 4, 5$ in directed graph.

6 Conclusion

This paper proposed a novel algorithms based on Nussbaum-type function to solve the consensus tracking of first-order linearly parameterized multi-agent with non-identical UCDs on connected undirected graphs or balanced and weakly connected graphs. The simulation results verifies the proposed algorithms can guarantee the agents achieve consensus. The proposed algorithms have two advantages compared with other researches on UCDs. One is that the model of multi-agent systems contains uncertainty, the other one is that the distributed control law can make multi-agent systems achieve consensus to arbitrary value. We intend to further research the adaptive consensus tracking of second-order or high-order multi-agent systems with UCDs and we will further consider the algorithms under the assumption which the network topology is a directed spanning tree in order to make the algorithm more general.

References

1. Olfati-Saber, R., Fax, J.A., Murray, R.M.: Consensus and cooperation in networked multi-agent systems. Proc. IEEE **95**(1), 215–233 (2007)
2. Li, H., Liao, X., Huang, T., Zhu, W.: Event-triggering sampling based leader-following consensus in second-order multi-agent systems. IEEE Trans. Autom. Control **60**(7), 1998–2003 (2015)
3. Wenwu, Y., Chen, G., Cao, M.: Some necessary and sufficient conditions for second-order consensus in multi-agent dynamical systems. Automatica **46**(6), 1089–1095 (2010)
4. Wen, G., Duan, Z., Ren, W., Chen, G.: Distributed consensus of multi-agent systems with general linear node dynamics and intermittent communications. Int. J. Robust Nonlinear Control **24**(16), 2438–2457 (2014)
5. Wenwu, Y., Ren, W., Zheng, W.X., Chen, G., Lü, J.: Distributed control gains design for consensus in multi-agent systems with second-order nonlinear dynamics. Automatica **49**(7), 2107–2115 (2013)
6. Chen, W., Li, X., Ren, W., Wen, C.: Adaptive consensus of multi-agent systems with unknown identical control directions based on a novel Nussbaum-type function. IEEE Trans. Autom. Control **59**(7), 1887–1892 (2014)

7. Du, J., Guo, C., Yu, S., Zhao, Y.: Adaptive autopilot design of time-varying uncertain ships with completely unknown control coefficient. IEEE J. Ocean. Eng. **32**(2), 346–352 (2007)

8. Astolfi, A., Hsu, L., Netto, M.S., Ortega, R.: Two solutions to the adaptive visual servoing problem. IEEE Trans. Robotics Autom. **18**(3), 387–392 (2002)

9. Yang, C., Ge, S.S., Lee, T.H.: Output feedback adaptive control of a class of nonlinear discrete-time systems with unknown control directions. Automatica **45**(1), 270–276 (2009)

10. Peng, J., Ye, X.: Cooperative control of multiple heterogeneous agents with unknown high-frequency-gain signs. Syst. Control Lett. **68**, 51–56 (2014)

11. Nussbaum, R.D.: Some remarks on a conjecture in parameter adaptive control. Syst. Control Lett. **3**(5), 243–246 (1983)

12. Ren, W., Beard, R.W.: Distributed Consensus in Multi-vehicle Cooperative Control. Springer, London (2008). https://doi.org/10.1007/978-1-84800-015-5

13. Slotine, J.J.E., Li, W.: Applied Nonlinear Control. Prentice Hall, Englewood Cliffs (1991)

14. Xudong, Y., Jingping, J.: Adaptive nonlinear design without a priori knowledge of control directions. IEEE Trans. Autom. Control **43**(11), 1617–1621 (1998)

15. Zhang, H., Lewis, F.L., Qu, Z.: Lyapunov, adaptive, and optimal design techniques for cooperative systems on directed communication graphs. IEEE Trans. Ind. Electron. **59**(7), 3026–3041 (2012)

16. Hong, Y., Jiangping, H., Gao, L.: Tracking control for multi-agent consensus with an active leader and variable topology. Automatica **42**(7), 1177–1182 (2006)

A Distributed Algorithm
Based on Multi-agent Network
for Solving Linear Algebraic Equation

Qingshan Liu[1(✉)], Jiang Xiong[2], Jing Zhong[2], Hong Ying[2], and Kaixuan Li[3]

[1] School of Mathematics, Southeast University, Nanjing 210096, China
qsliu@seu.edu.cn
[2] College of Computer Science and Engineering, Chongqing Three Gorges University,
Chongqing 404000, China
{xjcq123,zhongandy}@sohu.com, yinghok@163.com
[3] School of Automation, Huazhong University of Science and Technology,
Wuhan 430074, China
likaixuan@hust.edu.cn

Abstract. This paper presents a distributed discrete-time consensus algorithm based on multi-agent network to solve large-scale linear algebraic equation (LAE). The matrix in the LAE is divided into submatrices by the columns. Each agent in the network only has its own local data on the LAE and all the agents collaboratively find the solutions while they communicate with their neighbors. Based on the Lyapunov method for difference equation, the multi-agent network is analyzed to reach consensus at the solutions under some mild conditions. Compared with existing algorithms for LAE, the proposed algorithm is capable of solving large-scale distributed LAE problems with fixed step size.

Keywords: Linear algebraic equation (LAE) · Distributed algorithm
Multi-agent network · Convergence

1 Introduction

Recently, distributed algorithms have brought much attention to large-scale optimization in science and engineering, especially the algorithms designed based on multi-agent networks. As a special case, the linear algebraic equation can be considered as a feasibility problem of constrained optimization. The objective of distributed algorithm is to divide the large-scale problem into many small ones, and solve the problem in a parallel manner. To get the solutions, the primal-dual or Lagrangian method is generally used, then a consensus on the primal or dual variables are required to guarantee the optimality. In the literature, there are many consensus algorithms to be proposed for solving this kind of distributed optimization problems [1–5].

Q. Liu—This work was supported in part by the National Natural Science Foundation of China under Grant 61473333.

© Springer International Publishing AG, part of Springer Nature 2018
T. Huang et al. (Eds.): ISNN 2018, LNCS 10878, pp. 415–422, 2018.
https://doi.org/10.1007/978-3-319-92537-0_48

More recently, distributed optimization has been widely investigated based on the analysis method for multi-agent systems. By minimizing or maximizing additive functions with global or local constraints, distributed optimization can be utilized to a variety of engineering applications [6,7]. Many continuous-time multi-agent networks have been designed to solve distributed optimization problems with different design methods [4,8–10]. In [11], a distributed control protocol was designed for continuous-time distributed optimization problem with a coupling state set constraint. A second-order multi-agent network was proposed in [8] to solve bound-constrained distributed optimization problems. In [12], a collective neurodynamic approach, which was also described as distributed neurodynamic system, was investigated for solving distributed optimization problems with decoupling constraints.

In addition, some discrete-time distributed algorithms were proposed for constrained nonsmooth optimization. Based on the primal-dual method, the subgradient algorithm for constrained convex optimization was proposed in [1,13]. A distributed subgradient algorithm with diminishing step size was presented for unconstrained distributed optimization in [14]. Based on the stochastic transition matrix, the distributed multi-agent optimization with nonidentical constraints was proposed in [15,16]. In [17,18], the multi-agent networks with delays were investigated for continuous-time and discrete-time systems. Based on the cutting-plane consensus algorithm, the robust property was investigated for distributed optimization in [19]. The distributed projection algorithms for convex optimization were designed in [20] based on the stochastic subgradient errors.

In this paper, we are interested in designing distributed algorithm for solving linear algebraic equation. First, the matrix in the linear algebraic equation is decomposed to many submatrices such that the matrix multiplications can be processed in parallel. Then the optimization technique is used to solve the divided linear algebraic equation, and the corresponding optimal conditions are constructed. Finally, based on the Lyapunov theory, the convergence/consensus of the multi-agent system is analyzed.

The rest of the paper is as follows. The preliminaries and problem formulation are introduced in Sect. 2. In Sect. 3, the distributed algorithm is described and the convergence of the algorithm is analyzed. Next, an illustrative example shows the performance of the proposed algorithm in Sect. 4. Finally, Sect. 5 concludes the paper.

2   Preliminaries and Problem Formulation

2.1   Graph Theory

A weighted undirected graph is defined as $\mathcal{G} = (\mathcal{V}, \mathcal{E}, \mathcal{A})$ with order N, which consists of a vertex set $\mathcal{V} = \{v_1, v_2, \ldots, v_N\}$, an undirected edge set $\mathcal{E} \subseteq \mathcal{V} \times \mathcal{V}$ and an adjacency matrix $\mathcal{A} = \{a_{ij}\}_{N \times N}$ to denote the connected relationship between nodes. We define $a_{ij} = 1$ if $(v_i, v_j) \in \mathcal{E}$ and $a_{ij} = 0$ otherwise. So for undirected graph, the adjacency matrix $\mathcal{A}$ is a symmetric 0-1 matrix. Here we assume no self-connection in the graph; i.e., $a_{ii} = 0$. Let's define the degree of node v_i as $d(v_i) = \sum_{j=1, j \neq i}^{N} a_{ij}$ $(i = 1, 2, \ldots, N)$, then the graph's Laplacian matrix can be written as $L_N = D - \mathcal{A}$, where D is a diagonal matrix with the form $D = \text{diag}\{d(v_1), d(v_2), \ldots, d(v_N)\}$. For undirected graph, L_N is symmetric and positive semi-definite. If there exists a path between any pair of distinct nodes, we say that the graph is connected.

For the Laplacian matrix, there are many results to estimate the upper bound of the maximum eigenvalue, such as the one in the following lemma.

Lemma 1. *[21] Let $\mathcal{G}$ be a graph with degree sequence $d(v_1) \geq d(v_2) \geq \cdots \geq d(v_N)$. Then*

$$\lambda_{\max}(L_N) \leq 2 + \sqrt{[d(v_1) + d(v_2) - 2][d(v_1) + d(v_3) - 2]}.$$

Then the following corollary is derived directly from Lemma 1.

Corollary 1. *Let $\mathcal{G}$ be a δ-regular graph; i.e., the degree of any point is $d(v_i) = \delta$ $(i = 1, 2, \ldots, N)$. Then*

$$\lambda_{\max}(L_N) \leq 2\delta.$$

2.2 Problem Formulation

This paper is concerned with the following linear algebraic equation (LAE)

$$Ax = b, \tag{1}$$

where $x \in \mathbb{R}^n$, $A \in \mathbb{R}^{m \times n}$ and $b \in \mathbb{R}^m$. To solve the LAE in a distributed manner, the matrix A is divided to N sub-matrices, i.e., $A = (A_1, A_2, \ldots, A_N)$ with $A_i \in \mathbb{R}^{m \times n_i}$ $(n_1 + n_2 + \cdots + n_N = n)$, $x = (x_1^T, x_2^T, \ldots, x_N^T)^T$ with $x_i \in \mathbb{R}^{n_i}$, and $b = b_1 + b_2 + \cdots + b_N$ with $b_i \in \mathbb{R}^m$. Then the LAE in (1) can be written as

$$\sum_{i=1}^{N}(A_i x_i - b_i) = 0. \tag{2}$$

Then the distributed LAE in (2) is obviously equivalent to the following minimization problem

$$\begin{aligned} &\text{minimize } c, \\ &\text{subject to } \sum_{i=1}^{N}(A_i x_i - b_i) = 0, \end{aligned} \tag{3}$$

where c is a constant.

The Lagrange function of (3) is defined as

$$\Phi(x, z) = c + z^T \sum_{i=1}^{N}(A_i x_i - b_i), \tag{4}$$

where $z \in \mathbb{R}^m$ is the Lagrange multiplier.

From the Saddle Point Theorem [22], x^* is an optimal solution to (3), if and only if there exists $z^* \in \mathbb{R}^m$ such that (x^*, z^*) is a saddle point of the Lagrange function in (4); i.e., for any $x \in \mathbb{R}^n$, and $z \in \mathbb{R}^m$, (x^*, z^*) satisfies the following inequalities

$$\Phi(x^*, z) \leq \Phi(x^*, z^*) \leq \Phi(x, z^*).$$

That is to say (x^*, y^*) is also a solution to the following minimax problem

$$\min_{x \in \mathbb{R}^n} \max_{z \in \mathbb{R}^m} \Phi(x, z). \tag{5}$$

To solve the minimax problem (5) in a distributed manner, the Lagrange function in (4) is rewritten as

$$\tilde{\Phi}(x, \tilde{z}) = c + \tilde{z}^T(\bar{A}x - \bar{b}), \tag{6}$$

where $\tilde{z} = (z_1^T, z_2^T, \ldots, z_N^T)^T \in \mathbb{R}^{Nm}$ with $z_i \in \mathbb{R}^m$, $\bar{A} = \mathrm{diag}\{A_1, A_2, \ldots, A_N\}$ is a block diagonal matrix, and $\bar{b} = (b_1^T, b_2^T, \ldots, b_N^T)^T$. Here z_i is the ith estimate of the Lagrange multiplier of the ith agent.

Lemma 2. *Assume the graph of the multi-agent network to be connected. The minimax problem (5) is equivalent to the following one:*

$$\begin{aligned} &\min_{x \in \mathbb{R}^n} \max_{\tilde{z} \in \mathbb{R}^{Nm}} \tilde{\Phi}(x, \tilde{z}), \\ &\textit{subject to} \quad L\tilde{z} = 0, \end{aligned} \tag{7}$$

where $L = L_N \otimes I_m \in \mathbb{R}^{Nm \times Nm}$ with $L_N \in \mathbb{R}^{N \times N}$ being the Laplacian matrix of the graph, I_m being m-dimensional identity matrix and $\otimes$ being the Kronecker product.

Proof: Similar to the proof of Lemma 3 in [8], for connected graph, $L\tilde{z} = 0$ if and only if $\tilde{z} = 1_N \otimes z$ for some $z \in \mathbb{R}^m$; i.e., $z_1 = z_2 = \cdots = z_N = z$. Then the problems in (5) and (7) are equivalent due to the connectivity of the graph. $\square$

Theorem 1. *$(x^*, \tilde{z}^*)$ is an optimal solution to (7) if and only if there exists $y^* \in \mathbb{R}^{Nm}$ such that $(x^*, y^*, \tilde{z}^*)$ satisfies*

$$\begin{cases} \bar{A}^T \tilde{z}^* = 0, \\ L\tilde{z}^* = 0, \\ \bar{A}x^* - \bar{b} + \mu L y^* = 0, \end{cases} \tag{8}$$

where μ is a positive constant.

Proof: $(x^*, \tilde{z}^*)$ is a solution to (7) if and only if for any $(x, \tilde{z}) \in \Theta = \{(x, \tilde{z}) : x \in \mathbb{R}^n, L\tilde{z} = 0\}$, the following inequalities hold

$$\tilde{\Phi}(x^*, \tilde{z}) \leq \tilde{\Phi}(x^*, \tilde{z}^*) \leq \tilde{\Phi}(x, \tilde{z}^*). \tag{9}$$

From the right inequality in (9), x^* is a minimum point of $\tilde{\Phi}(x, \tilde{z}^*)$ on $\mathbb{R}^n$ if and only if $(x^*, \tilde{z}^*)$ satisfies $\nabla_x \tilde{\Phi}(x^*, \tilde{z}^*) = 0$; i.e., $\bar{A}^T \tilde{z}^* = 0$.

From the left inequality in (9), $\tilde{z}^*$ is a maximum point of $\tilde{\Phi}(x^*, \tilde{z})$ on $\tilde{z} \in \Theta' = \{\tilde{z} : L\tilde{z} = 0\}$. The Lagrange function of this maximum problem is

$$\tilde{\Phi}'(y, \tilde{z}) = \tilde{\Phi}(x^*, \tilde{z}) + \mu y^T L\tilde{z},$$

where $y \in \mathbb{R}^{Nm}$ is the Lagrangian multiplier and μ is a positive constant. From the Karush-Kuhn-Tucker conditions [22], $\tilde{z}^*$ is an optimal solution to this maximum problem, if and only if there exists $y^* \in \mathbb{R}^{Nm}$ such that $\nabla_y \tilde{\Phi}'(y^*, \tilde{z}^*) = 0$ and $\nabla_{\tilde{z}} \tilde{\Phi}'(y^*, \tilde{z}^*) = 0$; i.e., $L\tilde{z}^* = 0$ and $\bar{A}x^* - \bar{b} + \mu L y^* = 0$. □

3   Distributed Algorithm and Convergence Analysis

Next, the distributed algorithm for solving the LAE in (1) is proposed and its convergence is analyzed.

3.1   Distributed Algorithm

According to the equalities in (8), the distributed algorithm for solving (1) is proposed as the following difference equations:

$$\begin{cases} x(k+1) = x(k) - \sigma\bar{A}^T[\tilde{z}(k) + \bar{A}x(k) - \bar{b} + \mu L(y(k) - \tilde{z}(k))], \\ y(k+1) = y(k) - \tilde{z}(k) - \bar{A}x(k) + \bar{b} - \mu L(y(k) - \tilde{z}(k)), \\ \tilde{z}(k+1) = \tilde{z}(k) + \bar{A}x(k+1) - \bar{b} + \mu L(y(k) - \tilde{z}(k)), \end{cases} \tag{10}$$

where σ is the step size.

The distributed algorithm (10) can be equivalently expressed as the following component form:

$$\begin{cases} x_i(k+1) = x_i(k) - \sigma A_i^T[z_i(k) + A_i x_i(k) - b_i \\ \qquad\qquad +\mu \sum\limits_{j=1, j \neq i}^{N} a_{ij}(y_i(k) - y_j(k) - z_i(k) + z_j(k))], \\ y_i(k+1) = y_i(k) - z_i(k) - A_i x_i(k) + b_i \\ \qquad\qquad -\mu \sum\limits_{j=1, j \neq i}^{N} a_{ij}(y_i(k) - y_j(k) - z_i(k) + z_j(k)), \\ z_i(k+1) = z_i(k) + A_i x_i(k+1) - b_i \\ \qquad\qquad +\mu \sum\limits_{j=1, j \neq i}^{N} a_{ij}(y_i(k) - y_j(k) - z_i(k) + z_j(k)), \end{cases} \tag{11}$$

where a_{ij} is the connection weight between agents i and j in the graph of the multi-agent network.

For convenience of later discussions, we use the subscript to denote the iterations and let $x_k = x(k)$, $y_k = y(k)$ and $\tilde{z}_k = \tilde{z}(k)$. For simplicity, the algorithm in (10) can be rewritten as:

$$\begin{cases} x_{k+1} = x_k - \sigma\bar{A}^T[\tilde{z}_k + \bar{A}x_k - \bar{b} + \mu L(y_k - \tilde{z}_k)], \\ y_{k+1} = y_k - \tilde{z}_k - \bar{A}x_k + \bar{b} - \mu L(y_k - \tilde{z}_k), \\ \tilde{z}_{k+1} = \tilde{z}_k + \bar{A}x_{k+1} - \bar{b} + \mu L(y_k - \tilde{z}_k). \end{cases} \tag{12}$$

3.2 Convergence Analysis

According to Lemma 2, the solutions of the LAE in (1) is equivalent to the solutions of the minimax problem in (2) if the graph of the multi-agent network described as the distributed algorithm in (12) is connected. Therefore, the solutions of problem (1) can be guaranteed if only the network is connected and the iterations in (12) are convergent.

Theorem 2. *Assume that the graph corresponding to the multi-agent network is connected and undirected. The vector x_k of the distributed algorithm in (12) is globally convergent to a solution of (1) if $\sigma < 1/(2\lambda_{\max}(\bar{A}^T \bar{A}))$ and $\mu < 1/\lambda_{\max}(L)$, where $\lambda_{\max}$ is the maximum eigenvalue of a matrix.*

Proof: Since the proof is similar to that of Theorem 2 in [23], we omit it here due to the page limit. □

To make the algorithm (12) be convergent, the step size should satisfy $\sigma < 1/(2\lambda_{\max}(\bar{A}^T \bar{A}))$ and the coupling coefficient μ should satisfy $\mu < 1/\lambda_{\max}(L)$. Since $\bar{A}^T \bar{A} = \mathrm{diag}\{A_1^T A_1, A_2^T A_2, \ldots, A_N^T A_N\}$, the equivalent condition for the step size is $\sigma < 1/(2\max_i \lambda_{\max}(A_i^T A_i))$. In addition, since $L = L_N \otimes I_m$, it follows $\lambda_{\max}(L) = \lambda_{\max}(L_N)$, where $\lambda_{\max}(L_N)$ is the maximum eigenvalue of the Laplacian matrix of the graph. Then the following corollary can be derived directly from Theorem 2.

Corollary 2. *Assume that the graph corresponding to the multi-agent network is connected and undirected. The vector x_k of the distributed algorithm in (12) is globally convergent to a solution of (1) if $\sigma < 1/(2\max_i \lambda_{\max}(A_i^T A_i))$ and $\mu < 1/\lambda_{\max}(L_N)$.*

As a special case, if the graph of the multi-agent network is δ-regular, we have $\lambda_{\max}(L_N) \leq 2\delta$ from Corollary 1. Then the following corollary is obtained.

Corollary 3. *Assume that the graph corresponding to the multi-agent network is connected and δ-regular. The vector x_k of the distributed algorithm in (12) is globally convergent to a solution of (1) if $\sigma < 1/(2\max_i \lambda_{\max}(A_i^T A_i))$ and $\mu < 1/(2\delta)$.*

4   An Illustrative Example

In the example, the values of the elements of A and b are generated randomly in $[-1, 1]$. In the experiments, the matrix A is divided to blocks with equal columns and vector b is divided to b/N, where N is the number of the blocks in A. By taking different values of N, we give some comparisons of the performance of the distributed algorithm in Fig. 1, which shows the error of $\|Ax - b\|$. From it we can see that the algorithm has similar convergence rate for different values of N. However, with the larger N, the problem is divided to more partitions to get a better distributed computing.

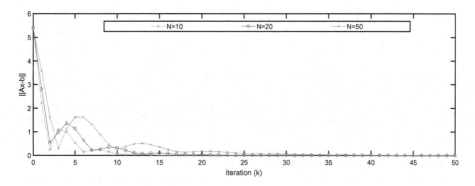

Fig. 1. Error function $\|Ax - b\|$ for different values of N.

5   Conclusion

This paper proposed a distributed algorithm based on continuous-time multi-agent network for linear algebraic equation. The linear algebraic equation was considered as a minimization problem and then the optimal conditions were constructed. Based on the optimal conditions, the distributed algorithm was designed after dividing the matrix into submatrices by the columns. Furthermore, the global convergence of the proposed distributed algorithm was analyzed to guarantee the solutions. Numerical example on a linear algebraic equation were presented to show the convergence of the algorithm. The potential advantages for the distributed algorithm included solving large-scale linear algebraic equations.

References

1. Nedic, A., Ozdaglar, A., Parrilo, P.A.: Constrained consensus and optimization in multi-agent networks. IEEE Trans. Autom. Control **55**, 922–938 (2010)
2. Yuan, D., Xu, S., Zhao, H.: Distributed primaldual subgradient method for multi-agent optimization via consensus algorithms. IEEE Trans. Syst. Man Cybern.-Part B: Cybern. **41**, 1715–1724 (2011)
3. Lu, J., Tang, C.Y.: Zero-gradient-sum algorithms for distributed convex optimization: the continuous-time case. IEEE Trans. Autom. Control **57**, 2348–2354 (2012)
4. Gharesifard, B., Cortés, J.: Distributed continuous-time convex optimization on weight-balanced digraphs. IEEE Trans. Autom. Control **59**, 781–786 (2014)
5. Mou, S.M., Liu, J., Morse, A.S.: A distributed algorithm for solving a linear algebraic equation. IEEE Trans. Autom. Control **60**, 2863–2878 (2015)
6. Boyd, S., Parikh, N., Chu, E., Peleato, B., Eckstein, J.: Distributed optimization and statistical learning via the alternating direction method of multipliers. Found. Trends Mach. Learn. **3**, 1–122 (2011)
7. Sundhar Ram, S., Nedić, A., Veeravalli, V.V.: A new class of distributed optimization algorithms: application to regression of distributed data. Optim. Methods Softw. **27**, 71–88 (2012)

8. Liu, Q., Wang, J.: A second-order multi-agent network for bound-constrained distributed optimization. IEEE Trans. Autom. Control **60**, 3310–3315 (2015)
9. Anderson, J., Papachristodoulou, A.: A decomposition/synchronization scheme for formulating and solving optimization problems. In: Proceedings of 1st IFAC Workshop on Distributed Estimation and Control in Networked Systems, pp. 96–101 (2009)
10. Lou, Y., Hong, Y., Wang, S.: Distributed continuous-time approximate projection protocols for shortest distance optimization problems. Automatica **69**, 289–297 (2016)
11. Qiu, Z., Liu, S., Xie, L.: Distributed constrained optimal consensus of multi-agent systems. Automatica **68**, 209–215 (2016)
12. Liu, Q., Yang, S., Wang, J.: A collective neurodynamic approach to distributed constrained optimization. IEEE Trans. Neural Netw. Learn. Syst. **28**, 1747–1758 (2017)
13. Wang, X., Hong, Y., Ji, H.: Distributed optimization for a class of nonlinear multiagent systems with disturbance rejection. IEEE Trans. Cybern. **46**, 1655–1666 (2016)
14. Nedic, A., Ozdaglar, A.: Distributed subgradient methods for multi-agent optimization. IEEE Trans. Autom. Control **54**, 48–61 (2009)
15. Lobel, I., Ozdaglar, A., Feijer, D.: Distributed multi-agent optimization with state-dependent communication. Math. Prog. **129**, 255–284 (2011)
16. Lin, P., Ren, W., Song, Y.: Distributed multi-agent optimization subject to nonidentical constraints and communication delays. Automatica **65**, 120–131 (2016)
17. Wang, H., Liao, X., Huang, T., Li, C.: Cooperative distributed optimization in multiagent networks with delays. IEEE Trans. Syst. Man Cybern. Syst. **45**, 363–369 (2015)
18. Yang, S., Liu, Q., Wang, J.: Distributed optimization based on a multiagent system in the presence of communication delays. IEEE Trans. Syst. Man Cybern. Syst. **47**, 717–728 (2017)
19. Bürger, M., Notarstefano, G., Allgöwer, F.: A polyhedral approximation framework for convex and robust distributed optimization. IEEE Trans. Autom. Control **59**, 384–395 (2014)
20. Ram, S.S., Nedić, A., Veeravalli, V.V.: Distributed stochastic subgradient projection algorithms for convex optimization. J. Optim. Theor. Appl. **147**, 516–545 (2010)
21. Grone, R., Merris, R.: The laplacian spectrum of a graph II. SIAM J. Discrete Math. **7**, 221–229 (1994)
22. Bazaraa, M., Sherali, H., Shetty, C.: Nonlinear Prog. Theor. Algorithms, 3rd edn. John Wiley & Sons, Hoboken, New Jersey (2006)
23. Liu, Q., Yang, S., Hong, Y.: Constrained consensus algorithms with fixed step size for distributed convex optimization over multiagent networks. IEEE Trans. Autom. Control **62**, 4259–4265 (2017)

Leader-Follower Tracking Problem for Multi-agent Systems with Directed Impulsive Communication

Changlin Tong, Wanli Jin, Hao Wang, Haijun Jiang$^{(\boxtimes)}$, and Zhiyong Yu

College of Mathematics and System Sciences, Xinjiang University,
Urumqi 830046, Xinjiang, China
jianghaijunxju@163.com

Abstract. The paper considers the tracking problem of multi-agent system with impulsive communication. Both the cases with fixed and switching directed networks are considered. By using Lyapunov stability theory and inequality techniques, the consensus tracking conditions are presented. Moreover, the coupling gain and a pinning strategy for choosing the nodes are carefully discussed, respectively. Finally, the validity of the protocol can be verified by some examples.

Keywords: Tracking problem · Switching communication
Directed network · Impulsive control

1 Introduction

Recently, the consensus problem has attached much attention due to its wide applications in the spacecraft formation flying [1], multiple robot coordination [2], flocking [3] and vehicle cooperative control [4]. A group of agents is called achieving consensus when they converge to a common value by interacting with each other. Hence, how to design distributed protocol such that all agents reach a common state is a major problem in the consensus control.

The pioneering work on consensus is [5]. After that, the consensus problem has been investigated in several fields, such as output feedback consensus, robust consensus, and adaptive consensus problems [6–8]. On the one hand, inspired by several-space craft formation flying problems, the leader-follower tracking (LFT) problem has been an active of research topic and there are many works on LFT [9–14]. On the other hand, although the continuous control can make all the agents reach the consensus, it will cost an enormous amount of energy. The impulsive control improve the efficiency. Moreover, since the impulsive control is

H. Jiang—This work was supported in part by the National Natural Science Foundation of China (Grants No. U1703262, No. 61473244), by the Excellent Undergraduate Innovation Program of Xinjiang Uyghur Autonomous Region under Grant 201710755047.

© Springer International Publishing AG, part of Springer Nature 2018
T. Huang et al. (Eds.): ISNN 2018, LNCS 10878, pp. 423–431, 2018.
https://doi.org/10.1007/978-3-319-92537-0_49

typically simpler and easier to implement than continuous-time control, various scientific communities have studied the impulsive control in the recent years.

Based on the above discussion, a protocol which solved the LFT problem of multi-agent system with directed impulsive communication is proposed in this paper. First, we investigate the LFT problem under fixed topology, then we find that if the strength of coupling and time interval satisfy some conditions, the LFT can be reached. Second, we consider the general condition that the control strength is a function decreasing with time. In addition, we use the method to popularize the conclusion in fixed topology to switching topologies.

The rest of this paper is organized as follows. In Sect. 2, the problem state and some assumptions are given. The main analyses for achieving LFT problem are presented in Sects. 3 and 4. Two examples are given to verify the effectiveness of the protocol in Sect. 5. In Sect. 6, a short conclusion is drawn.

2 Problem Formulation

Now, we consider a distributed multi-agent system with $N - 1$ agents and a leader. The nonlinear dynamics of the ith agent is described by

$$\dot{x}_i(t) = f(x_i(t), t) + u_i(t) \tag{1}$$

where $x_i(t) \in R$, $f(x_i(t), t)$ and $u_i(t)$ denote the agent state, the dynamic behavior and the control input, respectively.

The leader's dynamics is presented by

$$\dot{x}_0(t) = f(x_0(t), t) \tag{2}$$

where $x_0(t)$ is the state of the leader.

Definition 1. The LFT problem is said to be achieved in multi-agent system (1) if its solution satisfies

$$\lim_{t \to \infty} ||x_i(t) - x_0(t)|| = 0, \quad i = 1, 2, \cdots, N.$$

For investigating the LFT of (1) and (2), the following assumptions are given.

Assumption 1. There exists a nonnegative constant λ such that the following inequality holds for any x_i, x_j

$$|f(x_i(t)) - f(x_j(t))| \le \lambda |x_i(t) - x_j(t)|, \quad i, j = 1, 2, \cdots, N.$$

In the continuous control, the controller is working in a continuous process, while the controller works only at some time in the impulsive control, so it is a relatively more effective and better control method. Therefore, we propose the following protocol

$$u_i(t) = \alpha \sum_{k=1}^{\infty} \left(\sum_{j=1}^{N} a_{ij}(x_j(t) - x_i(t)) + d_i(x_i(t) - x_0(t)) \right) \delta(t - t_k) \tag{3}$$

where $\alpha > 0$ is constant which represent the coupling strength, d_i represents the control strength of the leader on the agent i, in which if $d_i > 0$, the leader control the agent i, else $d_i = 0$. The network structure is denoted by a directed graph $\mathcal{G} = \{\mathcal{V},\ \mathcal{E},\ \mathcal{A}\}$. The Dirac impulsive function $\delta(t)$ is defined:

$$\delta(t - t_k) = \begin{cases} 1, & t = t_k \\ 0, & t \neq t_k \end{cases} \tag{4}$$

where t_k is the impulsive sequence and $t_0 = 0,\ \lim_{k \to \infty} t_k = \infty$.

By the definition of $\delta(t)$, the impulsive control (3) is written as:

$$u_i(t) = \begin{cases} 0, & t \neq t_k \\ \alpha\bigg(\sum_{j=1}^{N} a_{ij}(x_j(t) - x_i(t)) + d_i(x_i(t) - x_0(t))\bigg), & t = t_k \end{cases} \tag{5}$$

Assumption 2. Suppose that the directed graph $\mathcal{G}$ has a directed spanning tree, and at least one follower agent can receive the leader's information.

Remark 1. Compared with the traditional controller, the impulsive controller is designed in the paper, which not only can clearly achieve target state but also greatly save resources.

3   Fixed Network Case

In this section, the LFT problem under fixed network is considered. With the impulsive control (3), the multi-agent system (1) is described by

$$\dot{x}_i(t) = f(x_i(t), t) + \alpha \sum_{k=1}^{\infty} \bigg(\sum_{j=1}^{N} a_{ij}(x_j(t) - x_i(t)) + d_i(x_i(t) - x_0(t))\bigg)\delta(t - t_k) \tag{6}$$

where the impulse time sequence $\{t_k\}_{k=1}^{\infty}$ satisfies $h_k = t_{k+1} - t_k$.

Assumption 3. The time interval h_k has lower and upper bounds, $\eta_1 \leq h_k \leq \eta_2$, where $\eta_1, \eta_2 > 0$.

Let $e_i(t) = x_i(t) - x_0(t)$ represent the tracking error, then the dynamics of the tracking error can be written as:

$$\begin{cases} \dot{e}_i(t) = f(x_i(t)) - f(x_0(t)), & t \neq t_k \\ \Delta e_i(t_k) = \alpha\bigg(\sum_{j=1}^{N} a_{ij}(x_j(t_k) - x_i(t_k)) + d_i(x_i(t_k) - x_0(t_k))\bigg), & t = t_k \end{cases} \tag{7}$$

Theorem 1. Suppose that Assumptions 1–3 hold. The systems (1) and (2) with the protocol (3) can achieve LFC if

$$\tilde{\rho} < e^{-2\lambda\eta_2} \tag{8}$$

where $\tilde{\rho}$ is the maximum eigenvalue of $[I - \alpha(L+D)]^T[I - \alpha(L+D)]$, η_2 represents upper bound of h_k.

Proof. Constructing the Lyapunov function as follows

$$V(t) = \sum_{i=1}^{N} e_i^2(t). \tag{9}$$

When $t \neq t_k$, it follows that

$$\dot{e}_i(t) = \dot{x}_i(t) - \dot{x}_0(t) = f(x_i(t)) - f(x_0(t)). \tag{10}$$

Based on Assumption 1 and (9)–(10), one can obtain that

$$\dot{V}(t) = 2 \sum_{i=1}^{N} e_i(t)\dot{e}_i(t) \leq 2\lambda \sum_{i=1}^{N} e_i^2(t). \tag{11}$$

Then,

$$\dot{V}(t) \leq 2\lambda \sum_{i=1}^{N} e_i^2(t) = 2\lambda V(t). \tag{12}$$

Hence, it has

$$V(t) \leq V(t_k)e^{2\lambda(t-t_k)}, \quad t \in [t_k, t_{k+1}). \tag{13}$$

When $t = t_k$, based on (7), it can obtain that

$$e_i(t_k^+) = -\alpha \sum_{j=1}^{N} l_{ij} e_j(t_k^-) + \alpha d_i e_i(t_k^-) + e_i(t_k^-). \tag{14}$$

Let $e(t) = (e_1(t), e_2(t), \cdots, e_N(t))$, then Eq. (14) is given by

$$e(t_k^+) = -\alpha(L+D)e(t_k^-) + e(t_k^-) = [I - \alpha(L+D)]e(t_k^-). \tag{15}$$

Therefore, we get

$$V(t_{k+1}^-) \leq V(t_k)e^{2\lambda h_k} \leq V(t_k)e^{2\lambda \eta_2}. \tag{16}$$

Combining with the Eq. (9), It has

$$V(t_{k+1}^+) = \sum_{i=1}^{N} e_i^2(t_{k+1}^+) \leq \tilde{\rho} \sum_{i=1}^{N} e_i^2(t_{k+1}^-) \tag{17}$$

where $\tilde{\rho} = \|I - \alpha(L+D)\|^2 = \lambda_{max}(I - \alpha(L+D))^T(I - \alpha(L+D))$, λ_{max} is the maximum eigenvalue of $[I - \alpha(L+D)]^T[I - \alpha(L+D)]$.

Based on (16) and (17). It follows that

$$V(t_{k+1}^+) \leq \tilde{\rho}e^{2\lambda \eta_2} V(t_k).$$

According to mathematical induction, one can obtain that

$$V(t_{k+1}^+) \leq [\tilde{\rho}e^{2\lambda \eta_2}]^k V(t_0). \tag{18}$$

Then from (8), we get $\lim_{t \to \infty} V(t) = 0$, which implies that the consensus problem is solved under fixed topology.

Corollary 1. Suppose that the network topology is undirected and Assumptions 1 and 3 hold. Then the systems (1) and (2) with protocol (3) can achieve the LFT problem if

$$\frac{1 - e^{-\lambda \eta_2}}{\rho_{min}} \leq \alpha \leq \frac{1 + e^{-\lambda \eta_2}}{\rho_{max}}$$

where ρ_{min} is the minimum eigenvalue of $(L + D)$, ρ_{max} is the maximum eigenvalue of $(L + D)$

Proof. Let ρ be the eigenvalue of $I - \alpha(L + D)$. There exists a matrix U which makes $U(I - \alpha(L + D))U^T = I - \alpha \hat{\Lambda}$, where $\hat{\Lambda} = diag(\rho_1, \cdots, \rho_N)$. Based on Theorem 1 and some simple calculations, it can easily derived.

Corollary 2. Suppose that the network topology is undirected and Assumptions 1 and 3 hold. Then the systems (1) and (2) with protocol (3) can achieve the LFT problem if

$$\alpha \geq n \frac{1 + e^{-\lambda \eta_2}}{tr(L) + tr(D)}. \tag{19}$$

Suppose the network is undirected, the following control method is given to control a set of nodes.

Step 1. Choosing α from (19).

Step 2. Finding $tr(D)$ which satisfies

$$tr(D) = \frac{n(1 + e^{-\lambda \eta_2})}{\alpha} - tr(L). \tag{20}$$

Step 3. Defining

$$\frac{n(1 + e^{-\lambda h_k})}{\alpha} - tr(L) = c.$$

Assuming that $d_i(t_k) = g(e_i(t_{k-1}))$ is a monotonically decrease function and it has an upper bound $\sup g_i(e_i(t_k)), i = k = 1, 2, \cdots, N$, then we order $\sup g_i(e_i(t_k))$ from large to small as following

$$\sup g_{i_1}(e_{i_1}(t_k)) > \sup g_{i_2}(e_{i_2}(t_k)) > \cdots$$
$$> \cdots > \sup g_{i_j}(e_{i_j})(t_k) > \cdots > \sup g_{i_n}(e_{i_n}(t_k)) \tag{21}$$

The point corresponding to $\sup g(e_{i_j}(x_{i_j}(t_k))$ is denoted as $v_{i_j}(t_k), j = 1, 2, \cdots, N$, then if

$$\sum_{j=1}^{m-1} \sup g_{i_j}(e_{i_j}(t_k)) < c, m = 2, 3, \cdots, N$$

at the same time,

$$\sum_{j=1}^{m} \sup g_{i_j}(e_{i_j}(t_k)) + \sup g_{i_m}(e_{i_m}(t_k)) > c$$

so, we can get the number of the manipulative notes are m.

Step 4. If α is not satisfactory, let $\alpha = \alpha + \epsilon_1$, where ϵ_1 is a small positive number. Repeating step 2 to step 4 until finding a proper α and the number of control numbers.

Remark 2. Although the control strength $d_i(t_k), i = k = 1, 2, \cdots, N - 1$ in corollary 2 can very large, we chose $d_i(t_k) = f(e_i(t_{k-1}))$ which become smaller with decreased of error system such that they are what we need the values in practice.

4   Switching Topologies Case

In this section, suppose that the information transmission network among agents is time-varying, which is described by the digraph $\mathcal{G}(t) = \{\mathcal{V}, \mathcal{E}(t), \mathcal{A}(t)\}$. Let $L_{\sigma(t)}$ denote the Laplace matrix of $\mathcal{G}(t)$, where the $\sigma(t)$ is the switching time that is calculated by using the function which is related with time intervals h_k. Similarly, the impulsive control input is given by:

$$u_i(t) = \alpha \sum_{k=1}^{\infty} \left(\sum_{j=1}^{N} a_{ij}(t)(x_j(t) - x_i(t)) + d_i(t)(x_i(t) - x_0(t)) \right) \delta(t - t_k) \quad (22)$$

where $i = 1, 2, \ldots, N$.

Similarly to the fixed network, under the impulsive controller (22), the multi-agent system (1) is donated by:

$$\begin{cases} \dot{x}_i(t) = f(x_i(t), t) - f(x_0(t), t)) & , t \neq t_k \\ \Delta x_i(t_k) = \alpha \left(\sum_{j=1}^{N} a_{ij}(t)(x_j(t) - x_i(t)) + d_i(x_i(t) - x_0(t)) \right), t = t_k \end{cases} \quad (23)$$

Assumption 4. There exists a directed spanning tree at each impulse interval and the switching frequency is greater than the impulse frequency, i.e., $T_{min} > h_k$, where $T_{min} = min\ [\hat{t}_k, \hat{t}_{k+1})$, $\hat{t}_k$ is switching time, and $h_k = t_k - t_{k-1}$.

Let $e_i(t) = x_i(t) - x_0(t)$ represent the tracking error, then the dynamics behavior of the tracking error system is written as:

$$\begin{cases} \dot{e}_i(t) = f(x_i(t)) - f(x_0(t)), & t \neq t_k \\ \Delta e_i(t_k) = \alpha(\sum_{j=1}^{N} a_{ij}(x_j(t_k) - x_i(t_k)) + d_i(x_i(t_k) - x_0(t_k))), t = t_k \end{cases} \quad (24)$$

Now, we introduce one of main results.

Theorem 2. For multi-agent systems (1) and (2) with the protocol (22), the LFT problem is achieved if the Assumptions 1, 3, and 4 hold and the following conditions are satisfied

$$\tilde{\rho}_{\sigma(t)} \leq e^{-2\lambda \eta_2} \quad (25)$$

$$\alpha \geq \frac{1 + e^{-\lambda \eta_2}}{tr(L_{\sigma(t)}) + tr(D_{\sigma(t)})} \quad (26)$$

where $\tilde{\rho}_{\sigma(t)}$ is the maximum eigenvalue of $[I - \alpha(L_{\sigma(t)} + D_{\sigma(t)(t)})]^T [I - \alpha(L_{\sigma(t)} + D_{\sigma(t)})]$.

Proof. The similar analysis can be found Theorem 1.

5   Numerical Examples

Showing the usefulness of the proposed consensus algorithms, the following two examples are presented.

Example 1. Considering the systems (1) and (2) with the protocol (3), the communication network is shown in Fig. 1. The agent dynamics is described by nonlinear function $f(x) = sin(x)$. The initial states are $x_1(0) = 1, x_2(0) = 5, x_3(0) = 3.5, x_4(0) = 8, x_5(0) = 0.005, x_6(0) = 2, x_7(0) = 4, x_8(0) = 6$. According to Theorem 1, the LCF can be achieved when $\alpha \geq 0.8$ as shown in Fig. 2, in which the agent x_2, x_3, x_4, x_5 need to be controlled.

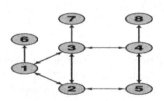

Fig. 1. The communication topology.   **Fig. 2.** The states of agents.

Example 2. Considering the systems (1) and (2) with the protocol (22), the communication topology are shown in Figs. 3, 4, 5 and 6. The agent dynamics is given by the function $f(x) = sin(x)$. The initial states are $x_1(0) = 1, x_2(0) = 5, x_3(0) = 3.5, x_4(0) = 0.0008, x_5(0) = 0.005, x_6(0) = 2, x_7(0) = 4, x_8(0) = 6$, then according to Theorem 2, the LFC can be achieved when the coupling strength $\alpha \geq 0.7835$ as shown in Fig. 7.

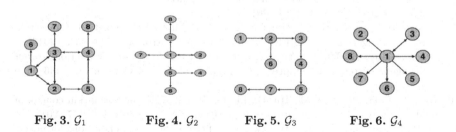

Fig. 3. $\mathcal{G}_1$ **Fig. 4.** $\mathcal{G}_2$ **Fig. 5.** $\mathcal{G}_3$ **Fig. 6.** $\mathcal{G}_4$

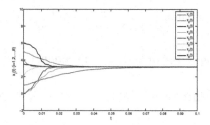

Fig. 7. The states of agents.

6 Conclusions

This paper studies the LFT problem of multi-agent systems via impulsive control. The convergence analyses of the proposed control protocols are considered for the fixed communication topology and switching topologies respectively. Two numerical examples are given to verify the feasibility of the results. The robust tracking consensus issue will be investigated in our future work.

References

1. Beard, R., Lawton, J., Hadaegh, F.: A coordination architecture for spacecraft formation control. IEEE Trans. Control Syst. Technol. **9**, 777–790 (2001)
2. Schneider-Fontan, M., Mataric, M.: Territorial multi-robot task division. IEEE Trans. Robotic. Autom. **14**, 815–822 (1998)
3. Vicsek, T., Czirok, A., Jacob, E., Cohen, I., Schochet, O.: Novel type of phase transition in a system of self-drive particles. Phys. Rev. Lett. **75**, 1226–1229 (1995)
4. Fax, J., Murray, R.: Information flow and cooperative control of vehicle formations. IEEE Trans. Autom. Control **49**, 1465–1476 (2004)
5. Olfati-Saber, R., Murray, R.: Consensus problems in networks of agents with switching topology and time-delays. IEEE Trans. Autom. Control **49**, 1520–1533 (2004)
6. Li, Z., Duan, Z., Chen, G.: Consensus of multi-agent systems and synchronization of complex networks: a unified viewpoint. IEEE Trans. Circuits Syst. I Reg. Papers **57**, 213–224 (2010)
7. Li, Z., Ren, W., Liu, X.: Consensus of multi-agent systems with general linear and Lipschitz nonlinear dynamics using distributed adaptive protocols. IEEE Trans. Autom. Control **58**, 1786–1791 (2013)
8. Trentelman, H., Takaba, K., Monshizadeh, N.: Robust synchronization of uncertain linear multi-agent systems. IEEE Trans. Autom. Control **58**, 1511–1523 (2013)
9. Yu, Z., Jiang, H., Hu, C., Yu, J.: Leader-following consensus of fractional-order multi-agent systems via adaptive pinning control. Int. J. Control **88**, 1746–1756 (2015)
10. Han, T., Guan, Z., Chi, M., Hu, B., Li, T., Zhang, X.: Multi-formation control of nonlinear leader-following multi-agent systems. ISA Trans. **69**, 140–147 (2017)
11. Li, P., Xu, S., Ma, Q., Chen, W., Zhang, Z.: Leader-following rendezvous for uncertain Euler-Lagrange multi-agent systems by output feedback. J. Franklin Inst. **354**, 4215–4230 (2017)

12. Zheng, T., He, M., Xi, J., Liu, G.: Leader-following guaranteed-performance consensus design for singular multi-agent systems with Lipschitz nonlinear dynamics. Neurocomputing **266**, 651–658 (2017)
13. Sun, F., Chen, J., Guan, Z., Ding, L., Li, T.: Leader-following finite-time consensus for multi-agent systems with jointly-reachable leader. Nonlinear Anal. Real. World Appl. **13**, 2271–2284 (2012)
14. Wang, X., Ni, W., Wang, X.: Leader-following formation of switching multirobot systems via internal model. IEEE Trans. Syst., Man, Cybern. B, Cybern. **42**, 817–826 (2012)

Event-Triggered Consensus of General Linear Multi-agent System with Time Delay

Yonghui Wu and Nankun Mu[✉]

The Chongqing Key Laboratory of Nonlinear Circuits and Intelligent Information Processing, Southwest University, Chongqing 400715, People's Republic of China
nankun.mu@qq.com

Abstract. This paper deals with the event-triggered consensus problem of general linear multi-agent system considering time delay under directed communication graph. The existence of a positive constant on inter-event interval is proved. Finally, the correctness of our results is illustrated by experiments.

Keywords: Event-triggered · Consensus · Multi-agent systems
Time delay

1 Introduction

Generally, multi-agent system consists of many agents with abilities such as computation and communication. The basic problem of this systems is consensus which means all agents' state of the systems can reach a common value by interaction or communication with their neighbor agents. Researches have successfully applied multi-agent system to a large number of practical problems such as unmanned aerial vehicle (UAV), distributed cooperation optimization and formation control and so on. As to the important problem, readers can refer to [3,10,14–18].

In traditional controllers design, the continuous communication between agents and update of controllers are often required for achieving the consensus, which must shorten the life span of system. To overcome the disadvantage, periodic sampling control scheme was proposed, leading to intermittent communication between agents and update of controllers. However, the control scheme also has its limitation, it may not make full use of the energy. As is proved, the event-triggered strategy outperforms periodic sampling control scheme for saving energy [1]. Due to this reasons, many studies about event-triggered consensus control scheme of this system appear [5,6,21].

Excluding Zeno behaviour, meaning without continuously exchanging information, is an important problem we should consider when analyzing the performance of event-triggered consensus algorithm for multi-agent system. For example, [2,3,7] all proved that event-triggered consensus of multi-agent system can

© Springer International Publishing AG, part of Springer Nature 2018
T. Huang et al. (Eds.): ISNN 2018, LNCS 10878, pp. 432–439, 2018.
https://doi.org/10.1007/978-3-319-92537-0_50

be achieved asymptotically under connected communication graph. But methods of them can not be used any more when communication graph is directed. However [13,22] addressed exclusion of Zeno behaviour, the performances of their algorithm are not perfect: the state error between agents converges to a constant Δ, rather than to 0. Hence, it is also significant and challenging for us to solve the problem under directed communication graph.

Time delay unavoidably emerges in dynamic systems [9] due to a signal processing and propagation. Hence, considering time delay has practical significance when designing the event-triggered control protocol. Up to now, there are only a few researches devoting to this issue [4,11,13]. Authors of [11] discussed single-integrator dynamics model under strongly connected communication graph. [4] studied the single-integrator dynamics model under the condition: directed communication network. In [13], authors dealt with the consensus of general linear model, but the consensus can not be fully achieved.

Based on the observation above, this paper addresses the event-triggered consensus of general linear multi-agent system with time delay under directed communication graph.

The main contributions are presented as follows.

1. The model of general linear multi-agent system, containing time delay fact which is not considered in [19,20], is studied for event-triggered scheme.
2. The existence of a positive constant on inter-event interval is ensured under more general conditions than [3,8]. The model of [3] is single-integrator and communication graph is undirected connected while [8] studied the case of undirected connected communication graph and time delay was not considered.

2   Preliminaries

Some notations to be used will be introduced throughout this paper. Let $\| \cdot \|$ stand for the Euclidean norm for vectors or the induced 2-norm for matrices. Let $A \in R^{m \times n}$ and $A \in C^{m \times n}$ represent a $m \times n$ real matrix and complex matrix, respectively. A^T describes transposed matrix of matrix A. Let $\lambda_i(A)$ stand for the ith eigenvalue of matrix A. $Re(\cdot)$ is used to denote real part of a complex number. Matrix $A \in C^{m \times n}$ is said to be Hurwitz if all its eigenvalues have strictly negative real parts.

The communication graph G in multi-agent system consists of three elements, the set of agents V, the set of edges between agents ξ and the weighted adjacency matrix A. For example, $(v_j, v_i) \in \xi$ is used to represent the agent i can obtain the information from agent j, then agent j is in-neighbor of agent i and agent i is out-neighbor of agent j. The element a_{ij} of A satisfies following conditions: $a_{ii} = 0, a_{ij} > 0$ if $(v_j, v_i) \in \xi$, otherwise $a_{ij} = 0$, $i, j = 1, 2, \ldots, N$. N_i describe the set of in-neighbors of agent i, meaning $N_i = \{j \in V | (v_j, v_i) \in \xi\}$. For all $i, j, 1, 2, \ldots, N, i \neq j$, if $(v_j, v_i) \in \xi$ always implies $(v_i, v_j) \in \xi$, the G is considered to be undirected communication graph otherwise directed. If there is a agent such that it can reach any other agents along the directed communication graph G, the G is said to contain a spanning tree and the agent is called root agent.

Consider following multi-agent system, whose dynamical behavior is described by

$$\dot{x}_i(t) = Ax_i(t) + Bu_i(t), i = 1, \ldots, N, \tag{1}$$

where $x_i(t) \in R^{n_i}$ and $u_i(t) \in R^{p_i}$ denote the state, input of agent i, respectively. $A \in R^{n_i \times n_i}$ and $B \in R^{n_i \times p_i}$ are constant matrices.

Definition 1. *By designing a proper controller u_i for each agent, the consensus of system (1) is said to be achieved if the following condition satisfies:*

$$\lim_{t \to +\infty} \|x_i(t) - x_j(t)\| = 0, i, j = 1, \ldots, N, \tag{2}$$

for any initial conditions.

We firstly introduce following assumptions when addressing consensus problem of systems (1).

Assumption 1. *(A, B) is stabilizable.*

Assumption 2. *The communication graph G between agents is directed containing a spanning tree.*

3   Event-Triggered Control Design

First, following lemma is derived for achieving our main result about the consensus of multi-agent system (1). Next, the event-triggered controller $u_i(t)$ considering time delay is presented, $i = 1, 2, \ldots, N$.

Lemma 1. *[20] If the matrix $A \in R^{n \times n}$ is Hurwitz, then following condition satisfies*

$$\| e^{At} \| \leq (n - 1) \| P_A \| \| P_A^{-1} \| c_A e^{a_A t}, t > 0, \tag{3}$$

where J_A is the Jordan canonical form of matrix A, P_A is a nonsingular matrix satisfying $P_A^{-1} A P_A = J_A$, $max_i Re(\lambda_i(A)) < a_A < 0$ and $c_A > 0$ obtaining value from $((\frac{d}{e(a_A - \lambda)})^d, +\infty)$. e, λ and d are defined in [20].

In the following, we will give the controller considering time delay for each agent.

$$u_i(t) = cK \sum_{j \in N_i} (e^{A(t - \tau - t_{k_i}^i)} x_i(t_{k_i}^i) - e^{A(t - \tau - t_{k_j}^j)} x_j(t_{k_j}^j)), \tag{4}$$

where $c > 0$ represents coupling gain, $K \in R^{p \times n}$ is the feedback gain matrix, $\{t_{k_0}^i, t_{k_1}^i, \ldots, t_{k_n}^i\}$ is triggering time sequence determined by event triggering mechanism, where $t_{k_0}^i = t_0 = 0$ is initial time, N_i is neighborhood set of agent i and τ represents time delay. We assume that communication delay and input delay are the same. $e^{A(t - \tau - t_{k_i}^i)} x_i(t_{k_i}^i)$ reflects the input delay between controller and actuator of agent i and $e^{A(t - \tau - t_{k_j}^j)} x_j(t_{k_j}^j)$ reflects communication delay between agents, $i, j = 1, 2, \ldots, N$.

Remark 1. When there exists the special case that root agent of a directed spanning tree receives no information from other agents, the problem become that of leader-following consensus. In this case, we set a triggering instant for the agent and the agent only triggers once. It is easy to know that the root agent only triggers one time throughout the process. This can be demonstrated by our computer simulations.

The measurement error is defined as

$$e_i(t) = e^{A(t-t^i_{k_i})}x_i(t^i_{k_i}) - x_i(t), t \in [t^i_{k_i}, t^i_{k_i+1}),$$ (5)

where $t^i_{k_i}$ is event-triggered instant determined by triggering function and it is given as follows:

$$f_i(t, e_i(t)) = \| e_i(t) \| - c_1 e^{-at},$$ (6)

where $c_1 > 0$ and α are positive constants to be determined. An event doesn't trigger for agent i until it satisfies $f_i(t, e_i(t)) = 0$. Because of time delay, its controller and neighbour agents receive the information and update the controllers at instant $t^i_{k_i} + \tau$. Other agents also work the same way. If the event doesn't occur, each agents run based on current controllers without communication with its neighbor agents.

Under Assumption 1 and 2, following steps are presented to choose the control parameters for addressing the consensus problem.

1. Find a solution matrix P for following linear matrix inequality to make sure it is a symmetric positive-definite. The feedback gain matrix K is set to be $K = -B^T P^{-1}$.

$$AP + PA^T - 2BB^T < 0.$$ (7)

2. The value of coupling gain c is chosen from $(\frac{1}{min_i Re(\lambda_i(L))}, +\infty)$, where $\lambda_i(L)$ represent nonzero eigenvalues of Laplacian matrix L.
3. Set parameter c_1 such that $c_1 > 0$ in (6).

Remark 2. Assumption 1 can make sure a symmetric positive-definite matrix solution P for linear matrix inequality (7) [20]. Under Assumption 2, we can obtain the value c and K based on step above such that the matrices $A + c\lambda_i(L)BK$, where $\lambda_i(L) \neq 0$, are all Hurwitz [12]. How to choose the parameter α will be explained in Theorem 1.

In the following, we present our main result.

Theorem 1. Under Assumption 1 and 2, system (1) can achieve the consensus exponentially under control strategy (4)(5)(6). The control parameters are determined according to the Step 1,2,3, and τ and α, respectively, are chosen such that their satisfy $\tau < \frac{-a_{11}}{c_{11}(k_3+k_4)}$ and $0 < \alpha < \alpha^*$, where α_{II}, c_{II}, k_3, k_4 and α^* are defined by A, B, L and c. Furthermore, there exists a positive constant lower bound on the inter-event time interval.

Proof. Combining with Lemma 1, the Inequality technique can be used to prove it.

Remark 3. When time delay is not considered, meaning $\tau = 0$, we can get result similar to [20], which implies our result is more general than that of [20].

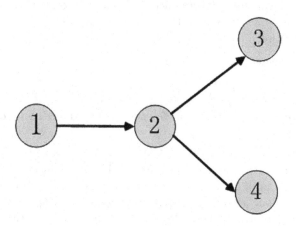

Fig. 1. Communication graph G

4   Simulation

In this part, experiment data is presented to illustrate the correctness of our results about the event-triggered consensus protocol of multi-agent system (1). Figure 1 is used to model communication network between agents. In this special case, the problem becomes leader-following consensus problem and agent 1 works as the leader agent triggering only once.

Table 1. Number of control update by event-triggered control scheme with time delay under directed graph

Control scheme	c_1	Time (s)	Update numbers of agents				
			1	2	3	4	*sum*
Event-triggered	0.4	39.527	0	21	66	49	136
	0.6	46.459	0	13	46	34	93
	1	58.833	0	17	58	38	113
	1.5	66.505	0	20	53	40	113
	2	77.872	0	21	68	47	136

The parameters are chosen as follows. $A = [0,1;-1,0]$, $B = [1,0;0,1]$. The Laplacian matrix of Fig. 1 $L = [0\ 0\ 0\ 0;\ -1\ 1\ 0\ 0;\ 0\ -1\ 1\ 0;\ 0\ -1\ 0\ 1]$ and nonzero eigenvalues of L are 1, 1, 1, respectively. Based on the step 1, 2, 3, choose

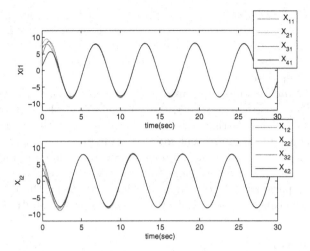

Fig. 2. State responds of the agents by event-triggered control

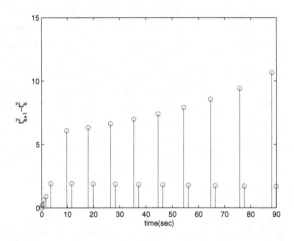

Fig. 3. Inter-event interval of agent 2 by event-triggered control within 90 s, $c_1 = 1$

Table 2. Number of communication by event-triggered control scheme with time delay under directed graph

Control scheme	c_1	Time (s)	Communication numbers of agents				
			1	2	3	4	*sum*
Event-triggered	0.4	39.527	1	40	0	0	41
	0.6	46.459	1	24	0	0	25
	1	58.833	1	32	0	0	33
	1.5	66.505	1	38	0	0	39
	2	77.872	1	40	0	0	41

$c = 1.9$ and $K = [-1/3, 0; 0, -1/3]$ and get $a_\Pi = -0.3167$. Hence, we can obtain $k_3 = 1.2235$, $k_4 = 1.4970$. $a_\Pi = -0.3167$, $\tau = 0.008$ and $a^* = 0.065$. Choose $\alpha = 0.06$ for simulation. The initial states are given by $X_1(0) = [6.733, 4.296]^T$, $X_2(0) = [7.727, 6.964]^T$, $X_3(0) = [4.231, 6.556]^T$ and $X_4(0) = [1.265, 1.343]^T$. The parameter c_1 works as a variable.

The term $'time'$ denotes the convergence time the agents take to satisfy the condition: $\sum_{j=2}^{4} \parallel x_1(t) - x_j(t) \parallel < 0.01$. From Fig. 2, the state consensus is achieved under our event-triggered control scheme. Also the result that there is a positive constant on inter-event interval is obvious to conclude from Fig. 3. In Tables 1 and 2, we record the number of controller update and number of communication between agents before convergence time, respectively.

In fact, the parameters τ, C and α also have effects on the performance of our algorithm, because of space limitation, this studies are omitted here.

5   Conclusion

This paper first has dealt with the event-triggered consensus of general linear multi-agent systems taking time delay into consideration under directed communication network. Next, Existing a positive constant on inter-event interval is proved by our method, even though our model is more complex than some existing literatures.

Acknowledgments. This work was supported in part by the National Key Research and Development Program of China under Grant 2016 YFB 0800601, in part by the National Natural Science Foundation of China under Grant 61472331.

References

1. Astrom, K.J., Bernhardsson, B.M.: Comparison of Riemann and Lebesgue sampling for first order stochastic systems. In: 2002 Proceedings of the IEEE Conference on Decision and Control, vol. 2, pp. 2011–2016 (2002)
2. Fan, Y., Feng, G., Wang, Y., Song, C.: Distributed event-triggered control of multi-agent systems with combinational measurements. Automatica **49**(2), 671–675 (2013)
3. Fan, Y., Liu, L., Feng, G., Wang, Y.: Self-triggered consensus for multi-agent systems with zeno-free triggers. IEEE Trans. Autom. Control **60**(10), 2779–2784 (2015)
4. Gao, L., Liao, X., Li, H., Chen, G.: Event-triggered control for multi-agent systems with general directed topology and time delays. Asian J. Control **18**(3), 945–953 (2016)
5. Garcia, E., Cao, Y., Casbeer, D.W.: Decentralized event-triggered consensus with general linear dynamics. Automatica **50**(10), 2633–2640 (2014)
6. Guo, G., Ding, L., Han, Q.L.: A distributed event-triggered transmission strategy for sampled-data consensus of multi-agent systems. Automatica **50**(5), 1489–1496 (2014)
7. Hu, W., Liu, L., Feng, G.: Consensus of linear multi-agent systems by distributed event-triggered strategy. IEEE Trans. Cybern. **46**(1), 148–157 (2016)

8. Hu, W., Liu, L., Feng, G.: Output consensus of heterogeneous linear multi-agent systems by distributed event-triggered/self-triggered strategy. IEEE Trans. Cybern. **PP**(99), 1–11 (2016)

9. Huang, H., Feng, G., Cao, J.: Robust state estimation for uncertain neural networks with time-varying delay. IEEE Trans. Neural Netw. **19**(8), 1329–1339 (2008)

10. Li, H., Liao, X., Huang, T., Zhu, W.: Event-triggering sampling based leader-following consensus in second-order multi-agent systems. IEEE Trans. Autom. Control **60**(7), 1998–2003 (2015)

11. Li, L., Ho, D.W.C., Lu, J.: Event-based network consensus with communication delays. Nonlinear Dyn. **87**(3), 1847–1858 (2017)

12. Li, Z., Duan, Z., Chen, G., Huang, L.: Consensus of multiagent systems and synchronization of complex networks: a unified viewpoint. IEEE Trans. Circuits Syst. I: Reg. Papers **57**(1), 213–224 (2010)

13. Mu, N., Liao, X., Huang, T.: Event-based consensus control for a linear directed multiagent system with time delay. IEEE Trans. Circuits Syst. II: Express Briefs **62**(3), 281–285 (2015)

14. Nowzari, C., Cortés, J.: Zeno-free, distributed event-triggered communication and control for multi-agent average consensus. In: 2014 American Control Conference (ACC), pp. 2148–2153. IEEE (2014)

15. Olfati-Saber, R., Murray, R.M.: Consensus problems in networks of agents with switching topology and time-delays. IEEE Trans. Autom. Control **49**(9), 1520–1533 (2004)

16. Ren, W.: On consensus algorithms for double-integrator dynamics. In: 2007 IEEE Conference on Decision and Control, pp. 2295–2300 (2008)

17. Ren, W., Atkins, E.: Distributed multi-vehicle coordinated control via local information exchange. Int. J. Robust Nonlinear Control **17**(10–11), 1002–1033 (2007)

18. Seyboth, G.S., Dimarogonas, D.V., Johansson, K.H.: Event-based broadcasting for multi-agent average consensus. Automatica **49**(1), 245–252 (2013)

19. Yang, D., Ren, W., Liu, X.: Decentralized consensus for linear multi-agent systems under general directed graphs based on event-triggered/self-triggered strategy. In: 2014 IEEE 53rd Annual Conference on Decision and Control (CDC), pp. 1983–1988. IEEE (2014)

20. Yang, D., Ren, W., Liu, X., Chen, W.: Decentralized event-triggered consensus for linear multi-agent systems under general directed graphs. Automatica **69**, 242–249 (2016)

21. Zhang, H., Feng, G., Yan, H., Chen, Q.: Observer-based output feedback event-triggered control for consensus of multi-agent systems. IEEE Trans. Ind. Electron. **61**(9), 4885–4894 (2014)

22. Zhu, W., Jiang, Z.P., Feng, G.: Event-based consensus of multi-agent systems with general linear models. Automatica **50**(2), 552–558 (2014)

Signal, Image and Video Processing

Robust Speaker Identification Algorithms and Results in Noisy Environments

Bulent Ayhan and Chiman Kwan[✉]

Signal Processing, Inc., Rockville, MD 20850, USA
bulentayhan@gmail.com, chiman.kwan@signalpro.net

Abstract. In this research, we have developed a robust speaker identification system, which involves mask estimation, gammatone features with bounded marginalization to deal with unreliable features, and Gaussian mixture model (GMM) for speaker identification. Extensive experiments using actual and synthesized conversations clearly demonstrated the performance of our algorithms under noisy conditions.

Keywords: Speaker identification · GMM · Gammatone · Noisy environment

1 Introduction

Robust speaker identification in noisy environments is always challenging. One group of approach is to apply microphone arrays and binaural processing techniques [1–8]. Motivated by recent advances in Computational Auditory Scene Analysis (CASA) [9], the objective of this research was to investigate the performance of a robust speaker identification system that can perform well in noisy environments. The first step is to estimate the ideal binary mask (IBM) of the noisy audio data. Based on estimated mask, gammatone features are extracted. Finally, the features are used in a Gaussian Mixture Model (GMM) for speaker identification. Extensive evaluations using actual and synthetic data clearly demonstrated the performance of the proposed system.

2 Technical Approach

2.1 System Architecture

Figure 1 outlines our proposed robust speaker identification algorithm. The first step is a mask estimation step. A "1" in a binary mask means that the given time-frequency unit is speech dominant. We propose to estimate this mask using a multilayer neural network. The second step is to deal with unreliable gammatone features in those noise dominant regions. We propose a technique known as bounded marginalization to deal with unreliable features. Finally, we propose to use Gaussian mixture model (GMM) in speaker identification.

© Springer International Publishing AG, part of Springer Nature 2018
T. Huang et al. (Eds.): ISNN 2018, LNCS 10878, pp. 443–450, 2018.
https://doi.org/10.1007/978-3-319-92537-0_51

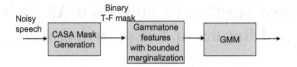

Fig. 1. Robust speaker identification scheme.

2.2   Auditory Features

In [10], gammatone filters were used to generate auditory features. A common practice is to use 64 filters with filter frequencies ranging from 50 Hz to 4,000 Hz. The gammatone filters' outputs are denoted by

$$G_m[i] = \left\| g|_{decimate}[i,m] \right\|^{1/3}, \ i = 0, \ldots, N-1, \ m = 0, \ldots, M-1, \tag{1}$$

where $N = 64$ denotes channel numbers and M is the number of frames.

A time slice of (1) is called the Gammatone Feature (GF). A discrete cosine transform (DCT) is usually applied to (1) to reduce the dimension of the features and decorrelate the features. The resulting coefficients are called the Gammatone Frequency Cepstral Coefficients (GFCC) [11, 12]. That is, $C[j]$, $j = 0 \ldots N - 1$, are given by,

$$C[j] = \sqrt{\frac{2}{N}} \sum_{i=0}^{N-1} G[i] \cos\left(\frac{j\pi}{2N}(2i+1)\right), j = 0, \ldots, N-1. \tag{2}$$

2.3   CASA Mask Generation

A binary T-F mask shows whether a T-F unit is dominated by target speech or background noise. An ideal binary mask (IBM) is a binary matrix defined as follows [13]:

$$IBM(t,f) = \begin{cases} 1, & \text{if } SNR(t,f) > 0 \\ 0, & \text{otherwise} \end{cases} \tag{3}$$

$IBM(t,f)$ is indexed by time t and frequency f. $SNR(t,f)$ refers to the local SNR (in dB) for the T-F unit in time frame t and frequency channel f.

To estimate the IBM from an input mixture, the first step is to estimate the pitch of at each frame [15]. Second, for each T-F unit, a 6-dimensional pitch-based feature vector is extracted [14]. These features become the inputs to an MLP (multilayer perceptron) classifier. The desired output during MLP training is the IBM.

Figure 2 shows an estimated IBM for a speech signal.

Figure 3 shows the IBM of one voice file and also the estimated mask using NN. The SNR here is 0 dB. We can see that the NN estimated mask is quite good.

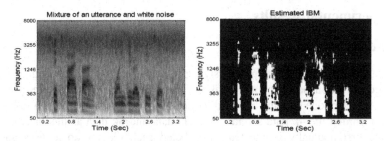

Fig. 2. Estimated IBM. Left: cochleagram of a noisy utterance at 0 dB SNR. Right: estimated IBM from the mixture with white indicating speech dominant regions.

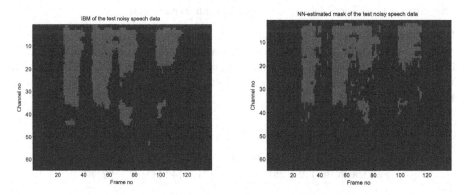

Fig. 3. Left: IBM; Right: NN estimated mask.

2.4   Marginalization to Deal with Unreliable Features

In [16], GMM was used to model the probability distribution of an extracted pitch vector X. Under noisy conditions, the speech segregation system in Sect. 2.3 produces a binary T-F mask. The speech dominant segments are reliable while the latter one is unreliable. Thus, the feature vector is represented as

$$X = \begin{bmatrix} X_r \\ X_u \end{bmatrix}. \tag{4}$$

where X_r and X_u denote the reliable and unreliable components, respectively.

The key idea behind marginalization is to generate decisions using reliable components. Consistent with [10], it was observed that bounded marginalization is better than that of full marginalization.

3 Experimental Results

3.1 Evaluation Using Data Set 1

Our data were from a data set previously supplied by the ONR. Each original file is a phone conversation between two speakers. Since the two speakers were at different sides of the telephone line, the bandwidth of each speaker's voice stream is either 4k or 8k. We regarded the 4k data as "far channel" data and 8k data as the "near channel" data. We first manually segmented and labeled each file for up to 60 s and then collected the voice streams from the same speaker to form a single wav file for each speaker. In all, 49 speakers' data were collected. Among them, only the speakers having either sufficient (>60 s) far channel data or near channel data were considered. Altogether, 10 speakers' data are employed in our experiments.

Training Set. The first 60 s, and full-length far channel data from the selected 10 speakers were used to train three sets of Gaussian mixture speaker models (GMM). Table 1 lists the full length of each speaker's data. Gaussian mixture model (GMM) was employed as speaker model and the covariance matrix of each model is a diagonal one with 16 components.

Table 1. Full length of each speaker's training data.

Speaker ID	01	03	04	07	14	17	26	38	43	44
Full length (sec)	97	255	87	159	171	114	133	117	97	81

Testing Set. Here we only show far channel data for testing. Each testing data was 20 s long. The far channel data set was created using the data starting from the 60th second of each speaker's far channel data file. Table 2 shows the number of testing data files created for each speaker.

Table 2. Number of testing data file for each speaker.

Speaker ID	01	03	04	07	14	17	26	38	43	44	Total
Testing data set (far channel set)	1	9	1	4	5	2	3	2	1	1	29

Voice Features. Two voice features were tested. They are MFCC and GFCC. The parameters used for each feature are described next. For MFCC and GFCC, the frame size was 25 ms. Frame generating rate (target rate) was 10 ms. The number of channels in each filterbank was 64. However, the first 10 channels were ignored as they correspond to very low frequencies. The final length of each feature vector was 22 after performing DCT and excluding the DC component.

Results. Our experimental results are summarized in Table 3. For each testing data, we added certain amount of white Gaussian noise with or without subsequent denoising process. The value shown inside each parenthesis was obtained with denoising applied. Our denoising algorithm is LogMMSE [17], which is a very popular method in denoising audio data.

Table 3. Speaker id performance (% of correct identification) for Data Set 1 of using sixty seconds of training data and 20 s of far-channel testing data.

SNR	Clean	18 dB	12 dB	6 dB	0 dB	−6 dB	−12 dB
MFCC	100 (100)	35 (55)	31 (38)	31 (34)	31 (31)	31 (31)	31 (31)
GFCC	100 (100)	76 (83)	59 (79)	41 (59)	21 (38)	7 (31)	0 (30)

From Table 3 and Fig. 4, we observed the following:

(a) MFCC is also very sensitive to the added white noise, even when the amount is not significant. The performance soon became unacceptable when SNR was 18 dB.

(b) GFCC has better performance as compared to MFCC under very small amount of noise. However, when SNR is less than 6 dB, its performance again became unacceptable.

(c) Denoising results are shown in parenthesis. It can be seen that GFCC features after denoising can significantly improve the speaker identification performance. For example, under 6 dB noise conditions, speaker id performance improved from 41% to 59%.

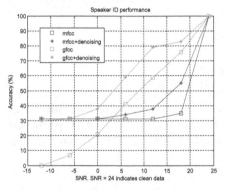

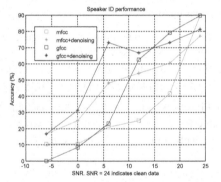

Fig. 4. Speaker id results using GFCC and MFCC under white noise conditions using Data Set 1. Both GFCC and MFCC did not incorporate any mechanisms to make them robust.

Fig. 5. Speaker id results using GFCC and MFCC under white noise conditions using Data Set 2. Both GFCC and MFCC did not incorporate any mechanisms to make them robust.

3.2 Evaluation Using Data Set 2

There are 12 speakers/files in Data Set 2, which also came from the ONR. This data set also comes from phone conversations. So we have far and near channels like Data Set 1. We used first 60 s as training data and the next 80 s as testing data. Each testing data is 20 s long. So there are a total of 48 testing files. Here we show only speaker id results using far channel data. Table 4 and Fig. 5 summarize the speaker id performance. The value shown inside each parenthesis was obtained with denoising applied. The background noise is white Gaussian and the denoising algorithm is logMMSE. We can observe the following:

(a) MFCC's performance drops quickly under mild noisy conditions. After denoising, the speaker id improves to certain extent, but not much.
(b) GFCC is more robust to noise. After denoising, even in 12 and 6 dB conditions, the speaker id can still achieve close to 70% correct identification, which is significantly better than that of MFCC.

Table 4. Speaker id performance (% of correct identification) for Data Set 2 of using sixty seconds of training data and 80 s of far-channel testing data.

SNR	Clean	18 dB	12 dB	6 dB	0 dB	−6 dB
MFCC	89.6 (77.1)	41.7 (60.4)	25 (54.2)	20.8 (47.9)	10.4 (25)	10.4 (16.7)
GFCC	89.6 (81.2)	79.2 (72.9)	62.5 (66.7)	22.9 (72.9)	8.3 (31.3)	0 (16.7)

3.3   More Intensive Studies

The two data sets mentioned earlier have limited files. In addition, it is very labor intensive to label the different segments. It takes about 15 min to label 1 min of data. So we decided to generate some synthesized data using RM1 database. In our synthetic data, we have:

- 78 speakers (male-male, male-female, female-female)
- 390 files total; used 195 files.
- White and babble noises were also considered
- SNR conditions: −12 dB, −6 dB, 0 dB, 6 dB, 12 dB, 18 dB.

Figures 6 and 7 show the baseline performance of speaker identification. Both GFCC and MFCC do not have any robustification mechanisms. GFCC performed quite well under white noise conditions whereas GFCC and MFCC have similar

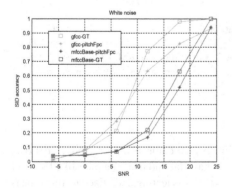

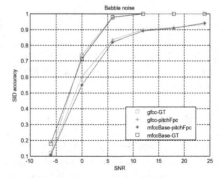

Fig. 6. Speaker id results using RM1 data. White noise. GFCC performed better.

Fig. 7. Speaker results using RM1 data. Babble noise. GFCC is slightly better.

performance in babble noise conditions. In addition, segmentation degrades the speaker id performance due to imperfect segmentation in noisy conditions.

Figures 8 and 9 show robust speaker identification results using RM1 data. It can be seen that our algorithm performs a lot better than a conventional method (MFCC-CMN) under low SNR conditions.

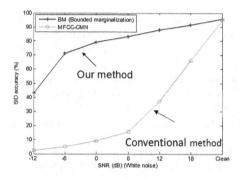

Fig. 8. Robust speaker id results using RM1 data. White noise. Our robust speaker id algorithms performs a lot better under low SNR conditions.

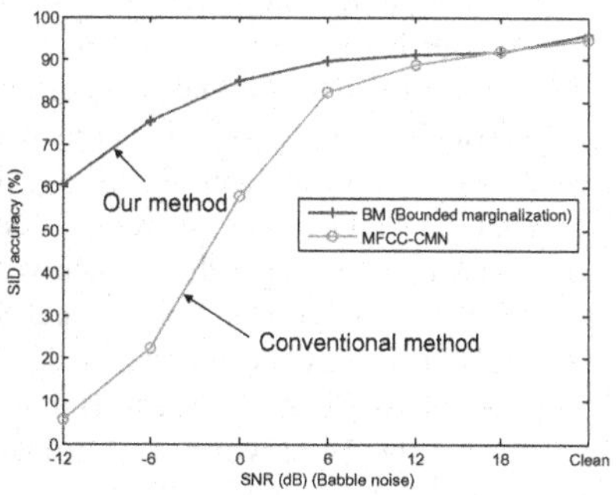

Fig. 9. Robust speaker id results using RM1 data. Babble noise. Our robust speaker id algorithms performs a lot better under low SNR conditions.

4 Conclusion

A robust speech identification system under noisy conditions was developed. Extensive simulations using actual and synthetic data were performed to demonstrate the performance of the proposed system.

One future direction of our research is to implement an accurate approach to estimating the IBM of the audio data.

Acknowledgments. This research was supported by ONR under contract N00014-12-M-0037. The authors would like to thank the ONR for providing some testing data sets. Some high level contributions from Prof. DeLiang Wang at the Ohio State University, who deserves to be a co-author, are duly acknowledged. Per Prof. Wang's request, we did not include him as a co-author and we are indebted to his support in this research.

References

1. Li, Y., Ho, K.C., Popescu, M.: A microphone array system for automatic fall detection. IEEE Trans. Biomed. Eng. **59**(5), 1291–1301 (2012)
2. Li, Y., Ho, K.C., Kwan, C.: Design of broad-band circular ring microphone array for speech acquisition in 3-D. In: International Conference on Acoustics, Speech, and Signal Processing, pp. 221–224 (2003)

3. Li, Y., Vicente, L., Ho, K.C., Kwan, C., Lun, D.P.K., Leung, Y.H.: A study of partially adaptive concentric ring array. J. Circuits, Syst. Sig. Process. **27**(5), 733–748 (2008)
4. Li, Y., Ho, K.C., Kwan, C.: A novel partial adaptive algorithm for broadband beamforming using concentric circular array. In: IEEE International Conference on Acoustics, Speech and Signal Processing, pp. 177–180 (2004)
5. Vicente, L.M., Ho, K.C., Kwan, C.: An improved partial adaptive narrow-band beamformer using concentric ring array. In: IEEE International Conference on Acoustics, Speech, and Signal Processing (2006)
6. Li, Y., Ho, K.C., Kwan, C., Leung, Y.H.: Generalized partially adaptive concentric ring array. In: IEEE International Symposium on Circuits Systems, pp. 3745–3748 (2005)
7. Li, Y., Ho, K.C., Kwan, C.: 3-D array pattern synthesis with frequency invariant property for concentric ring array. IEEE Trans. Sig. Process. **54**(2), 780–784 (2006)
8. Kwan, C., Mei, G., Zhao, X., Ren, Z., Xu, R., Stanford, V., Rochet, C., Aube, J., Ho, K.C.: Bird classification algorithms: theory and experimental results. In: IEEE International Conference on Acoustics, Speech, and Signal Processing, pp. 289–292 (2004)
9. Wang, D., Brown, G.: Computational Auditory Scene Analysis: Principles, Algorithms, and Applications. Wiley/IEEE Press, Hoboken (2006)
10. Patterson, R.D., Holdsworth, J., Allerhand, M.: Auditory models as preprocessors for speech recognition. In: Schouten, M.E.H. (ed.) The Auditory Processing of Speech: From Sounds to Words. Mouton de Gruyter, Berlin (1992)
11. Shao, Y., Srinivasan, S., Wang, D.L.: Incorporating auditory feature uncertainties in robust speaker identification. In: IEEE International Conference on Acoustics, Speech and Signal Processing, pp. 277–280 (2007)
12. Shao, Y., Wang, D.L.: Robust speaker identification using auditory features and computational auditory scene analysis. In: IEEE International Conference on Acoustics, Speech and Signal Processing, 1589–1592 (2008)
13. Williamson, D.S., Wang, D.L.: Speech dereverberation and denoising using complex ratio masks. In: IEEE International Conference on Acoustics, Speech and Signal Processing, pp. 5590–5594 (2017)
14. Lin, Z., Wang, D.L.: A supervised learning approach to monaural segregation of reverberant speech. IEEE Trans. Audio Speech Lang. Process. **17**, 625–638 (2009)
15. Lin, Z., Wang, D.L.: A multipitch tracking algorithm for noisy and reverberant speech. In: IEEE International Conference on Acoustics, Speech and Signal Processing (2010)
16. Reynolds, D.A., Quatieri, T.F., Dunn, R.B.: Speaker verification using adapted gaussian mixture models. Digit. Sig. Process. **10**, 19–41 (2000)
17. Ephraim, Y., Malah, D.: Speech enhancement using a minimum mean-square error log-spectral amplitude estimator. IEEE Trans. Acoust. Speech, Sig. Process. **33**(2), 443–445 (1985)

Marine Aquaculture Targets Automatic Recognition Based on GF-3 PolSAR Imagery

Jianchao Fan[1,2(✉)], Jianhua Zhao[1], Min Han[2], Xinxin Wang[1], and Bingnan Li[1]

[1] Department of Ocean Remote Sensing,
National Marine Environmental Monitoring Center,
Dalian 116023, China
{jcfan,jhzhao,xxwang,bnli}@nmemc.org.cn
[2] School of Control Science and Engineering,
Dalian University of Technology, Dalian 116024, Liaoning, China
minhan@dlut.edu.cn

Abstract. It is important that marine targets, including ships, oil spill and aquaculture etc., are detected precisely, which face large difficulty because of complex varied marine conditions. New launched GF-3 SAR satellite could provide long time series of SAR imagery for marine monitoring. More useful information can be obtained through the special polarimetric approach. Joint sparse representation classification approached are proposed to marine floating raft aquaculture recognition based on GF-3 polarimetric SAR (PolSAR) datasets. Experiment results demonstrate the superiority of GF-3 PolSAR images on the marine target recognition aspect.

Keywords: GF-3 SAR imagery · Marine aquaculture
Target recognition · Polarimetric decomposition

1 Introduction

GaoFen 3 (GF-3), as a full Polarimetric Synthetic Aperture Radar (PolSAR) satellite, had been launched by China in August 10, 2016. Its space resolution is 1–500 m, with three different imaging models, which has been tried to apply to the ocean, meteorology *etc.* fields. [1]. SAR satellite could overcome the cloudy and rainy weather commonly appearing the coastal area, compared with optical remote sensing imagery [2]. PolSAR imagery provide plenty of useful features for target recognition [3]. With the incasement of SAR satellites, large numbers of

J. Fan—The work described in the paper was supported by the National Key R&D Program of China (2016YFC1401007, 2017YFC1404902); National Natural Science Foundation of China (41706195, 61773087); National High Resolution Special Research (41-Y30B12-9001-14/16); Key Laboratory of Sea-Area Management Technology Foundation (201701).

© Springer International Publishing AG, part of Springer Nature 2018
T. Huang et al. (Eds.): ISNN 2018, LNCS 10878, pp. 451–458, 2018.
https://doi.org/10.1007/978-3-319-92537-0_52

remote sensing data need to be processed. Only experts explain cannot meet the data processing accuracy and speed requirements. There is now an increasing volume of fully polarimetric data due to the launch of GF-3 satellite, which could provide long time serial monitoring data. The need to proposed an automated interpretation method is necessary [4].

Recently, many researchers attempts to maximize the segmentation accuracy through different sets of features in PolSAR image segmentation. PolSAR features could be classified to two classes. One obtains polarimetric features from the basis scattering matrix, such as covariance matrix or coherence matrix. The other one is based on the target polarimetric decomposition theory, including Pauli [5], Cloude [6], Huynen [7], H-Alpha-Anisotropy [8], Freeman [9], Yamaguchi [10] methods *etc.* These different polarimetric approaches could extract different backscattering features of targets.

Marine floating raft aquaculture plays an important role in oceanic economy development, which is difficult to detect through optical remote sensing images [11]. Fan *et al.* [12] proposed a supervised classifier with weighted fusion-based representation for the floating raft target recognition. Hu *et al.* [13] present a modified statistical region merging algorithm to achieve superpixels segmentation of SAR images, which weakens the contamination of speckle noise. A supervised and contractive deep learning neural network, inspired by deep learning theory, was proposed to overcome the presence of speckle noises [14]. In this paper, new launched GF-3 PolSAR imagery are analyzed for marine target recognition, specially for the marine floating raft aquaculture. More useful information are obtained through the special polarimetric approach. A real GF-3 PolSAR image is utilized to verify the effectiveness.

The rest of this paper is organized as follows. Polarimetric SAR data processing is presented in Sect. 2. The joint sparse representation algorithm for GF-3 image is given in Sect. 3. The experimental results on MAFA recognition based on actual GF-3 PolSAR images are delineated in Sect. 4. Finally, concluding remarks are given in Sect. 5.

2   Polarimetric SAR Data Processing

PolSAR systems often have four different polarimetric channel and combine the complex matrix $[S]$, which is defined as

$$S = \begin{bmatrix} S_{hh} & S_{hv} \\ S_{vh} & S_{vv} \end{bmatrix} \tag{1}$$

Based on above PolSAR scattering matrix, the Pauli basis with orthogonal features $|S|_a = \frac{1}{\sqrt{2}} \begin{bmatrix} 1 & 0 \\ 0 & 1 \end{bmatrix}, |S|_b = \frac{1}{\sqrt{2}} \begin{bmatrix} 1 & 0 \\ 0 & -1 \end{bmatrix}, |S|_c = \frac{1}{\sqrt{2}} \begin{bmatrix} 0 & 1 \\ 1 & 0 \end{bmatrix}, |S|_d = \frac{1}{\sqrt{2}} \begin{bmatrix} 0 & -1 \\ 1 & 0 \end{bmatrix}$ are defined as,

$$S = \begin{bmatrix} S_{hh} & S_{hv} \\ S_{vh} & S_{vv} \end{bmatrix} = \alpha[S]_a + \beta[S]_b + \gamma[S]_c \tag{2}$$

where $\alpha = (S_{hh} + S_{vv})/\sqrt{2}$, $\beta = (S_{hh} - S_{vv})/\sqrt{2}$, $\gamma = \sqrt{2}S_{hv}$.

Furthermore, the eigenvectors-eigenvalue decomposition based on 3×3 Hermitian average polarimetric coherency $\langle[T_3]\rangle$ is performed as follows,

$$\langle[T_3]\rangle = \sum_{j=1}^{3} \lambda_i q_i q_i^{*\mathrm{T}} \tag{3}$$

where $\lambda_i > 0$, λ_i are real eigenvalues and the corresponding orthogonal eigenvectors q_i are

$$q_i = \sqrt{\lambda}\left[\cos\underline{\alpha} \ \sin\underline{\alpha}\cos\underline{\beta}e^{j\underline{\delta}} \ \sin\underline{\alpha}\cos\underline{\beta}e^{j\underline{\gamma}}\right]^T \tag{4}$$

where the average angles are defined in the same way

$$\underline{\alpha} = \sum_{i=1}^{3} q_i\alpha_i, \underline{\beta} = \sum_{i=1}^{3} q_i\beta_i, \underline{\delta} = \sum_{i=1}^{3} q_i\delta_i, \underline{\gamma} = \sum_{i=1}^{3} q_i\gamma_i \tag{5}$$

The total scattered power can be defined according to the relative eigenvalue,

$$SPAN = |S_{hh}|^2 + |S_{vv}|^2 + 2|S_{hv}|^2 = \sum_{k=1}^{3} \lambda_k \tag{6}$$

3   Joint Sparse Representation Classification

After polarimetric feature extraction, focusing on the marine floating raft aquaculture problem, a sparse representation of x_i with a given $B \times N$ dictionary D for two neighbor pixels x_i and x_j, is expressed as

$$x_i = D\alpha_i = \alpha_{i,\lambda_1}d_{\lambda_1} + \alpha_{i,\lambda_2}d_{\lambda_2} + \cdots + \alpha_{i,\lambda_K}d_{\lambda_K}, \tag{7}$$

where the index set $\Lambda_K = \{\lambda_1, \lambda_2, \cdots, \lambda_K\}$ indicates supporting atoms of the sparse vector α_i. Since x_i and x_j have similar characteristics, x_j can also be represented by the same set of training atoms $\{d_k\}_{k\in\Lambda_K}$, but with different coefficients $\{\alpha_{j,k}\}_{k\in\Lambda_K}$

$$x_j = D\alpha_j = \alpha_{j,\lambda_1}d_{\lambda_1} + \alpha_{j,\lambda_2}d_{\lambda_2} + \cdots + \alpha_{j,\lambda_K}d_{\lambda_K}, \tag{8}$$

where α_i and α_j have the same sparse level and non-zero elements with the same location.

Let $X' = [x_1\ x_2\ \cdots\ x_T]$ be a $B \times T$ matrix, where the vectors $\{x_t\}_{t=1,\cdots,T}$ are pixels in the search neighborhood. Thus, X' can be written as

$$X' = [x_1\ x_2\ \cdots\ x_T] = [D\alpha_1\ D\alpha_2\ \cdots\ D\alpha_T]$$
$$= D\underbrace{[\alpha_1\ \alpha_2\ \cdots\ \alpha_T]}_{S} = DS \quad, \tag{9}$$

The sparse vectors $\{\alpha_t\}_{t=1,\cdots,T}$ have the same support Λ, i.e. nonzero elements of sparse vectors that have the same location. The sparse matrix S only has $|\Lambda|$ nonzero rows. S can be recovered by solving the following optimization problem

$$\hat{S} = \arg\min \left\| X' - DS \right\|_F \quad s.t. \|S\|_{row,0} \leq K_0, \tag{10}$$

where $\|S\|_{row,0}$ is the number of nonzero rows of S, and $\|\cdot\|_F$ is the Frobenius norm. The objective (10) could be optimized through orthogonal matching pursuit algorithm.

4   Experiment Results

In order to verify the marine recognition capability of GF-3 PolSAR imagery, Changhai, Liaoning is chosen as the main research area, as shown in Fig. 1.

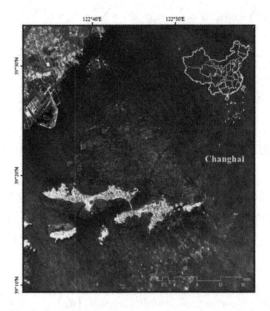

Fig. 1. The original SAR image of Changhai

From the above figure, there are various types of aquaculture such as oyster etc. The preprocess of SAR image includes speckle noises reduction, land mask, which is shown in Fig. 2. It could overcome the land interference to improve marine target recognition accuracy.

Color-code polarimetric decomposition image can reflect different target backscattering type. Here, $|\alpha|^2 \rightarrow$Red, $|\beta|^2 \rightarrow$Blue, and $|\alpha|^2 \rightarrow$Green, represent Bragg, double-bounce and even-bounce backscattering, respectively, as shown in Fig. 3. And the Freeman polarization decomposition result is shown as Fig. 4. It is seen that marine floating raft aquaculture can be detected intuitively.

Fig. 2. The land mask results of Changhai

Fig. 3. The Pauli decomposition results of Changhai (Color figure online)

Three area with different distribution are chosen as Fig. 5. Figure 6 present the true results of marine floating raft area. Adopting joint sparse representation algorithm, the recognition results are obtained in Fig. 7. To quantify the qualitative evaluation, the specifical overall accuracy and Kappa coefficient are tabulated in Table 1.

Fig. 4. The Freeman decomposition results of Changhai

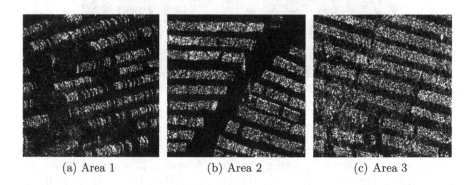

(a) Area 1   (b) Area 2   (c) Area 3

Fig. 5. Original PolSAR image of Changhai

Table 1. Results of three areas on PolSAR image recognition

	Overall accuracy	κ coefficient
Area 1	87.17%	0.6751
Area 2	88.01%	0.7544
Area 3	89.05%	0.7799

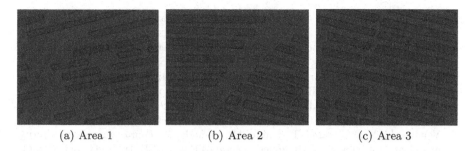

    (a) Area 1   (b) Area 2   (c) Area 3

Fig. 6. True results of marine floating raft aquaculture

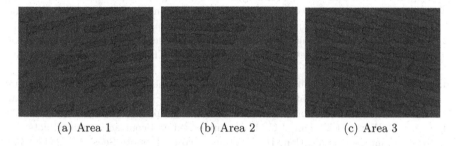

    (a) Area 1   (b) Area 2   (c) Area 3

Fig. 7. Recognition results of marine floating raft aquaculture

5   Conclusions

GF-3 PolSAR imagery can effective detect marine targets with appropriate polarimetric decomposition features and classification algorithm. The results of a actual Changhai study shows that the superiority in practical oceanic applications. In the future, more intelligent information extraction algorithm could be applied to process PolSAR imagery effectively.

References

1. Liu, J., Qiu, X., Hong, W.: Automated ortho-rectified SAR image of GF-3 satellite using Reverse-Range-Doppler method. In: 2016 IEEE International Geoscience and Remote Sensing Symposium, pp. 4445–4448, Beijing (2016)
2. Van Zyl, J.J., Arii, M., Kim, Y.: Model-based decomposition of polarimetric SAR covariance matrices constrained for nonnegative eigenvalues. IEEE Trans. Geosci. Remote Sens. **49**, 3452–3459 (2011)
3. Fan, J.C., Wang, J.: A two-phase fuzzy clustering algorithm based on neurodynamic optimization with its application for PolSAR image segmentation. IEEE Trans. Fuzzy Syst. **26**, 72–83 (2018)
4. Fan, J.C., Cao, K., Zhao, J.H., Jiang, D.W., Tang, X.L.: A hybrid particle swarm optimization algorithm for coastline SAR image automatic detection. In: 12th World Congress on Intelligent Control and Automation, pp. 822–825, Guilin (2016)
5. Cloude, S.R., Pottier, E.: A review of target decomposition theorems in radar polarimetry. IEEE Trans. Geosci. Remote Sens. **34**, 498–518 (1996)

6. Cloude, S.R.: Target decomposition theorems in radar scattering. Electron. Lett. **21**, 22–24 (1985)
7. Huynen, J.R.: Phenomenological theory of radar targets. Electromagn. Scatt. 653–712 (1978)
8. Cloude, S.R., Pottier, E.: An entropy based classification scheme for land applications of polarimetric SAR. IEEE Trans. Geosci. Remote Sens. **35**, 68–78 (1997)
9. Freeman, A., Durden, S.L.: A three-component scattering model for polarimetric SAR data. IEEE Trans. Geosci. Remote Sens. **36**, 963–973 (1998)
10. Yamaguchi, Y., Moriyama, T., Ishido, M., Yamada, H.: Four component scattering model for polarimetric SAR image decomposition. IEEE Trans. Geosci. Remote Sens. **43**, 1699–1706 (2005)
11. Fan, J.C., Chu, J.L. Geng, J. Zhang, F.S.: Floating raft aquaculture information automatic extraction based on high resolution SAR images. In: 2015 IEEE International Geoscience and Remote Sensing Symposium, pp. 3898–3901, Milan (2015)
12. Geng, J., Fan, J.C., Wang, H.Y.: Weighted fusion-based representation classifiers for marine floating raft detection of SAR images. IEEE Geosci. Remote Sens. Lett. **14**, 444–448 (2017)
13. Hu, Y.Y., Fan, J.C., Wang, J.: Target recognition of floating raft aquaculture in SAR image based on statistical region merging. In: 2017 Seventh International Conference on Information Science and Technology, pp. 429–432, Da Nang (2017)
14. Geng, J., Wang, H.Y., Fan, J.C.: Deep supervised and contractive neural network for SAR image classification. IEEE Trans. Geosci. Remote Sens. **55**, 2442–2459 (2017)

Video Server Deployment Using a Genetic Algorithm with Deterministic Initialization Strategy

Xin-Yi Hu, Yue-Jiao Gong[✉], Xin-Yuan Zhang, Yi-Ning Ma,
and Jun Zhang

School of Computer Science and Engineering,
South China University of Technology, Guangzhou 510006, China
gongyuejiao@gmail.com, junzhang@ieee.org

Abstract. Video server deployment problem (VSDP) is a crucial problem in enhancing video viewing experience. It is difficult for traditional deterministic optimization algorithm to solve VSDP because it is non-polynomial hard (NP-hard). Current server deployment patterns are challenged by the growing scale of networks, and it is therefore desirable to design appropriate optimization algorithm to cope with this issue. Owing to the promising performance in solving NP-hard problems, a genetic algorithm (GA)-based optimizer is developed in this paper. We propose a novel deterministic initialization strategy to deploy the GA population in promising initial positions for performance enhancement. In addition, by embedding the maximum cost minimum cost flow (MCMF) in the fitness evaluation, the algorithm optimizes the server deployment and the bandwidth allocation concurrently. This way, the proposed GA is comprehensive, which deals with different aspects involved in VSDP. Experimental results and the comparisons with other algorithms indicate that the proposed algorithm achieves superior performance in terms of solution quality and convergence rate.

Keywords: Video server deployment · Genetic algorithm (GA)
Deterministic initialization strategy · Improved fitness evaluation function
Maximum cost minimum cost flow (MCMF)

1 Introduction

Video server deployment (VSD) determines the viewing experience of end users and the cost of service providers. For video service providers, the deployment and bandwidth rental cost is expected to be minimized with constraints of corresponding bandwidth requirements. As for end users, they focus on viewing experience, i.e., sufficient bandwidth allocation. As the growing number of Internet users, the networks scale cannot meet users' requirements. Additional video servers are expected to be imbedded in the existing network. Due to the resources limitation of available resources, it becomes an urgent issue of how to deploy video servers in an efficient and profitable way. More concretely, the optimization is conducted at video service provider side ensuring that the cost of video server deployment and bandwidth rental is as

© Springer International Publishing AG, part of Springer Nature 2018
T. Huang et al. (Eds.): ISNN 2018, LNCS 10878, pp. 459–467, 2018.
https://doi.org/10.1007/978-3-319-92537-0_53

low as possible. The optimization also takes viewing experience of user side into consideration. User side requirement serves as an essential constraint of the optimization process.

Recent work on server deployment can be classified into two categories: (1) order allocation of multiple resources by a single server, and (2) allocation of multiple servers. The former focuses on minimizing the delay by arranging the order of the resources allocated to the server. Tassiulas and Ephremides [1] propose a queueing model to solve it. When given identical arrival and service statistics of different queues, it maximizes the throughput and minimizes the delay by using an allocation policy. As for the allocation of multiple servers, Nakrani and Tovey [2] propose a distributed bee algorithm. Shanthikumar and Yao [3, 4] propose two methods of server allocation in multiple center manufacturing systems. They summarize the nature of closed-queuing networks, and distribute servers and traffic by these natures, not by actual network needs.

Recent years, more work on server allocation policies have been done. Cameron et al. [5] propose a high-density model for server allocation and placement, which is a random deployment of servers without the limitations of existing network topologies. Palmer and Mitrani [6] pose a method that optimizing cloud providers revenues via energy efficient server allocation. This approach takes into account the server and traffic distribution, reducing costs by minimizing the cost of power consumption. Pussep and Abboud [7] also put forward an adaptive server allocation for peer-assisted video-on-demand, which focusses on a connected P2P network where users' service demand can be partially satisfied by other users.

Today, most of the work in this area is after the allocation of the servers, such as ten cooling solutions to support high-density server deployment [8].

The Genetic Algorithm (GA) has a good global search ability, which can quickly search out the global solution in the solution space without falling into the trap of rapid decline of the local optimal solution. Moreover, by virtue of its inherent parallelism, it is easy to carry out distributed computing, speed up the solution speed.

In this paper, a GA with deterministic initialization strategy (GA-DIS) is developed according to the formulation of VSDP. A novel initialization strategy is proposed in order to assign the GA population to promising original positions. A special fitness function is finely designed to speed up the convergence rate. We also employ the maximum cost minimum cost flow (MCMF) in the fitness evaluation, so as to concurrently optimize the server deployment and the bandwidth allocation. Nine practical VSDP instances are adopted to test the performance of the proposed algorithm.

The paper is structured as follows: formulation of VSDP is presented in Sect. 2. In Sect. 3, we introduce the server allocation approach and the details of GA-DIS. Performance investigation is conducted in Sect. 4. Finally, conclusions are drawn in Sect. 5.

2 Model

Video server deployment problem (VSDP) is highly correlated with user's viewing experience. The topology of video server network can be described as follows: the network structure is modeled as an undirected graph including several network nodes (e.g. routers, switches). Each node is connected to at least one other node via a network link. One node can transmit the received data over the network link to another connected node. The total bandwidth of each link is different to each other. The video transmission carried by each link charges the corresponding network rental fee according to the occupied bandwidth, while the rental fee per unit is different for each link. The total bandwidth occupied by a link cannot exceed the total bandwidth of the link.

Now we use a case to define the VSDP problem. Figure 1 shows a network topology; the number of nodes represents the node index. Red marked nodes are user nodes, the remaining nodes are potential server nodes that can be chosen to be VS. The link directly to the user's node is labeled $need_j$, indicates the video bandwidth consumption requirement of the jth user. Other links are marked (cap_i, $cost_i$), where cap_i indicates the link capacity limit for the ith link, $cost_i$ indicates the rental cost per unit of traffic on the ith link. VSDP is to select k nodes to deploy VS, in a network topology with m nodes, n users and e links, and meet the following requirements:

$$\min\left(k * deploymentCost + \sum cost_i * flow_i\right)$$
$$\text{s.t.} \begin{cases} flow_i < cap_i \\ \sum flow_j \geq need_j \end{cases} \tag{1}$$

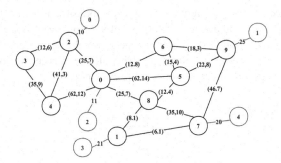

Fig. 1. A case of VSDP

Deployment scheme need to include not only the location of the nodes where the video content server is deployed, but also the network path between each consuming node and all video servers and the bandwidth consumed on the path.

3 Algorithm

We use a GA-DIS based algorithm to solve VSDP. After analysis of VSDP, we found that, the crux of the problem is to minimize the total VS deployment costs and bandwidth lease costs, while meeting users' traffic needs. At the same time, we found that, in a network where each edge has two attributes, capacity and cost, the maximum cost minimum cost flow (MCMF) can find a solution that maximizes the total flow which flow from source A to destination B, while keeping the total cost minimized, by reasonably choosing the path and flow through each edge. It can be noted that the minimum cost maximum flow algorithm is well suited to solve VSDP.

The core idea of the algorithm is that GA-DIS randomly generate possible solutions to determine the location of VS. MCMF is used as the fitness function of GA-DIS, in order to determine the amount of bandwidth each VS allocates to each node. The fitness function is also used to calculate the minimum cost and maximum flow of the possible solution, to determine whether it is the optimal solution.

3.1 Deterministic Initialization Strategy

In GA-DIS, each individual contains an array of chromosomes, a cost value, and a bandwidth value. Among them, the chromosome array represents a feasible solution. We denote the ith chromosome as (2), where N is the total number of nodes in the network. If $x_{i,\ j}$ is 1, jth node is chosen to be a video server, else if $x_{i,\ j}$ is 0, there is no video server on jth node.

$$X_i = (x_{i,1}, x_{i,2}, \ldots, x_{i,N}) \tag{2}$$

By analyzing the experimental data, we find that the servers are tend to be deployed on the network nodes which are directly connected to the user nodes. Figure 2 plots the best solution of case1, which represents an extreme situation that only one VS is ordinary network nodes, and other VSs all deployed on those nodes which directly connected to the user points. In order to speed up the convergence rate, the first individual is given a promising position where all the servers are deployed on the network nodes which are directly connected to user nodes.

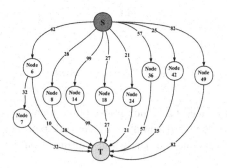

Fig. 2. The best solution result chart of case1

3.2 Preprocessing of the Input Map

As can be noted from Fig. 1, the number of VSs and user nodes are more than one. However, MCMF can only be applicable to single source point and single sink point graphs. Therefore, we transform the original network structure into a new one so that MCMF can be applicable to this scenario.

The transformation consists of three steps and is given as follows: First, build super source point S, super sink point T. Then, for each user node ID, establish a ID → T side. The cost of the side is 0, and the maximum capacity is the demand of this user node; for each VS node NID, establish a S → NID side. The cost of the side is 0, and the maximum capacity is the capacity of this VS node. After the transformation, user nodes and VS nodes can be regarded as ordinary nodes. The problem turns into finding the maximum cost minimum cost flow from S to T (Fig. 3).

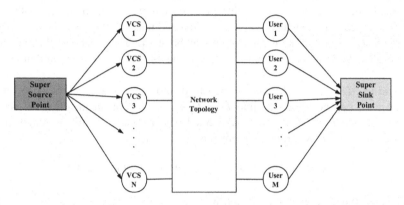

Fig. 3. Super source point and super sink point model

3.3   Design of Fitness Function

We use MCMF as the fitness function of GA-DIS. When using MCMF algorithm, we first find the minimum cost flow first, then try to get the maximum flow by expanding the chain. The specific steps can be seen in [9].

The first step of MCMF algorithm is to find the "shortest path", that is, the minimum cost flow. As Dijkstra algorithm is limited to the situation that the weight of the edge is not negative, the shortest path found by Dijkstra may be wrong. Bellman Ford can effectively find the "shortest path" in MCMF, but its efficiency is not high because of the excessive number of relaxation operations.

Therefore, we use SPFA, the improved algorithm for Bellman Ford. SPFA is based on the Bellman ford algorithm, but plus a queue optimization that reduces redundant relaxation operations. The idea is, since relaxation operations can only occur in nodes where "distance" changes, the scope for relaxation operations can be narrowed down, so we use queues record nodes to relaxation. The specific steps can be seen in [10].

We call the MCMF algorithm which use SPFA to find the "shortest path" as the fitness function1 (f_1). After that, we find a new way to replace SPFA to determine which path should be augmented, and the complexity of this new way is much lower. We call the MCMF algorithm with this new way as the fitness function2 (f_2).

Now we first analyze the principle of finding the shortest path algorithm. Take D_i be the shortest path from S to i. All the shortest path algorithm guarantees two conditions when algorithm ends.

$$\text{For any existing arc } (i, j), D_i + c_{i,j} \geq D_j \text{ is satisfied} \tag{3}$$

$$\text{There is at least one } i \text{ for each } j \text{ that can satisfied } D_i + c_{i,j} = D_j. \tag{4}$$

After the end of the algorithm, the edge just on the shortest path satisfies $D_j = D_i + c_{i,i}$. In the calculation of the minimum cost flow, we augment the path along $D_j = D_i + c_{i,j}$ each time, which will reduce flow and make some of the arc becomes no flow. This operation will not break (3) but may break (4). The usual cost-flow approach is to recalculate D for each augmentation, using SPFA, etc. This is undoubtedly a waste.

As in (3), $D_i + c_{i,j} \geq D_j$ can be translated into $D_i - D_j + c_{i,j} \geq, 0$. Also, in (4), $D_i + c_{i,j} = D_j$ can be translated into $D_i - D_j + c_{i,j} = 0$. For an identifier D, we can continue finding $D_i - D_j + c_{i,j} = 0$ augmented path by DFS. If DFS is failed, points collected by DFS are recorded as point sets V. Calculate

$$\Delta = \min\{D_i - D_j + c_{i,j}\} | i \in V, j \notin V, flow_{i,j} > 0 \tag{5}$$

Then for those points which is not in V,

$$D_i^\pi = D_i + \Delta \tag{6}$$

The new method only needs to augment, modify labels, but doesn't need BFS, queue, SPFA. As the new method saves the SPFA computing time, its complexity is very low.

4   Experiment

To thoroughly evaluate the performance of the proposed algorithm, we conducted a comparative experiment with five algorithms, such as BPSO-f_1, BPSO-DIS- f_1, GA- f_1, GA-DIS-f_1, GA-DIS-f_2, where A-f_1 and A-DIS represents the objective function of algorithm A is f_1 and initialization strategy of algorithm is the proposed deterministic initialization strategy. The number of iteration is set to 300, and the population size is fixed to 10. Table 1 shows the other parameter settings.

The main information of the nine test cases is shown in Table 2. These nine test cases can be divided into three dimensions according to the node number. The final results are shown in Table 3. The results show that GA-DIS-f_2 can get the best solution and run shorter time. The two GA models are more stable than the two BPSO models, while the two BPSO models run faster than the two GA models.

Table 1. Parameter configurations

Algorithm	Parameter configurations
BPSO-f_1	$\omega = 0.5 \sim 2$, $c_1 = 2 \sim 3$, $c_2 = 1 \sim 2$
BPSO-DIS-f_1	$\omega = 0.5 \sim 2$, $c_1 = 2 \sim 3$, $c_2 = 1 \sim 2$
GA-f_1	$pc = 0.7$, $pm = 0.07$
GA-DIS-f_1	$pc = 0.7$, $pm = 0.07$
GA-DIS-f_2	$pc = 0.8$, $pm = 0.09$

Table 2. Test cases information

Instance	Case	N	E_n	U_n
D1	C0	50	96	9
	C1	50	97	9
	C2	50	113	9
	C3	50	97	9
	C4	50	99	9
D2	C5	160	374	64
	C6	160	368	64
D3	C7	300	794	120
	C8	300	804	120

Here's some more explanation of the experimental results of case5–case8. The reason why BPSO-f_1, BPSO-DIS-f_1, GA-f_1, and GA-DIS-f_1 cannot get a solution is that SPFA is unable to solve the problem of cost flow with negative cycle. In a graph with n points, if a point gets into the queue more than n time, then there is a negative cycle in this graph. For instance, the source and sink points are isolated points, there is another negative cost, positive capacity circle. No matter what the initial label, simply by extension cannot eliminate this negative circle. Therefore, the SPFA algorithm will not terminate. In this case, the fitness function considers that the solution does not meet the user's needs and thus returns INF. So, the optimal solution is not available.

Table 3. Experiment results

Function		BPSO-f_1	BPSO-DIS-f_1	GA-f_1	GA-DIS-f_1	GA-DIS-f_2
Case 0	average time	7919.52	7803.96	8757.23	8106.04	5782.3
	minimum cost	2172	2172	2172	2092.6	2042
	average cost	2200.24	2109.45	2107.6	2172	2042
	maximum flow	303	303	303	303	303
Case 1	average time	8913.66	8739.42	9596.03	9035.33	6546.84
	minimum cost	2400	2400	2400	2400	2136
	average cost	2417.43	2411.1	2408.75	2405.66	2136
	maximum flow	382	382	382	382	382
Case 2	average time	9985.7	9539.3	11365.2	9720.8	7203.4
	minimum cost	1890	1890	1890	1890	1692
	average cost	1915.6	1910.2	1908.6	1894.8	1692
	maximum flow	431	431	431	431	431
Case 3	average time	14586.5	14501.9	15694.2	14589.7	13342.78
	minimum cost	2543	2543	2543	2543	2111
	average cost	2603.4	2593.1	2552.7	2547.86	2111
	maximum flow	340	340	340	340	340

(*continued*)

Table 3. (*continued*)

Function		BPSO-f_1	BPSO-DIS-f_1	GA-f_1	GA-DIS-f_1	GA-DIS-f_2
Case 4	average time	7846.4	7834.2	8727.3	8358.8	7433.8
	minimum cost	2160	2160	2160	2160	1967
	average cost	2270.4	2258.9	2263.7	2241.4	1967
	maximum flow	284	284	284	284	284
Case 5	average time	235056.7	269152.3	294624.8	253132.4	73045.3
	minimum cost	NA	NA	NA	NA	8961
	average cost	NA	NA	NA	NA	9323.7
	maximum flow	NA	NA	NA	NA	1975
Case 6	average time	255326.1	285910.7	269407.7	251439.2	68022.7
	minimum cost	NA	NA	NA	NA	9596
	average cost	NA	NA	NA	NA	9607.4
	maximum flow	NA	NA	NA	NA	1861
Case 7	average time	214724.8	247285.9	252467.6	253479.2	136392.5
	minimum cost	NA	NA	NA	NA	17974
	average cost	NA	NA	NA	NA	18992.9
	maximum flow	NA	NA	NA	NA	3698
Case 8	average time	263619.7	220637.4	212683.2	251239.4	145965.8
	minimum cost	NA	NA	NA	NA	19155
	average cost	NA	NA	NA	NA	19296.8
	maximum flow	NA	NA	NA	NA	3732

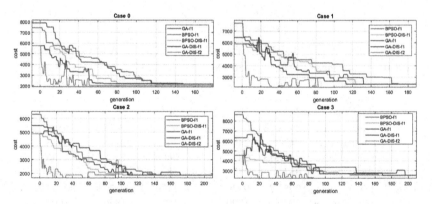

Fig. 4. Convergence curves of the five algorithms

The solve method in function2 is, forcing all negative cost side full flow, known as "backflow" operation. After doing so we destroyed the equilibrium conditions but satisfied the optimal conditions. Then we can seek feasible flow, and then seek the maximum flow. During this period, the optimal conditions have been maintained, the balance conditions and the maximum flow conditions could be gradually solved.

When comparing the convergence curves of the five algorithms, we find the reason why GA-DIS-f_2 can be the best one. For the three algorithms which has DIS, the DIS is equivalent to indicating a possible convergence direction when they initialize. From Fig. 4, it is easy to find that, BPSO-DIS-f_1, GA-DIS-f_1 and GA-DIS-f_2 start at the same number, while the other two algorithms may start from a number much larger.

5   Conclusions

In this paper, we give a rigorous analysis and formulation of VSDP. After that, we propose a GA based optimizer (GA-DIS) to cope with this problem. In order to speed up the convergence rate, a deterministic initialization strategy is proposed. A novel fitness function is designed to serve as a better guidance of the searching behavior. Experimental results indicate the effectiveness of the proposed deterministic initialization strategy and the new fitness function. GA-DIS shows superior performance in terms of solution quality and convergence rate.

References

1. Tassiulas, L., Ephremides, A.: Dynamic server allocation to parallel queues with randomly varying connectivity. IEEE Trans. Inf. Theory **39**, 466–478 (1993)
2. Nakrani, S., Tovey, C.: On honey bees and dynamic server allocation in internet hosting centers. Adapt. Behav. – Anim. Animat. Softw. Agents Robots Adapt. Syst. Arch. **12**, 223–240 (2004)
3. Shanthikumar, J.G., Yao, D.D.: On server allocation in multiple center manufacturing systems. Oper. Res. **36**, 333–342 (1988)
4. Shanthikumar, J.G., Yao, D.D.: Optimal server allocation in a system of multi-server stations. Manag. Sci. **33**, 1173–1180 (1987)
5. Cameron, C.W., Low, S.H., Wei, D.X.: High-density model for server allocation and placement. ACM SIGMETRICS Perform. Eval. Rev. – Meas. Model. Comput. Syst. **30**, 152–159 (2002)
6. Palmer, J., Mitrani, I.: Optimizing cloud providers revenues via energy efficient server allocation. Sustain. Comput.: Inform. Syst. **2**, 1–12 (2005)
7. Pussep, K., Abboud, O.: Adaptive server allocation for peer-assisted video-on-demand. In: IEEE International Symposium on Parallel & Distributed Processing, pp. 1–8. IEEE Press, New York (2010)
8. Hannaford, P.: Ten cooling solutions to support high-density server deployment. APC white paper #42 (2006)
9. Smith, D.K.: Network flows theory, algorithms, and applications. J. Oper. Res. Soc. **45**, 1340 (1994)
10. Duan, F.: A faster algorithm for the shortest-path problem called SPFA. J. Southwest Jiaotong Univ. **29**, 207–212 (1994)

R-RTRL Based on Recurrent Neural Network with K-Fold Cross-Validation for Multi-step-ahead Prediction Landslide Displacement

Jiejie Chen[1(✉)], Ping Jiang[2], Zhigang Zeng[3], and Boshan Chen[4]

[1] College of Computer Science and Technology, Hubei Normal University,
Huangshi 435002, China
chenjiejie118@gmail.com, chenjiejie118@126.com
[2] Computer School, Hubei PolyTechnic University, Huangshi 435002, China
[3] School of Automation, Huazhong University of Science and Technology,
Wuhan 430074, China
[4] College of Mathematics and Statistics, Hubei Normal University,
Huangshi 435002, China

Abstract. The reinforced real-time recurrent learning (R-RTRL) algorithm with K-fold cross-validation for recurrent neural networks (RNNs) are applied to forecast multi-step-ahead landslide displacement (K-R-RTRL). The proposed novel method is implemented to make two-and four-ahead forecasts in Liangshuijing landslide monitoring point ZJG24 in Three Gorges Reservoir area. Based on comparison purpose, two comparative neural networks are performed, one is RTRL, the other is back propagation through time neural network (BPTT). The proposed algorithm K-R-RTRL gets superior performance to comparative networks in the final numerical and experimental results.

Keywords: R-RTRL · K-fold cross-validation · RNNs · K-R-RTRL
BPTT

1 Introduction

There are a lot of natural disasters [1,2] in the world, such as earthquake, tsunami, landslide and so on. The effect of natural disasters are serious. And landslide brings serious threat to human life and production environment. Landslides as one of natural disasters, which frequently happen in Three Gorges Reservoir area in China. Then, it seriously influences people's production and living needs.

Landslide [3] not only have complex causes, but also have various and uncertainty effect factors. Many scholars devote their energies to find suitable ways to take measures and countermeasures for disaster prevention and reduction. The essence of landslide is similar to artificial neural networks [4–8], so multifarious

© Springer International Publishing AG, part of Springer Nature 2018
T. Huang et al. (Eds.): ISNN 2018, LNCS 10878, pp. 468–475, 2018.
https://doi.org/10.1007/978-3-319-92537-0_54

nonlinear algorithms are applied in landslide displacement. At present, most of scholars are prefer to use forward neural network to study one-step ahead landslide displacement. Then, some scholars try to use RNNs to study multi-step prediction in other nature disasters. RNNs [4–8] is a kind of neural network with fixed weights, external inputs and internal states. Inspired by this idea, the paper uses R-RTRL [4–8] with K-fold cross-validation [9] to forecast multi-step ahead landslide displacement.

The paper organization is listed as follow. The first section is an introduction to describe the background of this paper. Methods and materials about K-RTRL are presented in Sect. 2. A real case is listed in Sect. 3 to illustrate the availability of our model. Finally, Sect. 4 is a conclusion about this paper.

2   Methods and Materials

2.1   Cross-Validation

In order to detect the performance of a predictive model, then it prefers to produce to an unconnected data. Usually, this process is called cross-validation [9]. There are lots of various methods such as K-fold cross-validation, $K \times 2$ cross-validation, repeated random sub-sampling validation, leave-one-out cross-validation and so on, which are used in different aspects.

Considering different factors, K-fold cross-validation is selected for chosing parameters of model in this study. The core idea about K-fold cross-validation which is a technique of dividing the original sample into K sub-samples. Then, the validation data for testing the model uses only one sub-sample. The left K-1 sub-samples are regarded as training data for the model. These procedure can be repeated K times. Meanwhile, each of the K sub-samples is regarded only once as the validation data. A single estimation is computed by the K results from the folds.

2.2   R-RTRL NN

In order to store information for later use and to increase the efficiency of learning, RTRL algorithm [5–8] has marked traits for dynamic internal feedback loops. A RTRL in Fig. 1 has three layers, a concatenated input-output layer, a processing layer and an output layer.

Then, $x(t)$ stands for the M input vector to the network at discrete time t. And corresponding $K \times 1$ output vector is $z(t+1)$, $y(t+1)$ represents the corresponding $t+1$ vector one step later at time $M \times 1$ in the processing layer. The input $x(t)$ and one-step delayed output vector in the processing layer $y(t+1)$ are be linked to form the $(M+N) \times 1$. The i element is represented by $\mu_i(t)$.

All of these paper [5–8] have proposed a novel algorithm can repeatedly correct model parameters with the current information. These current information are used not only the latest observed values but also model's outputs.

R-RTRL NN adequately makes use of the antecedent information of the observations, and enhances their usefulness to alleviate time-lag phenomena in

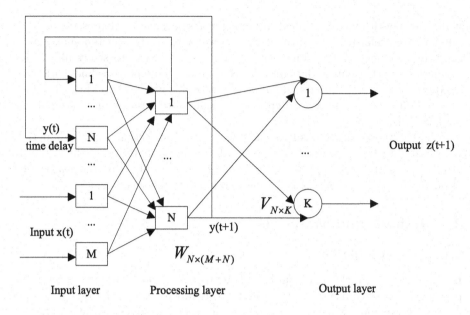

Fig. 1. Network architecture of RTRL

MSA prediction is used. Comparing with several models, R-RTRL NN does much better performance for MSA's forecasting.

At time $t + n$, the output layers'output through nonlinear system f is computed by

$$z(t+n) = f(net(t+n)) = f(\sum_j v_j(t+1)y_j(t+1)) \qquad (1)$$

At time $t + n$, define $d(t + n)$ as the target value. The time-varying error e and instantaneous error E is computed by

$$E(t+n) = 1/2e^2(t+n) = 1/2[d(t+n) - z(t+n)]^2 \qquad (2)$$

A time $t + n$, the weight adjustments can be defined by minimizing the instantaneous error.

$$\Delta v_j(t+1) = -\eta_1 \frac{\partial E(t+n)}{\partial v_j(t+1)} \qquad (3)$$

$$\Delta w_{ji}(t) = -\eta_2 \frac{\partial E(t+n)}{\partial w_{ji}(t)} \qquad (4)$$

where η_1 and η_2 are the learning-rata para at time $t + n$, so the weight adjustments can be defined ($z(t+n+1)$ to $z(t+2n-1)$) by minimizing the instantaneous error.

Then $z(t + \hat{n} + p)$ can be defined:

$$
\begin{aligned}
\hat{y}_j(t + p + 1) &= f(\hat{net}_j(t + p + 1)) \\
&= f\left(\sum_{i \in A \bigcup B} (w_{ji}(t) + \Delta w_{ji}(t)) \mu_i(t + p) \right)
\end{aligned} \tag{5}
$$

$$
\begin{aligned}
\hat{z}(t + n + p) &= f(\hat{net}_j(t + n + p)) \\
&= f\left(\sum_j (v_j(t + 1) + \Delta v_j(t + 1)) \hat{y}_j(t + p + 1) \right)
\end{aligned} \tag{6}
$$

Hence, the total reinforced error is computed by

$$
\hat{E} = \frac{1}{2} \sum_{p=1}^{n-1} \hat{e}^2 = \frac{1}{2} [\hat{z}(t + n + p) - z(t + n + p)]^2 \tag{7}
$$

The reinforced weight adjustments can be defined as

$$
\Delta \hat{v}_j(t + 1) = -\eta_3 \frac{\partial \hat{E}}{\partial v_j(t + 1)} \tag{8}
$$

where η_1 and η_2 are learning rate.

The reinforced weight adjustments can be considered as:

$$
W_{ji}(t + 1) = w_{ji}(t) + \Delta w_{ji}(t) + \Delta \hat{w}_{ji}(t) \tag{9}
$$

$$
v_j(t + 2) = v_j(t + 1) + \Delta v_j(t + 1) + \Delta \hat{v}_j(t + 1) \tag{10}
$$

2.3   R-RTRL NN

R-RTRL used K-fold cross-validation method to select the optimal number of hidden layer neurons at first. Then, the multi-step R-RTRL was used to multi step prediction of landslide displacement.

Step 1: It used 10-fold cross-validation to select the optimal number of hidden layer neurons. The number of neurons in the hidden layer was measured from 1 to 10.

Step 2: Set R-RTRL input variables by MI and PCC methods.

Step 3: Generated weights w and V randomly.

Step 4: Calculated difference between intermediate layer prediction $z(t + n)$ and target value $D(t + n)$. Then, it got weight Δw and Δv.

Step 5: Updated the weights of temporary RNNs, recalculated predicted value $\hat{z}(t + n + 1)$.

Step 6: Calculated intermediate layer prediction, the error value between $z(t+n+1)$ and $\hat{z}(t+n+1)$ is $\hat{e}(t+n+1)$.

Step 7: Calculated intermediate layer prediction, the error value between $z(t+n+2)$ and $\hat{z}(t+n+2)$ is $\hat{e}(t+n+2)$.

Step 8: If the time is not $t+n+2$, return 6, or continue.

Step 9: Update $\Delta\hat{w}$ and $\Delta\hat{v}$.

Step 10: If all data are computed, the process will be end or return step 4.

3   Application to Landslide Forecasting

3.1   Data Set

This paper's all experiments are based on MATLAB 2010b platform. The landslide is uncertainty, stability and complexity, so the formation of the landslide are extremely difficult to know. A case of Liangshuijing landslide in monitoring point 24 Three Gorges Reservoir area in China is proposed to illustrate the availability of our model.

3.2   Experiment and Results

Considering some other external factors rainfall and reservoir level, it uses two classical methods mutual information (MI) [10] and pearson cross correlation coefficients (PCC) to compute models' potential input variables. All data are divided into two groups to study. The training process contain 70% as the first group to set up the predicting model, and the rest recordings 30% are used to predict the displacement of landslide (see Tables 1 and 2). To make 2-, and 4- step ahead forecasts, it causes different lengths about results. Then, it uses K-fold cross-validation to obtain number of hidden layer neurons. In 2-head K-R-RTRL, the optimal number of neurons in the hidden layer is estimated to be 4, and the input parameter is 2. In 4-head K-R-RTRL, the optimal number of neurons in the hidden layer is estimated to be 5, and the input parameter is 2.

Four common methods [5–8] for evaluating the accuracy of prediction results mean absolute error (MAE), root mean square error (RMSE), relative error(RE) and correlation coefficient (R). Figures 2, 3 and Table 1 are described the value of Re about two-ahead and four-ahead. It is easily to get the predict results, the max of RE is 35.67%, the min of RE is 0.05%, and the min mean of RE is 7.26%. So it can be seen from the K-R-RTRL multi-step prediction is feasible and effective.

Then, we compare K-R-RTRL, RTRL and BPTT [5–8] according to RMSE, MAE and R. Table 2 has two input parameters and four hidden layer neurons. Table 3 has eight input parameters and five hidden layer neurons. In same condition, K-R-RTRL has the minimum MAE and RMSE, and the maximum R among three methods. Then, K-R-RTRL can solve up multi-step-ahead prediction landslide displacement problem. K-R-RTRL has more superiority in the weight adjustment, so the final result are better than the other methods.

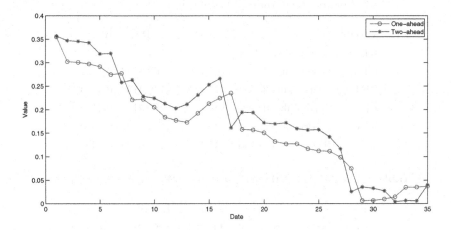

Fig. 2. K-R-RTRL's two step prediction of RE value

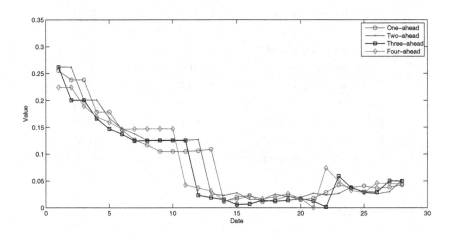

Fig. 3. K-R-RTRL's four step prediction of RE value

Table 1. Statistical data of RE

Variable	MIN	MAX	MEAN
Two-step ahead 1	0.0063	0.3551	0.1616
Two-step ahead 2	0.0040	0.3567	0.1816
Four-step ahead 1	0.0108	0.2554	0.0861
Four-step ahead 2	0.0157	0.2620	0.0870
Four-step ahead 3	0.0015	0.2617	0.0763
Four-step ahead 4	0.0005	0.2243	0.0810

Table 2. Comparison of three algorithms in the two step prediction

Variable	MAE	RMSE	R
RTRL two-step ahead 1	151.5080	174.5301	0.9319
RTRL two-step ahead 2	173.8630	202.8133	0.8122
BPTT two-step ahead 1	155.2981	177.4132	0.9103
BPTT two-step ahead 2	166.3599	189.3157	0.9176
K-R-RTRL two-step ahead 1	129.9981	145.1126	0.9359
K-R-RTRL two-step ahead 2	150.4751	171.6709	0.9304

Table 3. Comparison of three algorithms in the three step prediction

Variable	MAE	RMSE	R
RTRL four-step ahead 1	113.0197	126.1280	0.8901
RTRL four-step ahead 2	112.8539	124.6291	0.8938
RTRL four-step ahead 3	100.3440	110.5544	0.9171
RTRL four-step ahead 4	97.3896	107.4008	0.9261
BPTT four-step ahead 1	113.4523	132.5690	0.8156
BPTT four-step ahead 2	117.8957	132.8315	0.8615
BPTT four-step ahead 3	104.5090	121.6359	0.8906
BPTT four-step ahead 4	109.7865	125.6540	0.5892
K-R-RTRL four-step ahead 1	74.8256	89.3200	0.9533
K-R-RTRL four-step ahead 2	75.1500	91.7399	0.9541
K-R-RTRL four-step ahead 3	68.4461	84.4792	0.9538
K-R-RTRL four-step ahead 4	73.2015	88.0521	0.9485

4   Conclusions

It is imperative to find a credible and accurate prediction of future events. The K-R-RTRL networks are able to predict mutli-step ahead landslide forecast. And, it used BPTT and RTRL as comparison algorithm, our proposed methods are not only improve prediction accuracy but also enrich theoretical foundation for further landslide forecast research.

Acknowledgements. The work is supported by the Natural Science Foundation of China under Grant 61603129, the Natural Science Foundation of Hubei Province under Grant 2016CFC734.

References

1. Kilburn, C.R.J., Petley, D.N.: Forecasting giant, catastrophic slope collapse: lessons from Vajont, Northern Italy. Geomorphology **54**, 21–32 (2005)
2. Babu, G.L.S., Bijoy, A.C.: Appraisal of Bishop's method of slope stability analysis. Slope Stab. Eng. **1–2**, 249–252 (1999)
3. Lian, C., Zeng, Z.G., Yao, W., Tang, H.M.: Displacement prediction model of landslide based on a modified ensemble empirical mode decomposition and extreme learning machine. Nat. Hazards **66**, 759–771 (2013)
4. Chang, F.J., Hwang, Y.Y.: A self-organization algorithm for real-time flood forecast. Hydrol. Process. **13**(2), 123–138 (1999)
5. Chang, F.J., Chang, L.C., Huang, H.L.: Real-time recurrent learning neural network for stream-flow forecasting. Hydrol. Process. **16**, 2577–2588 (2002)
6. Chang, L.C., Chang, F.J., Chiang, Y.M.: A two step-ahead recurrent neural network for stream-flow forecasting. Hydrol. Process. **18**, 81–92 (2004)
7. Chang, L.C., Chen, P.A., Chang, F.J.: Reinforced two step-ahead weight adjustment technique for online training of recurrent neural networks. IEEE Trans. Neural Netw. Learn. Syst. **23**(8), 1269–1278 (2012)
8. Chen, P.A., Chang, L.C., Chang, F.J.: Reinforced recurrent neural networks for multi-step-ahead flood forecasts. J. Hydrol. **23**(8), 71–79 (2013)
9. Wiens, T.S., Dale, B.C., Boyce, M.S., Kershaw, G.P.: Three way k-fold cross-validation of resource selection functions. Ecol. Model. **212**(3–4), 244–255 (2008)
10. Kraskov, A., Stogbauer, H., Grassberger, P.: Estimating mutual information. Phys. Rev. E **69**(066138), 1–16 (2004)
11. Smith, T.F., Waterman, M.S.: Identification of common molecular subsequences. J. Mol. Biol. **147**, 195–197 (1981)
12. May, P., Ehrlich, H.-C., Steinke, T.: ZIB structure prediction pipeline: composing a complex biological workflow through web services. In: Nagel, W.E., Walter, W.V., Lehner, W. (eds.) Euro-Par 2006. LNCS, vol. 4128, pp. 1148–1158. Springer, Heidelberg (2006). https://doi.org/10.1007/11823285_121
13. Foster, I., Kesselman, C.: The Grid: Blueprint for a New Computing Infrastructure. Morgan Kaufmann, San Francisco (1999)
14. Czajkowski, K., Fitzgerald, S., Foster, I., Kesselman, C.: Grid information services for distributed resource sharing. In: 10th IEEE International Symposium on High Performance Distributed Computing, pp. 181–184, New York (2001)
15. Foster, I., Kesselman, C., Nick, J., Tuecke, S.: The physiology of the grid: an open grid services architecture for distributed systems integration. Technical report, Global Grid Forum (2002)
16. National Center for Biotechnology Information. http://www.ncbi.nlm.nih.gov

Personalized Response Generation for Customer Service Agents

Ma Cuihua[1], Ping Guo[1,2(✉)], and Xin Xin[1]

[1] School of Computer Science and Technology, Beijing Institute of Technology,
Beijing 100081, China
{chma,xxin}@bit.edu.cn
[2] Laboratory of Image Processing and Pattern Recognition,
Beijing Normal University, Beijing 100875, China
pguo@ieee.org

Abstract. Natural language generation is a critical component of dialogue system and plenty of works have proved the effectiveness and efficiency of sequence-to-sequence (seq2seq) model for generation. Seq2seq model is a kind of neural networks which usual require massive data to learn its parameters. For many small shops in customer service dialogue systems, there is not large dialogue dataset to be utilized to train this model, resulting in performance of trained model cannot meet real application requirements. In this work, we present the Tensor Encoder Generative Model (TEGM) collaborating data of many shops in customer service dialogue system, and expect to alleviate the disadvantage of data insufficiency. The generator fully trained from data can be capable of encoding personalized feature of each shop. Experimental results show that the TEGM indeed can improve performance compared to baseline.

Keywords: Generation · Dialogue system · seq2seq model
Neural network

1 Introduction

In recent years, as generation methods based on neural networks are of growing interest, neural response generation has received increasing attention. Generative models can automatically produce response word by word, making the dialogue more flexible and the response content more diverse. Due to the trained generative model would not need the support of massive historical dialogue data, when similar user questions cannot be found in historical data, responses produced by generative model are more general in all the cases. Hence, based on the previous work [1], the paper makes a further study to develop generative models for customer service dialogue system.

Most previous works, including dialogue system [2–4], Chinese couplet generation [5] and machine translation [6], are all based on neural networks and get good performance, which has proven that neural network methods are effective

© Springer International Publishing AG, part of Springer Nature 2018
T. Huang et al. (Eds.): ISNN 2018, LNCS 10878, pp. 476–483, 2018.
https://doi.org/10.1007/978-3-319-92537-0_55

to achieve response generation. However, these methods require a great deal of training data to generate text. Extensive historical dialogue data will help to model generative models in customer service dialogue system. Unfortunately, there is not a large dialogue dataset that can be used for training to get a good dialogue system for many small shops.

To solve the above issue, in this paper we propose Tensor Encoder Generative Model (TEGM) learned by common features digging out from dialogue text of many shops with the assumption that there are common features in dialogue text of many shops. Meanwhile the model learns personalized feature to describe personalized information of each shop. Finally, personalized dialogue text generation would be realized with insufficient data. Our work has three primary contributions:

1 *Dealing with insufficient data.* Assuming that there are common features in many dialogue systems, we learn generative model by common features digging out from dialogue data of many shops to solve data insufficiency problem.
2 *Personalized text generation.* It can be able to realize personalized dialogue text generation when we construct tensor in encoder to add personalized feature of each shop, then decode with attention to generate text.
3 *Evaluation.* We conduct the experiments with 168,000 dialogue text of 81 shops in one month provided by Easemob company. The results demonstrate that the proposed method outperforms seq2seq by 4.4% in perplexity.

2 Related Works

There are a lot of researchers in the past few decades who commit to response generation in dialogue systems. Common method is seq2seq model [7], which is based on encoder-decoder structure. Encoder can be used to map the input sentence to a vector of a fixed dimensionality, while decoder is used to generate the target sequence from the vector. Earlier, seq2seq model was applied to the task of machine translation [6]. Later, dialogue system [8,9] can be seen as mapping a sequence of words representing the question to a sequence of words representing the answer. Yao et al. [10] provided helpful response for customers on computer related issues using seq2seq model with intention and attention. Wen et al. [11] presented a LSTM-based seq2seq model for hotel and restaurant spoken dialogue systems. By successfully applied to a variety of tasks, generative model of seq2seq has been shown to be effective.

But response generation for customer service agents in shops is relatively unexplored. To the best of our knowledge, we are the first to suggest using dialogue text between customer service agents and clients to build dialogue systems to generate response content. Likewise, the customer service dialogue system can be treated as a source-to-target transduction problem and mapping rules can be learned between input messages and responses from a massive amount of training data. Furthermore, Serban et al. [12] proved that generating responses was considerably more difficult than translating between languages, likely due to the wide range of plausible responses and lack of phrase alignment between the question and the response.

3 Tensor Encoder Generative Model

3.1 Problem Definition

We treat dialogue system as sequence to sequence mapping task, then the goal of generative model is to learn the mapping rule. The input of model is word sequence of dialogue question and the output is word sequence of response. With vectorized representation, the problem can be summarized as follows.

As shown in Fig. 1, q_i denotes the vector of the ith word of input sentence, then $q_1, q_2, ..., q_m$ denote the vector representation of input sentence and m is the length of input sequence. Likewise, a_i denotes the vector of the ith word of target sentence, then $a_1, a_2, ..., a_n$ denote the vector representation of target output and n is the length of target sequence. The goal of generative model is to learn mapping rule f that can map input sequence q to target sequence a.

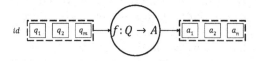

Fig. 1. Generation problem definition

After defining the goal to learn, we design the workflow for generating customer service response, as shown in Fig. 2. The triple *shopID, context, response* is the database to train model. Glossary contains all the words that make up a sentence and the size is L. Output sequence $a_1, a_2, ..., a_n$ generated by model needs the glossary to convert to text output. It is worth noting that, if the generative model is trained, the model can be used with only glossary and to generate response for customer service agents in one shop, no longer need the support of database of triples.

3.2 Tensor Encoder Generative Model

Figure 3 shows a visualization of sequence to sequence generation model. There are three parts: encoder, attention and decoder. While encoding in Tensor Encoder Generative Model (TEGM), it does not only encode input question, but also encode personalized vector representation of each shop by using tensor as weight parameter. The operation formula of encoder is as follows:

$$i_t = f(v_t^T \mathcal{W}_{xi} x_t + v_t'^T \mathcal{W}_{ih} h_{t-1} + b_i) \tag{1}$$

$$f_t = f(v_t^T \mathcal{W}_{xf} x_t + v_t'^T \mathcal{W}_{fh} h_{t-1} + b_f) \tag{2}$$

$$o_t = f(v_t^T \mathcal{W}_{xo} x_t + v_t'^T \mathcal{W}_{oh} h_{t-1} + b_o) \tag{3}$$

$$\hat{c}_t = g(v_t^T \mathcal{W}_{xc} x_t + v_t'^T \mathcal{W}_{ch} h_{t-1} + b_c) \tag{4}$$

$$c_t = f_t \odot c_{t-1} + i_t \odot \hat{c}_t \tag{5}$$

$$h_t = o_t \odot g(c_t) \tag{6}$$

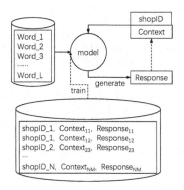

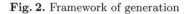

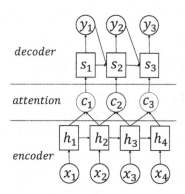

Fig. 2. Framework of generation

Fig. 3. Architecture of sequence to sequence model

v_t and v_t' both denote personalized vectors of each shop, so parameters $\mathcal{W}_{xi}$, $\mathcal{W}_{ih}$, $\mathcal{W}_{xf}$, $\mathcal{W}_{fh}$, $\mathcal{W}_{xo}$, $\mathcal{W}_{oh}$, $\mathcal{W}_{xc}$, $\mathcal{W}_{ch}$ are all tensor. Because of these tensors, the hidden state of encoder contains shop information and semantics of input question.

After encoding the input sentence into a vector in encoder progress, the vector would be used to generate sentence in decoder progress. In this paper we adopt decoder with attention mechanism [13]. According to the importance of each word in encoder, different weights are calculated with attention mechanism in different decoder progress. Decoder generates next word with different weights. The condition probability of decoder with attention mechanism is calculated as follows:

$$p(y_i|y_1,...,y_{i-1},c_i) = g(y_{i-1},s_i,c_i) \tag{7}$$

g denotes decode neural network, y_{i-1} denotes last generated word by decoder, s_i denotes ith hidden state in decode neural network and c_i is context vector. The probability represents possibility of target word generated according to different context vector c_i. Context vector c_i is a weighted average of the hidden state h_j of the encoder:

$$c_i = \sum_{j=1}^{T_i} \alpha_{ij} h_j \tag{8}$$

The calculation of context vector c_i depends on a series of encoding representation $(h_1, h_2, \ldots, h_j)$ of input sentence. Each h_j contains all the focus information of the jth word of the input sentence, indicating that the generated words are affected by different encoder words in decoder progress. The weights corresponding to each hidden state h_j are calculated as follows:

$$\alpha_{ij} = \frac{exp(e_{ij})}{\sum_{k=1}^{T_x} exp(e_{ik})} \tag{9}$$

$$e_{ij} = a(s_{i-1}, h_j) \tag{10}$$

e_{ij} is a alignment model that measures the alignment between the jth input and the ith output. The alignment model is different in different paper. In our paper, we use the activation output of feed forward neural network.

Given the input sequence x and the current time t, the probability of the next word to be generated, which is the same as kth word in glossary, is the output of last layer in decoder neural network:

$$p(y_t^k|x) = \frac{exp(y_t^k)}{\sum_{i=1}^{N} exp(y_t^i)} \tag{11}$$

We expect that the probability of generated words appearing in target sequence is larger. So our objective function is to maximize the product of probability of the words:

$$p(y|x) = \prod_{t=1}^{T} p(y_t|y_{t-1}, x) \tag{12}$$

also to minimize loss $\mathcal{L}$:

$$\mathcal{L} = -ln \prod_{t=1}^{T} p(y_t|y_{t-1}, x) \tag{13}$$

4   Experiments

4.1   Experimental Setup

Experimental dataset, which is the dialogue recording in customer service dialogue system of 81 shops during November 2015, is provided by Easemob company. Every dialogue has been processed to triples *shopID, context, response* with a total of 218 thousand dialogues. And the most of target responses are 3 to 6 words.

The system was implemented with tensorflow [14] and trained by partitioning collected corpus into a training, validation and testing set with the size of 168000, 25000 and 25000 respectively. The personalized vector is set to 10, and the vocabulary size is 70368. Seq2seq model is used as our baseline. Accurate evaluation of different models for dialogue system is still an open problem. Nevertheless, perplexity (PPL) is used for performance evaluation and has been suggested for generative dialogue models previously [12,15].

4.2   Evaluation

To test the adaptability of model for different training size, 20 shops are selected to use data of different size for training and the remaining data for testing, in collaboration with data of other shops. The experimental results are shown in

Table 1. Perplexity of methods with different training size

TrainingSize	200	1000	1500	2000	Overall
seq2seq	7.18	6.32	6.24	7.15	7.09
TEGM	6.89	6.06	5.90	6.98	6.78
Promotion	4.03%	4.14%	5.38%	2.38%	4.4%

Table 1. When there are 200 training data, the improvement of model is above 4%. As the training size increases, the effect of model gets better and better. When there are 2000 training data, the promotion is smaller. By carefully analyzing the results, we find that when the training size is 2000, the remaining data for testing is very small and may not represent all distribution of data, leading to the deviation of test results. And at the end of table there is a comparison of overall performance. The performance shows that TEGM is better than seq2seq, indicating that the personalized vector improves the ability of representing data and helps to represent question semantics while encoding.

Table 2. Rouge-L results of methods with different training size

TrainingSize	200	1000	1500	2000	Overall
seq2seq	63.97	63.57	66.94	64.78	41.76
TEGM	62.74	65.38	68.61	65.09	65.02

In order to comprehensively estimate the performance of our proposed method, we evaluate our model under Rouge-L metrics expected to be larger, and experimental results are shown in Table 2. By contrastively analyzing the results, similar conclusions can be gotten with Table 1.

To verify whether the generated responses are in accordance with the normal status of the customer service dialogue, we print the generated responses of two models in the test set and statistic the distribution of word number in generated responses, the results are shown in Fig. 4.

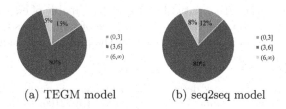

(a) TEGM model   (b) seq2seq model

Fig. 4. Distribution of word number in two models

From Fig. 4 , we can observe that the most responses are between 3 words and 7 words and the least are more than 6 words. Results indicate that the generated responses are relatively reasonable and consistent with the distribution of target responses.

In order to evaluate the reasonableness of the generated responses more intuitively and reduce the differences when scored by human, we have drafted an evaluation standard. The response is scored to be 1 when generated response contains core keywords or the same semantics with target response, 0 when generated response includes partial keywords or any other reasonable semantics and -1 when there is no semantic information or not the same semantics. And then choose 3 person to mark 300 responses according to the evaluation standard. Result of marked responses is shown in Fig. 5.

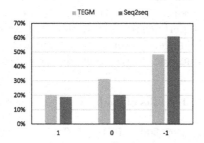

Fig. 5. Result of manual annotation

As shown in Fig. 5, result marked 0 of TEGM is better than that of seq2seq, indicating that TEGM has better scalability and ability of semantic representation. In terms of generating accurate responses, although our proposed TEGM does not significantly improve in comparison with seq2seq generation model, responses with some semantic information generated by TEGM is better than those generated by seq2seq largely.

5   Conclusions

In this paper, we propose Tensor Encoder Generative Model for customer service dialogue system collaborating data of many shops, capable of encoding personalized feature of each shop. Empirical performance of models was measured using perplexity, and experiments demonstrate that the proposed method outperforms seq2seq by 4.4%.

Acknowledgments. The work described in this paper was mainly supported by the National Nature Science Foundation of China (No. 61672100, 61375045), the Joint Research Fund in Astronomy under cooperative agreement between the National Natural Science Foundation of China and Chinese Academy of Sciences (No. U1531242), Beijing Natural Science Foundation (No. 4162054, 4162027).

References

1. Ma, C., Guo, P., Xin, X., Ma, X., Liang, Y., Xing, S., Li, L., Liu, S.: Collaborative response content recommendation for customer service agents. In: Cong, F., Leung, A., Wei, Q. (eds.) ISNN 2017. LNCS, vol. 10261, pp. 36–43. Springer, Cham (2017). https://doi.org/10.1007/978-3-319-59072-1_5
2. Ondřej, D., Filip, J.: A context-aware natural language generator for dialogue systems. In: Annual Meeting of the Special Interest Group on Discourse and Dialogue, pp. 185–190 (2016)
3. Wen, T.H., Gasic, M., Mrksic, N., et al.: Multi-domain neural network language generation for spoken dialogue systems. In: Conference of the North American Chapter of the Association for Computational Linguistics: Human Language Technologies, pp. 120–129 (2016)
4. Li, J., Monroe, W., Ritter, A., et al.: Deep reinforcement learning for dialogue generation. In: Empirical Methods in Natural Language Processing, pp. 1192–1202 (2016)
5. Yan, R., Li, C., Hu, X., et al.: Chinese couplet generation with neural network structures. In: Meeting of the Association for Computational Linguistics, pp. 2347–2357 (2016)
6. Sutskever, I., Vinyals, O., Le, Q.V.: Sequence to sequence learning with neural networks. In: Neural Information Processing Systems, pp. 3104–3112 (2014)
7. Dušek, O., Jurčíček, F.: Sequence-to-sequence generation for spoken dialogue via deep syntax trees and strings. In: Meeting of the Association for Computational Linguistics, pp. 45–51 (2016)
8. Serban, I., Klinger, T., Tesauro, G., et al.: Multiresolution recurrent neural networks: an application to dialogue response generation. In: Proceedings of the Thirty-First AAAI Conference on Artificial Intelligence, pp. 3288–3294 (2017)
9. Wen, T., Gasic, M., Kim, D., et al.: Stochastic language generation in dialogue using recurrent neural networks with convolutional sentence reranking. In: Annual Meeting of the Special Interest Group on Discourse and Dialogue, pp. 275–284 (2015)
10. Yao, K.S., Zweig, G., Peng, B.: Attention with intention for a neural network conversation model. Neural and Evolutionary Computing (2015)
11. Wen, T.H., Gasic, M., Mrksic, N., et al.: Semantically conditioned LSTM-based natural language generation for spoken dialogue systems. In: Empirical Methods in Natural Language Processing, pp. 1711–1721 (2015)
12. Serban, I.V., Sordoni, A., Bengio, Y., et al.: Building end-to-end dialogue systems using generative hierarchical neural network models. In: Proceedings of the Thirtieth AAAI Conference on Artificial Intelligence, pp. 3776–3783 (2016)
13. Bahdanau, D., Cho, K., Bengio, Y.: Neural machine translation by jointly learning to align and translate. In: International Conference on Learning Representations (2015)
14. Abadi, M., Agarwal, A., Barham, P., et al.: TensorFlow: large-scale machine learning on heterogeneous distributed systems. Distributed, Parallel, and Cluster Computing (2016)
15. Olivier, P., Helen, H.: A survey on metrics for the evaluation of user simulations. Knowl. Eng. Rev. 28(1), 59–73 (2013)

Tracking of Multiple Pixel Targets Using Multiple Cameras

Jin Zhou and Chiman Kwan[(⊠)]

Signal Processing, Inc., Rockville, MD, USA
ferrryzhou@gmail.com, chiman.kwan@signalpro.net

Abstract. Simultaneous tracking of multiple and small/pixel targets is important for many applications such as ship, aircraft, and vehicle tracking. This paper presents a practical and efficient framework for the above problem. The key ideas in the framework include 3D modeling of multiple cameras and the application of multiple Extended Kalman Filters (EKF) for multi-target tracking. Many practical issues such as multiple small targets, measurement noise, false targets, partial or missing target observations, multiple cameras, etc. have been addressed. Extensive experiments demonstrated the feasibility of the proposed framework.

Keywords: Target tracking · Kalman Filter · Pixel target

1 Introduction

There are many applications that require the tracking of small/pixel targets using multiple sensors. Image sensors (EO/IR) have many advantages over radars such as better mobility and lower cost. Hyperspectral imagers is another potential sensor that can be used for target detection and tracking.

In this project, it is assumed that a set of unmanned air vehicles (UAVs) or other platforms are used to detect and track multiple targets (vehicles or aircraft), which appear as pixel targets from long ranges in cameras. Each UAV carries one or more infrared cameras to capture heat emission from remote objects/aircraft. Figure 1 shows a sample scenario of target tracking using two cameras. In this scenario, two cameras are watching a remote site, where three targets are just taking off. In general, there can be many targets at the same or different times and we have many cameras to track them simultaneously.

Our pixel target tracking system consists of several key components. First, pixel targets are detected in each camera. Many algorithms can be used here, including anomaly detection algorithms [1–6] and foreground/background separation using sparsity [7]. Second, targets in multiple cameras are associated via a 3D camera geometric model. This model is very important for dealing with multiple targets in multiple cameras. Third, although sophisticated tracking algorithms such as [8–13] can be used, a simple and efficient target tracking algorithm based on Extended Kalman Filter (EKF) [16–18] is used to track the targets. Fourth, a number of practical algorithms have been utilized to address many practical issues such as false targets, partial or missing observations, coordination between multiple cameras, etc.

© Springer International Publishing AG, part of Springer Nature 2018
T. Huang et al. (Eds.): ISNN 2018, LNCS 10878, pp. 484–493, 2018.
https://doi.org/10.1007/978-3-319-92537-0_56

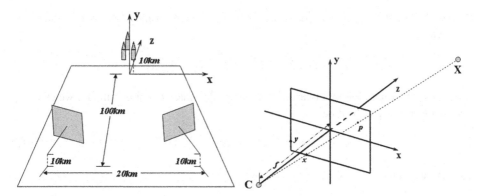

Fig. 1. Tracking multiple targets using multiple cameras.

Fig. 2. Geometric model of imaging.

Our tracking system is fully automatic, robust, flexible, scalable, efficient and practical for multiple pixel targets tracking. With all these capabilities, we believe that our multiple camera based tracking system is able to work in real world situations and provides a better solution than radar based tracking system in some complex scenario.

In the following, we first present the geometric model of camera and imaging process in Sect. 2. In Sect. 3, we then describe the geometric model based EKF for 3D target tracking from 2D camera observations. We combine multiple camera observations into a single observation vector so that all information can be used simultaneously. In this way, information from partial frames are effectively utilized. We further describe how we perform automatic new target state initialization based on triangulation. In addition, we will also present the strategy for multi-target and multi-group tracking, which involves automatic camera adjustment and multi-camera coordination. In Sect. 4, we demonstrate the capability of our tracking system with two simulation experiments, which includes observation noise, missing targets, false alarms, non-linear trajectory, multiple target groups, multiple sensors, and long video sequences. Finally, some remarks will be given in Sect. 5.

2   Geometric Models

Figure 2 shows the camera model. The symbols x, y and z denote the three axes of the camera. The letter C is the camera location. X is a 3D point and p is the corresponding image point. x and y are the image coordinate axes; the origin $(0, 0)$ is at bottom left. f is the focal length of the camera.

Given a 3D point X, its projection on image is p which can be computed by the following equation [14]

$$\hat{p} = KR[I| - C]\hat{X} \tag{1}$$

where $\hat{X}$ is the homogeneous coordinates of X and $\hat{p}$ is the homogeneous coordinates of p. That is,

$$p = \hat{p}(1:2)/\hat{p}(3) \text{ and } X = \hat{X}(1:3)/\hat{X}(4) \tag{2}$$

K is the camera internal matrix. R is the rotation matrix. For simplicity, we can use normalized image coordinates

$$\bar{p} = K^{-1}\hat{p}. \tag{3}$$

As a result,

$$\bar{p} = R[I|-C]\hat{X} = R(X-C). \tag{4}$$

In our simulation and tracking studies, we will use the above normalized image coordinates.

3 Multi-camera Tracking Based on Extended Kalman Filters

3.1 Tracking Using Extended Kalman Filter

We use Extended Kalman Filter (EKF) for its simplicity to perform the 3D object tracking based on 2D observations. The state vector is represented as

$$\mu = [x \quad y \quad z \quad v_x \quad v_y \quad v_z]^T \tag{5}$$

where $(x, y, z)^T$ is target's 3D location and $(v_x, v_y, v_z)^T$ is the speed vector. We use a linear motion model represented by

$$\mu_t = A\mu_{t-1}$$

where

$$A = \begin{bmatrix} 1 & 0 & 0 & \Delta t & 0 & 0 \\ 0 & 1 & 0 & 0 & \Delta t & 0 \\ 0 & 0 & 1 & 0 & 0 & \Delta t \\ 0 & 0 & 0 & 1 & 0 & 0 \\ 0 & 0 & 0 & 0 & 1 & 0 \\ 0 & 0 & 0 & 0 & 0 & 1 \end{bmatrix}.$$

The observation model is given by

$$\bar{p} = R(X - C) \tag{6}$$

where $X = \mu(1:3)$

$$p(i) = \bar{p}(i)/\bar{p}(3) = \frac{R_{i:}(X - C)}{R_{3:}(X - C)}$$

where $i = 1, 2$. $R_{i:}$ is the ith row of R and $[p(1), p(2)]$ are the normalized image coordinates.

For M cameras, we combine all the observations together to form a single measurement vector

$$Z = [p_1(1) \quad p_1(2) \quad p_2(1) \quad p_2(2) \quad \cdots \quad \cdots \quad p_M(1) \quad p_M(2)]^T. \tag{7}$$

In practice, due to missing pixels/frames or partial observations, it is possible that only a subset of the sensors have observations of the target. Therefore, the observation vector (Z) only contains the available information from a subset of the sensors [15].

3.2 Multi-target Tracking

To track multiple targets simultaneously, we maintain an EKF tracker for each target independently. To update each tracker with new observations, we use nearest neighbor strategy, i.e. for each image, the point which is closest to prediction position is assigned as new observation. To cope with missing pixels, we set a distance threshold. If the closest distance is larger than the threshold, we assume there is no new observation. If a tracker does not have any new observations for a long time, its covariance matrix will be large and we drop/stop it.

3.3 Automatic State Initialization for New Targets

The EKF tracker assumes there is an initial state to begin with. For image sensors, the 2D observations do not equal to the 3D positions and cannot be directly used as initial states. To initialize states, we use triangulation method to generate all possible 3D points based on the observations from multiple cameras. When there are many cameras and many false alarms, the number of all possible 3D points could be huge. We use re-projection error to eliminate a majority of the false targets.

3.4 Tracker Pruning

In the previous paragraph, we mentioned that even with initial tracker elimination based on re-projection error, there may still be a lot of false tracks. One way to get rid of false tracks is to use error covariance to measure the confidence of a tracker. If the covariance is large, the confidence is low. We use the inverse sum of the diagonal elements of the covariance matrix to indicate the confidence level. If the confidence level is below a threshold, we terminate the track and its associated EKF tracker. Usually, if a tracker cannot gain enough observation updates, its covariance will grow and finally terminate. Using the above technique, most of the false tracks and their corresponding trackers are eliminated as time goes on.

With enough time, all the survived tracks will merge to true targets. This leads to another issue: many tracks may become identical to each other. In practice, we do not need all of them. For each true target, we only need one tracker. To prune these redundant trackers, we measure similarity of the state vectors and if two trackers are too close, the one with lower confidence is terminated.

With tracker pruning, the number of total trackers will gradually converge to the number of true targets and the system speed will become very fast.

4   Simulations and Tracking Experiments

In this section, we use two simulations to demonstrate the effectiveness of our tracking system. The first simulation is a simple one, i.e. linear trajectory and single target group, and no need for camera adjustment. This simulation is used to demonstrate the basic functions of the tracking system such as robustness to noise, false alarms, missing target and the capability of automatic initialization. The second simulation is very challenging: non-linear trajectory, multiple groups, long time (say, 700 frames). This simulation is used to demonstrate advanced feature of the tracking system such as partial observation, active tracking, automatic multi-camera coordination, non-linear trajectory and tracker pruning. In both simulations, we used a simple target detection algorithm (Reed-Xiaoli Detector [2]) to detect the targets. Other sophisticated algorithms could be used as well where low false alarms can be achieved. However, the objective of these simulations is to demonstrate the proposed tracking system rather than target detection.

In the first simulation, we placed 4 cameras and generated 3 targets. The 3 targets are moving at a constant velocity. Figure 3 shows the simulation setup and the tracking process. Figure 4 shows the images highlighting the detected target pixel's locations. We simulated 30 frames and frame 1, 11, 16, and 26 are shown in Fig. 3. In each image, there are a random number (from 0 to 10) of false alarms. In addition, each target has a probability of 0.1 of missing in an image. The pixel locations are disturbed with random Gaussian noise with mean of 0.5 pixel. In Fig. 3, the camera is represented by 3 axes: red is z axis, blue is x axis and green is y axis. Image plane is in the end of z axis. Green circles represent target observations on images, which include true target's image and false alarms. Blue circles are 3 real targets in 3D space. Red crosses are estimated 3D targets in EKF tracker. Red circles represent the diagonal mean of EKF covariance matrix. In the beginning, there are 6 EKF trackers, only two of them are correct. In frame 11, one of the false target's track (the most right one in frame 1) disappears. Two false targets' tracks close to true targets merged to true target's location. Starting from frame 16, all false target trackers disappear and only 3 true target trackers exist and overlap with ground truth position.

In the second simulation, the experimental setup is as follows:

(1) There are 3 targets moving in circles. One target's speed is different from another two.
(2) There are 7 cameras.
(3) False alarms range from 0 to 5 for each image.
(4) There are 700 frames.

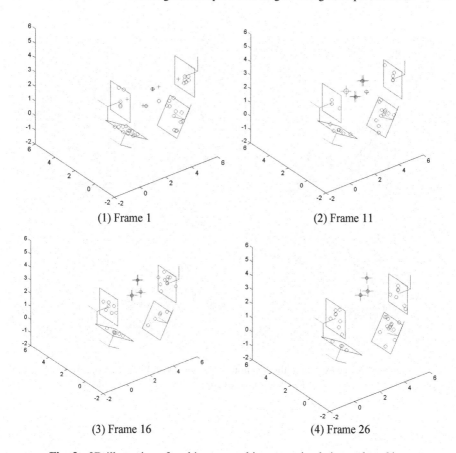

(1) Frame 1   (2) Frame 11

(3) Frame 16   (4) Frame 26

Fig. 3. 3D illustration of multi-target multi-camera simulation and tracking.

Other configuration parameters are the same as the previous simulation. Figure 5 shows trajectories of ground truth targets (in black circles) and EKFs (in lines). We can observe that all three real targets' trajectories are successfully captured. There are some false tracks. Most of them are terminated after a short time. Only 1 false track lasts more than 200 frames. Note that for one of the targets, there are two color lines, i.e. cyan and blue. This means that there are two corresponding tracks. In the beginning, the cyan track is tracking the target. However, after several hundred frames, it loses the target. Fortunately, our system can automatically recover the failed case by automatically initialize new targets. After several frames of failed tracking, a new blue tracker is created to track the target.

Figure 6 shows a realistic rendering of frame 500. The UAV network are coordinated to cover all targets. Note that for visualization, we highlight the target pixel as well as false alarms in the image. In reality, they are all single pixels.

Figure 7 shows a set of sample frames. In the beginning, there are many (more than 400) trackers that are initialized. After 10 frames, some trackers' confidence level becomes low (see big circles in the image). In frame 70, most false trackers are

Camera 1   Camera 2   Camera 3   Camera 4

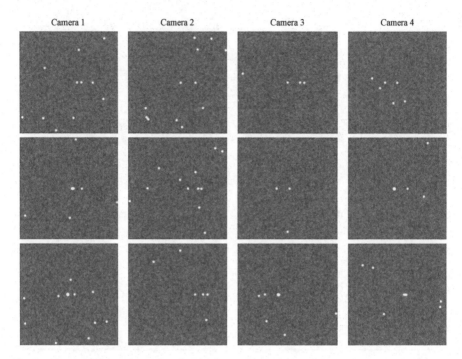

Fig. 4. Simulated images showing the locations of targets as well as false alarms. Columns are images from different cameras. Rows are images from time frame 1, 11, and 21.

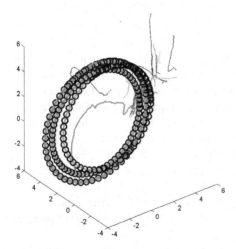

Fig. 5. Ground truth targets trajectory (in black circles) and EKF trackers' trajectory (in lines). (Color figure online)

Fig. 6. Frame 500 with realistic rendering. Three axes are the targets and red balls are EKF trackers. (Color figure online)

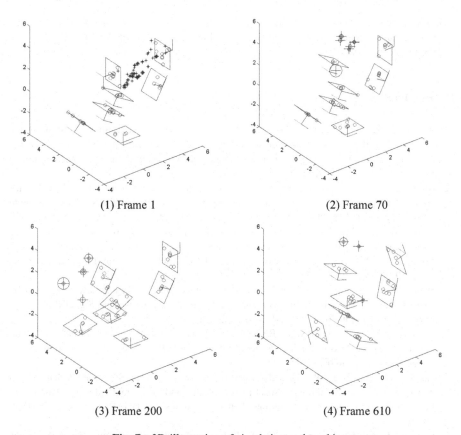

(1) Frame 1   (2) Frame 70

(3) Frame 200   (4) Frame 610

Fig. 7. 3D illustration of simulation and tracking.

eliminated. Note that in frame 70, the top camera changed its view angle to track the targets. In frame 200, most cameras changed their view angle. The top camera has changed at least twice. In frame 500, two target groups are totally separated due to different running speed. In this frame, both groups received enough attention. The two left cameras are watching the bottom group and other cameras are watching another group. Actually, the two right cameras can see both groups. So the bottom target is covered by 4 cameras and another two targets are covered by 5 cameras. Frame 610 has similar situation and all of the targets get enough coverage.

5   Conclusions

In this paper, we present a general framework for tracking multiple pixel targets using multiple cameras. Many practical issues such as missing pixels, partial observations, measurement noise, multiple targets, etc. have been addressed. Extensive simulations clearly demonstrated the performance of the framework.

Acknowledgments. This research was supported by MDA under contract # HQ0147-12-C-7883. Distribution Statement A. Approved for public release (17-MDA-9402 (31 Oct 17)); distribution is unlimited.

References

1. Ayhan, B., Kwan, C., Li, X., Trang, A.: Airborne detection of land mines using mid-wave infrared (MWIR) and laser-illuminated-near infrared images with the RXD hyperspectral anomaly detection method. In: Fourth International Workshop on Pattern Recognition in Remote Sensing, Hong Kong (2006)
2. Zhou, J., Kwan, C., Ayhan, B., Eismann, M.: A novel cluster Kernel RX algorithm for anomaly and change detection using hyperspectral images. IEEE Trans. Geosci. Remote Sens. **54**(11), 6497–6504 (2016)
3. Ayhan, B., Dao, M., Kwan, C., Chen, H., Bell, J.F., Kidd, R.: A novel utilization of image registration techniques to process mastcam images in mars rover with applications to image fusion, pixel clustering, and anomaly detection. IEEE J. Sel. Top. Appl. Earth Obs. Remote Sens. **10**, 4553–4564 (2017)
4. Wang, W., Li, S., Qi, H., Ayhan, B., Kwan, C., Vance, S.: Identify anomaly component by sparsity and low rank. In: IEEE Workshop on Hyperspectral Image and Signal Processing: Evolution in Remote Sensor (WHISPERS) (2015)
5. Li, S., Wang, W., Qi, H., Ayhan, B., Kwan, C., Vance, S.: Low-rank tensor decomposition based anomaly detection for hyperspectral imagery. In: IEEE International Conference on Image Processing (ICIP) (2015)
6. Qu, Y., Guo, R., Wang, W., Qi, H., Ayhan, B., Kwan, C., Vance, S.: Anomaly detection in hyperspectral images through spectral unmixing and low rank decomposition. In: International Geoscience and Remote Sensing Symposium (IGARSS), pp. 1855–1858 (2016)
7. Dao, M., Kwan, C., Ayhan, B., Tran, T.: Burn scar detection using cloudy MODIS images via low-rank and sparsity-based models. In: IEEE Global Conference on Signal and Information Processing, pp. 177–181 (2016)
8. Zhao, Z., Chen, H., Chen, G., Kwan, C., Li, X.: Comparison of several ballistic target tracking filters. In: Proceedings of American Control Conference, pp. 2197–2202 (2006)
9. Zhao, Z., Chen, H., Chen, G., Kwan, C., Li, X.: IMM-LMMSE filtering algorithm for ballistic target tracking with unknown ballistic coefficient. In: Proceedings of SPIE, Signal and Data Processing of Small Targets, p. 6236 (2006)
10. Kalal, Z., Mikolajczyk, K., Matas, J.: Tracking-learning-detection. IEEE Trans. Pattern Anal. Mach. Intell. **34**(7), 1409–1422 (2012)
11. Mei, X., Ling, H.: Robust visual tracking and vehicle classification via sparse representation. IEEE Trans. Pattern Anal. Mach. Intell. **33**(11), 2259–2272 (2011)
12. Yang, M.H., Zhang, K., Zhang, L.: Real-time compressive tracking. In: European Conference on Computer Vision (2012)
13. Ma, C., Huang, J.B., Yang, X., Yang, M.H.: Hierarchical convolutional features for visual tracking. In: Computer Vision (ICCV) (2015)
14. Hartley, R., Zisserman, A.: Multiple View Geometry in Computer Vision. Cambridge University Press, Cambridge (2003)
15. Song, B., Ding, C., Kamal, A., Farrell, J., Roy-Chowdhury, A.: Distributed camera networks: integrated sensing and analysis for wide area scene understanding. Sig. Process. Mag. **28**(3), 20–31 (2011)

16. Lewis, F.L.: Optimal Estimation. Wiley, Hoboken (1986)
17. Kwan, C., Chou, B., Kwan, L.M.: Comparison of deep learning and conventional object tracking approaches for low quality videos. In: 15th International Symposium on Neural Networks (2018)
18. Kwan, C., Lewis, F.L.: A note on Kalman filtering. IEEE Trans. Educ. **42**(3), 225–227 (1999)

A Comparative Study of Spatial Speech Separation Techniques to Improve Speech Recognition

Xinhui Zhou[1], Chiman Kwan[1(✉)], Bulent Ayhan[1], Chanwoo Kim[2], K. Kumar[2], and Richard Stern[2]

[1] Signal Processing, Inc., Rockville, MD, USA
zxinhui2001@gmail.com, chiman.kwan@signalpro.net,
bulentayhan@gmail.com
[2] Carnegie Mellon University, Pittsburg, PA, USA
chanwcom@gmail.com, kshitizk@andrew.cmu.edu,
rms@cs.cmu.edu

Abstract. Robust speech recognition in noisy and reverberant conditions is an important research area in recent years. Here we present a comparative study of several spatial speech separation methods. The main performance metric is word error rate (WER) under different signal-to-noise ratio (SNR) and reverberant conditions. Extensive simulations showed that one technique known as polyaural processing stood out as the best one.

Keywords: Speech recognition · Spatial speech separation · Reverberant

1 Introduction

Robust speech recognition in 1985 meant a good recognition rate in a quiet room using desktop microphones. Commercial products such as the IBM ViaVoice and Dragon Naturally Speaking system that can work reasonably well in office environments are the results of robust speech research in the 1980s. In recent years, speech researchers have significantly increased the standard for robust speech recognition that now includes recognition in a crowded room, over a cell phone in a car with the windows down, with the radio playing and at highway speeds.

In the above challenging situations, signal-to-noise ratio (SNR) is a major limiting factor for speech separation, speaker identification, and speech recognition. There are several viable approaches to addressing the above challenges. One is to apply microphone arrays and binaural processing techniques [1–6]. Another approach is to focus on monaural (single microphone) methods [7–9]. The third approach is a hybrid method combining the above two [10–16].

In this research, we performed extensive simulations to compare a number of spatial speech separation algorithms. Two of them were developed by Carnegie Mellon University (CMU). Three others were implemented by Signal Processing, Inc. (SPI). A simulation testbed was built. The testbed can emulate reverberant and multi-speaker environments. A well-known speech corpus (Resource Management) was used.

© Springer International Publishing AG, part of Springer Nature 2018
T. Huang et al. (Eds.): ISNN 2018, LNCS 10878, pp. 494–502, 2018.
https://doi.org/10.1007/978-3-319-92537-0_57

Extensive comparative studies were carried out to select the best features and the order of features for speech recognition. The feature types for comparison include Mel-Frequency Cepstral Coefficients (MFCC), Linear Predictive Coding (LPC), Short-Term Fourier Transform (STFT), and several others. It was found that the MFCC features with 7th order yielded the best performance. In addition, the language model and language weight were also optimally selected. It was found that the trigram model yielded very good performance. Comparison of the five spatial speech separation methods was performed under various signal-to-noise ratio (SNR) and reverberant conditions. It was found that the polyaural approach yielded the best performance. The WER can reach less than 10% even when the SNR is 0 dB. This is a very impressive performance.

This paper is organized as follows. Section 2 reviews the spatial speech enhancement framework. Various algorithms and modules will be briefly reviewed. Section 3 summarizes our extensive comparative studies and findings. Finally, concluding remarks will be given in Sect. 4.

2   Overview of the Speech Enhancement Framework

Speaker identification and speech recognition in clutter environments is extremely challenging for several reasons. First, voices from multiple speakers, background music, and noise (stationary and non-stationary) will all affect the performance of speaker identification and speech recognition. Second, signal-to-noise ratio (SNR) has been the limiting factor in speech separation, speech recognition, and speaker identification. This fact is well known among researchers in the speech community. For example, the 2006 Speech Separation Challenge was set up by researchers in England. For almost every study described on that website, the performance of speech separation drops drastically at low SNRs (<10 dB) to 20% or even low percentages. Third, in closed environments such as airport terminals, reverberation effects are serious issues limiting the performance of many speech processing algorithms.

To address the human computer interface in noisy environments, there are several viable approaches. The first one is a monaural approach that addresses the speech separation, speaker identification, and speech recognition by using a single microphone [17]. The second one focuses on the use of microphone arrays and binaural methods to reject background noise and to deal with reverberations. The third approach is a hybrid one, combining both monaural and microphone array techniques. Here, we focused on only the spatial speech separation using array processing.

We assume the intended speaker is in a noisy and reverberant environment. The noise is from the utterance of an interfering speaker. We also studied how to optimize the overall performance of speech recognition by choosing optimal acoustic features, language model, and other system parameters. The microphone array signal processing methods include polyaural [18], zero crossing amplitude estimate (ZCAE) [19], delay and sum (DS) beamforming, one microphone, interference rejection (IR) beamforming, and super-directive beamforming (SB). Word error rate (WER) in continuous automatic speech recognition has been compared at different signal-to-noise ratios (SNR)

(−20, −10, 0, 10, 20, inf dBs) and different reverberation times (0, 100, 200, 300, 400, 500, and 600 ms).

The DARPA Resource Management Continuous Speech Corpora (RM1) [20] has been used in this project to test our algorithms. It contains three sections: Speaker-Dependent (SD) training data, Speaker-Independent (SI) training data and test and evaluation data. But only the data in the last two sections have been used in this project. We have chosen 3200 utterances (half for target speakers and half for interfering speaker) from SI training data for training the acoustic models, and 1200 utterances (half for target speakers and half for interfering speaker) from test and evaluation data for the decoding.

CMU SPHINX-III speech recognition system has been used in this project. In addition to the two main parts: the acoustic model trainer and the decoder, Sphinx also has a module for the MFCC feature extraction. Along with the acoustic features such as MFCC, the pronunciation dictionary and the language model have to be provided for the training and decoding purposes. Word error rate (WER) is used to evaluate the performance of the speech recognition system under different circumstances.

The CMU-Cambridge Statistical Language Modeling Toolkit was developed to facilitate the construction and testing of bigram and trigram language models [21]. The feature extraction was done mainly by a function called melfcc.m in the toolbox developed by Professor Dan Ellis [22]. Also Sphinx has its own embedded function for feature extraction of MFCC, and ZCAE package also can be used as feature extractor.

The room dimensions and the locations of speakers and microphone arrays used in this project are illustrated in Fig. 1. There are many variants in SNR (−20 dB to clean) and reverberation (0–600 ms RT60)

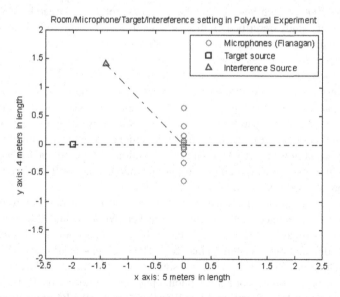

Fig. 1. Schematic of room dimensions and locations of speakers and the microphone array (same as in [18]).

3   Main Results

3.1   Selection of Acoustic Feature Type and Its Order

Different types of acoustic features have been tested to find the optimal one. Features, including mel-frequency cepstral coefficient (MFCC), Perceptual Linear Prediction (PLP), Relative Spectral Transform (RASTA), RASTA-PLP, Linear Predictive Coding (LPC), and Short Term Fourier Transform (STFT) at various orders ranging from 4 to 21, have been evaluated. We briefly describe these features below. Details of these acoustic features can be found in [23].

Among those acoustic features, MFCC and PLP yielded the best results. The minimum WERs are obtained in the case of the 7th order MFCC or the 9th order PLP. However, the 7th order MFCC is more robust to the noisy and reverberant environment as is shown in Fig. 2 and Fig. 3. The 7th order MFCC contains 7 MFCC coefficients, 7 derivatives of the coefficients, and 7 second-order derivatives of the MFCC coefficients. The frame length is 25 ms and the time shift of each frame is 10 ms.

For the rest of this project, the 7th order MFCC is used for all the speech recognition tasks.

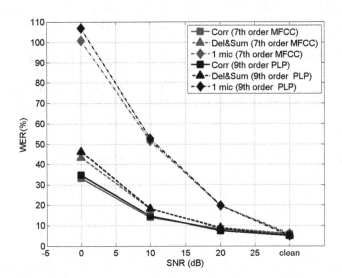

Fig. 2. WER obtained for polyaural processing in the presence of an interfering speech source as a function of SNR in the absence of reverberation. The language model is bigram for this figure.

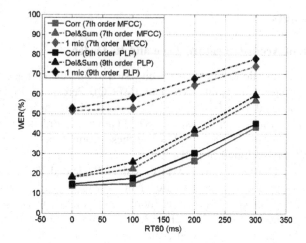

Fig. 3. WER obtained for polyaural processing in the presence of an interfering speech source as a function of reverberation with SNR 10 dB. The language model is bigram for this figure.

3.2   Selection of Language Model and Language Weight

Language model describes the probabilities between words. A bigram model describes the probability between two words and a trigram model describes the probabilities between three words.

Figure 4 shows the speech recognition accuracy obtained using bigram or trigram language models and at different language weights at the decoding stage. It shows that, for both the 7th order MFCC and the 9th PLP feature vector, the minimum WER is reached when the language weight is 13 along with the trigram language model.

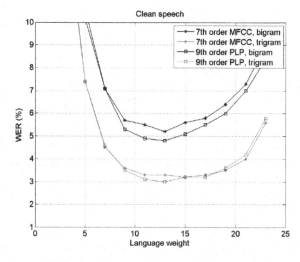

Fig. 4. The speech recognition accuracy using bigram or trigram language models and different language weights for the decoding stage.

Here, the decoder in the Sphinx system is used with the trigram language model, and a language weight 13.

3.3   Comparison of Various Methods Using Acoustic Models Trained from Clean Speech

Acoustic model is obtained by training a Hidden Markov Model (HMM). Unless one knows the noisy environment in advance, it is a normal practice to train the acoustic models using clean speech.

In the case that acoustic models are trained using clean speech, the corresponding WER results of a number of different microphone array signal processing methods are depicted with black lines in Figs. 5 and 6. The performance of all the methods for clean speech (SNR is inf dB which means no interfering utterances) are almost the same. However, with the decrease of SNR or the increase of reverberation time, the recognition performance degrades for all the methods.

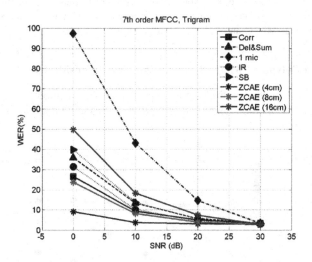

Fig. 5. WER obtained for polyaural (denoted as Corr) processing in the presence of an interfering speech source as a function of SNR in the absence of reverberation. Percentage The 7th order MFCC and trigram language model were used.

Among them, the most robust one in noisy and reverberant environment is the polyaural method, which is the bottom line in both Figs. 5 and 6 (denoted as Corr). The one-microphone method is the worst. Intuitively, more microphones used in the signal processing would lead to better performance in WER. It seems that the inter-microphone spacing also plays a big role in the ZCAE as can be noticed from Figs. 5 and 6.

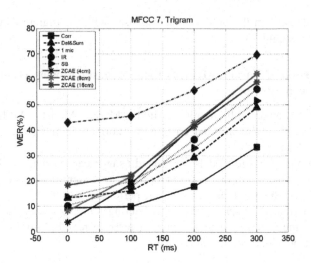

Fig. 6. Speech recognition accuracy obtained for polyaural (denoted as Corr) processing in the presence of an interfering speech source in the presence of reverberation. Here SNR is fixed at 10 dB. The 7th order MFCC and trigram language model were used.

3.4   WER in Polyaural Method for All the Cases Considered

Because polyaural method is the best among all the other methods, here we focus on only the polyaural method and evaluate its performance under various SNR and reverberant conditions.

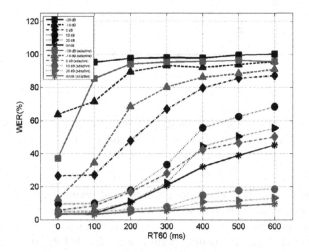

Fig. 7. Speech recognition accuracy obtained for polyaural processing in the presence of an interfering speech source as a function of reverberation with SNR −20 dB, −10 dB, 0 dB, 10 dB, 20 dB, and Inf dB. The 7th order MFCC and trigram language model were used. Black lines are based on clean speech trained acoustic models. Red lines are based on the corresponding noisy data trained acoustic models.

Figure 7 shows the WERs of the polyaural method for different SNRs and different reverberation times. It can be seen that for SNRs such as 10 dB, 20 dB, and Inf dB, the WERs are almost constant for the reverberation time up to 300 ms in the adaptive acoustic models. However, it degraded sharply when the SNR decreases to 0 dB at reverberation time 200 ms and 300 ms.

4 Conclusions

We have compared several spatial speech separation algorithms. Based on our extensive comparative studies, it was found that polyaural approach achieved the best performance under various SNR and reverberant conditions. We plan to compare the polyaural codes with other new developments such as deep learning in the near future.

Acknowledgments. This work was supported in part by National Science Foundation under grant IIP-0810012.

References

1. Kim, C., Menon, A., Bacchiani, M., Stern, R.M.: Sound source separation using phase difference and reliable mask selection. In: IEEE International Conference on Acoustics, Speech and Signal Processing (2018)
2. Dietz, M., Lestang, J.H., Majdak, P., Stern, R.M., Marquardt, T., Ewert, S.D., Hartmann, W. M., Goodman, D.: A framework for testing and comparing binaural models. J. Hear. Res. **360**, 92–106 (2017)
3. Li, Y., Vicente, L., Ho, K.C., Kwan, C., Lun, D.P.K., Leung, Y.H.: A study of partially adaptive concentric ring array. J. Circuits, Syst. Sig. Process. **27**(5), 733–748 (2008)
4. Vicente, L.M., Ho, K.C., Kwan, C.: An improved partial adaptive narrow-band beamformer using concentric ring array. In: IEEE International Conference on Acoustics, Speech, and Signal Processing (2006)
5. Li, Y., Ho, K.C., Kwan, C., Leung, Y.H.: Generalized partially adaptive concentric ring array. In: IEEE International Symposium Circuits System, pp. 3745–3748 (2005)
6. Kwan, C., Mei, G., Zhao, X., Ren, Z., Xu, R., Stanford, V., Rochet, C., Aube, J., Ho, K.C.: Bird classification algorithms: theory and experimental results. In: IEEE International Conference on Acoustics, Speech, and Signal Processing, pp. 289–292 (2004)
7. Wang, D., Brown, G.: Computational Auditory Scene Analysis: Principles, Algorithms, and Applications. Wiley/IEEE Press, Hoboken (2006)
8. Ephraim, Y., Malah, D.: Speech enhancement using a minimum mean-square error log-spectral amplitude estimator. IEEE Trans. Acoust. Speech Sig. Process. **33**(2), 443–445 (1985)
9. Kwan, C., Chu, S., Yin, J., Liu, X., Kruger, M., Sityar, I.: Enhanced speech in noisy multiple speaker environment. In: IEEE International Joint Conference on Neural Networks (IEEE World Congress on Computational Intelligence) (2008)
10. Deng, Y., Li, X., Kwan, C., Xu, R., Raj, B., Stern, R., Williamson, D.: An integrated approach to improve speech recognition rate for non-native speakers. In: Ninth International Conference on Spoken Language Processing, INTERSPEECH 2006 – ICSLP (2006)

11. Zhou, J., Ayhan, B., Kwan, C., Sands, O.S.: A high performance approach to minimizing interactions between inbound and outbound signals in helmet. In: SPIE Conference on Defense, Security, and Applications (2012)

12. Xu, R., Mei, G., Ren, Z., Kwan, C., Aube, J., Rochet, C., Stanford, V.: Speaker Identification and Speech Recognition Using Phased Arrays. In: Cai, Y., Abascal, J. (eds.) Ambient Intelligence in Everyday Life. LNCS (LNAI), vol. 3864, pp. 227–238. Springer, Heidelberg (2006). https://doi.org/10.1007/11825890_11

13. Kwan, C., Yin, J., Ayhan, B., Chu, S., Liu, X., Puckett, K., Zhao, Y., Ho, K.C., Kruger, M., Sityar, I.: An Integrated Approach to Robust Speaker Identification and Speech Recognition. IEEE International Joint Conference on Neural Networks (IEEE World Congress on Computational Intelligence) (2008)

14. Kwan, C., Zhou, J.: Compact Plug-In Noise Cancellation Device. Patent # 9,117,457 (2015)

15. Deng, Y., Li., X., Kwan, C., Raj, B., Stern, R.: Continuous feature adaptation for non-native speech recognition. Int. J. Comput. Control, Quantum Inf. Eng. 1, 1675–1682 (2007)

16. Kwan, C., Yin, J., Ayhan, B., Chu, S., Liu, X., Puckett, K., Zhao, Y., Ho, D., Kruger, M., Sityar, I.: Speech separation algorithms for multiple speaker environments. In: IEEE International Joint Conference on Neural Networks (2008)

17. Wang, D.: Computational auditory scene analysis: principles, algorithms and applications. Wiley, Hoboken (2006)

18. Stern, R., Gouvea, E., Kim, C., Kumar, K., Park, H.-M.: Binaural and multiple-microphone signal processing motivated by auditory perception. In: Proceedings of HSCMA Joint Workshop on Hands-Free Speech Communication and Microphone Arrays (2008)

19. Park, H.-M., Stern, R.M.: Spatial separation of speech signals using continuously-variable masks estimated from comparisons of zero crossings. In: Proceedings of IEEE International Conference on Acoustics, Speech, and Signal Processing (2006)

20. Bernstein, J., Price, P., Fisher, W.M., Pallett, D.S.: Resource Management RM1 2.0, Linguistic Data Consortium, Philadelphia (1993)

21. Clarkson, P.: Statistical language modeling using the cmu-cambridge toolkit. In: Proceedings of Eurospeech, pp. 2707–2710 (1997)

22. Ellis, D.P.W.: PLP and RASTA (and MFCC, and inversion) in Matlab (2005). http://labrosa.ee.columbia.edu/matlab/

23. Gold, B., Morgan, N.: Speech and Audio Signal Processing: Processing and Perception of Speech and Music. Wiley, New York (2001)

An Effective Object Detection Algorithm for High Resolution Video by Using Convolutional Neural Network

Denis Vorobjov[1]([✉]), Iryna Zakharava[1], Rykhard Bohush[1],
and Sergey Ablameyko[2]

[1] Polotsk State University, Blochin Street 29, Novopolotsk, Republic of Belarus
{d.vorobjov,i.zakharova,r.bogush}@psu.by
[2] Belarusian State University,
Nezavisimosti Avenue 4, Minsk, Republic of Belarus
ablameyko@bsu.by

Abstract. In this paper, an algorithm to detect small objects more accurately in high resolution video is proposed. For this task, an analysis of state-of-the-art algorithms in application to high resolution video processing, which can be implemented into modern surveillance systems is performed. The algorithm is based on CNN in application to high resolution video processing and it consists of the following steps: each video frame is divided into overlapping blocks; object detection in each block with CNN YOLO is performed; post processing for extracted objects in each block is done and merging neighbor regions with the same class probabilities is performed. The proposed algorithm shows better results in application to small objects detection on high resolution video than famous YOLO algorithm.

Keywords: Convolution Neural Networks · Video processing
YOLO · High resolution

1 Introduction

Video surveillance systems are used in fields such as pedestrian detection, robots, autopilots and etc. There are many video cameras which can record high resolution video. Such devices allow identification of object details to improve and increase the small objects detection probability.

In recent years, a big number of digital cameras have offered the ability to record 4 K high-resolution video. This notion refers to any digital image containing an X resolution of approximately 4000 pixels. The actual dimensions of the X and Y resolution of a 4 K image depends on the required aspect ratio of images. Positive side of using 4 K resolution systems is possibility to detect objects very precisely and accurately. Higher resolution can detect tiny objects without distortions, and also shows correct shape of large objects. At the same time 4 K resolution disadvantage is a big information capacity in every surveillance video frame. That is why real-time 4 K video processing system must have fast and effective image processing algorithms.

© Springer International Publishing AG, part of Springer Nature 2018
T. Huang et al. (Eds.): ISNN 2018, LNCS 10878, pp. 503–510, 2018.
https://doi.org/10.1007/978-3-319-92537-0_58

It is important to take into account that small objects detection percentage ratio can be varied at different resolutions. As an example, 80 × 80 pixels object takes in 0.69% of whole image in HDTV resolution, 0.3% for 2 K and 0.05% for 4 K. As results of these relations can be false negative detection results for small-sized objects.

To avoid described disadvantages, we think that the deep machine learning systems provide perfect performance for all challenges. All object detection systems have to dedicate following contributions: accuracy, precise extraction of regions of interest (RoIs) on frames or images and their classification with minimal deviation and speed, processing information in real-time.

A lot of interest in image processing and machine learning fields at this moment focused on convolutional neural networks (CNNs). Unlike traditional networks, CNNs provide reducing a number of extracting parameters and as an alternative of whole image processing we can process only extracted feature map, which take into account image topology and stable to affine transformation. But small objects on large scale images can being missed because scaling image or frame it is first preprocessing step almost at all image and video processing algorithms, and missing small objects on surveillance video tape can being a big problem.

At this moment, almost all systems do not take into account input image resolution. These systems make scaling by input layer size and in case of high resolution image or video frame small objects can be missed. In case of high resolution videos like 4 K, these systems are unsuitable for object detection. We propose a novel algorithm based on separating input frame into overlapping blocks. After that, CNN Yolo makes scaling, object detection and classification to each block. As a result we have bounding boxes are built around every detected object and class proposals for them. Finally we merge neighboring RoIs with the same class keeping in mind overlapping.

2 Related Works

At first, we analyze famous neural network architectures which use convolutional and maxpooling layers. CNN model AlexNet presented in [1] including 8 weighted layers. This CNN model has limitations with multiresolution analysis, and liable to overfitting according to side-supervision problem [2]. The main disadvantage that first network layer scale input image or frame and this lead to false negative small objects detection. Also this algorithm has big computational cost.

Another approach CNN model is R-CNN and it proposed that the previous RoIs extraction can make CNN work faster and more accurately. The main steps of R-CNN algorithm are preliminary extraction of RoIs using Selective Search algorithm, classification of extracted regions with AlexNet from [1], also, at the last stage, binary linear SVM classification model with Non-Maximum suppression to refine bounding boxes around RoIs, which belong to the one class. Comparison with initial AlexNet model shows that the R-CNN algorithm accomplishes better results in detection [3]. But R-CNN takes a long processing time per image and has almost all AlexNet disadvantages too. Trying to make R-CNN faster, in paper [4] it was proposed Fast

R-CNN which calculated convolutional features together with Selective Search and after that, each RoI is presented like convolutional feature map. New version is proposed in paper [5] and it is called Faster R-CNN. This network involves Region Proposal Network, which make proposals about RoIs location. This CNN works fast and accurate but low-resolution frames cannot be processed. Faster R-CNN is unsuitable for pedestrian detection on low resolution videos [6]. Also, according to proposed algorithm input image scaled to input layer size and small objects could be missed.

CNN GoogleNet [7] was contained about 100 layers, but fully connected layers were not used at all. Proposed architecture extracted 12 times less parameters than AlexNet and all architecture is used convolutional layers with different sizes. This approach allowed extracting various sized features. Previous RoIs extraction was improved by multibox method from [8]. The main disadvantage is the system did not take into account context image information and has big computational cost. Modified GoogLeNet with Inception v2 was proposed in [9]. With factorization convolutional layer into smaller convolutional kernels, computational speed became higher at 33%. Also, to avoid representational bottlenecks, half of features was gone to maxpooling layer and the next half was gone to the following convolutional layer simultaneously. For GoogLeNet Inception v3 modification was added Batch Normalization layer [10] instead of dropout technology. Inception v2 and Inception v3 took 2.5 computational time more than Inception. Also, all modifications were not taking into account input image resolution.

Proposed CNN topology ResNet in [11] was provided shortcut connection between repeated blocks and it helps to avoid detector degradation problem of deep neural networks. Top-5 error was 3.57%. But image scaling was preprocessing step yet.

Novel block Inception v4 proposed in [12], all CNN GoogLeNet trained on one PC. Also in [12], it is proposed GoogLeNet with Inception-ResNet v1 and Inception-ResNet v2. Proposed modifications do not take into account input image resolution.

Next approach presented in paper [13] and it is called CNN YOLO. YOLO showed the best result by computational cost. As disadvantage, we have to admit many localization errors especially for small objects, because this algorithm scale input image too. At paper [14], it is proposed YOLO v2, YOLO9000, modifications of YOLO. Better segmentation an classification was achieved by: batch normalization from [10]; high resolution classifier; convolutional with anchor boxes; using k-means; direct location prediction; RPN usage; fine-grained features; multi-scale training; novel classification model Darknet-19. Top-5 accuracy was 91.2% but proposed algorithm took a long of computational cost. Also multi-scale training gave better opportunity to detect small objects, but it is not enough for 4 K resolution systems.

YOLO favorably differentiates from other systems because it processes entire image without previous RoIs extraction. Also, as said at [13], YOLO is the fast object detection system which works better than Faster R-CNN. This is very important because we have to process a high-resolution video frames, and computational costs is very necessary parameter.

3 The Proposed Algorithm

Applying considered algorithms and methods for high resolution video frames demanding that input image scaling which lead to small-size objects are missing. For this problem evaluation we propose an algorithm that is based on CNN YOLO and consist of following steps: each video frame is divided into intersecting blocks; object detection in each block is performed with CNN YOLO; postprocessing is performed for extracted objects in each block and merging is done for neighbor regions with the same class probabilities.

Step 1. Frame separating. Input frame I with sizes $H \times W$ is divided into overlapping blocks $C_{i,j}$ with sizes $ch \times cw$, $i = \overline{0, H/ch - 1}$, $j = \overline{0, W/cw - 1}$. Step size is calculated like block size plus 10% overlapping. Overlap size can be vary by input frame resolution or object size.

Step 2. Blocks classification. Each block goes to YOLO. In this network, for block $C_{i,j}$ conditional class probabilities $Pr(Class_l|C_{i,j})$ is calculated for every class $Class_l$, where $l = \overline{0, classNumber - 1}$, $classNumber$ - the number of all classification classes. For each block $C_{i,j}$, the RoI $B_{i,j}^k$, $k = \overline{0, bbNumber - 1}$ is declared where $bbNumber$ - the number of RoIs for each block. In YOLO RoIs is frame fragment which is equal for every block and have center in the middle of them. Every RoI $B_{i,j}^k$ determines the followings values: $B_{i,j}^k(x, y)$ - the top left corner coordinates relative to the whole frame I; $B_{i,j}^k(w, h)$ - the width and height are predicted relative to the whole frame I; confidence prediction $Pr\left(B_{i,j}^k\right)$ - detection of object probability. If no object exists in that block, the confidence scores should be zero, $Pr\left(B_{i,j}^k\right) = 0$.

Step 3. Blocks postprocessing. The neighbor RoIs, which have combined overlapped region located closer than 10% from blocks edge, are searched. If these blocks are found, we calculate IoU (Intersection over Union) which describe two regions overlapping:

$$Iou = \frac{In}{B_{i0, j0}(w) \cdot B_{i0, j0}(h) + B_{i1, j1}(w) \cdot B_{i1, j1}(h) - In}, \tag{1}$$

where:

$$In = \left(\min\left(B_{i0, j0}(x) + B_{i0, j0}(w), \ B_{i1, j1}(x) + B_{i1, j1}(w)\right) - \max\left(B_{i0, j0}(x), \ B_{i1, j1}(x)\right)\right) \times \left(\min\left(B_{i0, j0}(y) + B_{i0, j0}(h), \ B_{i1, j1}(y) + B_{i1, j1}(h)\right) - \max\left(B_{i0, j0}(y), \ B_{i1, j1}(y)\right)\right) \tag{2}$$

where w and h - RoI width and height relative to the whole frame, x, y - represent the top left corner coordinates of the RoI.

If *Iou* > *T*, then RoIs $B_{i0,j0}$ and $B_{i1,j1}$ are combined, where *T* - coefficient which set identity degree for merged locations.

Figure 1 shows generalized algorithm that contains all steps described previously.

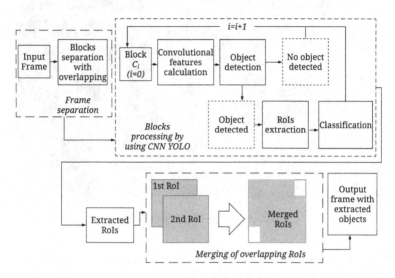

Fig. 1. The proposed algorithm

4 Experimental Results

For the proposed algorithm, training dataset PASCAL VOC [15], grid size $S = 7$, numbers of classes for each block *bbNumber = 2* and all classification classes number *classNumber = 20* were used. The classes names are: «bicycle», «bird», «boat», «bottle», «bus», «car», «cat», «chair», «cow», «dining table», «dog», «horse», «motorbike», «person», «potted plant», «sheep», «sofa», «train», «TV monitor» are used too. For experiments, the proposed algorithm was realized on C++ with GCC compiler and computer vision library OpenCV 3.1.

Table 1 shows that with increasing input frame resolution the proposed algorithm works more accurately than YOLO.

Table 1. Proposed algorithm and YOLO experimental results

Algorithm	Accuracy, δ_E, %			Time per frame, s		
	1024 × 1024	2048 × 2048	4096 × 3072	1024 × 1024	2048 × 2048	4096 × 3072
YOLO	57	48	31	0.11		
Proposed algorithm	49	47	42	0.46	1.72	2.64

Figure 2 shows RoIs localization for *3872 × 2592* resolution frame. If object parts are shift we can see that one object is separated into two parts, but accuracy that can be escalated by *bbNumber* value increasing.

Fig. 2. Extracted RoIs before merging

Figure 3 shows results after merging overlapped regions from Fig. 2.
For localization error calculation is used:

$$\delta_E = \sqrt{\frac{\sum\limits_{i=1}^{N}(X_{itr} - X_i)}{N}} \cdot 100\% \tag{3}$$

where i - frame index, N - objects on image number, Xitr - ground-truth coordinates, Xi - after processing coordinates.

Fig. 3. An example of merged RoIs

Examples of object detection based on our algorithm and YOLO shown at Fig. 4.
Experiments were conducted on PC with main characteristics: CPU i7 4.3 GHz, RAM 32 Gb. and GPU Nvidia GeForce GTX 1070. For experimental results showed at Fig. 4, video sequences with complex background and different range foreground

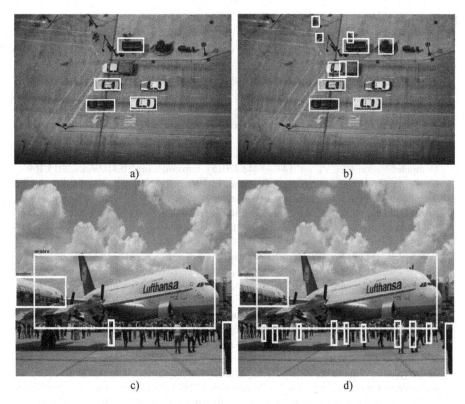

Fig. 4. Examples of object detection: (a,c) for YOLO; (b,d) for the proposed algorithm

objects numbers were used. In our approach, blocks were processed serially and it leads to bigger computational cost than YOLO but, in case of parallel processing, our algorithm can show results comparable to CNN YOLO.

5   Conclusions

We proposed objects detection algorithm for which main application is high-resolution surveillance video processing. The proposed algorithm more accurately detects small objects in high-resolution video. It is achieved by a fact that input frames are not scaled before frame division on blocks and also blocks overlapping gives higher precision. Block by block processing allows avoiding big computational cost. With our algorithm we achieve 35% higher results for 4 K video processing than YOLO algorithm. For PC with main parameters CPUi7 4.3 GHz, RAM 32 Gb, GPU Nvidia GeForce GTX 1070 one frame with 4 K resolution was processed at 2.64 s.

References

1. Krizhevsky, A., Sutskever, I., Hinton, G.E.: ImageNet classification with deep convolutional neural networks. In: Advances in Neural Information Processing Systems, vol. 25, pp. 1097–1105 (2012). https://doi.org/10.1007/978-3-319-46654-5_20
2. Han, X., Zhong, Y., Cao, L., Zhang, L.: Pre-trained alexnet architecture with pyramid pooling and supervision. Remote Sens. 9(8), 848 (2017). https://doi.org/10.3390/rs9080848
3. R-CNN for Object Detection. https://courses.cs.washington.edu/courses/cse590v/14au/cse590v_wk1_rcnn.pdf
4. Girshick, R.: Fast R-CNN. In: Proceedings of the 2015 IEEE International Conference on Computer Vision (ICCV), pp. 1440–1448 (2015). https://doi.org/10.1109/iccv.2015.169
5. Ren, S.Q., He, K.M., Girshick, R.B., Sun, J.: Faster R-CNN: towards real-time object detection with region proposal networks. ArXiv e-prints (2015)
6. Zhang, L., Lin, L., Liang, X., He, K.: Is faster R-CNN doing well for pedestrian detection? In: Leibe, B., Matas, J., Sebe, N. (eds.) ECCV 2016. LNCS, vol. 9906, pp. 443–457. Springer, Cham (2016). https://doi.org/10.1007/978-3-319-46475-6_28
7. Szegedy, C., Liu, W., Jia, Y. Q., Sermanet, P., Reed, S.E., Aguelov, D., Erhan, D., Vanhoucke, V., Rabinovich, A.: Going deeper with convolutions. In: IEEE Conference on Computer Vision and Pattern Recognition, pp. 1–9 (2015). https://doi.org/10.1109/cvpr.2015.7298594
8. Erhan, D., Szegedy, C., Toshev, A., Anguelov, D.: Scalable object detection using deep neural networks. In: CVPR 2014 Proceedings of the 2014 IEEE Conference on Computer Vision and Pattern Recognition, pp. 2155–2162 (2014). https://doi.org/10.1109/cvpr.2014.276
9. Szegedy, C., Vanhoucke, V., Ioffe, S., Shlens, J., Wojna, Z.: Rethinking the inception architecture for computer vision. In: Proceedings of IEEE Conference on Computer Vision and Pattern Recognition, pp. 2818–2826 (2016). https://doi.org/10.1109/cvpr.2016.308
10. Ioffe, S., Szegedy, C.: Batch normalization: accelerating deep network training by reducing internal covariate shift. In: Proceedings of the 32nd International Conference on Machine Learning, pp. 448–456 (2015)
11. He, K.M., Zhang, X.Y., Ren, S.Q., Sun, J.: Deep residual learning for image recognition. In: 2016 IEEE Conference on Computer Vision and Pattern Recognition (CVPR) (2016). https://doi.org/10.1109/cvpr.2016.90
12. Szegedy, C., Ioffe, S., Vanhoucke, V., Alemi, A.: Inception v4, Inception-ResNet and the impact of residual connections on learning. In: The Association for the Advancement of Artificial Intelligence Conference on Artificial Intelligence (AAAI), pp. 4278–4284 (2017)
13. Redmon, J., Divvala, S.K., Girshick, R.B., Farhadi, A.: You only look once: unified, real-time object detection. In: IEEE conference Computer Vision and Pattern Recognition (CVPR) (2017). https://doi.org/10.1109/cvpr.2016.91
14. Redmon, J., Farhadi, A.: YOLO9000: better, faster, stronger. In: 2017 IEEE Conference on Computer Vision and Pattern Recognition, pp. 6517–6525 (2017). https://doi.org/10.1109/cvpr.2017.690
15. Everingham, M., Gool, L.V., Williams, C.K.I., Winn, J.M., Zisserman, A.: The pascal visual object classes (VOC) challenge. Int. J. Comput. Vis. 88(2), 303–338 (2010)

Sound Signal Invariant DAE Neural Network-Based Quantizer Architecture of Audio/Speech Coder Using the Matching Pursuit Algorithm

Vladislav Avramov, Vadzim Herasimovich$^{(\boxtimes)}$,
and Alexander Petrovsky

Belarusian State University of Informatics and Radioelectronics, Minsk, Belarus
avramov.vladislav@gmail.com,
{gerasimovich,palex}@bsuir.by

Abstract. The paper is devoted to the quantization algorithm development based on the neural networks framework. This research is considered in the context of the scalable real-time audio/speech coder based on the perceptually adaptive matching pursuit algorithm. The encoder parameterizes the input sound signal frame with some amount of real numbers that are need to be compactly represented in binary form, i.e. quantized. The neural network quantization approach gives great opportunity for such a goal because the data quantized in whole vector but not in separate form and it can effectively use correlations between each element of the input coded vector. Deep autoencoder (DAE) neural network-based architecture for the quantization part of the encoding algorithm is shown. Its structure and learning features are described. Conducted experiments points out the big compression ratio with high recon-structed signal quality of the developed audio/speech coder quantization scheme.

Keywords: Neural network · Deep autoencoder · Audio/speech coding
Quantization · Stepwise activation function

1 Introduction

Continuous development and implementation of the new communication and multi-media technologies such as voice and music signals transmission in digital form (VoIP – Voice over Internet Protocol, VoLTE – Voice over LTE, DAB – Digital Audio Broadcasting); streaming media; and widespread use of the embedded systems requires the research and development of the new coding algorithms. Natural requirements for such algorithms are high quality with big compression ratio (CR), invariance towards the input audio signal type, real-time mode working and good scalability properties. Most of the modern popular coders can't produce all of them simultaneously. Vocoders are focused on the speech signals and unsatisfactorily work with music fragments [1]. Audio coders are suitable for high quality music signals but don't provide such CR for

© Springer International Publishing AG, part of Springer Nature 2018
T. Huang et al. (Eds.): ISNN 2018, LNCS 10878, pp. 511–520, 2018.
https://doi.org/10.1007/978-3-319-92537-0_59

speech as vocoders do [1] and most of them can't work in real-time mode. Some hybrid approaches consist of several models: for speech, and other type signals with real-time working ability, for example [2, 3]. Hence, development of the algorithm that can effectively work with all known types of signal is actual and essential research direction.

One of the most important part of the coding algorithm is the quantizer part that is responsible for the output information compression and the artifacts introduced in the processed signal. Quantization is a procedure of the mapping large set onto the smaller discrete sequence. There are two main types of the algorithm: scalar and vector quantization [4]. The first, processes each element in the input set separate, the second is a kind of clustering that uses codebooks for group of components processing. With scalar quantizer it can be achieved very high reconstructed signal quality when optimal quantization step is calculated. On the other hand, vector quantization (VQ) can be performed to the whole group of coded data and have compact representation as an index of vector in codebook. First approach cannot take into account internal characteristics of the processed information and linear and nonlinear properties in it. As for the VQ limitations, it is codebooks: their structure and size – they are constant and fixed from the moment they were trained. This work is devoted to the research of another approach to the quantization that is based on the deep autoencoder (DAE) neural network architecture. Using such algorithm as a core of the audio coder quantization stage [5] can fix limitations of the approaches mentioned above. Specifically, neural network-based quantizer does not limited with some codebook. There is a limitation in neuron quantity according to the network architecture, but the dimension of that space is much bigger than VQ codebooks. Another big advantage of the neural network approach is "generation" of the result vector based on the training information and input data.

Article briefly shows the structure of the developed audio/speech coding algorithm based on the sparse approximation with psychoacoustically adaptive time-frequency dictionaries. The main part of the work presents the research of the neural network based quantization block of the audio/speech coder. Architecture and learning algorithm of the developed DAE quantizer are shown. Experimental results and quality assessments of the reconstructed audio signals quantized with the neural network based quantizer display big capabilities of the developed approach.

2 Audio/Speech Coder Structure

The mathematical core that transforms and parameterizes an input signal frame is based on the matching pursuit (MP) algorithm [6] with perceptually adaptive wavelet packet (WP) based dictionary [7]. MP is a greedy algorithm performs sparse approximation i.e. signal representation with minimum amount of non-zero components. This is done through the mapping of an input frame onto a set of functions called atoms which are selected from the overcomplete dictionary. The proposed audio/speech coding algorithm, depicted in Fig. 1, consists of the two stages and works as follows. The first stage performs a psychoacoustically optimized WP decomposition [8]. Since the input signal is a sound, the information about human ear perception must be utilized for the efficient coding. WP optimization implemented using two cost functions: wavelet time entropy (*WTE*), which shows the WP coefficients information density for each level of the tree and perceptual entropy (*PE*), which gives the wavelet coefficients local perceptual information in each node of WP tree structure (WP subband) [9]. Both of them are calculated in wavelet domain.

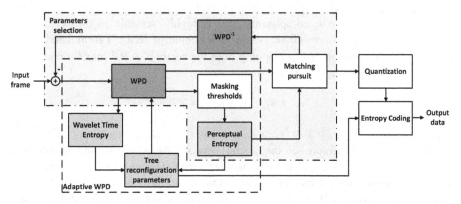

Fig. 1. Encoder algorithm structure

As results, the first stage returns a dictionary of atoms based on the calculated WP decomposition tree, simultaneous and time maskers and auditory excitation scalogram. At the second stage of the coding algorithm, the most perceptually relevant for the human ear components (atoms) that have maximum accordance with the modelled and original scalograms are selected [10]. MP algorithm stops when some stopping criterion is reached. It could be fixed number of selected atoms or residual energy threshold, for example. Result of the second stage (output of the "Matching pursuit" block in Fig. 1) of the coding algorithm is the frame atoms, which are strongly connected to their position in the WP tree because the decoding process occurs over the maximum reconstruction WP tree [10]. The atom structure looks as follows: the atom weight (real number), tree level, node number and the weight position in the vector (this three fields are natural numbers). The atom weights need to be quantized for compact representation and transmitting to the decoder part. The atom position cannot be distorted, so it is encoded only with entropy coding.

The decoder part performs dequantization and decoding of the atom weights and their position. For the output signal synthesis one WP reconstruction tree structure for all the frames is used because of the knowledge of the atoms location. It is necessary to arrange the weights in their positions and set to zero the empty nodes for the correct signal reconstruction.

3 DAE Based Quantization Algorithm

3.1 Motivation of the DAE Quantization Approach

The neural network quantization (NNQ) is a procedure of mapping a multidimensional space of vectors with real, continuous component amplitudes into some discrete set. In other words, NNQ is the joint quantization of the parameter vector. The process of NNQ allows eliminating redundancy due to the effective use of the interconnected properties of the vector parameters. Thus, NNQ offers several unique advantages over scalar quantization, including the ability to exploit the linear and nonlinear dependencies among the vector components, and is highly versatile in the selection of multidimensional quantizer cell shapes. The definition of NNQ is formulated as follows: NNQ of dimension M is a mapping from the vector $X \in \mathbb{R}^M$ into N-dimensional code vector Y containing K discrete output values:

$$NNQ : X \in \mathbb{R}^M \rightarrow Y,$$

where $X \in [x_1, x_2, \ldots, x_M]$; $Y \in [y_1, y_2, \ldots, y_N]$; $y_i \in [y_{i1}, y_{i2}, \ldots, y_{iK}], i = \overline{1, N}$.

The natural architecture of the neural network for implementing quantizer is autoencoder (AE) [5] – a feed forward network containing the input, code and output layers. The dimension of the input and output layers are equal. The main task of training such a neural network is to minimize the difference between output and input vectors.

A single-layer network described above is very limited in its computational capabilities, especially in case of solving NP-complete quantization task [11], which imposes discrete constraints on the internal representation. The amount of information stored and reproduced by a neural network of this type depends on the number of neurons and then it is obvious that the one hidden layer will not be enough, and the choice should be made in favor of a multilayer architecture DAE [5].

3.2 DAE Quantizer Learning Algorithm

It is a well-known fact that the training a multilayer neural networks by backpropagation algorithm causes the vanishing gradient problem [12], which leads to a low learning efficiency. The gradient calculation by the inverse error propagation method, cause its value decreases as it propagates from the output layer to the input one.

Greedy layer-wise training strategy [13, 14] was used to solve the problem described above. Thereby the training process of DAE is divided into the following two stages:

1. Pre-training – sequential pair learning of the neighboring layers of a neural network.
2. Fine-tuning – training the entire network using the backpropagation algorithm.

The basic idea of such training is that the weights of the multilayer network that were initialized by layer-wise pre-training will not need to be significantly changed in the learning process, and the problem of attenuation of the gradient will not so much affect the learning process.

In the current research, each layer of DAE was pre-trained using the single-layer AE. In its simplest form, AE consists of two parts: an encoder and a decoder part. The encoder part (1) is a function that maps the input $X \in \mathbb{R}^{N_x}$ to hidden representation $h \in \mathbb{R}^{N_h}$ and the decoder unit (2) maps it back to a reconstruction of the input data:

$$h = s(w_1 \cdot X + b_1), \tag{1}$$

$$X' = s(w_2 \cdot h + b_2), \tag{2}$$

where s is a nonlinear activation function; $w_1 \in \mathbb{R}^{N_h \times N_x}$, $w_2 \in \mathbb{R}^{N_x \times N_h}$ – weight matrices; $b_1 \in \mathbb{R}^{N_h}$, $b_2 \in \mathbb{R}^{N_x}$ – bias units; N_h and N_x are the number of hidden and input units respectively; X' is a reconstructed data vector. AE training process consists of learning the parameters $W = \{w_1, w_2\}$ and $B = \{b_1, b_2\}$ which are provide the smallest possible reconstruction error. Thus, the objective of AE training process is to optimize the following regularized objective function:

$$(f(W, B, X), X) = \frac{1}{N} \|X - f(W, B, X)\|^2 + \lambda \sum_{k=1}^{K} \|w_k\|^2, \tag{3}$$

where $f(W, B, X) = X'$ is the function implemented by the neural network; N – the number of the training samples; λ controls the strength of the L2 regularization; K – layers quantity; $W \in [w_1, \ldots, w_K]$, $B \in [b_1, \ldots, b_K]$ – the weight and bias matrices. The architecture of DAE quantizer experimentally was set as viewed in Fig. 2.

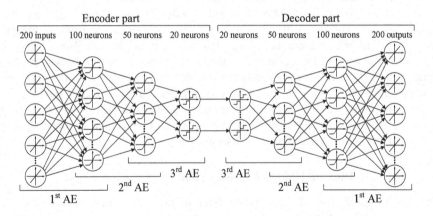

Fig. 2. DAE architecture quantizer. Bias units are not shown to simplify the structure

During the pre-training stage, the weights of DAE were initialized by the three single-layer AEs: $\{200 \times 100\}$, $\{100 \times 50\}$, $\{50 \times 20\}$. The first AE was trained on the prepared training set. Each subsequent AE was trained using the hidden layer outputs of each previous AE as input training data. The activation function of the hidden layers for the first two AEs is hyperbolic tangent, and for the code layer (third AE) stepwise activation function, which is described in the next subsection, was used.

Each data vector was normalized to unit variance, and then sorted in ascending order. Such a data representation breaks the structure and relationships in them, and makes all the vectors highly correlated. This approach makes the proposed DAE architecture invariant to the input sound signal. Sorting simplifies the structure of the input data, and lead to the reconstruction error reduction. The next section illustrates the reconstruction error comparison between sorted and unsorted input.

To perform the pre-training, dataset was divided into mini-batches, each containing 1000 cases, and the weights were updated after each mini-batch using the Adam optimization algorithm [15]. To determine when to stop the training process two stop criterions are used: minimum error deviation and monotonous error increase in the error analysis window. The length of the analysis window was set to 16 epochs. To avoid the saturation regions of the hyperbolic tangent function adaptive weight initialization scheme based on variance of the layer input data is used. Thereby the weights are initialized with small random values sampled from a zero-mean normal distribution with variance computed by the following equation:

$$V = \sqrt{1/(\sigma \cdot [N_{in} + N_{out}])}, \qquad (4)$$

where N_{in} and N_{out} are the number of the input and hidden units respectively, and σ is the computed standard deviation. When the pre-training stage is finished, it is necessary to connect every single level AE with each other to create a multilayer DAE whose encoder part is used to encode the input and whose decoder part is used in reverse order to decode the input (reconstruct it). This DAE is then fine-tuned using backpropagation algorithm to make its output as close as possible to its input.

At the fine-tuning stage DAE was trained with the same set of parameters and rules as at the pre-training stage with a maximum number of epochs set to 1000. To force the codes to be discrete, the outputs of the staircase units in the central code layer are rounded to the nearest flat region during the forward pass. However, backpropagation through discrete variables is generally not possible and making the model difficult to train efficiently. One approach to propagate the gradient through the code layer is to use the straight-through estimator [16] to compute gradient. The idea of this approach is simply to backpropagate through the hard stepwise function and ignore rounding of the outputs of the code layer during the backward pass.

3.3   Learning Discrete Hidden Representation

The outputs of the encoder part (code layer of the DAE) must be discrete. This constraint leads to a NP-hard optimization problem. There are a number of approaches to solve this task. The hashing methods based on the deep learning [17] are one of them. Most of hashing methods weaken the discrete constraint during the learning of hash functions. Thus, the continuous codes are learned first by introducing different constraints into the learning process. Then the codes are quantized to be binary with a chosen threshold. Another interesting approach to learn discrete hidden representation is to use staircase-like activation function [18] for the middle hidden layer (i.e. code layer). This function can be formulated by the following equation:

$$S(z) = \frac{1}{M-1} \sum_{i=1}^{M-1} \left(tanh\left(\alpha \left(z - \frac{2 \cdot i}{M} + 1 \right) \right) \right), \tag{5}$$

where parameter α – controls the transition rate from one level to the next and M is a number of steps. Parameter α must be a large value (in conducted research 100 is used) to make the hyperbolic tangent steps less smooth and closer to the hard stepwise function. This increases the proportion of the function flat regions and thereby maps most of the activations of the code layer neurons closer to one of 32 discrete values. The number of steps M experimentally was set to 32. Thereby the activation levels of the code layer outputs are quantized into M discrete values: $\frac{k-M}{M-1}, k = 1, 3, \ldots,$ $2 \cdot M - 1$. The stepwise activation function, which is used for the code layer naturally maps continuously distributed input data points into a number of discrete valued points (i.e. clusters) as shown in Fig. 3.

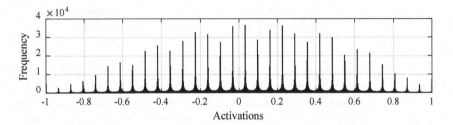

Fig. 3. Distribution of the code layer neurons activations

The resulting activation function and its derivative is shown in Fig. 4.

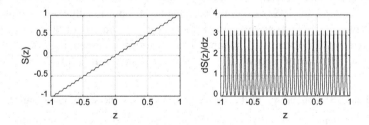

Fig. 4. Activation function of the units in the middle hidden layer and its derivative

The derivative of this function for backpropagation algorithm is calculated as the sum of the derivatives of each step by following equation:

$$\frac{dS(z)}{dz} = \frac{\alpha}{M-1} \sum_{i=1}^{M-1} \left(sech^2\left(\alpha \left(z - \frac{2 \cdot i}{M} + 1 \right) \right) \right). \tag{6}$$

4 Experimental Results

For the experiments, quantizer based on the DAE neural network was trained by the training set consists of about 36 min of the data such as speech of different speakers, music and other sound signals. As a test sequence, samples that were not included in the training set and shown in Table 1 were used. All sounds are one-channel signals with minimum duration of 7 s, 44.1 kHz sampling rate and 16-bit resolution.

Table 1. Test sequence description

Test item	Description	Test item	Description
es01	Vocal (Suzan Vega)	si01	Harpsichord
es02	German speech	si02	Castanets
es03	English speech	si03	Pitch pipe
sc01	Trumpet solo and orchestra	sm01	Bagpipes
sc02	Orchestra piece	sm02	Glockenspiel
sc03	Contemporary pop music	sm03	Plucked strings

The average bit budget for the quantized atoms weights and positions coding estimated as follows. The code layer of DAE for the 200 atoms input variant consists of 20 neurons with stepwise activation function. This function comprises 32 steps, so it is 5 bits per step. Multiplying bits amount for each neuron with their quantity will give 100 bit budget for the input 200 atoms representation. As for the position of the atoms Huffman entropy coding was implemented. It is necessary to add some bit budget to side information and multiplying all to the frames per second number for calculating total bitrate. For the 200 atoms variant approximate average bitrate is 10 kbps, it corresponds to the equivalent compression ratio (CR) about 70. For the other sets of atoms experiments the layers structure was changed proportionally their quantity grows (for example, for the 300 atoms variant the code layer consists of 30 neurons).

Comparison of normalizing the input data via sorting in ascending order in contrast of unsorted (approach, described in Subsect. 3.2) is shown in Table 2.

Table 2. MSE comparison of the normalization based on the sorted input and unsorted

Test item	es01	es02	es03	sc01	sc03	si01	si02
Sorted input MSE, $\cdot 10^{-6}$	7.17	29.39	35.11	17.38	37.76	4.67	3.24
Unsorted input MSE, $\cdot 10^{-3}$	2.8	13.9	18.5	6.4	16	1.7	1.5

As it seen from the table above the developed approach of the input data normalization gives big advantage (three orders of magnitude) in the output accuracy.

For the whole audio\speech coder algorithm (including DAE based quantizer) quality assessment, ITU-R Recommendation BS.1387-1 PEAQ (Perceptual Evaluation of Audio Quality) was used. This is a metric using for the perceptual distortion estimation based on the human ear auditory model. The output of PEAQ is the Objective

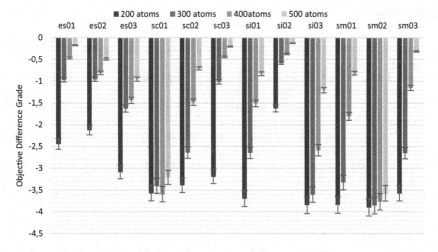

Fig. 5. Quality distribution of the test samples encoded by the proposed algorithm

Difference Grade (ODG). ODG scale is defined as follows: 0 – imperceptible impairment; −1 – perceptible, but not annoying; −2 – slightly annoying; −3 – annoying; −4 – very annoying impairment. Figure 5 shows the quality assessment results for the developed universal audio\speech coder presented DAE quantization approach.

As it can be seen from the figure above, there is no score below −4, so it means that all of the experimental items have "annoying impairment" or better even at the smallest atoms amount (i.e. the lowest bitrate). There is stable decrease of the ODG grade with growth of the atoms used for reconstruction for almost every test item except sc01. At the maximum bitrate used in the conducted experiments 9 out of 12 sounds have "imperceptible impairment" – their ODG grades are under −1. Comparison of the presented NNQ with the scalar quantization variant can be seen in [8], for example, but it is point to mention that DAE quantizer produce much deeper compression than the scalar quantization approach.

5   Conclusions

DAE neural network-based quantization algorithm for the scalable universal audio/speech coder using MP with perceptually adapted WP dictionary is proposed. This quantization method has all pros of the VQ like joint data group processing and using of the linear and nonlinear information properties. On the other hand, presented quantization approach fixes such VQ cons as static codebooks. Moreover, as it was shown in the article, DAE neural network-based quantizer absorbs perceptual information at the network training stage and uses it for the code word generation in the encoding mode. The objective quality assessment of the reconstructed audio and speech signals based on PEAQ metric shows good results with high CR (about 70 for 200 atoms variant) of the test sequence items.

References

1. Spanias, A., Painter, T., Atti, V.: Audio Signal Processing and Coding. Wiley, Hoboken (2007)
2. Valin, J.-M., Maxwell, G., Terriberry, T., Vos, K.: High-quality, low-delay music coding in the opus codec. In: AES 135th Convention (2013)
3. Vos, K., Sørensen, K.V., Jensen, S.S., Valin, J.M.: Voice coding with opus. In: AES 135th Convention (2013)
4. Chu, W.C.: Speech Coding Algorithms: Foundation and Evolution of Standardized Coders. Wiley, Hoboken (2003)
5. Sercov, V., Petrovsky, A.: Neural network quantizer of the parameters of the low bitrate vocoder with "speech + noise" speech formation model. In: Proceedings of the 4th International Conference "Digital signal processing and its applications", pp. 426–428 (2002)
6. Mallat, S., Zhang, Z.: Matching pursuits with time-frequency dictionaries. IEEE Trans. Sig. Process. **41**(12), 3397–3415 (1993)
7. Petrovsky, A., Petrovsky, A.: Matching pursuit algorithm with frame-based auditory optimized WP-dictionary for audio transient modelling. Electronica. Konstrukcje, technologie, zastosowania (4), 74–80 (2008)
8. Petrovsky, A., Herasimovich, V., Petrovsky, A.: Bio-inspired sparse representation of speech and audio using psychoacoustic adaptive matching pursuit. In: Ronzhin, A., Potapova, R., Németh, G. (eds.) SPECOM 2016. LNCS (LNAI), vol. 9811, pp. 156–164. Springer, Cham (2016). https://doi.org/10.1007/978-3-319-43958-7_18
9. Petrovsky, A., Krahe, D., Petrovsky, A.A.: Real-time wavelet packet-based low bit rate audio coding on a dynamic reconfiguration system. In: AES 114th Convention (2003)
10. Petrovsky, A., Herasimovich, V., Petrovsky, A.: Audio/speech coding using the matching pursuit with frame-based psychoacoustic optimized time-frequency dictionaries and its performance evaluation. In: 2016 Signal Processing: Algorithms, Architectures, Arrangements, and Applications (SPA), pp. 225–229 (2016)
11. Mumey, B., Gedeon, T.: Optimal mutual information quantization is NP-complete. In: Neural Information Coding Workshop (2003)
12. Bengio, Y., Simard, P., Frasconi, P.: Learning long-term dependencies with gradient descent is difficult. IEEE Trans. Neural Netw. **5**(2), 157–166 (1994)
13. Bengio, Y., Lamblin, P., Popovici, D., Larochelle, H.: Greedy layer-wise training of deep networks. In: Proceedings of the 19th International Conference on Neural Information Processing Systems (NIPS), pp. 153–160 (2006)
14. Hinton, G., Osindero, S., Teh, Y.W.: A fast learning algorithm for deep belief nets. Neural Comput. **18**(7), 1527–1554 (2006)
15. Diederik, K., Ba, J.: Adam: a method for stochastic optimization. In: Proceedings of the 3rd International Conference on Learning Representations (ICLR 2015) preprint: arXiv:1412. 6980 (2015)
16. Bengio, Y., Leonard, N., Courville, A.: Estimating or propagating gradients through stochastic neurons for conditional computation. preprint arXiv:1308.3432 (2013)
17. Do, T.-T., Doan, A.-D., Cheung, N.-M.: Learning to Hash with Binary Deep Neural Network. In: Leibe, B., Matas, J., Sebe, N., Welling, M. (eds.) ECCV 2016. LNCS, vol. 9909, pp. 219–234. Springer, Cham (2016). https://doi.org/10.1007/978-3-319-46454-1_14
18. Hecht-Nielsen, R.: Replicator neural networks for universal optimal source coding. Science **269**(5232), 1860–1863 (1995)

A Comparative Study of Conventional and Deep Learning Target Tracking Algorithms for Low Quality Videos

Chiman Kwan[(✉)], Bryan Chou, and Li-Yun Martin Kwan

Applied Research LLC, Rockville, MD, USA
chiman.kwan@signalpro.net,
choub90@gmail.com, martin.kwan97@gmail.com

Abstract. This paper presents a comparative study of several state-of-the-art target tracking algorithms, including conventional and deep learning ones, for low quality videos. A challenge video data set known as SENSIAC, which contains both optical and infrared videos at long ranges (1000 m–5000 m), was used in our investigations. It was found that none of the trackers can perform well under all conditions. It appears that the field of video tracking still needs some serious development in order to reach maturity.

Keywords: Deep learning · Target tracking · Low quality videos
Kalman filter

1 Introduction

Target tracking using optical and infrared imagers has many applications such as security monitoring and surveillance operations. Compared to radar [1, 2], multi-spectral [3, 4], and hyperspectral sensors [5, 6], optical and infrared imagers are low cost and easy to install and operate. In recent years, there are new tracking algorithms using track-learn-detect [7], compressive sensing [8, 9], deep learning [10], tracking by detection [11], and references therein. These algorithms have been proven to work well in benchmark data sets. However, the benchmark videos are of high resolution and high quality. In contrast, some realistic videos such as the SENSIAC videos [12] are of low quality in terms of resolution and environmental conditions.

One objective of this research is to compare some representative tracking algorithms in the literature using the SENSIAC data [12], which have both optical and infrared videos at various ranges. We do not have any preference on any particular tracking algorithms. In fact, we also include Kalman tracker [13–15], which is probably the oldest algorithm in the literature. Another objective is to see if deep learning approaches, due to recent hype in deep learning, are better than conventional algorithms.

This paper is organized as follows. In Sect. 2, we will briefly review the tracking algorithms in this study. Although the algorithms are not exhaustive, they are representative methods of many state-of-the-art algorithms in the literature. Section 3 focuses on an extensive comparative study using actual videos. Two performance metrics were used to compare different algorithms. Finally, some concluding remarks are included in Sect. 4.

© Springer International Publishing AG, part of Springer Nature 2018
T. Huang et al. (Eds.): ISNN 2018, LNCS 10878, pp. 521–531, 2018.
https://doi.org/10.1007/978-3-319-92537-0_60

2 Tracking Algorithms

The following approaches are by no means an exhaustive list of current methods. However, they are representative methods in target tracking in recent years. Some deep learning approaches were not included because our PCs do not have the necessary hardware or software to run them. We briefly outline the key ideas of each method below.

2.1 STAPLE Tracker [16]

For this algorithm, the histogram of oriented gradients (HOG) features are extracted from the most recent estimated target location and used to update the models of the tracker. Then a template response is calculated using the updated models and the extracted features from the next frame. To be able to estimate the location of the target, the histogram response is needed along with the template response. The histogram response is calculated by updating the weights in the current frame. Then the per-pixel score is computed using the next frame. This score and the weights, calculated before, are used to determine the integral image, and ultimately, the histogram response. Together, with the template and histogram response, the tracker is able to estimate the location of the target.

The STAPLE tracker [16] is able to successfully track the target of interest until the end of a video when there is no occlusion. Even with a camera that is not stationary, STAPLE [16] is able to keep a tight bounding box around the target and the bounding box appears to scale according to the target. However, the scaling of the bounding box is too little to be significant. There are some cases where the bounding box does not completely encase the entire target, but it will still follow and track the target when there is partial encasement by the bounding box. One major issue that STAPLE [16] suffers from is the case of occlusions. Once the target becomes occluded, STAPLE [16] is unable to redetect the target to track again after emerging from the occlusion. Overall, STAPLE [16] works well for targets that do not become occluded.

2.2 Long-Term Correlation Tracking (LCT) Tracker [17]

This algorithm starts by using the initial bounding box and expanding it to specify a search window. Features are then extracted from within the search window to estimate the target location. After the location has been computed, the scaling is then calculated for the bounding box. Then the program checks to make sure that the correct target is being tracked. If it is not, then the tracker performs redetection by finding possible states and chooses the most accurate state by comparing the confidence scoring for each state. After redetection, the appearance and motion model are updated. This update is performed regardless of whether or not the redetection module is performed. This cycle is continued until the end of the video.

The LCT tracker [17] is able to successfully track the target of interest until the end of the video. This algorithm has proven to be quite robust in that it is able to handle occlusions and a non-stationary camera. Although the LCT [17] is able to handle cases of light to moderate occlusion, it is unsuccessful when there is heavy occlusion. Such as when a target is under a heavy shadow that spans multiple frames. It has been found that the LCT [17] is unsuccessful because of the dramatic changes the shadows make on the appearance model of the target. Another minor fault of this algorithm is the dynamic scaling of the bounding box. When the orientation of the target changes and the bounding box is scaled, there are some cases when the bounding box becomes too large and covers more area around the target of interest than desired. Overall, the LCT [17] algorithm is robust and able to handle most cases of occlusion.

2.3   Fusion of STAPLE and LCT

The Fusion of STAPLE [16] and LCT [17] merges the two algorithms into one program. We implemented this fusion algorithm. The reasoning for this merge is to combine the best features of the two algorithms and resolve the main issues that each algorithm suffers as individual programs. It just so happens that the issues with STAPLE [16] can be resolved by the LCT [17] and the issues with the LCT [17] can be resolved with the STAPLE [16]. This Fusion tracker is able to successfully track the target of interest until the end of the video while keeping a tight fitting bounding box around the target. This includes cases with light to medium occlusion.

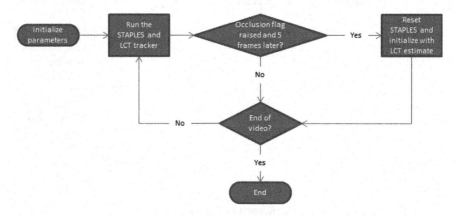

Fig. 1. Fusion of STAPLE and LCT tracking algorithms.

Figure 1 illustrates the fusion based tracker. The fusion tracker works by running the STAPLE [16] and LCT [17] trackers simultaneously. Since the bounding box information from the STAPLE [16] tracker has a more desirable result, STAPLE [16] is used to visualize the location of the target. The LCT [17] is used to detect occlusion and for redetection. Once occlusions are detected, a flag is raised and the program waits for 5 frames to pass so that the target has some time to emerge from the occlusion. Once the flag is raised and the 5 frames have passed, STAPLE [16] is reset and initialized with the location information from the LCT [17]. The purpose of resetting STAPLE [16] is to clear the history of the appearance and motion model. This cycle continues until the end of the video.

2.4   Kalman Tracker

Although Kalman tracker is easy to understand, we could not find a good Kalman tracker in the internet. So we implemented this by ourselves. The Kalman tracker is able to successfully track a moving target at close range until the end of the video if there are no occlusions and the camera is stationary. It has been found that the Kalman tracker has issues when the target is stationary because of its reliance on motion to be able to successfully track. Detection of motion is only performed every ten frames to ensure that there are notable differences between two frames. Overall, the Kalman tracker works for close range targets captured with a stationary camera.

Figure 2 illustrates the Kalman tracker. Given an initial position and velocity, a prediction of the next location is calculated for the first frame. Then, the same calculation is made for frames in between intervals of 10. For every other 10 frames, the Kalman filter parameters are updated using the motion of the target. More specifically, the measurement residual and Kalman gain are updated to predict a more accurate state estimate. This cycle continues until the end of the video.

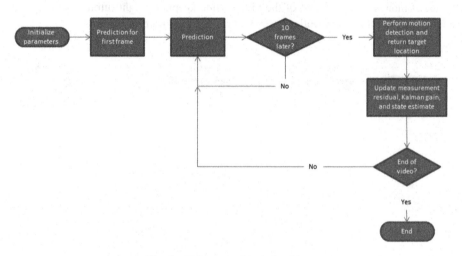

Fig. 2. Kalman tracking algorithm.

2.5   Hierarchical Convolutional Features for Visual Tracking (CF Tracker)

This is deep learning based tracker. As shown in Fig. 3, the CF tracker starts off the tracking by cropping out a search window from the first frame based on the initial position that is used as an input for the program. Once the search window has been established, convolutional features are extracted with spatial interpolation. Once this has been completed, a confidence score is computed for each VGG net layer. This score is used to estimate the closest target location for the next frame. Then another area is cropped out from the whole frame using the newest estimate and the convolutional features are extracted with interpolation to update the correlation filters for each layer. This cycle is repeated until the end of the video is reached.

The CF tracker performs similarly to the STAPLE and LCT tracker. It is able to track the target until the end of the video in most cases. This tracker is able to keep a bounding box around the target when the camera is not stationary and the scaling of the bounding box is adaptive, much like the STAPLE bounding box. However, the bounding box size changes are too small to be significant. One issue of this tracker is that the computational time is quite long. For one video of approximately 1,875 frames, the tracker takes about 30 min to complete. Although the tracker has not been tested on videos with occlusion, it appears that it would not handle occlusion very well due to the similar behavior with the STAPLE. Furthermore, the code does not have a function or algorithm for redetection.

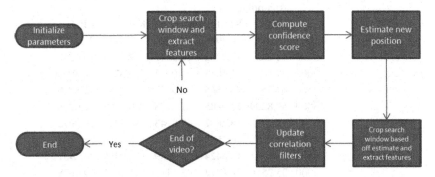

Fig. 3. Deep learning tracker.

3   Experiments

3.1   SENSIAC Database Description

All the tracking algorithms have been tested using the SENSIAC database [12], which contain different vehicles and human targets at multiple ranges. These videos are captured using both optical and mid-wave infrared (MWIR) cameras. This data set is available for purchase [12]. In this paper, we focus only on vehicles.

For vehicles, there are a total of nine targets. It is important to note that two targets were excluded because not all scenarios were available for the particular targets. These targets vary in size from a pickup truck to a tank. For each target, there are a total of 18 scenarios, nine for daytime and nine for night time. These nine daytime and nighttime scenarios vary in range from the target to the camera used to capture the video. The range starts from 1,000 m and ends at 5,000 m with an interval of 500 m. All the vehicles drive in a circular pattern at speeds specified within the ground truth files associated with each scenario. In total, there are 162 videos for vehicles.

3.2   Vehicle Tracking Results

Although there are quite a few performance metrics for evaluating different trackers in the literature, only two different performance metrics were performed on each of the scenarios. This is because only the ground truth center locations of the vehicles are available in the database. The first one was the distance precision (DP), which computes the average number of frames the estimate location was within range of the ground truth location. The second performance metric is the center location error (CLE), which computes the average distance between the ground truth location and the estimated location. The following tables are the averages of all targets for a particular range for each tracking algorithm.

Table 1. Averaged Center Location Error (CLE) for all cases. Optical videos.

CLE

			Algorithms				
			LCT	STAPLE	Fusion	Kalman	CF
Ranges	Day	1000	26.2451	24.3939	18.1098	**5.5431**	28.1734
		1500	18.3854	15.8202	12.5347	**7.1036**	16.0348
		2000	9.4061	11.1048	7.0533	**3.3757**	12.8006
		2500	67.3546	**38.8866**	61.0648	97.7282	45.8926
		3000	57.8209	**13.6605**	21.7178	80.7708	22.0208
		3500	19.1763	**14.2882**	49.8143	87.3758	26.9078
		4000	32.0739	**6.7583**	49.2002	105.4559	20.6885
		4500	31.1081	**17.6424**	23.9859	66.0445	23.2431
		5000	35.2556	**24.7713**	33.1415	51.2991	29.2628

Table 2. Averaged Distance Precision (DP) at threshold of 20 pixels for all cases.

DP (20 pixel threshold)

			Algorithms				
			LCT	STAPLE	Fusion	Kalman	CF
Ranges	Day	1000	0.3339	0.3574	0.5253	**0.9898**	0.3597
		1500	0.6352	0.6013	0.8247	**0.9860**	0.6350
		2000	0.9910	0.8650	**0.9998**	0.9986	0.8660
		2500	0.2700	**0.6502**	0.4535	0.2140	0.5336
		3000	0.3261	**0.9293**	0.7583	0.2536	0.7773
		3500	0.7830	**0.9100**	0.3890	0.2239	0.6539
		4000	0.4808	**0.9587**	0.3254	0.3459	0.7217
		4500	0.3591	**0.6466**	0.4985	0.1648	0.5196
		5000	0.3564	**0.5851**	0.4464	0.3192	0.5090

Optical Camera Results. Table 1 summarizes the averaged CLE of tracking results of different algorithms at different ranges. It should be noted that there are a number of vehicles at each range. Smaller CLEs mean better performance. It can be seen that Kalman tracker works well for ranges less than or equal to 2000 m. STAPLE works well for ranges longer than 2000 m. Table 2 shows the averaged Distance Precision

(DP) at threshold of 20 pixels for all cases. Again, it can be seen that the Kalman tracker works well for short ranges and STAPLE works well for long ranges. Compared to the conventional trackers, the deep learning based tracker (CF) only performs moderately well in long ranges. The fusion approach works well only when there are occlusions, which are not present in the SENSIAC videos. In terms of computational speed, Kalman and STAPLE are the fastest, followed the LCT, fusion, and CF.

Figure 4 shows the averaged DP at three ranges. The trends are similar to what we observe in Tables 1 and 2.

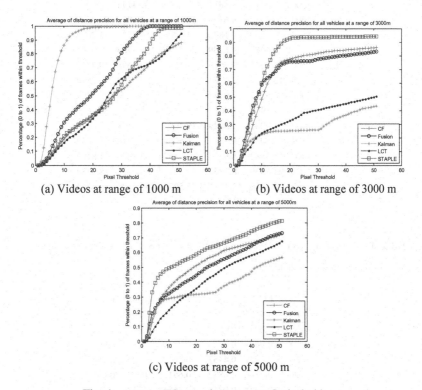

(a) Videos at range of 1000 m   (b) Videos at range of 3000 m

(c) Videos at range of 5000 m

Fig. 4. Average DP at various ranges. Optical videos.

Infrared Camera Results. Different from the optical videos that have only day time videos, the infrared videos have both day and night time videos. Table 3 shows the averaged CLE results for all cases. In both day and night time cases, STAPLE performs quite well for all ranges. All other algorithms do not perform that well. Similarly, Table 4 shows the averaged DP results for all cases. Again, STAPLE performs well in almost all cases. Figures 5, 6 and 7 plot the DP results for different ranges. We can observe the similar trends mentioned above. In terms of computational speed, Kalman and STAPLE are the fastest, followed the LCT, fusion, and CF.

Table 3. Averaged Center Location Error (CLE) for all cases. Infrared videos.

CLE							
			Algorithms				
			LCT	STAPLE	Fusion	Kalman	CF
Ranges	Day	1000	32.6376	**24.6038**	53.2527	89.1767	71.2136
		1500	22.6851	**13.9725**	17.5248	75.4930	63.8537
		2000	**10.2987**	15.5561	38.2592	59.2863	23.4091
		2500	55.6768	**47.5998**	56.6269	115.8784	52.7754
		3000	52.3696	24.0137	**23.8464**	85.4935	42.6051
		3500	29.5317	**8.5811**	50.1563	82.4144	39.9273
		4000	29.2585	**10.6956**	13.4652	45.4083	32.8579
		4500	25.9339	**21.1822**	25.3266	67.7747	42.2674
		5000	29.6687	**20.6289**	20.7262	132.2764	27.0285
	Night	1000	**18.0577**	29.7589	27.5016	80.0698	19.7410
		1500	12.5835	17.6375	17.2377	**8.9518**	12.2514
		2000	**7.5399**	11.9845	11.9410	7.9800	8.9405
		2500	37.1904	8.4052	**8.3242**	33.3183	72.2683
		3000	37.9731	**7.3029**	19.4694	51.0178	45.3617
		3500	24.5018	**6.8555**	25.5366	53.5819	31.9712
		4000	15.5882	**5.6554**	17.9157	33.1909	11.8107
		4500	23.6879	**8.3042**	19.2317	30.6024	18.9383
		5000	30.1010	**15.4727**	15.5971	158.9508	53.6705

Table 4. Averaged Distance Precision (DP) at threshold of 20 pixels for all cases.

DP (20 pixel threshold)							
			Algorithms				
			LCT	STAPLE	Fusion	Kalman	CF
Ranges	Day	1000	0.4533	0.3361	0.5508	**0.7006**	0.4058
		1500	**0.8022**	0.6575	0.7530	0.6873	0.3521
		2000	**0.9077**	0.7704	0.6330	0.5085	0.6684
		2500	0.2952	**0.4457**	0.3660	0.2935	0.2466
		3000	0.3306	0.6832	**0.6915**	0.0999	0.3058
		3500	0.5648	**0.9211**	0.3554	0.1018	0.2832
		4000	0.4543	**0.8544**	0.8038	0.1949	0.3678
		4500	0.4119	**0.6080**	0.4651	0.0276	0.3276
		5000	0.3751	0.5880	**0.5940**	0.2469	0.5035
	Night	1000	**0.5554**	0.3552	0.4456	0.4715	0.5247
		1500	0.7544	0.5654	0.6362	**0.9860**	0.8069
		2000	0.9620	0.7824	0.8503	0.9666	**1.0000**
		2500	0.5775	0.8954	**0.9027**	0.6246	0.4941
		3000	0.5303	**0.9304**	0.8347	0.4708	0.5638
		3500	0.6578	**0.9599**	0.7717	0.3769	0.5397
		4000	0.7932	**0.9619**	0.6293	0.4003	0.8157
		4500	0.5329	**0.8743**	0.5227	0.3767	0.6773
		5000	0.3797	**0.7411**	0.7426	0.0094	0.5394

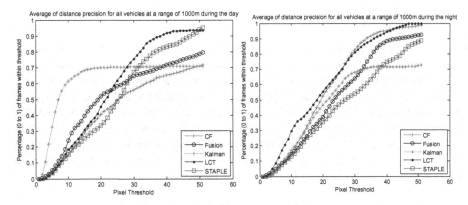

Fig. 5. Average distance precision for videos at range of 1000 m. Left: Infrared videos at day time; right: infrared videos at night time.

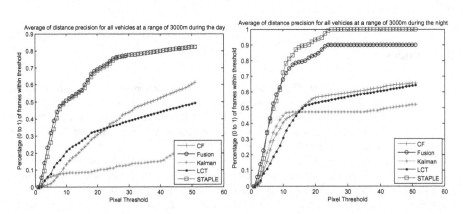

Fig. 6. Average distance precision for videos at range of 3000 m. Left: Infrared videos at day time; right: infrared videos at night time.

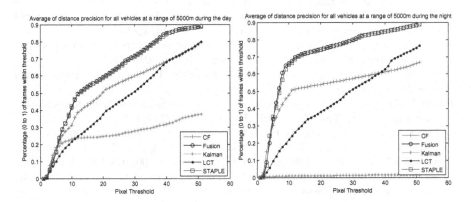

Fig. 7. Average distance precision for videos at range of 5000 m. Left: Infrared videos at day time; right: infrared videos at night time.

4 Conclusions

In this paper, we address target tracking for low quality videos. The low quality is caused by long range data acquisition as well as environmental conditions due to poor illumination and camera motions. Five representative trackers were used in our comparative study. Two performance metrics (center location error and distance precision) were used in our experiments. It was observed that one tracker known as STAPLE performed quite well whereas the deep learning based tracker did not work as well as STAPLE. A somewhat surprising results is that the Kalman tracker also works well up to 2000 m for optical videos. It is our belief that the field of target tracking still needs a lot of research, including deep learning based methods.

Acknowledgments. This research was supported by US Air Force under contract FA8651-17-C-0017. The views, opinions and/or findings expressed are those of the author(s) and should not be interpreted as representing the official views or policies of the Department of Defense or the U.S. Government.

References

1. Zhao, Z., Chen, H., Chen, G., Kwan, C., Li, X.: Comparison of several ballistic target tracking filters. In: Proceedings of American Control Conference, pp. 2197–2202 (2006)
2. Zhao, Z., Chen, H., Chen, G., Kwan, C., Li, X.: IMM-LMMSE filtering algorithm for ballistic target tracking with unknown ballistic coefficient. In: Proceedings of SPIE, Signal and Data Processing of Small Targets, vol. 6236 (2006)
3. Dao, M., Kwan, C., Koperski, K., Marchisio, G.: A joint sparsity approach to tunnel activity monitoring using high resolution satellite images. In: IEEE Ubiquitous Computing, Electronics & Mobile Communication Conference, pp. 322–328 (2017)
4. Perez, D., Banerjee, D., Kwan, C., Dao, M., Shen, Y., Koperski, K., Marchisio, G., Li, J.: Deep learning for effective detection of excavated soil related to illegal tunnel activities. In: IEEE Ubiquitous Computing, Electronics & Mobile Communication Conference, pp. 626–632 (2017)
5. Qu, Y., Qi, H., Ayhan, B., Kwan, C., Kidd, R.: Does multispectral/hyperspectral pansharpening improve the performance of anomaly detection? IEEE International Geoscience and Remote Sensing Symposium, pp. 6130–6133 (2017)
6. Zhou, J., Kwan, C., Ayhan, B.: Improved target detection for hyperspectral images using hybrid in-scene calibration. J. Appl. Remote Sens. **11**(3), 035010 (2017)
7. Kalal, Z., Mikolajczyk, K., Matas, J.: Tracking-Learning-Detection. IEEE Trans. Pattern Anal. Mach. Intell. **34**(7), 1409–1422 (2012)
8. Mei, X., Ling, H.: Robust visual tracking and vehicle classification via sparse representation. IEEE Trans. Pattern Anal. Mach. Intell. **33**(11), 2259–2272 (2011)
9. Zhang, K., Zhang, L., Yang, M.-H.: Real-time compressive tracking. In: Fitzgibbon, A., Lazebnik, S., Perona, P., Sato, Y., Schmid, C. (eds.) ECCV 2012. LNCS, vol. 7574, pp. 864–877. Springer, Heidelberg (2012). https://doi.org/10.1007/978-3-642-33712-3_62
10. Ma, C., Huang, J.B., Yang, X., Yang, M.H.: Hierarchical convolutional features for visual tracking. In: Computer Vision (ICCV) (2015)

11. Li, X., Kwan, C., Mei, G., Li, B.: A generic approach to object matching and tracking. In: Campilho, A., Kamel, M.S. (eds.) ICIAR 2006. LNCS, vol. 4141, pp. 839–849. Springer, Heidelberg (2006). https://doi.org/10.1007/11867586_76
12. SENSIAC. https://www.sensiac.org/external/products/list_databases.jsf
13. Lewis, F.L.: Optimal Estimation. Wiley, Hoboken (1986)
14. Zhou, J., Kwan, C.: Tracking of multiple pixel targets using multiple cameras. In: 15th International Symposium on Neural Networks (2018)
15. Kwan, C., Lewis, F.L.: A note on kalman filtering. IEEE Trans. Educ. **42**(3), 225–227 (1999)
16. Bertinetto, L., et al.: Staple: complementary learners for real-time tracking. In: Conference on Computer Vision and Pattern Recognition (2016)
17. Ma, C., Yang, X., Zhang, C., Yang, M.H.: Long-term correlation tracking. In: IEEE Conference on Computer Vision and Pattern Recognition (CVPR), Boston, MA, pp. 5388–5396 (2015)

Image Edge Detection for Stitching Aerial Images with Geometrical Rectification

Zhi-Xuan Liu, Qiu-Hua Lin[(⊠)], and Ying-Guang Hao

School of Information and Communication Engineering,
Dalian University of Technology, Dalian 116023, China
qhlin@dlut.edu.cn

Abstract. Changes of the flight attitude of unmanned aircraft cause nonlinear distortion in the aerial images. Stitching these images without geometric rectification may cause the problem of mismatching. However, the geometric rectification model produces invalid regions at the edge of images. A direct cutting for these invalid regions leads to removing lots of useful information, whereas a noisy seam is visible in the stitched image if the edge cutting is omitted. We propose a solution of edge detection for detecting invalid and noisy regions. More precisely, our method includes two passes of edge detection for images with geometric rectification. The first pass of image edge detection is to find the boundary between valid and invalid scenes. The second pass is to detect the noisy regions. The invalid and noisy regions are finally removed for image stitching, and the effective areas of the image are kept to the maximum extent. Experimental results demonstrate the efficacy of the proposed method.

Keywords: Image geometric rectification · Edge detection · Image stitching
Window function

1 Introduction

Unmanned aircraft have been widely applied in collecting aerial images, as it is flexible and the aerial images are with high resolution. The scene map stitched by aerial images can be used for the disaster management, agricultural monitoring, and reconnaissance and surveillance missions [1].

Due to unstable effects such as turbulence and self-vibration during flying, there are some changes of the flight attitude, including pitch angle, roll angle, yaw angle and altitude. Certain nonlinear geometric distortion is thus generated in the aerial images due to perspective transformation. Stitching these images without geometric correction may cause the problem of image mismatching. Therefore, many geometric rectification methods have been proposed. Some are based on ground control points (GCPs) [2–4]. Liew et al. examined the effects of different GCP distributions on the efficiency of rectification [2]. More and Pons studied the effect of the number of GCPs, and presented that a minimum of 25 GCPs was needed to achieve a root mean square error smaller than a pixel [3]. Bagheri and Sadeghian studied the GCP distribution and

© Springer International Publishing AG, part of Springer Nature 2018
T. Huang et al. (Eds.): ISNN 2018, LNCS 10878, pp. 532–540, 2018.
https://doi.org/10.1007/978-3-319-92537-0_61

number effects on different modeling methods such as rational functions, 3D polynomials and optimization artificial intelligent methods [4]. Some methods employ the reference image registration for rectification [5–7]. The SIFT algorithm was used to match the reference image and the distorted image to get the transformation matrix for correcting the image [5]. An automated geometric correction method was presented by introducing geometric distortions in the reference image using a global affine transformation function, prior to registering the reference image with the image to be geometrically corrected [6]. Image matching can be used to determine the geometric transformation that aligns the distorted image to the reference image [7]. There are also other methods based on camera imaging models [8–10]. Zhou developed a method based on photogrammetry model to determine the camera interior and exterior orientation parameters of each video frame [8]. Liu et al. optimized an error homograph matrix including the camera parameter error, perspective center error, image attitude error, and the error of projection plane [9]. A geometrical rectification model based on different flight attitude was proposed for unmanned aerial vehicle remote sensing images without control points [10]. In comparison with the methods based on GCPs and those based on the image registration needing reference images, the methods using flight attitude parameters to calibrate the images are straightforward and efficient.

However, for the geometric correction based on the camera imaging models, the interpolation method needs to be used. This leads to noisy regions at the edge of the corrected image, in addition to invalid regions with pixel values of zero. A simple cutting for the invalid and noisy regions may cause the removal of some valid regions. As such, we propose a method for detecting these regions via image edge detection, in an effort to keep the valid areas of the image to the maximum extent. Our method includes two passes of edge detection of the image. The first pass of image edge detection is to find the boundary between valid and invalid scenes. We use a window function and thresholding technique to detect invalid pixels. The second pass of image edge detection is to detect the noisy regions at the edge of the geometric corrected image. The same window function is used, and a criterion is presented for determining a pixel as a noisy pixel. The invalid and noisy regions are finally removed before stitching images.

The rest of this paper is organized as follows. Section 2 describes our proposed method for the two passes of image edge detection. Section 3 includes experiments and results. Conclusion is given in Sect. 4.

2   Proposed Method

2.1   Geometrical Corrected Images

In Fig. 1, the rectangle *ABCD* denotes the original aerial image, which has nonlinear distortion. The quadrangle *EFGH* represents an exampling image after geometric rectification. It includes noisy regions along edges due to the interpolation algorithm. The rectangle *IJKL* represents the minimum image containing *EFGH*. The area of *IJKL* excluding *EFGH*, called invalid regions, here including triangles *IEH*, *JFE*, *KGF*, and *LHG*. These invalid regions are filled with invalid pixels, the values of which are zero. The rectangle *MNOP* is the maximum intercepted image in *EFGH*. In this case, we have three choices for image stitching by using (1) the original aerial image *ABCD*, (2) the maximum intercepted image *MNOP* in *EFGH*, and (3) the minimum image *IJKL* containing *EFGH*. It is obvious to note that the first choice causes image mismatching; the second choice loses lots of image information; and the last choice results in invalid regions and irregular noisy edges at the stitching joints, but it retains the maximal effective areas of the original image. As such, we propose a method to detect the invalid and noisy regions.

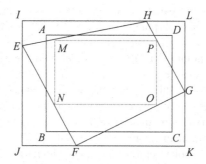

Fig. 1. Exampling images after geometric rectification

Our proposed method includes two passes of image edge detection for the minimum image *IJKL* containing *EFGH*. The first pass of image edge detection is to find the boundary between valid and invalid scenes. The second pass of image edge detection is to detect the noisy regions. The invalid and noisy regions are finally removed to obtain the image for image stitching.

2.2   The First Pass of Image Edge Detection

Figure 2 shows a sub-image for the first pass of image edge detection. The rectangular $S_1S_2S_3S_4$ represents a sub-image of *IJKL*, which is denoted as I_C for simplicity. The area $S_5S_6S_3S_4$ in grey represents the valid scene area, whereas the area $S_1S_2S_6S_5$ in white represents the invalid area. The boundary S_5S_6 is the edge of the sub-image. The rectangle $W_1W_2W_3W_4$, named as $W_{m \times m}$, denotes the window for image edge detection. Its size is $m \times m$, and m takes odd number of pixels such as 3, 5, or 7; we set $m = 5$ in Fig. 2(a). The numerical values in $W_{m \times m}$ show values of the pixels within the window. The pixel P with coordinate (x_0, y_0) is the pixel to be detected and is located at the center of $W_{m \times m}$. We calculate numbers of invalid pixels within $W_{m \times m}$ as follows:

$$Val(x,y)=\begin{cases} 1, & if \ I_C(x,y) \leq TH_n \\ 0, & others \end{cases} \tag{1}$$

$$n(x_0,y_0)= \sum_{i=x_0-\lfloor m/2 \rfloor}^{x_0+\lfloor m/2 \rfloor} \sum_{j=y_0-\lfloor m/2 \rfloor}^{y_0+\lfloor m/2 \rfloor} Val(i,j) \tag{2}$$

where $I_C(x,y)$ stands for the pixel value at (x,y) in I_C; TH_n, taking $1 \sim 5$ pixel(s), is a threshold for distinguishing invalid pixels from valid pixels. $Val(x,y)$ is the detected value for the pixel (x,y). If $Val(x,y)$ is equal to 1, the pixel (x,y) is judged as an invalid pixel. Otherwise, it is a valid pixel. The symbol $\lfloor \ \rfloor$ means the rounding down of a number, and $n(x_0,y_0)$ represents the total numbers of invalid pixels detected for $P(x_0,y_0)$.
The pixel $P(x_0,y_0)$ is judged as an invalid pixel if $n(x_0,y_0)$ satisfies Eq. (3):

$$m^2 - 2n(x_0,y_0) \leq 2m \tag{3}$$

Let U represent the set of pixels satisfying Eq. (3):

$$U = \left\{ (x_0,y_0) \middle| \ m^2 - 2n(x_0,y_0) \leq 2m, \quad (x_0,y_0) \in I_C \right\} \tag{4}$$

Let I_{C1} denote the resulting image of the first pass of image edge detection, the pixel value at (x,y) in I_{C1} is determined as follows:

$$I_{C1}(x,y) = \begin{cases} 0, & if \ (x,y) \in U \\ 255, & others \end{cases} \tag{5}$$

Figure 2(b) has the result. The rectangle $I_1 J_1 K_1 L_1$ represents I_{C1}. The white areas of I_{C1}, including the edge E-F-G-H and invalid pixels, are with values of 0. The grey area $EFGH$ corresponding to the valid regions, is with values of 255.

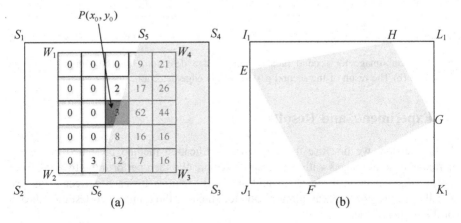

Fig. 2. A sub-image for the first pass of image edge detection. (a) The window for edge detection. (b) The result of the first pass of image edge detection.

2.3   The Second Pass of Image Edge Detection

The second pass of image edge detection is to determine the noisy regions on the basis of the resulting image I_{C1} in the first pass of image edge detection. As shown in Fig. 3 (a), the rectangle $S_1S_2S_3S_4$ represents a sub-image at the edge of I_{C1}. The pixel $\widetilde{P}$ with the coordinate $(\tilde{x}_0, \tilde{y}_0)$, located at the center of the detecting window $W_{m \times m}$, is the pixel to be detected in I_{C1}.

Let I_{C2} denote the result of the second pass of image edge detection. The new pixel value of $\widetilde{P}(\tilde{x}_0, \tilde{y}_0)$ in the image I_{C2} is obtained in the following way: Within the window $W_{m \times m}$, i.e., the area enclosed by $\tilde{x}_0 - \lfloor m/2 \rfloor$, $\tilde{x}_0 + \lfloor m/2 \rfloor$, $\tilde{y}_0 - \lfloor m/2 \rfloor$, and $\tilde{y}_0 + \lfloor m/2 \rfloor$, if there is one or more pixels, the pixel value of which is 0, $\widetilde{P}$ is judged as a noisy pixel, and the pixel value of $I_{C2}(\tilde{x}_0, \tilde{y}_0)$ is set to be 0. Otherwise, $\widetilde{P}$ is judged as a valid voxel belonging to the scene, and the pixel value of $I_{C2}(\tilde{x}_0, \tilde{y}_0)$ is set to be 255. After performing the detecting for all pixels in I_{C1}, we get the result I_{C2} $(I_2J_2K_2L_2)$ with the edge of E'-F'-G'-H', as shown in Fig. 3(b). The dark grey area within the quadrangle $E'F'G'H'$ is considered to be the valid region with less noises. The light grey area between the edges E-F-G-H and E'-F'-G'-H' is determined as the noisy regions which is to be removed before image stitching.

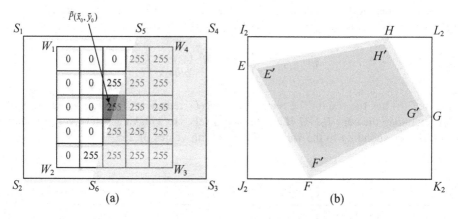

Fig. 3. A sub-image for second pass of image edge detection. (a) The window for edge detection. (b) The result of the second pass of image edge detection.

3   Experiments and Results

In this section, we first use the geometric rectification method presented in [10] to correct the aerial images with nonlinear distortion. We then perform the two passes of image edge detection to detect invalid and noisy regions for each corrected images. Finally, we present the exampling results for stitching three images to test the efficacy of the proposed method.

3.1   Image Edge Detection

Figure 4(a) shows an aerial image. The width is 1200 pixels and height is 1200 pixels. Figure 4(b) shows its geometric rectification image. Figure 4(c) illustrates the edge of an enlarged sub-image for showing the noisy regions at the edge of the geometric rectification image. It is observed from Fig. 4(c) that there are many discontinuous noisy pixels at the edges of the corrected image, which form the noisy regions.

In the experiment, we set $m = 7$, and $TH_n = 3$. Figure 5 shows the two boundaries detected by the two passes of image edge detection, and an enlarged sub-image showing the detected noisy regions between the two boundaries. It is seen that the detected noisy regions contain the discontinuous noisy pixels, as shown in Fig. 4(c).

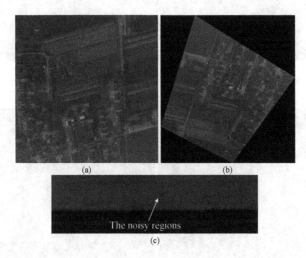

Fig. 4. An aerial image and its geometric rectification image. (a) The aerial image. (b) The geometric corrected image. (c) An enlarged sub-image showing the noisy regions at the edge of the corrected image.

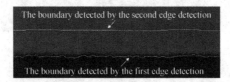

Fig. 5. An enlarged sub-image showing the detected noisy regions between the two boundaries of the two passes of image edge detection

3.2 Image Stitching

Figure 6 shows three geometric corrected images for three sequential aerial images used for image stitching. Figure 7(a) displays the stitched image by directly using the three geometric corrected images without removing the invalid and noisy edges. Figure 7(b) demonstrates the stitched image by using the proposed method, i.e., the

Fig. 6. Three geometric corrected images for three sequential aerial images used for stitching

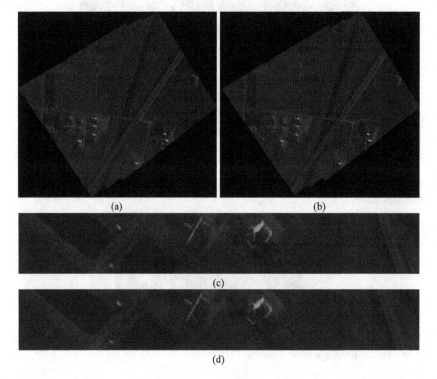

Fig. 7. The results of image stitching. (a) The stitched image without using the proposed method. (b) The stitched image using the proposed method. (c) An enlarged sub-image at the joint of the stitched image of (a). (d) An enlarged sub-image at the joint of stitched image of (b).

invalid and noisy regions at the edges of the three geometric corrected images are removed before image stitching. Figure 7(c) shows an enlarged sub-image at the joint of the stitched image of Fig. 7(a), whereas Fig. 7(d) shows that of Fig. 7(b). From Fig. 7(c), it is evident to find some black stripe due to the negative effects of the invalid and noisy regions. In contrast, we cannot find the black blocks in Fig. 7(d), the stitched image is seamless and of high quality. With the test of the other 101 images, it was found that the stitched image used our proposed method was also seamless and of high quality. In contrast, lots of blocks were found in the stitched image when omitting removal of the invalid and noisy edges.

4   Conclusion

We propose a method of two passes of image edge detection for detecting the invalid and noisy regions at the edges of aerial images after the geometric rectification. Our method can keep valid areas of the images for image stitching to the maximum extent, by only removing the invalid and noisy regions before image stitching. Experimental results show that the quality of the stitched image is better than a direct image stitching using the corrected images. Our future directions would be to improve the speed of the method or just use one pass of the image edge detection to get noiseless edges and regions.

References

1. Kim, J., Kim, T., Shin, D., Kim, S.: Fast and robust geometric correction for mosaicking UAV images with narrow overlaps. Int. J. Remote Sens. **38**(8–10), 2557–2576 (2017)
2. Liew, L.H., Lee, B.Y., Wang, Y.C., Cheah, W.S.: Simulation study on distribution of control points for aerial images rectification. In: Yeo, S.-S., et al. (eds.) Computer Science and its Applications. Lecture Notes in Electrical Engineering (LNEE), vol. 203, pp. 169–177. Springer, Dordrecht (2012). https://doi.org/10.1007/978-94-007-5699-1_18
3. More, G., Pons, X.: Influence of the nature and number of ground control points to the quality of remote sensing geometric corrections. In: International Geoscience and Remote Sensing Symposium (IGARSS), Munich, Germany, pp. 2356–2359 (2012)
4. Bagheri, H., Sadeghian, S.: Geometric rectification of high resolution satellite images using mathematical intelligent & classical modelling. In: Iranian Conference on Intelligent Systems (ICIS), Bam, Iran, pp. 1–6 (2014)
5. Deng, H., Wang, L., Liu, J., Li, D., Chen, Z., Zhou, Q.: Study on application of scale invariant feature transform algorithm on automated geometric correction of remote sensing images. In: Advances in Information and Communication Technology, IFIP AICT, vol. 393, PART 2, pp. 352–358 (2013)
6. Devaraj, C., Shah, C.A.: Automated geometric correction of landsat MSS L1G imagery. IEEE Geosci. Remote Sens. Lett. **11**(1), 347–351 (2014)
7. Brown, M., Lowe, D.G.: Automatic panoramic image stitching using invariant features. Int. J. Comput. Vis. **74**(1), 59–73 (2007)
8. Zhou, G.: Near real-time orthorectification and mosaic of small UAV video flow for time-critical event response. IEEE Trans. Geosci. Remote Sens. **47**(3), 739–747 (2009)

9. Liu, J., Gong, J., Guo, B., Zhang, W.: A novel adjustment model for mosaicking low-overlap sweeping images. IEEE Trans. Geosci. Remote Sens. **55**(7), 4089–4097 (2017)
10. Li, Z.: Geometrical Rectification for Unmanned Aerial Vehicle Remote Sensing Images without Control Points. Thesis, University of Electronic Science and Technology of China (in Chinese), pp. 9–29 (2010)

BP Neural Network with Regularization and Sensor Array for Prediction of Component Concentration of Mixed Gas

Lin Zhao[1,2], Jing Wang[2(✉)], and Xiuyu Chen[1]

[1] School of Computer Science and Technology,
Dalian Neusoft University of Information, Dalian 116023,
People's Republic of China
{zhaolin, chenxiuyu}@neusoft.edu.cn
[2] Faculty of Electronic Information and Electrical Engineering,
Dalian University of Technology, Dalian 116023, People's Republic of China
wangjing@dlut.edu.cn

Abstract. BP neural network with L_1 regularization is employed in this paper to solve the volatile organic compounds recognition problems. Recognition performance of neural networks is closely related to number of layers and number of nodes in each layer. The L_1 regularization makes some weights of the neural network approach zero, and helps to determine the nodes number of hidden layer in prediction of component concentrations in a gas mixture. Some rules of hidden layer node pruning are established by combining the function of regularization term, the response characteristics of sensors and composition of sensor array. The number of the hidden layer nodes determined by the pruning method gives better solution, and is close to the number of the hidden layer nodes determined by exhaustive experiments.

Keywords: BP neural network · Mixed gas recognition
Component concentration · L_1 regularization

1 Introduction

Volatile organic compounds (VOCs) including formaldehyde (HCHO), acetone, toluene, ethanol, 2-propanol (isopropyl alcohol) and limonene are emitted as gases from certain solids or liquids. Some of VOCs have adversely impact the people's health [1, 2]. They are also the biomarkers to detect human diseases [3]. There are many techniques to identify target gas in the mixture. Such as gas chromatographs, mass spectroscopy, FTIR analysis, electrochemistry sensors, semiconductor sensors, fluctuation enhanced sensing [4, 5], E-Nose [6] and some unmixing algorithms to mixtures if gas spectral signatures are available [7]. Semiconductor gas sensor possesses some advantages such as cheap to make and easy to use, and can convert the gas concentration directly to electrical signals. But one of disadvantages of semiconductor sensor is poor selectivity.

A sensor array with pattern recognition methods is a relatively convenient way to solve the problem of poor selectivity and recognize gas mixtures [8–10]. This method

T. Huang et al. (Eds.): ISNN 2018, LNCS 10878, pp. 541–548, 2018.
https://doi.org/10.1007/978-3-319-92537-0_62

has a wide range of applications, such as detecting explosive gas, controlling production processes and monitoring environmental pollutions, etc. [11, 12]. A semiconductor gas sensor array is used to acquiring signals. Pattern recognition methods convert signals into conclusion including gas classification and/or concentration prediction. In fact, the relationships between the sensor signals and conclusion are non-linear correlative. So pattern recognition is playing a crucial role in detecting characteristics of the sensor signals. Many existing pattern recognition methods were used in many applications [13–18]. Artificial neural networks (ANN) made an improvement in high accuracy and less processing time [19–22]. However, establishment of the neural network structure is still a difficult problem. A neural network is single or a multi hidden layer network, how many nodes are there in the input layer and output layer. What is more important is the number of nodes in the input layer.

In this paper, BP neural network with L1 regularization terms is employed. The nodes number of hidden layer in prediction of component concentrations for gas mixture were determined.

2   Experiments

2.1   BP Neural Network with Regularization

The BP neural network is a feedforward neural network, its basic idea is [23–25]: direction from input layer to output layer is defined as the forward direction, and direction of output layer to input layer is defined as the backward direction. Given training samples, the output of each layer is calculated in the forward direction until the output of output layer is obtained. The error of output layer results with the real value of samples is calculated. Then the parameters are modified by the backward direction according to the error. This process is repeated until network parameters meet requirements. It has been proved theoretically that the single hidden layer BP network can approximate all mapping functions [22].

When training accuracy of networks reaches a certain level, the simpler network structure is, the stronger generalization ability of the network is. And the more complex network structure is, the poorer generalization ability of the network is. In theory, it is still an open problem to calculate number of optimal nodes directly [26]. There are two kinds of methods for solving this problem: One is a growing method, starting with a small number of nodes in training process and keeping increasing new nodes; The other one is a pruning method, starting with a relatively large number of nodes in training process and then deleting nodes that are not needed. The neural network with regularization in the paper is a pruning method.

The regularization method [27–29] adds regularization term to error function, and then uses corresponding learning algorithm to train networks. In recent years, research of L_p regularization in neural network has attracted more and more scholars' attention, and it has been successfully applied to data processing, machine learning and other fields. At the same time, regularization method is also used to prune neural networks, and it is a more popular method. For the goal of pruning network structure, add a L_p

regularization term to error function in trained process. The output of each layer of a neural network is expressed as:

$$O = S(\sum_j (v_j * S(\sum_i w_{ij} x_i)))$$ (1)

where, x_i is the i-th component of the input vector, w_{ij} is the weight connecting the i-th component of the input node and the j-th hidden node, v_j is the weight connecting the output node and the j-th hidden nods, and $S(t)$ is a Sigmoidal function. The error function is as follows:

$$r = \frac{1}{2} \sum_m (O^m - y^m)^2$$ (2)

where y^m and O^m are the ideal output and the actual output of the m-the sample, respectively. The error function with regularization term is as follows:

$$r = \frac{1}{2} \sum_m (O^m - y^m)^2 + \lambda \|w\|_1^1$$ (3)

where w is the vector of all the weights. The last term in formula (3) is a regularization term, λ is a parameter, and

$$\|w\|_1^1 = |w_1| + |w_2| + \cdots + |w_n|$$ (4)

The derivative for the absolute value function is:

$$f(w) = |w|$$ (5)

$$f'(w) = (|w|)' = \left\{ \begin{array}{l} 1, w \geq 0 \\ -1, w < 0 \end{array} \right\}$$ (6)

2.2 Gas Mixtures Preparation and Measurement

The goal of this work is to prediction concentration components of VOCs gases mixtures. In the experiments, three 32 gas mixtures are prepared [30]. Each gas sample consists of four gases. They are formaldehyde, toluene, ethanol and acetone. Concentration of each single gas is 1 ppm, 2 ppm, 3 ppm, 4 ppm and 5 ppm. Gas samples are mixed with different concentrations of four gases.

The sensor array is consisted of four different semiconductor gas sensors [31]. Four sensors are sensitive to formaldehyde, toluene, ethanol and acetone. Table 1 shows the details of sensors.

Table 1. The details of sensors

Sensors	Manufacturers	Basic sensing materials	Doped sensing materials
1#	Our laboratory	SnO_2	Nothing
2#	Our laboratory	SnO_2	Pd
3#	Our laboratory	SnO_2	Zr
4#	Our laboratory	SnO_2	$La_{0.7}Sr_{0.3}FeO_3$

2.3 Pruning Rules of Nodes

The neural network is established and trained. According to the weight of input layer to hidden layer, some nodes in networks are removed. The rules of pruning are as follows:

(1) A node that connects single hidden layer with a weight of 0 is the node that can be deleted. It is mathematical meaning of regularization term.
(2) A node that can be deleted when the node has more than 50% of weights approaching to zero. In accordance with meaning of sensor array to delete this node, in the selection of sensor array, each sensor array can have a response value of every kind of mixed gas, if a node has more than 50% weight approaching to zero, sensors provide information does not meet the situation.
(3) Two weights of a node are more than 100 times different, the node can be deleted. Based on the weights of neural networks in gas mixture identification are basically balanced.
(4) A node's weight is less than the preset value, the node can be deleted. The set value is determined according to analysis of characteristics of the sensor.

2.4 The Process of Determining Nodes Number of Hidden Layer

The specific process of determining nodes number of hidden layer in neural networks is as follows:

(1) Establishing basic structure of neural networks. Determine the number of nodes in the input layer and output layer. Determine the initial parameters of neural networks, such as the learning rate.
(2) Select a relatively large number as the initial nodes number of hidden layer. Start training;
(3) Prune nodes of hidden layer, according to the pruning rules of nodes in hidden layer;
(4) Stop pruning until nodes of hidden layer can't be pruned, or the network meets requirements of experiment. Otherwise, number of nodes is reset according to the number of nodes after the last trimming, and restart from step (2).

3   Results and Discussion

In this paper, 24 gas samples were randomly selected to train BP neural network with and without L1 regularization, 8 gas samples were used as test samples. Two BP neural networks were single hidden layer networks. Nodes number of input layer was determined by the number of sensors in sensor array. The input layer had 4 nodes that corresponded to response values of the four sensors. Nodes number of output layer was determined according to gas components in gas samples. The output layer had 4 nodes that corresponded to four components in gas mixtures. Two BP neural networks had different node number of hidden layer. The neural network without regularization was a comparison of experimental results. The neural network with L2 regularization will makes all weights of the neural network approach zero, so the neural network with L1 regularization was employed in this paper.

Initial nodes number of hidden layer was determined to be 60. After completion of training, 20 nodes were deleted according to the pruning rule of nodes, and first test results of networks did not meet requirements. Nodes number of hidden layer was determined to be 40, second training was performed, 24 nodes were deleted according to the pruning rule of nodes, and final nodes number of hidden was 16.

The error is an important index to evaluate the performance of a neural network. The mean square error (MSE) is used as an evaluation method in concentration prediction. Formula is as follows:

$$MSE = \frac{1}{n} \sum_{i=1}^{n} (observed_i - predicted_i)^2 \qquad (7)$$

Figure 1 shows test error of BP neural network with nodes number of hidden layer from 4 to 20. The optimal number of nodes is 11, and the mean square error of neural network with 15 nodes and 17 nodes is small too. Nodes number of determined by the pruning method is 16. Difference of mean square error between them is 0.2. The pruning method can effectively determine nodes number of hidden layer.

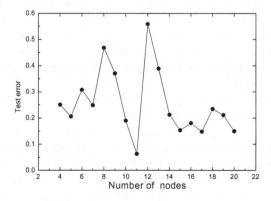

Fig. 1. Test error of BP neural network with nodes number of hidden layer

Predicting concentration of gas components in 8 test samples is given in Fig. 2(a–d) for formaldehyde, ethanol, acetone and toluene, respectively. The maximum difference of predicted value and true value of formaldehyde is 0.19 in Fig. 2(a). Prediction error of acetone is smaller, and the absolute error between the 5 test values of 1 ppm acetone is within 0.04 in Fig. 2(d).

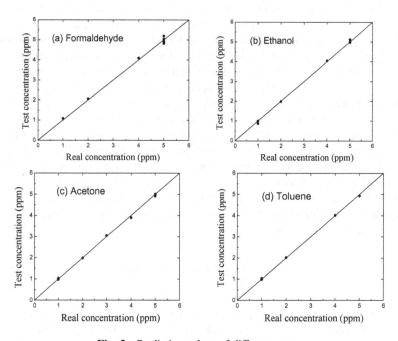

Fig. 2. Predictive values of different gases

4   Conclusion

In this paper, a sensor array is composed of four sensors, and 32 gas mixtures of four components containing formaldehyde, ethanol, acetone and toluene is made. Response data of sensor array to gas mixtures are analyzed by BP neural network, and each component concentration of gas mixtures is predicted. Experimental data show that the maximum error of prediction is not more than 0.19, and multiple predictive values to one component are stable.

Structure of networks is directly related to performance of networks. In this paper, the back propagation (BP) neural network with L1 regularization terms is employed. Characteristics of regularization terms are that the terms make partly weights approach to zero. According to this Characteristics combined with characteristics of sensor array, developed node pruning rules of hidden layer. Based on pruning rules, nodes number of hidden layer is determined by pruning method in a single hidden layer BP neural network. Nodes number of hidden layer determined by pruning method is a better solution, and nodes number is determined by several exhaustive methods is the interval optimal solution, the test mean square error for the same samples between two networks with different nodes number of hidden layer determined by two methods is 0.2.

Acknowledgement. The authors thank The National Natural Science Foundation of China (61574025) for financial support.

References

1. Koc, H., King, J., Teschl, G., Unterkofler, K., Teschl, S., Mochalski, P., Hinterhuber, H., Amann, A.: The role of mathematical modeling in VOC analysis using isoprene as a prototypic example. J. Breath Res. **5**(3), 037102 (2011)
2. Mirzaei, A., Leonardi, S.G., Neri, G.: Detection of hazardous volatile organic compounds (VOCs) by metal oxide nanostructures-based gas sensors: a review. Ceram. Int. **42**(14), 15119–15141 (2016)
3. Saalberg, Y., Wolff, M.: VOC breath biomarkers in lung cancer. Clin. Chim. Acta **459**, 5–9 (2016)
4. Ayhan, B., Kwan, C., Zhou, J., Kish, L.B., Benkstein, K.D., Rogers, P.H., Semancik, S.: Fluctuation enhanced sensing (FES) with a nanostructured, semiconducting metal oxide film for gas detection and classification. Sens. Actuators B Chem. **188**(11), 651–660 (2013)
5. Kwan, C., Schmera, G., Smulko, J., Kish, L.B., Heszler, P., Granqvist, C.G.: Advanced agent identification at fluctuation-enhanced sensing. IEEE Sens. J. **8**, 706–713 (2008)
6. Li, W., Leung, H., Kwan, C., Linnell, B.R.: E-nose vapor identification based on Dempster–Shafer fusion of multiple classifiers. IEEE Trans. Instrum. Meas. **57**(10), 2273–2282 (2008)
7. Kwan, C., Ayhan, B., Chen, G., Wang, J., Ji, B., Chang, C.I.: A novel approach for spectral unmixing, classification, and concentration estimation of chemical and biological agents. IEEE Trans. Geosci. Remote Sens. **44**(2), 409–419 (2006)
8. Ampuero, S., Bosset, J.O.: The electronic nose applied to dairy products: a review. Sens. Actuators B Chem. **94**(1), 1–12 (2003)
9. Krutzler, C., Unger, A., Marhold, H., Fricke, T., Conrad, T., Schütze, A.: Influence of MOS gas-sensor production tolerances on pattern recognition techniques in electronic noses. IEEE Trans. Instrum. Meas. **61**, 276–283 (2012)
10. Russo, D.V., Burek, M.J., Iutzi, R.M., Mracek, J.A., Hesjedal, T.: Development of an electronic nose sensing platform for undergraduate education in nanotechnology. Eur. J. Phys. **32**(32), 675 (2011)
11. Kim, H., Konnanath, B., Sattigeri, P., Wang, J., Mulchandani, A., Myung, N., Deshusses, M. A., Spanias, A., Bakkaloglu, B.: Electronic-nose for detecting environmental pollutants: signal processing and analog front-end design. Analog Integr. Circ. Sig. Process **70**(1), 15–32 (2012)
12. Hou, C., Li, J., Huo, D., Luo, X., Dong, J., Yang, M., Shi, X.J.: A portable embedded toxic gas detection device based on a cross-responsive sensor array. Sens. Actuators B Chem. **161** (1), 244–250 (2012)
13. Youn, C., Kawashima, K., Kagawa, T.: Concentration measurement systems with stable solutions for binary gas mixtures using two flowmeters. Meas. Sci. Technol. **22**(6), 065401 (2011)
14. Loui, A., Sirbuly, D.J., Elhadj, S., Mccall, S.K., Hart, B.R., Ratto, T.V.: Detection and discrimination of pure gases and binary mixtures using a dual-modality microcantilever sensor. Sens. Actuators, A: Phys. **159**(1), 58–63 (2010)

15. Lv, P., Tang, Z., Wei, G., Yu, J., Huang, Z.: Recognizing indoor formaldehyde in binary gas mixtures with a micro gas sensor array and a neural network. Meas. Sci. Technol. **18**(9), 2997 (2007)

16. Lewis, E., Sheridan, C., O'Farrell, M., King, D., Flanagan, C., Lyons, W.B., Fitzpatrick, C.: Principal component analysis and artificial neural network based approach to analysing optical fibre sensors signals. Sens. Actuators, A: Phys. **136**(1), 28–38 (2007)

17. Bahraminejad, B., Basri, S., Isa, M., Hambali, Z.: Application of a sensor array based on capillary-attached conductive gas sensors for odor identification. Meas. Sci. Technol. **21**(21), 085204 (2010)

18. Ehret, B., Safenreiter, K., Lorenz, F., Biermann, J.: A new feature extraction method for odour classification. Sens. Actuators B Chem. **158**(1), 75–88 (2011)

19. Argyri, A.A., Panagou, E.Z., Tarantilis, P.A., Polysiou, M., Nychas, G.J.E.: Rapid qualitative and quantitative detection of beef fillets spoilage based on fourier transform infrared spectroscopy data and artificial neural networks. Sens. Actuators B Chem. **145**(1), 146–154 (2009)

20. Alquraishi, A.A., Shokir, E.M.: Artificial neural networks modeling for hydrocarbon gas viscosity and density estimation. J. King Saud Univ. – Eng. Sci. **23**(2), 123–129 (2011)

21. Song, K., Wang, Q., Liu, Q., Zhang, H., Cheng, Y.: A wireless electronic nose system using a Fe_2O_3 gas sensing array and least squares support vector regression. Sensors **11**(1), 485–505 (2011)

22. Wu, W., Wang, J., Cheng, M., Li, Z.: Convergence analysis of online gradient method for BP neural networks. Neural Netw. **24**(1), 91–98 (2011)

23. Rumelhart, D.E., Hinton, G.E., Williams, R.J.: Learning representations by back-propagating errors. Nature **323**(6088), 399–421 (1988). Readings in Cognitive Science

24. Zhong, H., Miao, C., Shen, Z., Feng, Y.: Comparing the learning effectiveness of BP, ELM, I-ELM, and SVM for corporate credit ratings. Neurocomputing **128**(5), 285–295 (2014)

25. Liang, Y.C., Feng, D.P., Lee, H.P., Lim, S.P., Lee, K.H.: Successive approximation training algorithm for feedforward neural networks. Neurocomputing **42**(1), 311–322 (2002)

26. Stathakis, D.: How many hidden layers and nodes? Int. J. Remote Sens. **30**(8), 2133–2147 (2009)

27. Loone, S.M., Irwin, G.: Improving neural network training solutions using regularization. Neurocomputing **37**, 71–90 (2001)

28. Setiono, R.: A penalty-function approach for pruning feedforward neural networks. Neural Comput. **9**(1), 185–204 (1997)

29. Shao, H., Xu, D., Zheng, G., Liu, L.: Convergence of an online gradient method with inner-product penalty and adaptive momentum. Neurocomputing **77**(1), 243–252 (2012)

30. Zhao, L., Li, X., Wang, J., Yao, P., Akbar, S.A.: Detection of formaldehyde in mixed VOCs gases using sensor array with neural networks. IEEE Sens. J. **16**(15), 6081–6086 (2016)

31. Zhao, L., Wang, J., Li, X.: Identification of formaldehyde under different interfering gas conditions with nanostructured semiconductor gas sensors. Nanomater. Nanotechnol. **5**, 1 (2015)

Fusion of Laser Point Clouds and Color Images with Post-calibration

Xiao-Chuan Zhang, Qiu-Hua Lin[✉], and Ying-Guang Hao

School of Information and Communication Engineering,
Dalian University of Technology, Dalian 116023, China
qhlin@dlut.edu.cn

Abstract. Fusion of laser point clouds and color images has a great advantage in the photogrammetry, computer vision, and computer graphics communities. Most of existing methods estimate the projection matrix for mapping laser points to image pixels based on pre-calibration using checkboard patterns. We propose a method with post-calibration based on reference objects. We first generate an ideal projection matrix based on the pinhole camera model and the positional relationship between the laser scanner and the camera. We then correct the projection matrix based on the reference objects having longer vertical edges, as it is easy to detect the edge of the laser points. The horizontal coordinate offset is computed using the laser points and pixels at the vertical edges, and this is finally added to the projection matrix. Our method reduces the complexity of the data fusion. Experimental results verify the correctness of our method.

Keywords: Color point cloud · Laser · Image · Pinhole camera model
Post-calibration

1 Introduction

Laser scanning has developed rapidly in recent years and has become a new type of measurement technique. Laser scanner can obtain three-dimensional (3D) coordinates of a target quickly and accurately, and form 3D point clouds. Although laser point clouds lack of color information and texture information, the information can be provided by cameras. As such, the data fusion of the two sensors has become a hot topic. The 3D color point clouds can be specifically obtained by fusing laser point clouds and the image information, and they can be applied in various fields such as the photogrammetry, computer vision, and computer graphics communities [1].

The existing fusion methods mainly depend on the manual selection of the correspondences between the laser points and the image pixels. The basic principle is to find the corresponding points of checkboard patterns for the laser points and the camera pixels [2–7]. Zhang and Pless proposed a method using different poses of checkboard patterns and recording the corresponding points of the laser points and the image. Its core technology was to minimize an algebraic error and the rejection error by subsequent nonlinear refinement [2]. Ha proposed to use the triangular hole information and the line information to establish the correspondences [3]. Geiger et al. proposed a

© Springer International Publishing AG, part of Springer Nature 2018
T. Huang et al. (Eds.): ISNN 2018, LNCS 10878, pp. 549–556, 2018.
https://doi.org/10.1007/978-3-319-92537-0_63

method which needed more than one checkerboard patterns attached on the walls and the floors. The method identified planes from laser points by using segmentation, generated the transformation hypotheses by associating the planes randomly and refined the best ones to get the solution [4]. Khosravian et al. transformed the checkboard extraction into a combinatorial optimization problem, and performed optimization with a branch-and-bound technique [5]. There are also other methods, for example, image registration methods for fusing data based on a common reference frame and the line information [8].

In order to reduce the complexity of the data fusion, we focus on fusion of the laser points and the images without checkerboard patterns. We estimate the projection matrix based on pinhole camera model and the positional relationship between the laser scanner and the camera. We select objects with longer vertical edges as references to adjust the projection matrix, which is called post-calibration. The proposed method is flexible to adapt to a new sensors placement by measuring the new positional relationship and performing post-calibration to adjust the offset. Experimental testing is carried out using the KITTI dataset [9].

The rest of this paper is organized as follows. Section 2 describes the proposed method for estimating the projection matrix based on pinhole camera model and the positional relationship between sensors. Section 3 presents experiments and results. Section 4 is the Conclusion.

2   The Proposed Method

When the data are collected, the laser scanner and the camera are placed in fixed positions. Thus both sensors have constant absolute coordinates in each other's external coordinate system. Given the positional relationship for the laser scanner and the camera, we here map the laser points to the image pixels based on the pinhole camera model and the rigid coordinate transformation. A laser point is first mapped to a color pixel, and then the RGB value of the corresponding color pixel is added to the laser point. This is to maximally retain the spatial information obtained by the laser scanner, and to enhance the visualization in the meantime.

2.1   The Pinhole Camera Model

The proposed fusion method is to map a point in the 3D space into a pixel in the two-dimensional (2D) image. The pinhole camera model defines the relationship between a 3D spatial point and its imaging pixel. Figure 1 shows the pinhole camera model. In the Figure, $x_c - y_c - z_c$ is the camera coordinate system, the origin o_c of which is located at the focus of the camera, z_c is the optical axis; P is a 3D point with the coordinate of (x, y, z) in the camera coordinate system; $u - v$ is the imaging coordinate system; and (u, v) is the imaging coordinates of the point $P(x, y, z)$ in the image plane.

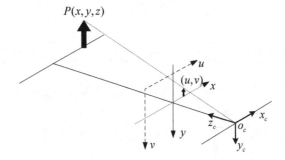

Fig. 1. The pinhole camera model

For the pinhole camera model shown in Fig. 1, the 3D point $P(x, y, z)$ is projected into the 2D image plane $u - v$ with the perspective transformation to form a view of the actual scene. According to the principle of triangular similarity, we have the following relationships [10]:

$$u = f * \frac{x_c}{z_c} + c_x \tag{1}$$

$$v = f * \frac{y_c}{z_c} + c_y \tag{2}$$

where f is the camera focal length in pixels, which is equal to the distance between o_c and the image plane; (c_x, c_y) is the image principal point. The above formula can be expressed as homogeneous coordinates [10]:

$$z_c \begin{bmatrix} u \\ v \\ 1 \end{bmatrix} = \begin{bmatrix} f & 0 & c_x & 0 \\ 0 & f & c_y & 0 \\ 0 & 0 & 1 & 0 \end{bmatrix} \begin{bmatrix} x_c \\ y_c \\ z_c \\ 1 \end{bmatrix} \tag{3}$$

By normalizing, the parameter z_c at the left side of Eq. (3) can be adjusted to 1. For simplicity, we omit z_c in the following.

2.2 Fusion of Laser Point Clouds and Color Images

Figure 2 shows the positional relationship for the laser scanner and the camera, which is based on the sensor setup for the KITTI dataset [9] used in our experiments. In Fig. 2, $x_c - y_c - z_c$ denotes the image coordinate system, whereas $x_l - y_l - z_l$ denotes the coordinate system of the laser points.

Assume the distances between the origins (o_l and o_c) of the two coordinate systems are dx, dy, and dz, respectively, referring to Fig. 2, we have:

$$x_c = -y_l + dy \tag{4}$$

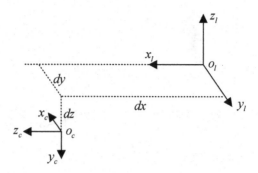

Fig. 2. The positional relationship for the laser scanner and the camera

$$y_c = -z_l - dz \tag{5}$$

$$z_c = x_l - dx \tag{6}$$

Rewriting Eqs. (4)–(6) in matrix, and taking Eq. (3) into account, we obtain the mapping matrix T_{l_c} between a laser point (x_l, y_l, z_l) and an image pixel (u, v):

$$
\begin{bmatrix} u \\ v \\ 1 \end{bmatrix} = \begin{bmatrix} f & 0 & c_x & 0 \\ 0 & f & c_y & 0 \\ 0 & 0 & 1 & 0 \end{bmatrix} \begin{bmatrix} -1 & 0 & 0 & dy \\ 0 & -1 & 0 & -dz \\ 0 & 0 & 1 & -dx \\ 0 & 0 & 0 & 1 \end{bmatrix} \begin{bmatrix} y_l \\ z_l \\ x_l \\ 1 \end{bmatrix} = T_{l\_c} \begin{bmatrix} y_l \\ z_l \\ x_l \\ 1 \end{bmatrix} \tag{7}
$$

2.3 Post-calibration Based on Reference Objects

Considering the projection matrix T_{l_c} is ideal, we next perform post-calibration for Eq. (7) using some objects in the image as references. Since it is easy to detect the edge of the laser image [11], and the scanning lines of the laser scanner are indeed arcs, we choose objects with longer vertical edges as references for post-correction.

Suppose there are N laser points along a vertical edge, and their corresponding image pixels, computed by Eq. (7), are $(u_1, v_1), (u_2, v_2), \ldots, (u_N, v_N)$. We calculate the average horizontal coordinate $\bar{u}_l$ of those points as:

$$\bar{u}_l = \sum_{i=1}^{N} u_i \Big/ N \tag{8}$$

After detecting the vertical edges for the reference object in the image, we select M points at longer edges determined by the Hough trasformation. Similarly, we calculate the average horizontal coordinate $\bar{u}_c$ of these M points:

$$\bar{u}_c = \sum_{i=1}^{M} u_c \Big/ M \qquad (9)$$

Then we have the horizontal coordinate offset for post-calibration:

$$\Delta u = \bar{u}_l - \bar{u}_c \qquad (10)$$

Referring to Eqs. (7) and (10), a simple way for post-calibration is to correct the projection as a whole:

$$\begin{bmatrix} u \\ v \\ 1 \end{bmatrix} = T_{l\_c} \begin{bmatrix} Y_l \\ Z_l \\ X_l \\ 1 \end{bmatrix} + \begin{bmatrix} \Delta u \\ 0 \\ 0 \end{bmatrix} \qquad (11)$$

Other approaches include sub-region correction by using distributed multiple reference objects. That is, multiple horizontal coordinate offsets can be calculated based on multiple reference objects. In this case, the post-calibration is nonlinear as it is composed of multiple sub-region linear correction.

3   Experiments and Results

3.1   Data and Fusion Results

We used the datasets from the KITTI Vision Benchmark Suite (http://www.cvlibs.net/datasets/kitti/) [9] to test the proposed method. The camera shooting frequency is

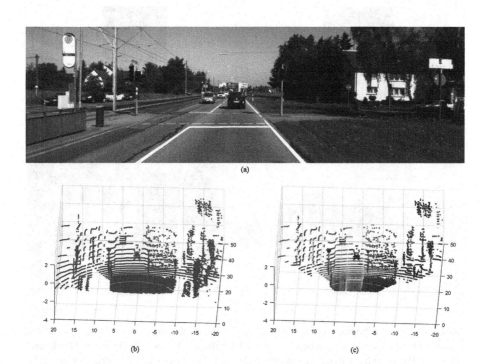

Fig. 3. One exampling fusion result of the proposed method. (a) A color image obtained by the camera; (b) The laser point cloud; (c) The color point cloud generated by the proposed method.

synchronous with the laser scanning frequency. The resolution of the uncompressed corrected image is 1242 × 375 pixels and the principal point (c_x, c_y) is (621, 187.5) (in pixel). The focal length f of the camera is 721.5377 pixels. The distances dx, dy, and dz between the origins of the two coordinate systems are 0.27 m, 0 m and 0.08 m, respectively.

One example of fusion results is shown in Fig. 3. Figure 3(a) shows a color image obtained by the camera. We selected the street lighting on the right side of the road as the reference object, as it has longer vertical edges. Figure 3(b) illustrates the laser point cloud sharing the same scene with Fig. 3(a). Figure 3(c) includes the fusion result of our method based on Eqs. (7)–(11). It can be seen that the 3D point cloud is correctly merged with the corresponding color information of the image.

Fig. 4. The post-calibration results. (a) The fusion result without post-calibration, candidate reference objects for post-calibration are marked by the red boxes; (b) The selected reference object; (c) The edge laser points (in red); (d) The detected edges of the reference object in the image (in red); (e) The post-calibration result (Color figure online)

3.2   Post-calibration Results

Figure 4(a) shows the preliminary result of mapping laser points onto the image without post-calibration. Candidate reference objects for post-calibration are marked by the red boxes. The mismatch between the laser points and the image pixels is visible in these boxes. We used the street lighting on the right side of the road, as shown Fig. 4 (b). We detected the edge points for the laser points in this region, and marked the points in red, as shown in Fig. 4(c). These points are the vertical edge points for post-calibration. The detected edges for the reference object in the image are marked as red lines, as shown in Fig. 4(d). By using Eqs. (8)–(10), we determined the horizontal coordinate offset for post-calibration, and $\Delta u = 10.6$ pixels. By using Eq. (11), we obtain the post-calibration result shown in Fig. 4(e). It is evident that the mismatch between the laser points and the image pixels is invisible after post-calibration, suggesting the correctness of our proposed post-calibration.

4   Conclusion

We proposed a fusion method for mapping laser points to the image pixels by combining the pinhole camera model and post-calibration based on reference objects. In contrast to the existing methods, our method does not require the complicated manual selection of correspondences. It only depends on the camera internal parameters and the positional relationship between the camera and the laser scanner, thus is flexible and easy to implement. Multiple reference objects can be used to perform region-specific post-calibration. In the future, we will study the methods for automatically selecting the areas for local correction.

References

1. Wang, R.: 3D building modeling using images and LiDAR: a review. Int. J. Image Data Fusion **4**, 273–292 (2013)
2. Zhang, Q., Pless, R.: Extrinsic calibration of a camera and laser range finder (improves camera calibration). In: IEEE/RSJ International Conference on Intelligent Robots and Systems, vol. 3, pp. 2301–2306 (2004)
3. Ha, J.-E.: Extrinsic calibration of a camera and laser range finder using a new calibration structure of a plane with a triangular hole. Int. J. Control Autom. Syst. **10**, 1240–1244 (2012)
4. Geiger, A., Moosmann, F., Car, O., Schuster, B.: Automatic camera and range sensor calibration a single shot. In: IEEE International Conference on Robotics and Automation, pp. 3936–3943 (2012)
5. Khosravian, A., Chin, T.-J., Reid, I.: A branch-and-bound algorithm for checkerboard extraction in camera-laser calibration. In: IEEE International Conference on Robotics and Automation, Singapore, pp. 6495–6502 (2017)
6. Unnikrishnan, R., Hebert, M.: Fast extrinsic calibration of a laser rangefinder to a camera. Carnegie Mellon University (2005)
7. Vasconcelos, F., Barreto, J.P., Nunes, U.: A minimal solution for the extrinsic calibration of a camera and a laser-rangefinder. IEEE Trans. Pattern Anal. Mach. Intell. **34**, 2097–2107 (2012)

8. Morgan, M., Habib, A., Al-Ruzouq, R., et al.: Photogrammetric and Lidar data registration using linear features. Photogram. Eng. Remote Sens. **71**, 699–707 (2005)

9. Geiger, A., Lenz, P., Stiller, C., Urtasun, R.: Vision meets robotics: the KITTI dataset. Int. J. Robot. Res. **32**, 1231–1237 (2013)

10. Hartley, R., Zisserman, A.: Multiple View Geometry in Computer Vision. Cambridge University Press, Cambridge (2006)

11. Xia, S., Wang, R.: A fast edge extraction method for mobile lidar point clouds. IEEE Geosci. Remote Sens. Lett. **14**, 1288–1292 (2017)

A Novel Color-Based Data Visualization Approach Using a Circular Interaction Model and Dimensionality Reduction

Jose Alejandro Salazar-Castro[1,2]([✉]), Paul D. Rosero-Montalvo[3,4,5],
Diego Fernando Peña-Unigarro[6], Ana Cristina Umaquinga-Criollo[3,4],
Zenaida Castillo-Marrero[5], Edgardo Javier Revelo-Fuelagán[6],
Diego Hernán Peluffo-Ordóñez[1,5], and César Germán Castellanos-Domínguez[2]

[1] Coorporación Universitaria Autónoma de Nariño, Pasto, Colombia
[2] Universidad Nacional sede Manizales, Manizales, Colombia
joasalazarca@unal.edu.co
[3] Universidad Técnica del Norte, Ibarra, Ecuador
[4] Universidad de Salamanca, Salamanca, Spain
[5] Yachay Tech, Urcuquí, Ecuador
[6] Universidad de Nariño, Pasto, Colombia

Abstract. Dimensionality reduction (DR) methods are able to produce low-dimensional representations of an input data sets which may become intelligible for human perception. Nonetheless, most existing DR approaches lack the ability to naturally provide the users with the faculty of controlability and interactivity. In this connection, data visualization (DataVis) results in an ideal complement. This work presents an integration of DR and DataVis through a new approach for data visualization based on a mixture of DR resultant representations while using visualization principle. Particularly, the mixture is done through a weighted sum, whose weighting factors are defined by the user through a novel interface. The interface's concept relies on the combination of the color-based and geometrical perception in a circular framework so that the users may have a at hand several indicators (shape, color, surface size) to make a decision on a specific data representation. Besides, pairwise similarities are plotted as a non-weighted graph to include a graphic notion of the structure of input data. Therefore, the proposed visualization approach enables the user to interactively combine DR methods, while providing information about the structure of original data, making then the selection of a DR scheme more intuitive.

Keywords: Data visualization · Dimensionality reduction
Interactive interface · Pairwise similarity

© Springer International Publishing AG, part of Springer Nature 2018
T. Huang et al. (Eds.): ISNN 2018, LNCS 10878, pp. 557–567, 2018.
https://doi.org/10.1007/978-3-319-92537-0_64

1 Introduction

Today, computer systems and technological advances are generating a great volume of information. Much of this information is often redundant, unnecessary or even contains erroneous data that at the time of processing can lead to misinterpretation and generate claims under wrong premises. The field of information visualization (IV) aims to generate more intelligible data representations, in such a way that users have a more visual and natural representation, facilitating the resulting data interpretation [8,9]. Broadly, in pattern recognition (PR), the quality of the training/learning stage depends highly on the quality of data [2]. Then, visualization-based preprocess alternatives result convenient, allowing both the generation of customized data representations while preserving the most meaningful information and the increasing the subsequent classification task accuracy [4]. In this sense, dimensionality reduction (DR) has been widely applied as a key stage in the IV and PR [2]. In general, a DR procedure seeks to extract low-dimensional data from a high-dimensional input data set [8,9]. This procedure generates a new data representation (embedded data), which contains the relevant information extracted by following a preestablished criterion, for instance: Preserving distance (as in Classic Multidimensional Scaling - CMDS) or by preserving the topology of the data (as in Locally Linear Embedding - LLE) [5]. More recent criterions as probability distributions divergence-based methods such as stochastic neighbors embedding (SNE) have been emerged [6]. As stated above, the visual data analysis can be improved by integrating DR methods with the interactivity and controllability properties (which comes from the field of IV) using models of user-machine interaction [5,10]. In general, with a more intuitive and natural the model, the better the interactivity as well as visual results [7]. In this work, a new alternative interaction model is proposed to generate representations according to the needs of the users [12]. Specifically, a geometric strategy is proposed to establish the weighting factors for linearly combining DR methods. To do this, we combine three conventional DR methods (CMDS, LLE and t-SNE) [4,6] to achieve an embedded data mix. A geometric approach allows the notion of mixing ratio to be given simply by running along the edges of a figure embedded in a circle. A chromatic approach visually shows the mixture as a color is associated with each method. In this way, the mixture allows to the user for finding adequately embedded data representations in a low-dimension space using a visual and intuitive frame. In this sense, also, artificial intelligence is integrated with the natural intelligence of human beings, generating a strong system for visual data analysis [9]. Finally, for the experiments, an artificial database is used.

The remaining of this paper is organized as follows: In Sect. 2, data visualization using dimensionality reduction is outlined. Section 3 introduces the proposed interactive data visualization scheme aimed at performing customized DR tasks. Section 4 presents the experimental setup and Sect. 5 shows the results. Finally, Sect. 6 gathers some final remarks as conclusions and future work.

2   Data Visualization Using Interactive Dimensionality Reduction

One of the main issues in PR and IV is the generation of appropriated representations for high-dimensional data especially in data with a complex structure. In this case, DR becomes a key stage for generating low-dimensional representations aimed to preserve the structure of data under certain criteria [3,10]. More technically, DR allows the extraction of lower dimensional, relevant information from big collections of data to improve the performance of a PR systems or enabling an intelligible data visualization. Some problems may contain thousands or, even, millions of explanatory variables, and therefore their analysis can involve a high computational burden. Besides, the system capability to generalize may be affected in the presence of noisy and/or irrelevant explanatory variables. DR is the process of discovering the explanatory variables that account for the greatest changes in the output response variable, DR can also be used to visualize data. Mathematically, the goal of dimensionality reduction is to embed a high dimensional data matrix $X = [x_i]_{1 \leq i \leq N}$, where $x_i \in \mathbb{R}^D$, into a low-dimensional, latent data matrix $Y = [y_i]_{1 \leq i \leq N}$ being $y_i \in \mathbb{R}^d$, where $d < D$ [4,5]. Then, given a high-dimensional input data set, the resultant embedding represents a realistic and intelligible visualization [9]. Figure 1 depicts an instance where a manifold (3D Swiss roll) is embedded into a 2D representation, which resembles to an unfolded version of the original manifold.

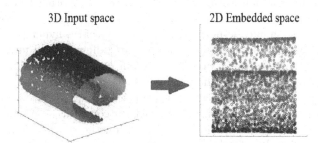

3D Input space   2D Embedded space

Fig. 1. Dimensionality reduction effect over an 3D artificial Swiss roll manifold, the 2D resultant embedded data is an attempt to unfolding the 3D original data.

From an interactive DR (iDR) approach, a traditional paradigm to perform IV using DR begins with the pre-setting of some criteria and parameters, then processing and finally presenting the data in a visual fashion [1]. In this sense, the user can only set initial parameters to obtain the results, so that they can be assessed regarding the requirements. Within this paradigm, users -even experts- might spend long time for setting parameters aimed to valid results. In our work, the user take control of the DR behavior by reconfiguring the algorithms in an iterative way [1] but by means of an interactivity model (as described in Sect. 3). So, the use of the proposed interface becomes more intuitive and interactive allowing even non-expert users readily analyze/explore data visually. The integration of natural intelligence of the human being with computational systems, instead of the use only of machine intelligence, allows to obtain better results.

3   Proposed Model for Interactive Data Visualization Scheme

In this section, the proposed method for interactive data visualization is outlined. Our interactivity model consists of a combination of two spectral, unsupervised methods and one divergence-based method for DR. Such combination is performed by mixing embedded data using a weighted sum. Since it is expected an interface with two relevant properties of information visualization, interactivity and controllability, we proposed a novel model based on a chromatic circle thus, the user can do the mixture by generating weights associated to each DR method. So do that, the user has to interact with a model of DR mixture to visualize X embedded into Y represented in a 2D scatter plot [11]. Let us suppose that the input matrix X is reduced by using M different DR methods, yielding a set of lower-dimensional representations: $\{Y^{(1)}, \cdots, Y^{(M)}\}$. Herein, we propose to perform a weighted sum in the form $\bar{Y} = \sum_{m=1}^{M} \alpha_m Y^m$, where $\{\alpha_1, \cdots, \alpha_M\}$ are the weighting factors. To make the selection of weighting factors intuitive, we use probability values so that $0 \le \alpha_m \le 1$ and $\sum_{m1=1}^{M} \alpha_m = 1$, and therefore all matrices $Y^{(m)}$ should be normalized to rely within a hypersphere of ratios. Hence, an intuitive, interactive interface for high-dimensional data representation into a low-dimensional representation can control such representation by using weights variation across the proposed model.

The Fig. 2 shows the general interface's scheme, that involve three main stages. The first one is the mixture of DR outcomes, the second one is the interactive DR in which the color selected within the color surface defines the embedded data. Finally, the third one carries out the data visualization in which structure information of the input high-dimensional space is added to the visual final representation.

3.1   Interactive, Chromatic-Circle Model

The most common way to represent the light reflected by the objects is the decomposition of the RGB color space in three primary colors red (R), green (G), and blue (B) (see Fig. 3). We can associate intensity values of the channels in a normalized image between 0 and 1 with the decomposition. The sense of vision allows to capture most of the information of the world. Hence, considering that the human beings have a visual nature, a chromatic-based model is proposed

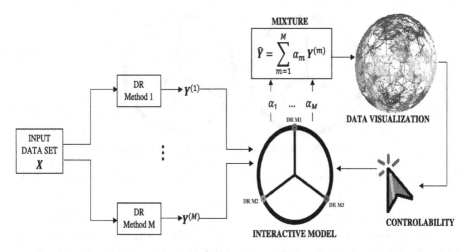

Fig. 2. General interface's scheme of proposed interactive data visualization using DR and similarity-based representations. Roughly speaking, it works as follows: first performs a mixture of resultant lower-dimensional representation spaces by taking advantage of conventional implementations of traditional DR methods. The interaction is provided through a interface that enables user to dynamically input the weighting factors for weighted mixture. A similarity-based model is used for visualizing the embedded data.

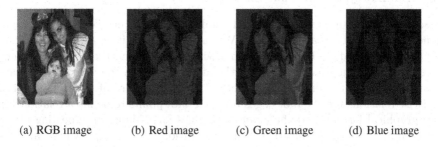

| (a) RGB image | (b) Red image | (c) Green image | (d) Blue image |

Fig. 3. RGB image decomposed into three channels: red (b), green (c), and blue (d). (Color figure online)

to take advantage of the RGB color space. In this paper, it is set to be 8 bits, meaning that every image has 256 intensity values (including the value 0), so the range of all possible intensity values are $\{I \mid 0 \leq I \leq 2^8 - 1\}$ where $I \in \mathbb{Z}$ [7].

In addition, the perception is approached as a fundamental mental activity and this makes it possible a logical decisions and inferences through mental representations. In this sense, the human vision tries to perceive and segment images through the identification of objects within an observed image. This process is done by identifying the edges of the figures or geometric bodies that the

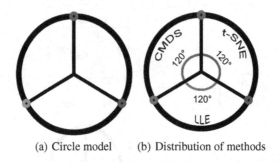

(a) Circle model   (b) Distribution of methods

Fig. 4. Proposed circle representation of the DR methods, each line is separate 120° with each other.

brain processes. Considering this, we propose an interactive model based on a segmented circle by three degrees lines separate 120 in which each section of the circle represent a DR method. The Fig. 4 depicts the proposed model and the Fig. 4(b) shows the distribution of the DR methods in the circle. To generate a novel model, we integrate the chromatic approach of perception with the geometric identification, generating a chromatic, geometric model by combining appropriately the selected DR methods called CMDS, LLE, and t-SNE.

3.2 Similarity-Based Visualization

A scatter plot is used to visualize de embedded data matrix Y of the high-dimensional input data matrix X. We use the similarity-based visualization approach proposed in [9], based on a pairwise similarity matrix $S \in \mathbb{R}^{N \times N}$, such that $S = [s_{ij}]$. The theory graph set the affinity between the i-th and j-th data point from Y as the entries s_{ij}. This holds the structure of X in topological pairwise relationship. We plot edges between data points to define a relationship in a graphical fashion and the amount of edges for making an appealing visual representations is constrained with the condition $s_{ij} > s_{max}$, where s_{max} is the maximum admissible similarity value, which is given by the users. In other words, our visualization approach consists of building a graph with constrained affinity values, the line width allows to generate an idea of how close the points are. If the line is thick, the points are close, on the other hand, if the line is thin, the points are far away.

4 Experimental Setup

4.1 Database, Parameter Settings and DR Methods

In order to visually evaluate the performance of the Chromatic-circle approach, we use both an artificial spherical shell (N = 1500 data points and D = 3) and an artificial Swiss roll (N = 3000 points and D = 3), as is depicted in Fig. 1. By the other hand, with the aim of capturing the local data structure for visualization, i.e. data points being neighbors, we utilize the gaussian similarity given by $s_{ij} = -exp(-0.5\|\boldsymbol{x}_{(i)} - \boldsymbol{x}_{(j)}\|^2/\sigma^2)$, where the parameter σ is a bandwidth value set as 0.1, being the 10% of the hypersphere ratio (applicable once matrices are normalized as discussed in Sect. 3.1). Finally, to perform the dimensionality reduction we consider two spectral DR methods, namely: CMDS and LLE, and one divergence-based method, called t-SNE. All of them are intended to obtain spaces in dimension $d = 2$.

4.2   Performance Measure

To quantify the performance of studied methods, the scaled version of the average agreement rate $R_{NX}(K)$ introduced in [3] is used, which is ranged within the interval $[0, 1]$. Since $R_{NX}(K)$ is calculated at each perplexity value from 2 to $N - 1$, a numerical indicator of the overall performance can be obtained by calculating its area under the curve (AUC). The AUC assesses the dimension reduction quality at all scales, with the most appropriate weights.

5   Results and Discussion

5.1   Interactive Interface

The whole content of the interface is related to pixels, in this way all the data points must be modify and changed only to positive points. Figure 5 depicts the final interface, it shows the interaction model and the possibility of selecting a 3D manifold to perform the iDR. In the upper right side there is a two-dimensional visualization of the input data. In order to give the perception of a 3D manifold to be processed, a turning effect is made on the original data. In the lower right corner, the data embedded in a 2D space is presented.

5.2   Interactive Dimensionality Reduction

As discussed in Sect. 2, the user takes control in a fashion that the DR methods are applied to an input data set by means of interactive adjustment of input parameters. Figure 6 depicts the way as the user can adjust these parameters using the proposed interactive model, for this purpose it is sufficient that the user moves one or all RGB spheres (red, green and blue) through the lines that segment the circle. The user moves only one sphere, the method associated with that sphere will be the only one used, if the user moves two spheres a weighted mixture of the two methods associated with each sphere will be given and if the user moves the three spheres then all methods will be mixed according to the weights related to the movement of the spheres on the lines. Figure 6(a) depicts the movement of the blue spheres for applying the t-SNE method, green

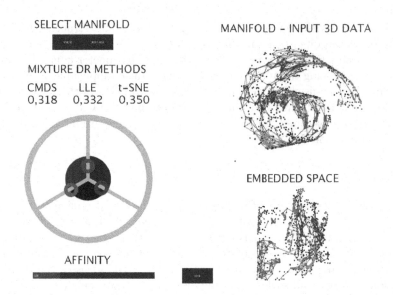

Fig. 5. Final interface for data visualization developed in processing.

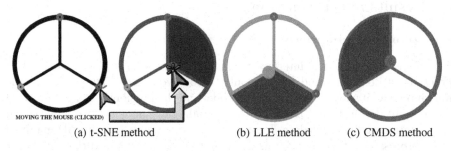

(a) t-SNE method   (b) LLE method   (c) CMDS method

Fig. 6. An example of interactivity the user can move the spheres along the lines that segment the circle for selecting a method. Methods selection through the model: CMDS method in (c), LLE method in (b) and t-SNE method in (a) (Color figure online)

for applying LLE (Fig. 6(b)) and red for applying CMDS (Fig. 6(c)). As discussed in Sect. 3.2, a quality measure allows comparison of results between each of the methods. Figure 7 shows how the combination of methods performs a low-dimension space. Figure 7(i) shows the quality curve that relates the representation of the three methods and the combination of them. This is done for the artificial Swiss roll.

5.3 Similarity Representation

Similarity representations can be made through the affinity section of the interface. To do this, the user must select points within the dedicated bar and this

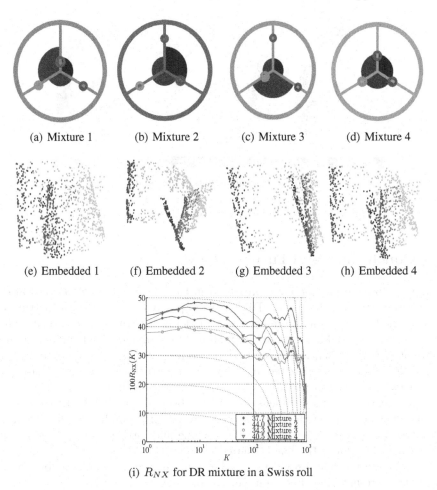

(a) Mixture 1   (b) Mixture 2   (c) Mixture 3   (d) Mixture 4

(e) Embedded 1   (f) Embedded 2   (g) Embedded 3   (h) Embedded 4

(i) R_{NX} for DR mixture in a Swiss roll

Fig. 7. Embedded Swiss roll representations. We apply mixture in different ways and obtained a representation in a low-dimensional space. (i) shows the R_{NX} for the fourth mixtures in the 3D Swiss roll.

will generate representations both in the entry space and in the low dimensional space. Figure 8 shows the affinity results for different selections. It can also be observed that the size of the lines that relate points represents the closeness or distance of these points. If the points are closer the line will be wider than if we have distant points.

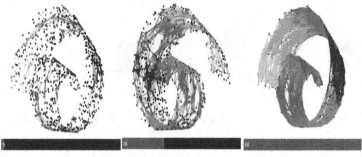

(a) Pairwise-similarities in a Swiss roll

Fig. 8. Pairwise similarity representation in a Swiss roll (a)

6   Conclusions and Future Work

The visualization methodology presented in this work represents a novel alternative way for IV. The use of iDR makes it possible to generate a mixture of DR methods through a chromatic-circle model in a friendly and intuitive way. The resulting embedded data can be modified by interactively changing the mix while it is performing, this ensures that the user selects a representation that suits the data analysis task required. By incorporating a visualization based on similarity, the user can related the data representations in the entry space with the representations of low dimension in the embedded space while these conserve their structure. For this purpose, the lines drawn corresponding to the k-nearest neighbors, the nearest points have a thick line and farthest points have a thin line while the color of the line is related to the color of the point neighborhood. Therefore, our interface provides a graphical, more natural and intelligible notion for data representation that preserves its topology after an iDR.

As future work, the aim is to explore other methods of reducing the dimensionality of data in order to generate low-dimension spaces while preserving the structure of the data and with the minor loss of information. These methods will be integrated into the interface so the circle will be segmented in $360/n$, where n is the number of methods to use for mixing.

Acknowledgments. This work is supported by the "Smart Data Analysis Systems - SDAS" group (http://sdas-group.com). Also, authors acknowledge to the research project "Desarrollo de una metodología de visualizaciń interactiva y eficaz de información en Big Data" supported by Agreement No. 180 November 1st, 2016 by VIPRI, as well as "Grupo de Investigación en Ingeniería Eléctrica y Electrónica - GIIEE", from Universidad de Nariño.

References

1. Díaz, I., Cuadrado, A.A., Pérez, D., García, F.J., Verleysen, M.: Interactive dimensionality reduction for visual analytics. In: Proceedings of the 22th European Symposium on Artificial Neural Networks, Computational Intelligence and Machine Learning (ESANN 2014), pp. 183–188. Citeseer (2014)
2. Fukunaga, K.: Introduction to Statistical Pattern Recognition. Academic Press, Cambridge (2013)
3. Lee, J.A., Renard, E., Bernard, G., Dupont, P., Verleysen, M.: Type 1 and 2 mixtures of Kullback-Leibler divergences as cost functions in dimensionality reduction based on similarity preservation. Neurocomputing **112**, 92–108 (2013)
4. Peluffo-Ordóñez, D.H., Lee, J.A., Verleysen, M.: Short review of dimensionality reduction methods based on stochastic neighbour embedding. In: Villmann, T., Schleif, F.-M., Kaden, M., Lange, M. (eds.) Advances in Self-Organizing Maps and Learning Vector Quantization. AISC, vol. 295, pp. 65–74. Springer, Cham (2014). https://doi.org/10.1007/978-3-319-07695-9_6
5. Peluffo-Ordóñez, D.H., Lee, J.A., Verleysen, M.: Generalized kernel framework for unsupervised spectral methods of dimensionality reduction. In: 2014 IEEE Symposium on Computational Intelligence and Data Mining (CIDM), pp. 171–177. IEEE (2014)
6. Peluffo Ordoñez, D.H., Lee, J.A., Verleysen, M., et al.: Recent methods for dimensionality reduction: a brief comparative analysis. In: 2014 European Symposium on Artificial Neural Networks, Computational Intelligence and Machine Learning (ESANN 2014) (2014)
7. Peña-Unigarro, D.F., Rosero-Montalvo, P., Revelo-Fuelagán, E.J., Castro-Silva, J.A., Alvarado-Pérez, J.C., Therón, R., Ortega-Bustamante, C.M., Peluffo-Ordóñez, D.H.: Interactive data visualization using dimensionality reduction and dissimilarity-based representations. In: Yin, H., et al. (eds.) IDEAL 2017. LNCS, vol. 10585, pp. 461–469. Springer, Cham (2017). https://doi.org/10.1007/978-3-319-68935-7_50
8. Peña-ünigarro, D.F., Salazar-Castro, J.A., Peluffo-Ordóñez, D.H., Rosero-Montalvo, P.D., Oña-Rocha, O.R., Isaza, A.A., Alvarado-Perez, J.C., Theron, R.: Interactive visualization methodology of high-dimensional data with a color-based model for dimensionality reduction. In: 2016 XXI Symposium on Signal Processing, Images and Artificial Vision (STSIVA), pp. 1–7. IEEE (2016)
9. Rosero-Montalvo, P., Diaz, P., Salazar-Castro, J.A., Peña-Unigarro, D.F., Anaya-Isaza, A.J., Alvarado-Pérez, J.C., Therón, R., Peluffo-Ordóñez, D.H.: Interactive data visualization using dimensionality reduction and similarity-based representations. In: Beltrán-Castañón, C., Nyström, I., Famili, F. (eds.) CIARP 2016. LNCS, vol. 10125, pp. 334–342. Springer, Cham (2017). https://doi.org/10.1007/978-3-319-52277-7_41
10. Salazar-Castro, J., Rosas-Narváez, Y., Pantoja, A., Alvarado-Pérez, J.C., Peluffo-Ordóñez, D.H.: Interactive interface for efficient data visualization via a geometric approach. In: 2015 XX Symposium on Signal Processing, Images and Computer Vision (STSIVA), pp. 1–6. IEEE (2015)
11. Sedlmair, M., Munzner, T., Tory, M.: Empirical guidance on scatterplot and dimension reduction technique choices. IEEE Trans. Vis. Comput. Graph. **19**(12), 2634–2643 (2013)
12. Ward, M.O., Grinstein, G., Keim, D.: Interactive Data Visualization: Foundations, Techniques, and Applications. CRC Press, Boca Raton (2010)

Bird Species Recognition Based on Deep Learning and Decision Fusion

Xuye Zhi and Chengan Guo[✉]

School of Information and Communication Engineering,
Dalian University of Technology, Dalian 116023, Liaoning, China
zhixuye@mail.dlut.edu.cn, cguo@dlut.edu.cn

Abstract. Bird species recognition is one of the most challenging tasks in fine-grained visual categorizations (FGVC) and has attracted wide attention in recent years. In this paper, we develop a bird recognition system that consists of three learning-type computational modules: the first one is for extracting the object and key parts from input images that is implemented by training a deep convolutional neural network (CNN) model, the second module is for feature extraction from the detected object and parts by using four other CNNs and further for computation of the high dimensional Gaussian descriptors based on the deep features, and the third module is for getting the final recognition result that is implemented by training four SVM classifiers with the Gaussian descriptors and integrating the outputs of the SVMs together with a decision fusion method. Experiment results obtained in the paper confirm the validity of the proposed approach.

Keywords: Bird species recognition · Convolutional neural network (CNN)
Object detection · High dimensional Gaussian descriptors

1 Introduction

With the deterioration of global ecological situation, birds have been more threatened than ever before. It is urgent to develop automatic bird recognition techniques for protecting birds and conserving the species diversity in the Earth. The computer vision-based bird species recognition is usually considered as a fine-grained visual categorization (FGVC) problem that is more elaborate than the generic image classification problems. The target of generic image classification is to distinguish basic-level categories such as bird and dog from each other while the FGVC is trying to distinguish subordinate-level categories, for example, to distinguish the gull and the tern from each other. Sometimes it is even more difficult since you need to tell an Arctic Tern from a Caspian Tern. Among all the FGVC challenges, the bird species recognition is one of the most complex tasks due to its high intra-class variance caused by changeable pose, occlusion or view point, and its low inter-class variance caused by similar subordinate categories.

In recent years, as a FGVC problem, bird species recognition has become a hot issue and attracted increasing interests with the development of image classification technology. One of the key techniques in bird recognition is the object and part

T. Huang et al. (Eds.): ISNN 2018, LNCS 10878, pp. 568–577, 2018.
https://doi.org/10.1007/978-3-319-92537-0_65

detection since the images of birds usually consist of many other background things in them and the discriminative features of a bird do not just lie on the whole image but also on some specific key parts of the object. Therefore, it is crucial to remove the background interferes and find the critical parts. Zhang et al. [1] proposed the part-based R-CNN that tried to localize the object and the key parts form the fine-grained categories by using the classic R-CNN detection model [2]. To fulfil the detection task in [2], the object and each of the critical parts are treated as independent categories in the classification stage of the R-CNN. In the training time, the ground truth bounding boxes of the object and parts are utilized. Then in the testing time, R-CNN can detect the object as well as the key parts automatically. With the CNN-based deep features for both the object level and part level, this method achieved the classification accuracy of 73.9% on the standard bird dataset Caltech-UCSD Bird Dataset (CUB200-2011) [3]. Huang et al. [4] proposed the part-stacked CNN (PS-CNN) method in which a fully convolutional network (FCN) [5] is adopted to fulfil the localization task and achieved the correct classification rate of 76.2% on the CUB200-2011 based on the deep CNN features. Peng et al. [6] proposed the object-part attention driven discriminative localization (OPADDL) which applied saliency extraction method CAM [7] for object detection and object-part spatial constraints for part detection. The CNN-based features are also used in [6] and the classification rate of 85.8% is obtained on the CUB200-2011.

Another key technique in bird recognition is feature extraction. Although CNN-based deep features are widely used for generic image classification, some other methods have shown better performance for FGVC problems, especially for the bird species recognition. Wang et al. [8] proposed a novel image descriptor called RAID-G which is based on the robust estimation of high dimensional Gaussian and is discriminative enough for bird recognition with the classification accuracy of 82.1% on CUB200-2011. Lin et al. [9] proposed Bilinear Convolutional Networks (B-CNN) that integrated two independent CNNs to extract features. Without any detection process, this method achieved 84.1% classification rate on CUB200-2011. Wei et al. [10] proposed the Mask-CNN method and used the FCN [5] to locate the key parts as well as to generate the weighted masks for selecting useful convolutional features, and, with this method, they have got the classification rate of 87.3% that is the best one among the results published so far on the CUB200-2011 database.

Basing on existing works, we develop a new bird species recognition system which is constituted with three computation modules: the first module is implemented by training a CNN model for detecting/localizing the object and key parts from the input bird image, the second module is composed of four other CNN models with which the deep features are extracted from the detected object and parts and then the deep features are used to compute the RAID-G descriptors, and the third module is for getting the final classification result from the RAID-Gs that is realized with four SVM classifiers and a decision fusion method. Many experiments have been conducted on the CUB200-2011 dataset for the new recognition system and the achieved classification rate is 86.2% that is in the advanced level among the results given by the state-of-the-art methods published in the literature.

The rest of the paper is organized as follows. Section 2 describes the proposed recognition system in detail. Section 3 presents experiment results obtained in the paper and compares them with others. Finally, Sect. 4 draws conclusions and points out the possible direction of the work.

2 Method

The proposed bird recognition system is illustrated in Fig. 1 that is composed of three computational modules: the object and part detection, the feature extraction, and the classification and decision fusion. Given an input image, the object, head and body of the bird in the image are detected/localized and then segmented through the detection module. Then the recognition system is divided into four branches including the branch for processing the original image, the branch for processing the object, the branches for processing the head and the body, respectively. Each branch contains a feature extraction process and a classifier. The intermediate results from different branches are fused to get the final classification result in the classification and decision fusion module. Details on the system will be given in the sequel sections.

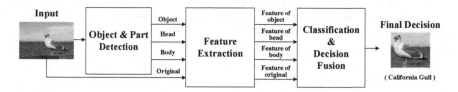

Fig. 1. Block diagram of the proposed method

2.1 Object and Part Detection

As mentioned in Sect. 1, it is crucial to localize the object and key parts of the bird in an input image for achieving a successful recognition. Therefore, the object and part detection module is designed and a deep CNN-based detection model, the single shot detector (SSD) [11], is introduced into the recognition system to fulfil the task. Figure 2 shows the architecture of the SSD used in this paper.

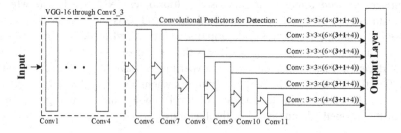

Fig. 2. Architecture of the SSD used in the object and part detection module

The SSD [11] is a fast detection model for predicting the locations of the multiple category objects in an image by using a deep CNN with default boxes. In the detection procedure of the proposed method, the object, head and body of a bird image are treated as different classes in order to localize the object and key parts of the bird image effectively. For the architecture of the SSD model used in this paper, it is modified by setting the channel numbers of the convolutional predictors to $m \times (3 + 1 + 4) = 8m$ to adapt the model to the bird detection problem of the work, where m is the number of default boxes.

2.2 Feature Extraction

As mentioned in Sect. 1, Wang et al. [8] proposed the new image descriptor RAID-G that has been proved to be more discriminative in bird recognition than the CNN features. The RAID-G is the high-dimension version of Gaussian descriptors which are based on the distribution of the local descriptors of an image, and is composed of the mean vector and the covariance matrix of the descriptor data.

In this paper, the RAID-G is introduced into the presented method for feature extraction. In order to obtain the high dimensional characteristics for the RAID-G, the CNN-based deep features are used as the original local descriptors from which the distribution is modeled with multivariate Gaussian. The block diagram of the feature extraction module is shown in Fig. 3 in which the object, head, and body are the image patches obtained from the object and part detection module, the original is the original input image, and X_i $(i = 1, \ldots, 4)$ are the CNN features output from the four VGG-16 networks [12].

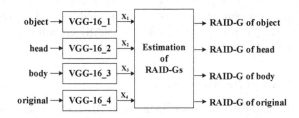

Fig. 3. Block diagram of the feature extraction module

In according to [8], the deep features need to be mapped into the reproducing kernel Hilbert space (RKHS) through a mapping function ϕ. Then RAID-G is estimated in RKHS as follows.

Given a set of features $X = \{x_1, \ldots, x_N | x_k \in R^d\}$, the mean vector μ and the sample covariance matrix S in RKHS can be computed by:

$$\mu = \frac{1}{N} \sum_{k=1}^{N} \phi(x_k) \tag{1}$$

$$S = \frac{1}{N} \sum_{k=1}^{N} (\phi(x_k) - \mu)(\phi(x_k) - \mu)^T \qquad (2)$$

In order to deal with the rank-deficient problem in estimating the covariance matrix S, the following regularized maximum likelihood estimation (MLE) method is used in [8] to re-estimate the covariance matrix by:

$$\sum = U \, diag(\lambda_k) \, U^T \qquad (3)$$

$$\lambda_k = \sqrt{(\frac{1-\alpha}{2\alpha})^2 + \frac{\delta_k}{\alpha}} - \frac{1-\alpha}{2\alpha} \qquad (4)$$

where $diag(\delta_k) = U^T S U$ with U the orthogonal matrix composed of eigenvectors and $diag(\delta_k)$ the diagonal matrix of the singular values in decreasing order, of S, and $\alpha \in (0, 1)$ is the regularized term.

After obtaining the mean vector μ and the matrix $\sum$ by above equations, a new matrix $G(\beta)$ is constructed in [8] by

$$G(\beta) = \begin{bmatrix} \sum + \beta^2 \mu \mu^T & \beta \mu \\ \beta \mu^T & 1 \end{bmatrix} \qquad (5)$$

where $\beta > 0$ is the weight parameter to balance the magnitude order of $\sum$ and μ.

Then the RAID-G feature vector is constructed with the upper triangular elements of $G(\beta)$ in [8]. As shown in Fig. 3, four RAID-G feature vectors are computed in this process for the three key parts (i.e., the object, head, and body of the bird image) and the original image, respectively, and then the four RAID-Gs will be used as the input data to train four SVM classifiers in the next module.

2.3   Classification and Decision Fusion

In the classification and decision fusion module, the RAID-G features are used as the image descriptors for making final classification of the bird in an input image. Figure 4 shows the block diagram of the module, in which four SVM-based classifiers are trained by using the RAID-Gs to obtain four intermediate classification results that are represented in score values (the score_obj, score_head, score_body, and score_orig).

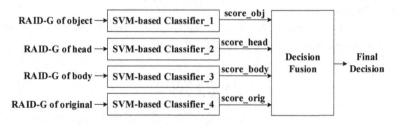

Fig. 4. Block diagram of the classification and decision fusion module

Based on the scores, the final decision (or classification) is made by a decision-level fusion strategy that will be given later in the section.

In the work, the SVM-based classifiers are designed with the one-versus-all version of the multi-class SVMs. Different from the commonly used one-versus-all SVM classifier that takes the highest output value as the final decision, here the linear output values of the SVMs are treated as the scores of different categories which are integrated with the following fusion method:

$$score\_final = w_1\,score\_orig + w_2\,score\_obj + w_3\,score\_head + w_4\,score\_body \quad (6)$$

where w_1, w_2, w_3 and w_4 are fusion weights, and $\sum_i w_i = 1$. The weight values can be determined by experiments in the training stage of the SVMs. For simplicity, the weights can also be set to equal, which means all the classifiers play the same role in the final decision.

As shown in Fig. 4, the four SVM classifiers are different from each other since they are trained by using different RAID-G data, i.e., the RAID-G of object, the RAID-G of head, and the RAID-G of body as well as the RAID-G of original image, respectively. Therefore, each classifier will give its classification results with different scores for a bird in an image. Based on the final scores obtained from the four SVM-based classifiers, the final decision of the fusion system is made for the category of the bird in the image by taking the highest final score in the following way:

$$final\ decision = \arg\max_{k \in N_C}\{\,score\_final\,(k)\,\} \quad (7)$$

where N_C is the number of the categories of the birds being classified.

3   Experiments

In this section, we present the experiment results obtained in the work and give comparison analyses between the proposed approach and the other existing state-of-the-art methods.

3.1   Implementation Settings

The proposed recognition system is implemented on a CPU+GPU platform with the CPU of the Intel®Core™ i7-7700@3.60 GHz and the GPU of the NVIDIA GeForce GTX 1080Ti, on which the experiments are conducted. The deep CNN networks including the SSD and the VGGs used in the recognition system are implemented with the open-source package Caffe [13]. The stochastic gradient descent (SGD) algorithm provided by VLFeat [14] is used to train the SVM classifiers. In the paper, all the experiments are conducted on the Caltech-UCSD Bird Dataset (CUB200-2011) [3] which is a widely-used fine-grained benchmark with total 11788 images for 200 categories of birds. Each image has detailed annotations including a subcategory label, an object bounding box and at most 15 points for part locations. For fair comparison, the experiments in training stage and testing stage are based on the dataset partition provided by the CUB200-2011 with 5994 images for training and 5794 images for testing, respectively.

In the implementation of the proposed method, in order to localize the object, head and body of the bird in an image automatically, the SSD model is trained by using the object bounding boxes and the part annotations provided by the CUB200-2011 so that it can fulfil the three-way detection task. In the feature extraction module, four VGG-16 models are exploited to generate the deep features, X_i $(i = 1, \ldots, 4)$, from their convolutional layer conv5_3, and then the deep features are used as the input arguments for generating the more discriminative RAID-G descriptors. The four VGG-16 models were pre-trained on ImageNet [15] and they are re-trained in the experiments by using the original bird image and the detected part images (the object, head and body), respectively. According to [8], the regularization parameter α in (4) is set to 0.75 and the parameter β in (5) is set to 0.3. In addition, the Hellinger mapping function (the element-wise square root function), $\phi_{Hel}(x_k) = \sqrt{x_k}$, is applied to map the original feature space into RKHS. And, in the implementation of the classification and decision fusion module, the fusion weights are set in different settings for getting better performance that will be discussed in Sect. 3.3.

3.2   Comparison Analysis

Table 1 gives the experiment results obtained in the paper and the results from several state-of-the-art methods published so far on the CUB200-2011 database. From Table 1, one can see that the recognition accuracy obtained by the proposed method is 86.2% that is at the position of top-2 among the results given by the existing methods. The result of top-1 is obtained by Wei et al. [10], in which the Mask-CNN model is combined with the ResNet-50 [16] that is a deeper and more effective network. As a comparison, the method of Mask-CNN with VGG-16 is also given in [10] by combining the Mask-CNN model with the VGG-16, in which the recognition accuracy is at top-4 among the results listed in the table.

Table 1. Comparison with the state-of-the-art methods tested on CUB200-2011

Method	Accuracy (%)
Part-based R-CNN [1]	73.9
PS-CNN [4]	76.2
RAID-G [8]	82.1
B-CNN [9]	84.1
Mask-CNN with VGG-16 [10]	85.7
OPADDL [6]	85.8
Proposed	**86.2**
Mask-CNN with ResNet-50 [10]	**87.3**

3.3 Evaluation on Fusion Strategy

As described in Sect. 2, the final recognition result of the proposed method is the fusion of the classification results from four branch classifiers that correspond to the branches of object, head, body, and original, respectively. In view that using different fusion strategy may generate different classification performance, the experiments on testing what fusion strategy is better are also conducted in the paper and Table 2 gives the experimental results in which the weight values in each fusion strategy are set to equal.

From Table 2, we can see the following points: (1) The object branch can give better performance than the original branch which means that the background in the original image may generate some interference with the recognition; (2) Both the head branch and the body branch have played important roles in the recognition system, especially when they are used together in the fusion process, although each of them cannot get a good enough result compared with the other branches when only using one of them; (3) The highest recognition rate is obtained when the branches of the object (or original), head and body are fused together. (4) The performance goes down a little bit while fusing all the four branches together, which shows that it may not be necessary to use both the object branch and the original branch together and one of them would be enough for the fusion method. However, more experiments need to be conducted for verification of this instance.

Table 2. Performance of different fusion strategies in the proposed method

Classifier branch				Fusion results
Original	Object	Part		Accuracy (%)
		Head	Body	
✓				81.0
	✓			82.9
		✓		80.5
			✓	76.8
		✓	✓	85.8
	✓	✓	✓	**86.2**
✓		✓	✓	**86.2**
✓	✓	✓	✓	86.0

4   Summary and Future Work

In this paper, we designed a bird species recognition system that is composed of three computational modules: the object and part detection, the feature extraction as well as the classification and decision fusion. The SSD model is introduced into the first module to localize the object and key parts of the bird in an input image. In the second module, four VGG-16 models are trained for extracting the deep features from the object, head, body, and original images, respectively, and then the more discriminative RAID-G descriptors are generated based on the learned deep features. In the classification and decision fusion module, four SVM classifiers with the four RAID-Gs as input data are trained to get the category information from their inputs. Finally, the category information from the four branch classifiers is fused to get the final recognition result about the input image. Many experiments have been conducted for the proposed approach by using the bird dataset CUB200-2011 in the work and the validity of the method has been confirmed by the experiment results.

In the presented method, both the second module and the third module contain four computation branches that brings about additional three times the computation load. It is noticed that efficient parallel algorithms can be developed for solving this problem, which is the future direction of the work.

References

1. Zhang, N., Donahue, J., Girshick, R., Darrell, T.: Part-based R-CNNs for fine-grained category detection. In: Fleet, D., Pajdla, T., Schiele, B., Tuytelaars, T. (eds.) ECCV 2014. LNCS, vol. 8689, pp. 834–849. Springer, Cham (2014). https://doi.org/10.1007/978-3-319-10590-1_54
2. Girshick, R., Donahue, J., Darrell, T., Malik, J.: Rich feature hierarchies for accurate object detection and semantic segmentation. In: IEEE Conference on Computer Vision and Pattern Recognition, pp. 580–587. IEEE Press, Columbia (2014)
3. Wah, C., Branson, S., Welinder, P., Perona, P., Belongie, S.: The Caltech-UCSD Bird-200-2011 dataset. Technical report CNS-TR-2011-001, Caltech (2011)
4. Huang, S., Xu, Z., Tao, D., Zhang, Y.: Part-stacked CNN for fine-grained visual categorization. In: IEEE Conference on Computer Vision and Pattern Recognition, pp. 1173–1182. IEEE Press, Las Vegas (2016)
5. Long, J., Shelhamer, E., Darrell, T.: Fully convolutional networks for semantic segmentation. In: IEEE Conference on Computer Vision and Pattern Recognition, pp. 3431–3440. IEEE Press, Boston (2015)
6. Peng, Y., He, X., Zhao, J.: Object-part attention driven discriminative localization for fine-grained image classification. arXiv:1704.01740v2 (2017)
7. Zhou, B., Khosla, A., Lapedriza, A., Oliva, A., Torralba, A.: Learning deep features for discriminative localization. In: IEEE Conference on Computer Vision and Pattern Recognition, pp. 2921–2929. IEEE Press, Las Vegas (2016)
8. Wang, Q., Li, P., Zuo, W., Zhang, L.: RAID-G: robust estimation of approximation infinite dimensional Gaussian with application to material recognition. In: IEEE Conference on Computer Vision and Pattern Recognition, pp. 4433–4441. IEEE Press, Las Vegas (2016)
9. Lin, T.Y., Roychowdhury, A., Maji, S.: Bilinear CNN models for fine-grained visual recognition. In: IEEE Conference on Computer Vision and Pattern Recognition, pp. 1449–1457. IEEE Press, Boston (2015)
10. Wei, X., Xie, C., Wu, J., Shen, C.: Mask-CNN: localizing parts and selecting descriptors for fine-grained bird species categorization. arXiv:1605.06878v1 (2016)
11. Liu, W., Anguelov, D., Erhan, D., Szegedy, C., Reed, S., Fu, C.-Y., Berg, Alexander C.: SSD: single shot multibox detector. In: Leibe, B., Matas, J., Sebe, N., Welling, M. (eds.) ECCV 2016. LNCS, vol. 9905, pp. 21–37. Springer, Cham (2016). https://doi.org/10.1007/978-3-319-46448-0_2

12. Simonyan, K., Zisserman, A.: Very deep convolutional networks for large-scale image recognition. In: International Conference on Learning Representations, pp. 1–14. San Diego (2015)
13. Jia, Y., Shelhamer, E., Donahue, J., Karayev, S., Long, J., Girshick, R., Guadarrama, S., Darrell, T.: Caffe: convolutional architecture for fast feature embedding. In: The 22nd ACM International Conference on Multimedia, pp. 675–678. ACM, Orlando (2014)
14. Vedaldi, A., Fulkerson, B.: VLFeat: an open and portable library of computer vision algorithms. In: The 18th ACM International Conference on Multimedia, pp. 1469–1472. ACM, Firenze (2010)
15. Deng, J., Dong, W., Socher, R., Li, L., Li, K., Li, F.: ImageNet: a large-scale hierarchical image database. In: IEEE Conference on Computer Vision and Pattern Recognition, pp. 248–255. IEEE Press, Miami (2009)
16. He, K., Zhang, X., Ren, S., Sun, J.: Deep residual learning for image recognition. In: IEEE Conference on Computer Vision and Pattern Recognition, pp. 770–778. IEEE Press, Las Vegas (2016)

Chinese News Text Classification of the Stacked Denoising Auto Encoder Based on Adaptive Learning Rate and Additional Momentum Item

Shuang Qiu[1], Mingyang Jiang[2(✉)], Zhifeng Zhang[2], Yinan Lu[3], and Zhili Pei[2(✉)]

[1] College of Mathematics, Inner Mongolia University for Nationalities, Tongliao, China
615339222@qq.com
[2] College of Computer Science and Technology, Inner Mongolia University for Nationalities, Tongliao, China
zhilipei@sina.com
[3] College of Computer Science and Technology, Jilin University, Changchun 130012, China

Abstract. In order to solve the problem of long training time that the Stacked Denoising Auto Encoder (SDAE) has. A kind of new SDAE is proposed which is based on adaptive learning rate and additional momentum term (LMSDAE). Finally, the LMSDAE is tested by Chinese News Text. The experimental results show that compared with the other three algorithms: SDAE, Sparse Denoising Auto Encoder (SPDAE) and Deep Belief Nets (DBN), the LMSDAE algorithm reduced the training times and increased the convergence rate. The accuracy of text classification can reach 87.95%.

Keywords: Stacked Denoising Auto Encoder · Adaptive learning rate
Additional momentum term · Text classification

1 Introduction

News information is an important component of social information resources. The classification of news is helpful to the realization of news order and news mining. With the rapid development of the Internet, people use news text classification frequently. But the growing dimension of the data make it difficult to deal with.

The powerful learning style and data-handling capacity of Denoising Auto Encoder which is proposed by Vincent [6] solve many recognition problems. DAE algorithm can reduce the noise interference and makes the features more robust. SDAE is a deep neural network consisting of multiple DAE. LMSDAE algorithm proposed in this paper adds adaptive learning rate and additional momentum term into SDAE algorithm, in order to improve the convergence rate of SDAE algorithm. And then this paper designs a weight training method based on LMSDAE which is tested by the classification of Chinese news text.

© Springer International Publishing AG, part of Springer Nature 2018
T. Huang et al. (Eds.): ISNN 2018, LNCS 10878, pp. 578–584, 2018.
https://doi.org/10.1007/978-3-319-92537-0_66

2 Correlation Theory

2.1 SDAE Algorithm

DAE algorithm is unsupervised learning. Unlike AE algorithm, the main idea of DAE algorithm is polluting sample data by add noise to the original data with a certain probability. It is the destruction of the original data. Then the data is input into a DAE. The polluted data is mapping to the hidden layer through activation function. And initial data is obtained by reconstruction error.

Compared with shallow neural networks, deep neural network is more efficient in learning features. But deep neural network is difficult to train, and its model is more complex. The basic idea of SDAE is: Take a DAE as a constituent part to build a deep neural network consist of many such DAE. The output of above layer is used as the input of following layer. During the course of training, the input must add the noise. And in the course of fine tuning, it must use initial data.

2.2 Adaptive Learning Rate

Learning rate has a great influence on the speed of convergence, it has a direct impact on training accuracy [1]. If the step is too small, it will lead to a slow learning process. Although high learning rate can accelerate the speed of learning, it may also cause the shock of learning process. This problem can be solved effectively if the learning rate can be adjust automatically during the learning process. A common adjustment formula of adaptive learning rate is:

$$\eta(k+1) = \begin{cases} 1.05\eta(k) & E(k+1) < E(k); \\ 0.7\eta(k) & E(k+1) > 1.04E(k); \\ \eta(k) & other. \end{cases} \tag{1}$$

$E(k+1)$ and $E(k)$ are the mean square error after the k + 1-th and the k-th iteration. This method ensures that the network is always trained at the maximum acceptable learning rate.

2.3 Additional Momentum Term

Additional momentum term [3] is to add a value to the change of each weight when the network correct the weight. The essence of additional momentum term is to transfer the influence of the last change of weight through a momentum factor. It makes the adjustment direction of the weight change to the average direction of the bottom instead of producing a big swing.

The weight adjustment formula of additional momentum term is:

$$\Delta w_{ij}(k+1) = (1 - mc)\eta\delta_i p_j + mc\Delta w_{ij}(k) \tag{2}$$

$$\Delta b_i(k+1) = (1 - mc)\eta\delta_i + mc\Delta b_i(k) \tag{3}$$

k is training times, p_j is input vector, mc is momentum factor, usually take about 0.9, δ_i is node error, η is learning rate.

When momentum factor is 1, the new change of weight is set to the latter, the variation produced by the gradient method is ignored. Thus, when the momentum term is added, the error of node δ_i becomes extremely small, that prevents $\Delta w_{ij}(k+1) \approx \Delta w_{ij}(k)$, thus $\Delta w_{ij}(k) = 0$. It is helpful for the network to jump out of local minimum of the error surface.

2.4   LMSDAE Algorithm

The adaptive learning rate algorithm can adjust the learning rate automatically, but the adjustment of the weight is regulated in a unified proportion, the difference between the weight adjustment of different layers is not taken into account. The additional momentum term algorithm makes up for the deficiency of the former. So this paper adopts the improved SDAE algorithm combined with adaptive learning rate and additional momentum (LMSDAE). Its weight correction formula is:

$$\Delta w_{ij}(k+1) = (1 - mc)\eta(k+1)\delta_i p_j + mc\Delta w_{ij}(k) \tag{4}$$

$$\Delta b_i(k+1) = (1 - mc)\eta(k+1)\delta_i + mc\Delta b_i(k) \tag{5}$$

3   Experimental Process

3.1   Text Preprocessing

Chinese expressions are made up of one or more words. Different forms of segmentation make different meanings of expressions. This improve the difficulty of the segmentation greatly. In this article, Jieba is used for text segmentation which is a Chinese segmentation method based on Python [5]. After the segmentation, there are still some stop words and a large number of punctuation marks that have little effect on the classification. This article sets up a full number of stop words, forms a stop words list and delete them.

3.2   Feature Extraction

After text preprocessing, we need to extract some representative words into the classification model to train. The feature extraction method used in this paper is the TF-IDF algorithm.

The idea of TF-IDF is that if a word appears more frequently in a certain class of text, and less in other class. Then it can be considered that this word has a great ability to classify. And it could be used for classification.

TF is Term Frequency, IDF is Inverse Document Frequency. Set the number of a certain key word is a. Set the total number of key words in the article is b. Set the total number of documents in the data set is x. Set the number of documents containing a certain key word is y. The formula are as follows:

$$TF = a/b \tag{6}$$

$$IDF = log(x/(y+1)) \tag{7}$$

$$TF - IDF = TF * IDF \tag{8}$$

This article preserves the TF-IDF value in the first 2000 words as the feature and put them into the LMSDAE model to train.

3.3 Structure of LMSDAE Classifier

Step 1. Determines the network structure of the hidden layer. For each text, feature words are entered one by one, and the network structure is 2000-200-100-9.

Step 2. Determines the initial parameters. The activation function of each hidden layer, the learning rate of gradient descent, the noise rate, the number of training iterations, and so on.

Step 3. Each hidden layer is forward calculated and trained layer by layer, where the activation function uses the ReLU activation function: $f(x) = \max(0, x)$.

Step 4. Calculates the mean square error E. The mean square error of the last iteration and the present iteration are compared, and the learning rate is adjusted according to the adaptive learning rate.

Step 5. Reverse calculation. The change of weight calculated by the additional momentum term algorithm, and put it into weight correction formula.

Step 6. If the mean square error satisfies the error precision, or the maximum number of training is reached, the training is over. Otherwise, return to Step 3.

4   Experimental Results

Two data set are used in this paper. There are a corpus of news text provided by Ronglu Li, Fudan University and Sogou news corpus. There are 20 categories in the data sets one. And 9 categories are selected as the data sets for this article, they are: computer, art, agriculture, economy, history, environment, politics, space and sports. There are 9000 articles in all, but they are not evenly distributed. 7000 of these 9000 articles are randomly selected as training sets, the remaining 2000 are used as test set. In data set two, there are 7 categories and 7000 articles in all, there are economy, healthy, military, tourism, sports, literature and campus. The computer configuration environment is: CPU is Intel (R) Core (TM) i3-4170 CPU@3.70 GHz, Windows 7 operating system.

Keep other parameters unchanged and set up $E < 0.1$, training times and convergence rate of LMSDAE algorithm are calculated which compared with the other three algorithms, there are: SDAE algorithm, Sparse Denoising Auto Encoder (SPDAE) [7] and Deep Belief Nets (DBNs), training times is the number of iterations when $E < 0.1$, convergence rate is the time that program run when $E < 0.1$, the results are as follows:

Table 1. Comparison of training times and convergence rate

	Algorithm	LMSDZE	SDAE	SPDAE	DBNs
DATE SET 1	Training times/times	62	360	219	225
	convergence rate/s	641.45	1201.70	835.97	1175.53
DATE SET 2	Training times/times	73	224	189	282
	convergence rate/s	659.55	865.84	741.65	1349.26

Table 1 shows that compared with compared with the other three algorithms, LMSDAE algorithm reduces the training times and increased the convergence rate with both two data sets. The faster the convergence rate is, the shorter the time that program runs. LMSDAE algorithm uses only half of the time taken by the SDAE algorithm to reach the terminating condition. This saves time efficiency.

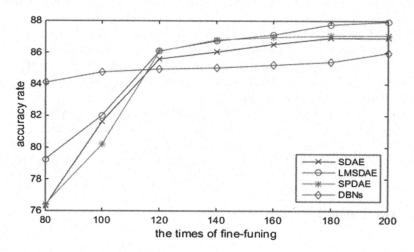

Fig. 1. Accuracy rate of data set 1

This paper also compares the accuracy rate and the recall rate of Chinese news classification by SDAE algorithm and LMSDAE algorithm. The results are as follows:

As shown in Figs. 1 and 2, the accuracy rate increase with the raise of the number of. At the 200th time, the LMSDAE algorithm can reach the accuracy of 87.95%, while the SDAE algorithm can only reach 86.9%. And in Table 2, the recall of LMSDAE also better than other algorithm. But as the number of fine-tuning increases, the operation time will increase doubly. Therefore, the time cost should be considered when setting the number of fine-tuning.

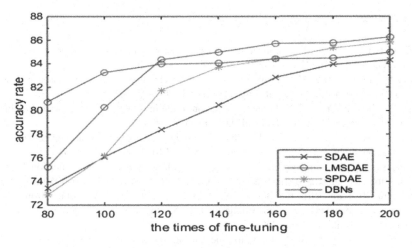

Fig. 2. Accuracy rate of data set 2

Table 2. Recall rate when fine-tuning times is 200

	LMSDZE	SDAE	SPDAE	DBNs
DATE SET 1	87.83	86.91	87.15	84.97
DATE SET 2	85.76	84.63	84.30	83.59

5 Conclusion and Prospect

This paper uses LMSDAE algorithm to classify Chinese News. Through comparison and verification, LMSDAE algorithm has a strong generalization ability, The advantages of LMSDAE are as follows:

(1) LMSDAE algorithm has strong robustness, and has good ability of self learning and fault tolerance.
(2) LMSDAE algorithm improves the accuracy and running time of SDAE.
(3) LMSDAE algorithm has a certain accuracy in Chinese news classification, and it can be widely used in life.

The shortcoming of this article is that only consider limited number of texts, the complex context of Chinese is not combined. And if the features can be extracted more accurately, more ideal results will be obtained and the reference value is greater.

Acknowledgements. This work is supported by the National Natural Science Foundation of China (61373067, 61672301), the Science and Technology Innovation Guide Project of Inner Mongolia Autonomous Region of china (KJCX2016, KJCX2017); the Information of Mongolian Medicine Based on Machine Learning Algorithm (MDXK004), the Research Program of science and technology at Universities of Inner Mongolia Autonomous Region (NJZY16177), the Natural Science Foundation of Inner Mongolia Autonomous Region of china (2016MS0624).

References

1. Zhao, J., Li, J., Zheng, R.: Application of adaptive learning rate method in power transformer fault diagnosis. J. Jilin Univ. (Inf. Sci. Ed.) **4**, 415–420 (2008)
2. Jia, W., Li, M., Zhu, M., Wang, J.: License plate character recognition based on stacked denoising autoencoder. Comput. Eng. Des. **37**(03), 751–756 (2016)
3. Ma, Y., Huo, Z., Yang, Z.: The implementation of the improved BP algorithm by adding the item of the momentum. Sci-Tech Inf. Dev. Econ. **8**, 157–158 (2006)
4. Qiao, J., Wang, G., Li, X., Han, H., Chai, W.: Design and application of deep belief network with adaptive learning rate. Acta Automatica Sin. **43**(8), 1339–1349 (2017)
5. Qiu, S., Jing, M., Zhang, Z., Lu, Y., Pei, Z.: Chinese short text classification based on denoising auto encoder. J. Inner Mongolia Univ. Natl. (Nat. Sci.) **5**, 400–405 (2017)
6. Vincent, P., Larochelle, H., Bengio, Y.: Extracting and composing robust features with denoising autoencoders. In: Proceedings of the 25th International Conference on Machine Learning, Helsinki, Finland (2008)
7. Zhang, C., Jiang, J.: Study on sparse de-noising auto-encoder neural network. J. Inner Mongolia Univ. Natl. (Nat. Chin. Ed.) **31**(1), 21–25 (2016)

Overcomplete Dictionary Pair for Music Super-Resolution

Lianqiang Li and Jie Zhu[✉]

School of Electronic Information and Electrical Engineering,
Shanghai Jiao Tong University, Shanghai, China
{sjtu_llq,zhujie}@sjtu.edu.cn

Abstract. With the development of society, people are going to pursue high quality music (HM). However, the Internet is filled with more generic music (GM) rather than HM. In this paper, we propose a novel algorithm called overcomplete dictionary pairs (ODP) algorithm. The ODP algorithm is able to recover HM from GM. The basic idea is to determine a set of elementary functions, called atoms, that efficiently capture music signal characteristics. There are mainly two steps. First, we employ K-SVD algorithm to jointly learn the overcomplete dictionary pairs of HM and GM frames. Then, we recovery HM via sharing the sparse representations of HM and GM. In order to validate the effectiveness of the ODP algorithm, the segment Signal-to-Noise Ratio performance and another objective parameter, perceptual objective listening quality assessment, which is introduced by the ITU are concerned. Experimental results show that the proposed algorithm is much better than conventional reconstruction method like shape-preserving piecewise cubic interpolation.

Keywords: High quality music · Sparse representation
Overcomplete dictionary pairs · K-SVD algorithm

1 Introduction

In the last decade, digital music has become more and more accessible and abundant over the Internet. When it comes to audio quality, high quality music (HM) usually means a better listening experience than generic music (GM) without considering the quality of headphones and other ingredients. Naturally, how to obtain HM from a given GM is an active object in audio signal processing [1–3]. In fact, GM is a down sampled version of HM. In other words, GM and HM are the same signals with different sampling rates. Recovering HM from a given GM is generally a severely ill-posed problem because of the insufficient number of bits. Our works are motivated by the research on sparse and redundant representation which suggests that signals could be well-presented as a sparse linear combination of atoms from an appropriately chosen overcomplete dictionary [4].

Sparse representation is widely used in audio and speech signal processing, such as sparse speech coding [5,6], speech recognition [7,8] and music retrieval

© Springer International Publishing AG, part of Springer Nature 2018
T. Huang et al. (Eds.): ISNN 2018, LNCS 10878, pp. 585–592, 2018.
https://doi.org/10.1007/978-3-319-92537-0_67

[9,10] et al. HM and GM are essentially the same audio signals with different sampling rates. As a result, there is high similarity between the sparse representations. In this paper, we adopt K-SVD [11] algorithm to jointly learn an overcomplete dictionary pair, D_g for GM frames and D_h for HM frames. On the condition that the sparse representation of a GM frame on D_g is the same with the sparse representation of the corresponding HM frame on D_h. For the purpose of recovering HM, we firstly obtain the sparse representations of GM frames by its dictionary D_g, then use those sparse representations to reconstruct corresponding HM frames according to HM dictionary D_h.

The rest of this paper is organized as follows. We describe the related works briefly in Sect. 2. Section 3 introduces how to recover high quality music with overcomplete dictionary pair in detail. Section 4 presents the experimental results and the evaluation of performance. Finally, we summarize the conclusions in Sect. 5.

2   Sparse Representation of Signals

Considering a real-valued, one-dimensional signal x with the length of $N \times 1$ and an overcomplete dictionary of M atoms $(M > N)$, denoted in terms of a $N \times M$ matrix D. Then x can be represented as a sparse linear combination with respect to D 's atoms as shown in Eq. (1):

$$x = Ds \tag{1}$$

where s is the $M \times 1$ sparse representation vector. It can be obtained by Eq. (2):

$$s = \arg \min \|x - Ds\|_2^2 + \lambda \|s\|_0 \tag{2}$$

where λ is a regularization parameter that controls the relative importance between error $(\|x - Ds\|_2^2)$ and sparsity $(\|s\|_0)$. Supposing $K\,(K \ll N)$ coefficients of s are nonzero or largest, and the $M - K$ remaining coefficients are zero or negligible, then s is called K-sparse.

Unfortunately, solving Eq. (2) is a non-deterministic polynomial (NP) hard problem. As a consequence, we change the ℓ_0 norm of sparse representations to ℓ_1 norm so that the computation in our algorithm becomes essentially a linear programming or convex optimization problem [11]. The Eq. (2) could be rewrited as following:

$$s = \arg \min \|x - Ds\|_2^2 + \lambda \|s\|_1 \tag{3}$$

Appling the overcomplete dictionaries to decompose signal into sparse coefficients is one of the most popular application in the state of the art sparse representation. In our paper, K-SVD algorithm is employed to learn effective dictionaries from a pre-prepared training database.

3 Recovering High Quality Music with Overcomplete Dictionary Pair

3.1 Joint Dictionary Training

We use a dictionary pair to recover HM in this paper. The dictionary pair consists of a GM dictionary and a HM dictionary. A traditional way to generate two coupled dictionaries, D_h for HM frames and D_g for GM frames is sampling the music frame pairs directly under the condition of preserving the correspondence between HM frames and GM frames. Since traditional method is expensively computational and result in large dictionaries, we manage to learn the dictionary pair simultaneously for the purpose of avoiding large database.

In order to learn an overcomplete dictionary pair, music frame pairs $P = \{H, G\}$ are pre-prepared as training database, where $H = \{h_1, h_2, h_3, \ldots, h_m\}$ are the set of HM frames and $G = \{g_1, g_2, g_3, \ldots, g_m\}$ are the corresponding set of GM frames. According to Eq. (2), we could deduce the sparse representations of GM and HM frames respectively as follows:

$$D_h = \arg \min_{\{D_h, S_h\}} \|H - D_h S_h\|_2^2 + \lambda \|S_h\|_1 \tag{4}$$

$$D_g = \arg \min_{\{D_g, S_g\}} \|G - D_g S_g\|_2^2 + \lambda \|S_g\|_1 \tag{5}$$

where, S_h is the sparse matrix of HM, and S_g is the sparse matrix of GM.

As we mentioned before, HM frames and GM frames are the same audio signals with different sampling rates. Therefore, the sparse representations of HM frames and the corresponding GM frames are highly similar to each other. To learn an overcomplete dictionary pair simultaneously, we combine Eqs. (4) and (5) together to force HM and GM representations share the same sparse matrix S_c, the process is shown in Eq. (6):

$$\begin{aligned} D_h, D_g = \arg \min_{\{D_h, D_g, S_c\}} \frac{1}{N_h} \|H - D_h S_c\|_2^2 \\ + \frac{1}{N_g} \|G - D_g S_c\|_2^2 \\ + \lambda(\frac{1}{N_h} + \frac{1}{N_g}) \|S_c\|_1 \end{aligned} \tag{6}$$

where N_h and N_g are the length of HM and GM frames respectively. We replace $\lambda(1/N_h + 1/N_g)$ with $\hat{\lambda}$ as a new balanced parameter, then we rewrite Eq. (6) as:

$$D_c = \arg \min_{\{D_c, S_c\}} \|P_c - D_c S_c\|_2^2 + \hat{\lambda} \|S_c\|_1 \tag{7}$$

where P_c and D_c are shown in the following:

$$P_c = \begin{bmatrix} H/\sqrt{N_h} \\ G/\sqrt{N_g} \end{bmatrix}, \qquad D_c = \begin{bmatrix} D_h/\sqrt{N_h} \\ D_g/\sqrt{N_g} \end{bmatrix} \tag{8}$$

In Eq. (7), since both $\boldsymbol{D}_c$ and $\boldsymbol{S}_c$ are unknown, we fix either of them to make equation convex, and then solve the other. Then we utilize K-SVD algorithm to learn the overcomplete dictionary pair $\boldsymbol{D}_c$ of size $N \times M$ with initial dictionary $\boldsymbol{D}_0$ which is constructed with an $N \times N$ DCT matrix and $M - N$ Gaussian random atoms ($N \times 1$ vector), where $N = N_h + N_g$.

3.2 Recovering High Quality Music

In this subsection, we will illustrate how to recover the HM from a given GM. We have the overcomplete dictionary pair, $\boldsymbol{D}_h$ and $\boldsymbol{D}_g$, by implementing the plans which have been arranged in the last section. Moreover, we could obtain $\boldsymbol{G} = \boldsymbol{\Psi}\boldsymbol{H}$ because GM is regarded as a down sampled version of HM, where $\boldsymbol{\Psi}$ is a down sampling matrix. We firstly reconstruct a coarse HM $\boldsymbol{H}_c$ from the shared sparse matrix and then refine it by following reconstruct constraint:

$$\boldsymbol{H}_r = \arg\min_{\boldsymbol{H}_r}\|\boldsymbol{G} - \boldsymbol{\Psi}\boldsymbol{H}_r\|_2^2 + \rho\|\boldsymbol{H}_r - \boldsymbol{H}_c\|_2^2 \tag{9}$$

where $\boldsymbol{H}_r$ is the refined HM and ρ is a regularization parameter. The entire recovering process is illustrated in Algorithm 1.

Algorithm 1. Recovering HM from a given GM via overcomplete dictionary pair

---

Require: Dictionary pair $\boldsymbol{D}_h$ and $\boldsymbol{D}_g$; A given GM $\boldsymbol{G}$; Frame overlap ϕ; Downsampling matrix $\boldsymbol{\Psi}$.
Ensure: Corresponding HM $\boldsymbol{H}$.
1: Enframe: Dividing $\boldsymbol{G}$ into several frames of length N_g with the consideration of the frame overlap ϕ.
2: **for** each frame $\boldsymbol{g}_i$ of $\boldsymbol{G}$ **do**
3:    Solving the optimization problem to obtain the sparse presentations $\boldsymbol{s}_i$ of $\boldsymbol{g}_i$: $\boldsymbol{s}_i = \arg\min_{\boldsymbol{s}_i}\|\boldsymbol{g}_i - \boldsymbol{D}_g\boldsymbol{s}_i\|_2^2 + \lambda\|\boldsymbol{s}_i\|_1$.
4:    Recovering correponding HM frame $\boldsymbol{h}_i = \boldsymbol{D}_h\boldsymbol{s}_i$ of length N_h and then save $\boldsymbol{h}_i$.
5: **end for**
6: Reconstructing the coarse high quality music $\boldsymbol{H}_c$ from all recovered HM frames $\{\boldsymbol{h}_i\}$.
7: Obtaining refined high quality music $\boldsymbol{H}_r$ which statisfies:$\boldsymbol{H}_r = \arg\min_{\boldsymbol{H}_r}\|\boldsymbol{G} - \boldsymbol{\Psi}\boldsymbol{H}_r\|_2^2 + \rho\|\boldsymbol{H}_r - \boldsymbol{H}_c\|_2^2$.
8: **return** $\boldsymbol{H} = \boldsymbol{H}_r$.

---

4   Experimental Results

To evaluate the performance of our proposed algorithm, several experiments have been carried out. We use *Greatest Maksim*, which is the eighth studio album by Maksim Mrvica, as our data set. All music in this album are sampled at 44.1 KHz and recorded at 16-bit depth. First of all, we prepare HM frames. We select

200 HM segments of length 16000 from all music randomly. Furthermore, each segment is divided into about 1000 frames of length 160, thus we generate about 200,000 HM frames in total. Next, we prepare the corresponding GM frames to compose the frame pairs. We down sample all 200 HM segments by 4 times and obtain 200 GM segments of length 4000, and then these GM segments are divided into GM frames of length 40 in the same way as before. So that we get about 200,000 pairs of HM and GM frames for constructing a training set which would be used to jointly learn an overcomplete dictionary pair of 1024 atoms by K-SVD algorithm. The default configuration of parameters is summarized as follows: overlap rate ϕ is 50%, length of GM frames N_g is 40, length of HM frames N_h is 160, the number of dictionary atoms M is 1024, λ is 0.15 (recommended value is between 0.1 and 0.2), and ρ is 0.15 as well.

The shape-preserving piecewise cubic interpolation (SPCI) is selected as the referenced algorithm to compare with the proposed ODP algorithm. As far as the objective metrics are concerned, the latest ITU standard POLQA (perceptual objective listening quality assessment) [12,13] is introduced as a objective metric with its higher accuracy for wide-band signals. POLQA is the successor of PESQ (ITU-T Rec. P.862). It avoids weaknesses of the current P.862 model and is extended towards handling of higher bandwidth audio signals. The other objective metric is segmental SNR (segSNR). The segSNR metric is defined in Eq. (10).

$$
segSNR = 10 \cdot \log\left(\frac{\|\boldsymbol{H}_{seg}\|_2^2}{\|\boldsymbol{H}_{seg} - \hat{\boldsymbol{H}}_{seg}\|_2^2} \right) \tag{10}
$$

where $\boldsymbol{H}_{seg}$ denotes the HM segment, and the variable with hat denotes the recovered results. segSNR metric would be computed by segmenting the segments using 160 points duration Hamming windows with 50% overlap between adjacent frames. To validate our recovering algorithm, we down sample the 17-th music *Croatian Rhapsody* by 4 times as the testing GM (testing data). Following the procedure of Algorithm 1, we recover HM from the given GM.

The waves of HM segments and some zoomed frames both on original condition and reconstructed condition are shown in Fig. 1. We can find that the reconstructed HM segments by ODP algorithm are quite similar to the original HM segments. There is very little loss between them. And we could also see that the zoomed frames recovered by ODP algorithm are more smooth than those in original ones.

The performance of ODP algorithm and SPCI algorithm with respect to POLQA scores are shown in Fig. 2. We can find that the ODP algorithm gains better performance as far as POLQA is concerned. It's clear the POLQA scores of ODP algorithm is always larger than those in SPCI algorithm. In fact, the former's scores are about 0.0072 to 0.1991 larger than those in SPCI algorithm on the whole.

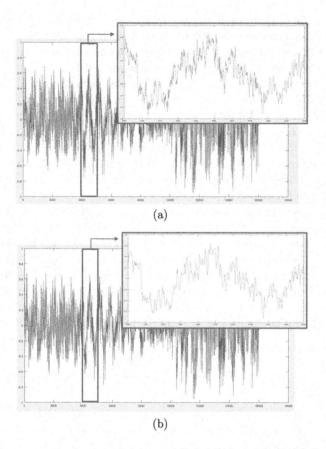

Fig. 1. HM segments and zoomed frames: (a) Original segment; (b) Reconstructed segment

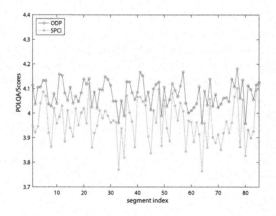

Fig. 2. Performance comparison in terms of POLQA

Table 1 lists the average, standard deviation, maximum and minimum values of both segSNR and POLQA scores. We can find that the ODP algorithm has bigger average and smaller standard deviation segSNR than those in SPCI. Besides, the performance based on POLQA scores almost agree with that based on segSNR. More specifically, average segSNR of ODP is 0.3722 dB bigger than that of SPCI, and average POLQA score of ODP is 0.1152 higher than that of SPCI.

Table 1. Comparison on the performance in term of POLQA and segSNR

	segSNR/dB		POLQA/Scores	
	ODP	SPCI	ODP	SPCI
Average	**23.6540**	22.4718	**4.0790**	3.9638
Standard deviation	2.7733	**2.8348**	0.0026	**0.0066**
Maximum	**33.3674**	32.3195	**4.1804**	4.1194
Minimum	**21.5661**	20.1845	**3.9585**	3.7648

5 Conclusion

In this paper, we propose a new algorithm called overcomplete dictionary pairs (ODP) algorithm for recovering high quality music (HM) from a given generic music (GM) via an overcomplete dictionary pair which were learned jointly by K-SVD algorithm. Experimental results show that the proposed ODP algorithm is able to recover HM with very little loss. In addition, when comparing with conventional reconstruction method like shape-preserving piecewise cubic interpolation, the OPD algorithm achieves almost 0.4 dB improvement in terms of segSNR and 0.2 improvement in terms of POLQA score.

Acknowledgments. This work is supported by the National Key Research Project of China under Grant No. 2017YFF0210903 and the National Natural Science Foundation of China under Grant Nos. 61371147 and 11433002.

References

1. Cho, N., Kuo, C.C.J.: Sparse music representation with source-specific dictionaries and its application to signal separation. IEEE Trans. Audio Speech Lang. Process. **19**(2), 326–337 (2011)
2. Guichaoua, C.: Dictionary learning for audio inpainting. HAL Robotics [cs. RO] (2012)
3. Le Roux, J., Kameoka, H., Ono, N., De Cheveigne, A., Sagayama, S.: Computational auditory induction as a missing-data model-fitting problem with Bregman divergence. Speech Commun. **53**(5), 658–676 (2011)

4. Yang, J., Wright, J., Huang, T.S., Ma, Y.: Image super-resolution via sparse representation. IEEE Trans. Image Process. **19**(11), 2861–2873 (2010)
5. Petrovsky, A., Herasimovich, V., Petrovsky, A.: Bio-inspired sparse representation of speech and audio using psychoacoustic adaptive matching pursuit. In: Ronzhin, A., Potapova, R., Németh, G. (eds.) SPECOM 2016. LNCS (LNAI), vol. 9811, pp. 156–164. Springer, Cham (2016). https://doi.org/10.1007/978-3-319-43958-7_18
6. Xie, Y., Huang, J., He, Y.: One dictionary vs. two dictionaries in sparse coding based denoising. Chin. J. Electron. **26**(2), 367–371 (2017)
7. Dighe, P., Asaei, A., Bourlard, H.: Sparse modeling of neural network posterior probabilities for exemplar-based speech recognition. Speech Commun. **76**, 230–244 (2016)
8. Zong, Y., Zheng, W., Cui, Z., Li, Q.: Double sparse learning model for speech emotion recognition. Electron. Lett. **52**(16), 1410–1412 (2016)
9. Vaizman, Y., McFee, B., Lanckriet, G.: Codebook-based audio feature representation for music information retrieval. IEEE/ACM Trans. Audio Speech Lang. Process. **22**(10), 1483–1493 (2014)
10. Adler, A., Emiya, V., Jafari, M.G., Elad, M., Gribonval, R., Plumbley, M.D.: Audio inpainting. IEEE Trans. Audio Speech Lang. Process. **20**(3), 922–932 (2012)
11. Aharon, M., Elad, M., Bruckstein, A.: K-SVD: an algorithm for designing overcomplete dictionaries for sparse representation. IEEE Trans. Signal Process. **54**(11), 4311–4322 (2006)
12. Beerends, J.G., Schmidmer, C., Berger, J., Obermann, M., Ullmann, R., Pomy, J., Keyhl, M.: Perceptual objective listening quality assessment (POLQA), the third generation ITU-T standard for end-to-end speech quality measurement part I - temporal alignment. J. Audio Eng. Soc. **61**(6), 366–384 (2013)
13. Beerends, J.G., Schmidmer, C., Berger, J., Obermann, M., Ullmann, R., Pomy, J., Keyhl, M.: Perceptual objective listening quality assessment (POLQA), the third generation ITU-T standard for end-to-end speech quality measurement part II - perceptual model. J. Audio Eng. Soc. **61**(6), 385–402 (2013)

Multi-column Spatial Transformer Convolution Neural Network for Traffic Sign Recognition

Jin Zhang, Shukai Duan[✉], Lidan Wang, and Xianli Zou

National and Local Joint Engineering Laboratory of Intelligent Transmission
and Control Technology, Brain-Inspired Computing and Intelligent Control
of Chongqing Key Lab, School of Electronic and Information Engineering,
Southwest University, Chongqing 400715, China
duansk@swu.edu.cn

Abstract. Traffic sign recognition is an important research area in intelligent transportation, which is especially important in autopilot system. Convolutional Neural Network (CNN) is the main research method of traffic sign recognition. However, the convolution neural network is easily affected by the spatial diversity of the image. With regard to this, in this paper, a multi-column spatial transformer convolution neural network named MC-STCNN is proposed to solve the problem when Convolutional Neural Network (CNN) can't adapt to the spatial diversity of the image very well. The MC-STCNN network consisted of CNN and STN is formed by training pictures of different sizes. It can be well adapted to the spatial diversity and the images input of different sizes. It achieves an accuracy of 99.75% on GTSRB traffic sign recognition, exceeding the current highest accuracy of 99.65%.

Keywords: Deep learning · Traffic sign recognition
Convolution neural network · Spatial transformation network

1 Introduction

Fast and accurate identification of traffic signs is the guarantee of safe driving for unmanned vehicles. Common methods for identification of traffic signs include HOG feature extraction, support vector machine (SVM), extreme learning machine (ELM), deep learning and so on [1]. Akatsuka and Imai firstly used the template matching algorithm to identify the speed signs in traffic signs [2]. Kellmeyer and Zwahlen used BP neural networks to identify the warning signs in high-speed road sections [3]. Ren et al. achieved a 95% recognition accuracy on traffic sign recognition by using the feature extraction [4]. Prisacariu et al. realized the real-time identification and tracking of traffic signs using support vector machines [5]. Liu et al. used log-polar mapping and visual codebook to identify the Speed limit sign [6]. Stallkamp et al. created the traffic sign database GTSRB and compared various methods in the form of competition [7]. So far, the CNN method adopted by Ciresan et al. achieved the highest accuracy of 99.46% in the GTSRB competition [8]. Jin et al. achieved 99.65% accuracy on the GTSRB database by improving the convolutional neural network [9]. Huang et al.

© Springer International Publishing AG, part of Springer Nature 2018
T. Huang et al. (Eds.): ISNN 2018, LNCS 10878, pp. 593–600, 2018.
https://doi.org/10.1007/978-3-319-92537-0_68

obtained 99.56% accuracy by using ELM combined with HOG [10]. Aghdam et al. achieved 99.61% accuracy for classifying traffic signs in real-time [11].

Compared with the traditional machine learning, the Convolutional Neural Network has higher accuracy in the recognition of traffic signs and it has become the main research method of traffic sign recognition. However, the convolution neural network is easily affected by the spatial diversity of the image. The appearance of spatial transform network solves these problems [12].

In this paper, a multi-column spatial transformer convolution neural network named MC-STCNN is proposed. The MC-STCNN network consisted of CNN and STN is formed by training pictures of different sizes. It can be well adapted to the spatial diversity and the images input of different sizes. Compared with the other models for Traffic Sign Recognition, it has higher accuracy.

2   MC-STCNN Model

2.1   Model Architecture

The proposed network structure of the multi-column spatial transformation convolution neural network model MC-STCNN is shown in Fig. 1. The MC-STCNN network is composed of Input, Distributor, multi-column ST-CNN networks, Averaging and Output.

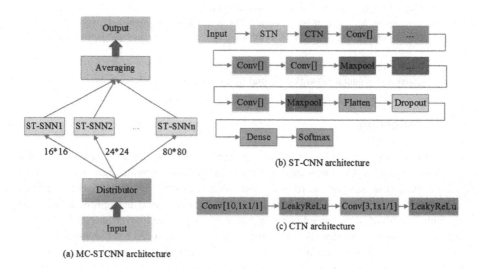

Fig. 1. MC-STCNN model

The architecture of the MC-STCNN is shown in Fig. 1. The images from Input are reshaped to different sizes by Distributor. There are multi-column ST-CNN networks behind Distributor and different ST-CNN networks use different sizes of pictures as input. Different ST-CNN models are trained separately. The output is obtained by averaging the sum of outputs of all ST-CNN networks.

The structure of a single ST-CNN network is shown in Fig. 1. After the input image is adjusted by the STN network, the CTN network [13] is used to extract the color features. The features are extracted using multiple convolution layers, and flattening the feature map into a one-dimensional vector through Flatten. Some neurons are randomly inactivated by Dropout. Finally, the output results are obtained by multiple fully connected layers (Dense layer) and a softmax function.

The CTN network is shown in Fig. 1. It is composed of two convolution layers with convolution kernels of 1×1. The two convolutional layers output the number of features of 10 and 3 respectively. The activation functions are all Leaky RELU and the CTN network can extract the color features of color images which increase the accuracy of traffic signs recognition.

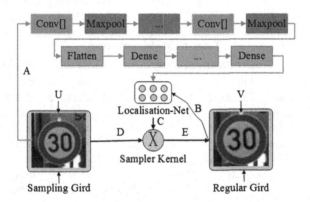

Fig. 2. ST-CNN network

The ST-CNN network is shown in Fig. 2. U is input feature map and V is input feature map. The concept of coordinate grid is introduced in ST-CNN network. Sampling Gird preserves the coordinate grid $\left(x_i^u, y_i^u\right)$ corresponding to the input feature map's pixels, and Regular Gird preserves the coordinate grid $\left(x_i^v, y_i^v\right)$ of the corresponding output feature map pixels.

STN-CNN network can obtain its output feature map according to the order of the operation ABCDE. Firstly, make the input feature map as input, after several layers of convolution, pooling and fully connected, 6 parameters of affine transform matrix can be get, and then perform the first-step operation, regarding the Regular Gird's coordinates $\left(x_i^v, y_i^v\right)$ and affine transform matrix T_θ as the input of the Localisation-Net, the output feature map's coordinates corresponding to the input feature map's coordinates $\left(x_i^u, y_i^u\right)$ can be obtained as

$$\begin{bmatrix} x_i^u \\ y_i^u \end{bmatrix} = T_\theta \begin{bmatrix} x_i^v \\ y_i^v \\ 1 \end{bmatrix} = \begin{bmatrix} \theta_{11} & \theta_{12} & \theta_{13} \\ \theta_{21} & \theta_{22} & \theta_{23} \end{bmatrix} \begin{bmatrix} x_i^v \\ y_i^v \\ 1 \end{bmatrix} \tag{1}$$

Operation of the input feature map's coordinates corresponding input feature pixels through bilinear interpolation to obtain the target pixel sampling operation, the operation will be copied to the target pixel output feature map coordinates the output characteristics of grid map, then complete the space network transformation operation.

This section describes the network structure of the MC-STCNN. Specific parameter configuration see the next section.

2.2 Model Parameters

In this paper, the MC-STCNN network consists of 5 ST-CNN networks. The Distributor reshapes the input image to 16, 24, 32, 64 and 80 pixels for training. The parameters of each ST-CNN network is shown in Table 1.

Table 1. Model parameters

		ST-CNN1	ST-CNN2	ST-CNN3	ST-CNN4	ST-CNN5
Input		16	24	32	64	80
STN	Conv	32,(5,5)/2	32,(5,5)/2	64,(7,7)/2	32,(7,7)/2	32,(7,7)/2
	Maxpool	(2,2)/2	(2,2)/2	(2,2)/2	(2,2)/2	(2,2)/2
	Conv	64,(3,3)/1	(3,3)/1	96,(5,5)/2	64,(5,5)/2	64,(5,5)/2
	Maxpool	(2,2)/2	(2,2)/2	(2,2)/2	(2,2)/2	(2,2)/2
	Conv	128,(2,2)/1	128,(2,2)/1	128,(2,2)/2	128,(3,3)/1	128,(3,3)/1
	Maxpool	(2,2)	(3,3)	(2,2)	(4,4)	(5,5)
	Dense	64/6	64/6	128/64/6	64/6	64/6
CTN						
Conv		16,(3,3)/1	32,(5,5)/1	32,(5,5)/1	32,(3,3)/1	—
Conv		32,(3,3)/1	64,(5,5)/1	64,(5,5)/1	64,(3,3)/1	64,(5,5)/1
Conv		64,(3,3)/1	96,(5,5)/1	96,(5,5)/1	96,(3,3)/1	96,(5,5)/1
Conv		96,(3,3)/1	128,(5,5)/1	128,(5,5)/1	128,(3,3)/1	128,(5,5)/1
Conv		128,(3,3)/1	—	192,(5,5)/1	192,(3,3)/1	192,(5,5)/1
Conv		—	—	256,(5,5)/1	256,(3,3)/1	—
Maxpool		—	—	—	(3,3)/2	—
Conv		—	—	512,(5,5)/1	512,(3,3)/1	—
Maxpool		—	—	(2,2)/2	(3,3)/2	(2,2)/2
Conv		256,(3,3)/1	192,(5,5)/1	256,(5,5)/1	256,(3,3)/1	256,(5,5)/1
Maxpool		(3,3)/2	(2,2)/2	(2,2)/2	(3,3)/2	(2,2)/2
Conv		128,(3,3)/1	128,(5,5)/1	128,(5,5)/1	128,(3,3)/1	128,(5,5)/1
Maxpool		(2,2)/2	(2,2)/2	(2,2)/2	(3,3)/2	(2,2)/2
Conv		64,(3,3)/1	64,(2,2)/1	64,(5,5)/1	64,(3,3)/1	64,(5,5)/1
Maxpool		(4,4)	(6,6)	(4,4)	(4,4)	(10,10)
Flatten						
Dropout		0.6	0.6	0.6	0.6	0.6
Dense		43	43	43	43	43
Softmax						

Table 1 shows the network parameters of MC-STCNN. Input represents the picture size that the Distributor outputs to each ST-CNN network, STN represents the network connection method of generating six parameters in the affine matrix by the spatial transformation network. "Conv 32,(5,5)/2" denote the convolution operation with a convolution kernel of 5×5, a step size of 2, and the number of output feature maps is 32. "Maxpool (2,2)/2" represents a pooling operation with a window size of 2×2 and a step size of 2. "Dense 64/6" represents a fully connected layer with 64 neurons is connected to a fully connected layer with 6 neurons. "Dropout 0.6" represents 60% of the neurons are inactivated. "—" represents no such operation.

In this paper, the convolution part Conv [] is composed of convolution, activation function and data normalization in series. In the STN network, exponential linear unit (ELU) is used as the activation function behind the convolution, while in the CTN section, Leaky RELU as the activation function behind the convolution. The activation function of other parts uses RELU behind the convolution.

When the model is trained, the loss function adopts the cross entropy, and Adam is used as the optimization algorithm. The learning rate is 0.001, the exponential decay rate of first moment estimation is 0.9, the exponential Decay Rate of Second Moment Estimation is 0.999, the initial time step is 0.01, and the minimum constant for numerical stability is 10^{-8}.

3   Experiments and Results

3.1   Database Selection

GTSRB database has become the most widely used traffic identification database. This article uses the GTSRB database as training and testing sample.

(a) Speed limit signs   (b) Other   (c) Derestriction signs   (d) Mandatory signs
                          prohibitory signs

(e) Danger signs   (f) Unique signs

Fig. 3. GTSRB database

The GTSRB database is shown in Fig. 3. There are 43 kinds of traffic signs in the GTSRB database, which are divided into six main categories: speed limit signs, other prohibitory signs, derestriction signs, mandatory signs, danger signs and unique signs. GTSRB database contains 39,209 train images and 12,569 test images.

3.2 Experimental Environment

We use a system with a Core i7-7700 K, 16 GB DDR4 and a graphics card of type GTX 1080. The operating system is Ubuntu14.04. The programming language is Python and the deep learning framework is Keras.

3.3 Experimental Results

The MC-STCNN network consists of ST-CNN1, ST-CNN2, ST-CNN3, ST-CNN4 and ST-CNN5. The five networks are connected together according to Fig. 1. The parameters of the 5 ST-CNN networks are shown in Table 1. The accuracy of the MC-STCNN network and the 5-columns ST-CNN network on the GTSRB test set is shown in Table 2.

Table 2. The accuracy of 5 ST-CNN networks

	Average	Speed limits	Prohibitions	Derestriction	Mandatory	Danger	Unique
ST-CNN1	96.86	97.00	98.76	97.39	96.40	95.50	95.32
ST-CNN2	99.05	99.10	99.55	99.37	97.32	99.16	**100.0**
ST-CNN3	99.66	99.33	99.80	**99.58**	99.79	**99.94**	100.0
ST-CNN4	99.49	**99.59**	99.80	99.42	**100.0**	99.49	94.88
ST-CNN5	99.25	98.84	99.85	99.05	**100.0**	99.33	97.58
MC-STCNN	**99.75**	**99.59**	**99.95**	99.47	**100.0**	99.87	**100.0**

The accuracy of six categories of traffic signs (speed limit signs, other prohibitory signs, derestriction signs, mandatory signs, danger signs and unique signs) is shown in the Table 2. The table shows that the accuracy of ST-CNN1 to ST-CNN5 is 96.86%, 99.05%, 99.66%, 99.49%, and 99.25%. Due to the inconsistency of the network structure, the accuracy does not increase with the increase of the size of the input image. The network structure of ST-CNN3 is better set, with a higher accuracy of 99.66%. The MC-STCNN network's accuracy is 99.75%, which is higher than any single ST-CNN network. It validates the effectiveness of MC-STCNN network.

The prediction results of each model and each type of traffic signs are statistically calculated to obtain the classification accuracy of 43 traffic signs classes, as shown in Fig. 4.

In Fig. 4. Coordinates in x-axis and y-axis denote 43 traffic sign classes. From A to F denote speed limit signs, other prohibitory signs, derestriction signs, mandatory signs, danger signs and unique signs. As shown in Fig. 4. The MC-STCNN network can eliminate some of the prediction error values through the connection of multiple ST-CNN networks, which enhances the generalization capability of the network and improves the prediction accuracy.

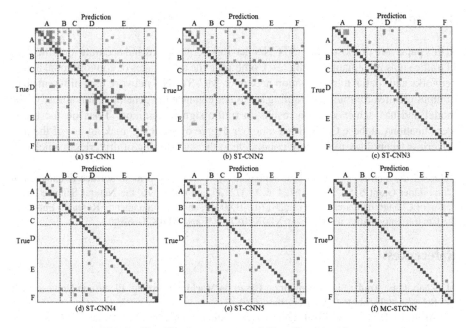

Fig. 4. Classification accuracy of 43 traffic signs classes

3.4 Experimental Results Comparison and Analysis

This paper compares the MC-STCNN model, the single ST-CNN model with the models tested by other researchers in the traffic identification database GTSRB. The experimental results are shown in Table 3.

Table 3. Recognition accuracy for categories on GTSRB dataset

	Average	Speed limits	Prohibitions	Derestriction	Mandatory	Danger	Unique
MC-STCNN	**99.75**	**99.59**	99.95	99.47	**100.0**	99.87	**100.0**
ST-CNN	99.66	99.33	99.80	99.58	99.79	**99.94**	**100.0**
Jin et al. [9]	99.65	—	—	—	—	—	—
Aghdam et al. [11]	99.61	—	—	—	—	—	—
Huang et al. [10]	99.56	99.54	**100.0**	98.33	99.94	98.96	99.95
Committee of CNNs [8]	99.46	99.47	99.93	**99.72**	99.89	99.07	99.22
Human (Best) [7]	99.22	98.32	99.87	98.89	**100.0**	99.21	**100.0**
Human (average) [7]	98.84	97.63	99.93	98.89	99.72	98.67	**100.0**

In Table 3. We can understand that CNN has become the most important method of traffic sign recognition research. In this paper, the highest accuracy of the single ST-CNN network is up to 99.66%. The MC-STCNN model accuracy is 99.75%. It is higher than the other models and the maximum recognition accuracy of 99.22% in humans, proving the validity of the MC-STCNN network model.

4   Conclusion

In this paper, we propose a MC-STCNN network for the rapid and accurate identification of traffic signs in unmanned vehicles. Combining the advantages of convolutional neural networks and spatial transformation networks, MC-STCNN network uses different sizes of input pictures for multiple training to further enhance the generalization ability of the model and has achieved good results in traffic sign recognition. Tests on the traffic identification database GTSRB get a higher degree of accuracy, making use of them in driverless technology to be more conducive to the safe driving of driverless vehicles.

Acknowledgements. This work was supported by the National Natural Science Foundation of China under Grant 61571372, 61672436, 61372139 and 61601376, the Natural Science Foundation of Chongqing under Grant cstc2017jcyjBX0050, and the Fundamental Research Funds for the Central Universities under Grant XDJK2017A005 and XDJK2016A001.

References

1. Zhao, G.F.: Traffic Sign Recognition Based on Machine Learning. Electronic University Of Science & Technology Of Hangzhou (2015)
2. Akatsuka, H., Imai, S.: Road signposts recognition system. In: The International Conference on SAE Vehicle Highway Infrastructure: Safety Compatibility, pp. 189–196 (1987)
3. Kellmeyer, D.L., Zwahlen, H.T.: Detection of highway warning signs in natural video images using color image processing and neural networks. In: IEEE World Congress on Computational Intelligence, vol. 7, pp. 4226–4231 (1994)
4. Ren, F.X., Huang, J.S., Jiang, R.Y., Klette, R.: General traffic sign recognition by feature matching. In: Proceedings of the 24th International Conference Image and Vision Computing, pp. 409–414 (2009)
5. Prisacariu, V.A., Timofte, R., Zimmermann, K., Reid, I., Van Gool, L.J.: Integrating object detection with 3D tracking towards a better driver assistance system. In: 20th International Conference on Pattern Recognition (ICPR), pp. 3344–3347 (2010)
6. Liu, B., Liu, H., Luo, X., Sun, F.C.: Speed limit sign recognition using log-polar mapping and visual codebook. In: 9th International Symposium on Neural Networks (ISNN), pp. 247–256 (2012)
7. Stallkamp, J., Schlipsing, M., Salmen, J., Igel, C.: The German traffic sign recognition benchmark: a multi-class classification competition. In: IEEE International Joint Conference on Neural Networks, pp. 1453–1460 (2011)
8. Ciresan, D., Meier, U., Masci, J., Schmidhuber, J.: Multi-column deep neural network for traffic sign classification. Neural Netw. **32**, 333–338 (2012)
9. Jin, J.Q., Fu, K., Zhang, C.S.: Traffic sign recognition with hinge loss trained convolutional neural networks. IEEE Trans. Intell. Transp. Syst. **15**(5), 1991–2000 (2014)
10. Huang, Z.Y., Yu, Y.L., Gu, J.S.: An efficient method for traffic sign recognition based on extreme learning machine. IEEE Trans. Cybern. **47**(4), 920–933 (2016)
11. Aghdam, H.H., Heravi, E.J., Puig, D.: A practical and highly optimized convolutional neural network for classifying traffic signs in real-time. Int. J. Comput. Vis. **122**(2), 246–269 (2017)
12. Jaderberg, M., Simonvan, K., Zisserman, A., Kavukcuoglu, K.: Spatial transformer networks. In: Advances in Neural Information Processing Systems (2015)
13. Mishkin, D., Sergievskiy, N., Matas, J.: Systematic evaluation of CNN advances on the ImageNet. In: arXiv (2016)

Real-Time Key Frame Extraction in a Low Lighting Condition

Tao Shen, Zhan-Li Sun[✉], Fu-Qiang Han, and Ya-Min Wang

School of Electrical Engineering and Automation, Anhui University, Hefei, China
zhlsun2006@126.com

Abstract. In a low lighting condition, the key frame extraction is an intractable problem due to the degraded video quality. Aimed at this issue, an effective real-time key frame extraction method is proposed to deal with the video captured in a low lighting condition. Firstly, we invert the image and turn the low-dark background into a fog-like scene. Then, we construct the atmospheric scattering model, and reconstruct the enhanced low-light image by removing the haze and inverting the image. Furthermore, a selection strategy based on hash criterion is designed to determine whether the transmission map needs to be recalculated to improve the processing speed. Moreover, an improved vibe algorithm is presented to model and extract foreground objects. Finally, according to the ratio of the foreground object to the whole image, we judge whether there is a moving object in a frame. The experimental results on some typical videos demonstrate the feasibility of the proposed method.

Keywords: Key frame extraction · Low lighting enhancement
Dehazing · Hash index · Guided filter

1 Introduction

The purpose of key frame extraction is to express the main content of relevant video stream with fewer video frames. Due to its universality and effectiveness, it has attracted many domestic and foreign experts and scholars to study, and has achieved remarkable research results. Tonomura et al. [1] firstly proposed the idea of key frames, and set the first frame as the key frame. Zhuang et al. [2] proposed the strategy of selecting the key frame according to the inter-frame change. They calculated the difference between the representative frame and other frames, and selected the frame that difference is greater than the threshold.

Z.-L. Sun—The work was supported by a grant from National Natural Science Foundation of China (No. 61370109), a key project of support program for outstanding young talents of Anhui province university (No. gxyqZD2016013), a grant of science and technology program to strengthen police force (No. 1604d0802019), and a grant for academic and technical leaders and candidates of Anhui province (No. 2016H090).

© Springer International Publishing AG, part of Springer Nature 2018
T. Huang et al. (Eds.): ISNN 2018, LNCS 10878, pp. 601–610, 2018.
https://doi.org/10.1007/978-3-319-92537-0_69

Sun [3] divided each frame of video sequence into foreground and background, and selected key frames according to the ratio of foreground to background. However, the precision of key frame extraction under complex background is difficult to improve, such as in low lighting conditions. It is a challenge for background modeling. If we cannot capture the moving object precisely, it will seriously affect our analysis of video content, which makes it difficult to extract the key frames. The accuracy of video synopsis cannot be guaranteed.

In view of the above problems, we propose a low lighting enhancement method by combining dark channel [4] and guided filtering [5], which greatly improve the accuracy of key frame extraction under low lighting conditions. We design a strategy based on the hash criterion, to judge whether the transmission map need to be recalculated, which greatly improve the processing speed. The feasibility of the algorithm was proved by the experiments on the various low lighting videos. We design a strategy to eliminate the "ghost" of vibe (Visual Background Extractor) [6], which optimize the background modeling algorithm. Experimental results show that the accuracy and recall of key frame extraction are improved.

2　Methodology

2.1　Enhancement of Low Lighting Videos

We find that each RGB color channel in the sky and background region of the inverted image has a high brightness. Non-sky areas, such as buildings, vehicles and so on, have at least one channel with very low brightness, which is very similar to hazy images. So the idea of dehazing can be used.

Based on the above observations, we propose a low lighting video enhancement algorithm. First, the pixels of each frame of the input video are inverted according to the following formula:

$$R^z(x) = 255 - I^z(x), \tag{1}$$

where z represents one of the RGB color channels, $I^z(x)$ denotes the low lighting image. $R^z(x)$ represents the corresponding output image. In order to get rid of the haze, we need to construct the atmospheric scattering model [7]:

$$I(x) = J(x)t(x) + A(1 - t(x)), \tag{2}$$

where $I(x)$ represents an image that needs to be dehazed. $J(x)$ is the fogless image. A is the atmospheric light component. $t(x)$ is the transmission map. Let's say A is known. In order to restore the non-hazy image, only the transmission map is required according to the above atmospheric scattering model. We use the dark channel priori theory to find the transmission map. Dark channel priori theory refers to the fact that some pixels always have at least one color channel with very low values in most non-sky local areas. That is, the minimum value of light intensity in the area is a very small number.

In the real world, there is always some particulate matter or dust in the air. So it is necessary to preserve a certain amount of haze. The restriction factor ω is introduced. Based on the dark channel priori theory, the preestimate of transmission is derived using [4]:

$$t(x) = 1 - \omega \min_{y \in \Omega(x)} (\min_z \frac{I^z(y)}{A^z}), \tag{3}$$

where ω is 0.85 and z is one of RGB channels. We reconstruct the image using [4]:

$$J(x) = \frac{R(x) - A}{t(x)} + A. \tag{4}$$

Finally, we invert the dehazed image using Eq. (1) and the enhanced low lighting image will be obtained.

2.2 Optimize Transmission Map with Guided Filter

Transmission map is obtained directly according to the dark channel theory, so the halo effect can be found in the image. In this paper, we propose to further process the image by using the guided filter to obtain a more accurate transmission map $\bar{t}$. We use the input image I as the guided graph to get the cost function [5]:

$$E(a_k, b_k) = \sum_{i \in \omega_k} ((a_k I_i + b_k - t)^2 + \varepsilon a_k^2), \tag{5}$$

where t is a rough estimate of the transmission map, ε is the regularization parameter, ω_k is the neighborhood in which the pixel point k is the center. (a_k, b_k) is constant in neighborhood ω_k.

The transmission map $\bar{t}(x)$ optimized by the guided filter can be expressed as [5]:

$$\bar{t}(x) = \frac{1}{|\omega|} \sum_{ki \in \omega_k} (a_k I_i + b_k), \tag{6}$$

where $|\omega|$ is the pixel count in the neighborhood of ω_k.

2.3 The Transmission Selection Strategy Based on Hash Criterion

The transmission map is calculated for each pixel in each image, and this slows the operation speed of the algorithm. Based on the hash criterion, we design a selection strategy of transmission calculation, and guarantee the real-time processing of videos.

Each frame is divided into N 8 * 8 blocks, respectively calculating the grayscale average of 64 pixels of each adjacent frame. The grayscale of each pixel is then compared with the mean value. If it's greater than or equal to the average, we set it to 1; If it's less than the average, we set it to 0. Combining the results together makes up a 64-bit integer, which is the fingerprint of this small block. Hamming distance of the two frames is calculated. If the hamming distance is less than the threshold value (a predetermined threshold value), we say the two small pieces of high similarity. In this case, the transmission of $8*8$ is replaced by the perspective of the corresponding position in one frame, or to recalculate the current frame of this small piece of transmission. Considering the subtle changes in the background may not be detected, the transmission map is forced to be updated every 50 frames.

2.4   Foreground Extraction and Background Modeling

In order to ensure real-time processing, the improved vibe algorithm is used to model the background of enhanced low lighting video. Vibe is based on a small number of samples for background modeling, so the operation efficiency is high, and there is a certain robustness to small noises. However, because it uses the first frame to initialize the background model, there will be a "ghost" problem. The so-called "ghosting" problem refers to the fact that the algorithm will take the first frame of a video sequence as the background of the moving object in the scene. So that this object will be viewed as a foreground for a long time after it leaves the scene. Next we introduce the specific steps of the motion object detection algorithm proposed in this chapter. Because adjacent pixels have similar pixel values. For the first pixel, we randomly select the pixel values of the neighborhood as its model sample values. The mathematics can be expressed as [6]:

$$M^0(x) = \{v^0(y|y \in N_G(x))\}, \tag{7}$$

where $N_G(x)$ stands for adjacent pixels. y represents the random selection of adjacent pixels as the model sample values.

The background model stores a sample value for each background point, and each new pixel value is compared with the sample value to determine whether it belongs to the background. The specific method is to calculate the direct distance between the sample set and the new pixel value. If the distance is less than the threshold (the threshold is set in advance), the approximate number of sample points will be increased. Otherwise, the new pixel point is considered as the background. The number of samples N is 20, threshold min is 2, and the threshold value of the same distance R is 20.

2.5   Updating of the Background Model

The update strategy of the background model is to update the sample values of the model with the probability of $\frac{1}{\varphi}$ at each background pixel. At the same time, there is $\frac{1}{\varphi}$ probability to update the model sample values of its neighborhood pixels. We take advantage of the spatial propagation characteristics of pixel values to update the neighborhood sample values. The background model gradually spreads outward, which is also conducive to the identification of "ghost" area. When the number of foreground pixels reaches the critical value, it becomes the background. There is a probability of $\frac{1}{\varphi}$ to update the sample values of the model.

When selecting the samples in the sample set to be replaced, we randomly select a sample to be updated to ensure a smooth life cycle of the samples. Because the updating is random, the probability that a sample is not updated at time t is $\frac{N-1}{N}$. If the time is continuous, then the probability that the samples are still retained after time can be expressed as [6]:

$$P(t, t + dt) = (\frac{N-1}{N})^{(t+dt)-t}. \tag{8}$$

The above expression indicates whether a sample is replaced with t in the model, and the random strategy is appropriate. Not every frame needs to update the background model, but to update the background model according to certain update rate. When a pixel is determined as the background, it has a probability of 1/rate updating the background model. The rate is the time sampling factor, and the general value is 16.

3   Experimental Results

In our experiments, we use Windows PC with Intel Core i5-3330 with 8G of RAM, Windows10 operating system. The images' resolution is 640 * 480.

In order to validate and evaluate the validity of the key frame extraction algorithm proposed in this paper, we first verify the effectiveness of the image enhancement algorithm. We test the images in the public photography dataset [8]. We have selected eight kinds of pictures, namely, Aquarium, Architecture, Street and Theater. All eight of these images have a dark background and a lack of exposure.

We compared with LDR [9], LIME [10] and RBF [11] respectively. Figure 2 shows the effect of the algorithm comparison. We can see that RBF, LIME and our algorithm have a good visual effect. It is better to restore the real scene. Our algorithm also enhances the contrast of images and improves the visual effect of human eyes.

We will continue to analyze the algorithm running time and image quality. In the Sect. 2, we propose a strategy of transmission selection based on hashing criterion, which can greatly improve the efficiency of the algorithm. Figure 1 shows the difference between the use of a hash criterion to simplify the transmission calculation. On the left is the original image, in the middle is the enhanced diagram without the hash criterion, and on the right is the enhanced diagram using the hashing criterion. Table 1 shows the time of running a frame for the algorithm. Table 2 compares our algorithm's time with other algorithms to run a frame. It can be seen that while improving the efficiency of the algorithm, the quality of the image did not decrease too much, even the naked eye could not see the image quality decline.

In order to measure the low lighting image enhancement algorithm proposed in this paper excellent more objectively. We use HDR datasets [12] with ground truth as test sets. And we calculate the PSNR and SSIM [13] of the enhanced image and ground truth.

Fig. 1. Left: the original image. Middle: without hash criterion. Right: hash criterion.

Table 1. The influence of transmission selection strategy on algorithm running time.

Time (ms)	No optimization	Optimization
OURS	376.0	31.2

Figure 3 is the comparison of PSNR and SSIM between our algorithm and other algorithms such as RBF, LDR and LIME. It can be seen that the PSNR and SSIM values of our algorithm are higher than others'. The enhanced image is closer to the real value. Figure 4 is an intuitive comparison between the image and the real value after our algorithm is processed.

In order to visually demonstrate the effectiveness of the low lighting video enhancement algorithm proposed in this chapter to improve the accuracy of video synopsis. Figure 5 shows the binarization diagram for foreground extraction, where the left represents the original image, the middle represents the unenhanced image, and the right represents the enhanced image.

In order to objectively judge the accuracy in our video synopsis algorithm, we compared the vibe, mixed Gaussian algorithm [14], frame difference method. The accuracy(P) and recall(R) rate of the four data sets are calculated respectively using:

$$P = \frac{TP}{TP + FP}, R = \frac{TP}{TP + FN},\tag{9}$$

where (TP) means predicting the positive class as positive, (FP) means predicting the negative class as positive, (FN) means predicting the original positive class as negative. It can be seen from Table 3 that the accuracy of video concentration algorithm in this paper is obviously superior to other algorithms.

Table 2. Comparison of run time of low lighting enhancement algorithm runs a frame.

Time (ms)	Aquarium	Architecture	Street	Theater
LDR	62.4	58.4	61.8	243.6
LIME	743.8	316.2	361.6	305.6
RBF	7610.5	7541.8	7536.1	7481.6
OURS	**31.1**	**31.0**	**30.0**	**29.2**

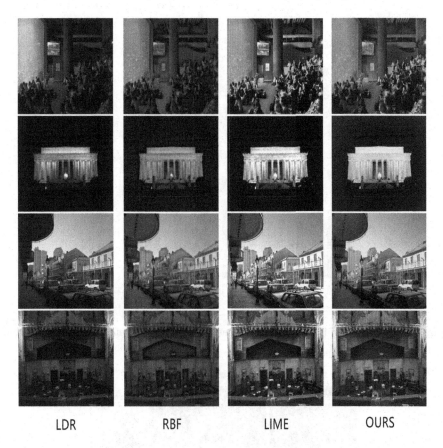

LDR   RBF   LIME   OURS

Fig. 2. Comparison of the visual effect of low lighting enhancement algorithm.

Table 3. Precion and recall of key frame extraction algorithm.

Precion/recall	Video1	Video2	Video3	Video4
Vibe	1.00/0.002	1.00/0.12	0.94/0.11	1.00/0.13
GMM	0.92/0.09	1.00/0.09	1.00/0.08	1.00/0.10
Dif	0/0	1.00/0.003	1.00/0.01	1.00/0.09
OURS	**0.80/0.28**	**1.00/0.52**	**0.95/0.35**	**1.00/0.63**

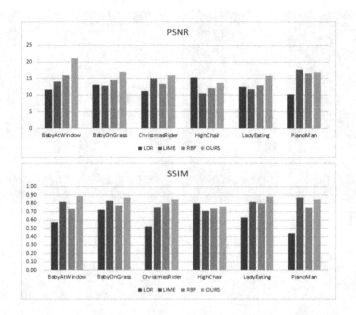

Fig. 3. Comparison of PSNR and SSIM between low lighting enhancement algorithm.

Fig. 4. Left: low lighting image. Middle: ground truth. Right: the effect of our algorithm.

Fig. 5. Left: original image. Middle: binarization diagram of original image. Right: binarization diagram of enhanced image.

4   Conclusions

In this paper, we have presented a novel, real-time, effective low lighting key frame extraction method. We improve accuracy through image enhancement. We designed a method of transmission selection based on hash criterion, which improves the speed of the algorithm. The improved vibe algorithm is used to detect moving objects and keep the frame of the moving objects as the key frame. In the later stage, we consider the combination of moving object detection and target identification, and selectively preserve the frame of a certain kind of object.

References

1. Tonomura, Y., Akutsu, A., Otsuji, K., Sadakata, T.: VideoMAP and VideoSpacelcon: tools for anatomizing video content. In: Conference on Human Factors in Computing Systems, pp. 131–136 (1993)
2. Zhang, H.J., Wu, J., Zhong, D., Smoliar, S.W.: An integrated system for content-based video retrieval and browsing. Pattern Recognit. **30**(4), 643–658 (1997)
3. Sun, Z.: Combination of color-and object-outline-based method in video segmentation. In: Storage and Retrieval Methods and Applications for Multimedia, pp. 61–69 (2003)
4. He, K., Sun, J., Tang, X.: Single image haze removal using dark channel prior. In: IEEE Conference on Computer Vision and Pattern Recognition, pp. 1956–1963 (2009)
5. He, K., Sun, J., Tang, X.: Guided image filtering. In: Daniilidis, K., Maragos, P., Paragios, N. (eds.) ECCV 2010. LNCS, vol. 6311, pp. 1–14. Springer, Heidelberg (2010). https://doi.org/10.1007/978-3-642-15549-9_1
6. Barnich, O., Droogenbroeck, M.V.: Vibe: a powerful random technique to estimate the background in video sequences. In: IEEE International Conference on Acoustics, Speech and Signal Processing, pp. 945–948 (2009)
7. Eric, B., Fabrice, N.: Precomputed atmospheric scattering. Comput. Graph. Forum **27**(4), 1079–1086 (2008)
8. http://mcl.korea.ac.kr/projects/LDR/LDR_TEST_IMAGES_DICM.zip

9. Lee, C., Lee, C., Kim, C.S.: Contrast enhancement based on layered difference representation of 2D histograms. IEEE Trans. Image Process. **22**(12), 5372–5384 (2013)
10. Guo, X., Li, Y., Ling, H.: LIME: low-light image enhancement via illumination map estimation. IEEE Trans. Image Process. **26**(2), 982–993 (2016)
11. Elad, M.: Retinex by two bilateral filters. In: Kimmel, R., Sochen, N.A., Weickert, J. (eds.) Scale-Space 2005. LNCS, vol. 3459, pp. 217–229. Springer, Heidelberg (2005). https://doi.org/10.1007/11408031_19
12. Sen, P., Shechtman, E., Shechtman, E., Shechtman, E., Shechtman, E., Shechtman, E.: Robust patch-based HDR reconstruction of dynamic scenes. ACM Trans. Graph. **31**(6), 203 (2012)
13. Wang, Z., Bovik, A.C., Sheikh, H.R., Simoncelli, E.P.: Image quality assessment: from error visibility to structural similarity. IEEE Trans. Image Process. **13**(4), 600–612 (2004)
14. Stauffer, C., Grimson, W.E.L.: Adaptive background mixture models for real-time tracking. In: IEEE Conference on Computer Vision and Pattern Recognition, vol. 2, pp. 2246 (1999)

Moving Cast Shadow Removal
Based on Texture Feature
and Color Space

Chao Zheng, Zhan-Li Sun$^{(\boxtimes)}$, Nan Wang, and Xin-Yuan Bao

School of Electrical Engineering and Automation, Anhui University, Hefei, China
zhlsun2006@126.com

Abstract. Moving cast shadow detection is an essential and pivotal problem in image processing. One problem is that many existed moving cast shadow detection methods are only suitable for some specific situations. In order to solve this problem, a cast shadow detection and elimination algorithm based on the combination of texture feature and YUV color space is proposed in this paper. Firstly, we detect moving object using PBAS algorithm which suppress ghost region. Furthermore, a part of cast shadow candidate region is obtained by texture detection. Then, the other cast shadow candidate region is obtained by shadow detection based on YUV color space. Finally, two parts of the cast shadow candidate regions are screened and merged by the shadow feature. Experimental results show that the proposed method has higher detection rates and discrimination rates compared to some well-known methods.

Keywords: Cast shadow · Color space · Moving object detection
Texture detection

1 Introduction

Currently the moving cast shadow is one of the fundamentally interference factors of the moving object detection. Most of the moving object detection algorithms have mistakes that cast shadow region are seen as moving object. This phenomenon occurred is owing to shadows share the same movement characteristics as the objects and also typically differ from the background.

Many approaches for moving cast shadows detection and removal have been proposed over the past decades. For example, the HSV approach introduced by Cucchiara et al. [1] is one of the most famous methods have been presented. Sun

---

Z.-L. Sun—The work was supported by a grant from National Natural Science Foundation of China (No. 61370109), a key project of support program for outstanding young talents of Anhui province university (No. gxyqZD2016013), a grant of science and technology program to strengthen police force (No. 1604d0802019), and a grant for academic and technical leaders and candidates of Anhui province (No. 2016H090).

© Springer International Publishing AG, part of Springer Nature 2018
T. Huang et al. (Eds.): ISNN 2018, LNCS 10878, pp. 611–618, 2018.
https://doi.org/10.1007/978-3-319-92537-0_70

et al. [2,3] according to the c1c2c3 color space characteristics of objects and their
shadows, appropriate threshold thresholds of luminance and chroma are set to
eliminate shadows. Lee et al. [4] using Laplace operator to detect foreground and
background edge to realize shadow detection. Some algorithms using geometric
models to describe the cast shadow of moving object such as Hsieh et al. [5].
However, many of the above-mentioned moving shadow detection methods use
general-purpose image feature descriptors to detect cast shadows. These feature
descriptors maybe suitable for shadow detection in specific situations and often
fail to detect shadow region from the foreground object in other situations.

In this paper, we present a new method that builds on texture features and
color features. This new method detects cast shadow by combining texture features and color features can suitable for most of the problematic situations.

2   PBAS Moving Object Detection

PBAS algorithm [6] is a moving object detection algorithm which combining
the advantages of ViBE [7] algorithm and SACON [8] algorithm, having greatly
illumination robustness and high foreground detection rate. In this algorithm,
firstly establishes the initialization background model. Then, the pixel point is
detected by a given threshold parameter. Background pixels update the background model with the decision threshold $R(x_i)$ and the learning rate $T(x_i)$.
Finally, the update factor that the decision threshold $R(x_i)$ and the learning
rate $T(x_i)$ is updated. The update factor $T(x_i)$ and $R(x_i)$ of PBAS algorithm
is dynamic update, which is better than ViBE algorithm, which also makes the
robustness of PBAS algorithm better.

2.1   Suppression of Ghost Shadow by Frame Difference Method

When the background model initialization process is performed using the original
PBAS algorithm, a ghost phenomenon occurs if there is a foreground object
and the like. In view of the phenomenon of ghost, a method of eliminating
ghost region based on frame difference method is proposed. Using $I_n(x_i)$ and
$I_{n-1}(x_i)$ to represent the pixels of the current frame image and the previous
frame, respectively. $d_n(x_i)$ is absolute value of the post subtract image, then
$d_n(x_i)$ can be expressed as:

$$d_n(x_i) = |I_n(x_i) - I_{n-1}(x_i)|, i = 1, 2, \cdots . \tag{1}$$

In general, when $d_n(x_i) = 0$, there means non moving object is expressed,
in contrast, when $d_n(x_i) \neq 0$, then the corresponding pixel is a moving object.
However, in practice, due to noise and other factors interference, the value will
not be so absolute, so we need to set the threshold T to judge the moving object:

$$R_n = \begin{cases} 255 \ if d_n(x_i) \geq T \\ 0 \ \ if d_n(x_i) < T \end{cases} . \tag{2}$$

If the $d_n(x_i)$ is greater than or equal to the threshold value T, it is judged to be a moving object, and its gray pixel value is 255, else it is not a moving object with a gray pixel value of 0. The region with a pixel value of 255 is defined as the foreground moving object region.

2.2 Union and Post-processing

Because the foreground detected by frame difference method will not appear Ghost region, nevertheless may appear false detection. So judging whether the foreground pixel detected by frame difference method are also foreground pixels detected by PBAS algorithm, the gray pixel is 255 pixels, otherwise it is 0. Then post-processing is necessary, which includes open/close morphology processing and filling for small holes. For best result, the foreground pixels which have been morphological process and foreground pixels $F(x_i)$ were obtained with the PBAS union.

3 Moving Cast Shadow Removal

The our method of cast shadow region detection and elimination consists of two main stages, namely, pixel-texture shadow Removal and pixel-spaces shadow detection. Here is build that the foreground has been extracted and the background frames are available. First of all, the initial shadow detection and elimination are realized by gradient algorithm. The candidate region S_1 of moving object is obtained by removing cast shadow region. This algorithm is based on the gradient feature of the object, so it is not affected by the change of pixel value. Secondly, the shadow is detected and eliminated by YUV color space [9] transformation, and the candidate region S_2 of moving object after eliminating cast shadow is obtained. At last, the two candidate regions are fused according to the shadow features to obtain the complete moving object after the final elimination of the cast shadow.

3.1 Pixel-Texture Shadow Removal

Texture detection for the detected foreground object and its corresponding background, here utilized the Scharr gradient operator. Scharr operator model can be conveyed as follows:

$$\begin{bmatrix} -3 & 0 & 3 \\ -10 & 0 & 10 \\ -3 & 0 & 3 \end{bmatrix}, \begin{bmatrix} -3 & -10 & -3 \\ 0 & 0 & 0 \\ 3 & 10 & 3 \end{bmatrix}. \tag{3}$$

Firstly, Scharr gradient operators are used to calculate the each pixel(x,y)of gradient vector of the background, respectively in two directions that horizontal $g_{f,1}(x,y)$ and vertical directions $g_{f,2}(x,y)$, which formula can be factorized as [4]:

$$g_{f,i}(x,y) = f(x,y) * H_i(x,y), i = 1, 2, \tag{4}$$

where $f(x,y)$ is coordinates (x,y) pixel values, $H_i(x,y)$ is Scharr gradient operators of horizontal and vertical directions. Secondly, using scharr gradient operators to calculate the each pixel (x,y) of gradient vector of the foreground of the current frame, respectively in two directions that horizontal $g_{c,1}(x,y)$ and vertical directions $g_{c,2}(x,y)$, which formula can be factorized as [4]:

$$g_{c,i}(x,y) = f(x,y) * H_i(x,y), i = 1,2. \qquad (5)$$

Thirdly, calculation of the difference d between the foreground gradient of the current image frame and the gradient of its corresponding background image, percent [4]:

$$d = \|g_{c,i}(x,y) - g_{f,i}(x,y)\| = \sum_{i=1}^{2} |g_{c,i}(x,y) - g_{f,i}(x,y)|. \qquad (6)$$

Afterward, a series of morphological operations such as contour extraction, hole filling, image filtering and so on are carried out to determine the region of shadow elimination S_1.

3.2 Shadow Detection Based on YUV Color Space

YUV color space is a color coding method, where Y denotes brightness and gray value of image U and V represent color difference U and V are two components of color. The conversion formula between YUV color space and RGB color space is [9]:

$$\begin{bmatrix} Y \\ U \\ V \end{bmatrix} = \begin{bmatrix} 0.299 & 0.587 & 0.114 \\ -0.147 & -0.289 & 0.436 \\ 0.615 & -0.515 & 0.100 \end{bmatrix} \begin{bmatrix} R \\ G \\ B \end{bmatrix}. \qquad (7)$$

The color difference between luminance Y and UV is mutual independence, and the projection shadow region has the following characteristics in YUV color space. In the first place, the pixel brightness of the projection area is lower than the pixel brightness of its corresponding background and foreground. In the second place, the background pixels color pixel color projection area and its corresponding is very similar. The YUV shadow region M_1 is detected according to the above two characteristics. Shadow region M_1 formula can be factorized as [9]:

$$M_1 = \begin{cases} y_{min} < y_f - y_b < y_{max} \\ v_{min} < v_f - v_b < v_{max} \end{cases}, \qquad (8)$$

where y_f and y_b respectively represent Y component values of the foreground and the corresponding background, v_f and v_b represent V component values of the foreground and the corresponding background, respectively. y_{min}, y_{max}, v_{min}, v_{max} respectively represent component values of limited threshold. Detection the shadow region by the set threshold which made above.

3.3 Shadow Region Fusion

Both the pixel-texture shadow removal algorithm and the base on YUV color space shadow detection algorithm have their own limitations. Pixel-texture shadow removal algorithm also appears the phenomenon of the missing of foreground region while removing the shadow. At the same time, base on YUV color space shadow detection algorithm has a poor effect on deep value of shadows and is prone to false detection or missing detection. Thus, according to the specific characteristics of shadow, the shadow region fusion removed by the two algorithms can compensate for the defects of a single algorithm. At first, the pixel value of the shadow region of the moving object is smaller than the pixel value of corresponding to the background. Second, in that there is no direct light source in the projection region and only air scattering, the shadow region of moving objects will change blue relative to the chromatic shadow region. The standard of fusion is the RGB channel pixel values in the foreground area are all smaller than the RGB channel pixel values of the corresponding background and the difference between the foreground and the corresponding background R channel and G channel pixel difference is greater than that of the B channel.By this standard to fuse two parts of the shadow region. At last, getting the final region of moving object.

4   Experiments

The performance evaluation for the proposed method is conducted under various environments. Four challenging datasets for indoor and outdoor environments are used in the experiment, including highway, cubicle, pedestrians and bungalows provided for the Change Detection Challenge [10]. Table 1 represents a summary of the technical details of various publicly available datasets for indoor and outdoor situations. All experiments in this paper have been carried out using a PC running Microsoft Visual Studio 2013 and Opencv 2.4.11 on Inter(R) Core(tm)i5-3470 Eight-Core Processor at 3.2 GHz with 8 GB RAM.

Table 1. Technical details of datasets

	Scene type	Number of frame	Size
Highway	Outdoor	1700	320*240
Bungalows	Outdoor	1700	360*240
Cubicle	Indoor	7400	352*240
Pedestrians	Outdoor	1100	360*240

The first sequence is highway, exhibits quite a few heavy traffic condition with strong and large size cast shadows. The bungalows sequence shows a traffic scene captured with a narrow-angle camera. This sequence is a good example of having chromatic shadows, non-textured surfaces and foreground-shadow camouflage. Cubicle is a typical indoor environment in which a strong camouflage exists between parts of a walking person and the background. Pedestrians shows an outdoor environment for different light conditions and different sizes of objects and shadows. It represents cases of having most of the problematic situations.

The qualitative and quantitative results from the proposed method have been evaluated and compared with those obtained by three well-known methods, namely, chromaticity, physical and geometry. The chromaticity-based approach assumes that the area under the cast shadow has a lower intensity but maintains the same chroma as the original area. The physical method attempts to model the specific appearance of the shadow pixel. Geometry-based methods predict the direction, size, and shape of shadows for light sources, object shapes, and ground planes.

Figure 1 shows shadow detection results using the ours method and four other methods, namely, the chromaticity method(Chr) [11], physical method(phy) [5] and geometry methods(geo) [12]. In the first row of Fig. 1, a challenging frame from each dataset is shown. The ground truth images are given in the second column. The shadow detection results using our, chr, geo and phy method are shown in the third, fourth, fifth and sixth column, respectively.

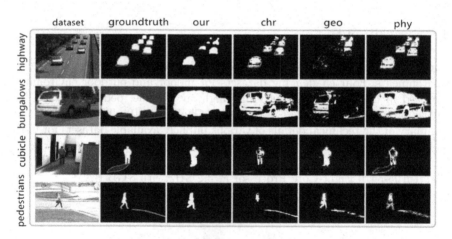

Fig. 1. Qualitative shadow removal results for the four methods. The shadow detection results using our, chr, geo and phy method are shown in the third, fourth, fifth and sixth column.

Table 2 represents the overall quantitative performance of the seven methods using three metrics, namely, the shadow detection rate, the shadow discrimination rate, and the speed. The shadow detection rate η measures the percentage of shadow points correctly detected as shadows and the shadow discrimination rate ξ measures the percentage of object points correctly detected as objects. They are calculated as follows:

Table 2. Performance analysis

Datasets	Highway			Bungalows			Cubicle			Pedestrians		
	η	ξ	θ	η	ξ	θ	η	ξ	θ	η	ξ	θ
our	0.77	0.80	0.79	0.90	0.94	0.92	0.70	0.77	0.73	0.76	0.81	0.79
geo	0.51	0.88	0.63	0.43	0.81	0.57	0.54	0.65	0.61	0.71	0.81	0.76
chr	0.48	0.85	0.61	0.67	0.81	0.73	0.61	0.63	0.62	0.69	0.80	0.74
phy	0.65	0.71	0.67	0.68	0.79	0.72	0.39	0.42	0.41	0.37	0.60	0.46

$$\eta = \frac{TP_s}{TP_s + FN_s}, \tag{9}$$

$$\xi = \frac{TP_f}{TP_f + FN_f}, \tag{10}$$

where the subscript s stands for shadow and f for foreground. TF_s and TP_f are on behalf of the number of true positive pixels with respect to either shadow or foreground objects. FN_s and FN_f represent the number of false negative pixels with respect to either shadow or foreground objects. All the two values η and ξ are the larger the better. In this paper, we use the comprehensive θ as a single performance measure.

$$\theta = \frac{2\eta\xi}{\eta + \xi}. \tag{11}$$

It can be seen that the our method outperforms the other three methods in terms of the cast shadow detection rate from the indoor and outdoor video sequences for qualitative comparisons. It can be seen from the results that the algorithms proposed in this paper are all the best.

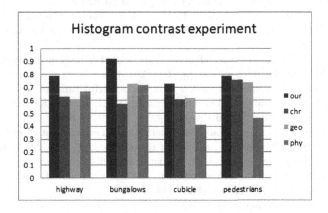

Fig. 2. Histogram contrast experiment of θ

At the same time, we also present a quantitative analysis of the results, utilizing the evaluate metric θ. The quantitative analysis can provide the persuasive shadow removal performance. As illustrated in Fig. 2, whether evaluate our approach in a qualitative way or in a quantitative way, the our method obtains better performance than other three methods: the chromaticity method(Chr), physical method(phy) and geometry methods(geo), especially for outdoor scenes such as bungalows and highway which are much more challenging.

5   Conclusion

In this paper, we proposed an effective method for detecting and removal moving shadows in indoor and outdoor environments. A combination of two features, namely, pixel-texture shadow removal and color-spaces shadow detection is introduced and formulated to improve the shadow detection results in various problematic situations. Experimental results on various datasets show the robustness of the proposed method and superior performance over three well-known methods in terms of shadow detection rate.

References

1. Cucchiara, R., Grana, C., Piccardi, M., Prati, A.: Detecting moving objects, ghosts, and shadows in video streams. IEEE Trans. Pattern Anal. Mach. Intell. **25**(10), 1337–1342 (2003)
2. Sun, B., Li, S.: Moving cast shadow detection of vehicle using combined color models. In: Pattern Recognition, pp. 1–5 (2010)
3. Golchin, M., Khalid, F., Abdullah, L.N., Davarpanah, S.H.: Shadow detection using color and edge information. J. Comput. Sci. **9**(11), 1575–1588 (2013)
4. Lee, B.E., Nguyen, T.B., Sun, T.C.: An efficient cast shadow removal for motion segmentation. In: WSEAS International Conference on Signal Processing, Computational Geometry and Artificial Vision, pp. 83–87 (2009)
5. Hsieh, J.W., Hu, W.F., Chang, C.J., Chen, Y.S.: Shadow elimination for effective moving object detection by Gaussian shadow modeling. Image Vis. Comput. **21**(6), 505–516 (2003)
6. Sun, B., Li, S.: Moving cast shadow detection of vehicle using combined color models. In: Pattern Recognition, pp. 1–5 (2010)
7. Barnich, O., Droogenbroeck, M.V.: ViBe: a powerful random technique to estimate the background in video sequences. In: IEEE International Conference on Acoustics, Speech and Signal Processing, pp. 945–948 (2009)
8. Wang, H., Suter, D.: Background subtraction based on a robust consensus method. In: International Conference on Pattern Recognition, pp. 223–226 (2006)
9. Joshi, A.J., Atev, S., Masoud, O., Papanikolopoulos, N.: Moving shadow detection with low-and mid-level reasoning. In: 2007 IEEE International Conference on Robotics and Automation, pp. 4827–4832 (2007)
10. http://www.changedetection.net/
11. Huang, J.B., Chen, C.S.: Moving cast shadow detection using physics-based features. In: IEEE Conference on Computer Vision and Pattern Recognition, pp. 2310–2317 (2009)
12. Leone, A., Distante, C.: Shadow detection for moving objects based on texture analysis. Pattern Recognit. **40**(4), 1222–1233 (2007)

A Novel Low Level Feature Normalization Method for Content Based Image Retrieval

Trung Xuan Hoang[1(✉)], Tuyet Van Dao[2,3], Nguyen Trinh Nguyen[4],
Huy Hoang Ngo[5,6], and Ablameyko Sergey[2,7]

[1] Hanoi University of Business and Technology, Hanoi, Vietnam
trungvnit@gmail.com
[2] Belarusian State University, Minsk, Belarus
daovt@bsu.by, ablameyko@bsu.by
[3] Vietnam National Space Center, Vietnam Academy of Science
and Technology, Hanoi, Vietnam
dvtuyet@vnsc.org.vn
[4] Nong Lam University Hochiminh City, Linh Trung Ward, Thu Duc District,
Hochiminh City, Vietnam
nguyentrinhnguyen@hcmuaf.edu.vn
[5] Electric Power University of the Vietnam Ministry of Industry and Trade,
Hanoi, Vietnam
[6] Institute of Information Technology, Vietnam Academy of Science
and Technology, 18 Hoang Quoc Viet, Hanoi, Vietnam
huyngo3i@gmail.com
[7] United Institute of Informatics Problems, National Academy
of Sciences of Belarus, 6, Surganova Street, 220012 Minsk, Belarus

Abstract. In CBIR, images are represented by certain low-level features that describe their color, texture and shape. The combination of different image features in a global distance measurement requires normalized feature vectors. Nowaday, several normalization methods have been proposed for CBIR such as min-max, 3-sigma, and 3sigma-FCM. In this paper, we propose another method which is an upgrade from the 3sigma-FCM method. Experimentation has shown the effectiveness and efficiency of the proposed algorithm for normalizing low-level image features. The dynamic range of each component of the normalized vectors within $[-1, 1]$ is wider than that of the 3sigma-FCM. The experiment also demonstrates that our method increases CBIR quality when combined with algorithms to define the similarity measure of images such as the EMR.

Keywords: CBIR · Low level features · FCM · 3sigma-FCM
3sigma-opt · EMR

1 Introduction

Content-Based Image Retrieval (CBIR) has become an important research area in recent years. These systems often retrieve the visual representations of the image and define the functions to measure the similarity, search, and match the relation for retrieval on demand[1–8].

© Springer International Publishing AG, part of Springer Nature 2018
T. Huang et al. (Eds.): ISNN 2018, LNCS 10878, pp. 619–627, 2018.
https://doi.org/10.1007/978-3-319-92537-0_71

In general, the Content-Base Image Retrieval system requires the inclusion of descriptive information about color, texture, and shape feature at the same time. Each visual feature vector extracted from an image has the numerical components which belong to different intervals. Therefore, when combining multiple representational features for images to form a similarity measurement of a pair of images, we need to standardize the vector feature data such that all components of the normalized vectors belong to the same interval, namely the [0, 1] (see [1, 2]).

Recently, in [3] the authors proposed a normalization method called 3sigma-FCM (3σ-*FCM*). This method is an extension of the well-known 3-sigma normalization, which is used extensively in the field of CBIR [2, 6]. The 3sigma-FCM has been effectively applied in CBIR, however, the components of normalized vectors still fall into a narrower interval within the [−1, 1] interval. This reduces the generalization of the 3sigma-FCM to apply this method to other domains, where the normalized data is required to spread over the entire normalization interval, such as to construct the similarity measure between a couple of individual image based on the Choquet integral in [7].

In this paper, we propose a method *of upgrading from the 3σ-FCM* that is considered a linear transformation of *3σ-FCM* with linear coefficients estimated automatically and optimally from the image feature database. These differences are presented in Sects. 3 and 4.

The rest of the paper is organized as follows. Section 2 describes some research related to using the specific combinations, normalized features. The Sect. 3 presents the proposed normalization method for image feature vectors. Experimental results are given in Sect. 4. Conclusion and future research direction are in the Sect. 5.

2 Background

2.1 Low-Level Features in CBIR

In different CBIR applications, we usually have to combine low-level features that describe about colors, textures, and shapes of images [2, 6–10] to define a similarity measurement between images. Below we list some specific low-level features: vector color Moments (Color feature type); vector LBP and Gabor Wavelets Texture (Texture feature type); vector Edge and GIST (Shape feature types). In general, image representation models by low-level feature require the normalization of features into the numeric interval [0, 1] to compensate for the discrepancy between the feature components defined in a global similarity measure of images.

2.2 Normalization of the Low-Level Feature Vector Components

Normalization of the low-level features affects the effectiveness of CBIR systems [3]. Recently, in [3] the authors have presented an extended normalization method based on the 3-sigma to overcome the limitation of requiring that each component of the low-level features should have Gauss distribution. Given a low-level feature vector database, using the standard FCM algorithm (about FCM, see [11]), we segment the feature vectors into C clusters as follows:

Give $\{E_{t,i}\}_{1 \leq i \leq n}$, where $E_{t,i}$ is the t-th tuple of raw feature vector of the i-th image and constants $p = p(t) > 1$, $C = C(t) \in N^+$, $C \geq 2$, $m_t = \dim(E_{t,i})$, $\forall 1 \leq i \leq n$, the FCM minimizes the following objective function:

$$J(V, \eta) = \sum_{i=1}^{n} \sum_{c=1}^{C} \eta_{c,i}^p \left\| E_{t,i} - V_c \right\|^2 \rightarrow \min, \tag{1}$$

with the Euclidean distance measure, $\left\| E_{t,i} - V_{t,c} \right\|^2 = \sum_{j=1}^{m_t} (E_{t,i,j} - V_{t,c,j})^2$ and the variable constraints are given by:

(i) $\eta_{c,i} \in [0,1], \forall 1 \leq i \leq n, 1 \leq c \leq C$,

(ii) $\sum_{c=1}^{C} \eta_{c,i} = 1, \forall 1 \leq i \leq n$ \hfill (2)

the 3σ-FCM normalization operator [3] is given as follows:

Let $x = \{x_{t,j}\}_{j=1}^{m_t}$, $\forall t$, $1 \leq t \leq T$, $1 \leq j \leq m_t$ be an input data vector with m_t dimension for each t-th tuple $(1 \leq t \leq T)$, the 3σ-FCM normalization vector of vector **x** is a vector $x_{norm} = \{x_{norm,t,j}\}_{j=1}^{m_t}$, $\forall t$, $1 \leq t \leq T$, $1 \leq j \leq m_t$ defined by:

$$x_{norm,t,j} \overset{def}{=} \frac{\min\limits_{1 \leq c \leq C}\left\{\frac{x_{t,j}-V_{t,c,j}}{3\sigma_{t,c,j}}\right\} + \max\limits_{1 \leq c \leq C}\left\{\frac{x_{t,j}-V_{t,c,j}}{3\sigma_{t,c,j}}\right\}}{C+1} \tag{3}$$

where C is the desired cluster number of *data vectors* $\{E_{t,i}\}_{1 \leq i \leq n}$ *of t-th tuple by using the FCM clustering algorithm*, $V_{t,c,j}$ $(1 \leq t \leq T, 1 \leq c \leq C, 1 \leq j \leq m_t)$ *is the j-th component of the c-th center of the clusters obtained by FCM for* $\{E_{t,i}\}_{1 \leq i \leq n}$ *and* $\sigma_{t,c,j}$ $(1 \leq t \leq T, 1 \leq c \leq C, 1 \leq j \leq m_t)$ *is the standard deviation of j-th component of feature t-th for c-th cluster.*

Besides, $\sigma_{t,c,j}$ $(1 \leq t \leq T, 1 \leq c \leq C, 1 \leq j \leq m_t)$ *is calculated by:*

$$\forall 1 \leq j \leq m_t, \; \sigma_{t,c,j} \overset{def}{=} \sqrt{\sum_{i=1}^{n} \eta_{c,i}^p (E_{t,i,j} - V_{t,c,j})^2 \Big/ \sum_{i=1}^{n} \eta_{c,i}^p}$$

$$= \sqrt{(\sum_{i=1}^{n} \eta_{t,c,i}^p (E_{t,i,j})^2 \Big/ \sum_{i=1}^{n} \eta_{t,c,i}^p) - V_{t,c,j}^2} \tag{4}$$

Properties of 3σ-FCM including:

(P.1) No need to assume that the input vector components follow the Gaussian distribution.

(P.2) Preservesing the order of each component of the vector and most values of each vector component are in $[-1, 1]$.

(P.3) For each tuple t, the parameters of the normalization operator in individual dimension are related to each other.

However, 3σ-FCM still has some limitations, that are:

(L.1) The dynamic range of the vector components obtained by 3σ-FCM can still be narrower than $[-1, 1]$.

(L.2) The 3σ-FCM is still influenced by the parameter C.

In Sect. 3, we propose an extension method of 3σ-FCM which still keeps the advanced properties P.1–P.3, and overcomes the limitations L.1 and L.2.

2.3   The Proposed Objective Index and Definition

Let $E = \left\{E_{t,i}\right\}_{1 \leq i \leq n}$ be the database of feature vectors and TN be a normalization operator applied for feature vectors.

Denote $E_{norm} = \left\{E_{norm,t,i}\right\}_{1 \leq i \leq n}$, where $E_{norm,t,i} = TN(E_{t,i}) \; \forall t, 1 \leq t \leq T, 1 \leq i \leq n$.

Our proposal index to evaluate the effectiveness of a normalization operator TN defined by:

$$RMS \stackrel{def}{=} \sqrt{\frac{\sum\limits_{i=1}^{n} \sum\limits_{1 \leq j \leq \; \dim \; E_{t,i} \wedge E_{norm,t,i,j} \in [-1,1]} E_{norm,t,i,j}^2}{n^* \dim E_t}} \tag{5}$$

The larger the RMS, the better the normalization in the sense of the wider dynamic variation range within interval $[-1, 1]$ of individual normalized vector component of the database $\left\{E_{t,i,j}\right\}, j = \overline{1, \dim(\vec{E}_t)}$.

By using the FCM, after clustering the low-level feature vectors of t-th tuple (such as, t∈{*Color moment, LBP, Gabor Wavelet texture, Edge, GIST*} of the image database $E = \left\{E_{t,i}\right\}_{1 \leq i \leq n}$, we receive center vectors $\left\{\vec{V}_{t,c}\right\}_{1 \leq c \leq C(t)}$ and the two-dimensional matrix of membership values in $[0,1]$ which are $\left\{\eta_{t,j,c}\right\}_{1 \leq j \leq m_t, 1 \leq c \leq C(t)}$. Instead of using the scaling factor $a = 1/(C + 1)$ and $b = 0$ as in 3σ-FCM, we will use a general linear transformation $x_j \mapsto a_j x_j + b_j$, where $a = a\left(\left\{E_{t,i}\right\}_{1 \leq i \leq n}\right) \in [0, 1], b = b\left(\left\{E_{t,i}\right\}_{1 \leq i \leq n}\right)$ estimated automatically from the database $E = \left\{E_{t,i}\right\}_{1 \leq i \leq n}$ such that the a and b coefficients satisfy the following two conditions:

(C.1) For each vector component $1 \leq j \leq \dim(E_t)$ of t-th tuple, there is not over $(100 * \alpha_{out})\%$ vectors of the database $E = \left\{E_{t,i}\right\}_{1 \leq i \leq n}$ which have the j-th component falls outside of the interval $[-1,1]$.

(C.2) RMS index value is the largest.

Definition: 3sigma-opt (3σ-opt) normalization operator with optimal parameters.

Let $x = \{x_{t,j}\}_{j=1}^{m_t}, \forall t, 1 \leq t \leq T, 1 \leq j \leq m_t$ be an input data vector with m_t dimension for each t-th tuple ($1 \leq t \leq T$), the 3σ-opt normalization vector of vector $\mathbf{x}$ is a vector $x_{norm} = \{x_{norm,t,j}\}_{j=1}^{m_t}, \forall t, 1 \leq t \leq T, 1 \leq j \leq m_t$ defined by:

$$x_{norm,j} \stackrel{def}{=} a_{opt}\left(\min_{1 \leq c \leq C}\left\{\frac{x_j - V_{t,c,j}}{3\sigma_{t,c,j}}\right\} + \max_{1 \leq c \leq C}\left\{\frac{x_j - V_{t,c,j}}{3\sigma_{t,c,j}}\right\} \right) + b_{opt}, \forall j = \overline{1, m_t} \quad (6)$$

where a_{opt}, b_{opt} are two coefficients that satisfy:

(i) $0 < a_{opt} < 1, -0.5 \leq b_{opt} \leq 0.5$
(ii) a_{opt}, b_{opt} are the solution of the following objective function:

$$F_t(a,b) = \cfrac{1}{1 + \sqrt{\cfrac{\sum\limits_{i=1}^{n} \sum\limits_{1 \leq j \leq \ \dim E_{t,i} \wedge ad_{t,i,j} + b \in [-1,1]} (ad_{t,i,j} + b)^2}{n^* \dim E_t}}}$$
$$+ \#\left\{j \in \overline{1, \dim(E_t)}/\#\{i \in \overline{1,n}/ad_{t,i,j} + b \notin [-1,1]\} > n * \alpha_{out}\right\} \rightarrow \min$$
$$(7)$$

and

$$d_{t,i,j} \stackrel{def}{=} \min_{1 \leq c \leq C}\left\{\frac{E_{i,j} - V_{t,c,j}}{3\sigma_{t,c,j}}\right\} + \max_{1 \leq c \leq C}\left\{\frac{E_{i,j} - V_{t,c,j}}{3\sigma_{t,c,j}}\right\}, t = \overline{1,T}, i = \overline{1,n}, j = \overline{1, \dim(E_t)}$$
$$(8)$$

$\alpha_{out} \in (0,1)$ is the threshold for the number of elements of the j-th vector component $j = \overline{1, \dim(E_t)}$ of t-th tuple of feature vectors of the database $E = \{E_i\}_{i=1}^{n}$ which fall out of $[-1,1]$.

3   The Proposed Algorithm

By the definition 1 of the 3σ-opt above, we obtain the following results:

Remark 1: The function $F_t(a,b)$ is designed based on the principle of adding a value of 1.0 to each component $j \in \overline{1, \dim(E_t)}$ which is bigger than $(100 * \alpha_{out})\%$ vector of a database of a low-level feature tuple t at each vector falling outside of the interval [−1, 1]. Thus, F_t (a, b) will increase when there are many components $j \in \overline{1, \dim(E_t)}$ of t-th tuple of low-level feature vectors that fall outside of the interval [−1, 1].

Remark 2: If $F_t(a,b) < 1$ then with each j-th component in t-th tuple of feature vectors, $j = \overline{1, \dim(E_t)}$, the number of vectors of t-th tuple of feature vectors in the database

$\{E_{t,i}\}_{1 \le i \le n}$ after transforming according to formula (7) which falls outside the $[-1,1]$ not exceed to n * α_{out}.

Algorithm: 3σ-opt normalization operator with optimal parameters.

Input: The database $\{E_{t,i}\}_{1 \le i \le n}$ of t-th tuple of feature vectors ($1 \le t \le T$), constant p = p(t) > 1,

$C = C(t) \in N^+, C \ge 2$, $m_t = \dim(E_{t,i}^F), \forall i = \overline{1,n}$.

Percentage thresholds falling out [-1, 1] after normalizing: α_{out}

Output: The database $\{E_{t,i}^{Norm}\}_{1 \le i \le n}$ of normalized feature vectors where most of j-th

component of the t-th tuple $\{E_{t,i}^{Norm}\}_{1 \le i \le n}$ are in the interval [0, 1], the center vectors

$\{V_{t,c}\}_{1 \le c \le C_t}$ of cluters, $\{\sigma_{t,c,j}\}_{1 \le c \le C_t, 1 \le j \le m_t}$ and the optimal parameters a$_{opt}$, b$_{opt}$ of 3σ-opt.

Step 1: Do $FCM(C_t, {}_t)(\{E_{t,i,c}\}_{1 \le i \le n, 1 \le t \le T}, p_t)$, obtain $\{V_{t,c}\}_{c=1}^{C_t}$,

$\{\eta_{t,c,i}\}_{1 \le c \le C_t, 1 \le i \le n}$, according to formula (2) and (3)

Step 2: Calculate $\{\sigma_{t,c,j}\}_{1 \le c \le C_t, 1 \le j \le m_t}$ according to formula (5)

Step 3: Calculate $\{d_{t,c,j}\}_{1 \le c \le C_t, 1 \le j \le m_t}$ according to formula (8)

Step 4: Solve $F_t(a,b) \to \min$ with a $\in$ (0, 1) and b $\in$ [-0.5, 0.5] where F$_t$(a,b) determined by formula (7) as the following sub steps:

 4.1: Start $a = \dfrac{1}{C+1}$, $b = 0$.

 4.2: Repeat, change a and b such that F$_t$(a,b) reaches the approximate value of the idea smallest value (The method to solve this problem, see [12])
 4.3: Stop, obtain a$_{opt}$ = a, b$_{opt}$ = b.

Step 5: Normalization in [-1, 1]:

Repeat to each tuple t of each feature vector $\{\vec{E}_{t,i}\}$:

 5.1: Repeat with each component j $j = \overline{1, m_t}$ of $\vec{E}_{t,i}$, calculate $E_{t,i,j}^{norm}$ according to formula (6).
 5.2: Normalization in [0,1] (to apply for CBIR):

 Calculate $E_{t,i,j}^{norm} = \min\left\{\dfrac{\max\{E_{t,i,j}^{norm}, -1\} + 1}{2}, 1\right\}$.

Return: $\{\vec{E}_{t,i}^{norm}\}_{1 \le i \le n}$, $\{\vec{V}_{t,c}\}_{1 \le c \le C_t}$, $\{\sigma_{t,c,j}\}_{1 \le c \le C_t, 1 \le j \le m_t}$, a$_{opt}$, b$_{opt}$.

---

4   Experimental Results

We performed experiments on two datasets Corel10 K [13] and Oliva [14]. These are the standard datasets that are widely used to evaluate the performance of CBIR systems. These datasets are organized into semantic classes based on how people perceive similarity. Each class represents a different semantic theme, images in the same class are considered related to one another.

The first data set, Corel10 K, is a subset of the Corel photo gallery database. It consists of 10000 images divided into 100 layers with 100 images per layer. The Oliva second data set consists of 2600 images organized into 8 classes: Coast & Beach, open country, forest, mountain, high way street, city center, tall building, each class has 260 to 409 images.

In our experiments, we used five global features to describe an image: Color Moments, LBP, Gabor Wavelets Texture, Edge, and GIST. All of these features are normalized so that each vector component is within the $[-1, 1]$ (and then they will be normalization in $[0, 1]$) based on the algorithm 1. The Euclid distance will be used to calculate the distance between the feature vectors.

4.1   Calculated Optimal Parameters and the RMS Index Values

The 3σ-FCM strongly depends on the number of clusters of segmented vectors. However, 3σ-opt does not have this limitation as 3σ-FCM, because it is defined for maximizing the dynamic range of the vector components in $[-1, 1]$ through the objective function $F_t (a, b)$ in formula (7) (Table 1).

Table 1. Optimal parameters of 3σ-opt, RMS values of 3σ-opt and 3σ-FCM for the low-level feature vectors of Corel10 K dataset with the desired number of clusters C = 10, $\alpha_{out} = 0.02$

Feature data	a_{opt}	b_{opt}	RMS 3σ-FCM	RMS 3σ-opt
Color Moments	0.5138	0.0096	0.065946	**0.36407**
LBP	0.2315	0.0037	0.11644	**0.28731**
Gabor Wavelets	0.4290	−0.2294	0.089657	**0.3881**
Edge	0.0755	0.500	0.12538	**0.53337**
GIST	0.3377	−0.4953	0.060937	**0.54033**

4.2   Experimental Comparisons in CBIR

For comparison, we used the EMR algorithm [15] (the modules are as follows: Training module. Feature extraction. Learning and Classification) to evaluate the effectiveness of our proposed algorithm against with [3]. Experiments with top 100 images rated based on the EMR over 10% of retrieval images selected randomly from the Corel10 K and Oliva datasets, both gave higher average results of 3σ-opt compared to those of 3σ-FCM (Table 2).

Table 2. Compare effectiveness of image retrieval of 3σ-opt and 3σ-FCM using the Corel10 K and the Oliva datasets.

Image dataset	Average accuracy (3σ-FCM)	Average accuracy (3σ-opt)
Corel10 K	65,3%	**69,1%**
Oliva	73,3%	**75,4%**

The above empirical results show that 3σ-opt is more effective than 3σ-FCM. When the low-level feature vectors are normalized by the proposed 3σ-opt, the effectiveness of the image retrieval EMR has been improved.

5   Conclusions

The paper presents a method for normalizing low-level feature vectors of images extending from the 3σ-FCM method. It also preserves the order of the vector components as the 3σ-FCM, moreover it is independent of the cluster number used in the clustering step by the FCM algorithm. Especially, the proposed method has the advantage of a wider dynamic range of normalized feature vector components than the 3σ-FCM ones. Experiments in image retrieval with image databases that are widely used in CBIR such as the Corel (10000 images) and the Oliva datasets have showcased the effectiveness of the proposed method in comparison to the 3σ-FCM.

Acknowledgments. This research is supported by the Vietnam Academy of Science and Technology under the grant VAST01.05/15-16.

References

1. Bai, C., Kpalma, K., Ronsin, J.: Color textured image retrieval by combining texture and color features. In: 2012 Proceedings of the 20th European Signal Processing Conference (EUSIPCO). IEEE Press (2012)
2. Rui, Y., et al.: Relevance feedback: a power tool for interactive content-based image retrieval. IEEE Trans. Circuits Syst. Video Technol. **8**(5), 644–655 (1998)
3. Van Hieu, V., Huy, N.H., Tao, N.Q., Quynh, N.H.: A novel method normalized data and refine weights for combination features in content-based image retrieval. Vietnam. RD-ICT J. Res. Dev. Appl. Inf. Commun. Technol. **1**(35), 63–75 (2016)
4. Ortega, M., et al.: Supporting similarity queries in MARS. In: Proceedings of the Fifth ACM International Conference on Multimedia. ACM (1997)
5. Giang, N.T., Tao, N.Q., Dung, N.D., Huy, N.H.: Learning interaction measure with relevance feedback in image retrieval. J. Comput. Sci. Cybern. **32**(2), 113–131 (2016)
6. Deng, Y., et al.: An efficient color representation for image retrieval. IEEE Trans. Image Process. **10**(1), 140–147 (2001)
7. Jose, S., Joseph, P.: Content based image retrieval system with watermarks and relevance feedback. Int. J. Comput. Appl. **99**(11), 1–6 (2014)

8. Rui, Y., Huang, T.S., Mehrotra, S.: Content-based image retrieval with relevance feedback in MARS. In: 1997 Proceedings of International Conference on Image Processing, vol. 2. IEEE Press (1997)
9. Tamura, H., Mori, S., Yamawaki, T.: Textural features corresponding to visual perception. IEEE Trans. Syst. Man Cybern. **8**(6), 460–473 (1978)
10. Ojala, T., Pietikainen, M., Harwood, D.: A comparative study of texture measures with classification based on feature distributions. Pattern Recognit. **29**(1), 51–59 (1996)
11. Bezdek, J.C.: Pattern Recognition with Fuzzy Objective Function Algorithms. Springer Science & Business Media, Heidelberg (2013). https://doi.org/10.1007/978-1-4757-0450-1
12. https://www.mathworks.com/help/matlab/math/optimizing-nonlinear-functions.html
13. https://sites.google.com/site/dctresearch/Home/content-based-image-retrieval
14. Hoi, S.C.H., Lyu, M.R., Jin, R.: A unified log-based relevance feedback scheme for image retrieval. IEEE Trans. Knowl. Data Eng. **18**(4), 509–524 (2006)
15. Xu, B., Bu, J., Chen, C., Wang, C., Cai, D., He, X.: EMR: a scalable graph-based ranking model for content-based image retrieval. IEEE Trans. Knowl. Data Eng. **27**(1), 102–114 (2015)

An Effective Algorithm for Determining Pitch Markers of Vietnamese Speech Sentences

Thai Yen Ta[1(✉)], Hung Van Nguyen[2], Tuyet Van Dao[3,4],
Huy Hoang Ngo[5], and Ablameyko Sergey[3,6]

[1] Hanoi University of Business and Technology, Hanoi, Vietnam
tayenthai@gmail.com
[2] Military Institute of Science and Technology, Hanoi, Vietnam
Nvhnt73@gmail.com
[3] Belarusian State University, Minsk, Belarus
{daovt, ablameyko}@bsu.by
[4] Vietnam National Space Center, Vietnam Academy of Science
and Technology, Hanoi, Vietnam
dvtuyet@vnsc.org.vn
[5] Electric Power University, Vietnam Ministry of Industry and Trade,
235 Hoang Quoc Viet Street, Hanoi, Vietnam
huyngo3i@gmail.com
[6] United Institute of Informatics Problems of the National Academy of Sciences
of Belarus, 6, Surganova Street, Minsk 220012, Belarus

Abstract. Synthesizing Vietnamese tone plays an important role in Vietnamese text-to-speech systems. To accomplish this, the first important step is to determine the pitch-markers of voice utterances and this technique is still an open issue. In this paper, we propose a simple and efficient algorithm that locates the pitch-markers at the peaks of the cumulative signal of each voiced part of the input utterance. The experimentation has shown that the proposed algorithm presents pitch-markers with high accuracy and based on this obtained result, we have already synthesized Vietnamese complex tones such as the drop and the broken tones for isolated syllables with clear hearing.

Keywords: Pitch markers · Tones · Cumulative signal · Voiced/unvoiced

1 Introduction

The Vietnamese language is a monosyllabic and tonal language with six tones, every syllable must be expressed with a tone. The tone has a function of distinguish the meaning of the word. At the acoustic level, we can characterize each tone by fundamental frequency F0 contours.

To convert a speech of a syllable with the level tone into a speech of the same syllable but with a different tone such as the rising tone, firstly we need to determine the pitch markers (PM-Pitch Marker) of the original speech syllable [1–11]. Secondly, we have to stylized F0 contour of the rising tone and finally use a tool such as PSOLA algorithm [12] to create a target speech syllable with the rising tone (Fig. 1).

© Springer International Publishing AG, part of Springer Nature 2018
T. Huang et al. (Eds.): ISNN 2018, LNCS 10878, pp. 628–636, 2018.
https://doi.org/10.1007/978-3-319-92537-0_72

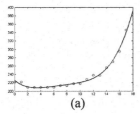 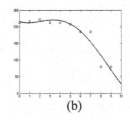 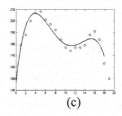

(a)   (b)   (c)

Fig. 1. The typical F0 contours shape of some tones of Vietnamese isolated syllables (a) rising tone (b) broken tone and (c) the drop tone.

2 Proposed

In this section, we propose a multi-phase pitch-mark detection algorithm for Vietnamese speech sentences.

2.1 The Cumulative Signal of a Voiced Segment

Let $x = \{x_j\}_{1 \leq j \leq N}$ be a voiced segment (in the time domain or frequency domain, without loss of generality assumed that the signal x is sampled from an interval [−a, a] with some a > 0), we define the cumulative signal $s = \{s_j\}_{1 \leq j \leq N}$ of x by

$$s_1 = x_1, \ \forall j = \overline{2, N}, s_j \overset{\text{def}}{=} s_{j-1} + x_j = \int_1^j x_t dt. \tag{1}$$

Thus, $x_t = \frac{\partial s}{\partial t}$ ($\forall t$, $X_t = S_t - S_{t-1}$).

In order to segment the input utterance into voiced/unvoiced parts we will use zero-crossing rate and the short time energy of a speech signal, in which they are defined as follows:

$$Z_x(m) = \frac{1}{M} \sum_{n=m-M+1}^{m} \frac{|sign(x_n) - sign(x_{n-1})|}{2}, m = \overline{M+1, N} \tag{2}$$

where M is the parameter (Fig. 2).

The $Z_x(m)$ values are used to determine whether the speech sample x_m belong to the voiced or unvoiced part, when $Z_x(m) > \alpha_z$ then sample x_m is in the voiced part and vice versa, The parameter α_z is determined empirically (for example, $\alpha_z = 0.17$) (Fig. 3).

 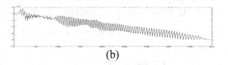

(a)   (b)

Fig. 2. (a) The sentence "Trời nghe trở gió ầm ầm trên mặt nước" ("God make the rumbling wind on the water") extracted in the Vietnamese book "Adventures of a Cricket". (b) The cumulative signal of the voiced part / gió/ (/wind/). The pitch-markers (marked by small circles) of the original voice segment are located "appropriately" in the signal points changing from positive to negative, respectively, as the peaks of the cumulative signal.

(a) The pitch-markers are located at the points in which the voice signal changes from positive to negative.

(b) The corresponding peaks of the cumulative signal.

Fig. 3. The relationship between signal points changes from positive to negative and the peaks of the correspondent cumulative total signal.

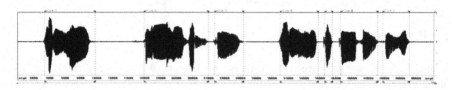

Fig. 4. Automatically dividing into 7 voiced segments of the recording sentence "*Đừng lo, xem mây vận trời đêm nay có cơ đổi gió.*" ("*Do not worry, looking at the clouds, the wind may change direction tonight.*") – extracted in the Vietnamese book "Adventures of a Cricket", each segment is shown in a pair of red-blue dashed lines. (Color figure online)

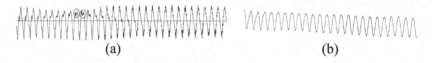

(a)   (b)

Fig. 5. (a) The partial signal of the second segment in the voiced segments. (b) The corresponding cumulative signal.

In Fig. 5b, the peaks of the cumulative signal are more visible than the original voice signal. The pitch markers located at peaks of the original voice signal are indistinguishable in amplitude from points surrounding them. In the details, the peaks having higher amplitude than the surrounding ones, usually also are PMs of the cumulative signal. From here, we propose a new approach, instead of locating pitch markers based on the original speech wave, we determine the pitch markers in the peak set of the cumulative signal of the speech.

The algorithm determining the PMs based on the cumulative signal is as follows:

Algorithm: EPM (Estimating the PMs of speech waves).

Input: Voice signal sequence $\{x_m\}_{1 \leq m \leq N}$ in time domain.

Parameter $\alpha_e, \alpha_z \in (0,1)$: The decisive thresholds of remove silence and

voiced/unvoiced .

Sampling frequency value : f_s

$[f_{0,min}, f_{0,max}]$ is the range of F0 values and M is the number of samples of a short time frame.

Output: Number of voiced segments K, Pitch markers according to four types
$$\left\{pm_{k,j}^+\right\}_{1\le k\le K, 1\le j\le n_k^+}, \left\{pm_{k,j}^-\right\}_{1\le k\le K, 1\le j\le n_k^-}, \left\{p_{k,j}^-\right\}_{1\le k\le K, 1\le j\le n_{k,2}^-}, \left\{p_{k,j}\right\}_{1\le k\le K, 1\le j\le n_{k,2}^+},$$
where $\left\{pm_{k,j}^+\right\}_{1\le k\le K, 1\le j\le n_k^+}, \left\{pm_{k,j}^-\right\}_{1\le k\le K, 1\le j\le n_k^-}$ are the two traditional Pitch makers.

Step 1: Segment the signal $\{x_m\}_{1\le m\le N}$ into voiced segments.

1.1: Determine the zero crossing rate $\{Z_x(m)\}$ according to the formula (2)

1.2: Divide the signal segment $\{x_m\}_{1\le m\le N}$ into no-overlapping frames with M samples for each frame. Determine the energy E_t of each frame$_t = \{x_m\}_{(t-1)M+1\le m\le tM}$, where $E_t = \sum_{m=(t-1)M+1}^{tM} x_m^2$.

1.3: Remove silence: Obtain K and the segment of speech signals $\{x_m\}_{M*t_{k,1}\le m\le M*t_{k,2}}, k = \overline{1,K}$ according to the energy threshold $\alpha_e*\max\{E_t\}$, where $t_{k,1}, t_{k,2}$ are the smallest frame index at the start and largest at the end of each segment k, so that the $E_{t_{k,1}} \ge \alpha_e \max\{E_t\}, E_{t_{k,2}} \ge \alpha_e \max\{E_t\}$.

1.4: With each non-silence segment $\{x_m\}_{M*t_{k,1}\le m\le M*t_{k,2}}, k = \overline{1,K}$, extract the voiced segment $\{x_m\}_{N_{k,1}\le m\le N_{k,2}}$, where $x_{N_{k,1}}, x_{N_{k,2}}$ are the first sample x_n and the last sample x_n of the k-th signal such that $Z_x(n) < \alpha_z$.

Step 2 : $T_{min} = f_s/f_{0,max}$, $T_{max} = f_s/f_{0,min}$

Step 3:   Repeat on each voiced segment $\{x_m\}_{N_{k,1}\le m\le N_{k,2}}, k = \overline{1,K}$,

3.1:   Calculate the cumulative signal $S_k = \{s_m\}_{N_{k,1}\le m\le N_{k,2}}, k = \overline{1,K}$ following the formula (1)

3.2:   Determine the peak of S_k, compute the average amplitude at the peak of S_k:
$$mean_k = \frac{\sum_{n\in peak\{S_k\}} |S_{k,n}|}{\# peak\{S_k\}}$$

3.3:   Determine the first suitable peak of S_k, $p_{k,1}$ is the first n-th peak that $S_{k,n}$ over the threshold $mean_k$; $p_{k,1} = \arg\min_{n\in peak\{S_k\}} \left\{|S_{k,n}| \ge mean_k\right\}$,

3.4. Remove the peak $n \in peak\{S_k\}, n < p_{k,1}$

3.5: Only keep the peak $p_{k,j} \in peak\{S_k\}, p_{k,j} - p_{k,j-1} \in [T_{k,min}, T_{k,max}]$

3.6: Continue to remove the peaks with small amplitude (the second close to the peaks with large amplitude), which mean removing the peaks $p_{k,j}$ that

$$p_{k,j} < \min\left\{p_{k,j-1} \cdot p_{k,j+1}\right\}$$

3.7: Remove the peak $\dfrac{fs}{p_{k,j+1}-p_{k,j}} > 0.5 * \left(\dfrac{fs}{p_{k,j}-p_{k,j-1}} + \dfrac{fs}{p_{k,j+2}-p_{k,j+1}}\right)$ (Eliminates the points of the F0 contour rising from the nearest point on the left and right).

3.8: Insert a peak:

$$m \in peak(S_k), p_{k,j} < m < p_{k,j+1}, \left| P_m - \frac{p_{k,j} + p_{k,j+1}}{2} \right| \rightarrow \min \quad \text{when}$$

$$\frac{fs}{p_{k,j+1}-p_{k,j}} < 0.5 * \left(\frac{fs}{p_{k,j}-p_{k,j-1}} + \frac{fs}{p_{k,j+2}-p_{k,j+1}}\right)$$

(Inserts a rejected peak at the point of F0 contour being lower than the nearest point on the left and right.)

3.9: Let $peak_R\{S_k\}$ be the set of the trim peaks of segment S_k.

Step 4: Repeat, on each voiced segment $\{x_m\}_{N_{k,1}\leq m \leq N_{k,2}}, k = \overline{1,K}$,

4.1: Calculate the F0 value on each segment $[p_{k,j},\ p_{k,j+1}]$ of $\{x_m\}_{N_{k,1}\leq m \leq N_{k,2}}$,

$$f_{0,k,j} = \frac{f_s}{p_{k,j+1} - p_{k,j}}, j = \overline{1, \# peak_R\{S_k\} - 1}$$

4.2: Determine the pitch markers according to the local maximum point criterion of the segment $\{x_m\}_{N_{k,1}\leq m \leq N_{k,2}}$

$$pm_{k,j}^+ = max\left\{peak\{x_n\}_{p_{k,j}\leq n \leq p_{k,j+1}}\right\}$$

4.3: Determine the pitch markers according to the local minimum point criterion of the voiced part $\{x_m\}_{N_{k,1}\leq m \leq N_{k,2}}$, $pm_{k,j}^- = min\left\{peak\{-x_n\}_{p_{k,j}\leq n \leq p_{k,j+1}}\right\}$

Step 5: Determining Pulse Points for Praat type [8], the same as step 3 but taking the local minimum point of the cumulative signal, we get $\left\{p_{k,j}^-\right\}$ on each voiced part

$\{x_m\}_{N_{k,1}\leq m \leq N_{k,2}}, k = \overline{1,K}$

Step 6: End

Return: Number of voiced segments K, the pitch markers for four types

$$\left\{pm_{k,j}^+\right\}_{1\leq k \leq K, 1\leq j \leq n_k^+}, \left\{pm_{k,j}^-\right\}_{1\leq k \leq K, 1\leq j \leq n_k^-}, \left\{p_{k,j}^-\right\}_{1\leq k \leq K, 1\leq j \leq n_{k,2}^-}, \left\{p_{k,j}\right\}_{1\leq k \leq K, 1\leq j \leq n_{k,2}^+}$$

Comment: From the PMs we find out a rough estimate of the values of F0, according to the formula in step 4.1 of Algorithm 1, However, to have a good estimate of the values of F0 contours, many post-processing are required, such as the smoothing step for F0 values (Fig. 6).

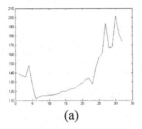 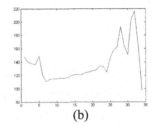

(a)   (b)

Fig. 6. F0 contour rough, not smooth $\{f_s/(p_{j+1} - p_j)\}$ of sound /bốn/(/four/), (a) {pj} is the pulse points computed by Praat [8], and (b) are the signal points that change from negative to positive by proposed Algorithm 1.

3 Experiment

3.1 Experimental Data

In order to experiment the Algorithm 1, a single speaker story reading corpus was created, uttered by a female speaker of standard Vietnamese voice. The entire size of the corpus is 5 h. To this effect, the recordings were cut manually at the sentence level. Phones were labeled by means of forced alignment and manual refinement and then syllable labels created. Break indices were marked manually. There are 567 sentences, 7,724 syllables and 23,482 phonemes in the corpus. The corpus contains 1,088 of the 2,587 legal Vietnamese syllables as the illustration in the Fig. 4.

3.2 Experiment to Determine the PMs

The formulas show that Algorithm 1 has a smaller computational complexity than dynamic programming-type algorithm [5] because it does not require the steps to segment the whole speech utterance into short time frames and choose a suitable time point of each short time frame that gives high autocorrelation value. For the reliability of Algorithm 1, we will compare Algorithm 1 with the Talkin-type algorithm implemented in software Praat [8]. The parameter f0min = 50 Hz, f0max = 550 Hz and the silence removal threshold $\alpha_e = 0.2$ and the voiced/unvoiced decision threshold $\alpha_z = 0.17$.

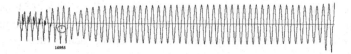

Fig. 7. A PM (called a Pulse point) is determined by Praat [8]

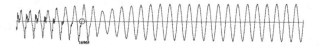

Fig. 8. A PM is determined by the Algorithm 1.

As we can see, the PMs determined by the Algorithm 1 are more noticeable than the result of Praat when directly observing by eyes the speech signals as shown in Figs. 7 and 8 above.

We will apply the method to identify the pitch markers to synthesize tones of Vietnamese isolated syllables. To stylized tones, we use Xu's model, which has been widely used for Mandarin [13] to model F0 contours of the tones (for tonal languages).

$F(t) \approx \alpha^* e^{-\lambda t} + a^* t + b$, such that a F0 contour is created from the combination of the two components: the linear approximation $a^* t + b$ and the non-linear approximation $\alpha^* e^{-\lambda t}$.

The computing of the coefficients of the model, given trend-line F0 value also uses the least squares method, instead of finding the coefficients a, b, α, λ we determine a, b, k ($k = e^{-\lambda}$) by minimize the objective function:

$$\sum_{i=1}^{n-1} \left(F_{0,i+1} - a^* (i+1) - b - k^* \left(F_{0,i} - a^* i - b \right) \right)^2 \to \min \qquad (3)$$

Where n is the number of speech frames, $\{F_{0,i}\}_{i=1}^{n}$ is a F0 sequence of each frame corresponding. The stylized method using Xu model is built as follows:

Step 1: Select syllables with Level tone, Drop tone with syllables ending p-t-c/ch, determine F0 contour of them.

Step 2: Determine the PMs of this wave of tone by Algorithm 1.

Step 3: Using least squares method to fit Xu model's parameters as a, b, k. Generate target F0 contour by the Xu model.

Step 4: Using PSOLA algorithm to synthesize a syllable with the target tone.

The results for synthesizing tones for Vietnamese syllables have been shown that synthetic speech is produced in a clearly audible quality (Fig. 9).

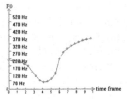

Fig. 9. Converting F0 contour for synthesizing broken tone from a syllable with level tone

4 Conclusions

The paper proposes an algorithm to determine the pitch markers of the original voice signal in a time domain based on the cumulative signal. The Algorithm is simple, with no need to divide a voiced segment into short segments (frames) as other methods, achieving high accuracy with the synthesized input signal for synthesizing Vietnamese tones. With the Vietnamese speech data of the lexical tones and the phonetics tested, the full coverage of the Vietnamese phonetics was included. The results of calculating the pitch markers according to the new approach proved to be correct, equivalent and more accurate than the Praat calculation approach.

References

1. A short guide to pitch-marking in the festival speech synthesis system and recommendations for improvements. Local Language Speech Technology Initiative (LLSTI) Reports (2004). http://www.llsti.org
2. Legát, M., Matoušek, J., Tihelka, D.: On the detection of pitch marks using a robust multi-phase algorithm. Speech Commun. **53**(4), 552 (2011)
3. Bořil, H., Pollák, P.: Direct time domain fundamental frequency estimation of speech in noisy conditions. In: EUSIPCO, pp. 1003–1006 (2004)
4. Wang, D., Hansen, J.H.L.: F0 estimation for noisy speech by exploring temporal harmonic structures in local time frequency spectrum segment. In: 2016 IEEE International Conference on Acoustics, Speech and Signal Processing, ICASSP. IEEE Press (2016)
5. Talkin, D.: A robust algorithm for pitch tracking (RAPT). In: Kleijn, W.B., Paliwal, K.K. (eds.) Speech Coding and Synthesis. Elsevier (1995)
6. Chen, J.-H., Kao, Y.-A.: Pitch marking based on an adaptable filter and a peak-valley estimation method. Comput. Linguist. Chin. Lang. Process. **6**(2), 1–12 (2001)
7. Legát, M., Tihelka, D., Matoušek, J.: Pitch marks at peaks or valleys? In: Matoušek, V., Mautner, P. (eds.) TSD 2007. LNCS (LNAI), vol. 4629, pp. 502–507. Springer, Heidelberg (2007). https://doi.org/10.1007/978-3-540-74628-7_65
8. PRAAT: doing phonetics by computer. http://www.Praat.org
9. Kounoudes, A., Naylor, P.A., Brookes, M.: The DYPSA algorithm for estimation of glottal closure instants in voiced speech. In: IEEE International Conference on Acoustics, Speech, and Signal Processing, ICASSP. IEEE Press (2002)
10. Babacan, O., Drugman, T., d'Alessandro, N., Henrich, N., Dutoit, T.: A quantitative comparison of glottal closure instant estimation algorithms on a Large Variety of Singing Sounds. In: Acoustics, Speech, and Signal Processing, IEEE International Conference on ICASSP. IEEE Press (2013)

11. Yin Pitch Estimator (2012). http://audition.ens.fr/adc/sw/yin.zip. Accessed 27 Nov 2012
12. Charpentier, F., Stella, M.: Diphone synthesis using an overlap-add technique for speech waveforms concatenation. In: IEEE International Conference on Acoustics, Speech, and Signal Processing, ICASSP 1986. IEEE Press (1986)
13. Xu, C.X., Xu, Y., Luo, L.-S.: A pitch target approximation model for F0 contours in Mandarin. In: ICPHS99 (1999)

An Effective Facial Image Verification Based Attendance Management System

Zeng-Mei Li, Hui-Na Dai, Zhan-Li Sun[(✉)], and Xia Chen

School of Electrical Engineering and Automation, Anhui University, Hefei, China
zhlsun2006@126.com

Abstract. In this paper, we present an effective facial image verification based automated attendance management system (FIV-AMS). The proposed system can be divided into three main components: face detection, image pre-processing, and face recognition. The core step of our attendance management system is the Gist feature extraction based face recognition, which can achieve three functions. Experimental results demonstrate the validity and feasibility of the proposed system by using the statical model and the dynamic model.

Keywords: Facial image verification · Gist feature
Attendance management system · Statical model · Dynamic model

1 Introduction

Attendance management system is an important component to establish the modern enterprise information management mechanisms which provides the basis for availability assessment of staff or students attendance. All kinds of the earliest methods including biometric identification and artificial identification based attendance equipments, such as manual sign-in, magnetic card and fingerprint attendance [1,2], made by different manufacturers have been appeared over the last several decades.

In [3], a biometrics based wireless fingerprint attendance management system was devised to solve the issue of spurious attendance and laying the corresponding network. An automatic attendance system based on ZigBee technology was proposed by using fingerprint verification technique to extract the minutiae information of taking attendance automatically in [4]. However, the two biggest disadvantages of these traditional approaches are that they are generally time consuming and hard to avoid cheating.

Recently, some novel techniques, such as iris detection, face recognition [5], voice print, and handprint, based attendance management system have been proposed [6–9]. A wireless iris recognition based attendance management system was designed to solve the problem of cheating in [6]. In [7], a attendance system combining the attendance recording and dormitory management based on MySQL and featured was designed for students. An automated attendance management

© Springer International Publishing AG, part of Springer Nature 2018
T. Huang et al. (Eds.): ISNN 2018, LNCS 10878, pp. 637–644, 2018.
https://doi.org/10.1007/978-3-319-92537-0_73

system based on face recognition technique was proposed to achieve attendance recording by using modified Viola-Jones algorithm and alignment-free partial in [8]. In [9], a biometric voice recognition technology using voiceprints of an individual was proposed to authenticate for people having difficulty in using hands and other biometric traits. However, these system are sensitive to background information and may not reliable when some images are collected under different circumstances.

To overcome these disadvantages mentioned above, an effective facial image verification based automated attendance management system (FIV-AMS) is given in this paper. The proposed system can be divided into three main steps: face detection, image pre-processing, and face recognition. Our attendance management system can accomplish three functions including identifying the face in the input image belongs to whom, whether the face to be identified is from a real person and whether the person has already registered. Experimental results on several widely used feature extraction methods by using the statical and dynamic model prove the effectiveness and feasibility of the proposed method.

The remainder of the paper is organized as follows. The proposed method is derived in Sect. 2, followed by experiments in Sect. 3. Finally, conclusions are made in Sect. 4.

2   Methodology

In this section, we clearly introduce our facial image verification based attendance management system. Our attendance management system can be divided to three main steps: face detection, image pre-processing and face recognition.

The person to be identified should be facing the camera of our attendance management system, followed by clicking the dynamic model button to begin recording the dynamic images. Then, two different images with the same person, named I_1 and I_2, can be gathered by our attendance management system from the recording video clip automatically. It should be pointed out that at least one photo contains a full face, which will appear on the GUI of our attendance management system.

2.1   Face Detection

In order to eliminate the interference of background information of the captured images, such as passing faces, a face detection step should first be given to get face area of input images. A machine learning approach is adopted in our face detection step because of its ability to process images extremely rapidly and achieve high detection accuracy [10].

Taking I_1, which contains a frontal face, as an example. The integral image of the original image I_1 is first given as [10]:

$$II(x, y) = \sum_{x' \le x, y' \le y} I_1(x', y')$$

(1)

where $\mathbf{II}$ is the integral image. The coordinates (x, y) and (x', y') both denote the location of a pixel. Then, the two-rectangle feature, three-rectangle feature, and four-rectangle feature can be computed rapidly according to the integral image.

Furthermore, a best single rectangle feature can be chosen to separate the positive and negative examples by applying a weak learning algorithm described as [10]:

$$h_j(x) = \begin{cases} 1 & \text{if } p_j f_j(x) < p_j \theta_j \\ 0 & \text{otherwise} \end{cases} \tag{2}$$

where f_j, θ_j and p_j represent a feature, a threshold and a parity, respectively. The x denotes a 24×24 pixel sub-window of an image. In order to achieve increased detection performance and radically reduce computation time, an attentional cascade algorithm is used for the above classifiers.

Finally, we can obtain two images by removing background information, once a frontal face is detected in each original images. To facilitate feature extraction, we set the size of the images to $m \times m$, where $m = 200$ in our experimental. The nearest neighbor interpolation algorithm is chosen in the zoom process, which can also be replaced by other interpolation algorithm.

2.2   Image Pre-processing

In order to eliminate the influence of the illumination intensity and improve the accuracy of face recognition, the images need to be pretreated. The preprocessing consists of image enhancement and texture extraction.

When the two images are captured in low-light conditions, the details of the images can not be reflected. Therefore, the light enhancement should be used to improve the visibility. A low-light image enhancement (LIME) method is chosen because of its good performance [11]. The maximum value in R, G, and B channels is first sought out, followed by estimating the illumination of each pixel individually. Then, the final illumination map can be achieved accordingly by refining the initial illumination map when a structure prior is imposed.

On the other hand, extracting texture features can further remove the influence of illumination on human face. Here, we use the following method, instead of the histogram equalization algorithm. For a given $m \times m$ face image $\mathbf{I}_1$ [16]:

$$\mathbf{I}_{11} = \frac{\mathbf{I}_1}{\left(\frac{\sum_{i,j=1}^{m} |\mathbf{I}_{ij}|^a}{m \times m}\right)^{\frac{1}{a}}} \tag{3}$$

$$\mathbf{I}_{12} = \frac{\mathbf{I}_{11}}{\left(\frac{\sum_{i,j=1}^{m} min(trim, |\mathbf{I}_{ij}|)^a}{m \times m}\right)^{\frac{1}{a}}} \tag{4}$$

$$\mathbf{I}_{13} = trim \times tanh(\frac{\mathbf{I}_{12}}{trim}) \tag{5}$$

where $trim = 10$, $a = 1$ in our experiment. $\mathbf{I}_{13}$ is the texture extracted image.

2.3   Face Recognition

We first give some definitions before introducing face recognition. Let $\mathbf{T}$ and $\mathbf{P}_i$ represent the test image and the face image of ith person, respectively. $\mathbf{S}_{ij}$ denotes the jth sample of the ith person. $\mathbf{F}_{ijk}$ and $\mathbf{UF}_k$ express the features detected by the kth Gabor filter, where the former comes from the jth sample of the ith person and the latter is the unidentified face. $\mathbf{R}_{ijk}$ is a result by comparing the corresponding kth Gabor filter of the test face and the jth sample of the ith person. $Vote_{kj}$ denotes the result of the jth sample of the kth Gabor filter. And $i = 1, 2, \ldots, N_i$, $j = 1, 2, \ldots, N_j$, and $k = 1, 2, \ldots, N_k$.

In this section, we assume that we can always find a face match to the input image whether the input face belongs to face database. We first extract gist features from the input images before face recognition [12]. Figure 1 shows the flowchart of our face recognition. This face recognition system can implement three functions.

(1) To identify the face in the input image belongs to whom.
   Having generated the gist feature images based on the kth Gabor filters for all the training face images and test images, we calculate the distance between corresponding features as:

$$\mathbf{R}_{ijk} = \|\mathbf{UF}_k - \mathbf{F}_{ijk}\|_F^2, \quad i = 1, 2, \ldots, P_i. \tag{6}$$

   The person correspond to the smallest $\mathbf{R}_{ijk}$ is taking as the result of this round denoted as $Vote_{kj}$. Then, we can obtain $P_j \times P_k$ votes. We finally believe that the input face belongs to the person with the most votes.
(2) To identify whether the face to be identified is from a real person.
   The main idea of this function is that there should exist some differences between the input two images if the face to be identified comes from a real person. Let $\mathbf{D}_1$ denotes the difference of the gist feature between $\mathbf{I}_1$ and $\mathbf{I}_2$. The average of these two images is represented by $\mathbf{M}_1$. We believe that it is a real person to be identified as long as $\mathbf{D}_1$ is not less than a given threshold, named c_1, times $\mathbf{M}_1$.
(3) To Identify whether the person has been registered or not.
   We first need to find all the samples that correspond to the result of (1). Then, calculating the average difference between the first sample and the rest samples, denoted as $\mathbf{M}_2$. Next, we calculate the difference between the input image and the first sample, denote as $\mathbf{D}_2$. The input person has been registered in the database when $\mathbf{D}_2$ is not lager than c_2 times $\mathbf{M}_2$.

3   Experimental Results

In this section, two means including dynamic model and statical model are adopted to demonstrate the validity and feasibility of the proposed facial image verification based attendance management system (denoted as FIV-AMS). These two patterns differ only in image acquisition. The test images used by the former are captured by a camera, while the latter is obtained by the face database.

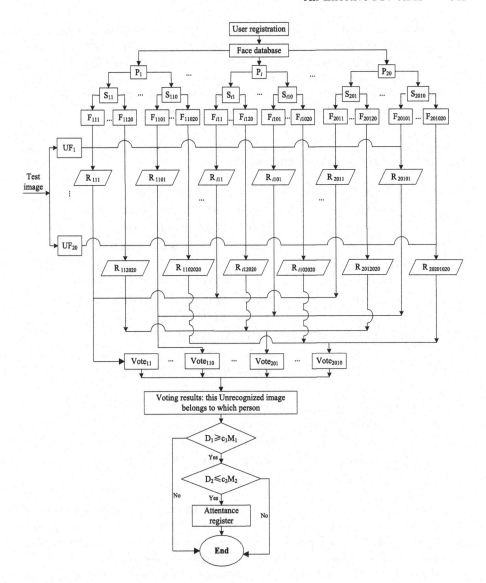

Fig. 1. Flowchart of our face recognition.

We set $N_i = 13$, $N_k = 20$, and the sample sizes N_j varying from 10 to 80 in the experiment of statical model. The samples are divided into two parts: half of samples are training data and the rest are testing data. Note that there is no limit to facial expressions of these samples taken by the same device for the same person. The core of our attendance management system is the face recognition step, which is based on feature extraction. To investigate the effect of samples N_j on the performances of our proposed FIV-AMS approach, Table 1 tabulate the average, standard deviation and times of the proposed statical model by using four different feature extraction methods Gist [12], SRC [13], LDA [14], and FLDA [15], respectively. From these tables, we can see that FIV-AMS based on Gist feature has a better performance than the other three feature extraction methods for different sample sizes under the same condition. The left image of Fig. 2 shows the result of statical model based on the Gist feature.

Table 1. The average, standard deviation and times of the proposed statical model based on SRC, LDA, FLDA and GIst, respectively.

SRC	Number of sample	10	20	40	60	80
	Aver	0.6954	0.8377	0.9277	0.9633	0.9671
	Stdev	0.1075	0.0239	0.0141	0.0097	0.0078
	Time	1.321	2.9184	5.6564	8.1711	12.051
LDA	Number of sample	10	20	40	60	80
	Aver	0.9200	0.9815	0.9954	0.9962	0.9985
	Stdev	0.0547	0.0163	0.0040	0.0035	0.0012
	Time	1.0785	2.4811	3.7082	6.2133	7.8394
FLDA	Number of sample	10	20	40	60	80
	Aver	0.8769	0.9923	1	1	1
	Stdev	0.1267	0.0243	0	0	0
	Time	7.742	36.73	56.76	120.0	200.4
Gist	Number of sample	10	20	40	60	80
	Aver	0.9616	1	1	1	1
	Stdev	0.0543	0	0	0	0
	Time	1.377	2.993	7.839	13.82	19.25

In dynamic model, N_i, N_j and N_k are set to 20, 10, and 20, respectively. In this model, those samples taken by the same device for the same person maybe collected under different environments and illumination except the facial expressions. This is similar to the actual conditions. We can see from Table 2 that the accuracy of Gist feature are more higher than those of the other three methods. Finally, the results of dynamic model based on four different features shown in the right image of Fig. 2. This indicates that our dynamic model based on the Gist feature is a more robust approach.

Table 2. The results of dynamic model based on four different features.

Method	GIST	FLDA	LDA	SRC
Accuracy	0.9500	0.8500	0.7000	0.2500

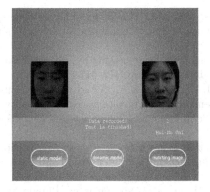 

Fig. 2. The results of our attendance management system by using the statical model (the left image) and dynamic model (the right image), respectively.

4   Conclusions

Our proposed facial image verification based attendance management system can be divided into three mainly steps: face detection, image pre-processing and face recognition. Face recognition is the major step in this system which can achieve three functions. The experimental results containing statical model and dynamic model demonstrated the feasibility and effectiveness of the proposed facial image verification based attendance management system.

Acknowledgments. The work was supported by a grant from National Natural Science Foundation of China (No. 61370109), a key project of support program for outstanding young talents of Anhui province university (No. gxyqZD2016013), a grant of science and technology program to strengthen police force (No. 1604d0802019), and a grant for academic and technical leaders and candidates of Anhui province (No. 2016H090).

References

1. Maltoni, D., Maio, D., Jain, A.K., Prabhakar, S.: Handbook of Fingerprint Recognition. Springer, London (2009). https://doi.org/10.1007/978-1-84882-254-2
2. Kaur, M., Singh, M., Girdhar, A., Sandhu, P.S.: Fingerprint verification system using minutiae extraction technique. In: Proceedings of World Academy of Science Engineering and Technology, p. 497 (2008)
3. Zhang, Y., Ji, L.: The design of wireless fingerprint attendance system. In: International Conference on Communication Technology, pp. 1–4 (2006)
4. Li, J.P., Zhu, X.N., Xue, L., Zhang, Z.M., Sui, J.S.: Wireless fingerprint attendance system based on zigbee technology. In: International Workshop on Intelligent Systems and Applications (ISA), pp. 1–4 (2010)
5. Sun, Z.L., Lam, K.M., Dong, Z.Y., Wang, H., Gao, Q.W., Zheng, C.H.: Face recognition with multi-resolution spectral feature images. PLoS One 8(2), e55700 (2013)
6. Kadry, S., Smaili, M.: Wireless attendance management system based on iris recognition. Sci. Res. Essays 5(12), 1428–1435 (2013)

7. Fan, F., Hou, L., Fu, J., Chen, S., Feng, R., Wang, J.: The design of high-efficiency and synergetic attendance system. In: International Conference on Information Engineering for Mechanics and Materials (2015)
8. Jayant, N.K., Borra, S.: Attendance management system using hybrid face recognition techniques. In: Advances in Signal Processing, pp. 412–417 (2016)
9. Rashid, R.A., Mahalin, N.H., Sarijari, M.A., Aziz, A.A.A.: Security system using biometric technology: design and implementation of voice recognition system (VRS). In: International Conference on Computer and Communication Engineering, pp. 898–902 (2008)
10. Viola, P., Jones, M.: Rapid object detection using a boosted cascade of simple features. In: IEEE Computer Society Conference on Computer Vision and Pattern Recognition, p. 511. IEEE Press (2001)
11. Guo, X., Li, Y., Ling, H.: LIME: low-light image enhancement via illumination map estimation. IEEE Trans. Image Process. Publ. IEEE Sig. Process. Soc. **26**(2), 982–993 (2017)
12. Oliva, A., Torralba, A.: Modeling the shape of the scene: a holistic representation of the spatial envelope. Int. J. Comput. Vis. **42**(3), 145–175 (2001)
13. Deng, W., Hu, J., Guo, J.: Extended SRC: undersampled face recognition via intraclass variant dictionary. IEEE Trans. Pattern Anal. Mach. Intell. **34**(9), 1864–1870 (2012)
14. Lu, J., Plataniotis, K.N., Venetsanopoulos, A.N.: Face recognition using LDA-based algorithms. IEEE Trans. Neural Netw. **14**(1), 195 (2003)
15. Gao, Q.X., Zhang, L., Zhang, D.: Face recognition using FLDA with single training image per person. Appl. Math. Comput. **205**(2), 726–734 (2008)
16. https://blog.csdn.net/hlx371240/article/details/49308245

Intelligent Control, Robotics and Hardware

Estimation of Distribution Algorithm for Autonomous Underwater Vehicles Path Planning

Run-Dong Liu, Zhi-Hui Zhan[✉], Wei-Neng Chen, Zhiwen Yu, and Jun Zhang[✉]

Guangdong Provincial Key Lab of Computational Intelligence and Cyberspace Information, School of Computer Science and Engineering, South China University of Technology, Guangzhou 510006, China
zhanapollo@163.com

Abstract. Path planning is that given the start point and target point, finding out a shortest or smallest cost path. In recent years, more and more researchers use evolutionary algorithms (EAs) to solve path planning problems, such as genetic algorithms (GAs) and particle swarm optimization (PSO). Estimation of distribution algorithms (EDAs) belong to a kind of EAs that can make good use of global statistic information of the population. However, EDAs are seldom used to solve path planning problems. In this paper, we propose an EDA variant named adaptive fixed-height histogram (AFHH) algorithm to make path planning for autonomous underwater vehicles (AUVs). The proposed AFHH algorithm can adaptively shrink its search space to make good use of computational resource. We use a regenerate approach to avoid getting stuck in local optimum. We also measure the ability of fixed-height histogram (FHH) algorithm for path planning. We simulate a 3-D environment to measure the ability of the proposed AFHH algorithm. The results show that AFHH has a good convergence rate and can also get better performance.

Keywords: Estimation of distribution algorithm (EDA)
Autonomous underwater vehicles (AUVs) · Path planning
Adaptive fixed-height histogram (AFHH)

1 Introduction

Path planning is one of the most significant methods to make some robots more intelligent such as unmanned vehicles. Autonomous underwater vehicles (AUVs) are a kind of underwater robots [1]. They can work underwater according to humans' predefined commands. During the working period, they don't need to communicate with humans. Therefore, in some dangerous underwater environment such as contaminated areas, they can complete missions instead of humans [2]. Due to the widely application of AUVs, path planning for AUVs has become a very significant research topic. Although path planning problems (PPP) have been widely studied in the literatures, many of them don't need to consider too many conditions. For example, the traveling

© Springer International Publishing AG, part of Springer Nature 2018
T. Huang et al. (Eds.): ISNN 2018, LNCS 10878, pp. 647–655, 2018.
https://doi.org/10.1007/978-3-319-92537-0_74

salesman problem (TSP) which is also a kind of PPPs, just needs to find a shortest path without considering complex environment [3].

According to study in [4], path planning algorithm can be divided into two groups. One is the resolution complete algorithms, and the other one is the probabilistic resolution complete algorithms. The A* approach is resolution complete algorithm. Garau *et al.* [5] used A* approach to make path planning for AUVs in complex environment. EAs are a kind of probabilistic resolution complete algorithms. In recent years, many researchers use EAs to solve some kinds of PPPs. Shih *et al.* [6] proposed a genetic-based effective approach to solve the PPP for AUVs. Zhang *et al.* [7] used an adaptive differential evolution (ADE) algorithm to make path planning for AUVs.

In this paper, we propose an adaptive fixed-height histogram (AFHH) algorithm to make path planning for AUVs in 3-D environment. The fixed-height histogram (FHH) algorithm is a kind of EDAs. It is also a kind of EAs. The proposed AFHH algorithm can adaptively shrink search space in the course of evolution. We randomly generate new individuals with the current search space every T generations to make the algorithm avoid getting stuck in local optimum. Furthermore, we use a 3-D environment model to check out whether AFHH has a good path planning ability.

The rest of this paper is organized as follows. Section 2 introduces the background knowledge of EDAs and environment modeling of AUVs path planning. Section 3 describes the proposed AFHH algorithm for path planning in detail. Section 4 presents results of experiments. Section 5 makes a conclusion of this paper.

2   Background Knowledge

2.1   Environment Modeling for AUVs Path Planning

To make path planning for AUVs, the first step is constructing an environment model. Environment underwater in some area is very complex. The shape of seabed is not smooth. It maybe changes sharply in different areas. Besides, some floating obstacles make the environment more complex. In this paper, we use a 3-D static environment which is constructed in [7] to model the PPP for AUVs.

Herein, we consider the path planning in 3-D space with length, width, and depth. As shown in Fig. 1(a), the X axis, Y axis, and Z axis represent the environment's length, width and depth respectively. In Fig. 1(a), spheres represent floating obstacles, and the others represent seabed.

The 3-D environment model is split to 40 parallel sections along the y axis. The section is a profile of the 3-D environment. The section is shown in Fig. 1(b). The red areas represent obstacles. Each section is formed with a 20×20 grid. Besides, a $40 \times 20 \times 20$ array is used to save all sections. If there are obstacles in some areas, then the corresponding grids will be set as 1. Otherwise, they will be set as 0.

In each section, a feasible waypoint will be found. The trajectory is formed with 40 waypoints which are respectively generated in 40 sections. After that, we use a cost function to evaluate the path's quality according to its length, variation of depth, turning radius, and safety. The cost function is defined as:

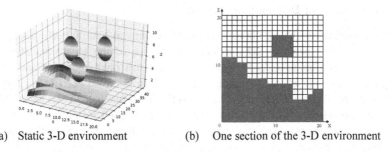

(a)   Static 3-D environment   (b)   One section of the 3-D environment

Fig. 1. The environment models of path planning for AUVs.

$$F_{cost} = C_{length} + C_{depth} + C_{smooth} + C_{block} \tag{1}$$

where C_{length} represents the length of a path. C_{depth} represents the variation of a path's depth. C_{smooth} represents a path's smooth degree. C_{block} represents the safety of a path. C_{length} is defined as:

$$C_{length} = 1 - \frac{L_{PsPt}}{L_{path}}, C_{length} \in (0,1) \tag{2}$$

where L_{PsPt} is the Euclidean distance between start point and stop point. L_{path} is the length of the whole path. C_{depth} is defined as:

$$C_{depth} = \frac{D_{max} - D_{min}}{D}, C_{depth} \in (0,1) \tag{3}$$

where D_{max} is the max depth of the path, and D_{min} is the min depth of the path. D is the max depth of the 3-D environment model. C_{smooth} is defined as:

$$C_{smooth} = \begin{cases} 2 + \frac{N_{unable}}{N_{segment}}, & N_{unable} > 0 \\ 0, & N_{unable} = 0 \end{cases}, C_{smooth} \in 0 \cup (2,3) \tag{4}$$

where N_{unable} is the number of path segments whose turning radius beyond the motion ability of AUVs. If the length of one path segment larger than a predefined value θ, then N_{unable} will increase. We set θ as 1.75. $N_{segment}$ is the number of all path segments. C_{block} is defined as:

$$C_{block} = \begin{cases} 2 + \frac{N_{block}}{N_{space}}, & N_{block} > 0 \\ 0, & N_{block} = 0 \end{cases}, C_{block} \in 0 \cup (2,3) \tag{5}$$

where N_{block} is the number of unfeasible waypoints. N_{space} is the number of sections.

2.2   Estimation of Distribution Algorithm

EDA is a kind of stochastic algorithms which belongs to EAs. It performs better than GA in most case because EDA makes a good use of the global statistics. EDA's procedure is similar to GA. However, EDA doesn't have mutation and crossover procedures. Tsutsui *et al.* [8] proposed two histogram based EDAs, one is the fixed-width histogram (FWH) algorithm, and the other one is the FHH algorithm. Xiao *et al.* [10] proposed a histogram-based EDA which is used for processing continuous optimization problems. Yang *et al.* [11] proposed an improved EDA which can process multimodal problems.

3   Proposed AFHH Algorithm

In this section, we describe the proposed AFHH algorithm for path planning in detail. We first choose the organization of individual's structure, which is proposed in [7]. As shown in Eq. (6), the individual's structure is made of waypoints. Each waypoint is a tuple which contains 3-D positional information. The X axis and Z axis values are generated in each section. The Y axis values are known. That is, $y_j = j$, where j is the index of sections. The x and z values are updated with the same procedure.

$$individual = \begin{bmatrix} x_1, x_2, \ldots, x_{Dim} \\ y_1, y_2, \ldots, y_{Dim} \\ z_1, z_2, \ldots, z_{Dim} \end{bmatrix} \tag{6}$$

In traditional FHH algorithm's model building step, search space of each variable is divided into K bins. All bins have the same height. Each bin's width will change in each generation. Let $X_i = \{x_1, x_2, \ldots, x_{Dim}\}$, where Dim is the number of variables, i is the index of individuals. First, select S best individuals and sort them according to the value of the jth variable. Then, use Eqs. (7) and (8) to update bins.

$$Bin\_lower_m = \begin{cases} lower, & \text{if } m = 0 \\ \left(x_{m \cdot S/K} + x_{m \cdot S/K - 1}\right)/2, & \text{otherwise} \end{cases} \tag{7}$$

$$Bin\_upper_m = \begin{cases} Bin\_lower_{m+1}, & \text{if } m < K - 1 \\ upper, & \text{otherwise} \end{cases} \tag{8}$$

where Bin_lower_m is the lower value of the mth bin, Bin_upper_m is the upper value of the mth bin, *lower* and *upper* represent search space's lower bound and upper bound respectively.

When sampling new individuals, each variable will select a bin randomly. Then use the bin's lower bound and upper bound to generate a value randomly. As shown in Fig. 2, during evolution, the bin's width is continuously changing. Figure 2(b) shows that the first bin and the last bin have larger width than others. It is little help for finding global optimum when using them to generate new individuals.

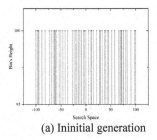

(a) Ininitial generation

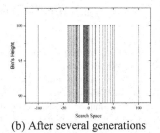

(b) After several generations

Fig. 2. Bin's distribution in search space of one variable in different generations

In AFHH's model building step, all individuals are sorted according to the value of the jth variable. Then record the smallest value and the largest value of the jth variable with *intervalLower[j]* and *intervalUpper[j]* respectively, where *intervalLower* and *intervalUpper* are arrays whose length is *Dim*. After that, if AFHH finds a feasible path, which means the cost function's value is less than 2.0, parameter p_m which is defined as Eq. (9) will be used to control whether to change search space's size of the jth variable [9]. Then, AFHH will use Eqs. (7) and (8) to update current bins.

$$p_m = 0.01 + 0.99 \cdot \frac{\exp\left(\frac{10 \cdot g}{G}\right) - 1}{\exp(10) - 1} \in [0.01, 1.00] \tag{9}$$

where g is the current generation, G is the maximum iteration. p_m is a nonlinear parameter. When change the search space's size, we use the mean of *intervalLower [j]* and Bin_lower_0 as search space's lower bound, and use the mean of *intervalUpper [j]* and Bin_upper_{k-1} as search space's upper bound. The procedure of updating bins and sampling are the same as traditional FHH algorithm. It is illustrated in Fig. 3.

4 Experiments and Results

4.1 Experiments Setup

The real underwater environment is simulated like the ones in Fig. 4. The area is 20 m long, 40 m width and 20 m depth. Four scenarios are used to measure AFHH's performance. AFHH, FHH, PSO, enhance differential evolution with random walk (RWDE) [12], and ADE [7] are used to make a comparison of their ability on path planning [7]. For the FHH and AFHH algorithms, bins size K is set as 50, and S is set as 100. The PSO is a conventional global topology PSO variant, whose w is set as 0.5. c_1 and c_2 are both set as 2.0. For the RWDE algorithm, two pairs of fixed parameters are used ($F = 0.5$, $CR = 0.1$; $F = 0.1$, $CR = 0.5$). All algorithms use the same maximum function evaluations (FEs) 5000000, and the same population's size 200. All results are got after 30 times independently run. All algorithms are implemented on a PC with Intel core i7 processor running 3.6 GHz, RAM of 8 GB.

```
Procedure of AFHH's Model Building
01 Begin
02   Load current scenario's map;
03   Initialize the population;
04   While (Not Stop)
05     //model building
06     While (j < Dim)
07       Find the biggest and smallest values from jᵗʰ variables;
08       intervalUpper[j] = biggest value;   intervalLower[j] = smallest value;
09       Sort S best individuals' jᵗʰ variable from small to large;
10       //Decide whether to shrink the search space of jᵗʰ variable
11       If ((current best fitness value < 2.0) and (random(0,1)<pₘ))
12         lower[j] = intervalLower[j];   upper[j] = intervalUpper[j];
13       End of If
14       Use Eq. (7) and Eq. (8) to update jᵗʰ variable's bins;
15     End of While
16     //generate New Individuals
17     If ((gen%T == 0) and (gen != 0))
18       Use current search space randomly generate new individuals;
19     Else
20       While (i < NP)
21         Randomly select a bin for each variable to generate new variable;
22         Use new variables to form the iᵗʰ individual;
23         Calculate the iᵗʰ individual's cost function's value;
24       End of While
25     End of If
26     Select NP best individuals to form new population;
27   End of While
28 End
```

Fig. 3. Procedure of the proposed AFHH algorithm for path planning

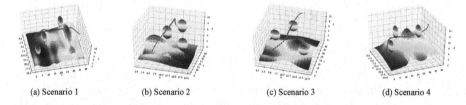

(a) Scenario 1   (b) Scenario 2   (c) Scenario 3   (d) Scenario 4

Fig. 4. The 3-D static environment models we simulate.

4.2   Results Comparisons

In Table 1, the first column represents different scenario, the second column fills with start points and target points. The mean and standard deviation of 30 independently runs of a path are calculated. Values in brackets are standard deviation. Results in Table 1 show that the proposed AFHH algorithm performs better than other algorithms in most cases. Besides, it is steadier in all independent runs. If a path is feasible, the value of cost function will be less than 2.0, and the smaller the better. As shown in

Table 2, although the AFHH algorithm can obtain high quality paths, it runs slowest in all scenarios. Because AFHH needs more time to construct probability model. PSO runs fastest in all scenarios, but it can't obtain feasible paths.

As shown in Fig. 5, AFHH converge faster than other algorithms in all scenarios. It has steady performance in all scenarios. Besides, AFHH not only converges faster, but also gets better results. The FHH can also get feasible paths, but it needs more iterations. Moreover, it is not steady sometimes. PSO performs worst, it can't find feasible path in all scenarios. The ADE can find feasible path. However, it needs more generations. Moreover, it is not steady sometimes. The RWDE with different parameters can also get good results in all scenarios, but it needs more iterations.

Table 1. Experimental results on AFHH, FHH, PSO, RWDE, and ADE with different scenarios

Scenario	Start point Target point	Cost function value					
		AFHH	FHH	PSO	RWDE (F = 0.5, CR = 0.1)	RWDE (F = 0.1, CR = 0.5)	ADE
1	S:(12,0,4) T:(10,39,6)	**0.33(6.18E−02)**	1.00(0.98)	3.56(0.29)	0.56(0.69)	0.39(9.25E−02)	0.94(1.10)
	S:(11,0,4) T:(3,39,6)	**0.32(3.47E−02)**	2.84(0.36)	3.29(0.32)	0.80(0.89)	0.40(0.14)	2.10(0.85)
	S:(9,0,6) T:(13,39,8)	0.25(4.75E−02)	0.74(0.87)	3.19(0.25)	**0.24(4.01E−02)**	0.27(6.42E−02)	0.97(1.01)
2	S:(7,0,7) T:(14,39,10)	**0.19(2.15E−02)**	0.50(0.68)	3.28(0.24)	0.28(3.17E−02)	0.24(6.75E−02)	0.54(0.68)
	S:(8,0,6) T:(17,39,10)	**0.26(1.97E−02)**	1.59(1.06)	3.25(0.31)	0.55(0.65)	0.53(0.71)	1.65(1.06)
	S:(6,0,5) T:(10,39,7)	**0.28(5.28E−02)**	1.02(0.97)	3.23(0.28)	0.79(0.86)	0.37(9.07E−02)	1.18(1.02)
3	S:(6,0,7) T:(12,39,11)	**0.23(1.36E−02)**	0.28(3.46E−02)	3.41(0.21)	0.27(4.21E−02)	0.32(6.54E−02)	0.75(0.87)
	S:(5,0,7) T:(11,39,8)	**0.22(1.43E−02)**	0.46(0.61)	3.05(0.15)	0.29(5.26E−02)	0.28(6.10E−02)	1.02(1.17)
	S:(3,0,8) T:(12,39,9)	0.22(1.42E−02)	0.60(0.83)	3.16(0.29)	0.68(0.83)	**0.20(7.47E−02)**	1.30(1.09)
4	S:(7,0,9) T:(15,39,10)	**0.17(6.97E−03)**	0.64(0.88)	3.22(0.23)	0.27(4.86E−02)	0.26(3.73E−02)	0.47(0.71)
	S:(15,0,8) T:(10,39,12)	**0.32(4.67E−02)**	1.14(1.05)	3.05(0.23)	0.54(0.62)	0.51(0.60)	0.97(0.99)
	S:(12,0,6) T:(13,39,12)	0.44(5.14E−02)	0.81(0.84)	3.33(0.18)	0.61(0.66)	**0.39(5.60E−02)**	1.06(0.96)

Table 2. Computation time of AFHH, FHH, PSO, RWDE, and ADE in different scenarios

Scenario	Start point Target point	Computation time (Sec)					
		AFHH	FHH	PSO	RWDE (F = 0.5, CR = 0.1)	RWDE (F = 0.1, CR = 0.5)	ADE
1	S:(12,0,4) T:(10,39,6)	72.09	61.02	**36.76**	57.45	45.28	40.54
2	S:(7,0,7) T:(14,39,10)	72.04	60.98	**37.82**	56.46	44.96	37.94
3	S:(6,0,7) T:(12,39,11)	72.02	60.95	**35.89**	56.49	45.00	37.26
4	S:(7,0,9) T:(15,39,10)	72.19	60.79	**35.39**	56.31	44.73	37.55

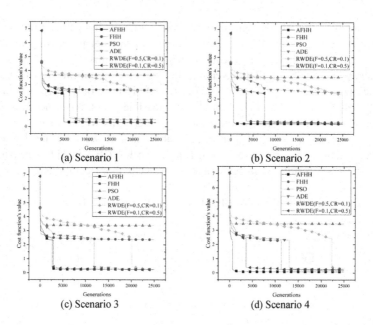

Fig. 5. All algorithms' convergence property in different scenarios

5   Conclusions

In this paper, we propose the AFHH algorithm, which has good convergence rate and better performance. Many earlier works used GA, DE and PSO to make path planning. We find that EDAs can also complete this mission well. Maybe when use EDAs to solve path planning problems, parameters or properties of EDAs should change corresponding to problems. As the results shown in Sect. 4, AFHH needs more computation time to obtain high quality paths. This weakness is to be optimized in future works. Besides, the ability of EDAs to make path planning in dynamic environment should be checked.

Acknowledgments. This work was partially supported by the National Natural Science Foundations of China (NSFC) with Nos. 61772207 and 61332002, the Natural Science Foundations of Guangzhou Province for Distinguished Young Scholars with No. 2014A030306038, the Project for Pearl River New Star in Science and Technology with No. 201506010047, the GDUPS (2016), and the Fundamental Research Funds for the Central Universities.

References

1. Blidberg, D.: The development of autonomous underwater vehicles (AUV); a brief summary. In: Proceedings of the International Conference on Robotics and Automation (ICRA), Seoul, South Korea, May 2001
2. Wang, B., Yu, L., Deng, Z., Fu, M.: A particle filter-based matching algorithm with gravity sample vector for underwater gravity aided navigation. IEEE/ASME Trans. Mechatron. **21**(3), 1399–1408 (2016)
3. Arango, M.D., Serna, C.A.: A memetic algorithm for the traveling salesman problem. IEEE Lat. Am. Trans. **13**(8), 2674–2679 (2015)
4. Zeng, Z., Lian, L., Sammut, K., He, F., Tang, Y., Lammas, A.: A survey on path planning for persistent autonomy of autonomous underwater vehicles. Ocean Eng. **110**, 303–313 (2015)
5. Garau, B., Alvarez, A., Oliver, G.: Path planning of autonomous underwater vehicles in current fields with complex spatial variability: an A* approach. In: Proceedings of the IEEE Conference on Robotics and Automation, Barcelona, Spain, pp. 546–556, April 2005
6. Shih, C.-C., Horng, M.-F., Pan, T.-S., Pan, J.-S., Chen, C.-Y.: A genetic-based effective approach to path-planning of autonomous underwater glider with upstream-current avoidance in variable oceans. Soft. Comput. **21**(18), 5369–5386 (2017)
7. Zhang, C., Gong, Y., Li, J.J., Lin, Y.: Automatic path planning for autonomous underwater vehicles based on an adaptive differential evolution. In: Proceedings of the ACM Genetic and Evolutionary Computation Conference, Canada, pp. 89–96, July 2014
8. Tsutsui, S., Pelikan, M., Goldberg, D.E.: Evolutionary algorithm using marginal histogram models in continuous domain. IlliGAL Report, vol. 2001019, no. 999, p. 1050 (2001)
9. Zhan, Z.H., Liu, X.F., Zhang, H., Yu, Z., Weng, J., Li, Y., Gu, T., Zhang, J.: Cloudde: a heterogeneous differential evolution algorithm and its distributed cloud version. IEEE Trans. Parallel Distrib. Syst. **28**(3), 704–716 (2017)
10. Xiao, J., Yan, Y., Zhang, J.: HPBILc: a histogram-based EDA for continuous optimization. Appl. Math. Comput. **215**(3), 973–982 (2009)
11. Yang, P., Tang, K., Lu, X.: Improving estimation of distribution algorithm on multimodal problems by detecting promising areas. IEEE Trans. Cybern. **45**(8), 1438–1449 (2015)
12. Zhan, Z.-H., Zhang, J.: Enhance differential evolution with random walk. In: International Conference on Genetic and Evolutionary Computation Conference Companion, pp. 1513–1514. ACM, New York (2012)

Fault Diagnosis Method of Diesel Engine Based on Improved Structure Preserving and *K*-NN Algorithm

Yu Li[1], Min Han[1(✉)], Bing Han[2], Xinyi Le[3], and Shunshoku Kanae[4]

[1] Faculty of Electronic Information and Electrical Engineering,
Dalian University of Technology, Dalian 116023, China
minhan@dlut.edu.cn
[2] State Key Laboratory of Navigation and Safety Technology,
Shanghai Ship and Shipping Research Institute, Shanghai 200135, China
hanbing@sssri.com
[3] School of Mechanical Engineering,
Shanghai Jiao Tong University, Shanghai 200240, China
lexinyi@sjtu.edu.cn
[4] Department of Medical Engineer, Faculty of Health Sciences,
Junshin Gakuen University, Fukuoka, Japan
Kanae.s@junshin-u.ac.jp

Abstract. The diesel engine fault data is nonlinear and it's difficult to extract the characteristic information. Kernel Principal Component Analysis (KPCA) is used to extract features of nonlinear data, only considering global structure. Kernel Locality Preserving Projection (KLPP) considers the local feature structure. So an improved algorithm for global and local structure preserving is proposed to extract the feature of data. The improved feature extraction algorithm combining KPCA and KLPP, avoids the loss of information considering the global and local feature structure and then uses the modified *K*-NN algorithm for fault classification. In this paper, the software AVL BOOST is used to simulate the faults of diesel engine. The simulation experiments indicate the proposed method can extract the feature vectors effectively, and shows good classification performance.

Keywords: Diesel engine fault diagnosis · Feature extraction
Kernel Principal Component Analysis · Locality structure preserving
Modified *K*-NN

1 Introduction

Diesel engine is widely used in engineering and its fault diagnosis has attracted much attention [1]. If we can extract the effective characteristics accurately, we can classify and diagnose the faults. Currently, the fault diagnosis methods based on data driven [2] include Principal Component Analysis (PCA) [3], Independent Component Analysis (ICA) [4], Fisher Discriminant Analysis (FDA) [5], Wavelet Transform [6], Support Vector Machine (SVM) [7], etc. Besides, the manifold learning can extract the intrinsic

© Springer International Publishing AG, part of Springer Nature 2018
T. Huang et al. (Eds.): ISNN 2018, LNCS 10878, pp. 656–664, 2018.
https://doi.org/10.1007/978-3-319-92537-0_75

properties from high nonlinear data including Locally Linear Embedding (LLE), Locality Preserving Projection (LPP), Kernel Local Preserving Projection (KLPP) [8], etc. The structural characteristics of data include the local structural characteristics and the global structural characteristics [9]. The former reflects the intrinsic properties, and the latter reflects the external shape. KPCA maps the input space to high-dimensional feature space and mainly describes the global structure characteristics of data. KLPP realizes the linear computation while maintaining the local structure features.

In the statistical methods, many achievements have been achieved by using FDA for fault diagnosis [10]. But it still needs to be further improved to solve the following problems: (1) In projective space, data aliasing for different classes appears; (2) The boundary data is far from the center of the class, resulting in the classification fuzzy. Therefore, we propose an improved method in this paper. First, we use local and global feature extraction method to solve the data aliasing problem. Then we use the modified K-NN method to reduce the classification error rate. To verify the effectiveness of our proposed method, it has been simulated on the diesel engine fault data which is simulated by the diesel engine simulation professional software AVL BOOST [11]. The simulation results show that our proposed method has good performance on the feature extraction and fault classification. It provides a basis for fault diagnosis and classification of actual marine diesel engine.

2 Improved Structure Preserving Algorithm

The improved global and local structure preserving algorithm (GLSP) integrates the global structural characteristics of KPCA and KLPP. The basic ideas are as follows: KPCA uses the linear PCA to extract the features and realizes the maximization of the variance, and KLPP maintains the local structure of data set by constructing near neighbor graph, and maintains the nonlinear manifold low-dimensional local characteristics.

2.1 The Objective Function of Local Structure Preserving

The dataset $X^{\mathrm{T}} = \{x_1, x_2, \ldots, x_n\} \in R^n$ is mapped to high-dimensional space by nonlinear mapping $\boldsymbol{\Phi}$. $J_{local}(w)$ aims to find a projection vector w, which can make the projection $y_i = (\boldsymbol{\Phi}(x_i))^T w$ maintain the neighbor structure of dataset. The local structure preserving objective function can be written as follows:

$$
\begin{aligned}
J_{local}(w) &= \min_{w} \sum_{i=1}^{n} \sum_{j=1}^{n} \left\| y_i - y_j \right\|^2 s_{i,j} \\
&= \min_{w} \sum_{i=1}^{n} \sum_{j=1}^{n} \left\| (\boldsymbol{\Phi}(x_i))^T w - (\boldsymbol{\Phi}(x_j))^T w \right\|^2 s_{i,j} \\
&= \min_{w} \left\{ w^{\mathrm{T}} (\boldsymbol{\Phi}(x_i))^{\mathrm{T}} (D - S) \boldsymbol{\Phi}(x_j) w \right\}
\end{aligned}
\tag{1}
$$

where $s_{i,j}$ is the weight parameter, indicating the neighbor relationship between data points; S is the weight matrix; $D_{ii} = \sum\limits_{j=1}^{n} s_{i,j}$ is the diagonal matrix.

$$s_{i,j} = \begin{cases} \exp\left(-\|x_i - x_j\|^2\right)/t & x_i \in \Omega_{x_j}^k, x_j \in \Omega_{x_i}^k \\ 0, & \text{other} \end{cases} \tag{2}$$

Introduce the kernel function $K = \Phi(x_i)^T \Phi(x_j)$ and there exists a coefficient $\alpha_i (i = 1, 2, \ldots, n)$, which can present the sample as $w = \sum\limits_{i=1}^{n} \alpha_i \Phi(x_i)$. The objective function of KLPP is converted as follows:

$$\begin{aligned} J_{local}(\alpha) &= \min_{\alpha} \left\{ \alpha^T \Phi(x_i) \left(\Phi(x_j)\right)^T (D - S) \Phi(x_i) \left(\Phi(x_j)\right)^T \alpha \right\} \\ &= \min_{\alpha} \alpha^T KLK\alpha = \min_{\alpha} \alpha^T L_1 \alpha \end{aligned} \tag{3}$$

where $L = D - S$ represents *Laplacian* matrix; $L_1 = KLK$.

2.2   The Objective Function of Maximizing the Structure Variance

The KPCA objective function can be written as follows:

$$J_{global}(w) = \max_{w} \sum_{i=1}^{n} y_i^2 = \max_{w} \left((\Phi(x_i))^T w \right)^2 \tag{4}$$

where $w^T w = 1$.

Introduce the kernel function and the objective function is translated as follows:

$$\begin{aligned} J_{global}(\alpha) &= \max_{w} \sum_{i=1}^{n} \left(\alpha(\Phi(x_i))^T \Phi(x_j) \right)^2 \\ &= \max_{w} \alpha^T KK\alpha = \max_{w} \alpha^T C\alpha \end{aligned} \tag{5}$$

where $\alpha^T K\alpha = 1$; $C = KK$.

2.3   Improved Global Objective Function

Combining the idea of KPCA objective function and KLPP objective function, the local and global objective function is constructed as follows:

$$\begin{aligned} J(\alpha) &= \max_{\alpha} \left(J_g(\alpha) - J_l(\alpha) \right) \\ &= \max_{\alpha} \left(\alpha^T C\alpha - \alpha^T L_1 \alpha \right) \\ &= \max_{\alpha} \left(\alpha^T (C - L_1)\alpha \right) \end{aligned} \tag{6}$$

However, the two objective functions are difficult to achieve the best effect at the same time. Therefore, a weight parameter β is introduced to balance the two objective functions.

$$\beta_C = \frac{\rho(C)}{\rho(C) + \rho(L_1)}, \beta_{L_1} = 1 - \beta_C \tag{7}$$

where $\rho(\cdot)$ is the spectral radius of the correlation matrix. So the improved global objective function is converted as follows:

$$\begin{aligned} J(\alpha) &= \max_{\alpha} \left(\alpha^T \left(\beta_C C - \beta_{L_1} L_1 \right) \alpha \right) \\ &= \max_{\alpha} \alpha^T M \alpha \end{aligned} \tag{8}$$

where $M = \beta_C C - \beta_{L_1} L_1, 0 \leq \beta_C \leq 1, 0 \leq \beta_{L_1} \leq 1$.

After determining the value of β, the Lagrange multiplier method can be used to solve the vector α.

$$L = \alpha^T M \alpha - \lambda(\alpha^T K \alpha - 1) \tag{9}$$

Where λ is the Lagrange multiplier. When $\frac{\partial L}{\partial \alpha} = 0$, we can get

$$M\alpha = \lambda K \alpha \tag{10}$$

We can get the eigenvalues arranging by size and the eigenvectors $A = (\alpha_1, \alpha_2, \ldots, \alpha_n)$ corresponding to eigenvalues. The contribution rate is usually set more than 85%.

3   Improved Kernel Fisher Discriminant Analysis Algorithm

FDA is a linear dimensionality reduction technique aiming to maximize the separation between classes and minimize the separation within classes. To solve the problems of nonlinear data, the kernel function method has been introduced to FDA.

3.1   Kernel Fisher Discriminant Analysis

The dataset is mapped to high-dimensional space by non-linear mapping Φ.

$$m_i = \frac{1}{N_i} \sum_{j=1}^{N_i} \Phi(x_j) \tag{11}$$

where N_i is the number of observations of class C_i. The between-class-scatter matrix S_B and the within-class-scatter matrix S_W are as follows:

$$S_B = \frac{1}{N} \sum_{i=1}^{C} N_i (m_i - m)(m_i - m)^{\mathrm{T}} \tag{12}$$

$$S_W = \frac{1}{N} \sum_{i=1}^{C} \sum_{j=1}^{N_i} \left[\Phi\left(x_i^j\right) - m_i\right] \left[\Phi\left(x_i^j\right) - m_i\right]^{\mathrm{T}} \tag{13}$$

where m_i is the mean vector of class i; m is the mean vector of the dataset.

The FDA vector can be determined as:

$$J(w) = \max \frac{w^{\mathrm{T}} S_B w}{w^{\mathrm{T}} S_W w} \tag{14}$$

where w is the optimal projection vector. Then we introduce the kernel function K_{ij} and the objective function of KFDA is as follows:

$$J(\alpha) = \max \frac{\alpha^{\mathrm{T}} K_B \alpha}{\alpha^{\mathrm{T}} K_W \alpha} \tag{15}$$

where K_B and K_W can be computed as follows:

$$\begin{cases} K_B = \dfrac{1}{C(C-1)} \sum_{i,j=1}^{C} \left(\mu_i - \mu_j\right)\left(\mu_i - \mu_j\right)^{\mathrm{T}} \\ \mu_i = \left(\dfrac{1}{N_i}\sum_{j=1}^{N_i} K\left(x_1, x_i^j\right), \ldots, \dfrac{1}{N_i}\sum_{j=1}^{N_i} K\left(x_N, x_i^j\right)\right)^{\mathrm{T}} \end{cases} \tag{16}$$

$$\begin{cases} K_W = \dfrac{1}{C}\sum_{i=1}^{C} \dfrac{1}{N_i}\sum_{j=1}^{N_i} \left(\xi_j - \mu_i\right)\left(\xi_j - \mu_i\right)^{\mathrm{T}} \\ \xi_j = \left(K\left(x_1, x_j\right), K\left(x_2, x_j\right), \ldots, K\left(x_N, x_j\right)\right)^{\mathrm{T}} \end{cases} \tag{17}$$

The question can be translated to solve the eigenvalues and eigenvectors of the equation $K_W^{-1} K_B$. Radial Basis Function (RBF) is used as kernel function in this paper.

3.2   Improvement of Fault Classification

The FDA calculates the Euclidean Distance between two projection vectors. But Mahalanobis Distance is not affected by dimension. It can exclude the correlation interference among different variables. The discriminate rule is as follows:

$$(y - \bar{y}_i)^{\mathrm{T}} \Sigma_i^{-1} (y - \bar{y}_i) = \min_{1 \le h \le C} (y - \bar{y}_h)^{\mathrm{T}} \Sigma_h^{-1} (y - \bar{y}_h) \tag{18}$$

where y is the projection vector; Σ_i is the covariance matrix of the class i projection.

Mahalanobis Distance has an error rate for fault classification on boundary points, so we consider using the modified K nearest neighbor (K-NN) algorithm for classification. But there are also some problems, for example: (1) The K-NN algorithm needs to store all training samples with complex distance calculation. (2) The K-NN algorithm does not take the distance into account, and it may lead to an error of classification. To solve these problems, the improved measures are put forward as follows:

(1) **Find the boundary points.** Calculate the Mahalanobis Distance $dis_1, dis_2, \ldots,$ dis_C and sort the distance $dis_1', dis_2', \ldots, dis_C'$ from order.

$$\left| \frac{dis_1' - dis_2'}{dis_1'} \right| \le \varepsilon, \varepsilon \in (0, 1) \tag{19}$$

(2) **Use weighted method to improve the K-NN algorithm accuracy.** For the boundary points, the distance between the nearest K sample points and the pending points is $dis_1, dis_2, \ldots, dis_K$. A function $V(dis_i) = 1/dis_i$ is set to represent the weighted value between the boundary points and the sample points.

4 Simulations

This paper takes the 13500TEU marine diesel engine as the research object, and uses the software AVL BOOST to simulate four types of different conditions in Table 1. The relative error between simulation result and bench test is not more than 1%, so we can think that the results of the AVL BOOST simulation experiment are accurate.

Table 1. The one normal condition and three fault types

No.	Fault types	Data dimension
1	Normal	960×15
2	Fault1_Insufficient cooling of diesel engine air cooler	960×15
3	Fault2_Diesel engine exhaust blockage	960×15
4	Fault3_Low diesel engine turbocharging efficiency	960×15

4.1 Comparison of Data Aliasing with Improved Global Objective Algorithm

We use 480 samples as training data, and the other 480 samples as testing data. The first 3 dimension feature vectors are extracted by KPCA, KLPP and GLSP. And the simulation results are shown in Figs. 1, 2 and 3.

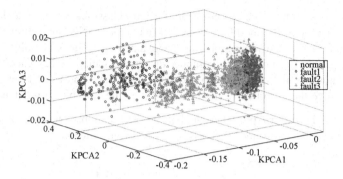

Fig. 1. Feature extraction based on KPCA

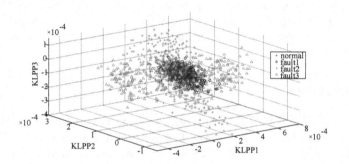

Fig. 2. Feature extraction based on KLPP

As shown in Figs. 1 and 2, KPCA can separate the fault 1 and the fault 3 partly, but there is a crossover between normal condition and fault 2. KLPP cannot effectively separate the normal condition and fault 1. The performance of GLSP is shown in Fig. 3. The four types are effectively separated and the clustering ability is good.

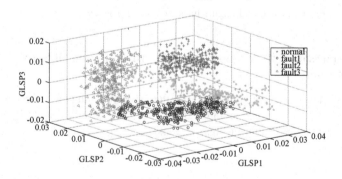

Fig. 3. Feature extraction based on global objective algorithm

4.2   Comparison of Fault Data Classification Fuzzy

After the feature extraction based on GLSP, there is still a problem of fuzzy classification. The modified K-NN algorithm is used for classification. The simulation results are shown in Fig. 4.

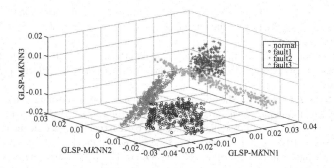

Fig. 4. Fault classification based on modified K-NN algorithm

Table 2. Fault diagnosis results

No.	Model	Test accuracy%
1	ELM	62.26
2	SVM	66.86
3	RVM	68.53
4	GLSP-MKNN	76.35

To verify the validity of the proposed method, ELM, SVM, RVM and the modified K-NN algorithm are used for comparing. The accuracy of the fault diagnosis is shown in Table 2. The results show that our proposed method has the highest accuracy.

5   Conclusions

In this paper, we proposed GLSP method, and the method can extract the sensitive feature information of the diesel engine nonlinear fault data. It has more accurate fault classification effect. On the other hand, the modified K-NN algorithm can separate fault boundary points well by introducing the boundary parameter. The simulation results demonstrates the effectiveness of the proposed method. Besides, the efficiency of fault detection radio still needs to be improved for further study in terms of real diesel engine fault diagnosis.

Acknowledgments. This work was supported by the National Natural Science Foundation of China (No. 61773087) and the Fundamental Research Funds for the Central Universities (DUT17ZD216) and Shanghai Rising-Star Program (15QB1400800).

References

1. Yang, Y., Ming, A., Zhang, Y., Zhu, Y.: Discriminative non-negative matrix factorization (DNMF) and its application to the fault diagnosis of diesel engine. Mech. Syst. Sig. Process. **95**, 158–171 (2017)
2. Cai, B., Zhao, Y., Liu, H., Xie, M.: A data-driven fault diagnosis methodology in three-phase inverters for PMSM drive systems. IEEE Trans. Power Electron. **32**(7), 5590–5600 (2016)
3. Garcia-Alvarez, D., Fuente, M.J., Sainz, G.I.: Fault detection and isolation in transient states using principal component analysis. J. Process Control **22**(3), 551–563 (2012)
4. Han, M., Jiang, L.: Endpoint prediction model of basic oxygen furnace steelmaking based on PSO-ICA and RBF neural network. In: Proceedings of the International Conference on Intelligent Control Information Process, vol. 39, no. 1, pp. 388–393 (2010)
5. Dufrenois, F.: A one-class kernel fisher criterion for outlier detection. IEEE Trans. Neural Netw. Learn. Syst. **26**(5), 982–994 (2015)
6. Pradhan, B., Jebur, M.N., Shafri, H.Z.M., Tehrany, M.S.: Data fusion technique using wavelet transform and Taguchi methods for automatic landslide detection from airborne laser scanning data and quickbird satellite imagery. IEEE Trans. Geosci. Remote Sens. **54**(3), 1610–1622 (2016)
7. Wang, X.Z., Han, M., Yang, X.L., Lin, D.: Calculating lime input quantity by alkalinity deviation estimation based on support-vector-machines. Control Theory Appl. **26**(12), 1415–1418 (2009)
8. Deng, X.G., Tian, X.M.: Sparse kernel locality preserving projection and its application in nonlinear process fault detection. Chin. J. Chem. Eng. **21**(2), 163–170 (2013)
9. Zhang, M., Ge, Z., Song, Z., Fu, R.: Global-local structure analysis model and its application for fault detection and identification. Ind. Eng. Chem. Res. **50**(11), 6837–6848 (2011)
10. Shi, H.T., Liu, J.C., Wu, Y.H., Zhang, K., Zhang, L.X., Xue, P.: Fault diagnosis of nonlinear and large-scale processes using novel modified kernel Fisher discriminant analysis approach. Int. J. Syst. Sci. **47**(5), 1095–1109 (2016)
11. Kahveci, N.E., Impram, S.T., Genc, A.U.: Boost pressure control for a large diesel engine with turbocharger. In: IEEE Proceedings of the American Control Conference, pp 2108–2113 (2014)

NN - Sliding Mode Control Design
for Trajectory Tracking and Roll Reduction
of Marine Vessels

Cheng Liu, Jingqi Li$^{(\boxtimes)}$, Rong Zhao, and Tieshan Li

Navigation College, Dalian Maritime University, Dalian, China
Lassieliucheng@163.com, LiJingQi_surprise@163.com,
18840864289@163.com, tieshanli@126.com

Abstract. Both trajectory tracking (TT) and fin roll reduction (FRR) are fundamental marine applications, and they are usually studied separately in previous studies. Actually, the roll motion often occurs during the trajectory tracking in waves; therefore, they should be studied together. In this work, we consider the trajectory tracking and fin roll reduction of marine vessel as an integral system. It includes three system inputs, namely, the force in surge, the control moment in roll, and the control torque in yaw, while four degrees of freedom (DoF), i.e., position, roll angle and yaw angle are needed to be controlled. Through combining the hierarchical sliding mode approach and neural network technique, a novel control algorithm is proposed. The neural network is introduced to deal with model uncertainty. Lyapunov stability theorem ensures stability of the close-loop system, and various simulations are provided to validate the effectiveness and performance of the proposed algorithm.

Keywords: Trajectory tracking · Underactuated marine vessels
Fin roll reduction · Neural network

1 Introduction

Trajectory tracking problem of underactuated marine vessels, which attracts considerable attention from control community, is tricky, attractive, as well as challenging. A global coordinate transformation approach was proposed to achieve homogeneity of the system, and a continuous periodic time-varying feedback law was presented to stabilize the marine vessel to the origin [1]. An algorithm with respect to the tracking control of underactuated marine vessels was presented by assuming that the velocity in surge was always positive based on backstepping technique [2], however, the orientation was not controlled. Time-invariant discontinuous feedback laws were constructed to achieve asymptotic stability of the closed-loop system and reach the expected configuration with exponential convergence rates [3]. The underactuated model was converted into a triangular-like form through a coordinate transformation approach, which made the integrator backstepping scheme applicable and a semi-global result was finally obtained [4]. A time-varying global solution was proposed with respect to two degrees of freedom of stabilizing the kinematic model [5], however, it

© Springer International Publishing AG, part of Springer Nature 2018
T. Huang et al. (Eds.): ISNN 2018, LNCS 10878, pp. 665–676, 2018.
https://doi.org/10.1007/978-3-319-92537-0_76

was only suit for straight line occasions. Smooth time-varying state feedback was proposed to make an underactuated marine vessel globally uniformly asymptotical stable to the origin relied on backstepping approach [6]. Two systematic controllers were developed based on the passivity approach and cascade-backstepping approach [7]. However, the method suffers from persistent excitation (PE) condition where the straight line cannot be tracked, which would be pretty restrictive from a practical standpoint. Most works discussed above have not taken the external disturbance into account, which widely exists in seaway [8, 9]. With the reference of related results on cascade systems, a global solution was finally achieved [10] with the tracking error dynamics of the system divided into a cascade of two linear subsystems which can be controlled independently. The stability analysis of the system was conducted based on linear time-varying theory, and this work also suffered from PE condition. Multivariable controllers were proposed to stabilize the underactuated marine vessel and reduce the roll and pitch simultaneously [11]. Only linear course occasion was covered in this work. A global solution was finally achieved based on the cascade approach under a weaker PE condition [12]. Three smooth global time-varying controllers designed for the stabilization of underactuated marine vessels were proposed with different techniques [13]. Many different kinds of control methods have been proposed to solve trajectory tracking problem, such as sliding mode control [14, 16], backstepping technique [17], predictive control [18], etc.

To the authors' best knowledge, all the works mentioned above except Do et al. [11] did not consider the fin roll reduction simultaneously. However, Do et al. [11] only covered the case of a linear course, which is rather limited. As a matter of fact, roll motion often occurs during trajectory tracking, which has negative influences on ship motion in seaway, including cargo damage, and limiting the crew's operation performance etc. Thus, it is appropriate to study trajectory tracking and fin roll reduction simultaneously from practical perspective.In our work, trajectory tracking problem of under-actuated marine vessels with fin roll reduction is studied. A four-degree-of-freedom (4-DoF) mathematical model of ship motion is taken into account, which contains surge, sway, roll and yaw. The force in surge, the control moment in roll, and the control torque in yaw are perceived as the system inputs, and it is the position, orientation, and roll angle of ships that need to be controlled. It is obvious to see that the degrees of control inputs are fewer than the degrees that need to be controlled, which means the system under study is a class of underactuated system. Trajectory tracking of under-actuated marine vessel requires the ship to arrive certain pinpoint location at the specific time we predetermined. Meanwhile, ship motion suffers from strong nonlinearities like large inertia and time-delay. Trajectory tracking of under-actuated marine vessels with fin roll reduction turns to be a rather difficult and challenging problem.

To solve the above problems, controllers for trajectory tracking of underactuated marine vessels with fin roll reduction are proposed based on hierarchical sliding mode and neural networks [19]. Hierarchical sliding mode technique is employed so that underactuation property can be dealt with. The neural network here is introduced to deal with uncertainties of the model [20]. Random waves are involved so that robustness of proposed control algorithm can be testified. Furthermore, Lyapunov stability theorem is employed to conduct stability analysis of closed-loop system.

Finally, various numerical simulations are provided to validate the effectiveness and performance of the designed controllers.

2 Preliminaries and Problem Formulation

2.1 Radial Basis Function (RBF) Neural Network

In our work, the RBF neural network is introduced to work as a tool used for approximating nonlinear function. It belongs to a class of linearly parameterized neural networks and can be represented as [21]

$$f_n(Z) = W^T H(Z) \tag{1}$$

where $Z \in \Omega_z \subset R^n$ represents the input vector, $W \in R^l$ represents the weight vector, and l represents the weight number. Besides, the basis function vector is given as

$$H(z) = [h_1(z), h_2(z), \ldots, h_l(z)]^T \in R^l \tag{2}$$

Select RBFs as the Gaussian functions with the form of

$$h_i(z) = \exp(-\frac{\|z - \mu_i\|}{2\delta_i^2}), \quad (i = 1, 2, \ldots l) \tag{3}$$

where $\mu_i = [\mu_{i1}, \mu_{i2}, \ldots, \mu_{in}]^T$ is the center of the receptive field and δ_i is the width of the Gaussian function. It has been proved that system (1) can approximate any continuous function on a compact set $\Omega_z \subset R^l$ to arbitrary accuracy as

$$f(Z) = W^{*T}H(Z) + \varepsilon, \quad \forall Z \in \Omega_z \tag{4}$$

where W^* represents the ideal constant weights, and ε is introduced to represent the approximation error. The ideal weight vector W^* of the neural network can be defined as the value of W that minimizes $|\varepsilon|$ for all $Z \in \Omega_z \subset R^n$, namely

$$W^* \triangleq \arg \min_{W \in R^l} \left\{ \sup_{z \in \Omega_z} |f(z) - W^T H(z)| \right\}. \tag{5}$$

2.2 Mathematical Model of Marine Vessels

A class of 4-DoF underactuated marine vessels with fin stabilizer to reduce roll motion is considered in our work. The mathematical model of the marine vessels is given in the following form [22, 23]

$$\dot{x} = u\cos\psi - v\cos\phi\sin\psi, \dot{y} = u\sin\psi + v\cos\phi\cos\psi, \dot{\phi} = p$$
$$\dot{\psi} = r\cos\phi, \dot{u} = f_u + \frac{1}{m_{11}}\tau_1, \dot{v} = f_v, \dot{p} = f_p + \frac{1}{m_{33}}\tau_2 + \tau_w, \dot{r} = f_r + \frac{1}{m_{44}}\tau_3 \quad (6)$$

where x and y are used to represent the longitudinal and lateral displacement, respectively. ψ and ϕ are used to represent the yaw and roll angle, respectively. u and v are the longitudinal and lateral velocity, p and r are used to represent the roll rate and yaw rate, respectively. τ_w is used to represent the random wave. τ_1, τ_2, τ_3 are the control inputs. And $f_u = \frac{m_{22}}{m_{11}}vr - \frac{d_{11}}{m_{11}}u^2, f_v = -\frac{m_{11}}{d_{11}}ur - \frac{m_{22}}{d_{22}}v, f_p = -\frac{d_{33}}{m_{33}}p - l\phi, f_r = \frac{m_{11}-m_{22}}{m_{44}}uv - \frac{d_{44}}{m_{44}}r$. $m_{ii}, d_{ii}(i=1,2,3,4)$ are model parameters. For the purpose of simplifying the control design process, some assumptions are required.

Assumption 1: The external disturbances are $|\tau_w| \leq E_d$.

Assumption 2: The functions f_u, f_v, f_p, f_r are smooth and unknown.

2.3   Problem Statement

The expected trajectory is generated by a virtual ship model in the following form

$$\dot{x}_d = u_d\cos\psi_d - v_d\sin\psi_d x, \dot{y}_d = u_d\sin\psi_d + v_d\cos\psi_d, \dot{\psi} = r_d,$$
$$\dot{u}_d = \frac{m_{22}}{m_{11}}v_d r_d - \frac{d_{11}}{m_{11}}u_d^2 + \frac{1}{m_{11}}\tau_{1d}, \dot{v}_d = -\frac{m_{11}}{m_{22}}u_d r_d - \frac{d_{22}}{m_{22}}v_d,$$
$$\dot{r}_d = \frac{m_{11}-m_{22}}{m_{44}}u_d v_d - \frac{d_{44}}{m_{44}}r_d + \frac{1}{m_{44}}\tau_{3d} \quad (7)$$

where the meaning of symbols is similar to those in Subsect. 2.2. Employ the following coordinate transformation, we have

$$z_1 = x\cos\psi + y\sin\psi, z_2 = -x\sin\psi + y\cos\psi, z_3 = \phi, z_4 = \psi \quad (8)$$

Similarly, we can obtain

$$z_{1d} = x_d\cos\psi_d + y_d\sin\psi_d, z_{2d} = -x_d\sin\psi_d + y_d\cos\psi_d, z_{3d} = \phi_d = 0, z_{4d} = \psi_d \quad (9)$$

Define the error system

$$z_{1e} = z_1 - z_{1d}, z_{2e} = z_2 - z_{2d}, z_{3e} = z_3, z_{4e} = z_4 - z_{4d} \quad (10)$$

Thus, tracking control for underactuated marine vessels is transformed into the problem of stabilization control of system given by (10). Let $z_{1d} = z_{2d} = z_{3d} = z_{4d} = 0$, the trajectory tracking of underactuated marine vessels can be transformed into the stabilization case.

3 Control Design and Stability Analysis

First, the third subsystem for system given by (10) is stabilized by employing a common sliding mode method. Then, the second and fourth subsystem is stabilized by using a hierarchical sliding mode approach. Finally, the first subsystem is stabilized by employing a common sliding mode method too. We employ four RBF neural networks in order to obtain approximation of f_u, f_v, f_p and f_r, respectively. For the purpose of expressing the design procedure explicitly, the stability analysis is incorporated into the control design procedure. The process of the control design mainly include three steps as follows.

Step 1: Define a common sliding mode surface as

$$S_1 = c_1 z_{3e} + \dot{z}_{3e} \tag{11}$$

where c_1 is a positive constant. Differentiating Eq. (11), we have

$$\dot{S}_1 = c_1 p + f_p + \frac{1}{m_{33}} \tau_2 + \tau_w \tag{12}$$

By using RBF neural network to obtain the approximation of f_p

$$\hat{f}_p = \hat{W}_1^T H_1(Z) \tag{13}$$

where $\hat{f}_p$ is the estimated value of f_p, and $\hat{W}_1$ is the estimated value of W_1^*.
The equivalent control law for the third subsystem is designed as

$$\tau_{2eq} = m_{33}(-c_1 p - \hat{f}_p) \tag{14}$$

and the switch control law of the third subsystem is designed as

$$\tau_{2sw} = m_{33}(-\eta_1 \mathrm{sgn}(S_1) - k_1 S_1) \tag{15}$$

where η_1 and k_1 are both positive parameters.
Then, the total control law for roll moment can be expressed as

$$\tau_2 = \tau_{2eq} + \tau_{2sw} \tag{16}$$

Consider the first Lyapunov candidate function as below

$$V_1 = \frac{1}{2} S_1^2 + \frac{1}{2\gamma_1} \tilde{W}_1^T \tilde{W}_1 \tag{17}$$

where $\tilde{W}_1 = W_1^* - \hat{W}_1$, γ_1 is a positive parameter.
Differentiating Eq. (17), then we can obtain

$$\dot{V}_1 \le \tilde{W}_1^T (S_1 H_1(Z) - \frac{1}{\gamma}\dot{\hat{W}}_1) - \eta_1|S_1| - k_1 S_1^2 + (E_d + \varepsilon_1)S_1 \tag{18}$$

Let $\dot{\hat{W}}_1 = \gamma_1 S_1 H_1(Z)$, we have

$$\dot{V}_1 \le -k_1 S_1^2 - \eta_1|S_1| + (\varepsilon_1 + E_d)S_1 \tag{19}$$

Step 2: The hierarchical sliding mode includes two first-order sliding mode surfaces which we have designed firstly. Then, we synthesize the first-order sliding mode surfaces on certain ratio to design a second-order sliding mode surface.

Define the first first-order sliding surface as

$$\sigma_1 = c_2 z_{2e} + \dot{z}_{2e} \tag{20}$$

where c_2 is a positive constant. Differentiating Eq. (20), then we can obtain

$$\dot{\sigma}_1 = c_2(v\cos\phi - z_1 r\cos\phi - \dot{z}_{2d}) + f_v\cos\phi - vp\sin\phi$$
$$- (u + z_2 r\cos\phi)r\cos\phi - z_1\cos\phi(f_r + \frac{1}{m_{33}}\tau_3) + z_1 rp\sin\phi - \ddot{z}_{2d} \tag{21}$$

Employing RBF neural network to approximate f_v and f_r, similar to Eq. (13), we can obtain

$$\hat{f}_v = \hat{W}_2^T H_2(Z) \tag{22}$$

$$\hat{f}_r = \hat{W}_3^T H_3(Z) \tag{23}$$

where $\hat{f}_v$ and $\hat{f}_r$ are the estimations of f_v and f_r; $\hat{W}_2$ and $\hat{W}_3$ are the estimations of W_2^* and W_3^*, respectively. Define first first-order equivalent sliding mode surface as

$$\sigma_1 = c_2 z_{2e} + \dot{z}_{2e} \tag{24}$$

where c_2 is a positive constant. Differentiating Eq. (24), then we can obtain

$$\dot{\sigma}_1 = c_2(v\cos\phi - z_1 r\cos\phi + \dot{z}_{2d}) - f_v\cos\phi - z_1\cos\phi(\frac{\tau_3}{m_{33}})$$
$$vp\sin\phi - (u + z_2 r\cos\phi)r\cos\phi - z_1 f_r\cos\phi + z_1 rp\sin\phi - \ddot{z}_{2d}] \tag{25}$$

Then the first first-order equivalent control law is designed as

$$\tau_{31eq} = -\frac{m_{33}}{z_1\cos\phi}\left[-c_2(v\cos\phi - z_1 r\cos\phi + \dot{z}_{2d}) - \hat{f}_v\cos\phi\right.$$
$$\left. + vp\sin\phi + (u + z_2 r\cos\phi)r\cos\phi + z_1\hat{f}_r\cos\phi - z_1 rp\sin\phi + \ddot{z}_{2d}\right] \tag{26}$$

Define second first-order equivalent sliding mode surface as

$$\sigma_2 = c_3 z_{4e} + \dot{z}_{4e} \tag{27}$$

where c_3 is a positive constant. Differentiating Eq. (27), then we can obtain

$$\dot{\sigma}_2 = c_3(r \cos \phi - \dot{z}_{4d}) + (f_r + \frac{1}{m_{44}} \tau_3) \cos \phi - rp \sin \phi - \ddot{z}_{4d} \tag{28}$$

Then the second first-order equivalent law can be designed as

$$\tau_{32eq} = \frac{m_{44}}{\cos \phi} \left[-c_3(r \cos \phi - \dot{z}_{4d}) - \hat{f}_r \cos \phi + rp \sin \phi + \ddot{z}_{4d} \right] \tag{29}$$

Define the second order sliding mode surface as

$$S_2 = a\sigma_1 + b\sigma_2 \tag{30}$$

where a and b are both the sliding mode parameters. Differentiating Eq. (30), we can obtain

$$\dot{S}_2 = a\dot{\sigma}_1 + b\dot{\sigma}_2 \tag{31}$$

The switched control law can be designed as below

$$\tau_{3sw} = \frac{-\eta_2 \operatorname{sgn}(S_2) - k_2 S_2 + a \frac{z_1 \cos \phi}{m_{44}} \tau_{32eq} - b \frac{\cos \phi}{m_{44}} \tau_{31eq}}{b \frac{\cos \phi}{m_{44}} - a \frac{z_1 \cos \phi}{m_{44}}} \tag{32}$$

where η_2, k_2 are both positive parameters. Then, the total control law of the yaw moment can be written as

$$\tau_3 = \tau_{31eq} + \tau_{32eq} + \tau_{3sw} \tag{33}$$

Consider the second Lyapunov candidate function as

$$V_2 = \frac{1}{2} S_2^2 + \frac{1}{2\gamma_2} \tilde{W}_2^T \tilde{W}_2 \tag{34}$$

where γ_2 is a positive parameter, $\tilde{W}_2 = W_2^* - \hat{W}_2$. Differentiating Eq. (34), then we can obtain

$$\dot{V}_2 = S_2(a(\tilde{f}_v \cos \phi + z_1 \cos \phi \tilde{f}_r - \frac{z_1 \cos \phi}{m_{44}} \tau_{32eq} - \frac{z_1 \cos \phi}{m_{44}} \tau_{3sw}) \\ + b(\tilde{f}_r \cos \phi + \frac{\cos \phi}{m_{44}} \tau_{31eq} + \frac{\cos \phi}{m_{44}} \tau_{3sw})) - \frac{1}{\gamma_2} \tilde{W}_2^T \dot{\hat{W}}_2 \tag{35}$$

where $\tilde{f}_v = f_v - \hat{f}_v$, $\tilde{f}_r = f_r - \hat{f}_r$ are the estimation errors. Substituting Eqs. (26), (29) and (32) into Eq. (35), we have

$$\dot{V}_2 = S_2(az_1\tilde{f}_r \cos\phi + b\tilde{f}_r \cos\phi) + S_2\left[a\cos\phi(\tilde{W}_2^T H_2(Z) + \varepsilon_2)\right] - \eta_2|S_2| - k_2 S_2^2$$
$$- \frac{1}{\gamma_2}\tilde{W}_2^T \dot{\hat{W}}_2 \tag{36}$$

Let $\dot{\hat{W}}_2 = \gamma_2 S_2 H_2(Z)a\cos\phi$, it can be obtained

$$\dot{V}_2 = S_2(az_1\tilde{f}_r \cos\phi + b\tilde{f}_r \cos\phi) - k_2 S_2^2 + a\cos\phi\varepsilon_2 S_2 - \eta_2|S_2| \tag{37}$$

Step 3: The first subsystem can be stabilized by employing a common sliding mode

$$S_3 = c_4 z_{1e} + \dot{z}_{1e} \tag{38}$$

where c_4 is a positive constant. Differentiating Eq. (38), then we can obtain

$$\dot{S}_3 = c_4(u + z_2 r\cos\phi - \dot{z}_{1d}) + f_u + \frac{1}{m_{11}}\tau_1 + (v\cos\phi - z_1 r\cos\phi)r\cos\phi$$
$$+ z_2\cos\phi(f_r + \frac{1}{m_{44}}\tau_3) - z_2 rp\sin\phi - \ddot{z}_{1d} \tag{39}$$

Employing RBF neural network to approximate f_u

$$\hat{f}_u = \hat{W}_4^T H_4(Z) \tag{40}$$

where $\hat{f}_u$ is the estimated value of f_u, $\hat{W}_4$ is the estimated value of W_4^*. The equivalent control law can be obtained as

$$\tau_{1eq} = m_{11}\big(-c_4(u + z_2 r\cos\phi - \dot{z}_{1d}) - \hat{f}_u - (v\cos\phi - z_1 r\cos\phi)r\cos\phi$$
$$- z_2\cos\phi(\hat{f}_r + \frac{1}{m_{44}}\tau_3) + z_2 rp\sin\phi + \ddot{z}_{1d}\big) \tag{41}$$

The switch control law of surge force can be expressed as

$$\tau_{1sw} = m_{11}(-\eta_3 \operatorname{sgn}(S_3) - k_3 S_3) \tag{42}$$

where η_3 and k_3 are both positive parameters. Then, the total control law of surge force can be written as

$$\tau_2 = \tau_{2eq} + \tau_{2sw} \tag{43}$$

Consider the third Lyapunov candidate function as

$$V_3 = \frac{1}{2}S_3^2 + \frac{1}{2\gamma_4}\tilde{W}_4^T \tilde{W}_4 \tag{44}$$

where γ_4 is a positive parameter, $\tilde{W}_4 = W_4^* - \hat{W}_4$. Differentiating Eq. (44), and substituting Eqs. (41) and (42) into the resulted equation, then we can get

$$\dot{V}_3 = S_3(z_2\tilde{f}\cos\phi_r) + S_3(\tilde{W}_4^T H_4(Z) + \varepsilon_4) - \eta_3|S_3| - k_3S_3^2 - \frac{1}{\gamma_4}\tilde{W}_4^T\dot{\hat{W}}_4 \tag{45}$$

Let $\dot{\hat{W}}_4 = \gamma_4 S_3 H_4(Z)$, we have

$$\dot{V}_3 = S_3(z_2\tilde{f}_r\cos\phi) - \eta_3|S_3| - k_3S_3^2 + \varepsilon_4 S_3 \tag{46}$$

Consider the total Lyapunov function as follows

$$V = \sum_{i=1}^{3} V_i + \frac{1}{2\gamma_3}\tilde{W}_3^T\tilde{W}_3 \geq 0 \tag{47}$$

where γ_3 is a positive parameter, $\tilde{W}_3 = W_3^* - \hat{W}_3$.

Let $\dot{\hat{W}}_3 = \gamma_3(aS_2z_1\cos\phi + bS_2\cos\phi + z_2S_3\cos\phi)H_3(Z)$, and differentiate Eq. (47), we have

$$\dot{V} \leq -\sum_{i=1}^{3}(k_iS_i^2 + \eta_i|S_i|) + (\varepsilon_1 + E_d)S_1 + a\cos\phi\varepsilon_2 S_2$$
$$+ \varepsilon_3(aS_2z_1\cos\phi + bS_2\cos\phi + z_2S_3\cos\phi) + \varepsilon_4 S_3 \tag{48}$$

Let $\eta_1 \geq \varepsilon_1 + E_d, \eta_2 \geq a\varepsilon_2\cos\phi + a\varepsilon_3 S_2 z_1\cos\phi + b\varepsilon_3\cos\phi, \eta_3 \geq \varepsilon_3 z_2 S_3\cos\phi + \varepsilon_4 S_3$, we have

$$\dot{V} \leq -\sum_{i=1}^{3} k_i S_i^2 \tag{49}$$

From Eqs. (47) and (49), we will reach the conclusion that the system under control is stable based on Lyapunov stability theorem [24].

4 Simulation Results

In this section, simulation result is provided to validate the effectiveness and performance of the designed controllers. The ship model is a container ship model, whose parameters are [22]: $m_{11} = 0.00103, m_{22} = 0.0150, m_{33} = 0.000021, m_{44} = 0.0050, d_{11} = 0.0004226, d_{22} = 0.0116, d_{33} = 0.0000075, d_{44} = 0.0022, l = 3.8537$. The control parameters are $c_1 = 10, c_2 = 1, c_3 = 1, c_4 = 1, a = 0.001, b = 100, k_1 = k_2 = k_3 = 100, \eta_1 = \eta_2 = \eta_3 = 0.001$. Parameters for the neural network are selected as $\mu_i = 0.5, \delta_i = 5, \gamma_i = 1, (i = 1, \ldots, 5)$. The initial values are selected as $x_0 = 1, y_0 = 0.87, \phi_0 = 0, \psi_0 = \pi/4, u_0 = 0, v_0 = 0, p_0 = 0, r_0 = 0$. Figure 1 shows the tracking performance of the designed algorithm. The red dot represents the desired trajectory and the blue line is the track trajectory. It is obvious to see that the tracking trajectory will fit the desired trajectory very well. Figure 2 gives the variation curves for the yaw angle and roll angle. From Fig. 2, we can see the roll angle is very small under very high disturbances. We can conclude the proposed controllers are robustness to external disturbances. Figure 3 depicts the system inputs of the force in surge, the control moment in roll and the control torque in yaw, respectively.

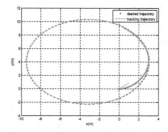

Fig. 1. The tracking performance of position (Color figure online)

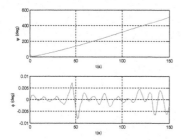

Fig. 2. The yaw angle and roll angle

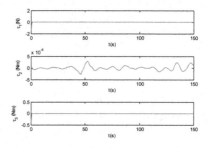

Fig. 3. The control inputs of three controller

5   Conclusions

In our work, three controllers, i.e., the force in surge, the control moment in roll and the control torque in yaw, are designed for trajectory tracking of underactuated marine vessels with fin roll reduction based on hierarchical sliding mode approach and neural network. The hierarchical sliding mode approach is used to address the underactuation, and the RBF neural networks are employed to obtain approximation of the nonlinear functions. The proposed controllers are robust to extreme waves through combining the hierarchical sliding mode and neural networks. Lyapunov stability theorem has guaranteed stability of the closed-loop system. The simulations have validated the effectiveness and performance of the designed controllers.

Acknowledgments. This work is supported in part by the National Natural Science Foundation of China (Nos. 51179019, 61374114), the Fundamental Research Program for Key Laboratory of the Education Department of Liaoning Province (LZ2015006), the Natural Science Foundation of Liaoning (20170580081), and the Fundamental Research Funds for the Central Universities under Grants 3132016313, 3132017114 and 3132016311, Postdoctoral innovation talent support plan (BX201700041).

References

1. Pettersen, K.Y., Egeland, O.: Exponential stabilization of an underactuated surface vessel. In: Proceedings of the 35th Conference on Decision and Control, pp. 967–972. IEEE Press, Japan (1996)
2. Godhavn, J.M.: Nonlinear tracking of underactuated surface vessels. In: Proceedings of the 35th Conference on Decision and Control, pp. 975–980. IEEE Press, Kobe (1996)
3. Reyhanoglu, M.: Exponential stabilization of an underactuated autonomous surface vessel. Automatica 33(12), 2249–2254 (1997)
4. Pettersen, K.Y., Nijmeijer, H.: Tracking control of an underactuated surface vessel. In: Proceedings of the 37th IEEE Conference on Decision and Control, pp. 4561–4566. IEEE Press, USA (1998)
5. Indiveri, G., Aicardi, M., Casalino, G.: Nonlinear time-invariant feedback control of an underactuated marine vehicle along a straight course. In: Proceedings of the IFAC Conference on Manoeuvring and Control of Marine Craft, Aalborg, Denmark, pp. 221–226 (2000)
6. Mazenc, F., Pettersen, K.Y., Nijmeijer, H.: Global uniform asymptotic stabilization of an underactuated surface vessel. IEEE Trans. Autom. Control 47(10), 1759–1762 (2002)
7. Jiang, Z.P.: Global tracking control of underactuated ships by Lyapunov's direct method. Automatica 38(2), 301–309 (2002)
8. Do, K.D., Jiang, Z.P., Pan, J.: Underactuated ship global tracking under relaxed conditions. IEEE Trans. Autom. Control 47(9), 1529–1536 (2002)
9. Do, K.D., Jiang, Z.P., Pan, J.: Universal controllers for stabilization and tracking of underactuated ships. Syst. Control Lett. 47(4), 299–317 (2002)
10. Lefeber, E., Pettersen, K.Y., Nijmeijer, H.: Tracking control of an underactuated ship. IEEE Trans. Control Syst. Technol. 11(1), 52–61 (2003)
11. Do, K.D., Pan, J., Jiang, Z.P.: Robust adaptive control of underactuated ships on a linear course with comfort. Ocean Eng. 30(17), 2201–2225 (2003)
12. Lee, T.C., Jiang, Z.P.: New cascade approach for global κ-exponential tracking of underactuated ships. IEEE Trans. Automatic Control 49(12), 2297–2303 (2004)
13. Dong, W., Guo, Y.: Global time-varying stabilization of underactuated surface vessel. IEEE Trans. Autom. Control 50(6), 859–864 (2005)
14. Aguiar, A.A., Hespanha, J.P.: Trajectory-tracking and path-following of underactuated autonomous vehicles with parametric modeling uncertainty. IEEE Trans. Autom. Control 52(8), 1362–1379 (2007)
15. Dong, W., Guo, Y.: Nonlinear tracking control of underactuated surface vessel. In: American Control Conference, pp. 4351–4356. IEEE Press, USA (2005)
16. Cheng, J., Yi, J., Zhao, D.: Design of a sliding mode controller for trajectory tracking problem of marine vessels. IET Control Theory Appl. 1(1), 233–237 (2007)

17. Chwa, D.: Global tracking control of underactuated ships with input and velocity constraints using dynamic surface control method. IEEE Trans. Control Syst. Technol. **19**(6), 1357–1370 (2011)
18. Yan, Z., Wang, J.: Model predictive control for tracking of underactuated vessels based on recurrent neural networks. IEEE J. Oceanic Eng. **37**(4), 717–726 (2012)
19. Wang, W., Yi, J., Zhao, D., Liu, D.: Design of a stable sliding-mode controller for a class of second-order underactuated systems. IEE Proc. Control Theory Appl. **151**(6), 683–690 (2005)
20. Ge, S.S., Hang, C.C., Lee, T.H., Zhang, T.: Stable Adaptive Neural Network Control, vol. 13. Springer, New York (2001). https://doi.org/10.1007/978-1-4757-6577-9
21. Ge, S.S., Wang, C.: Adaptive NN control of uncertain nonlinear pure-feedback systems. Automatica **38**(4), 671–682 (2002)
22. Fossen, T.I.: Handbook of Marine Craft Hydrodynamics and Motion Control. Wiley, Hoboken (2011)
23. Perez, T.: Ship Motion Control. Springer, London (2005). https://doi.org/10.1007/1-84628-157-1
24. Haddad, W.M., Chellaboina, V.: Nonlinear Dynamical Systems and Control: A Lyapunov-Based Approach. Princeton University Press, Princeton (2008)

Supplementary Frequency Control for Multi-machine Power System Based on Adaptive Dynamic Programming

Zhan Shi, Zhanshan Wang$^{(\boxtimes)}$, Yanhong Luo, and Dan Ye

School of Information Science and Engineering,
Northeastern University, Shenyang 110819, China
shizhan_neu@163.com, zhanshan_wang@163.com,
neuluo@gmail.com, yedan@ise.neu.edu.cn

Abstract. Power system is a nonlinear high-dimension complex system with dynamic uncertainties, how to carry out frequency regulation effectively in the event of disturbance is a difficult problem to be solved urgently. In this paper, a robust adaptive dynamic programming (robust ADP) based supplementary frequency controller for each generator is designed to solve multi-machine power system frequency regulation problem. The control policy iteration of each subsystem controller only uses their own state and input information for learning, without knowing the whole system dynamics. MATLAB and PSAT are used to establish the New England 10-machine 39-bus test system to verify the effective of the proposed control scheme. The simulation results show that the designed controller can effectively adapt to changes in the power system and make the system frequency recover to the reference value quickly.

Keywords: Power system · Frequency control · Distributed control

1 Introduction

With the continuous expansion of system scale and a large number of renewable energy contained uncertainty access to it, the challenge to security and stability of power system has become more severely. In the actual alternating current (AC) power network with large capacity units, the power balance is usually achieved by adjusting the system frequency [1]. Traditionally, it can be accomplished through adjusting power generation (primary) droop control and (secondary) automatic generation control (AGC) [2]. In addition, supplementary frequency control (SFC) is added for better frequency regulation in some power system [3, 4].

Actually, it's difficult to make independent operation of the whole system frequency regulation [5]. If the system frequency is not properly controlled, it may cause power network to collapse which seriously affect people's daily life and bring huge economic losses. Therefore, to the safe and stable operation of power system, it must be effectively controlled.

The traditional frequency controllers are designed based on a single-machine infinite-bus (SMIB) power system simplified model which is linearized at partial specific operating points. However, this method is difficult to attempt satisfactory

© Springer International Publishing AG, part of Springer Nature 2018
T. Huang et al. (Eds.): ISNN 2018, LNCS 10878, pp. 677–685, 2018.
https://doi.org/10.1007/978-3-319-92537-0_77

optimal control over the entire operating range of system. In recent years, nonlinear models are used to solve this problem instead of approximate linear model. However, nonlinear controllers have a more complicated structure. Particularly in multi-machine power systems, it's very difficult to implement.

The emergence of adaptive dynamic programming (ADP) provides a feasible and effective method to solve the nonlinear controller design problem. As a new nonlinear optimal control method, it may not need the model of controlled object, also not need the accurate cost function, so bring it into power system may afford a new solution of nonlinear optimal control [6]. Until now, ADP has been used in many aspects of power systems, such as the excitation controller design [7] and automatic voltage regulator design [8]. ADP can also apply to a multi-machine power system [9].

However, using ADP method to design controller is usually needed the whole system state information. This process takes a long time to calculate. In addition, multi-machine power system is a nonlinear high-dimension complex system with dynamic uncertainties. The state information collected by the above system for ADP design may affect the effect of controller.

In order to avoid the deficiencies of ADP method in multi-machine frequency controller design, we use a new computational intelligence method called robust adaptive dynamic programming (robust ADP) to design frequency controller [10]. The robust ADP is built on the techniques of ADP to solve the decentralized or distributed controller design of large-scale systems which have the existence of unknown parameters, dynamic uncertainties, and the limited information of state variables.

In this paper, we assume that power system is already equipped with droop controller, and we focus on designing the supplementary controller of each subsystem synchronous generator through robust ADP method. During the iteration of designed control policy, each subsystem supplementary controller only utilizes local state variables, without knowing the system dynamics. Simulation results on the New England 10-machine 39-bus test system show the effective of designed controller.

2 Multi-machine Power System Model

We consider a multi-machine power system which has N synchronous generators. This lossless high voltage transmission grid with topology induced by susceptance matrix $B_{ij} \in \mathbb{R}^{n \times n}$ is an adjacency matrix represent the power transmission line connection between node i and node j (the transmission line reactances are neglected). The system buses υ can be divided to synchronous generators υ_G and loads υ_L. The model is described by the following Differential Algebraic Equation (DAE) [1, 11]:

$$
\begin{aligned}
\Delta\dot{\theta}_i &= \Delta\omega_i \\
M_i\Delta\dot{\omega}_i/\omega_0 + D_i\Delta\omega_i &= P_{mi} - P_{ei} + u_i, \ i \in \nu_G \\
D_i\Delta\omega_i &= P_i - P_{ui} + u_i, \ i \in \nu_L \\
P_{ei} &= \sum\nolimits_{j\in\nu_G, j\neq i} E_i E_j B_{ij} \sin(\theta_i - \theta_j) \\
P_{ui} &= \sum\nolimits_{j\in\nu_L, j\neq i} U_i U_j B_{ij} \sin(\theta_i - \theta_j)
\end{aligned}
\tag{1}
$$

where, θ_i and ω_i are the phase angle and the frequency respectively at bus i, θ_0 and ω_0 are the nominal phase angle and the nominal frequency respectively. Also, there are $\Delta\theta_i = \theta_i - \theta_0$, $\Delta\omega_i = \omega_i - \omega_0$. $M_i > 0$ is the inertial time constant of i - th generators. $D_i > 0$ is the primary droop control coefficient of generator or the damping of frequency dependent devices or loads. u_i is the supplementary control input for each bus. P_{mi} is the mechanical power of generator, P_{ei} is the electromagnetic power of generator, P_i is positive constant power for sources and negative constant power for loads. E_i is the transient electromotive force of i - th generators, U_i is the voltage at bus i.

Remark 1: During a disturbance, the oscillation of θ_i is superimposed on ω_0, but $\Delta\omega_i$ is very smaller than ω_0. Therefore, the generator speed is practically equal to ω_0, and the air-gap torque is considered equal to the air-gap power in per unit [11]. So, we will use P_{mi} and P_{ei} instead of mechanical torque T_{mi} and electromagnetic torque T_{ei}.

Consider each synchronous generator of the N - th machine power system with speed regulation controllers [11]

$$\dot{P}_{mi}(t) = [-P_{mi}(t) + u_{mi}]/T_i \tag{2}$$

where T_i is the governor time constant, u_{mi} is the control input of represents deviation of the valve opening.

3 Supplementary Frequency Control

3.1 Problem Formulation

Equations (1) and (2) can be rewritten in a matrix form if we choose to control generators as the main method of frequency adjustment:

$$\begin{bmatrix} \Delta\dot{\theta}_i(t) \\ \Delta\dot{\omega}_i(t) \\ \Delta\dot{P}_{mi}(t) \end{bmatrix} = \begin{bmatrix} 0 & 1 & 0 \\ 0 & -D_i/2H_i & \omega_0/2H_i \\ 0 & 0 & -1/T_i \end{bmatrix} \begin{bmatrix} \Delta\theta_i(t) \\ \Delta\omega_i(t) \\ \Delta P_{mi}(t) \end{bmatrix} + \begin{bmatrix} 0 \\ 0 \\ -1/T_i \end{bmatrix} u_i(t) \tag{3}$$

where

$$\Delta P_{mi}(t) = P_{mi}(t) - P_{ei}(t)$$

$$u_i(t) = u_{mi}(t) - P_{ei}(t) - E_i(t) \sum_{j=1,j\neq i}^{N} \{E_j(t)B_{ij}\cos[\theta_i(t) - \theta_j(t)]\}$$

If we define $x_i = [\Delta\theta_i(t) \; \Delta\omega_i(t) \; \Delta P_{mi}(t)]^T$ as the subsystem state vector and $y_i = \Delta\omega_i(t)$ as the subsystem output, then the i - th subsystem $(1 \leq i \leq N)$ of multi-machine power system with dynamic uncertainties is described as follow

$$\dot{x}_i = A_i x_i + B_i \hat{u}_i$$
$$y_i = C_i x_i \tag{4}$$

where $\hat{u}_i = u_i + \phi_i(y)$, $x_i \in \mathbb{R}^{ni}$, $y_i \in \mathbb{R}^{qi}$, and $\hat{u}_i \in \mathbb{R}^{mi}$ are state, output, and supplementary control input for i-th subsystem; $A_i \in \mathbb{R}^{ni \times ni}$ and $B_i \in \mathbb{R}^{ni \times mi}$ are i - th subsystem of multi-machine power system matrices, $C_i \in \mathbb{R}^{1 \times ni}$ is an uncertain system matrices. Output $y = [y_1, y_2, \ldots y_N]^T$ and $\phi_i(\cdot) : \mathbb{R}^q \rightarrow \mathbb{R}^{mi}$ for all $y \in \mathbb{R}^q$ is an unknown interconnection. It is also assumed that (A_i, B_i) is stabilizable and (A_i, C_i) is observable [12].

3.2 Principle of Robust ADP Method

Now, we are interested to find a control policy of each subsystem (4) in the form of

$$\hat{u}_i = -K_i x_i \tag{5}$$

to minimize the following quadratic cost index [13]

$$J_i = \int_0^\infty (x_i^T Q_i x_i + \hat{u}_i^T R_i \hat{u}_i) d\tau = x_i^T P_i x_i \tag{6}$$

where K_i is the feedback gain; $Q_i = Q_i^T \geq 0$, $R_i = R_i^T > 0$, $(Q_i^{1/2}, A_i)$ is observable.

According to linear optimal control theory [12], when both A_i and B_i are known accurately, the solution of above optimal control problem is solved by (5) with

$$K_i = R_i^{-1} B_i^T P_i \tag{7}$$

where P_i is a unique positive definite solution to algebraic Riccati equation (ARE)

$$(A_i - B_i K_i)^T P_i + P_i (A_i - B K_i) + Q_i + K_i^T R_i K_i = 0 \tag{8}$$

The structure of controller design by using robust ADP method for the controlled system with unknown environment is presented in Fig. 1.

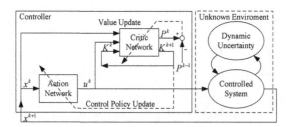

Fig. 1. Structure of the robust ADP learning scheme

Its components include action network and critic network. At time k, the system state x^k is the input of action network and the control policy u^k in the current state is its output. Both of them with the feedback gain K^k are the inputs of critic network which role is to solve the matrix P^k and the new feedback gain K^{k+1} at time $k+1$.

A. *Critic network*

The function of critic network is to calculate the new feedback gain with (8) by using Kleinman's algorithm [13]. Let given K_i^0 of the i-th subsystem with $A_i - B_i K_i^0$ is Hurwitz for all $k \in \mathbb{Z}_+$, then the solution matrix P_i^k and feedback gain matrix K_i^k can calculated by the follow:

$$0 = (A_i^k)^T P_i^k + P_i^k A_i^k + Q_i^k$$
$$K_i^{k+1} = R_i^{-1} B_i^T P_i^k \qquad (9)$$

where $A_i^k = A_i - B_i K_i^k$ and $Q_i^k = Q_i + (K_i^{k+1})^T R_i K_i^k$.

Figure 2 shows the structure of the critic network of robust ADP. The output K_i^{k+1} is the updated feedback gain to the control policy of the action network. The other output of the critic network P_i^k is the value index (function).

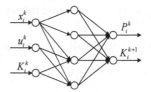

Fig. 2. Structure of the critic network

The critic network does value update when the following condition are not satisfied

$$|K_i^{k+1} - K_i^k| \le \varepsilon \qquad (10)$$

where $\varepsilon > 0$ is the threshold of the iterative algorithms' stopping criterion.

Remark 2: In practice, we cannot make infinite calculations. To obtain a more approximation result of optimal solution, the threshold ε is chosen sufficiently small.

Thus, the critic network of each subsystem can be represented as:

$$P_i^k = P(x_i^k, u_i^k, K_i^k, W_{ci}) \qquad (11)$$

where W_{ci} is the weight of i-th subsystem critic network.

Remark 3: If we repeat above Eq. (9) until (10) is satisfied for all $k \ge 1$ [13], we can get $u_i = -K_i^k x_i$ as the optimal control input to the i-th synchronous generator.

B. *Action network*

Figure 3 shows the structure of the action network of robust ADP.

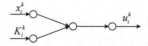

Fig. 3. Structure of the action network

The function of action network is to calculate the new control policy based on new state and feedback gain. When the condition (10) is not satisfied, the input of action network K_i^k is updated to K_i^{k+1} by control policy update. Then, the action network use new system state x_i^{k+1} and new feedback gain K_i^{k+1} to calculate new control policy u_i^{k+1}.

Thus, the action network of each subsystem can be represented as:

$$u_i^k = u(x_i^k, K_i^k, W_{ai}) \tag{12}$$

where W_{ai} is the weight of i-th subsystem action network.

3.3 Supplementary Frequency Controller Design by Robust ADP

Similar to (5), we consider the following control policy

$$\hat{u}_i = -K_i^k x_i + e \tag{13}$$

where artificial noise e is a sum signal for the purpose of online learning to add.

Taking the time derivative of $x_i^T P_i^k x_i$ with (4) and (13), we can get

$$d(x_i^T P_i^k x_i)/dt = -x_i^T Q_i^k x_i + 2(\hat{u}_i + K_i^k x_i)^T R_i (K_i^{k+1}) x_i \tag{14}$$

For the i-th subsystem, by integrating both sides of (14) on any given interval $[t, t + \Delta t]$ [13], we have it follows that

$$x_i^T(t + \Delta t) P_i^k x_i(t + \Delta t) - x_i^T(t) P_i^k x_i(t) =$$
$$- \int_t^{t+\Delta t} x_i^T Q_i^k x_i d\tau + 2 \int_t^{t+\Delta t} (\hat{u}_i + K_i^k x_i)^T R_i (K_i^{k+1}) x_i d\tau \tag{15}$$

Considering computational simplicity without losing any information, applying the Kronecker product representation [14], Eq. (15) can be converted to

$$x_i^T \otimes x_i^T \big|_t^{t+\Delta t} \text{vec}(P_i^k) = 2 \left(\int_t^{t+\Delta t} x_i^T \otimes x_i^T d\tau \right) (I_{nn} \otimes (K_i^k)^T R_i) \text{vec}(K_i^{k+1})$$
$$+ 2 \left(\int_t^{t+\Delta t} x_i^T \otimes \hat{u}_i^T d\tau \right) (I_{nn} \otimes R_i) \text{vec}(K_i^{k+1})$$
$$- \left(\int_t^{t+\Delta t} x_i^T \otimes x_i^T d\tau \right) \text{vec}(Q_i^k) \tag{16}$$

Then, we can get the following matrix form

$$\Lambda_i^k [\, \text{vec}(P_i^k) \quad \text{vec}(K_i^{k+1}) \,]^T = \Gamma_i^k [\text{vec}(Q_i^k)] \tag{17}$$

where

$$\Lambda_i^k = \begin{bmatrix} x_i^T \otimes x_i^T \big|_t^{t+\Delta t} & -2(\int_t^{t+\Delta t} x_i^T \otimes x_i^T d\tau)(I_{nn} \otimes (K_i^k)^T R_i) \\ & -2(\int_t^{t+\Delta t} x_i^T \otimes \hat{u}_i^T d\tau)(I_{nn} \otimes R_i) \end{bmatrix} \tag{18}$$

$$\Gamma_i^k = -(\int_t^{t+\Delta t} x_i^T \otimes x_i^T d\tau)$$

Remark 4: According to (17) and (18), in the process of solving feedback gain, inexact parameters and dynamic uncertainties of the system itself are not used, only choose the initial Q_i and R_i to calculate. Comparing with other design methods, the proposed algorithm only use the state and input information of their own subsystem during the iteration for learning, and it takes a short time to calculate. We can find that this algorithm can be implemented in parallel without interact each subsystem.

Remark 5: At each interval step k in (17) and (18), the algorithm needs to take enough sample data for calculation. Each given integration interval $[t, t + \Delta t]$ can be divided into $l + 1$ sampling intervals $(t, t_1), (t_1, t_2), \ldots, (t_l, t + \Delta t)$. Then, we obtain a set of equations with subsystem own data that can be used to solve P_i^k and K_i^{k+1}.

4 Simulation

In simulation, we use MATLAB and PSAT to establish the New England 10-machine 39-bus system to verify the effective of the proposed method. Generator 39 (G39) is used as the reference generator. The supplementary frequency controllers are installed at generators 30–38 (G30-G38). The nominal frequency f is denoted by 60 Hz. The system topology diagram is shown in Fig. 4.

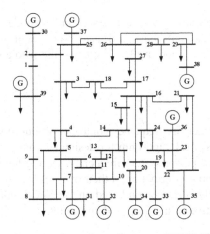

Fig. 4. The network topology diagram of IEEE-39 system

Simulation duration choose 0 to 14 s. From t = 0 s to 2 s, all the generators are in stable operation. At t = 2 s, an impulse disturbance was added on the power load to and simulating to 6 s. Then, each generator frequency starts oscillating. In order to restore the frequency to the nominal value and improve the whole power system dynamic performance, the algorithm is conducted from t = 6 s to 8 s. The control policies after iterative calculation are applied from t = 8 s to the end of the simulation.

Figure 5 shows the results comparison between our method and the reference [3] method. The cyan line represents the frequency variation curve without using SFC. The blue line and the red line represent the variation of the frequency curve using proposed and [3] method, respectively. It can be seen that after using control policy which calculation by separate methods, the oscillation of frequencies in this paper has been significantly reduced and frequencies quickly returned to the nominal value; the amplitude of oscillation for each frequency variation curve in [3] decreases gradually, and all frequencies return to the nominal value after a period of time. This simulation results show that the supplementary frequency controllers designed by proposed approach for the multi-machine power system can get better control.

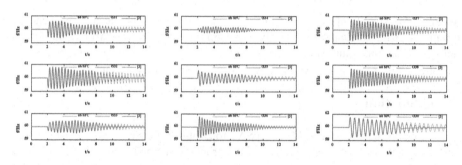

Fig. 5. Frequency variation result comparison between proposed method and [3] method (Color figure online)

Remark 6: For a large-scale system with uncertainties, under the same conditions of time, each controller based on robust ADP using subsystem own information can get better control effect than method in [3, 4] by using the whole system information.

5 Conclusion

In this paper, the supplementary frequency controller of multi-machine power system is designed. We use robust ADP algorithm for designing controllers of each subsystems to control multi-machine power system frequency. During the iteration, the algorithm only use the state and input information of their own for learning, without knowing the system dynamics. Finally, a simulation based on the New England 10-machine 39-bus system shows the effective of the proposed controller.

Acknowledgments. This work was supported in part by the National Natural Science Foundation of China (Grant Nos. 61473070, 61433004, 61627809).

References

1. Dörfler, F., Grammatico, S.: Gather-and-broadcast frequency control in power systems. Automatica **79**, 296–305 (2017)
2. Tang, Y., Yang, J., Yan, J., Zeng, Z.: Frequency control using on-line learning method for island smart grid with EVs and PVs. In: International Joint Conference on Neural Networks (IJCNN), pp. 1440–1446. IEEE Press, New York (2014)
3. Guo, W.T., Liu, F., Mei, S.W., Si, J., He, D.W., Harley, R.: Approximate dynamic programming based supplementary frequency control of thermal generators in power systems with large-scale renewable generation integration. In: IEEE PES General Meeting—Conference & Exposition, pp. 1–5. IEEE Press, New York (2014)
4. Malla, N., Shrestha, D., Ni, Z., Tonkoski, R.: Supplementary control for virtual synchronous machine based on adaptive dynamic programming. In: IEEE Congress on Evolutionary Computation (CEC), pp. 1998–2005. IEEE Press, New York (2016)
5. Milligan, M., Frew, B., Kirby, B., Schuerger, M., Clark, K., Lew, D., Denholm, P., Zavadil, B., O'Malley, M., Tsuchida, B.: Alternatives no more: wind and solar power are mainstays of a clean, reliable, affordable grid. IEEE Power Energy Mag. **13**(6), 78–87 (2015)
6. Werbos, P.J.: Approximate dynamic programming for real-time control and neural modeling. In: Handbook of Intelligent Control: Neural, Fuzzy and Adaptive Approaches, pp. 493–525. Van Nostrand Reinhold, New York (1992)
7. Lin, X.F., Wang, J.: The application of action-dependent heuristic dynamic programming in excitation system of synchronous generator. Electr. Autom. **33**(2), 20–23 (2011)
8. Park, J.W., Harley, R.G., Venayagamoorthy, G.K.: Adaptive-critic-based optimal neuro-control for synchronous generators in a power system using MLP/RBF neural networks. IEEE Trans. Ind. Appl. **39**(5), 1529–1540 (2003)
9. Venayagamoorthy, G.K., Harley, R.G., Wunsch, D.C.: Dual heuristic programming excitation neurocontrol for generators in a multimachine power system. IEEE Trans. Ind. Appl. **39**(2), 382–394 (2003)
10. Jiang, Y., Jiang, Z.P.: Computational adaptive optimal control for continuous-time linear systems with completely unknown dynamics. Automatica **48**(10), 2699–2704 (2012)
11. Kundur, P., Balu, N.J., Lauby, M.G.: Power System Stability and Control. McGraw-Hill, New York (1994)
12. Vrabie, D., Pastravanu, O., Abu-Khalaf, M., Lewis, F.L.: Adaptive optimal control for continuous-time linear systems based on policy iteration. Automatica **45**(2), 477–484 (2009)
13. Kleinman, D.: On an iterative technique for Riccati equation computations. IEEE Trans. Autom. Control **13**(1), 114–115 (1968)
14. Horn, R.A., Johnson, C.R.: Matrix Analysis, 2nd edn. Cambridge University Press, Cambridge (2013)

Task Assignment Based on a Dual Neural Network

Jiasen Wang[1,2(✉)] and Jun Wang[1,2]

[1] Department of Computer Science, City University of Hong Kong,
Hong Kong, China
jiasewang2-c@my.cityu.edu.hk, jwang.cs@cityu.edu.hk
[2] Shenzhen Research Institute, City University of Hong Kong, Shenzhen, China

Abstract. In this paper, task assignment, such as target assignment and parcel dispatching, for multi-agent systems is addressed. The problems are formulated as the linear assignment problem and its extensions. A dual neural network is used for solving them. Simulation results are reported on assigning multiple agents to multiple targets and dispatching parcels to given destinations using multiple agents.

Keywords: Neural network · Autonomous vehicle · Task assignment

1 Introduction

Task assignment problems [1,2] are to assign multi-agents to multi-tasks in an optimal way. Their applications include weapon-target assignment [3], target assignment for autonomous vehicles [4], etc. Recent years witness increased importance of task assignment problems because of widely deployment of autonomous vehicles.

Target assignment and parcel dispatching are two special cases of task assignment. Target assignment is an important problem for unmanned ports, where vessels are supposed to move from ports to others. In an open sea area, formation restructuring of autonomous surface vehicles (ASVs) also needs target assignment. Parcel dispatching is a logistics problem, where the optimal configuration of agents minimizes the cost of parcel delivering.

Many methods are available in the literature for various task assignment problems in applications. An algorithm for weapon-target assignment is presented in [3]. A variable-swarm auction algorithm is provided in [4] to fulfill the assignment from multiple unmanned aerial vehicles (UAVs) to multiple targets. Two cooperative task assignment methods for UAVs are presented in [5] and [6], respectively. A game-theoretical formulation of autonomous vehicle-target assignment is presented in [7]. For multi-vehicle multi-task allocations, a distributed heuristic algorithm is presented in [8]. A greedy algorithm for task

This work was supported in part by the Research Grants Council of the Hong Kong Special Administrative Region of China, under Grants 14207614 and 11208517, and in part by the National Natural Science Foundation of China under grant 61673330.

allocation of UAVs is proposed in [9]. For task assignment of UAVs under uncertain environments, a robust approach is presented in [10]. For task assignment in distributed computing systems, an heuristic algorithm is proposed in [11]. A task assignment algorithm based on particle swarm optimization is proposed in [12]. Nevertheless, in general, task assignment problems are NP-hard.

In this paper, target assignment and parcel dispatching problems are formulated as the linear assignment problem and its extensions. Specifically, target assignment problem is formulated as the linear assignment problem, where the number of agents equals to the number of tasks. Parcel dispatching problems are formulated as extensions of the linear assignment problem, where the number of agents and the number of tasks are not equal. A one-layer dual neural network proposed in [13] for the linear assignment problem is adopted for solving the formulated problems.

2   Problem Formulations

Let n and m denote the number of agents and the number of tasks, respectively. Let c_{ij} denote the cost of assigning the ith agent to the jth task.

2.1   Target Assignment

Target assignment for a multi-agent system is to find the optimal pairing from a set of agents to a set of targets. To fulfill the assignment, each target must be assigned to only one agent and each agent must be assigned to only one target. The decision variable is defined as

$$x_{ij} = \begin{cases} 1 & \text{if agent } i \text{ is assigned to target } j, \\ 0 & \text{otherwise.} \end{cases}$$

Consider n agents and n targets; i.e., $n = m$. The target assignment problem can be formulated as the linear assignment problem as follows

$$\mathrm{P}_1: \quad \min \sum_{i=1}^{n} \sum_{j=1}^{n} c_{ij} x_{ij} \tag{1}$$

$$\text{s.t.} \sum_{i=1}^{n} x_{ij} = 1, \tag{2}$$

$$\sum_{j=1}^{n} x_{ij} = 1, \tag{3}$$

$$x_{ij} \in \{1, 0\}. \tag{4}$$

Equation (2) ensures that one target can be assigned to only one agent. Equation (3) ensures that one agent can be assigned to only one target. Based on the assumption that the optimal solution is unique and total unimodularity property [1], $x_{ij} \in \{0, 1\}$ can be equivalently replaced by $x_{ij} \geq 0$. Thus the problem becomes a linear program with equality and non-negative constraints.

2.2   Parcel Dispatching

For parcel dispatching, agents should go to warehouses to take parcels to their destinations. The decision variable is defined as

$$x_{ij} = \begin{cases} 1 & \text{if agent } i \text{ is assigned to deliver parcel } j, \\ 0 & \text{otherwise.} \end{cases}$$

When $n \leq m$ (i.e., the number of agents is less than or equal to the number of parcels), the parcel dispatching problem can be formulated as

$$P_2: \quad \min \sum_{i=1}^{n} \sum_{j=1}^{m} c_{ij} x_{ij} \tag{5}$$

$$\text{s.t.} \sum_{i=1}^{n} x_{ij} \leq p, \tag{6}$$

$$\sum_{j=1}^{m} x_{ij} = 1, \tag{7}$$

$$x_{ij} \in \{1,0\}. \tag{8}$$

Equation (6) ensures that one parcel can be assigned to at most p ($p \geq 1$) agents. Equation (7) ensures that one agent can be assigned to deliver only one parcel. By introducing non-negative slack variables $s_1, ..., s_m$, (6) can be equivalently replaced by

$$1 - \sum_{i=1}^{n} x_{ij} = s_j.$$

When $n \geq m$ (i.e., the number of agents is greater than or equal to the number of parcels), the dispatching problem can be formulated as

$$P_3: \quad \min \sum_{i=1}^{n} \sum_{j=1}^{m} c_{ij} x_{ij} \tag{9}$$

$$\text{s.t.} \sum_{j=1}^{m} x_{ij} \leq q, \tag{10}$$

$$\sum_{i=1}^{n} x_{ij} = 1, \tag{11}$$

$$x_{ij} \in \{1,0\}. \tag{12}$$

Equation (10) ensures that one agent can be assigned to deliver at most q ($q \geq 1$) parcels. Equation (11) ensures that one parcel can be assigned to only one agent. By introducing non-negative slack variables $s_1, ..., s_n$, (10) can be equivalently replaced by

$$1 - \sum_{j=1}^{m} x_{ij} = s_i.$$

Based on the assumption that the optimal solution is unique and total unimodularity property [1,2], $x_{ij} \in \{0,1\}$ in P$_2$ and P$_3$ can also be equivalently replaced by $x_{ij} \geq 0$. Thus problems P$_2$ and P$_3$ become a linear program with equality and non-negative constraints.

The formulated problems are in linear program forms as follows

$$\min_{x} c^T x, \text{ s.t. } Ax = b, x \geq 0, \tag{13}$$

where $x = [x_{11}, ..., x_{nm}]^T \in R^{mn}$, $c = [c_{11}, ..., c_{nm}]^T \in R^{mn}$, $A \in R^{(m+n) \times d}$, with $d = nm$, $nm + n$, $nm + m$ for problems P$_1$, P$_2$ and P$_3$, respectively. The dual problem of (13) is given by

$$\max_{y} b^T y, \text{ s.t. } A^T y \leq c.$$

3   A Dual Neural Network

It is possible to solve problem (13) efficiently via neurodynamic methods. For example, the primal and the dual assignment networks [14], the primal-dual assignment network [15], the improved dual networks [16] are proposed. In particular, a one-layer dual neural network (DNN) for solving problem (13) is proposed in [13] with the following dynamic equation:

$$\epsilon \frac{dy}{dt} \in -\sigma Ag(A^T y - c) + b, \tag{14}$$

where ϵ is a time constant, σ is a positive gain parameter, g is a discontinuous activation function defined as

$$g(v) = \begin{cases} 1 & v > 0, \\ [0,1] & v = 0, \\ 0 & v < 0. \end{cases}$$

It is proven in [13] that the DNN in (14) is convergent to the optimal dual solution in finite time provided that σ satisfies the following condition:

$$\sigma > \frac{\|b\|_2}{\min_{A\gamma \in \Delta} \|A\gamma\|_2},$$

where Δ is the largest compact set in $A\Gamma \setminus \{0\}$, $\Gamma = \{\gamma : \gamma = [\gamma_1, \gamma_2, ..., \gamma_n]^T, 0 \leq \gamma_i \leq 1$ and at least one $\gamma_i = 1\}$, $A\Gamma = \{A\gamma : \gamma \in \Gamma\}$. The primal optimal solution is obtained by decoding the steady state of (14) via the following decoding equation [14]:

$$x = \delta(A^T y - c), \tag{15}$$

where

$$\delta(v) = \begin{cases} 1 & v = 0, \\ 0 & v \neq 0. \end{cases}$$

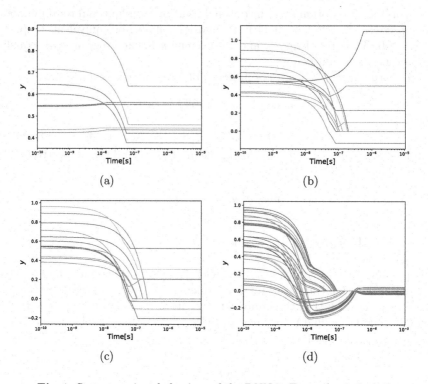

Fig. 1. State transient behaviors of the DNN in Examples 1, 3, 4, 5.

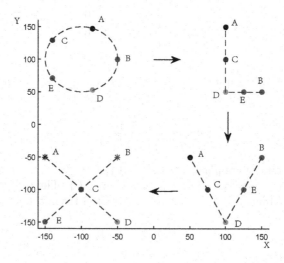

Fig. 2. Formation of five ASVs in Example 2.

Table 1. Coordinates on X-Y plane

	"O"	"L"	"V"	"X"
1	$(-50.0, 100.0)$	$(150, 50)$	$(150, -50)$	$(-50, -50)$
2	$(-84.5, 147.5)$	$(125, 50)$	$(125, -100)$	$(-100, -100)$
3	$(-140.4, 129.3)$	$(100, 50)$	$(100, -150)$	$(-150, -50)$
4	$(-140.4, 70.6)$	$(100, 100)$	$(75, -100)$	$(-150, -150)$
5	$(-84.5, 52.4)$	$(100, 150)$	$(50, -50)$	$(-50, -150)$

4   Simulation Results

In this section, five examples are discussed to illustrate the results. In all the following examples, the parameters are set as $p = q = 1$, $\epsilon = 10^{-5}$, and $\sigma = 5$.

Example 1. Consider a problem of four agents and four targets (i.e., $m = n = 4$ in P_1). The cost matrix is

$$C = \begin{bmatrix} 1 & 2 & 3 & 4 \\ 2 & 4 & 3 & 1.1 \\ 3 & 0.8 & 2 & 4 \\ 3 & 2 & 1 & 5 \end{bmatrix}.$$

The optimal solution is $x_{11} = x_{24} = x_{32} = x_{43} = 1$. Figure 1(a) depicts the state convergent behaviors of the DNN. The optimal solution is matched by decoding steady state of the DNN using (15). The *cvxopt* toolbox[1] is also used to solve this problem, but it returns an infeasible solution.

Example 2. Consider a problem of five ASVs to be assigned to five formation locations sequentially. Specifically, the ASVs should be assigned from formations "O" to "L", "L" to "V" and "V" to "X" in an order in the horizontal plane. In every assignment, $m = n = 5$. So the problem belongs to P_1, but in a sequential manner. Figure 2 depicts assignment results. From formation "O" to "L", the assignment result is $[1, 5, 4, 2, 3]$, which means that the 1st location in "O" is assigned to the 1st location in "L", the 2nd location in "O" is assigned to the 5th point in "L" and so on (see Table 1 for location details). From formation "L" to "V", the assignment result is $[1, 2, 3, 4, 5]$. From formation "V" to "X", the assignment result is $[1, 4, 5, 2, 3]$ or $[3, 4, 5, 2, 1]$. Note that "A" location in "V" can be assigned to "A" location or "B" location in "X"; i.e., the solution is not unique. It can be handled by arbitrary selection.

Example 3. Consider a problem of four agents to deliver eight parcels (i.e., $n = 4$, $m = 8$ in P_2). The cost matrix is

$$C = \begin{bmatrix} 0.1 & 2 & 3 & 4 & 5 & 6 & 7 & 8 \\ 2 & 1 & 3 & 0.1 & 0.8 & 6 & 7 & 8 \\ 3 & 0.5 & 1 & 4 & 5 & 6 & 7 & 8 \\ 4 & 3 & 1.1 & 4 & 5 & 6 & 7 & 8 \end{bmatrix}.$$

---

[1] http://cvxopt.org/.

The optimal solution is $x_{11} = x_{24} = x_{32} = x_{43} = 1$. Figure 1(b) depicts the state convergent behaviors of the DNN. The optimal solution is matched by decoding the steady state of the DNN using (15).

Example 4. Consider a problem of eight agents to deliver four parcels (i.e., $n = 8$, $m = 4$ in P_3). The cost matrix is

$$C^T = \begin{bmatrix} 0.1 & 0.7 & 3 & 3 & 3 & 3 & 3 & 3 \\ 2 & 1 & 0.2 & 0.9 & 2 & 2 & 2 & 2 \\ 3 & 3 & 5 & 0.5 & 3 & 3 & 3 & 3 \\ 4 & 0.1 & 6 & 4 & 6 & 6 & 6 & 6 \end{bmatrix}.$$

The optimal solution is $x_{11} = x_{24} = x_{32} = x_{43} = 1$. Figure 1(c) depicts the state convergent behaviors of the DNN. The decoding result of the steady state of the DNN matches the optimal solution.

Example 5. Suppose that 1000 parcels need to be delivered in Hong Kong. These parcels are stored in ten warehouses. Each warehouse stores 100 parcels. Destinations of parcels are obtained from [17]. Suppose at each round that ten agents are used, and two parcels are offered by each warehouse for delivering. To fulfill the task, 100 rounds of delivering are needed. For the first 99 rounds $n = 10$ and $m = 20$, for the last round $n = m = 10$. So the task is a combination of problem P_1 and P_3. Figure 1(d) depicts state convergent behaviors of the DNN in a snapshot (the first round). Figure 3 depicts the optimal objective values in each round of dispatching.

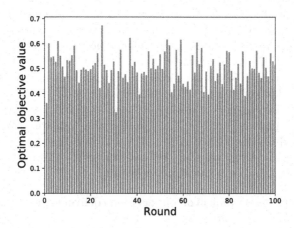

Fig. 3. Optimal objective values for each round dispatching in Example 5.

5   Conclusions

In this paper, two classes of task assignment problems are formulated: target assignment problem is formulated as the linear assignment problem; and parcel dispatching problems are formulated as the extensions of the linear assignment problem. A one-layer dual neural network is adopted for solving these problems. Five examples on target assignment and parcel dispatching are discussed to substantiate the efficacy of the neurodynamics-based task assignment.

References

1. Luenberger, D.G.: Linear and Nonlinear Programming. Addison-Wesley, Boston (1984)
2. Bertsekas, D.P.: Network Optimization: Continuous and Discrete Models. Citeseer, Princeton (1998)
3. Lee, Z.-J., Su, S.-F., Lee, C.-Y.: Efficiently solving general weapon-target assignment problem by genetic algorithms with greedy eugenics. IEEE Trans. Syst. Man Cybern. Part B (Cybern.) **33**(1), 113–121 (2003)
4. Morgan, D., Subramanian, G.P., Chung, S.-J., Hadaegh, F.Y.: Swarm assignment and trajectory optimization using variable-swarm, distributed auction assignment and sequential convex programming. Int. J. Robot. Res. **35**(10), 1261–1285 (2016)
5. Jin, Y., Minai, A.A., Polycarpou, M.M.: Cooperative real-time search and task allocation in UAV teams. In: Proceedings of 42nd IEEE Conference on Decision and Control, vol. 1, pp. 7–12 (2003)
6. Beard, R.W., McLain, T.W., Goodrich, M.A., Anderson, E.P.: Coordinated target assignment and intercept for unmanned air vehicles. IEEE Trans. Robot. Autom. **18**(6), 911–922 (2002)
7. Arslan, G., Marden, J.R., Shamma, J.S.: Autonomous vehicle-target assignment: a game-theoretical formulation. J. Dyn. Syst. Meas. Control **129**(5), 584–596 (2007)
8. Zhao, W., Meng, Q., Chung, P.W.: A heuristic distributed task allocation method for multivehicle multitask problems and its application to search and rescue scenario. IEEE Trans. Cybern. **46**(4), 902–915 (2016)
9. Oh, G., Kim, Y., Ahn, J., Choi, H.-L.: Task allocation of multiple UAVs for cooperative parcel delivery. In: Dołęga, B., Głębocki, R., Kordos, D., Żugaj, M. (eds.) Advances in Aerospace Guidance, Navigation and Control, pp. 443–454. Springer, Cham (2018). https://doi.org/10.1007/978-3-319-65283-2_24
10. Alighanbari, M., How, J.P.: A robust approach to the UAV task assignment problem. Int. J. Robust Nonlinear Control **18**(2), 118–134 (2008)
11. Lo, V.M.: Heuristic algorithms for task assignment in distributed systems. IEEE Trans. Comput. **37**(11), 1384–1397 (1988)
12. Salman, A., Ahmad, I., Al-Madani, S.: Particle swarm optimization for task assignment problem. Microprocess. Microsyst. **26**(8), 363–371 (2002)
13. Liu, Q., Wang, J.: A one-layer dual recurrent neural network with a heaviside step activation function for linear programming with its linear assignment application. In: Honkela, T., Duch, W., Girolami, M., Kaski, S. (eds.) ICANN 2011. LNCS, vol. 6792, pp. 253–260. Springer, Heidelberg (2011). https://doi.org/10.1007/978-3-642-21738-8_33
14. Wang, J.: Primal and dual assignment networks. IEEE Trans. Neural Netw. **8**(3), 784–790 (1997)

15. Wang, J., Xia, Y.: Analysis and design of primal-dual assignment networks. IEEE Trans. Neural Netw. **9**(1), 183–194 (1998)
16. Hu, X., Wang, J.: Solving the assignment problem using continuous-time and discrete-time improved dual networks. IEEE Trans. Neural Netw. Learn. Syst. **23**(5), 821–827 (2012)
17. Open street map (2018). https://www.openstreetmap.org/

Dependence of Critical Temperature
on Dispersion of Connections in 2D Grid

Boris V. Kryzhanovsky[1(✉)], Iakov M. Karandashev[1,2],
and Magomed Yu. Malsagov[1]

[1] Scientific Research Institute for System Analysis, RAS, Moscow, Russia
kryzhanov@gmail.com,
{Karandashev,malsagov}@niisi.ras.ru
[2] Peoples Friendship University of Russia (RUDN University), Moscow, Russia

Abstract. The calculation of probabilities in many problems of computer vision and machine learning is reduced to the finding of a normalizing constant (partition function). In the paper we evaluate the normalizing constant for a two-dimensional nearest-neighboring Ising model with almost constant average interaction between neighbors with a little noise. The two-dimensional Ising model is a perfect object for investigation. Firstly, a plane grid can be regarded as a set of image pixels. Secondly, the statistical physics offers an exact analytical solution obtained by Onsager for identical grid elements. We carry out numerical experiments to compute the normalizing constant for the case in which the noise in grid elements grows smoothly, analyze the results and compare them with Onsager's solution.

Keywords: The normalizing constant · Two-dimensional grid
Nearest-neighbors interaction · Critical temperature · Noise of grid elements

1 Introduction

Today's tendencies in the field of neural networks mostly suggest the development of supervised learning methods. However, there are problems that involve few or no labeled data. In such cases the learning without a teacher is the only applicable approach. The unsupervised learning goes together with data dimensionality reduction and clustering. The demonstrative example of the approach is autoencoders. Regrettably, the interest to them has dropped significantly with the advent of fast optimization methods for feedforward neural networks. Such networks generate a one-way function whose inverse is very difficult to build.

One of the first learning methods for deep autoencoders (e.g. the restricted Boltzmann machine) engages the maximization of the likelihood function of a Bayesian neural network. The computation of the likelihood function gradient comes down to the finding of the normalizing constant by approximate methods like contrastive divergence (CD) [1, 2].

In most cases it is impossible to compute the normalizing constant precisely. In fact, there are just a few models that permit us to do that. Here we deal with one of such models, the two-dimensional Ising model without an external field. This model presents

© Springer International Publishing AG, part of Springer Nature 2018
T. Huang et al. (Eds.): ISNN 2018, LNCS 10878, pp. 695–702, 2018.
https://doi.org/10.1007/978-3-319-92537-0_79

a perfect object of investigation. First, a plane grid can be regarded as a collection of image pixels. Second, for this model the statistical physics offers the exact analytical solution known as Onsager's solution [3] for constant couplings. Moreover, the Fisher-Kasteleyn algorithm [4–7] allows a numerical solution for any finite dimensional 2D-grid with any interaction coefficients.

In this paper, we have calculated the free energy for planar graphs, when the interaction between neighbors has a constant average value with a small noise. We found that with the increasing noise of interactions the peak of the second derivative of the free energy goes farther and farther from Onsager's prediction until it disappears at all.

The analysis of the heat capacity showed that when noise variations are small, the critical temperature shifts linearly with the growing noise dispersion. We used the n-vicinities method [8] to compute the free energy, which allowed us to find an approximate relationship between the shift of critical temperature and the growth of noise dispersion, which agrees well with the experimental data.

2 The Problem Statement

It is best to use the terms of physics for our purposes. Let there be a set of N binary spins described by the Hamiltonian

$$E = -\frac{1}{2N} \sum_{i,j=1}^{N} J_{ij} s_i s_j, \quad s_i = \pm 1. \tag{1}$$

This functional is often used in problems of machine learning and image processing. Quantities $s_i = \pm 1$ mean the belongingness to one of two pixel classes (background or object) or the neuron activity in a Bayesian neural network. Given a particular temperature, the possibility of the system staying in state s is defined by the formula

$$P(s) = \frac{1}{Z} e^{-\beta E(s)} \tag{2}$$

where β is the inverse temperature, and $Z = \sum_s e^{-N\beta E(s)}$ is the normalizing constant (partition function), the sum over all possible configurations s. As seen from (2), to evaluate the probability of a particular configuration, we need to know the normalizing constant, which is not so simple. It is the usual practice to find the specific free energy of the system rather than the constant Z itself:

$$f(\beta) = -\frac{\ln Z}{N} \tag{3}$$

The knowledge of the free energy also allows us to compute the major measurable physical parameters of the system:

$$U = \frac{\partial f}{\partial \beta}, \quad \sigma^2 = -\frac{\partial^2 f}{\partial \beta^2}, \quad C = -\beta^2 \frac{\partial^2 f}{\partial \beta^2}, \tag{4}$$

where internal energy $U = \bar{E}$ is the ensemble average for given β, $\sigma^2 = \overline{E^2} - \bar{E}^2$ is the energy dispersion, and $C = \beta^2 \sigma^2$ is the specific heat capacity. It should be noted that the dispersion σ^2 and heat capacity C differ only by factor β^2, the heat capacity being a more popular term in physics.

In the paper we study a planar model in which spins form a square grid, interacting only with four nearest neighbors.

If we limit ourselves to the case when the interaction with the nearest neighbors is given by a constant $J_{ij} = J = 1$, then we get Onsager's solution [3] derived for $N \to \infty$ and periodic boundary conditions:

$$f(\beta) = -\frac{\ln 2}{2} - \ln(\cosh 2\beta J) - \frac{1}{2\pi} \int_0^\pi \ln\left(1 + \sqrt{1 - k^2 \cos^2 \theta}\right) d\theta \tag{5}$$

$$U = -\coth 2\beta \cdot \left[1 + \frac{2}{\pi} E_1(k)(2\tanh^2 2\beta - 1)\right] \tag{6}$$

$$C = \frac{4\beta^2}{\pi \tanh^2 2\beta} \cdot \left\{ E_1(k) - E_2(k) - \left(1 - \tanh^2 2\beta\right) \left[\frac{\pi}{2} + \left(2\tanh^2 2\beta - 1\right) E_1(k)\right] \right\} \tag{7}$$

where

$$k = \frac{2\sinh 2\beta}{\cosh^2 2\beta}, \tag{8}$$

$E_1 = E_1(k)$ and are complete elliptic integrals of first and second order correspondingly:

$$E_1(x) = \int_0^{\pi/2} (1 - x^2 \sin^2 \phi)^{-1/2} \, d\phi, \quad E_2(x) = \int_0^{\pi/2} (1 - x^2 \sin^2 \phi)^{1/2} \, d\phi . \tag{9}$$

Onsager's solution (5)–(7) describes the asymptotic behavior for an infinite grid. It follows from these formulae that the heat capacity C should demonstrate logarithmic divergence at a critical temperature:

$$\beta_{ONS} = \frac{1}{2}\ln\left(1 + \sqrt{2}\right) \approx 0.4407 \tag{10}$$

It was shown in paper [9] that there is no logarithmic divergence for finite grids. Instead, there is a peak at temperatures around β_{ONS}, the height of the peak growing logarithmically with the grid size.

It can be assumed that logarithmic growth with increasing dimensionality is a consequence of the fact that all matrix elements J_{ij} in the grid are equal to each other. Thus, a kind of coherence arises, leading to an unlimited increase in the specific heat with increasing grid size. To avoid this kind of coherence, we investigate the case in which the value of the interaction coefficients varies about unit just slightly:

$$J_{ij} = 1 + \varepsilon, \quad \varepsilon \in (-\eta, \eta) \tag{11}$$

ε stands for the additive noise, which is uniform over the interval and whose maximum amplitude is equal to parameter η.

3   Experimental Results

In computational experiments we used the Kasteleyn-Fisher algorithm [4–7]. Enabling the calculation of free energy for any planar models, the algorithm allowed us to analyze the behavior of free energy and its derivatives (internal energy U and heat capacity C) for different grids of dimension $N = L \times L$. It is to be noted that the algorithm is applicable to planar grids only. It means that we consider only grids with free boundary conditions because a grid with periodic boundary conditions, as well as a two-dimensional model subjected to an external field, is not a planar graph.

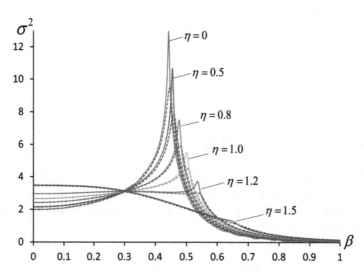

Fig. 1. Energy dispersion σ^2 as a function of inverse temperature β for different noise amplitudes η. The dashed and solid lines represent data for $L = 100$ and $L = 400$, correspondingly.

We carried out a few experiments with grids whose dimension ranged from $L = 100$ to $L = 400$, noise amplitude η varying from 0 to 1.5.

Since our major interest was the behavior of the critical temperature, its second derivative (energy dispersion) σ^2 rather than the free energy itself provided us most information. Figure 1 shows the results of our experiments.

It is seen from the Fig. 1 that the dispersion peak moves smoothly to the right, i.e. towards greater values of β, with the noise amplitude η. The height of the peak decreases until it becomes almost invisible at $\eta = 1.5$ ($L = 400$) and disappears at all with small grid dimensions ($L < 100$).

It is worth noticing that there is a point near $\beta \approx 0.3$ in Fig. 1 where all the curves intersect. We don't know if this observation bears any physical significance, but the intersection looks like a sharp point only at small noise amplitudes ($\eta < 1.5$), it spreads out with higher noise amplitudes.

Figure 1 permits the conclusion that the peak disappears at all starting from a particular noise amplitude. It is probable that the phase transition, which is typical of the two-dimensional Ising model, disappears in the same manner as the dispersion peak does.

Besides the temperature dependence of thermodynamic properties, we investigated the effect of added noise on the spectral characteristics of the system. Let's define the probability of the system being in a particular energy state as:

$$P(E) = \frac{e^{N\Psi(E)}}{2^N}, \tag{12}$$

where $\Psi(E)$ is the spectral density of the energy state distribution. It is simple to show [10] that spectral density $\Psi(E)$ is related to the free energy and its derivatives by the following implicit formulae:

$$E = \frac{df(x)}{dx}, \quad \Psi(E) = xE - f(x), \tag{13}$$

where $f(x)$ results from $f(\beta)$ by substituting β by x. Here we introduce a variable x to point out that the spectral density is not related to the temperature variable. Varying x from 0 to ∞, we go over the whole energy spectrum: expressions (13) allow energy E and density $\Psi(E)$ to be found for each value of x. The first and second derivatives of the spectral density are also determined by implicit formulae:

$$\partial\Psi/\partial E = -x, \tag{14}$$

$$\partial^2\Psi/\partial E^2 = -\sigma^{-2}(x). \tag{15}$$

The plot of the spectral density itself holds little information because it is almost independent of noise of matrix elements. More information can be obtained from the plot of the second derivative of $\Psi(E)$ with respect to energy (see Fig. 2).

It is clear that the higher the dispersion peak σ^2, the nearer $\partial^2\Psi/\partial E^2$ approaches zero (see Eq. (15)). When $N \to \infty$, dispersion $\sigma_c^2 \to \infty$ at the critical point, and the

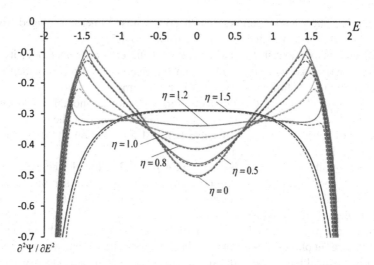

Fig. 2. The second derivative of the distribution density as a function of energy E for different noise amplitudes η. The dashed and solid lines represent data for $L = 100$ and $L = 400$, correspondingly.

curve $\partial^2 \Psi / \partial E^2$ comes close to zero. With finite dimensions, the dispersion is always finite. For this reason, $\partial^2 \Psi / \partial E^2$ also stays a finite distance off zero.

When the noise is added, the structure of the spectrum changes gradually, which is clearly seen in Fig. 2. When $\eta < 1.2$, we can see a noticeable sag in the middle of the plot. When $\eta > 1.5$, there is no sag, which may mean a qualitative change of the system.

4 Analytics

Let us consider the relationship between the critical temperature and scatter of matrix elements. Since Onsager's solution doesn't hold such information, let us use the approximation based on so-called n-vicinities method [8]. After some simplifications the equation of state from [8] takes the form:

$$\ln \frac{1+m}{1-m} = 8mb \left[\frac{2-b}{2+\sigma_\eta^2} - b \left(\frac{1}{2} - m^2 \right) \right] \tag{16}$$

where variable m is the magnetization, σ_η^2 is the noise dispersion of matrix elements, b is the dimensionless parameter related to β as:

$$\beta = \frac{\pi b}{\sqrt{2} \left(2 + \sigma_\eta^2 \right)} \tag{17}$$

Finding the critical point is reduced to the numerical solution of (16) for given parameters b and σ_η^2. When b is small, Eq. (16) has a unique solution $m = 0$. When b is greater than critical value b_c, there is another solution $m \neq 0$. Substituting b_c in (17) gives the critical value of inverse temperature $\beta = \beta_c$, at which the phase transition occurs.

Table 1 gives β_c for different σ_η^2: the first row holds experimental values of β_c, and the second row carries the values obtained by solving Eq. (16) numerically.

Table 1. The relationship between β_c and σ_η^2: experiment and theory.

η	0.0	0.2	0.5	0.8	1.0	1.2
$\sigma_\eta^2 = \eta^2/3$	0.000	0.013	0.083	0.213	0.333	0.480
β_c experiment	0.442	0.444	0.454	0.476	0.500	0.536
β_c theory	0.440	0.442	0.452	0.477	0.501	0.534

It is seen that theoretical and experimental values differ by less than 0.5%, which corresponds to the experimental accuracy. It can be noticed that within the given range of dispersion σ_η^2 dependence $\beta_c = \beta_c(\sigma)$ can be approximated accurately enough by the expression:

$$\beta_c = \beta_{\text{ONS}} \left(1 + \frac{1}{2}\sigma_\eta^2 \right), \tag{18}$$

where β_{ONS} is Onsager's critical value (10). The curves $\beta_c = \beta_c(\sigma_\eta)$ are presented in Fig. 3. It is seen that critical value β_c grows with σ_η^2 almost linearly.

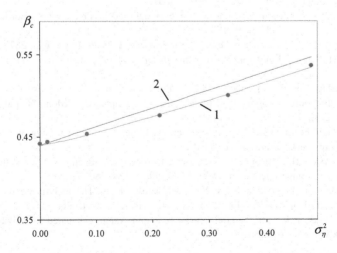

Fig. 3. Dependence $\beta_c = \beta_c(\sigma_\eta)$: the rhombi stand for experimental points; 1 is the theoretical curve; 2 is the approximation curve (18).

5 Conclusion

The research has dual purpose.

First, it was interesting for us to know how the adding of noise to interaction elements changes the system and its thermodynamic properties. The conventional Onsager model, in which all elements are strictly units, seems to be rather far from practice. We have showed that a small addition of noise does not bring about sharp changes. Rather it leads to smooth changes of thermodynamic properties such as heat capacity and spectral density. At the same time, starting with a certain value of the noise amplitude, a qualitative rearrangement of the system is likely, perhaps even a disappearance of the phase transition. However, judging about the presence of phase transition in finite-dimension systems is rather a problem.

Second, we tested the earlier developed n-vicinities method. This approximation method showed excellent agreement with the results of the numerical experiment, which gives us reasons to look forward to its further development and application in machine vision and image processing. The primary goal of further research is the addition of an external field to the model.

We believe that the described methods for estimating and calculating the partition function for the case of random connections will be useful in training Bayesian neural networks.

References

1. Krizhevsky, A., Hinton, G.E.: Using very deep autoencoders for content-based image retrieval. In: European Symposium on Artificial Neural Networks ESANN-2011, Bruges, Belgium (2011)
2. Hinton, G.E., Salakhutdinov, R.R.: Reducing the dimensionality of data with neural networks. Science 313(5786), 504–507 (2006)
3. Onsager, L.: Crystal statistics. I. a two-dimensional model with an order–disorder transition. Phys. Rev. 65(3–4), 117–149 (1944)
4. Kasteleyn, P.: Dimer statistics and phase transitions. J. Math. Phys. 4(2), 287–293 (1963)
5. Fisher, M.: On the dimer solution of planar Ising models. J. Math. Phys. 7(11), 1776–1781 (1966)
6. Karandashev, Ya.M., Malsagov, M.Yu.: Polynomial algorithm for exact calculation of partition function for binary spin model on planar graphs. Opt. Mem. Neural Netw. (Inf. Opt.) 26(2) (2017). https://arxiv.org/abs/1611.00922
7. Schraudolph, N., Kamenetsky, D.: Efficient exact inference in planar Ising models. In: NIPS (2008). https://arxiv.org/abs/0810.4401
8. Kryzhanovsky, B., Litinskii, L.: Generalized bragg-williams equation for system with an arbitrary long-range interaction. Dokl. Math. 90(3), 784–787 (2014)
9. Karandashev, I.M., Kryzhanovsky, B.V., Malsagov, M.Yu.: The analytical expressions for a finite-size 2D Ising model. Opt. Mem. Neural Netw. (Inf. Opt.) 26(3), 165–171 (2017)
10. Kryzhanovsky, B.V.: The spectral density of a spin system calculated for solvable models. http://arxiv.org/abs/1704.01351

Boundedness and Stability for a Class of Timescale-Type Time-Varying Systems

Qiang Xiao[1,2(✉)], Shiping Wen[1,2], Zhigang Zeng[1,2(✉)], and Tingwen Huang[3]

[1] School of Automation, Huazhong University of Science and Technology,
Wuhan 430074, China
{xq1620128,zgzeng}@hust.edu.cn, wenshiping226@126.com
[2] Key Laboratory of Image Processing and Intelligent Control of Education Ministry
of China, Wuhan 430074, China
[3] Department of Mathematics, Texas A&M University at Qatar, Doha, Qatar
tingwen.huang@qatar.tamu.edu

Abstract. This paper investigated a class of time-varying systems on
time scales. Based on the general theory of time scales, the ultimate
boundedness and asymptotic stability of the system is studied. Two
examples illustrate the validity of the obtained results.

Keywords: Boundedness · Asymptotic stability
Time-varying system · Time scale

1 Introduction

In the paper, we are concentrated on the timescale-type time-varying system
with its boundedness and asymptotic stability

$$x^{\Delta}(t) = f(t, x(t)), \ t \in \mathbb{T}, \ x(0) = x_0 \in \mathbb{R}^n, \tag{1}$$

where $x(t) \in \mathbb{R}^n$ is the state of the system, $f : \mathbb{T} \times \mathbb{R}^n \to \mathbb{R}^n$ is a rd-continuous
function satisfying $f(t, 0) = 0$ for all $t \in \mathbb{T}$.

Let $\mathbb{T} = \mathbb{R}$, system (1) represents the following ordinary differential system

$$\dot{x}(t) = f(t, x(t)), \ t \in \mathbb{R}, \ x(0) = x_0. \tag{2}$$

Let $\mathbb{T} = \mathbb{Z}$, then system (1) reduces to the following ordinary difference system
with its initial value

$$x(k + 1) = x(k) + f(k, x(k)), \ k \in \mathbb{Z}, \ x(0) = x_0. \tag{3}$$

In [1], Raffoul formulated some sufficient criteria to ensure the uniformly
bounded stability of all solutions of system (2), and in [2], new stability conditions for a class of time-varying systems were established. In [3], Islam and
Raffoul studied the exponential stability of zero solution of system (3). In effect,
the stability of systems (2) and (3) have been considered separately in a quite

© Springer International Publishing AG, part of Springer Nature 2018
T. Huang et al. (Eds.): ISNN 2018, LNCS 10878, pp. 703–710, 2018.
https://doi.org/10.1007/978-3-319-92537-0_80

frequent manner. Also, many neural network models also have been modeled separately by continuous and discrete-time equations frequently [4–8]. However, by using the time scale theory, systems (2) and (3) could be discussed in a unification fashion, depicted by system (1).

Time scale theory was proposed in 1989 by Stefan Hilger, which initially aimed to unify the differential and difference equations, and then mainly developed in [9,10]. In recent years, dynamic equations on time scales have been widely developed due to its basic characterization of unification and extension [11–17]. In [11], the authors developed the stability conditions for a class of timescale-type time-invariant linear systems. Later, Gard and Hoffacker in [12] studied the stability criteria of time-varying scalar dynamic timescales-type equations, and also it was the first time that the behaviors of time-varying dynamic timescales-type equations were investigated. In additions, plenty of work have been published based on time scales recently, such as the stabilization and synchronizing of neural networks, pinning control for complex networks [18–22]. Specifically, the results in [21] discussed the multiperiodicity and activating set for a class of linear threshold networks which contains conditions in both [7] and [23]. Moreover, when we consider the dynamics of system (1) on a specific time domain, like $\cup_{k=0}^{+\infty}[2k, 2k+1]$ or $\cup_{k=0}^{+\infty}[2k, 2k+1-1/(k+2)]$, the common methods are not applicable to deal with. Therefore, it deserves to be further studied on time scales. As far as the authors' knowledge, only a few works have been done on the boundedness and asymptotic stability for system (1), and there remains much room for further investigations.

The rest of this paper is as follows. Basic concepts of time scales and essential definitions are given in Sect. 2. Section 3 gives the main results. Two numerical examples are given to illustrate the validity of the main results in Sect. 4, followed by Conclusions in Sect. 5.

2   Preliminaries

$\mathbb{T}$ represents a time scale which is an arbitrary nonempty closed subset of the real set $\mathbb{R}$. σ, ρ, μ denote the forward, backward jump operators and graininess function, respectively. C_{rd} denotes the set of rd-continuous functions; $\mathcal{R}$ and $\mathcal{R}^+$ denote the set of regressive and positive regressive functions; In general, for a function f, $f^\sigma(t) = f(\sigma(t))$; $f^\Delta(t)$ denotes the Δ-derivative of f at $t \in \mathbb{T}$; $e_p(t, s)$ is the timescale-type exponential function. For the detailed definitions or properties of these concepts, one can refer to [9,10].

Remark 1. Given two special time scales $\mathbb{R}$ and $h\mathbb{Z}(h \neq 0)$, and a regressive constant c, for the timescale-type exponential function, we have

(a) Let $\mathbb{T} = \mathbb{R}$, then $e_c(t, 0) = \exp(ct)$ for any $t \in \mathbb{R}$.
(b) Let $\mathbb{T} = h\mathbb{Z}$, then $e_c(t, 0) = (1 + ch)^{t/h}$ for any $t \in h\mathbb{Z}$.
(c) Let $\mathbb{T} = \mathbb{P}_{1,1}$, then $e_c(t, 0) = \exp\{k\}(1 + c)^k \exp\{t \bmod 2\}$ for any $t \in [2k, 2k+1]$, $k \in \mathbb{Z}$.

Definition 1. System (1) is said to be:

1. *Bounded* if for any initial value x_0, there exists a positive scalar $\delta = \delta(x_0)$ such that $\|x(t)\| \leq \delta$ for all $t \in \mathbb{T}$.
2. *Lyapunov stable* if for an arbitrary $\varepsilon > 0$, there exists $\delta(\varepsilon, t_0)$ such that $\|x(0)\| < \delta \Rightarrow \|x(t)\| < \varepsilon, \forall t \in \mathbb{T}$.
3. *Asymptotically stable* if it is Lyapunov stable, and there is a constant $c = c(x_0) > 0$ such that $x(t) \to 0$ as $t \to \infty$, for all $\|x_0\| < c$.

Notations. Throughout this paper, $\mathbb{R}$ ($\mathbb{R}^+$) and $\mathbb{Z}$ denote the (nonnegative) real number set and the integer number set, resp. $\|\cdot\|$ denotes the Euclidean norm. For any $x \in \mathbb{R}$, $\langle x \rangle_{\inf} = \inf\{\tilde{x} \in \mathbb{T} | \tilde{x} > x\}$. Without other statements, we always assume that $\min\{\mathbb{T}\} = 0$.

3   Boundedness and Stability Conditions for Time-Varying Systems on Time Scales

This section addresses the main results via the concept of exponential function and integral on time scales.

Theorem 1. Consider system (1). Given $x_0 \neq \mathbf{0}$. Suppose that there exist a rd-continuous differentiable function $V : \mathbb{R}_{\mathbb{T}}^+ \times \mathbb{R}^n \to \mathbb{R}^+$ with $V(t, 0) = 0$ for all $t \in \mathbb{R}_{\mathbb{T}}^+$, a $\mathcal{K}$-class function α, and a regressive function $g : \mathbb{R}^+ \to \mathbb{R}$ such that

(i) $\alpha(\|x(t)\|) \leq V(t, x)$,
(ii) $V^{\Delta}(t, x) \leq g(t)V(t, x)$ with $\int_0^{\infty} g(t)\Delta t \leq \lambda$,

for $t \in \mathbb{R}_{\mathbb{T}}^+$, then the solution of system (1) is ultimately bounded above, and the ultimate upper-bound (UUB) is $\alpha^{-1}(V(0, x_0)e^{\lambda})$. Moreover, if $\lambda = -\infty$, then it is asymptotically stable.

Proof. From condition (ii), one gets

$$V(t, x(t)) \leq V(0, x_0)e_{g(t)}(t, 0) = V(0, x_0) \exp\left(\int_0^t \xi_{\mu(\tau)}(g(\tau))\Delta\tau\right) \quad (4)$$

For any point t on any time scale $\mathbb{T}^k$, t is either *right-dense* or *right-scattered*. In what follows, we introduce an auxiliary discrete time scale $\mathbb{T}_{aux} \triangleq \{t_k^2\}_{k=1}^{\infty}$, where t_i^2 is the i-th *right-scattered* point of $\mathbb{T}$. Unless $\mathbb{T}$ is $\mathbb{R}$, then $\mathbb{T}_{aux}$ is non-empty, and $\mathbb{T} = [0, t_1^2] \cup_{k=1}^{\infty} [\sigma(t_k^2), t_{k+1}^2]$.

Therefore,

$$\exp\left(\int_0^t \xi_{\mu(\tau)}(g(\tau))\Delta\tau\right)$$

$$= \exp\left(\int_0^{t_1^2} \xi_{\mu(\tau)}(g(\tau))\Delta\tau + \int_{t_1^2}^{\sigma(t_1^2)} \xi_{\mu(\tau)}(g(\tau))\Delta\tau\right.$$

$$\left. + \sum_{k=1}^{\infty}\left[\int_{\sigma(t_k^2)}^{t_{k+1}^2} \xi_{\mu(\tau)}(g(\tau))\Delta\tau + \int_{t_{k+1}^2}^{\sigma(t_{k+1}^2)} \xi_{\mu(\tau)}(g(\tau))\Delta\tau\right]\right).$$

For any $t_k^2 \in \mathbb{T}_{aux}$,

$$\int_{t_k^2}^{\sigma(t_k^2)} \xi_{\mu(\tau)}(g(\tau)) \Delta\tau = \mu(t_k^2)\xi_{\mu(t_k^2)}(g(t_k^2)) = \text{Log}(1 + g(t_k^2)\mu(t_k^2))$$

$$\leq g(t_k^2)\mu(t_k^2) = \int_{t_k^2}^{\sigma(t_k^2)} g(\tau)\Delta\tau$$

and

$$\int_{\sigma(t_k^2)}^{t_{k+1}^2} \xi_{\mu(\tau)}(g(\tau))\Delta\tau = \int_{\sigma(t_k^2)}^{t_{k+1}^2} g(\tau)\Delta\tau.$$

Then we have

$$V(t, x(t)) \leq V(0, x_0)e_{g(t)}(t, 0) = V(0, x_0)\exp\left(\int_0^t g(\tau)\Delta\tau\right). \qquad (5)$$

Therefore, $V(t, x(t)) \leq V(0, x_0)e^\lambda$, i.e., the solution of system (1) is ultimately bounded above, and its UUB is $\alpha^{-1}(V(0, x_0)e^\lambda)$. For the case of $\lambda = -\infty$, we perform the proof with two steps.

Step 1: *Lyapunov stable.* Let $G(t) = \int_0^t g(\tau)\Delta\tau$. From the definition of g and condition (ii) that $G(t)$ is rd-continuous and $G(t) \to -\infty$ as $t \to +\infty$, which means that for any $M < 0$, there exists a $T(T \geq 0, T \in \mathbb{T})$ such that $G(t) \leq M$ for all $t \geq T, t \in \mathbb{R}_\mathbb{T}^+$. Let $A = \max_{t \leq T, t \in \mathbb{R}_\mathbb{T}^+}\{G(t)\}$ and $B = \max\{M, A\}$, then for any $t \geq 0, t \in \mathbb{R}_\mathbb{T}^+$, one has

$$V(t, x) \leq V(0, x_0)\exp(G(t)) \leq V(0, x_0)\exp(B). \qquad (6)$$

Given an arbitrary $\varepsilon > 0$, there exists a scalar $\delta = \delta(\varepsilon)$ such that for any $\|x_0\| \leq \delta$

$$V(0, x_0)\exp(B) \leq \alpha(\varepsilon). \qquad (7)$$

Together with (6)–(7) and condition (i), one gets

$$\|x(t)\| \leq \varepsilon, \ t \in \mathbb{T}$$

which implies the Lyapunov stability of system (1).

Step 2: *Asymptotic convergence.* It can be directly deduced from (5) and condition (ii) that $V(t, x) \to 0$, as $t \to +\infty$, i.e., $x \to 0$ as $t \to +\infty$, which implies the asymptotic convergence of system (1).

Remark 2. In Theorem 1, the function $V(t, x)$ is not required to be monotone decreasing, which is different from most of the works before.

Here, we have the following two special cases for systems (2) and (3).

Corollary 1. Consider system (2). Given $x_0 \neq 0$. Suppose that there exist a continuous differentiable function $V : \mathbb{R}^+ \times \mathbb{R}^n \to \mathbb{R}^+$ with $V(t, 0) = 0$ for all $t \in \mathbb{R}^+$, a $\mathcal{K}$-class function α, and a continuous function $g : \mathbb{R}^+ \to \mathbb{R}$ such that

(i) $\alpha(\|x(t)\|) \leq V(t, x)$,
(ii) $\dot{V}(t, x) \leq g(t)V(t, x)$ with $\int_0^\infty g(t)dt \leq \lambda$,

for $t \in \mathbb{R}^+$, then the solution of system (2) is ultimately bounded above, and the UUB is $\alpha^{-1}(V(0, x_0)e^\lambda)$. Moreover, if $\lambda = -\infty$, then it is asymptotically stable.

Remark 3. Recently, Chen and Yang in [2] established some new stability conditions for (2), it is obvious that one of the main results in [2] is the same as Corollary 1, which shows the generality of the obtained results in this paper.

Corollary 2. Consider system (3). Given $x_0 \neq 0$. Suppose that there exist a function $V : \mathbb{Z}^+ \times \mathbb{R}^n \to \mathbb{R}^+$ with $V(k, 0) = 0$ for all $k \in \mathbb{Z}^+$, a $\mathcal{K}$-class function α, and a function $g : \mathbb{Z}^+ \to \mathbb{R}$ such that

(i) $\alpha(\|x(k)\|) \leq V(k, x)$,
(ii) $V(k + 1, x) \leq [1 + g(k)]V(k, x)$ with $\sum_0^\infty g(k) \leq \lambda$,

for $k \in \mathbb{Z}^+$, then the solution of system (3) is ultimately bounded above, and the UUB is $\alpha^{-1}(V(0, x_0)e^\lambda)$. Moreover, if $\lambda = -\infty$, then it is asymptotically stable.

4 Numerical Examples

Two examples are given to illustrate the validity of the main results.

Example 1. Consider the linear time-varying system described by

$$x^\Delta(t) = \frac{1}{(t+1)^2}x(t), \ t \in \mathbb{R}_{\mathbb{T}}^+, \tag{8}$$

where $x_0 = x(0) = 2$. Let $V(t, x) = x^2(t)$, $\alpha(s) = s^2$.

Case 1: Let $\mathbb{T}_1 = \mathbb{R}$, $g(t) = \frac{2}{(t+1)^2}$, then we have $V^\Delta(t, x) = \frac{2}{(t+1)^2}x^2(t) = g(t)V(t, x)$, with $\int_0^\infty g(t)\Delta t = 2$, therefore, by Theorem 1, system (8) is ultimately bounded above with the UUB $= 5.4366$.

Case 2: Let $\mathbb{T}_2 = h\mathbb{Z}$, $g(t) = \frac{2}{(t+1)^2} + \frac{h}{(t+1)^4}$, then we have $V^\Delta(t, x) = \left(\frac{2}{(t+1)^2} + \frac{h}{(t+1)^4}\right)x^2(t) = g(t)V(t, x)$. Table 1 depicts λ, UUB estimated by Theorem 1, and real UUB for system (8) on the different time scale $\mathbb{T}_2$.

Case 3: Let $\mathbb{T}_3 = \mathbb{P}_{1,1}$, $g(t) = \frac{2}{(t+1)^2} + \frac{\mu(t)}{(t+1)^4}$. Then we have $V^\Delta(t, x) = \left(\frac{2}{(t+1)^2} + \frac{\mu(t)}{(t+1)^4}\right)x^2(t) = g(t)V(t, x)$, and

$$\int_0^\infty g(t)\Delta t = \int_0^\infty \frac{2}{(t+1)^2}\Delta t + \int_0^\infty \frac{\mu(t)}{(t+1)^4}\Delta t$$

$$= \sum_{k=0}^\infty \int_{2k}^{2k+1} \frac{2\Delta t}{(t+1)^2} + \sum_{k=0}^\infty \int_{2k+1}^{2k+2} \frac{2\Delta t}{(t+1)^2} + \sum_{k=0}^\infty \int_{2k+1}^{2k+2} \frac{\Delta t}{(t+1)^4}$$

$$= \sum_{k=0}^\infty \int_{2k}^{2k+1} \frac{2dt}{(t+1)^2} + \sum_{k=0}^\infty \frac{1}{2(k+1)^2} + \sum_{k=0}^\infty \frac{1}{4(k+1)^4} = 1.7862.$$

Therefore, system (8) is ultimately bounded above with the UUB $= 4.8854$.

Table 1. The comparisons of λ, UUB estimated by Theorem 1, and real UUB for different time scales $\mathbb{T}_2$.

$\mathbb{T}_2$	λ	UUB by Theorem 1	Real UUB
$h \equiv 1$	4.3721	17.8000	3.6761
$h \equiv 0.1$	2.1420	5.8366	5.1088
$h \equiv 0.01$	2.0134	5.4371	5.4007
$h \equiv 0$	2.0000	5.4366	5.3343

Table 2. The comparisons of λ, UUB estimated by Theorem 1, and real UUB for different time scales $\mathbb{T}_2$.

$\mathbb{T}_2$	λ	UUB by Theorem 1	Real UUB
$h \equiv 1$	-2.2075	0.6633	1.0000
$h \equiv 0.1$	-2.0647	0.7123	0.7608
$h \equiv 0.01$	-2.0066	0.7333	0.7383
$h \equiv 0$	-2.0000	0.7358	0.7352

Example 2. Consider the next linear time-varying system given by

$$x^{\Delta}(t) = -\frac{1}{(t+1)^2} x(t), \ t \in \mathbb{R}_{\mathbb{T}}^+, \tag{9}$$

where $x_0 = x(0) = 2$. Let $V(t,x) = x^2(t)$, $\alpha(s) = s^2$.

Case 1: Let $\mathbb{T}_1 = \mathbb{R}$, $g(t) = -\frac{2}{(t+1)^2}$, then we have $V^{\Delta}(t,x) = -\frac{2}{(t+1)^2}x^2(t) = g(t)V(t,x)$, with $\int_0^{\infty} g(t)\Delta t = -2$, therefore, by Theorem 1, system (9) is ultimately bounded above with the UUB $= 0.7358$.

Case 2: Let $\mathbb{T}_2 = h\mathbb{Z}$, $g(t) = -\frac{2}{(t+1)^2} + \frac{h}{(t+1)^4}$, then we have $V^{\Delta}(t,x) = \left(-\frac{2}{(t+1)^2} + \frac{h}{(t+1)^4}\right)x^2(t) = g(t)V(t,x)$. Table 1 depicts λ, UUB estimated by Theorem 1, and real UUB for system (9) on the different time scale $\mathbb{T}_2$.

Case 3: Let $\mathbb{T}_3 = \mathbb{P}_{1,1} = \cup_{k=0}^{\infty}[2k, 2k+1]$, $g(t) = -\frac{2}{(t+1)^2} + \frac{\mu(t)}{(t+1)^4}$. Then we have $V^{\Delta}(t,x) = \left(-\frac{2}{(t+1)^2} + \frac{\mu(t)}{(t+1)^4}\right)x^2(t) = g(t)V(t,x)$, and by the similar calculation as in Example 1, we get $\int_0^{\infty} g(t)\Delta t = -1.2450$. Therefore, system (9) is ultimately bounded above with the UUB $= 1.7032$.

Remark 4. From Table 1, one can see that with the decreasing of the graininess function $\mu(t)$, the UUB estimated by Theorem 1 is decreasing, while it is increasing from Table 2. The opposite trend for the estimated UUB in Tables 1 and 2 comes from the different monotonicity of the function V in Examples 1 and 2.

5   Conclusions

This paper addresses the boundedness and asymptotic stability for a class of time-varying systems on time scales. A new timescale-type criterion guaranteeing the boundedness and asymptotic stability of the addressed nonlinear system has been given. When the time scale is $\mathbb{R}$, the timescale-type results yield results for a continuous-time system. On the other hand, when the time scale is $\mathbb{Z}$, the same timescale-type results yield results for a discrete-time system. The obtained criteria unify and improve some existing results. Two numerical examples are given to depict the validity of the theoretical results.

Acknowledgments. This research was supported by National Priority Research Project NPRP 8-274-2-107, funded by Qatar National Research Fund <http://www.qnrf.org/>.

References

1. Raffoul, Y.N.: Boundedness in nonlinear differential equations. Nonlinear Stud. **10**, 343–350 (2003)
2. Chen, G.P., Yang, Y.: New stability conditions for a class of linear time-varying systems. Automatica **71**, 342–347 (2016)
3. Islam, M.N., Raffoul, Y.N.: Exponential stability in nonlinear difference equations. J. Differ. Equ. Appl. **9**, 819–825 (2003)
4. Huang, T.W., Li, C.D., Yu, W.W., Chen, G.R.: Synchronization of delayed chaotic systems with parameter mismatches by using intermittent linear state feedback. Nonlinearity **22**, 569–584 (2009)
5. Huang, T.W., Li, C.D., Duan, S.K., Starzyk, J.A.: Robust exponential stability of uncertain delayed neural networks with stochastic perturbation and impulse effects. IEEE Trans. Neural Netw. Learn. Syst. **23**, 866–875 (2012)
6. Zhang, X.M., Han, Q.L., Zeng, Z.G.: Hierarchical type stability criteria for delayed neural networks via canonical Bessel-Legendre inequalities. IEEE Trans. Cybern. **48**, 1660–1671 (2018). https://doi.org/10.1109/TCYB.2017.2776283
7. Yi, Z., Tan, K.K.: Multistability of discrete-time recurrent neural networks with unsaturating piecewise linear activation functions. IEEE Trans. Neural Netw. **15**, 329–336 (2004)
8. Shen, T., Petersen, L.R.: Linear threshold discrete-time recurrent neural networks: stability and globally attractive sets. IEEE Trans. Autom. Control **61**, 2650–2656 (2016)
9. Bohner, M., Peterson, A.: Dynamic Equations on Time Scales: An Introduction with Applications. Birkhäuser, Boston (2001)
10. Bohner, M., Peterson, A.: Advances in Dynamic Equations on Time Scales. Birkhäuser, Boston (2002)
11. Pötzsche, C., Siegmund, S., Wirth, F.: A spectral characterization of exponential stability for linear time-invariant systems on time scales. Disc. Cont. Dyn. Syst. **9**, 1223–1241 (2003)
12. Gard, T., Hoffacker, J.: Asymptotic behavior of natural growth on time scales. Dyn. Syst. Appl. **12**, 131–147 (2003)
13. DaCunha, J.J.: Stability for time varying linear dynamic systems on time scales. J. Comput. Appl. Math. **176**, 381–410 (2004)

14. Siegmund, S., Son, D.T., Kalauch, A.: Exponential stability of linear time-invariant systems on time scales. Nonlinear Dyn. Syst. Theory **9**, 37–50 (2009)

15. Doan, T.S., Kalauch, A., Siegmund, S., Wirth, F.R.: Stability radii for positive linear time-invariant systems on time scales. Syst. Control Lett. **59**, 173–179 (2010)

16. Taousser, F.Z., Defoort, M., Djemai, M.: Region of exponential stability of switched linear systems on time scales. IFAC-PapersOnLine **48**, 93–98 (2015)

17. Shah, S.O., Zada, A.: Uniform exponential stability for time varying linear dynamic systems over time scales. J. Anal. Number Theory **5**, 115–118 (2017)

18. Xiao, Q., Huang, Z.K.: Consensus of multi-agent system with distributed control on time scales. Appl. Math. Comput. **277**, 54–71 (2016)

19. Xiao, Q., Zeng, Z.G.: Scale-limited lagrange stability and finite-time synchronization for memristive recurrent neural networks on time scales. IEEE Trans. Cybern. **47**, 2984–2994 (2017)

20. Xiao, Q., Zeng, Z.G.: Lagrange stability for T-S fuzzy memristive neural networks with time-varying delays on time scales. IEEE Trans. Fuzzy Syst. https://doi.org/10.1109/TFUZZ.2017.2704059

21. Huang, Z.K., Raffoul, Y.N., Cheng, C.Y.: Scale-limited activating sets and multi-periodicity for threshold-linear networks on time scales. IEEE Trans. Cybern. **44**, 488–499 (2014)

22. Huang, Z.K., Bin, H.H., Cao, J.D., Wang, B.Y.: Synchronizing neural networks with proportional delays based on a class of q-type allowable time scales. IEEE Trans. Neural Netw. Learn. Syst. https://doi.org/10.1109/TNNLS.2017.2729588

23. Zhang, L., Yi, Z., Yu, J.L.: Multiperiodicity and attractivity of delayed recurrent neural networks with unsaturating piecewise linear transfer functions. IEEE Trans. Neural Netw. **19**, 158–167 (2008)

The Design of Ureteral Renal Interventional Robot for Diagnosis and Treatment

Junbin Li[1], Qi Chen[2], Le Xie[1,3(✉)], Fan Feng[3], Wei Xue[2],
Baijun Dong[2], Hesheng Wang[4], and YunHui Liu[5]

[1] School of Biomedical Engineering, Shanghai Jiao Tong University,
Shanghai, China
lexie@sjtu.edu.cn
[2] Renji Hospital Affiliated to School of Medicine of Shanghai Jiao Tong
University, Shanghai, China
[3] National Digital Manufacturing Technology Center,
Shanghai Jiao Tong University, Shanghai, China
[4] The School of Electronic Information and Electrical Engineering,
Shanghai Jiao Tong University, Shanghai, China
[5] The Department of Mechanical and Automation Engineering, Chinese
University of Hong Kong, Hong Kong, China

Abstract. In the process of ureteral renal surgery, the surgeon needs to stand and hold ureteroscope for operation, which can easily make surgeon tired, decreasing the accuracy of surgeon's operation, so master-slave mode of operation was adopted to develop ureteral minimally invasive surgical robot. Surgeon can sit in front of operational console and perform surgery, which can improve operation quality, alleviate labor intensity, and, at the same time, allow the surgeon to avoid X-ray damage with this technique. The magnetic navigation electronic element is integrated in self-developed ureteroscope to help surgeon with identification reduce the difficulty of surgery, and shorten operation time. When haemorrhage, causing the unclear vision, might happen during surgery, it is likely to flush with increasing pressure, but high stress can increase the risk of complications. Therefore, the development of pressure guide wire is helpful to monitor pressure and precaution the surgery to avoid complication.

Keywords: Master-slave · Ureteroscope · Robot

1 Introduction

Ureteral renal interventional surgery, with minimally invasive, safe, rapid recovery, high efficiency of treatment, can diagnose kidney stone, ureteral calculus and upper urinary tract tumor under the direct vision, it can be used in lithotripsy and tumorectomy with the help of laser. However, there are many challenges in traditional ureteric renal surgery, the main problems include the difficulty of the structural identification of

---

J. Li and Q. Chen—Contributed equally to this paper.

T. Huang et al. (Eds.): ISNN 2018, LNCS 10878, pp. 711–718, 2018.
https://doi.org/10.1007/978-3-319-92537-0_81

the renal space, lack of real-time warning about the intrarenal pressure, and the imperfection in the degree of operational refinement. Moreover, it demands high operation performance of the surgeon, referring to specific and skilled endovascular techniques, and the surgeon's operating posture can easily lead to fatigue, which means it is hard to finish by oneself and requires the help of the assistant. Therefore, the development of surgical robot is expected to solve those problems [1–3].

At present, Da Vinci robot is the world's most successful robot, which has succeeded in prostate cancer surgery, but is not suitable for ureteral renal interventional surgery [4, 5].

Avicenna Roboflex by Turkish company ELMED is the most representative ureteroscopic robot with master-slave structure. Surgeon can perform ureteral renal surgery through remote control, but this robot is unable to offer the force feedback function [6–9].

Ureteral renal interventional treatment with the two-dimensional endoscopic image guidance can't do precise positioning and control. In recent years, magnetic navigation technology combined with the imaging, as a new interventional therapy technology, can be more accurately to locate the lesion [10, 11]. It is proposed to develop and integrate the magnetic navigation function in ureteroscopy to guide interventional surgery.

High intrarenal pressure can increase the risk of complications during surgery, so the function of pressure measurement seems to be crucial. It is proposed to develop intrarenal pressure guide wire to reduce the risk of surgical complications.

This article tends to introduce how to develop a ureteral renal interventional robot for diagnosis and treatment, the mainly functions of which involve operational refinement, real-time navigation, intrarenal pressure warning, endoscopic assisted diagnosis and treatment operation. We used the Denavit-Hartenberg (D-H) method to build kinematics model, the bi-directional control strategy and neural network based on the error back propagation for PD control was adopted. The robotic system will improve the effects of diagnosis and treatment in clinically kidney stone, ureteral stone and upper urinary tract tumor operation.

2   The Function Design of System

The mechanical design of ureteral renal interventional system is based on the kinematics, statics and elastic mechanics models, realizing flexible height adjustment of ureteroscopic, forward and backward motion, rotary motion and the front-end bending motion.

The research and optimization of control system is the master-slave interaction technology about force feedback. To achieve the high-precision localization and real-time tracking of surgical instruments, magnetic navigation system was integrated into ureteroscopic to guide interventional surgery. The real-time magnetic navigation of the robot can be realized by image-guided positioning.

The urinary system is maintained at a certain pressure range. Keeping high or low pressure for a long time can cause a series of complications and lead to death eventually. Therefore, it is important to measure the cavitary pressure accurately and real-timely, especially when it comes to the diagnosis and treatment of diseases in these systems. This paper also plans to study the problem of pressure measurement in ureter and renal pelvis.

3   The Realization Scheme of the Robot System

3.1   The Realization of the Mechanical System

The design and implementation of mechanical structure to manipulate precisely is the basis of this project. Mainly including elevating platform, linear guide, rotary mechanism and carrying platform.

The carrying platform is mainly included servo motor, flange coupling, auxiliary knob and ureteroscope base. The base is fixed with a ureteroscope, then the auxiliary knob is connected with the servo motor through flanged coupling, on the other end of knob is connected with button to control the bending of ureteroscope, and the bending can be realized by servo motor.

Elevating platform is used to adjust the height of the ureteroscope before surgery, we chose linear guide about 600 mm to meet the requirements of the horizontal motion.

The ureteroscope's axial movement is implemented by the ball screw and linear guide, we installed the linear guide on the elevating platform to realize the elevating movement. In order to ensure smooth and accurate work, we use high precision and stiffness elevating platform, screw and linear guide, which can meet the design requirements of the ureteral renal interventional treatment. Axial motion principle: First, the servo motor drives the screw to rotate, then the screw's circular rotation drives the linear movement of the nut. Second, the moving nut is connected with a movable base, the base is mounted on the linear guide, so the nut's linear movement converts into linear movement of the movable base. The rotation mechanism is mounted separately on the moving base. Therefore, this mechanism can achieve the axial linear movement of the ureterscope. The positive and negative rotation of the ball screw can control the forward or backward of the soft ureteroscope.

A u-shaped frame is designed to control the bending of the ureteroscope, the ureteroscope has a u-shaped part to control the bending, so this u-shaped frame can be matched with it. The servo motor can rotate in two directions, which is connected with u-shaped frame, achieving the bending movement.

Figure 1 shows the three-dimensional diagram of the mechanical structure and u-shaped frame.

The rotary mechanism is separately mounted on the linear guide, when the servo drives the linear guide, the rotary mechanism only perform linear movement. So those design can prevent the linear movement from the rotation and bending movement.

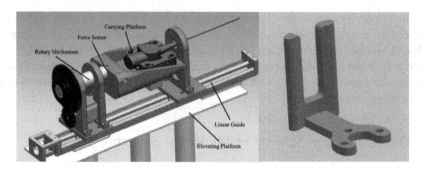

Fig. 1. The three-dimensional diagram of the mechanical structure and u-shaped frame

As shown in Fig. 1, force sensor is installed between the carrying platform and rotational axis, which is used to collect the force during the operation of ureteroscope. Force sensor and ureteroscope are to stay within the same relative position, therefor, during the movement of the ureteroscope, the force and torque can be transmitted to the carrying platform, then it will be transmitted to the force sensor. The information is collected by the data acquisition card. Finally, force information will be calculated by the program.

3.2   The Realization of the Control System

For purpose of the research and optimization of master-slave interaction control technology, the master-slave model of robot based on force feedback was established. A force feedback information collected and processed system, exerting impacts real-timely, stably and accurately and realizing interactive control optimization, was developed. We focus on master-slave bi-directional control, trajectory optimization based on prior knowledge.

Kinematics Solution

The slave manipulator of robot includes four joints: elevating joint, forward-backward joint, rotation joint and bending joint. However, the elevating joint is adjusted in the specified location before the operation, so according to the Denavit-Hartenberg (D-H)

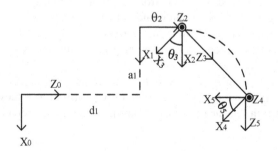

Fig. 2. D-H coordinate of slave manipulator

Table 1. D-H parameters of slave manipulator

Link	Θ	d	A	α
1	0	d_1	a_1	0
2	θ_2	0	0	90°
3	θ_3	0	0	−90°
4	0	d_4	0	90°
5	θ_5	0	0	−90°

method, we just need to build kinematics model about the forward-backward, rotary and bending joint. As shown in Fig. 2, the coordinate of bending joint is based on the method which is presented by Hannan [12].

Table 1 shows the D-H parameters of slave manipulator, θ_2 is the rotation angle, $\theta_3 = \theta_5$.

According to the D-H method, Then we get the Jacobian matrix of the robot.

$$J = \begin{bmatrix} 0 & \frac{1}{2\theta_3}\sin(\theta_2) - \frac{1}{2\theta_3}\sin(\theta_2)cos(2\theta_3) & \frac{1}{2\theta_3^2}\cos(\theta_2) - \frac{1}{2\theta_3^2}cos(\theta_2)cos(2\theta_3) - \frac{1}{\theta_3}\cos(\theta_2)sin(2\theta_3) \\ 0 & \frac{1}{2\theta_3}\cos(\theta_2) - \frac{1}{2\theta_3}\cos(\theta_2)cos(2\theta_3) & \frac{1}{2\theta_3^2}\sin(\theta_2) - \frac{1}{2\theta_3^2}sin(\theta_2)cos(2\theta_3) - \frac{1}{\theta_3}\sin(\theta_2)\sin(2\theta_3) \\ 1 & 0 & -\frac{1}{2\theta_3^2}\sin(2\theta_3) + \frac{1}{\theta_3}\cos(2\theta_3) \end{bmatrix}$$

(1)

Master-Slave Control Strategy

The bi-directional control strategy in teleoperation is shown in Fig. 3. When the surgeon operates the master manipulator (the Geomagic touch force feedback device as the master manipulator). Firstly, the PC obtains the space coordinate parameters of the force feedback device in real time. Secondly, the speed of the master manipulator is calculated by the Jacobian matrix, then the speed of the slave manipulator is obtained through master-slave mapping. Thirdly, the angular velocity of the respective joints can get by the inverse Jacobian matrix, Finally, the angular velocity information is converted into servo motor motion parameters to drive the movement. In order to achieve stable control, the position error from the robot is corrected according to the PD control based on neural network. At the same time, the force value is measured by the force sensor and produced by the Geomagic touch device.

Neural network based on the error back propagation for PD control is used in this paper, the displacement sensor obtained the location information of slave, then we can get the error by comparing with location information of mater mapping, According to the Eq. (2) and the performance index function 3, the weighting coefficient will be revised, finally, we get the new k_p and k_d parameters to achieve stable control, u_k is the input value from the slave, k is the current time error, r_k is the input value of the neural network, y_k is the output value of the displacement sensor.

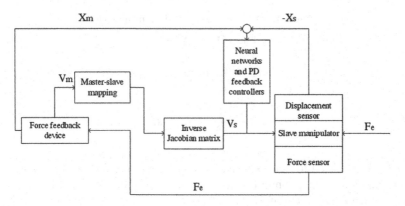

Fig. 3. Bi-directional control strategy

$$u_k = k_p(e_k - e_{k-1}) + k_d(e_k - 2e_{k-1} + e_{k-2}) \tag{2}$$

$$E_k = \frac{1}{2}(rk - y_k)^2 \tag{3}$$

3.3   The Realization of Navigable and Manometric Function

A silicon piezoresistive pressure sensor based on MEMS technology is applied to be a unit in the pressure monitoring, the Wheatstone bridge is composed of semiconductor which can transform the force into electric signal, and the silicon piezoresistive pressure sensor has high-precision, low-power, low-cost and other advantages.

The miniature pressure sensor is installed on the front-end of the guide wire. During the operation, the pressure guide wire is inserted into the working channel of the ureteroscope to measure the pressure in the kidney real-timely. When the pressure exceeds the safety threshold, the alarm can remind the surgeon.

Magnetic navigation system can accurately and real-timely measure three-dimensional space under the situation of occlusion, which uses tiny sensor coils to track and measure surgical instruments.

The magnetic navigation system and the puncture needle with sensor. Through the modification of the surgical instruments, combined with the intelligent navigation software, the magnetic navigation system realizes the spatial location and three-dimensional display of the lesion area.

4   Summary

The Fig. 4 shows the spatial relationship between the patient and robot.

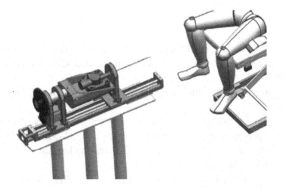

Fig. 4. Spatial relationship between the patient and robot

Our prototype is shown in Fig. 5, This paper tries to study the problems including: the easily tired of surgeon, the difficulty of the structural identification of the renal space and lack of real-time warning about the intrarenal pressure, so we designed a ureter renal interventional robot for diagnosis and treatment, the mainly functions of which involve operational refinement, real-time navigation, intrarenal pressure warning, endoscopic assisted diagnosis and treatment operation. Our prototype improved the effects of diagnosis and treatment in clinically kidney stone, ureteral stone and upper urinary tract tumor operation.

Fig. 5. The prototype of the mechanical structure

Acknowledgements. This work was supported by Natural Science Foundation of China (No. 61672341), The project of Science and Technology Commission of Shanghai municipality (No. 17441903800), The project of major program of National Natural Science Foundation of China (No. 61190124, 61190120), Key Project of SJTU Medical and Engineering Cross Research Fund (YG2017ZD03).

References

1. Li, J., Wang, S., Chen, R., et al.: Comparative study of holmium laser lithotripsy under ureteroscope and open surgery for ureteral calculi. Pract. J. Card. Cereb. Pneumal Vasc. Dis. **25**, 21–22 (2017)
2. Chew, B.H., Lange, D.: The future of ureteroscopy. Minerva Urol. E Nefrol. **68**(6), 592–597 (2016)
3. Geavlete, P., Multescu, R., Geavlete, B.: Pushing the boundaries of ureteroscopy: current status and future perspectives. Nat. Rev. Urology **11**(7), 82–373 (2014)
4. Szabó, F.J., de Alexander, L.T.: Robotic surgery - the modern surgical treatment of prostate cancer. Magy. Onkol. **58**(3), 173–181 (2014)
5. Tian, X.M., Wang, D., Ren, Z.J.: Comparison of clinical effect of Da Vinci robotic surgery and laparoscopic surgery for prostate cancer. J. Laparosc. Surg. **22**(7), 486–489 (2017)
6. Saglam, R., Koruk, E., Kabakci, A.S., et al.: Robotic use of the commercially available flexible ureterorenoscopes with a new user friendly control system. Eur. Urol. Suppl. **11**(1), e387–e387a (2012)
7. Saglam, R., Muslumanoglu, A.Y., Tokatlı, Z., et al.: A new robot for flexible ureteroscopy: development and early clinical results (IDEAL stage 1-2b). Eur. Urol. **66**(6), 1092–1100 (2014)
8. Desai, M.M., Grover, R., Aron, M., et al.: Robotic flexible ureteroscopy for renal calculi: initial clinical experience. J. Urol. **186**(2), 563–568 (2011)
9. Talari, H.F., Monfaredi, R., Wilson, E., et al.: Robotically assisted ureteroscopy for kidney exploration. In: Spie Medical Imaging, pp. 1–6 (2017)
10. Ramcharitar, S., van Geuns, R.J., Patterson, M., et al.: A randomized comparison of the magnetic navigation system versus conventional percutaneous coronary intervention. Catheter. Cardiovasc. Interv. **72**(6), 761–770 (2008)
11. Yoshida, K., Yokomizo, A., Matsuda, T., et al.: The advantage of a ureteroscopic navigation system with magnetic tracking in comparison with simulated fluoroscopy in a phantom study. J. Endourol. **29**(9), 76–88 (2015)
12. Hannan, M.W., Walker, I.D.: Kinematics and the implementation of an elephant's trunk manipulator and other continuum style robots. J. Field Robot. **20**(2), 45–63 (2003)

Nonlinear Disturbance Observer Based Adaptive Integral Sliding Mode Tracking Control of a Quadrotor

Ning Wang$^{(\boxtimes)}$, Qi Deng, and Yongpeng Weng

School of Marine Electrical Engineering, Dalian Maritime University, Dalian, China
n.wang.dmu.cn@gmail.com

Abstract. In this paper, the nonlinear observer based tracking control is addressed for a quadrotor with system uncertainties and external disturbances. Main contributions are as follows: (1) A nonlinear observer is employed to estimate complex unknowns including unmodelled dynamics and external disturbances for a quadrotor, and thereby enhancing robustness of the closed-loop system; (2) An adaptive integral sliding mode based control scheme is then employed to handle tracking control problem of a quadrotor, and achieves high-accuracy tracking performance; (3) The global asymptotic stability of the closed-loop tracking system can be guaranteed rigorously via Lyapunov approach. Finally, simulation results demonstrate the effectiveness of the proposed control scheme.

Keywords: Integral sliding mode control · Adaptive control
Nonlinear disturbance observer · Quadrotor

1 Introduction

The quadrotor is an unmanned helicopter that has the capability of vertical taking off and landing in space. Because of its simple structure, easy operation and other characteristics, it is widely used in military and civilian fields [1,2]. The quadrotor has four rotors fixed on a cross configuration. By changing the speed of different motors, you can make the quadrotor produce different movements. Due to its flexible nature, quadrotor has attracted the attention of numerous researchers.

As an under-actuated system, quadrotor has four independent inputs and six outputs. the simplicity for construction and favorable maneuverability also lead to great challenges in controller design. Recent years, there are some approaches

N. Wang—This work is supported by the National Natural Science Foundation of P. R. China (under Grants 51009017 and 51379002), the Fund for Dalian Distinguished Young Scholars (under Grant 2016RJ10), the Innovation Support Plan for Dalian High-level Talents (under Grant 2015R065), and the Fundamental Research Funds for the Central Universities (under Grant 3132016314).

© Springer International Publishing AG, part of Springer Nature 2018
T. Huang et al. (Eds.): ISNN 2018, LNCS 10878, pp. 719–726, 2018.
https://doi.org/10.1007/978-3-319-92537-0_82

to deal with underactuation as well as stabilization [3]. Backstepping is an efficient method for dealing with under-actuated systems [4,5]. In paper [6], backstepping based techniques are utilized to design a nonlinear adaptive controller to compensate for the mass uncertainty of the quadrotor. However, it requires a full knowledge of the model, which it is prone to instability for any uncertainty. The quadrotor system is divided into a fully-actuated subsystem and an under-actuated subsystem in paper [7], and a sliding mode control was proposed to stabilized the class of cascade under-actuated systems, but this paper did not consider the external disturbances. In paper [8], a robust backstepping controller based on integral sliding mode method is proposed for quadrotor subject to smooth bounded disturbances. Recently, fuzzy control is an attractive candidate for quadrotor system because of its ability to generate high performance tracking in the presence of unmodelled dynamics [9,10].

As a very effective technique for dealing with disturbances, disturbance observation has received extensive attention. The nonlinear disturbance observer was first proposed in [11], it is used for friction estimation and compensation for a two-link robotic manipulator. In addition, Chen gave a systematic and comprehensive overview of the perturbation observer in [12], and a comparative study of how to deal with external disturbances and system uncertainties.

This organization of this paper is as follows. In Sect. 2, the quadrotor model are addressed. The nonlinear disturbance observer is designed in Sect. 3. An adaptive integral sliding mode tracking control scheme is proposed and stability analysis is presented in Sect. 4. Some simulation results are conducted in Sect. 5. Finally, some conclusions are written in Sect. 6.

2   Quadrotor Model

The quadrotor is an underactuated system which has six outputs, but only four independent inputs. From [8], the simplified quadrotor state model can be obtained as

$$
\begin{cases}
\dot{x}_{11} = x_{21} \\
\dot{x}_{21} = -g + (C_{x_{14}}C_{x_{15}})\frac{u_1}{m} + d_1 \\
\dot{x}_{12} = x_{22} \\
\dot{x}_{22} = (C_{x_{14}}S_{x_{15}}C_{x_{16}} + S_{x_{14}}S_{x_{16}})\frac{u_1}{m} + d_2 \\
\dot{x}_{13} = x_{23} \\
\dot{x}_{23} = (C_{x_{14}}S_{x_{15}}S_{x_{16}} - S_{x_{14}}C_{x_{16}})\frac{u_1}{m} + d_3 \\
\dot{x}_{14} = x_{24} \\
\dot{x}_{24} = x_{25}x_{26}a_1 + x_{25}a_2\omega + b_1u_4 + d_4 \\
\dot{x}_{15} = x_{25} \\
\dot{x}_{25} = x_{24}x_{26}a_3 + x_{24}a_4\omega + b_2u_5 + d_5 \\
\dot{x}_{16} = x_{26} \\
\dot{x}_{26} = x_{24}x_{25}a_5 + b_3u_6 + d_6
\end{cases}
$$

where the state vector $X = [x_{11}, x_{21}, x_{12}, \ldots, x_{26}]^T$ are defined as

$$x_{11} = z, x_{21} = \dot{z}, x_{12} = x, x_{22} = \dot{x}$$
$$x_{13} = y, x_{23} = \dot{y}, x_{14} = \phi, x_{24} = \dot{\phi}$$
$$x_{15} = \theta, x_{25} = \dot{\theta}, x_{16} = \psi, x_{26} = \dot{\psi}$$

and angular velocity of the propeller blades is $\omega = \omega_1 - \omega_2 + \omega_3 - \omega_4$, d_i, $(i = 1, 2 \ldots 6)$ are the unknown disturbance that contains system uncertainties and other external factors, a_i $(i = 1, 2, \ldots, 5)$ and b_i $(i = 1, 2, 3)$ are the normalized parameters, u_1, u_2, u_3, u_4 are the control input, these parameters are defined as

$$a_1 = \frac{I_y - I_z}{I_x}, a_2 = \frac{J_r}{I_x}, a_3 = \frac{I_z - I_x}{I_y}$$
$$a_4 = -\frac{J_r}{I_x}, a_5 = \frac{I_x - I_y}{I_z}, b_1 = \frac{l}{I_x}$$
$$b_2 = \frac{l}{I_y}, b_3 = \frac{d}{I_z}$$

$$\begin{cases} u_1 &= b(\omega_1^2 + \omega_2^2 + \omega_3^2 + \omega_4^2) \\ u_4 &= b(\omega_3^2 - \omega_1^2) \\ u_5 &= b(\omega_4^2 - \omega_2^2) \\ u_6 &= d(\omega_1^2 - \omega_2^2 + \omega_3^2 - \omega_4^2) \end{cases}$$

with I_x, I_y and I_z are the inertia moments of the quadrotor system and J_r is the inertia moments of the propeller blades. l is the distance between the center of the quadrotor and the center of a propeller. b and d are scale factors related to air density, rotor angle and drag coefficient.

In this paper, we design the controller to achieve the tracking control of the quadrotor with the external disturbances. In other words, the controller can allow the quadrotor to track the desired trajectory (z_d, x_d, y_d, ψ_d). Because the quadrotor is an underactuated system, it has six outputs $(z, x, y, \phi, \theta, \psi)$, but only has four inputs (u_1, u_4, u_5, u_6). Therefore, we can not control all of the states at the same time. To solve this problem, we control (z, x, y, ψ) tracking desired signals (z_d, x_d, y_d, ψ_d), and enable (ϕ, θ) stable to zero simultaneously. We introduce two virtual control inputs (u_x, u_y), which represent the relation between pitch and x motion, roll and y motion respectively.

$$\begin{cases} u_x = (\cos\phi \sin\theta \cos\psi + \sin\phi \sin\psi) \\ u_y = (\cos\phi \sin\theta \sin\psi - \sin\phi \cos\psi) \end{cases} \tag{1}$$

then, transforming the Eq. (1) we have

$$\begin{cases} \phi_d = \arcsin(u_x \sin\psi - u_y \cos\psi) \\ \theta_d = \arcsin(\frac{u_x \cos\psi + u_y \sin\psi}{\cos\phi_d}) \end{cases} \tag{2}$$

In addition, part of the state space model related to (x, y) can be written as follows:

$$
\begin{cases}
\dot{x}_{12} = x_{22} \\
\dot{x}_{22} = u_x \frac{u_1}{m} + d_2 \\
\dot{x}_{13} = x_{23} \\
\dot{x}_{23} = u_y \frac{u_1}{m} + d_3
\end{cases}
\tag{3}
$$

Next, in order to facilitate the controller design, the state model is simplified as

$$
\begin{cases}
\dot{x}_{1i} = x_{2i} \\
\dot{x}_{2i} = f_i(x) + g_i(x)u_i + d_i
\end{cases}
\tag{4}
$$

where the control input vector is $U = [u_1, u_2, u_3, u_4, u_5, u_6]^T$. In the state model, $f_i(x)$ and $g_i(x)$ are the smooth nonlinear functions $(i = 1, 2, 3, 4, 5, 6)$, can be written as

$$
f_1(x) = -g, g_1(x) = \frac{\cos x_{14} \cos x_{15}}{m}
$$
$$
f_2(x) = 0, g_2(x) = \frac{u_1}{m}
$$
$$
f_3(x) = 0, g_3(x) = \frac{u_1}{m}
$$
$$
f_4(x) = x_{25}x_{26}a_1 + x_{25}a_2\omega, g_4(x) = b_1
$$
$$
f_5(x) = x_{24}x_{26}a_3 + x_{24}a_4\omega, g_5(x) = b_2
$$
$$
f_6(x) = x_{24}x_{25}a_5, g_6(x) = b_3
$$

Assumption 1. The control inputs command and its first derivative with time exist and are bounded.

Assumption 2. To avoid singularity problems, the attitude angles are limited to $(-\frac{\pi}{2} \leq \phi \leq \frac{\pi}{2})$, $(-\frac{\pi}{2} \leq \theta \leq \frac{\pi}{2})$ and $(-\pi \leq \psi \leq \pi)$.

Assumption 3. The unknown disturbance term d_i are bounded, and the bounds are unknown, $|d| < \delta$.

3   Nonlinear Disturbance Observer Design

It is easy to cause the system output unstable by directly design the controller because of external disturbance and system uncertainty. Therefore, in this section, we first design an nonlinear disturbance observer to observe the external disturbance of the system. The nonlinear disturbance observer is designed and an auxiliary variable α is introduced as follows [11]:

$$
\begin{cases}
\alpha = \hat{d}_i - p(x) \\
\dot{\alpha} = -L(x)\alpha + L(x)\left[-p(x) - g(x)u - f(x)\right]
\end{cases}
\tag{5}
$$

with d_i is the unknown external disturbance, $p(x)$ is the nonlinear function to be designed, and $L(x)$ is the gain of the nonlinear observer. Usually, we choose a constant $L(x) = a, a > 0$ and design $p(x) = ax_{2i}$. Here, $p(x)$ is satisfied:

$$\dot{p}(x) = L(x)\dot{x}_{2i} \tag{6}$$

Defining the observation error of nonlinear observer

$$\tilde{d}_i = d_i - \hat{d}_i \tag{7}$$

Generally, there is no prior knowledge of derivative of d_i, assuming that $\dot{d}_i = 0$. Then, from (7) we have the observer error dynamic system:

$$\begin{aligned}
\dot{\tilde{d}}_i &= \dot{d}_i - \dot{\hat{d}}_i \\
&= -\dot{\alpha} - \dot{p}(x) \\
&= -L(x)\tilde{d}_i
\end{aligned} \tag{8}$$

From the Eq. (8), we can make the observation error converge exponentially by choosing $L(x) > 0$ appropriately. Therefore, the choice of $p(x)$ is crucial, design

$$u_{i,d} = -\frac{1}{g_i(x)}\hat{d}_i \tag{9}$$

where $g_i(x)$ is the gain of the controller, $u_{i,d}$ as the part of the controller.

4   Controller Design

In this section, we design integral sliding mode control scheme for the quadrotor nonlinear system using the developed disturbance observer.

Theorem 1. *Consider the quadrotor state model under the tracking control law as follows:*

$$u_i = -\frac{1}{g_i}\left[c_i\dot{e}_i + f_i - \ddot{x}_{1id} + k_ie_i + \hat{d}_i + h_is_i + \hat{\delta}_i sign(s_i)\right] \tag{10}$$

where e_i, $i = 1, 2, 3, 4, 5, 6$ is the tracking error defined as

$$e_i = x_{1i} - x_{1id} \tag{11}$$

and s_i is the sliding surface as follows:

$$s_i = c_ie_i + \dot{e}_i + k_i\int e_i \tag{12}$$

with design parameters $c_i > 0$ and $k_i > 0$. In this control law, h_i is chosen as positive constants, $\hat{\delta}$ is estimated value of the upper bound of the unknown uncertainty d_i, and the adpative law for $\hat{\delta}$ as

$$\dot{\hat{\delta}} = \gamma_i|s_i|, \gamma_i > 0 \tag{13}$$

we also have the error between δ and $\hat{\delta}$ as

$$\tilde{\delta} = \delta - \hat{\delta} \tag{14}$$

Then, under this control scheme, the quadrotor system can achieve asymptotic stability.

Proof. Consider the Lyapunov function for each subsystem candidate:

$$V_i = \frac{1}{2}s_i^2 + \frac{1}{2\gamma_i}\tilde{\delta}_i^{\,2} + \frac{1}{2}\tilde{d}_i^{\,2} \tag{15}$$

The time derivative of V_i along (8), (12) and (13) is

$$\dot{V}_i = s_i\dot{s}_i + \frac{1}{\gamma_i}\tilde{\delta}_i\dot{\tilde{\delta}}_i + \tilde{d}_i\dot{\tilde{d}}_i$$

$$= s_i\left(c_i\dot{e}_i + \ddot{e}_i + k_ie_i\right) - \frac{1}{\gamma_i}\tilde{\delta}_i\dot{\hat{\delta}}_i + \tilde{d}_i\dot{\tilde{d}}_i$$

$$= s_i\left(c_i\dot{e}_i + f_i + g_iu_i + d_i - \ddot{x}_{1id} + k_ie_i\right) - \frac{1}{\gamma_i}\tilde{\delta}_i\dot{\hat{\delta}}_i + \tilde{d}_i\dot{\tilde{d}}_i \tag{16}$$

Combining with control law (14) and the adaptive law (13), we have

$$\dot{V}_i = s_i\left(d_i - \hat{d}_i - h_is_i - \hat{\delta}_i sign(s_i)\right) - \tilde{\delta}_i|s_i| - L_i\tilde{d}_i^{\,2}$$

$$= \tilde{d}_is_i - h_is_i^{\,2} - \hat{\delta}_i|s_i| - \tilde{\delta}_i|s_i| - L_i\tilde{d}_i^{\,2}$$

$$= \tilde{d}_is_i - h_is_i^{\,2} - \delta_i|s_i| - L_i\tilde{d}_i^{\,2}$$

$$\leq \delta_i|s_i| - h_is_i^{\,2} - \delta_i|s_i| - L_i\tilde{d}_i^{\,2}$$

$$= -h_is_i^{\,2} - L_i\tilde{d}_i^{\,2} \tag{17}$$

We can guarantee $\dot{V}_i \leq 0$ by selecting the appropriate parameters. For the entire system, the Lyapunov function can chosen as

$$V = \frac{1}{2}\sum_{i=1}^{6}\left(s_i^2 + \frac{1}{\gamma_i}\tilde{\delta}_i^{\,2} + \tilde{d}_i^{\,2}\right) \tag{18}$$

and the time derivative of V can be given as

$$\dot{V} = \sum_{i=1}^{6}\left(-h_is_i^{\,2} - L_i\tilde{d}_i^{\,2}\right) \tag{19}$$

We can see that the quadrotor system is asymptotic stability under this control scheme. This completes the proof.

5   Simulation Studies

In this section, simulations are conducted to prove the effectiveness of the presented adaptive integral sliding mode controller and nonlinear disturbance observer. The nominal parameters of the quadrotor are chosen as $m = 2\,\mathrm{kg}$, $l = 0.5\,\mathrm{m}$, $b = 3.16 \times 10^{-5}$, $d = 7.32 \times 10^{-7}$, inertia parameters I_x, I_y, I_z are chosen as $I_x = I_y = 6.114 \times 10^{-3}\,\mathrm{kgm}^2$, $I_z = 1.223 \times 10^{-2}\,\mathrm{kgm}^2$, $J_r = 1.55 \times 10^{-5}\,\mathrm{kgm}^2$. The external disturbances in state model are governed by $d_i = cos(0.5t)$, $i = 1, 2, \ldots, 6$. The desired trajectory are used by $(z_d = 2, x_d = cos(0.5t), y_d = sin(0.5t), \psi_d = 0.1)$. Where the controller parameters are chosen as $c_1 = 2, c_2 = 2, c_3 = 1, c_4 = 5, c_5 = 5, c_6 = 5$, $k_1 = 5, k_2 = 0.1, k_3 = 5, k_4 = 0.1, k_5 = 0.1, k_6 = 1$, $h_1 = h_2 = h_3 = h_4 = h_5 = h_6 = 1$. The gains of adaptive laws are chosen as $\gamma_i = 10, i = (1, 2, \ldots, 6)$. The disturbance observer parameters are designed as $L_i(x) = 15, i = (1, 2, \ldots, 6)$.

Simulations results are presented in Figs. 1, 2, 3 and 4. It can be clear seen from Fig. 1 that the actual trajectory can track the desired one in (z, x, y, ψ)

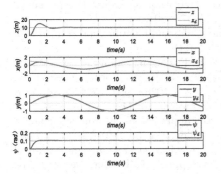

Fig. 1. Desired and actual trajectories for $z(t), x(t), y(t), \psi(t)$.

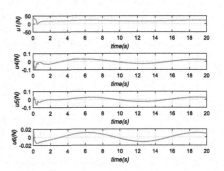

Fig. 2. Quadrotor outputs.

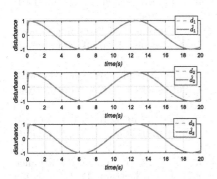

Fig. 3. Observation of disturbance for d_1, d_2, d_3.

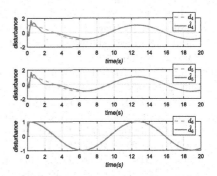

Fig. 4. Observation of disturbance for d_4, d_5, d_6.

respectively. Figure 2 shows the actual outputs (u_1, u_4, u_5, u_6) tend to be steady after the initial tremble. Figure 3 and Fig. 4 show the disturbance observers can quickly estimate the actual disturbance.

6 Conclusion

In this paper, to pursue trajectory tracking of a quadrotor in the presence of external disturbance, a integral sliding mode based nonlinear disturbance observer scheme has been proposed. Under the control scheme, not only that unknown disturbances can be completely estimated but also trajectory tracking exactly can be achieved, and thereby the robustness of the system has been improved. In addition, comprehensive simulation studies have also been proved the effectiveness of the proposed control strategy.

References

1. Kendoul, F.: Survey of advances in guidance, navigation, and control of unmanned rotorcraft systems. J. Field Robot. **29**(2), 315–378 (2012)
2. Zhang, X., Li, X., Wang, K.: A survey of modelling and identification of quadrotor robot. Abstr. Appl. Anal. **10**(23), 991–1002 (2014)
3. Wang, Y., Wang, N., Lv, S., Yin, J., Er, M.J.: Fuzzy uncertainty observer based filtered sliding mode trajectory tracking control of the quadrotor. In: Cong, F., Leung, A., Wei, Q. (eds.) ISNN 2017. LNCS, vol. 10262, pp. 137–147. Springer, Cham (2017). https://doi.org/10.1007/978-3-319-59081-3_17
4. Das, A., Lewis, F., Subbarao, K.: Backstepping approach for controlling a quadrotor using lagrange form dynamics. J. Intell. Robot Syst. **56**(1–2), 127–151 (2009)
5. Kuljaca, O., Swamy, N., Lewis, F.L., Kwan, C.: Design and implementation of industrial neural network controller using backstepping. IEEE Trans. Ind. Electron. **50**(1), 193–201 (2003)
6. Huang, M., Xian, B., Diao, C.: Adaptive tracking control of underactuated quadrotor unmanned aerial vehicles via backstepping, pp. 2076–2081 (2010)
7. Xu, R., Ozguner, U.: Sliding mode control of a quadrotor helicopter. In: IEEE Conference on Decision and Control, pp. 4957–4962 (2006)
8. Ramirez, R.H., Parra, V.V., Sanchez, O.A., et al.: Robust backstepping control based on integral sliding modes for tracking of quadrotors. J. Intell. Robot Syst. **73**(1–4), 51–66 (2014)
9. Wang, N., Er, M.J.: Direct adaptive fuzzy tracking control of marine vehicles with fully unknown parametric dynamics and uncertainties. IEEE Trans. Control Syst. Technol. **24**(5), 1845–1852 (2016)
10. Wang, N., Sun, J.C., Liu, Y.C.: Direct adaptive self-structuring fuzzy control with interpretable fuzzy rules for a class of nonlinear uncertain systems. Neurocomputing **170**(5), 1640–1645 (2016)
11. Chen, W.H., Ballance, D.J., Gawthrop, P.J., et al.: A nonlinear disturbance observer for robotic manipulators. IEEE Trans. Ind. Electron. **47**(4), 932–938 (2000)
12. Chen, W.H., Yang, J., Guo, L.: Disturbance-observer-based control and related methods: an overview. IEEE Trans. Ind. Electron. **63**(2), 1083–1095 (2016)

On Speed Controller Neural Tuner Application to Compensate PMSM Mechanics Inertia Moment Drift

Yuri I. Eremenko⊙, Anton I. Glushchenko$^{(\boxtimes)}$⊙,
Vladislav A. Petrov⊙, and Aleksandr V. Molodykh⊙

A.A. Ugarov Stary Oskol Technological Institute (branch), NUST "MISIS",
Stary Oskol, Russia
a.glushchenko@ieee.org

Abstract. A problem of adaptive control methods application to a speed vector control system of a Permanent Magnet Synchronous Motor (PMSM) with time varying mechanical parameters is considered. Such methods analysis is made to select the most appropriate one for the problem under consideration. As a result, a neural tuner is chosen. A synchronous motor mathematical model is shown, and the vector based control system of the motor is described. The neural tuner structure and its operation principle are presented. It is applied to adjust the speed controller of the PMSM. Experiments are conducted using the mathematical model of a PMSM Siemens 1FK7103, in which the mechanical inertia moment value is changed gradually during the modeling process. The tuner application as an augmentation to the speed controller allows to keep the required transient quality during the experiment despite the drive nonstationarity in contrast to a P-controller with the constant parameter value. This results in avoidance of, firstly, the transient time increase when the inertia moment is higher than its nominal value and, secondly, the speed overshoot in vice versa case.

Keywords: Synchronous motor · PMSM · Speed control · Adaptive control
Neural tuner · Mechanics value drift

1 Introduction

Nowadays permanent magnet synchronous motors (PMSM) are becoming more and more widely used in different branches of industry because of the development of vector control algorithms. They allow to keep the required torque and speed of the drive with the high accuracy [1]. For this reason, these motors are used for applications, where correct functioning is critical for final product quality. For an instance, they are applied to sawing and lathe machines. However, PMSM P and PI controllers must be tuned appropriately to provide the required accuracy [1], since a control system of the mentioned drive is sensitive to changes of its parameters [2].

© Springer International Publishing AG, part of Springer Nature 2018
T. Huang et al. (Eds.): ISNN 2018, LNCS 10878, pp. 727–735, 2018.
https://doi.org/10.1007/978-3-319-92537-0_83

Considering the above mentioned problem, there have been a lot of attempts to replace the linear control algorithms with regulators based on other approaches: fractional order control [3]; adaptive control [4], robust control [5], predictive control [6]. However, the number of their applications to industrial plants is rather low, since the PMSM parameters variation can rarely be predicted and is difficult to be limited [7].

Therefore, the PMSM are controlled with the P and PI regulators in the majority of cases, since they are simply implemented, have high efficiency and clear functioning algorithms. In this connection, the development of the adaptive systems, which are based on these control principles and adjust their parameters in real time, seems to be more promising from the point of view of their future industrial application. A number of approaches, which are based on the drive mathematical model, have been developed to implement mentioned controller tuning [8, 9]. But these methods application is limited due to the great dependence of their performance on the accuracy of both the data measurements from the plant and the drive models.

Some methods of adaptive P and PI controllers tuning are able to function without the drive model. Considering the PMSM, it is a gradient descent method [10], which main disadvantage is a problem of selection of an adaptation step value. Artificial intelligence methods, in particular, neural networks (NN) [11, 12] and fuzzy logic (FL) [13, 14], do not also require the drive model to be used to solve the problem under consideration. The FL allows to use expert knowledge to adjust the controller, but there is an unsolved problem of choice and subsequent tuning of normalization coefficients values for the input and output signals of a fuzzy tuner. The NN can be trained online and are able to approximate data from a training set [15, 16]. These advantages make them be one of the most promising approaches comparing to all mentioned methods. However, the problem of a learning rate value selection is not solved, since this value depends on the current transient quality and the stability of the control system during online training process. At the same time, a method of development of a neural tuner for a speed controller of a DC drive is proposed in [17]. It is based on simultaneous application of the neural networks and the expert knowledge allowing to avoid the above mentioned disadvantages and having the following advantages. The tuner does not require neither the drive model, nor off-line training. The learning rate of its on-line training is limited to keep the control system stable.

The scope of this research is both to apply this tuner to control the PMSM under the condition of drift of the drive mechanics inertia moment value and demonstrate its effectiveness comparing to the control system with a conventional speed P-controller.

2 Problem Formulation

2.1 Control Scheme Description

First of all, the PMSM speed vector control system is considered [11] (Fig. 1). Here θ is the mechanical rotor angle, $\omega = d\theta/dt$ is the mechanical rotor angular speed, ω_{ref} is ω setpoint, i_{ds} is the d-axis stator current, i_{qs} is the q-axis stator current, $i_{ds\ ref}$ is the d-axis stator current setpoint, $i_{qs\ ref}$ is the q-axis stator current setpoint, PWM is the pulse width modulation, d-q is the rotating reference frame direct and quadrature axis, a-b-c is the three-phase stationary reference frame, i_a is the a-phase stator current, i_b is the b-phase stator current, i_c is the c-phase stator current. A transformation of the coordinates from q-d to a-b-c and vice versa is made with the help of the orthogonal Park/Clarke method.

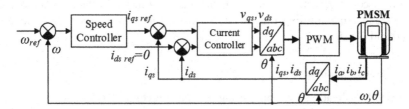

Fig. 1. Block diagram of vector PMSM control system

In this case the task is to keep the required drive speed ω_{ref} with the help of the speed P-controller, which calculates the setpoint value for the stator current projection onto q-axis of the rotating reference frame. Its value for the d-axis projection $i_{ds\ ref}$ is usually equaled to nil for the PMSM. The "Current Controller" block contains two PI-controllers for the above mentioned stator current projections. The outputs of these controllers are q-axis stator voltage v_{qs} and d-axis stator voltage v_{ds}, which are then transformed into the three-phase stationary reference frame a-b-c and sent to the motor through the PWM. In their turn, the phase currents i_a, i_b, i_c are measured from the motor and transformed into the projections i_{qs} and i_{ds}. The mechanical rotor angle θ and the mechanical rotor angular speed ω are measured from the motor.

The following paragraph contains a mathematical description of the PMSM.

2.2   Mathematical Model of PMSM

A non-salient PMSM can be described as follows [18]:

$$v_{ds} = R_s i_{ds} - \omega_r L_S i_{qs} + L_S \frac{di_{ds}}{dt}, \tag{1}$$

$$v_{qs} = R_s i_{qs} + \omega_r L_S i_{ds} + \omega_r \psi_f + L_S \frac{di_{qs}}{dt}, \tag{2}$$

where R_s is the stator resistance, ω_r is the angular rotor speed in electrical degrees, L_S is the stator inductance, ψ_f is the excitation flux linkage.

$$\omega_r = P \cdot \omega/2 \tag{3}$$

P is the number of poles. The torque equation is

$$T_e = (3/2) \cdot (P/2) \cdot \psi_f \cdot i_{qs}. \tag{4}$$

The mechanical equation of the motor is

$$T_e - T_L = J \cdot (d\omega/dt) + B \cdot \omega. \tag{5}$$

B is the viscous friction coefficient; J is the rotational inertia, T_L is the load torque. In this research modeling experiments are conducted using the following conditions – $T_L = 0$ and $B = 0$.

2.3   Problem Statement

The PMSM is already functioning using the speed P-controller. Its current settings are known, and they provide the required quality of the speed transient processes for the nominal values of the drive parameters from the point of view of an overshoot and oscillations. At the same time, J value is gradually changed during experiments. The task is to adjust K_P parameter of the speed P-controller to keep the required transients quality, despite the specified J value drift. The neural tuner is to be applied to solve this task. It has no information about the parameters values of the drive model.

3   Neural Tuner

In this research the PMSM adaptive control scheme (Fig. 2) is arranged using the neural tuner. Comparing to the scheme in Fig. 1, this one allows to compensate J value variation by K_P adjustment in real time. The tuner is called every Δt seconds and obtains data (ω_{ref}, ω, i_{qsd}) from the conventional control system. It consists of a neural network, which is trained online only, and a rule base, which reflects the expert knowledge. The base is responsible for both determination of the time moments when to train the network and the learning rate value calculation. So it makes an assessment of the situation, and if any of the rules triggers, then the neural network is trained. In any case, the network output (K_P) is calculated using the above mentioned data.

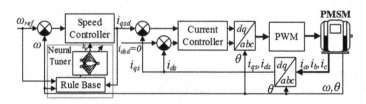

Fig. 2. Block diagram of vector PMSM control system with speed controller neural tuner

The structure of the neural network (Fig. 3) for the tuner is calculated using formulas from [19] and enough to tune a P-controller. The rule base to train this network online is shown in [17] and implemented with the help of the Matlab Script Language. Rules conditions contain a description of the situations when the quality of the transient process does not meet the requirements.

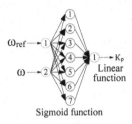

Fig. 3. Tuner neural network structure

Their consequences include empirical formulas to calculate the speed of the neural network training. Too high values of this speed are prevented with the help of the developed method to assess the sustainability of the control system with the tuner [19]. Δt value is calculated using [17].

4   Experimental Results

The mathematical model of the PMSM Siemens 1FK7103 (Table 1) being a typical drive of such kind has been developed (Fig. 4) in order to conduct the experiments, which results are shown in Fig. 5. They were made as follows. The setpoint was a sequence of these values (Fig. 5A): zero rad/s – 314 rad/s (the drive nominal speed) – zero rad/s – minus 314 rad/s – zero rad/s. The acceleration of the electric drive was equaled to $2.8 \cdot 10^3$ rad/s^2 due to existing limitations on the stator current, so this value was also the speed of the setpoint value change. The overshoot of the speed loop transients was 0.104% when the drive parameters nominal values were used. So the required overshoot limits were determined as [0.075%; 0.216%]. The inertia moment (J) was changed during the experiments as a sine wave signal (Fig. 5B). Δt was calculated as 0.01 ms. The neural network of the tuner was trained online only, so its performance is shown in Fig. 5. Using the rule base, the tuner adjusted K_P value (Fig. 5C).

The form of the curve in Fig. 5C is generally the same as for the curve of the inertia moment change (Fig. 5B). So the tuner compensated the drive nonstationarity. The tuner was able to keep the value of the overshoot for the speed loop close to the initial value (0.104%) throughout the experiment (Fig. 5D, red line) contrary to the system without the tuner (Fig. 5D, blue line).

The neural tuner kept the overshoot value in the range of [0.075%; 0.216%], whereas the maximum and minimum overshoot values for the system with the conventional P-controller were 0.307% and 0% respectively. This indicated that: (1) the

Table 1. Table captions should be placed above the tables.

Parameter name	Value
Optimum power P_{opt}, kW	5.37
Voltage, V	400
Rated speed n_N, rpm	3000
Max. permissible speed n_{max}, rpm	5000
No. of poles P	8
Efficiency η, %	93
Rated torque M_N, N·m	14
Moment of inertia J, kg·m^2	0.0118
Rated current I_N, A	12
Max. current I_{max}, A	84
Stall current I_0, A	27.5
Winding resistance at 105°C Rs, Ohm	0.1206
Stator inductance L_S, mH	2
Mechanical time constant T_{mech}, ms	1.55

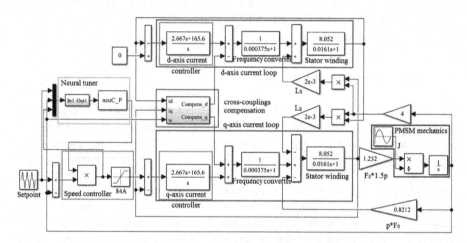

Fig. 4. PMSM mathematical model (L_S is the stator inductance, F_0 is the initial magnetic flux, p is the number of the poles pairs)

transient time increased for the control system without the tuner when J was higher than the nominal value, (2) the overshoot and the number of oscillations (Fig. 5E) were reduced by the tuner when J was lower than the nominal value (the maximum over-shoot for the system without the tuner was 30% higher than for the system with it). That allowed the control system with the tuner to improve the energy efficiency of the drive by 3% comparing to the system without it.

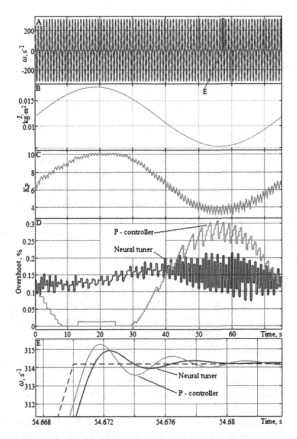

Fig. 5. Compensation of PMSM mechanics parameters drift with neural tuner and P-controller (ω is the rotor mechanical speed, J is the inertia moment, K_P is the adjustable parameter) (Color figure online)

5   Conclusion

In this research, as a result of the analysis of the adaptive control methods, the neural tuner was selected to be applied to adjust the speed P-controller of the PMSM.

The numerical experiments were conducted using the PMSM model. Taking all obtained results into consideration, the conclusion can be made that the application of the developed adaptive control system allowed to keep the required speed transient quality for the PMSM. Under the conditions of the drift of the inertia moment value (J) the tuner allowed to provide both the required acceleration of the electric drive when J was higher than its nominal value and the required overshoot when J was lower than its nominal value. In the course of the experiments the neural tuner made it possible to reduce the overshoot by 30% and increase the drive energy efficiency by 3% comparing to the system without the controller adjustment.

The scope of future research is to use the neural tuner to reject disturbances acting on the PMSM. In order to achieve that, the rule base of the tuner is to be improved.

Acknowledgements. This research was supported by the Russian Federation Ministry of Science and Education, grant no. 14.575.21.0133 (RFMEFI57517X0133).

References

1. Tursini, M., Parasiliti, F., Zhang, D.: Real-time gain tuning of PI controllers for high-performance PMSM drives. IEEE Trans. Ind. Appl. **4**(38), 1018–1026 (2002)
2. Pillay, P., Krishnan, R.: Control characteristics and speed controller design for a high performance permanent magnet synchronous motor drive. IEEE Trans. Power Electron. **2**(5), 151–159 (1990)
3. Zhang, B.T., Pi, Y.: Robust fractional order proportion-plus-differential controller based on fuzzy inference for permanent magnet synchronous motor. IET Control Theory Appl. **6**(6), 829–837 (2012)
4. Li, S.H., Liu, Z.G.: Adaptive speed control for permanent magnet synchronous motor system with variations of load inertia. IEEE Trans. Ind. Electron. **8**(56), 3050–3059 (2009)
5. Zhang, X., Sun, L., Zhao, K., Sun, L.: Nonlinear speed control for PMSM system using sliding-mode control and disturbance compensation techniques. IEEE Trans. Power Electron. **3**(28), 1358–1365 (2013)
6. Preindl, M., Bolognani, S.: Model predictive direct speed control with finite control set of PMSM drive systems. IEEE Trans. Power Electron. **2**(28), 1007–1015 (2013)
7. El-Sousy, F.F.M.: Intelligent optimal recurrent wavelet Elman neural network control system for permanent-magnet synchronous motor servo drive. IEEE Trans. Ind. Inform. **4**(9), 1986–2003 (2013)
8. Skoczowski, S., Domek, S., Pietrusewicz, K., Plater, B.B.: A method for improving the robustness of PID control. IEEE Trans. Ind. Electron. **6**(52), 1669–1676 (2005)
9. Xi, X., Yongdong, L., Min, L.: Performance control of PMSM drives using a self-tuning PID. In: 2005 IEEE International Conference on Electric Machines and Drives, pp. 1053–1057. IEEE, San Antonio (2005)
10. Jung, J.W., Leu, V.Q., Do, T.D., Kim, E.K., Choi, H.H.: Adaptive PID speed control design for permanent magnet synchronous motor drives. IEEE Trans. Power Electron. **2**(30), 900–908 (2014)
11. Kumar, V., Gaur, P., Mittal, A.P.: ANN based self tuned PID like adaptive controller design for high performance PMSM position control. Expert Syst. Appl. **17**(41), 7995–8002 (2014)
12. Zhang, L., Xu, B.J., Wen, K.L., Li, Y.H.: The study of permanent magnetic synchronous motor control system through the combination of BP neural network and PID control. In: Juang, J., Huang, Y.C. (eds.) Intelligent Technologies and Engineering Systems. Lecture Notes in Electrical Engineering, vol. 234, pp. 311–320. Springer, New York (2013). https://doi.org/10.1007/978-1-4614-6747-2_38
13. Wang, L., Tian, M., Gao, Y.: Fuzzy self-adapting PID control of PMSM servo system. In: 2007 IEEE International Conference on Electric Machines & Drives Conference, pp. 860–863. IEEE, Antalya (2007)
14. Hsu, S.C., Liu, C.H., Liu, C.H., Wang, N.J.: Fuzzy PI controller tuning for a linear permanent magnet synchronous motor drive. In: 27th Annual Conference of the IEEE Industrial Electronics Society, pp. 1661–1666. IEEE, Denver (2001)

15. Kwan, C., Lewis, F.L.: Robust backstepping control of induction motors using neural networks. IEEE Trans. Neural Netw. **5**(11), 1178–1187 (2000)
16. Kwan, C., Lewis, F.L.: Robust backstepping control of nonlinear systems using neural networks. IEEE Trans. Syst. Man Cybern. – Part A: Syst. Hum. **6**(30), 753–766 (2000)
17. Glushchenko, A.I., Petrov, V.A.: On neural tuner application to adjust speed P-controller of rolling mill main DC drive. In: 2017 IEEE International Siberian Conference on Control and Communications, pp. 1–5. IEEE, Astana (2017)
18. De Doncker, R., Pulle, D.W.J., Veltman, A.: Advanced Electrical Drives: Analysis, Modeling, Control. Springer Science & Business Media, Heidelberg (2011). https://doi.org/10.1007/978-94-007-0181-6
19. Glushchenko, A.I.: Method of calculation of upper bound of learning rate for neural tuner to control DC drive. In: Kryzhanovsky, B., Dunin-Barkowski, W., Redko, V. (eds.) NEUROINFORMATICS 2017. SCI, vol. 736, pp. 104–109. Springer, Cham (2018). https://doi.org/10.1007/978-3-319-66604-4_16

Nonlinear Observers for a Class of Neuronal Oscillators in the Presence of Strong Measurement Noise

Julio Pérez[1], Yu Tang[2(✉)], and Ileana Grave[2]

[1] Faculty of Mechanical Engineering, Institute of Automatic Control,
Technical University of Munich, 85748 Munich, Garching, Germany
j.perez@tum.de
[2] Faculty of Engineering, National Autonomous University of Mexico,
04360 Mexico City, Mexico
tang@unam.mx, ileanaangelica@gmail.com

Abstract. The objective of this paper is to design observers for a class of neuronal oscillators on the one hand, and to give a comparative study of the observer performance as the number of synchronized observer increases, on the other hand. More specifically, we apply the methodology of observer design in [4] for a class of neural oscillators. Contraction tool [7] is applied to obtain an exponentially convergent reduced-order observer, which serves as a building-block to construct a complete-order observer when the output is corrupted by moderate level of noise. In presence of strong measurement noise, several identical complete-order observers are coupled to synchronize.

Keywords: Observer · Neuro-oscillator · Contraction theory
Synchronization

1 Introduction

Measurement noise is inevitable in control systems. When high precision is required, the noise effect must be taken into account in the control system design. The celebrate Kalman filter design provides a systematic solution to this issue for linear systems when the noise has a known power density distribution. Although the extended Kalman filter design may work for nonlinear systems, the stability margin for the linear system is no longer maintained [1]. High-gain observers with constant gain [6] or with adaptive gain [9] have been used to reduce the noise level when the output measurements are noisy. However, this scheme can be applied only for systems represented in triangular form and may be affected by the *peaking* phenomena.

This work was supported in part by CONACyT 253677 and PAPIIT-UNAM IN113418.

© Springer International Publishing AG, part of Springer Nature 2018
T. Huang et al. (Eds.): ISNN 2018, LNCS 10878, pp. 736–744, 2018.
https://doi.org/10.1007/978-3-319-92537-0_84

In a recent work [11], it is claimed that synchronization may protect from the noise in neuro-systems in the sense that the clean (in the absence of external noise) system trajectory may be recovered by a group of identical and synchronized systems when the noise is present. Relying on this interesting finding, it was proposed an observer design in [4] to deal with the noisy measurements in the depth estimation in a perspective vision system. It was shown that the performance of the complete-order observer for the noise-free case may be recovered asymptotically as the number of coupled complete-order observers tends to infinite. This result sets a theoretical limit of performance in the presence of measurement noise.

The objective of this paper is two fold: to design observers for a class of neuro-oscillators on the one hand, and to give a comparative study of the observer performance as the number of synchronized observer increases, on the other hand. More specifically, we apply the methodology of observer design in [4] for a class of neuronal oscillators. Contraction analysis [7] is applied to obtain an exponentially convergent reduced-order observer, which serves as a building-block to construct a complete-order observer. In presence of strong measurement noise, several identical complete-order observers are coupled to synchronize. The developed schemes were applied to a FitzHughC-Nagumo neuro-oscillator and verified by means of simulation. The results show that the noise attenuation is significant even with a few coupled complete-order observers.

Recent evidence indicates that synchronous neural oscillations reveal much about the origin and nature of cognitive processes such as memory, attention and consciousness [13]. This oscillatory activity of the brain has been described by a large number of mathematical models where the nonlinear oscillator networks are included [2,10]. In almost all cases, the nonlinear equations are related to the membrane potential and the slow and fast ion currents in the neuron. The behavior of the neuron membrane potential expressed by this models is greatly similar to the signals measured in an electroencephalography (EEG) [3], while the slow and fast diffusive ion currents remain unmeasurable. In brain – computer applications [5], especially based-model control systems [14], it is needed not only to have free-noise measurements, but also an accurate estimation of the unmeasurable states in order to obtain a more suitable control law.

The rest of the paper is organized as follows. In Sect. 2 the problem is formulated and a brief overview of contraction theory is introduced. Section 3 is related to the designs of the reduced-order, complete-order and synchronized complete-order observers. In Sect. 4 the performance of such designs is tested under noisy measurements via numerical simulations. Concluding remarks are drawn in Sect. 5.

2   Preliminaries and Problem Formulation

In order to be used in the observer designs, the following contraction results are introduced.

2.1   Contraction Theory

Theorem 1 (Contraction [8]). *Consider the nonlinear system*

$$\dot{\mathbf{x}} = \mathbf{f}(\mathbf{x}, t), \tag{1}$$

where $\mathbf{f}$ *is an* $n \times 1$ *nonlinear vector function and* $\mathbf{x}$ *is the* $n \times 1$ *state vector. If the symmetric part of the Jacobian matrix is uniformly negative define, i.e, for some* $\lambda > 0$

$$\mathbf{J}_s = \frac{1}{2}\left(\frac{\partial \mathbf{f}}{\partial \mathbf{x}} + \frac{\partial \mathbf{f}}{\partial \mathbf{x}}^\top\right) \leq -\lambda \mathbf{I}, \quad \forall t \geq 0 \tag{2}$$

then the system (1) is contracting with converge rate upper bounded by λ. *If a dynamic system verifies the contraction property, it can be then concluded that all neighboring trajectories converge to each other, regardless of initial conditions.*

Theorem 2 (Partial contraction [12]). *The smooth nonlinear system*

$$\dot{\mathbf{x}} = \mathbf{f}(\mathbf{x}, \mathbf{x}, t), \tag{3}$$

is said to be partially contracting if the associate virtual system

$$\dot{\mathbf{x}}_v = \mathbf{f}(\mathbf{x}_v, \mathbf{x}, t), \tag{4}$$

is contracting respect to $\mathbf{x}_v$ $\forall \mathbf{x}$ *uniformly in* t. *Moreover, if a particular solution of the auxiliary system* $\mathbf{x}_v$ *verifies a smooth specific property, then all trajectories of the original* $\mathbf{x}$ *system verify this property exponentially.*

2.2   Neuronal Oscillator Model

Consider a nonlinear oscillator described as

$$\dot{\mathbf{v}} = \mathbf{f}_1(\mathbf{v}, \mathbf{y}, \mathbf{u}, t), \tag{5a}$$
$$\dot{\mathbf{y}} = \mathbf{f}_2(\mathbf{v}, \mathbf{y}, \mathbf{u}, t), \tag{5b}$$

where $\mathbf{u} \in \mathbb{R}^p$ is the system input, $\mathbf{v} \in \mathbb{R}^{n_v}$ and $\mathbf{y} \in \mathbb{R}^{n_y}$ are the unmeasurable and measurable state vectors with $\mathbf{f}_1$ and $\mathbf{f}_2$ the $n_v \times 1$ and $n_y \times 1$ vector functions, respectively. Our main goal is to obtain an estimate of the process governed by (5a) using the available information given by (5b) in presence of strong measurement noise. To achieve this, the following assumptions are made.

Assumption 1. *The nonlinear vector function is of the form* $\mathbf{f}_2(\mathbf{v}, \mathbf{y}, \mathbf{u}, t) = P(\mathbf{y}, t)\mathbf{v} + g(\mathbf{y}, \mathbf{u})$.

Assumption 2. *The dimension of the unmeasurable and measurable states is the same, i.e,* $n_v = n_y$ *with* $P(\mathbf{y}, t) = P^\top(\mathbf{y}, t) > 0$, $\forall t \geq 0$.

Under these assumptions, system (5a, 5b) is redefined as

$$\dot{\mathbf{v}} = \mathbf{f}_1(\mathbf{v}, \mathbf{y}, \mathbf{u}, t), \tag{6a}$$

$$\dot{\mathbf{y}} = P(\mathbf{y}, t)\mathbf{v} + g(\mathbf{y}, \mathbf{u}). \tag{6b}$$

A wide range of neuronal oscillators can be rewritten as in (6a, 6b), *e.g*, the Morris–Lecar and FitzHugh–Nagumo models. As an example, consider the well known van der Pol (VP) nonlinear oscillator model expressed as

$$\dot{v} = -(y^2 - 1)v + h(y, t),$$

$$\dot{y} = v.$$

Notice that for this case $P(y, t) = 1$ and $g(y, u) = 0$. Hence, in the following sections we formulate a general methodology for the design of contracting-based observers for systems of the form (6a, 6b).

3   Observer Designs

The last system structure given by (6a, 6b) helps us to easily obtain an observer design whose trajectories converge exponentially to those of a target system. In the above subsections, analysis is taken first over the non-implementable expressions. Afterward the implementable designs are presented.

3.1   Reduced-Order

Consider the next virtual (non-implementable) observer

$$\dot{\hat{\mathbf{v}}} = \mathbf{f}_1(\hat{\mathbf{v}}, \mathbf{y}, \mathbf{u}, t) + K_v(\mathbf{y}, t)(\mathbf{v} - \hat{\mathbf{v}}), \tag{7}$$

where the matrix $K_v(\mathbf{y}, t)$ is the estimation gain. The observer has $\hat{\mathbf{v}} = \mathbf{v}$ as a particular solution and it is also contracting by choosing the K_v such that

$$\mathbf{J}_s = [\frac{\partial \mathbf{f}_1(\hat{\mathbf{v}}, \mathbf{y}, \mathbf{u}, t)}{\partial \hat{\mathbf{v}}} - K_v(\mathbf{y}, t)]_s \leq -\lambda \mathbf{I}. \tag{8}$$

Thus, the reduced-order estimated states converge exponentially to the unmeasurable dynamics (6a) in noise-free environments by Theorems 1 and 2. This simple design can be transformed into an implementable observer if we first select the gain as $K_v(\mathbf{y}, t) = KP(\mathbf{y}, t)$ with $K = K^\top > 0$. Then

$$\dot{\hat{\mathbf{v}}} = \mathbf{f}_1(\hat{\mathbf{v}}, \mathbf{y}, \mathbf{u}, t) - KP(\mathbf{y}, t)\hat{\mathbf{v}} + KP(\mathbf{y}, t)\mathbf{v}. \tag{9}$$

Taking into account (6b), the unavailable term $P(\mathbf{y}, t)\mathbf{v}$ in (9) is replaced by $P(\mathbf{y}, t)\mathbf{v} = \dot{\mathbf{y}} - g(\mathbf{y}, \mathbf{u})$ we obtain

$$\dot{\hat{\mathbf{v}}} = \mathbf{f}_1(\hat{\mathbf{v}}, \mathbf{y}, \mathbf{u}, t) - KP(\mathbf{y}, t)\hat{\mathbf{v}} + K\dot{\mathbf{y}} - Kg(\mathbf{y}, \mathbf{u}). \tag{10}$$

Rearranging (10) by moving $K\dot{\mathbf{y}}$ to the left side of the equation it results

$$\frac{d}{dt} \underbrace{(\hat{\mathbf{v}} - K\mathbf{y})}_{\bar{\mathbf{v}}} = \mathbf{f}_1(\hat{\mathbf{v}}, \mathbf{y}, \mathbf{u}, t) - Kg(\mathbf{y}, \mathbf{u}) - KP(\mathbf{y}, t)\hat{\mathbf{v}}.$$

Finally, the dynamic of the implementable reduced-order observer is given by

$$\dot{\bar{\mathbf{v}}} = \mathbf{f}_1(\hat{\mathbf{v}}, \mathbf{y}, \mathbf{u}, t) - K[g(\mathbf{y}, \mathbf{u}) + P(\mathbf{y}, t)\hat{\mathbf{v}}], \tag{11a}$$
$$\hat{\mathbf{v}} = \bar{\mathbf{v}} + K\mathbf{y}. \tag{11b}$$

Recalling the van der Pol oscillator, the reduced-order contracting observer is of the form

$$\dot{\bar{v}} = - (y^2 - 1)\hat{v} + h(y, t) - K\hat{v},$$
$$\hat{v} = \bar{v} + Ky.$$

3.2   Complete-Order

Consider the complete-order observer for system (6a, 6b)

$$\dot{\hat{\mathbf{v}}} = \mathbf{f}_1(\hat{\mathbf{v}}, \mathbf{y}, \mathbf{u}, t) + K_v(\mathbf{y}, t)(\mathbf{v} - \hat{\mathbf{v}}) + P^\top(\mathbf{y}, t)(\mathbf{y} - \hat{\mathbf{y}}), \tag{12a}$$
$$\dot{\hat{\mathbf{y}}} = P(\mathbf{y}, t)\hat{\mathbf{v}} + g(\mathbf{y}, \mathbf{u}) + K_y(\mathbf{y} - \hat{\mathbf{y}}), \tag{12b}$$

with $K_y = K_y^\top \geq K_0$. The dynamic of the observer used to estimate the unmeasurable states maintains the same form as in the reduced-order observer plus a new term related to the measurable vector $\mathbf{y}$. Let $\mathbf{x} = \begin{bmatrix} \mathbf{v}^\top & \mathbf{y}^\top \end{bmatrix}^\top$ and $\hat{\mathbf{x}}$ the associate estimate vector. Then, the particular solution $\hat{\mathbf{x}} = \mathbf{x}$ is verified. The Jacobian matrix of (12a, 12b) has the form

$$\mathbf{J} = \begin{bmatrix} \dfrac{\partial \mathbf{f}_1(\hat{\mathbf{v}}, \mathbf{y}, \mathbf{u}, t)}{\partial \hat{\mathbf{v}}} - K_v(\mathbf{y}, t) & -P^\top(\mathbf{y}, t) \\ P(\mathbf{y}, t) & -K_y \end{bmatrix}, \tag{13}$$

and its symmetric part is given below by

$$\mathbf{J}_s = \mathrm{diag}([\dfrac{\partial \mathbf{f}_1(\hat{\mathbf{v}}, \mathbf{y}, \mathbf{u}, t)}{\partial \hat{\mathbf{v}}} - K_v(\mathbf{y}, t)]_s, -K_y) \leq -\lambda\mathbf{I}, \tag{14}$$

where $\lambda = \min(K, K_y)$. Hence, it follows from Theorems 1 and 2 that (12a, 12b) converges exponentially with contracting rate λ to the target system. Recurring to the same procedure as in the reduced-order observer, the implementable complete-order observer is obtained as

$$\dot{\bar{\mathbf{v}}} = \mathbf{f}_1(\hat{\mathbf{v}}, \mathbf{y}, \mathbf{u}, t) - K[g(\mathbf{y}, \mathbf{u}) + P(\mathbf{y}, t)\hat{\mathbf{v}}] + P^\top(\mathbf{y}, t)(\mathbf{y} - \hat{\mathbf{y}}), \tag{15a}$$
$$\dot{\hat{\mathbf{y}}} = P(\mathbf{y}, t)\hat{\mathbf{v}} + g(\mathbf{y}, \mathbf{u}) + K_y(\mathbf{y} - \hat{\mathbf{y}}), \tag{15b}$$
$$\hat{\mathbf{v}} = \bar{\mathbf{v}} + K\mathbf{y}, \tag{15c}$$
$$\hat{\mathbf{v}}_s = \bar{\mathbf{v}} + K\hat{\mathbf{y}}, \tag{15d}$$

where $\hat{\mathbf{v}}_s$ is taken as the observer output in order to reduce the impact of a possible noisy signal $\mathbf{y}$, being replaced by the estimate $\hat{\mathbf{y}}$.

3.3 Synchronized Observer

Now, consider a noisy system described by the Itô stochastic differential equations

$$dv = f_1(v, y)dt, \tag{16a}$$

$$dy = f_2(v, y)dt, \tag{16b}$$

$$y_i = y + \sigma_w w_i, \quad i = 1, \dots, N, \tag{16c}$$

where y_i denotes the i-th measurement of the output y corrupted by white noise w_i with intensity σ_w. It has been shown [4] that if (16a 16b, 16c) is contracting for some $\lambda > 0$, then the square distance between each synchronized complete-order observer of the form

$$d\hat{v}_i = [f_1(\hat{v}_i, y_i) + K_s \sum_j (\hat{v}_j - \hat{v}_i)]dt, \tag{17a}$$

$$d\hat{y}_i = [f_2(\hat{v}_i, y_i) + K(t)(y_i - \hat{y}_i) + K_s \sum_j (\hat{y}_j - \hat{y}_i)]dt, \tag{17b}$$

with $j = 1, \dots, N$ and K_s the synchronization gain, and the mean value $\bar{x} = \frac{1}{N} \sum_i \hat{x}_i$ is upper bounded by (see [4] for details)

$$\|\bar{x} - \hat{x}\|^2 \leq \frac{N(N-1)}{4N^2} \frac{H_{bd}(k_{max}^2 + l_F^2 \sigma_w^2)}{\lambda_f + K_s N} + \frac{(k_{max}^2 + l_F^2 \sigma_w^2)}{N}. \tag{18}$$

Notice the left side of (18) can be reduced as the number of synchronized observers is increased, $i.e.$, as $N \to \infty$ and by Theorem 9 of [4] the synchronized observer recovers the estimation of both measurable and unmeasurable states as the noise free case. Thus, a modified version of (17) based on the complete-order observer presented above is proposed as

$$d\bar{v}_i = [f_1(\hat{v}_i, y_i, u, t) - K[g(y_i, u) + P(y_i, t)\hat{v}_i] + P^\top(y_i, t)(y_i - \hat{y}_i) + K_s \sum_j (\hat{v}_j - \hat{v}_i)]dt, \tag{19a}$$

$$d\hat{y}_i = [P(y_i, t)\hat{x}_i + g(y_i, u) + K_y(y_i - \hat{y}_i) + K_s \sum_j (\hat{y}_j - \hat{y}_i)]dt, \tag{19b}$$

$$\hat{v}_i = \bar{v}_i + Ky_i, \tag{19c}$$

$$\hat{v}_s = \bar{v}_i + K\hat{y}_i. \tag{19d}$$

4   Simulation

In this section we illustrate the behavior of all the observers schemes developed in the last sections over two different nonlinear models. The first one is the aforementioned VP oscillator followed by the FN neuron model given by

$$\dot{v} = -\frac{1}{c}(y - a + bv), \tag{20a}$$

$$\dot{y} = -\frac{1}{3}y^3 + y + v + I, \tag{20b}$$

where y represents the rate of change of the neuron membrane potential and v is related to the ion current in the neuron. a, b, c are constant parameters and the input value I determines the excitation output mode of the model, either spiking or quiet. In this case, one immediately verifies that $g(y, t) = -\frac{1}{3}y^3 + y + I$ and $P(y, t) = 1$. In both cases the output signals are corrupted by gaussian noise with standard deviation $\sigma_w = 0.2$ and mean $\mu = 0$. All the initial conditions of the observers were fixed equal to zero and those for the targets models were established as $v(0) = 0.5$ and $y(0) = -0.5$. The corresponding values of the gains are $K_s = 10$, $K = 15$, $K_y = 30$. The parameters of the FN model were selected as $a = 0.7$, $b = 0.1$, $c = 3.5$ and $I = 0.5$ (spiking mode). In the case of the van der Pol oscillator, the function h is of the form $h(y, t) = -3y + \frac{t}{t+1}y^2 + y\,sin(t)$ and the number of synchronized observers was established as $N = 50$. In order to quantify the error reduction, the reduced (11a, 11b), complete (15a, 15b, 15c, 15d) and synchronized (19a, 19b, 19c, 19d) RMS estimation error is calculated over steady state $t \in [10, 25](sec)$ and enlisted in Table 1. Performance improvement of the synchronized and the complete order observer is showed in Fig. 1 for the van der Pol and FitzHugh-Nagumo models, respectively. Notice that the reduced-order observer amplifies the noisy output measurements through the term $K\mathbf{y}$ used in the calculation of $\hat{\mathbf{v}}$. The large RMS

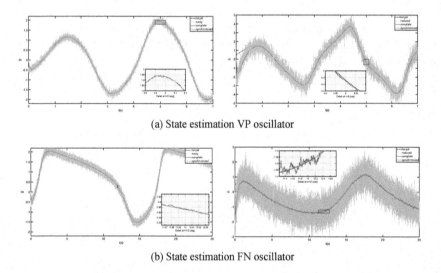

(a) State estimation VP oscillator

(b) State estimation FN oscillator

Fig. 1. The target dynamic is given in black (dashed), the reduced-order observer response and the noisy output measurements are in green (dotted), the complete-order one is given in blue (solid) and the synchronized observer is in red (dash-dotted). (Color figure online)

errors in Table 1 related to this case confirm the noise amplification. Nevertheless, these errors are significantly reduced if the estimation of $\mathbf{v}$ is made by the use of the output estimation $\hat{\mathbf{y}}$ instead of the original output corrupted by noise. As Table 1 indicates, further noise reduction is achieved with the synchronization of several complete-order observers over a single one.

Table 1. RMS Errors of VP and FN Observers for $t \in [10, 25](sec)$

Oscillator	Error	Reduced	Complete	Synchronized
van der Pol	$v - \hat{v}$	38.2077	0.1314	0.0584
	$y - \hat{y}$	–	0.0005	0.000026
FitzHugh-Nagumo	$v - \hat{v}$	38.1254	0.0802	0.0087
	$y - \hat{y}$	–	0.00048	0.000016

5   Conclusions

In this paper, we have presented a new design scheme of observers for neuronal oscillators whose rate of convergence has been proved to be exponential in a noise-free environment. Moreover, when the output measurements are corrupted by noise, synchronized complete-order observers have been developed in order to reduce the noise impact on both measurable and unmeasurable states. Simulations are provided to show a gradual improvement of estimation performance on the reduced, complete and synchronized observers in this last scenario. Finally, the results presented in this paper could be extended to study systems with unknown parameters and to the case where the measurable states are described as a nonlinear function of the unmeasurable dynamics, in order to include a more extensive class of nonlinear oscillators.

References

1. Dani, A., Chung, S.J., Hutchinson, S.: Observer design for stochastic nonlinear systems via contraction-based incremental stability. IEEE Trans. Autom. Control **60**(3), 700–714 (2015)
2. Fairhurst, D., Tyukin, I., Nijmeijer, H., van Leeuwen, C.: Observers for canonic models of neural oscillators. Math. Model. Nat. Phenom. **5**, 146–184 (2010)
3. Ghorbanian, P., Ramakrishnan, S., Whitman, A., Ashrafiuon, H.: A phenomenological model of EEG based on the dynamics of a stochastic Duffing-van der Pol oscillator network. Biomed. Sig. Process. Control **15**, 1–10 (2015)
4. Grave, I., Tang, Y.: A new observer for perspective vision systems under noisy measurements. IEEE Trans. Autom. Control **60**(2), 503–508 (2015)
5. Hinterberger, T., Kbler, A., Kaiser, J., Neumann, N., Birbaumer, N.: A braincomputer interface (BCI) for the locked-in: comparison of different EEG classifications for the thought translation device. Clin. Neurophysiol. **114**(3), 416–425 (2003)
6. Khalil, H.: Nonlinear Systems. Prentice Hall, Upper Saddle River (2002)

7. Lohmiller, W., Slotine, J.J.: On metric observers for nonlinear systems. In: Proceedings of the 1996 IEEE International Conference on Control Applications. pp. 320–326, September 1996
8. Lohmiller, W., Slotine, J.J.: On contraction analysis for non-linear systems. Automatica **34**(6), 683–696 (1998)
9. Sanfelice, R., Praly, L.: On the performance of high-gain observers with gain adaptation under measurement noise. Automatica **47**(10), 2165–2176 (2011)
10. Steur, E., Tyukin, I., Nijmeijer, H.: Semi-passivity and synchronization of diffusively coupled neuronal oscillators. Phys. D: Nonlinear Phenom. **238**(21), 2119–2128 (2009)
11. Tabareau, N., Slotine, J.J., Pham, Q.C.: How synchronization protects from noise. PLoS Comput. Biol. **6**(1), e1000637 (2010)
12. Wang, W., Slotine, J.J.: On partial contraction analysis for coupled nonlinear oscillators. Biol. Cybern. **92**(1), 38–53 (2005)
13. Ward, L.: Synchronous neural oscillations and cognitive processes. Trends Cognit. Sci. **7**(12), 553–559 (2003)
14. Wolpaw, J., Birbaumer, N., McFarland, D., Pfurtscheller, G., Vaughan, T.M.: Braincomputer interfaces for communication and control. Clin. Neurophysiol. **113**(6), 767–791 (2002)

Residence Time Regulation in Chemical Processes: Local Optimal Control Realization by Differential Neural Networks

Tatyana Poznyak[1], Isaac Chairez[2(✉)], and Alexander Poznyak[3]

[1] Superior School of Chemical Engineering and Extractive Industries, IPN,
Mexico City, Mexico
tpoznyak@ipn.mx
[2] Professional Interdsciplinary Unit of Biotechnology, IPN, Mexico City, Mexico
jchairezo@ipn.mx
[3] Automatic Control Department, CINVESTAV-IPN, Mexico City, Mexico
apoznyak@ctrl.cinvestav.mx

Abstract. A new method to design local optimal controller for uncertain system governed by continuous flow transformations (CFT) is presented. The on-line solution of the adaptive gains adjusting a linear control form yields the calculus of the sub-optimal controller. A special performance index, oriented to solve the transient evolution of CFT systems, is proposed. The class of systems considered in this study is highly uncertain: some components of chemical reactions are no measurable on line and then, they cannot be used in the controller realization. The recovering of this information was executed by a differential neural network (DNN) structure. The ozonation process of a single contaminant (as the particular example of CFT) is evaluated in detail using the control design proposed here.

Keywords: Differential Neural Networks · Local optimal control
Uncertain systems · Ozonation processes

1 Introduction

Sequential as well as simultaneous chemical and biochemical transformations characterize the dynamics of a relevant majority of industrial processes. These transformations may occur in diverse reaction regimes including batch, continuous or semi-batch. Semi-batch is a class of hybrid regimen where some reactants stay in the reactor during the entire reaction and some other reactants flow continuously through the reactor but still participate in the chemical transformations. Oxygen in the aerobic microbiological transformation is an example of such compounds that flows continuously, yielding the concept of continuous flow transformations (CFT) [4].

© Springer International Publishing AG, part of Springer Nature 2018
T. Huang et al. (Eds.): ISNN 2018, LNCS 10878, pp. 745–756, 2018.
https://doi.org/10.1007/978-3-319-92537-0_85

The semi-batch regimen offers several advantages compared to other reaction regimes (such as safer and environment friendly chemistry). It also increases mass and heat transfer, provides a higher degree of control of the process, etc. In consequence, the process time, needed to complete the reaction, can be decreased. Therefore, the reaction rate can be augmented to its maximum theoretical value.

The concept of *flash chemistry*, emerged recently to characterize reactions and it involves consecutive and simultaneous CFT, yielding reactive intermediates, competing reaction pathways, exothermic transformations and undesired accumulation of by-products [10].

Effective flash chemical reactions require the implementation of robust (against perturbations and modeling uncertainties) but precise regulation of the residence time for the reactant flowing in the reactor. The precise control of the reaction requires mixing executed in a period of time smaller than the residence time. Therefore, efficient mixers are needed in the reactor configuration.

Usually, CFT can be modeled by gathering the characteristics of mass transfer and kinetic processes (including the presence of reaction accelerators such as catalysts). Mass transfer may consider the injection of an external gaseous compound that regulates the kinetic reaction (oxygen, ozone, carbon dioxide, etc.). This reagent participates actively in the flash CFT and its *residence time* in the reactor is a primary reaction condition that should be controlled precisely. In general, the residence time of this reagent depends on two operation conditions: gas flow $W_g, L \cdot s^{-1}$ and its concentration with respect to the carrier gas $c_{g,in}, mole \cdot L^{-1}$. The product of these two variables defines the mass flow $(mole \cdot s^{-1})$ of the reactant entering into the reactor which is passively limited by the mass transfer coefficient $k_L a, s^{-1}$. In consequence, the residence time is strictly defined by the product of W_g and $c_{g,in}$ [7].

In general, there is an intrinsic relationship between W_g or $c_{g,in}$. The adjustment of one of these variables affects the value of the other one. This effect introduces a challenging design process for the operation conditions, if a specific mass transfer is needed to regulate the residence time. Even more, if an optimal regimen (theoretical solution) is desired in the reactor operation, the strict optimal control of these two interconnected variables is mandatory.

A large number of optimal control solutions has been obtained in a wide diversity of science and engineering fields since the 1950s [5]. Two principal theories have been used to get the optimal close-loop control designs: *Maximum Principle* and *Dynamic Programming*. In both cases, analytic solutions are rarely obtained in closed-loop form because there is a necessity of solving complex partial differential equations (the so-called Hamilton-Jacobi-Bellman-Isaacs equation) that yields to the calculus of the control law ensuring the global and perhaps unique optimal solution, even in the presence of some control and state constraints. Another important restriction of these classical methods is the requirements of the complete knowledge of the model and on-line access to all states of the process.

Nowadays, there is a fast increment in researching efforts devoted to designing intelligent control systems which are not optimal at all, but offers good transient as well as stable steady state behaviors. The application of such controllers on diverse practical systems is restricted because no optimal (even local) behavior can be ensured. This is a major drawback in extending the class of systems that can be controlled by such artificial intelligent solutions. The so-called intelligent optimal control designs are usually exhibiting a local solution because the approximation needed to represent the system that should be controlled. Nowadays, there are diverse options to realize the non-parametric approximation of the uncertain systems governed by CFT.

Artificial neural networks (ANN) are used as primary tools to design reliable solutions in the process control framework [1]. These solutions are used mainly in situations where there is poor knowledge of the system or just a few of its variables can be measured on-line [8]. There is a plenty of process control researchers who have replaced conventional control solutions (which demonstrated inefficiency because the number of assumptions that must be fulfilled before they can be applied in real systems) with alternative solution which used ANN or some similar methods as the key element in the controller [9]. Moreover, some classical problems in systems theory like modeling of dynamic systems, parameter identification, optimization and trajectory tracking are now performed using such adaptive algorithms in a simpler and usually more effective manner, when compared to the solutions obtained by classical techniques. *Dynamic neural network* (DNN) is used as a control trajectory priming system with learning, generalization and encapsulating capabilities [6]. This adaptive modeling technique seems to be a natural option to produce reliable approximation of the uncertain system that should be controlled. This approximation can be used eventually as part of the optimization solution realized by the Local Optimal concept [3]. The locality of the solution is enforced since the validity of the approximation (produced by the DNN) is sustained only in a bounded region of the state space.

The contributions of this study are:

- the design of a local optimal controller is based on the DNN approximation of the uncertain system;

- the control actions are realized by the on-line minimization of a feasible performance index characterizing the gas mass, consumed during the reaction, as well as the current concentration of each compound.

The challenges of designing the controller include the necessity of proposing new learning laws that can enforce the convergence of the identification error to the origin. Even more, the close-loop controller using the DNN estimation introduces the necessity of estimating the variation of the performance index.

The *organization of this manuscript* is the follows. In Sect. 2, we present the concept of LOC and explain how it can be applied for the class of systems governed by CFT. The Sect. 3 describes the nonlinear optimization problem based on LOC. Also, the same section shows the application of DNN to reconstruct the non-measurable variables of the system that were eventually used in the sub-optimal control design. Simulation results are given in Sect. 4 for the control design detailed in this study. Section 5 closes the paper with some final remarks.

2 Local Optimal Control for Processes Regulated by CFT

The determination of optimal experimental conditions of processes, controlled by CFT under several uncertain factors, constitutes the basic optimization problem considered in this study. Optimization problems of dynamic processes are typically quite challenging for real-time applications. Even more challenging are the on-line control applications that must satisfy strict real-time state constraints. Many systems regulated by CFT are hardly optimized. Moreover, in real practice, the vast majority of CFT governed processes deals with multimodal performance indexes that must be optimized considering the presence of the uncertainties or perturbations. This is the reason because these solutions lead to sub-optimal controllers.

The successful optimization of CFT processes requires the consideration of the following topics: (a) laminar flow synthesis, (b) mass and energy balances, (c) equipment sizing, (d) process simulation and (e) controller designing that provides the fulfilling of some objective aims. Sometimes, some economic evaluations are required additionally to justify the suggested sub-optimal control. Nevertheless, an accurate model of the process is crucial for achieving good economical performance. Even more, the control and states restrictions must be considered in the sub-optimal control design. This is a main condition because of the strict relationships between $c_{g,in}$ and W_g with the residence time.

Admissible Set of Control Actions. The first step in the sub-optimal control designing for CFT governed processes is the definition of admissible control functions. Usually, the relationship between both elements $c_{g,in}$ and W_g for the reactant c_g in the control design is established in the following manner:

1. Fixing the gas flow-rate $W_g = u_1$ ($L \cdot s^{-1}$) in the reactor, the desired reactant concentration $c_{g,in} = u_2/u_1$ at the reactor input can be established by adjusting an additional characteristic in the device used to produce/inject the reactant. For example, the corresponding selection of the power discharge voltage u_0 ($k \cdot V$) of the ozone generator, that is:

$$u_2 = u_1 c_{g,in}(u_0, u_1) = \varphi(u_0, u_1) u_1$$

   where the function φ is a specific mapping for each individual device.

2. Fixing the value of u_0, an hence, fixing the desired concentration $c_{g,in}(u_0, u_1) = u_2/u_1$, one can change the properties of the CFT varying the flow-rate $W_g = u_1$, i.e.,

$$u_1 = u_2/c_{g,in}(u_0, u_1) \tag{1}$$

One example of the function $\varphi(u_0, u_1)$ is depicted in Fig. 1.

Notice that admissible set of possible control variables $u_1 = W_g$ and $u_2/u_1 = c_{g,in}$ are

$$W_g^- := u_1^- \leq u_1 \leq u_1^+ =: W_g^+$$
$$\varphi^-(u_1) := c_{g,in}^-(u_1) \leq \varphi(u_0, u_1) \leq c_{g,in}^+(u_1) := \varphi^+(u_1) \tag{2}$$

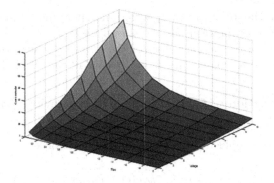

Fig. 1. Example of the functional relationship between the flow and concentration of the reagent $c_{g,in}$ entering into the reactor regulated by CFT.

Then, $u_1^- \leq u_1 \leq u_1^+$, $u_2^- := \max_{u_1} u_1 \varphi^-(u_1) \leq$, $u_1 c_{g,in}(u_0, u_1) = u_2 \leq$, $\max_{u_1} u_1 \varphi^+(u_1) =: u_2^+$. By the physical sense, both low constraints are equal to zero, that is, $u_1^- = u_2^- = 0$.

2.1 CFT System as an Uncertain Plant

We are interested in the solution optimization problem for the CFT process, represented by

$$\frac{d}{dt}x(t) = f(x(t), u(t)) + \xi(x(t), t) \tag{3}$$

where $x = [c_g, Q/V_{liq}, c_1, ..., c_N]^{\top}$. Here $Q, mole$ is the mass amount of ozone dissolved in the liquid phase with a volume V_{liq}, L and $c_j, mole \cdot L^{-1}$, $j = 1, ..., N$ represents the concentration of compound j that reacts with c_g with a bimolecular reaction rate $k_j, L \cdot mole^{-1} \cdot s^{-1}$. The term ξ describes the non-modeled elements in the reaction (internal uncertainties) or the external perturbations for the model. These perturbations are represented by satisfy the boundedness condition given by

$$\|\xi_t\|^2 \leq \xi^+ \ \forall t \geq 0, \ \xi^+ \in \mathbb{R}^+$$

Usually, this model is uncertain because the kinetic parameters k_j are unknown and the only measurable on-line output of the system is $y = c_{g,in}$. These factors force the design to consider the reaction system as *an uncertain plant* whose mathematical model contains both uncertain parameters and non-measurable states Q and c_j.

The application of the DNN theory permits to obtain the estimates of the non measurable states. The corresponding information can be obtained without the strict mathematical expression of the reaction system (3). In view of the state reconstruction method, based on DNN, it is possible to assume that

$$\hat{Q}(t) \simeq Q(t) \text{ and } \hat{c}_j(t) \simeq c_j(t) \ (j = \overline{1, N})$$

where $\hat{Q}$ is the estimate of Q and $\hat{c}_j$ is the corresponding estimate of c_j. Therefore, the optimization problem can be solved using the estimated variables by the DNN instead of the actual values of the Q and c_j. Now, the local optimal control may be realized based on the application of the DNN observers.

2.2   Reconstruction of Contaminant Concentrations by DNN

The estimation of unmeasured variables of the uncertain CFT system (3) can be obtained by the application of the following DNN observer:

$$\frac{d}{dt}\hat{x}(t) = \hat{f}\left(\hat{x}(t), u(t), W(t), V(t)\right) + L_1 e(t) + L_2 \text{sign}\left(e(t)\right) + L_3\left(e(t) - e(t-h)\right)$$
(4)

where $\hat{x} = \left[\hat{c}_g, \hat{Q}/V_{liq}, \hat{c}_1, \ldots, \hat{c}_N\right]^\top$ is the estimated state and $u = [u_1, u_2]^\top$. Each variable in $\hat{x}$ corresponds to the estimated state of (3). The function $\hat{f}$ describes the approximated function represented by the DNN and it is given by

$$\hat{f}(\hat{x}) = A\hat{x} + W_1\sigma(\hat{x}) + W_2\phi_1(\hat{x})u_1 + W_3\phi_2(\hat{x})u_2.$$

Define $W = [W_1, W_2, W_3]$ and $V = [V_1, V_2, V_3]$. The matrices W and V describe the weights of the output and hidden layer in the DNN structure. The variables σ, ϕ_1 and ϕ_2 are the activation vectors functions. The matrices L_1, L_2 and L_3 describe the correction gains of the observer based on DNN for the linear term, the discontinuous term and the delayed approximation of derivative term, respectively. The learning laws providing the weights adjustment is suggested as:

$$\left.\begin{array}{l} \dfrac{d}{dt}W(t) = \Phi\left(W(t), V(t), \hat{x}(t), y(t), u(t), t\right) \\[2mm] \dfrac{d}{dt}V(t) = \Psi\left(V(t), W(t), \hat{x}(t), y(t), u(t), t\right) \end{array}\right\}$$
(5)

The detailed structure of both functions Φ and Ψ can be consulted in [6]. Based on this description, the estimation of c_g, Q and c_j are

$$\left.\begin{array}{l} \dfrac{d}{dt}\hat{c}^g\left(t\right) = A_g\left(t\right) + B_{1,g}\left(t\right)u_1\left(t\right) + B_{2,g}\left(t\right)u_2\left(t\right) \\[2mm] \dfrac{d}{dt}\hat{Q}\left(t\right) = A_Q\left(t\right) + B_{1,Q}\left(t\right)u_1\left(t\right) + B_{2,Q}\left(t\right)u_2\left(t\right) \\[2mm] \dfrac{d}{dt}\hat{c}_j\left(t\right) = A_{c_j}\left(t\right), \ j=\overline{1,N} \end{array}\right\}$$
(6)

where the terms A_g, $B_{1,g}$ and $B_{2,g}$ are given by

$$A_g = a_{1,1}\hat{c}_g + a_{1,2}\hat{Q}/V_{liq} + \sum_{i=1}^N a_{1,2+i}\hat{c}_i + H_1^\top\left[W_1\sigma(V_1\hat{x}) + L_1 e + L_2\text{sign}\left(e\right) + L_3\left(e - e_{-h}\right)\right]$$
$$B_{1,g} = H_1^\top W_2\Phi_1(V_2\hat{x}), \quad B_{2,g} = H_1^\top W_3\Phi_2(V_3\hat{x})$$
(7)

The terms included in the estimation of Q are:

$$\frac{A_Q}{V_{liq}} = a_{2,1}\hat{c}_g + \frac{a_{2,2}\hat{Q}}{V_{liq}} + \sum_{i=1}^{N} a_{2,2+i}\hat{c}_i + H_2^{\top}\left[W_1\sigma(V_1\hat{x}) + L_{1,2}e + L_{2,2}\text{sign}(e) + L_{3,2}(e - e_h)\right],$$
$$B_{1,Q} = H_2^{\top}W_2\Phi_1(V_2\hat{x}), \quad B_{2,Q} = H_2^{\top}W_3\Phi_2(V_3\hat{x})$$

$$(8)$$

The elements used to estimate the dynamics of variables for the concentrations c_j are:

$$A_{c_i} = a_{2+i,1}\hat{c}_g + \frac{a_{2+i,2}\hat{Q}}{V_{liq}} + \sum_{s=1}^{N} a_{2+i,2+s}\hat{c}_s +$$
$$H_{2+i}^{\top}\left[W_1\sigma(V_1\hat{x}) + L_{1,2+i}e + L_{2,2+i}\text{sign}(e) + L_{3,2+i}(e - e_h)\right]$$

$$(9)$$

Here $H_l \in \mathbb{R}^{N+2}$, $H_l = 1$ in the l component and $H_l = 0$ otherwise.

3   Integral Optimization Method

3.1   Main Optimization Criteria for the LOC Designing

Optimal control is an extension of the calculus of variations and consists of a mathematical optimization method for deriving control policies. Classical optimal control theory deals with *exact (non-approximative) models of the processes* with the final aim of deriving a feedback law realizing the extreme value of the considered cost functional. Then, this theory cannot be applied if the model is uncertain or the variables are not available on-line. That is the reason that justifies the application of the so-called, *Local Optimal Control Method* [2,3,6] which is simpler (but not exact) than classical optimal control and admit justifiable practical realization. Notice that for the case of systems regulated by CFT, besides of the model uncertainty, the *multi-criterion character* of the optimization problem must be taken into account: the LOC action should realize two main tasks in the reaction simultaneously:

- *Maximal contaminants decomposition*, corresponding to the most efficient decomposition effect in the reactor;
- *Minimal concentration at the rector output of the injected reactant*, realizing the most effective regime of CFT with the minimal fraction of unused reactant c_g which may reduce the economical efficiency of the process.

The next section details the optimization criterion described above.

3.2   Joint Weighted Optimization Functional

For each time $t \geq 0$, let us define the *joint weighted performance index*:

$$F(\hat{c}^g(t), \hat{c}(t)) := \frac{1}{2}\left(\lambda_0[\hat{c}^g(t)]^2 - \sum_{s=1}^{N}\lambda_s\left([\hat{c}_s(t)]^2 - [\hat{c}_s(0)]^2\right)\right) + \rho \quad (10)$$

where $\rho > 0$ and λ_i $\left(i = \overline{0, N}\right)$ are weighting parameters. These weights characterize the relative *importance* of the corresponding component in the optimization process. These weights satisfy the so-called simplex-conditions: $\sum\limits_{s=0}^{N} \lambda_s = 1$, $\lambda_s \geq 0$ $\left(s = \overline{0, N}\right)$. Since the initial contaminant concentrations $\hat{c}_s(0)$ are always greater than the concentrations $\hat{c}_s(t)$ (assuming the decomposition of such compounds), it follows that for all $t \geq 0$, $F\left(\hat{c}^g(t), \hat{c}(t)\right) \geq \rho > 0$ where $\hat{c}$ is the vector formed by the set concentrations $\hat{c}_j$. Then, the performance index F is strictly positive.

Remark 1. Notice that the local aims for the control design are:
  - to minimize the term $\left[\hat{c}^g(t)\right]^2$ that corresponds to reduce as much as possible the quantity of unused reactant c_g in the reaction,

  - to maximize the term $\sum\limits_{s=1}^{N} \lambda_s \left[\hat{c}_s(t)\right]^2$, or equivalently, minimize $\left(-\sum\limits_{s=1}^{N} \lambda_s \left[\hat{c}_s(t)\right]^2\right)$, providing the maximal contaminant decomposition effect.

The global criterion of the *averaged losses minimization* on the time-interval $[0, T]$ can be formulated as follows:

$$J\left(u\left(\cdot\right)\right) := \limsup_{t \to \infty} \frac{1}{t + \varepsilon} \int\limits_{\tau=0}^{t} F\left(\hat{c}^g(\tau), \hat{c}(\tau)\right) d\tau, \ \varepsilon > 0 \qquad (11)$$

Optimal control actions $u^*(t) = \left(u_1^*(t), u_2^*(t)\right)^\top$ correspond to the solution of the following optimization problem

$$J\left(u\left(\cdot\right)\right) \to \min_{u^*(t) \in U_{adm}} \qquad (12)$$

where $U_{adm} = \left\{u \in \mathbb{R}^2 : u_1^- \leq u_1 \leq u_1^+, \ u_2^- \leq u_2 \leq u_2^+\right\}$ is the admissible set of all possible control action and variables $\hat{c}^g(t)$, $\hat{c}(t)$ are obtained by the approximation provided by the differential neural network.

3.3   Minimization of Local Losses

The exact solution of the problem (11) requires the application of the *OC methods* [5] which solution is too complex from mathematical and practical point of views. Then, by the local optimal concept instead of minimizing (11) let minimize the local losses $F\left(\hat{c}_g(t), \hat{c}(t)\right)$, given in (10) within a given class of controllers , namely, linear controllers with time-varying gain parameters. The time-derivative of the local cost-functional $F\left(\hat{c}_g(t), \hat{c}(t)\right)$ (10) satisfies:

$$\frac{d}{dt} F\left(\hat{c}_g(t), \hat{c}(t)\right) = \lambda_0 \hat{c}_g(t) \frac{d}{dt} \hat{c}_g(t) - \sum\limits_{s=1}^{N} \lambda_s \hat{c}_s(t) \frac{d}{dt} \hat{c}_s(t) =$$

$$\lambda_0 \hat{c}_g(t) \left[A_g(t) + B_{1,g}(t) u_1(t) + B_{2,g}(t) u_2(t)\right] - \sum\limits_{s=1}^{N} \lambda_s \hat{c}_s(t) A_{c_i}(t)$$

Select the applied controllers $u_1(t)$, $u_2(t)$ such that they fulfill the relations

$$\lambda_0 \hat{c}_g(t) B_{1,g}(t) u_1(t) = -k_1 \lambda_0 [\hat{c}_g(t)]^2, \quad k_1 > 0$$

$$\lambda_0 \hat{c}_g(t) A_g(t) + \lambda_0 \hat{c}_g(t) B_{2,g}(t) u_2(t) - \sum_{s=1}^{N} \lambda_s \hat{c}_s(t) A_{c_i}(t)$$

$$= \frac{k_1}{2} \sum_{s=1}^{N} \lambda_s \left([\hat{c}_s(t)]^2 - [\hat{c}_s(0)]^2 \right) + \rho$$

(13)

Such control actions, realizing the local optimal control are:

$$u_1(t) = -\frac{k_1}{2} B_{1,g}^{-1}(t) \hat{c}^g(t) \quad u_2(t) = \begin{cases} v_2(t) \text{ if } v_2(t) \le u_2^+ \\ u_2^+ \text{ if } v_2(t) > u_2^+ \end{cases}$$

(14)

where

$$v_2(t) = (B_{2,g}(t))^{-1} \left[(\lambda_0 \hat{c}^g(t))^{-1} \sum_{s=1}^{N} \lambda_s \hat{c}_s(t) \left[\frac{k_1}{2} \hat{c}_s(t) + A_{c_i}(t) \right] - A_g(t) \right]$$

(15)

Usually, the ozonation reaction is executed in the regime when $v_2(t) \le u_2^+$. The application of these controllers and in view of that $F(\hat{c}^g(t), \hat{c}(t)) \ge 0$ one gets:

$$\frac{d}{dt} F(\hat{c}_g(t), \hat{c}(t)) = -k_1 F(\hat{c}_g(t), \hat{c}(t)) \le -k_1 \rho < 0$$

which means that local loss function $F(\hat{c}_g(t), \hat{c}(t))$ monotonically decreases and therefore, tends to its minimal value. To fulfill the constraint $0 = u_1^- \le u_1 \le u_1^+$ it is sufficient to take

$$k_1 = 2u_1^+ \left[\left(\left| B_{1,g}^{-1}(t) \right| + \varepsilon \right) W_g^+ \right]^{-1}$$

(16)

4   Numerical Results

The majority of chemical processes and, in particular, ozonation can be described in a general format characterized by CFT. The resulting system of ordinary equations gathers both the ozone mass transfer and its kinetic reaction with the initial contaminants, their by-products formed and decomposed along the ozonation. In this particular process, the ozone dissolved in the aqueous phase is $Q, mole$ which is transferred from the gaseous phase (with a given ozone concentration c_g). This Q is consumed by the reaction with the contaminants as well as the corresponding by-products. The initial contaminants $(c_j, mole \cdot L^{-1}, j \in [1, N])$ are decomposed by the reaction with the dissolved ozone.

The vector $u \in \mathbb{R}^2$ describes the variables used to represent the control elements that adjust the ozonation dynamics, that is $u = [u_1, u_2]^\top$ is formed by the ozone flow injected into the reactor and gas concentration fixed at the reactor's input produced by the ozone generator. A more realistic model must consider the presence of external perturbations that may affect the ozonation and that cannot be included as part of the reactions occurring in the reactor. The nominal model f can be represented as follows:

$$
f = \begin{bmatrix} -V_g^{-1} \left[c_{g,in} W_g - u + k_{sat}(Q_{\max} - Q)\text{-}Q \sum_{i=1}^{N} k_i c_i \right] \\ k_{sat}(Q_{\max} - Q)\text{-}Q \sum_{i=1}^{N} k_i c_i \\ -k_1 \dfrac{Q}{V_{liq}} c_1 \\ \vdots \\ -k_N \dfrac{Q}{V_{liq}} c_N \end{bmatrix} \tag{17}
$$

In the nominal model (17), V_g (L) is the volume of the gaseous phase, W_g $(L \cdot s^{-1})$ is the ozone flow entering the ozonation reactor, k_{sat} (s^{-1}) is the saturation constant of ozone in water, $Q_{\max}$ $(mole)$ represents the maximum amount of ozone in the saturation state of the liquid phase at a fixed temperature, k_i $(L \cdot mole^{-1} \cdot s^{-1})$ is the reaction rate constant of the corresponding initial contaminant c_j with the ozone dissolved in the aqueous phase and V_{liq} (L) is the volume of the aqueous phase. All the reaction considered in (17) can be considered CFT because they are ruled by the interaction between ozone and the organics in the reactor.

The model (17) possesses several characteristics that may be considered in the observer design: (a) assumption of bilinear interaction with respect to the components of the state-vector, (b) not all the parameters of this model are known, (c) the contaminants concentrations can be measured using special and expensive laboratory equipment such as UV-Vis spectrophotometer, High Performance Liquid Chromatography, Gel Chromatography, Infrared spectroscopy, Nuclear Magnetic Resonance, etc. and (d) only some of components (frequently only one) of the state-vector can be measured during the process: in the case of ozonation it is the current concentration c_g of ozone in the gas-phase, $y = c_g$. Notice that the control actions are bounded and measurable. Also, the function f is locally Lipschitz, which is a technical issue that must be fulfilled if the observer described in this study should be designed. Also, the chemical nature of the states justify the assumption that all of them are bounded from above.

4.1   Variables Which Can Be Considered as Control Actuators

Recall that the mathematical model of ozonation in presence of several contaminants is given by the collection of Ordinary Differential Equation (17). Reconstruction of non-measurable variables $Q(t)$ and $c_j(t)$ is realized by the application of the DNN Observers (DNNO) (8) and (9). In ODE (17) the main parameters, which can significantly change the behavior of the process and, therefore, can be considered as the *principal control actions*, are: W_g is the gas flow-rate $(L \cdot s^{-1})$ in the ozone reactor, so that,$v_1 := W_g$, $c_{g,in}$ is the ozone concentration at the reactor input $(mole \cdot L^{-1})$, that is, $v_2 := c_{in,g}$. Notice also that in the model of the process (17) both control variables v_1 and v_2 participate as the bilinear form proposed in the introduction section, that is $u_1 := v_1 = W_g$ and $u_2 := v_1 v_2 = W_g c_{g,in}$. In this new control variables, the bilinear control term becomes to be linear one: $W_g (c_{g,in} - c_g) = v_1 v_2 - c_g v_1 = u_2 - c_g u_1$. Then, the DNN form proposed for the function $\hat{f}$ is clearly justified.

4.2 Computer Simulations

Traditionally, researchers have a priory information on the following process parameters: a) $V_g = 0.3L$ the volume of the gas phase, b) $k_{sat} = 0.2 s^{-1}$ the saturation constant of ozone in water, c) $Q_{max} = 0.05\,mol$ the maximum amount of ozone in the saturation state of the liquid phase at a fixed temperature and d) $Q_0 = Q_0 mole$ the initial amount of ozone in liquid phase. In this study, only one contaminant was considered and the constant reaction rate was ($k_1 = 1934.0L \cdot mole^{-1} \cdot s^{-1}$). This rate constant corresponds to the result obtained for phenol in [7].

Figure (2a) demonstrates the variation of ozone gas concentration c_g, Fig. (2b) shows the variation of the ozone dissolved in the liquid phase while

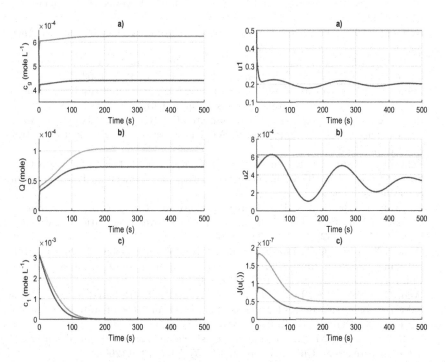

Fig. 2. Temporal behavior of the states c_g, Q and x_1 considered in the system ruled by CFT. Evaluation of the control actions u_1 and u_2 as well as the performance index J. The lines in blue represent the variables obtained with fixed values of the controllers and the lines in red corresponds to the variables obtained with the sub-optimal controller. (Color figure online)

Fig. (2c) depicts the variation of the contaminant concentration. The comparison of all the variables with respect to the values obtained when both controllers used the common constant values $u_1 = 0.5L \cdot s^{-1}$ and $u_2 = 15.0\,mg \cdot L^{-1}$.

5 Conclusions

The local optimal control developed in this study minimized the performance index, designed specially for the class of uncertain systems governed by CFT. The linear controllers with the special adaptive gains are shown to enforce the optimization process. A new adaptive observer, using the structure of DNN with additional linear, discontinues and error delayed correction terms successfully recuperate the behavior of the non-measurable states of systems. Based on the application of the reconstructed states, the evaluation of LOC with DNN observations has been successfully completed.

References

1. Haykin, S.: Neural Networks and Learning Machines. Prentice Hall, Upper Saddle River (2009)
2. Kelmans, G.K., Chernitser, A.V., Poznyak, A.: Adaptive locally optimal control. Int. J. Syst. Sci. **12**(2), 235–254 (1981)
3. Kelmans, G.K., Poznyak, A.: Chernitser: locally optimal control of plants with unknown parameters. Autom. Remote Control **43**(10), 1293–1303 (1982)
4. Mándity, I.M., Ötvös, S.B., Fülöp, F.: Strategic application of residence-time control in continuous-flow reactors. ChemistryOpen **4**(3), 212–223 (2015)
5. Pontryagin, L.S., Boltyansky, V.G., Gamkrelidze, R.V., Mishenko, E.F.: Mathematical Theory of Optimal Processes. Wiley Interscience, New York (1969). (translated from Russian)
6. Poznyak, A., Sanchez, E., Yu, W.: Differential Neural Networks for Robust Nonlinear Control (Identification, State Estimation and Trajectory Tracking). World Scientific, Singapore (2001)
7. Poznyak, T., Bautista, G.L., Chairez, I., Cordova, R.I., Rios, E.: Decomposition of toxic pollutants in landfill leachate by ozone after coagulation treatment. J. Hazard. Mater. **152**(3), 1108–1114 (2008)
8. Wen, G.X., Chen, C.P., Liu, Y.J., Liu, Z.: Neural-network-based adaptive leader-following consensus control for second-order non-linear multi-agent systems. IET Control Theory Appl. **9**(13), 1927–1934 (2015)
9. Wen, G., Chen, C.P., Liu, Y.J., Liu, Z.: Neural network-based adaptive leader-following consensus control for a class of nonlinear multiagent state-delay systems. IEEE Trans. Cybern. **47**(8), 2151–2160 (2017)
10. Yoshida, J.I., Nagaki, A., Yamada, T.: Flash chemistry: fast chemical synthesis by using microreactors. Chem.-A Eur. J. **14**(25), 7450–7459 (2008)

A Time-Varying-Constrained Motion Generation Scheme for Humanoid Robot Arms

Zhijun Zhang$^{(\boxtimes)}$, Lingdong Kong$^{(\boxtimes)}$, and Yaru Niu

School of Automation Science and Engineering,
South China University of Technology, Guangzhou 510641, China
`auzjzhang@scut.edu.cn`, `scutkld@foxmail.com`

Abstract. An efficient time-varying gesture-determined dynamical (TV-GDD) scheme is proposed for motion planning of redundant dual-arms manipulation. Motion planning for such tasks on humanoid robots with a high number of degrees-of-freedom (DOF) requires computationally efficient approaches to generate the expected joint configuration when given the end-effector tasks. To do so, we investigate a time-varying joint-limits constrained quadratic-programming (QP) approach and an efficient numerical computing method. This strategy provides feasible solutions at a low computation cost within physical limits. In addition, the joint configuration can be adjusted dynamically according to the expected gestures and tasks. Comparative simulations and experimental results on a humanoid robot demonstrate the effectiveness and feasibility of the scheme.

Keywords: Humanoid robot · Dual arms · Motion generation
Quadratic programming · Redundancy resolution

1 Introduction

Humanoid robots can help people immerse themselves in environments of peer-to-peer cooperation and are thus increasingly welcomed in various applications [1]. Dual-arms of humanoid robots can not only fulfill manipulation tasks [2], but also perform important components of the body language [3]. In contrast to the single-arm system, multi-arm systems can be more efficient by performing motions simultaneously [4]. The early multi-arm system can trace back to Goertz's remote manipulators for handling of radioactive goods in the 1940's [5]. From the late 1950's to the early 1970's, dual-arms teleoperation was developed because of the deep-sea and deep-space exploration [6].

In recent years, due to the fast development of humanoid robots [2], dual-arm applications attract researchers and engineers' interests again. Humanoid robots require dual-arms to perform daily work naturally in home environment autonomously or semi-autonomously [7]. They can also improve the sociability with displaying emotional body language [8]. To perform daily tasks with

© Springer International Publishing AG, part of Springer Nature 2018
T. Huang et al. (Eds.): ISNN 2018, LNCS 10878, pp. 757–767, 2018.
https://doi.org/10.1007/978-3-319-92537-0_86

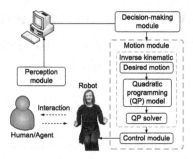

Fig. 1. System architecture of the female humanoid robot.

dual-arms of humanoid robots, the dual-arms motion planning should be considered. One of the basic problems is the inverse kinematic problem. Nunez *et al.* presented an analytic solution to humanoid robot arms [9], of which each arm has three DOF. However, most humanoid robot arms in actual applications have more DOF and are thus redundant. This redundancy improves the flexibility when the robot implement end-effector tasks [10], and inevitably increases computation difficulties. Traditional redundancy-resolution methods are pseudoinverse-based schemes. Wang and Li proposed a closed-loop inverse kinematics based on pseudoinverse method, which is used to dual-arms on a mobile platform [10]. Note that the above methods have to compute the matrix inverse, then QP methods are preferred recently. Kanoun *et al.* proposed a QP-based task priority framework to resolve the kinematic-redundancy problem [11]. Zhang and Zhang performed QP-based methods on a physical planar manipulator [12]. To solve the redundant-resolution problem effectively, two redundancy-resolution schemes are presented and their equivalence relationship was proved [13]. However, most existing optimization methods focus on a single manipulator, and only a few consider dual-arms of humanoid robots [11]. Inspired by the above works, a QP-based online generation scheme is proposed in this paper to generate expected gestures of dual-arms. The gestures are movements or positions of the hand, arm, body which express idea, intention, opinion, emotion, etc. To obtain the optimization solutions of the designed QP scheme, a discrete numerical method is presented to control the robot to finish not only tasks of end-effectors but also some expected subtasks. The architecture of this system is shown in Fig. 1. It allows an easier coordination of interaction between two arms. Before ending this section, the main contributions of this paper are as follows:

- A time-varying gesture-determined dynamical (TV-GDD) scheme for dual-arms coordinated motion generation is proposed and applied to an actual humanoid robot.
- Different from the pseudoinverse methods or QP-based methods focusing on single or planar dual arms, together with the numerical QP solver, the proposed TV-GDD scheme can on-line generate behaviors for humanoid robots.

- To enable generating expected arm configurations, a novel TV-GDD function is designed, proposed and discussed in details, which can make the arms move according to the expected gesture.

2   General Quadratic Programming Model

The presented robot in this paper is a humanoid robot with a sitting posture. It is able to display realistic facial and body expressions. It has two arms and the dual arms have 14 DOF (7 of each arm). The origin of Frame {0} is chosen at the waist (i.e., the base). The forward kinematics of the dual arms is that given the left/right joint-space vectors θ_L and θ_R, the end-effector position vectors r_L and r_R can be obtained as follows:

$$r_L = f_L(\theta_L), \ r_R = f_R(\theta_R) \tag{1}$$

where $f_L(\cdot)$ and $f_R(\cdot)$ are smooth nonlinear functions. Generally, Eq. (1) can be obtained when the structure of the robot is known. One fundamental issue for redundant robots is the inverse kinematics problem, i.e., to obtain the joint vectors with given end-effector trajectories.

The classical approaches to solving the redundancy-resolution problem are pseudoinverse methods. Specifically, at the joint-velocity level, the pseudoinverse type solution can be formulated as

$$\dot{\theta}_L = \mathcal{J}_L^{\dagger}(\theta_L)\dot{r}_L + (\mathcal{I} - \mathcal{J}_L^{\dagger}(\theta_L)\mathcal{J}_L(\theta_L))w_L \tag{2}$$

$$\dot{\theta}_R = \mathcal{J}_R^{\dagger}(\theta_R)\dot{r}_R + (\mathcal{I} - \mathcal{J}_R^{\dagger}(\theta_R)\mathcal{J}_R(\theta_R))w_R \tag{3}$$

where $\mathcal{J}_L^{\dagger}(\theta_L) \in \mathbb{R}^{n \times m}$ and $\mathcal{J}_R^{\dagger}(\theta_R) \in \mathbb{R}^{n \times m}$ denote the pseudoinverse of the Jacobian matrices $\mathcal{J}_L(\theta_L)$ and $\mathcal{J}_R(\theta_R)$; $\mathcal{I} \in \mathbb{R}^{n \times n}$ is the identity matrix; $w_L \in \mathbb{R}^n$ and $w_R \in \mathbb{R}^n$ are arbitrary vectors selected for optimization criteria.

The traditional pseudoinverse approaches (2)-(3) need to compute inverse matrices and do not properly consider the inequality problems [12]. Inspired by the previous work [13,14], an online optimization technique which resolve the redundancy problem is designed as follows:

(1) QP-based left and right arm schemes are exploited and formulated as

$$\text{minimize} \quad \dot{\theta}_L^{\mathrm{T}} \mathcal{Q} \dot{\theta}_L / 2 + b_L^T \theta_L \tag{4}$$

$$\text{subject to} \quad \mathcal{J}_L(\theta_L)\dot{\theta}_L = \dot{r}_L + \mathcal{K}_L(r_L - f_L(\theta_L)) \tag{5}$$

$$\theta_L^- \leqslant \theta_L \leqslant \theta_L^+ \tag{6}$$

$$\dot{\theta}_L^- \leqslant \dot{\theta}_L \leqslant \dot{\theta}_L^+ \tag{7}$$

$$\text{minimize} \quad \dot{\theta}_R^{\mathrm{T}} \mathcal{W} \dot{\theta}_R / 2 + b_R^{\mathrm{T}} \theta_R \tag{8}$$

$$\text{subject to} \quad \mathcal{J}_R(\theta_R)\dot{\theta}_R = \dot{r}_R + \mathcal{K}_R(r_R - f_R(\theta_R)) \tag{9}$$

$$\theta_R^- \leqslant \theta_R \leqslant \theta_R^+ \tag{10}$$

$$\dot{\theta}_R^- \leqslant \dot{\theta}_R \leqslant \dot{\theta}_R^+ \tag{11}$$

where $\mathcal{Q} \in \mathbb{R}^{n \times n}$ and $\mathcal{W} \in \mathbb{R}^{n \times n}$ are coefficients of the quadratic terms; while b_L and b_R are those pertaining to the linear terms; $\mathcal{J}_L$ and $\mathcal{J}_R$ are the Jacobian matrices of the left/right arms, defined as $\mathcal{J} = \partial f(\theta)/\partial \theta$. Eqs. (5) and (9) express linear relations between the left/right end-effector velocities $\dot{r}_L \in \mathbb{R}^m$ and $\dot{r}_R \in \mathbb{R}^m$, and joint velocities $\dot{\theta}_L \in \mathbb{R}^n$ and $\dot{\theta}_R \in \mathbb{R}^n$; $\mathcal{K}_L(r_L - f_L(\theta_L))$ and $\mathcal{K}_R(r_R - f_R(\theta_R))$ are position-error feedbacks, where $\mathcal{K}_L$ and $\mathcal{K}_R$ are positive-definite symmetric (typically diagonal) $m \times m$ feedback-gain matrices. Eqs. (6) and (10) are bound constraints of joint-angle limits. Eqs. (7) and (11) are bound constraints of joint-velocity limits.

(2) To solve the above two QP problems simultaneously, (4)-(11) should be converted to a standard QP form. The criteria (4) and (8) are integrated as

$$\text{minimize} \begin{bmatrix} \dot{\theta}_L \\ \dot{\theta}_R \end{bmatrix}^T \begin{bmatrix} W & \mathbf{0}_{n \times n} \\ \mathbf{0}_{n \times n} & Q \end{bmatrix} \begin{bmatrix} \dot{\theta}_L \\ \dot{\theta}_R \end{bmatrix} + \begin{bmatrix} b_L \\ b_R \end{bmatrix}^T \begin{bmatrix} \dot{\theta}_L \\ \dot{\theta}_R \end{bmatrix}. \tag{12}$$

(3) Forward kinematics equations of left and right arms (5) and (9) are combined together as

$$\begin{bmatrix} \mathcal{J}_L & \mathbf{0}_{3 \times 7} \\ \mathbf{0}_{3 \times 7} & \mathcal{J}_R \end{bmatrix} \cdot \begin{bmatrix} \dot{\theta}_L \\ \dot{\theta}_R \end{bmatrix} = \begin{bmatrix} \dot{r}_L \\ \dot{r}_R \end{bmatrix} + \begin{bmatrix} k_L(r_L - f_L(\theta_L)) \\ k_R(r_R - f_R(\theta_R)) \end{bmatrix} \in \mathbb{R}^{2m \times 2n}. \tag{13}$$

(4) Joint-angle and joint-velocity limits of left and right arms (6) and (10) are combined as

$$\begin{bmatrix} \theta_L^- \\ \theta_R^- \end{bmatrix} \leqslant \begin{bmatrix} \theta_L \\ \theta_R \end{bmatrix} \leqslant \begin{bmatrix} \theta_L^+ \\ \theta_R^+ \end{bmatrix} \in \mathbb{R}^{2n}, \quad \begin{bmatrix} \dot{\theta}_L^- \\ \dot{\theta}_R^- \end{bmatrix} \leqslant \begin{bmatrix} \dot{\theta}_L \\ \dot{\theta}_R \end{bmatrix} \leqslant \begin{bmatrix} \dot{\theta}_L^+ \\ \dot{\theta}_R^+ \end{bmatrix} \in \mathbb{R}^{2n}. \tag{14}$$

(5) Hence, the QP formulations (4)-(7) and (8)-(11) can be reformulated as

$$\text{minimize} \quad \dot{\vartheta}^T \mathcal{M} \dot{\vartheta}/2 + b^T \vartheta \tag{15}$$
$$\text{subject to} \quad \jmath(\vartheta)\dot{\vartheta} = \dot{\Upsilon} + \mathcal{K}(\Upsilon - f(\vartheta)) \tag{16}$$
$$\vartheta^- \leqslant \vartheta \leqslant \vartheta^+ \tag{17}$$
$$\dot{\vartheta}^- \leqslant \dot{\vartheta} \leqslant \dot{\vartheta}^+ \tag{18}$$

where $\vartheta = [\theta_L^T; \theta_R^T]^T \in \mathbb{R}^{2n}$; $b = [b_L^T; b_R^T]^T$; $\vartheta^- = [\theta_L^{-T}, \theta_R^{-T}]^T \in \mathbb{R}^{2n}$; $\vartheta^+ = [\theta_L^{+T}, \theta_R^{+T}]^T \in \mathbb{R}^{2n}$; $\dot{\vartheta} = d\vartheta/dt = [\dot{\theta}_L^T, \dot{\theta}_R^T]^T \in \mathbb{R}^{2n}$; $\dot{\vartheta}^- = [\dot{\theta}_L^{-T}, \dot{\theta}_{R-T}]^T \in \mathbb{R}^{2n}$; $\dot{\vartheta}^+ = [\dot{\theta}_L^{+T}, \dot{\theta}_R^{+T}]^T \in \mathbb{R}^{2n}$; $\dot{\Upsilon} = [\dot{r}_L^T; \dot{r}_R^T]^T \in \mathbb{R}^{2n}$; matrices $\mathcal{M} \in \mathbb{R}^{2n \times 2n}$, $\jmath \in \mathbb{R}^{2m \times 2n}$, and $\mathcal{K} \in \mathbb{R}^{2m \times 2m}$ are

$$\mathcal{M} = \begin{bmatrix} \mathcal{W} & \mathbf{0}_{n \times n} \\ \mathbf{0}_{n \times n} & Q \end{bmatrix}, \jmath = \begin{bmatrix} \mathcal{J}_L & \mathbf{0}_{m \times n} \\ \mathbf{0}_{m \times n} & \mathcal{J}_R \end{bmatrix}, \mathcal{K} = \begin{bmatrix} \mathcal{K}_L & \mathbf{0}_{m \times m} \\ \mathbf{0}_{m \times m} & \mathcal{K}_R \end{bmatrix}$$

with matrix $\mathcal{M}$ and vector b being determined by a specific redundancy-resolution scheme. $\mathcal{K}$ is the feedback gain and determined by the actual effect. In actual applications, if $\mathcal{M} = [\mathcal{H}_L, 0; 0, \mathcal{H}_R]$ with $\mathcal{H}$ denoting the inertia matrix and $b = 0$, Eqs. (15)-(18) constitute a minimum-kinetic-energy (MKE) scheme.

If $\mathcal{M}$ is set as an identity matrix and $b = [\lambda(\theta_L - \theta_L(0)); \lambda(\theta_R - \theta_R(0))]$, Eqs. (15)-(18) would be a repetitive motion planning (RMP) scheme. If $\mathcal{M}$ is set as an identity matrix, and $b = 0$, Eqs. (15)-(18) correspond to a minimum-velocity-norm (MVN) scheme. For simplicity and without causing loss of generality, the latter scheme will be used in the following sections.

3 TV-GDD Scheme and Solver

Humanoid robots not only need to perform end-effector tasks, but also desire to act as human would, like emulating human movement and adopting natural-looking postures. Therefore, a corresponding TV-GDD scheme is proposed, and it is solved by a discrete numerical solver.

3.1 TV-GDD Scheme

To enable the robot to generate expected gestures, some joints must be adjusted dynamically according to the tasks with time passing by. For QP methods, the physical limits of a joint are described as two bounds of inequality constraints. Therefore, we can find an appropriate function that can adjust the bounds of desired values. Mathematically, the function which adjusts the joints to the expected states and uses to generate desired gestures dynamically is as follows:

$$\vartheta_{\text{new}}^{\pm}(t) = \vartheta^{\pm} + \frac{\vartheta_{\text{diff}}^{\pm}}{1 + e^{-(t - \mathcal{T}_{\text{SP}})/c_{\text{tuning}}}} \qquad (19)$$

where $\vartheta_{\text{diff}}^{\pm} = \vartheta_{\text{goal}}^{\pm} - \vartheta^{\pm}$ with $\vartheta_{\text{goal}} = [\vartheta_{\text{goalL}}^{\text{T}}, \vartheta_{\text{goalR}}^{\text{T}}]^{\text{T}}$ is the expected joint configuration; $0 < c_{\text{tuning}} \leqslant 1$ is a time-tuning parameter, which tunes the variation tendency; $\mathcal{T}_{\text{SP}} = \mathcal{T}_d/N$, with $\mathcal{T}_d$ denoting the task execution duration, and $N \geqslant 1$ influences the proximity between the adjusted values and the initial value/target values. Figure 2 shows that the TV-GDD function (19) can regulate the ith initial joint value $\vartheta_i^{\pm}$ into target joint value $\vartheta_{\text{goal}i}^{\pm}$ gradually and smoothly. Without loss of generality, consider $i = 3$ as an example. If $\vartheta_{\text{goal3}}^{-} = \vartheta_{\text{goal3}}^{+} = 5$, the function can adjust the lower/upper limits of the third joint to 5 after a period of time. Given that the robot arms are redundant, kinematic task can still be performed while one or more of the joints is adjusted into an expected configuration.

Consider the TV-GDD function (19), the joint constraint (17) becomes

$$\vartheta_{\text{new}}^{-}(t) \leqslant \vartheta \leqslant \vartheta_{\text{new}}^{+}(t). \qquad (20)$$

Given that the redundancy-resolution method is performed at the velocity level, the new joint limit (20) should be formulated using the constraint of $\dot{\vartheta}$ as

$$\nu(\vartheta_{\text{new}}^{-}(t) - \vartheta) \leqslant \dot{\vartheta} \leqslant \nu(\vartheta_{\text{new}}^{+}(t) - \vartheta) \qquad (21)$$

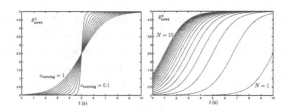

Fig. 2. New joint bounds $\theta_{\mathrm{new}i}^{\pm}$ profiles with different c_{turning} and N ($\theta_{\mathrm{goal}i}^{\pm} = 5$ and $\theta_i^{\pm} = 0$). $\theta_{\mathrm{new}i}^{\pm}$ profiles with different c_{turning} ($N = 2$, $\theta_{\mathrm{goal}i}^{\pm} = 5$, and $\theta_i^{\pm} = 0$); $\theta_{\mathrm{new}i}^{\pm}$ profiles with different N ($c_{\mathrm{turning}} = 0.9$, $\theta_{\mathrm{goal}i}^{\pm} = 5$ and $\theta_i^{\pm} = 0$), respectively.

where parameter $\nu > 0$ is used to scale the feasible region of $\dot{\vartheta}$. In this paper, ν is set as 2. For the ith element, constraints (17) and (18) can be written as

$$\max\{\dot{\vartheta}_i^-, \nu(\vartheta_{\mathrm{new}i}^-(t) - \vartheta_i)\} \leqslant \dot{\vartheta}_i \leqslant \min\{\dot{\vartheta}_i^+, \nu(\vartheta_{\mathrm{new}i}^+(t) - \vartheta_i)\}. \tag{22}$$

With $\zeta_{\mathrm{new}i}^-(t) = \max\{\dot{\vartheta}_i^-, \nu(\vartheta_{\mathrm{new}i}^-(t) - \vartheta_i)\}$ and $\zeta_{\mathrm{new}i}^+(t) = \min\{\dot{\vartheta}_i^+, \nu(\vartheta_{\mathrm{new}i}^+(t) - \vartheta_i)\}$, the TV-GDD scheme can be formulated as

$$\text{minimize} \quad \dot{\vartheta}^{\mathrm{T}} \mathcal{M} \dot{\vartheta}/2 + b^{\mathrm{T}} \vartheta \tag{23}$$

$$\text{subject to} \quad \jmath(\vartheta)\dot{\vartheta} = \dot{\Upsilon} + k(\vartheta - f(\vartheta)) \tag{24}$$

$$\zeta_{\mathrm{new}}^-(t) \leqslant \dot{\vartheta} \leqslant \zeta_{\mathrm{new}}^+(t). \tag{25}$$

Kinematic tasks and gestures are performed simultaneously by solving QP problem (23)–(25). Specifically, the gesture model formulated in (19) is integrated into inequality (25) as the bounds, and the kinematic tasks described by the end-effector paths $\dot{r}_{\mathrm{L}}$ and $\dot{r}_{\mathrm{R}}$ are integrated into (5), (9) and (24) as the right-hand sides. Subsequently, the QP-based TV-GDD scheme (23)–(25) is formulated. The scheme is then solved by a discrete QP solver, and the results are further mapped into the robot-controllable value domain. Finally, the control data are sent to the robot controller, which drives the robot to execute the end-effector tasks.

3.2   TV-GDD Scheme Solver

Equations (23)–(25) can be converted to a linear variational inequality (LVI) [12], which is further equivalent to the following linear projection equation:

$$\Phi_\Omega(u - (\Gamma u + q)) - u = 0 \tag{26}$$

where $\Phi_\Omega(\cdot) : \mathbb{R}^{2n+2m} \to \Omega$ is a projection operator, $\Omega = \{u|u^- \leqslant u \leqslant u^+\} \subset \mathbb{R}^{2n+2m}$, $1_\iota := [1, \cdots, 1]^{\mathrm{T}} \in \mathbb{R}^\iota$

$$u := \begin{bmatrix} \vartheta \\ \iota \end{bmatrix}, \quad u^+ := \begin{bmatrix} \zeta_{\mathrm{new}}^+(t) \\ \omega 1_\iota \end{bmatrix} \in \mathbb{R}^{2n+2m}, \quad u^- := \begin{bmatrix} \zeta_{\mathrm{new}}^-(t) \\ -\omega 1_\iota \end{bmatrix} \in \mathbb{R}^{2n+2m},$$

$$\Gamma := \begin{bmatrix} \mathcal{M} & -\jmath^{\mathrm{T}}(\vartheta) \\ \jmath(\vartheta) & 0 \end{bmatrix} \in \mathbb{R}^{(2n+2m) \times (2n+2m)}, \quad q := \begin{bmatrix} 0 \\ -\dot{\Upsilon} \end{bmatrix} \in \mathbb{R}^{2n+2m}.$$

In addition, $u \in \mathbb{R}^m$ is the primal-dual decision vector, $u^- \in \mathbb{R}^m$ and $u^+ \in \mathbb{R}^m$ are the lower and upper bounds of u, respectively, and ϖ is set as a sufficiently large value (e.g., in the simulations and experiments, $\varpi = 10^{10}$).

To solve Eq. (26), by defining $\varepsilon(u) := u - \Phi_\Omega(u - (\Gamma u + q))$, the following iterative algorithm causes $\varepsilon(u) \to 0$. Supposing that the initial primal-dual decision variable vector is set as $u^0 \in \mathbb{R}^{2n+2m}$, for iteration number $k = 0, 1, 2, \cdots$, if $u^k \notin \Omega^*$, then [15]

$$u^{k+1} = u^k - \frac{\|\varepsilon(u^k)\|_2^2 \sigma(u^k)}{\|\sigma(u^k)\|_2^2} \tag{27}$$

where $\varepsilon(u^k) = u^k - \Phi_\Omega(u^k - (\Gamma u^k + q))$ and $\sigma(u^k) = (\Gamma^T + I)\varepsilon(u^k)$. For the numerical calculation, $\varepsilon(u^k) = 10^{-5}$.

4 Simulations and Experiments

In this section, the scheme on the physical humanoid robot is performed. The end-effector task is to play a ball game. In the simulations, the initial joints of the left/right arms are $\vartheta_L(0) = [\pi/40, -\pi/10, \pi/30, 0, -131\pi/360, \pi/3, 11\pi/36]^T$ (rad) and $\vartheta_R(0) = [-\pi/40, \pi/10, -\pi/30, \pi, -131\pi/360, \pi/3, -25\pi/36]$ (rad), respectively. This task requires the speeds of both hands to be equal to each other; i.e., $\dot{r}_L = \dot{r}_R$. The execution duration is $T_d = 6T = 18$ s. The upper/lower limits of the joint velocities of the dual arms are 6 rad/s and -6 rad/s, respectively.

4.1 Synthesized by Pseudoinverse Scheme

For comparison, the pseudoinverse scheme (2)–(3) are applied to the redundancy problem of the dual arms. The end-effector task is to move the ball up, left, down, and then move back. This is to match the latter experiment which tries to move the ball from one cup to another. To illustrate these problems clearly, joint values and velocities of the dual arms synthesized by the pseudoinverse method are shown in Figs. 3 and 4, respectively. Evidently, the generated joint values synthesized by the traditional pseudoinverse scheme (2)–(3) run out of the expected values. That is to say, it cannot accomplish the expected gesture-configuration task. In summary, from the above analysis, the traditional pseudoinverse scheme (2)–(3) is unexpected in actual applications. Specifically, one problem is some joint values or velocities may exceed their physical limits. Another problem is the hands cannot hold the rod stably and the hand gesture would be very strange due to the free rotation of the forearms and wrist.

4.2 Synthesized by TV-GDD Scheme

The TV-GDD scheme is employed to complete the same end-effector task. To keep the forearms and waists moving as little as possible and finally go to an expected gesture, the TV-GDD function (19) is employed. Specifically, $T_{SP} =$

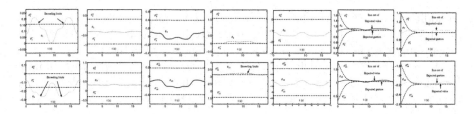

Fig. 3. Dual-arms joint values of the humanoid robot synthesized by pseudoinverse scheme (2)-(3). The ith joint value $\vartheta_{\mathrm{new}i}$ and the bounds $\vartheta_{\mathrm{new}i}^{\pm}$ with $i = 1, 2, ..., 14$.

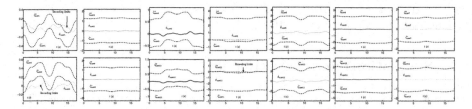

Fig. 4. Joint-velocities synthesized by pseudoinverse scheme (2)-(3) that exceed their limits. The ith joint velocity $\dot{\vartheta}_{\mathrm{new}i}$ subject to $\zeta_{\mathrm{new}i}^{\pm}$ with $i = 1, 2, \ldots, 14$, respectively.

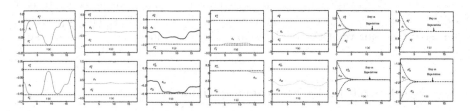

Fig. 5. Dual-arms joint values of the humanoid robot synthesized by TV-GDD scheme (23)-(25). The ith joint value $\vartheta_{\mathrm{new}i}$ subject to $\vartheta_{\mathrm{new}i}^{\pm}$ with $i = 1, 2, \ldots, 14$, respectively.

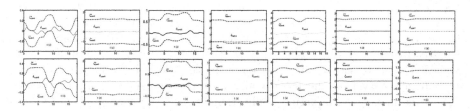

Fig. 6. Dual-arms joint velocities of the humanoid robot synthesized by TV-GDD scheme (23)-(25). The ith joint velocity $\dot{\vartheta}_{\mathrm{new}i}$ subject to $\zeta_{\mathrm{new}i}^{\pm}$ with $i = 1, 2, \ldots, 14$.

0.75 s, $c_{\mathrm{tuning}} = 1$, $\vartheta_{\mathrm{goalL}}^{+} = [9\pi/180, \pi/10, 22.5\pi/180, \pi/2, 0, \pi/3, 55\pi/180]^{\mathrm{T}}$ rad, $\vartheta_{\mathrm{goalL}}^{-} = [0, -54\pi/180, -10.5\pi/180, 0, -131\pi/180, \pi/3, 55\pi/180]^{\mathrm{T}}$ rad, $\vartheta_{\mathrm{goalR}}^{+} = [0, 54\pi/180, 10.5\pi/180, \pi, 0, \pi/3, -25\pi/36]^{\mathrm{T}}$ rad, $\vartheta_{\mathrm{goalR}}^{-} = [-9\pi/180, -18\pi/180, -22.5\pi/180, \pi/2, -131\pi/180, \pi/3, -25\pi/36]^{\mathrm{T}}$ rad.

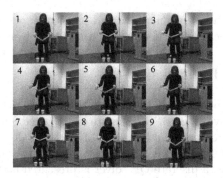

Fig. 7. Snapshots of task execution when the humanoid robot plays with a ball.

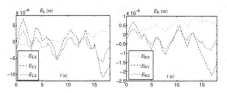

Fig. 8. Positioning-errors of end-effectors (hands) synthesized by the TV-GDD scheme.

To illustrate the effectiveness of the combined time-varying constraint (25) in the scheme, the joint values and velocities of the dual arms during the execution of the task are shown in Figs. 5–6. As shown in Fig. 5, with (19), the upper/lower joint limits tend to overlap after approximately 5 s. This drives joints ϑ_6, ϑ_7, ϑ_{13} and ϑ_{14} to an expected configuration. Furthermore, it also avoids the unexpected rotation of the forearm and wrist at later stages. Figure 6 shows that all the generated joint values never exceed their physical limits and thus that this scheme is applicable. To examine the computational cost, the average computing time within each sampling interval ($\mathcal{T}_{\text{Ave}}$), and the total computing time within each experiment ($\mathcal{T}_{\text{Sum}}$), are measured. While the robot plays with the ball, $\mathcal{T}_{\text{Ave}} = 0.001$ s and $\mathcal{T}_{\text{Sum}} = 1.12$ s, which are both very small compared with the total task execution time $\mathcal{T}_{\text{d}} = 18$ s, thus validating that the computing task can be completed within each sampling interval during the ball-playing experiment. The snapshots during the task execution is shown in Fig. 7. The dual arms lift a yellow ball through a "V" shape stick. It moves the ball along a straight path, places it in another cup, and then move back. During the experiment, the robot moves the ball very well, and keep its hand gesture as expected. Figure 8 shows the positioning-errors of the left/right end-effectors (hands). The errors are measured by the deviations of the generated end-effector trajectories from the desired end-effector paths; i.e., $E = \Upsilon - f(\vartheta)$. It is worth mentioning that the MAE is just 2.1832×10^{-5} m, all AAE are less than 6.2×10^{-6} m, and the RMSE are less than 8.41×10^{-6} m. These tiny errors demonstrate further the accuracy of the TV-GDD scheme in solving the redundancy-resolution problem.

In summary, the above simulations and physical experiment verify that the proposed TV-GDD scheme is effective, accurate and physically realizable.

5   Concluding Remarks

A novel time-varying-constrained scheme for dual-arms motion generation has been proposed and investigated. To generate an expected motion configuration, a time-varying gesture-determined dynamical function is designed. Based on such function, a TV-GDD scheme is derived. To solve such a scheme so as to generate the expected motions, a discrete QP solver is presented and used. These generated optimal solutions are used to control the physical humanoid robot. Both the computer simulations and physical experiments demonstrate the effectiveness and feasibility of the proposed TV-GDD scheme.

Acknowledgments. This work was supported in part by the National Natural Science Foundation under Grants 61603142 and 61633010, the Guangdong Foundation for Distinguished Young Scholars under Grant 2017A030306009, the Science and Technology Program of Guangzhou under Grant 201707010225, the Fundamental Research Funds for Central Universities under Grant 2017MS049.

References

1. Bouyarmane, K., Kheddar, A.: On weight-prioritized multi-task control of humanoid robots. IEEE Trans. Autom. Control **pp**, 1 (2017)
2. Liu, Z., Chen, C., Zhang, Y., Chen, C.L.: Adaptive neural control for dual-arm coordination of humanoid robot with unknown nonlinearities in output mechanism. IEEE Trans. Cybern. **45**, 521 (2015)
3. Xiao, Y., Zhang, Z., Beck, A., Yuan, J., Thalmann, D.: Human-robot interaction by understanding upper body gestures. Presence: Teleoperators Virtual Environ. **23**(2), 133–154 (2014)
4. Shin, S., Kim, C.: Human-like motion generation and control for humanoid's dual arm object manipulation. IEEE Trans. Ind. Electron. **62**, 2265–2276 (2015)
5. Goertz, R.C.: Fundamentals of general purpose remote manipulators. Nucleonics **10**(11), 36–42 (1952)
6. Fletcher, T.: The Undersea Mobot, Nuclear Electronics Laboratory of Hughes Aircraft Company. Technical Report, January 1960
7. Kuindersma, S., Scott, R., Robin, F., Maurice, V.: Optimization-based locomotion planning, estimation, and control design for the atlas humanoid robot. Auton. Robot. **40**, 429–455 (2016)
8. Lyubova, N., Ivaldi, S., Filliat, D.: From passive to interactive object learning and recognition through self-identification on a humanoid robot. Auton. Robot. **40**, 33–57 (2016)
9. Nunez, J.V., Briseno, A., Rodriguez, D.A., Ibarra, J.M., Rodriguez, V.M.: Explicit analytic solution for inverse kinematics of bioloid humanoid robot. In: Robotics Symposium and Latin American Robotics Symposium, pp. 33–38. IEEE (2012)
10. Wang, J., Li, Y.: Inverse kinematics analysis for the arm of a mobile humanoid robot based on the closed-loop algorithm. In: International Conference on Information and Automation, pp. 516–521. IEEE (2009)

11. Kanoun, O., Lamiraux, F., Wieber, P.-B.: Kinematic control of redundant manipulators: generalizing the task-priority framework to inequality task. IEEE Trans. Robot. **27**(4), 785–792 (2011)
12. Zhang, Z., Zhang, Y.: Acceleration-level cyclic-motion generation of constrained redundant robots tracking different paths. IEEE Trans. Syst. Man Cybern. Part B (Cybern.), **42**(4), 1257–1269 (2012)
13. Zhang, Z., Zhang, Y.: Equivalence of different-level schemes for repetitive motion planning of redundant robots. Acta Autom. Sinica **39**(1), 88–91 (2013)
14. Cheng, F., Chen, T., Sun, Y.: Resolving manipulator redundancy under inequality constraints. IEEE Trans. Robot. Autom. **10**, 65–71 (1994)
15. He, B.: A new method for a class of linear variational inequalities. Math. Program. **66**, 137–144 (1994)

Robust Control Design of Uncertain Strict Feedback Systems Using Adaptive Filters

Yong-Hua Liu[✉] and Chun-Yi Su

Guangdong Key Laboratory of IoT Information Technology, School of Automation,
Guangdong University of Technology,
Guangzhou 510640, Guangdong, People's Republic of China
liuyonghua1042@gmail.com, chunyi.su@gmail.com

Abstract. This paper concerns on the tracking problem of uncertain strict feedback systems. By employing the adaptive filters, a robust state feedback control scheme is derived, where a common compensator is utilized to eliminate the effects induced by each filters. Compared with the existing results using standard dynamic surface control approach, the closed loop stability does not depend on small filter time constants. Finally, the correctness of the developed methodology is demonstrated via a numerical example.

Keywords: Strict feedback · Nonlinear systems
Dynamic surface control · Robust control · Adaptive filter

1 Introduction

During the past several years, adaptive nonlinear control of uncertain systems has attracted much attention [1]. Particularly, as a powerful design tool, backstepping approach has been investigated extensively for control design of large classes of nonlinear lower triangular systems with uncertainties [6–10]. Nevertheless, the backstepping approach suffers from the "explosion of complexity" issue, which is induced by the repeated differentiations of virtual control variables [11,12].

To avoid the obstacle of "explosion of complexity" in the procedure of recursive design, a new constructive approach, called as dynamic surface control (DSC), was proposed for nonlinear strict feedback systems in [11,12], where the virtual control law is passed through a linear low pass filter at each design step, so that the time derivative of virtual controllers is removed. Consequently, the DSC technique was suggested for designing simplified adaptive controllers for uncertain nonlinear systems [14,15]. However, as revealed by [16], owing to the use of linear low pass filters, boundary layer errors are introduced into DSC systems resulting in large tracking error bounds and degraded tracking accuracy, which implies that the DSC schemes are sensitive to the filter time constants.

© Springer International Publishing AG, part of Springer Nature 2018
T. Huang et al. (Eds.): ISNN 2018, LNCS 10878, pp. 768–774, 2018.
https://doi.org/10.1007/978-3-319-92537-0_87

To improve the tracking error performance, an adaptive DSC approach was proposed recently [17], where the adaptive filters are employed to cancel the "explosion of complexity" issue, and a compensator at each step is introduced to eliminate the effects raised by boundary layer errors.

In this paper, based on the results of [17], we present a novel robust DSC scheme for uncertain nonlinear strict feedback systems. Instead of utilizing the linear low pass filters, we employ the adaptive filters to remove the "explosion of complexity" issue. Besides, a common compensator is introduced to cancel the effects raised by boundary layer errors. It is proven rigorously that the closed loop stability are guaranteed. Finally, the developed methodology of this paper is validated via a simulation study.

2   Problem Formulation

Consider the following class of nonlinear strict feedback systems with parametric uncertainties as follows:

$$\dot{x}_i = \theta_i f_i(\bar{x}_i) + x_{i+1}, i = 1, ..., n - 1,$$
$$\dot{x}_n = \theta_n f_n(\bar{x}_n) + u,$$
$$y = x_1, \tag{1}$$

where $\bar{x}_i = [x_1, \cdots, x_i]^T \in R^i$, $i = 1, \cdots, n$; $\bar{x}_n \in R^n$ is the system state vector, $u \in R$ and $y \in R$ are the input and out of system, respectively; θ_i, $i = 1, ..., n$ are unknown constant parameters; $f_i(\cdot) : R^n \to R$, $i = 1, ..., n$ are known differentiable functions.

The main objective of this paper is to develop a robust adaptive control law u for system (1) such that the output y tracks a reference signal y_r, and guarantees the boundedness of all the closed loop signals.

Assumption 1. *The reference signal y_r and its derivatives $\dot{y}_r$ and $\ddot{y}_r$ are available and bounded.*

Lemma 1 [18]. *For any $\epsilon > 0$ and for any $z \in R$, the following inequality holds*

$$0 \leq |z| - \frac{z^2}{\sqrt{z^2 + \epsilon^2}} < \epsilon \tag{2}$$

3   Robust Control Design

The proposed robust DSC scheme, similar to the backstepping technique, contains n steps as follows.

Step 1: Define the first surface error $z_1 = x_1 - y_r$, we have

$$\dot{z}_1 = \theta_1^T f_1 + x_2 - \dot{y}_r \tag{3}$$

The virtual controller α_1 and the adaptive law for $\hat{\theta}_1$ are chosen as

$$\alpha_1 = -k_1 z_1 - \hat{\theta}_1 f_1 + \dot{y}_r \tag{4}$$

$$\dot{\hat{\theta}}_1 = \gamma_1 (z_1 f_1 - \lambda_1 \hat{\theta}_1) \tag{5}$$

where $k_1 > 0$, $\gamma_1 > 0$ and $\lambda_1 > 0$ are design parameters, $\hat{\theta}_1$ is an estimate of θ_1, $\tilde{\theta}_1 = \theta_1 - \hat{\theta}_1$.

Define the Lyapunov function V_1 as

$$V_1 = \frac{1}{2} z_1^2 + \frac{1}{2\gamma_1} \tilde{\theta}_1^2 \tag{6}$$

In view of (3)–(5), one has

$$\dot{V}_1 = \dot{z}_1 z_1 - \frac{1}{\gamma_1} \tilde{\theta}_1 \dot{\hat{\theta}}_1$$

$$= -k_1 z_1^2 + g_1 (x_2 - \alpha_1) z_1 + \lambda_1 \tilde{\theta}_1 \hat{\theta}_1 \tag{7}$$

To avoid the "explosion of complexity" issue, let α_1 pass through the following adaptive filter to obtain a new filtered signal s_1:

$$\tau_1 \dot{s}_1 = -e_1 - \frac{\tau_1 \hat{M}^2 e_1}{\sqrt{\hat{M}^2 e_1^2 + \sigma^2}} - \tau_1 g_1 z_1, \, s_1(0) = \alpha_1(0) \tag{8}$$

where $e_1 := s_1 - \alpha_1$ denotes the first boundary layer error, $\hat{M}$ is an estimate of M, which will be clarified later; τ_1 is a filter time constant, σ is a positive constant.

Step $i (i = 2, \cdots, n-1)$: Define the ith surface error $z_i = x_i - s_{i-1}$, it has

$$\dot{z}_i = \theta_i f_i + x_{i+1} - \dot{s}_{i-1}$$

$$= \theta_i f_i + x_{i+1} + \frac{\hat{M}^2 e_{i-1}}{\sqrt{\hat{M}^2 e_{i-1}^2 + \sigma^2}} + z_{i-1} + \frac{e_{i-1}}{\tau_{i-1}} \tag{9}$$

The virtual controller α_i and the adaptive law for $\hat{\theta}_i$ are chosen as

$$\alpha_i = -k_i z_i - 2z_{i-1} - \hat{\theta}_i f_i - \frac{\hat{M}^2 e_{i-1}}{\sqrt{\hat{M}^2 e_{i-1}^2 + \sigma^2}} - \frac{e_{i-1}}{\tau_{i-1}} \tag{10}$$

$$\dot{\hat{\theta}}_i = \gamma_i (z_i f_i - \lambda_i \hat{\theta}_i) \tag{11}$$

where $k_i > 0$, $\gamma_i > 0$ and $\lambda_i > 0$ are design parameters, $\hat{\theta}_i$ is an estimate of θ_i, $\tilde{\theta}_i = \theta_i - \hat{\theta}_i$.

Define the Lyapunov function V_i as

$$V_i = V_{i-1} + \frac{1}{2} z_i^2 + \frac{1}{2\gamma_i} \tilde{\theta}_i^2 \tag{12}$$

Along with (9)–(11), the time derivative of V_i is

$$\dot{V}_i = \dot{V}_{i-1} + \dot{z}_i z_i - \frac{1}{\gamma_i}\tilde{\theta}_i\dot{\hat{\theta}}_i$$

$$= -\sum_{j=1}^{i} k_j z_j^2 + \sum_{j=1}^{i-1} z_j e_j + (x_{i+1} - \alpha_i)z_i + \sum_{j=1}^{i} \lambda_i \tilde{\theta}_i \hat{\theta}_i \tag{13}$$

Let α_i pass through the following nonlinear filter to obtain a filtered virtual controller s_i:

$$\tau_i \dot{s}_i = -e_i - \frac{\tau_i \hat{M}^2 e_i}{\sqrt{\hat{M}^2 e_i^2 + \sigma^2}} - \tau_i z_i, \; s_i(0) = \alpha_i(0) \tag{14}$$

where $e_i := s_i - \alpha_i$ denotes the ith boundary layer error; τ_i is a filter time constant.

Step n: Define the nth surface error $z_n = x_n - s_{n-1}$, it has

$$\dot{z}_n = \theta_n f_n + u - \dot{s}_{n-1}$$

$$= \theta_n f_n + u + \frac{\hat{M}^2 e_{n-1}}{\sqrt{\hat{M}^2 e_{n-1}^2 + \sigma^2(t)}} + z_{n-1} + \frac{e_{n-1}}{\tau_{n-1}} \tag{15}$$

The actual controller u and the adaptive laws for $\hat{\theta}_n$ and $\hat{M}$ are chosen as

$$u = -k_n z_n - 2z_{n-1} - \hat{\theta}_n f_n - \frac{\hat{M}^2 e_{n-1}}{\sqrt{\hat{M}^2 e_{n-1}^2 + \sigma^2}} - \frac{e_{n-1}}{\tau_{n-1}} \tag{16}$$

$$\dot{\hat{\theta}}_n = \gamma_n(z_n f_n - \lambda_n \hat{\theta}_n) \tag{17}$$

$$\dot{\hat{M}} = \beta\left(\sum_{i=1}^{n-1} |e_i| - \chi\hat{M}\right) \tag{18}$$

where $k_n > 0$, $\gamma_n > 0$, $\lambda_n > 0$, $\beta > 0$ and $\chi > 0$ are design parameters, $\hat{\theta}_n$ is an estimate of θ_n, $\tilde{\theta}_n = \theta_n - \hat{\theta}_n$.

Define the Lyapunov function V_n as

$$V_n = V_{n-1} + \frac{1}{2}z_n^2 + \frac{1}{2\gamma_n}\tilde{\theta}_n^2 + \sum_{i=1}^{n-1}\frac{1}{2}e_i^2 + \frac{1}{2\beta}\tilde{M}^2 \tag{19}$$

From (15)–(18), it is obtained that

$$\dot{V}_n = \dot{V}_{n-1} + \dot{z}_n z_n - \frac{1}{\gamma_n}\tilde{\theta}_n\dot{\hat{\theta}}_n + \sum_{i=1}^{n-1} e_i \dot{e}_i - \frac{1}{\beta}\tilde{M}\dot{\hat{M}}$$

$$= -\sum_{j=1}^{n} k_j z_j^2 + \sum_{j=1}^{n-1} z_j e_j + \sum_{j=1}^{n} \lambda_i \tilde{\theta}_i \hat{\theta}_i + \sum_{i=1}^{n-1} e_i \dot{e}_i - \frac{1}{\beta}\tilde{M}\dot{\hat{M}} \tag{20}$$

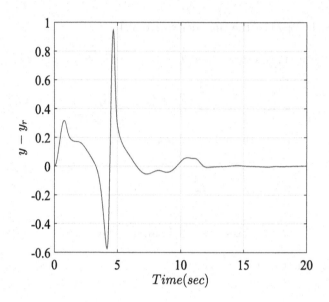

Fig. 1. Tracking performance.

Theorem 1. *Consider the closed loop system consisting of the plant (1), the nonlinear filters (8), (14) with a common compensator (18), the control signal (16), and the adaptive laws (5), (11), (17). Suppose that Assumptions 1-2 hold, for any initial conditions satisfying $V_n(0) \leq p$, where p is a given positive constant, then there exist design parameters k_i, γ_i, λ_i, $i = 1, ..., n$, τ_j, $j = 1, ..., n-1$, β, χ such that all the closed loop signals are semi-globally uniformly ultimately bounded.*

Proof. The detailed proof is omitted here owing to the limited space, which can be referred in [17].

4   A Simulation Study

To verify the feasibility of the proposed findings, in this section, the following second order nonlinear system is considered:

$$\dot{x}_1 = \theta_1 x_1 e^{-0.5x_1} + x_2$$
$$\dot{x}_2 = \theta_2 x_1 x_2 + u$$
$$y = x_1 \tag{21}$$

where θ_1 and θ_2 are unknown constant parameters. The control objective is to design a robust controller u such that y tracks the reference signal $y_r = \sin(t)$.

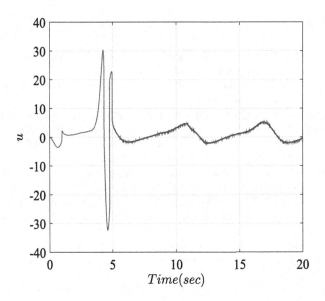

Fig. 2. Control signal u.

For simulation purpose, the unknown parameters are assumed as $\theta_1 = 2$, $\theta_2 = 1$. The design parameters are chosen as $k_1 = 5$, $k_2 = 1$, $\gamma_1 = \gamma_2 = 4$, $\lambda_1 = \lambda_2 = \chi = 0.001$, $\beta = 5$, $\tau_1 = 0.5$, $\sigma = 0.01$. The initial conditions for simulation study are set as $[x_1(0), x_2(0)]^T = [0, 1]^T$, $\hat{\theta}_1(0) = 0$, $\hat{\theta}_2(0) = 1$, $\hat{M}(0) = 0$. The simulation results are displayed in Figs. 1 and 2. Figure 1 presents the output tracking error. The control signal u is shown in Fig. 2. As stated in Figs. 1 and 2, it is shown that all signals of the closed loop system are bounded.

5   Conclusion

In this paper, a robust DSC strategy has been developed for a class of nonlinear uncertain systems in strict feedback form. Instead of utilizing the linear filters, the nonlinear filters with a common compensator are employed to cancel the "explosion of complexity" issue in the recursive technique. It is proven that, based on the proposed DSC scheme, the semi-globally boundedness of all closed loop signals are guaranteed. Finally, the correctness of the developed methodology is demonstrated with a numerical example.

Acknowledgments. This work was supported by the National Natural Science Foundation of China under Grant No. 61733006.

References

1. Isidori, A.: Nonlinear Control Systems, 2nd edn. Springer, New York (1989). https://doi.org/10.1007/978-3-662-02581-9
2. Krstic, M., Kanellakopoulos, I., Kokotovic, P.V.: Nonlinear and Adaptive Control Design. Wiley, New York (1995)
3. Astolfi, A., Karagiannis, D., Ortega, R.: Nonlinear and Adaptive Control with Applications. Springer, Berlin (2007). https://doi.org/10.1007/978-1-84800-066-7
4. Utkin, V.I.: Sliding Modes in Control and Optimization. Springer, New York (1992). https://doi.org/10.1007/978-3-642-84379-2
5. Li, H., Wu, C., Jing, X., Wu, L.: Fuzzy tracking control for nonlinear networked systems. IEEE Trans. Cybern. **47**(8), 2020–2031 (2017)
6. Cai, Z., de Queiroz, M.S., Dawson, D.M.: Robust adaptive asymptotic tracking of nonlinear systems with additive disturbance. IEEE Trans. Autom. Control **51**(3), 524–529 (2006)
7. Zhang, Z., Xu, S., Zhang, B.: Asymptotic tracking control of uncertain nonlinear systems with unknown actuator nonlinearity. IEEE Trans. Autom. Control **59**(5), 1336–1341 (2014)
8. Zhao, X., Zheng, X., Niu, B., Liu, L.: Adaptive tracking control for a class of uncertain switched nonlinear systems. Automatica **52**, 185–191 (2015)
9. Zhao, X., Shi, P., Zheng, X., Zhang, L.: Adaptive tracking control for switched stochastic nonlinear systems with unknown actuator dead-zone. Automatica **60**, 193–200 (2015)
10. Li, Y.X., Yang, G.H.: Adaptive asymptotic tracking control of uncertain nonlinear systems with input quantization and actuator faults. Automatica **72**, 177–185 (2016)
11. Swaroop, D., Hedrick, J.K., Yip, P.P., Gerdes, J.C.: Dynamic surface control for a class of nonlinear systems. IEEE Trans. Autom. Control **45**(10), 1893–1899 (2000)
12. Yip, P.P., Hedrick, J.K.: Adaptive dynamic surface control: a simplified algorithm for adaptive backstepping control of nonlinear systems. Int. J. Control **71**(5), 959–979 (1998)
13. Wang, D., Huang, J.: Neural network-based adaptive dynamic surface control for a class of uncertain nonlinear systems in strict-feedback form. IEEE Trans. Neural Netw. **16**(1), 195–202 (2005)
14. Liu, Y.H., Huang, L., Xiao, D.: Adaptive dynamic surface control for uncertain nonaffine nonlinear systems. Int. J. Robust Nonlin. Control **27**(4), 535–546 (2017)
15. Liu, Y.H.: Saturated robust adaptive control for uncertain non-linear systems using a new approximate model. IET Control Theory Appl. **11**(6), 870–876 (2017)
16. Pan, Y., Yu, H.: Dynamic surface control via singular perturbation analysis. Automatica **57**, 29–33 (2015)
17. Liu, Y.H.: Adaptive dynamic surface asymptotic tracking for a class of uncertain nonlinear systems. Int. J. Robust Nonlin. Control **28**(4), 1233–1245 (2018)
18. Zuo, Z., Wang, C.: Adaptive trajectory tracking control of output constrained multi-rotors systems. IET Control Theory Appl. **8**(13), 1163–1174 (2014)

Analysis of Influencing Factors on Humanoid Robots' Emotion Expressions by Body Language

Zhijun Zhang$^{(\boxtimes)}$, Yaru Niu$^{(\boxtimes)}$, Shangen Wu, Shuyang Lin, and Lingdong Kong

School of Automation Science and Engineering,
South China University of Technology, Guangzhou 510641, China
auzjzhang@scut.edu.cn, auchrisniu@mail.scut.edu.cn

Abstract. In addition to speech, nonverbal behaviors of the human like facial expressions and body languages can also express emotions in socializing. It is expected to be known whether humanoid robots can also express their emotions in Human-Robot Interaction (HRI). This is a basic research problem since the humanoid robots are expected to be the members of our society. In this paper, we present humanoid robots' capabilities of expressing emotions by body language and discuss the facts that may influence the emotion expression through questionnaire surveys and the statistic analysis. The research is carried out on the Nao robot and the results show that the expression of emotion is affected by the ambiguity of the body language and the joint limits of the robot.

Keywords: Humanoid robot · Emotion · Body language

1 Introduction

The global population of people aged over 60 years old will be more than 2 billion by 2050 according to the World Health Organization [1]. Social robots may play a significant role in interaction and companionship with aged and disabled people in the future. In HRI, the more vividly and naturally robots behave, the more comfortable and pleased humans feel. Enabling the robots to express their emotions naturally is an effective way to improve the lifelikeness of robots and the quality of interaction. There is no doubt that speaking is a direct way of emotion expressions whereas humans and robots can express complex or delicate emotions indirectly by nonverbal manners including facial expressions [2,3] and body language [4–6].

Facial Action Coding System (FACS) is an universal standard for categorizing the facial emotion expression. It was firstly developed by a Swedish anatomist Hjortsjö [7] and adopted and published by Ekman in 1977 [8]. Based on computer science, FACS has been made into a system that can track face, extract face features and produce temporal files automatically to overcome the original limitation of time costs and extensive training requirements [9].

© Springer International Publishing AG, part of Springer Nature 2018
T. Huang et al. (Eds.): ISNN 2018, LNCS 10878, pp. 775–785, 2018.
https://doi.org/10.1007/978-3-319-92537-0_88

Some robots that have the appearance of the human are created to be anthropomorphic and support facial expressions. In [10], a robot called Albert HUBO was designed by combining the Einstein-like head and the body modified with HUBO robot. The head had smooth skin and numerous motors to support a large range of facial expressions. Hiroshi Ishiguro et al. built a humanoid robot Geminoid F who had delicate artificial skin and hair which was hard to distinguish from human [11]. Its rich facial expressions also make communication more attractive. However, according to uncanny valley theory [12], familiarity will suddenly drop when the human likeness of robot increases to a certain extent so that we cannot simply consider that the quality of HRI will improve as the robot is more human-like.

What is more, most humanoid robots at present only have fixed faces so that facial expressions are not appropriate for them to convey emotions. Therefore, body language may be a better approach for them to express emotions. Also, humanoid robots usually have numerous degrees of freedom which provides them with the advantage of displaying various complicated postures.

Although there is still no research pointing out which posture stands for which specific emotion, it has been proved that body language is able to convey emotions. Darwin and Prodger [13] figured out a functional link between postural responses and emotions through the experiments by Electromyography (EMG). The researchers found differences in four muscles when the participants were in anger or fear, suggesting that when emotions expressed, the corresponding muscles would have some reactions.

In [14], experiments were designed to compare people's identification for body language performed by an actor and artificial agents. A professional actor was asked to perform 10 emotions with body language. The motions were recorded by a human motion capture device and then regenerated by animation. The face and hands of the human and the animation were removed to avoid uncanny valley effect and volunteers were asked to choose an emotion from Geneva Emotion Wheel for the posture display. They concluded that artificial agents can express emotions by body language and discussed several facts that could affect the expression. Besides, they also investigated the effect of the head position on the emotion expression using the Nao robot.

In this paper, two surveys were conducted to investigate whether Nao is able to convey emotions by static postures. We established emotional posture library containing six basic emotions through Internet searching and image processing. These postures were regenerated by the Nao robot. Volunteers were asked to recognize the emotion expressed by the body language of the human and the Nao robot in two questionnaires. Two facts that may affect the emotion expressions of the robot, which are the ambiguity of the postures and the joint limits of the robot, were figured out by analyzing the statistical result. They were finally verified by the method of hypothesis testing conducted in SPSS, a software used for statistical analysis.

Fig. 1. An example of the initial picture, the processed picture and the corresponding photo of Nao (Posture 36 in survey 1).

2   Surveys

First of all, a set of emotional postures was established and six basic emotions [15], including anger, disgust, fear, happiness, sadness and surprise, were selected. We searched pictures of these six basic emotions through Google and tried to find non-repeated postures with evident differences to avoid confusion. 42 postures were finally obtained including 10 anger, 8 disgust, 6 fear, 7 happiness, 5 sadness and 6 surprise.

Since what we care about is body language, in the first survey, the face in each picture was removed to eliminate the influence of facial expressions. Then the processed pictures were placed out of sequence in the questionnaire and there were 8 options for participants to evaluate the emotion that a posture expressed, including six emotions mentioned above, "neutral", and "other". Participants were asked to make a choice after watching a posture as soon as possible to ensure that the choices were made by the first impression. 29 participants were invited to finish the questionnaires.

In the second survey, Nao's joints were moved to perform the similar posture according to each one in the picture mentioned above. The positions and directions of the robot's limbs were set as similar as possible to those in the pictures. Then 42 postures of the robot were obtained. Each posture of Nao was recorded in Choregraphe, a simulator platform for Nao. The postures were performed by the robot and photographed. Then the photos were placed out of sequence in the questionnaire and each photo was followed by 8 options that were the same as the first survey. Because Nao's facial expression kept unchanged, it would not influence the conclusion. An example of the initial picture, the processed picture and the corresponding photo of Nao is shown in Fig. 1.

The statistical result of the first survey is shown in Table 1(a), in which "s1" denotes the sequence number of the human's posture in the first survey, "a" denotes anger, "d" denotes disgust, "f" denotes fear, "h" denotes happiness, "sa" denotes sadness, "su" denotes surprise, "n" denotes neutral, and "o" denotes other. The rest of the table is about the ratio of each option for each posture. Because a small amount of participants did not make a choice for some postures in their questionnaire, some of the total ratios in one row do not reach 100%.

Table 1. The results of the surveys (out of sequence).

(a) The ratio of each option corresponding to each picture of human's posture									(b) The ratio of each option corresponding to each photo of robot's posture								
s1	a	d	f	h	sa	su	n	o	s2	a	d	f	h	sa	su	n	o
1	0.069	0.103	0.000	0.000	0.138	0.483	0.069	0.103	1	0.000	0.150	0.000	0.050	0.150	0.500	0.100	0.050
2	0.034	0.069	0.103	0.069	0.483	0.000	0.069	0.138	2	0.050	0.550	0.100	0.150	0.000	0.050	0.050	0.050
3	0.103	0.000	0.069	0.069	0.000	0.759	0.000	0.000	3	0.100	0.100	0.350	0.000	0.400	0.000	0.000	0.050
4	0.000	0.000	0.069	0.069	0.414	0.069	0.345	0.034	4	0.400	0.000	0.000	0.500	0.000	0.000	0.050	0.000
5	0.000	0.000	0.034	0.759	0.000	0.207	0.000	0.000	5	0.000	0.150	0.000	0.000	0.850	0.000	0.000	0.000
6	0.034	0.034	0.103	0.345	0.034	0.379	0.069	0.000	6	0.200	0.000	0.000	0.300	0.000	0.000	0.250	0.200
7	0.103	0.414	0.241	0.138	0.000	0.000	0.069	0.034	7	0.050	0.000	0.500	0.000	0.050	0.050	0.150	0.150
8	0.000	0.207	0.379	0.034	0.034	0.276	0.000	0.069	8	0.100	0.150	0.100	0.000	0.300	0.000	0.200	0.100
9	0.000	0.000	0.345	0.000	0.655	0.000	0.000	0.034	9	0.050	0.250	0.100	0.100	0.000	0.000	0.350	0.100
10	0.000	0.000	0.966	0.000	0.000	0.000	0.034	0.000	10	0.050	0.050	0.000	0.300	0.000	0.350	0.150	0.100
11	0.759	0.034	0.000	0.034	0.000	0.069	0.069	0.034	11	0.150	0.000	0.550	0.050	0.250	0.000	0.000	0.000
12	0.000	0.000	0.000	0.000	1.000	0.000	0.000	0.000	12	0.100	0.100	0.150	0.050	0.050	0.100	0.200	0.250
13	0.034	0.414	0.207	0.034	0.000	0.000	0.241	0.034	13	0.000	0.000	0.000	0.800	0.000	0.100	0.000	0.100
14	0.000	0.000	0.034	0.034	0.483	0.000	0.379	0.069	14	0.000	0.000	0.000	0.050	0.000	0.650	0.200	0.100
15	0.069	0.000	0.000	0.586	0.000	0.310	0.034	0.000	15	0.050	0.100	0.350	0.100	0.150	0.000	0.150	0.100
16	0.724	0.138	0.000	0.000	0.000	0.000	0.103	0.034	16	0.200	0.100	0.000	0.050	0.000	0.000	0.500	0.150
17	0.103	0.034	0.000	0.828	0.000	0.000	0.000	0.034	17	0.100	0.050	0.400	0.000	0.000	0.450	0.000	0.000
18	0.000	0.000	0.138	0.345	0.000	0.069	0.276	0.172	18	0.000	0.150	0.050	0.150	0.000	0.150	0.400	0.100
19	0.000	0.034	0.483	0.000	0.207	0.241	0.034	0.000	19	0.050	0.050	0.050	0.000	0.150	0.000	0.500	0.200
20	0.000	0.034	0.000	0.000	0.931	0.000	0.000	0.034	20	0.050	0.250	0.150	0.050	0.000	0.200	0.200	0.100
21	0.000	0.000	0.000	0.103	0.000	0.828	0.034	0.034	21	0.050	0.050	0.150	0.050	0.000	0.050	0.500	0.150
22	0.276	0.034	0.000	0.621	0.069	0.000	0.000	0.000	22	0.050	0.250	0.300	0.050	0.000	0.300	0.050	0.000
23	0.103	0.241	0.379	0.000	0.069	0.138	0.000	0.069	23	0.050	0.050	0.150	0.000	0.000	0.300	0.350	0.100
24	0.586	0.000	0.034	0.103	0.000	0.000	0.172	0.103	24	0.050	0.200	0.050	0.050	0.450	0.000	0.150	0.050
25	0.034	0.000	0.000	0.483	0.000	0.345	0.103	0.034	25	0.400	0.000	0.000	0.100	0.000	0.200	0.150	0.150
26	0.069	0.000	0.034	0.862	0.000	0.000	0.000	0.034	26	0.150	0.400	0.100	0.000	0.000	0.100	0.050	0.200
27	0.138	0.034	0.000	0.724	0.000	0.069	0.034	0.000	27	0.000	0.150	0.300	0.100	0.050	0.000	0.400	0.000
28	0.276	0.034	0.034	0.448	0.069	0.000	0.103	0.034	28	0.300	0.100	0.050	0.350	0.000	0.000	0.100	0.100
29	0.621	0.103	0.103	0.000	0.034	0.000	0.069	0.034	29	0.350	0.000	0.150	0.200	0.150	0.050	0.100	0.000
30	0.000	0.655	0.310	0.000	0.000	0.000	0.000	0.034	30	0.000	0.050	0.100	0.000	0.750	0.000	0.050	0.050
31	0.966	0.034	0.000	0.000	0.000	0.000	0.000	0.000	31	0.000	0.100	0.450	0.050	0.050	0.050	0.200	0.100
32	0.034	0.655	0.207	0.000	0.000	0.000	0.000	0.103	32	0.000	0.300	0.000	0.000	0.450	0.100	0.000	0.150
33	0.000	0.621	0.310	0.000	0.000	0.000	0.000	0.069	33	0.000	0.100	0.700	0.100	0.000	0.000	0.000	0.100
34	0.034	0.000	0.034	0.690	0.000	0.000	0.069	0.172	34	0.150	0.000	0.000	0.650	0.000	0.050	0.100	0.050
35	0.379	0.034	0.000	0.069	0.000	0.000	0.276	0.241	35	0.000	0.450	0.200	0.000	0.000	0.250	0.100	0.000
36	0.069	0.379	0.448	0.000	0.034	0.000	0.034	0.034	36	0.000	0.450	0.350	0.050	0.000	0.050	0.050	0.050
37	0.379	0.138	0.103	0.000	0.241	0.000	0.000	0.138	37	0.000	0.000	0.100	0.400	0.000	0.000	0.250	0.250
38	0.000	0.069	0.828	0.000	0.000	0.103	0.000	0.000	38	0.700	0.100	0.000	0.000	0.000	0.100	0.050	0.050
39	0.862	0.034	0.000	0.103	0.000	0.000	0.000	0.000	39	0.000	0.000	0.000	0.500	0.000	0.400	0.100	0.000
40	0.000	0.034	0.069	0.000	0.862	0.000	0.034	0.000	40	0.650	0.050	0.000	0.100	0.000	0.000	0.150	0.050
41	0.897	0.000	0.000	0.034	0.000	0.034	0.034	0.000	41	0.000	0.450	0.350	0.000	0.000	0.000	0.200	0.103
42	0.000	0.414	0.207	0.000	0.034	0.276	0.034	0.034	42	0.000	0.050	0.050	0.300	0.000	0.150	0.350	0.100

Similarly, the statistical result of the second survey is shown in Table 1(b), in which "s2" denotes the sequence number of the robot's posture in the second survey.

3   Analysis and Hypothesis

In Table 1(a) and (b), the option with highest ratio for each posture would be considered as the best choice to represent the emotion expressed by the posture. The robot's postures of happiness are depicted as an example in Fig. 2. The best choices of emotions for the human's postures and the robot's postures respectively are put together with the keywords of these human's postures searched in Google in Table 2 for comparison. Through analysis and comparison, we build two hypotheses of the influencing factors on humanoid robots' emotion expression by body language.

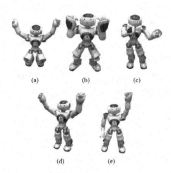

Fig. 2. The chosen robot's postures of happiness.

3.1   Hypothesis of Influencing Factor 1: Ambiguity

If the best emotion choice of a human's posture and that of the corresponding Nao's posture are consistent, there are two cases to consider.

The first case is that the search keyword is consistent with the best emotion choice for the human's posture. Using the sequence numbers in the first survey as reference, for example, the search keyword, the best choice for corresponding human's posture and the best choice for corresponding Nao's posture of the first posture are all surprises. Similarly, there are 22 other postures of the same case. Their sequence numbers are 2, 3, 10, 11, 12, 14, 17, 19, 20, 22, 23, 26, 27, 30, 32, 33, 34, 37, 39, 40, 41, 42, respectively.

In the second case, the keyword is different from the best choice for human's posture. For example, the 36th human posture is recognized as fear whereas its corresponding search keyword is disgust. It suggests that human and Nao can convey the same emotion by the similar body language but the body language itself is unable to express a certain emotion independently. Obviously, this is due to the effect of facial expressions. Without facial expressions, body language cannot express emotions properly and adequately in this case, which means the body language is of ambiguity. Therefore, the ambiguity is supposed as an influencing factor.

Table 2. Comparison of emotions expressed by the initial picture, corresponding body language of the human and body language of NAO.

s1	Initial	Human	Nao	s2	s1	Initial	Human	Nao	s2
1	surprise	surprise	surprise	1	22	happiness	happiness	happiness	4
2	sadness	sadness	sadness	5	23	fear	fear	fear	15
3	surprise	surprise	surprise	17	24	anger	anger	happiness	6
4	fear	sadness	other	12	25	surprise	happiness	surprise	14
5	happiness	happiness	surprise	10	26	happiness	happiness	happiness	28
6	surprise	surprise	neutral	23	27	happiness	happiness	happiness	13
7	fear	disgust	neutral	9	28	anger	happiness	neutral	16
8	disgust	fear	disgust	26	29	anger	anger	neutral	27
9	fear	sadness	fear	11	30	disgust	disgust	disgust	36
10	fear	fear	fear	31	31	anger	anger	neutral	18
11	anger	anger	anger	38	32	disgust	disgust	disgust	36
12	sadness	sadness	sadness	30	33	disgust	disgust	disgust	2
13	disgust	disgust	fear&surprise	22	34	happiness	happiness	happiness	34
14	sadness	sadness	sadness	8	35	anger	anger	neutral	21
15	surprise	happiness	disgust	20	36	disgust	fear	fear	33
16	anger	anger	neutral	19	37	anger	anger	anger	29
17	happiness	happiness	happiness	37	38	disgust	fear	fear	7
18	happiness	happiness	neutral	42	39	anger	anger	anger	40
19	fear	fear	fear	3	40	sadness	sadness	sadness	24
20	sadness	sadness	sadness	32	41	anger	anger	anger	25
21	surprise	surprise	happiness	39	42	disgust	disgust	disgust	35

3.2   Hypothesis of Influencing Factor 2: Joint Limits

If the best emotion choice of a human's posture is consistent with the search keyword, similarly, there are also two cases.

The first case is that the emotions are consistent in three corresponding pictures, which has been discussed above. The second one is that the best emotion choices are different between the human's and the Nao's postures. In this case, the factors causing the difference may exist in the robot itself, concretely and mainly, the limitations of Nao's joints. For example, the 5th posture's keyword and the best choice of human's posture are both happinesses but the best choice for Nao's posture is surprise. As can be seen from Fig. 3, Nao cannot perform the similar posture as the human because of its joint limits. There are other 9 postures in the same situation with the sequence numbers of 6, 13, 16, 18, 21, 24, 29, 31, 35. Therefore, the joint limit is hypothesized as another influencing factor.

Fig. 3. The posture of the robot (Posture 5) is restricted by joint limits.

4 Hypothesis Testing

It has been pointed out in the above section that the emotion expression of Nao's postures may be affected by the inherent ambiguity of the postures and the joint limits of the robot. In this section, the assumptions will be verified through two experiments using the method of hypothesis testing.

4.1 Preparation for Verification

In this paper, a posture is considered ambiguous when the selected times of its best choice do not exceed twice the selected times of its second best choice according to the general rule found in survey 1. For example, 12 participants thought that the 7th posture expressed the emotion of disgust while 7 participants chose the option of fear. The selected ratios of this two emotions are relatively close, which means that the posture itself cannot convey a certain emotion accurately. 42 Nao postures can be divided into the ambiguous type and the non-ambiguous type according to this definition. Also, the postures also can be divided into two types according to joint limits.

Therefore, we obtain four groups of postures, including 9 postures with ambiguity and without joints limits (Group 1), 12 postures without ambiguity and with joint limits (Group 2), 12 postures without both of them (Group 3) and 9 postures with both of them (Group 4).

4.2 Experiment 1: Verification of Ambiguity

Group 3 and Group 1 were used to verify the effect of the ambiguity of postures on robots' emotion expression. Defining the emotions chosen by most participants as the correct emotions, we got the accuracy of the recognizing emotion for each posture of NAO which was the sample for T-test. The result of normality test is shown in Table 3. The first row is for Group 3 and the second row is for Group 1. The statistics of these two groups are normally distributed since Sig.>0.05. Then T-test could be conducted and its result is shown in Table 4. In the Levene's test, Sig. is larger than 0.05, suggesting that two samples have similar variances. The Sig. in the first line is less than 0.05, so we can conclude

Table 3. The result of normality test in experiment 1.

VAR0001		Kolmogorov-Smirnov			Shapiro-Wilk		
		Statistic	df	Sig.	Statistic	df	Sig.
VAR0002	1.000	0.173	12	0.200	0.939	12	0.480
	2.000	0.193	9	0.200	0.903	9	0.269

Table 4. The result of T-test in experiment 1.

		Levene's test for equality of variances		t-test for equality of means						
		F	Sig.	t	df	Sig.(2-tailed)	Mean differ-ence	Std. error dif-ference	95% Conference interval of the difference	
									Lower	Upper
VAR0002	Equal variances assumed	0.783	0.387	3.892	19	0.001	0.315278	0.081005	0.145733	0.484823
	Equal variances not assumed			3.679	13.284	0.003	0.315278	0.85698	0.130541	0.500014

that the accuracies of these two group are significantly different. According to the box plot depicted in Fig. 4, the non-ambiguous group have higher accuracies of the emotion expression than the ambiguous group generally.

4.3 Experiment 2: Verification of Joint Limits

Group 3 and Group 2 were used to verify whether joint limits affect the emotion expression of the robot. Before verification, we should make sure that there is no significant difference between the accuracies of the emotion expressions of human's postures corresponding to these two groups of NAO's postures. Similar to experiment 1, normality test and T-test were conducted and the results are shown in Tables 5 and 6. Two groups of samples obey the normal distribution and

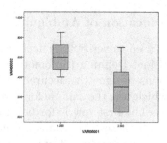

Fig. 4. The box plot for Nao's postures with ambiguity (Group1, on the right) and without ambiguity (Group3, on the left).

Table 5. The result of normality test for human's postures in experiment 2.

VAR0001		Kolmogorov-Smirnov			Shapiro-Wilk		
		Statistic	df	Sig.	Statistic	df	Sig.
VAR0002	1.000	0.119	12	0.200	0.953	12	0.684
	2.000	0.180	12	0.200	0.939	12	0.481

Table 6. The result of T-test for human's postures in experiment 2.

		Levene's test for equality of variances		t-test for equality of means						
		F	Sig.	t	df	Sig.(2-tailed)	Mean differ-ence	Std. error dif-ference	95% Conference interval of the difference	
									Lower	Upper
VAR0002	Equal variances assumed	1.602	0.219	−1.172	22	0.254	−0.069083	0.058927	−0.191291	0.053124
	Equal variances not assumed			−1.172	19.765	0.255	−0.69083	0.058927	−0.192097	0.053930

the accuracies of these two groups are basically the same according to the results which suggested that the postures of the samples are similarly not ambiguous. The corresponding box plot is depicted in Fig. 5(a).

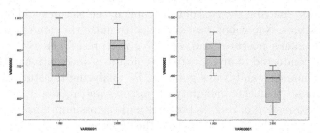

(a) The box plot for human's postures in experiment 2. (b) The box plot for Nao's postures in experiment 2.

Fig. 5. Box plots in experiment 2 (Group 3 on the left, Group 2 on the right).

Then normality test for the accuracies of these two group was conducted and its result in Table 7 shows that the data of these two groups are not normally distributed. Therefore, nonparametric test was adopted instead of T-test. In SPSS, Mann-Whitney U test, one method of nonparametric test, was conducted automatically. The result in Table 8 shows that the null hypothesis is rejected, in other words, the accuracies of emotional expressions of the group with joint limits

Table 7. The result of normality test for Nao's postures in experiment 2.

VAR0001		Kolmogorov-Smirnov			Shapiro-Wilk		
		Statistic	df	Sig.	Statistic	df	Sig.
VAR0002	1.000	0.173	12	0.200	0.939	12	0.480
	2.000	0.212	12	0.143	0.843	12	0.030

Table 8. The result of Mann-Whitney U test for Nao's postures in experiment 2.

Null hypothesis	Test	Sig.	Decision
The distribution of VAR00002 is the same across categories of VAR00001	Independent-Samples Mann-Whitney U Test	0.000	Reject the null hypothesis

are significantly different from those of the group without joint limits. According to Fig. 5(b), the accuracies of emotion expressions of the group without joint limits are generally higher than the group with joint limits.

5   Conclusions

In this paper, the questionnaire survey and hypothesis testing were conducted to investigate what factors may affect the emotion expression of robot's postures. First the emotional postures library was established by searching pictures on the Internet. After removing the face of the people in the pictures and only reserving the body postures, Nao robot was controlled to make the same postures so that we got 42 human's postures and 42 Nao's postures. Then two questionnaire surveys were conducted to investigate the volunteers' recognition of the emotions expressed by human's and Nao's postures. By analyzing the statistic results, we made hypotheses that the ambiguity of postures and robots' joint limits affect the emotion expression of robot's postures and the assumptions were verified by hypothesis testing. The result shows that the hypotheses are tenable. Besides, the emotion can be conveyed more correctly without the ambiguity of postures and joint limits. Hence, these two factors should be avoided in practical application.

Acknowledgments. This work was supported in part by the National Natural Science Foundation under Grants 61603142 and 61633010, the Guangdong Foundation for Distinguished Young Scholars under Grant 2017A030306009, the Science and Technology Program of Guangzhou under Grant 201707010225, the Fundamental Research Funds for Central Universities under Grant 2017MS049.

References

1. World Health Organization. http://www.who.int/mediacentre/news/releases/2015/older-persons-day/en/
2. Adăscălitei, F., Doroftei, I., Lefeber, D., et al.: Controlling a social robot performing nonverbal communication through facial expressions. In: Advanced Materials Research, vol. 837, pp. 525–530. Trans Tech Publications (2014)
3. Hsu, S.C., Huang, H.H., Huang, C.L.: Facial expression recognition for human-robot interaction. In: IEEE International Conference on Robotic Computing, pp. 1–7. IEEE (2017)
4. Xu, J., Broekens, J., Hindriks, K., et al.: Robot mood is contagious: effects of robot body language in the imitation game. In: Proceedings of the 2014 International Conference on Autonomous Agents and Multi-agent Systems, pp. 973–980. International Foundation for Autonomous Agents and Multiagent Systems (2014)
5. Embgen, S., Luber, M., Becker-Asano, C., et al.: Robot-specific social cues in emotional body language. In: RO-MAN, pp. 1019–1025. IEEE (2012)
6. McColl, D., Jiang, C., Nejat, G.: Classifying a persons degree of accessibility from natural body language during social human-robot interactions. IEEE Trans. Cybern. **47**(2), 524–538 (2017)
7. Hjortsjö, C.H.: Man's Face and Mimic Language. Studen litteratur (1969)
8. Ekman, P.: Facial Action Coding System (1977)
9. Hamm, J., Kohler, C.G., Gur, R.C., et al.: Automated facial action coding system for dynamic analysis of facial expressions in neuropsychiatric disorders. J. Neurosci. Methods **200**(2), 237–256 (2011)
10. Oh, J.H., Hanson, D., Kim, W.S., et al.: Design of android type humanoid robot Albert HUBO. In: 2006 IEEE/RSJ International Conference on Intelligent Robots and Systems, pp. 1428–1433. IEEE (2006)
11. Becker-Asano, C., Ishiguro, H.: Evaluating facial displays of emotion for the android robot Geminoid F. In: 2011 IEEE Workshop on Affective Computational Intelligence, pp. 1–8. IEEE (2011)
12. Mori, M.: The uncanny valley. Energy **7**(4), 33–35 (1970)
13. Darwin, C., Prodger, P.: The Expression of the Emotions in Man and Animals. Oxford University Press, New York (1998)
14. Beck, A., Stevens, B., Bard, K.A., et al.: Emotional body language displayed by artificial agents. ACM Trans. Interact. Intell. Syst. **2**(1), 2 (2012)
15. Dalgleish, T., Power, M.: Handbook of Cognition and Emotion. Wiley, Hoboken (2000)

Bio-signal, Bioinformatics and Biomedical Engineering

Increasing Stability of EEG Components Extraction Using Sparsity Regularized Tensor Decomposition

Deqing Wang[1,2], Xiaoyu Wang[1], Yongjie Zhu[1,2], Petri Toiviainen[3], Minna Huotilainen[4], Tapani Ristaniemi[2], and Fengyu Cong[1,2(✉)]

[1] Department of Biomedical Engineering, Faculty of Electronic Information and Electrical Engineering, Dalian University of Technology, Dalian 116024, China
deqing.wang@foxmail.com, xiaoyu.wang0207@foxmail.com,
yongjie.zhu@foxmail.com, cong@dlut.edu.cn
[2] Faculty of Information Technology,
University of Jyväskylä, Jyväskylä 40100, Finland
tapani.e.ristaniemi@jyu.fi
[3] Department of Music, Art and Culture Studies, Faculty of Humanities and Social Sciences, University of Jyväskylä, Jyväskylä 40700, Finland
petri.toiviainen@jyu.fi
[4] CICERO Learning Network and Cognitive Brain Research Unit, Faculty of Educational Sciences, University of Helsinki, Helsinki 00014, Finland
minna.huotilainen@helsinki.fi

Abstract. Tensor decomposition has been widely employed for EEG signal processing in recent years. Constrained and regularized tensor decomposition often attains more meaningful and interpretable results. In this study, we applied sparse nonnegative CANDECOMP/PARAFAC tensor decomposition to ongoing EEG data under naturalistic music stimulus. Interesting temporal, spectral and spatial components highly related with music features were extracted. We explored the ongoing EEG decomposition results and properties in a wide range of sparsity levels, and proposed a paradigm to select reasonable sparsity regularization parameters. The stability of interesting components extraction from fourteen subjects' data was deeply analyzed. Our results demonstrate that appropriate sparsity regularization can increase the stability of interesting components significantly and remove weak components at the same time.

Keywords: Tensor decomposition · Sparse regularization
Nonnegative constraints · Ongoing EEG · Stability analysis

1 Introduction

In recent years, tensor decomposition [1] has gained more and more popularity for EEG data processing [2]. By time-frequency representation, multi-channel EEG data can be converted into a third-order (time × frequency × channel) tensor. In some EEG

© Springer International Publishing AG, part of Springer Nature 2018
T. Huang et al. (Eds.): ISNN 2018, LNCS 10878, pp. 789–799, 2018.
https://doi.org/10.1007/978-3-319-92537-0_89

experiments, a seventh-order tensor may be generated potentially [2]. But sometimes basic tensor decompositions on EEG data can't guarantee meaningful factors. For example, the third-order EEG tensor mentioned above is a nonnegative tensor essentially. The extracted temporal components should be energy series which are nonnegative. The spectral components should be spectra which are nonnegative and usually very sparse. The spatial components are topographies which are sometimes also sparse. Constrained and regularized tensor decomposition can make the results meaningful and interpretable [1].

Nonnegativity is often achieved by constrained optimization methods. Nonnegative constrains can naturally give sparse results [3], but this sparsity is only a side effect and not controllable. l_1-norm regularization is an effective and widely applied method to impose sparsity explicitly [4], and has been employed for sparse and nonnegative tensor decomposition [5–7]. But these works regarding sparse regularization in tensor decomposition [5–7] only tested a few groups of sparsity regularization parameters, and demonstrated that their model can successfully impose sparsity on factors. No work, as far as we know, has studied how the change of sparsity level affects the results of tensor decomposition and the physical meanings in real application.

In this study, ongoing EEG tensor data under naturalistic modern tango music stimulus are analyzed. Sparse nonnegative CANDECOMP/PARAFAC decomposition is employed to extract groups of interesting components whose temporal components are highly correlated with music features and hose spatial components have dipolar topographies. In order to reveal a clear picture of EEG components' properties at different sparsity level, a large range of sparsity regularization parameters are tested. We propose a method to select reasonable regularization parameters that can best balance the data fitting and sparsity. We find that when sparsity regularization is imposed on tensor decomposition, the stability of interesting components is increased significantly. In our results, appropriate sparsity regularization can also remove weak components and elements on nonzero sparse components such as spectra.

2 Sparse Nonnegative CANDECOMP/PARAFAC Decomposition

2.1 Notation

In this paper, a boldface lowercase letter, such as x, denotes a vector; a boldface uppercase letter, such as X, denotes a matrix; and a boldface Euler script letter, such as $\mathcal{X}$, denotes a high order tensor. Operator $\circ$ denotes outer product of vectors, and $[\![\,]\!]$ denotes Kruskal operator. $\|\cdot\|_F$ represents Frobenius norm, and x_1 represents l_1-norm of vector x. We call sparse nonnegative CANDECOMP/PARAFAC decomposition "sparse NCP" and the version without sparsity regularization "NCP" for short.

2.2 Mathematical Model

Given a tensor $\mathcal{X} \in \mathbb{R}^{I_1 \times I_2 \times \cdots \times I_N}$, sparse NCP is to solve the following problem:

$$\min_{A^{(1)}, \cdots, A^{(N)}} \frac{1}{2} \left\| \mathcal{X} - [\![A^{(1)}, \cdots, A^{(N)}]\!] \right\|_F^2 + \sum_{n=1}^{N} \beta_n \sum_{j=1}^{K} \left\| a_j^{(n)} \right\|_1 \qquad (1)$$

$$\text{s.t.}\, A^{(n)} \geq 0 \text{ for } n = 1, \cdots, N,$$

where $A^{(n)} \in \mathbb{R}^{I_n \times K}$ for $n = 1, \cdots, N$ are estimated factors, and $a_j^{(n)}$ represents the jth column of $A^{(n)}$. β_n for $n = 1, \cdots, N$ are parameters of sparsity regularization items. K is the selected rank-1 tensor number, and the estimated factors in Kruskal operator can be represented by sum of K rank-1 tensors in outer product form:

$$[\![A^{(1)}, \cdots, A^{(N)}]\!] = \sum_{j=1}^{K} a_j^{(1)} \circ \cdots \circ a_j^{(N)} \qquad (2)$$

2.3 Model Solution

Sparse NCP in (1) is a highly nonlinear and nonconvex model, which is non-trivial to solve and converge. Recently, Xu applied an efficient alternating proximal gradient (APG) method to solve nonnegative matrix and tensor decomposition [8]. Later, Xu extended APG method to solve nonnegative Tucker decomposition with l_1-norm sparsity regularizations [7]. Inspired by Xu's work [7], we utilize the same updating method in block coordinate descend (BCD) framework to solve problem (1).

Supposing $\widehat{A}^{(n)}$ is an extrapolated point, $\widehat{G}^{(n)}$ is the block-partial gradient at $\widehat{A}^{(n)}$ and $L^{(n)}$ is a Lipschitz constant, factor matrix $A^{(n)}$ is updated by

$$A^{(n)} \leftarrow \underset{A^{(n)} \geq 0}{\operatorname{argmin}} \left[\left\langle \widehat{G}^{(n)}, A^{(n)} - \widehat{A}^{(n)} \right\rangle + \frac{L^{(n)}}{2} \left\| A^{(n)} - \widehat{A}^{(n)} \right\|_F^2 + \beta_n \sum_{j=1}^{K} \left\| a_j^{(n)} \right\|_1 \right] \qquad (3)$$

which can be written in the closed form

$$A^{(n)} \leftarrow \max \left(0, \widehat{A}^{(n)} - \frac{\widehat{G}^{(n)}}{L^{(n)}} - \frac{\beta_n 1_{I_n \times K}}{L^{(n)}} \right) \qquad (4)$$

The detailed solution and convergence properties of APG can be found in [7, 8].

3 Materials and Methods

3.1 EEG Data and Music Signal

Data Description. The data in this study are ongoing EEG of fourteen right-handed and healthy adults under continuous and naturalistic modern tango music stimulus.

Short-time Fourier transform (STFT) was applied to the EEG data, and a third-order tensor was created for each subject with size of $510 \times 146 \times 64$ on temporal, spectral and spatial mode respectively. In this paper, we represent the estimated factors of the third-order EEG tensor as $A^{(\text{Temporal})}$, $A^{(\text{Spectral})}$ and $A^{(\text{Spatial})}$.

Acoustic Features. Five long-term acoustic features, including two tonal features (Mode, Key Clarity) and three rhythmic features (Pulse Clarity, Fluctuation Centroid, Fluctuation Entropy), were extracted from the tango music [9]. STFT was also used for feature extraction and one acoustic feature temporal series contains 510 samples.

The detailed data collection experiment paradigm and data preprocessing procedures can be found in [10, 11]. Detailed acoustic features can be found in [9].

3.2   Correlation Analysis

According to previous studies [9, 10], we hypothesize that acoustic features (tonal and rhythmic components) can activate certain brain areas. We performed correlation analyses (by Pearson's correlation coefficient) between the time series of long-term acoustic features and the time series of temporal components from EEG tensor decomposition to find stimulus-related activations. Monte Carlo method and permutation tests were employed to compute the threshold of correlation coefficient [9, 10]. In the results of EEG tensor decomposition, the temporal components significantly correlated (at level $p < 0.05$) with any of the five acoustic features, and their corresponding spectral and spatial components were recorded for further investigations.

3.3   Sparsity Parameter Selection

When applying sparse NCP model to decompose EEG tensor, a key point is the selection of sparsity regularization parameters β_n in model (1), which balance the data fitting and sparsity level. Data fitting at iteration k is defined by

$$\text{Fit}_k = 1 - \frac{\left\| \mathcal{X} - \left[\!\left[A_k^{(1)}, \cdots, A_k^{(N)} \right]\!\right] \right\|_F}{\|\mathcal{X}\|_F}, \tag{5}$$

which is a measure of similarity of estimated factors to original data tensor. The sparsity level of estimated factor $A_k^{(n)}$ at iteration k is defined by

$$\text{Sparsity}_{A_k^{(n)}} = \frac{\#\left\{ A_k^{(n)}(i,j) < T_s \right\}}{I_n \times K}, \tag{6}$$

where $\#\{\cdot\}$ means the number of elements in factor $A_k^{(n)}$ that satisfy the assumption. Strictly speaking, the factor sparsity should be measured by the number of elements that equal to zero. But in practice it is better to select a small positive sparsity threshold T_s. In this study, we select $T_s = 1e - 6$.

In order to reveal a broad picture of data properties and results at different sparsity levels, we tested a large range of sparsity regularization parameters of β_ns for sparse NCP. The procedures are shown in the following steps.

Step 1. For the temporal and spatial factor, select $\beta_{\text{temporal}} = \beta_{\text{spatial}} = e^{\lambda_1}$ and $\beta_{\text{spectral}} = e^{\lambda_2}$. λ_1 and λ_2 contain N_1 and N_2 linearized numbers, then there will be $N_1 \times N_2$ different groups of parameter combinations $[\beta_{\text{temporal}}, \beta_{\text{spectral}}, \beta_{\text{spacial}}]$ β_{temporal} and β_{spatial} are set by small numbers, and don't have high sparsity effects. They are made the same in order to reduce the parameter group number.

Step 2. Using each group of parameters, run sparse NCP 10 times, and record the average nonzero components number of spectral factor, the average fitting value using (5), and the average sparsity level of spectral factor using (6). Because the spectral components are usually very sparse, only the spectral factor is considered.

Step 3. Reorder all of groups of results based on spectral factor sparsity level in ascend order with in $[0, 1]$, and generate the 'Fit-Sparsity' curve which reveal the fitting change at different spectral sparsity value.

Step 4. According to the 'Fit-Sparsity' curve, identify the maximum effective sparsity level based on the relative fitting change (slope) defined as

$$\text{slope} = \frac{\Delta \text{Fit}}{\Delta \text{Sparsity}} = \frac{\text{Fit}(\text{Sparsity}_1) - \text{Fit}(\text{Spasity}_2)}{\text{Sparsity}_1 - \text{Sparsity}_2}. \tag{7}$$

When the slope at some sparsity point is very close to 0.5, the sparsity value and its corresponding sparsity parameters group β_n s are selected. We assume that the slope should not be less than -0.5, because after that the fitting value become poor dramatically and the tensor decomposition results may be not accurate.

3.4 Stability Analysis

By correlation analysis introduced in Sect. 3.2, we can find the interesting components which are assumed to be stimulus-related activations. Tensor decomposition models of NCP with and without sparsity regularization were evaluated respectively. We evaluated the stability of these components using the following steps.

Step 1. Run sparse NCP 5 times for one subject's EEG tensor, and record those groups of temporal, spectral and spatial components whose temporal courses are significantly correlated with any of five music features. Keep those groups of components whose topographies (spatial components) are dipolar as templates [10]. We assume 5 times or more may yield more accurate templates. One group components of template can be represented by a rank-1 tensor of their outer product:

$$\mathcal{T} = t^{(\text{Temporal})} \circ t^{(\text{Spectral})} \circ t^{(\text{Spatial})}$$

Step 2. Based on (2), after the tensor decomposition, K rank-1 tensors in outer product form will be obtained. Supposing it is the rth time decomposition, according to [12], the correlation coefficient of the jth rank-1 tensor and the template is

$$\rho(j,r) = \mathrm{corr}\left(a_j^{(\text{Temporal})}, t^{(\text{Tempral})}\right) \times \mathrm{corr}\left(a_j^{(\text{Spectral})}, t^{(\text{Spectral})}\right)$$
$$\times \mathrm{corr}\left(a_j^{(\text{Spatial})}, t^{(\text{Spatial})}\right) \tag{8}$$

where $\mathrm{corr}(\cdot, \cdot)$ is the calculation of Pearson's correlation coefficient, $j = 1, \cdots, K$ and $\rho(j,r) \in [0,1]$. Then, calculate the maximum correlation coefficient [12] of the K rank-1 tensors with the template as:

$$P(r) = \max_{j=1,\cdots,K} \rho(j,r) \tag{9}$$

Step 3. Run sparse NCP 100 times, and record all $P(r)$, $r = 1, \cdots, 100$. Make a histogram of the 100 $P(r)$ values. Because $P(r) \in [0,1]$, the number of occurrences within $[0.95, 1]$ is recorded as stability measurement criterion for further analysis. The higher this criterion number is, the more stable sparse NCP performs.

Step 4. Within the 5 times runs in Step 1 many groups of templates that have very similar temporal, spectral and spatial components will be found. The highest criterion number of these templates after 100 times test will be kept.

4 Experiments and Results

4.1 Tensor Decomposition Implementation

Factor Initialization. All the factors were initialized using normally distributed rand numbers as in [8].

Stop Criteria. We stopped the iteration during tensor decomposition by criterion of relative residual change (fit change) according to (5), when the following condition between two iterations are satisfied:

$$T_{\text{stop}} = |\text{Fit}_k - \text{Fit}_{k+1}| < \epsilon, \tag{10}$$

where, $\epsilon = 1e - 6$ in this study.

Components Number Selection. Before decomposing each participant's EEG tensor, we should determine the components number for sparse NCP (1). A simple and convenient way was employed in this study. We made spatial mode unfolding of the third-order EEG tensor yielding a 64×74460 matrix where temporal and spectral modes were merged. Then we performed PCA along spatial mode on this matrix and recorded the principal components number that give 99% explained variance for each subject's EEG tensor. The numbers for 14 subjects' EEG tensor are listed in Table 1.

Table 1. Components number selection of 14 subjects' EEG tensors

Subject	#1	#2	#3	#4	#5	#6	#7	#8	#9	#10	#11	#12	#13	#14
Number	37	44	52	34	38	34	51	38	45	31	57	40	53	43

4.2 Sparsity Regularization Parameters

For the temporal and spatial factor, we selected $\beta_{\text{temporal}} = \beta_{\text{spatial}} = e^{\lambda_1}$, where vector $\lambda_1 = [-Inf, -5 : 0.2 : 0]$ in MATLAB format; for the spectral factor, we selected $\beta_{\text{spectral}} = e^{\lambda_2}$, where $\lambda_2 = [-Inf, -5 : 0.2 : 1]$. The linear ranges of λ_1 and λ_2 were selected by try and error method, and can be adjusted for different data. In our EEG data test, we found that using exponential form of a linearized vector parameters, the spectral factor sparsity level were approximately uniformly distributed within $[0, 1]$, which helps to analyze the fitting change at different sparsity levels. Vector λ_1 contains 27 numbers, and λ_2 contains 32 numbers, so there will be $27 \times 32 = 864$ groups of parameters. We expect to add strong sparsity parameters on spectral factor and weak sparsity parameters on temporal and spatial factors. All groups of parameters with $\lambda_1 > \lambda_2$ were removed, and finally, 509 groups were kept for test.

Each of the 509 parameter groups were tested 10 times on sparse NCP, and the average nonzero components number of spectral factor, tensor fitting value, and sparsity level of spectral factor were recorded. Figure 1 shows the results of subject #1's tensor data after all the steps in Sect. 3.4. From Fig. 1(a) we can find that, when more sparsity is added to spectral factor, some components become zeros, which are weak signal components. Figure 1(b) shows the tensor decomposition fitting changes at different spectral factor sparsity levels. When sparsity increases, fitting value decreases gradually, because some weak components are removed. But after some sparsity point, the fitting value drops dramatically. In order to find this point, we smoothed the fitting curve in (b) by low-pass filter, as is shown in (c). Next, we computed the slope according to Eq. (7), as is shown in (d). Based on curve (d), the largest sparsity level value 0.85 before slope -0.5 was selected. Then we searched in all groups of sparsity regularization parameters and found the group $[\lambda_1, \lambda_2, \lambda_1] = [-2.8, 0.2, -2.8]$ could attain the sparsity level 0.85 best. All subjects' results are shown in Table 2.

4.3 Sparsity and Stability Comparison

From Table 2 we identified the sparsity regularization parameters group $[\beta_{\text{temporal}}, \beta_{\text{spectral}}, \beta_{\text{spacial}}] = [e^{\lambda_1}, e^{\lambda_2}, e^{\lambda_1}]$ for each subject's tensor data, using which we run tensor decomposition model (1). In order to make a comparison, we also tested the original NCP without any sparsity regularizations by setting $[\beta_{\text{temporal}}, \beta_{\text{spectral}}, \beta_{\text{spacial}}] = [0, 0, 0]$.

Figure 2 shows two templates of subject #1 whose temporal components are both correlated with fluctuation centroid music feature series. One template has sparsity regularization imposed, while another doesn't. The histograms of stability analyses are also included. The template in Fig. 2(a) is selected from the 5th run of NCP and the

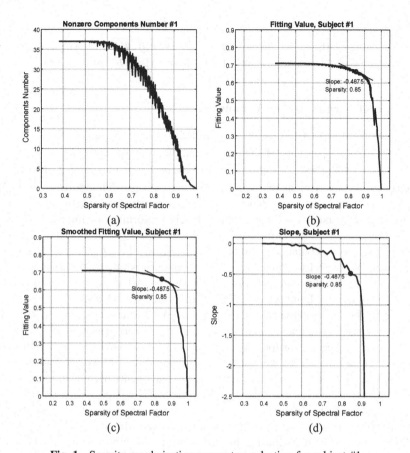

Fig. 1. Sparsity regularization parameters selection for subject #1

14th rank-1 components, and has the highest stability measurement number (the number between $[0.95, 1]$ on histogram) than other similar templates in the 5 runs.

The template in Fig. 2(b) is selected from the 5th run of sparse NCP and the 23th rank-1 components. All of the results for 14 subjects are summarized in Table 3 with selected templates and stability analyses[1]. The selected pairs of templates for comparison have very similar topographies and spectra, and appear in both situations with and without sparsity imposed on spectral components.

Comparing the histograms in Fig. 2(a) and (b), we find that, with sparsity regularization the stabilities of selected templates components have obvious increases. Table 3 further demonstrates that, for most of the subjects, when sparsity regularization is imposed on NCP for EEG data, the stability of extracting interesting components highly correlated with some certain music features are improved significantly.

---

[1] The stability was measured by number of maximum correlation coefficient within $[0.95, 1]$. But there are two exceptions of "#11-FlucCentroid" and "#13-FlucCentroid", which were measured within $[0.9, 0.95]$, because no significant value appeared within $[0.95, 1]$.

Table 2. Results of sparsity regularization parameters selection

Subject	Identified sparsity	Nonzero comps	Fitting value	$[e^{\lambda_1}, e^{\lambda_2}, e^{\lambda_1}]$	$[\lambda_1, \lambda_2, \lambda_1]$
#1	0.85	20.4	0.6667	[0.0608, 1.2214, 0.0608]	[−2.8, 0.2, −2.8]
#2	0.87	28.5	0.6991	[0.0123, 0.3012, 0.0123]	[−4.4, −1.2, −4.4]
#3	0.86	42.5	0.6726	[0.0000, 2.7183, 0.0000]	[−Inf, 1.0, −Inf]
#4	0.84	28.7	0.7683	[0.0183, 0.2466, 0.0183]	[−4.0, −1.4, −4.0]
#5	0.90	18.4	0.7241	[0.0150, 0.1653, 0.0150]	[−4.2, −1.8, −4.2]
#6	0.86	17.4	0.8084	[0.0123, 0.0907, 0.0123]	[−4.4, −2.4,−4.4]
#7	0.90	31.8	0.8095	[0.0067, 0.1353, 0.0067]	[−5.0, −2.0, −5.0]
#8	0.89	24.5	0.6870	[0.0183, 1.8221, 0.0183]	[−4.0, 0.6, −4.0]
#9	0.88	28.8	0.6811	[0.0334, 0.3679, 0.0334]	[−3.4, −1.0, −3.4]
#10	0.88	19.5	0.7435	[0.0498, 0.6703, 0.0498]	[−3.0, −0.4, −3.0]
#11	0.93	37.2	0.7188	[0.0498, 0.4493, 0.0498]	[−3.0, −0.8, −3.0]
#12	0.90	19.8	0.7110	[0.0150, 1.4918, 0.0150]	[−4.2, 0.4, −4.2]
#13	0.92	33.4	0.6992	[0.0224, 0.2466, 0.0224]	[−3.8, −1.4, −3.8]
#14	0.90	20.4	0.6899	[0.0123, 0.6703, 0.0123]	[−4.4, −0.4, −4.4]

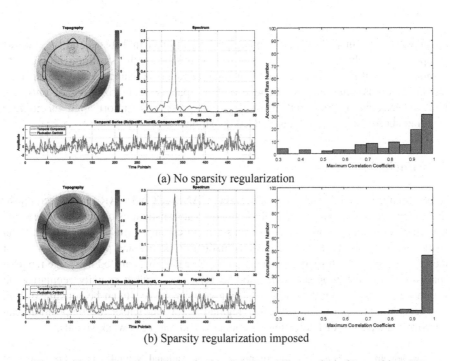

(a) No sparsity regularization

(b) Sparsity regularization imposed

Fig. 2. Fluctuation centroid templates and their stability analysis from subject #1

From Fig. 1(a) we observe that when high sparsity regularization is imposed on spectral factor, more components of full zeros appear. This is a general phenomenon for

Table 3. Stability analyses of sparsity regularization for all subjects

Subject	Music feature	No sparsity regularization		With sparsity regularization	
		Template index	Stability	Template index	Stability
#1	PulseClarity	[Run#5, Comp#14]	42%	[Run#5, Comp#23]	**74%**
	FlucCentroid	[Run#2, Comp#12]	31%	[Run#3, Comp#34]	**46%**
#4	FlucCentroid	[Run#3, Comp#9]	86%	[Run#1, Comp#24]	**97%**
#7	Key	[Run#1, Comp#21]	57%	[Run#2, Comp#30]	**63%**
#8	Mode	[Run#4, Comp#35]	29%	[Run#1, Comp#33]	**60%**
	Mode	[Run#5, Comp#3]	16%	[Run#3, Comp#15]	**68%**
	Key	[Run#2, Comp#37]	17%	[Run#1, Comp#22]	**57%**
#9	Mode	[Run#3, Comp#37]	10%	[Run#4, Comp#23]	**54%**
#10	PulseClarity	[Run#4, Comp#27]	48%	[Run#2, Comp#25]	**49%**
	Key	[Run#4, Comp#1]	**57%**	[Run#2, Comp#20]	51%
#11	FlucCentroid	[Run#5, Comp#55]	14%	[Run#3, Comp#40]	**55%**
	Mode	[Run#3, Comp#1]	**73%**	[Run#1, Comp#56]	48%
#13	FlucEntropy	[Run#2, Comp#17]	29%	[Run#1, Comp#34]	**58%**
	FlucCentroid	[Run#1, Comp#5]	16%	[Run#5, Comp#52]	**37%**
	Key	[Run#3, Comp#51]	30%	[Run#2, Comp#20]	**72%**

all subjects according to the nonzero components number in Table 2 and the selected components numbers in Table 1. By carefully observing the spectrum in Fig. 2(b) compared to that in (a), we also find that small elements are suppressed when sparsity regularization is imposed. We believe adding sparsity regularization not only can remove weak components but also help to suppress weak information on nonzero components for nonnegative tensor decomposition.

5   Conclusion

In this study, we applied sparse nonnegative CANDECOMP/PARAFAC decomposition to ongoing EEG tensor data collected under naturalistic music stimulus. Interesting temporal components correlated with music features and corresponding spectral and spatial components were extracted. Mathematical properties and physical meanings of the decomposition with sparsity regularization were deeply analyzed in a large range of sparsity levels. We proposed a method to select reasonable sparsity regularization parameters based on the derivative of fitting-sparsity curve. It can be concluded from our results that appropriate sparsity regularization on tensor decomposition can improve the stability of interesting components and suppress weak signals.

Acknowledgements. This work was supported by the National Natural Science Foundation of China (Grant No. 81471742), the Fundamental Research Funds for the Central Universities [DUT16JJ(G)03] in Dalian University of Technology in China, and the scholarships from China Scholarship Council (Nos. 201600090043 and 201600090042).

References

1. Sidiropoulos, N.D., De Lathauwer, L., Fu, X., et al.: Tensor decomposition for signal processing and machine learning. IEEE Trans. Sig. Process. **65**(13), 3551–3582 (2017)
2. Cong, F., Lin, Q.-H., Kuang, L.-D., et al.: Tensor decomposition of EEG signals: a brief review. J. Neurosci. Methods **248**, 59–69 (2015)
3. Lee, D.D., Seung, H.S.: Learning the parts of objects by non-negative matrix factorization. Nature **401**(6755), 788–791 (1999)
4. Donoho, D.L.: For most large underdetermined systems of linear equations the minimal L1-norm solution is also the sparsest solution. Commun. Pure Appl. Math. **59**(6), 797–829 (2006)
5. Mørup, M., Hansen, L.K., Arnfred, S.M.: Algorithms for sparse nonnegative Tucker decompositions. Neural Comput. **20**(8), 2112–2131 (2008)
6. Liu, J., Liu, J., Wonka, P., et al.: Sparse non-negative tensor factorization using columnwise coordinate descent. Pattern Recogn. **45**(1), 649–656 (2012)
7. Xu, Y.: Alternating proximal gradient method for sparse nonnegative Tucker decomposition. Math. Program. Comput. **7**(1), 39–70 (2015)
8. Xu, Y., Yin, W.: A block coordinate descent method for regularized multiconvex optimization with applications to nonnegative tensor factorization and completion. SIAM J. Imaging Sci. **6**(3), 1758–1789 (2013)
9. Alluri, V., Toiviainen, P., Jääskeläinen, I.P., et al.: Large-scale brain networks emerge from dynamic processing of musical timbre, key and rhythm. Neuroimage **59**(4), 3677–3689 (2012)
10. Cong, F., Alluri, V., Nandi, A.K., et al.: Linking brain responses to naturalistic music through analysis of ongoing EEG and stimulus features. IEEE Trans. Multimedia **15**(5), 1060–1069 (2013)
11. Wang, D., Cong, F., Zhao, Q., et al.: Exploiting ongoing EEG with multilinear partial least squares during free-listening to music. In: 2016 IEEE 26th International Workshop on Machine Learning for Signal Processing (MLSP), Salerno, Italy, pp. 1–6. IEEE (2016)
12. Cong, F., Phan, A.H., Zhao, Q., et al.: Benefits of multi-domain feature of mismatch negativity extracted by non-negative tensor factorization from EEG collected by low-density array. Int. J. Neural Syst. **22**(6), 1250025 (2012)

The Aftereffects of Visual Illusions (Ponzo and Müller-Lyer): Hand-Dependent Effects in Sensorimotor Domain

Valeria Karpinskaia[1], Vsevolod Lyakhovetskii[2,3],
Alla Cherniavskaia[1(✉)], and Yuri Shilov[4]

[1] St. Petersburg State University, St. Petersburg, Russia
v.karpinskaya@spbu.ru, alla.cherman@gmail.com
[2] RAS Institute of Physiology, St. Petersburg, Russia
v_la2002@mail.ru
[3] Russian Scientific Center for Radiology and Surgical Technologies,
St. Petersburg, Russia
[4] Samara University, Samara, Russia
shilov0ll0@yandex.ru

Abstract. We examined the effects of perceptual set on Ponzo and Müller-Lyer illusions, revealing the existence of the illusory aftereffect in a sensorimotor domain. Our findings demonstrate that the effects of exposure to illusory stimuli in a sensorimotor domain are hand dependent and that there is a correlation between the direction of the aftereffect and the variant of illusion as well as a correlation between the speed of the hand movements over the neutral stimuli during test trials and the type of visual illusion shown during the exposure phase. The results support our hypotheses that: (i) the different illusions have their origins at different stages of the processing of visual information and (ii) effects of illusory perceptual set depend on hemispheric-specific mental representations, which might be activated by the movements of the right or the left hand.

Keywords: Ponzo · Müller-Lyer · Aftereffect · Sensorimotor domain

1 Introduction

Since Uznadze and Piaget, perceptual aftereffects have been investigated using pairs of stimuli that really differ from one from another at a perceptual set stage, e.g. different loads for right and left hand [1, 11]. However, eliciting stimuli that are equal to each other have rarely been used. Typically, the aftereffects of such stimuli were studied using verbal responses [8, 17]. More recently, Milner and Goodale have shown that the responses to visual illusions in the sensorimotor domain (e.g. using grasping tasks) are fundamentally different from the verbal responses due, the authors have claimed, to the activation of the dorsal rather than the ventral stream [13]. In our recent work [12] we have studied the aftereffects of Ponzo and Müller-Lyer illusions using a pointing task with just the right hand. However, the influence of the hand used (right or left) on the aftereffect is also of great interest because the movements sequences of the right hand

© Springer International Publishing AG, part of Springer Nature 2018
T. Huang et al. (Eds.): ISNN 2018, LNCS 10878, pp. 800–806, 2018.
https://doi.org/10.1007/978-3-319-92537-0_90

are activated by regions of the left hemisphere in the brain, while the movements sequences of the left hand are activated by regions of both hemispheres [5]. Thus, the aim of the present study is to investigate the influence of the hand used on aftereffects in the sensorimotor domain.

2 Methods

One hundred participants took part in the study, all students of the St. Petersburg State University, with normal or corrected vision, right-handed, according to the Edinburgh handedness inventory [15]. They were divided onto ten groups: eight experimental and two control groups. Five of the groups of participants (four experimental and one control) executed the task using their right hand and five - their left hand.

Stimuli of the Ponzo illusions ((1) inverted version, (2) classical one) as well as stimuli of the Müller-Lyer illusion ((3) with outgoing fins on the lower shaft, (4) with outgoing fins on the upper shaft) were used (Fig. 1a, b, c, d). Stimuli of different shaft length (from 4.5 to 11.5 cm with a 1.5 cm interval) were presented ten times to the eight experimental groups during the exposure phase on the touch-screen. Different variants of the corresponding illusion types were shown to each of the eight different groups of participants. In exposure trials, the size of the shafts was varied to avoid a situation when participants remember the length of shafts. However, we expected the participants to produce the perceptual set with the general rule "longer-shorter".

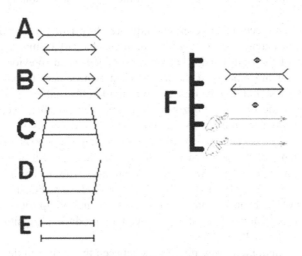

Fig. 1. Stimuli and methods

Neutral stimuli were demonstrated thirty times during the subsequent test trials. In addition it should be mentioned that the control groups observed the neutral stimuli (two equal length lines without flanks, 6 cm length) during all phases of the experiment. The equal length of these stimuli in all test trials allowed us to estimate the resistance of a perceptual set [9, 10].

The distance was 80 cm (between the touch screen and the participant). Each time, after disappearance of stimulus, participants were asked to track their hand across a touch screen to reproduce lengths of the each shaft of that stimulus. First, we asked them to track the hand along a top shaft. After that participants track the same hand along a lower shaft. Each participant moved his or her hand from left side to the right side, according to instructions (Fig. 1f). There was no feedback in the experiment. The start and the end points of a trajectory of their movements of the hand as well as the duration of each hand movement were monitored. As a result we could observe any deviation of the participant's visual perception of the neutral stimuli during the test trials.

We used the Mann-Whitney U test to measure the significance of the aftereffect sizes, as the responses were not normally distributed, and R2010b Matlab (version 7.11.0.584, Matworks Inc.).

3   Results and Discussion

In previous studies, we used the two illusions (Ponzo and Müller-Lyer) because they have similar visual effect (two lines of equal size look like different) but, according to some theoretical perspectives, they could have different mechanisms. The Ponzo illusion is classified as a "cognitive contrast illusion" while the Müller-Lyer illusion is classified as an "overestimation illusion" [3]. Our previous studies [6, 7] have revealed the existence of the effect of perceptual set in the sensorimotor domain for right hand movements.

The mean aftereffects in the present study are shown in Fig. 2. All values were expressed as the difference of the length of stimuli shafts (%). Comparing the results of the movements of the right hand, (that were examined in our previous studies [12]), with the results of movements of the left hand, it is necessary to point out that the number of illusory stimuli that cause a significant aftereffect differs. For the right hand movements, only the classical Ponzo illusion results in an aftereffect (positive and prolonged) that we can indicate as significant. For movements of a left hand, an inverted version, a classical version of the Ponzo as well as one version (outgoing fins on the upper shaft) of the Müller-Lyer illusions resulted in distortions to the motor responses of subsequently-presented neutral stimuli. The mean aftereffects were $7.14 \pm 0.81\%$, $9.04 \pm 0.94\%$ and $4.93 \pm 1.31\%$ respectively. For the left hand, only the participants of the control group and one experimental group (outgoing fins on the lower shaft) of the Müller-Lyer illusion failed to produce a significant aftereffect ($-0.89 \pm 0.64\%$ and $0.40 \pm 0.63\%$).

For the right hand, there were differences between the groups in the distribution of the hand movements speeds in test trials. The slowest hand movements were found after exposure to the inverted version of Ponzo illusion over neutral stimuli (their central parts). We need to mention, that the fastest hand movements were found also for neutral stimuli after exposure to (i) the classical version of Ponzo illusion and (ii) the neutral stimuli. The speed of the movements over neutral stimuli (their central parts) was found to be similar to each other after exposure to two different versions of Müller-Lyer

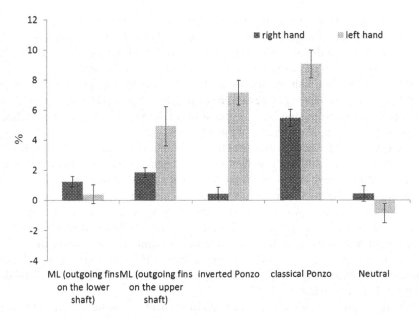

Fig. 2. The strength of the aftereffects for the right and left hands, %

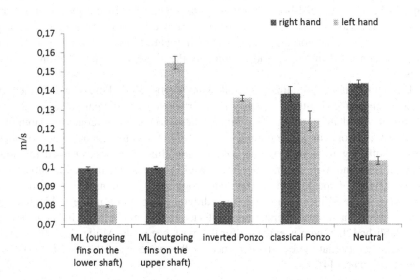

Fig. 3. The mean speeds of the right and left hand movements, m/s

illusion. In the same time it was faster significantly than the speed of the movements over the neutral stimuli after exposure to the inverted version of the Ponzo (Fig. 3).

For the left hand, the slowest movements over the central shafts were found after exposure to the Müller-Lyer illusion (outgoing fins on the lower shaft) (0,07 ± 0,012 m/s and 0,08 ± 0,001 m/s respectively), during both the acquisition trials and the test trials.

The fastest movements over the central shafts were found after exposure to the Müller-Lyer illusion (outgoing fins on the upper shaft) (0,15 ± 0,006 m/s; 0,15 ± 0,006 m/s). A similar difference in speeds during acquisition and test trials was found for the group exposed to the Ponzo inverted illusion (0,13 ± 0,007 m/s; 0,13 ± 0,005 m/s). Comparing these data with the speeds for the control group (exposed to the neutral stimuli), we conclude that exposure to both versions (inverted and classical) of the Ponzo and one version (outgoing fins on the upper shaft) of the Müller-Lyer illusion resulted in increases in the speed of movement of the left hand.

There was no difference in movements over the shafts (the upper part as well as the lower part) of neutral stimuli. This fact indicates the absence of any bias to the wrong estimation of the upper as well as of the lower parts of the stimuli by participants. In visual domain, visual illusions generally unaffected the sensitivities, such as just noticeable differences (thresholds) [14], which may be evaluated by looking at dispersion (variance) in the responses of the participants. All groups showed approximately equal SEs of estimate in case of the neutral stimuli as well as of the illusory effects, thus confirming the results of Morgan et al. (1990) in sensorimotor domain: exposure to an illusion has an effect on the lengths of movements of the hand and does not affect their dispersion.

During the presentation of the test stimuli movements of the hand were not planned feed-forward. Otherwise the speed of the hand movements did not depend on the stimulus variant. On the contrary the hand movements were under constant conscious control (the constant feed-back). Moreover, the speed of the hand movements during the test phase was influenced by the stimuli presented previously during the set stage. Here we suggest that for the simplest stimuli (neutral) used in the experiment the conscious control is minimal. And presumably the aftereffect is possible only in these cases.

Different patterns of aftereffect following exposure to Ponzo and Müller-Lyer illusions suggest that aftereffects may have originated at different stages of the processing of visual information. The clinical data showing a difference in strength of these two illusions in schizophrenic and autistic patients support this hypothesis. Persons suffering from schizophrenia for a short time were less inclined to show a Ponzo illusion and more inclined to show a Müller-Lyer one compared to subjects that had no history of mental illness [16]. The cognitive operations that underlie global processing in the Müller-Lyer illusion are different from those in the Ebbinghaus and Ponzo illusions, and these operations are affected in autism [2]. Also, in haptic domain, it is established that there is evidence for the existence of the Müller-Lyer illusion, but it is contradictory that there is the evidence for the existence of the classical version of the Ponzo illusion [4].

4   Conclusions

The results of our experiment show that prior exposure to both versions (classical and inverted) of the Ponzo and one version (out-going fins on the upper shaft) of the Müller-Lyer illusions for the left hand, and the prior exposure to the classical Ponzo illusion for the right hand result in distortions of the motor responses of subsequently-presented neutral stimuli as well as in increases in the speed of hand movements for the correspondent cases.

Our findings demonstrate the existence of hand-dependent illusory aftereffect during motor response at visual illusions. The direction of the aftereffect depends on the variant of illusion, thereby defending our hypotheses that: the different illusions have their origins at different stages of the processing of visual information and the effects of illusory perceptual set depend on hemispheric-specific mental representations, which might be activated by the movements of the right or the left hand.

Acknowledgements. Russian Humanitarian Scientific Fund 16-36-01008.

References

1. Bjalava, I.T.: Psychology of Set and Cybernetics, 251 p. Nauka, Moscow (1965) (in Russian)
2. Chouinard, P.A., Noulty, W.A., Sperandio, I., Landry, O.: Global processing during the Muller-Lyer illusion is distinctively affected by the degree of autistic traits in the typical population. Exp. Brain Res. **230**(2), 219–231 (2013)
3. Coren, S., Girgus, J.S., Erlichman, H., Hakstian, A.R.: An empirical taxonomy of visual illusions. Percept. Psychophys. **20**, 129–137 (1976)
4. Gentaz, E., Hatwell, Y.: Geometrical haptic illusions: the role of exploration in the Müller-Lyer, vertical-horizontal, and Delboeuf illusions. Psychon. Bull. Rev. **11**(1), 31–40 (2004)
5. Grafton, S.T., Hazeltine, E., Ivry, R.B.: Motor sequence learning with the nondominant left hand. A PET functional imaging study. Exp. Brain Res. **146**, 369–378 (2002)
6. Karpinskaia, V., Lyakhovetskii, V.: The differences in the sensorimotor estimation of the illusions Ponzo and Müller-Lyer. Exp. Psichol. **7**, 3 (2014). (in Russian)
7. Karpinskaia, V., Lyakhovetskii, V., Allakhverdov, V., Shilov, Y.: The peculiarities of perceptual set in sensorimotor illusions. In: Cheng, L., Liu, Q., Ronzhin, A. (eds.) ISNN 2016. LNCS, vol. 9719, pp. 706–711. Springer, Cham (2016). https://doi.org/10.1007/978-3-319-40663-3_81
8. Kasatov, A.P., Obvinceva, A.V.: Qualitative features of perceptual set, measured by estimation of the magnitude, and crossmodal selection. Psychol. Bull. Ural State Univ. **2**, 163–169 (2001). (in Russian)
9. Kostandov, E.A., Kurova, N.S., Cheremushkin, E.A., Iakovenko, I.A.: The role of unconscious sets formed on the basis of the perception of concrete visual stimuli and of illusory representations in conscious cognitive activity. Zh. Vyssh. Nerv. Deiat. Im. I. P. Pavlova **48**(3), 438–448 (1998). (in Russian)
10. Kostandov, E.A.: Formation of the perceptual set on the basis of illusory representations and at perception of concrete visual stimuli. Hum. Physiol. **25**(1), 5–14 (1999). (in Russian)
11. Leontiev, A.N., Zaporogec, A.V.: The Restoration of Movements, 231 p. Soviet Science, Moscow (1945). (in Russian)
12. Lyakhovetskii, V., Karpinskaia, V.: The aftereffects of Müller-Lyer and Ponzo illusions: differences revealed in sensorimotor domain. Proc. Latvian Acad. Sci. **71**(5), 352–358 (2017)
13. Milner, D., Goodale, M.: Visual Brain in Action. Oxford University Press, Oxford (1995)

14. Morgan, M.J., Hole, G.J., Glennerster, A.: Biases and sensitivities in geometrical illusions. Vis. Res. **30**(11), 1793–1810 (1990)
15. Oldfield, R.C.: The assessment and analysis of handedness: the edinburgh inventory. Neuropsychologia **9**, 97–113 (1971)
16. Shoshina, I.I., Perevozchikova, I.N., Konkina, S.A., Pronin, S.V., Shelepin, Iu.E., Bendera, A.P.: Features of perception of length of segments under conditions of Ponzo and Müller-Lyer illusions in schizophrenia. Zh. Vyssh. Nerv. Deiat. Im. I.P. Pavlova **61**(6), 697–705 (2011). (in Russian)
17. Valerjev, P., Gulan, T.: The role of context in Müller-Lyer illusion: the case of negative Müller-Lyer illusion. Rev. Psychol. **20**, 29–36 (2013)

Network Study on SecA – A Component of Sec Secretion System in Bacteria *Pseudomonas Aeruginosa*

Shaomin Yan and Guang Wu[✉]

State Key Laboratory of Non-food Biomass and Enzyme Technology,
National Engineering Research Center for Non-food Biorefinery,
Guangxi Key Laboratory of Bio-refinery, Guangxi Academy of Sciences,
98 Daling Road, Nanning 530007, Guangxi, China
hongguanglishibahao@yahoo.com

Abstract. *Pseudomonas aeruginosa* is a Gram-negative bacterium and infects plants, animals and humans. Secretion systems in *P. aeruginosa* play an important role in infections. Sec secretion system has eight components, of which SecA is an ATPase. However, gene network study on how SecA functions under different experimental conditions has yet to be done. In this study, network is used to analyze *P. aeruginosa* genes under four types of experimental conditions, i.e. stress, habitat, nutrition and mutation. Special attention is given to (i) how many clusters form under control and experimental conditions, (ii) how many genes in SecA cluster, (iii) how many genes change their membership together with SecA, and (iv) which gene connects with SecA under control and experimental conditions, and their functions. The results demonstrate how genes reorganize under experimental conditions, and discussion is given to the reasons for such reorganizations.

Keywords: Network · *Pseudomonas aeruginosa* · Secretion system

1 Introduction

Pseudomonas aeruginosa is a Gram-negative bacterium living in soil and water. It can infect plants [1], animals [2], and humans including eye [3], burn wound [4], acute and chronic pulmonary infections, especially cystic fibrosis [5], which is associated with substantial morbidity and mortality [6]. Besides, *P. aeruginosa* is the major bacterium developing drug resistance in clinic [7].

Gram-negative bacteria have seven secretion systems [8], which secrete toxins, degradative enzymes, and others leading to damages and death of host cells [9]. Because Gram-negative bacteria have outer and inner membranes, the secretion process is carried out in two steps: (i) type II secretion system operates across outer membrane [10], and (ii) Sec system operates across inner membrane [11].

Sec system is composed of SecA, which is an ATP-dependent motor protein [12]; SecB, which is chaperone brings protein precursors to Sec system [13]; SecYEG, which is a complex of SecY, SecE and SecG forming a gated pore in the inner

© Springer International Publishing AG, part of Springer Nature 2018
T. Huang et al. (Eds.): ISNN 2018, LNCS 10878, pp. 807–814, 2018.
https://doi.org/10.1007/978-3-319-92537-0_91

membrane [14]; SecDF, which is composed of SecD and SecF facilitating protein secretion [15]; YajC and YidC, whose function is related to protein insertion [16].

SecA is important because it converts ATP into a mechanical force to drive proteins to go through Sec secretion system across the inner membrane [17]. However, it is not clear how SecA interacts with other genes in *P. aeruginosa*, especially under different circumstances. A way to address this question is to combine all available transcriptomic data and look at how SecA gene network functions under various experimental conditions. Currently, the most transcriptomic studies on *P. aeruginosa* are done using platform GPL84, and their results are documented in public domain, Gene Expression Omnibus (GEO) [18]. To our knowledge, network has not been used to investigate SecA, therefore this study was designed to analyze the gene network of SecA from *P. aeruginosa* under different experimental conditions.

2   Materials and Methods

2.1   Data

Platform GPL84 contains 5549 *P. aeruginosa* PAO1 genes [19], of which SecA, SecB, SecD, SecE, SecF, SecG, SecY and YajC are PA4403, PA5128, PA3821, PA4276, PA3820, PA4747, PA4243, and PA3822, respectively. Of the transcriptomic data in GEO [18], the experimental conditions can be classified into four types: mutation in *P. aeruginosa*, changing habitat, environmental stress and starvation.

2.2   Gene Network

In this study, each gene corresponds to a node, and the edge between two nodes is determined according to correlation between transcriptomic data for these two genes. When two genes work together under the same condition, their transcriptomic profiles can be correlated. In this way, network can reveal how genes organize under the control condition and how genes reorganize under experiment conditions [20]. Network analysis was conducted using iGraph R package [21] and Pajek [22].

3   Results and Discussion

Of various stresses on *P. aeruginosa* such as azithromycin [23], ciprofloxacin [24], hydrogen peroxide (H_2O_2) is important because H_2O_2 plays crucial roles in release of extracellular DNA [25], DNA repair proteins, catalases, intracellular iron transport, bacterial adaption to oxidative stress, pyocins, glycolysis [26, 27]. Figure 1 shows the gene network of *P. aeruginosa* under control (left panel) and stress (right panel) experimental conditions, i.e. *P. aeruginosa* PAO1 exposed to H_2O_2 [26]. In this type of figures, each symbol represents a gene, the line between two symbols indicates a good correlation in transcriptomic data between two genes, and the same colored symbols construct a cluster. Actually, each panel includes all 5549 *P. aeruginosa* PAO1 genes.

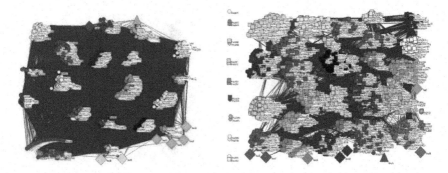

Fig. 1. Gene network of *P. aeruginosa* under control (left panel) and H_2O_2 (right panel) conditions. Triangle symbols represent SecA, diamond symbols represent the rest of Sec genes, circle symbols represent the rest 5541 genes under control condition, and square symbols represent the rest 5541 genes under experimental condition. The data are GSE3090 in GEO [18, 26]. (Color figure online)

Of various habitats for *P. aeruginosa* such as plant [28], biofilms [29], animal gut [30], burn wounds of humans [31], *P. aeruginosa* in cystic fibrosis is most important [32] because most cystic fibrosis patients have infection of *P. aeruginosa* [33] although cystic fibrosis is an inherited disease [34]. Figure 2 displays the gene network of *P. aeruginosa* from planktonic culture (left panel) and from clonal isolate of cystic fibrosis (right panel).

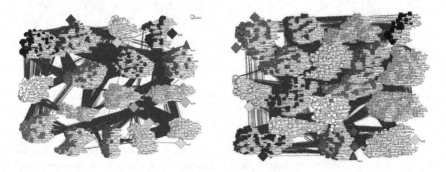

Fig. 2. Gene network of *P. aeruginosa* from planktonic culture (left panel) and from clonal isolate of cystic fibrosis (right panel). The data are GSE10304 in GEO [18, 32]. (Color figure online)

Of variety of nutrition in *P. aeruginosa* such as iron starvation [35], sulfate starvation [36], low oxygen tension [37], phosphate abundance [38], iron is very important for the growth of *P. aeruginosa*. Figure 3 demonstrates the gene network of *P. aeruginosa* without supplement of PQS (left panel) and with PQS (right panel).

Of various mutations in *P. aeruginosa* such as mutations in quorum sensing [40], in regulation of fatty acid [41], in biofilm formation [42], in cell-surface signalling

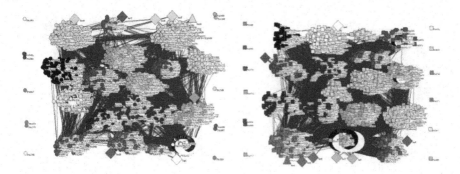

Fig. 3. Gene network of *P. aeruginosa* without supplement of PQS (left panel) and with PQS (right panel). The data are GSE3836 in GEO [18, 39]. (Color figure online)

systems [43], in agmatine and putrescine catabolism [44], the mutation in cystic fibrosis is clinically most important [45]. Figure 4 illustrates the gene network of *P. aeruginosa* from non-clonal isolate (left panel) and clonal isolate with mutation (right panel).

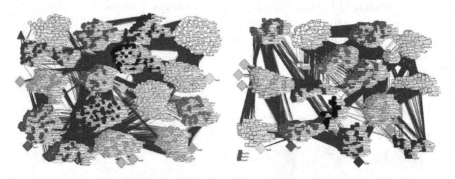

Fig. 4. Gene network of *P. aeruginosa* from non-clonal isolate (left panel) and clonal isolate with mutation (right panel). The data are GSE6122 in GEO [18, 45]. (Color figure online)

Interestingly, Sec components, i.e. SecA, SecB, SecD, SecE, SecF, SecG, SecY, and YajC, belong to different clusters, and not many connections exist between them in these figures, although they all work for Sec secretion system. These suggest that the regulation of Sec secretion system could work differently for each component.

How 5549 genes from *P. aeruginosa* organize and reorganize in terms of correlation network can be further elaborated in Table 1. At first, the number of cluster (row 1) and number of genes in SecA cluster (row 3) are different in control groups, which is plausible because the samples of *P. aeruginosa* come from different sources.

In the first row in Table 1, H_2O_2 has strong influence on the number of clusters. This is reasonable since bacteria often face various reactive oxygen species during their lifetime and *P. aeruginosa* has a defense system against reactive oxidants [26]. Along the third row in Table 1, the number of genes in SecA cluster is quite different one from another. As a cluster indicates that the genes in the cluster have similar transcriptomic

Table 1. Network statistics (No. A: Number of cluster, No. B: Number of genes in SecA cluster, No. C: Number of genes changing their numbership with SecA, Color: color of SecA cluster)

Group	Figure 1		Figure 2		Figure 3		Figure 4	
	Control	Stress	Control	Habitat	Control	Nutrition	Control	Mutation
No. A	19	35	17	17	27	29	16	18
Color	Lime green	Cadet blue	Cadet blue	Red	Pink	Orange	Purple	Lime green
No. B	398	258	348	437	360	391	314	545
No. C	22		28		26		58	

profiles, so it is more likely that these genes could function simultaneously with SecA. It is interesting to note that the number of genes in SecA cluster decreases in Fig. 1 whereas the number of genes in SecA cluster increases in Figs. 2, 3 and 4. This suggests that *P. aeruginosa* mobilizes more genes for secretion together with SecA under habitat, nutrition and mutation conditions. Furthermore, the fourth row in Table 1 indicates how many genes change their membership together with SecA. Evidently, mutation leads more genes to change their membership together with SecA because a single mutation could change the metabolic pathway completely [45].

It is intriguing to look at which gene connects with SecA in these figures. For Fig. 1, ten genes (PA4626, PA4718, PA5026, PA5163, PA5320, PA5358, PA5387, PA5459, PA5539, PA5563) and two genes (PA4791, PA4993) connect with SecA in control and experimental groups. For Fig. 2, twelve genes (PA4410, PA4605, PA4703, PA4729, PA4766, PA4810, PA4968, PA5007, PA5069, PA5189, PA5473, PA5565) and six genes (PA4627, PA4749, PA4852, PA4937, PA5010, PA5301) connect with SecA in control and experimental groups. For Fig. 3, two genes (PA4512, PA4619) and three genes (PA4729, PA5268, PA5500) connect with SecA in control and experimental groups. For Fig. 4, six genes (PA4782, PA5099, PA5241, PA5268, PA5391, PA5485) and sixteen genes (PA4574, PA4680, PA4723, PA4776, PA4835, PA4865, PA4872, PA4917, PA5019, PA5065, PA5067, PA5091, PA5214, PA5244, PA5281, PA5316) connect with SecA in control and experimental groups.

When look at these genes according to *Pseudomonas* proteins classification [46], a general patterns can be observed. For control groups, the connected genes are mainly related to (i) coenzyme transport and metabolism, (ii) cell cycle control, cell division, chromosome partitioning, (iii) cell wall/membrane/envelope biogenesis, (iv) energy production and conversion, and (v) inorganic ion transport and metabolism. For experimental groups, the connected genes are mainly related to (i) amino acid transport and metabolism, (ii) carbohydrate transport and metabolism, (iii) translation, ribosomal structure and biogenesis, and (iv) inorganic ion transport and metabolism.

It is reasonable that SecA connects with the genes related to transport and metabolism under both control and experimental conditions because Sec secretion system secretes proteins; related to cell division/wall/membrane/envelope biogenesis under control condition because SecA is located in inner membrane; related to energy production and conversion because SecA itself is an ATPase under control condition. However, it is not clear why the genes related to inorganic ion transport appear in both control and experimental groups, because SecA is not involved in ion transport. This should be a point for pursuit in future. Interestingly enough, a recent study shows that SecA interacts ribosomes [47], which could explain why SecA connects with genes related to translation, ribosomal structure and biogenesis under experimental condition.

In conclusion, we conduct a network study on transcriptomic data from *P. aeruginosa* under four types of experimental conditions, demonstrate how genes reorganize under experimental conditions, and discuss the reasons for such reorganizations.

Acknowledgements. This study was partly supported by National Natural Science Foundation of China (31460296 and 31560315), and Special Funds for Building of Guangxi Talent Highland.

References

1. Sitaraman, R.: *Pseudomonas* spp. as models for plant-microbe interactions. Front. Plant Sci. **6**, 787 (2015)
2. Rahme, L.G., Ausubel, F.M., Cao, H., Drenkard, E., Goumnerov, B.C., Lau, G.W., Mahajan-Miklos, S., Plotnikova, J., Tan, M.W., Tsongalis, J., Walendziewicz, C.L., Tompkins, R.G.: Plants and animals share functionally common bacterial virulence factors. Proc. Natl. Acad. Sci. U.S.A. **97**, 8815–8821 (2000)
3. Willcox, M.D.: *Pseudomonas aeruginosa* infection and inflammation during contact lens wear: a review. Optom. Vis. Sci. **84**, 273–278 (2007)
4. Church, D., Elsayed, S., Reid, O., Winston, B., Lindsay, R.: Burn wound infections. Clin. Microbiol. Rev. **19**, 403–434 (2006)
5. Elborn, J.S.: Cystic fibrosis. Lancet **388**(10059), 2519–2531 (2016)
6. Klockgether, J., Tümmler, B.: Recent advances in understanding *Pseudomonas aeruginosa* as a pathogen. F1000Res. **6**, 1261 (2017)
7. Buhl, M., Peter, S., Willmann, M.: Prevalence and risk factors associated with colonization and infection of extensively drug-resistant *Pseudomonas aeruginosa*: a systematic review. Expert Rev. Anti. Infect. Ther. **13**, 1159–1170 (2015)
8. Yan, S., Wu, G.: Secretory pathway of cellulase: a mini-review. Biotechnol. Biofuels **6**, 177 (2013)
9. Cianciotto, N.P., White, R.C.: Expanding role of type II secretion in bacterial pathogenesis and beyond. Infect. Immun. **85** pii, e00014–e00017 (2017)
10. Costa, T.R., Felisberto-Rodrigues, C., Meir, A., Prevost, M.S., Redzej, A., Trokter, M., Waksman, G.: Secretion systems in Gram-negative bacteria: structural and mechanistic insights. Nat. Rev. Microbiol. **13**, 343–359 (2015)
11. Tsirigotaki, A., De Geyter, J., Sostaric, N., Economou, A., Karamanou, S.: Protein export through the bacterial Sec pathway. Nat. Rev. Microbiol. **15**, 21–36 (2017)
12. Sardis, M.F., Economou, A.: SecA: a tale of two protomers. Mol. Microbiol. **76**, 1070–1081 (2010)
13. Yan, S., Wu, G.: Large-scale evolutionary analyses on SecB of bacterial Sec system. PLoS ONE **10**, e0120417 (2015)
14. Beckwith, J.: The Sec-dependent pathway. Res. Microbiol. **164**, 497–504 (2013)
15. Yan, S., Wu, G.: Evolutionary evidence on suitability of SecD as a target for development of antibacterial agents against *Staphylococcus aureus*. Ecol. Evol. **6**, 1393–1410 (2016)

16. Komar, J., Alvira, S., Schulze, R.J., Martin, R., Lycklama, A., Nijeholt, J.A., Lee, S.C., Dafforn, T.R., Deckers-Hebestreit, G., Berger, I., Schaffitzel, C., Collinson, I.: Membrane protein insertion and assembly by the bacterial holo-translocon SecYEG-SecDF-YajC-YidC. Biochem. J. **473**, 3341–3354 (2016)

17. Kusters, I., Driessen, A.J.: SecA, a remarkable nanomachine. Cell. Mol. Life Sci. **68**, 2053–2066 (2011)

18. Barrett, T., Wilhite, S.E., Ledoux, P., Evangelista, C., Kim, I.F., Tomashevsky, M., Marshall, K.A., Phillippy, K.H., Sherman, P.M., Holko, M., Yefanov, A., Lee, H., Zhang, N., Robertson, C.L., Serova, N., Davis, S., Soboleva, A.: NCBI GEO: archive for functional genomics data sets–update. Nucleic Acids Res. **41**, D991–D995 (2013)

19. http://www.affymetrix.com/support/technical/byproduct.affx?product=paeruginosa

20. Yan, S., Wu, G.: Reorganization of gene network for degradation of polycyclic aromatic hydrocarbons (PAHs) in *Pseudomonas aeruginosa* PAO1 under several conditions. J. Appl. Genet. **58**, 545–563 (2017)

21. http://igraph.org/

22. de Nooy, W., Mrvar, A., Batagelj, V.: Exploratory Social Network Analysis with Pajek: Revised and Expanded Second Edition, Structural Analysis in the Social Sciences 34. Cambridge University Press, Cambride (2011)

23. Nalca, Y., Jänsch, L., Bredenbruch, F., Geffers, R., Buer, J., Häussler, S.: Quorum-sensing antagonistic activities of azithromycin in *Pseudomonas aeruginosa* PAO1: a global approach. Antimicrob. Agents Chemother. **50**, 1680–1688 (2006)

24. Cirz, R.T., O'Neill, B.M., Hammond, J.A., Head, S.R., Romesberg, F.E.: Defining the *Pseudomonas aeruginosa* SOS response and its role in the global response to the antibiotic ciprofloxacin. J. Bacteriol. **188**, 7101–7110 (2006)

25. Das, T., Manefield, M.: Phenazine production enhances extracellular DNA release via hydrogen peroxide generation in *Pseudomonas aeruginosa*. Commun. Integr. Biol. **6**, e23570 (2013)

26. Chang, W., Small, D.A., Toghrol, F., Bentley, W.E.: Microarray analysis of *Pseudomonas aeruginosa* reveals induction of pyocin genes in response to hydrogen peroxide. BMC Genom. **6**, 115 (2005)

27. Deng, X., Liang, H., Ulanovskaya, O.A., Ji, Q., Zhou, T., Sun, F., Lu, Z., Hutchison, A.L., Lan, L., Wu, M., Cravatt, B.F., He, C.: Steady-state hydrogen peroxide induces glycolysis in *Staphylococcus aureus* and *Pseudomonas aeruginosa*. J. Bacteriol. **196**, 2499–2513 (2014)

28. Weir, T.L., Stull, V.J., Badri, D., Trunck, L.A., Schweizer, H.P., Vivanco, J.: Global gene expression profiles suggest an important role for nutrient acquisition in early pathogenesis in a plant model of *Pseudomonas aeruginosa* infection. Appl. Environ. Microbiol. **74**, 5784–5791 (2008)

29. Mikkelsen, H., Bond, N.J., Skindersoe, M.E., Givskov, M., Lilley, K.S., Welch, M.: Biofilms and type III secretion are not mutually exclusive in *Pseudomonas aeruginosa*. Microbiology **155**, 687–598 (2009)

30. Koh, A.Y., Mikkelsen, P.J., Smith, R.S., Coggshall, K.T., Kamei, A., Givskov, M., Lory, S., Pier, G.B.: Utility of in vivo transcription profiling for identifying *Pseudomonas aeruginosa* genes needed for gastrointestinal colonization and dissemination. PLoS ONE **5**, e15131 (2010)

31. Bielecki, P., Puchałka, J., Wos-Oxley, M.L., Loessner, H., Glik, J., Kawecki, M., Nowak, M., Tümmler, B., Weiss, S., dos Santos, V.A.: In-vivo expression profiling of *Pseudomonas aeruginosa* infections reveals niche-specific and strain-independent transcriptional programs. PLoS ONE **6**, e24235 (2011)

32. Manos, J., Arthur, J., Rose, B., Tingpej, P., Fung, C., Curtis, M., Webb, J.S., Hu, H., Kjelleberg, S., Gorrell, M.D., Bye, P., Harbour, C.: Transcriptome analyses and biofilm-forming characteristics of a clonal *Pseudomonas aeruginosa* from the cystic fibrosis lung. J. Med. Microbiol. **57**, 1454–1565 (2008)

33. Kumar, V., Abbas, A.K., Aster, J.: Robbins Basic Pathology. Elsevier, New York (2017)

34. O'Sullivan, B.P., Freedman, S.D.: Cystic fibrosis. Lancet **373**, 1891–1904 (2009)

35. Zheng, P., Sun, J., Geffers, R., Zeng, A.P.: Functional characterization of the gene PA2384 in large-scale gene regulation in response to iron starvation in *Pseudomonas aeruginosa*. J. Biotechnol. **132**, 342–352 (2007)

36. Tralau, T., Vuilleumier, S., Thibault, C., Campbell, B.J., Hart, C.A., Kertesz, M.A.: Transcriptomic analysis of the sulfate starvation response of *Pseudomonas aeruginosa*. J. Bacteriol. **189**, 6743–6750 (2007)

37. Alvarez-Ortega, C., Harwood, C.S.: Responses of *Pseudomonas aeruginosa* to low oxygen indicate that growth in the cystic fibrosis lung is by aerobic respiration. Mol. Microbiol. **65**, 153–165 (2007)

38. Zaborin, A., Gerdes, S., Holbrook, C., Liu, D.C., Zaborina, O.Y., Alverdy, J.C.: *Pseudomonas aeruginosa* overrides the virulence inducing effect of opioids when it senses an abundance of phosphate. PLoS ONE **7**, e34883 (2012)

39. Bredenbruch, F., Geffers, R., Nimtz, M., Buer, J., Häussler, S.: The *Pseudomonas aeruginosa* quinolone signal (PQS) has an iron-chelating activity. Environ. Microbiol. **8**, 1318–1329 (2006)

40. Lequette, Y., Lee, J.H., Ledgham, F., Lazdunski, A., Greenberg, E.P.: A distinct QscR regulon in the *Pseudomonas aeruginosa* quorum-sensing circuit. J. Bacteriol. **188**, 3365–3370 (2006)

41. Kang, Y., Nguyen, D.T., Son, M.S., Hoang, T.T.: The *Pseudomonas aeruginosa* PsrA responds to long-chain fatty acid signals to regulate the fadBA5 beta-oxidation operon. Microbiology **154**, 1584–1598 (2008)

42. Attila, C., Ueda, A., Wood, T.K.: PA2663 (PpyR) increases biofilm formation in *Pseudomonas aeruginosa* PAO1 through the psl operon and stimulates virulence and quorum-sensing phenotypes. Appl. Microbiol. Biotechnol. **78**, 293–307 (2008)

43. Llamas, M.A., Mooij, M.J., Sparrius, M., Vandenbroucke-Grauls, C.M., Ratledge, C., Bitter, W.: Characterization of five novel *Pseudomonas aeruginosa* cell-surface signalling systems. Mol. Microbiol. **67**, 458–472 (2008)

44. Chou, H.T., Kwon, D.H., Hegazy, M., Lu, C.D.: Transcriptome analysis of agmatine and putrescine catabolism in *Pseudomonas aeruginosa* PAO1. J. Bacteriol. **190**, 1966–1975 (2008)

45. Manos, J., Arthur, J., Rose, B., Bell, S., Tingpej, P., Hu, H., Webb, J., Kjelleberg, S., Gorrell, M.D., Bye, P., Harbour, C.: Gene expression characteristics of a cystic fibrosis epidemic strain of *Pseudomonas aeruginosa* during biofilm and planktonic growth. FEMS Microbiol. Lett. **292**, 107–114 (2009)

46. Winsor, G.L., Griffiths, E.J., Lo, R., Dhillon, B.K., Shay, J.A., Brinkman, F.S.: Enhanced annotations and features for comparing thousands of *Pseudomonas* genomes in the *Pseudomonas* genome database. Nucleic Acids Res. **44**, D646–D653 (2016)

47. Huber, D., Jamshad, M., Hanmer, R., Schibich, D., Döring, K., Marcomini, I., Kramer, G., Bukau, B.: SecA cotranslationally interacts with nascent substrate proteins *in vivo*. J. Bacteriol. **199**, pii: e00622–e00616 (2016)

A Prediction Model for the Risk of Osteoporosis Fracture in the Elderly Based on a Neural Network

Yong Wang[1], Zhiqiang Zhang[1], Nanchuan Cai[2(✉)], Yousheng Zhou[1], and Di Xiao[3]

[1] College of Computer Science and Technology, Chongqing University of Posts and Telecommunications, Chongqing 400065, China
[2] Chongqing the Seventh People's Hospital, Chongqing 400054, China
389962417@qq.com
[3] College of Computer Science, Chongqing University, Chongqing 400044, China

Abstract. A prediction model for the risk of osteoporosis fractures in the aged people is proposed based on a neural network system. A back propagation (BP) neural network is used as the key component in the prediction model. In our prediction model, not only the bone mineral density (BMD), but also some conventional medical examination data from renal function test (RFT), routine blood test (RBT) and liver function test (LFT) are considered. About 5,000 sample data are extracted from more than 20,000 cases in the Seventh People's Hospital of Chongqing, China. The BP neural network is trained by a 10-fold cross validation method. Then, the well trained BP neural network is used to predict the risk of osteoporosis fractures. Moreover, we also test the performance of the proposed model in the condition of privacy preservation by hiding gender and age. The experiment results show that the prediction accuracy of the proposed model is more than 70%. Therefore, the model has the high potential to auxiliary diagnose the possibility of osteoporosis fractures.

Keywords: BP neural network · Osteoporosis fractures · Prediction model
Medical care

1 Introduction

With the arrival of an aging society, the number of patients with osteoporosis gradually increases in China. The osteoporotic fractures and its complication is becoming one of the common diseases for the aged people in China. For any diseases, the prevention is always an important and effective way. Now, the BMD detection is an important method to diagnose and predict the osteoporotic fractures. However, some studies show that the prediction accuracy of osteoporosis fracture is not high if only depending on BMD [1].

In the process of disease diagnosis and treatments, there are some very complex nonlinear connections between detected information and results. It is not easy or even impossible to establish an explicit expression between the detected information and

© Springer International Publishing AG, part of Springer Nature 2018
T. Huang et al. (Eds.): ISNN 2018, LNCS 10878, pp. 815–823, 2018.
https://doi.org/10.1007/978-3-319-92537-0_92

results. On the other side, artificial neural network (ANN) is an effective method to deal with the nonlinear relations between variables [2]. In medical field, the etiology of most diseases is not clear and the manifestations of various diseases are varied. Thus, the conventional ways to diagnose diseases are mainly based on doctor's experience, symptoms, and medical examination results. To enhance the accuracy of medical diagnosis, some novel methods based on neural network, deep learning technology, and artificial intelligence are becoming a new trend.

In this paper, we construct a prediction model based on a BP neural network to seek the relationship between osteoporosis fracture and some routine medical examination data. The model focuses on predicting the risk of osteoporosis fracture in aged population. The test results show the proposed prediction model is simple and effective, and has high potential to be applied to inspect osteoporosis fracture.

2   Osteoporosis Fracture in the Elderly

Osteoporosis is a common geriatric disease, which is the most common reason for a broken bone among the elderly [3]. The Osteoporosis owns the following characteristics: the bone mass and bone strength are decreased; the fibrous structure of bone tissue is degenerated; the bone brittleness is increased. Thus, bones may weaken to such a degree that a break may occur with minor stress or spontaneously. Until a broken bone occurs there are typically no symptoms [4]. According to the epidemiological survey, there are about 1.5 million fractures per year caused by osteoporosis in the United States [5]. With the growing of the world population and the coming of global population ages, the number of people suffered osteoporosis fracture will rise to 2.6 million in 2025 and 6.3 million in 2050 [5]. The bone broken is an important factor for the aged people to lead to disability, or even death [6]. The effect of osteoporotic fracture can last five years when it happened. The death risk for the aged people suffered hip fracture in three months is 5–8 times higher than that of the normal aged people [6].

The main reason for osteoporosis fracture in the elderly is the decrease of bone strength. Bone strength is a combination of bone density and bone mass. Now, BMD detection is the best way to assess bone strength and is also a reliable method for early diagnosis of osteoporosis. However, according to the clinical observations, some patients suffered bone fracture but their BMDs are not in the condition of osteoporosis. Meanwhile, some patients show the opposite results, that is, they are in a very low BMD status but they do not suffer bone broken. Some studies show that about 10%–44% of osteoporosis fractures occur in the people whose BMD match the standard of osteoporosis [7]. Only using BMD cannot predict the osteoporotic fracture accurately. This method probably omits some patients with high risk of bone fracture but their BMD is in a normal level. As we know, the risk assessment of bone broken is of great significance for the prevention and treatment of osteoporosis fracture. Therefore, it is attracting more and more interests for the researcher in medical care and computer science to how to effectively identify the patient group with the high risk of osteoporosis fracture.

3   The Proposed Prediction Model

In the conventional method, only BMD is used to evaluate the risk of osteoporosis fracture. However, the accuracy rate of this method is about 45%, which is hard to satisfy the requirement of health [7]. Here, we proposed a prediction model to evaluate the risk of bone broke based on a BPANN. BPANN is one of the most widely used neural network models, as shown Fig. 1, which consists of an input layer, several hidden layers and an output layer. To achieve a comprehensive result, more medical indexes are used in the proposed model. Moreover, to avoid excessive medical examination, we only choose the indexes in the common medical examination.

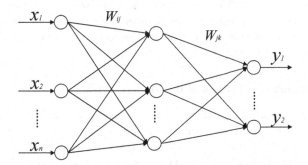

Fig. 1. The general structure of BPANN

3.1   The Inputs of the Model

Firstly, some basic data are selected as the inputs of the BPANN, which are listed as follows:

- Gender: the value of gender is 0 or 1. Here, 0 is for male and 1 is for female.
- Age: the data type for age is integer.
- Height: the unit for height is centimeter (cm).
- Weight: the unit for weight is kilogram (kg).

Secondly, since BMD is an important index to evaluate the risk of bone broken, it is also selected as an input of the BPANN.

Thirdly, some mineral indexes from RFT, RBT and LFT are used as the input variables. They are albumin (Alb), calcium(Ca), phosphorus(P), and alkaline phosphatase (Alp). All of them are important mineral materials of constructing bones. Moreover, the numbers of hemoglobin (Hb) and lymphoctyte(Lym) in RBT are chosen as two another input variables. They are both related to the nutritional status of bones.

Since 11 variables are considered in our model, the number of input layer nodes is also set as 11. These 11 variables are divided into two types. One type is for the 0/1 variable and the other is for the numeric variable.

3.2   The Output of the Model

The purpose of constructing this model is predicting the bone broke. If the bone broken happened, the output of the model is 1. Otherwise, the result is 0. According to the return value and its format, only one node is needed in the output layer.

3.3   The Hidden Layer of the Model

The key issue for the hidden layer is determining the number of nodes in it. Here, we determine the number of nodes in the hidden layer by an experiment method. According to experiences, the number of nodes in the hidden layer is initialized as 100 and the prediction results are calculated in a sample dataset. Then, we adjust the number of nodes and calculate the results again. We repeat adjusting the nodes for some times. Finally, we select the node number corresponding to the best prediction results as the final number of nodes in the hidden layer. The details on the selection of nodes in hidden layer will be described in Sect. 5.2.

3.4   The Computation Process of the Model

In the proposed model, the numbers of inputs, neurons in hidden layer and output neuron are 11, 100, and 1, respectively. Define v_{ij} $(i = 0, 1, 2, \ldots, 11; j = 1, 2, \ldots, 100)$ and $w_{jk}(j = 1,2,\ldots, 100; k = 1)$ as the weight parameters between input layer and hidden layer, and between hidden layer and output layer, respectively. Denote $a_j(j = 1, 2, \ldots, 11)$, $b_j(j = 1, 2, \ldots, 100)$ and $c_j(j = 1)$ as the threshold values of neurons in the hidden layer and output layer, respectively. For a training sample $X(x_1, x_2, \ldots, x_{11})$, we can get the output result as below:

$$I_j = \sum_{i=1}^{11} v_{ij}x_i + a_i, \quad j = 1, 2, \ldots, 100 \tag{1}$$

$$y_j = f_1(I_j) = f_1(\sum_{i=1}^{11} (v_{ij}x_i + a_j)), \quad j = 1, 2, \ldots, 100 \tag{2}$$

$$I_k = \sum_{j=1}^{100} (w_{jk}y_j + b_j), \quad k = 1 \tag{3}$$

$$Z_k = f_2(I_k) = f_2(\sum_{j=1}^{100} (w_{jk}y_j + b_j)), \quad k = 1 \tag{4}$$

where z_k is the output value corresponding to sample X; f_1 and f_2 are the activation functions. When z_k is computed, we can adjust the weight parameters in the model by the backpropagation of errors. After finish the training, the model can be used to predict.

4 Data Collection and Preprocessing

4.1 Data Collection

In this section, the proposed prediction model is evaluated on a real dataset from Chongqing 7th People's Hospital. All the data used in this study are collected from electronic health record in Chongqing 7th People's Hospital. We firstly collected the records from January 2016 to December 2017, which includes 21,631 cases. We do a preliminary screening about the data and delete the data that does not meet the requirement of experiment. Moreover, some bone broken cases caused by traffic accident and violence are removed. Finally, the 5,230 cases were obtained, including 788 positive cases. In the final 5,230 cases, most of them include the 11 medical examination indexes described in Sect. 3.1. A part of the dataset is shown in Table 1.

Table 1. A part of the dataset

Gender	Age	Height	Weight	BMD	Alb	Ca	P	Alp	Hb	Lym
1	69	168	66	−0.6346	40.8	2.14	0.96	107.68	1.42	115.63
0	51			−1.2825	46.4	2.49	1.09	151.6	1.59	148.5
1	71	165	74	−0.7323					1.82	141
0	69	172	79	−1.5923	40.5	2.34	1.18	108.5	2.17	137
0	84	150	42	−3.2427	42.8	2.44	1.3	89.7	1.01	117
0	76			−3.3952	37.23	2.11	0.94	140.5	1.76	122.75
0	85			−3.2941	29.77	1.98	0.67	94.5	0.73	88.89
0	64	158	55	−3.6052	39.75			98.1	0.88	97
0	71	150	50	−3.0520	46.5	2.34	1.14	77.2	1.66	130
1	74	167	59	−1.0450	40.9	2.28	0.75	84.7	1.39	125.67
1	86	160	65	−0.8104	43.3	2.32	1.16	71.1	1.49	119.67
0	89	150	35	−2.8167	41.5	2.27	1.16	97.4	1.52	113
1	57				44.6	2.32	0.73	114.5		
0	82				29.75	1.98	1.95	129.88	2.1	110.14

4.2 Data Preprocessing

The general operations on data preprocessing are performed to make the dataset satisfy the requirement of the prediction. The following steps are executed orderly.

Step 1. Fill the missing data. As we know, different patients have different illness condition. The medical examinations for them are different. It is not necessary for some patients to take all the medical examinations related to our prediction model. Thus, in the dataset, some data are missing. In order to make the dataset more suitable for classifier learning, we used the mean value to fill the missing data values.

Step 2. Rescale the data. There are 11 indexes in our dataset. They have quite different measurement units. Since the BPANN is sensitive to the scale of measurement, we need to rescale all the data in a same measurement unit. Here, we scale all the indexes into the interval [0, 1] by using the 'Min-Max-Scaler' method. Step 3. In order to avoid overfitting and to make training stable and fast, we used L_2 norm to normalize and regularize.

Step 4. Relieve the oversampling problem. There are totally 5,230 cases in our dataset. Only 880 cases among them are positive. The negative cases are much more than the positive ones. Thus, the SMOTE algorithm is used to balance the positive cases and the negative cases [8].

5   Results

5.1   Evaluation Metrics

In general, the five metrics are used to evaluate the performance of the classifier, i.e. accuracy, area under curve(AUC), precision, true positive rate(TPR), and false positive rate(FPR). The formulas for these five metrics are listed below [9]:

$$Accuracy = \frac{TP + TN}{TP + FP + TN + FN} \tag{5}$$

$$Precision = \frac{TP}{TP + FP} \tag{6}$$

$$TPR = \frac{TP}{TP + FN} \tag{7}$$

$$FPR = \frac{FP}{TN + FP} \tag{8}$$

$$AUC = \frac{\sum_{i \in positiveClass} rank_i - \frac{M(1+M)}{2}}{MN} \tag{9}$$

where TP is the number of true positives, TN is the number of true negatives, FP is the number of false positives, FN is the number of false negatives. M and N are the numbers of positive samples and negative samples, respectively. $rank_i$ is the rank value corresponding to the score of the positive-negative pair.

5.2   Experiment Results and Analysis

Since the number of cases in the dataset is not enough large, a 10-fold cross validation strategy is used in our experiment. In the BPANN, the Relu function shown in Eq. (10) is set as the hidden layer activation function $f1$. The learning rate and the number of training are respectively set to 0.001 and 1000. The sigmoid function shown in Eq. (11) is chosen as the activation function $f2$ of output layer. The classification threshold is 0.5. The number of nodes in the hidden layers is determined by a trial and error method. We set different nodes for the hidden layer and compute the corresponding

ROC results, which is shown in Fig. 2. Since the difference of ROCs with different nodes in hidden layer is very small, we zoom in the ROC curves. According to Fig. 2, it can be conclude that the hidden layer with 100 nodes has the better result. Therefore, the number of nodes is set as 100.

$$f(x) = \max(0, x) \tag{10}$$

$$f(x) = \frac{1}{1 + e^{-x}} \tag{11}$$

We firstly obtain the prediction results by using all the input data described in Sect. 3.1. The statistics results for the performance of our model are shown in Fig. 3. As we know, the age and gender are the two important factors related to the person privacy. From the view of privacy preservation, we remove the age, or gender, or both of them from the model inputs. To convenience of description, the condition without using age is defined as NA. Similarly, NG is for the condition without using gender. NGA is for the lack of both age information and gender information. The prediction results in NG, NA and NGA are computed and compared with the normal condition. To the convenience of comparison, the evaluate metrics for the results in the privacy preservation conditions are also shown in Fig. 3, too.

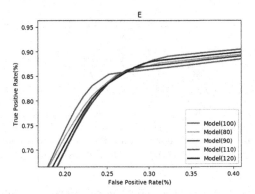

Fig. 2. The ROCs with different nodes in the hidden layer

According to Fig. 3A, the accuracies of normal condition, NG, NA, NGA are all higher than 77% Meanwhile, the precisions of normal condition and NG, NA, NGA are all higher than 78% (Fig. 3B). The high accuracy and precision show that the BPANN is a promising way to predict the risk of osteoporosis fracture. Moreover, the effect on prediction result is very small by the removing age and gender from the inputs. The reduction of accuracy and precision caused by ignoring age and gender is about 2 percent. It implies that it is possible to remove the private information (age and gender) and keep the prediction in a high accurate level.

Based on the results shown in Fig. 3C to D, we have that all AUCs are larger than 0.78. The TPRs and FPRs of the four conditions are respectively higher than over 84%

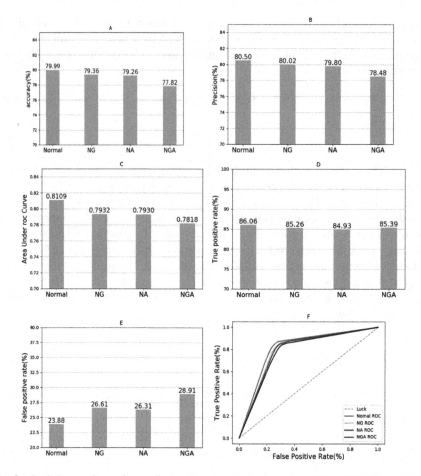

Fig. 3. Statistics results on the prediction Performance in normal condition, NG, NA and NGA. (A) Accuracy (B) Prediction (C) AUC (D) TPR (E) FPR (F) ROC.

and lower than 29%. It means that the proposed model has high prediction performance. Finally, according to the ROC curves shown in Fig. 3F, we can get the normal condition has better prediction result than NG, NA, and NGA.

6   Conclusion

Based on the routine medical examination data, a neural network model is presented to predict the risk of osteoporosis fractures in the elderly. The BPANN with one hidden layer is the core method to establish the pathological diagnosis model. The experiment results show that our method is simple and effective. Moreover, from the view of privacy preservation, we also test the prediction result by removing two input information: age and gender. The test result indicates that age and gender have some effect on the prediction result. The prediction results in NA, NG and NAG are still acceptable in order to achieve privacy preservation.

It is just a trial to predict the risk of osteoporosis fracture based on a neural network model. But it is promising method to aid doctors to diagnose the possibility of bone broken in the elderly. Further work can be done in two areas. Firstly, more data should be collected to further check the validity of the proposed model. Secondly, more methods especially in machine learning field can be applied to design the prediction model.

Acknowledgments. The work described in this paper was supported by grants from the National Natural Science Foundation of China (no. 61472464) and the Social Science Foundation of Chongqing (Nos. 2014SKZ02, 2015SKZ09).

References

1. He, Y.X., Wei, Q.Z., Xiong, Q.L., et al.: Research progress of the relationship between osteoporotic fractures and bone mineral density. Chin. J. Osteoporos. **20**(2), 219–224 (2014)
2. Zhang, Y.F., Yu, Y., Zhao, Y., et al.: Application of artificial neural network in clinical medicine. Beijing Biomed. Eng. **35**(3), 318–324 (2016)
3. Paskins, Z., Jinks, C., Mahmood, W., et al.: Public priorities for osteoporosis and fracture research: results from a general population survey. Arch. Osteoporos. **12**(1), 45 (2017)
4. White, S.C., Atchison, K.A., Gornbein, J.A., et al.: Risk factors for fractures in older men and women: the leisure world cohort study. Gend. Med. **3**(2), 110–123 (2006)
5. Dennison, E., Mohamed, M.A., Cooper, C.: Epidemiology of osteoporosis. Rheum. Dis. Clin. N. Am. **32**(4), 617–629 (2006)
6. Rd, M.L.: Adverse outcomes of osteoporotic fractures in the general population. J. Bone Miner. Res. **18**(6), 1139 (2003)
7. Stone, K.L., Seeley, D.G., Lui, L.Y., et al.: BMD at multiple sites and risk of fracture of multiple types: long-term results from the Study of Osteoporotic Fractures. J. Bone Miner. Res. **18**(11), 1947–1954 (2003)
8. Chawla, N.V., Bowyer, K.W., Hall, L.O., et al.: SMOTE synthetic minority over-sampling technique. J. Artif. Intell. Res. **16**(1), 321–357 (2011)
9. Gönen, M., Alpaydın, E.: Multiple kernel learning algorithms. J. Mach. Learn. Res. **12**, 2211–2268 (2011)

Patients' EEG Analysis Based on Multi-indicator Dynamic Analysis Measure for Supporting Brain Death Determination

Yao Miao$^{(\boxtimes)}$ and Jianting Cao

Graduate School of Engineering, Saitama Institute of Technology, Fukaya, Japan
{e6006gxp,cao}@sit.ac.jp

Abstract. It is crucial to analyze coma and quasi-brain-death patients' EEG (electroencephalography) by using different signal processing methods, in order to provide reliable scientific references for supporting BDD (brain death determination). In this paper, we proposed the multi-indicator dynamic analysis measure which was by combining Dynamic 2T-EMD (turning tangent empirical mode decomposition) and Dynamic ApEn (approximate entropy) to comprehensively analyze offline coma and quasi-brain-death patients' EEG from dynamic EEG energy and dynamic complexity. Firstly, 60s EEG randomly selected from 36 cases of patients' EEG (coma: 19; quasi-brain-death: 17) were analyzed to show the overall dynamic energy and complexity distribution for 2 groups. Secondly, one coma patient's EEG, one quasi-brain-death patient's EEG, and one special patient's EEG which was from coma to quasi-brain-death state were processed to present individual characteristics. Results show intuitively that patients in coma state have higher dynamic EEG energy and lower complexity distribution than patients in quasi-brain-death state.

Keywords: Dynamic multi-indicator · Patient's EEG
Dynamic EEG energy · Dynamic complexity

1 Introduction

The human brain consists of medulla oblongata, pons, midbrain, cerebellum, diencephalon, and telencephalon, among which oblongata, pons and midbrain are called brainstem [1]. The concept of brain death was firstly proposed in 1959 [2]. There are three different definitions of brain death so far, which are total brain death, brainstem death and diffuse cortical death, after being constantly revised. The first BDD standard in human history was proposed in 1968, which was the complete, irreversible and permanent loss of brain and brainstem function [3].

In the clinic practice of BDD, professional physicians need to carry out a number of strict conformation tests, which might take risks such as the risk

© Springer International Publishing AG, part of Springer Nature 2018
T. Huang et al. (Eds.): ISNN 2018, LNCS 10878, pp. 824–833, 2018.
https://doi.org/10.1007/978-3-319-92537-0_93

resulted by apnea test and risk caused by taking long time during whole tests process. So it is important to use advanced signal processing methods to process EEG, in order to provide reliable and objective scientific criteria and to avoid misjudgment for supporting clinic judgment of BDD.

Some signal processing methods were applied to process EEG from different perspectives. For example, ICA (independent component analysis) was applied to remove noise and artifacts and extract weak brain activity components from EEG in the project of BDD [4]. And some complexity methods were applied to obtain statistic features of EEG signals [5]. And information fusion via fission based on EMD was used to differentiate coma and brain-death EEG [6]. Moreover, EMD based methods were applied to process EEG signals from mono-channel static EEG energy indicator [7].

In this paper, we proposed the multi-indicator dynamic analysis measure to comprehensively process patients' EEG from dynamic EEG energy and dynamic complexity aspects, which was based on by combining Dynamic 2T-EMD (turning tangent empirical mode decomposition) algorithm and Dynamic ApEn (approximate entropy) algorithm. There were 2 parts of work included. Firstly, the principle of the multi-indicator dynamic analysis measure, the Dynamic 2T-EMD algorithm and the Dynamic ApEn algorithm were briefly illustrated. Secondly, two experiment measures were conducted from both overall and individual perspectives. Specifically, from the overall perspective, 60s EEG data were selected randomly from every of 36 cases of coma and quasi-brain-death patients' EEG, and analyzed by the multi-indicator dynamic measure proposed to get the dynamic EEG energy and dynamic complexity trend characteristics for coma group and quasi-brain-death group. And from individual perspective, 60s EEG data from every of two typical EEG and one special EEG were selected randomly and processed by the measure. Here the two typical EEG were from two patients that including one coma patient and one quasi-brain-death patient, and one special EEG came from one patient who was from coma state to quasi-brain-death state. Results show obviously that the distribution of dynamic EEG energy of coma patients' EEG are higher than that of brain-death patients' EEG, and at the same time the trend of dynamic complexity of coma patient's EEG are lower than that of brain-death patient's EEG from both overall and individual perspectives, which is helpful to provide more reliable and more accurate results for supporting BDD.

2   Methods

2.1   The Multi-indicator Dynamic Analysis Measure

The multi-indicator dynamic analysis measure was used to study the dynamic distribution characteristics of EEG from multi-perspective for every time window, which was conducted through a combination of different dynamic algorithms.

The key of the measure lied in dynamics and different indicators. Firstly, compared with static EEG analysis, dynamic EEG analysis has the following two advantages [8]. (i) Dynamic EEG analysis can observe changes of vital signs, and help physicians evaluate and predict patients' state trend [9]. (ii) The accuracy and reliability of results can be improved by dynamic analysis.

The brief principle is shown in Fig. 1. In Fig. 1, a segment of off-line raw EEG signals was divided into multiple time windows by introducing the time window and the time step. And as the time window and time step sliding, EEG data were analyzed by applying Dynamic 2T-EMD and Dynamic ApEn algorithms to obtain the dynamic EEG energy distribution and dynamic complexity distribution in time domain.

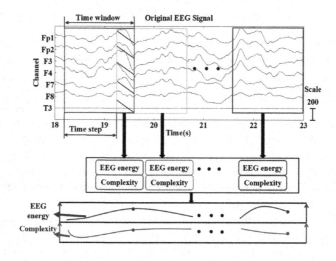

Fig. 1. The principle of multi-indicator dynamic analysis measure.

2.2   Dynamic 2T-EMD Algorithm

2T-EMD is a fully data-driven algorithm of signal processing for single and multiple channels signals. It can decompose a given signal $s(t)$ into a finite set of IMFs (Intrinsic Mode Functions) $\sum_{n=1}^{N} IMF_n$ from low frequency to high frequency and a monotonic residual signal $r(t)$, shown in (1) [10].

$$s(t) = \sum_{n=1}^{N} IMF_n + r(t) \tag{1}$$

Dynamic 2T-EMD algorithm is the extended form of 2T-EMD by introducing time window Δt and time step $\Delta \lambda$, and it's used to analyze EEG data to obtain dynamical EEG energy distribution with the time window Δt and time step $\Delta \lambda$ sliding [11]. Here EEG energy is defined as the value by multiplying power spectrum within the frequency band by corresponding recording time. Specifically, take the simple case as an example, when $\Delta t = \Delta \lambda$, for a multivariate signal with n components from T_1 to T_2

$$\{\overrightarrow{s}(k \cdot \Delta t)\}_{k=0}^{K} = \{\overrightarrow{s}(0 \cdot \Delta t), \overrightarrow{s}(1 \cdot \Delta t), \ldots, \overrightarrow{s}(K \cdot \Delta t)\} \tag{2}$$

Where T_1 is the start time of signal processing, and then

$$T_2 = T_1 + K \cdot \Delta t = T_1 + K \cdot \Delta \lambda \tag{3}$$

And K is the number of time windows in the given time from T_1 to T_2. Then after processed by Dynamic 2T-EMD, we can obtain results shown in following formula.

$$\{\overrightarrow{s}(k \cdot \Delta t)\}_{k=0}^{K} = \left\{ \sum_{i=1}^{N} \overrightarrow{IMF}_i(k \cdot \Delta t) + \overrightarrow{r}_N(k \cdot \Delta t) \right\}_{k=0}^{K} \tag{4}$$

2.3 Dynamic ApEn Algorithm

The approximate entropy is defined as a similarity vector that continues to maintain a similar conditional probability over a certain threshold when the dimension increases from m to $m+1$ [12]. And its physical meaning is the probability that the time series produces a new pattern when the dimension changes. Specifically, the smaller the approximate entropy is, the lower the complexity is, the smaller the probability that the time series produces new patterns is, that is to say, it has a certain regularity and predictability [13].

More specifically, compute the time series $\overrightarrow{x}(n) = \{x(1), x(2)\ldots, x(N)\}$, $(n = 1, 2, \ldots, N)$ to obtain the ApEn($\overrightarrow{x}(n)$, m, r) of the sequence, where m is the length of the series of vectors, r is threshold. And m-dimensional vectors $\overrightarrow{v}(k) = \{x(k), x(k+1), \ldots, x(k+m-1)\}$ is firstly constructed from $\overrightarrow{x}(n)$, and then use $\overrightarrow{v}(i)$ and $\overrightarrow{v}(j)$ $(i, j \leq N - m + 1)$ to represent $\overrightarrow{x}(n)$. The distance between $\overrightarrow{v}(i)$ and $\overrightarrow{v}(j)$ can be represent as shown below, where d is the maximum norm.

$$d[\overrightarrow{v}(i), \overrightarrow{v}(j)] = max_{k=1,2,\ldots m}[\|x(i+k-1) - x(j+k-1)\|] \tag{5}$$

Given a threshold r, $B^{m,r}(i)$ is defined as the number of $\overrightarrow{v}(i)$ and $\overrightarrow{v}(j)$ in the threshold for each $i \leq N - m + 1$. Then we define $C^{m,r}(i)$ as the conditional probability that $\overrightarrow{v}(i)$ and $\overrightarrow{v}(j)$ are similar at the threshold.

$$C^{m,r}(i) = \frac{B^{m,r}(i)}{N - m + 1} \tag{6}$$

Where $i \leq N - m + 1$, and $\phi^{m,r}$, the average of $C^{m,r}(i)$, which is also the entropy average is expressed as below.

$$\phi^{m,r} = \frac{1}{N - m + 1} \sum_{i=1}^{N-m+1} \log C^{m,r}(i) \tag{7}$$

Then $ApEn(\overrightarrow{x}(n), m, r)$ can be expressed as below.

$$ApEn(\overrightarrow{x}(n), m, r) = \phi^{m,r} - \phi^{m+1,r} \tag{8}$$

Dynamic ApEn algorithm is the extension of existing ApEn algorithm by introducing a running window Δt, which can reflect the dynamic complexity change of the whole recording time and avoid the loss of detail information.

2.4   The EEG Recording

The EEG data we used in the paper were recorded in EEG preliminary examination in a Chinese hospital from June 2004 to March 2006, with the permission of patients' families [14]. During the EEG recording, patient was lying on the bed in the ICU. And the EEG data was detected by the portable NEUROSCAN ESI-64 system and a laptop computer. Six exploring electrodes (Fp1, Fp2, F3, F4, F7, F8) as well as one ground electrode (GND) were placed on the forehead, and two reference electrodes (A1, A2) were placed on earlobes. And the sampling frequency was 1000 Hz and the electrode resistance was lower than $8\,K\Omega$. The placement of electrodes was shown in Fig. 2. In this paper, the EEG of 35 coma and quasi-brain-death patients (male: 21; female: 14) with a total of 36 cases of EEG (coma: 19; quasi-brain-death: 17), in which there were one case of EEG in coma and one case of EEG in quasi-brain-death included in the same special patient whose state was from coma in the first EEG recording process to quasi-brain-death state in the second EEG recording process after 10 h. And since the recording time for each case of EEG was different, 60s EEG data were selected randomly from 36 cases of EEG to process in order to unify the time of EEG being processed in the dynamic analysis.

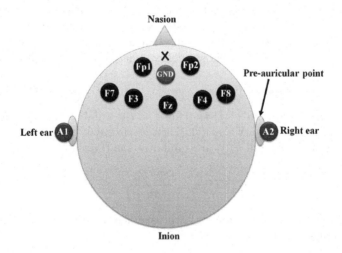

Fig. 2. The placement of 9 electrodes.

3   Results and Discussion

There were 2 parts in this section. Firstly, in order to give an overall dynamic
distribution results for coma group and quasi-brain-death group, we selected
randomly 60s EEG data from every of 36 cases of coma and quasi-brain-death
EEG, and analyzed by the multi-indicator dynamic measure proposed. Secondly,
two typical cases of EEG from two different patients who were in coma and
quasi-brain-death state respectively, and one special patient whose EEG was
from coma state to quasi-brain-death state were processed to give the 3 cases of
individual dynamic distributions.

3.1   Results and Discussion for 2 Groups

In this part, 19 cases of EEG data for coma group and 17 cased of EEG data for
quasi-brain-death group were analyzed by the multi-indicator dynamic measure
based on Dynamic 2T-EMD and Dynamic ApEn. Here the time window of both
Dynamic 2T-EMD and Dynamic ApEn were set to 1 s and no overlap among
time windows. Then we took mean value of every second for channels averaged
for coma group and quasi-brain-death group respectively due to the two group
were not balanced. As shown in Fig. 3, it is obviously observed that the range of
mean dynamic EEG energy for channels averaged for coma group is 2.3×10^4–
4.5×10^4, is higher than that for quasi-brain-death group which is 4.0×10^3–
4.7×10^3, and at the same time the mean dynamic complexity distribution for
channels averaged for coma group is lower than that of quasi-brain-death group,
in which the range of dynamic complexity for coma group and quasi-brain-death
group are 0.328–0.5 and 0.999–1.101 respectively. Moreover, the overall mean
value and standard deviation of EEG energy for coma group and quasi-brain-
death group are $2.9 \times 10^4 \pm 3.6 \times 10^3$ and $4.4 \times 10^3 \pm 2.0 \times 10^2$, respectively;
and that of ApEn for coma and quasi-brain-death group are 0.4048 ± 0.0390,
1.0499 ± 0.0219, separately. That can be observed there exists larger individual
differences.

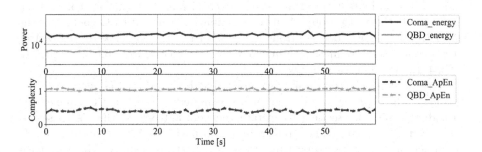

Fig. 3. Dynamic mean EEG and complexity distribution of average channel for coma
group and quasi-brain-death group.

And as shown in Fig. 4, we also analyzed the dynamic EEG energy distribution for every channel (Fp1, Fp2, F3, F4, F7 and F8) for both coma group and quasi-brain-death group. The mean dynamic EEG energy and dynamic ApEn distributions characteristics for every channel for coma and quasi-brain-death group are consistent with the distributions of average channels for 2 groups, in which the fluctuation range of dynamic EEG energy for 2 groups at 6 channels are 2.4×10^4–5.5×10^4, 2.2×10^4–4.8×10^4, 2.6×10^4–4.9×10^4, 2.2×10^4–4.1×10^4, 1.8×10^4–4.0×10^4 and 1.7×10^4–3.3×10^4 respectively, while that for quasi-brain-death group are 3.3×10^3–4.6×10^3, 3.7×10^3–5.0×10^3, 3.9×10^3–5.3×10^3, 4.4×10^3–5.4×10^3, 3.6×10^3–5.7×10^3 and 4.2×10^3–6.2×10^3 respectively, no more than 1.0×10^4, and the fluctuation range of dynamic complexity for coma group at 6 channels are 0.2696–0.4806, 0.2986–0.5209, 0.2859–0.4769, 0.3466–0.5360, 0.3031–0.5044 and 0.3455–0.5594 respectively, no more than 0.6, and the fluctuation range of dynamic complexity for quasi-brain-death group at 6 channels are 0.9874–1.1473 and 0.9645–1.1330, 1.0138–1.1479, 1.0348–1.1754, 0.9731–1.1245 and 0.8802–1.0338 respectively.

3.2 Results and Discussion for 3 Cases

In this part, we selected 60s EEG data from the coma patient's EEG with recording time of 937 s as well as 60s EEG data from the brain-death patient's EEG with recording duration of 905 s. As is shown in Fig. 5, it is intuitively observed the dynamic change of EEG energy and ApEn for the two typical cases. The range of dynamic EEG energy of the coma patient's EEG is 3.5×10^4–1.1×10^5, while it's 1.8×10^3–4.1×10^3 for the brain-death patient's EEG. At the same time, the results show that the ApEn of coma patient's EEG fluctuate in the range of 0.0128–0.1764, and no more than 1, while the ApEn of brain-death patient's EEG changes in the range of 0.6194–1.4176. Moreover, the special patient' EEG whose state was from coma to quasi-brain-death state was processed, in which 60s EEG data from coma EEG segment and 60s EEG data from quasi-brain-death segment were selected to analyzed by the measure proposed. It is shown that for the same patient, the EEG energy and complexity distribution characteristics for coma state and quasi-brain-death state are consistent with that for coma group and quasi-brain-death group. And the distribution range of EEG energy for the special patient' EEG decrese from 1.7×10^4–4.1×10^4 to 2.4×10^3–5.8×10^3, at the same time the fluctuate range of comlexity increse from 0.0725–0.3045 to 0.9304–1.3178. As shown in Fig. 6.

The more obvious the brain activity is, The higher the EEG energy is. And the lower the ApEn is, the lower of the complexity is, then the smaller the probability that the sequence generate the new pattern is, that is to say, it has a certain regularity and predictability. So it can be infer that there exists brain activity for coma group while there is almost no brain activity for quasi-brain-death group since the dynamic EEG energy distribution for coma group is obviously higher than that for quasi-brain-death group. Moreover, And it can be also infer that there exists the brain activity rhythm in EEG for coma group while there are almost disorder noise in EEG for quasi-brain-death group as

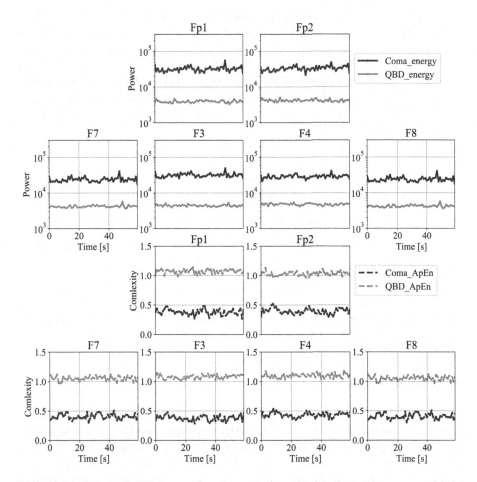

Fig. 4. Dynamic mean EEG energy and complexity of 6 channels for coma group and quasi-brain-death group.

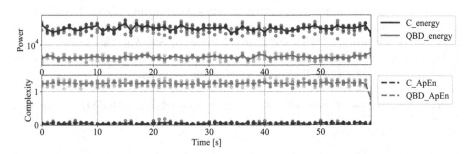

Fig. 5. Dynamic EEG energy and complexity distribution of average channel for one coma patient and one quasi-brain-death patient.

the dynamic ApEn distribution for coma group is lower than that for quasi-brain-death group. And dynamic distribution can provide more accurate and reliable results compared with static values. Furthermore, since the BDD is a serious issue, it is necessary to use different methods to improve the accuracy of results. For example, measures of synchronization for EEG has been widely used to analyzed real EEG [15], and especially applied in Alzheimer's disease EEG analysis [16]. This can be used as another EEG processing methods for supporting BDD in the future.

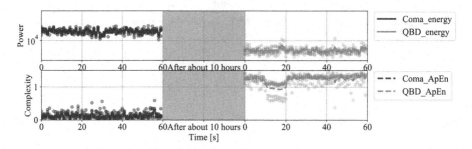

Fig. 6. Dynamic EEG energy and complexity distribution of average channel for the patient who was from coma to quasi-brain-death state.

4   Conclusion

In this paper, The multi-indicator dynamic analysis measure was proposed, which was by combining Dynamic 2T-EMD algorithm and Dynamic ApEn algorithm to comprehensively analyze patients' EEG signals from dynamic EEG energy and dynamic complexity indicators. And 36 cases of coma and quasi-brain-death patients' EEG were analyzed to show the overall dynamic distribution characteristics for coma group and quasi-brain-death group. Then 3 patients' EEG including one coma patient's EEG, one quasi-brain-death patient's EEG and one patient' EEG from which was from coma to quasi-brain-death state were processed from individual perspective. Results show intuitively that patients in coma state have higher EEG energy and lower complexity at the same time than patients in brain-death state from dynamic aspect. And this work can provide more accurate and reliable results for supporting BDD and also helpful to develop real-time EEG preliminary examination systems.

Acknowledgments. This work was partly supported by KAKENHI (25420417, 15H04002 and 17K00326).

References

1. Chen, Z., et al.: Brian Death: Modern Thanatology. Chinese Science Press, Beijing (2008)
2. Mollaret, P., Goulon, M.: Le Coma dpass. Revue Neurol. **101**, 5–15 (1959)
3. Becheer, H.K., et al.: Report of the Ad hoc committee of the Harvard medical school to examine the definition of brain death: a definition of irreversible coma. JAMA **205**, 337–340 (1968)
4. Cao, J.: Analysis of the quasi-brain-death EEG data based on a robust ICA approach. In: Gabrys, B., Howlett, R.J., Jain, L.C. (eds.) KES 2006. LNCS (LNAI), vol. 4253, pp. 1240–1247. Springer, Heidelberg (2006). https://doi.org/10.1007/11893011_157
5. Chen, Z., Cao, J., Cao, Y., et al.: Qualitative evaluation and quantitative EEG analysis in brain death diagnosis for adults: an empirical study. Cogn. Neurodyn. **2**(3), 257–271 (2008)
6. Li, L., Saito, Y., Looney, D., et al.: Data fusion via fission for the analysis of brain death. In: Evolving Intelligence Systems: Methodology and Applications, pp. 279–320. Springer, Heidelberg (2008)
7. Shi, Q., Cao, J., Tanaka, T., Wang, R., Zhu, H.: EEG data analysis based on EMD for coma and quasi-brain-death patient. J. Exp. Theor. Artif. Intell. **23**, 97–110 (2011)
8. Ni, L., Cao, J., Wang, R.: Analyzing EEG of quasi-brain-death based on dynamic sample entropy measures. Comput. Math. Methods Med. (2013)
9. Zhang, T., Xu, K.: Multifractal analysis of intracranial EEG in epilepticus rats. In: Lu, B.-L., Zhang, L., Kwok, J. (eds.) ICONIP 2011. LNCS, vol. 7062, pp. 345–351. Springer, Heidelberg (2011). https://doi.org/10.1007/978-3-642-24955-6_42
10. Fleureau, J., Nunes, J.-C., Kachenoura, A., Albera, L., Senhadji, L.: Turning tangent empirical mode decomposition: a framework for mono- and multivariate signals. IEEE Trans. Sig. Process. **59**, 1309–1316 (2011)
11. Miao, Y., Wang, D., Cui, G., Zhu, L., Cao, J.: Analyzing patients' EEG energy for brain death determination based on Dynamic 2T-EMD. Int. J. Comput. Technol. **16**, 717–720 (2017)
12. Pincus, S.M.: Approximate entropy (ApEn) as a measure of system complexity. Proc. Natl. Acad. Sci. **88**, 110–117 (1991)
13. Ni, L.: Decision support for brain death diagnosis based on EEG signal processing on complexity and power feature. East China University of Science and Technology, China (2016)
14. Cao, J., Chen, Z.: Advanced EEG signal processing in brain death diagnosis. In: Mandic, D., Golz, M., Kuh, A., Obradovic, D., Tanaka, T. (eds.) Signal Processing Techniques for Knowledge Extraction and Information Fusion, pp. 275–298. Springer, Boston (2008). https://doi.org/10.1007/978-0-387-74367-7_15
15. Jalili, M., Barzegaran, E., Knyazeva, M.G.: Synchronization of EEG: bivariate and multivariate measures. IEEE Trans. Neural Syst. Rehabil. Eng. **22**(2), 212–221 (2014). A Publication of the IEEE Engineering in Medicine & Biology Society
16. Knyazeva, M.G., Jalili, M., Brioschi, A., et al.: Topography of EEG multivariate phase synchronization in early Alzheimer's disease. Neurobiol. Aging **31**(7), 1132–1144 (2010)

A New Epileptic Seizure Detection Method Based on Fusion Feature of Weighted Complex Network

Hanyong Zhang[1,2], Qingfang Meng[1,2(✉)], Mingmin Liu[1,2],
and Yang Li[1,2]

[1] School of Information Science and Engineering,
University of Jinan, Jinan 250022, China
ise_mengqf@ujn.edu.cn
[2] Shandong Provincial Key Laboratory of Network Based Intelligent
Computing, Jinan 250022, China

Abstract. Epileptic seizure detection plays an important role in the diagnosis of epilepsy. High-performance automatic detection method of epilepsy can reduce the workload of medical workers clinically, which has important clinical research significance. In this paper, we propose a new epileptic seizure detection method based on the statistic fusion feature of complex network. Firstly, we convert electroencephalogram (EEG) signals into complex network using horizontal visibility graph and weighted horizontal visibility graph. Then, we extract the average degree square and average weighted degree of complex network. Finally, the weighted sum of this two features is calculated as a single dimensional feature to classify the epileptic EEG signals. Experimental results show that the classification accuracy based on the feature fusion is up to 99%. It indicates that the classification accuracy of the single feature based on feature fusion is very high and the proposed method is effective to classify EEG signals.

Keywords: Complex network · Horizontal visibility graph
Weighted horizontal visibility graph · Average degree · Weighted degree

1 Introduction

Epilepsy is a widespread brain neuropathy and about 37 million people in the world are suffering from epilepsy. Clinically, electroencephalography (EEG) is the most common and important tool for the diagnosis and treatment of epilepsy [1]. In the beginning, professional doctors detected the epilepsy by recognizing EEG with their eyes. But this way has disadvantages of consuming a lot of manpower, lower efficiency and consuming more time. Therefore, the automatic detection method of epilepsy EEG has important significance for clinical research.

With deep research on brain, people found that the human brain is a complex non-linear dynamics system. The analysis of nonlinear dynamics of EEG signals has become an important research method. Kannathal [2] proposed a detection method utilizing the approximate entropy and confirmed that different EEG signals have different entropies. Song used optimized sample entropy [3, 4], which achieved better

© Springer International Publishing AG, part of Springer Nature 2018
T. Huang et al. (Eds.): ISNN 2018, LNCS 10878, pp. 834–841, 2018.
https://doi.org/10.1007/978-3-319-92537-0_94

classification results. Spectral entropy and some other entropy were introduced to epilepsy detection in [5, 6]. Results of conventional non-linear methods are not satisfactory, which can't meet the actual situation needs. In recent years, complex network theory provides a new perspective for time series analysis. Analyzing the time series by transforming it into a graph becomes a powerful method for signal processing [7, 8]. Lacasa et al. [9] first proposed the visibility graph (VG) algorithm, which could convert arbitrary time series into a graph. Then, Lacasa et al. [10] proposed the horizontal visibility graph (HVG) algorithm.

VG and HVG algorithms have been widely used in biological signal processing. They were used to the analysis of EEG and ECG signals in [11, 12]. Tang et al. [13] analyzed VGs from higher band frequencies of epilepsy EEGs and showed that it was more effective than that of the entropy method in seizure detection. Zhu et al. [14] also implemented VG-based features to classify epileptic EEGs. Considering the connection weights between nodes, Zhu et al. [15] proposed a weighted horizontal visibility algorithm. However, they used only average weighted degree of WHVG as the feature of the weighted complex network and did not get a good classification result.

In this paper, we improve the method that convert EEG time series into WHVG mentioned by Zhu et al. [15]. The rest of this paper is organized as follows: our proposed method are described in the next section. Experiment results and analysis are in the third section. The last section includes the conclusions of our work.

2 Methodology

Figure 1 shows a block diagram of the method proposed in this paper, which includes construction of WHVG, extraction of the feature, and the classification based on this feature.

2.1 Feature Extracted Method Based on Horizontal Visibility Graph

In our proposed methodology, firstly we convert EEG time series data into horizontal visibility graph. The specific algorithm of horizontal visibility graph is described below. For mapping the time series data into HVG, each data sample point of time series is considered as a node of the graph. Considering a time series $\{x_1, x_2, \ldots, x_i, \ldots x_n\}$, x_i is the i_{th} sample point and is considered as a node n_i of graph $G(V, E)$, where V is the node set, $V = \{n_i\}$, $i = 1, 2, \ldots, N$. E is the edge set and E_{ij} is 1 if edges of two nodes exist. The edge between two nodes are determined on the basis of the following equation:

$$n_k < min(n_i, n_j) \; \forall k, \quad i < k < j \tag{1}$$

where n_i is the i_{th} node in HVG. It means that the edge between n_i and n_j exists if one can draw a line from the vertex of the smallest of the two points but cutting no intermediate date n_k.

In the theory of complex network, degree is the most basic and important feature of complex network. The degree of a node in complex network is the number of edges the node has to other nodes. The equation of degree is as follows:

$$D_i = \sum_{j \in B(i)} E_{ij} \tag{2}$$

where, $B(i)$ is the neighborhood of node i. The average degree is defined as:

$$AD = \frac{1}{N} \sum_{i=1}^{N} D_i \tag{3}$$

where, N is total number of nodes in the network. The average degree reflects the connection strength of nodes. The network with more connected nodes has a larger average degree. In order to clearly reflect the difference of degree between different networks, we improve this network characteristic of degree. Based on degree, we calculate the square of average degree. It makes the difference between the connection strength more obvious. We propose a new HVG feature called average degree square (ADD), which is defined as:

$$ADD = \left(\frac{1}{N} \sum_{i=1}^{N} D_i \right)^2 \tag{4}$$

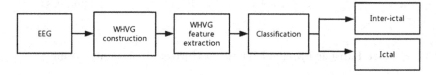

Fig. 1. The block diagram of the proposed method

2.2   Feature Extraction Method Based on Weighted Horizontal Visibility Graph

In Sect. 2.1, we extract a new feature using HVG. HVG has some limitations because it doesn't consider the edge weight between the nodes of complex network. The weight between the nodes of a complex network reacts the dynamic information of the original time series and it is an important topological structure of complex network. There are still many details of WHVG for improvement, so we utilize the WHVG by using a new edge weight. In this paper, we use the below Eq. (5) to calculate the edge weight:

$$w_{ij} = \left| \frac{n_j - n_i}{j - i} \right| \tag{5}$$

where, w_{ij} is the absolute value of the slope between node i and j.

In the theory of weighted complex network, weighted degree is the most basic and significant feature of complex network. The weighted degree of the node i is the total weights of all the edges attached to node i which is represented by:

$$W_{(i)} = \sum_{j \in B(i)} w_{ij} \tag{6}$$

where, $B(i)$ is the neighborhood of node i. The average weighted degree (AW) is defined as:

$$AW = \frac{1}{N} \sum_{i=1}^{N} W(i) \tag{7}$$

where, N is total number of nodes in the graph. It should be emphasized that due to sudden changes in seizure epilepsy EEG signals, the edge weight of different signals will have obvious differences.

2.3   Feature Fusion

In this paper, we propose the method of feature fusion of complex network. After adjusting the value of the above two features, we add *ADD* and *AW* as the final classification feature named average degree weight (ADW), which is defined as:

$$ADW = 50 * ADD + AW \tag{8}$$

Since the value of the two features is not an order of magnitude and the importance of each feature is also different, we use different parameters.

3   Experimental Result and Analysis

In this study, we use a clinical epileptic EEG data set from the University of Bonn, Germany. Although there are five sets in the dataset, only two sets were used in this study: interictal (set D) and ictal (set E). This two sets are the key point to find epilepsy seizure. Each set contains 100 segments of single channel EEG with 23.6 s duration. Every EEG datum is sampled at a rate of 173.61 Hz, and has 4096 points. In this experiment, the length of each sample datum we adopt is 1024, which will make computation faster. All the simulations are tested on the MATLAB 2016b.

Degree describes the internal information of the EEG signal and reflects some information of original time series. In addition, it reflects the regularity of complex network. According to the Eq. 4, we calculate the improved average degree of HVG. Then we calculate the average of the feature values of each sample as a feature. Finally, the 200 features extracted from 200 samples are inputted into a linear classifier. The classification accuracy is 96.5%. In order to observe the classification result visually, Fig. 2 plots the best classification result with the square of average degree. In Fig. 2, each '+' presents the ictal signal and each '*' presents the interictal signal.

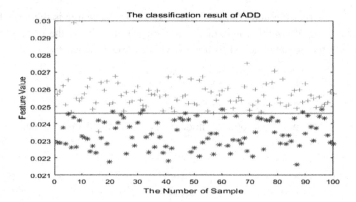

Fig. 2. The classification result using feature ADD

From Fig. 2, we find some sample points are classified wrongly but more sample points are classified correctly. It means that this feature can be used for classification of EEG signals. As we all know, when seizures occur, complex network becomes more irregular, so the degree of ictal signal is larger than that of interictal signal. This is consistent with our experimental results.

In the second step, we verify the effectiveness of the average weighted degree. After putting it into a linear classifier, it achieves a classification accuracy of 97%. Figure 2 plots the best classification result with the average weighted degree. In Fig. 3, each '+' presents the ictal signal and each '*' presents the interictal signal. From the Fig. 3, we find that most sample points can be classified correctly except for a few sample points. The proposed feature of the weighted horizontal visibility graph called AW can fully distinguish differences between the two EEG signals. It can be concluded that weighted degree is a significant feature of the weighted complex network and can be used for the classification of EEG signals.

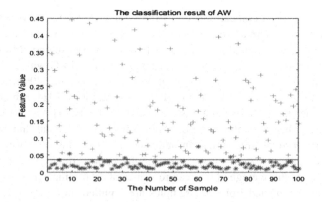

Fig. 3. The classification result using feature AW

Finally, considering feature fusion, according to Eq. 8, we put the sum of this two features as a new single feature into linear classifier to obtain higher classification accuracy. From Fig. 3, we can clearly find that the values of the ictal are higher than the interictal generally. It means that the single feature proposed in this paper can become an excellent classification feature, so we can classify the EEG signals by studying the different values of ADW of complex network. The classification accuracy of ictal and interictal EEG signals using ADW is up to 99%. Figure 4 plots the final classification result of ADW. In Fig. 4, each '+' presents the ictal signal and each '*' presents the interictal signal as before.

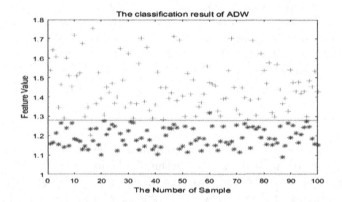

Fig. 4. The classification result using feature ADW

From the Fig. 3, we find that most sample points can be classified correctly except for two sample points. Compared with other complex network features, the feature proposed in this paper can obtain better performance in classifying EEG signals. It means that a preeminent classification feature can achieve a good classification result. Table 1 shows the accuracy of this two proposed feature and the last single fusion feature. It proves that feature fusion achieves a good result. We can draw a conclusion that the fusion feature obtains more time series dynamic information so that it obtains a better classification accuracy.

Table 1. The classification results of the proposed features

Feature	Sensitivity (%)	Specificity (%)	ACC (%)
Improved average degree	99	94	96.5
Weighted degree	95	99	97
Fusion feature	99	99	99

Table 2 shows the classification accuracy of epileptic EEG based on the fusion feature of improved weighted horizontal visibility graph and other methods. It can be seen from the table that the accuracy classification by the extracted single feature based on WHVG is significantly higher than that of other methods. It means that our method can get more information of the EEG time series. The novelty of this method is that it proposes a new HVG-based feature and introduces a new edge weight of WHVG. What's more, the proposed method provides a new idea for the feature extraction of complex network and it will help the development of complex network theory. There is a reason to believe that our method are helpful to the diagnosis and treatment of clinical epilepsy.

Table 2. The classification results of the proposed method and other existing methods

Methods	Data length	Feature	ACC (%)
Proximity network [16]	1024	NEED	96.5
Proximity network [17]	2048	Pclu	94.5
Clustering technique [18]	4096	CT feature	93.6
Weighted HVG [15]	1024	wdr	93.0
Proposed method	1024	AWE	99.0

4 Conclusions

Many methods have been proposed for discriminating interictal and ictal activities in the EEG signals. In this study, a fusion feature of the improved weighted horizontal visibility graph called ADW was introduced. In the proposed method, first, we transformed the original EEG time series into complex network by using the weighted horizontal visibility graph algorithm. Then,the ADW were extracted from WHVGs, which is used as a single feature of the classification of interictal and ictal EEGs. The classification accuracy is 99%. The result shows that the feature has a perfect classification performance. This accuracy, which was obtained using just one fusion feature, is higher than those obtained by several previous methods. Based on experimental results, we can reach the conclusion that the method proposed in this study can distinguish ictal EEG from interictal EEG with high accuracy. With the increasing incidence of epilepsy, the detection methods are helpful to the diagnosis and treatment of epilepsy patients.

Acknowledgments. This work was supported by the National Natural Science Foundation of China (Grant No. 61671220, 61201428), the Project of Shandong Province Higher Educational Science and Technology Program, China (Grant No. J16LN07), the Shandong Province Key Research and Development Program, China (Grant No. 2016GGX101022).

References

1. Hazarika, N., Chen, J.Z., Tsoi, A.C., Sergejew, A.: Classification of EEG signals using the wavelet transform. Sig. Process. **59**, 61–72 (1997)
2. Kannathal, N., Lim, C.M., Acharya, U.R., Sadasivan, P.K.: Entropies for detection of epilepsy in EEG. Comput. Methods Programs Biomed. **80**, 187–194 (2005)

3. Song, Y., Crowcroft, J., Zhang, J.: Automatic epileptic seizure detection in EEGs based on optimized sample entropy and extreme learning machine. J. Neurosci. Method. **210**, 132–146 (2012)
4. Lake, D.E., Richman, J.S., Griffin, M.P., Moorman, J.R.: Sample entropy analysis of neonatal heart rate variability. Am. J. Physiol.-Regul. Integr. Comp. Physiol. **283**, 789–797 (2002)
5. Acharya, U.R., Molinari, F., Sree, S.V., Chattopadhyay, S., Ng, K.H., Suri, J.S.: Automated diagnosis of epileptic EEG using entropies. Biomed. Sig. Process. Control **7**, 401–408 (2012)
6. Mirzaei, A., Ayatollahi, A., Gifani, P., Salehi, L.: EEG analysis based on wavelet-spectral entropy for epileptic seizures detection. In: 2010 3rd International Conference on Biomedical Engineering and Informatics, pp. 878–882. IEEE Press, New York (2010)
7. Zhang, J., Small, M.: Complex network from pseudoperiodic time series: topology versus dynamics. Phys. Rev. Lett. **96**, 238701 (2006)
8. Donner, R.V., Small, M., Donges, J.F., Marwan, N., Zou, Y., Xiang, R., Kurths, J.: Recurrence-based time series analysis by means of complex network methods. Int. J. Bifurcat. Chaos **21**, 1019–1046 (2011)
9. Lacasa, L., Luque, B., Ballesteros, F., Luque, J., Nuno, J.C.: From time series to complex networks: the visibility graph. Proc. Natl. Acad. Sci. U.S.A. **105**(13), 4972–4975 (2008)
10. Luque, B., Lacasa, L., Ballesteros, F., Liuque, J.: Horizontal visibility graphs exact results for random time series. Phys. Rev. E **80**, 046103 (2009)
11. Ahmadlou, M., Adeli, H., Adeli, A.: New diagnostic EEG markers of the Alzheimer's disease using visibility graph. J. Neural Transm. **117**, 1099–1109 (2010)
12. Shao, Z.G.: Network analysis of human heartbeat dynamics. Appl. Phys. Lett. **96**, 073703 (2010)
13. Tang, X., Xia, L., Liao, Y., Liu, W., Peng, Y., Gao, T., Zeng, Y.: New approach to epileptic diagnosis using visibility graph of high-frequency signal. Clin. EEG Neurosci. **44**, 150–156 (2013)
14. Zhu, G., Li, Y., Wen, P.: Analyzing epileptic EEGs with a visibility graph algorithm. In: 5th International Conference on Biomedical Engineering and Informatics, pp. 432–436. IEEE Press, New York (2012)
15. Zhu, G., Li, Y., Wen, P.P.: Epileptic seizure detection in EEGs signals using a fast weighted horizontal visibility algorithm. Comput. Methods Programs Biomed. **115**, 64–75 (2014)
16. Wang, F., Meng, Q., Zhou, W., Chen, S.: The feature extraction method of EEG signals based on degree distribution of complex networks from nonlinear time series. In: Huang, D.-S., Bevilacqua, V., Figueroa, J.C., Premaratne, P. (eds.) ICIC 2013. LNCS, vol. 7995, pp. 354–361. Springer, Heidelberg (2013). https://doi.org/10.1007/978-3-642-39479-9_42
17. Wang, F., Meng, Q., Chen, Y., Zhao, Y.: Feature extraction method for epileptic seizure detection based on cluster coefficient distribution of complex network. WSEAS Trans. Comput. **13**, 351–360 (2014)
18. Li, Y., Wen, P.P.: Clustering technique-based least square support vector machine for EEG signal classification. Comput. Methods Programs Biomed. **104**, 358–372 (2011)

Epileptic Detection Based on EMD and Sparse Representation in Clinic EEG

Qingfang Meng[1,2(✉)], Lei Du[1,2], Shanshan Chen[1,2],
and Hanyong Zhang[1,2]

[1] School of Information Science and Engineering,
University of Jinan, Jinan 250022, China
ise_mengqf@ujn.edu.cn
[2] Shandong Provincial Key Laboratory of Network Based Intelligent
Computing, Jinan 250022, China

Abstract. The sparse representation has gained considerable attention in pattern classification recently. A new method is designed to detect seizure EEG signals by empirical mode decomposition (EMD) and sparse representation. First of all, the EMD method is used to process EEG signals for generating IMFs. Then frequency features of IMFs are extracted as the dictionary in sparse representation based classification (SRC) scheme to realize reduction of the data dimension and calculation cost. Finally, the KSVD is exploited to optimize dictionary. It has been showed that the algorithm can well detect the seizure EEG signals and the accuracy is up to 99%. Furthermore, the quick speed makes the method practical for the treatment of epilepsy in practice.

Keywords: Seizure EEGs · Classification · EMD · Spares representation
KSVD

1 Introduction

Epilepsy is a kind of disease which is characterized by the dysfunction of the central nervous system caused by the repeated and sudden over discharge of brain. The EEG (Electroencephalogram) has been an effective tool to diagnose the epileptic seizures. The traditional epilepsy detection for long-term EEGs which meanly rely on vision is very inconvenient and the cost of time is high. Epileptic detection plays a significant role in the diagnosis of epilepsy while in clinic.

Many techniques have been developed to identify epilepsy in several years. The time-frequency analysis and nonlinear dynamical methods of EEG signals were performed widely [1–4]. Subband nonlinear parameters and genetic algorithm [2], approximate entropy based on discrete wavelet transform (DWT) [3] are all used for automatic seizure detection. Besides, various effective classifiers (i.e. artificial neural network [4, 5], support vector machine [6], extreme learning machine [7], etc.) improve the performance of classification.

It has been reported that when analysing nonstationary signals empirical mode decomposition (EMD) [8] plays well [9, 10]. Using EMD method a EEG signals can be decomposed into a serious of components named intrinsic mode functions (IMFs). The

© Springer International Publishing AG, part of Springer Nature 2018
T. Huang et al. (Eds.): ISNN 2018, LNCS 10878, pp. 842–849, 2018.
https://doi.org/10.1007/978-3-319-92537-0_95

self-adaptive capacity of this method makes it extensively used to research the bio-logical [8, 11].

Recently, an algorithm called sparse representation has been popular, which has been highly used in blind speech signals separation [13], face recognition [12], image super-resolution [14], EEG signals detection [15]. Wright etc. developed a approach based on the sparse representation based classification (SRC) [12], in which the sparse representation of a testing EEG sample is obtained from training samples set. The dictionaries which are more usually employed in sparse representation include Principal Component Analysis, the Fast Fourier Transform, wavelets and dictionary learning methods, i.e. fisher discrimination dictionary learning (FDDL) model [16] and KSVD [17].

In this work, a sparse representation and EMD based novel method for seizure recognition is found out. Firstly, decompose the training and test EEG signals into several IMFs through EMD method. Then, the four features of IMFs are extracted to reduce data dimension and computational cost. The feature vectors of training dataset constitute the dictionary. The KSVD algorithm is exploited to optimize dictionary. Finally, a sparse linear combination of the training samples represents the test sample in the framework of SRC. The feature's combination of IMFs and KSVD dictionary optimization has strong performance of epileptic EEG detection.

2 Seizure Detection Based on EMD and SRC Methods

2.1 Dataset

The data set used come form the University of Bonn Medical Centre. Each of these five sets (i.e. Z, O, N, F, and S) contain 100 single-channel EEG signals with sampling frequency of 173.61 Hz. We chose two sets (Set F, measured interictal EEG intracranially from the epileptogenic zone and Set S, ictal EEG from the epileptogenic zone) to validate our method. All of the 100 epochs of each sets are grouped into four segments, whose length is 1024 points.

2.2 Empirical Mode Decomposition

EMD is an adaptive and efficient method that automatically decomposes a non-stationary signal into a serious of functions called Intrinsic Mode Functions (IMFs). Two conditions that must obey for every IMF: at any data point, the upper and lower envelope must be zero on average; and in anytime, the difference between the number of extreme and zero crossings must the same, or diff one at most. The EMD algorithm for the signal $x(t)$ can be described as:

(1) Find the extreme (including local maximum and minimum) of $x(t)$, then interpolate the maximum and the minimum by cubic spline function, generating the upper and lower envelops: U_{max} and U_{min}.

(2) Compute the average value

$$m_1 = \frac{U_{\max} + U_{\min}}{2} \tag{1}$$

(3) The first component h_1 is calculated as

$$h_1 = x(t) - m_1 \tag{2}$$

(4) Regard h_1 as new $x(t)$ and to determine if h_1 is an IMF, if not, repeat the above steps, otherwise, get the first IMF, determine it as $c_1 = h_1$.

(5) Designated the residue r_1 as subtracting c_1 from $x(t)$

$$r_1 = x(t) - c_1 \tag{3}$$

(6) Regarding the residue r_1 as a new data and the sifting process will continue to find the other IMFs until c_1 or r_1 is smaller enough, or r_1 is a monotone function. Thus, after getting all of the IMFs, the signal $x(t)$ can be expressed as

$$x(t) = \sum_{i=1}^{m} c_i + r_m \tag{4}$$

2.3   Feature Extraction

For epileptic EEG, feature extraction can make vector dimension and computational cost lower. In the work, four specific features, fluctuation index, coefficient of variation, relative amplitude and relative energy are computed from the first five IMFs. The characteristic of interictal EEG and ictal EEG are different, which makes it practical to classify the seizure EEGs. The traditionally linear analysis for long-term high-dimensional data cannot fully describe the behaviours of EEG signals due to the non-linearity and non-stationary. Furthermore, the nonlinear methods via phase space reconstruction for the long-term high-dimensional signals are usually complexity of computation. Select less than 4-D features can make computation easy and reduce data dimension.

2.4   Classification Based on Sparse Representation

The algorithm of sparse representation comes from compressed sensing and it breaks the limit of the Nyquist sampling rate in the field of signal processing. It provides a new method for signal analysis.

2.4.1   Sparse Representation Based Classification (SRC)

The sparse representation based classification (SRC), whose basic principle is to process the input test sample. In addition, the samples are represented as a combination of the training samples. It has exhibited good result in face recognition [12]. Suppose we have K object classes, denote by the serious of training samples $A = [A_1, A_2, \cdots, A_k]$ as the dictionary from all the K classes. Assuming we have a training set that the ith class is considered as a matrix $A_i = [s_{i1}, s_{i2}, \cdots, s_{in}] \in \Re^{m \times n_i}$, where $v_{i,j}, j = 1, 2, \cdots, n_i$ is an m-dimensional vector and it is extended by the jth sample of class i. In terms of the test sample $y \in \Re^m$ from corresponding class, y should be approximate represented as the weighted combination of the training samples and it is calculated as:

$$y = \sum_{j=1}^{n_i} \alpha_{ij} s_{ij} = A_i a_i \tag{5}$$

The $a_i = [a_{i1}, a_{i2}, \cdots, a_{in}]^T \in \Re^n$ are its coefficients. So, if the test sample y is a part of class i, the weight vector of all the training samples should be $a = [a_1; a_2; \cdots; a_k] = [0, \cdots, 0, \alpha_{i1}, \alpha_{i2}, \cdots, \alpha_{in_i}, 0, \cdots, 0]^T$. Namely, identities of test samples can be effectively coded with the sparse non-zero entries in a_i. When the solution a is quite sparse, the sparsest solution $y = Aa$ can be summarized as l_0-optimization question:

$$\hat{a} = \arg\min\|a\|_0 \ subject \ to \ Aa = y \tag{6}$$

However, the algorithm of solving the sparsest problem is NP-hard and it is difficult to completed. With the development of compressed sensing theory and sparse representation algorithm, there are more evidences that the sparsest solution can be expressed as the following equation:

$$\hat{a} = \arg\min\|a\|_1 \ subject \ to \ Aa = y \tag{7}$$

Through Eq. 7, the test sample may not be represented by training samples, because real data will have noise pollution. Through resolving the following steady l_1-minimization problem, the sparse solution a could be improved well:

$$\hat{a} = \arg\min\|a\|_1 \ subject \ to \ \|Aa - y\|_2 \leq \varepsilon \tag{8}$$

A new vector δ_i that whose nonzero points are related to the class i in $\hat{a}$ is defined for classification. Using the vector, the test sample can be reconstructed as

$$\tilde{y} = A\delta_i(\hat{a}) \tag{9}$$

If the residue between y and $\tilde{y}$ is smaller, the probability that y belongs to the ith class would be bigger. Test sample y can be judged to be part of the class whose $\tilde{y}$ has least residue with y.

$$\min_i r_i(y) = \|y - A\delta_i(\hat{a})\| \ for \ i = 1, 2, \cdots, k \tag{10}$$

2.4.2 Dictionary Learning (DL)

Dictionary is important in sparse representation. KSVD algorithm is an iterative dictionary learning (DL) method, used to optimize a dictionary initialized by the training dataset. The algorithm encompasses two principal stages: (1) Fixed A, update the sparse coefficient a; (2) Fixed a, update dictionary A and coefficient a. The dictionary is updated by largest singular value corresponding eigenvectors. The objective function is

$$\|y - Aa\|_F^2 = \left\| (y - \sum_{i \neq k} A_i a_i) - A_k a_k \right\|_F^2 = \|E_k - A_k a_k\| \tag{5}$$

E_k is solved by singular value decomposition (SVD), $E_k = U \Delta U^{-1}$. The column of U is the feature vector, Δ is diagonal matrix and the dictionary is optimized as $a = U(:, 1)$.

3 Analysis of Experiment Results

For test the performance of the method, respectively divided the two classes of EEG signals (F and S) into two groups with the same sample size to form the training set and the test set (both of the training and test set have 200 samples of ictal EEGs and 200 samples of interictal EEGs). EEG signals are processed into IMFs first. The frequency of IMFs are shown in Fig. 1. IMF1–3 component contain the most frequencies of ictal EEG.

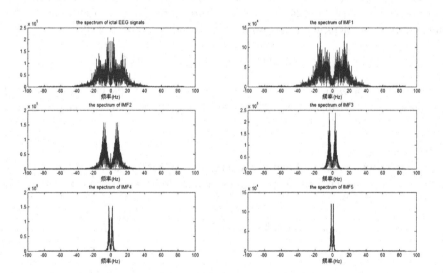

Fig. 1. The spectrum of IMFs of an ictal EEG signal

Compute the four features of the IMFs, and the complex EEG signals can be mapped to the linear feature space. The training samples and test samples are replaced by the characteristics of IMF components.

In the framework of SRC, the test sample could be precisely represented sparsely by training samples, a very important problem is how to determine the tolerance parameter of reconstruction error in (8), which gives great effect on the result of identification. The l_1-minimization problem can be solved by the CVX toolbox. The classification accuracy of IMFs with different parameter ε are shown in Table 1.

Table 1. Classification accuracy of IMFs with different parameter ε

ε	0.85	0.65	0.45	0.25	0.15	0.1	0.05	0.035	0.025	0.015	0.01	0.005	0.001
EEG	0.885	0.88	0.875	0.87	0.875	0.875	0.875	0.875	0.88	0.88	0.885	0.885	0.885
IMF1	0.935	0.935	0.935	0.935	0.94	0.945	0.945	0.95	0.955	**0.965**	0.96	0.945	0.945
IMF2	0.945	0.94	0.93	0.94	0.945	0.94	0.94	0.94	0.94	0.94	0.94	0.945	0.94
IMF3	0.89	0.885	0.89	0.885	0.895	0.89	0.895	0.895	0.895	0.895	0.89	0.89	0.89
IMF4	0.76	0.75	0.745	0.75	0.745	0.74	0.725	0.725	0.725	0.74	0.735	0.73	0.735
IMF5	0.62	0.615	0.62	0.625	0.665	0.655	0.625	0.63	0.635	0.62	0.59	0.575	0.595

From Table 1, the classification results of IMF1-3 based on SRC is greater than the raw EEGs. And the IMF1 linear feature can improve the accuracy up to 96.5% ($\varepsilon = 0.015$). To make the classification accuracy better, the higher frequency IMF components are combined to build the feature vector.

The recognition results of combined IMF components are shown in Table 2. Compared with SVM, the classification performance of sparse representation is no longer dependent on selection and computation of features entirely. The comparison of SRC and SVM for seizure detection is summarized in Table 3. Each EEG epochs with duration of 23.6 s contain 4097 points. For real time seizure detection, the time consumed by one EEG sample should be not more than 5.9 s. For combined IMF123 components of one EEG sample, the average computing time of 12-D feature vector in SRC is 0.51 s.

Table 2. The classification performance of combined IMF components

Components	Sensitivity(%)	Specificity(%)	Accuracy (%)
IMF12 + SRC	95.00	96.00	95.50
IMF123 + SRC	99.00	96.00	97.50
IMF12 + SRC + DL	100	96.00	98.00
IMF123 + SRC + DL	100	98.00	99.00

Table 3. The comparison of SRC and SVM for seizure detection

Method	Sensitivity(%)	Specificity(%)	Accuracy(%)	Time(s)
EMD + SVM	97.00	96.25	96.60	1.40
Kernel SRC	99.00	98.00	98.50	2.0
This method	100.00	98.00	99.00	0.51

4   Conclusion

This paper has proposed an automated detection method of seizure EEGs using SRC to recognize the two classes of EEGs (i.e. epileptic ictal EEG and interictal EEG). EMD was used to get more information for analyse the epileptic EEG. Then four features of IMFs are extracted as the dictionary in SRC scheme to reduce data dimension and computational cost. Finally, the KSVD is exploited to optimize dictionary and performs well. The higher recognition rate and faster test time show that for real time detection of clinical epileptic EEGs the idea reported in this work will be potential.

Acknowledgments. This work was supported by the National Natural Science Foundation of China (Grant No. 61671220, 61201428), the Project of Shandong Province Higher Educational Science and Technology Program, China (Grant No. J16LN07), the Shandong Province Key Research and Development Program, China (Grant No. 2016GGX101022).

References

1. Acharya, U.R., Chua, K.C., Lim, T.C., Dorithy, Suri, J.S.: Automatic identification of epileptic EEG signals using nonlinear parameters. J. Mech. Med. Biol. **9**, 539–553 (2009)
2. Kai, C.H., Sung, N.Y.: Detection of seizures in EEG using subband nonlinear parameters and genetic algorithm. Comput. Biol. Med. **40**, 823–830 (2010)
3. Ocak, H.: Automatic detection of epileptic seizures in EEG using discrete wavelet transform and approximate entropy. Expert Syst. Appl. **36**, 2027–2036 (2009)
4. Guo, L., Rivero, D., Seoane, J., Pazos, A.: Classification of EEG signals using relative wavelet energy and artificial neural networks. In: The First ACM/SIGEVO Summit on Genetic and Evolutionary Computation, pp. 177–183. ACM Press, Shanghai (2009)
5. Ubeyli, E.D.: Combined neural network model employing wavelet coefficients for EEG signals classification. Digit. Sig. Process. **19**, 297–308 (2009)
6. Zhao, J.L., Zhou, W.D., Liu, K., Cai, D.M.: EEG signal classification based on SVM and wavelet analysis. J. Comput. Appl. Softw. **28**, 114–116 (2011)
7. Yuan, Q., Zhou, W.D., Li, S.F., Cai, D.M.: Epileptic EEG classification based on extreme learning machine and nonlinear features. Epilepsy Res. **96**, 29–38 (2011)
8. Braun, S., Feldman, M.: Decomposition of non-stationary signals into varying time scales: some aspects of the EMD and HVD methods. Mech. Syst. Sig. Process. **25**, 2608–2630 (2011)
9. Li, S.F., Zhou, W.D., Cai, D.M., Liu, K., Zhao, J.L.: EEG signal classification based on EMD and SVM. J. Biomed. Eng. **28**, 891–894 (2011)
10. Pachori, R.B., Bajaj, V.: Analysis of normal and epileptic seizure EEG signals using empirical mode decomposition. Comput. Methods Programs Biomed. **104**, 373–381 (2011)
11. Tafreshi, A.K., Nasrabadi, A.M., Omidvarnia, A.H.: Epileptic seizure detection using empirical mode decomposition. In: 8th IEEE International Symposium on Signal Processing and Information Technology, pp. 238–242. IEEE Press, New York (2008)
12. Wright, J., Yang, A.Y., Ganesh, A., Sastry, S.S., Ma, Y.: Robust face recognition via sparse representation. IEEE Trans. Pattern Anal. Mach. Intell. **31**, 210–227 (2009)
13. Georgiev, P., Theis, F., Cichocki, A.: Sparse component analysis and blind source separation of underdetermined mixtures. IEEE Trans. Neural Netw. **16**, 992–996 (2005)

14. Yang, J., Wright, J., Huang, T., Ma, Y.: Image super-resolution as sparse representation of raw patches. In: Proceedings of the IEEE International Conference on Computer Vision and Pattern Recognition, pp. 1–8. IEEE Press, New York (2008)
15. Faust, O., Acharya, U.R., Adeli, H., Adeli, A.: Wavelet-based EEG processing for computer-aided seizure detection and epilepsy diagnosis. Seizure **26**, 56–64 (2015)
16. Yang, M., Zhang, L., Feng, X.C., Zhang, D.: Sparse representation based fisher discrimination dictionary learning for image classification. Int. J. Comput. Vision **109**, 209–232 (2014)
17. Chen, Z.H., Zuo, W.M., Hu, Q.H., Lin, L.: Kernel sparse representation for time series classification. Inf. Sci. **292**, 15–26 (2015)

Dynamical Analysis of a Stochastic Neuron Spiking Activity in the Biological Experiment and Its Simulation by $I_{Na,P} + I_K$ Model

Huijie Shang[1], Zhongting Jiang[1], Dong Wang[1,2(✉)], Yuehui Chen[1,2],
Peng Wu[1,2], Jin Zhou[1,2], and Shiyuan Han[1,2]

[1] School of Information Science and Engineering,
University of Jinan, Jinan 250022, China
ise_wangd@ujn.edu.cn
[2] Shandong Provincial Key Laboratory of Network Based Intelligent Computing,
University of Jinan, Jinan 250022, China

Abstract. An irregular on-off like spiking activity is observed in the rat neural pacemaker experiment with the changes of extracellular calcium concentration. The spiking activity is simulated using a minimal model, the stochastic $I_{Na,P} + I_K$ model. The nonlinear time series analysis on ISI series shows the similar stochastic dynamical features of both experimental and simulated results. The power spectrum and SNR analysis suggests that this spiking activity is the autonomous stochastic resonance induced by noise near a subcritical Hopf bifurcation. Thus, it becomes easy for us to compare different stochastic firing patterns observed in the same experiment and stimulated under one same model. Besides, some deterministic-like characteristics by the analysis results on ISI series were also explained in this paper.

Keywords: Spiking neuron · Neurodynamics · Stochastic firing pattern
$I_{Na,P} + I_K$ model

1 Introduction

The nervous system coordinates body actions by transmitting information with the shape of neural discharge activities [1, 2]. For a long time, the related knowledge was obtained from biological experiments. Since the late 1950's, numerical simulation with math models and nonlinear time series analysis were widely used to reveal the nature of neural events. [3, 4]. A neuron is the basic unit of the nervous system. Various dynamical phenomena of a single neuron could be found in both the experiment and simulation [5–8]. In these previous studies, chaotic firing patterns and stochastic firing patterns were often confused with each other [6, 7]. Several chaotic patterns with irregular rhythm were re-recognized as the stochastic firing pattern, such as integer multiples firing pattern and on-off firing pattern. These researches suggested that internal and external noise played important roles in inspiring new stochastic firing patterns [7–10].

© Springer International Publishing AG, part of Springer Nature 2018
T. Huang et al. (Eds.): ISNN 2018, LNCS 10878, pp. 850–859, 2018.
https://doi.org/10.1007/978-3-319-92537-0_96

However, uncertain identification of the stochastic firing pattern still exits and should be careful to be dealt with. If possible, the bifurcation analysis of the randomicity may be helpful to the stochastic firing pattern identification [12]. In addition, some neuron models were usd to stimulate the stochastic firing pattern before, like Chay model, FitzHugh–Nagumo model, and Morris–Lecar model [7, 9, 10]. There was little research with the minimal models, those having minimal sets of currents that enable the models to generate various action potentials. As well known, with the minimal models, we will see that the behavior of the models depends not so much on the ionic currents as on the relationship between (in)activation curves and the time constants.

In the present study, typical on-off like spiking activities were recorded in the neural pacemaker experiment. With the changes of experimental parameters, this bursting was found to be generated between resting state and period one period firing. We then used $I_{Na,P} + I_K$ model to simulate the experimental observations and analyze the underlying dynamics. The rest of the present Letter is organized as follows: Sect. 2 presents the experimental methods, theoretical model and analysis method. Section 3 gives the experimental analysis results. Section 4 presents similarity between the results of numerical simulation and experimental observation. Section 5 provides the discussion and conclusion.

2 Models and Methods

2.1 Experimental Model

The real biological system in the present paper employed an experimental neural pacemaker model. It was widely applied to study the neural firing activities and helpful to understand the spontaneous discharges of injured nerve. The operation principles and processes are introduced in Ref. [11].

2.2 Theoretical Model

The $I_{Na,P} + I_K$ model, which is one of the most fundamental models in computational neuroscience, was employed to numerically simulate the experimental firing activities. We can obtain his minimal model by removing the leakage current and the gating variable from the Hodgkin-Huxley model. Then, the resulting model consists of a fast Na^+ current and a relatively slower K^+ current [13]. Its deterministic form contains the following two simultaneous differential equations:

$$C\dot{V} = I - g_L(V - E_L) - g_{Na}m_\infty(V)(V - E_{Na}) - g_K n(V - E_K) \tag{1}$$

$$\dot{n} = (n_\infty(V) - n)/\tau(V) \tag{2}$$

The variables and parameters were introduced particularly the previous study [13]. Besides, the stochastic $I_{Na,P} + I_K$ model, in which a Gaussian white noise $\xi(t)$ was directly added to the right hand of Eq. (1), was also studied here, as shown in Eq. (3).

$$C\dot{V} = I - g_L(V - E_L) - g_{Na}m_\infty(V)(V - E_{Na}) - g_K n(V - E_K) + \xi(t) \qquad (3)$$

The stochastic factor possesses the statistical properties as $<\xi(t)> = 0$; $<\xi(t)$, $\xi(t')> = 2D\,\delta(t - t')$; where D is the noise density and δ is the Dirac δ-function.

In both deterministic and stochastic model, I is chosen as bifurcation parameter and others are as follow: $C = 1.0$; $E_L = -78.0$; $g_L = 1.0$; $g_{Na} = 4.0$; $g_K = 4.0$; $V_m = -30.0$; $Vn = -45.0$; $K_m = 7.0$; $K_n = 5.0$; $\tau(V) = 8.0$; $E_{Na} = 60.0$; $E_k = 90.0$. Models are solved by Mannelle numerical integrate method [14] with integration time step being 10^{-3} s. Upstrokes of the voltage reached the amplitude of -25.0 mV are counted as spikes.

In our previous work, we use $I_{Na,P} + I_K$ model successfully simulated the integer multiples firing pattern also observed in the neural pacemaker experiment.

2.3   Analysis Methods

In this paper, the method of phase space reconstruction, surrogate data, nonlinear prediction (NPE), approximate entropy, Complexity, autocorrelation coefficient (ACC) analysis, power spectrum analysis, and Signal to Noise Ratio (SNR) analysis, were used to carry on analysis on the experimental and simulated data. The algorithms of all the analysis methods were particularly described in the previous studies [15–20]. To avoid repetition, it's not described here.

3   Experimental Analysis Results

In 27 experimental pacemaker units, when the *extracellular* calcium concentration $([Ca^{2+}]_o)$ was gradually changed, a type of irregular spiking activity was generated. As shown in Fig. 1(a), the spike trains of bursting exhibited obvious non-periodic. This spiking activity would be changed to resting state with the increase of $([Ca^{2+}]_o)$, while to period 1 spiking with the decrease of $([Ca^{2+}]_o)$.

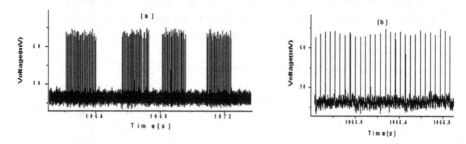

Fig. 1. On-off like spiking activity in experimental neural pacemakers. (a) Spike trains. (b) Part of (a), indicating the spiking train in the continuous discharge period.

The simple statistical characteristics of this pattern were as follows: Continuous fast bursting discharge occurs alternately with long resting period; the average ISI value of the continuous discharge is 0.0566 ± 0.0045 s with a low variability 7.88%, which could be approximated as period 1 spiking, as shown in Fig. 1(b); the average duration of resting period is 0.285 ± 0.188 s, which is far greater than that of continuous discharge ISI.

These statistical characteristics are very similar to those of on-off firing pattern in previous reports.

The nonlinear time series analysis results of this firing activity also showed its on-off pattern like characteristics. ISI series and ISI histogram were showed as Fig. 2(a) and (b). Most points gathered to form the basic ISI point-belt at a relatively low position in Fig. 2(a), corresponding to the first extra high peak in ISIH shown in Fig. 2 (b). It further confirmed the period 1 spiking was continuous in discharge period. The point sets of the first return map of the ISI series exhibited a 'right angle-like' structure, with two 'sides' composed of two groups of point clusters parallel to the x-coordinate and the y-coordinate, respectively, as shown in Fig. 2(c). The same structure also appeared in the first return map of the surrogate data of the ISI series, without any significant difference from its raw data, as shown in Fig. 2(d). With increasing of the lag, ACC of the ISI series only vibrated around zero when the value of lag was not zero, as shown in Fig. 2(e). NPE of ISI series could not be predicted either in a short step or in a long step, as shown in Fig. 2(f).

Although the results above exhibited the stochastic features, the results of approximate entropy and complexity on ISI series was 0.2130 and 0.2187 respectively, implying this ISI series had low complexity and high orderliness.

4   Numerical Simulation Results and Analysis

With the deterministic $I_{Na,P} + I_K$ model, there was no pattern as same as that in the experiment. Then, the stochastic $I_{Na,P} + I_K$ model mentioned above was applied to simulate. In the deterministic $I_{Na,P} + I_K$ model, the equilibrium bifurcation of the system has stable equilibrium point when I from 40 to 50, is shown in Fig. 3(a). s of the system. When $I = 42.2310$, the system generated the saddle-node bifurcation. When $I = 48.9016$, the system generated the subcritical Hopf bifurcation. Thus, when I is more than 42.2310 and less than 48.9016, the resting stable equilibrium points coexists with the limit cycle attractors. This is also reflected in the V-n phase plane, as shown in Fig. 3(b).

Taking $I = 45$ and $D = 1$ for example, we simulated the on-off like spiking trains similar to those in the experiment, as shown in Fig. 4.

The nonlinear time series analysis results of the simulated firing activity also

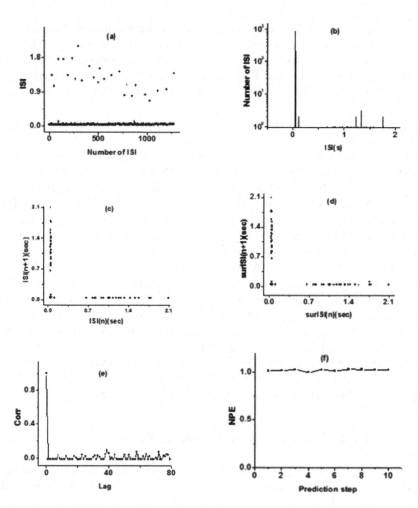

Fig. 2. Time series methods analysis on the ISI series of the on-off pattern like spiking activity in the experimental neural pacemaker. (a) ISI series. (b) ISI histogram. (c) First return map of ISI. (d) First return map of surrogate data of ISI. (e) ACC of ISI. (f) NPE of ISI.

showed similar dynamical characteristics similar to that in the experiment, as shown in Fig. 5.

The results of Approximate Entropy and Complexity on stimulated ISI series was 0.1999 and 0.2461 respectively, also implying this stimulated ISI series had low complexity and high orderliness.

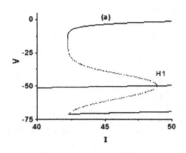

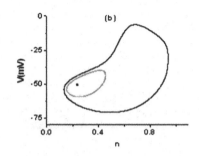

Fig. 3. (a) Equilibrium points bifurcation diagram of the deterministic $I_{Na,P} + I_K$ model when I is from 42.2310 to 48.9016, while solid lines represent the amplitude of stable limit cycles and the dotted lines represent the amplitude of unstable limit cycles. (b) When I = 45, there is a coexistence of equilibrium and limit cycle attractors in the V-n phase plane, while black dot solid represents a stable equilibrium point, the red line represents a unstable limit cycle, and the black line represents a stable limit cycle. (Color figure online)

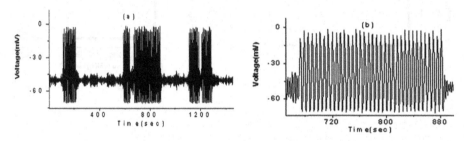

Fig. 4. On-off like spiking activity simulated by the stochastic $I_{Na,P} + I_K$ model (I = 45 and D = 1). (a) Spike trains. (b) Part of (a), indicating the spiking train in the continuous discharge period.

In fact, when I was gradually changed near the subcritical Hopf bifurcation, the behavior of the stochastic $I_{Na,P} + I_K$ model system was also between resting state and period 1 firing, similar to the course in the experiment, as shown in Fig. 6.

The power spectrum analysis and SNR analysis with different value of D were also carried on to study the roles of the noise. The power spectrum density $p(f)$, the peak value of the power spectrum, and the two eigen values of SNR, β_1 and β_2, all showed similar change characters with the increase of noise density. All of them increased firstly and then decreased. There was a noise intensity, about D = 30, could make the four indicators reach the maximum values, as shown in, as shown in Fig. 7.

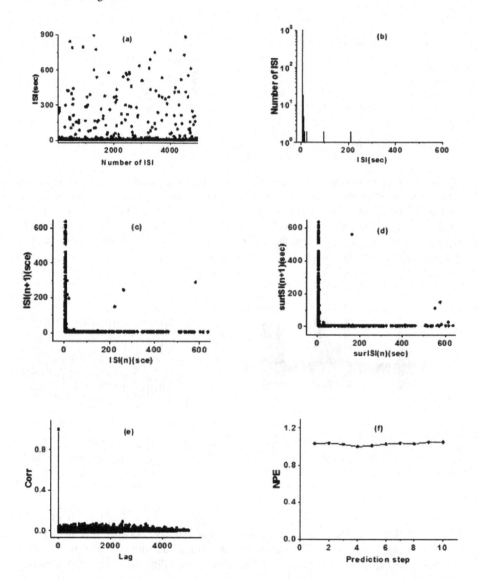

Fig. 5. Time series methods analysis on the ISI series of the on-off pattern like spiking activity simulated by the stochastic $I_{Na,P} + I_K$ model ($I = 45$ and $D = 1$). (a) ISI series. (b) ISI histogram. (c) First return map of ISI. (d) First return map of surrogate data of ISI. (e) ACC of ISI. (f) NPE of ISI.

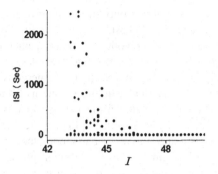

Fig. 6. Bifurcation diagrams of ISI about the parameter I in the stochastic $I_{Na,P} + I_K$ model ($D = 1$).

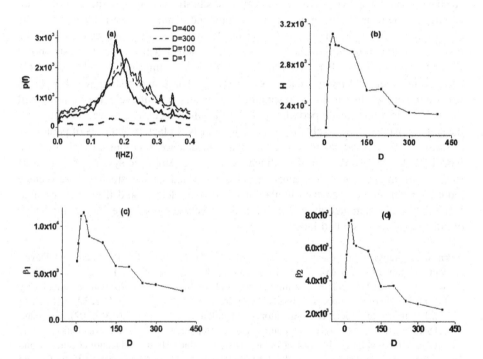

Fig. 7. Power spectrum analysis and SNR analysis with different noise density of the stochastic $I_{Na,P} + I_K$ model ($I = 45$). (a) The power spectrum. (b) The height of power spectrum. (c) β_1. (d) β_2.

5   Discussion and Conclusions

Power spectrum analysis and SNR analysis were always used as the standards to indentify whether the stochastic resonance occurred. In this article, there was no sources of external noise. So, the results of power spectrum analysis and SNR analysis suggested that the irregular spiking activity in this investigation was the autonomous stochastic resonance induced by stochastic noise. In fact, stochastic resonance and autonomous stochastic resonance are both the common phenomena in neural firing. Previous studies revealed that, except for the negative roles, the noise could also play positive and key roles in information processing of the nervous system. However, it is still difficult to accurately identify stochastic firing patterns from complex neural firing rhythm, especially as similar to chaotic firing pattern. In this study, nonlinear time series analysis and bifurcation analysis were employed to reveal the dynamical features of the irregular on-off like spiking activity. What's more, the minimal model, stochastic $I_{Na,P} + I_K$ model, was used to simulate the experiment phenomenon. Because of the same dynamical bifurcation scenarios as the experimental data, these results were credible. This also provide a new idea for the identify the dynamical features of the rich neural firing patterns by simple neuron models. Most of the results suggest that this is s stochastic spiking activity. However, why a stochastic pattern has the deterministic features by the result of the approximate entropy and complexity on ISI series? By the equilibrium bifurcation of the deterministic $I_{Na,P} + I_K$ model, we can anwser the question by two aspects. On the one hand, being affected by inner stochastic noise fluctuations, the system behavior transiting between the limit cycle and fixed stable equilibrium point is random, that is, when the discharge and resting will happen is uncertain. On the other hand, corresponding to the stable limit cycle, the period 1 still maintain their deterministic periodicity in the transition metioned above, meaning that the spiking may be more likely to appear continuously. In fact, by analysis of parameter interval in which noise takes part, there is a "coexistence zone" in the deterministic model. That is the expression of nonlinearity in the deterministic systems. In previous studies, the integer multiple firing was also identified as the stochastic resonance induced by the noise with the simulation in other models. Could the same minimal model be used to simulate the two firing activies between discharge and resting? This question need to be studied later.

Acknowledgments. This research was supported by the National Key Research And Development Program of China (No. 2016YFC0106000), the Natural Science Foundation of China (Grant No. 61302128), and the Youth Science and Technology Star Program of Jinan City (201406003), although supported by NSFC (Grant No. 61573166, 61572230, 61671220, 61640218), the Natural Science Foundation of Shandong Province (ZR2013FL002), the Shandong Distinguished Middle-aged and Young Scientist Encourage and Reward Foundation, China (Grant No. ZR2016FB14), the Project of Shandong Province Higher Educational Science and Technology Program, China (Grant No. J16LN07), the Shandong Province Key Research and Development Program, China (Grant No. 2016GGX101022).

References

1. Bao, W., Huang, Z., Yuan, C.A., Huang, D.S.: Pupylation sites prediction with ensemble classification model. Int. J. Data Min. Bioinform. **18**(91), 91–104 (2017)
2. Khurana, V., Kumar, P., Saini, R., Roy, P.P.: EEG based word familiarity using features and frequency bands combination. Cogn. Syst. Res. **49**, 33–48 (2018)

3. Ren, W., Hu, S.J., Zhang, B.J., Wang, F.Z., Gong, Y.F., Xu, J.X.: Period-adding bifurcation with chaos in the inter-spike intervals generated by an experimental neural pacemaker. Int. J. Bifurcat. Chaos **7**, 1867–1872 (1997)
4. Gu, H.G., Yang, M.H., Li, L., Liu, Z.Q., Ren, W.: Chaotic and ASR induced firing pattern in experimental neural pacemaker. Dyn. Contin. Discret. Impuls. Syst. (Ser. B: Appl. Algorithms) **11**, 19–24 (2004)
5. Levine, D.S.: Modeling the instinctive-emotional-thoughtful Mind. Cogn. Syst. Res. **45**, 82–94 (2017)
6. Li, Y., Gu, H.-G.: The distinct stochastic and deterministic dynamics between period-adding and period-doubling bifurcations neural bursting patterns. Nonlinear Dyn. **87**, 2541–2562 (2016)
7. Petrov, S.: Dynamics properties of knowledge acquisition. Cogn. Syst. Res. **47**, 12–15 (2018)
8. Yang, M.H., An, S.C., Gu, H.G., Liu, Z.Q., Ren, W.: Understanding of physiological neural firing patterns through dynamical bifurcation machineries. NeuroReport **17**(10), 995–999 (2006)
9. Braun, H.A., Wissing, H., Schafer, K., Hirsch, M.C.: Oscillation and noise determine signal transduction in shark multimodal sensory cells. Nature **367**, 270–273 (1994)
10. Jia, B., Gu, H.G., Xue, L.: A basic bifurcation structure from bursting to spiking of injured nerve fibers in a two-dimensional parameter space. Cogn. Neuro dyn. **11**(2), 189–200 (2017)
11. Li, Y.Y., Gu, H.G.: The distinct stochastic and deterministic dynamics between period-adding and period-doubling bifurcations of neural bursting patterns. Nonlinear Dyn. **87**(4), 2541–2562 (2016)
12. Zhao, Z.G., Jia, B., Gu, H.G.: Bifurcations and enhancement of neuronal firing induced by negative feedback. Nonlinear **86**(3), 1549–1560 (2016)
13. Börgers, C.: An Introduction to Modeling Neuronal Dynamics, pp. 111–115. Springer International Publishing. Springer, Cham (2017). https://doi.org/10.1007/978-3-319-51171-9
14. Jia, B., Gu, H.G.: Identifying type I excitability using dynamics of stochastic neural firing patterns. Cogn. Neurodyn. **6**, 485–497 (2012)
15. Gu, H.G., Zhang, H.M., Wei, C.L., Yang, M.H., Liu, Z.Q., Ren, W.: Coherence resonance induced stochastic neural firing at a saddle-node bifurcation. Int. J. Mod. Phys. B **25**, 3977–3986 (2011)
16. Gu, H.G., Zhao, Z.G., Jia, B., Chen, S.G.: Dynamics of on-off neural firing patterns and stochastic effects near a sub-critical Hopf bifurcation. PLoS ONE **10**(4), e0121028 (2015)
17. Xing, J.L., Hu, S.J., Xu, H., Han, S., Wan, Y.H.: Subthreshold membrane oscillations underlying integer multiples firing from injured sensory neurons. NeuroReport **12**, 1311–1313 (2001)
18. Chay, T.R.: Chaos in a Three-variable Modle of an Excitable Cell. Phys. D **16**, 233–242 (1985)
19. Mannella, R., Palleschi, V.: Fast and precise algorithm for computer simulation of stochastic differential equations. Phys. Rev. A **40**, 3381–3386 (1989)
20. Wiesenfeld, K., Pierson, D., Pantazelo, E.: Stochastic resonance on a circle. Phys. Rev. Lett. **72**(14), 2125–2129 (1994)

Blinks Identification Using the GMM Classification Method of Polynomial Modeling of EEG Signals

Rim Somai[1]([✉]), Meriem Riahi[2], and Faouzi Moussa[1]

[1] El Manar University, FST, Tunis, Tunisia
rimsomai@gmail.com, faouzimousssa@gmail.com
[2] Tunis University, ENSIT, Tunis, Tunisia
meriem.riehi2013@gmail.com

Abstract. Nowadays, people who suffer from sever motor handicap like amyotrophic lateral sclerosis (ALS) can take a profit from the commercialization of brain computer interface (BCI). This technology progress contributes on the integration of ALS people in the society by giving them the possibility to command machine only by the power of brain signals (EEG signals). Therefore, the BCI system can be based on deferent paradigms. Our main objective here, is to detect the blinks in the EEG signals in order to command machine. In this paper, we propose a new blink detection approach based on unsupervised clustering of the blink regression parameters using the Gaussian mixture model (GMM). Our approach is mainly based on learning and prediction phases. The learning phase aims to apply GMM clustering on blink curve parameters which are approximated by polynomial regression. After the automatic segmentation process, the prediction phase aims to classify the curve approximated parameters related to each of the unknown EEG segments. We experimented our approach based on 50 collected blinks from five different subjects. We obtained encouraging results with 0.9310 as a recognition accuracy score...

Keywords: BCI · EEG signals · GMM · Blinks
Polynomial regression

1 Introduction

The idea of the brain computer was focused on the use of brain waves in order to control a machine. The BCI based system can be a solution for people who suffered from multiple handicaps. However, the majority of different types of BCI system needs a large users learning period. We are looking for a simple interface based system with no necessary training period. The voluntary blinks based systems was used to command machines. Practically, the disabled user can easily start to use such system. The blinks can be detected in the EEG signals. In the literature, we find some systems controlled by voluntary blinks. Ma

© Springer International Publishing AG, part of Springer Nature 2018
T. Huang et al. (Eds.): ISNN 2018, LNCS 10878, pp. 860–867, 2018.
https://doi.org/10.1007/978-3-319-92537-0_97

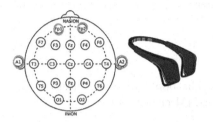
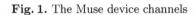
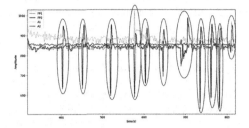

Fig. 1. The Muse device channels

Fig. 2. Manual blink selection (Color figure online)

et al. proposed a BCI system controls a multi-functional humanoid robot and four mobile robots. This hybrid BCI system used both the Electrooculography i.e. eye movements (EOG) and the EEG signals [1]. Ferreira et al. employed the blinks to control a robotic Wheelchair [2]. The blink in an EEG recorded signal can be easily recognized by expert. Therefore, in a real time system commanded by blinks, this task must be automatized. Ochoa surveyed four most known methods to detect blinks in the EEG signals: The Blind Source Separation (BSS) method, the classical rejection or removal method, the bandpass FIR filters and the neural networks [3]. The majority of BSS based methods used the Independent Component Analysis (ICA). Gao et al. proposed a peak detection methods of ICA combined with SVM classifier [4]. Gebrehiwot et al. work used the FastICA, band-pass filtering and thresholding steps [5]. Also, Gupta et al. used the statistical methods for artifacts detection [6]. Abo et al. proposed an algebraic method that represent each piecewise signal by a second degree polynomial. Each coefficient is considered as an output of a FIR filter. Then, the blinks are detected by the algebraic spike detection method [7]. Some deletion approaches are based on neural networks [8]. In this paper, we focus on the voluntary blink detection in order to command a system. We propose a novel approach for automatic blinks detection using the GMM classification method of polynomial EEG signals modeling.

2 The Proposed Approach

As mentioned in the introduction, many methods and techniques were proposed to solve the blink detection problem, but none of them admit a blink signal signature based on blink trajectories shape. While, the Electrocardiography (ECG) signal curve has its known signature [9]. Also, We have to improve the recognition accuracy score in order to make the voluntary blink based system effective. The first step of a BCI system is the EEG signals acquisition. We used the $Muse^1$ which integrate four channels: A1, A2, Fp1 and Fp2 as shown in the Fig. 1. In this section, we present our approach named GMM classification of polynomial

---

[1] http://www.choosemuse.com/.

EEG models. It is composed by two main phases: The learning phase and the predicting phase.

2.1   The Learning Phase

In this phase, three sub steps are provided: The blink segments selection, the polynomial regression and the unsupervised GMM classification.

The Blink Segments Selection: Our laboratory expert examines subjects for the aim to identify blinks. He specifies the exact segment containing each blink. In this phase, we are based on an expert in order to guarantee correct blink segments. As shown in Fig. 2, the selected EEG blink signals in deferent bounded intervals on the four channels are surrounded with the blue circle.

The Polynomial Regression: Our approach is based on polynomial regression in order to fit blink curves. The polynomial is with n degree (Eq. 1). The $(n+1)$ polynomial coefficients are determined as follow: We consider finished set of **p** points in the selected segment with $p > n$.

$$P_n(x) = a_n x^n + a_{(n-1)} x^{(n-1)} + \cdots + a_1 x + a_0; P(x_i) = \sum_{k=0}^{n} a_k x_i^k \quad (1)$$

The adjustment of the approximated coefficients (a_i with $0 \preceq i \preceq n$ and x is the indeterminate) of the polynomial involves the minimization of the residual sum of squares (RSS) (Eq. 2) [10]:

$$\min RSS = \min \sum_{i=1}^{p} \epsilon^2 = \min \sum_{i=1}^{p} \left[y_i - \sum_{k=0}^{n} a_k x_i^k \right]^2 \quad (2)$$

We should determine each of a_k values which put the partial derivative of $\sum_{i=0}^{p} \epsilon^2$ over a_k to 0. Furthermore, for $q = 0 \ldots n$, we have the Eq. 3:

$$\frac{\partial P}{\partial a_q} = 2 \sum_{i=1}^{p} \left\{ -\left[y_i - \sum_{k=0}^{n} a_k x_i^k \right] x_i^q \right\} = \sum_{q}^{n} \left[a_k \sum_{i=1}^{p} x_i^{k+q} \right] = 0 \quad (3)$$

We vary the polynomial degree n in order to choose the degree that maximize the coefficient of determination R2 score between the initial and the approximated signals. R2 measure the proportion of the variance in the dependent variable that is predictable from the independent variable(s). Whenever R2 score is nearest of 1, it gives an idea about the success of predicting of the dependent variable from the independent variables. In our case, the choice of n depends on R2 score. The R2 is stable from degree 5 for the majority of blinks.

The Unsupervised GMM Classification: Once we have the polynomial coefficients adjusted to the blink curves, we will proceed to a unsupervised classification. The unsupervised classification allows the automating of the blink recognition procedure. We specify that we need exactly two class $k = 2$: A class for the blinks and the other class for the not blinks. A coefficients matrix representing the blinks and the not blinks signals is generated. It is then learned to the blink recognition system using Gaussian mixture model (GMM) [11]. Gaussian model, is based on the density With x_p: is the vector of the curve parameters, n: is the dimension of the x_p, μ_p: is the average vector with n dimension, $\sum_k$: is the covariance matrix with $n*n$ dimension, $|\sum_k|$: is the determinant of $\sum_k$ and $\frac{1}{(2\Pi)^{n/2}|\sum_k|^{1/2}}$ is a normalization constant. The function of Gaussian distribution defined as follows:

$$N(x_p|\mu_k,\sigma_k^2) = \frac{1}{(2\Pi)^{n/2}\,|\sum_k|^{1/2}} e^{-\frac{1}{2}(x_p-\mu_k)^t \sum_k^{-1}(x_p-\mu_k)} \tag{4}$$

With x_p: is the vector of the curve parameters, n: is the dimension of the x_n, μ_n: is the average vector with n dimension, $\sum_k$: is the covariance matrix with $n*n$ dimension, $|\sum_k|$: is the determinant of $\sum_k$ and $\frac{1}{(2\Pi)^{n/2}|\sum_k|^{1/2}}$ is a normalization constant. To identify the blinks signals represented by polynomial parameters, we can't restricted on the use a single Gaussian model defined in Eq. 4. The solution is to use the linear combination of $K = 2$ Gaussian models our unsupervised classification problem as presented in the Eq. 5):

$$f(x_p|\theta_k) = \sum_{k=1}^{M} \pi_k N(x_p|\mu_k,\sigma_k^2) \tag{5}$$

With $\pi_k \in 1..M$: is the set of weight values, $\mu_k \in 1..M$: is the set of averages, $\sigma_k^2 \in 1..M$: is the set of co-variance matrix, $\theta_k = \pi_k, \mu_k, \sigma_k^2$.
The function $f(x_p|\theta_k)$ depends on π_k, μ_k and σ_k^2 parameters. Many methods try to estimate those parameters. The most used method is the maximum likelihood known as Expectation-Maximization algorithm (EM) [12]. It's a three-step iterative algorithm: The parameters initialization $(\pi_k, \mu_k$ and $\sigma_k^2)$ and the loop until the convergence:

- **Expectation step:** Calculate the conditional probabilities $t_{(i,k)}$ of the sample i of the k = 2 component as in the Eq. 6:

$$t_{(i,k)} = \frac{\pi_k N(x_i|\mu_k,\sigma_k^2)}{\sum_{j=1}^{m} \pi_j N(x_i|\mu_j,\sigma_j^2)} \tag{6}$$

With $j \in 1,..,m$: Gaussian set.

- **Maximization step:** Update the parameters by maximizing the quantity Q according to the different parameters of the model (apply the Eq. 7)

$$\tilde{\theta}_k = argmax_{\theta_k} Q\left(\theta_k,\theta_k^{old}\right) \tag{7}$$

2.2   The Predicting Phase

The prediction phase aims to distinguish the voluntary blinks from the other signals. It is composed by three steps: The automatically segmentation of the input signals, the polynomial regression of the segments curves and the GMM prediction of the polynomial coefficients vector.

The Signal Segmentation: The input signals contains local maximas and local minimas. A local minimas must be smaller than its immediate neighbor points respectively a local maximas should be greater than its immediate neighbor points. The peaks detection in EEG data is based on their amplitude. We detect the segments containing three successive local minimas represented by green points. As it's shown in the Fig. 3, the segments bounds are represented by the blue dashed lines. They are not necessarily equals.

The Polynomial Regression: In this step we proceed with the same polynomial regression of the previous phase. We fit a vector of polynomial coefficients for each segment. We use the same degree n of the learning phase. So we obtain a Matrix that contain the blinks and the not blinks to be used as input to the GMM prediction algorithm.

The GMM Prediction: In this step, we try to estimate to each signal its parameters $(\pi_k, \mu_k$ and $\sigma_k^2)$. We apply the Expectation-Maximization algorithm (EM) seen in the learning phase. The obtained parameters can then determine the function $f(x_p|\theta_k)$ of the Eq. 5. We can then determine the class of the signal i.e. predict it is a Blink or not Blink.

3   Experimentation

3.1   Material, Experimental Configuration and Data Acquisition

We used the headband $Muse^2$ to record EEG signals. The tests was done using a simple GUIs presented in Fig. 4. It contains a colored panel and a select button. Each 5 s, a random color appears on the panel. The user sitting in front of a screen without other external stimulus. If the user wishes to select a color, he has only to blink. Five adult subjects (one Man is 34 years old and four women aged 30, 69, 50 and 54) accepted to test our system. Voluntarily, the subjects blink. We counted approx an average of 20 blinks for each subject. We are interested to signals from the channels FP1 and FP2 because of its proximity to the eyes. The signal thus acquired is sent via bluetooth to a mobile application. The application sends the EEG signals to the principal program written in python language. The detection of the peaks was based on the peak function of scipy library. The polynomial regression function of the segments was developed using the numpy library. The GMM and the performance measures using the sklearn api [13].

3.2   Results and Discussion

The Polynomial Regression: The choice of the polynomial degrees influence the quality of classification, the recognition rate continue to increase until degree

---

[2] http://www.choosemuse.com/.

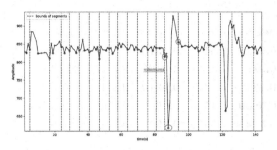

Fig. 3. The segments (Color figure online)

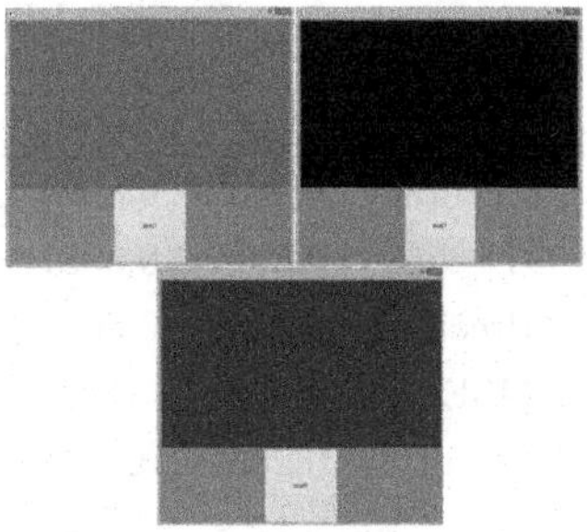

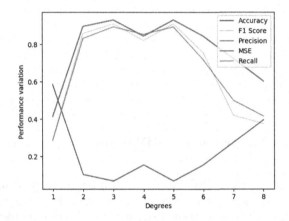

Fig. 4. The segments (Color figure online)

Fig. 5. The performance variation with polynomial degrees 1 to 8

is equal to 5. After, all metrics measure begin to decrease so we can conclude that it's an over-learning of polynomial parameters, like it's presented in the Fig. 5.

The GMM Classification: As a classification method, the performance are measured with a lot of metrics, we note the accuracy, f1 score, precision, mean square error, recall, specificity, sensitivity, cross correlation coefficient, etc. [14]. In our case, we measure different scores illustrated in the Table 1. On a representative basis, we applied the PCA as a linear dimensionality reduction [13] to represent the six classified polynomial coefficients by the GMM. The coefficients was projected to a lower dimensional space (2D). In the Fig. 6, the projected blink parameters representation are regrouped, they are very close in the space. Respectively for the not blinks.

Comparative Study: To evaluate our approach, we have to compare it to other existing methods. This approaches don't only use the same EEG data but also do not shared their datasets. For the reason that the blink signals of the

Table 1. Performance values

Metrics	deg = 1	deg = 2	**deg = 3**	deg = 4	**deg = 5**	deg = 6	deg = 8
Accuracy	0.4137	0.8965	**0.9310**	0.8448	**0.9310**	0.8448	0.6034
f1 score	0.2926	0.8587	**0.9100**	0.8214	**0.9100**	0.7559	0.3763
Precision	0.4137	0.8965	**0.9310**	0.8448	**0.9310**	0.8448	0.6034
MSE	0.5862	0.1034	**0.0689**	0.1551	**0.0689**	0.1551	0.3965
Recall	0.2857	0.8318	**0.8943**	0.8541	**0.8943**	0.7187	0.4166

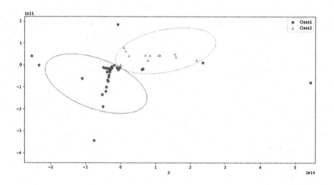

Fig. 6. The GMM classification

eyes are so similar in every EEG signals, we think that comparison can be done based on the recognition metrics. Comparing to [15] with an accuracy of signal classification about 90%, our method surpass it [16]. On a representative basis, we applied the PCA as a linear dimensionality reduction [13] to represent the six classified polynomial coefficients by the GMM. The coefficients was projected to a lower dimensional space (2D). In the Fig. 5, the projected blink parameters representation are regrouped, they are very close in the space. Respectively for the not blinks.

4   Conclusion

An EEG Expert can recognize a blink signal of any subject. In real time application this task must be automatized. The previous works try to separately study each subject signals. In this paper, the goal was to identify the blink curve whatever the subject. So, we can therefore talk about a blink signature. We try to automatically recognize the blink by recognizing its polynomial modeling. Then, we classed the extracted signals polynomial parameters using the GMM method. The experimental study confirmed the advantage of our approach. Despite the small dataset learned to our system, the recognition rate of the blink in the EEG signal was good. The objective of our future research is to generalize our approach for detecting the different excitation signals and establishing a various classification methods comparison of the regularized signals polynomial parameters.

References

1. Ma, J., Zhang, Y., Cichocki, A., Matsuno, F.: A novel EOG/EEG hybrid human-machine interface adopting eye movements and ERPs: application to robot control. IEEE Trans. Biomed. Eng. **62**(3), 876–889 (2015)
2. Ferreira, A., Silva, R., Celeste, W., Bastos Filho, T.F., Sarcinelli Filho, M.: Human-machine interface based on muscular and brain signals applied to a robotic wheelchair. J. Phys.: Conf. Ser. **90**, 012094 (2007)
3. Ochoa, J.B.: EEG signal classification for brain computer interface applications. Ecole Polytechn. Fed. Lausanne **7**, 1–72 (2002)
4. Gao, J.F., Yang, Y., Lin, P., Wang, P., Zheng, C.X.: Automatic removal of eye-movement and blink artifacts from EEG signals. Brain Topogr. **23**(1), 105–114 (2010)
5. Gebrehiwot, T., Paprocki, R., Gradinscak, M., Lenskiy, A.: Extracting blink rate variability from EEG signals. Int. J. Mach. Learn. Comput. **6**(3), 191 (2016)
6. Gupta, M., Beckett, S.A., Klerman, E.B.: On-line EEG denoising and cleaning using correlated sparse signal recovery and active learning. Int. J. Wirel. Inf. Netw. **24**, 1–15 (2017)
7. Tiganj, Z., Mboup, M., Pouzat, C., Belkoura, L.: An algebraic method for eye blink artifacts detection in single channel EEG recordings. In: Supek, S., Sušac, A. (eds.) Biomag 2010. IFMBE, vol. 28, pp. 175–178. Springer, Springer (2010). https://doi.org/10.1007/978-3-642-12197-5_38
8. Hu, J., Wang, C.S., Wu, M., Du, Y.X., He, Y., She, J.: Removal of EOG and emg artifacts from EEG using combination of functional link neural network and adaptive neural fuzzy inference system. Neurocomputing **151**, 278–287 (2015)
9. Gawde, G.S., Pawar, J.: Turning function based distance measure for searching similar ECG trajectories (2017)
10. Draper, N.R., Smith, H., Pownell, E.: Applied Regression Analysis, vol. 3. Wiley, New York (1966)
11. McLachlan, G., Peel, D.: Finite Mixture Models. Wiley, Hoboken (2004)
12. Dempster, A.P., Laird, N.M., Rubin, D.B.: Maximum likelihood from incomplete data via the EM algorithm. J. R. Stat. Soc. Ser. B (Methodol.) **39**, 1–38 (1977)
13. Buitinck, L., Louppe, G., Blondel, M., Pedregosa, F., Mueller, A., Grisel, O., Niculae, V., Prettenhofer, P., Gramfort, A., Grobler, J., Layton, R., VanderPlas, J., Joly, A., Holt, B., Varoquaux, G.: API design for machine learning software: experiences from the scikit-learn project. In: ECML PKDD Workshop: Languages for Data Mining and Machine Learning, pp. 108–122 (2013)
14. Forman, G.: An extensive empirical study of feature selection metrics for text classification. J. Mach. Learn. Res. **3**, 1289–1305 (2003)
15. Dawaga, M.E.: Automatic detection of eye blinking using the generalized ising model. PhD thesis, The University of Western Ontario (2016)
16. Wang, G., Teng, C., Li, K., Zhang, Z., Yan, X.: The removal of EOG artifacts from EEG signals using independent component analysis and multivariate empirical mode decomposition. IEEE J. Biomed. Health Inf. **20**(5), 1301–1308 (2016)

Author Index

Printed in the United States
By Bookmasters